NX 2506 For Beginners

Tutorial Books

NX 2506 For Beginners

NX 2506 For Beginners

Download Resource Files from:
www.tutorialbooks.weebly.com

Write to us at ***online.books999@gmail.com*** *for any technical support*

Contents

Introduction

Welcome to the *NX 2506 for Beginners* book. This book is written to assist students, designers, and engineering professionals. It covers the important features and functionalities of NX using relevant examples and exercises.

This book is written for new users, who can use it as a self-study resource to learn NX. In addition, it can also be used as a reference for experienced users. The focus of this book is part modeling, assembly modeling, drawings, sheet metal, and surface design.

Topics covered in this Book

- Chapter 1, "Getting Started with NX," introduces NX. The user interface and terminology are discussed in this chapter.
- Chapter 2, "Sketch Techniques," explores the sketching commands in NX. You will learn to create parametric sketches.
- Chapter 3, "Extrude and Revolve features," teaches you to create basic 3D geometry using the Extrude and Revolve commands.
- Chapter 4, "Placed Features," covers the features, which can be created without using sketches.
- Chapter 5, "Patterned Geometry," explores the commands to create patterned and mirrored geometry.
- Chapter 6, "Additional Features and Multibody Parts," covers additional commands to create complex geometry. In addition, the multibody parts are also covered.
- Chapter 7, "Modifying Parts," explores the commands and techniques to modify the part geometry.
- Chapter 8, "Assemblies," explains you to create assemblies using the bottom-up and top-down design approaches.
- Chapter 9, "Drawings," covers how to create 2D drawings from 3D parts and assemblies.
- Chapter 10, "Sheet Metal Design," covers how to create sheet metal parts and flat patterns.
- Chapter 11, "Surface Design," covers how to create complex shapes using surface design commands.
- Chapter 12, "NX Realize Shape," helps you to create complex shapes using freeform modeling.

Chapter 1: Getting Started with NX

Introduction to NX

NX is a parametric and feature-based system that allows you to create 3D parts, assemblies, and 2D drawings. The design process in NX is shown below.

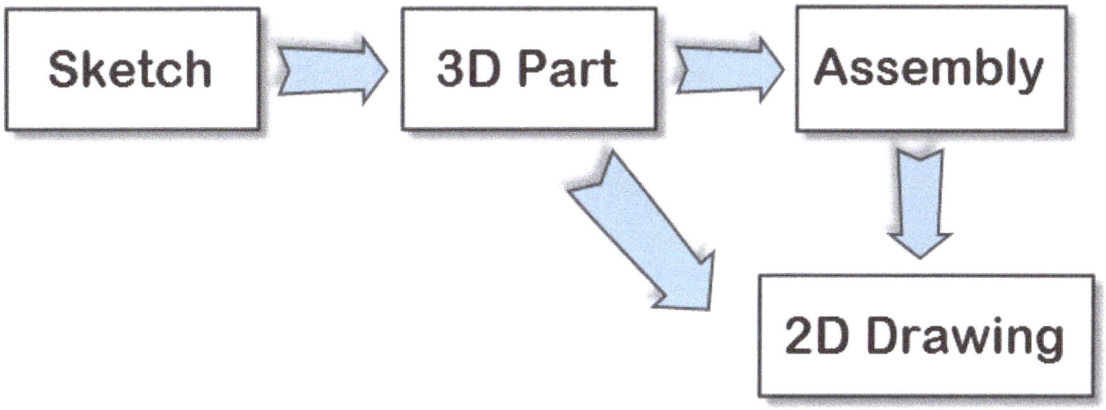

In NX, parameters, dimensions, or relations control everything. For example, if you want to change the position of the hole shown in the figure, you need to change the dimension or constraint that controls its position.

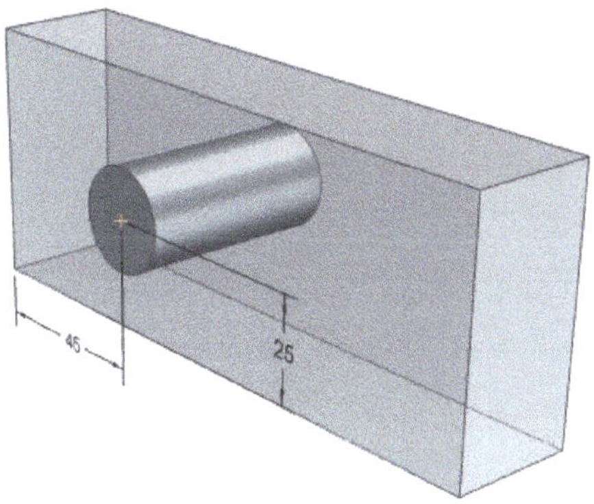

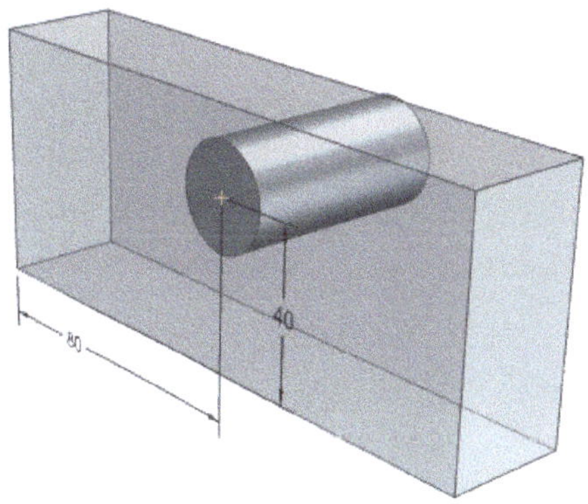

The parameters and relation allow you to have control over the design intent. The design intent describes the way your 3D model will behave when you apply dimensions and relations to it. For example, if you want to position the hole at the center of the block, one way is to add dimensions between the hole and the adjacent edges. However, when you change the size of the block, the hole will not be at the center.

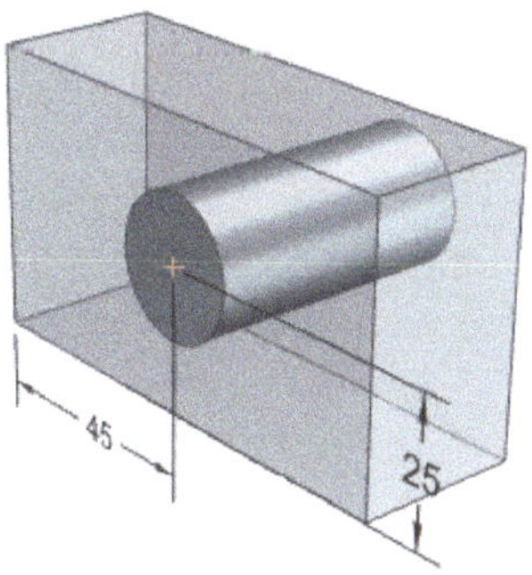

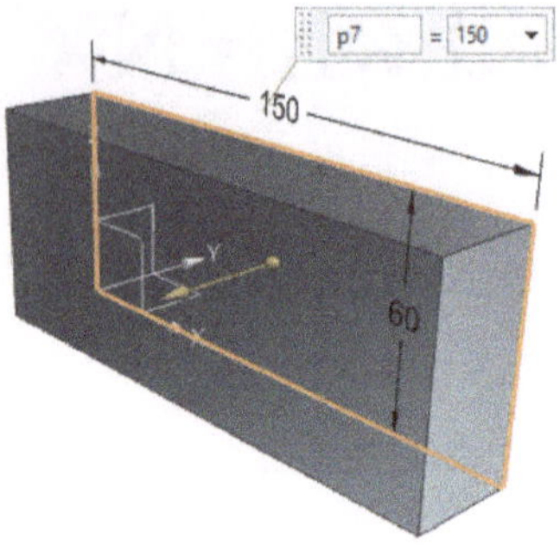

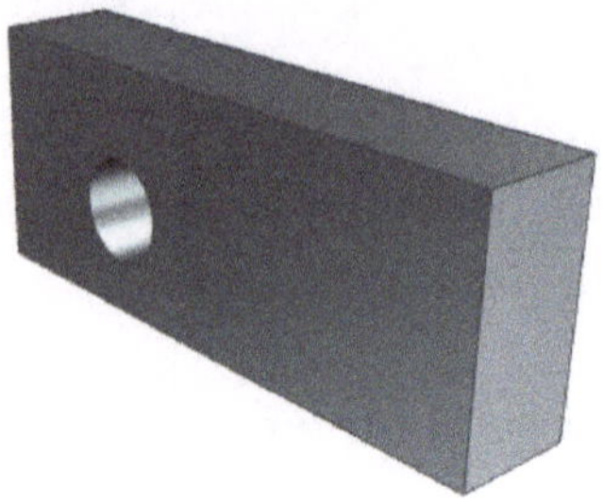

You can make the hole to be at the center, even if the size of the block changes. To do this, you need to delete the dimensions. Next, include the horizontal and vertical edges of the face. Apply the **Make Midpoint Aligned** relationships between the hole point and the horizontal and vertical edges. Now, even if you change the size of the block, the hole will always remain at the center.

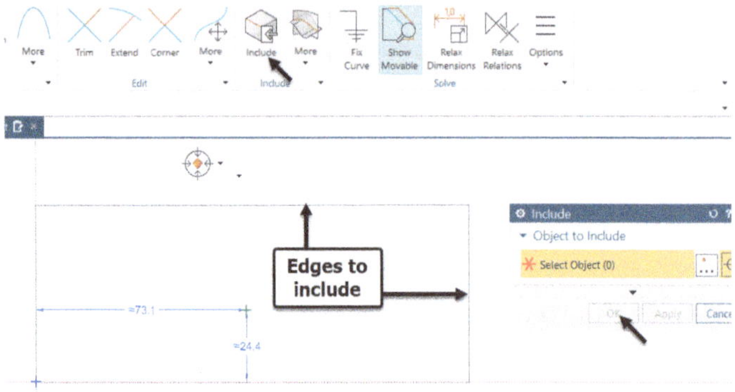

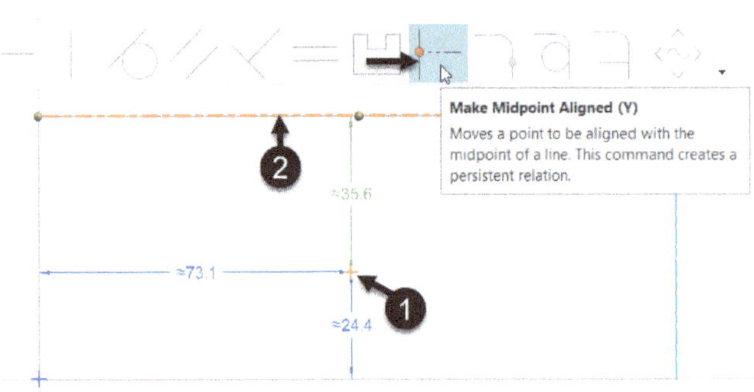

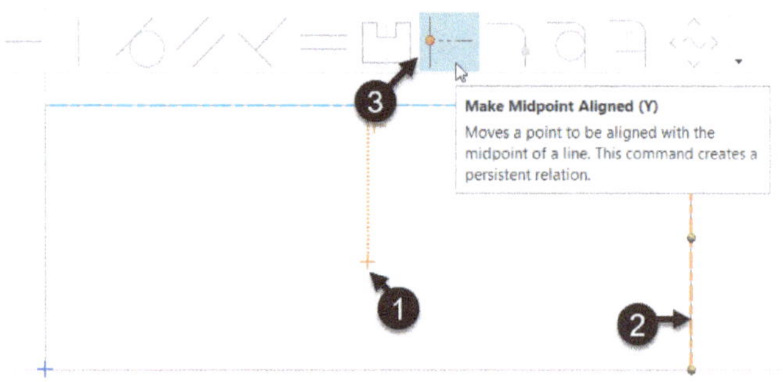

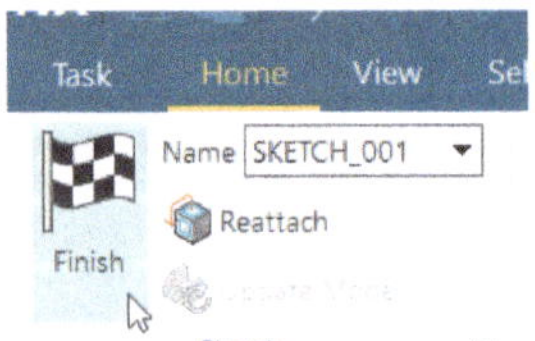

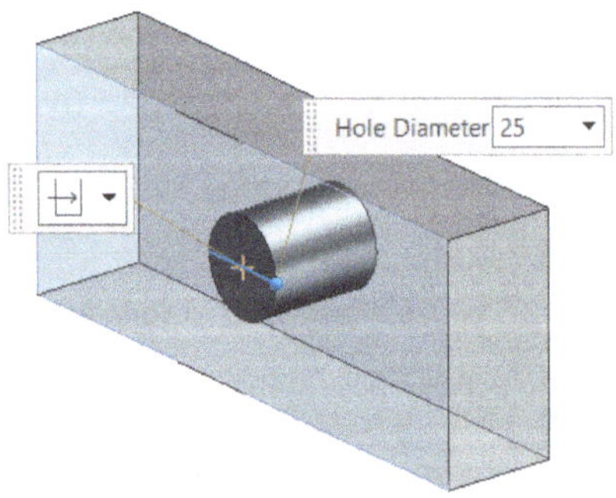

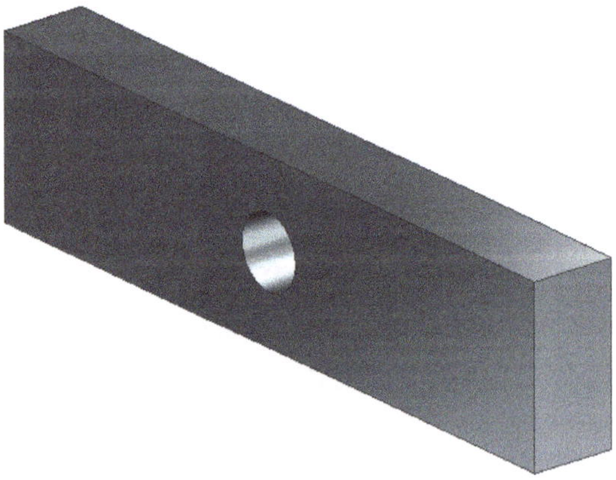

The other big advantage of NX is the associativity between parts, assemblies, and drawings. When you make changes to the design of a part, the changes will take place in any assembly that it is a part of. In addition, the 2D drawing will update automatically.

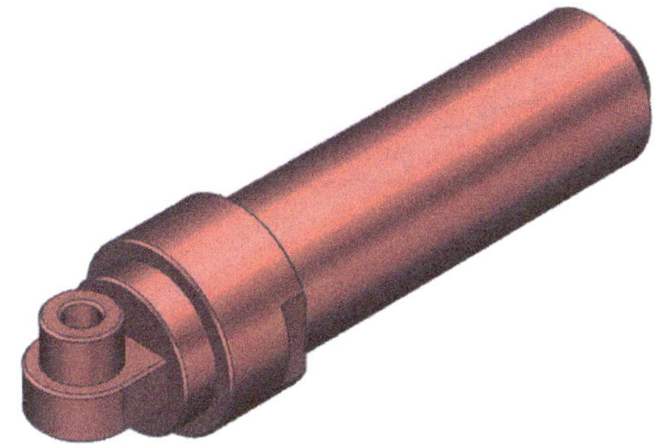

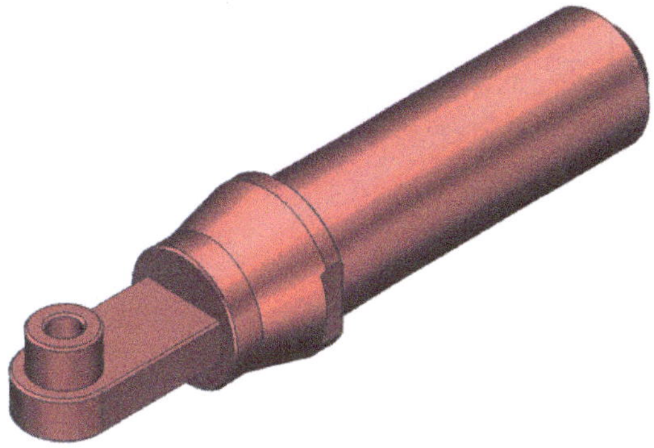

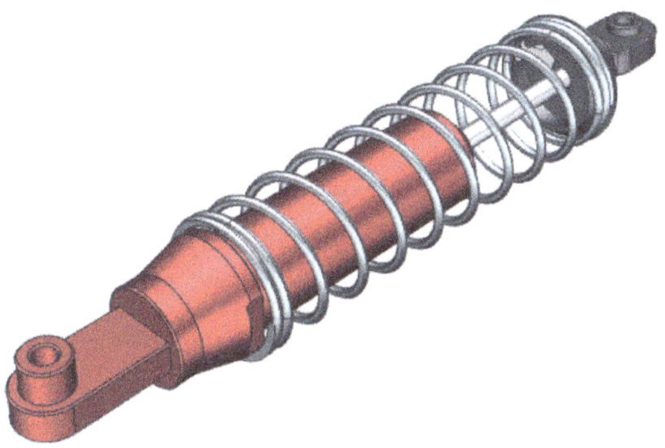

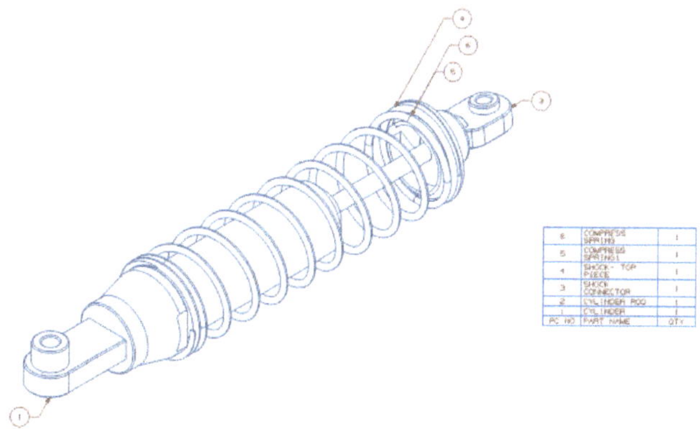

Starting NX

To start **NX**, type **NX** in the search box available on the taskbar. Select NX from the search results; the NX application window appears. On the Application Window, click **Home > New** to open the **New** dialog. On this dialog, click the **Model** template, and then click **OK**. The files created in NX have an extension *.prt*.

User Interface

The following image shows the **NX** application window.

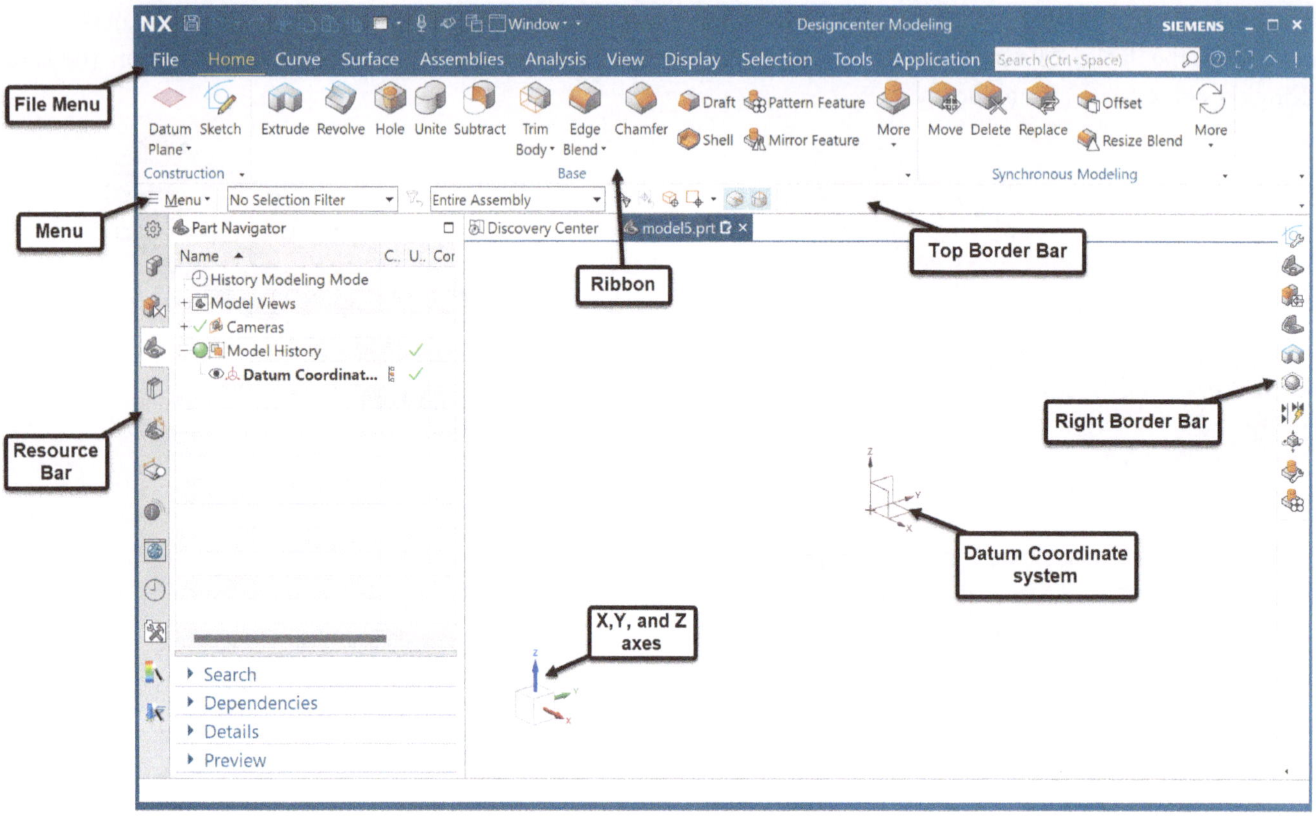

Various components of the user interface are:

Quick Access Toolbar

The Quick Access Toolbar is located on the top left corner. It has some commonly used commands such as **Save**, **Undo, Redo, Copy**, and so on. You can add more commands to the **Quick Access Toolbar** by clicking on the down-arrow next to it, and then selecting commands from the pop-up menu.

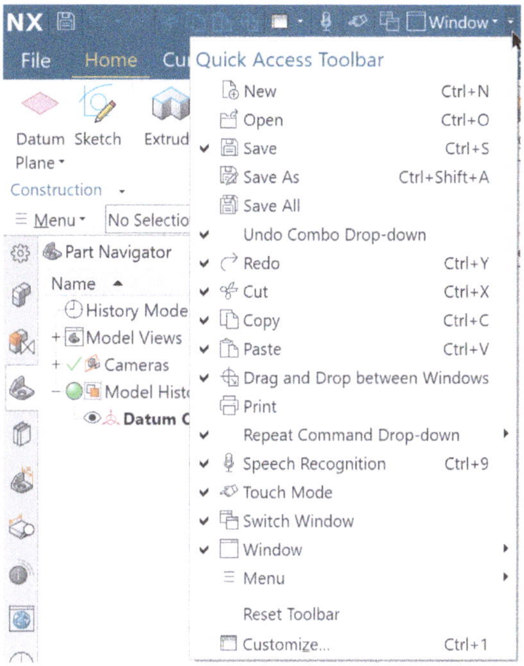

File Menu

The **File Menu** appears when you click on the **File** button located at the top left corner of the window. The **File Menu** has a list of self-explanatory menus. You can see a list of recently opened documents under the **Recently Opened Parts** section. You can also switch to different applications of NX using the File Menu.

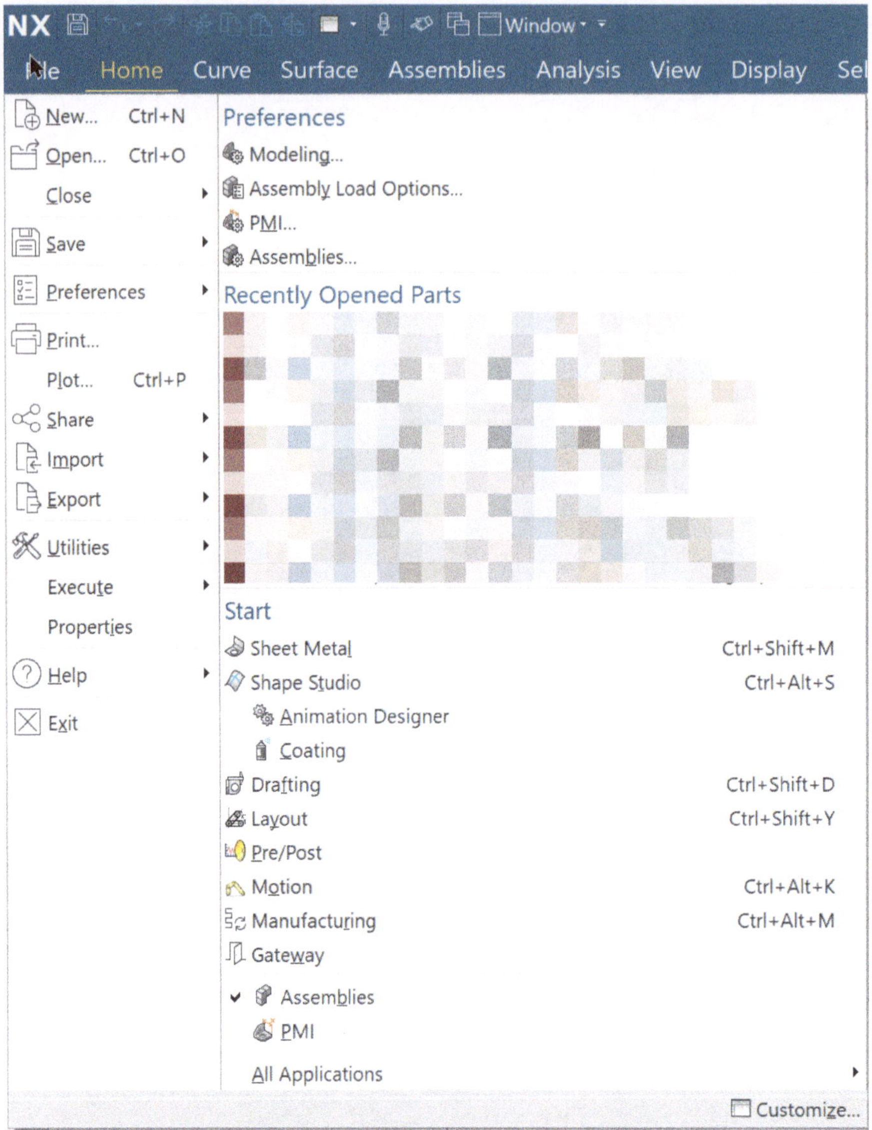

Ribbon

A ribbon is a set of commands, which help you to perform various operations. It has tabs and groups. Various tabs of the ribbon are:

Home tab

This ribbon tab contains commands such as **New**, **Open**, **Help,** and so on.

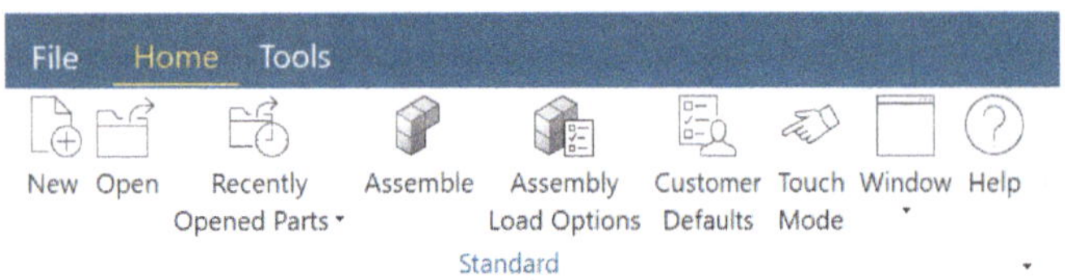

Home tab in the Model template

This ribbon tab has the commands to construct 2D and 3D features.

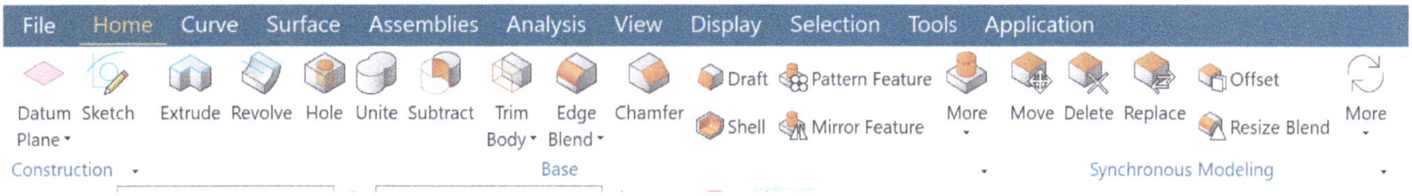

Analysis tab

This ribbon tab has commands to measure objects. It also has commands to analyze the draft, curvature, and surface of the model geometry.

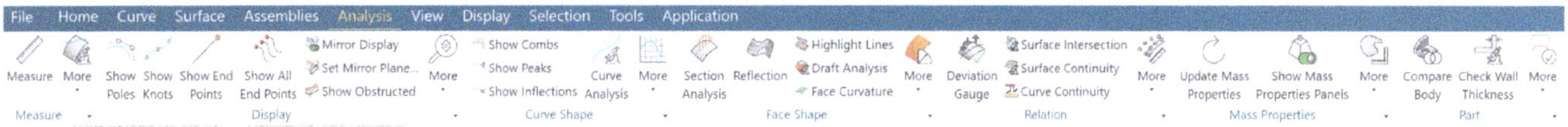

Home tab in Sketch Task environment

This ribbon tab has all the sketch commands. It is available in a separate environment called the Sketch Task environment.

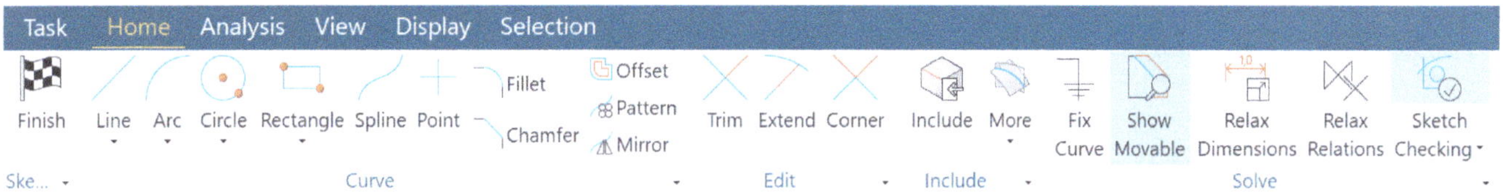

Tools tab

This ribbon tab has the commands to create expressions, part families, movies, fasteners.

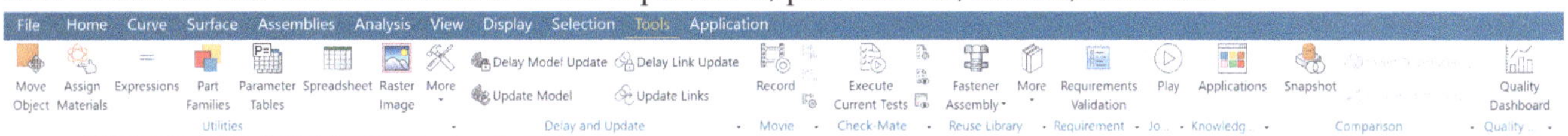

View tab

This ribbon tab has the commands to modify the display of the model and user interface.

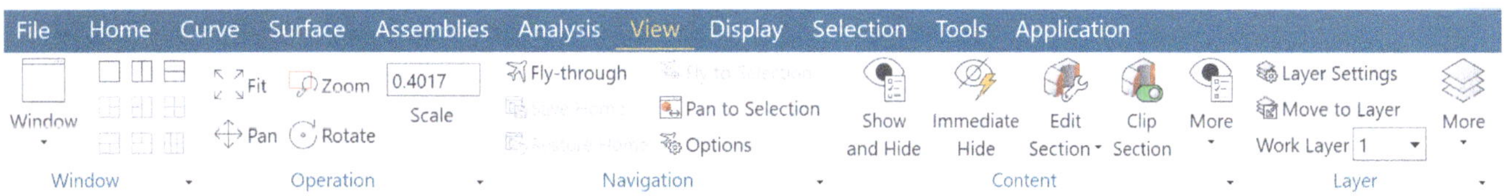

Display tab

This ribbon tab has the commands for controlling the visual appearance of your model, from basic display styles to advanced, photorealistic rendering and virtual reality environments.

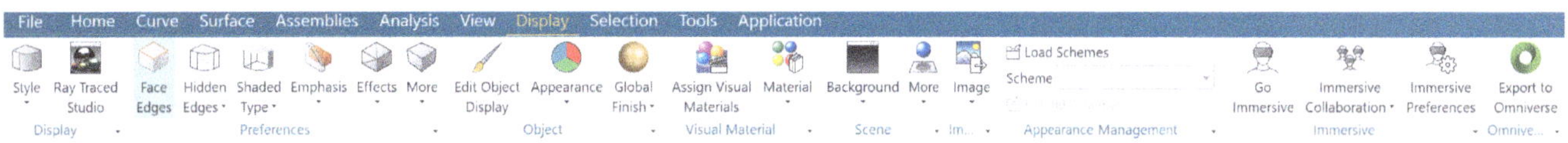

Assemblies tab

This tab contains the commands to construct an assembly.

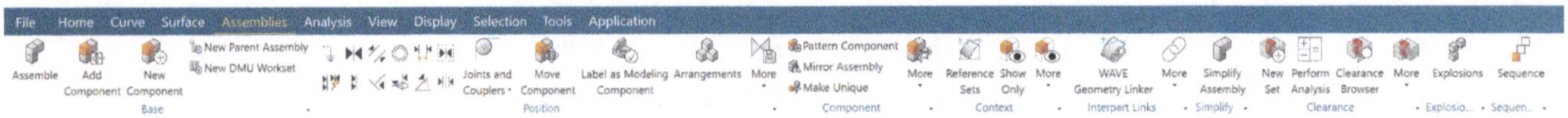

Drafting template ribbon

In the **Drafting** template, you can generate orthographic views of the 3D model. The ribbon tabs in this template contain commands to generate 2D drawings.

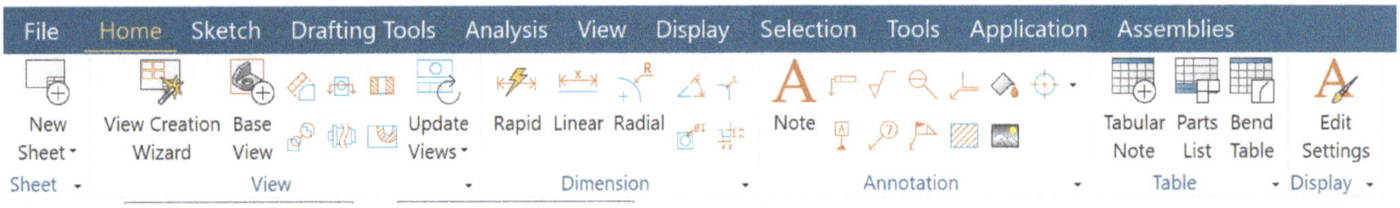

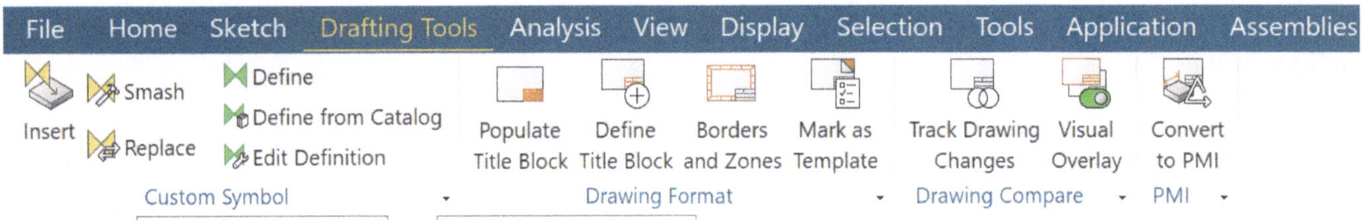

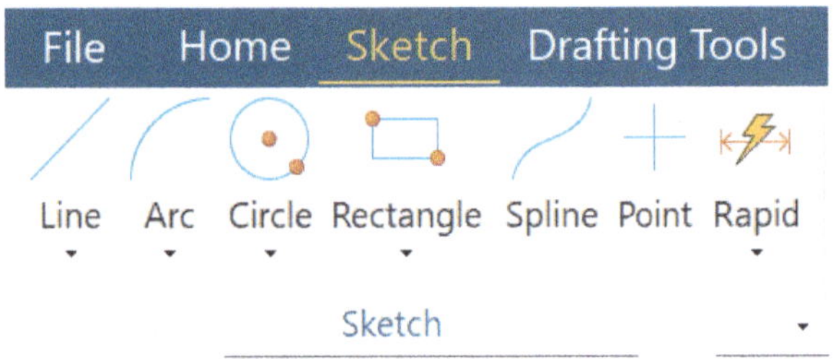

Sheet Metal ribbon

The commands in this ribbon help you to construct sheet metal components.

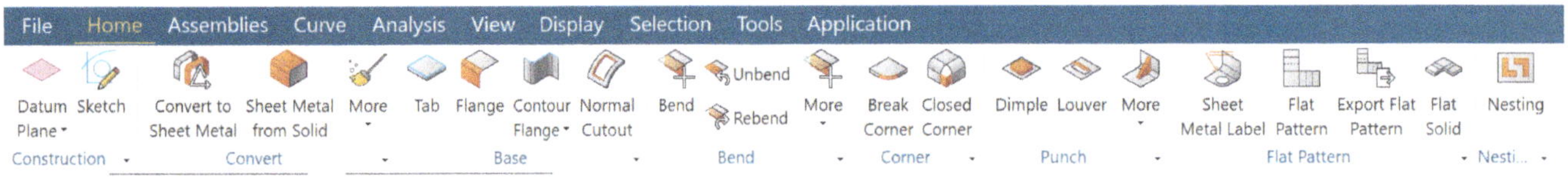

Some tabs are not visible by default. To display a particular tab, right-click on the ribbon and select the tab name from the list displayed.

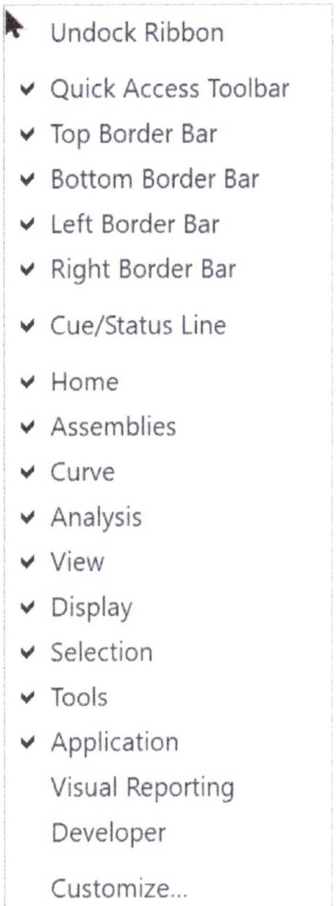

You can also add a ribbon tab by opening the **Customize** dialog.

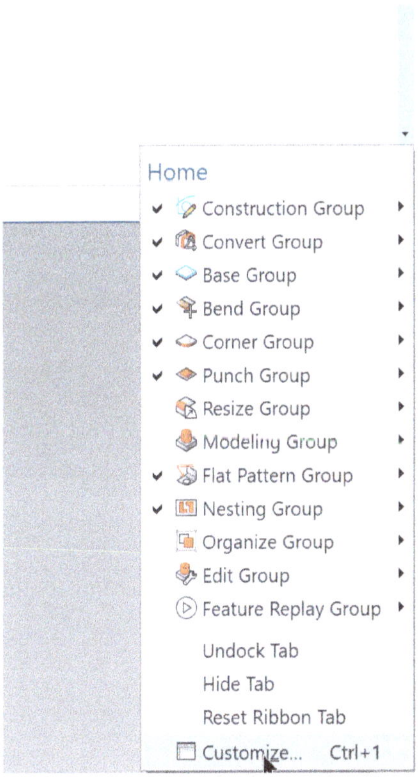

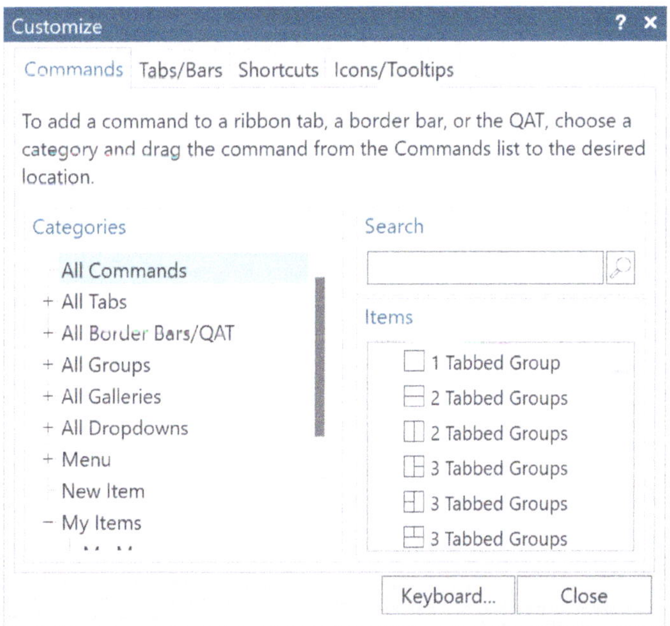

Ribbon Groups and More Galleries

The commands on the ribbon are arranged in various groups depending upon their use. Each group has a **More Gallery**, which contains additional commands. Click on the **More** option of a group to display the gallery.

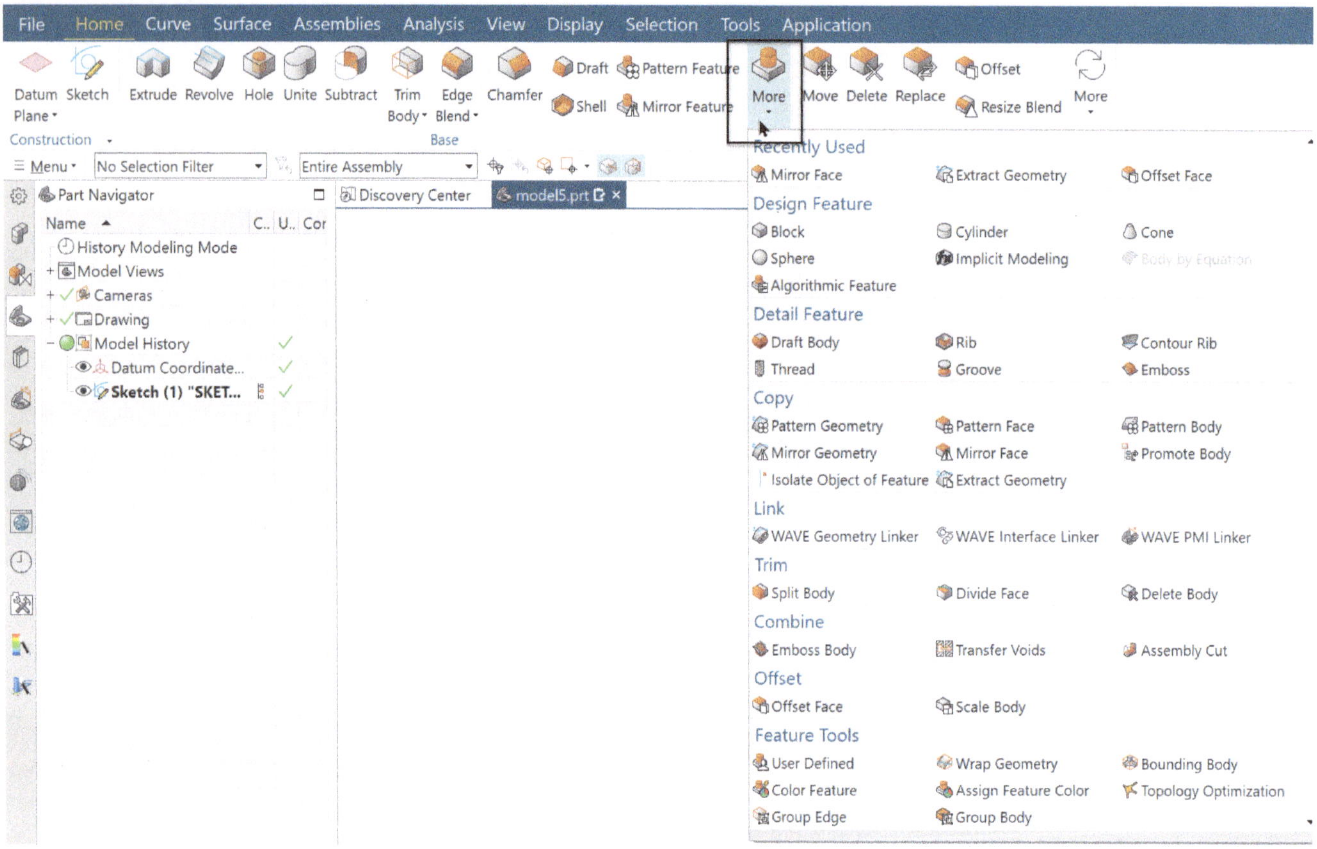

You can add more commands to a ribbon group by clicking the arrow located at the bottom right corner of a group; a drop-down appears. Select the name of the command to be added to the group.

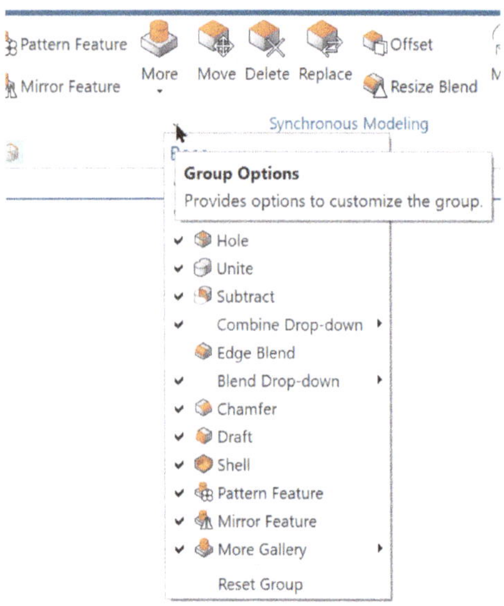

Command Finder

The **Command Finder** bar is used to search for any command. You can type any keyword in the **Command Finder** bar and find a list of commands related to it.

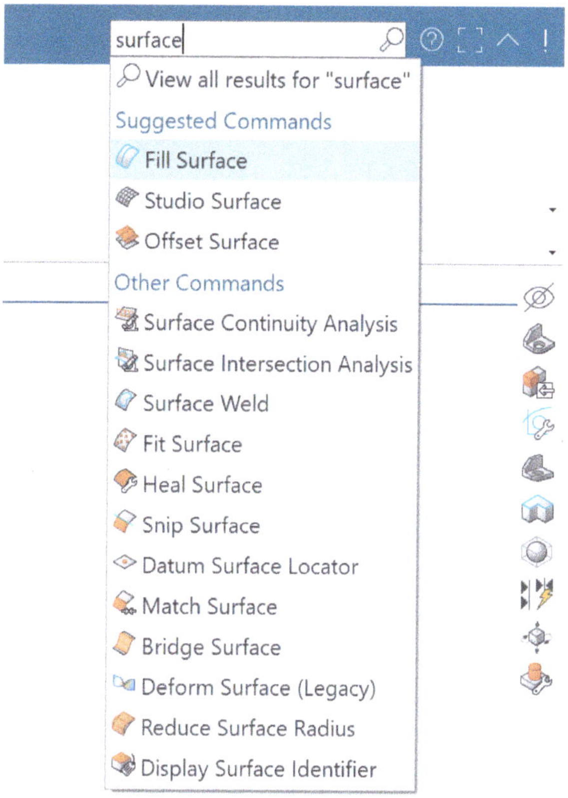

Top Border Bar

The Top Border Bar is available below the ribbon. It has all the options to filter the objects that you can select from the graphics window. It also has some options to change the display of the model in the graphics window.

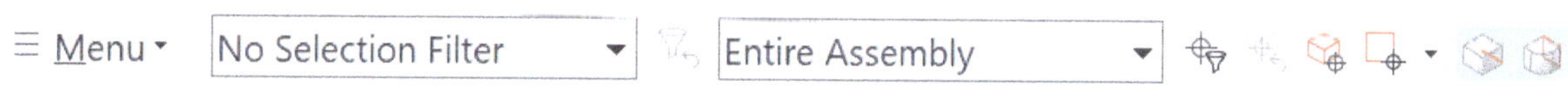

Menu

The Menu is located on the Top Border Bar. It has various options (menu titles). When you click on a menu title, a drop-down appears. Select an option from this drop-down.

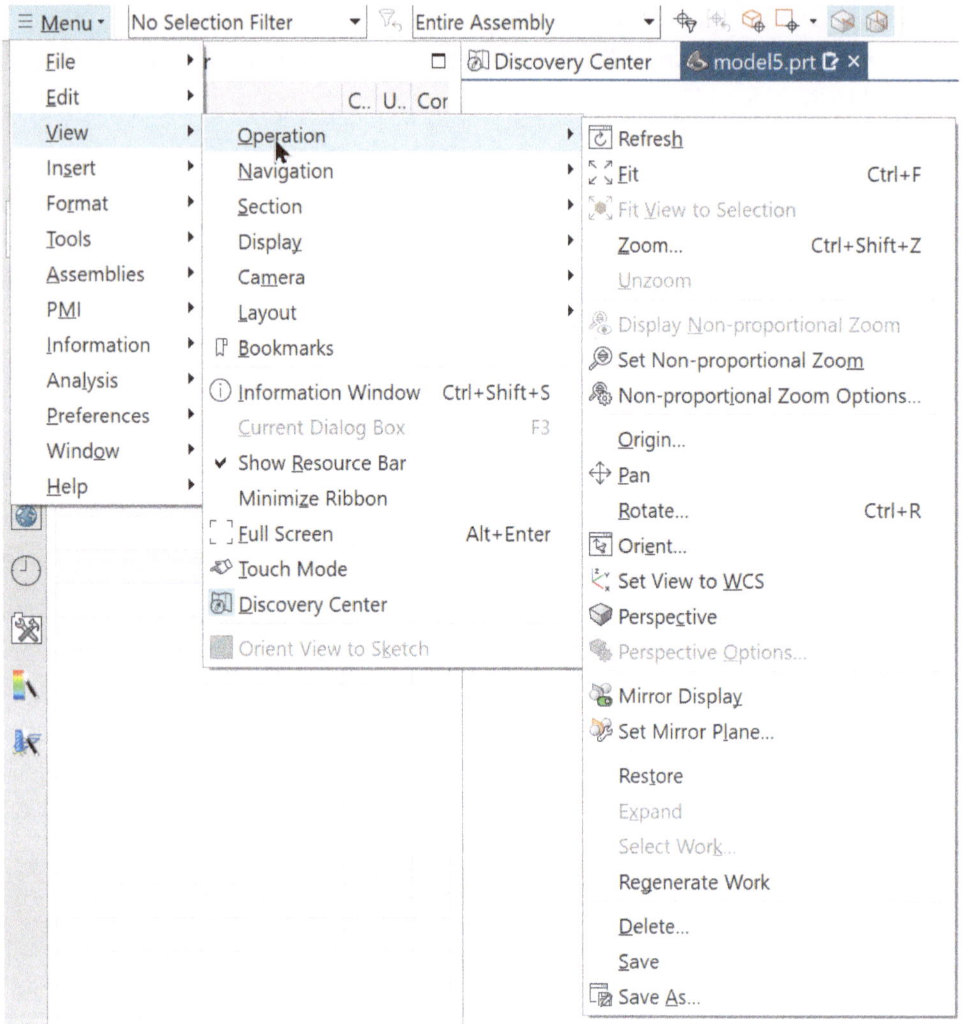

Status bar

The Status bar is available below the graphics window. It shows the prompts and the action taken while using the commands.

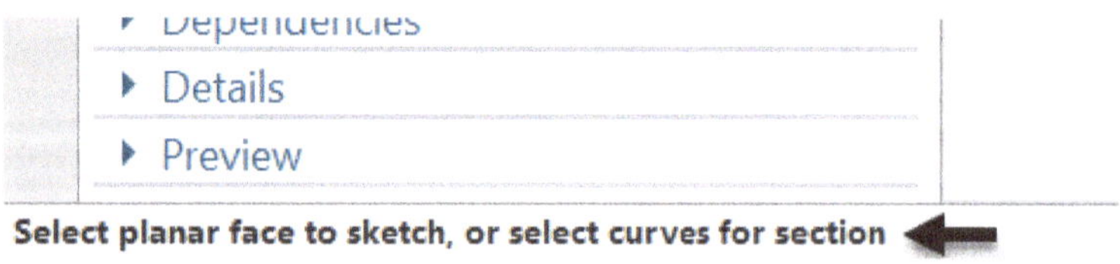

Resource Bar

The Resource Bar is located on the left side of the window. It has all the navigator windows such as Assembly Navigator, Constraint Navigator, Part Navigator, and so on.

Part Navigator

It contains the list of operations carried while constructing a part model.

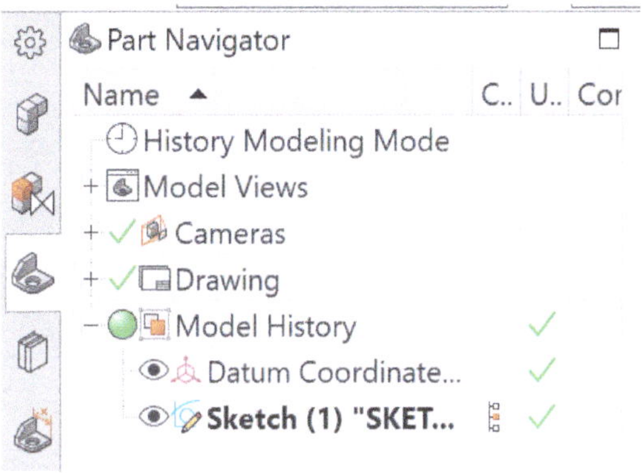

Roles Navigator

The **Roles** Navigator has a list of system default and industry-specific roles. There are two types of roles: **Content** and **Presentation**. A content role is a set of commands and ribbon tabs customized for a specific application. For example, the **CAM Essentials** role has a set of commands used for performing manufacturing operations. This textbook uses the **Advanced** content role.

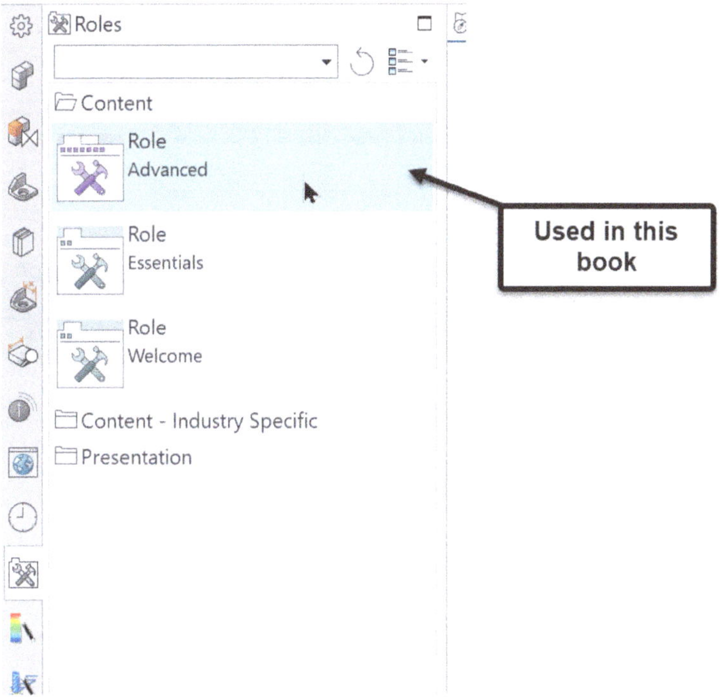

A Presentation role is an arrangement of the commands in the user interface. NX provides you with three Presentation roles: **Default**, **Touch Panel**, and **Touch Tablet** roles. This textbook uses the **Default** presentation role. The other two roles help you to use NX on a Touch screen PC or tablet.

Touch Panel role

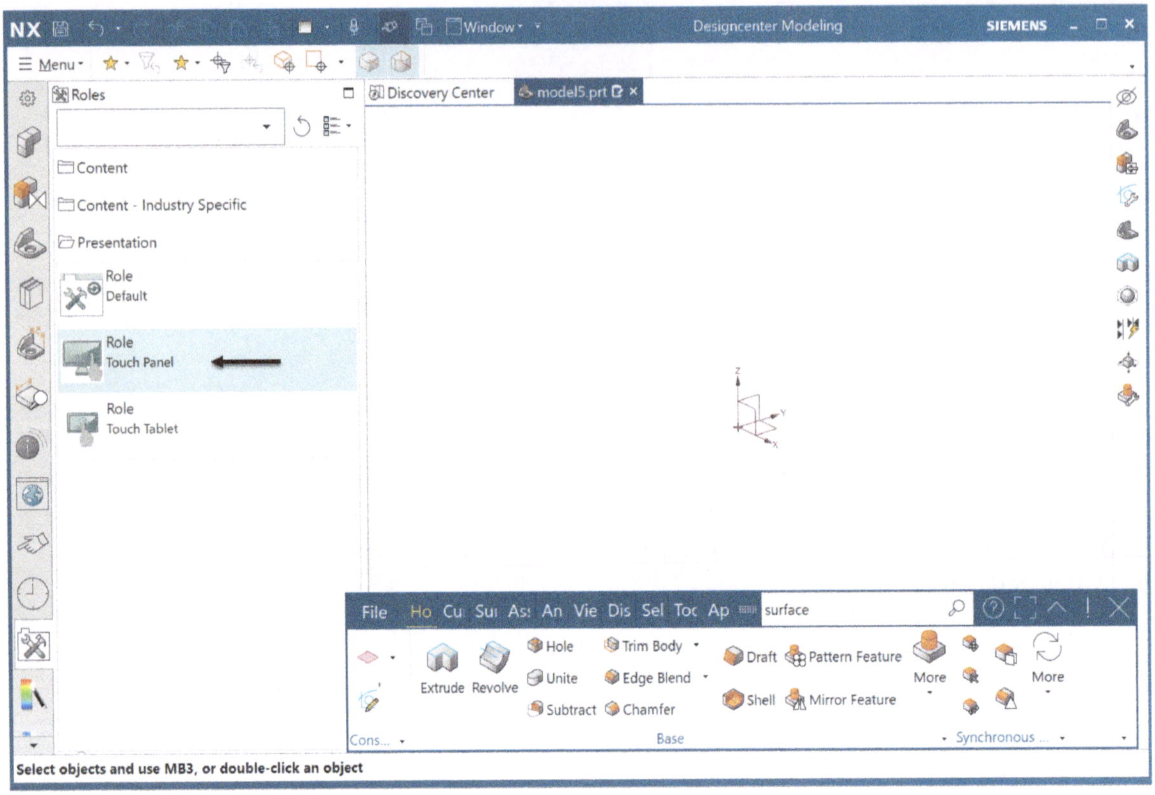

Touch Tablet role

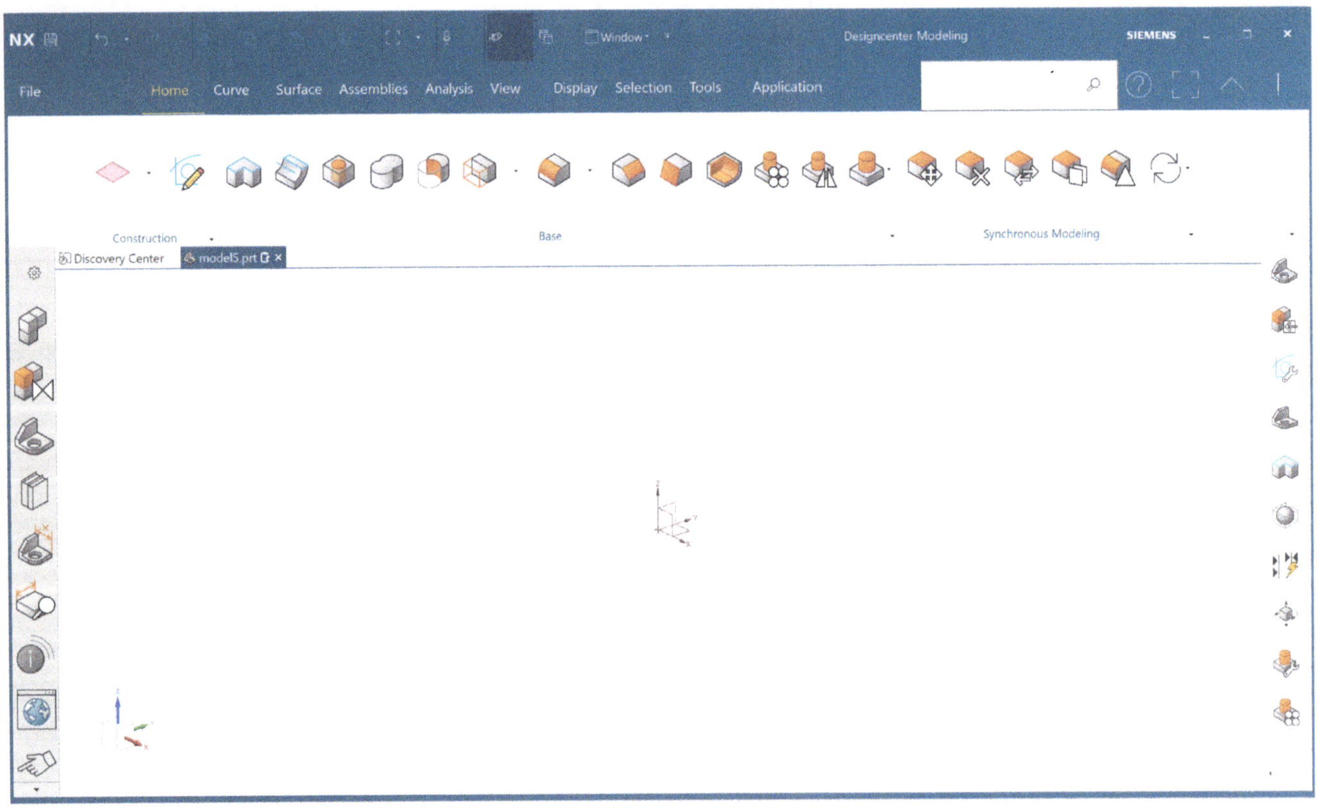

Dialogs

When you execute any command in NX, the dialog related to it appears. A dialog has various options. The following figure shows various components of a dialog.

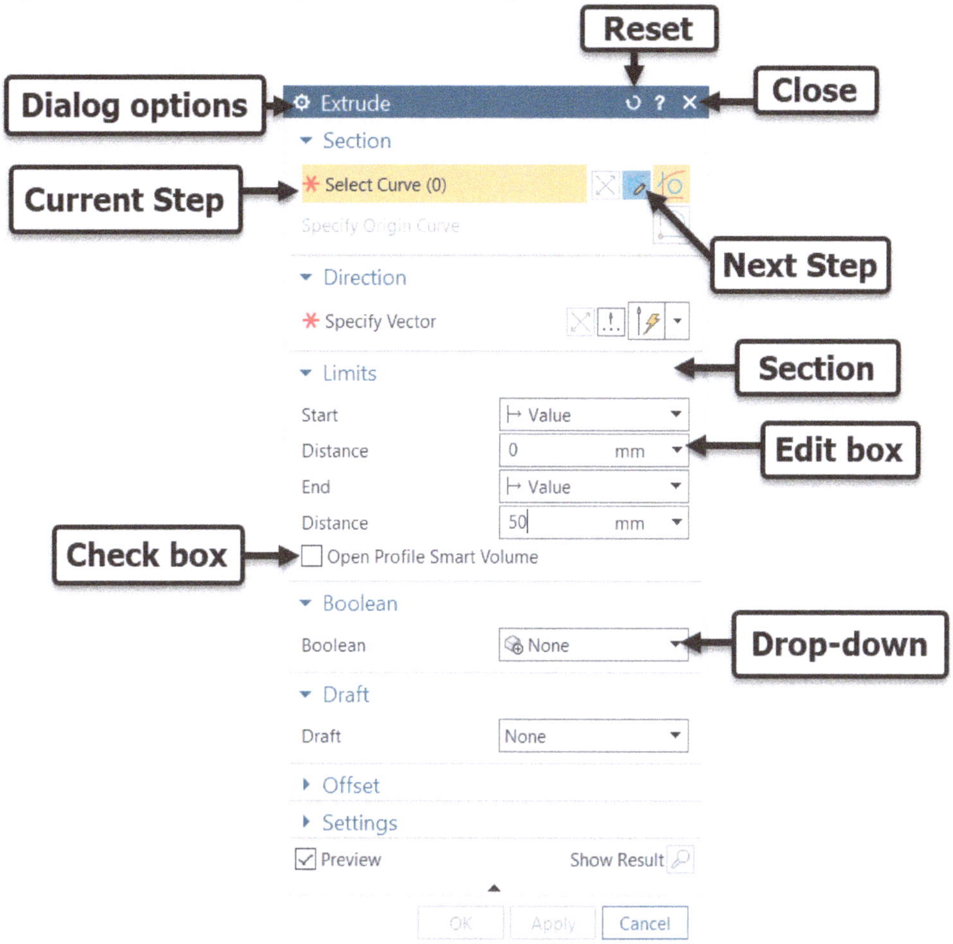

This textbook uses the default options on the dialog. If you have made any changes to a dialog, click the **Reset** button on the dialog; the default options appear.

Mouse Functions

Various functions of the mouse buttons are:

Left Mouse button (MB1)

When you double-click the left mouse button (MB1) on an object, the dialog related to the object appears. Using this dialog, you can edit the parameters of the objects.

Middle Mouse button (MB2)

Click this button to execute the **OK** command.

Right Mouse button (MB3)

Click this button to open the shortcut menu. The shortcut menu has some selection filters and options to modify the display of the model.

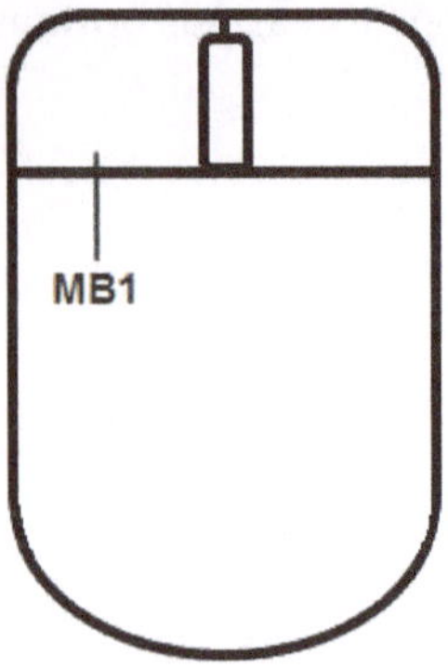

Select

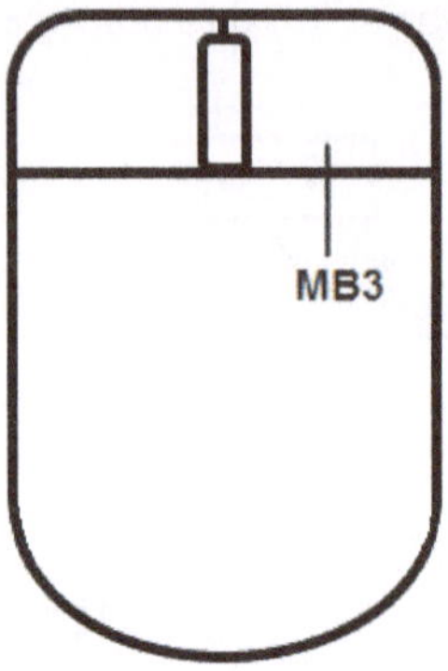

Shortcut Menu

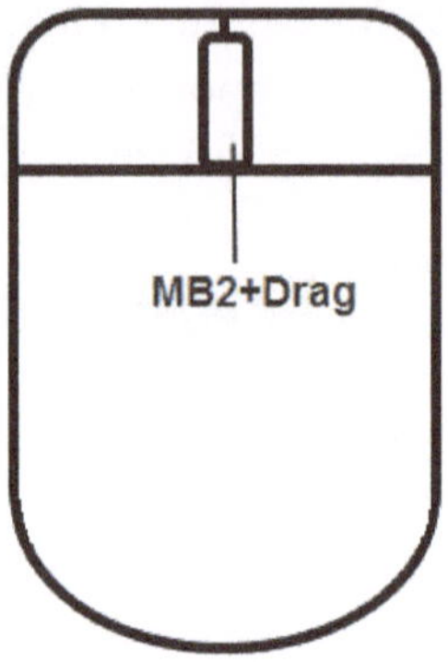

Rotate

The other functions with a combination of the three mouse buttons are:

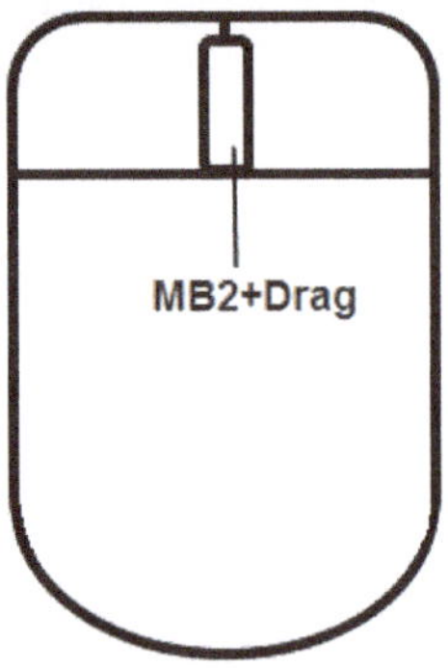

Rotate

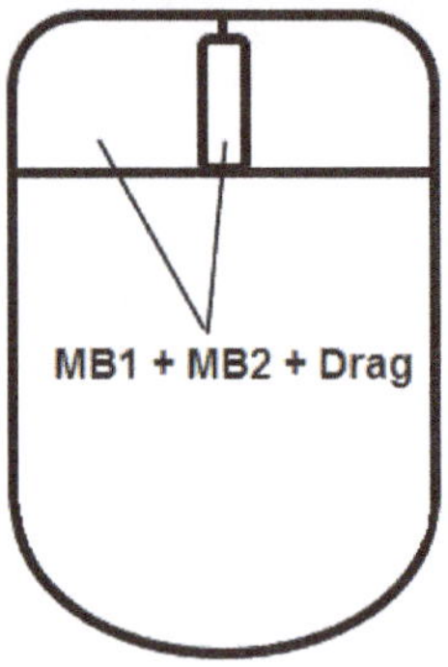

Zoom In/Out

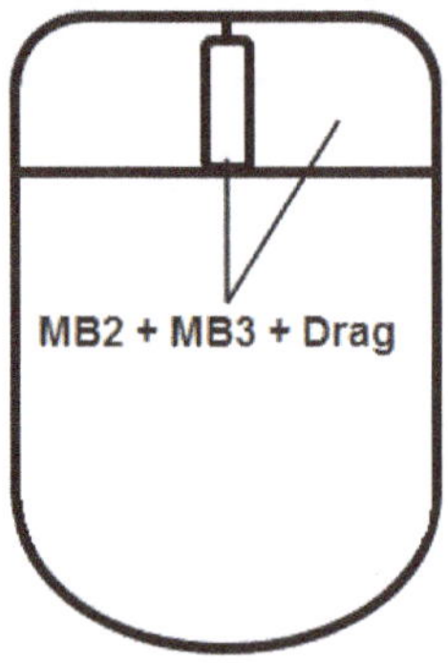

Pan

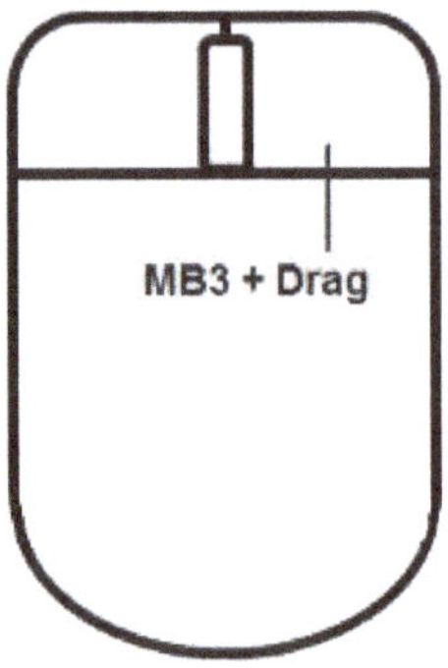

Box Menu

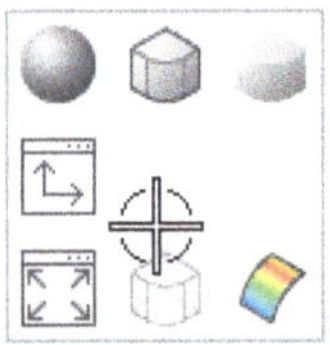

Edit Background

To change the background color of the window, click **Display > Scene > Background** drop-down > **White** on the ribbon.

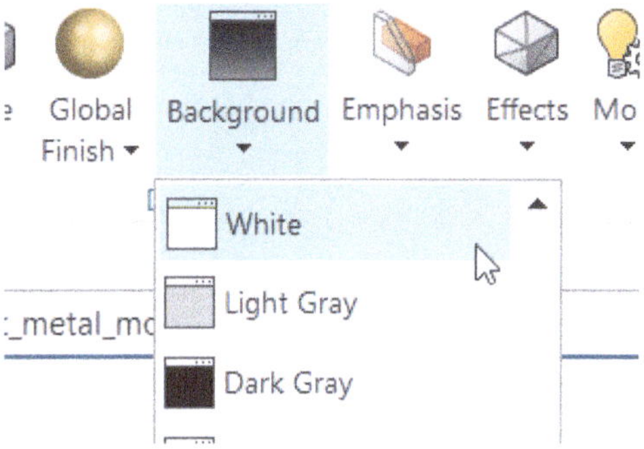

Shortcut Keys

CTRL+Z	(Undo)
CTRL+Y	(Redo)
CTRL+S	(Save)
F5	(Refresh)
F1	(NX Help)
CTRL + SHIFT + Z	(Zoom)
CTRL + R	(Rotate)
CTRL+M	(Starts the Modeling environment)
CTRL+SHIFT+D	(Starts the Drafting environment)
CTRL+SHIFT+M	(Starts the NX Sheet Metal environment)
CTRL+ALT+M	(Starts the Manufacturing environment)
X	(Extrude)
CTRL+1	(Customize)
CTRL+D	(Delete)
CTRL+N	(New File)
CTRL+O	(Open File)
CTRL+P	(Plot)

NX Help

NX offers you the help system that goes beyond basic command definition. You can access NX help by using any of the following methods:

- Press the F1 key.
- Click on the **On Context Help** option on the right side of the window.

Questions

1. Explain how to customize the Ribbon.
2. What is the design intent?
3. Give one example of where you would establish a relationship between a part's features.
4. Explain the term 'associativity' in NX.
5. List any two procedures to access NX Help.
6. How can you change the background color of the graphics window?
7. How can you activate the Box Menu?

8. How is NX a parametric modeling application?

Chapter 2: Sketch Techniques

This chapter covers the methods and commands to create sketches used in the part-modeling environment. The commands and methods are discussed in the context of the part-modeling environment. In NX, you can create sketches in two environments: Part and Sketch task environment. You will learn to create sketches in both environments.

In NX, you create a rough sketch, and then apply dimensions and relations that define its shape and size. The dimensions define the length, size, and angle of a sketch element, whereas relations define the relations between sketch elements.

The topics covered in this chapter are:

- Sketching in the Sketch Task Environment
- Use relations and dimensions to control the shape and size of a sketch
- Learn sketching commands
- Learn commands and options that help you to create sketches easily

Sketching the Sketch Task environment

Creating sketches in the Sketch Task environment is very easy. You have to activate the **Sketch** command, and then define a plane on which you want to create the sketch. To do this, click **Home > Construction > Sketch** on the ribbon. Next, click on any of the Principal Planes located at the center of the graphics window. On the **Create Sketch** dialog, the Show Principal Planes option is selected by default. As a result, the principal planes are displayed on the Coordinate System. The principal planes allow you to select a correct the plane to define the orientation of the sketch. Also, the 'Sketch' text is displayed on the selected principal plane. Next, click **OK** on the **Create Sketch** dialog to start the sketch. You can now start drawing sketches on the selected plane. After creating the sketch, click **Home > Sketch > Finish Sketch** on the ribbon to finish the sketch.

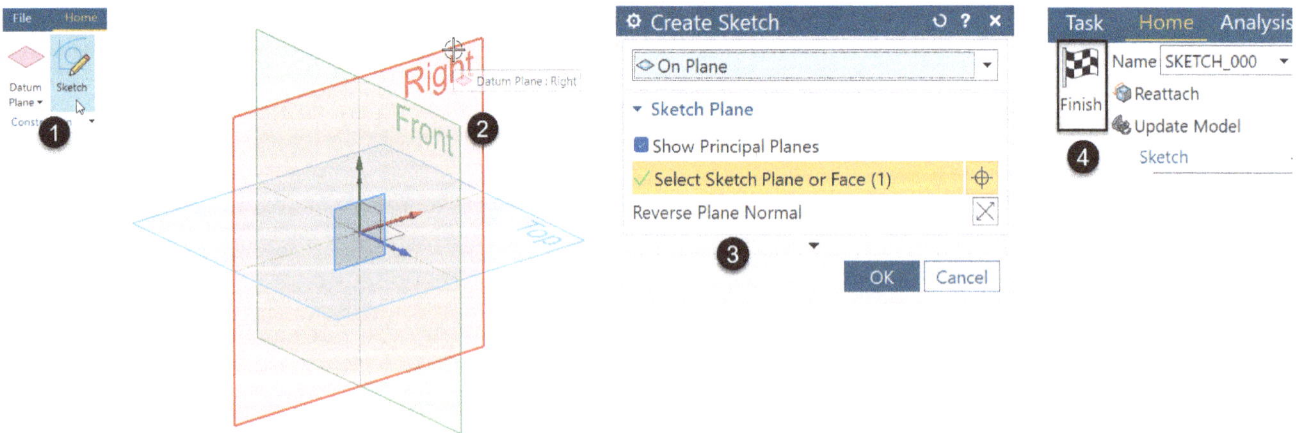

Draw Commands

NX provides you with a set of commands to create sketches. These commands are located on the **Curve** panel of the **Home** ribbon.

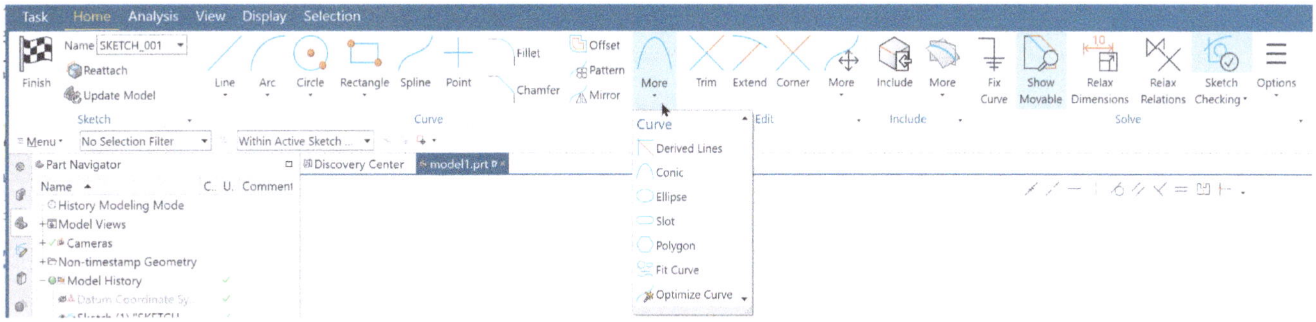

The Line Command

The **Line** command is one of the most commonly used commands while creating a sketch. To activate this command, you need to click **Home > Curve > Line** on the ribbon. Notice that the mouse pointer changes to a pencil glyph indicating that the drawing command is active. Also, the **Line** dialog appears. Click in the graphics window to specify the first point of the line. Move the pointer and click to define the endpoint of the line segment.

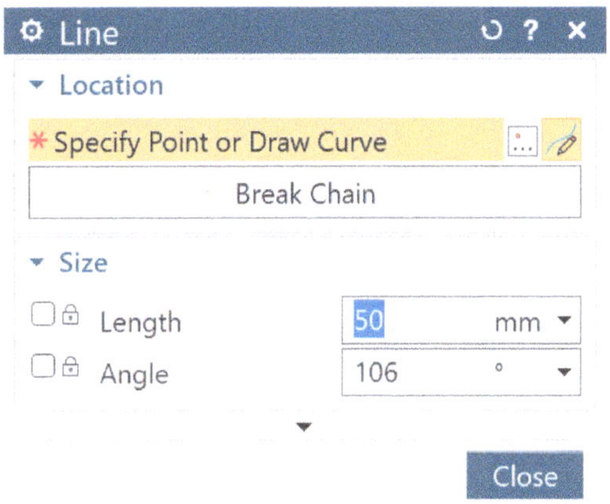

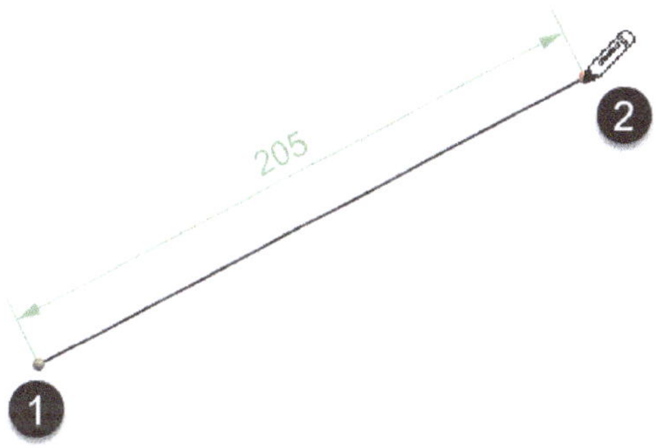

Move the pointer and pause until the **Perpendicular relation glyph** appears between the first line and the rubber-band line attached to the pointer. A dotted guide line is then displayed, showing the perpendicular direction. Move the pointer along this dotted line, which is aligned perpendicular to the first line. The relation defines the behavior of the sketch element (relations are explained later in this chapter). Click to create the second line, which is automatically assigned a **Perpendicular relation** with the first line.

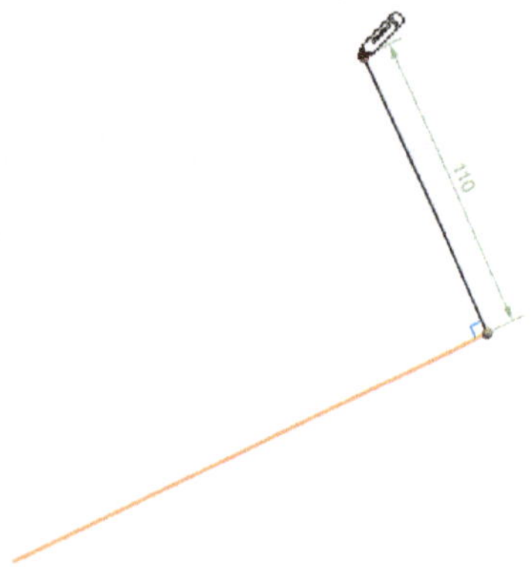

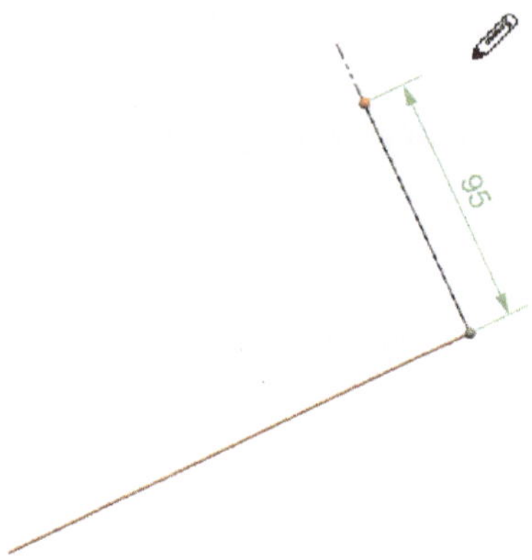

Move the pointer along the dotted line, which is collinear to the second line. The **Collinear** relation appears next to the line. Click to create a line collinear to the second line.

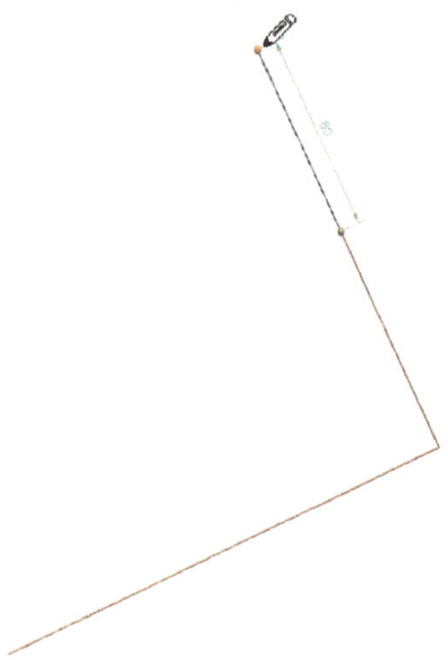

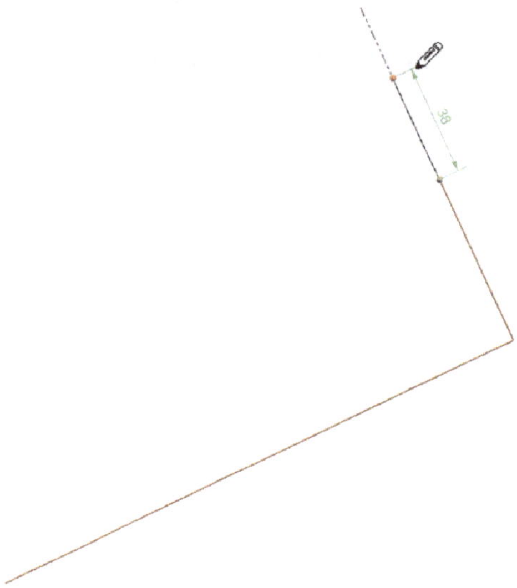

Move the pointer horizontally toward the left and notice the **Horizontal** relation next to the line. Click to create the horizontal line.

Move the pointer vertically downward and notice the **Vertical** relation. Click to create the vertical line.

Move the pointer and notice that the **Parallel** relation appears. Also, a line is highlighted. Click to create a line parallel to the highlighted line.

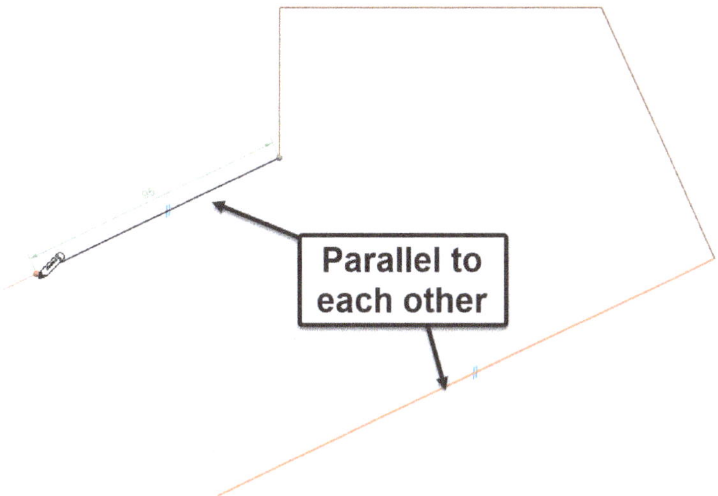

Move the pointer to the first line's midpoint; a dotted line appears between the midpoint and the pointer. Click to specify the endpoint of the line. Notice that no relation is created between the midpoint and endpoint. However, this helps you to specify the points quickly.

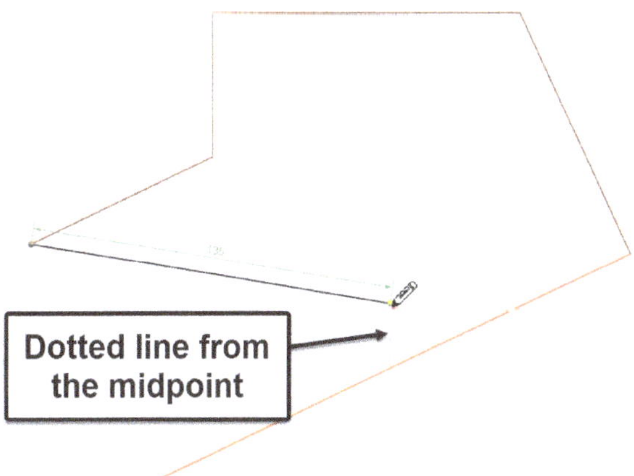

Right-click and select **Break Chain** from the shortcut menu; the line chain is stopped. Notice that the **Line** command is still active.

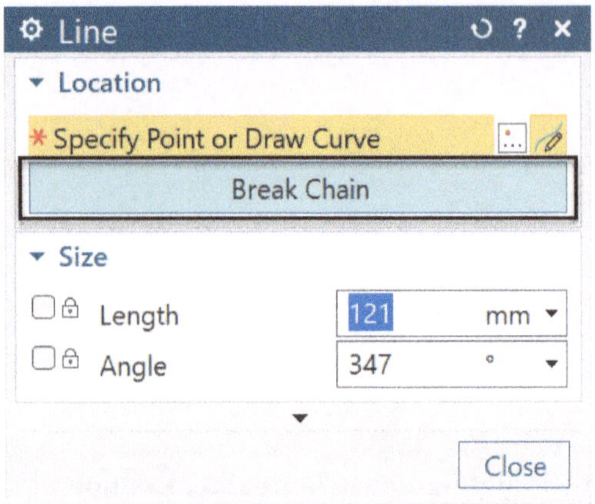

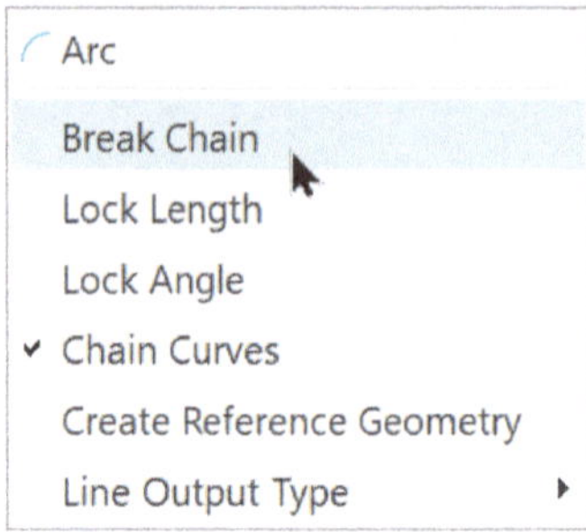

The **Line** command can also be used to draw arcs continuous with lines. Click in the graphics window, move the pointer horizontally toward the right and click. Right-click and select **Arc** from the shortcut menu.

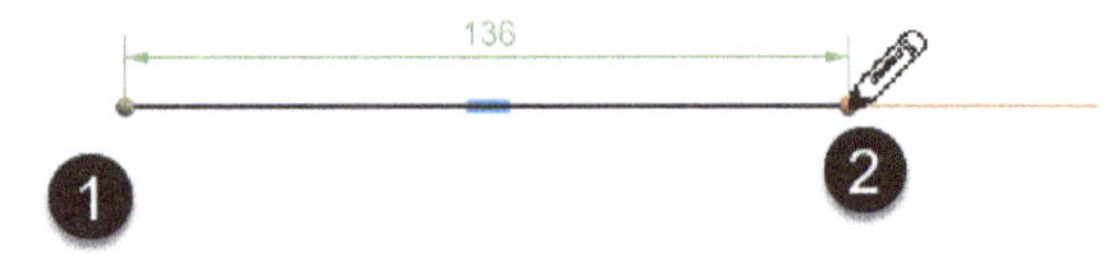

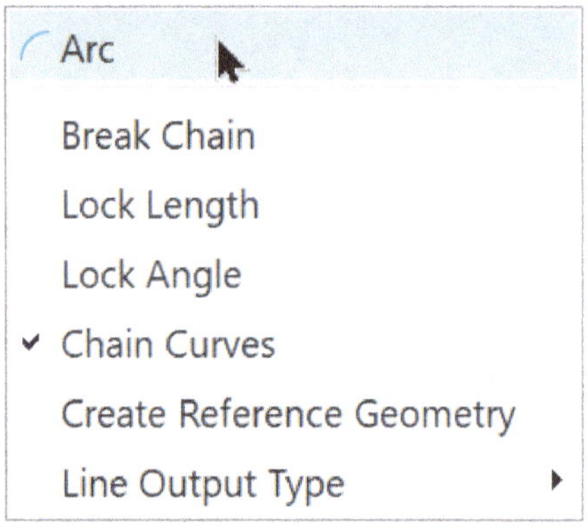

Move the pointer to the right and then upward, and click when the **Tangent relation glyph** (a small vertical tick mark) appears on the connected horizontal line. Next, move the pointer along the arc and click again when the **Tangent relation glyph** is displayed, establishing tangency with the horizontal line.

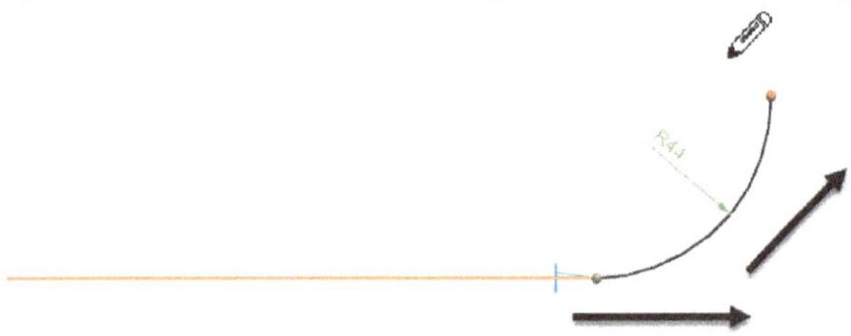

Move the pointer toward right; the arc appears normal to the previous arc. Click to specify the endpoint of the arc. Move the pointer and click to specify the direction of the arc. Next, press Esc to deactivate the **Line** command.

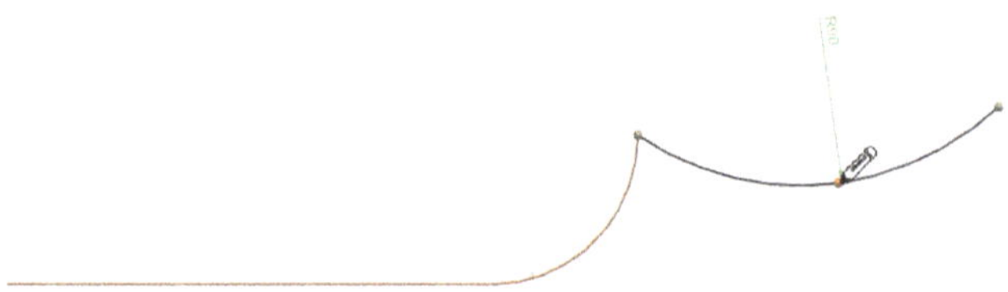

To delete a line, select it and press the **Delete** key. To select more than one line, press and hold the **Alt** key and then click on the line segments; the lines will be highlighted. You can also select multiple lines by dragging a box from right to left. Press and hold the left mouse button and drag a box from right to left; the lines inside or crossing the box boundary will be selected. Dragging a box from left to right will only select the lines that are inside the box.

Creating a Midpoint Line

You can create a midpoint line using the **Line from Midpoint** command (on the ribbon, click **Home** > **Curve** > **Line** drop-down > **Line from Midpoint**). Next, specify the midpoint of the line, and then move the pointer. Click to specify the endpoint of the line.

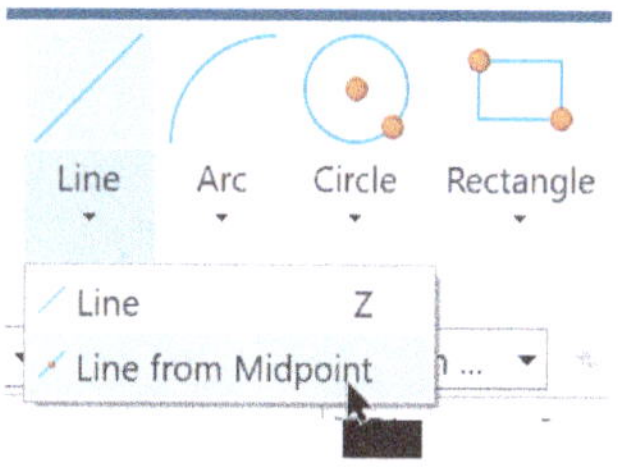

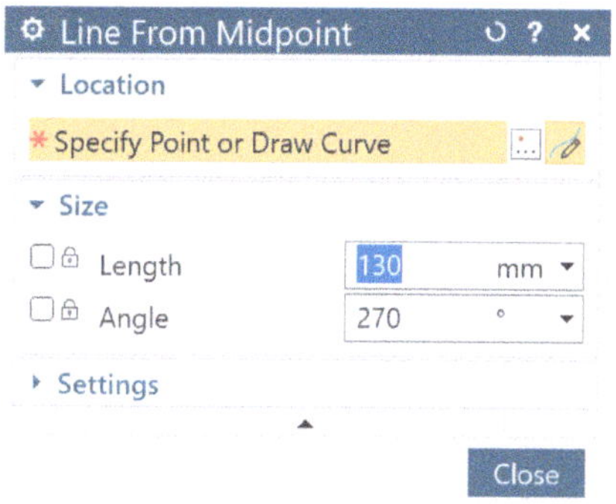

Creating arcs

You can create an arc using two command: **Arc** and **Arc by Center**.

Arc command

This command creates an arc by defining its start, end, and radius. Activate the **Arc** command (click **Home > Curve > Arc** on the ribbon). Click to define the start point of the arc. Click again to define the endpoint. After defining the start and end of the arc, you need to define the radius and position of the arc. Move the pointer and click to define the radius and position of the arc.

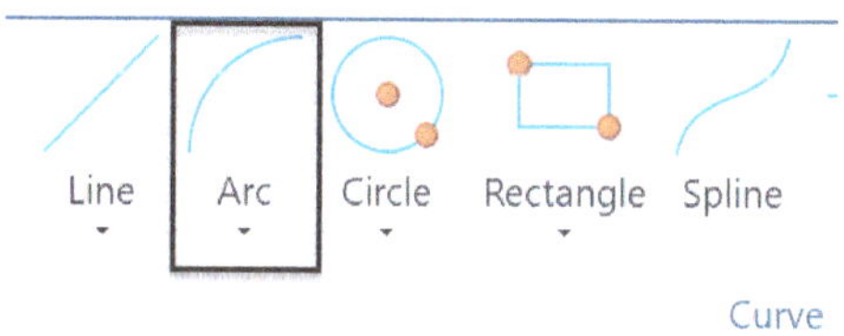

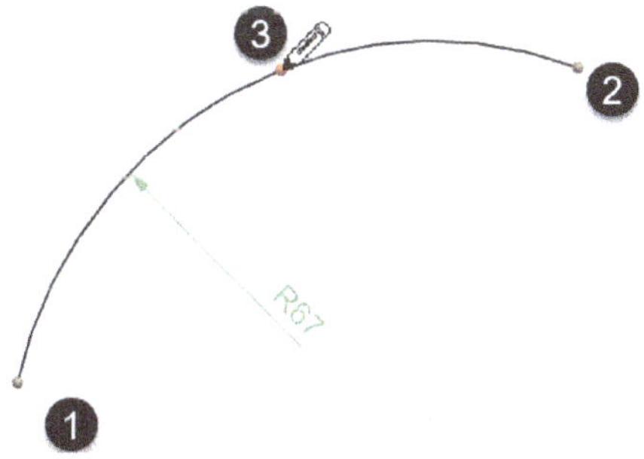

Arc by Center command

This command creates an arc by defining its center, start, and end. click **Home > Curve > Arc** drop-down > **Arc by Center** on the ribbon. Click to define the center point. Next, move the pointer, and you will notice that a dotted line appears between the center and the pointer. This line is the radius of the arc. Now, click to define the start point of the arc and move the pointer; you will notice that an arc is drawn from the start point. Once the arc appears the way you want, click to define its endpoint.

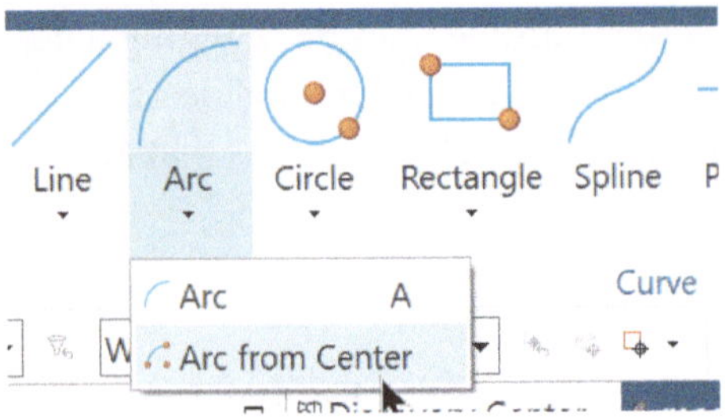

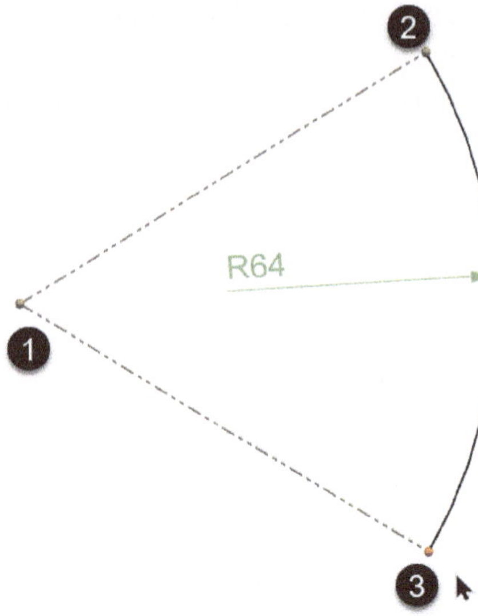

Creating Rectangles

You can create a rectangle using three different commands: **Rectangle**, **Rectangle by Three Points**, and **Rectangle From Center**.

Rectangle Command

This command creates a rectangle by defining its diagonal corners. Activate the **Rectangle** command (On the ribbon, click **Home > Curve > Rectangle**). Click to define the first corner. Drag the pointer and click to define the second corner. You can also type-in values in the **Width** and **Height** boxes attached to the pointer.

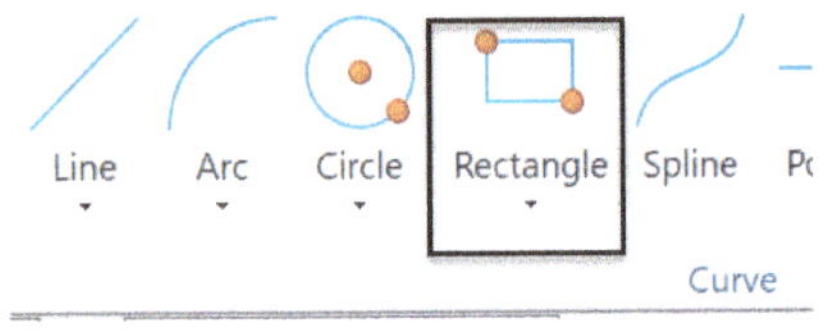

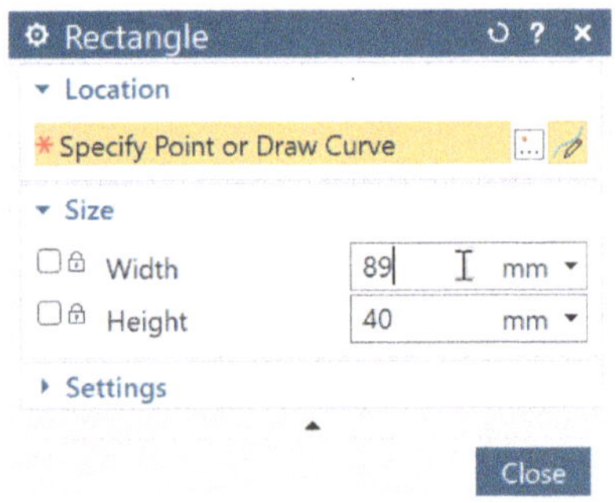

Rectangle by Three Points command

This command creates an inclined rectangle. The first two points define the width and inclination angle of the rectangle. The third point defines its height.

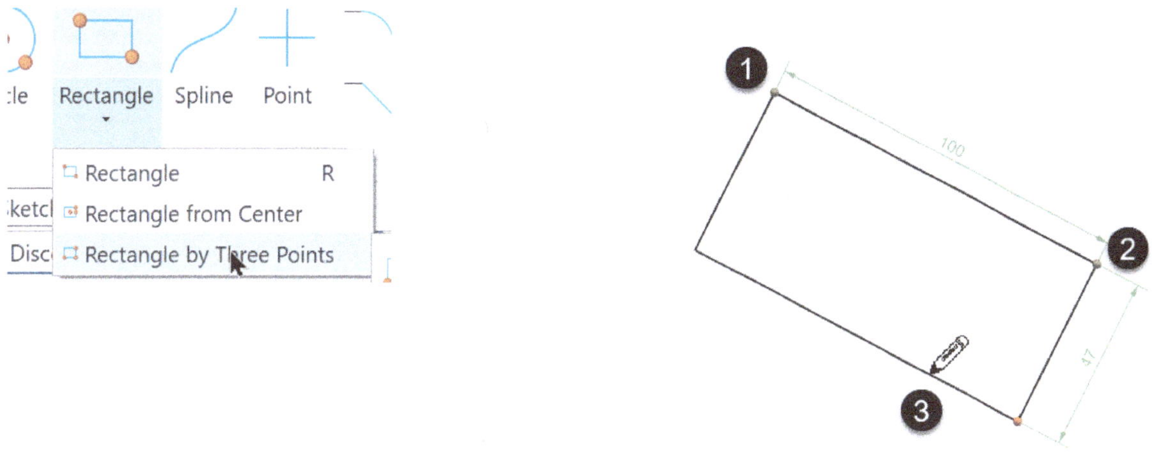

The other procedure to create a three points rectangle is to specify the first corner. Next, type-in a value in the **Angle** box. Press the Tab key and type-in values in the **Width** and **Height** boxes. Click on the graphics window to create the rectangle.

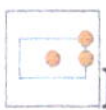Rectangle From Center command

This method creates a rectangle by defining three points: center of the rectangle, and mid and endpoints of the height. On the ribbon, click **Home > Curve > Rectangle** drop-down > **Rectangle From Center**. Specify the centerpoint of the rectangle, move the pointer, and click to define the width and orientation angle of the rectangle. Move the pointer and click to define the height of the rectangle.

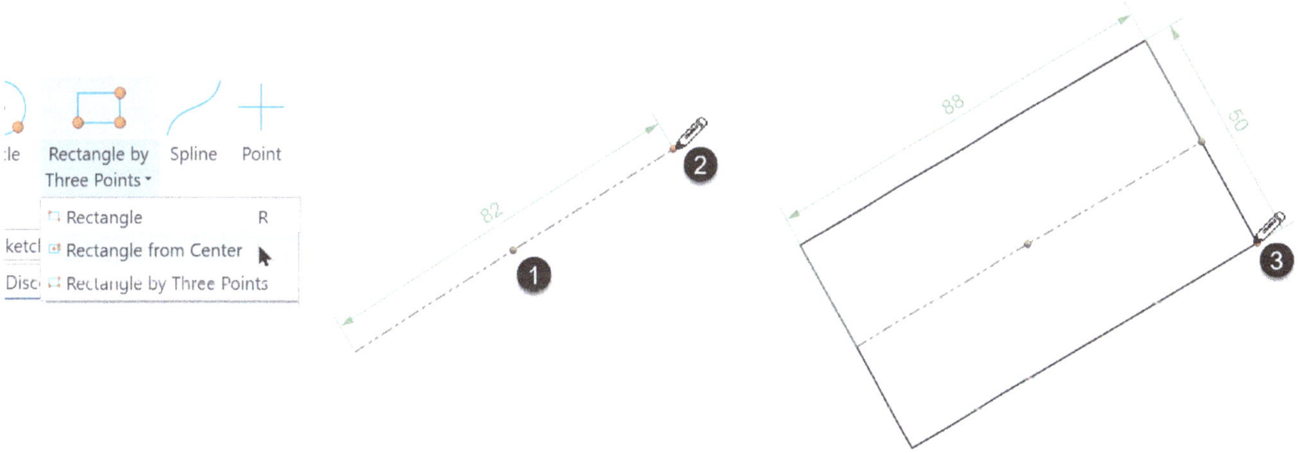

Creating Circles

You can a circle using two commands: **Circle** and **Three Point Circle.**

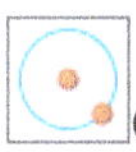Circle

This is the most common way to draw a circle. Activate the **Circle** command (click **Home > Curve > Circle** on the ribbon). Click to define the center point of the circle. Drag the pointer, and then click again to define the diameter of the circle.

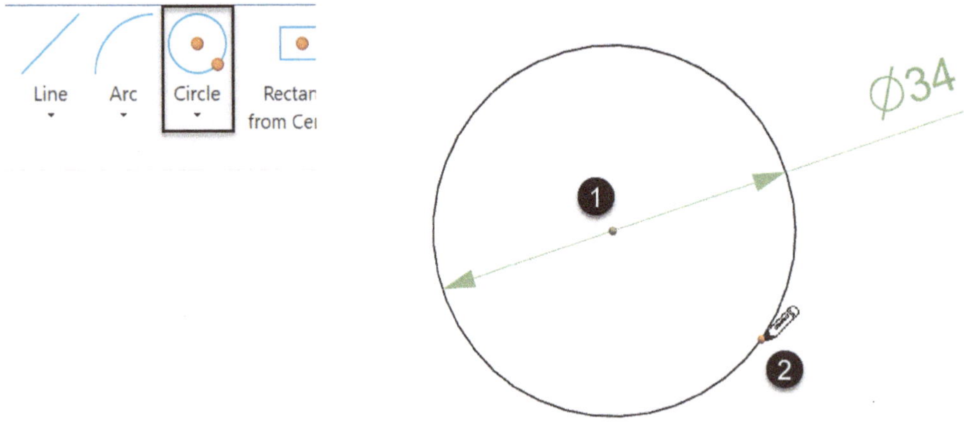

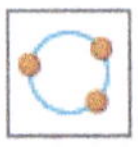 **Three Point Circle command**

This method creates a circle by using three points. Click **Home > Curve > Circle > Three Point Circle** on the ribbon. Select three points from the graphics window. You can also select existing points from the sketch geometry. The first two points define the location of the circle, and the third point defines its diameter.

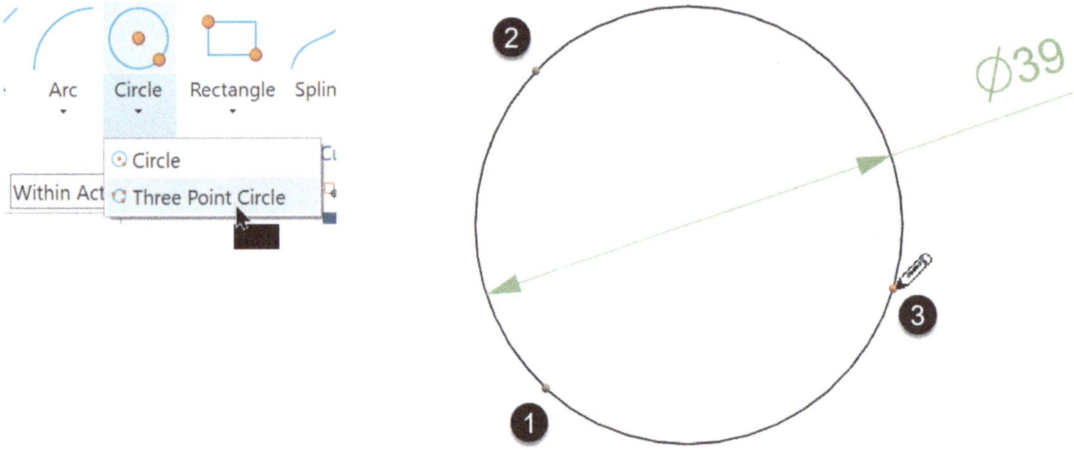

Polygon command

This command provides a simple way to create a polygon with any number of sides. This command is available in the **More Curve** gallery on the **Curve** group. To display the More Curve gallery, click the down arrow located on the bottom right corner of the **Curve** group. Next, select the **More Curve** gallery.

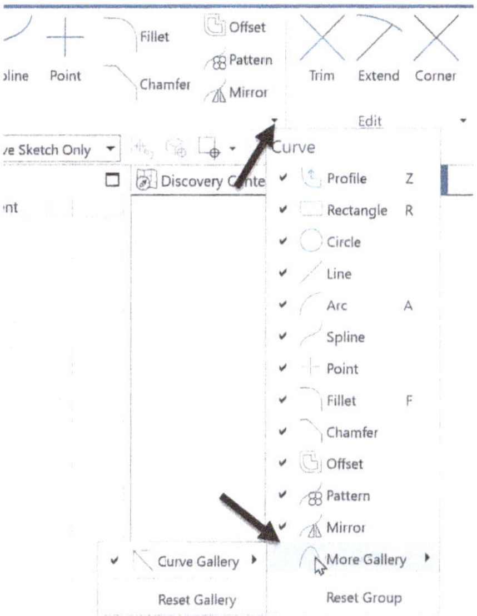

Activate the **Polygon** command (On the ribbon, click **Home > Curve > More > Polygon**) and click in the graphics window to define the center of the polygon. As you move the pointer away from the center, you will see a preview of the polygon. To change the number of sides of the polygon, click in the **Number of Sides** box on the dialog and enter a new number. Next, press the ENTER key to update the preview.

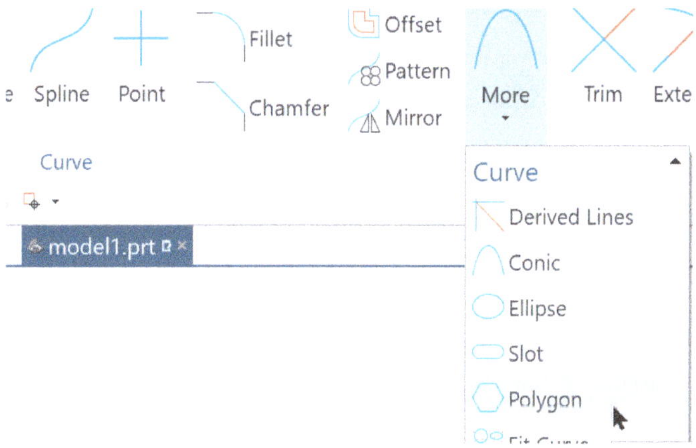

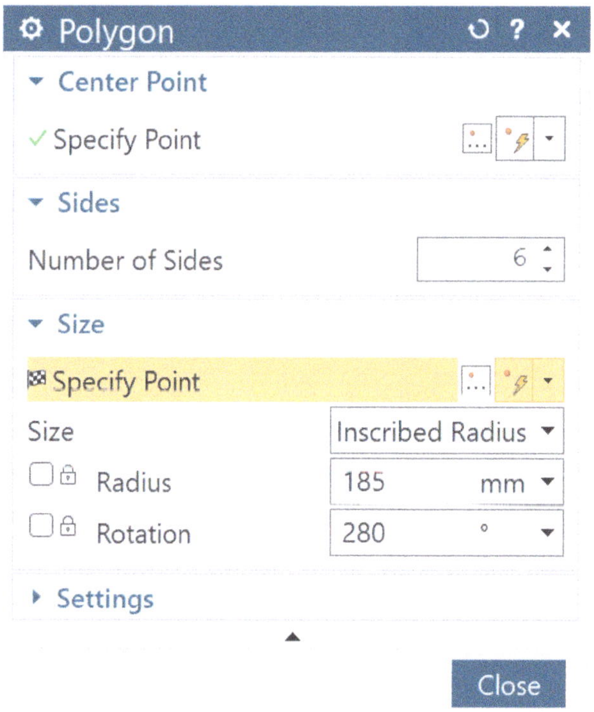

Now, you have to define the size of the polygon. On the dialog, the **Size** menu has three options to define the size of the polygon: **Inscribed Radius**, **Circumscribed Radius**, and **Side Length**. If you select **Inscribed Radius**, the pointer will be on one of the flat sides of the polygon. If you select **Circumscribed Radius**, a vertex of the polygon will be attached to the pointer. Click on the window to define the size and angle of the polygon. You can also define the size and angle of the polygon by entering values in the **Radius** and **Rotation** boxes on the dialog.

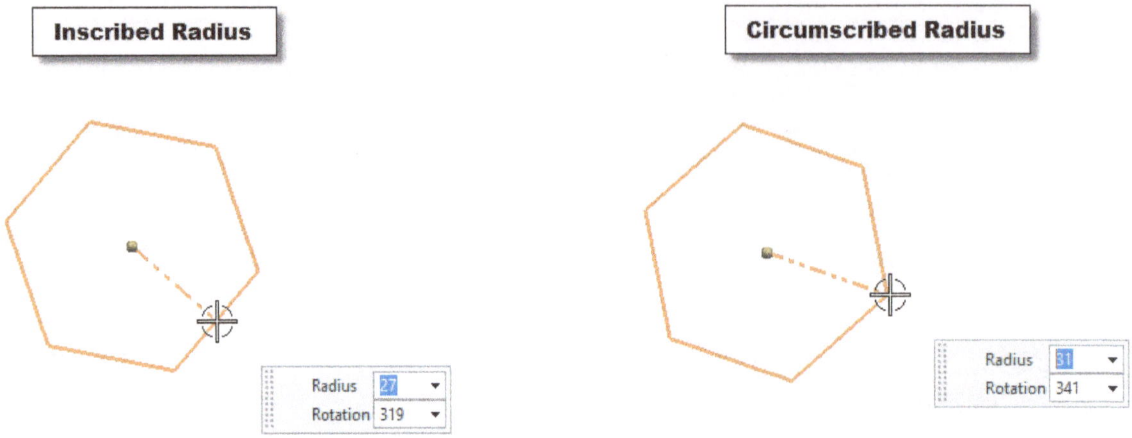

If you select **Side Length**, then you have to define the length and angle of one side, a polygon. Type-in values in the **Length** and **Rotation** boxes and press Enter to create the polygon.

Ellipse command

This command creates an ellipse using a center point, and major and minor axes. Activate this command (On the ribbon, click **Home > Curve > More > Ellipse**) and click to define the center of the ellipse. On the **Ellipse** dialog, type-in values in the **Major Radius** and **Minor Radius** boxes. You can also drag the arrows attached to the ellipse to define the major and minor radius.

On the dialog, type-in a value in the **Angle** box or drag the angle modifier on the ellipse to define the rotation angle of the ellipse. On the dialog, click **OK** to create the ellipse.

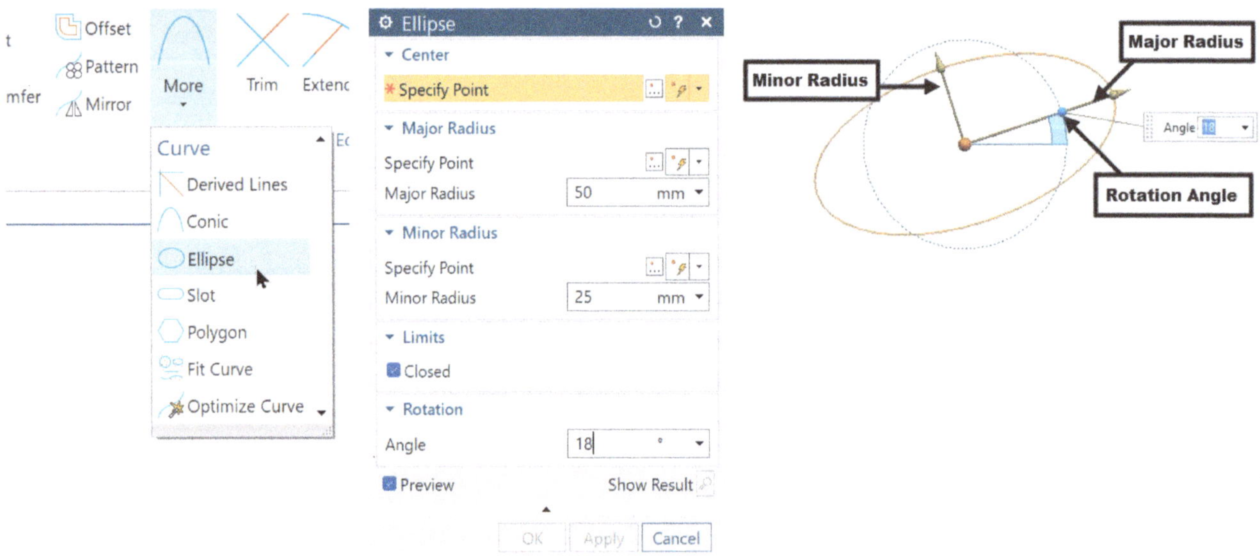

Studio Spline command

The **Studio Spline** command (on the ribbon, click **Home > Curve > Spline**) creates a smooth B-spline curve using two different methods: **Through Points** and **By Poles**. B-Splines are non-uniform curves, which are used to create smooth shapes.

The **Through Points** method creates a smooth spline passing through the points you select.

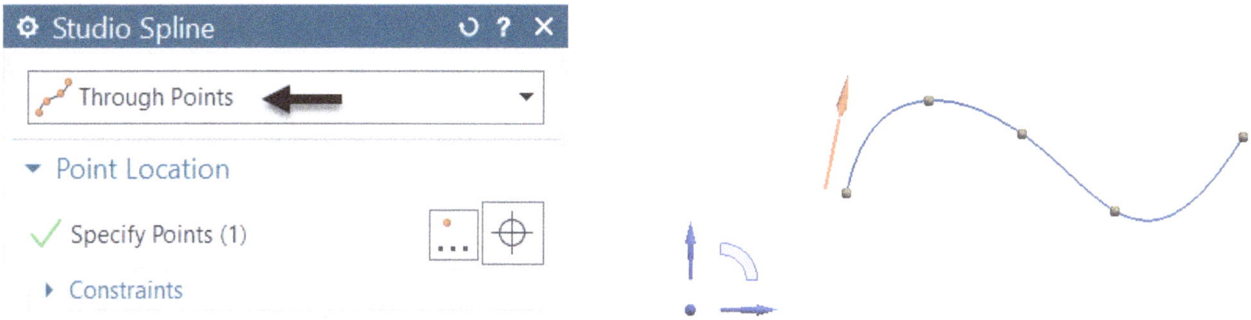

In the **By Poles** method, you will define various points called as poles. As you define the poles, grey lines are created connecting them. The spline will be drawn a tangent to these lines.

You can also use the **Close Curve** option to create a closed curve.

On the dialog, click **OK** to complete the studio spline.

Adding Dimensions to the Sketch

It is generally considered a good practice to ensure that every sketch you create is fully-constrained before creating solid features. The term 'fully-constrained' means that the sketch has a definite shape and size. You can fully-constrain a sketch by using dimensions and relations. When you select a sketch element, some dimensions will be displayed on them. These dimensions are called relaxed dimensions, and they do not have any control over the sketch geometry. If you want these dimensions to control the shape and size of the sketch geometry, you have to convert them into Driving dimensions. Driving dimensions are so named because they drive the geometry of the sketch.

You can add Driving dimensions to a sketch by selecting a sketch element, and then clicking on the dimensions attached to it. You can use this method to add all types of dimensions, such as length, angle, and diameter, and so on. The dimensions are displayed based on the geometry you select. For instance, to dimension a circle, click on the circle and select the diameter dimension attached to it; you will notice that a box pops up. Type-in a value in this box, and then press Enter to update the dimension.

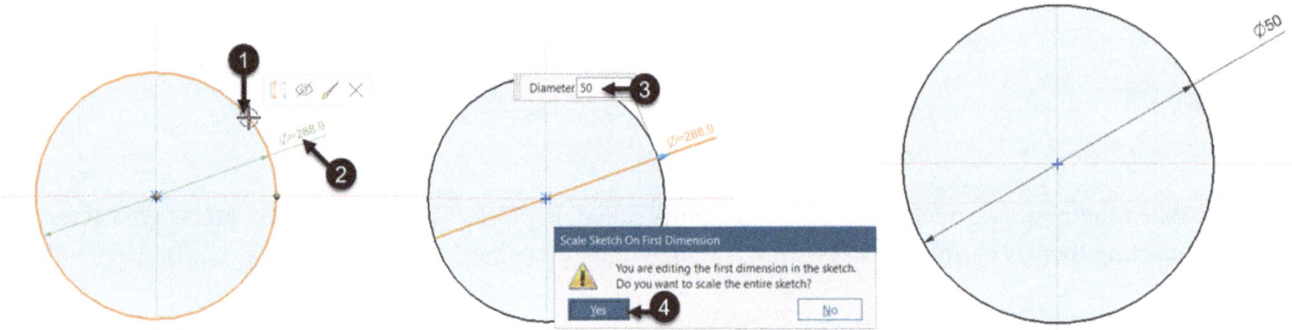

Click on a line if you want to add a dimension to it. Next, select the dimension attached to the line, and then type-in a value and press Enter; the dimension will be updated.

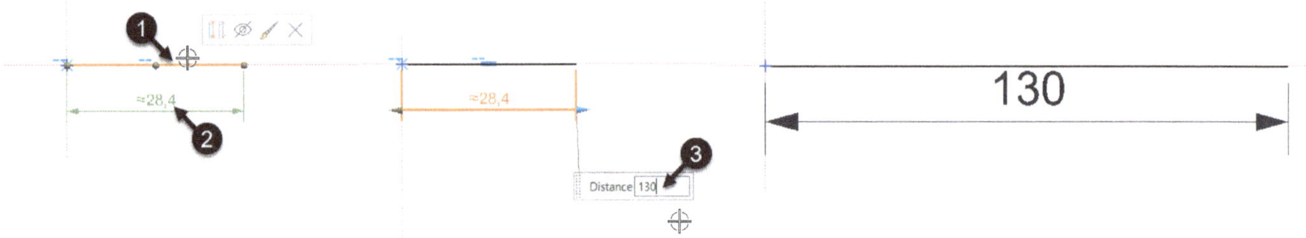

Linear Dimensions

NX allows you to create various types of linear dimensions. Select a line and click on the horizontal dimension. Next, type-in a value in the Dimension box and press ENTER; a horizontal dimension is created.

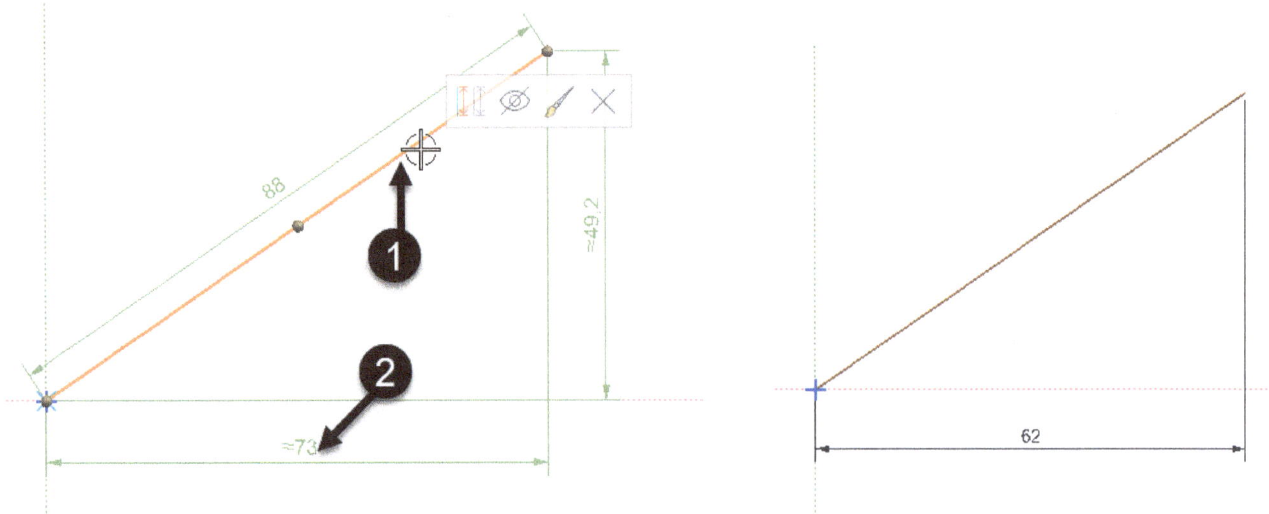

Select a line and click the vertical dimension. Next, type the dimension value and press ENTER; a vertical dimension will be created.

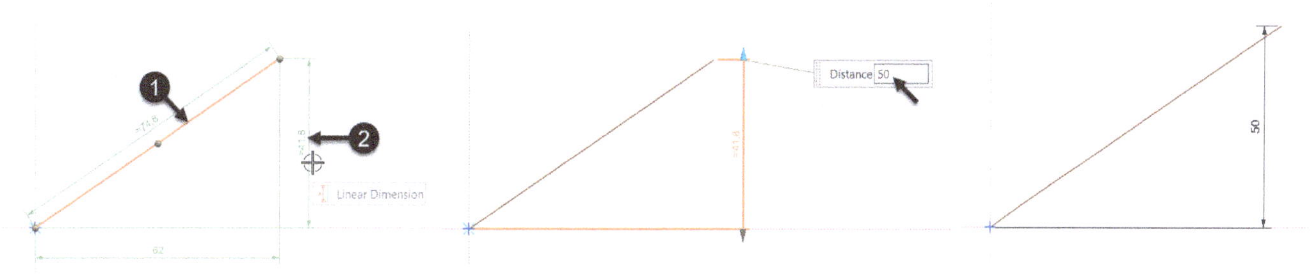

If you want the true length of the line, select the line and click on the parallel dimension. Next, double-click on the dimension, type-in a value in the box, and press Enter; the dimension is updated.

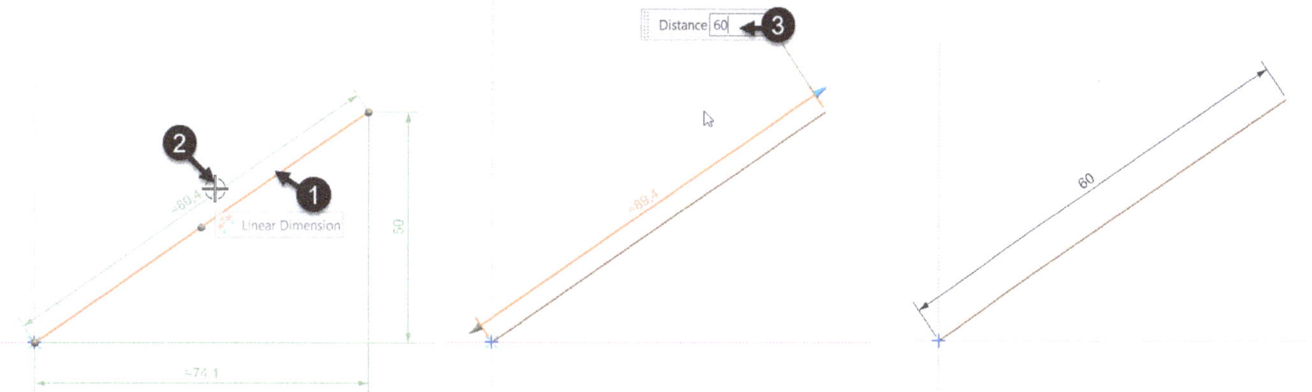

Angular Dimension

The procedure to create an angular dimension is similar to that of linear dimensions. Select two lines that are positioned at an angle to each other. Click on the angular dimension. Next, type-in a value, and press Enter.

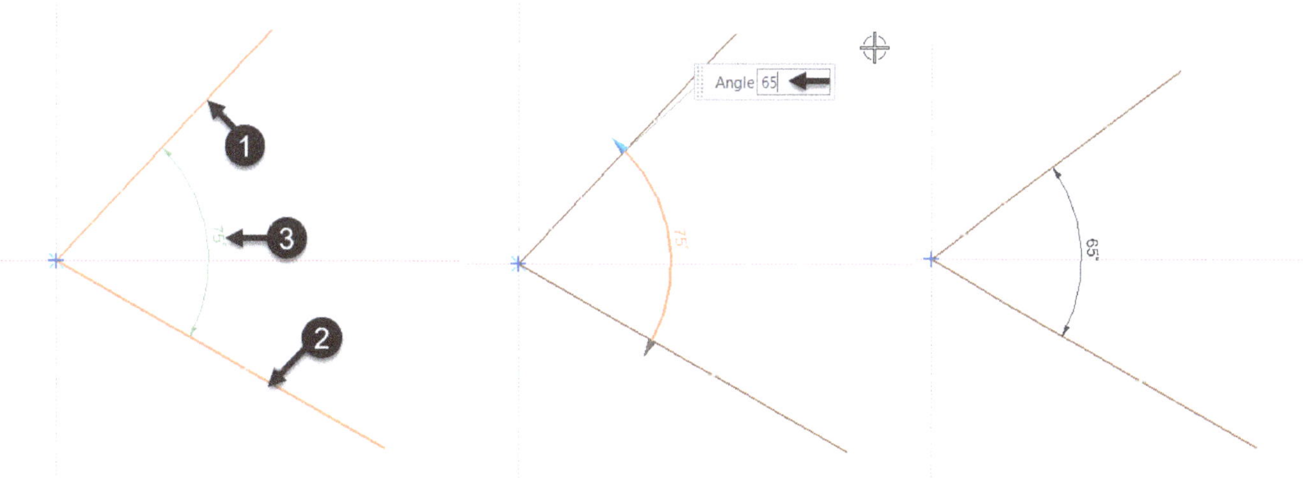

Over-constrained Sketch

When creating sketches for a solid or surface feature, NX will not allow you to over-constrain the geometry. The term 'over-constrain' means adding more dimensions than required. The following figure shows a fully constrained sketch. If you add another dimension to this sketch (e.g., diagonal dimension), the **Edit Dimension Value** message pops up. It shows that the dimension could not be edited, try relaxing the dimensions. Next, click

OK on the message box. The diagonal dimension will remain as the relaxed dimension, which means that the dimension value changes when you change the other dimensions.

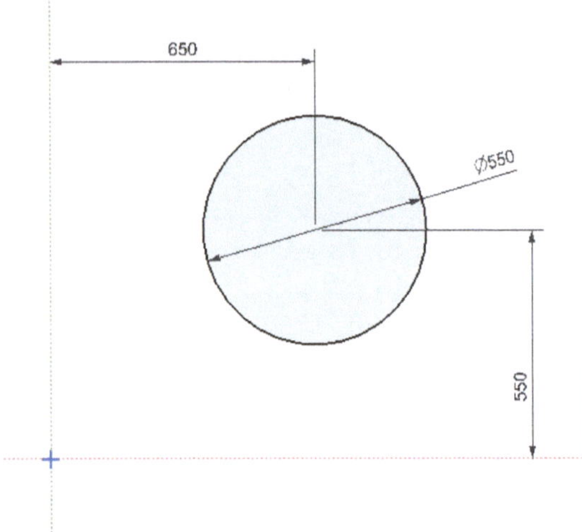

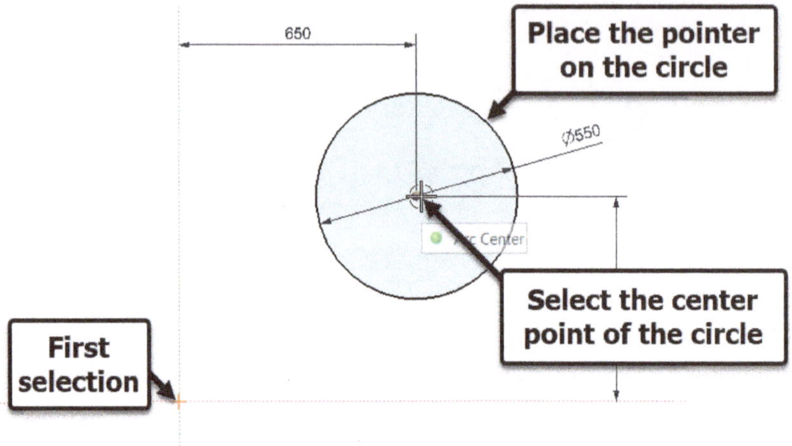

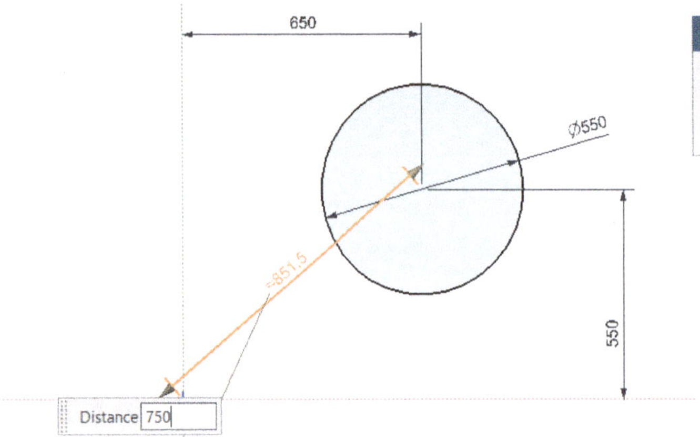

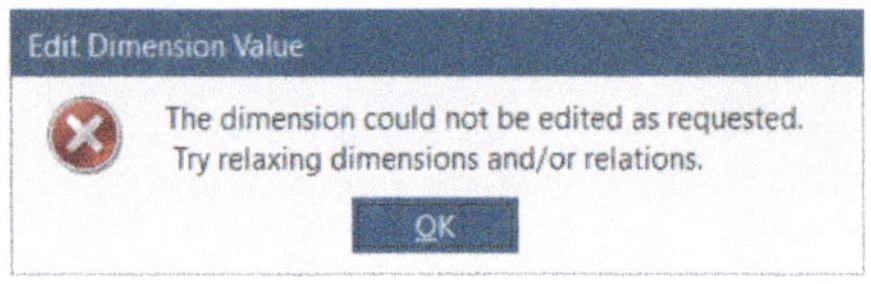

You can also make one of the dimensions as a Reference dimension. Click on the diagonal dimension and select **Convert to Reference** on the contextual toolbar. The reference dimension will be in brown. Now, if you change the value of the horizontal or vertical dimension, the reference dimension, along with the diagonal distance updates automatically. Also, note that the dimensions which are initially created will be driving dimensions, whereas the dimensions created after fully defining the sketch are driven dimensions.

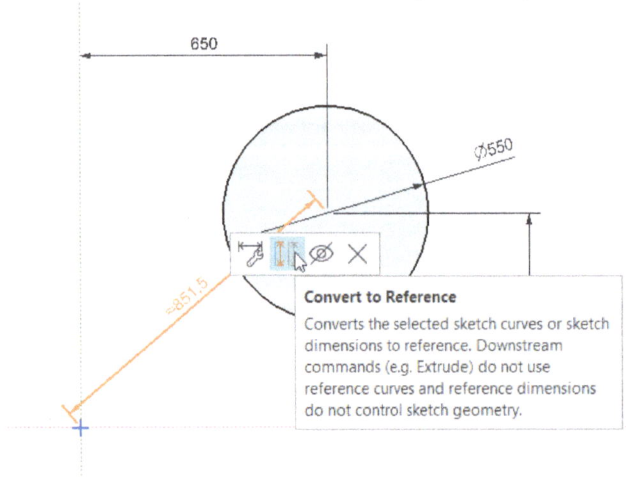

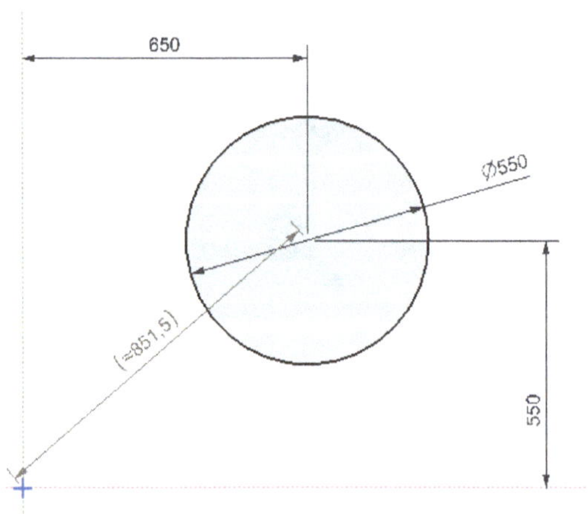

Geometric Relations

Geometric Relations are used to control the shape of a drawing by establishing relationships between the sketch elements. These geometric relations can be applied using the **Sketch Scene bar** displayed below the ribbon.

Make Coincident

This relation connects a point with another point. Select the points to be made coincident and click the **Make Coincident** icon on the **Sketch Scene bar**; the selected points will be connected.

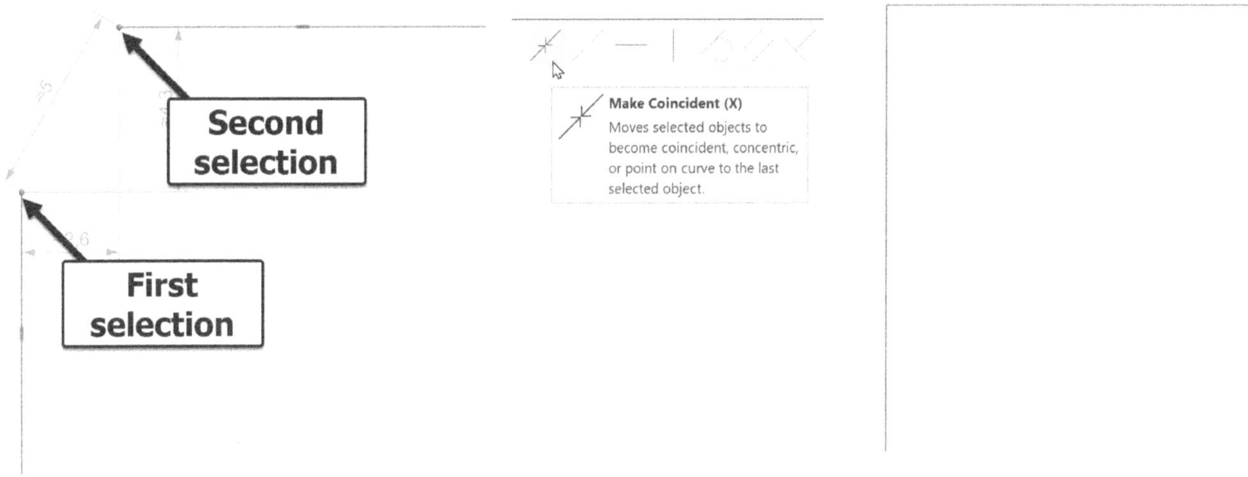

The **Make Coincident** relation can also be used to make a vertex or a point to be on a line, curve, arc, or circle. Select a curve and point and click the **Make Coincident** icon on the **Sketch Scene bar**. The point will lie on the curve or the curve extension.

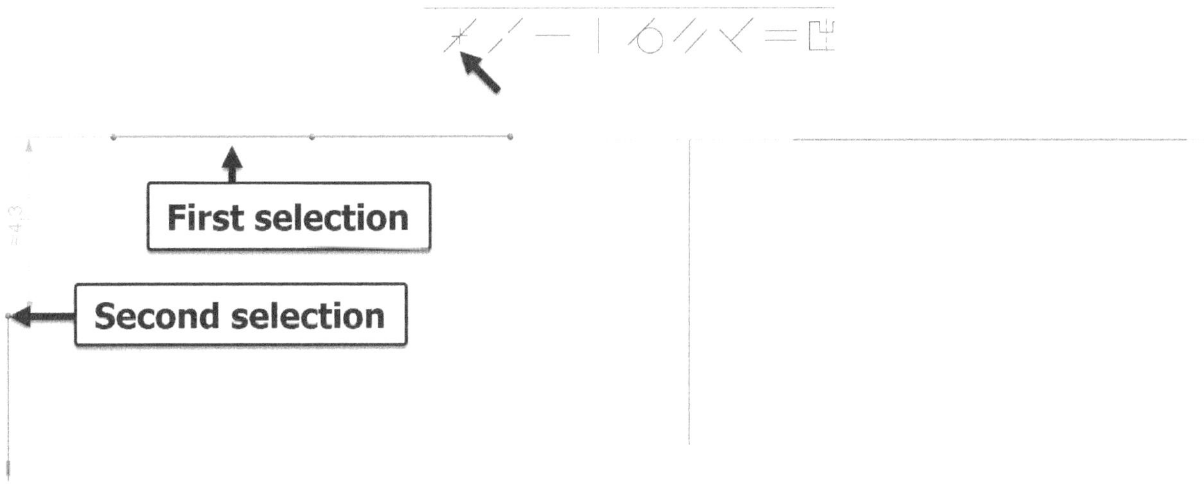

The **Make Coincident** relation can also be used to make the center points of arcs, circles, or ellipses coincident. Select a circle or arc from the sketch. Select another circle or arc, and then click **Make Coincident** on the **Sketch Scene bar**. The first circle/arc will be concentric with the second circle/arc.

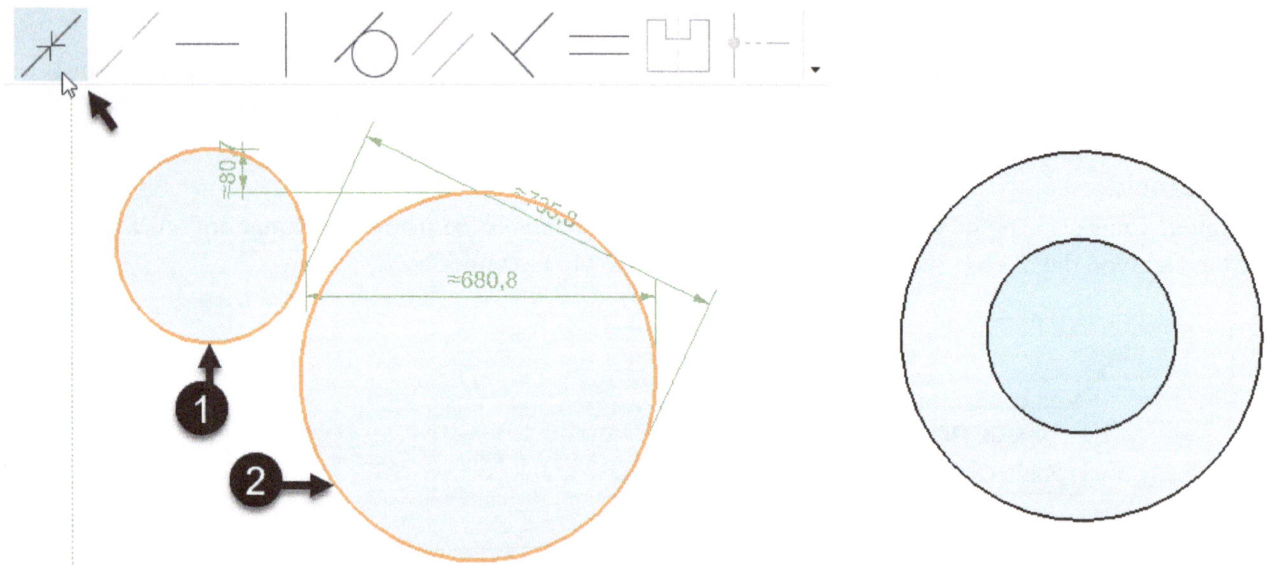

Make Tangent

This relation makes an arc, circle, or line tangent to another arc or circle. Select a circle, arc, or line. Select another circle, arc, or line. On the **Sketch Scene bar**, click the **Make Tangent** button; both the elements become tangent to each other.

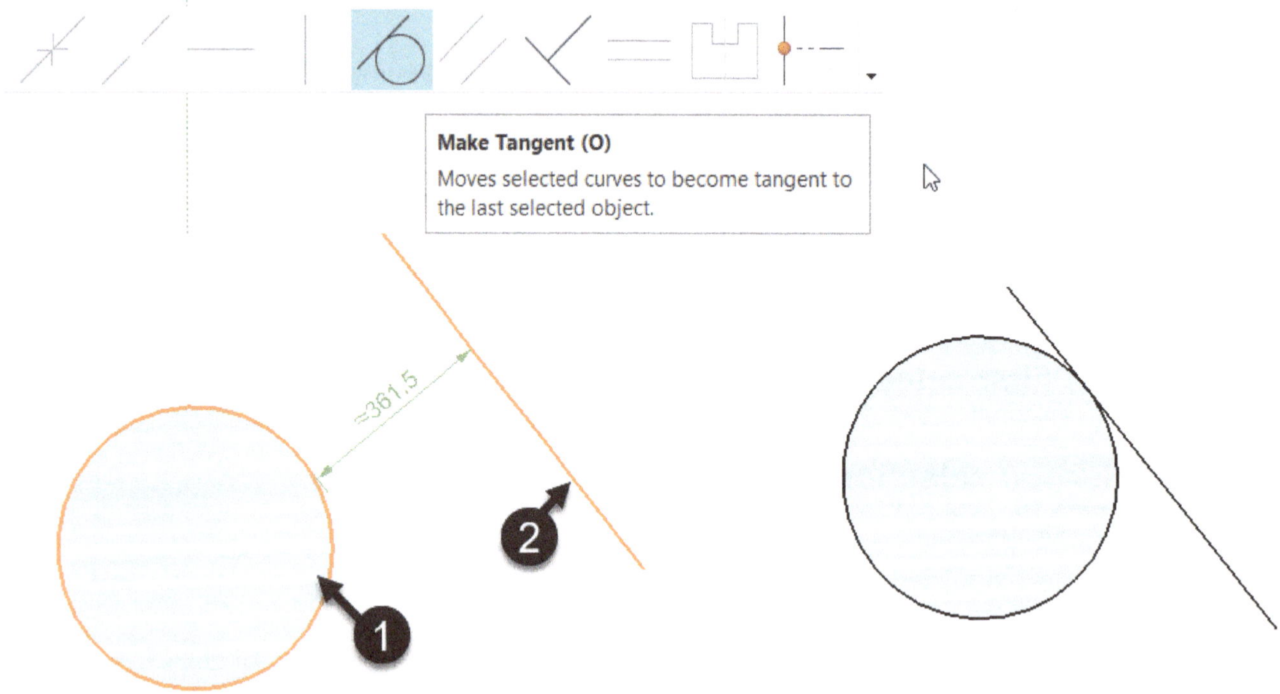

Make Parallel

This relation makes two lines parallel to each other. Select two lines from the sketch and click **Make Parallel** on the **Sketch Scene bar**. The under-constrained line is made parallel to the constrained line. For example, if you select a line with vertical relation and a free to move line, the free-to-move line becomes parallel to the vertical line.

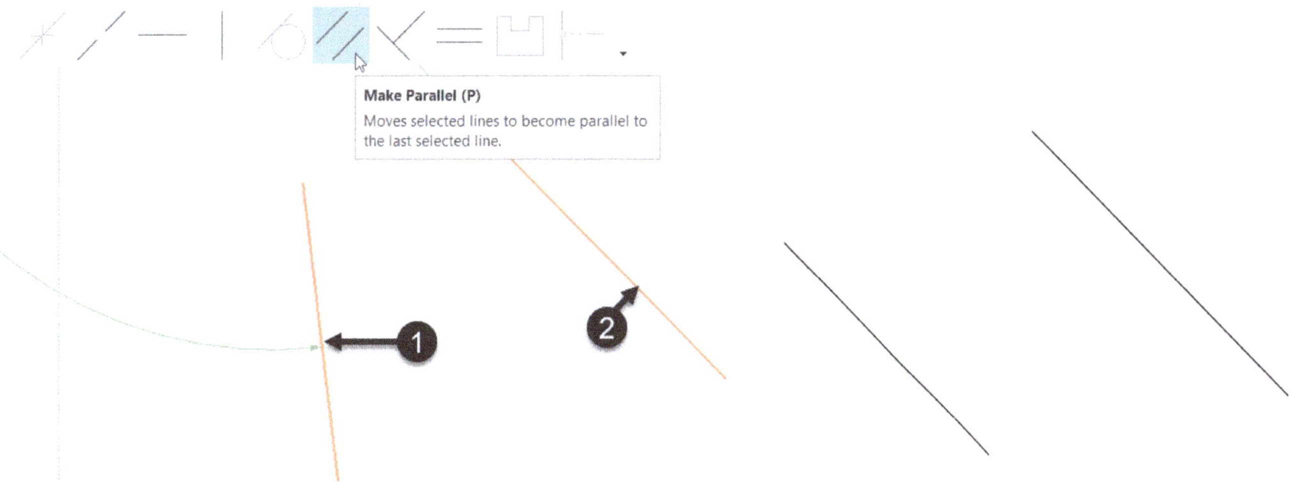

Make Horizontal

This relation makes a line horizontal. Select a free-to-move line, and then click **Make Horizontal** on the **Sketch Scene bar**; the line is made horizontal.

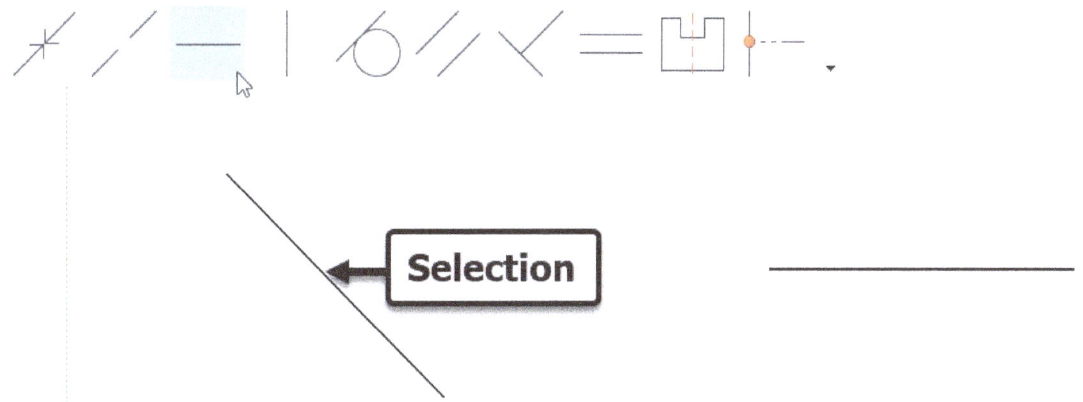

The **Make Horizontal** relation aligns the two selected points horizontally. Select the points to align horizontally, and then click the **Make Horizontal** button on the **Sketch Scene bar**.

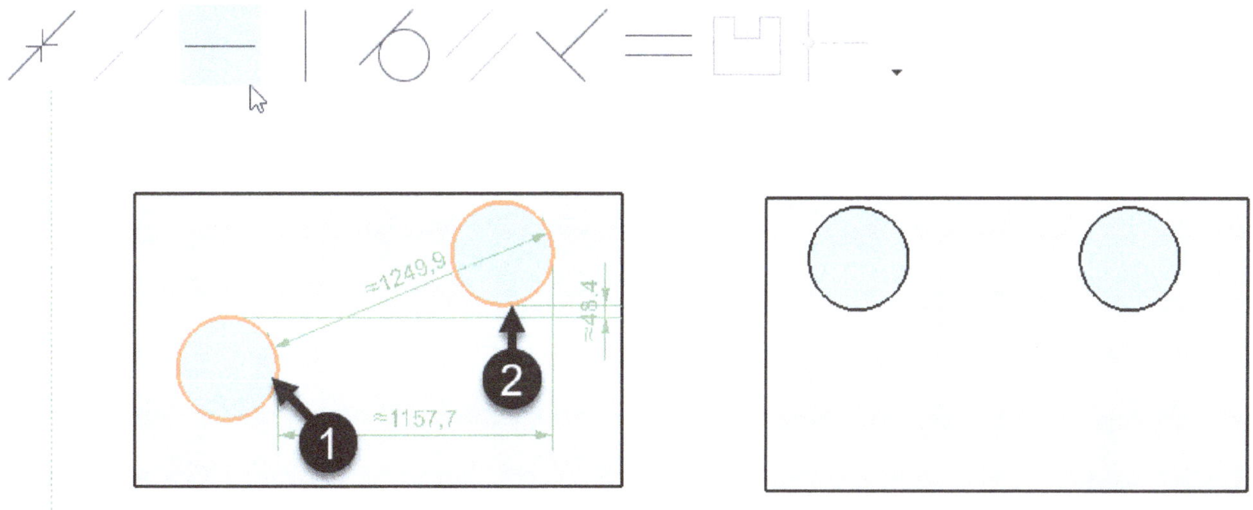

Make Vertical

This relation makes a line vertical. Select an under-constrained line, and then click **Make Vertical** on the **Sketch Scene bar**.

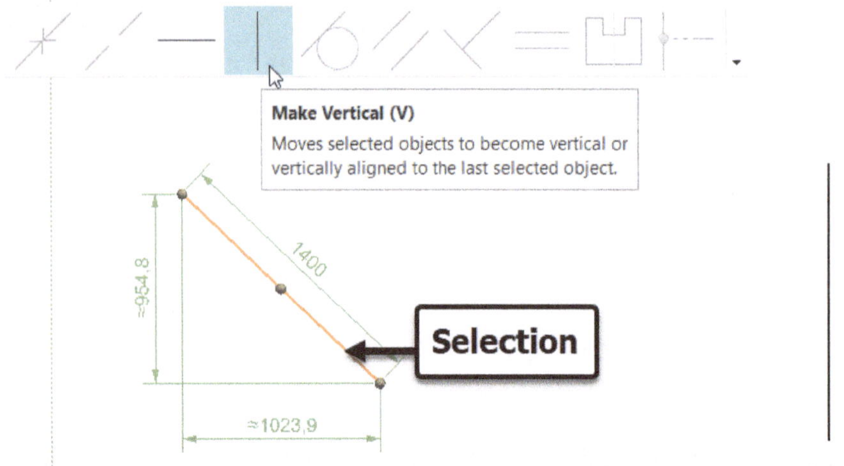

The **Make Vertical** relation aligns the two selected points vertically. Select the points to align vertically, and then click the **Make Vertical** button on the **Sketch Scene bar**.

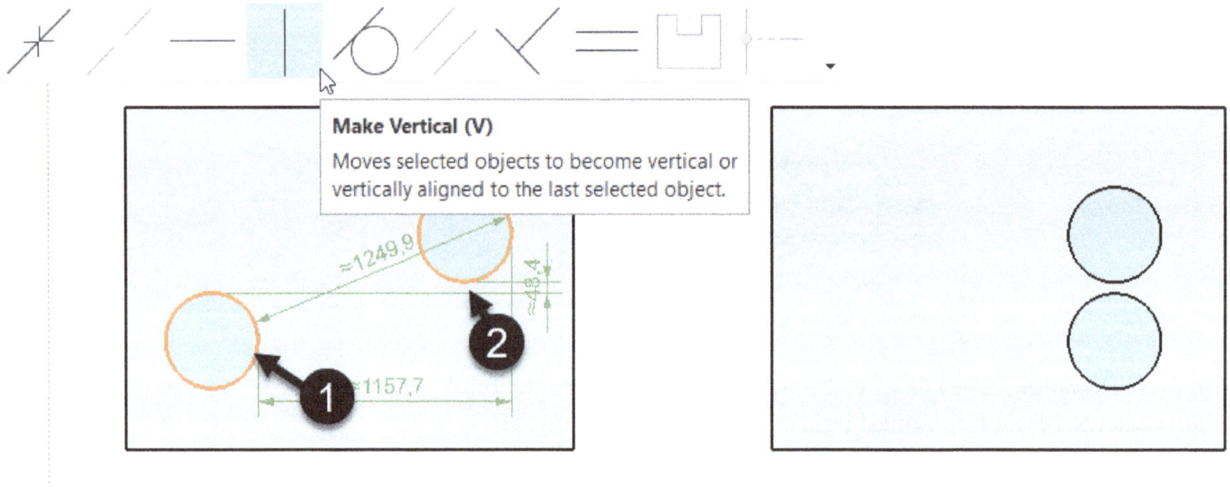

Make Equal

This relation makes two lines equal in length.

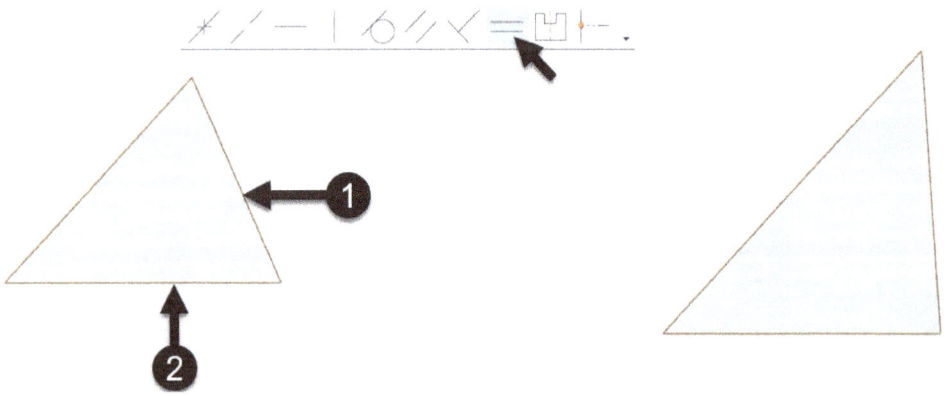

You can also make two circles or arcs equal in radius.

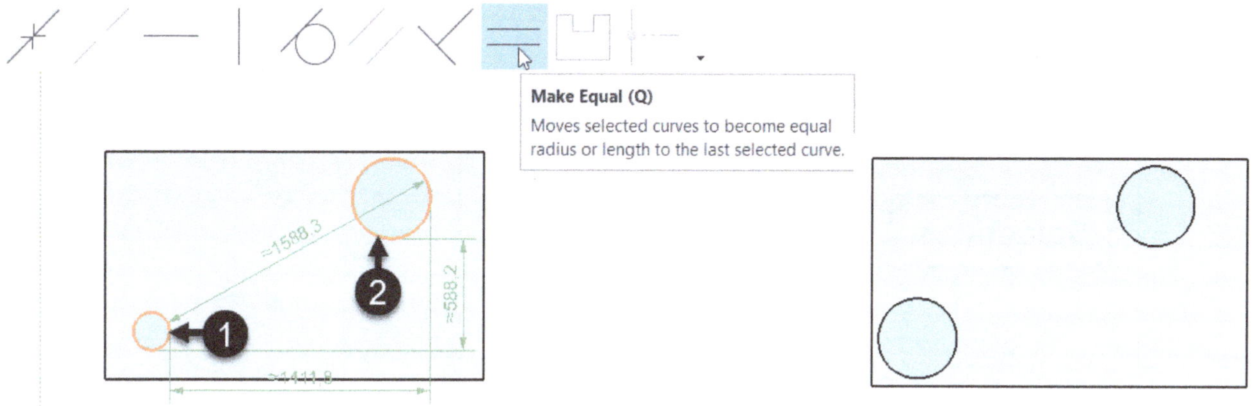

Make Perpendicular

This relation makes two lines perpendicular to each other. Select two lines from the sketch, and click the **Make Perpendicular** icon on the **Sketch Scene bar**. The two lines will be made perpendicular to each other.

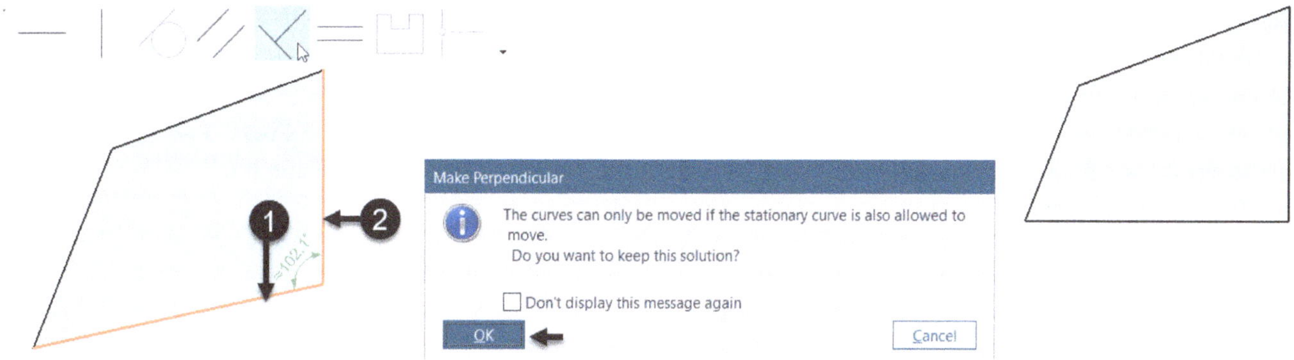

Make Collinear

This relation forces a line to be collinear to another line. The lines are not required to touch each other.

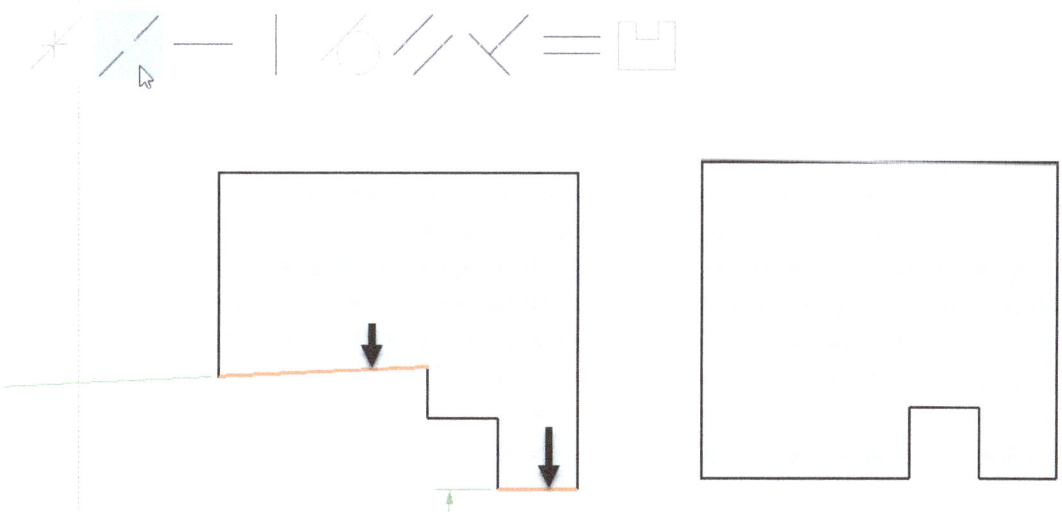

Make Midpoint Aligned

This relation forces a point or vertex to be aligned with the midpoint of a line. Click on a point or vertex, and then click on a line. Select **Make Midpoint Aligned** from the **Sketch Scene bar**.

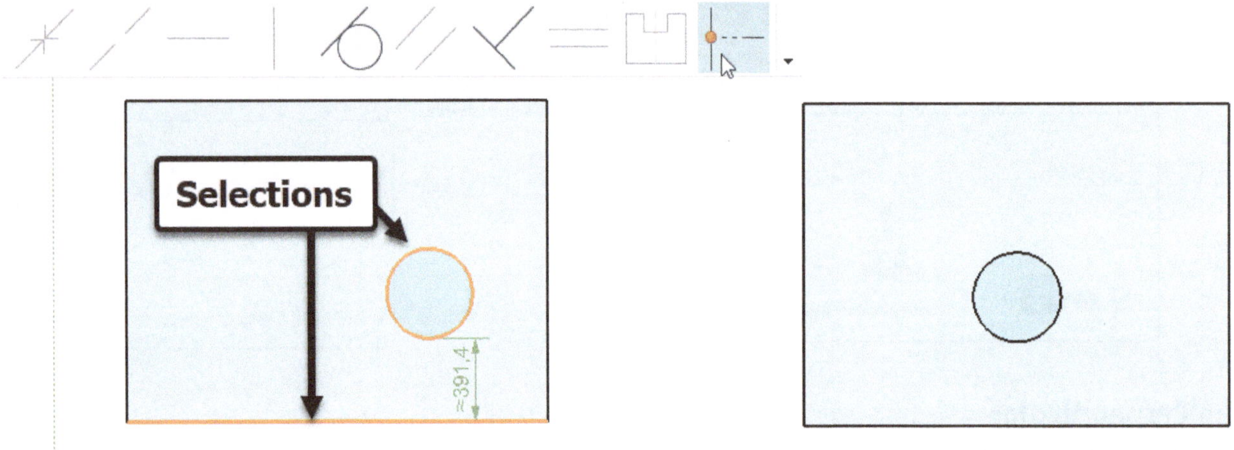

Make Uniform scale

This relation scales a spline in both horizontal and vertical direction. By default, this relation is not displayed on the **Sketch Screen bar**. You need to turn ON the **Create Persistent Relations** option to display this relation on the **Sketch Screen bar**. To do this, click the down-arrow locate on the **Solve** group and select the **Options** option; the **Options** gallery is displayed on the **Solve** group. Next, click **Home > Solve > Options > Create Persistent Relations** on the ribbon. Select a spline and click **Make Uniform scale** on the **Sketch Scene Bar**.

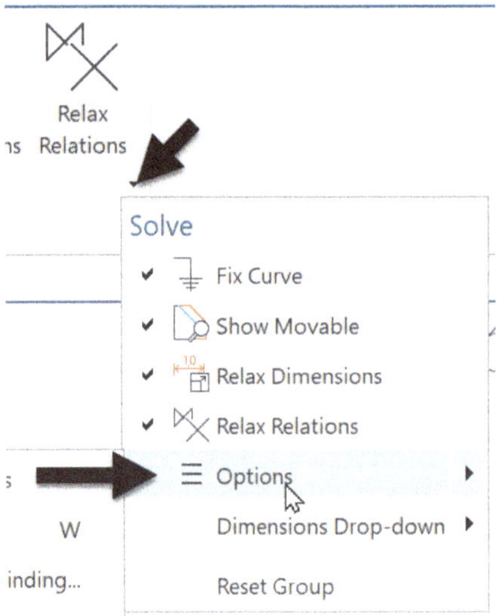

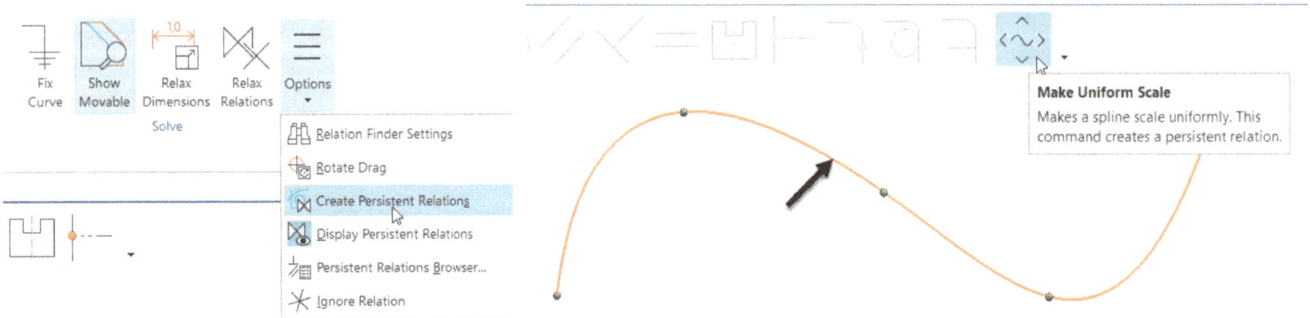

Select the two end points of the spline and change the dimension value; the spline is scaled uniformly in both horizontal and vertical directions.

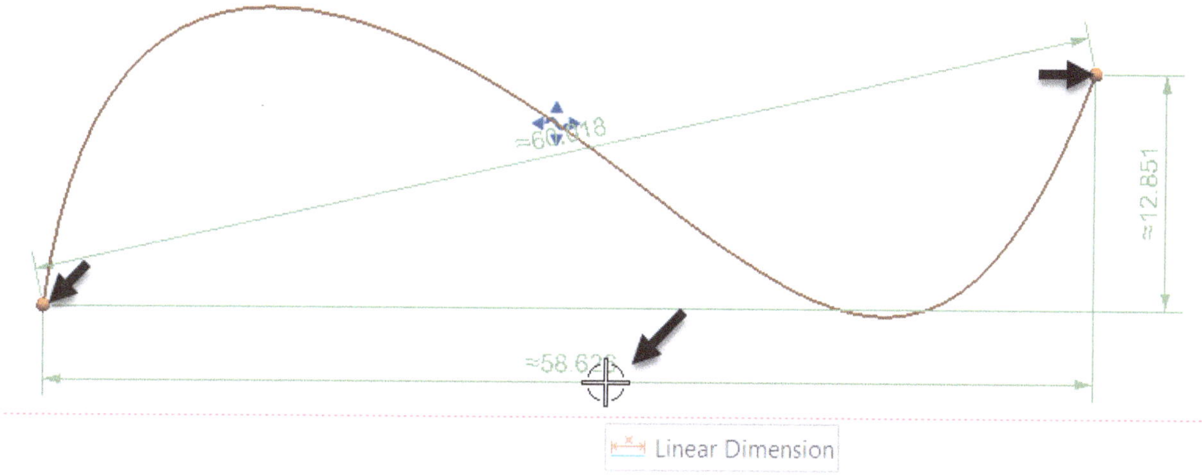

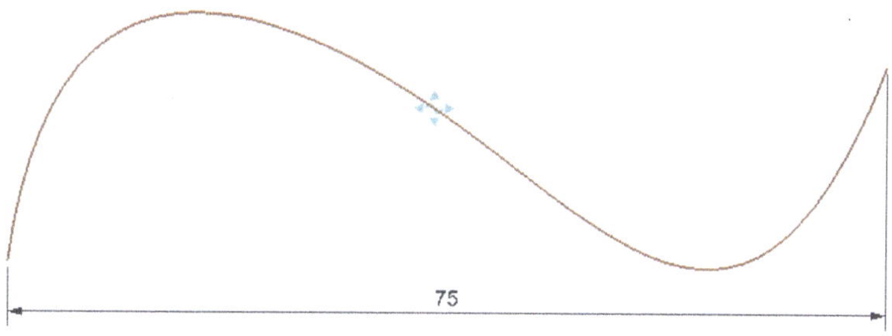

Make Symmetric

This command makes two objects symmetric about a line. The objects will have the same size, position, and orientation about a line. Click on the first and second objects. Next, select the line of symmetry. On the **Sketch Scene bar**, click the **Make Symmetric** icon. The two objects will be made symmetric about the line of symmetry. Also, the line of symmetry is converted into a reference object.

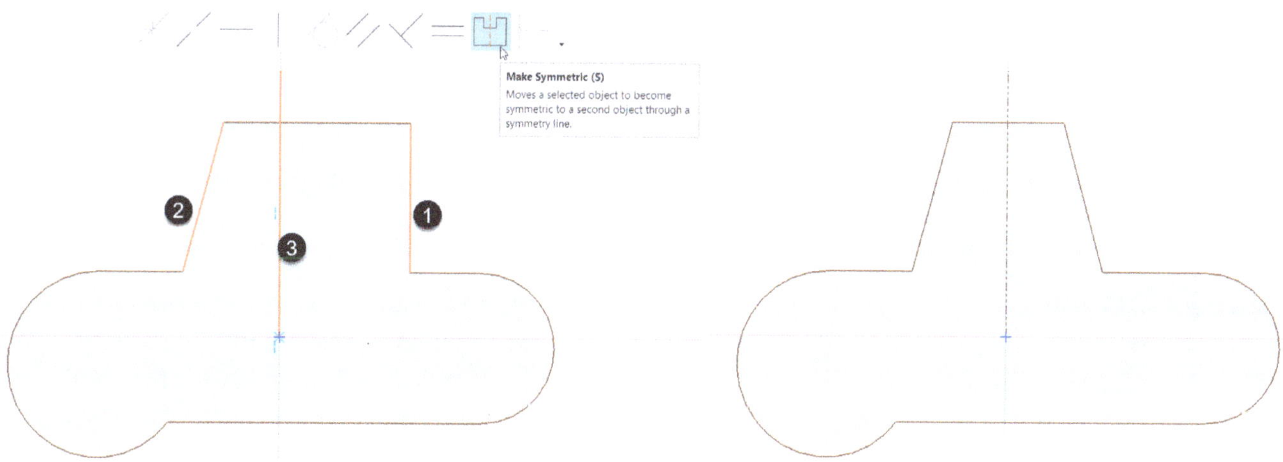

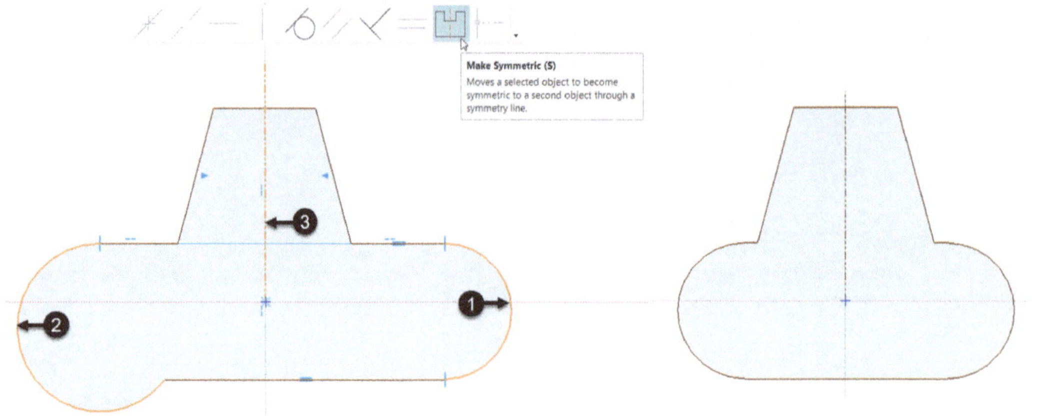

Relax Dimensions

The **Relax Dimensions** command allows you to change the dimension values without affecting the relations. For example, if you want to drag the small circle in the figure given below, click the **Relax Dimensions** button in the **Solve** group of the **Home** ribbon tab. Next, click and drag the small circle and notice that the linear dimension associated with it changes its value without affecting the relations.

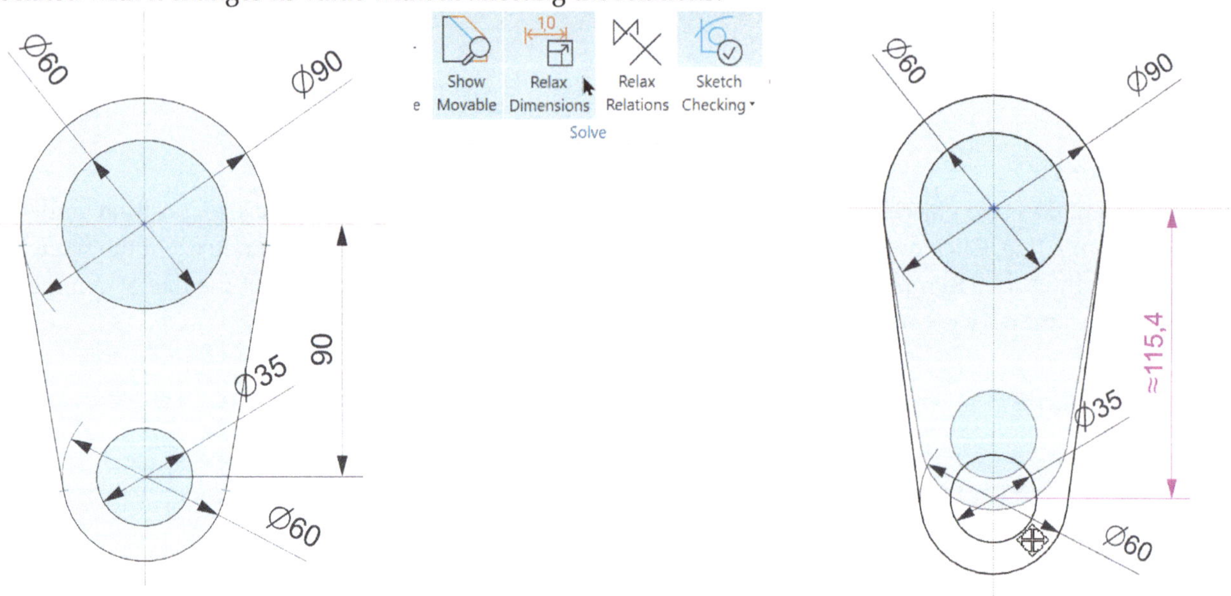

Relax Relations

The **Relax Relations** command allows you to make changes to the sketch without affecting the dimensions. However, when you modify the sketch, the relations are affected. For example, if you want to drag the small circle in the figure given below, click the **Relax Relations** button in the **Solve** group of the **Home** ribbon tab. Next, click and drag the small circle and notice that the **Coincident** relation associated with the circle is ignored. However, the linear dimension remains unaffected.

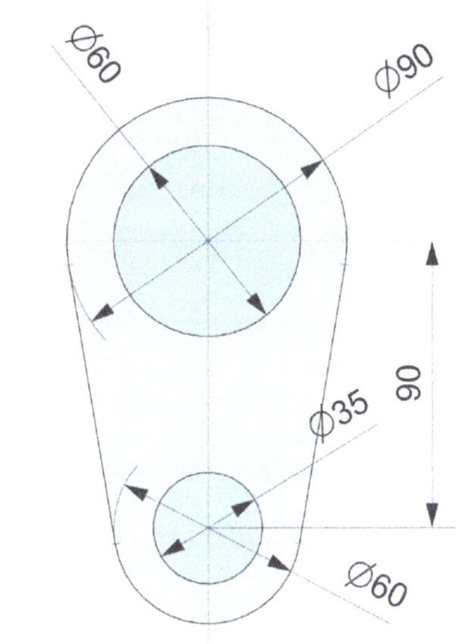

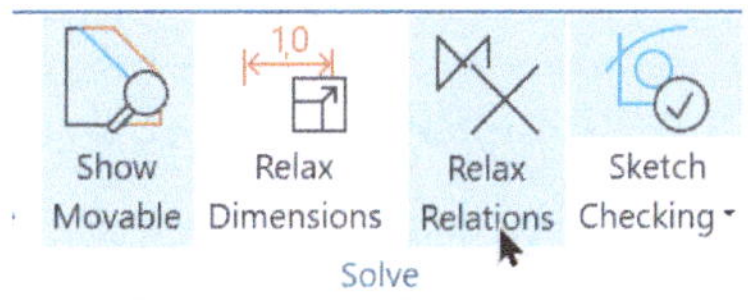

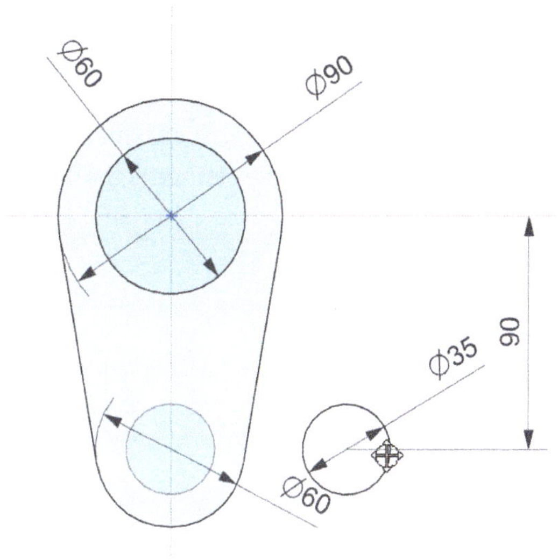

Show Movable

The **Show Movable** command identifies which elements of a sketch are **under-constrained** and can still move. This helps you check the level of constraint in your sketch and ensures that it is properly defined before moving into 3D features.

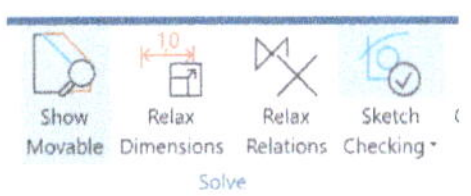

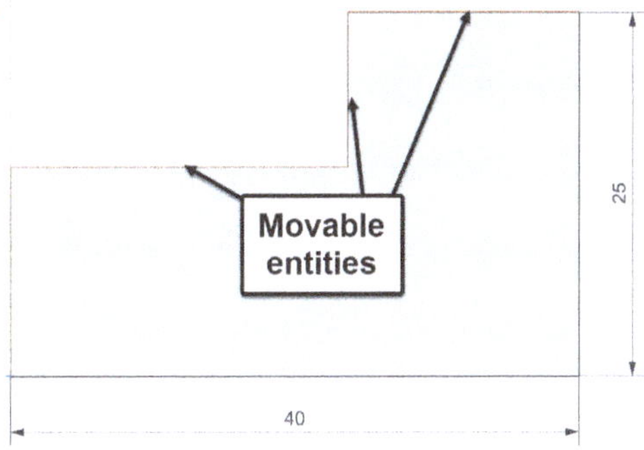

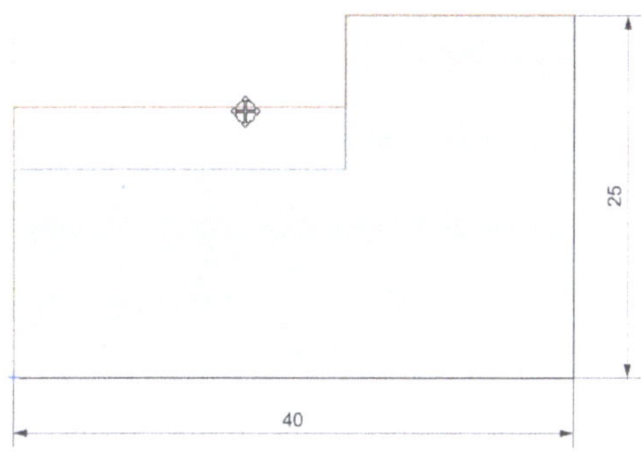

Convert to Reference

This command converts a sketch element into a reference element. Reference elements support you in creating a sketch of the desired shape and size. To convert a sketch element to the reference element, click on it and select **Convert to Refcrcncc** on the contextual toolbar. You can also convert it back to a sketch element by clicking on it and selecting **Convert from Reference**.

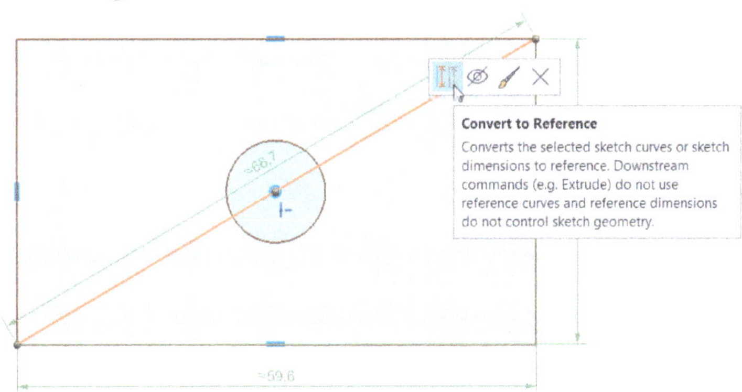

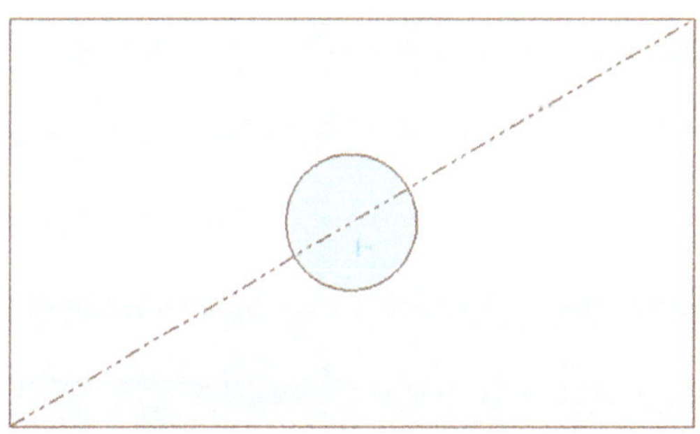

The Fillet command

This command rounds off sharp corners formed by the intersection of two lines, arcs, circles, and vertices of rectangles or polygons. To activate this command, go to the ribbon and click on **Home > Curve > Fillet**. Next, select the ends of the elements that you want to fillet. Enter a value for the radius in the '**Radius**' box and press Enter on your keyboard. Note that the elements to be filleted need not necessarily touch each other

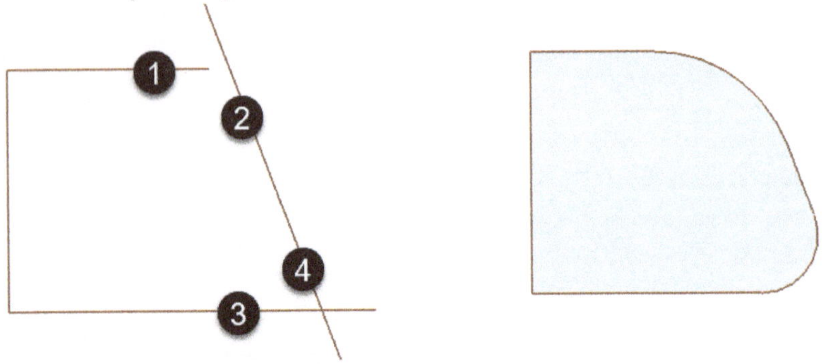

To apply a fillet to the elements, you can drag the pointer across them.

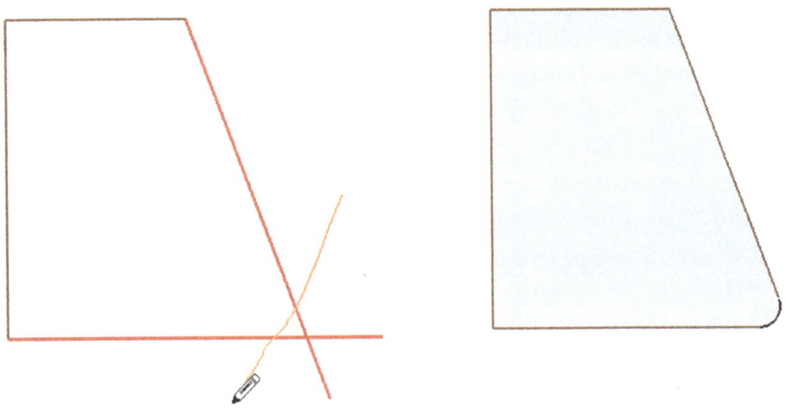

By default, the fillet radius extends or trims the elements as necessary. However, if you prefer not to trim or extend the elements, select the **Untrim** option on the dialog. Then, choose the elements forming a corner, move the pointer, and create the fillet by clicking. Note that the elements are not trimmed at the corner.

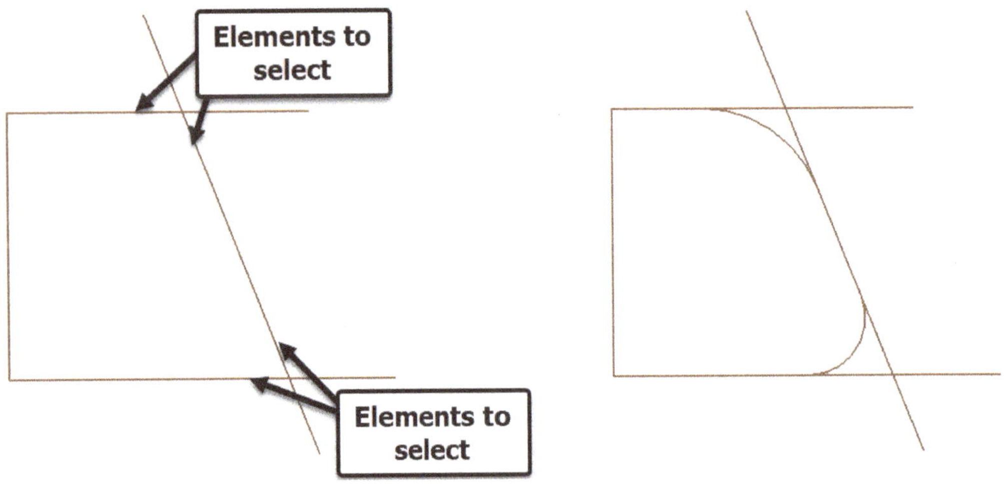

Use the **Delete Third Curve** option, if you want to create the fillet between three curves.

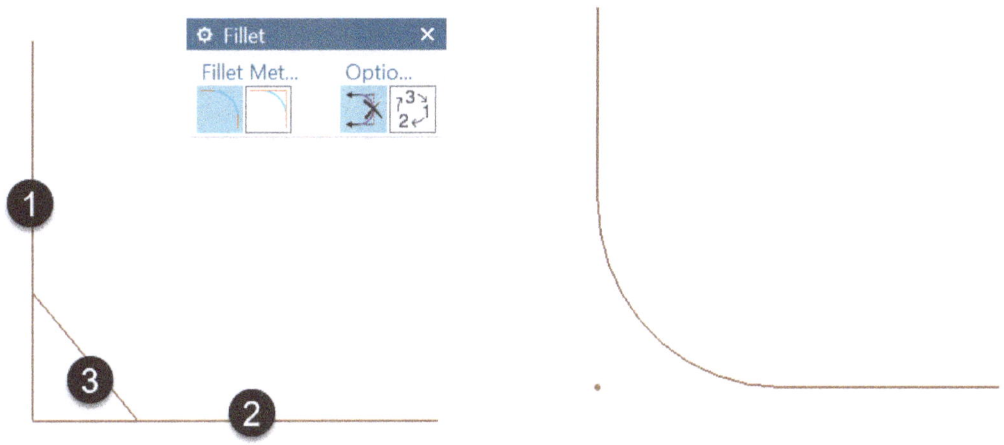

Use the **Create Alternate Fillet** option, if you want an alternative solution.

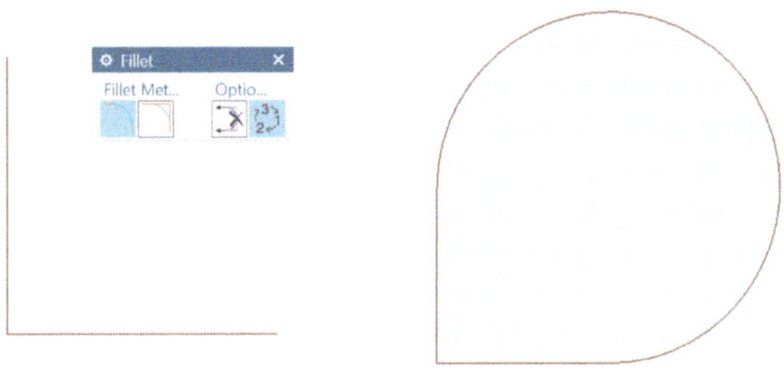

The Chamfer command

This command replaces a sharp corner with an angled line. Activate this command (On the ribbon, click **Home > Curve > Chamfer**) and select the elements' ends to be chamfered. Type-in the chamfer angle in the **Distance** box and press Enter on the Keyboard.

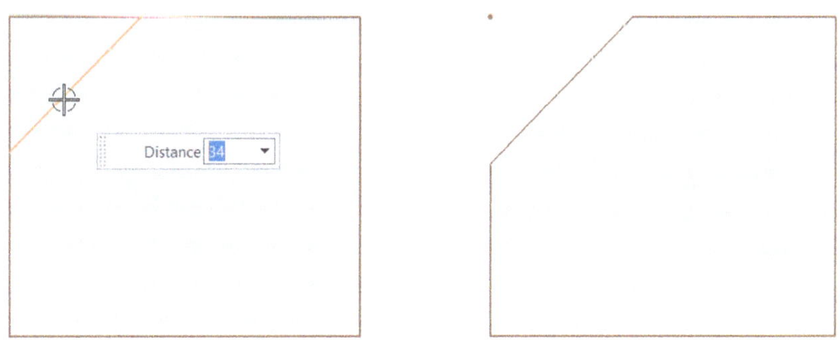

The Extend command

This command extends elements such as lines, arcs, and curves until they intersect another element called the boundary edge. Activate this command (On the ribbon, click **Home > Edit > Extend**) and click on the element to extend. It will extend up to the next element.

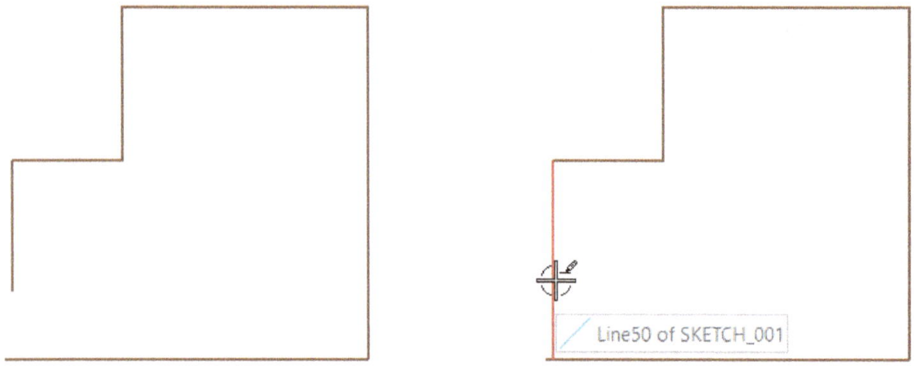

The Trim command

This command trims the end of an element back to the intersection of another element. Activate this command (On the ribbon, click **Home > Edit > Trim**) and click on the element or elements to trim. You can also drag the pointer across the elements to trim.

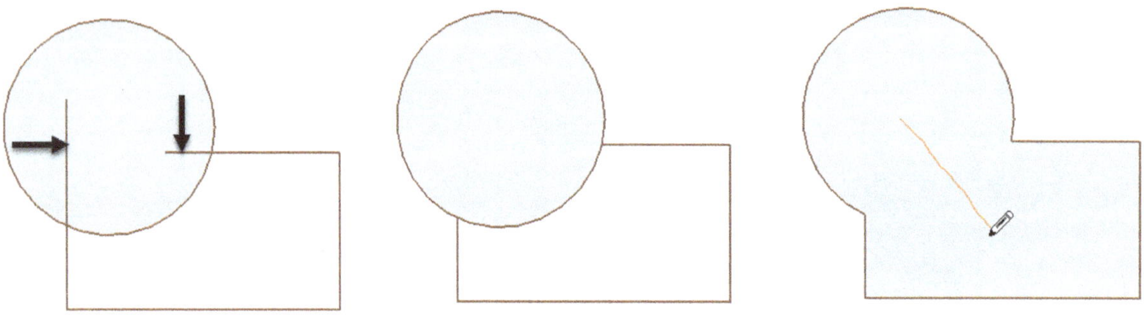

The Corner command

This command trims and extends elements to form a corner. Activate this command (On the ribbon, click **Home > Edit > Corner**) and select two intersecting elements. The selected elements are trimmed and extended to form a closed corner.

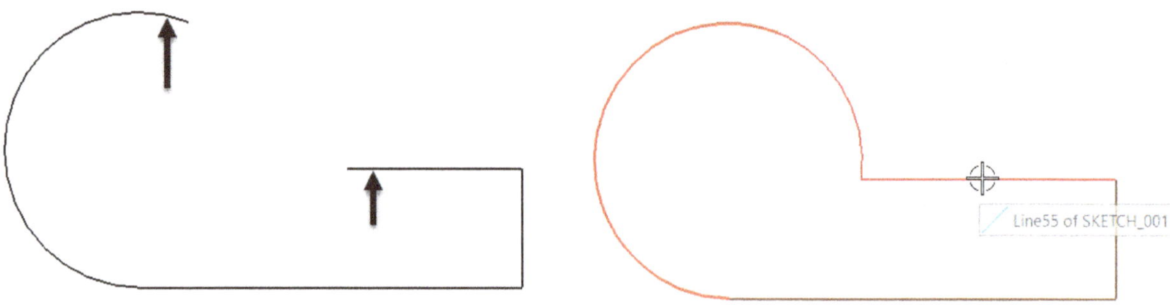

The Offset command

This command creates a parallel copy of a selected element or chain of elements. Activate this command (on the ribbon, click **Home > Curve > Offset**) and select an element or chain of elements to offset. After selecting the element(s), type a value in the **Distance** box. On the **Offset Curve** dialog, click the **Reverse Direction** button to reverse the side of the offset. Check the **Symmetric Offset** option to create a parallel copy on both sides. Set the **Cap Options** to **Arc Cap** to create arcs at the corners. Check the **Create Persistent Relation** option under the **Settings** section if you want to maintain a relation between the original and the offset curve. You can also enable the **Create Dimension** option to automatically place a dimension showing the offset distance in the sketch. Finally, click **OK** and the parallel copy of the selected elements will be created.

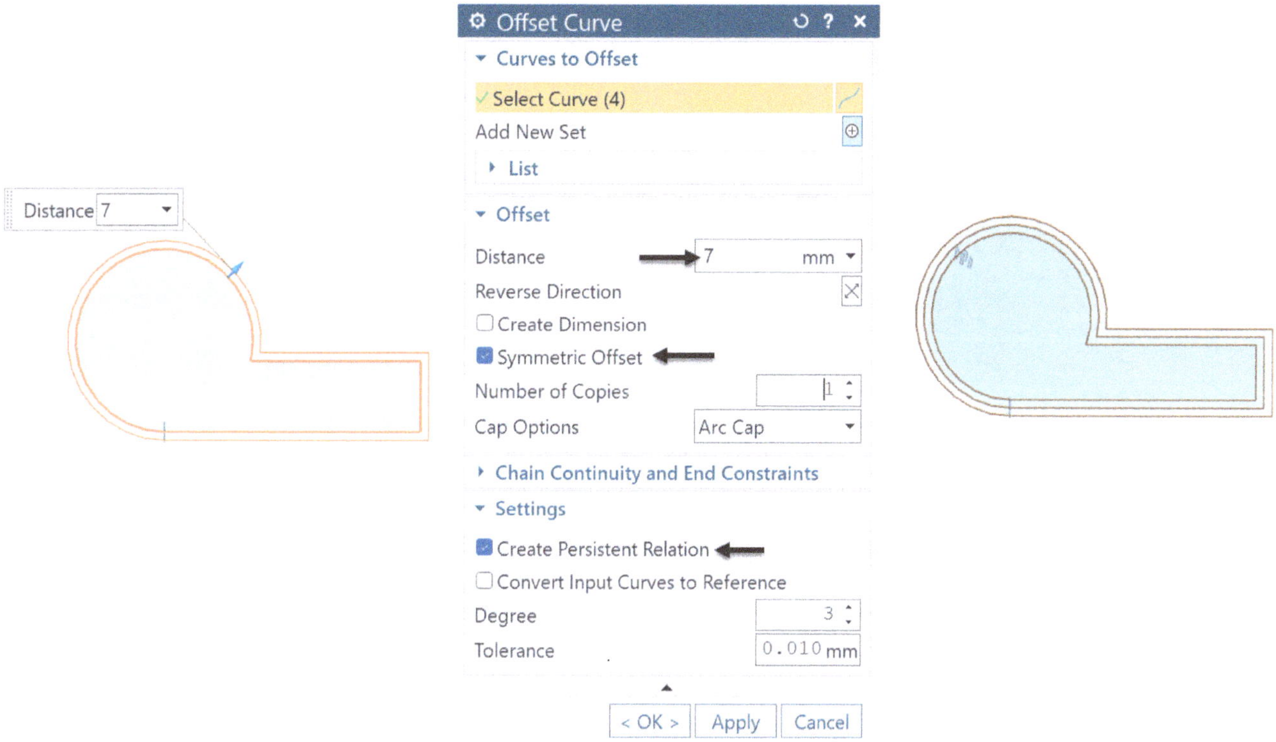

Examples

Example 1 (Millimeters)

In this example, you draw the sketch shown below.

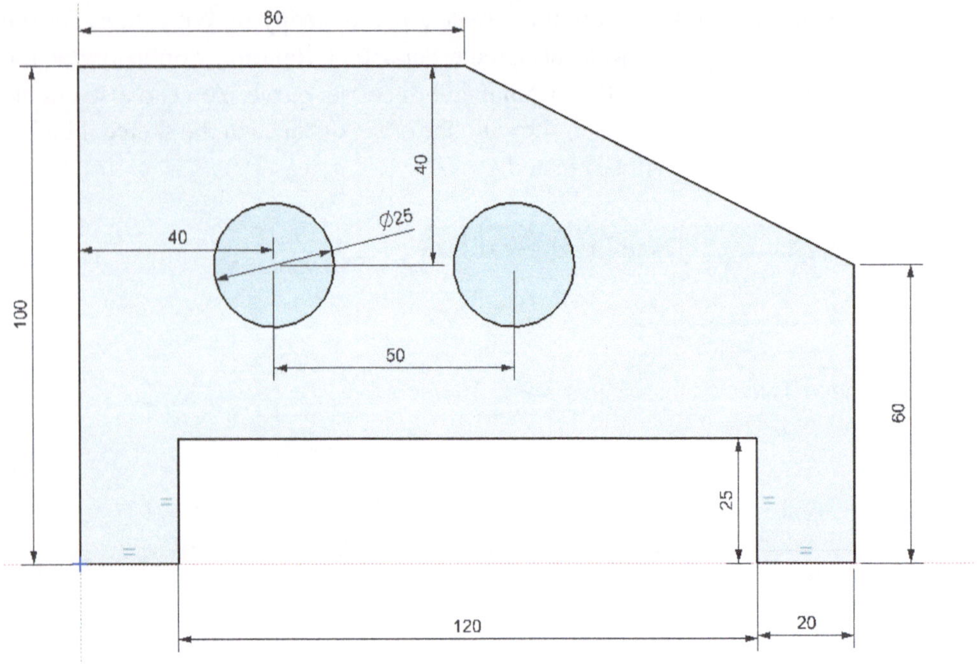

1. Start **NX** by clicking the **NX** icon on your desktop.
2. On the ribbon, click **Home** tab > **Standard** panel >**New**.
3. On the **New** dialog, set **Units** to **Millimeters**. Click **Model**, and then click **OK**. A new NX file starts in the **Modeling** mode.
4. To start a new sketch, click **Home > Construction > Sketch** on the ribbon.
5. On the Datum Coordinate System, click on the Front plane.
6. On the **Create Sketch** dialog, click **OK** to start the sketch.
7. On the ribbon, click **Home > Curve > Line**.
8. Click on the origin point to define the first point of the line.

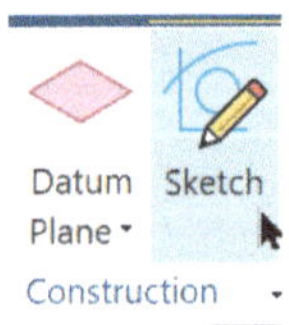

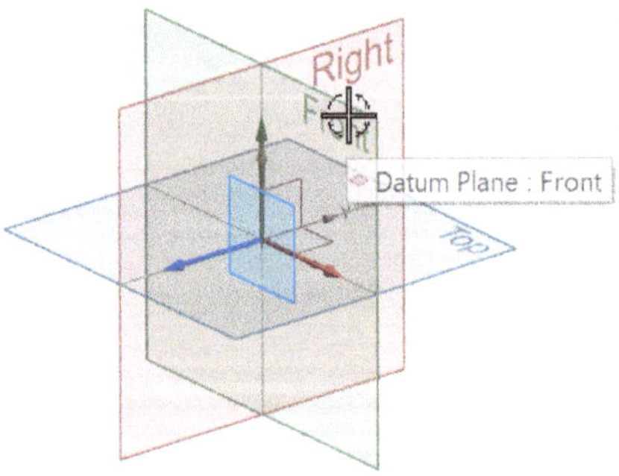

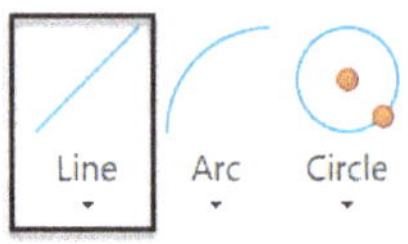

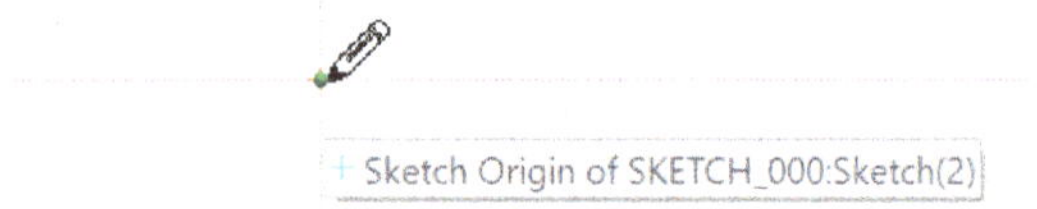

9. Move the pointer horizontally toward the right.
10. Click to define the endpoint of the line.
11. Move the pointer vertically upwards. Click to draw the second line.

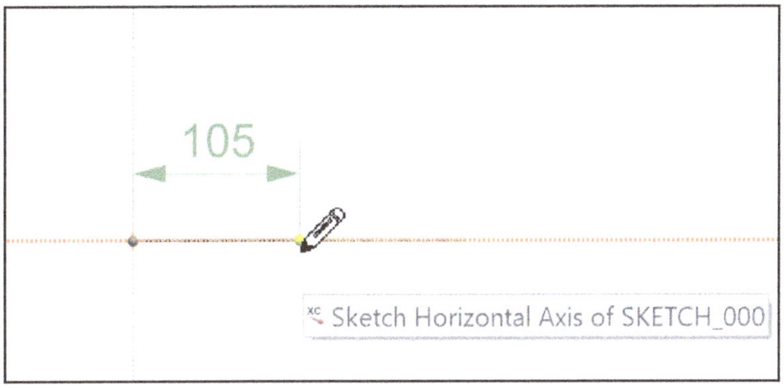

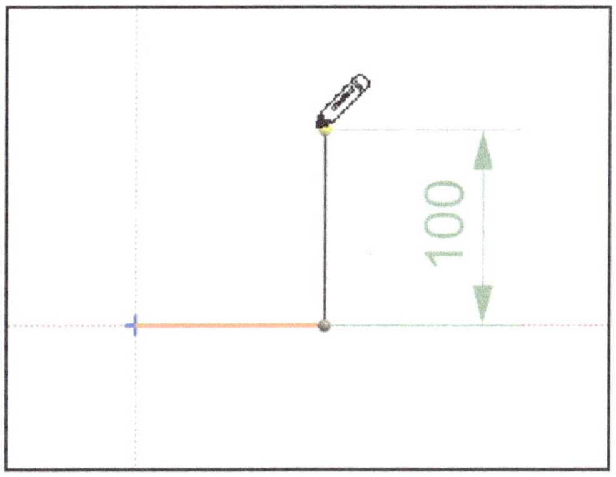

12. Move the pointer horizontally toward the right and click.
13. Move the pointer vertically downward and click when the horizontal trace-lines appear from the sketch origin.

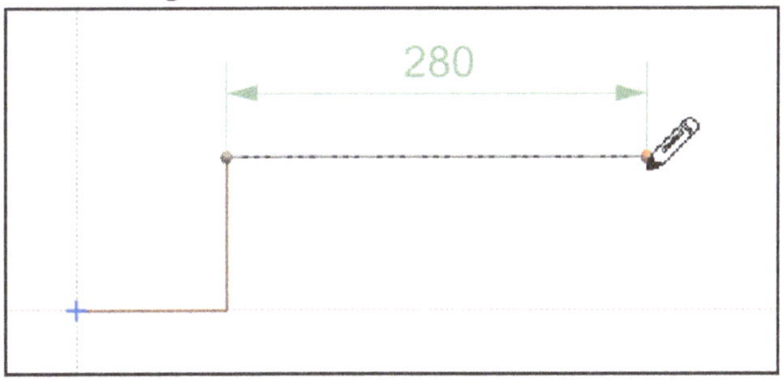

14. Move the pointer horizontally toward the right up to a short distance, and then click.
15. Move the pointer vertically upward and click.

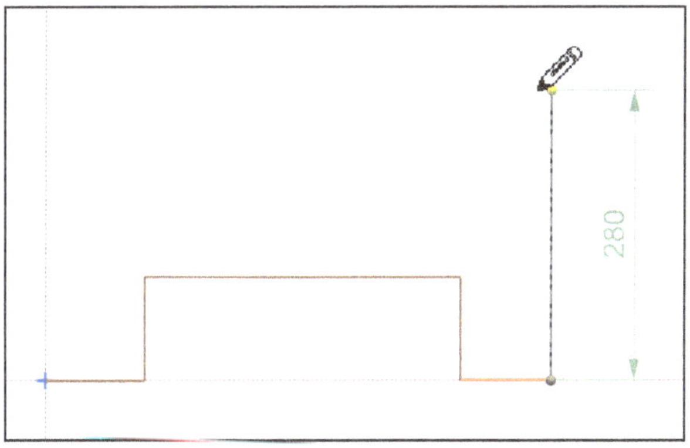

16. Move the pointer in the top-left direction and click.
17. Move the pointer horizontally towards the left and click when vertical trace-lines appear from the origin.

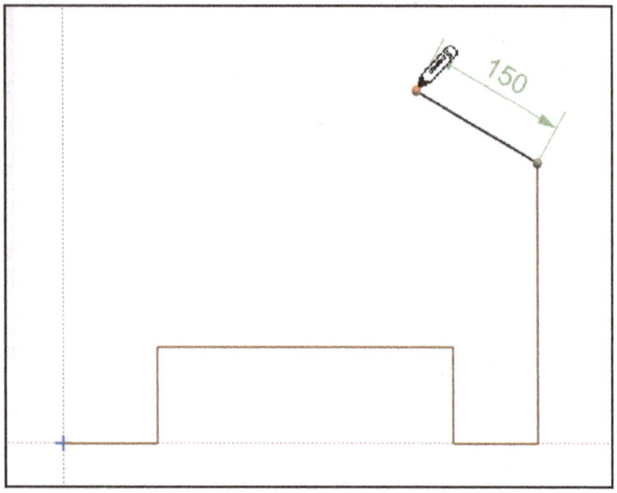

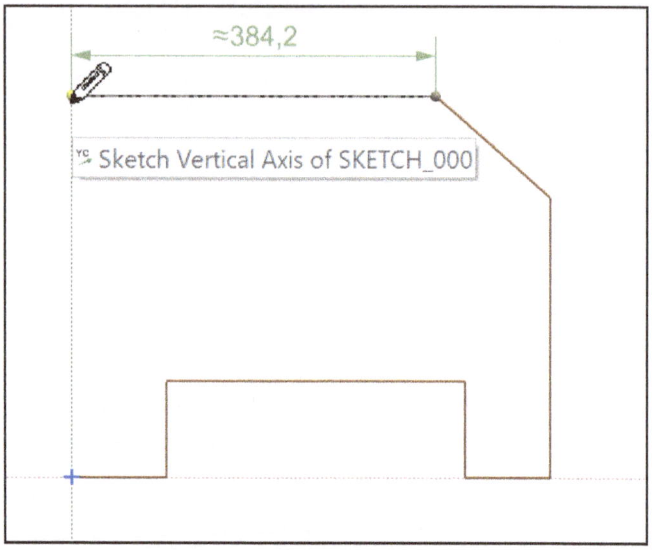

18. Select the start point of the sketch to create a closed loop. Notice the shade inside the region.

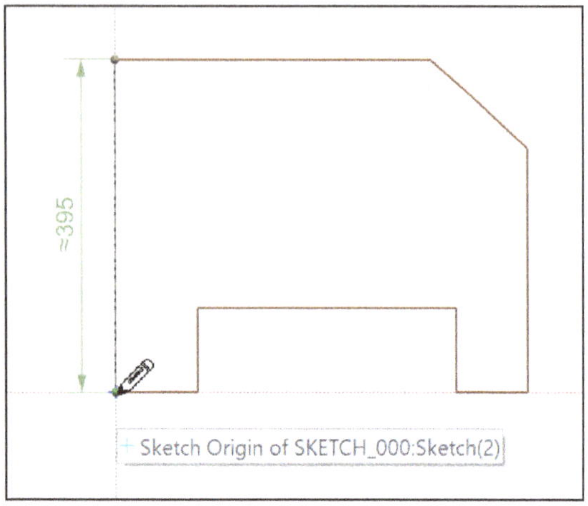

19. Press Esc to deactivate the **Line** command.
20. Select the line on the left side and click the **Make Vertical** icon on the **Sketch Scene bar**.

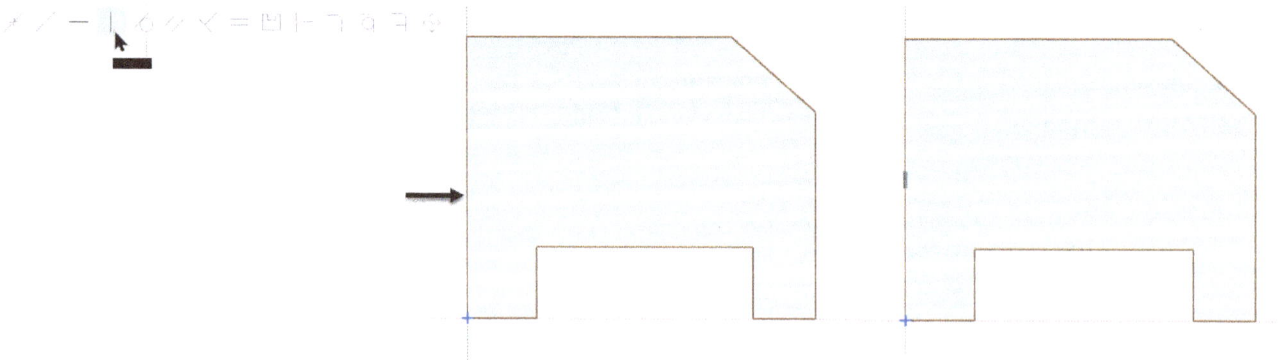

21. Select the top horizontal line and click the **Make Horizontal** icon on the Sketch Screen bar.
22. Click on the two horizontal lines at the bottom. Select **Make Equal** from the Sketch Screen bar; they become equal in length.

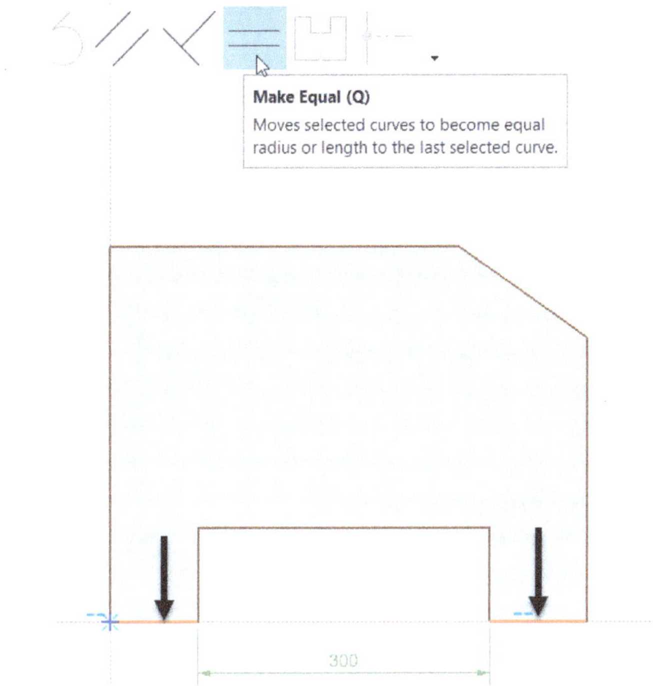

23. Select the small vertical lines, and then click the **Equal Length** icon to make their lengths equal.

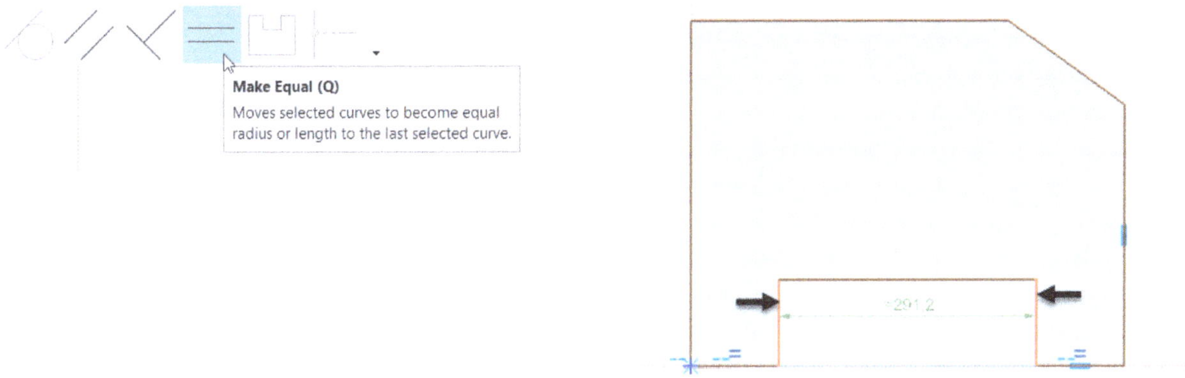

24. Select the lower right horizontal line. Next, select the dimension attached to the selected line.
25. Type-in **20** in the dimension box and press Enter on the Keyboard.
26. Click **OK** on the **Scale Sketch On First Dimension** message box; the sketch is scaled to the first dimension.
27. On the ribbon, click **View > Operation > Fit**; the sketch is fitted in the graphics window.

28. Select the small vertical line, and then click on the dimension attached to it.
29. Type-in **25** in the dimension box and press Enter on the Keyboard. Next, press ESC.
30. Likewise, change the dimension values of the right vertical line to **60**. Press ESC.

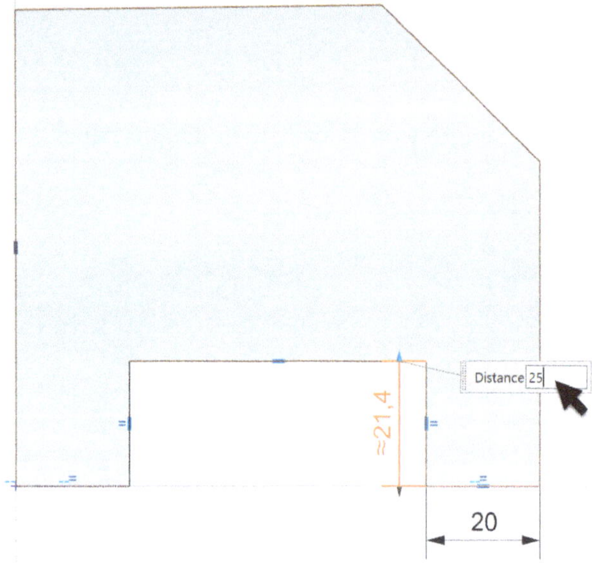

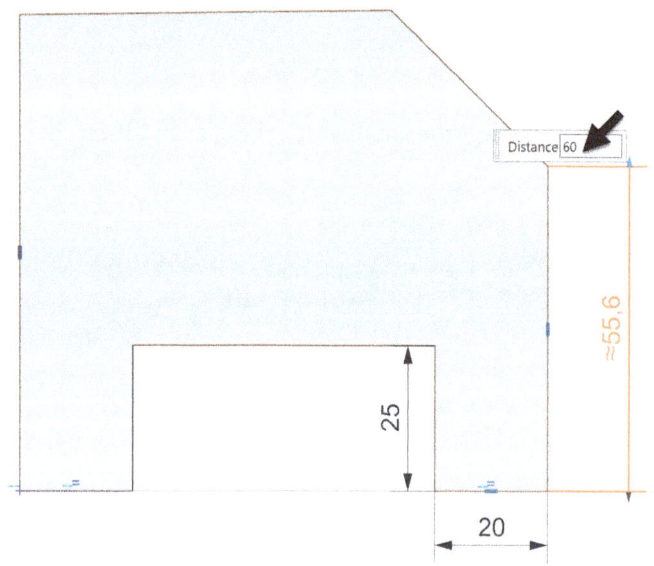

31. Likewise, apply the remaining dimensions, as shown.

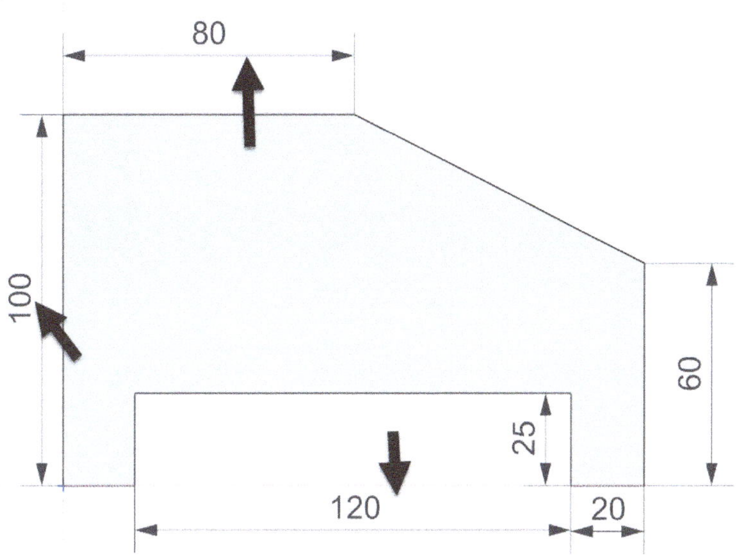

32. On the ribbon, click **Home > Curve > Circle**. Click inside the sketch region to define the center point of the circle. Move the pointer and click to define the diameter. Likewise, create another circle.

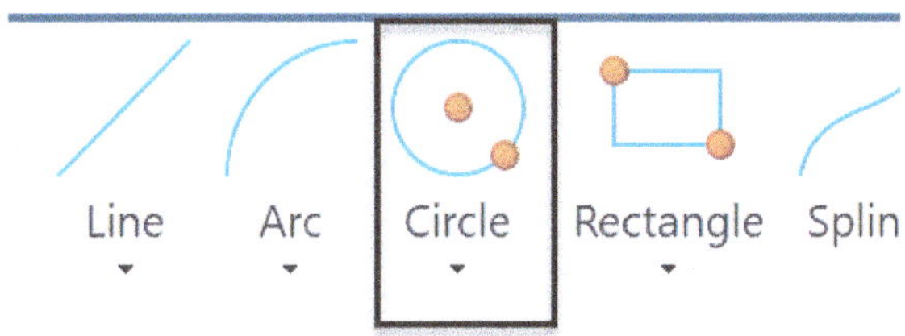

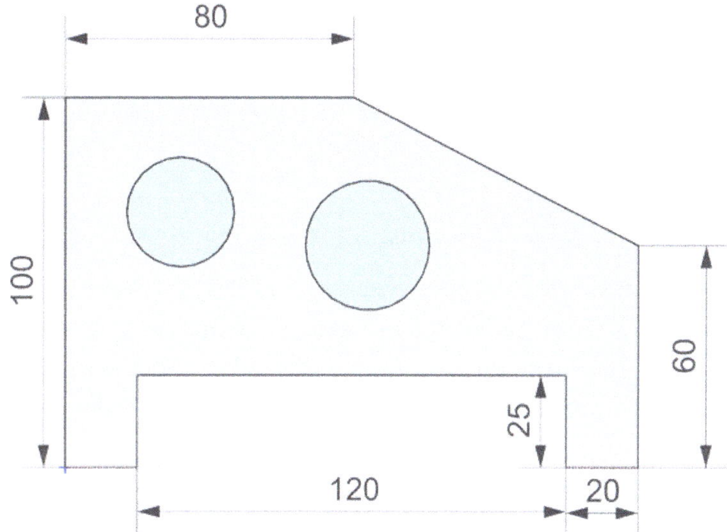

33. Select the two circles and click **Make Equal** on the **Sketch Screen bar**. The diameters of the circles will become equal.
34. Select the two circles and click **Make Horizontal** on the **Sketch Screen bar**. The centerpoints of the two circles are aligned horizontally.

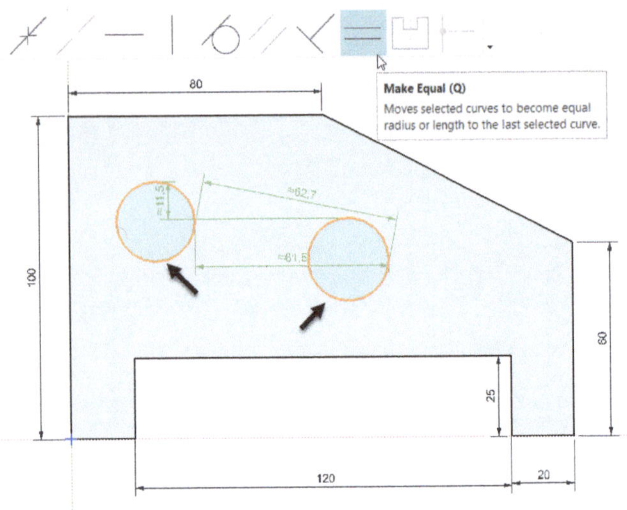

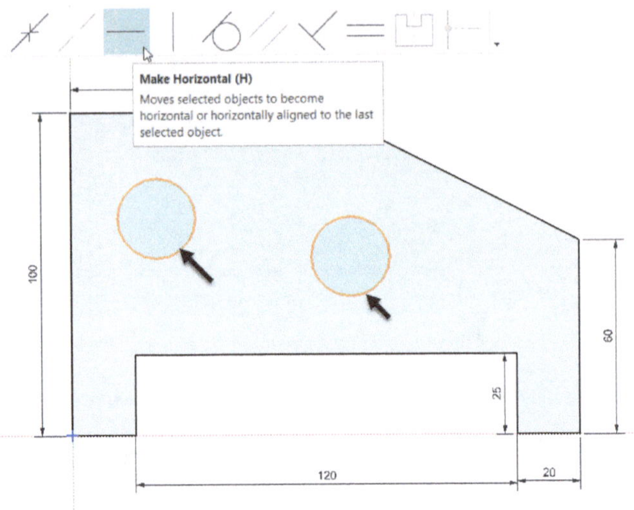

35. Select anyone of the circle, and then click on the dimension attached to it.
36. Type 25 and press ENTER. Next, press ESC.
37. Place the pointer on anyone of the circle. Next, select its centerpoint.
38. Likewise, select the centerpoint of the other circle. Next, select the dimension displayed between the two centerpoints.
39. Type 50 and press ENTER.

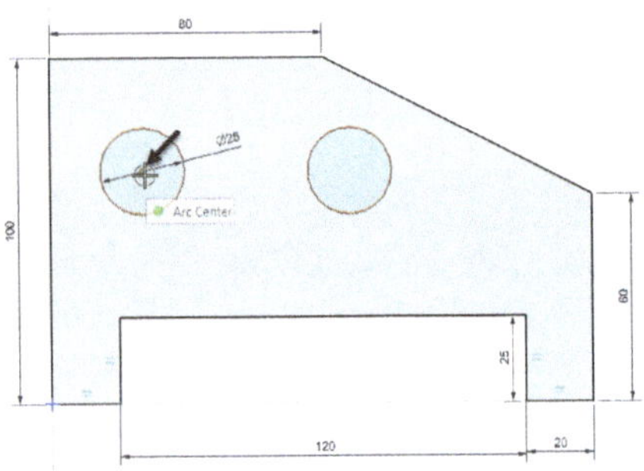

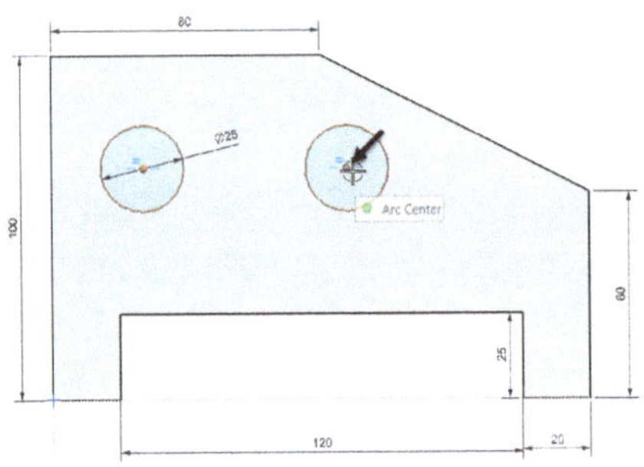

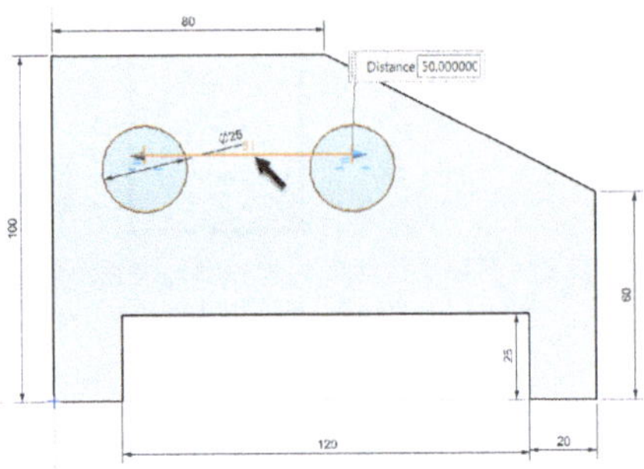

40. Likewise, create other dimensions between the circles and the adjacent lines, as shown below.
41. On the ribbon, click **Home > Sketch > Finish Sketch**.

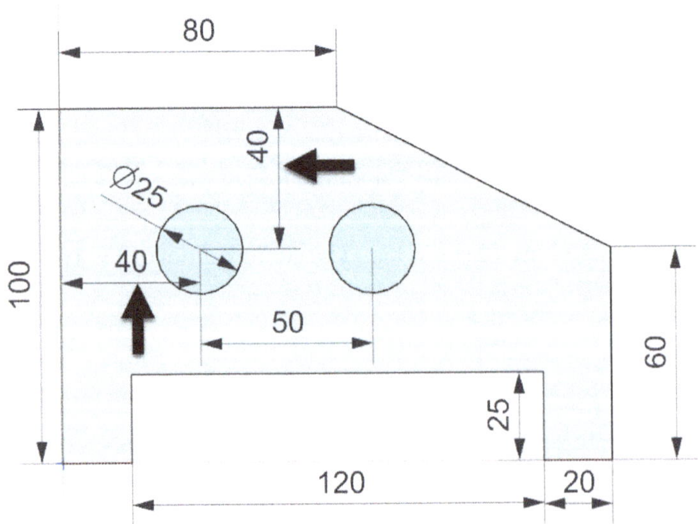

42. Click the **Save** icon on the **Quick Access Toolbar**.

43. On the **Name Parts** dialog, type-in **C2_example1** in the **Name** box and click the folder icon. Define the location and file name, and then click **OK** twice to save the part file.
44. Click the **Close** button below the Top Border bar to close the part file.

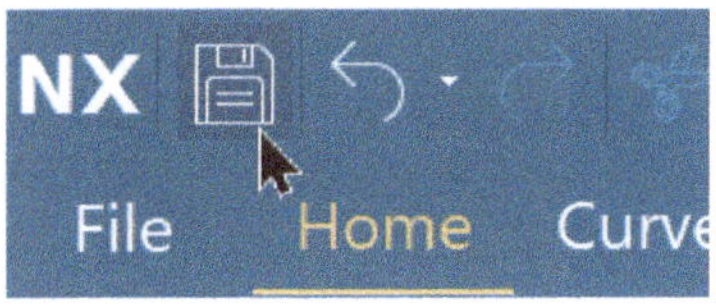

Example 2 (Inches)

In this example, you will draw the sketch shown below.

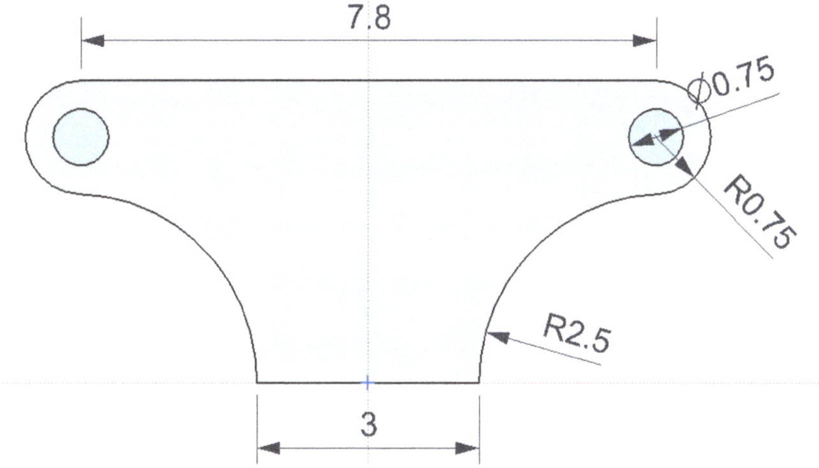

1. Start **NX** by clicking the **NX** icon on your desktop.
2. On the **Quick Access Toolbar**, click the **New** icon.
3. On the **New** dialog, set the **Units** to **Inches** and select the **Model** template. Click **OK** to start a new part file.
4. To start a new sketch, click **Home > Construction > Sketch** on the ribbon.
5. On the **Datum Coordinate System**, click on the Top Plane. Click **OK** to start the sketch.

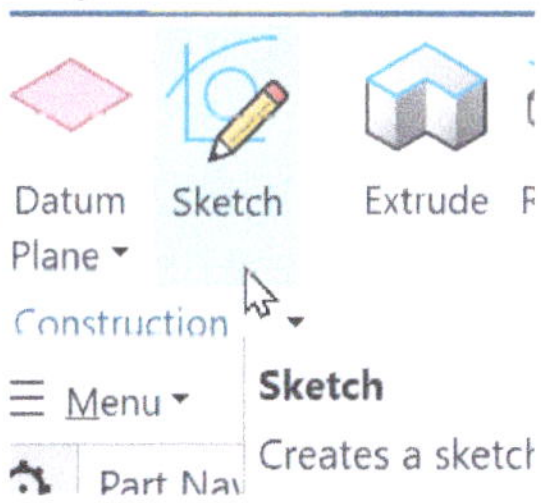

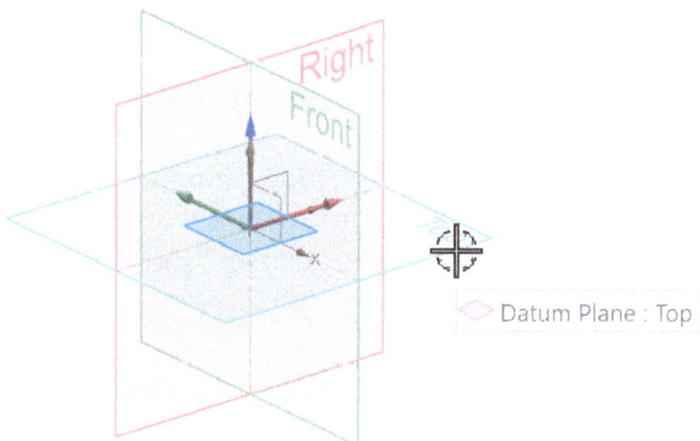

6. Activate the **Line** command (On the ribbon, click **Home > Curve > Line**).
7. Click on the second quadrant of the coordinate system to define the start point of the profile. Drag the pointer horizontally and click to define the endpoint.
8. Right-click and select **Arc** from shortcut menu.

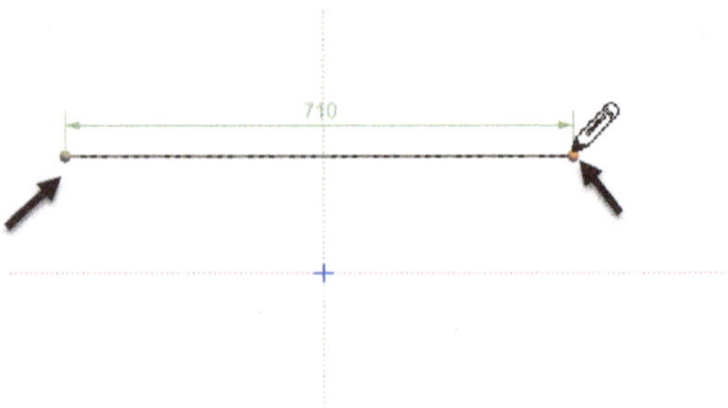

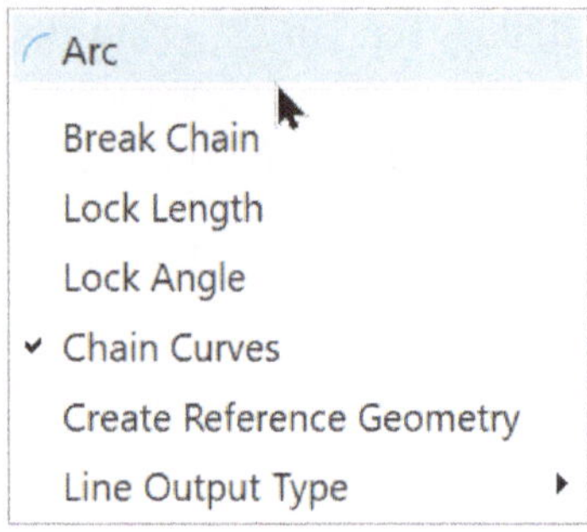

9. Move the pointer in the upward right direction. Click to specify the endpoint of the arc.
10. Move the pointer along the arc and click when a small tick is displayed on horizontal line; the arc is created tangent to the horizontal line.

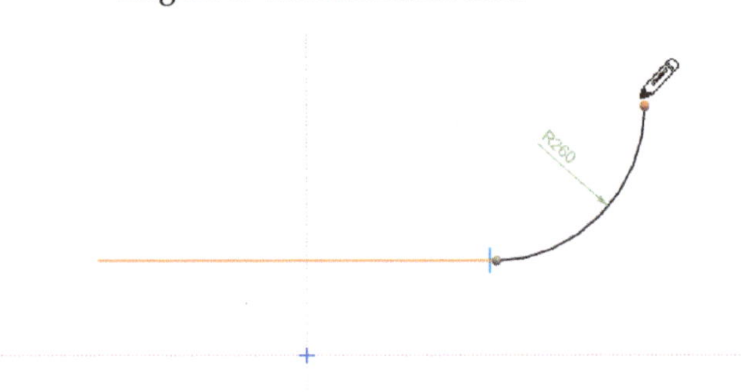

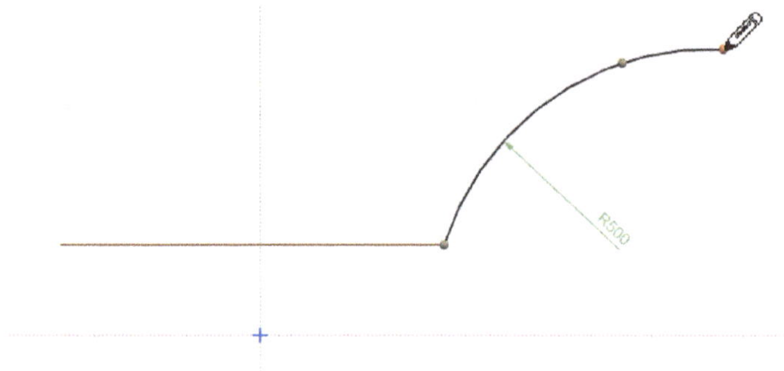

11. Move it upwards right.
12. Move the pointer toward the left and click when a vertical dotted line appears, as shown below.

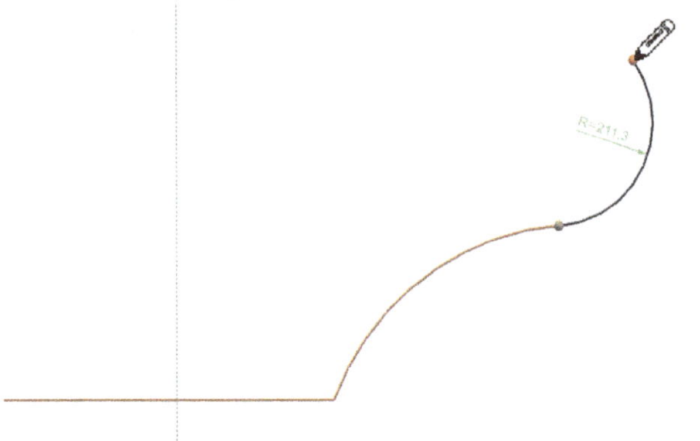

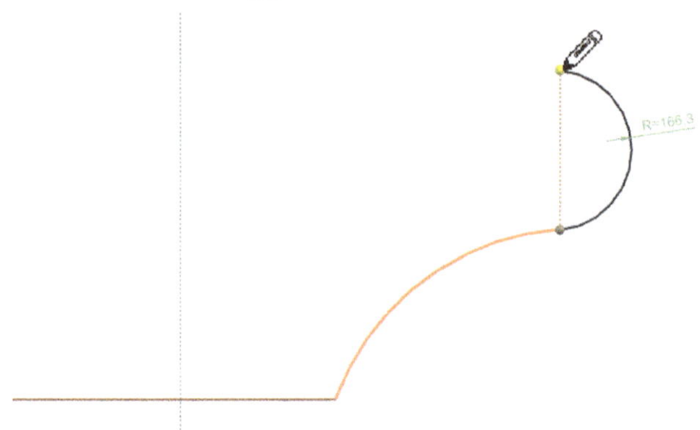

13. Right-click and select **Line** from shortcut menu.
14. Move the pointer toward the left and click to create a horizontal line.
15. Right-click and select **Arc** from shortcut menu. Next, move the pointer vertically downward and click.

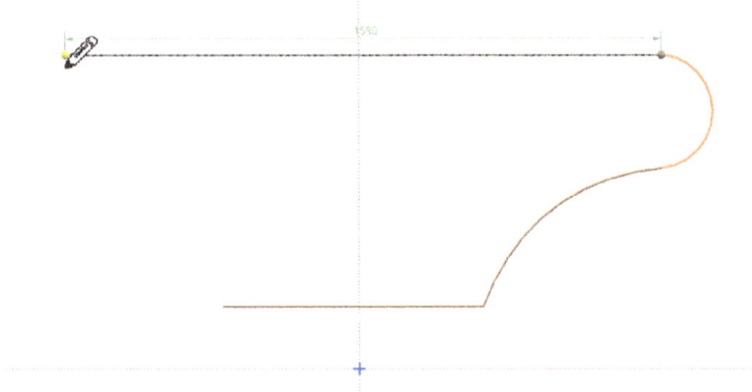

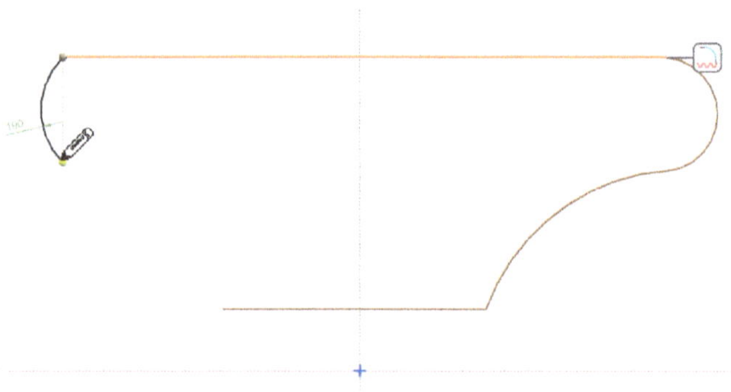

16. Move the pointer toward left and click when a small tick (tangent relation glyph) is displayed on the horizontal line.
17. Move the pointer toward the downward right and click on the start point to close the sketch.

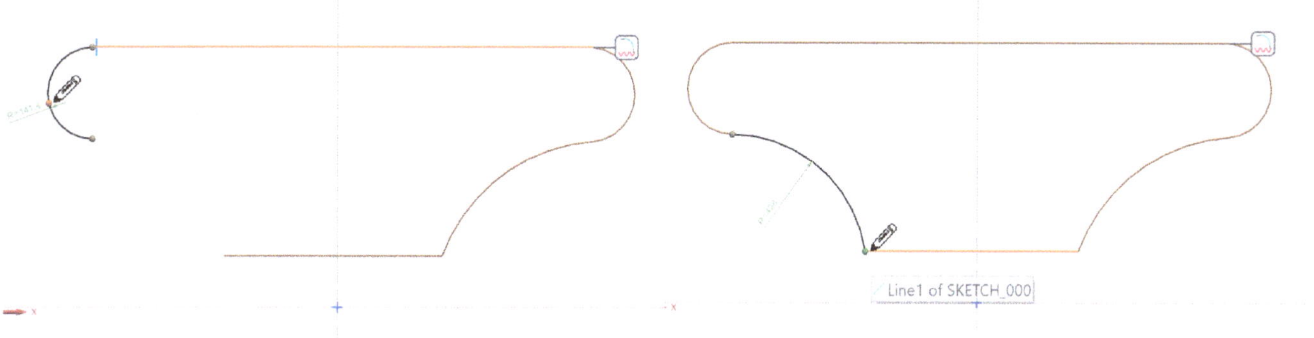

18. Press ESC.
19. Activate the **Circle** command and draw a circle inside the loop. Next, press ESC.
20. Click on the circle and the small arc. Click **Make Coincident** on the Sketch Screen bar. The circle and arc are made concentric.

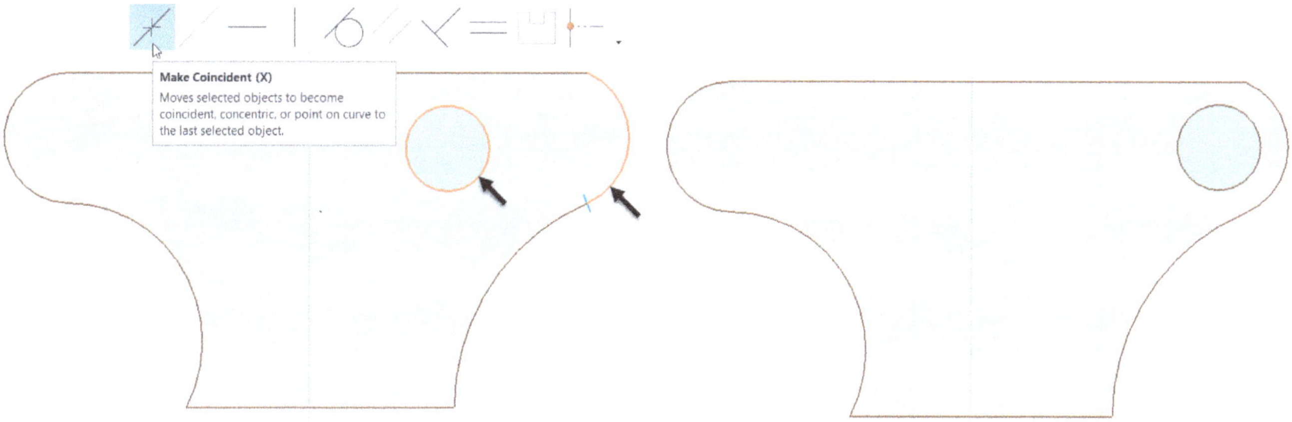

21. Likewise, create another circle concentric to the small arc located on the left side.

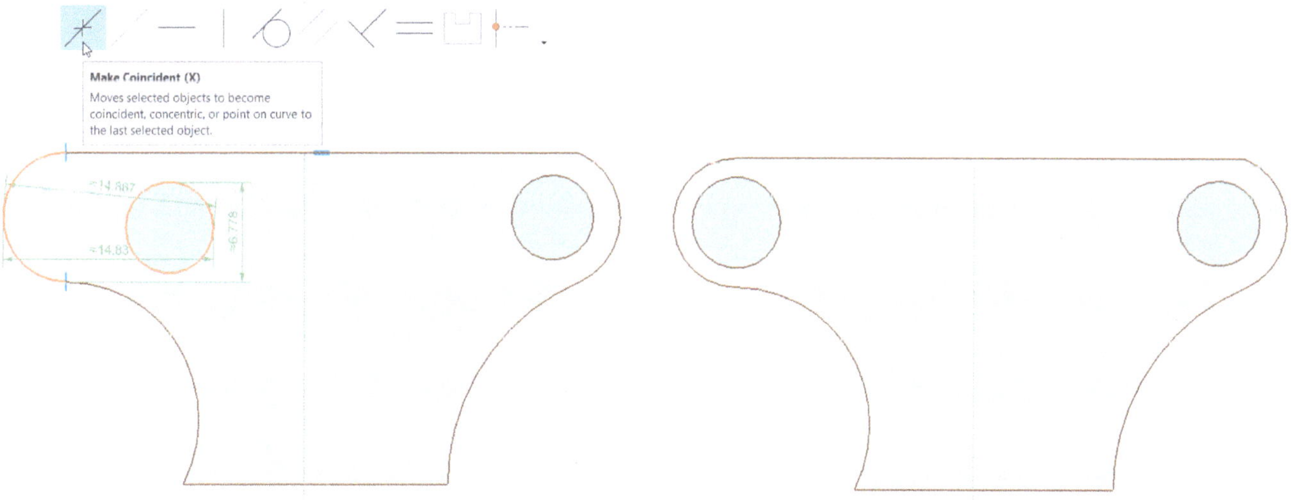

22. Click on the large arcs on both sides of the vertical axis.
23. Click on the vertical axis located at the center.

24. Click the **Make Symmetric** icon on the **Sketch Screen bar**. The arcs are made symmetric about the vertical axis.

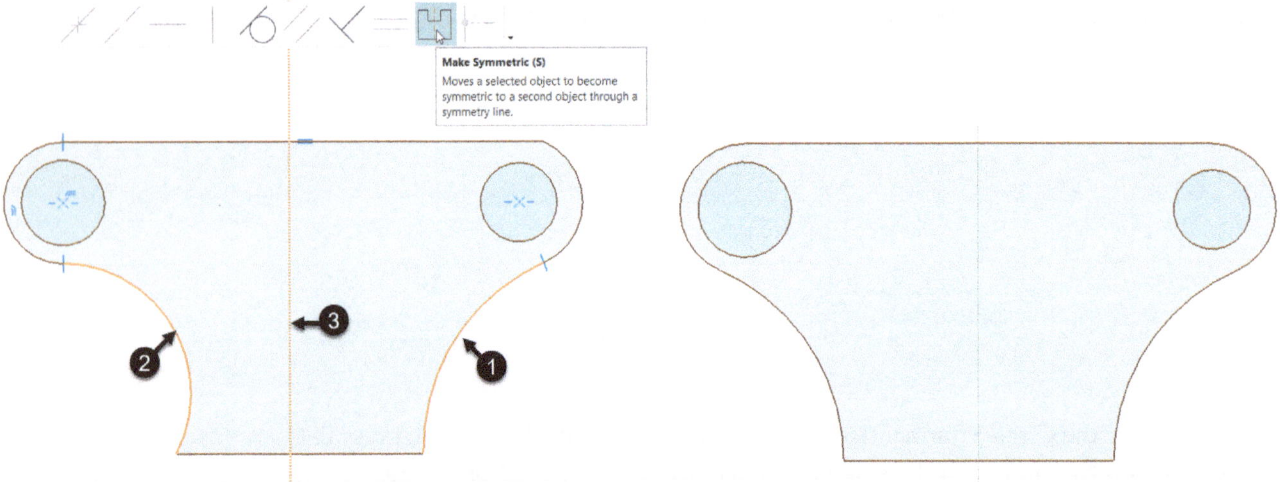

25. Likewise, make the small arcs and circles symmetric about the Y-axis.

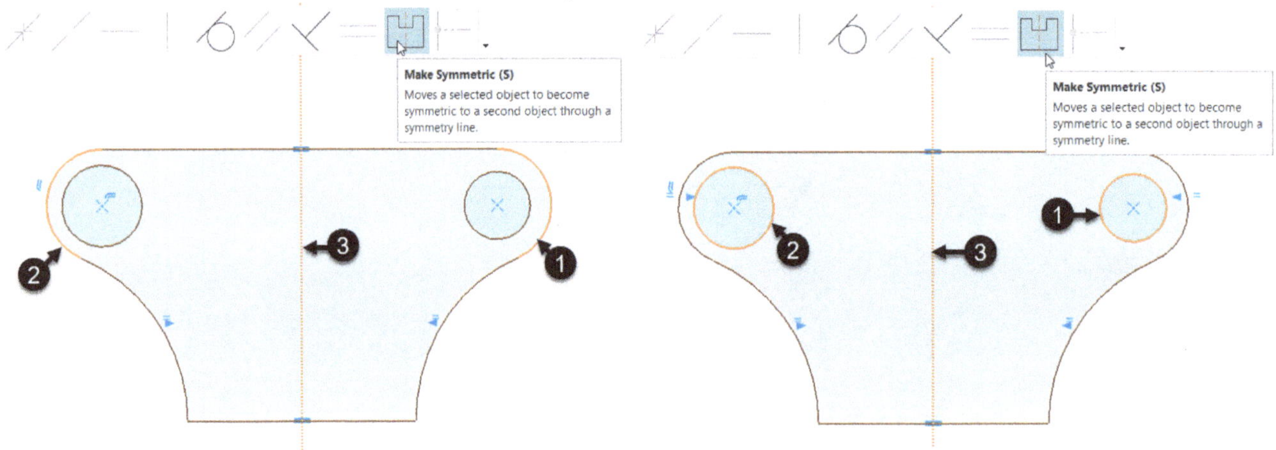

26. Apply the **Make Equal** relation between the two circles.
27. Apply the **Make Collinear** relation between the bottom horizontal line and the horizontal axis.

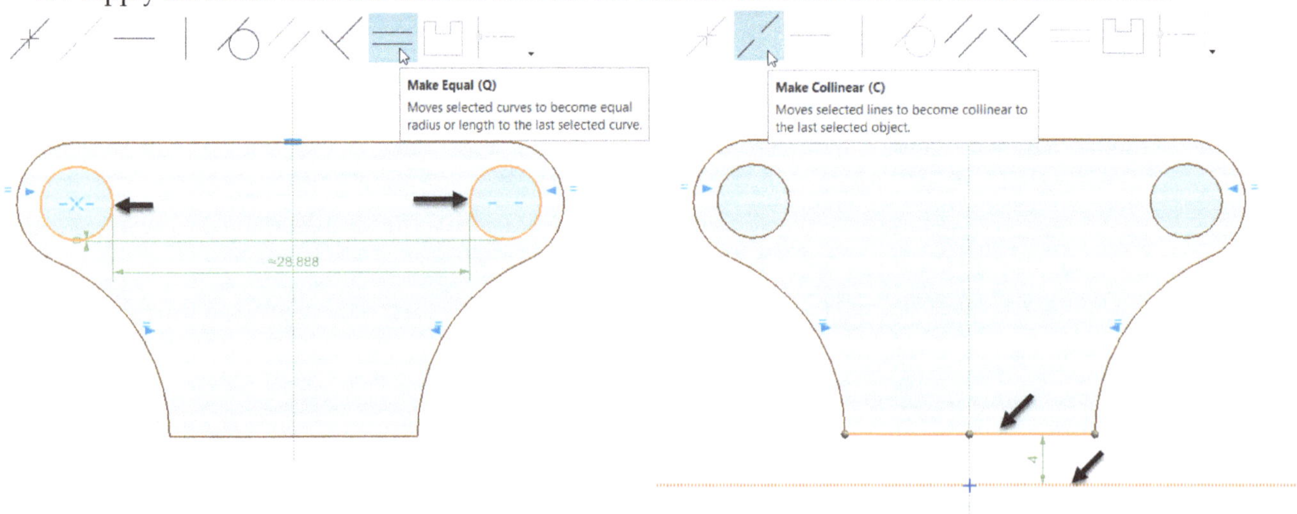

28. Apply dimensions to the sketch, as shown below.

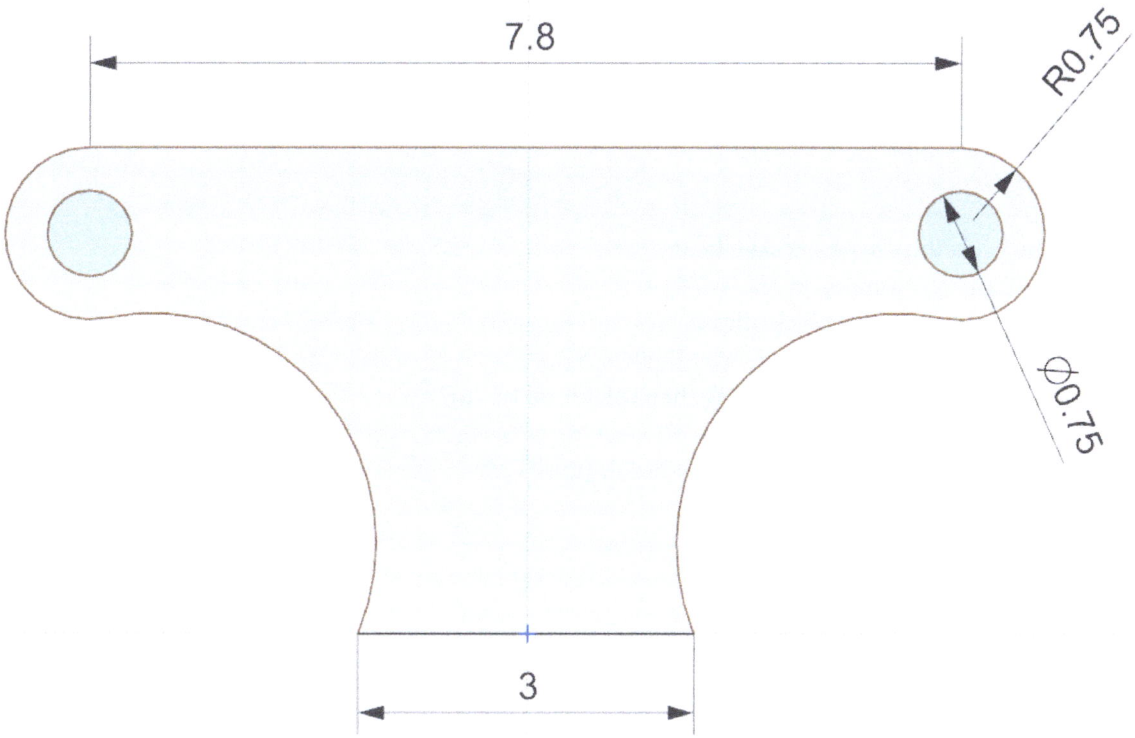

29. Place the pointer on the large arc and select its centerpoint.
30. Select the horizontal axis and click the **Make Coincident** icon on the **Sketch Scene Bar**.

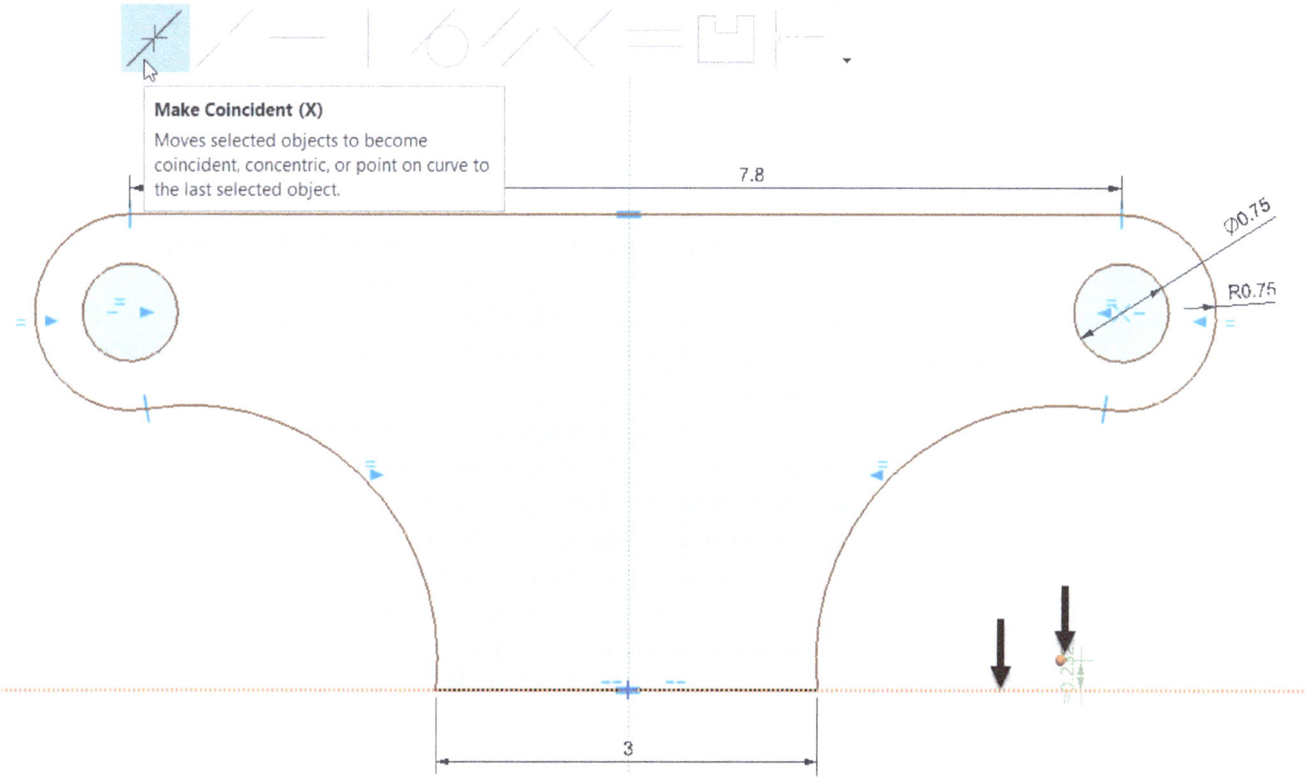

31. Select the large arc and click on the dimension attached to it. Type 2.5 and press ENTER.
32. On the ribbon, click **View > Operation > Fit** to fit the drawing in the graphics window.

33. Click **Finish** on the ribbon to complete the sketch.
34. To save the file, click **File > Save > Save**.
45. On the **Name Parts** dialog, type-in **C2_example2** in the **Name** box and click the folder symbol. Define the location, file name, and click **OK** twice to save the part file.
35. To close the file, click **File > Close > All Parts**.

Questions

1. What is the procedure to create sketches?
2. List any two sketch relations in NX.
3. Describe the method to create an ellipse.
4. How do you define the shape and size of a sketch?
5. How do you create a tangent arc using the **Profile** command?
6. List any two methods to create circles.
7. How do you create a fillet with an alternate solution?

Exercises

Exercise 1

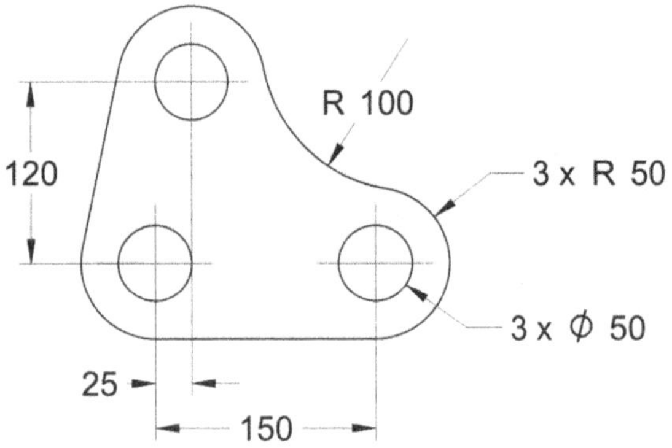

Exercise 2

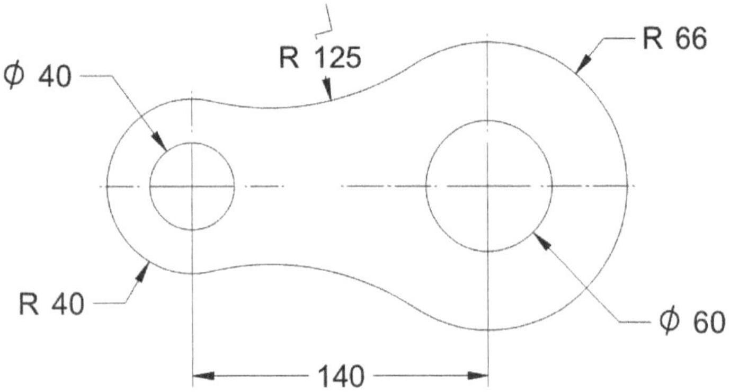

Exercise 3 (Inches)

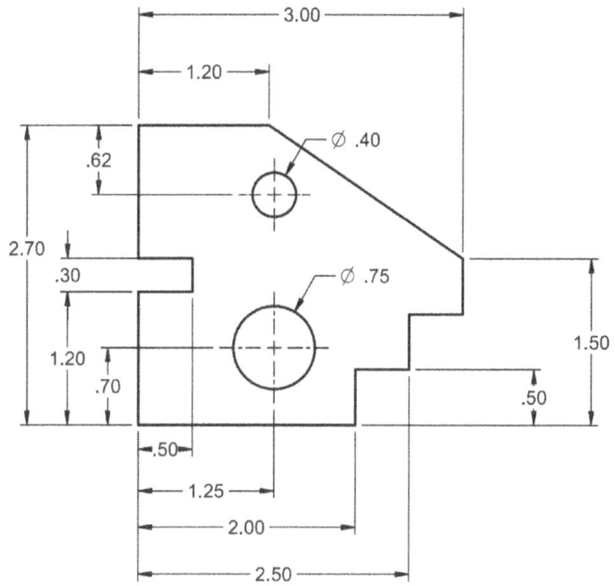

Chapter 3: Extrude and Revolve Features

Extrude and revolve features are used to create basic and simple parts. Most of the time, they form the base for complex parts, as well. These features are easy to create and require a single sketch. Now, you will learn the commands to create these features.

The topics covered in this chapter are:

- *Constructing Extrude and Revolve features in the Modeling template*
- *Creating Reference Planes*
- *Additional Options in the Extrude and Revolve commands*

Extrude Features

Extrude is the process of taking a two-dimensional profile and converting it into 3D by giving it some thickness. A simple example of this would be taking a circle and converting it into a cylinder. Once you have created a sketch profile or profiles you want to *Extrude*, activate the **Extrude** command (On the ribbon click **Home > Base > Extrude**). Click on the sketch profile to add thickness to the sketch. Type-in a value in the **End** box and press Enter to create the *Extrude* feature.

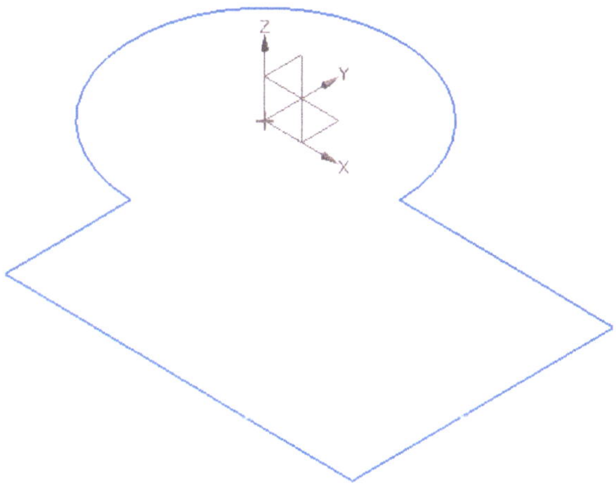

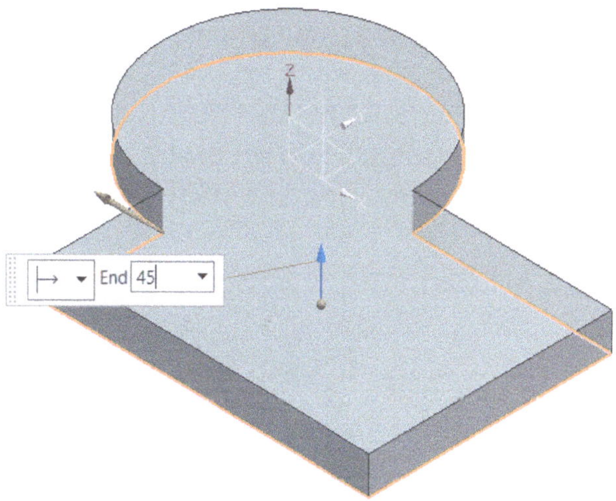

You can use the **Symmetric Value** option on the dialog to add equal thickness on both sides of the sketch.

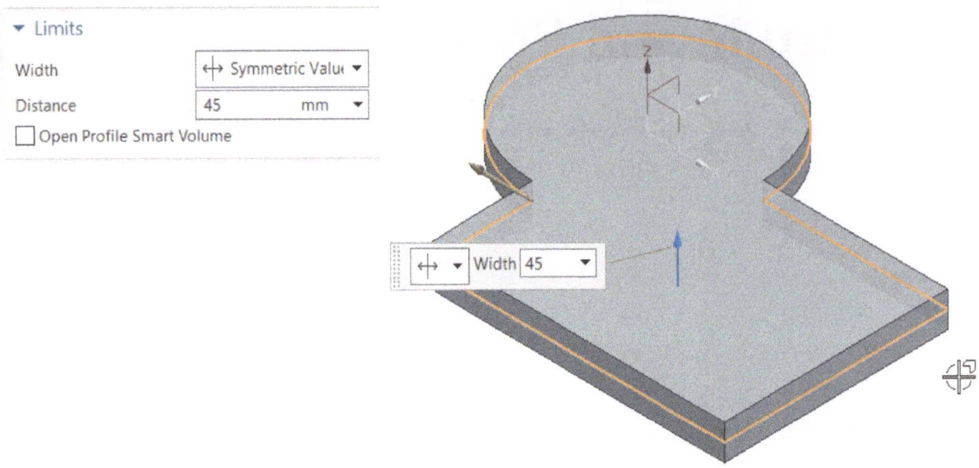

On the dialog, click **OK** to complete the *Extrude* feature. You will learn about the options available on the Extrude dialog later in this chapter.

Revolve Features

Revolve is the process of taking a two-dimensional profile and revolving it about a centerline to create a 3D geometry (shapes that are axially symmetric). While creating a sketch for the *Revolve* feature, it is important to think about the cross-sectional shape that will define the 3D geometry once it is revolved around an axis. For instance, the following geometry has a hole in the center. This could be created with a separate *Cut* or *Hole* feature. But to make that hole part of the *Revolve* feature, you need to sketch the axis of revolution using a reference line so that it leaves a space between the profile and the axis. By default, the reference elements of the sketch are not displayed in the Modeling window. To display the reference line, click the right mouse button on the sketch in the **Part Navigator** and then select **Settings**. On the **Sketch Settings** dialog, check the **Display Reference Curves** option in the **Inactive Sketch** section. Next, click **OK** to display the reference line.

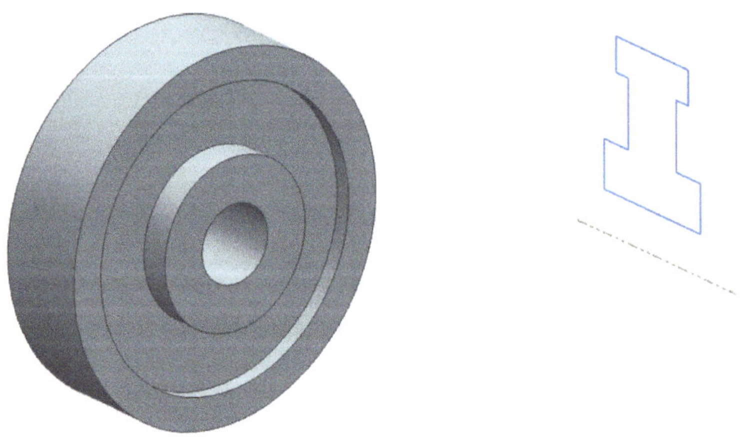

After completing the sketch, activate the **Revolve** command (On the ribbon, click **Home >Base > Revolve**). Click on the sketch to define the section of the *Revolve* feature. On the dialog, click **Specify Vector** under the **Axis** section. Click on a line to define the axis of revolution. The sketch will be revolved around a full 360 degrees. If you want to enter an angle of revolution, type-in a value in the **End** box attached to the preview and press Enter on the Keyboard. On the dialog, click **OK** to complete the *Revolve* feature.

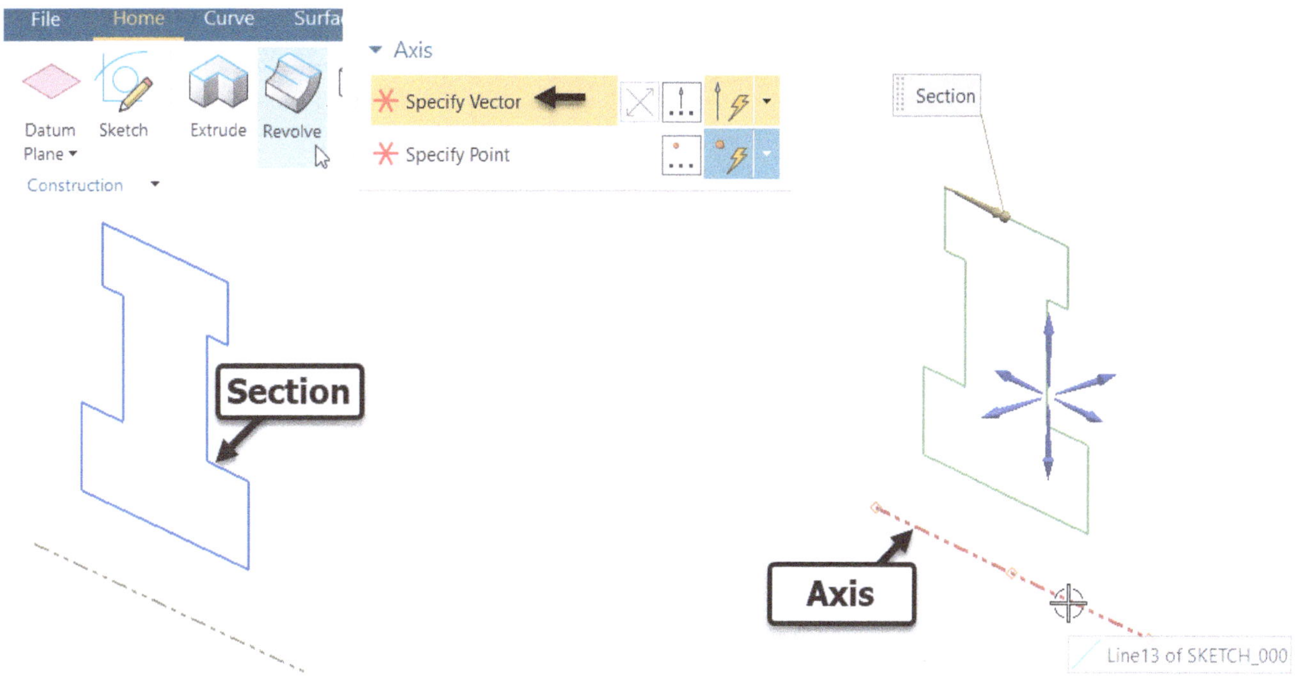

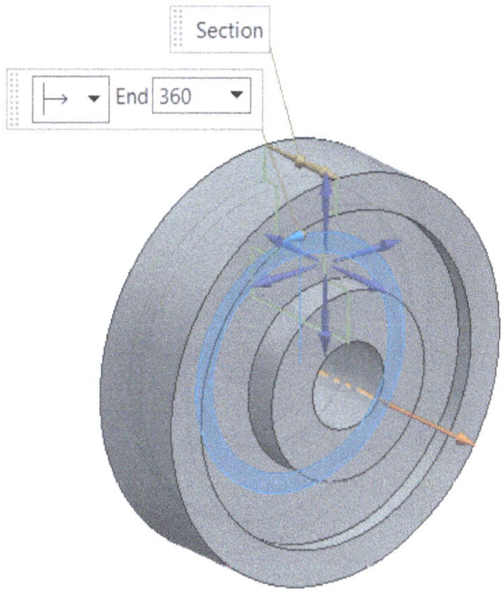

Datum Planes

Each time you start a new part file, NX creates default Datum planes along with the Datum coordinate system, automatically. Planes and coordinate systems make up a specific type of feature in NX, known as Datum features. These features act as supports to your 3D geometry. In addition to the default Datum features, you can create your own additional planes and coordinate systems too. Until now, you have known how to create sketches on any of the default datum planes. If you want to create sketches and geometry at locations other than default datum planes, you can create new datum planes manually. You can do so by using the **Datum Plane** command.

At Distance

This method creates a datum plane, which will be parallel to a face or another plane. Activate the **Datum Plane** command (click **Home > Construction > Datum Plane** on the ribbon). On the **Datum Plane** dialog, set the **Type** to **At Distance** and select a flat face. Click and drag the arrow that appears on the plane (or) type-in a value in the **Distance** box and press Enter on the Keyboard. On the dialog, click the **Reverse Direction** button to flip the plane to the other side of the model face. If you want to create more than one parallel plane, then type-in a value in the **Number of Planes** box on the dialog.

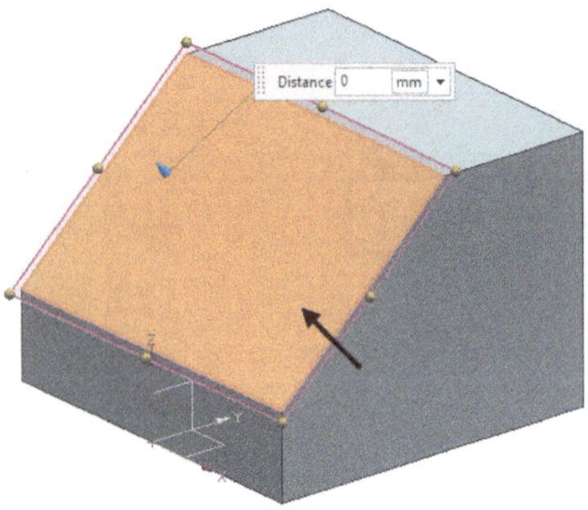

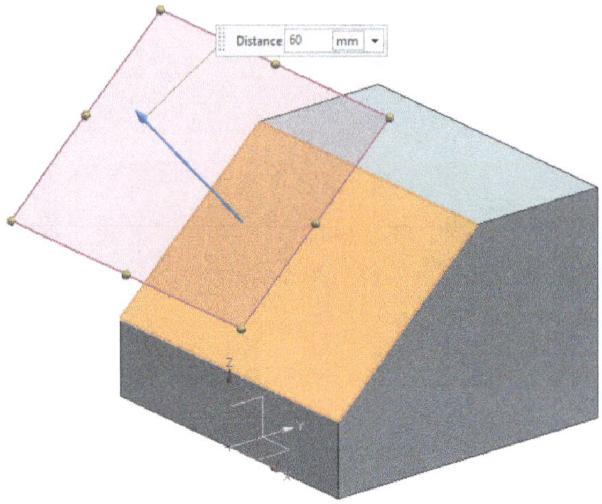

On the dialog, click **OK** to create the **At Distance** plane.

At Angle

This method creates a plane, which will be positioned at an angle to a face or plane. Activate the **Datum Plane** command and select **Type > At Angle** on the **Datum Plane** dialog. Select a flat face or plane. Next, click on the edge of the part geometry to define the rotation axis. Type-in a value in the **Angle** box and press Enter on the Keyboard.

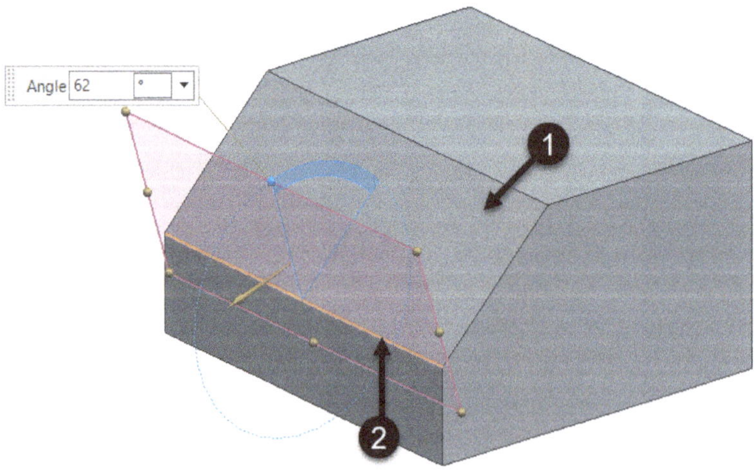

On the dialog, select **Angle Option > Perpendicular** to create a plane perpendicular to the selected face. Select **Angle Option > Parallel** to create a plane parallel to the selected face.

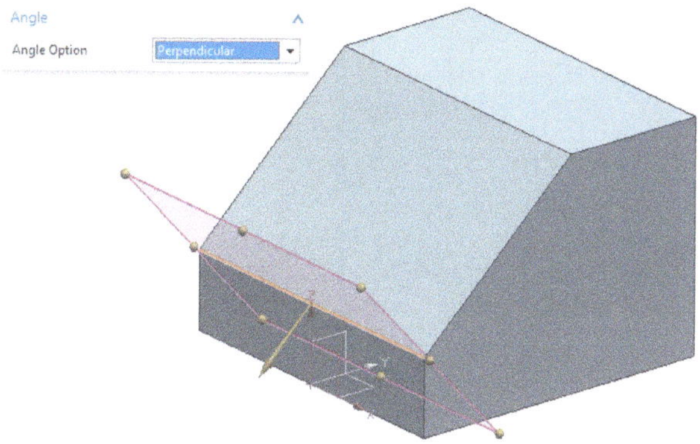

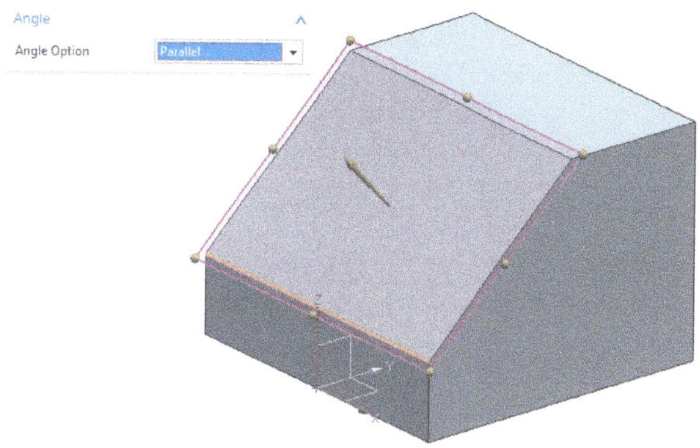

Bisector

This method creates a plane, which lies at the midway between two selected faces. You can also create a plane passing through the intersection point of the two selected planes or faces. Activate the **Datum Plane** command and select **Type > Bisector** on the **Datum Plane** dialog. Click on two faces of the model geometry, which are parallel to each other. Click **OK** to create the bisector plane.

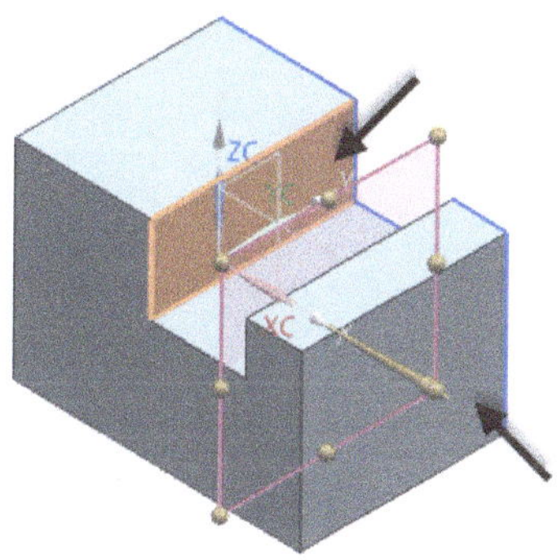

Activate the **Datum Plane** command select **Type > Bisector** on the **Datum Plane** dialog. Select two intersecting faces or plane from the graphics window; the preview of the bisector plane appears. On the dialog, expand the **Plane Orientation** section and click the **Alternate Solution** button; the plane orientation changes. Click **OK** to create the bisector plane.

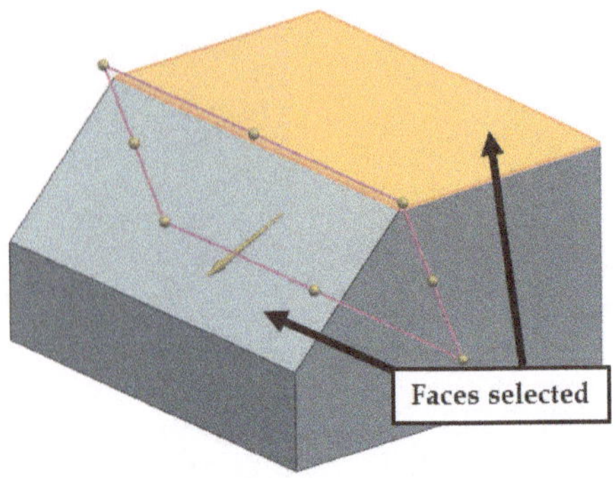

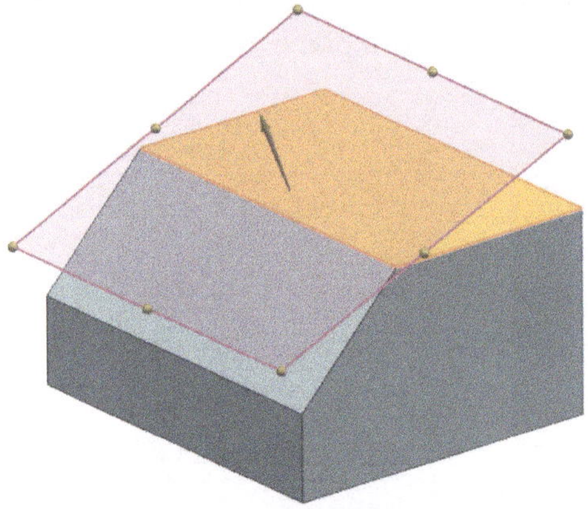

Alternate Solution

Curves and Points

This method creates a datum plane passing through a points and curves using different subtype methods. These methods are discussed next. Activate the **Datum Plane** and select **Type > Curves and Points** on the **Datum Plane** dialog. Next, select **Subtype > Curves and Points** from the **Curves and Points Subtype** section. Select a point from the graphics window. Next, select line or planar face. A datum plane will be created passing through the selected point and the line. Note that if you select a planar face as the second selection, the datum plane will be created parallel to the selected face and passing through the selected point.

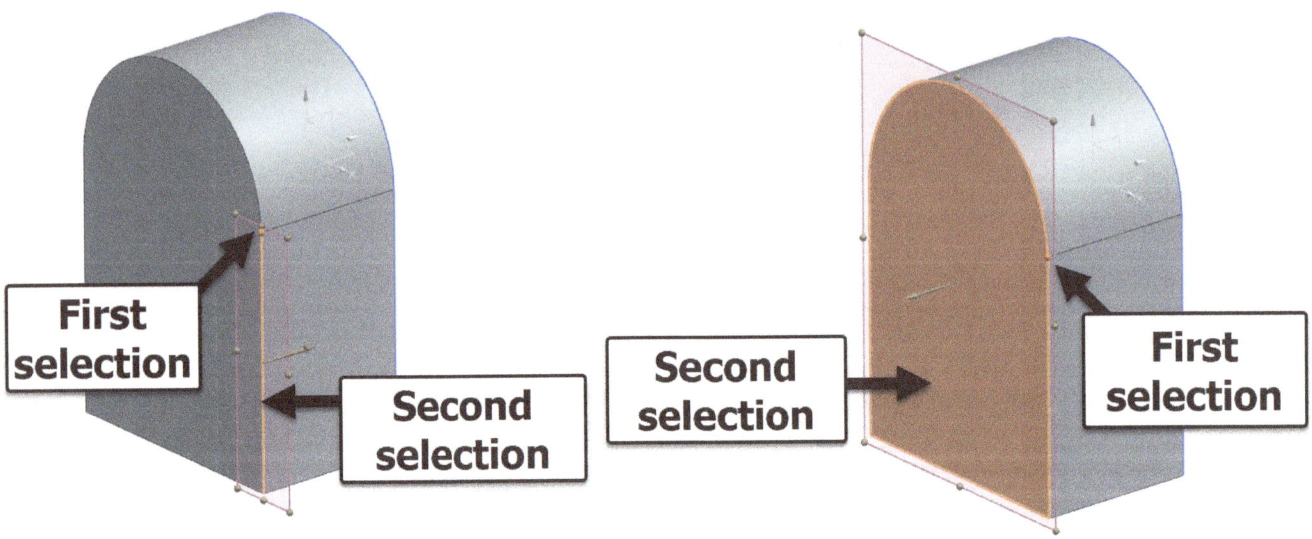

Select **Subtype > One Point** and select a point from the graphics window; the datum plane will be created passing through the single selected point.

Select **Subtype > Two Points** and select two points from the graphics window; the datum plane will be created passing through the first selected point and perpendicular to the second selected point.

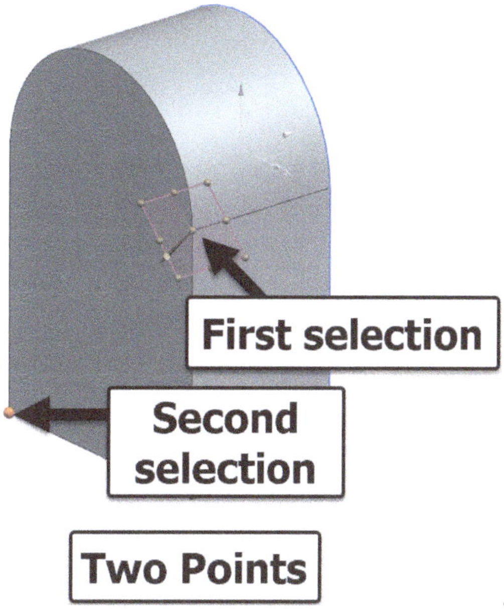

Select **Subtype > Three Points** and select three points from the model geometry. A plane will be placed passing through these points.

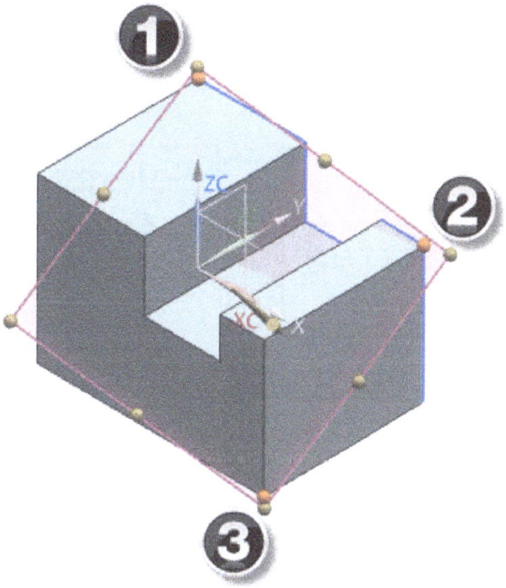

Select **Subtype > Point and Curve/Axis** and select a point. Next, select linear object or axis; the datum plane is created passing through the selected point and linear object.

Select **Subtype > Point and Plane/Face** and select a point. Next, select a planar face or plane; the datum plane is created passing through the selected point and parallel to the selected face.

Tangent

This option creates a plane tangent to a curved face using different subtype methods. On the **Datum Plane** dialog, click **Type > Tangent** . Next, select **Subtype > One Face** from the **Tangent Subtype** section and select a curved face. A plane tangent to the selected face appears.

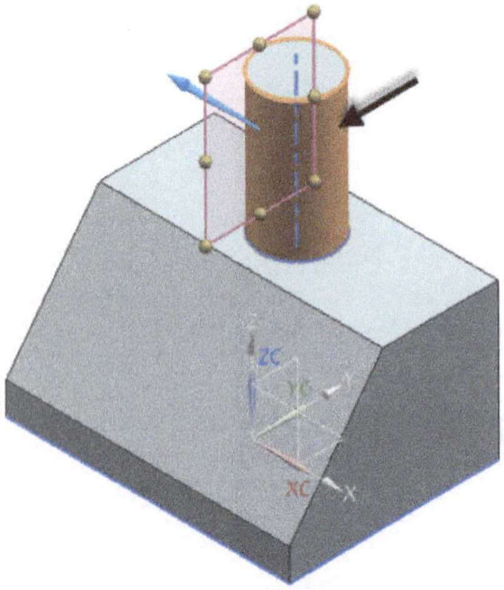

Select **Subtype > Through Point** and select a cylindrical face from the graphics window. Next, click **Specify point** in the **Reference Geometry** section and select a point (Note that you can use the options in the **Specify Point** drop-down available in the **Reference Geometry** section to define a point); the datum plane will be created passing through the selected point and tangent to the selected cylindrical face.

Select **Subtype > Through Line** and select a cylindrical face from the graphics window. Next, click **Select Linear Object** in the **Reference Geometry** section and select a line or linear edge; the datum plane will be created passing through the selected line and tangent to the selected cylindrical face.

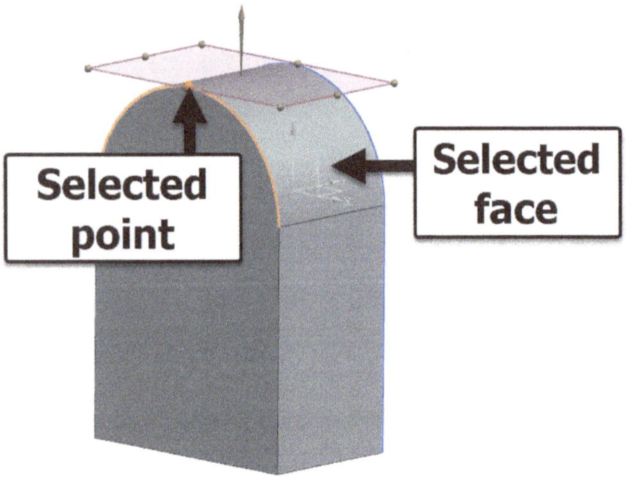

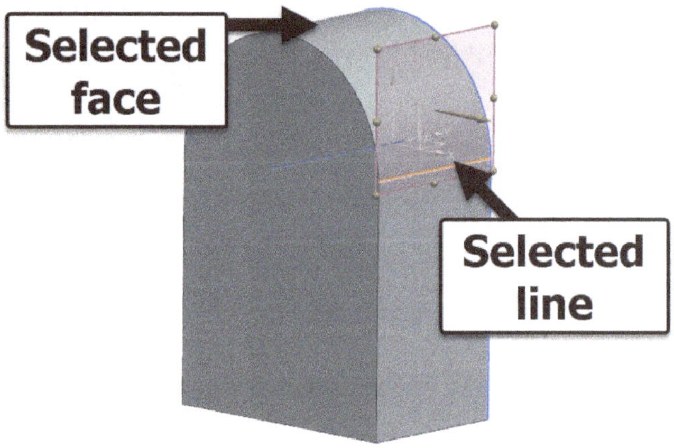

Select **Subtype > Two Faces** and select a cylindrical face from the graphics window. Next, click **Select Object** in the **Reference Geometry** section and select another cylindrical face; the datum plane will be created tangent to the two selected cylindrical faces. Next, expand the **Plane Orientation** section and click the **Alternate Solution** 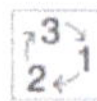 button to switch the alternate solution of the tangent plane. Click the **Alternate Solution** button until the desired solution is displayed. Expand the **Offset** section and check the **Offset** option to offset the newly created datum plane. You can change the offset distance by entering a value in the **Distance** box. Click **OK** to create the plane tangent to the two selected cylindrical faces.

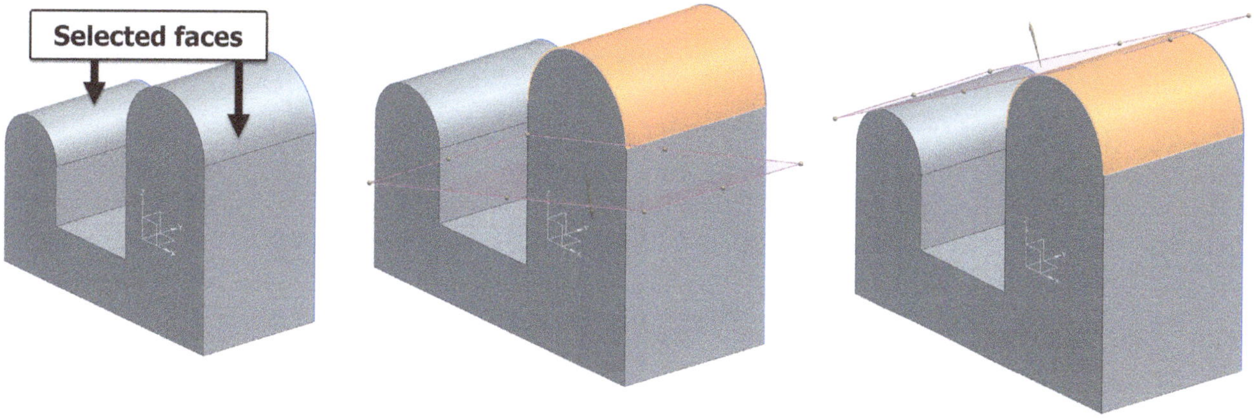

Select **Subtype > Angle to Plane** and select a cylindrical face from the graphics window. Next, click **Select Planar Object** in the **Reference Geometry** section and select planar face or plane; a datum plane will be displayed tangent to the selected cylindrical face. Also, the angle manipulator displayed along with the datum plane. Click and drag the angle manipulator (or) type-in a value in the **Angle** box; the datum plane will the positioned at the specified angle from the selected planar face.

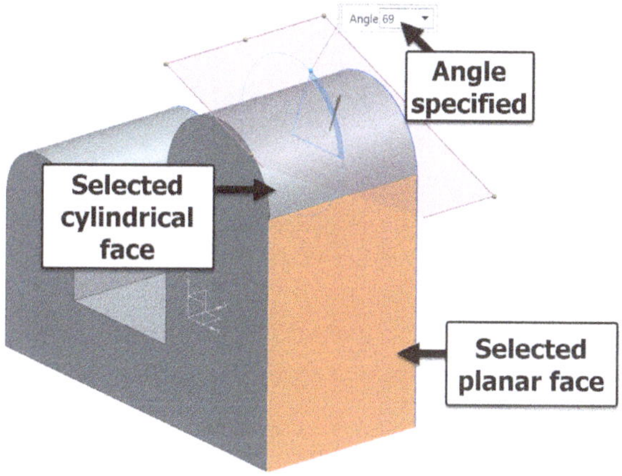

Select **Subtype > Tangent** to create a datum plane tangent to a cylindrical face using all the above methods.

Two Lines

This method helps you to create a datum plane by using two lines. . On the **Datum Plane** dialog, click **Type > Two Lines**  and select two coplanar lines; the datum plane will be created passing through the two selected lines or edges.

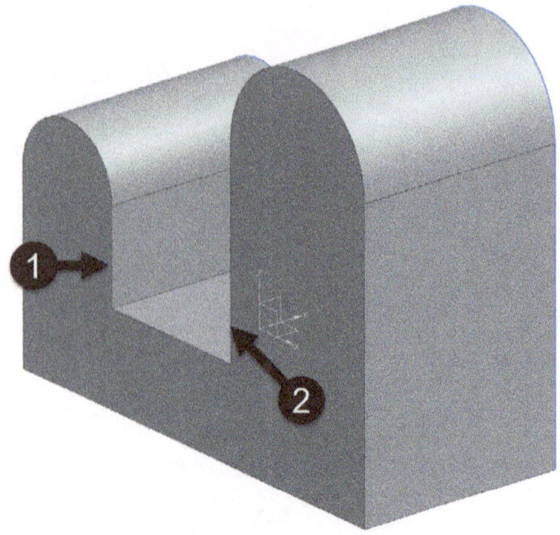

Click the **Alternate Solution** button on the **Plane Orientation** section of the **Datum Plane** dialog to make the datum plane pass through the first selected line or edge and perpendicular to the second selection. Again, click the **Alternate Solution** button on the **Plane Orientation** section to make the datum plane pass through the second selection and perpendicular to the first selection.

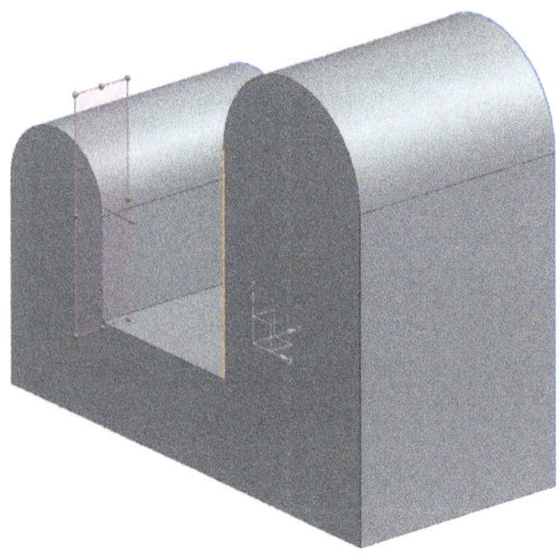

Select **Type > Two Lines** and select two lines or edges that are perpendicular to each other. The datum plane passing through the first selection and perpendicular to the second line is created. Click the **Alternate Solution** button to make the datum plane pass through the second line and perpendicular to the first line.

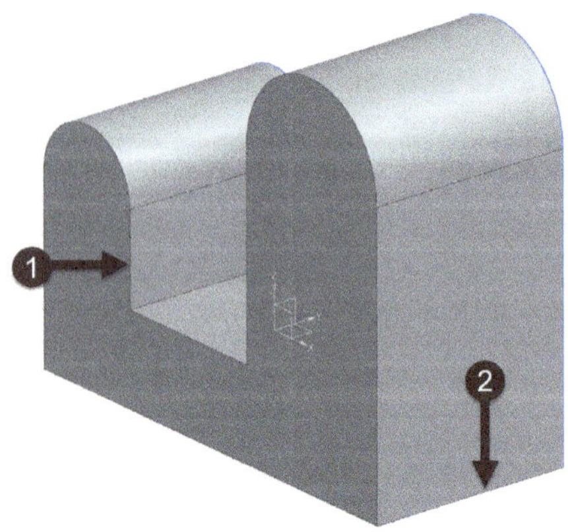

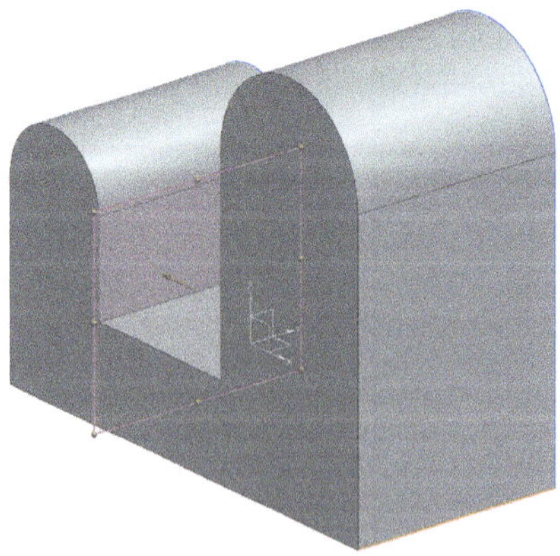

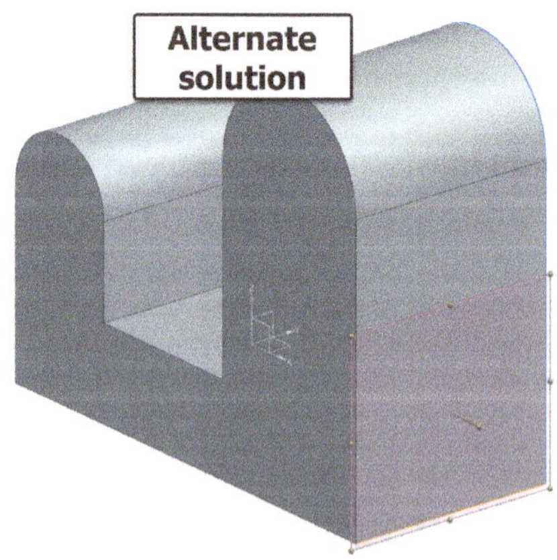

Select **Type > Two Lines** and select two lines or edges that are non-parallel and non-perpendicular to each other. The datum plane will be created passing through the first selection and parallel to the second selection. Click the **Alternate Solution** button to make the datum plane pass through the second line and parallel to the first line.

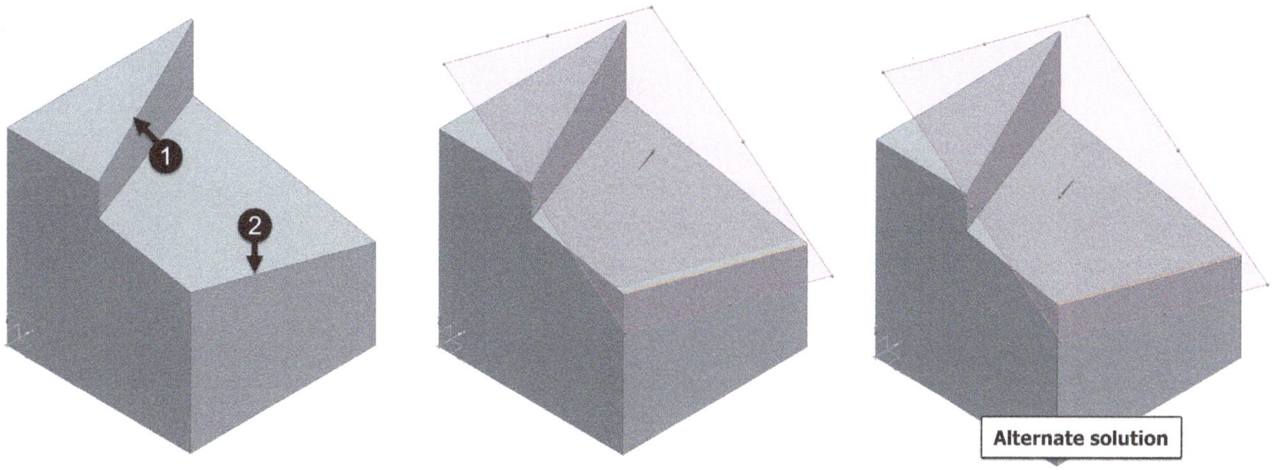

Through Object

This method creates a datum plane passing through a selected curve, edge, face, plane, or CSYS. On the **Datum Plane** dialog, click **Type > Through Object** and select an edge, line, curve, face, plane, or CSYS. A datum plane is created passing through the selection. Note that if you select a spherical or cylindrical face, the datum plane will be create passing through center or axis of cylinder, respectively.

On Curve

This method creates a datum plane, which will be normal (perpendicular) to a line, curve, or edge. On the **Datum Plane** dialog, click **Type > On Curve** and select an edge, line, curve, arc, or circle. Next, select an option from the **Location** drop-down (For example, **Arc Length**). Drag the pointer and click on a point to define the location of the plane (or) type-in a value in the **Arc Length** box and press Enter.

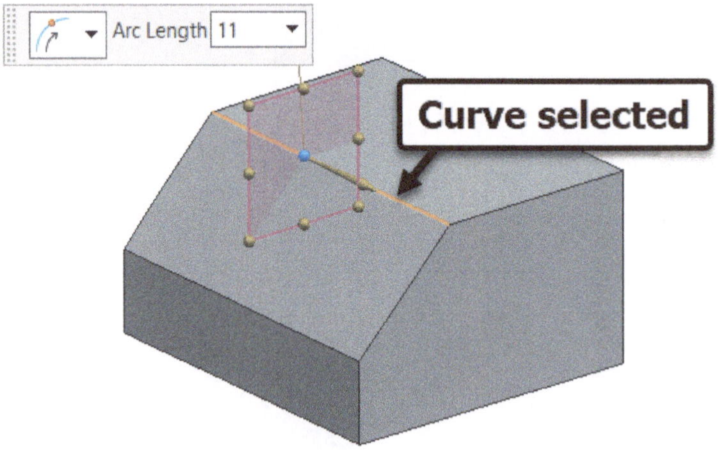

Point and Direction

This method creates a datum plane by defining its position and orientation with precision. On the **Datum Plane** dialog, click **Type > Point and Direction** and select a point on an existing feature or click the **Point Dialog** button and input the precise coordinates of a specific location within your design. This point serves as a reference to the datum plane. Next, click **Specify Vector** in the **Normal Direction** section and select Vector axis from the triad displayed. You can also select a line or edge to define the orientation of the datum plane.

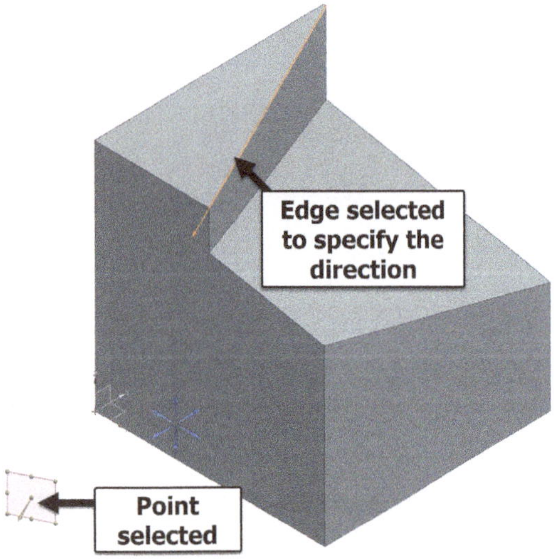

Datum CSYS

This command creates a new coordinate system in addition to the default one. Activate this command (click **Home > Construction > Datum/Point Drop-down > Datum CSYS**  on the ribbon). The Dynamic WCS appears on the default coordinate system. Click on the Translate handle (arrow) and drag the pointer. Click on a point to position the coordinate system.

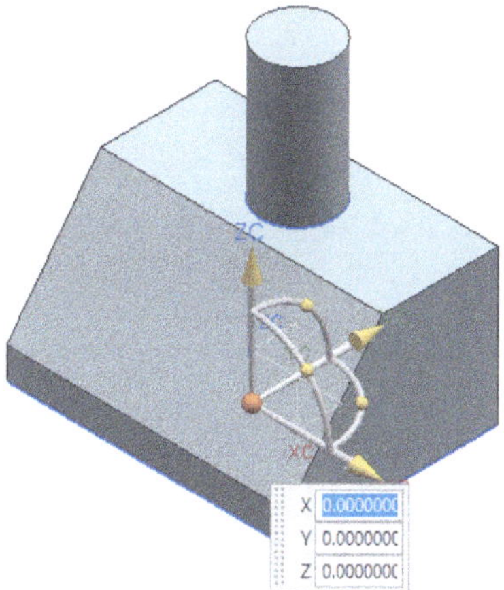

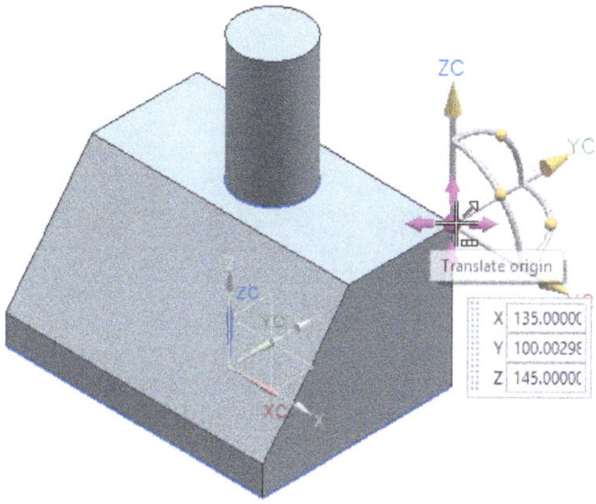

Drag the XC, YC, or ZC handles to translate the Dynamic WCS along X, Y, or Z-axis, respectively. Drag the small dots on the coordinate system to rotate it about X, Y, or Z-axis, respectively. On the dialog, click **OK** to create a new datum coordinate system.

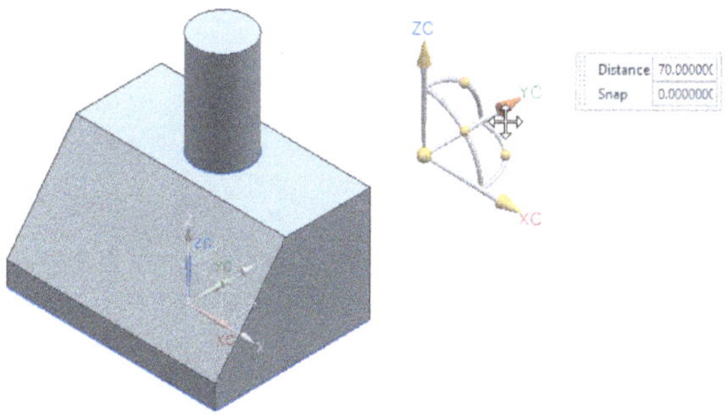

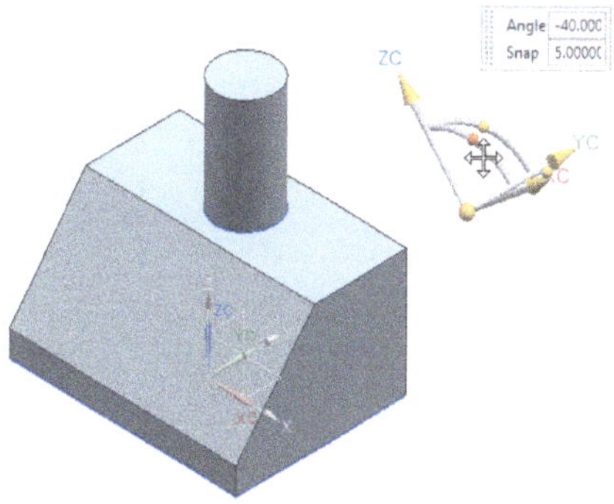

Additional options of the Extrude command

The **Extrude** command has some additional options to create a 3D geometry, complex features, and so on.

Boolean

When you extrude a sketch, the **Boolean** options determine whether the material is added, subtracted, or intersected from an existing solid body.

Inferred

This option adds or removes material from the part geometry. If you extrude a sketch into the part geometry, the material will be removed. Likewise, if you extrude the sketch in the direction away from the part geometry, the material will be added.

Unite

This option adds material to the geometry.

Subtract

This option removes material from the geometry.

Intersect

This option creates a solid body containing the volume shared by two separate bodies.

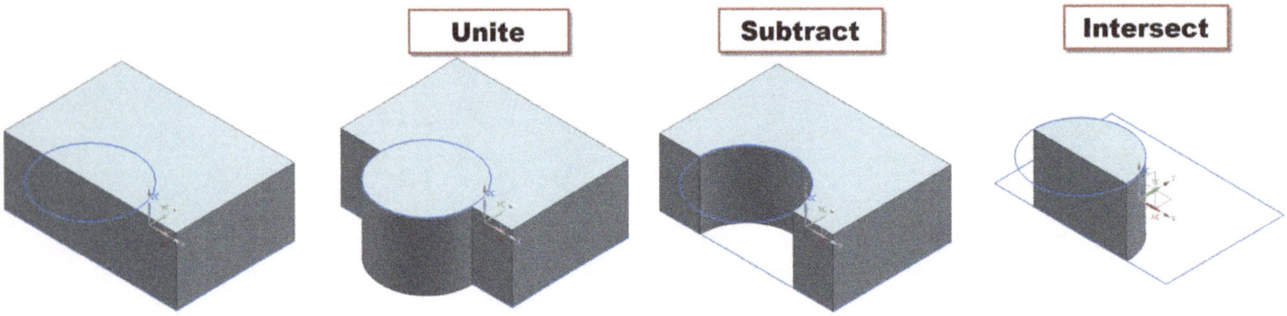

None

This option creates a separate solid body. This will be helpful while creating multi-body parts.

Limits

On the **Extrude** dialog, the **Limits** section has various options to define the start and end limits of the *Extrude* feature. These options are **Value, Symmetric Value, Until Next, Until Selected, Until Extended,** and **Through All.**

The **Until Next** option extrudes the sketch through the face next to the sketch plane.

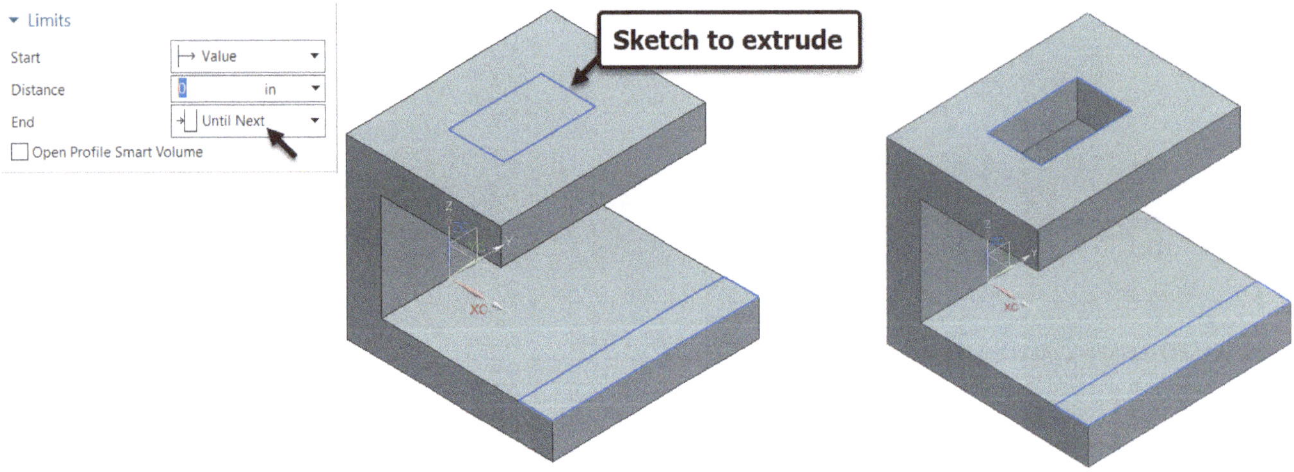

The **Until Selected** option extrudes the sketch up to a selected face. Note that this option only works if the select face or plane will completely intersect the extruded body. Ensure that the sketch will lie on the selected face if projected.

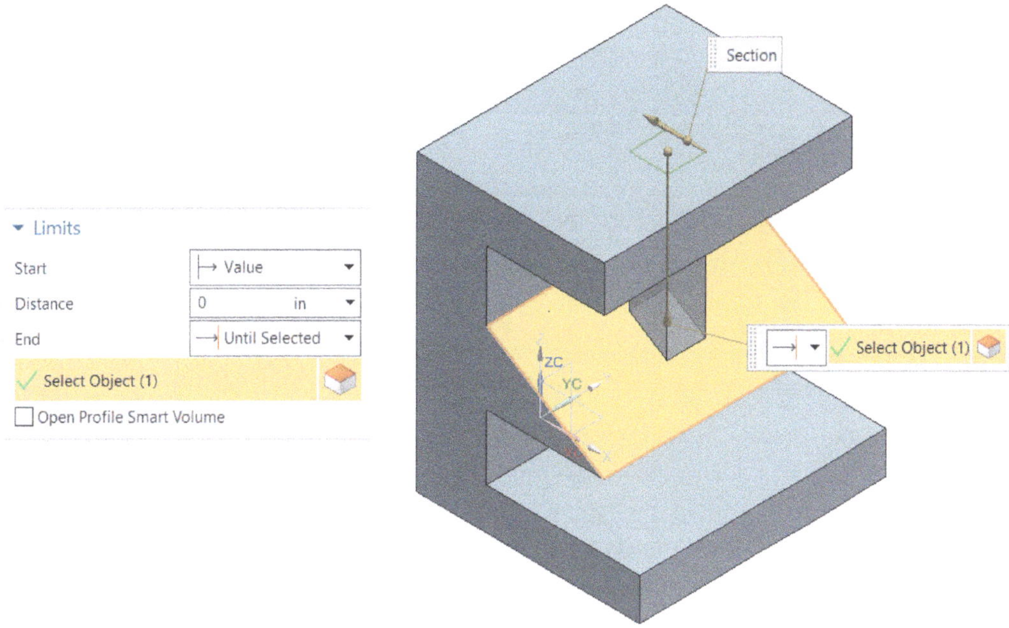

The **Until Extended** option extrudes the sketch from the sketch plane up to the extended portion of the selected face. This option functions even if the extruded body and the chosen face or plane only partially intersect or do not intersect at all.

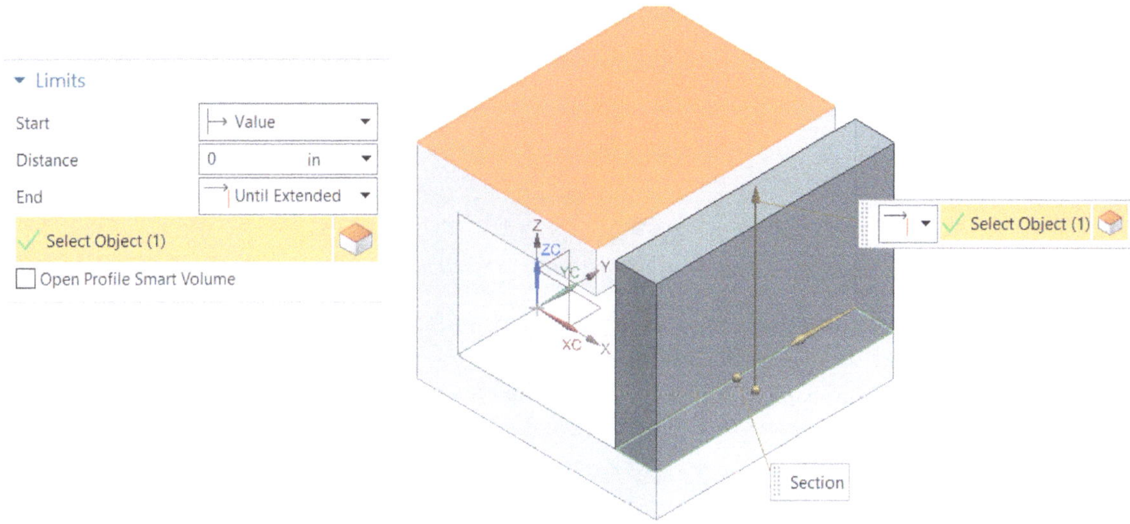

The **Through All** option extrudes the sketch throughout the 3D geometry. Note that on selecting the **Through All** option, it may require more time to process compared to the other options, particularly for complex models.

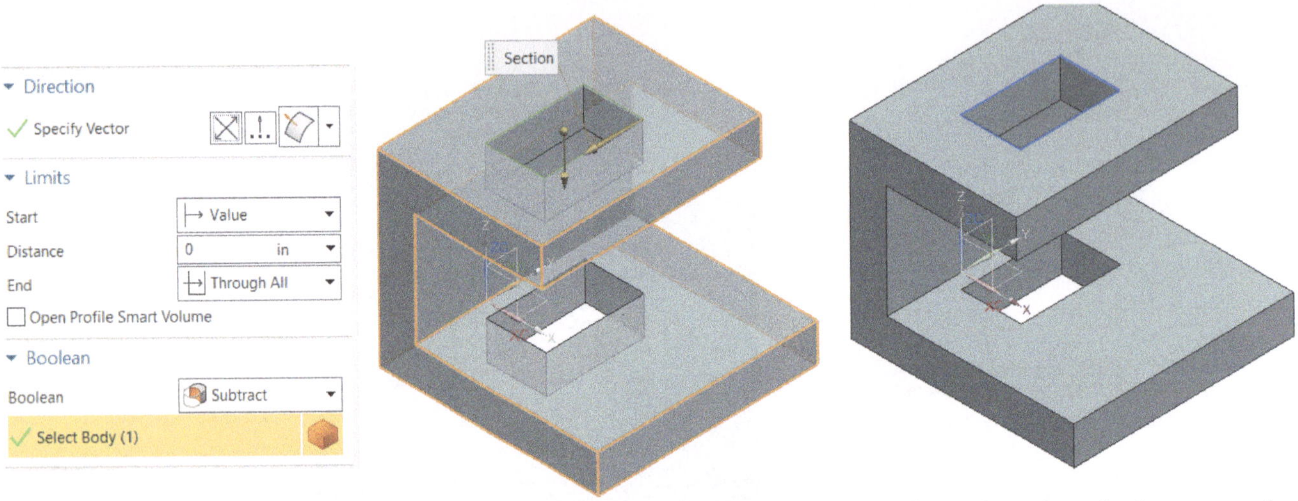

The **Offset from Selected** option extrudes the sketch up to a distance offset from the selected plane or surface. Activate the **Extrude** command and select the sketch to be extruded. Next, select the **Offset from Selected** option from the **End** drop-down. Select a plane or surface, and then type-in a value in the **Distance** box.

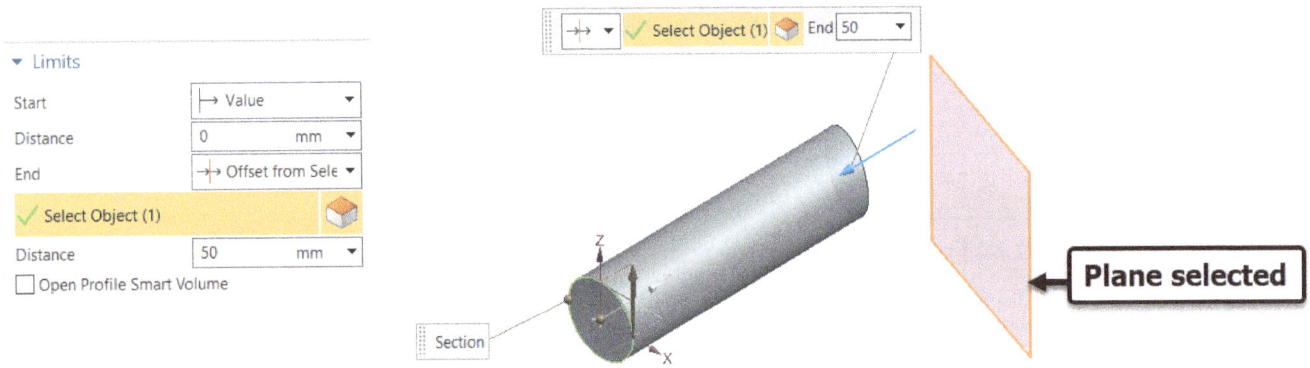

Open Profile Smart Volume

This option creates an *Extrude* feature using an open profile. It extends the profile to meet the adjacent edges. Activate the **Extrude** command, and then click on the open profile. On the dialog, select **Limits > Open Profile Smart Volume** and set the **Boolean** type to **Subtract.** Under the **Direction** section, click the **Reverse Direction** button.

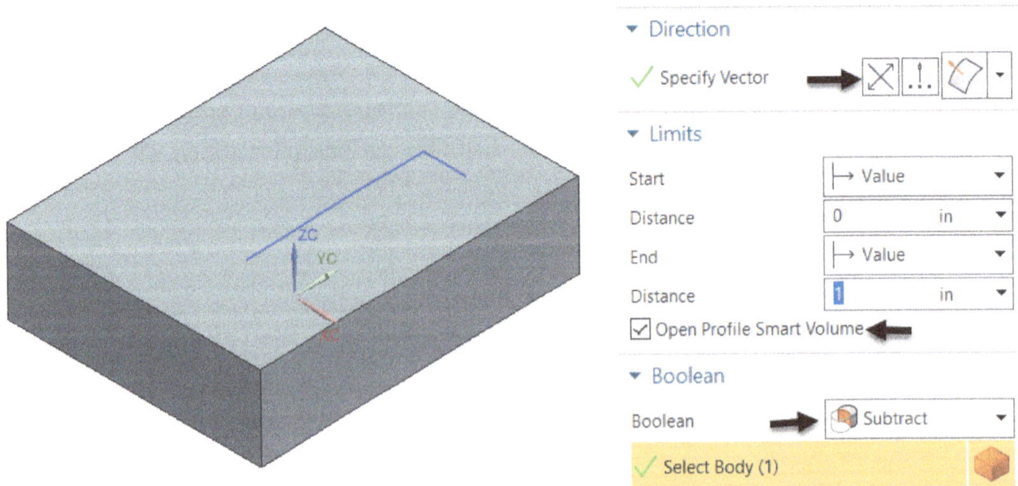

A preview of the *Extrude* feature appears. Double-click on the horizontal arrow to change the material side. On the dialog, type-in a value in the **End Distance** box and press Enter.

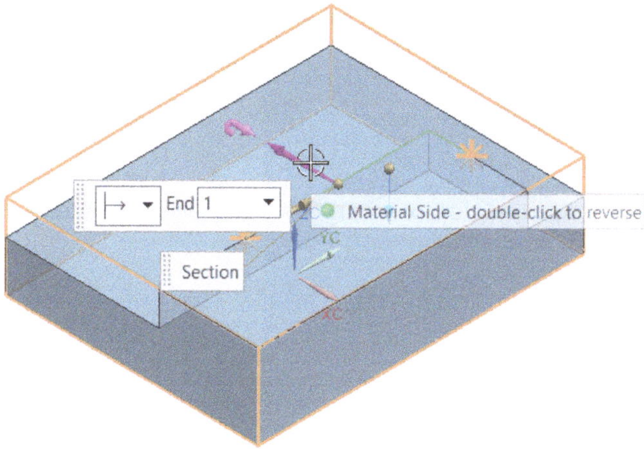

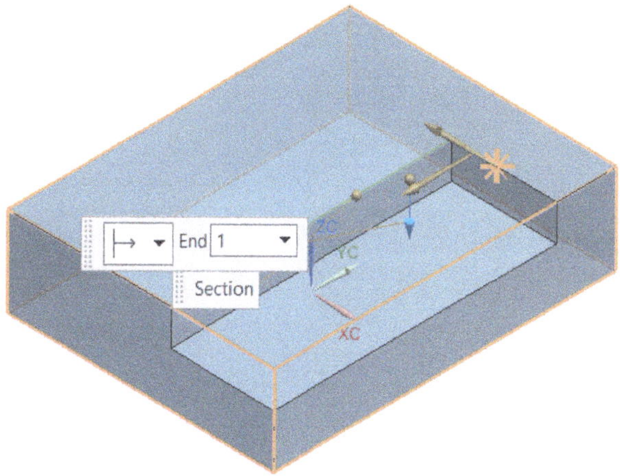

Draft options

The **Draft** options will help you to apply a draft to the extrusion. There are five draft options under the **Draft** section of the **Extrude** dialog: **From Start Limit**, **From Section**, **From Section-Asymmetric Angle**, **From Section-Symmetric Angle**, and **From Section-Matched Ends**. Note that the last three options are available only when you extrude the sketch on both sides of the sketch plane.

The **From Start Limit** option applies a draft to the extrusion from the start limit. Note that the sketch plane and Start Limit are not required to be the same. You can change the start limit of the extrusion by entering a value in the Distance box below the Start drop-down. The draft angle can be changed dynamically using the arrow that appears on the geometry. A positive angle applies an inward draft, and a negative angle applies an outward draft.

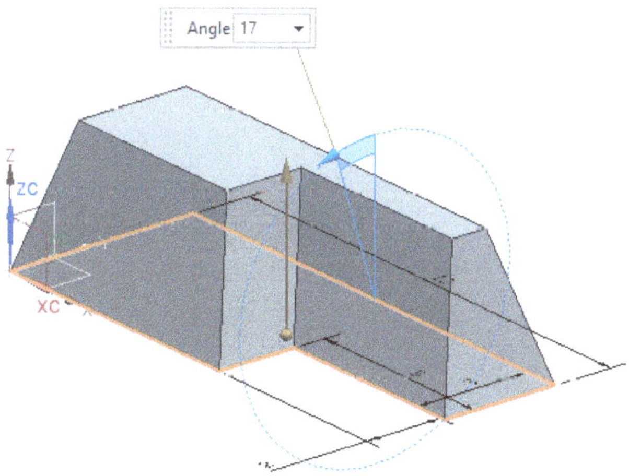

The **From Section** option applies a draft to the extrusion from the sketch plane. In addition, different draft angles can be applied to multiple faces of the extrusion. Select **Angle Option > Multiple**, and you will notice that multiple arrows appear on the side faces of the extrusion. Different angles can be applied dynamically using these arrows.

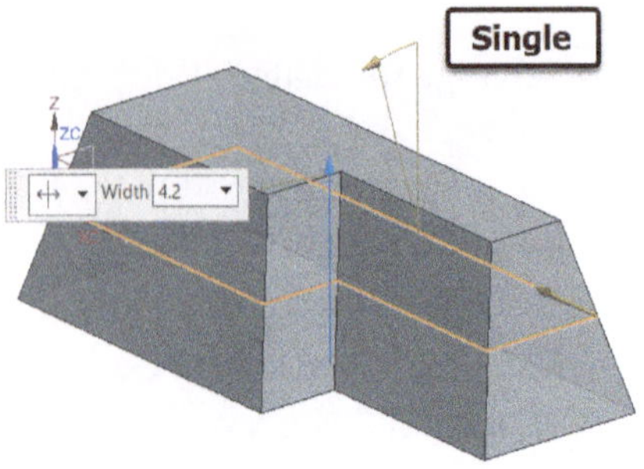

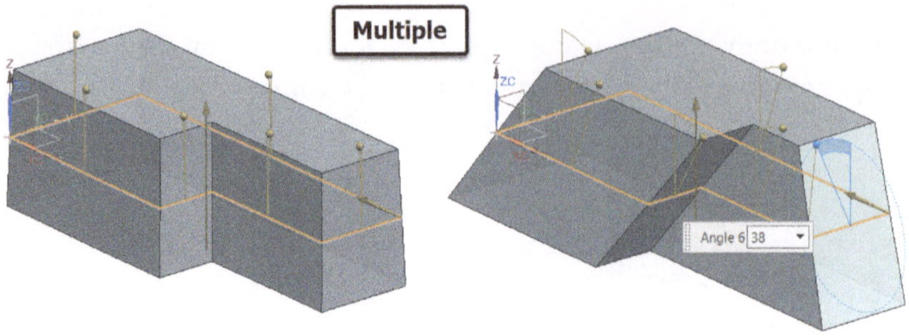

The **From Section-Asymmetric Angle** option applies different draft angles to either side of the sketch plane.

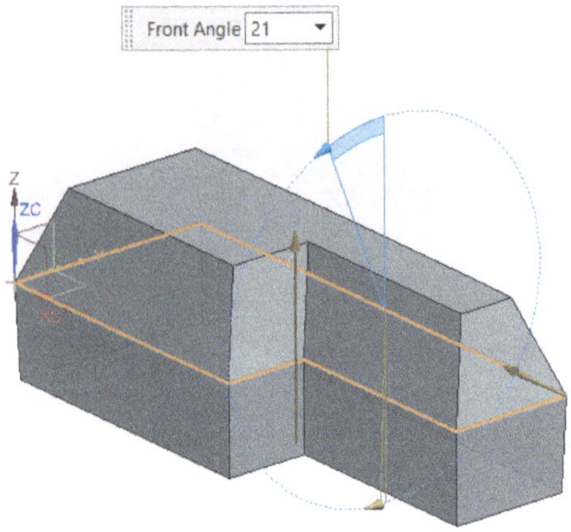

The **From Section-Symmetric Angle** option applies a draft symmetrically on both sides of a sketch plane.

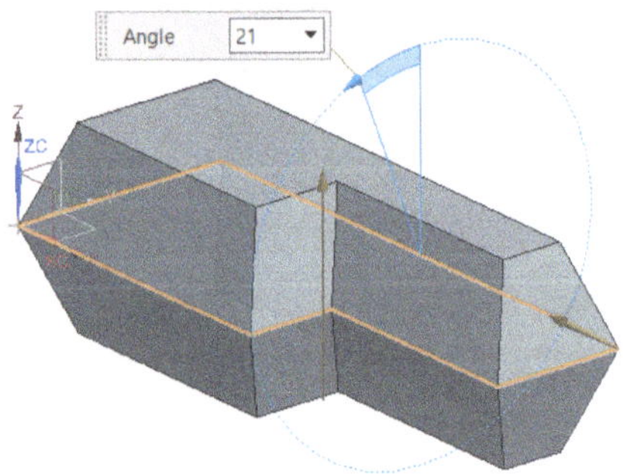

The **From Section-Matched Ends** option applies a draft to both sides of the extrusion such that the top and bottom faces match each other.

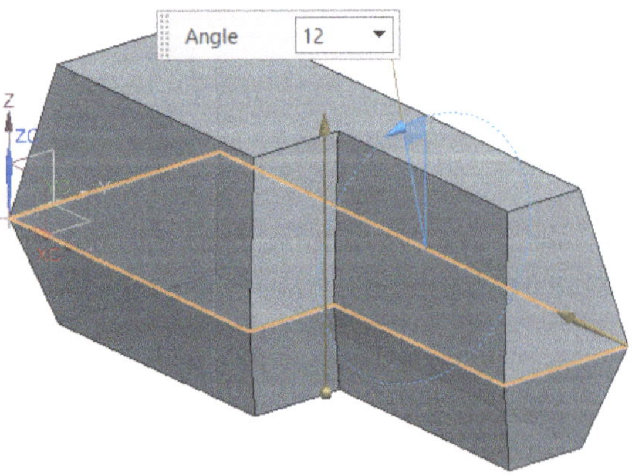

Offset options

The **Offset** options will help you add thickness to the selected sketch. There are three offset options: **Single-Sided**, **Two-Sided**, and **Symmetric**. These three types of offsets are explained in the images shown next.

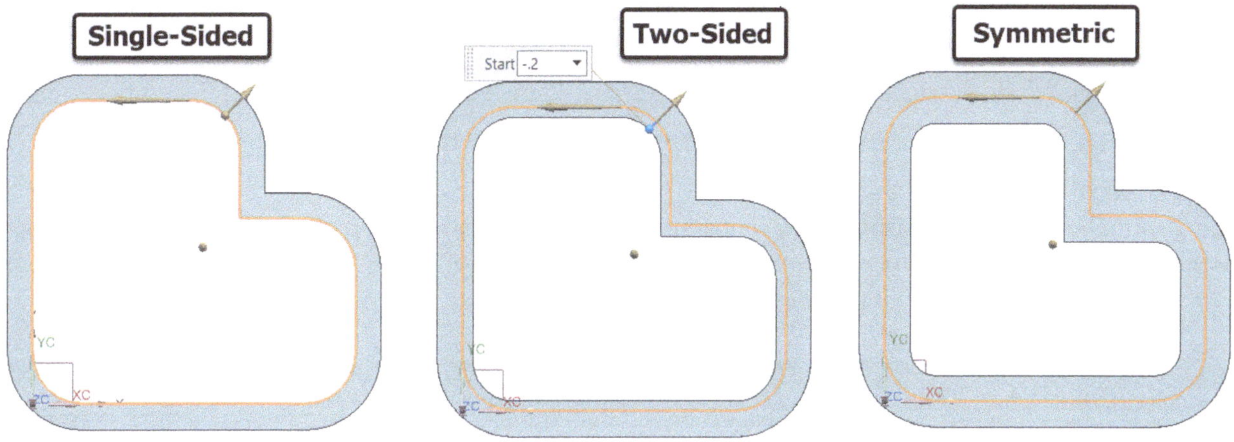

View Modification commands

The model display in the graphics window can be determined using various view modification commands. Most of these commands are located on the **View** tab on the ribbon. These commands can also be accessed from the shortcut menu, or box menu in the graphics window. The following are some of the main view modification commands:

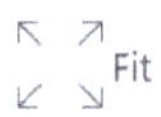	**Fit**	The model will be fitted in the current size of the graphics window so that it will be visible completely.
	**Pan**	Activate this command and press the left mouse button. Drag the pointer to move the model view on the plane parallel to the screen.
	**Rotate**	Activate this command and press the left mouse button. Drag the pointer to rotate the model view. You can select the model edges or curves to rotate about them. You can also type-in a rotation angle.
	**Zoom**	Activate this command and drag a rectangle. The contents inside the rectangle will be zoomed.
	**Fit View to Selection**	This command fits the selected objects in the graphics window. It is available in the **More** gallery of the **Operations** group of the **View** ribbon tab.

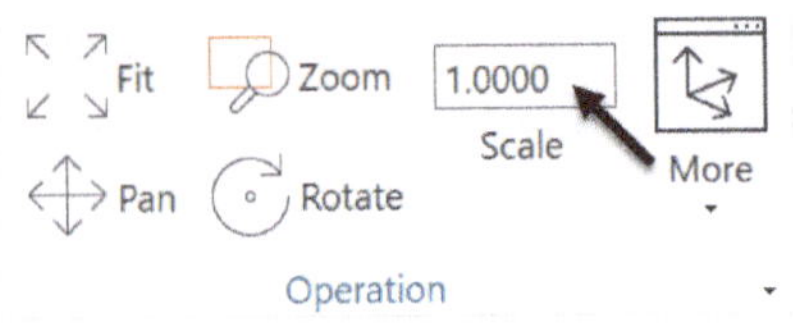	**Zoom Scale**	Type-in a value in this box and press Enter; the model view is zoomed in or out based on the value that you entered. Note that this box is available only on the **View** tab of the ribbon.

Visualization commands

You can control how a model is displayed by choosing from different visualization options available on the **Display** tab of the ribbon. These commands allow you to switch between perspective and parallel projection, apply shading with or without edges, or display the model in various wireframe styles.

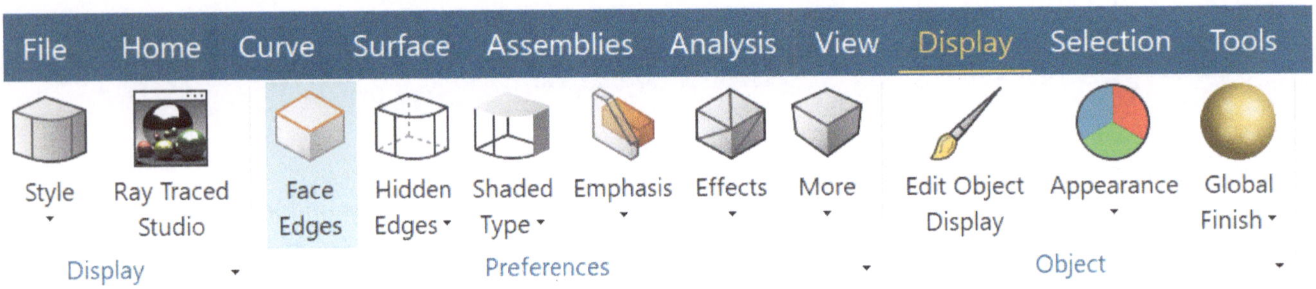

Perspective

This command is available in the **Preferences** group. It allows you to switch between **perspective projection** and **parallel projection** of the model.

In **perspective projection**, the model is displayed as it would appear to the human eye. Objects that are farther from the viewpoint appear smaller, while closer objects appear larger. This gives a realistic 3D view, which is useful when you want to visualize how the model would look in a real-world setting.

In **parallel projection**, all objects are displayed at their true size, regardless of distance from the viewpoint. There is no sense of depth, and parallel lines remain parallel instead of converging. This mode is often used for technical drawings and measurements, where accuracy and proportions must be preserved.

Perspective OFF

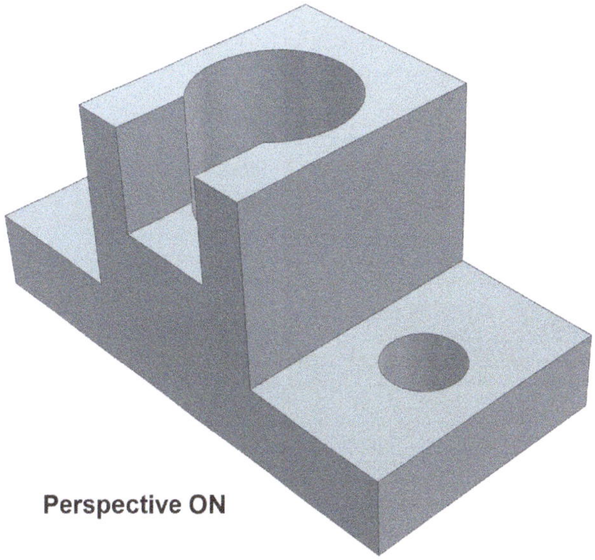

Perspective ON

Style

This drop-down is available in the **Display group**. It allows you to switch between different display styles of the model, such as **Shaded**, **Wireframe**, and **Studio**.

Shaded

The model is displayed with solid surfaces filled in using colors and material properties.

Wireframe

The model is represented using only its edges and curves. Surfaces are transparent, making all internal and external edges visible.

Studio

This style enhances the shaded display with more realistic lighting, reflections, and rendering effects.

Shaded

Wireframe

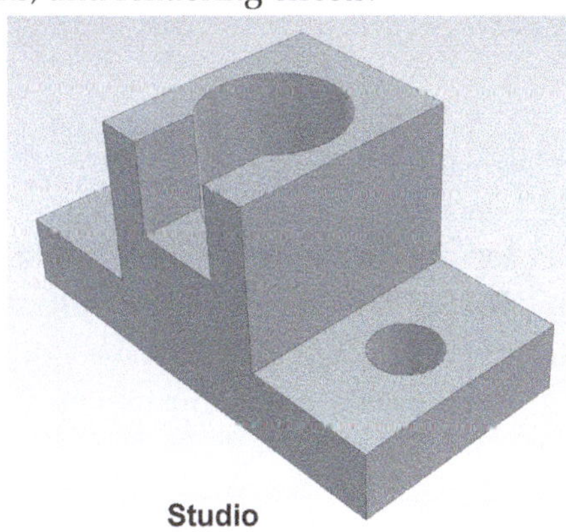

Studio

Orient View drop-down

This drop-down is used to change the orientation of the model. It is available on the **Top Border Bar**. If it is not visible, click the down arrow on the right side of the Top Border Bar and enable the **View group** option.

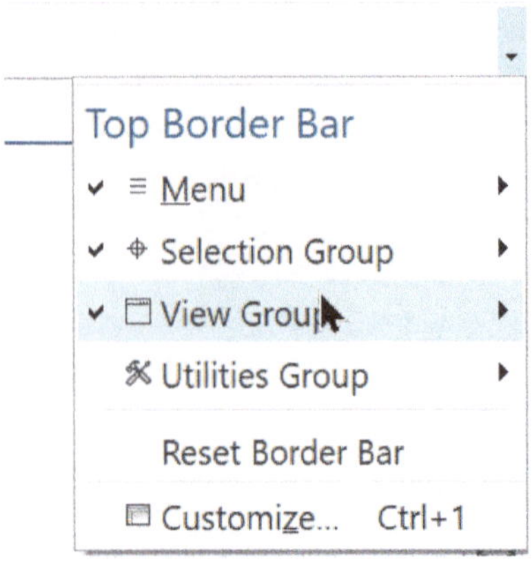

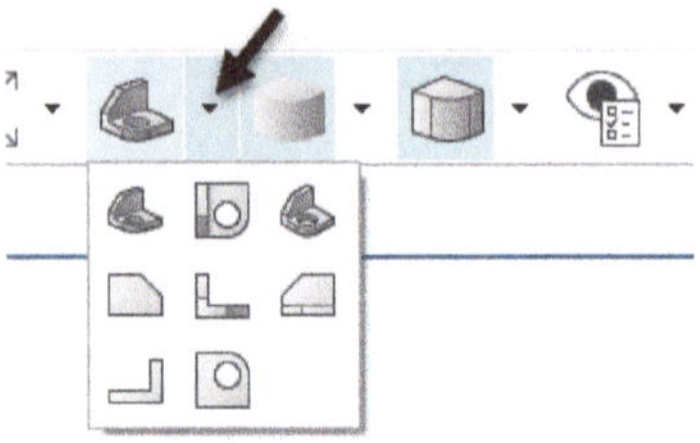

Examples

Example 1 (Millimeters)

In this example, you will create the part shown below.

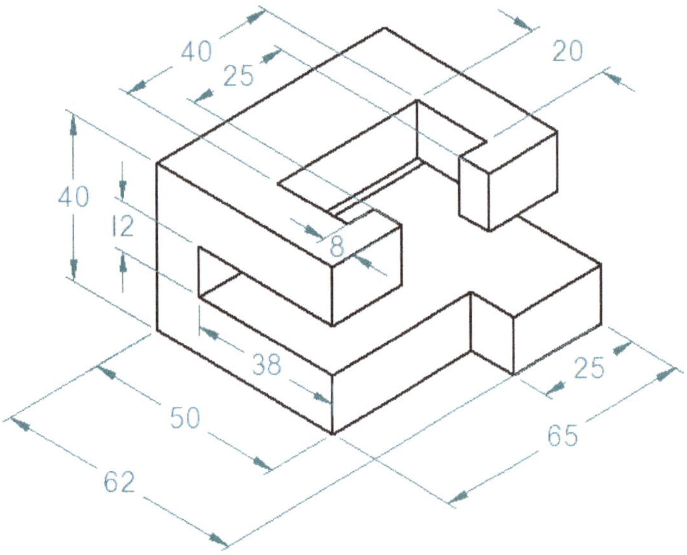

Creating the Base Feature

1. Start **NX**.
2. On the ribbon, click **Home > Standard > New**.
3. On the **New** dialog, select **Units > Millimeters**. Click the **Model** template, and then click **OK**.
4. On the ribbon, click **Home > Construction > Sketch**.
5. On the Datum coordinate system, click the Front plane. Click **OK** on the **Create Sketch** dialog.

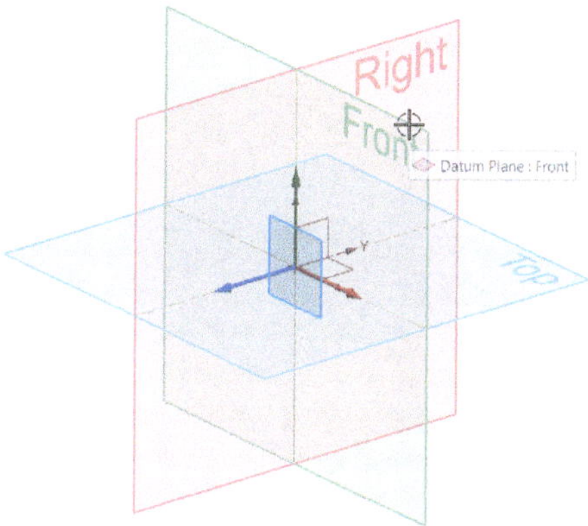

6. On the ribbon, click **Home > Curve > Rectangle** .
7. Click the origin point to define the first corner of the rectangle.
8. Move the pointer toward the top right corner and click to define the second corner. Press ESC.
9. Select the horizontal line of the rectangle, and then click on the dimension attached to it.
10. Type **50** in the dimension box and press Enter on the Keyboard.
11. Click **OK** on the **Scale Sketch on First Dimension** message box. Next, press ESC.
12. Select the vertical line of the rectangle, and then click on the dimension attached to it.
13. Type 40 in the dimension box and press Enter on the Keyboard. Next, press ESC.

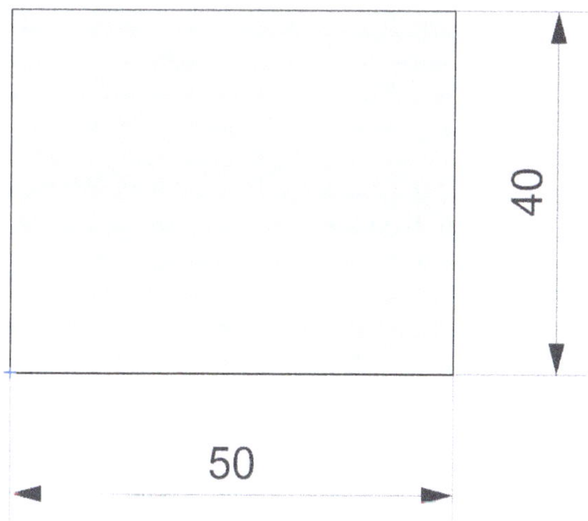

14. On the ribbon, click **Home > Sketch > Finish**.
15. On the ribbon, click **Home > Base> Extrude**. Select the sketch if not already selected.
16. On the **Extrude** dialog, under the **Limits** section, click **Start > Symmetric Value**.
17. On the dialog, type-in **65** in the **Distance** box and press Enter on the Keyboard. Click **OK** on the **Extrude** dialog to complete the *Extrude* feature.

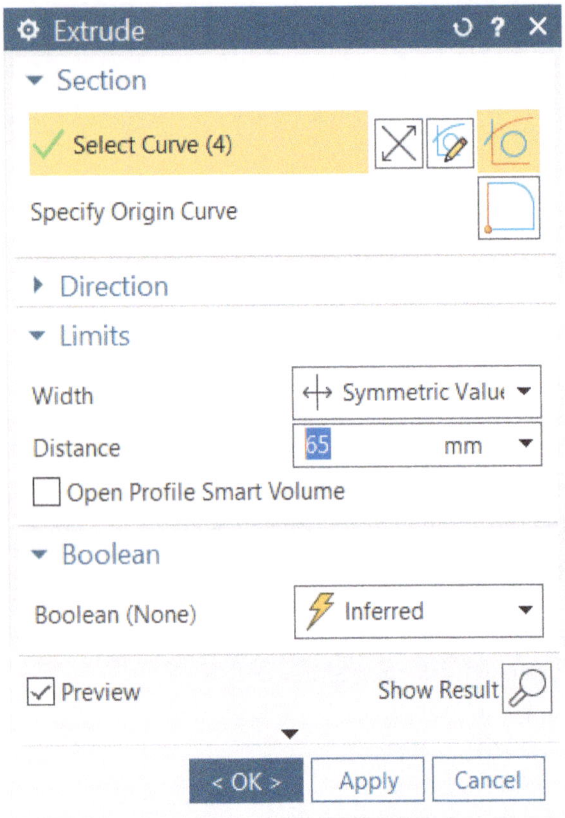

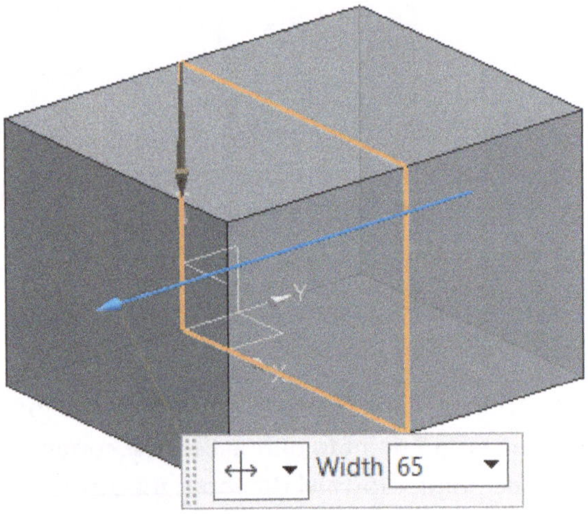

Creating the Cut throughout the body

1. Activate the **Extrude** command and click on the front face of the part geometry. Make sure that you click near the lower-left corner. This defines sketch origin at the lower-left corner.

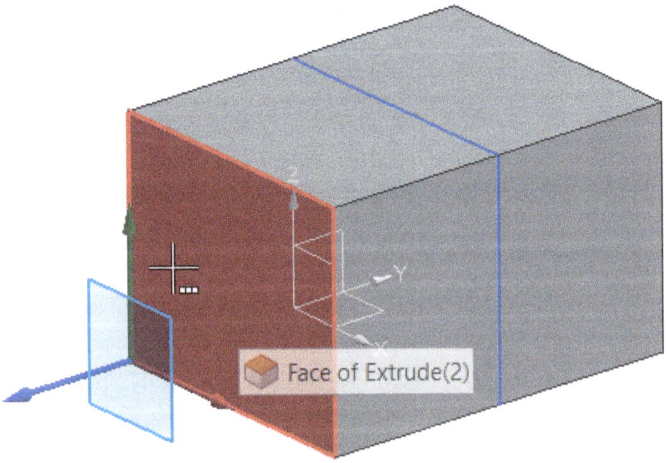

2. On the ribbon, click **Home > Include > Include**. Next, click on the right vertical edge and click **OK**.

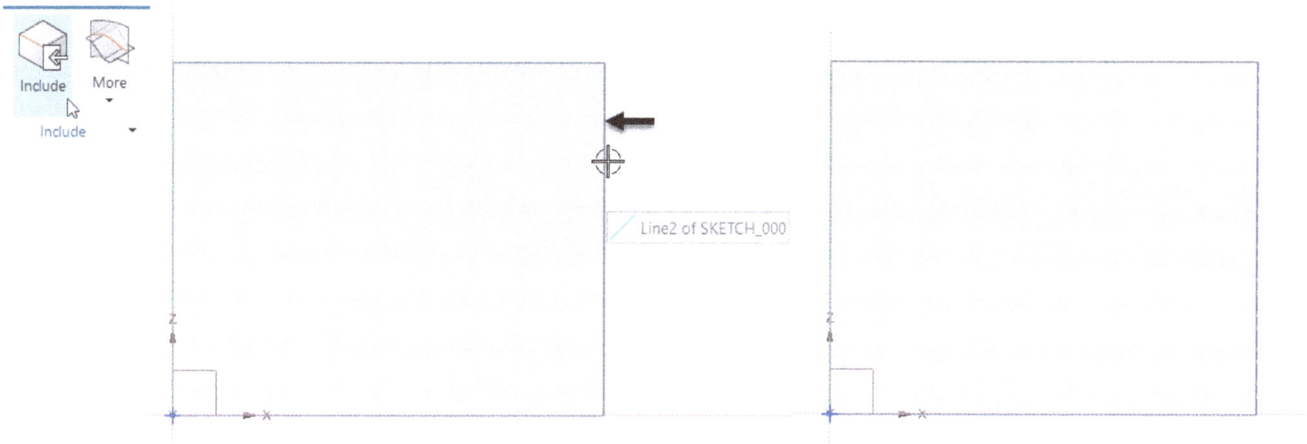

3. On the ribbon, click **Home > Curve > Rectangle**  .
4. Click on the upper portion of the included vertical edge.
5. Move the pointer diagonally toward bottom-left, and then click. Next, press ESC.

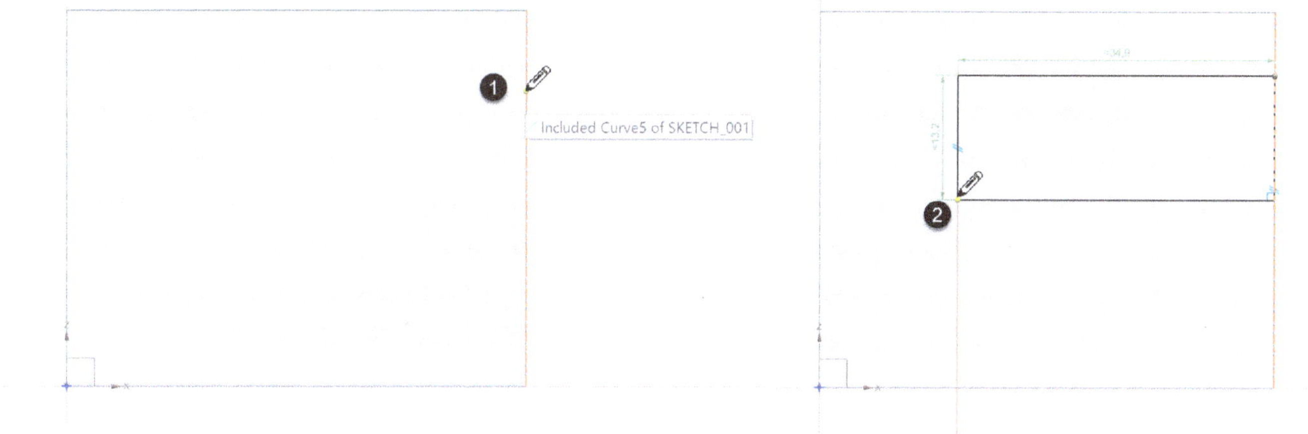

6. Select the horizontal line of the sketch, and click on the dimension attached to it.
7. Type 38 in the **Dimension** box and press Enter on the Keyboard. Next, press ESC.
8. Select the vertical line of the sketch, and click on the dimension attached to it.
9. Type 12 in the **Dimension** box and press Enter on the Keyboard.
10. Select the left vertical line of the rectangle, and then select its midpoint.
11. Select the included vertical edge.
12. On the Sketch Screen Bar, click the **Make Midpoint Aligned** icon; the midpoint of the left vertical line of the rectangle is aligned to the midpoint of the included edge.

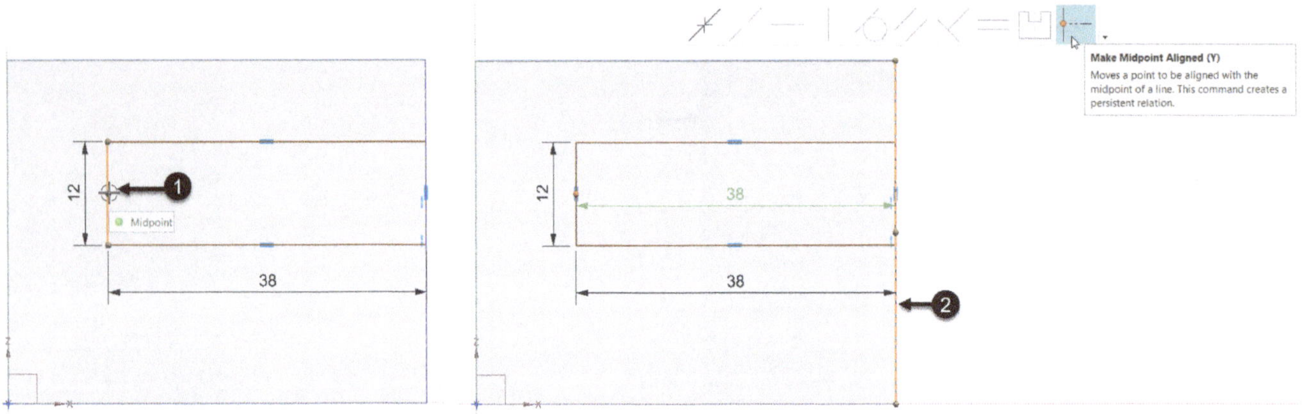

13. On the ribbon, click **Home > Sketch > Finish**.
14. On the dialog, select **End > Through All**. Under the **Boolean** section, select **Boolean > Subtract**.
15. If the extrude handle points toward the front, then click the **Reverse Direction**  button under the **Direction** section.
16. Click **OK** to create the cut throughout the part geometry.

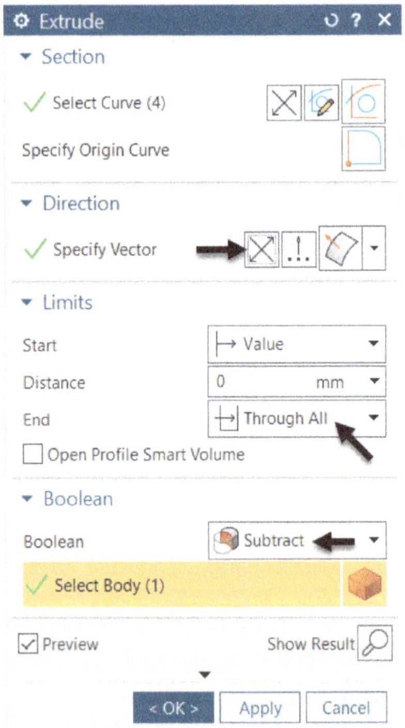

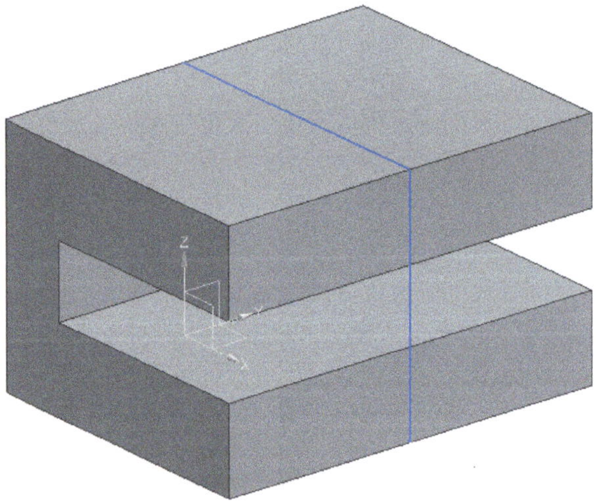

Creating the Cut up to the surface next to the sketch plane

1. Activate the **Extrude** command and click on the top face of the part geometry. Make sure that you click near the lower-left corner. This defines the sketch origin at the lower-left corner.

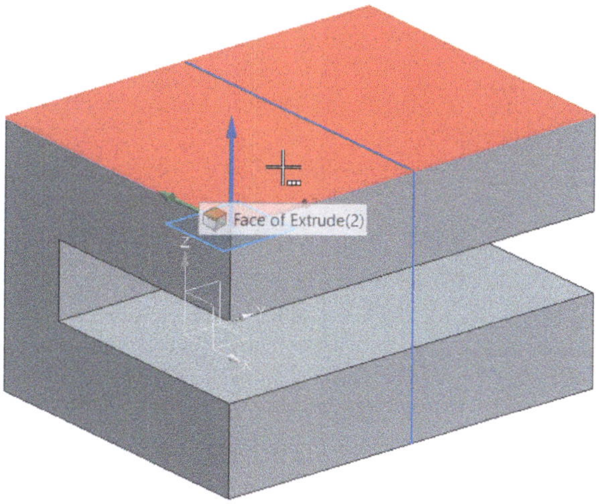

2. Activate the **Line** command and click the horizontal axis, as shown.
3. Move the pointer horizontally toward the right and click.

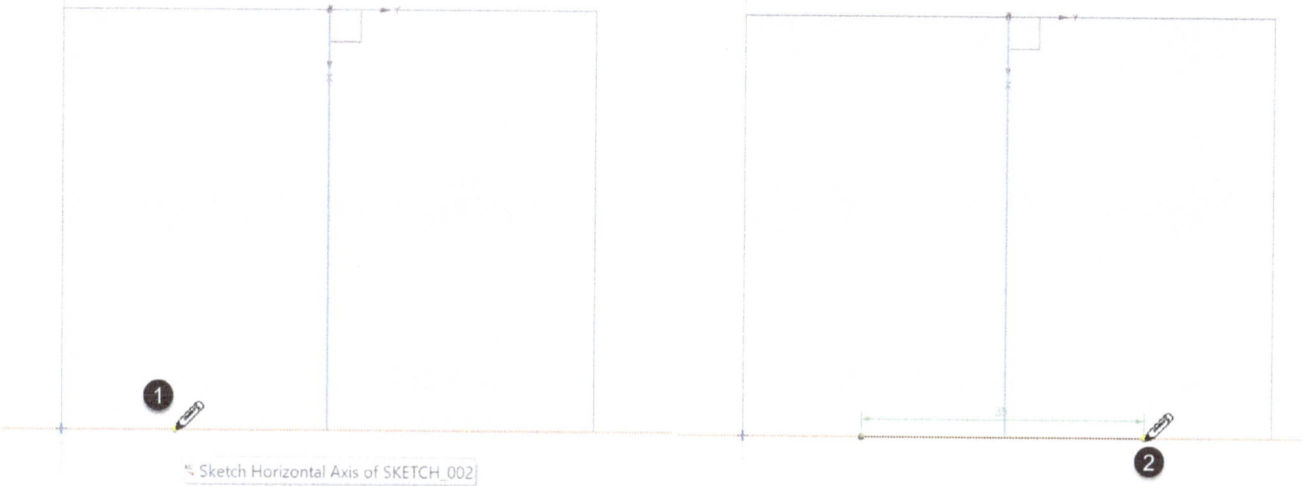

4. Move the pointer vertically upward and click when a dimension value of 8 is displayed.
5. Move the pointer horizontally toward the right and click.

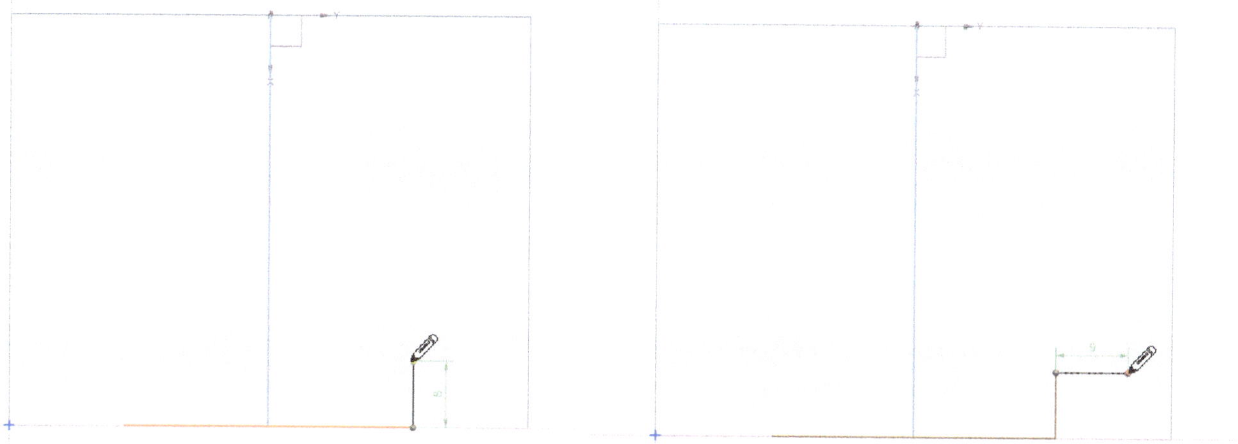

6. Move the pointer vertically upward and click when a dimension value of 20 is displayed.

7. Move the pointer toward the left and click.

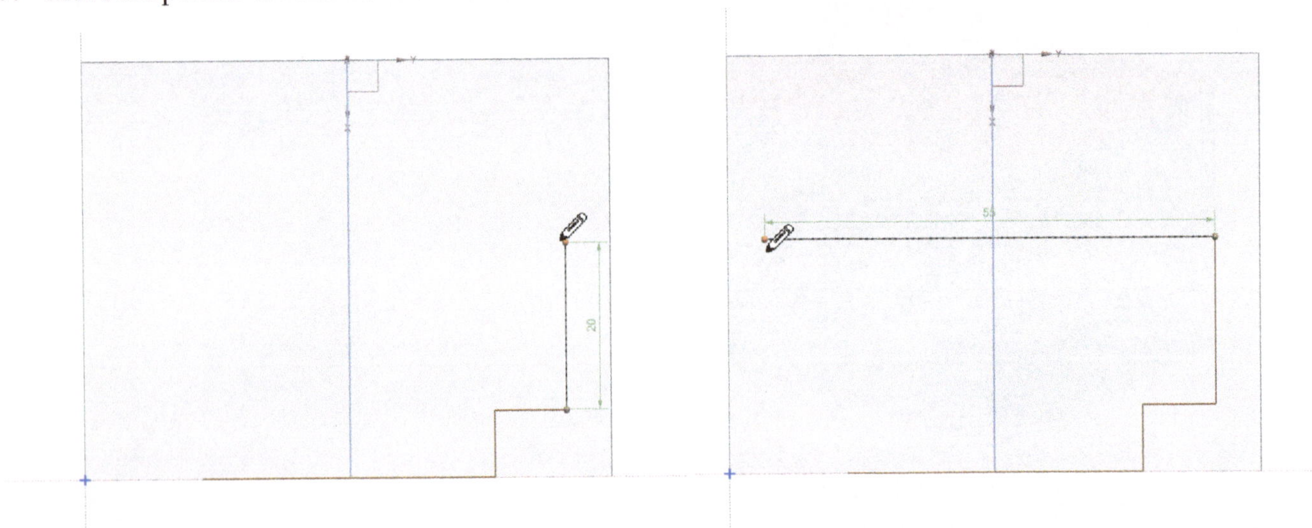

8. Likewise, create the other two lines, as shown. Close the **Line** dialog.

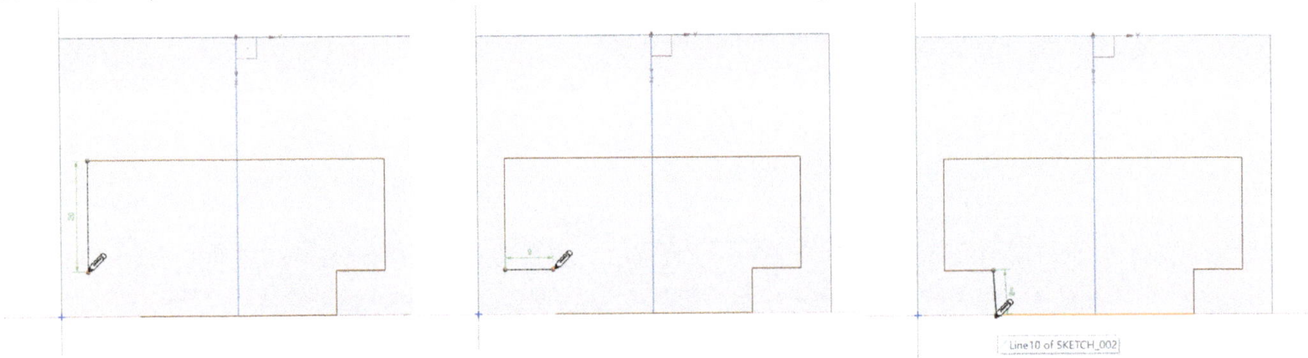

9. Select the two horizontal lines, as shown. Select the **Make Equal** relation from the Sketch Scene Bar.
10. Select the two lines, as shown. Select the **Make Equal** relation from the Sketch Scene Bar.

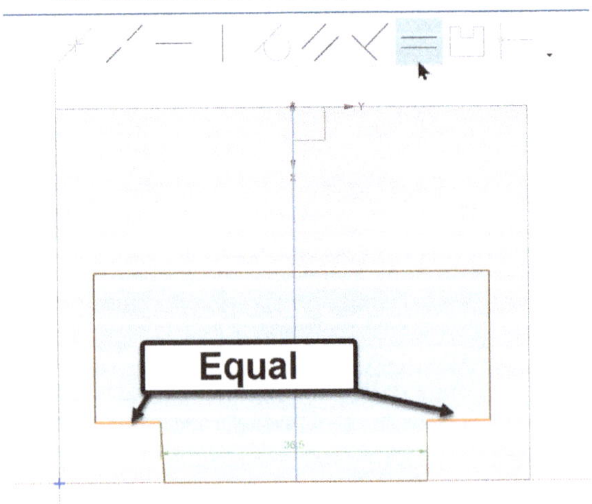

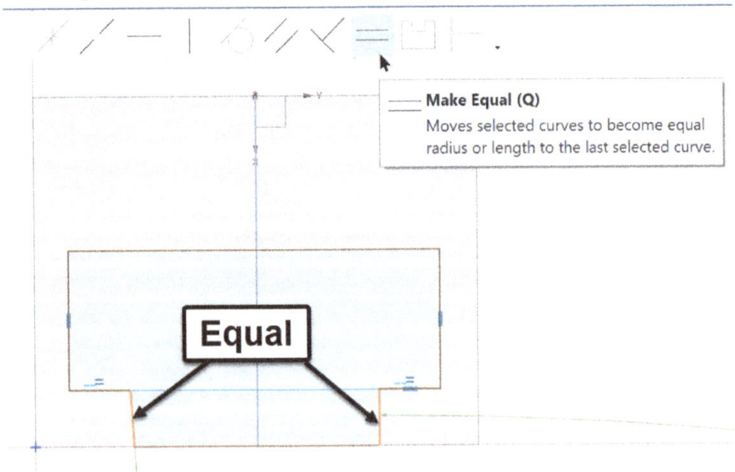

11. Select the line, as shown. On the Sketch Scene Bar, select the **Make Vertical** relation (leave this step if the **Vertical** relation is already applied).

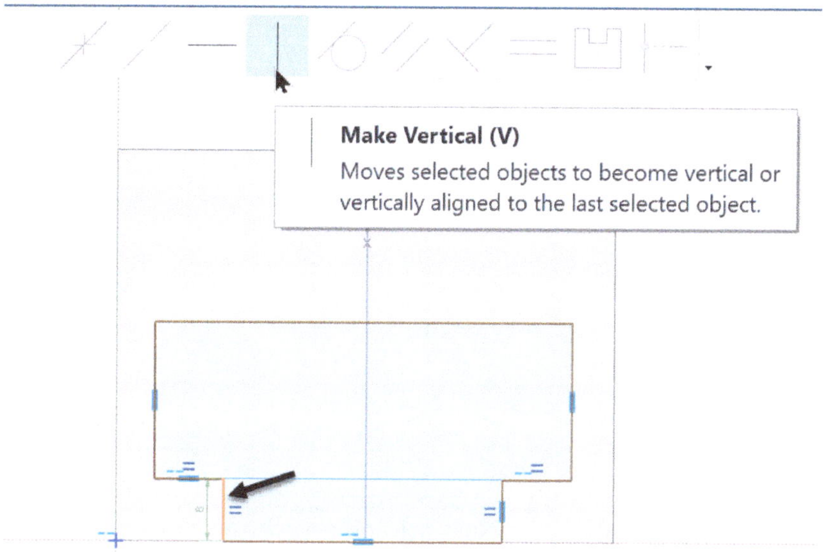

12. Select the bottom horizontal line of the sketch, and click on the dimension attached to the line.
13. Type 24 in the **Dimension** box and press Enter. Click **OK** on the **Scale Sketch on First Dimension** message box. Next, press ESC.
14. Select the top horizontal line of the sketch, and click on the dimension attached to the line.
15. Type 40 in the **Dimension** box and press Enter. Next, press ESC.

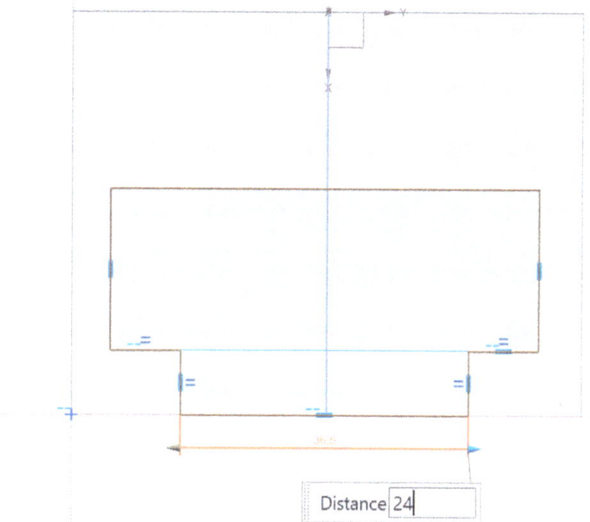

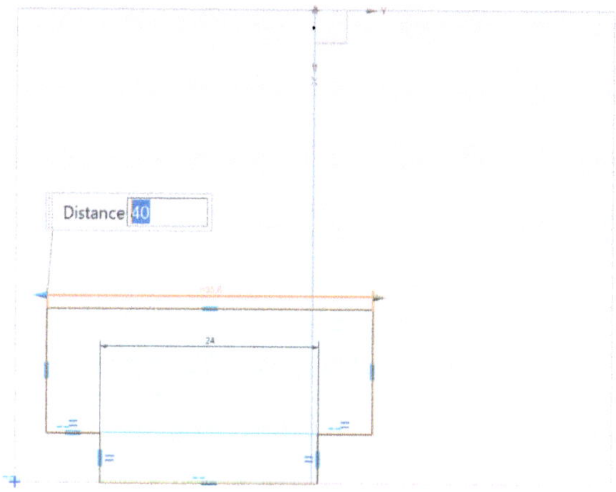

16. Likewise, add the two vertical dimensions, as shown.

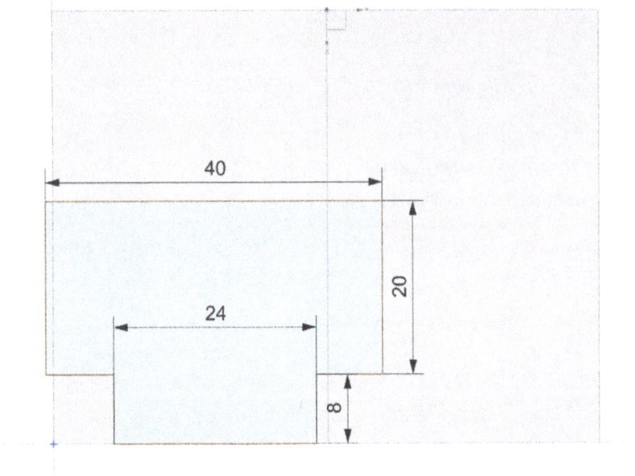

17. On the ribbon, click **Home > Include > Include**  . Next, select the top horizontal edge of the model.
18. Click **OK** to include the selected edge.
19. Select the top horizontal line of the sketch. Next, select the midpoint of the selected line.
20. Select the included horizontal edge and click the Make Midpoint Aligned icon on the Sketch Scene Bar.

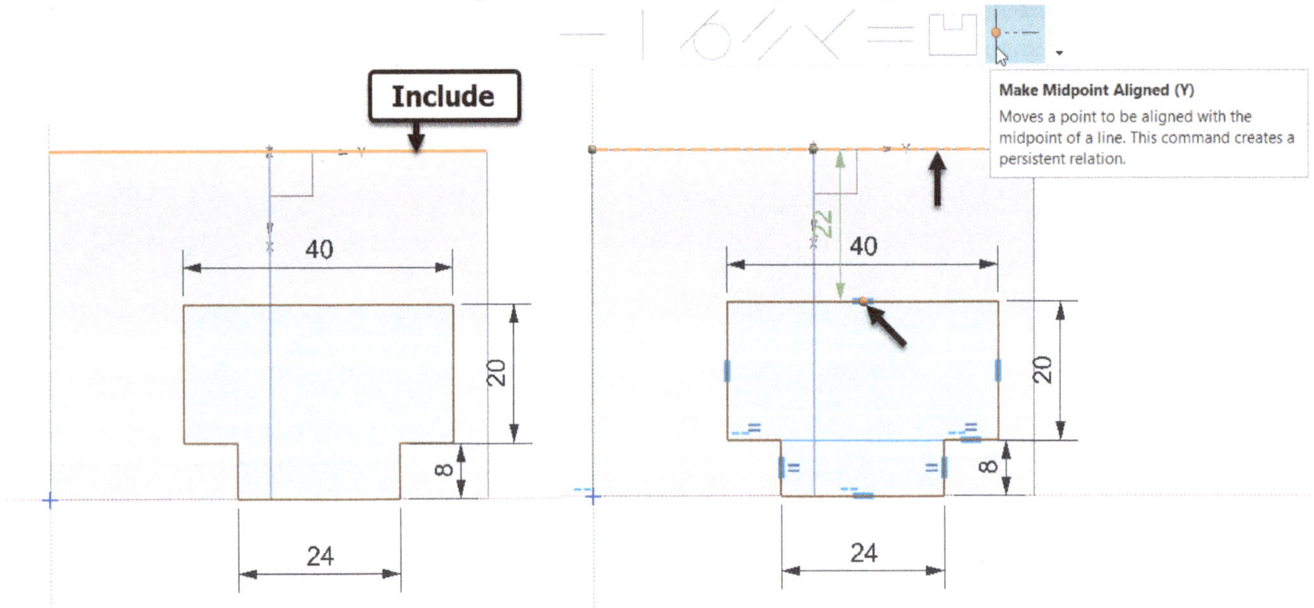

21. On the ribbon, click **Home > Sketch > Finish.**
22. On the **Extrude** dialog, click **End** > **Until Next**. Under the **Direction** section, click the **Reverse Direction** button.
23. Under the **Boolean** section, click **Boolean > Subtract**. Click **OK** to create the cut-out feature until the surface next to the sketch plane.

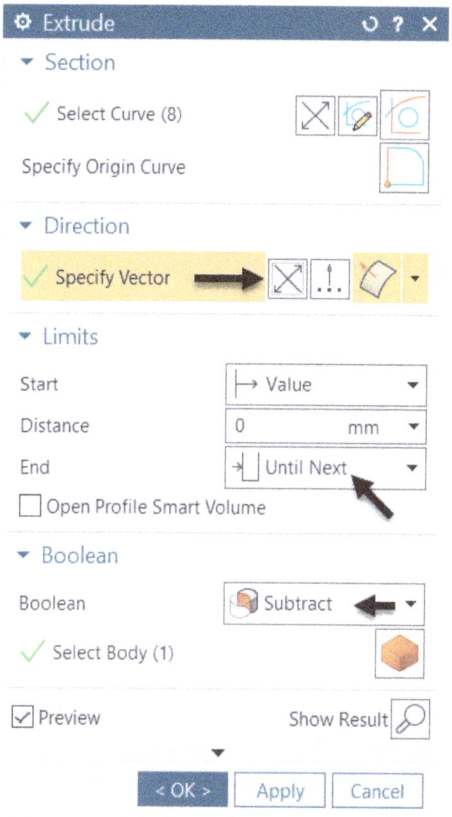

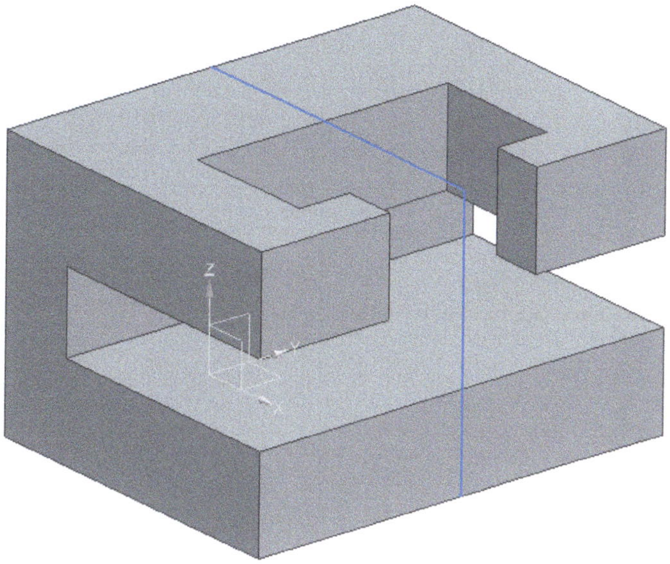

Extruding the sketch up to the Extended Surface

1. Activate the **Extrude** command and click on the horizontal face, as shown in the figure. Make sure that you click near the lower right corner. This defines the sketch origin at the lower right corner.
2. Draw a rectangle. Apply dimensions and finish the sketch.

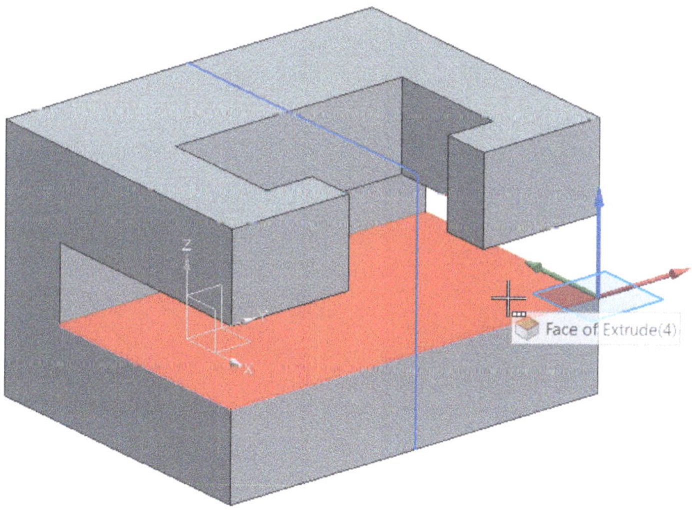

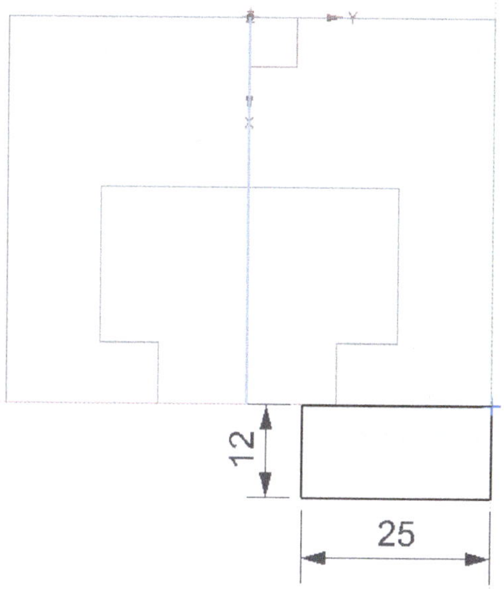

3. On the **Extrude** dialog, click **Boolean > Unite**.
4. Click **End > Until Extended** and select the bottom face of the part geometry.

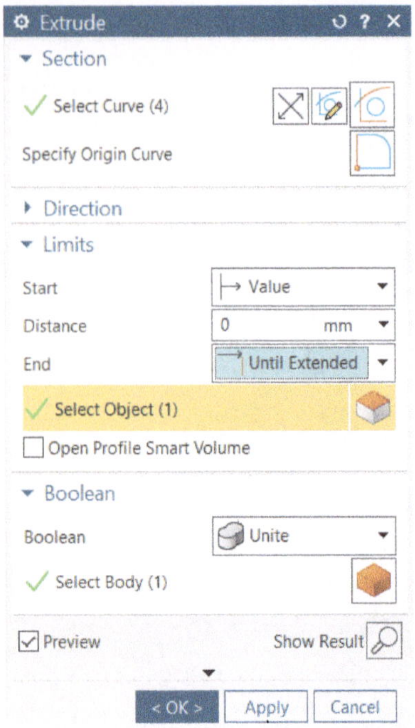

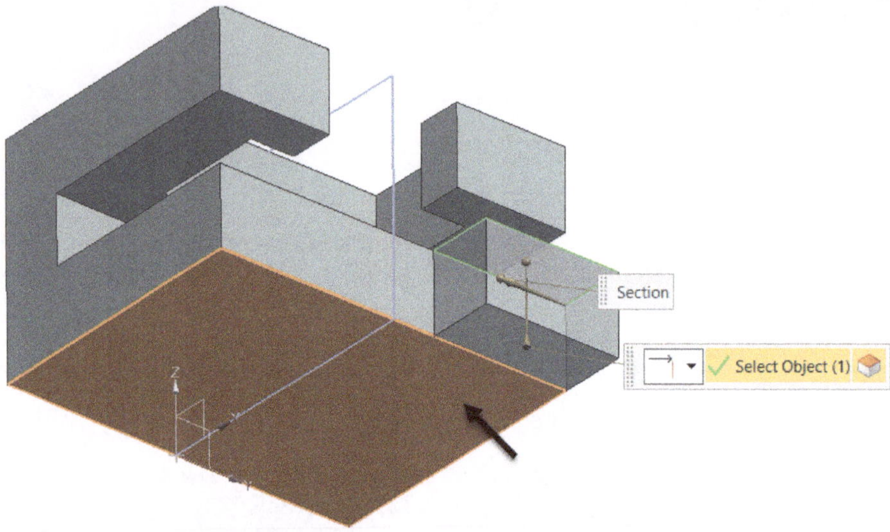

5. Click **OK** to complete the part.
6. On the ribbon, click **View > Content > Show and Hide**.
7. On the **Show and Hide** dialog, click the **Hide** icon next to **Sketches**. Close the dialog.

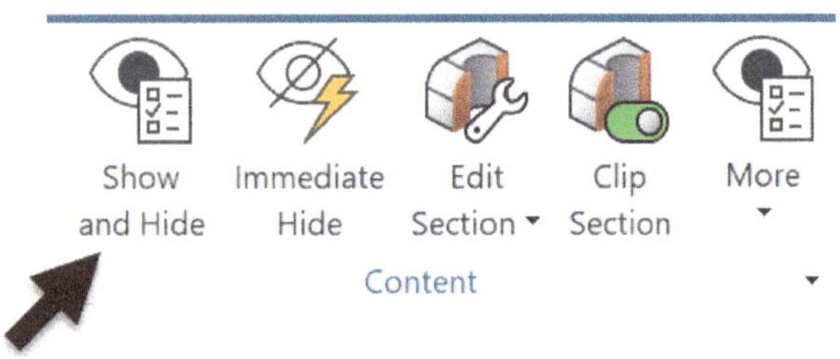

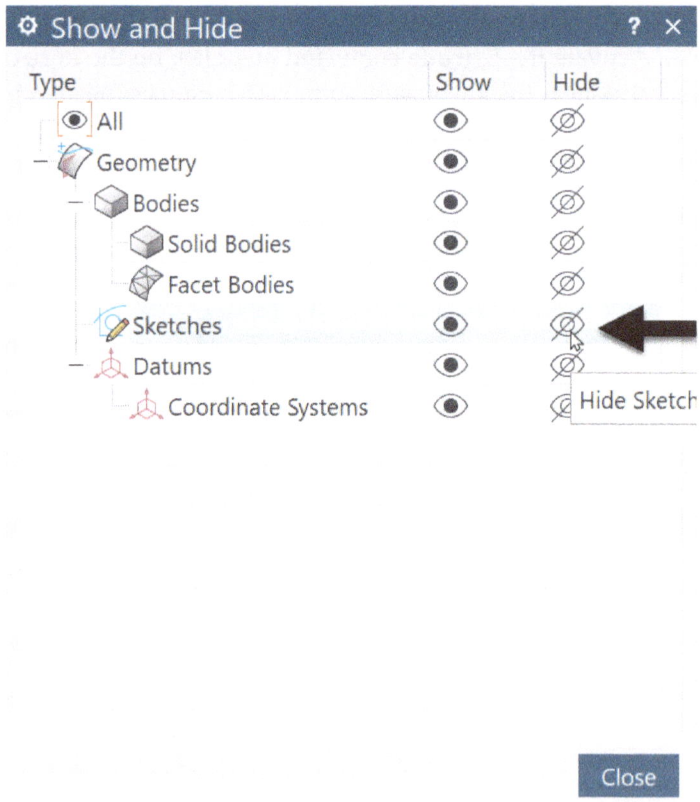

8. Right-click and select **Orient View > Isometric**.

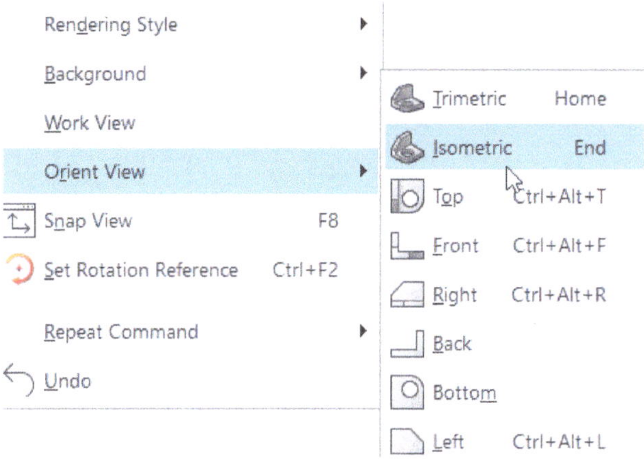

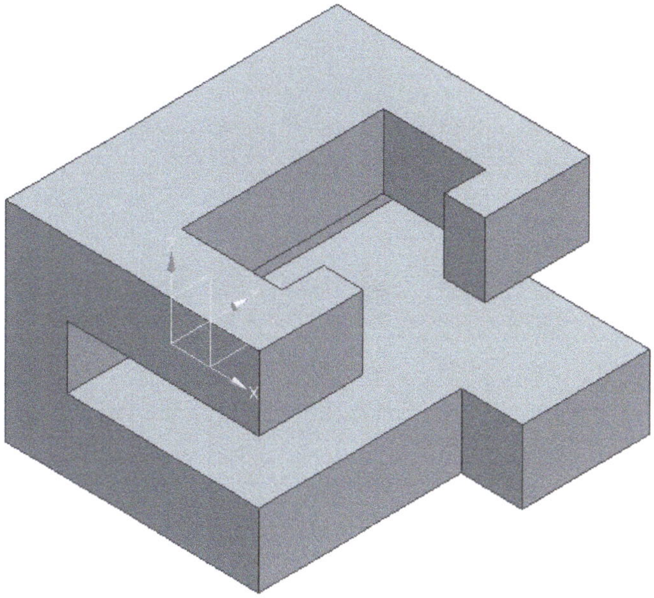

9. Save and close the file.

Example 2 (Inches)

In this example, you will create the part shown below.

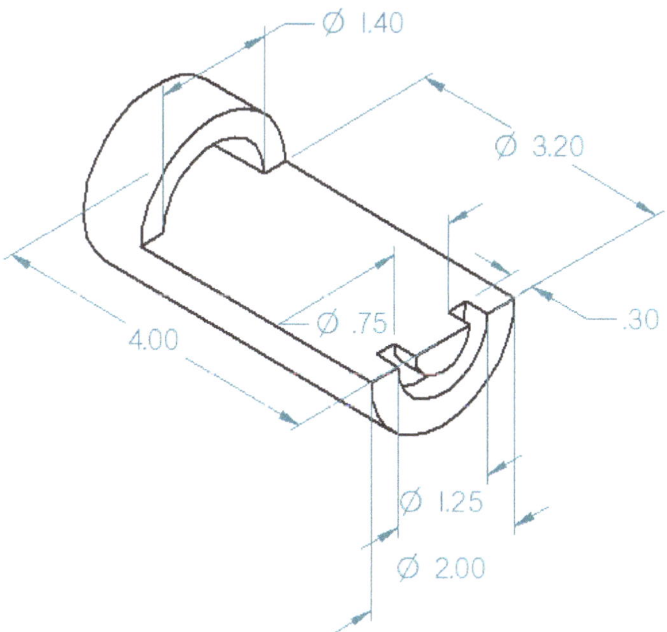

Creating the Revolved Solid Feature

1. Start **NX**.
2. On the **Quick Access Toolbar**, click **New**; the **New** dialog appears.
3. On the **New** dialog, click **Units > Inches** and select the **Model** template. Click **OK** to close the dialog.
4. On the ribbon, click **Home > Construction > Sketch**.
5. Select the Top plane from the Datum Coordinate System. Click **OK** on the **Create Sketch** dialog.

6. On the ribbon, click **Home > Curve > Rectangle From Center** icon. Specify the three points of the rectangle, as shown. Close the **Rectangle from Center** dialog.

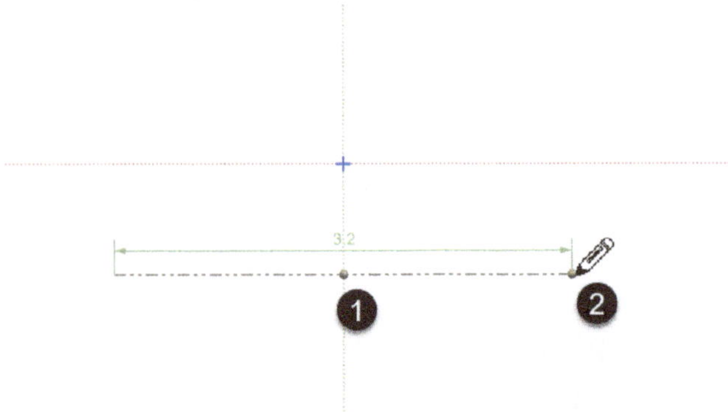

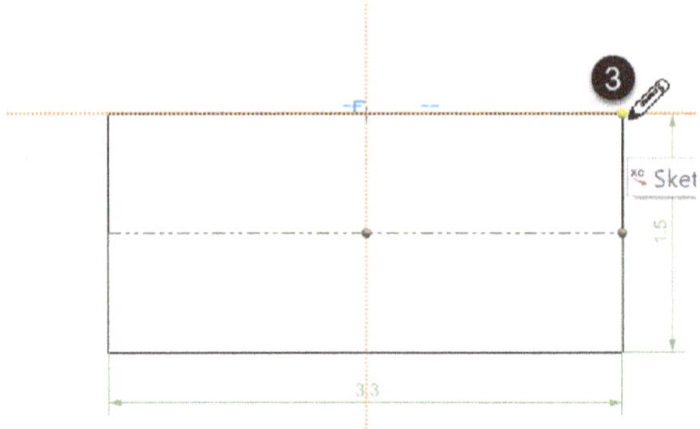

7. Apply dimensions to the sketch, as shown.

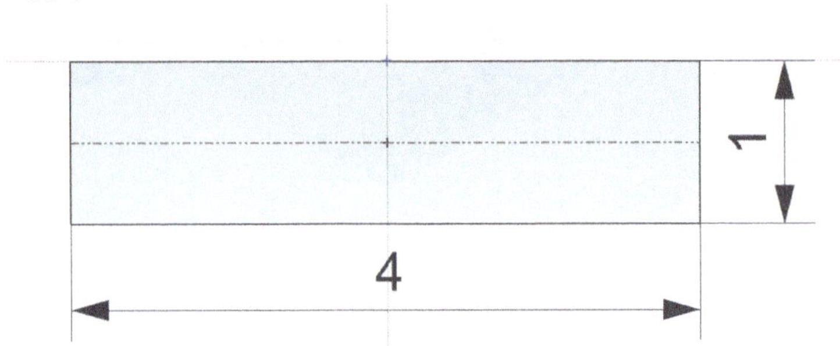

8. Click **Home > Sketch > Finish** on the ribbon.
9. Activate the **Revolve** command (On the ribbon, click **Home > Base > Revolve**) and click on the sketch.
10. On the **Revolve** dialog, click **Specify Vector** and click on the line passing through the XC-axis.
11. On the **Revolve** dialog, under the **Limits** section, type-in **180** in the **Angle** box below the **End** drop-down. Click the **Reverse Direction** button under the **Axis** section, if required. Click **OK** to create the *Revolve* feature.

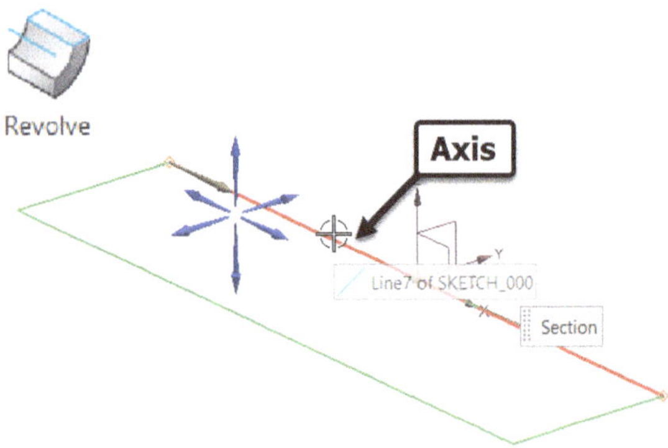

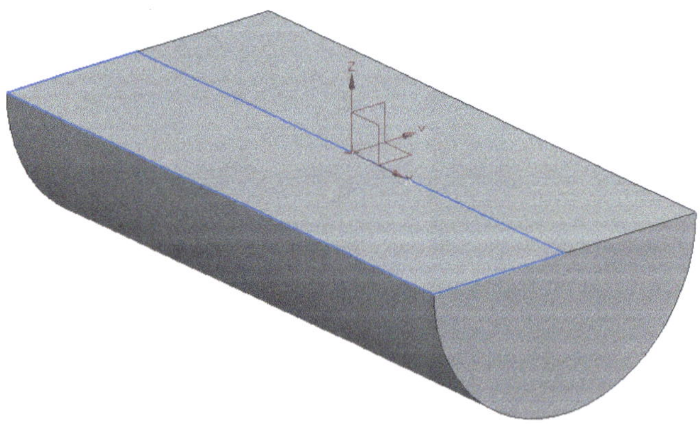

Creating the Revolved Cut

1. Activate the **Revolve** command and click on the top face of the part geometry.
2. Draw the sketch on the top face and apply dimensions. Finish the sketch.

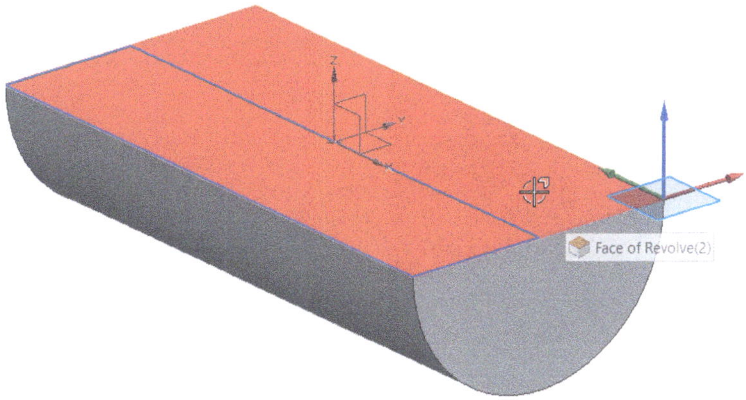

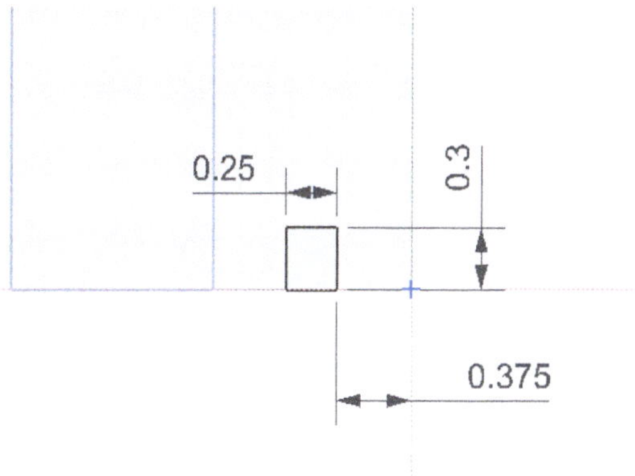

3. Click on the X-axis vector to define the axis of the revolution.
4. Click on the origin of the datum coordinate system to define the axis origin.
5. Type-in **180** in the **End** box and click the **Reverse Direction** button under the **Direction** section.
6. Under the **Boolean** section, click **Boolean > Subtract**.
7. Click **OK** to create the revolved cut-out.

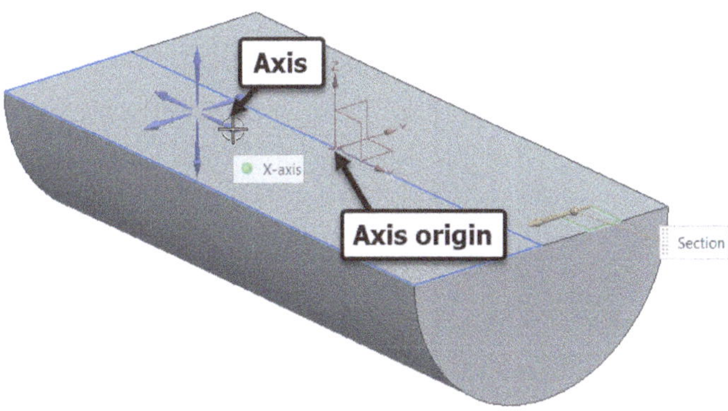

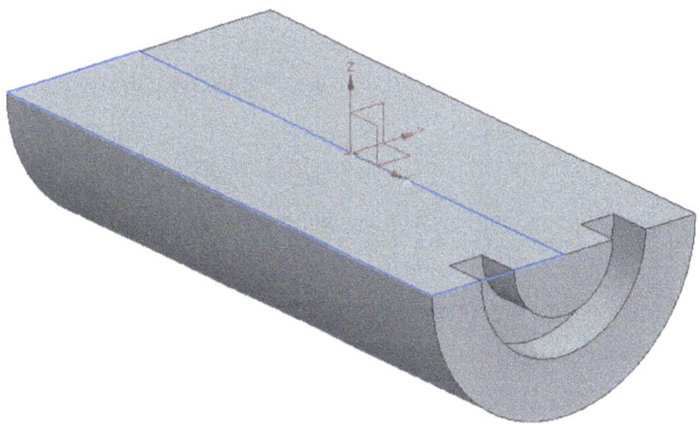

Adding a Revolved Feature to the model

1. Activate the **Revolve** command and click on the top face of the part geometry.
2. Draw a sketch and click **Finish** on the ribbon.
3. On the ribbon, click **Boolean > Unite**.
4. Click on the **Specify Vector** option under the **Axis** section of the **Revolve** dialog. Click on the X-axis of the triad to define the axis of rotation and click on the origin to define the axis origin.

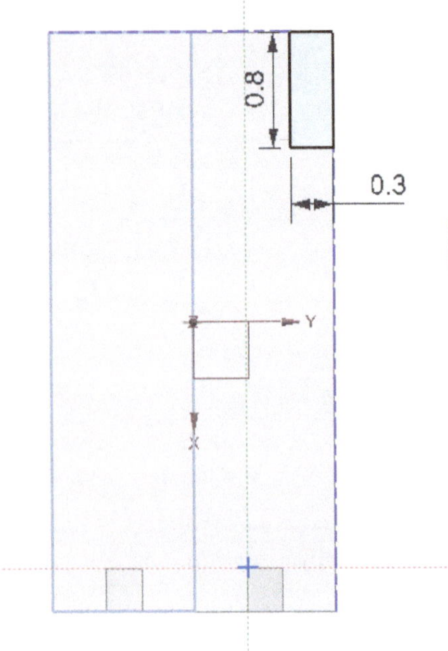

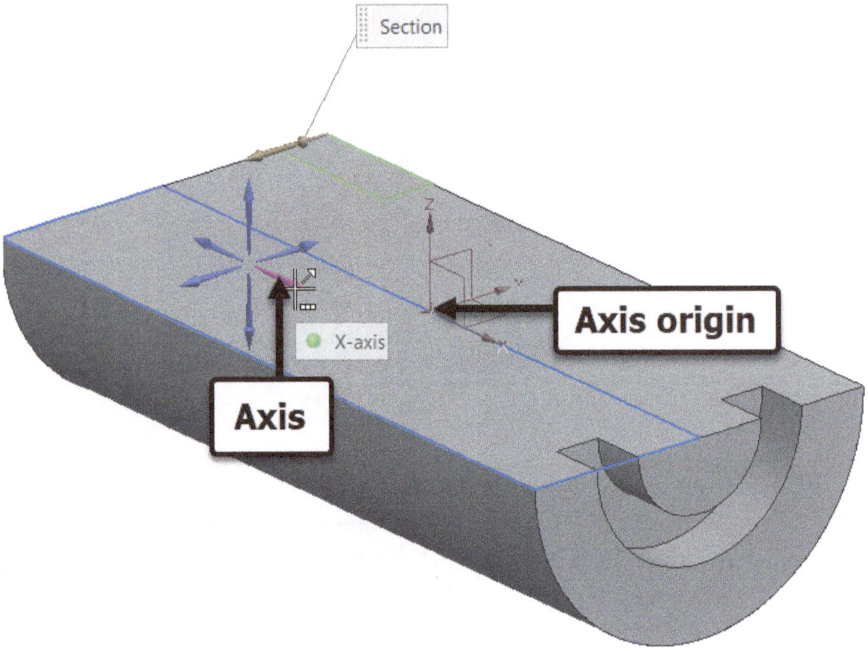

5. Type-in **180** in the **End** box and click **OK** to add the *Revolve* feature to the geometry.
6. On the ribbon, click **View > Content > Immediate Hide**.

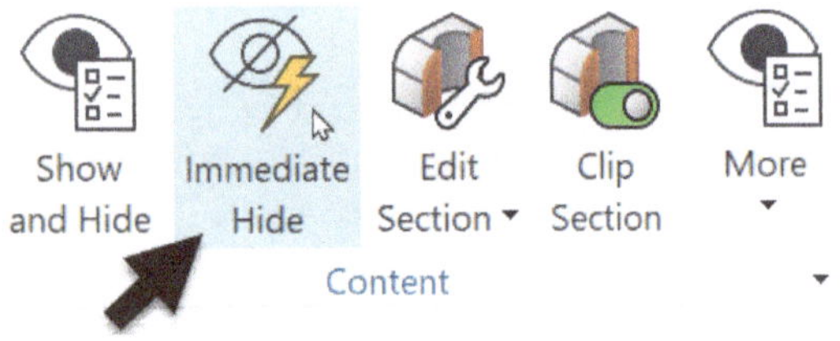

7. Click on the sketch that lies on the part geometry. It will be hidden immediately. Close the **Immediate Hide** dialog.

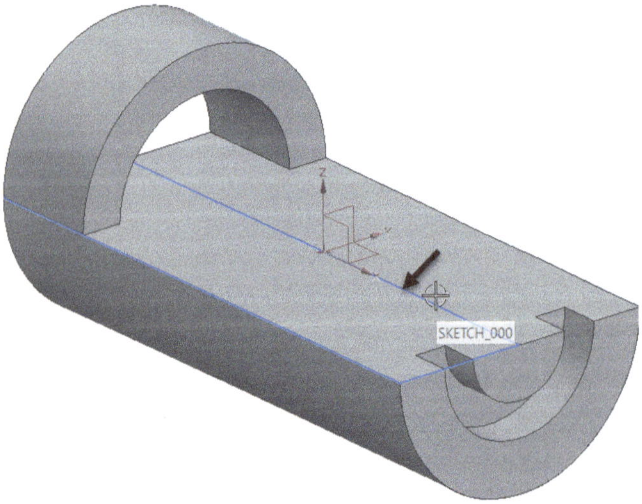

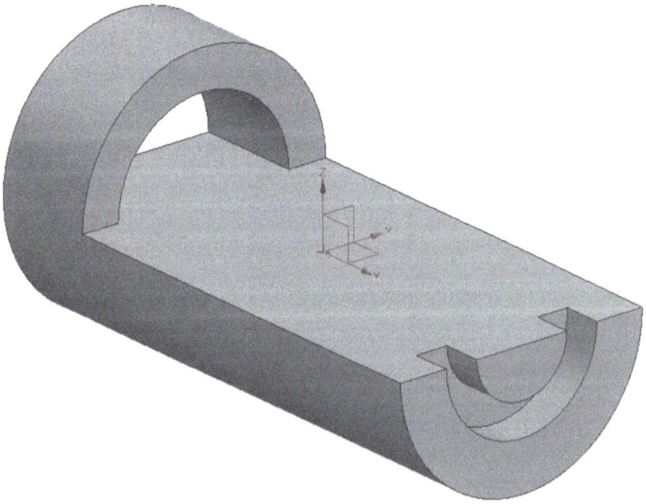

8. Save and close the file.

Questions

1. How to create parallel planes in NX?
2. What are the **Draft** options available on the **Extrude** dialog?
3. List any two **Limit** types available on the **Extrude** dialog.
4. How to extrude an open profile in NX?
5. List any two Boolean operations.
6. How to create angled planes in NX?

Exercises

Exercise 1 (Millimeters)

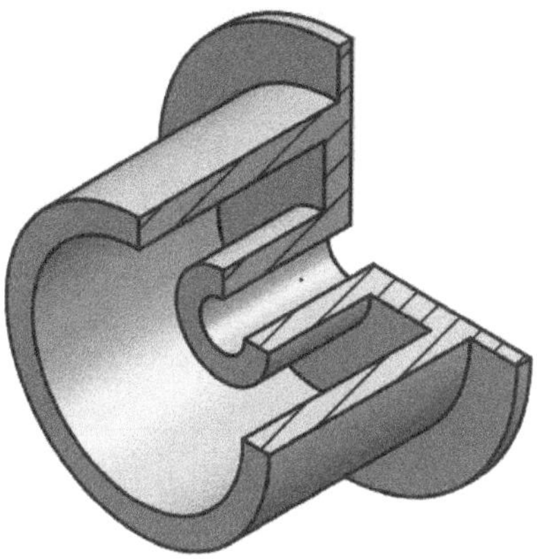

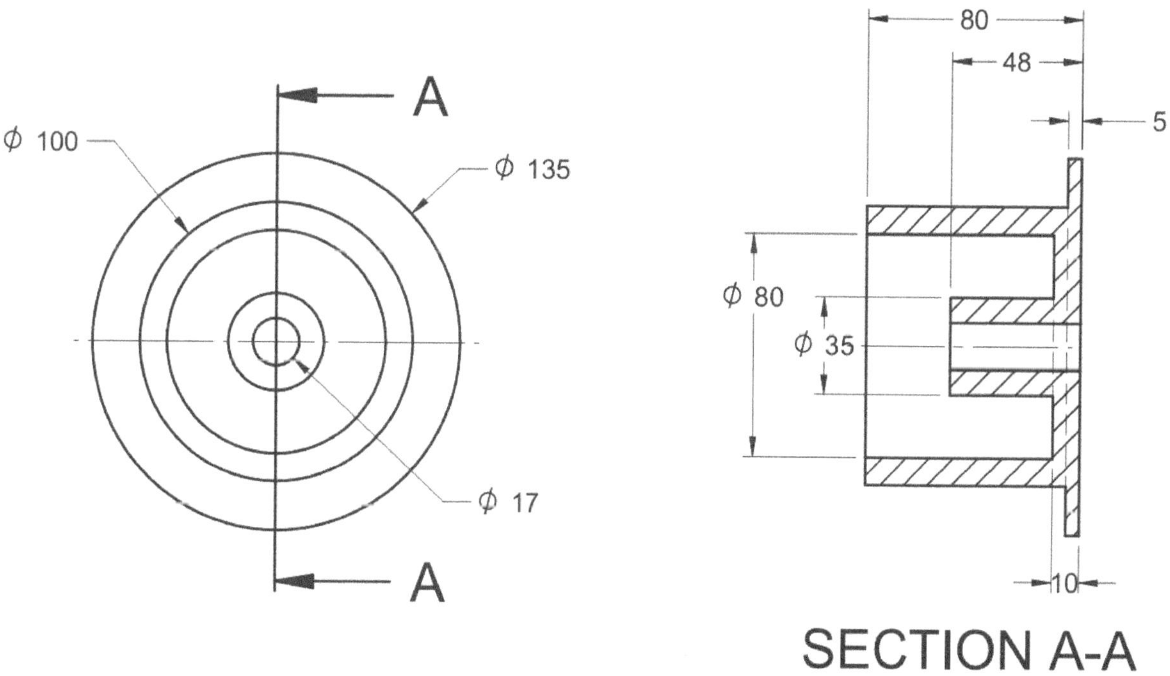

Exercise 2 (Inches)

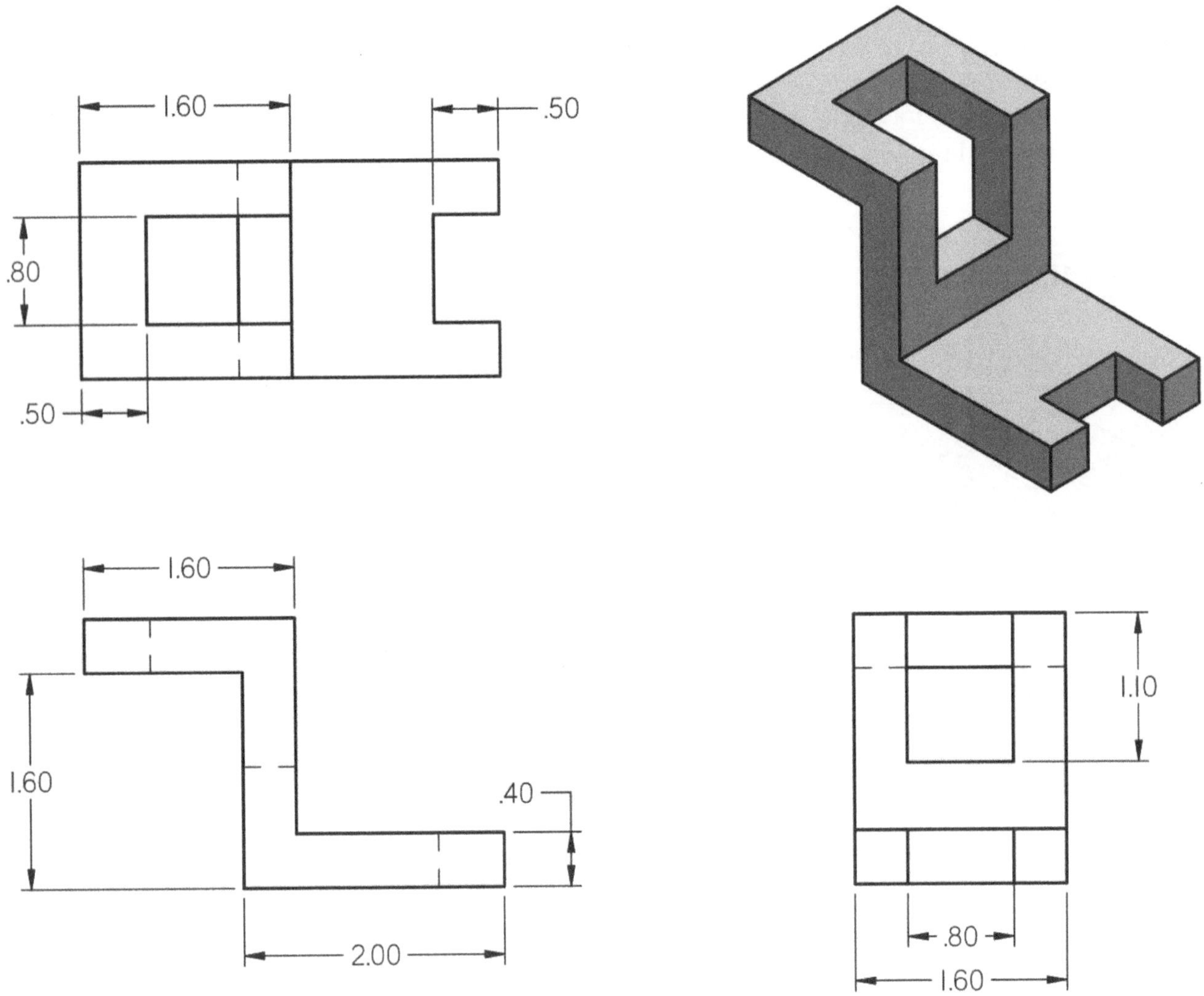

Exercise 3 (Millimeters)

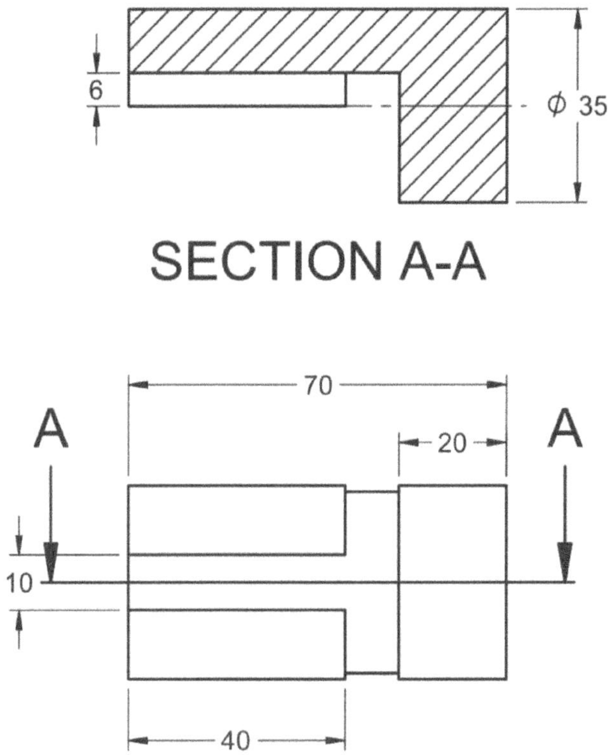

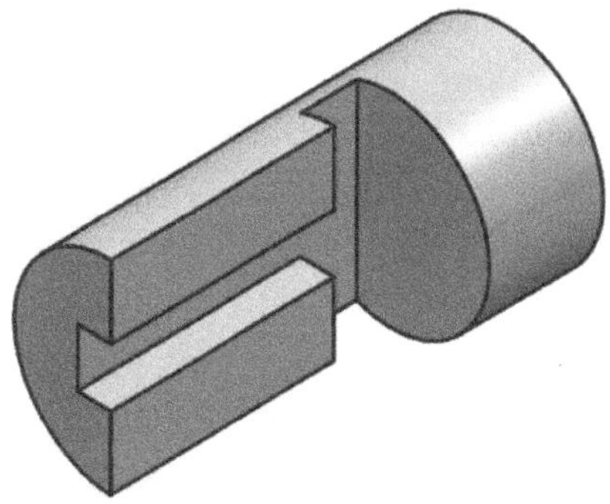

Chapter 4: Placed Features

So far, all of the features that were covered in the previous chapter were based on two-dimensional sketches. However, there are certain features in NX that do not require a sketch at all. Features that do not require a sketch are called placed features. You can simply place them on your models. However, to do so, you must have some existing geometry. Unlike a sketch-based feature, you cannot use a placed feature for a first feature a model. For example, to create a *Blend* feature, you must have an already existing edge. In this chapter, you will learn how to add placed features to your design.

The topics covered in this chapter are:

- *Holes*
- *Threads*
- *Slots*
- *Blends*
- *Chamfers*
- *Drafts*
- *Shells*

Hole

As you know, it is possible to use the *Extrude* command to create cuts and remove material. But, if you want to drill holes that are of standard sizes, the **Hole**  command is a better way to do this. The reason for this is it has many hole types already predefined for you. All you must do is choose the correct hole type and size. The other benefit is when you are going to create a 2D drawing, NX can place the correct hole annotation automatically. Activate this command (Click **Home > Base > Hole** on the ribbon), and you will notice that a dialog pops up. There are options in this dialog that make it easy to create different types of holes.

Simple Hole

To create a simple hole feature, select **Type > Simple** on the **Hole** dialog.

Specifying the Hole Size and Form

Select an option from the **Hole Size** drop-down (**Custom**, **Drill Size**, or **Screw Clearance**). Select the **Custom** option from the **Hole Size** drop-down. Next, type-in a value in the **Hole Diameter** box. Expand the **Chamfer** sub-section in the **Form** section, and then check the **Start Chamfer** and **End Chamfer** options, if you want to apply chamfer to the ends of the hole.

(or)

Select the **Drill Size** option from the **Hole Size** drop-down and specify the hole **Standard**. Next, select the hole size from the **Size** drop-down. After specifying the hole size, select an option from the **Fit** drop-down (**Exact** or **Custom**). The fit is specified automatically if you select the **Exact** option. You need to specify the Hole Diameter manually, if you select the **Custom** option from the **Fit** section.

(or)

Select the **Screw Clearance** option from the **Hole Size** drop-down and specify the hole **Standard.** Next, select the **Screw Type**, **Screw Size**, and **Fit**. The **Screw Clearance** option helps create holes that allow screws to fit smoothly without getting stuck or causing too much friction. It provides space or allowance for easy assembly and movement of the screws.

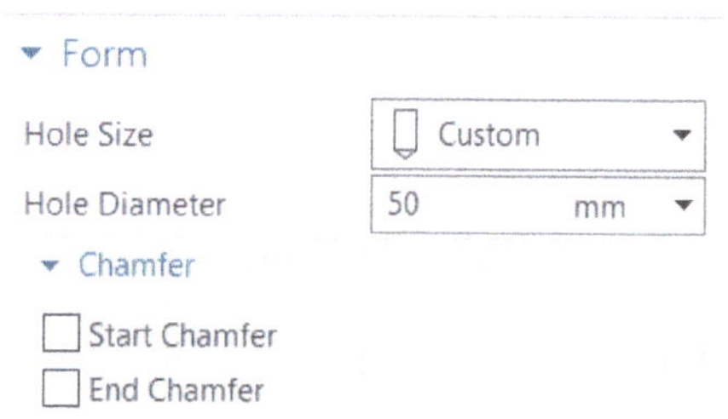

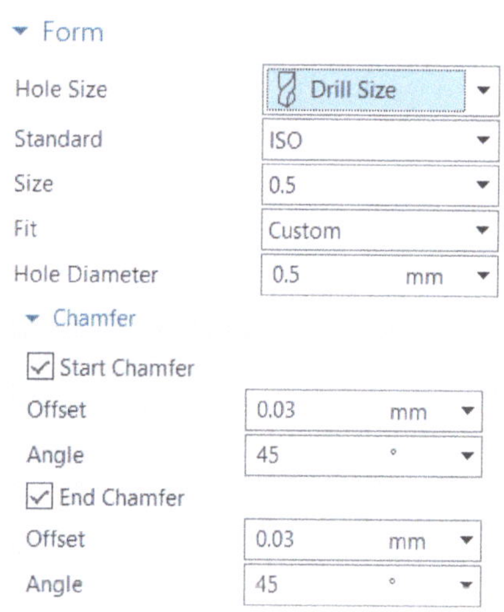

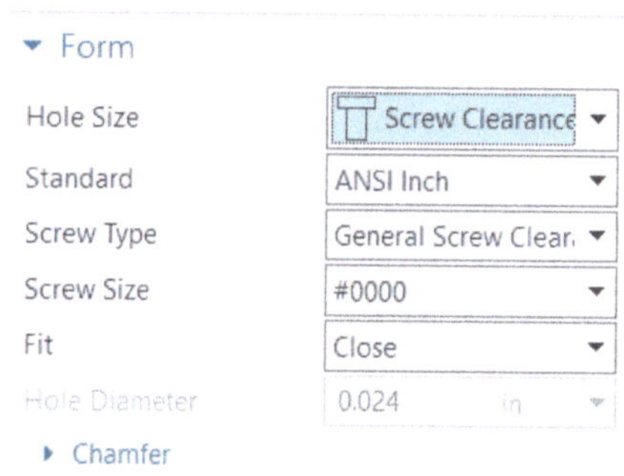

Specifying the Hole Depth

Under the **Limits** section, select the **Depth Limit** type. If you want a through-hole, select **Depth Limit > Through Body**. If you want the hole only up to some depth, then select **Depth Limit > Value**, and then type-in a value in the **Hole Depth** box. The **Depth To** drop-down has two options to define the depth of the hole: **Shoulder** and **Tip**. The **Shoulder** option applies the **Depth** value to the cylindrical portion of the hole. The **Tip** option applies the **Depth** value to the entire hole up to the bottom tip. The **Tip Angle** box defines the angle of the cone tip at the bottom.

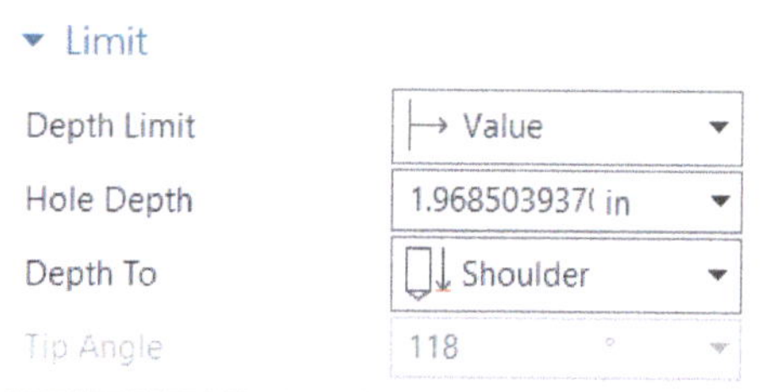

Specifying the Location of the Hole

In the **Position** section, click **Specify Point**, and then click on a face. Likewise, click to specify more hole locations.

Next, click on the location dimensions and change the values. However, you can also click the **Sketch Section** icon in the **Position** section to activate the Sketch Task environment. Next, modify the location dimensions. On the ribbon, click **Home > Sketch > Finish**.

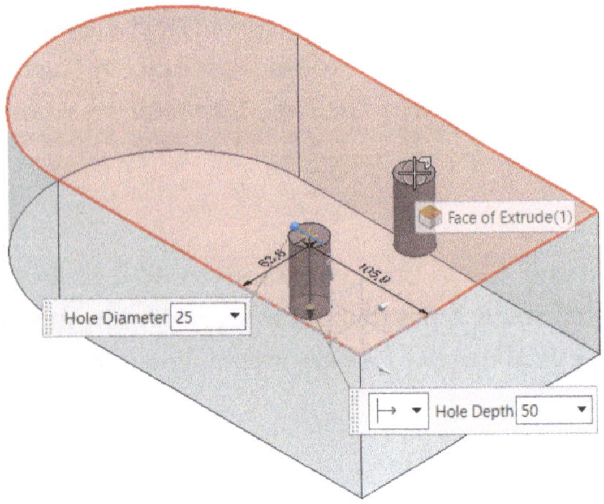

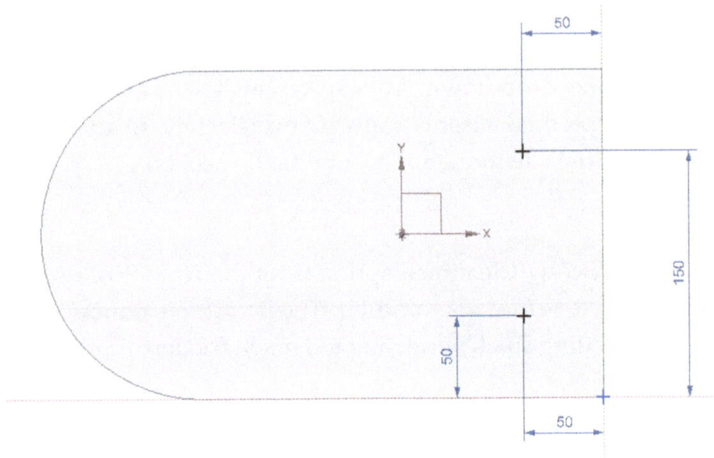

Specifying the Hole Direction

The holes will be created normal to the selected face. If you want to create holes at an angle or along a specified vector, then set the **Hole Direction** to **Along Vector**. Select the **Two Points** option from the drop-down next to the **Specify Vector** option. Next, select two points from the graphics window. Click **OK** to create the holes.

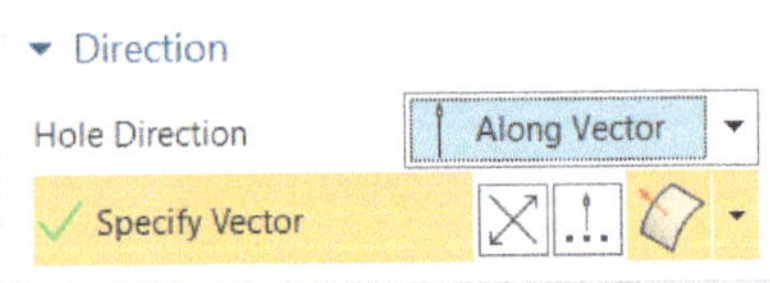

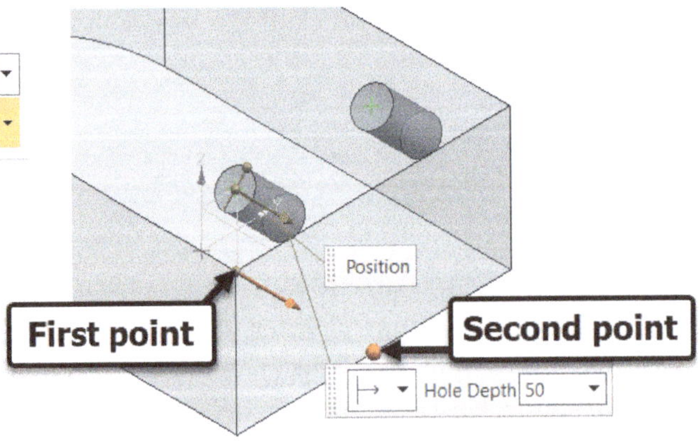

Counterbored Hole

A counterbore hole is a large diameter hole added at the opening of another hole. It is used to accommodate a fastener below the level of the work piece surface. To create a counterbore hole, select **Type > Counterbored**. Next, define the Hole Diameter, C-Bore diameter, and C-Bore Limit, and C-Bore Depth values. Specify the settings in the **Limit** section. Type-in, a value in the **Tip angle** box, to define the angle of the V-bottom.

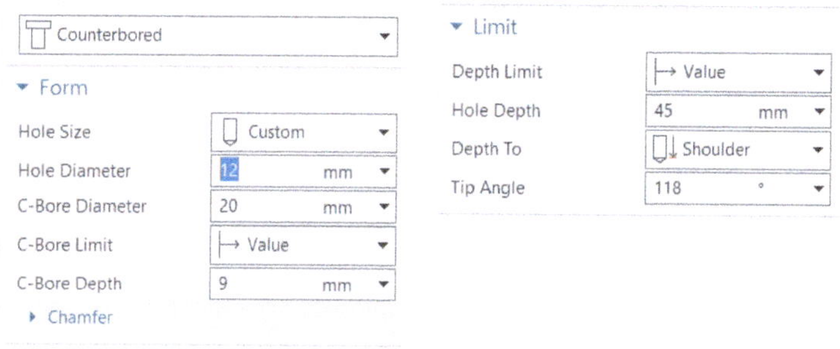

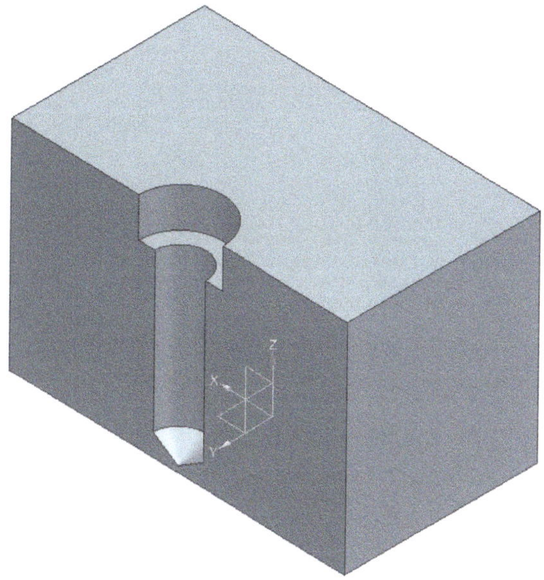

Countersunk Hole

A countersunk hole has an enlarged V-shaped opening to accommodate the fastener below the level of the work piece surface. To create a countersunk hole, set the hole **Type** to **Countersunk**. Type-in values in the **Hole Diameter**, **C-Sink Diameter**, and **C-Sink Angle** boxes. Set the hole depth and end condition.

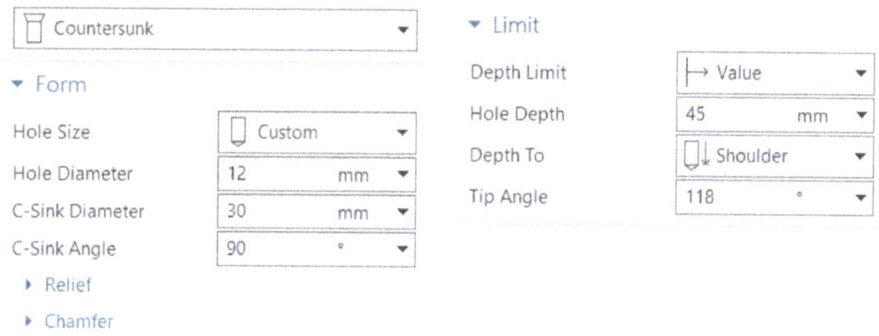

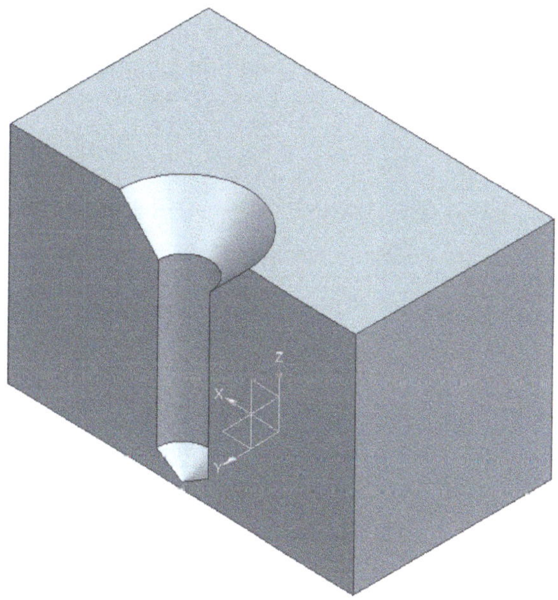

Tapered Hole

Tapering is the process of decreasing the hole diameters toward one end. A tapered hole has a smaller diameter at the bottom. To create a tapered hole, set the hole **Type** to **Tapered**. Type-in a value in the **Hole Diameter** box, and then enter the taper angle in the **Taper Angle** box. After defining the taper, specify the hole depth.

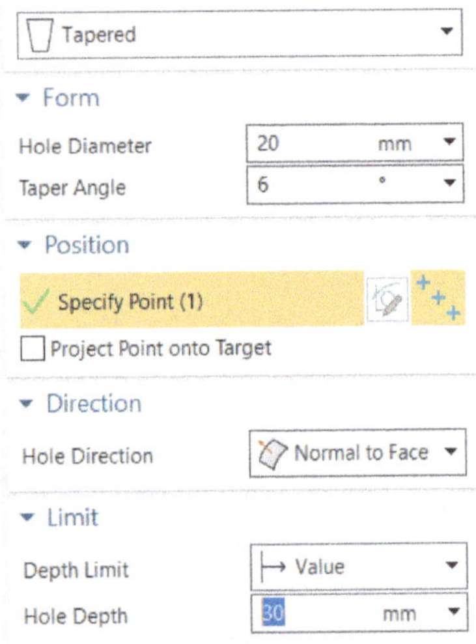

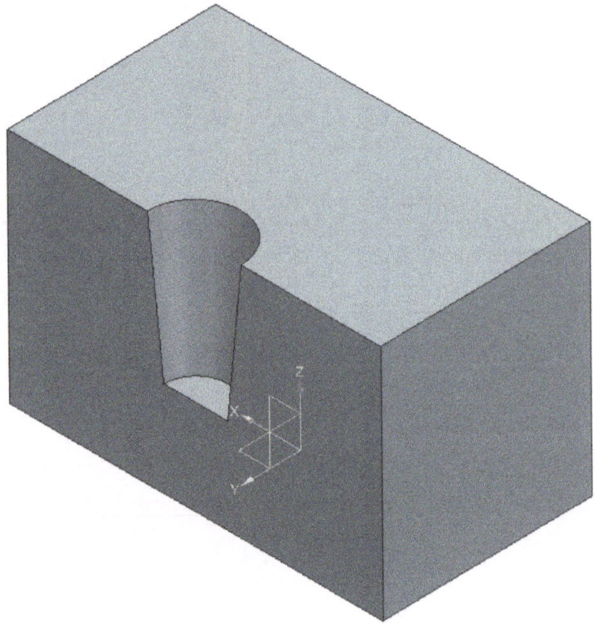

Threaded Hole

To create a threaded hole feature, set the hole **Type** to **Threaded Hole**. Under the **Form** section, set the **Thread Dimensions** settings and thread **Handedness**. Set the hole limits and end condition in the **Limit** section. If you want to provide relief, then expand the **Relief** sub-section and check the **Apply Relief** option. Likewise, enable or disable the **Start Chamfer** and **End Chamfer** options.

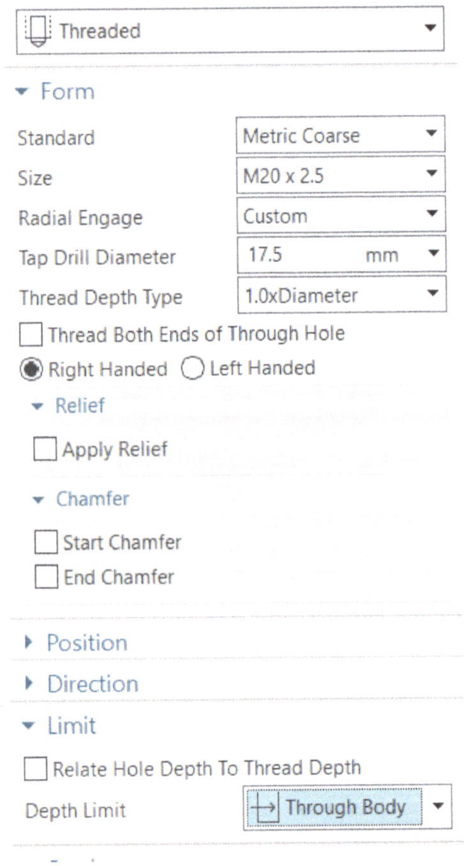

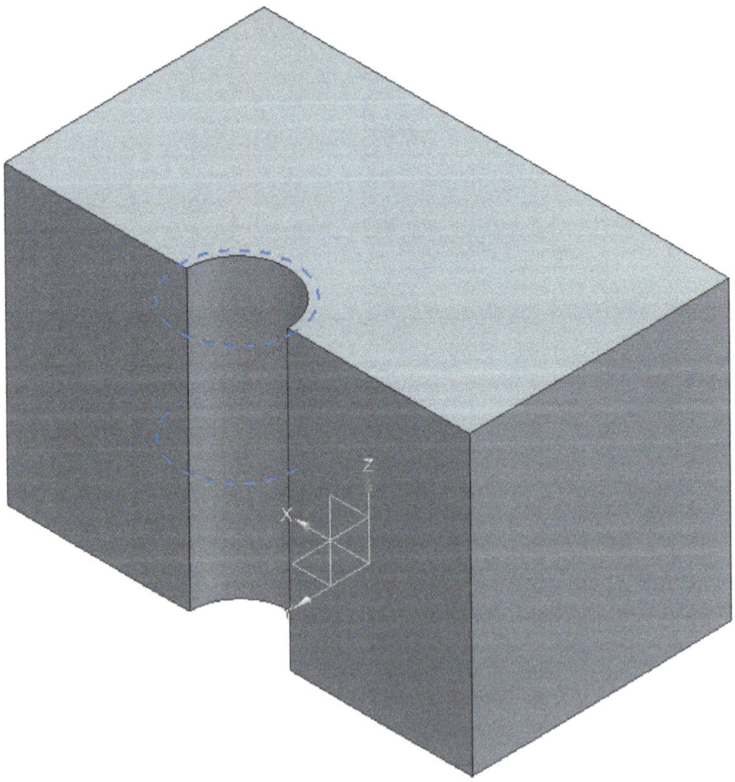

Thread

This command adds a thread feature to a cylindrical face. The thread features are added to a 3D geometry so that when you create a 2D drawing, NX can automatically place the correct thread annotation. Activate this command (click **Home > Base > More > Detail Feature > Thread** on the ribbon). The **Thread** dialog pops up on the screen. To create a symbolic thread, set the **Thread Type** to **Symbolic** and click on a cylindrical face of the part geometry. The thread parameters are automatically updated in the **Form** section of the **Thread** dialog.

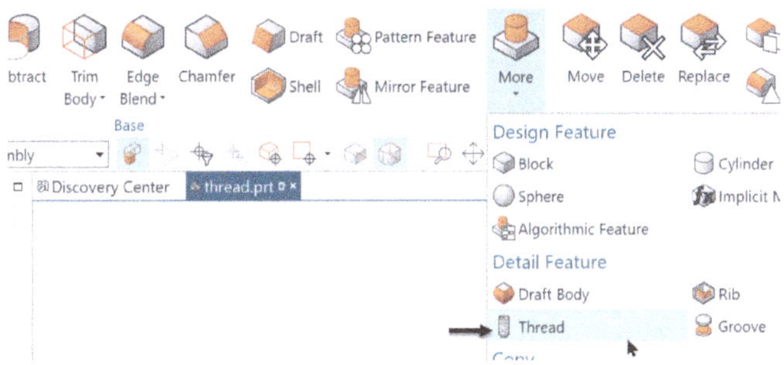

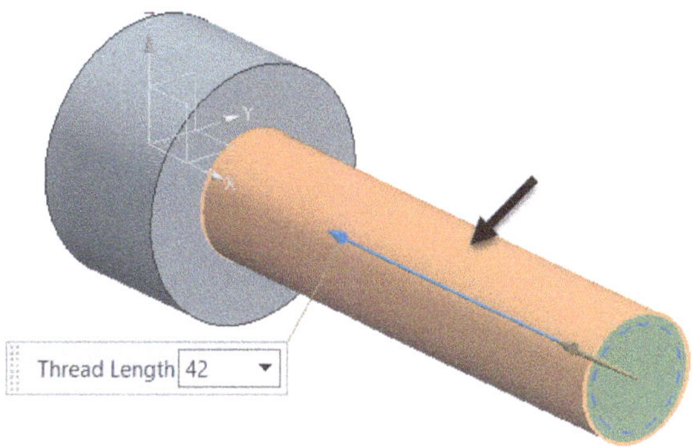

If you want to change the thread parameters, then select an option from the **Input** drop-down. You can select the **Thread table** or **Manual** option. If you select the **Thread Table** option, then select a standard from the **Thread Standard** drop-down available in the **Form** section. Note that you need to select a standard thread that matches the diameter of the cylindrical face. Next, specify the parameters in the **Form** section such as Thread Size, Handedness, Number of Starts, and Method. If you select the **Manual** option from the **Input** drop-down, you need to manually specify the thread parameters such as **Shaft Diameter**, **Major Diameter**, **Minor Diameter**, **Pitch**, and **Angle**.

Next, specify the thread length in the **Limit** section. You can specify the thread length using anyone of the three options available in the **Thread Limit** drop-down: **Value**, **Full**, **Short of Full**. If you select the **Value** option, then you need to specify the **Thread Length** value. The **Full** option specifies the thread length up to the full length of the selected cylinder. The **Short of Full** option specifies the thread using an offset from the end of the cylinder. In the **Pitch Multiple** box, you can specify the offset value in terms of multiples of the pitch. Click **OK** to apply the symbolic thread.

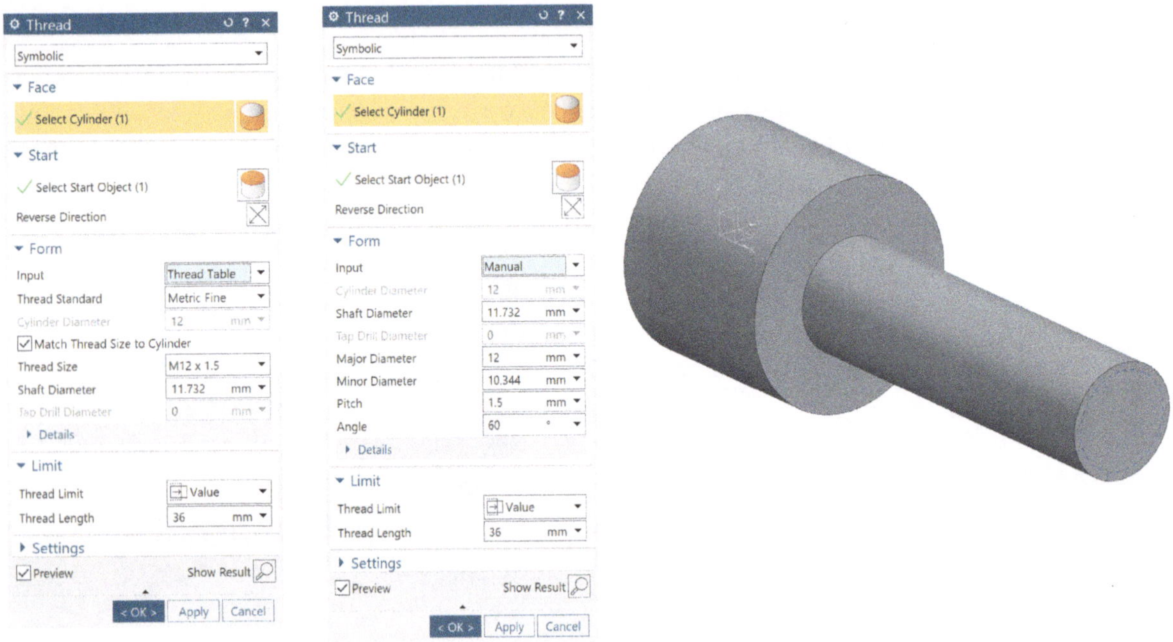

To create a detailed thread, set the **Thread Type** to **Detailed** and click on the cylindrical face. On the **Thread** dialog, define the thread parameters and rotation. Click **OK** to complete the thread feature.

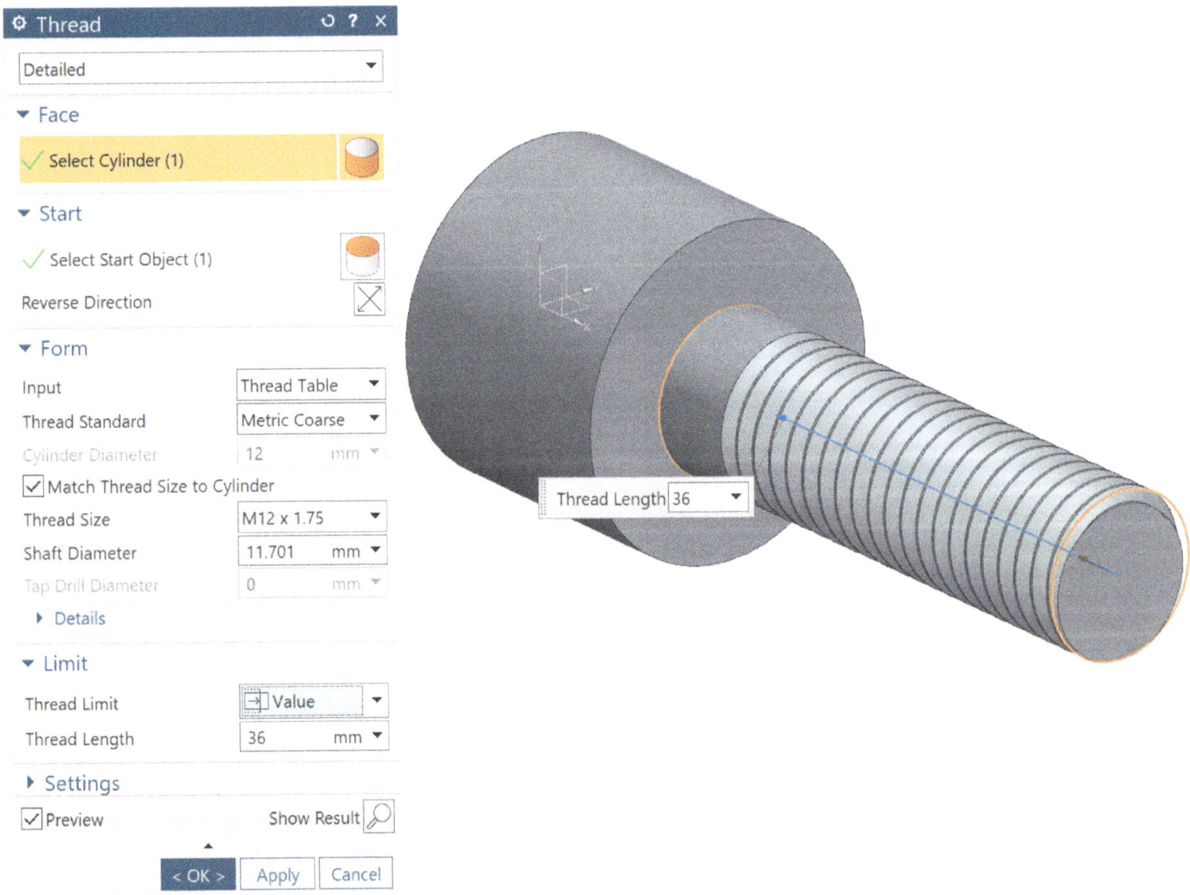

Edge Blend

This command breaks the sharp edges of a model and blends them. You do not need a sketch to create a blend. All you need to have is model edges. Activate this command (click **Home > Base > Edge Blend** on the ribbon) and select edges. As you start selecting edges, you will see a preview of the geometry. You can select the edges, which are located at the back of the model without rotating it. To do this, activate the **Allow Selection of Hidden Wireframe** button on the Top Border Bar. By mistake, if you have selected the wrong edge, you can deselect it by holding the Shift key and selecting the edge again. You can change the radius by typing a value in the **Radius 1** box displayed on the selected edge. As you change the radius, all the selected edges will be updated. It is because they are all part of one instance. If you want the edges to have different radii, you must create blends in separate instances. Select the required number of edges and click **OK** to finish this feature. The *Edge Blend* feature will be listed in the Part Navigator.

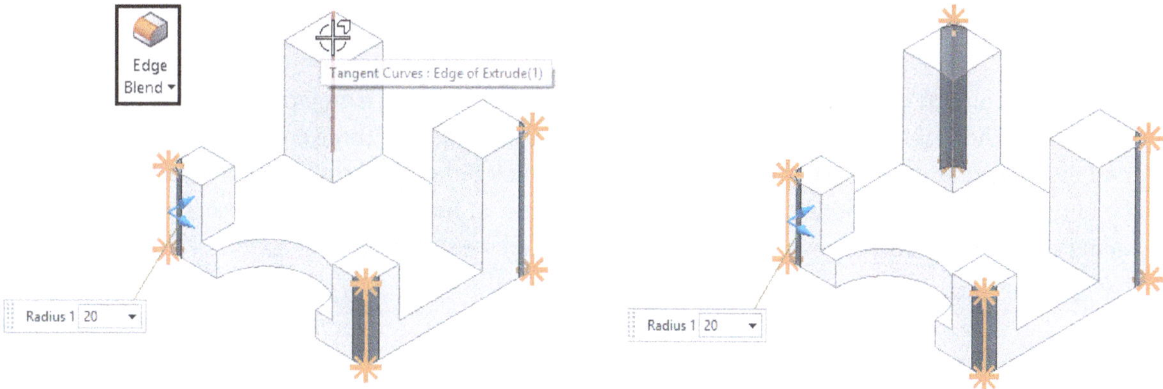

Curvature Continuous Blends

By default, the edge blends are tangent to adjacent faces. However, if you want to create a blend that is curvature continuous with the adjacent faces, then select the **G2 (Curvature)** option from the **Continuity** drop-down on the dialog. Next, type-in a value in the **Radius 1** and **Rho 1** boxes. The edge blends with different rho values are shown below.

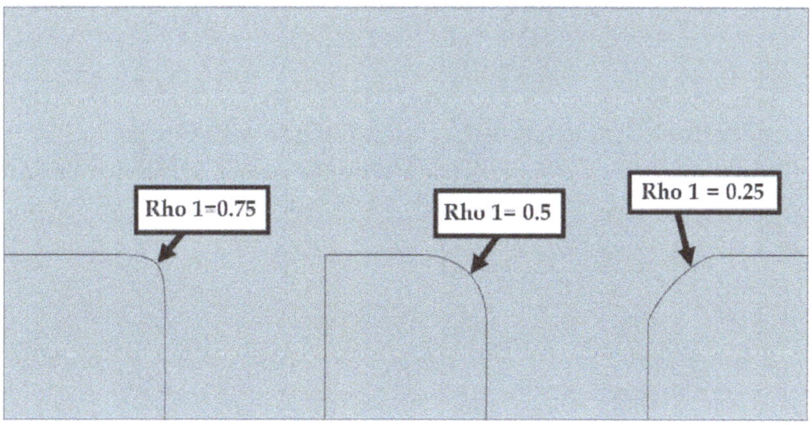

Variable Radius Blend

NX allows you to create a blend with a varying radius along the selected edge. Activate the **Edge Blend** command and click on edge to blend. On the **Edge Blend** dialog, expand the **Variable Radius** section and click **Specify Radius Point**. Define the variable radius points on the selected edge. Drag the arrows to change the radius value at each location. Check the **Soft Radius change at End** option, if you want a smooth transition between the variable radius points.

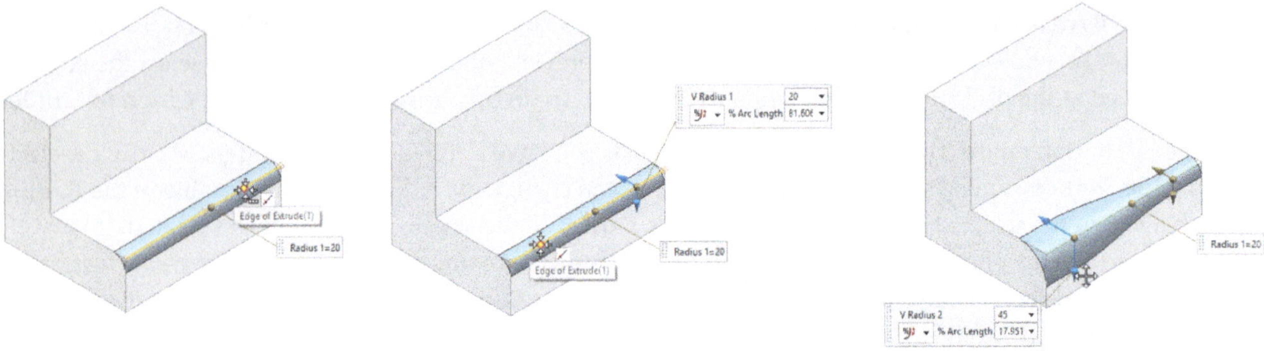

Corner Setback

If you create an edge blend on three edges that come together at a corner, you have the option to control how these three blends are blend together. Activate the **Edge Blend** command and select the three edges that meet at a corner. On the **Edge Blend** dialog, expand the **Corner Setback** section and click **Select End Point**. Now, click on the vertex where the three blends meet. You will notice that three arrows appear at the corner. Drag these arrows to change the setback distances dynamically (or) type-in values in the individual setback boxes.

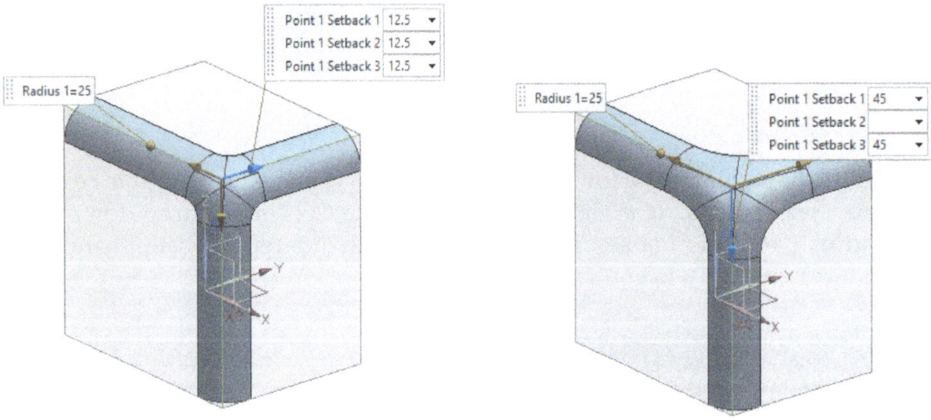

The **Corner Setback** drop-down in the **Corner Setback** section has two options: **Include with Corner** and **Separate from Corner**. The **Include with Corner** option includes the setback with the corner. The **Separate from Corner** option creates a separate setback from the corner, as shown.

Include with Corner

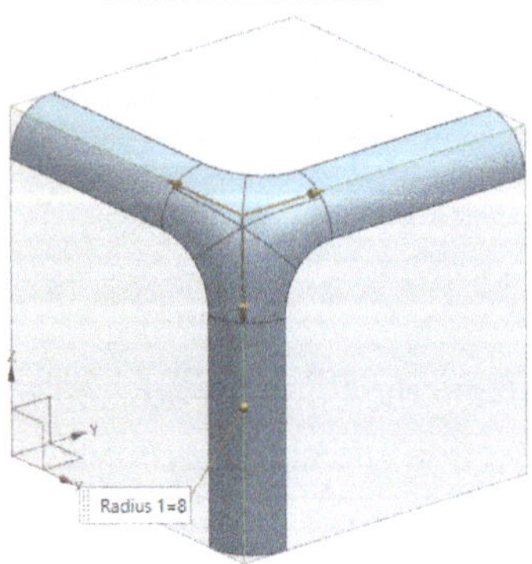

Separate from Corner

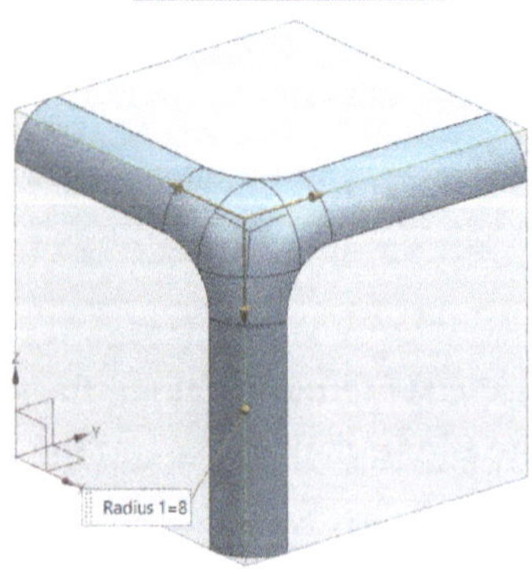

Stop Short of Corner

If you want the edge blend to stop short of the corner, then expand the **Stop Short of Corner** section and click **Select End Point**. Click on a corner vertex of the selected edge and drag the mouse. The blend will be stopped at a distance specified by dragging the mouse.

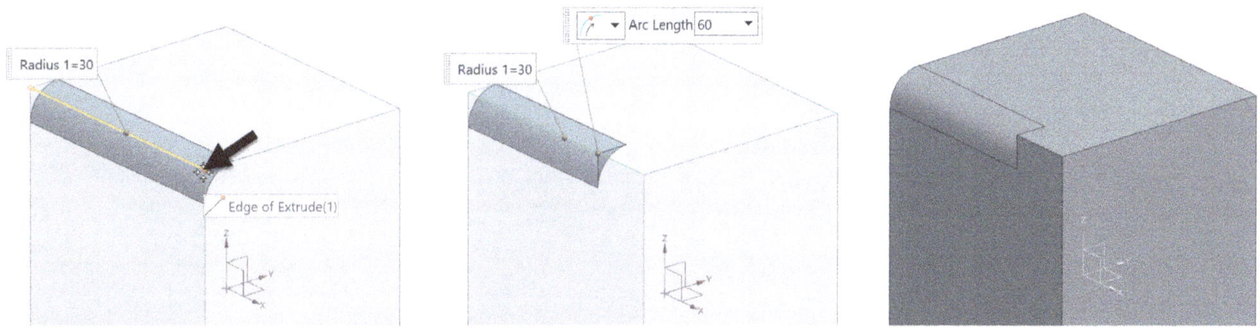

The **Limit** drop-down in the **Stop Short of Corner** section has two options: **Distance** and **Blend Intersection**. The **Distance** option is used to limit a blend up to a selected point. The **Blend Intersection** option is used to stop two blends from intersecting at a corner. You need to select the intersection point of the two blends, as shown.

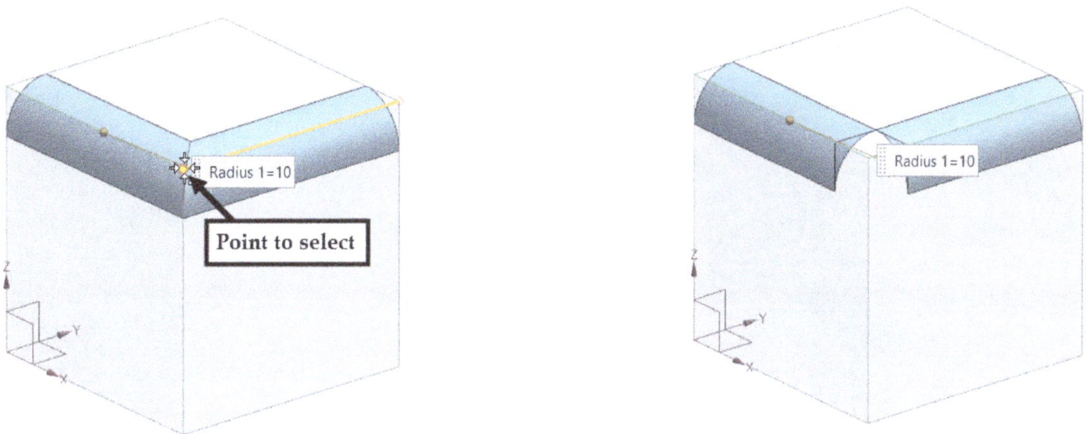

Length Limit

NX allows you to limit the length of an edge blend using a limiting object. To do this, expand the **Length Limit** section and check the **Enable Length Limit** option. Next, select an option from the **Limit Object** drop-down. You can select **Plane, Face** or **Edge** from this drop-down. For example, select the **Plane** option, and then click on edge selected to create the blend; a plane appears on edge at the selected point. Click and drag the center point of the plane to define its position. You can also type-in a value in the **Arc Length** box that appears on selecting the centerpoint of the plane.

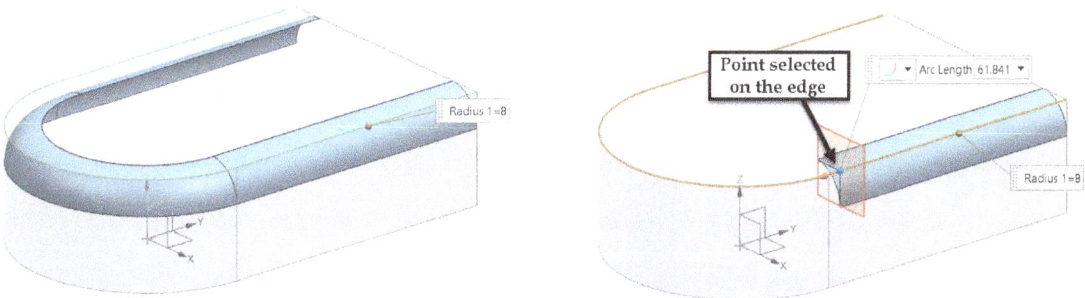

If the limiting plane intersects the blend at multiple points, then click the **Specify Trim Location Point** option in the **Length Limit** section, and then click on the portion to keep.

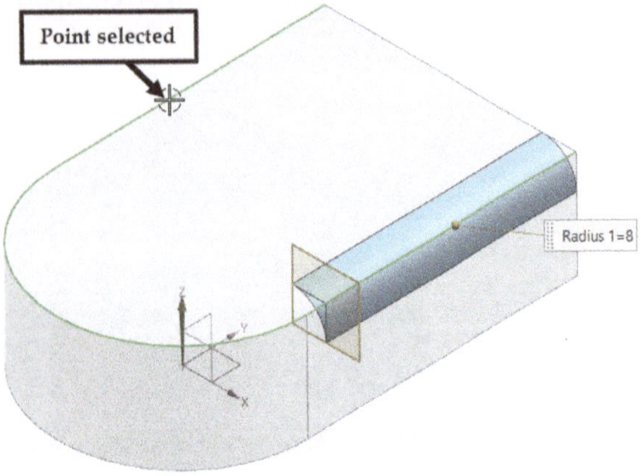

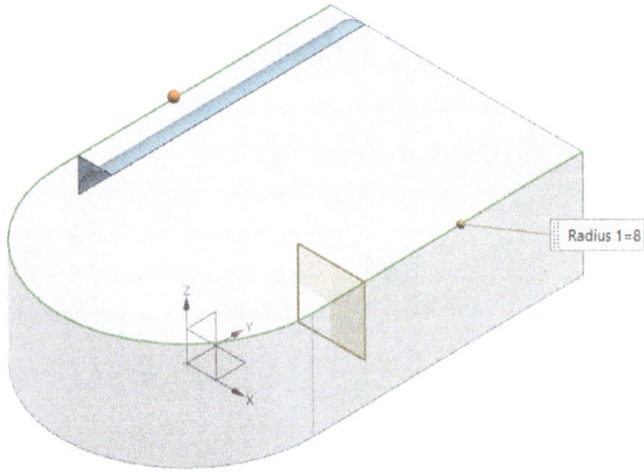

If you select the **Edge** option from the **Limit Object** drop-down, you need to select an edge to define the limit object. The edge blend will be limited up to the selected edge.

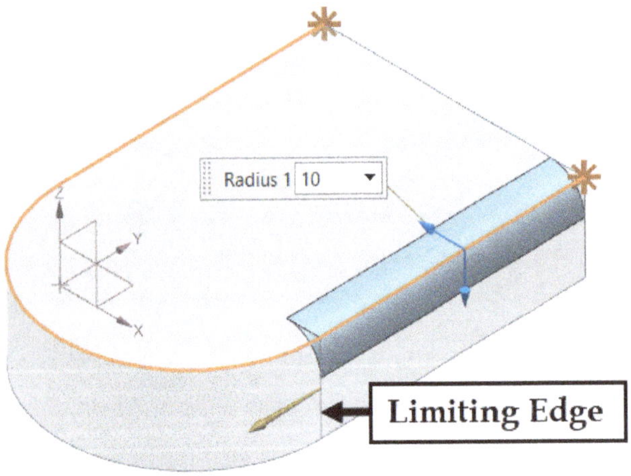

If you select the **Face** option from the **Limit Object** drop-down, then select a face from the model geometry.

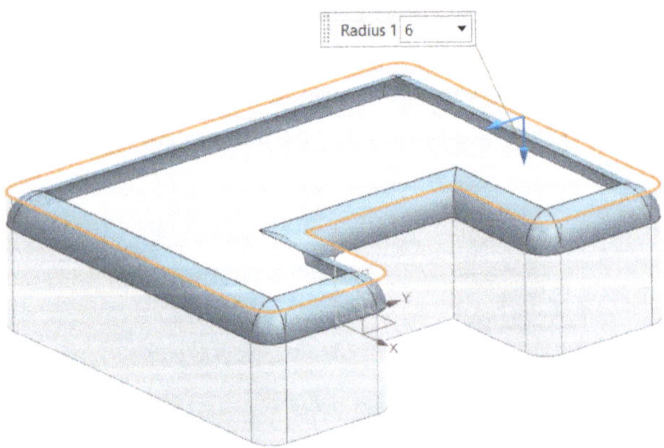

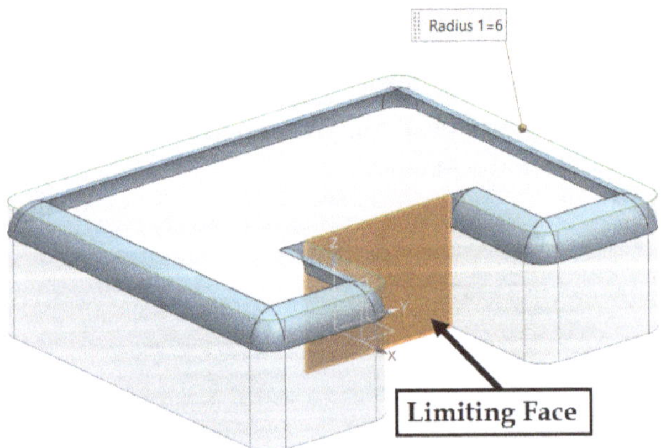

Chamfer

The **Chamfer** and **Edge Blend** commands are commonly used to break sharp edges. The difference is that the **Chamfer** command adds a bevel face to the model. A chamfer is also a placed feature. Activate this command (click **Home > Base > Chamfer** on ribbon) and select **Cross Section > Symmetric**. Select the edge to chamfer and type-in a value in the **Distance** box and press Enter to create the chamfer. Click **OK** to complete the chamfer.

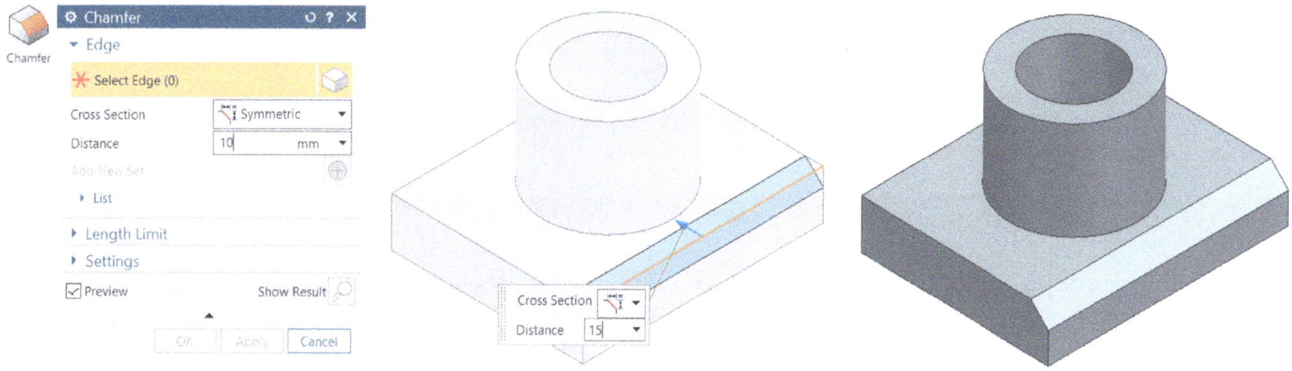

Asymmetric chamfer

If you want a chamfer to have different setbacks on both sides of the edge, then select **Cross Section > Asymmetric** on the dialog. Type-in values in the **Distance 1** and **Distance 2** boxes on the dialog and select the edge to chamfer. If you want to switch the setback distance, then click the **Reverse Direction** button on the dialog.

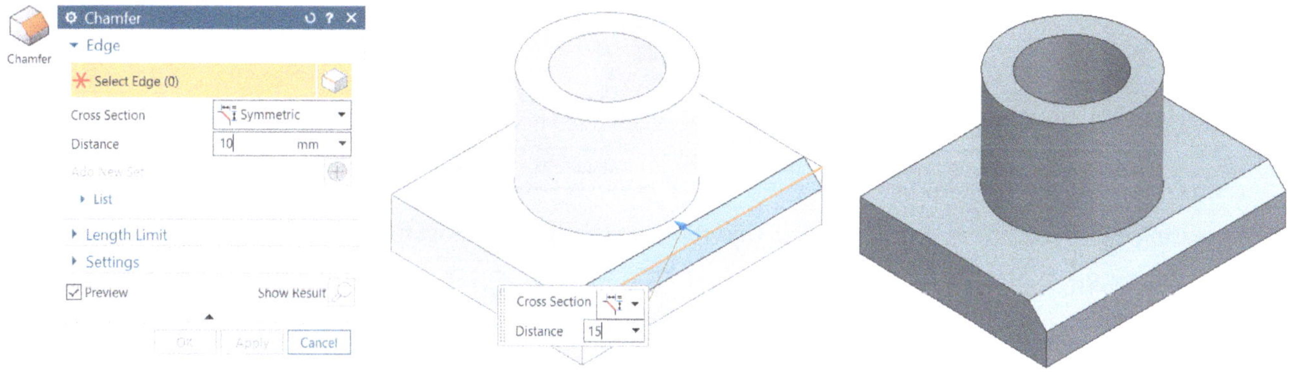

Offset and Angle chamfer

This option lets you create a chamfer by defining its distance and angle values. On the **Chamfer** dialog, select **Cross Section > Offset and Angle** and click on edge to chamfer. Type-in values in the **Distance** and **Angle boxes** and click **OK**.

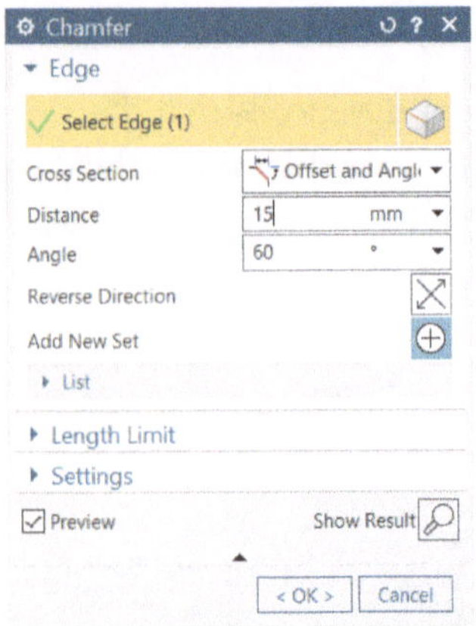

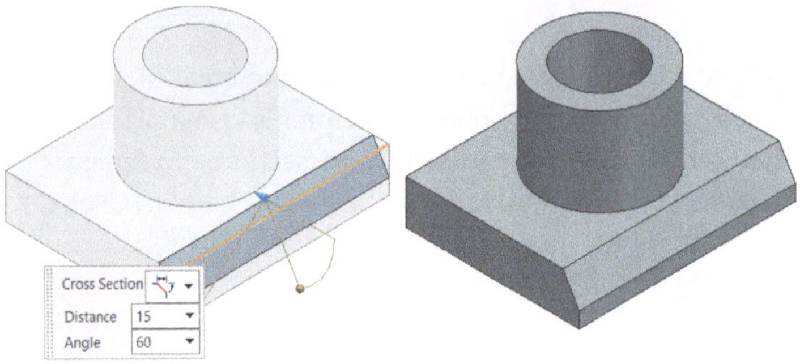

Draft

When creating cast or plastic parts, you are often required to add a draft on them so that they can be molded easily. A draft is an angle or taper applied to the faces of components so that they can be removed from the mold easily. The following illustration shows a molded part with and without a draft.

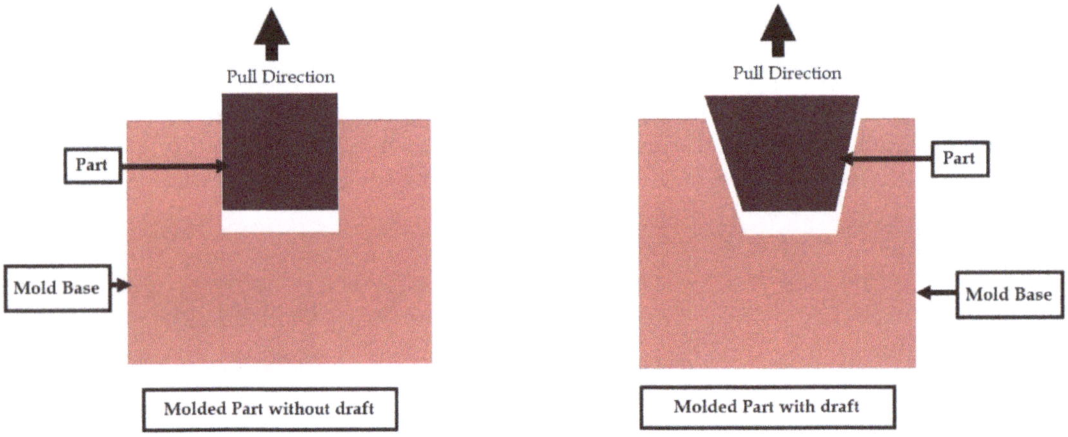

When creating *Extrude* features, you can predefine the draft angle. But most of the time, it is easier to apply the draft after the features are created. Activate the **Draft** command (On the ribbon, click **Home > Base > Draft**). On the **Draft** dialog, select **Type > Face** and click on the X, Y, or Z-axis to define the draft direction.

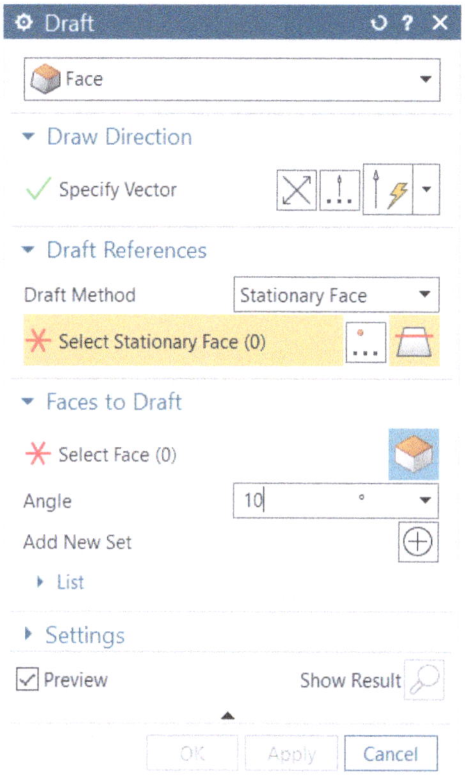

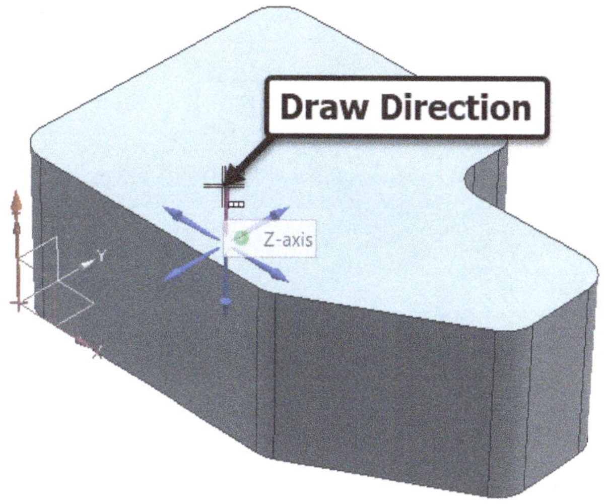

On the **Draft** dialog, select **Draft Method > Stationary Face**. Select a face, which will act as a reference plane (stationary face) for the draft. The draft angle will be measured with reference to this face. After selecting the reference plane (stationary face), click **Faces to Draft > Select Face**. Select the faces to draft and type-in a value in the **Angle 1** box. If you want to flip the draft direction, then click the **Reverse Direction** icon under the **Draw Direction** section. Next, click **OK** to add the draft.

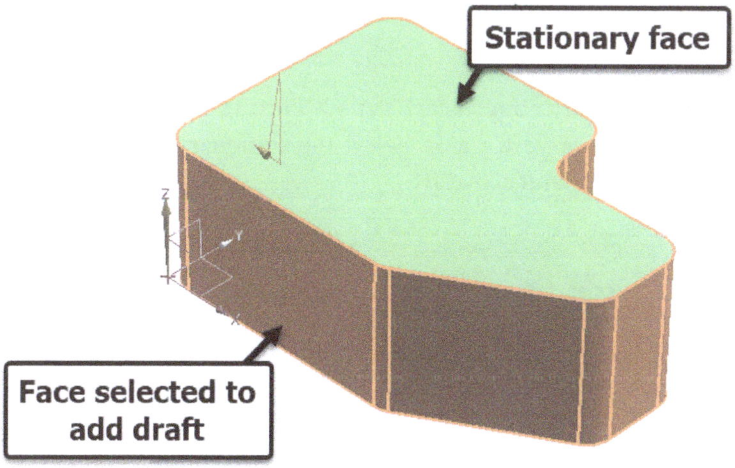

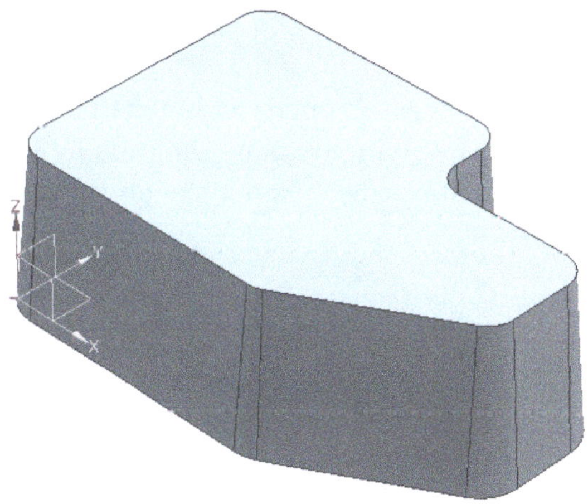

Edge Draft

The **Edge** option adds a draft to the using a stationary edge. Select **Type > Edge** on the **Draft** dialog. Next, specify the Draw Direction by selecting an edge or vector axis. Select the edges of the faces to be drafted. Next, type-in a value in the **Angle 1** box and click **OK**.

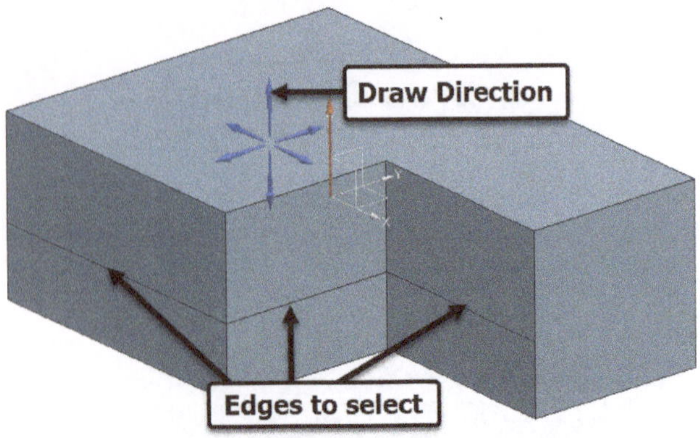

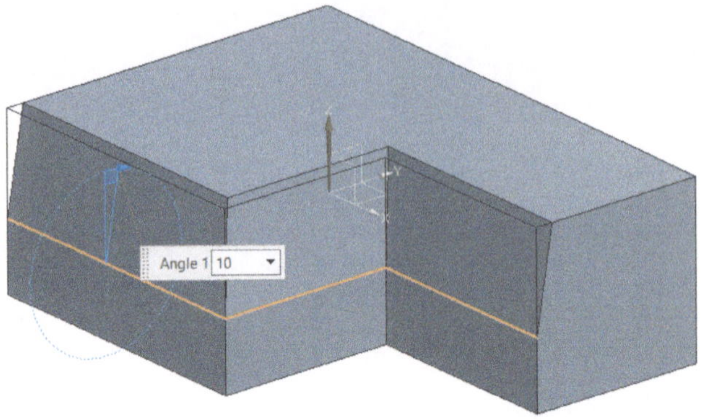

Tangent to Face Draft

The **Tangent to Face** option adds a draft to the faces that are tangent to the selected face. Select **Type > Tangent to Face** on the **Draft** dialog. Next, specify the Draw Direction by selecting an edge or vector axis. Select the face tangent to the faces to be drafted. Next, type-in a value in the **Angle 1** box and click **OK**.

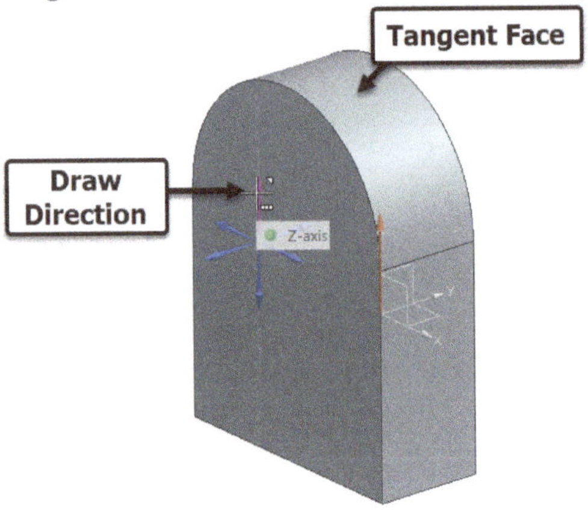

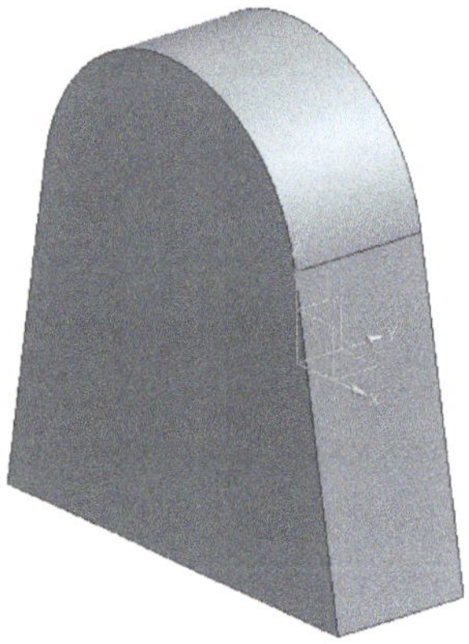

Parting Edge Draft

The **Parting Edge** option adds a draft to the using a stationary edge. Select **Type > Parting Edge** on the **Draft** dialog. Next, specify the Draw Direction by selecting an edge or vector axis. Select the stationary face, and then select the parting edges. Next, type-in a value in the **Angle 1** box and click **OK**.

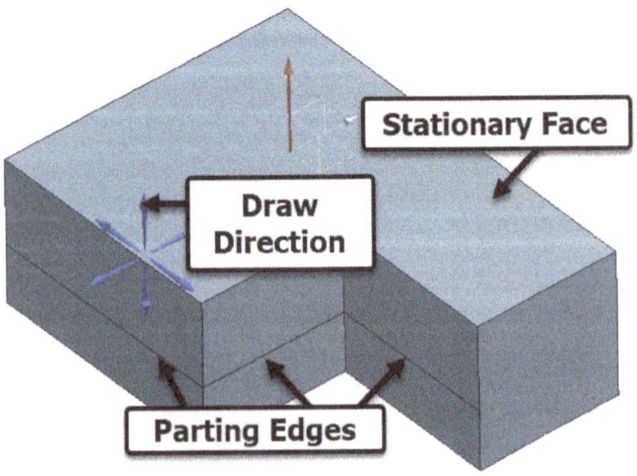

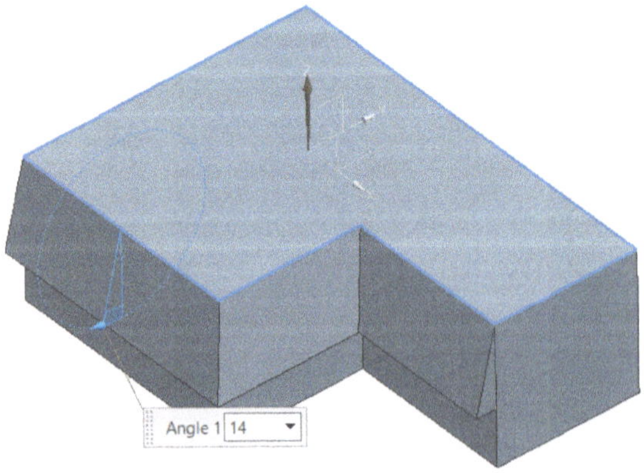

Shell

Shell is another useful command that can be applied directly to a solid model. It allows you to take a solid geometry and make it hollow. This can be a powerful and timesaving technique when designing parts that call for thin walls such as bottles, tanks, and containers. This command is easy to use. You should have a solid part to use this command. Activate this command from the **Base** group (On the ribbon, click **Home > Base > Shell**). On the **Shell** dialog, select **Type > Open**, and select the faces to remove. Type-in the wall thickness in the **Thickness** box that appears on the model. Click the **Reverse Direction** button to specify whether the thickness is added inside or outside the model. Click **OK** to finish the feature.

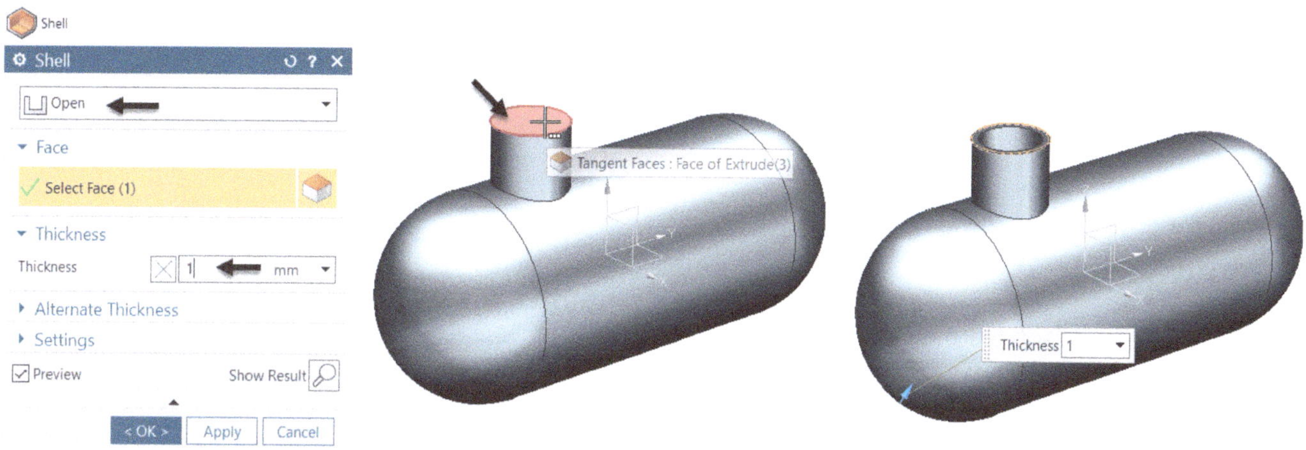

If you want to shell a portion with a different thickness value, expand the **Alternate Thickness** section, and click **Select Face**. Select the outer face of the portion to which you want a different thickness value. Type the alternate thickness value in the **Thickness 1** box.

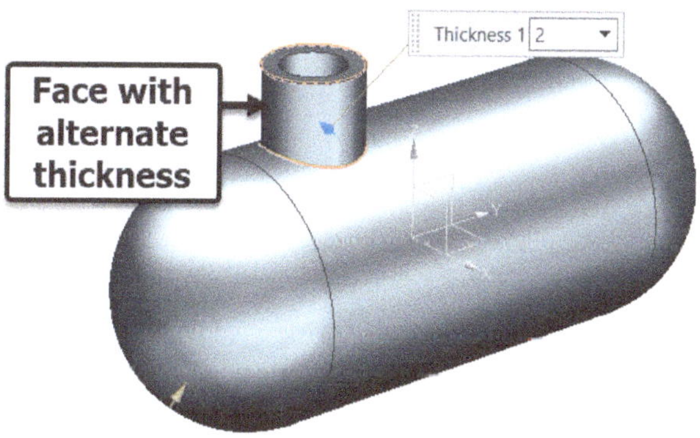

If you want to shell the solid body without removing any faces, then select **Type > Closed** on the dialog. Click on the solid body and type-in a value in the **Thickness** box.

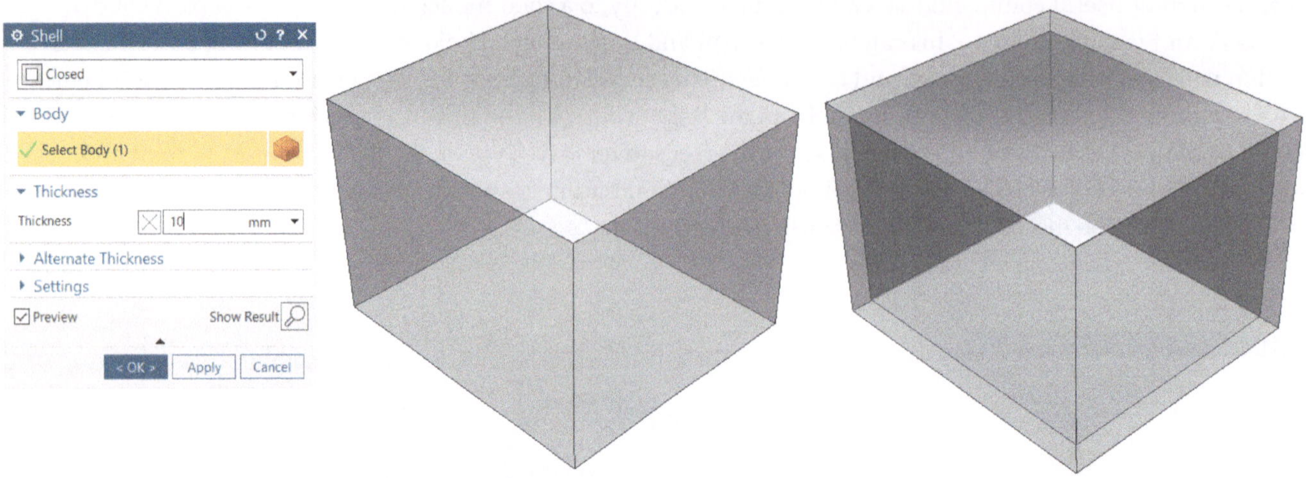

Examples

Example 1 (Millimetres)

In this example, you will create the part shown below.

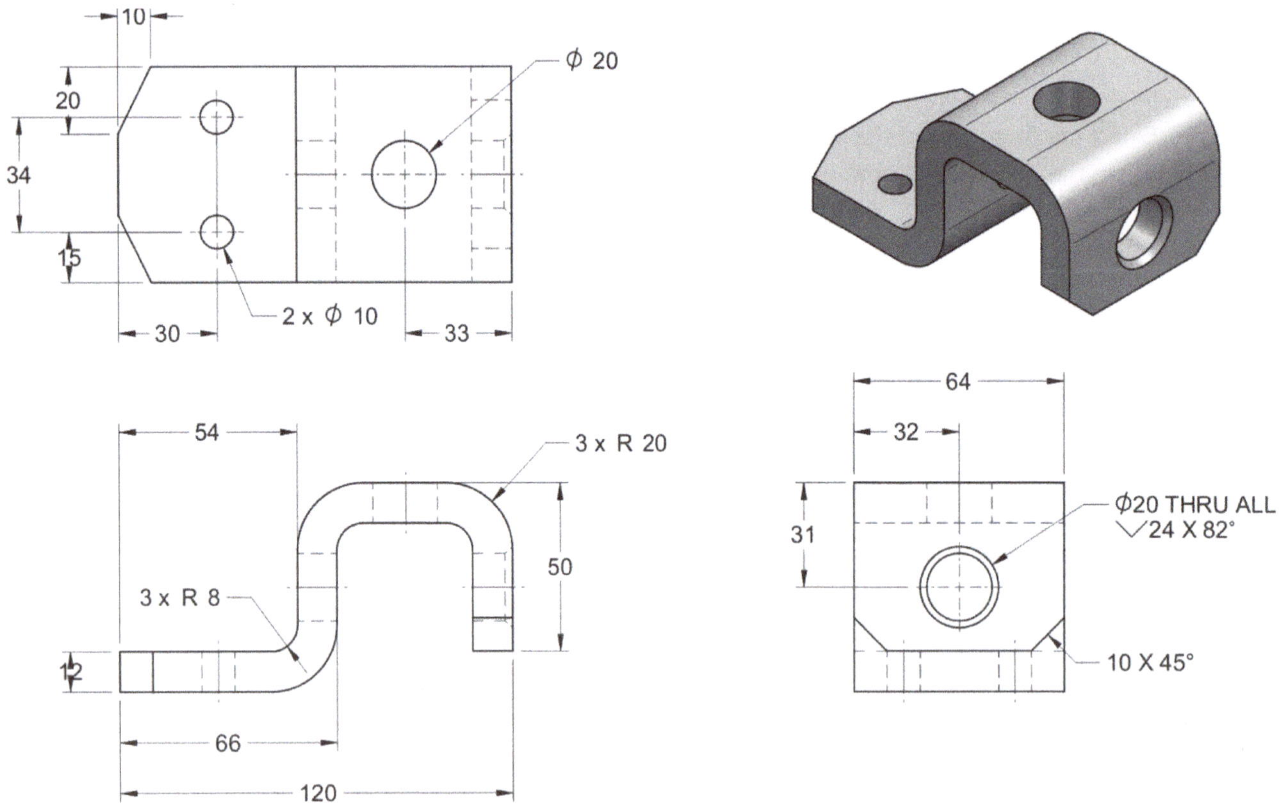

1. Start **NX**.
2. On the ribbon, click **New**. On the **New** dialog, select **Units > Millimeters** and double-click the **Model** template.
3. On the ribbon, click **Home > Base > Extrude**.

4. On the Datum Coordinate System, select the XZ plane. Draw the sketch shown in the figure and create the Extrude feature of 64 mm thickness.

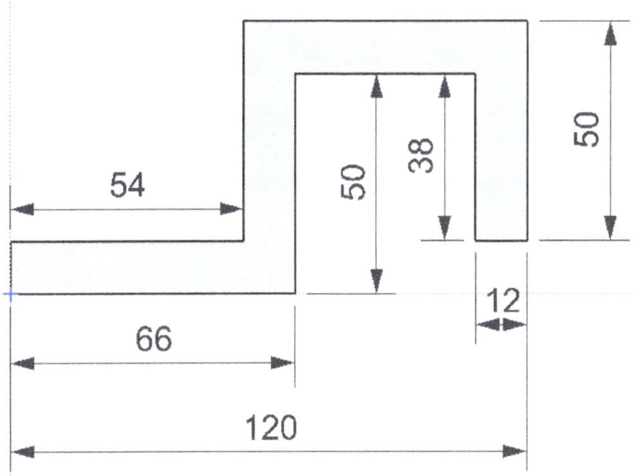

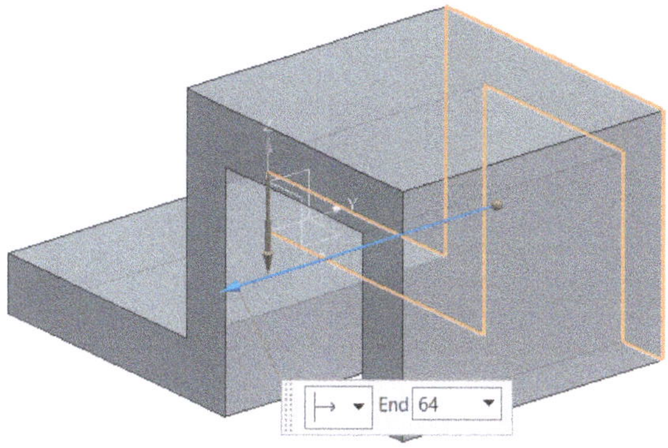

5. On the ribbon, click **Home > Base > Hole**.
6. On the **Hole** dialog, select **Type > Countersunk**.
7. Set the **C-Sink Diameter** and **C-Sink Angle** values to **24** and **82**, respectively.
8. Set the **Hole Diameter** value to **20** mm.
9. Set the **Depth Limit** value to **Through Body**.
10. Click on the right-side face of the part geometry. A point is placed on the selected face.

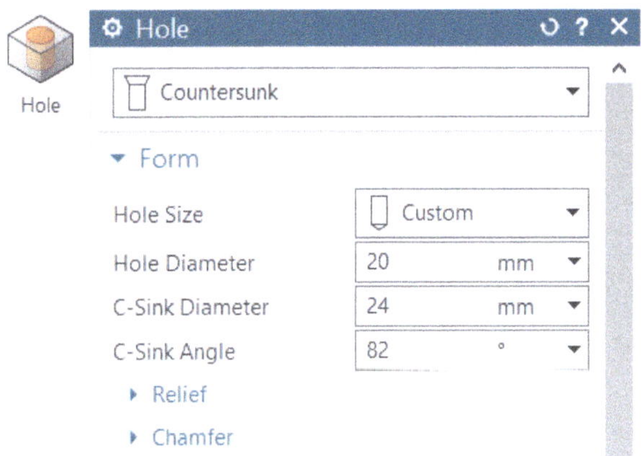

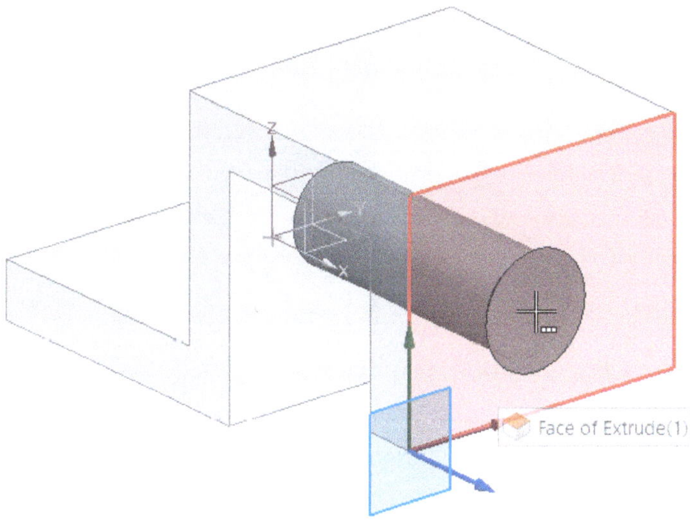

11. Change dimensions defining the point location. Next, click **OK** to complete the hole feature.

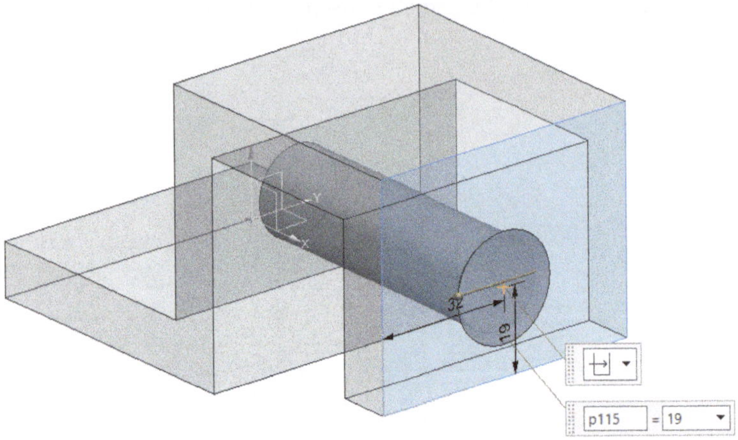

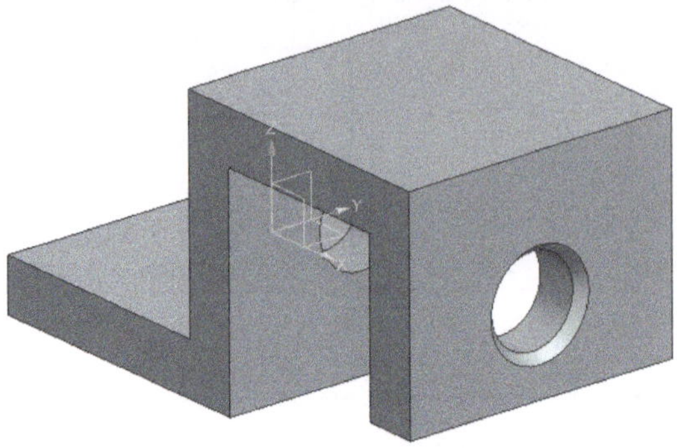

12. Activate the **Hole** command and select **Type > Simple** on the **Hole** dialog.
13. Set the **Hole Diameter** value to 20 mm.
14. Set the **Depth Limit** type to **Through Body** under the **Limit** section. Click on the top face of the part geometry.
15. Change the dimensions defining the location of the hole by clicking on them.

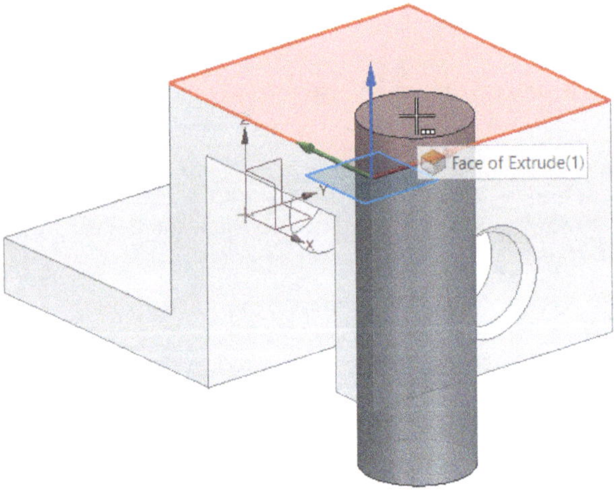

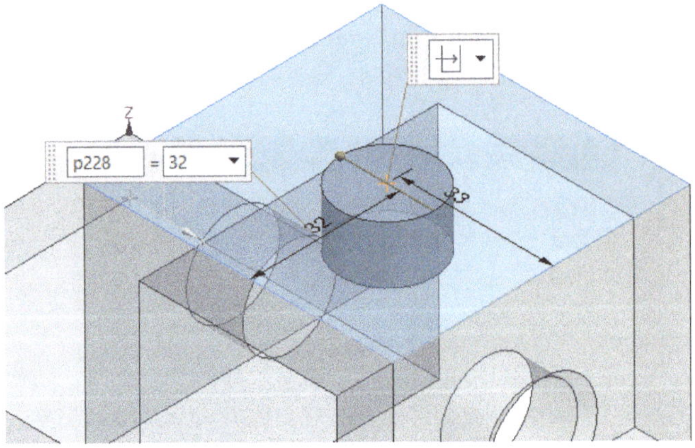

16. Click **OK** to close the dialog.

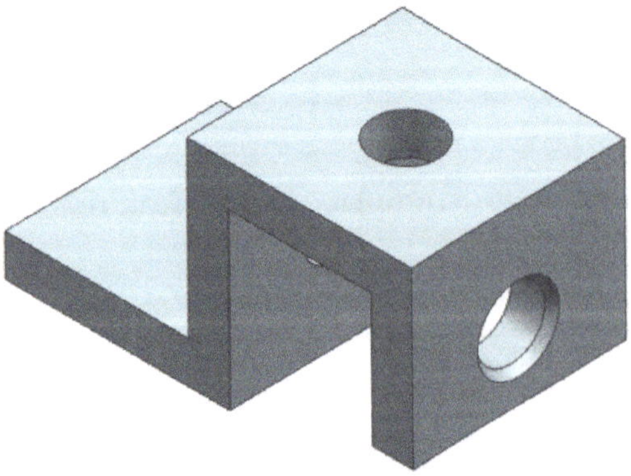

17. On the bottom-left corner of the graphic window, click the Z-axis of the coordinate system and set the **Angle** value to 90. This changes the view orientation of the model.

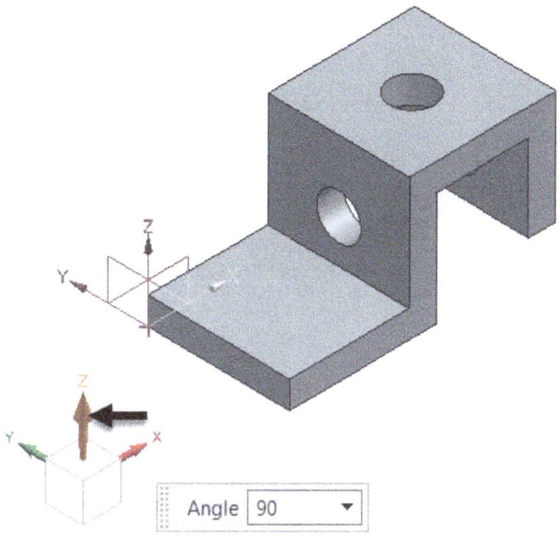

18. Activate the **Hole** command. On the **Hole** dialog, select **Type > Simple** and type-in **10** in the **Hole Diameter** box.
19. Click on the lower top face to place a point for the hole location.
20. Click once again to place another hole. Next, change the dimensions defining the location of the holes

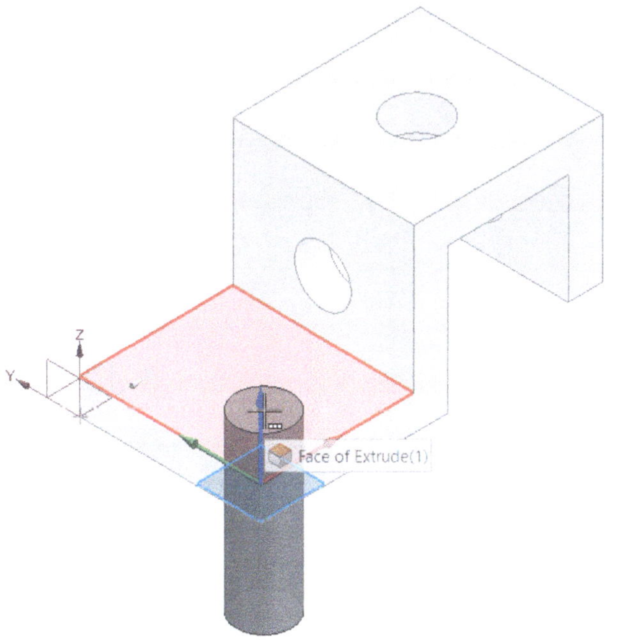

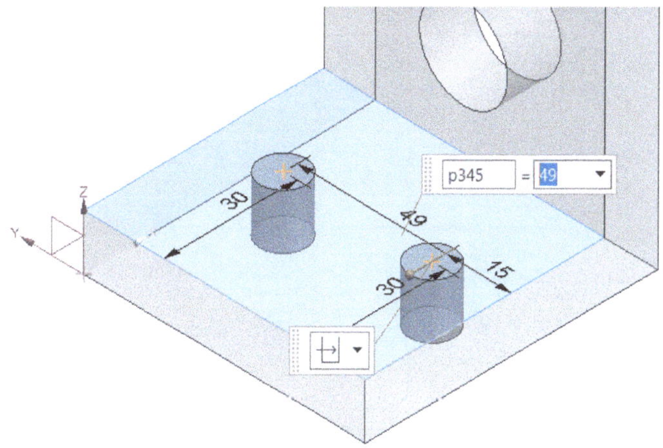

21. Click **OK** to complete the hole feature.

22. Click **Home > Base > Chamfer** on the ribbon.
23. On the **Chamfer** dialog, select **Cross Section > Asymmetric**.
24. Set the **Distance 1** and **Distance 2** values to **10** and **20**, respectively.
25. Click on the side edge of the selected face, as shown in the figure.
26. Click **Apply** on the dialog.

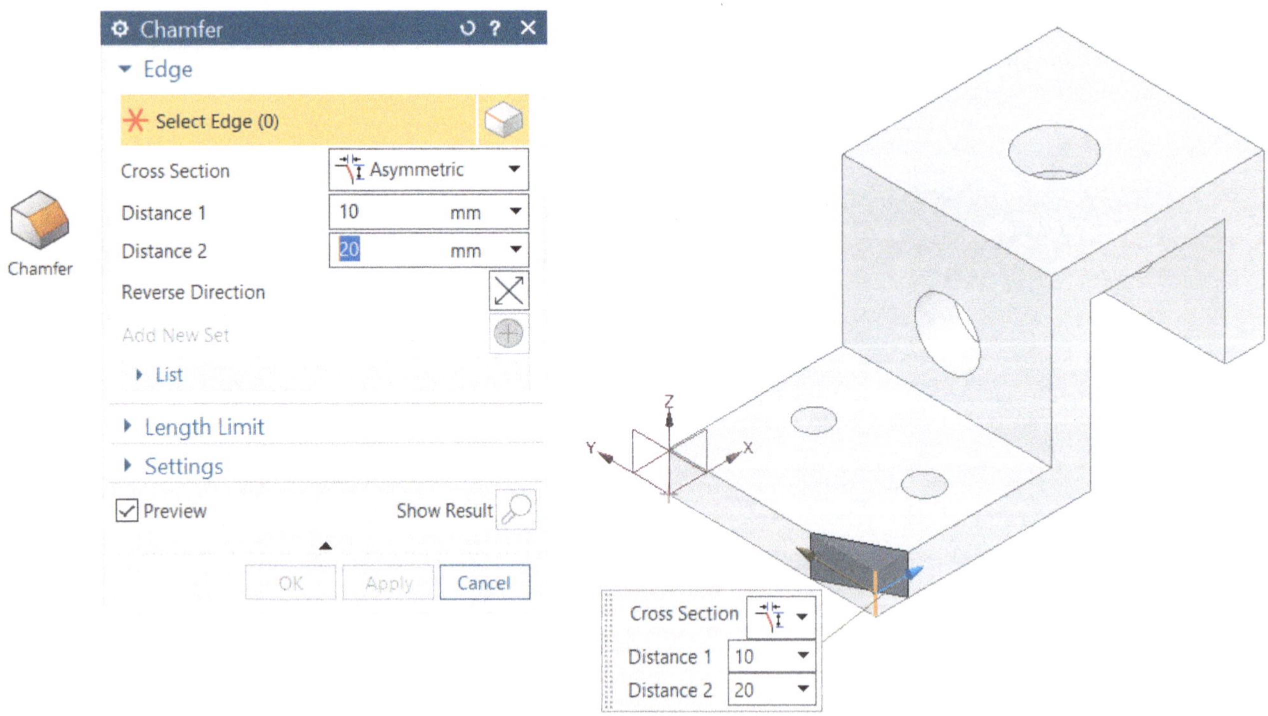

27. Click on the rare side edge and click the **Reverse Direction**  button.
28. Click **OK** to apply the chamfer.

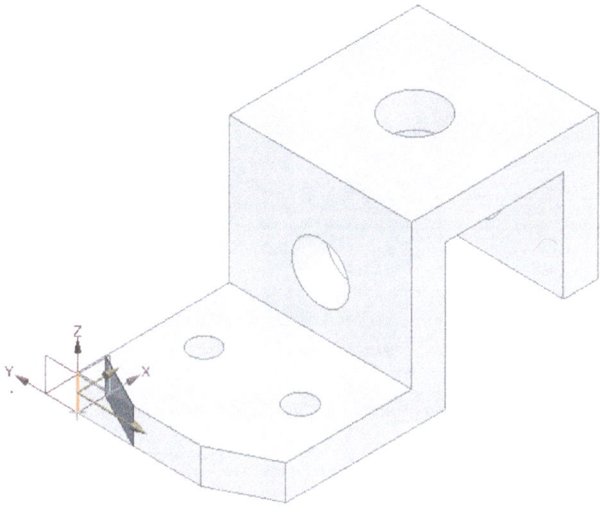

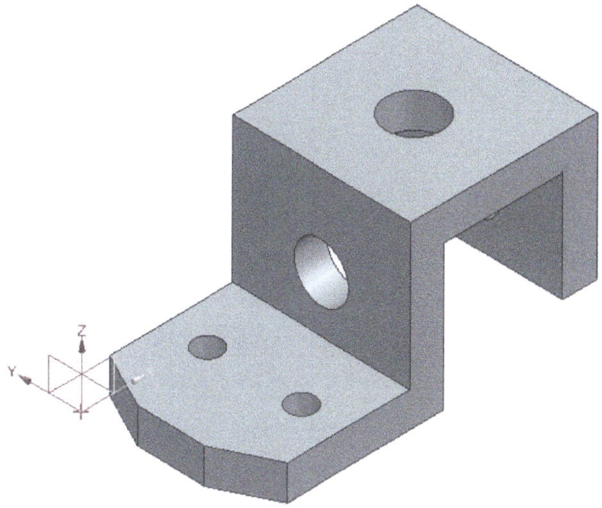

29. Click **Home > Base > Edge Blend** on the ribbon.
30. On the **Edge Blend** dialog, select **Shape > Circular** and type-in **8** in the **Radius 1** box.
31. Select **Continuity > G1 (Tangent)** from the **Edge** section of the dialog.
32. On the Top Border Bar, activate the **Allow Selection of Hidden Wireframe** icon.

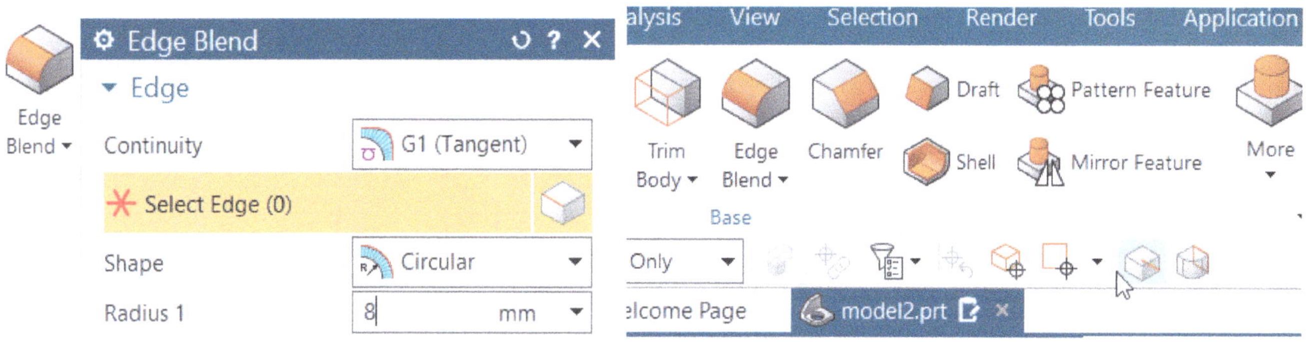

33. Click on the horizontal edges of the geometry, as shown below.
34. Click **Apply** on the dialog and type-in 20 in the **Radius 1** box.

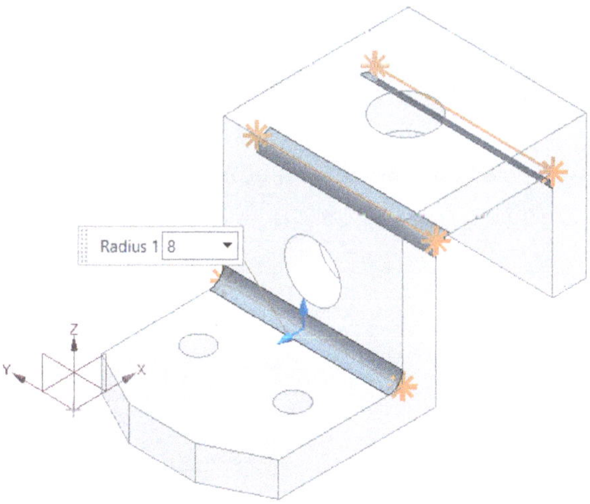

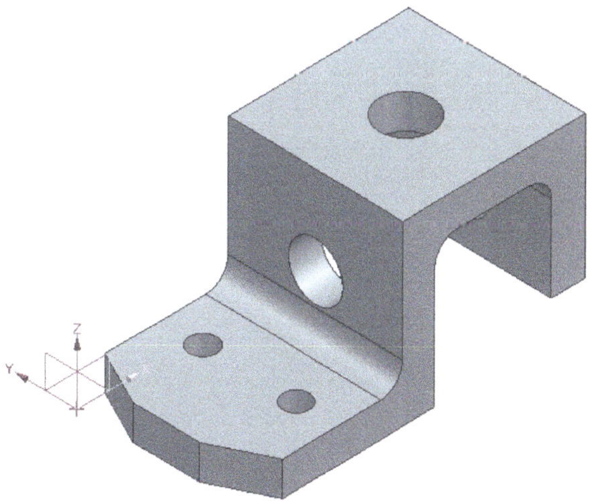

35. Click on the outer edges of the model, as shown below. Click **OK** to complete the edge blend feature.

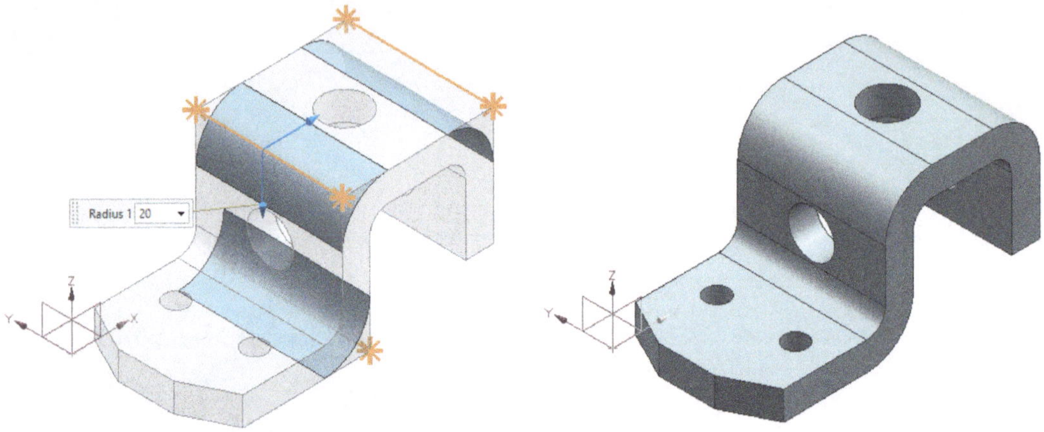

36. Press the **Home** key on your keyboard to change the orientation of the model view to Trimetric.
37. Click **Home > Base > Chamfer** on the ribbon.
38. On the **Chamfer** dialog, select **Cross Section > Symmetric**.
39. Click on the lower corners of the part geometry.
40. Type-in **10** in the **Distance** box and press Enter on the Keyboard. Click **OK** to chamfer the edges.

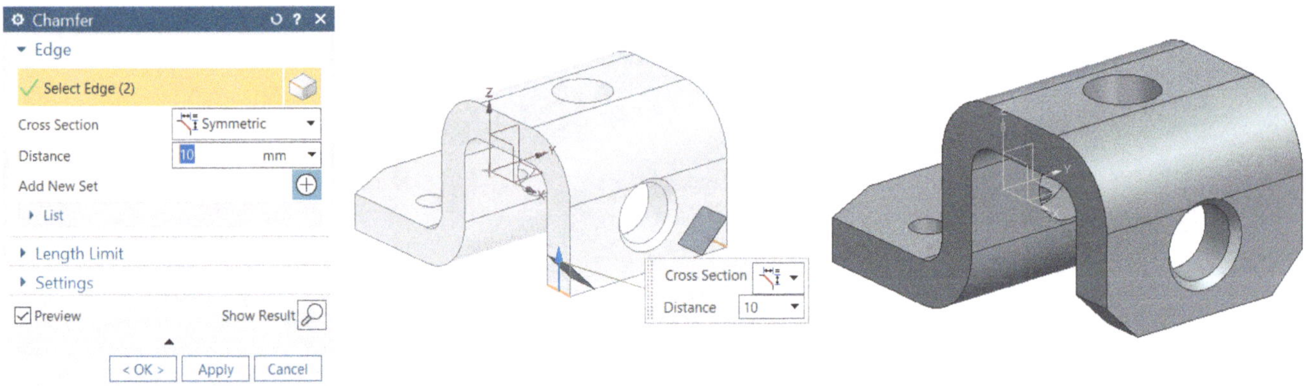

41. Save and close the file.

Questions

1. What are placed features?
2. Which option allows you to create a chamfer with unequal setbacks?
3. Which option allows you to create a variable radius blend?
4. When you create a thread on a cylindrical face, the thread diameter will be calculated automatically or not?

Exercises

Exercise 1 (Millimetres)

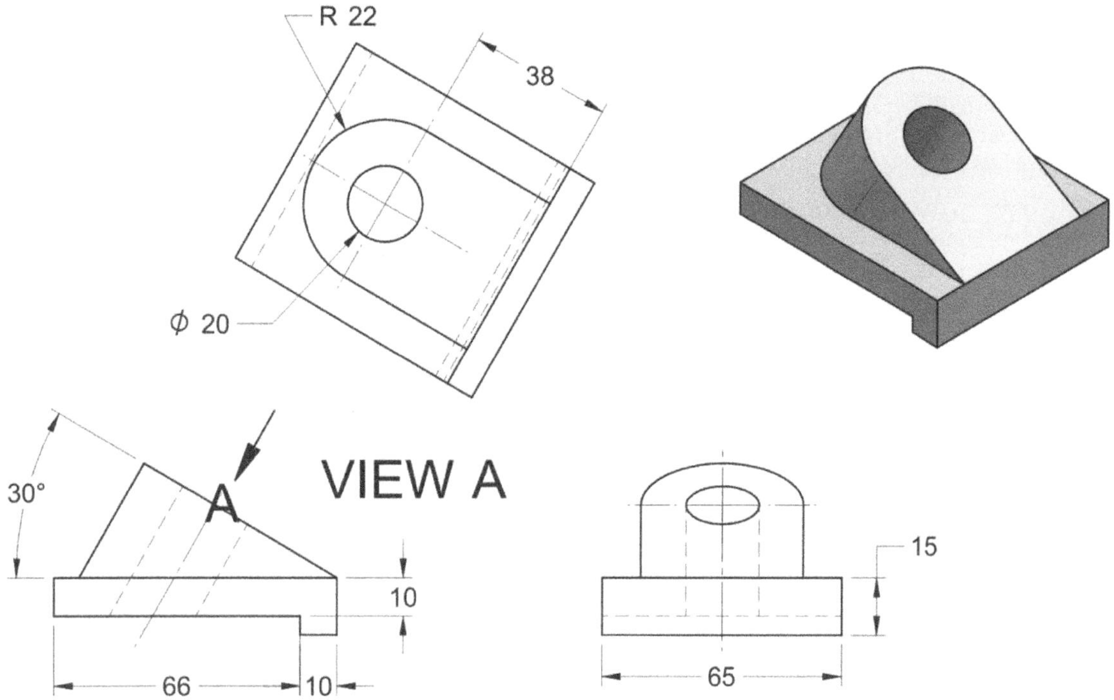

Exercise 2 (Inches)

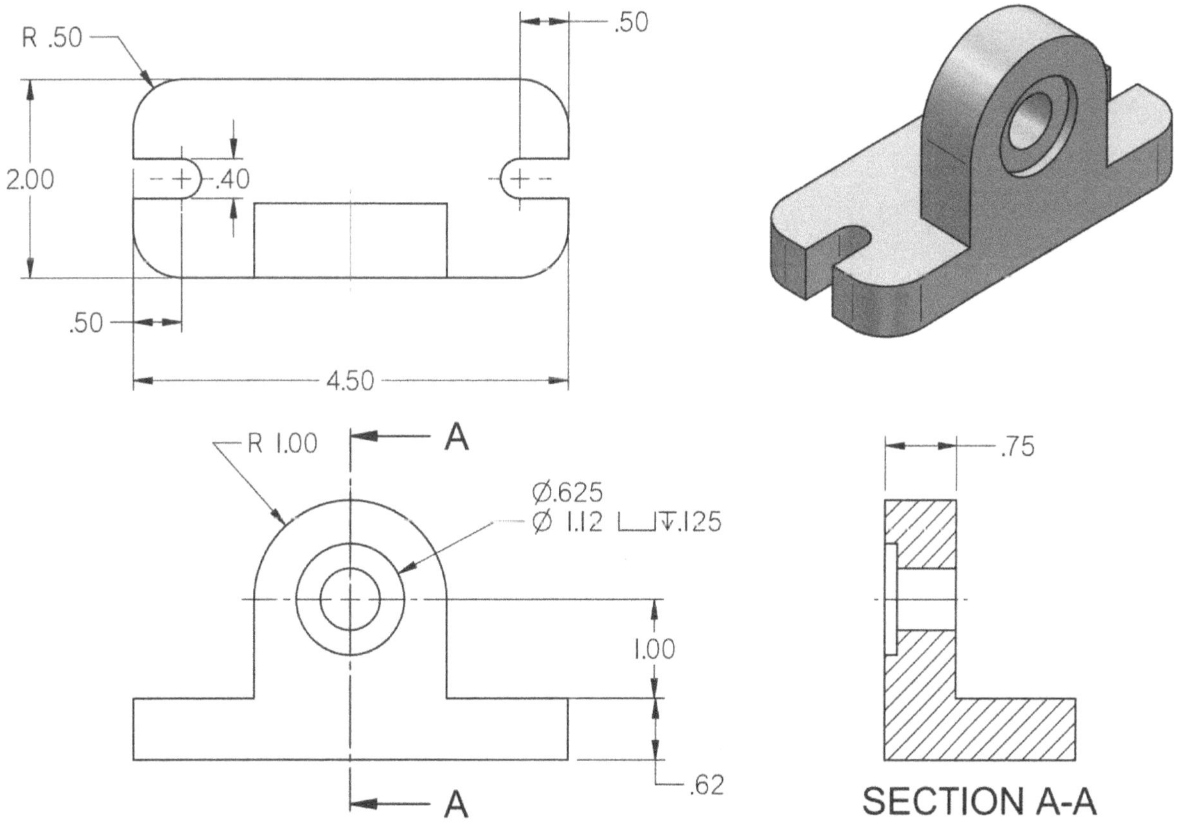

Chapter 5: Patterned Geometry

When designing a part geometry, often, there are elements of symmetry in each part, or there are at least a few features that are repeated multiple times. In these situations, NX offers some commands that save you time. For example, you can use mirror features to design symmetric parts, which makes designing the part quicker. This is because you only have to design a portion of the part and use the mirror feature to create the remaining geometry.

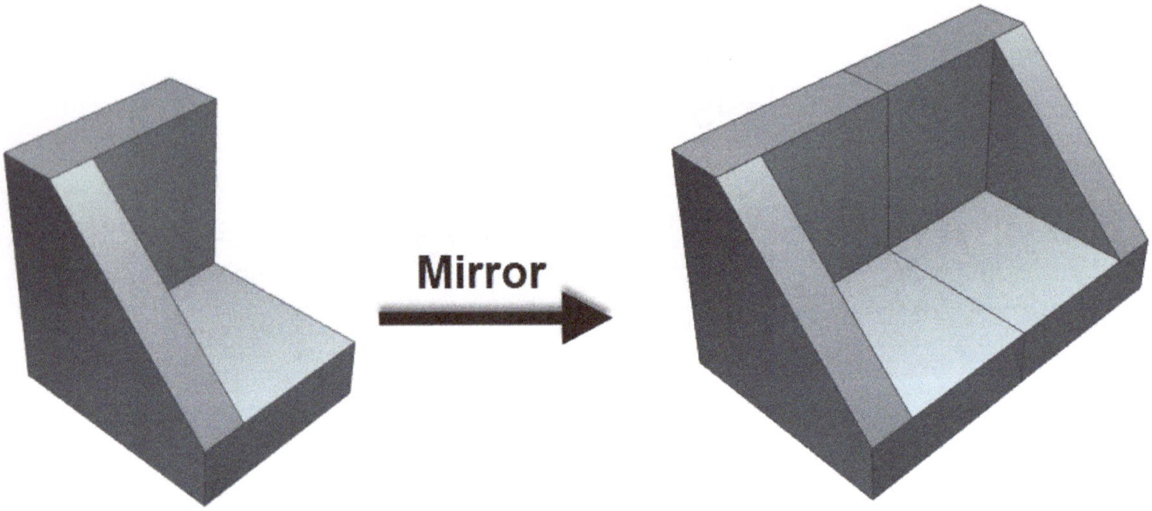

In addition, there are some pattern commands to replicate a feature throughout the part quickly. They save you time from creating additional features individually and help you modify the design easily. If the design changes, you only need to change the first feature, and the rest of the pattern features will update automatically. In this chapter, you will learn to create mirrored and pattern geometries using the commands available in NX.

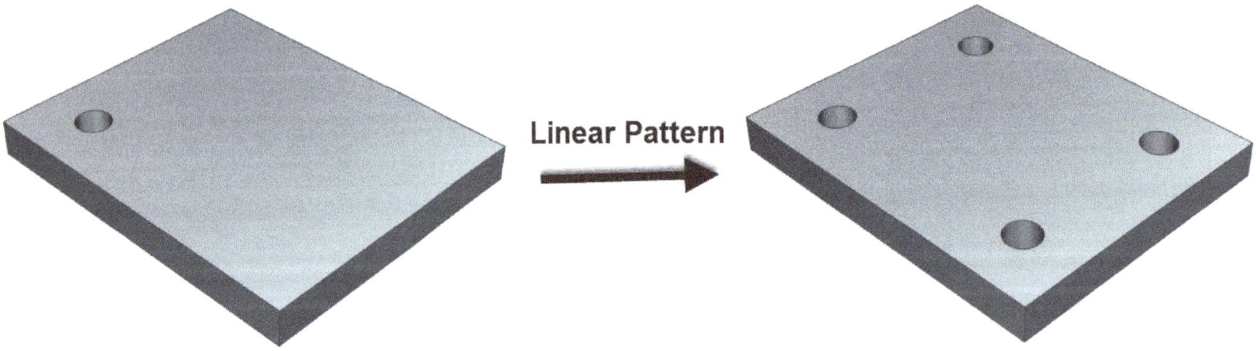

The topics covered in this chapter are:

- *Mirror* features
- *Linear Patterns*
- *Circular Patterns*
- *Along Curve Patterns*
- *Helical Patterns*

Mirror Feature

If you are designing a symmetric part, you can save time by using the **Mirror Feature**  command. Using this command, you can replicate the individual features of the entire body. To mirror features (3D geometry), you need to have a face or plane to use as a reference. You can use a model face, default plane, or create a new plane if it does not exist where it is needed.

Activate the **Mirror Feature** command (click **Home > Base > Mirror Feature** on the ribbon). On the part geometry, click on the features to mirror, and then click **Select Plane** on the **Mirror Feature** dialog. Now, select the reference plane about which the features are to be mirrored.

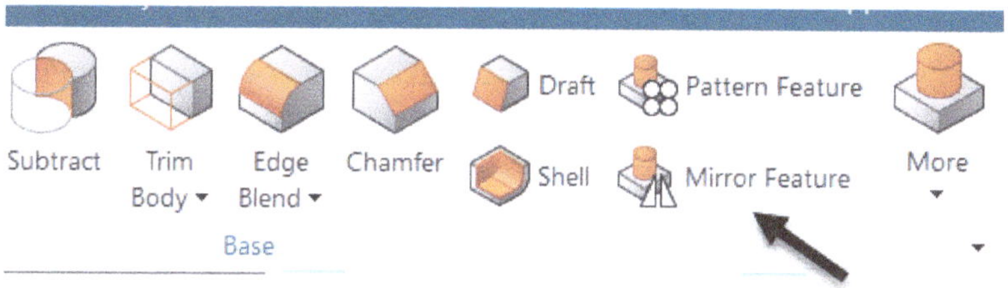

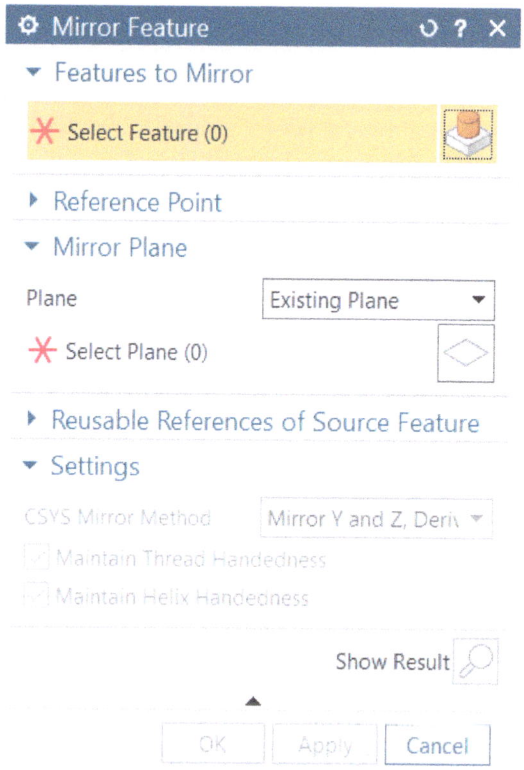

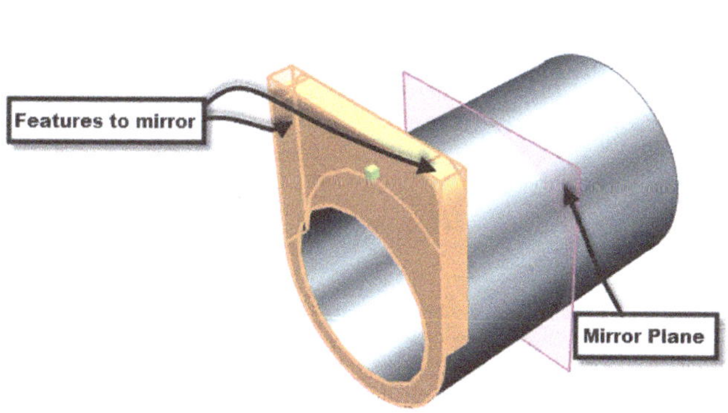

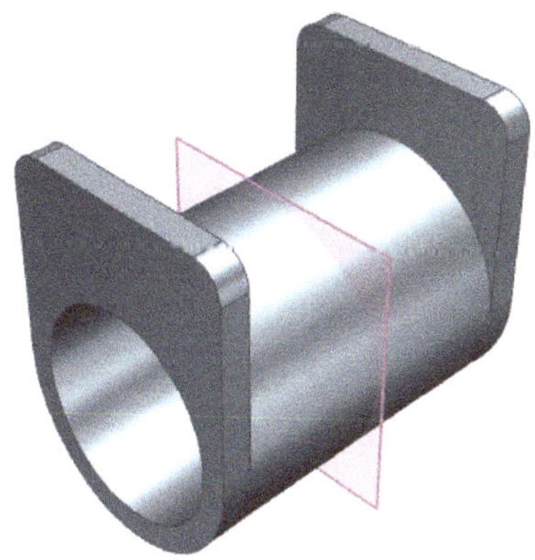

Now, if you make changes to the original feature, the mirrored feature will be updated automatically.

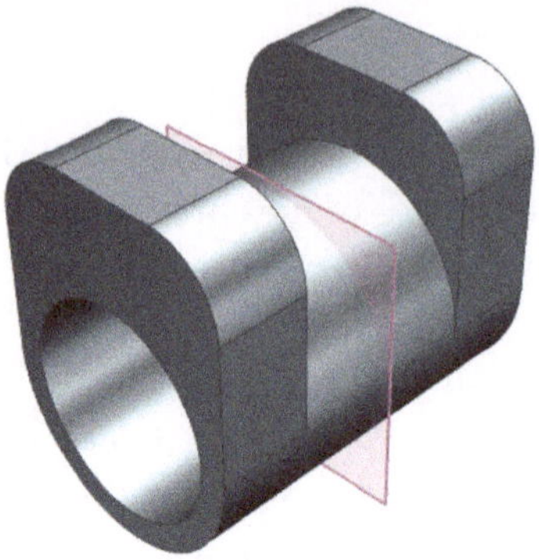

Mirror Geometry

If the part you are creating is completely symmetric, you can save more time by creating half of it and mirroring the entire geometry rather than individual features. You can accomplish this by using the **Mirror Geometry** command. Activate this command (On the ribbon, click **Home > Base > More > Copy > Mirror Geometry**) and click on the solid part. On the **Mirror Geometry** dialog, click **Specify Plane** and select the face about which the geometry is to be mirrored. Click **OK** to complete the mirror geometry.

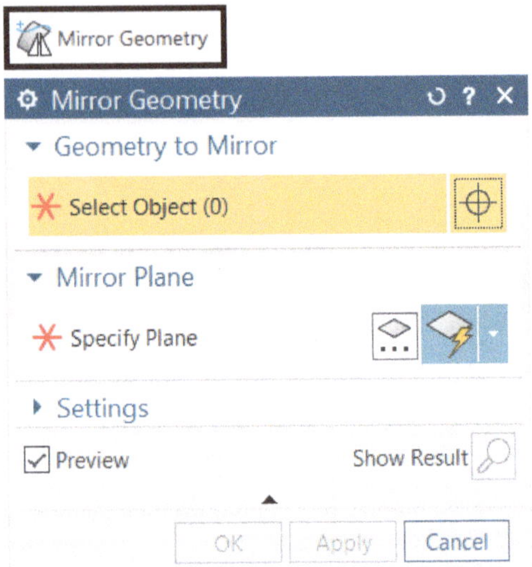

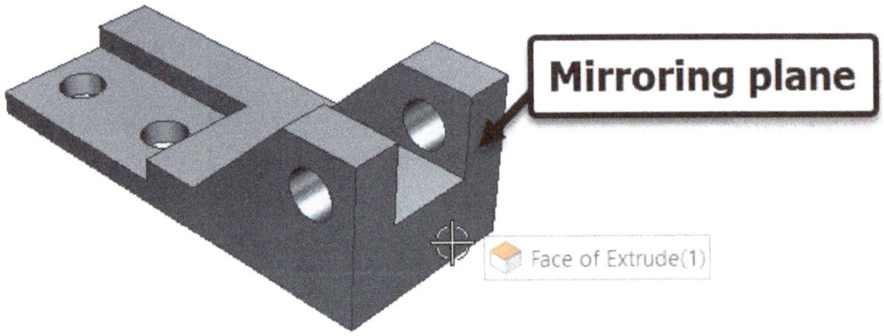

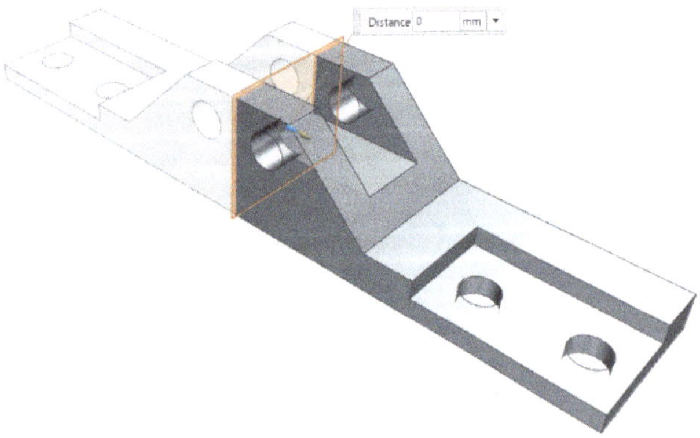

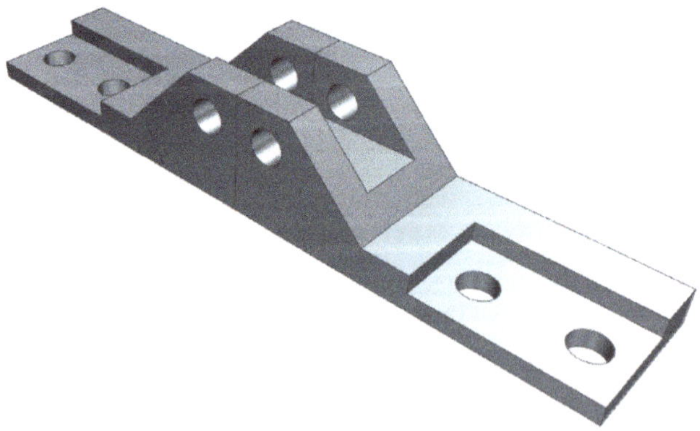

Pattern Feature

This command replicates a feature using different layouts such as linear, circular, polygonal, spiral, along a curve, and randomly arranged points. Activate this command (on the ribbon, click **Home > Base > Pattern Feature**). The following sections explain the different pattern layouts that can be created using the **Pattern Feature** command.

Linear Layout

To create a pattern in a linear layout, you must first activate the **Pattern Feature** command (On the ribbon, click **Home > Base > Pattern Feature**). On the **Pattern Feature** dialog, under the **Pattern Definition** section, select **Layout > Linear** . Select the feature to pattern from the model geometry and select **Direction 1 > Specify Vector**. On the part geometry, click on edge (or) select the X, Y, or Z-axis to define the direction 1 of the linear pattern. You will notice that a pattern preview appears on the model. Now, select **Spacing > Count and Pitch** on the dialog and set the parameters of the pattern (**Count** and **Pitch Distance**). Check the **Symmetric** option if you want to pattern the feature on both sides.

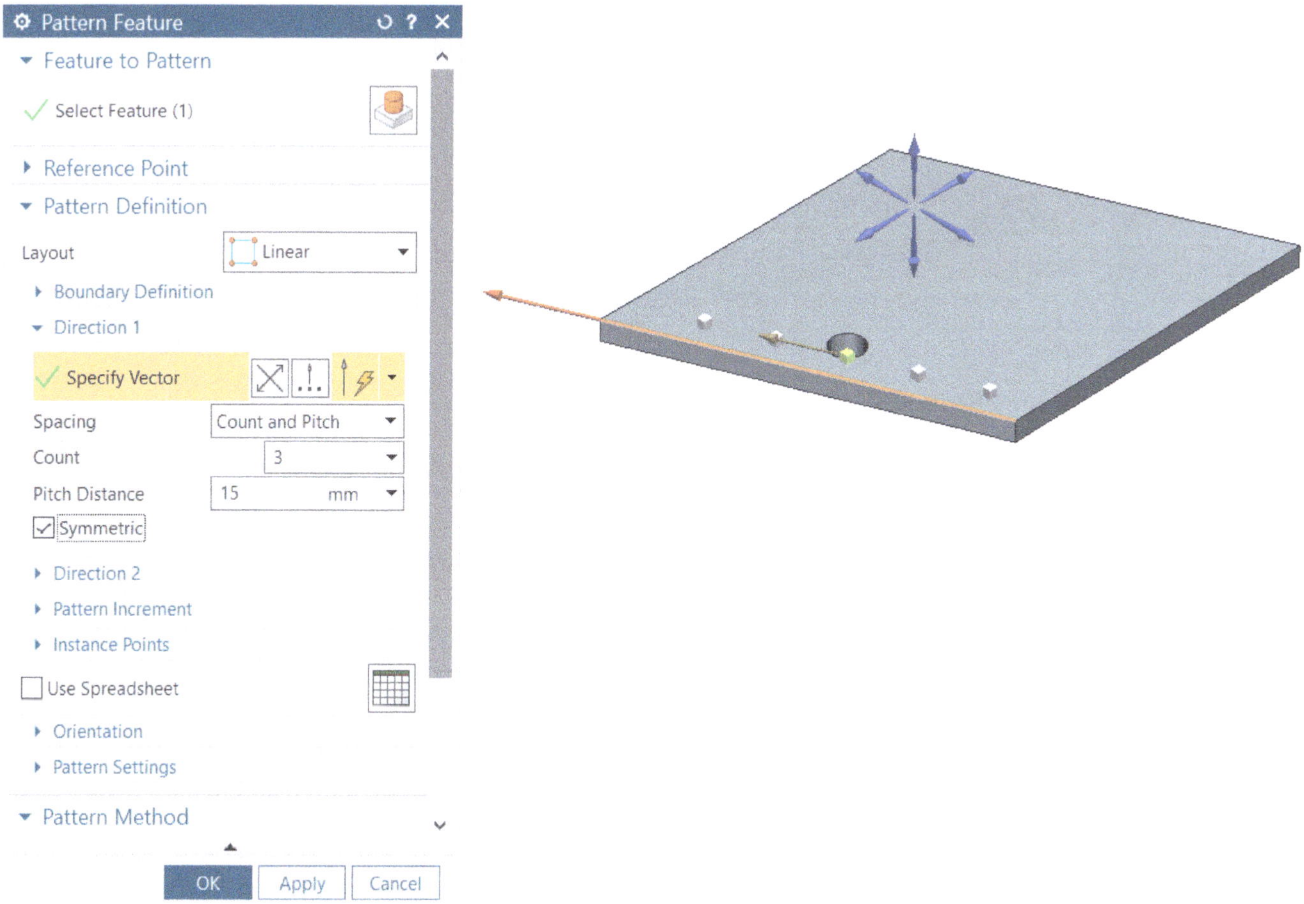

Under the **Direction 2** section, check the **Use Direction 2** option to pattern the feature in the second direction as well. Click on edge to define the second direction of the pattern. Set the parameters (**Count** and **Pitch Distance**) of the pattern in direction 2.

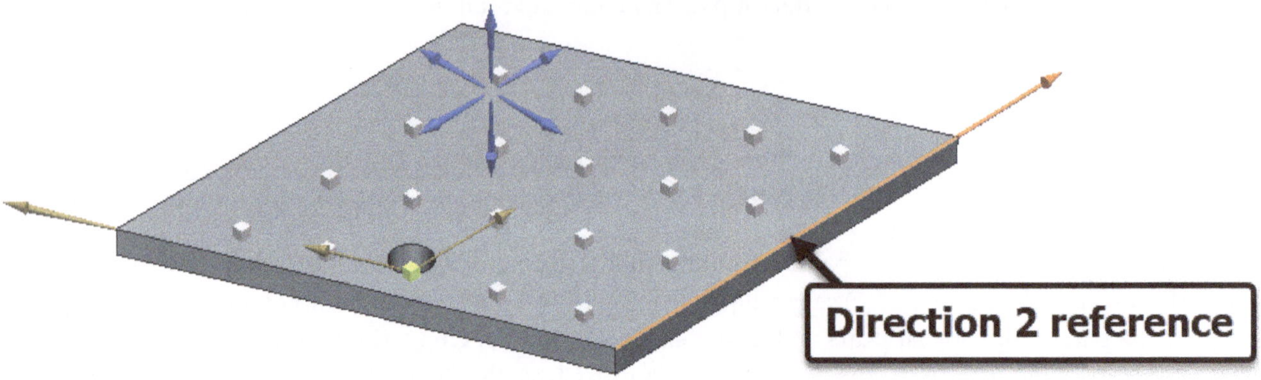

If you want to suppress an instance of the pattern, click the right mouse button on it and select **Suppress**.

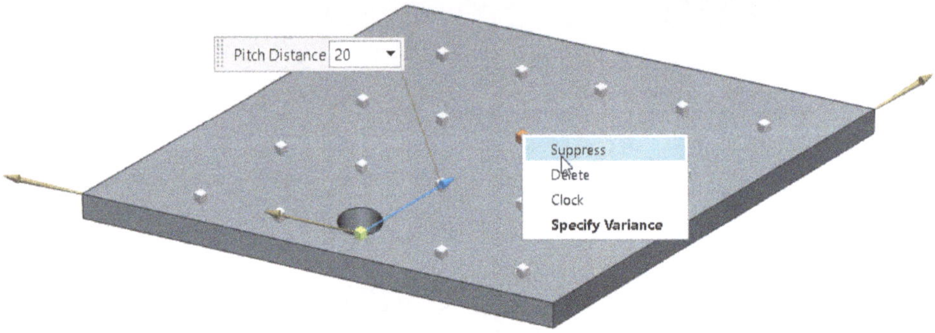

Select **Spacing > Count and Span** on the **Pattern Feature** dialog, if you want to enter the instant count and total spacing along the direction 1 or direction 2.

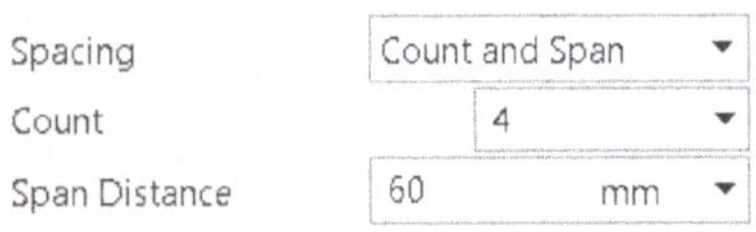

Select **Spacing > Pitch and Span**, if you want to enter the distance between individual instances of the pattern and total spacing along the directions.

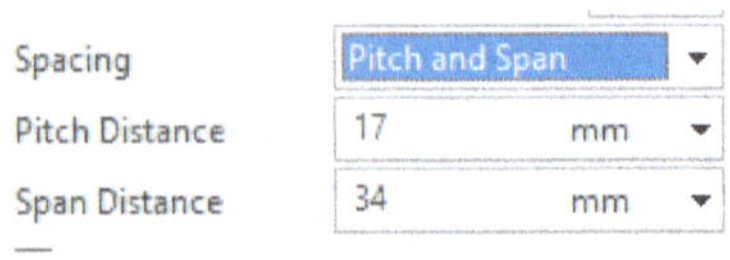

Select **Spacing > List** and add multiple sets of instances along a single direction using the **Add New Set**  button. You can define different spacing value for each set.

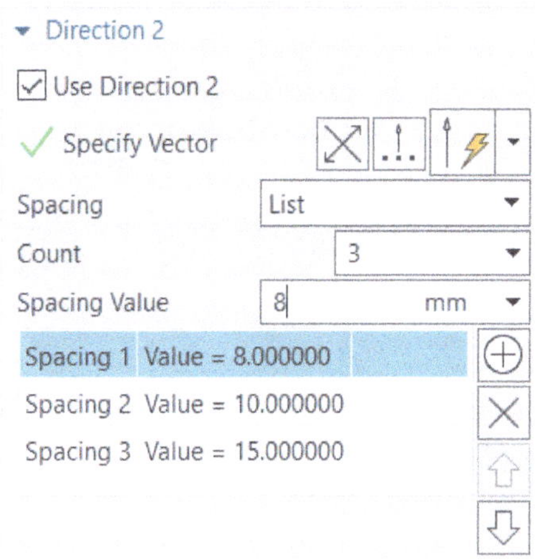

Select **Spacing > Points** and select multiple points from the graphics window to specify the location of the instances along the single direction.

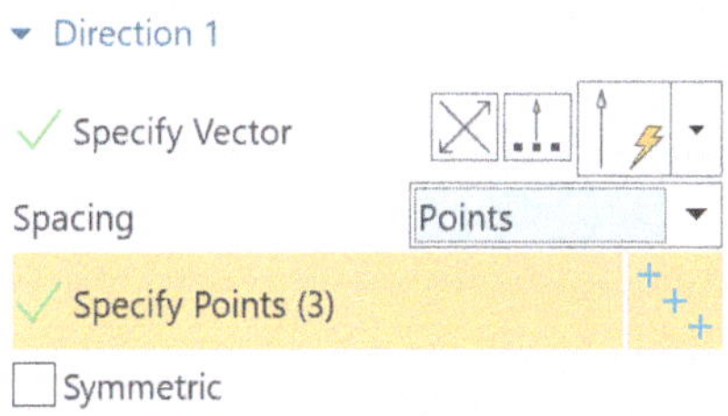

On the **Pattern Feature** dialog, click **OK** to complete the pattern.

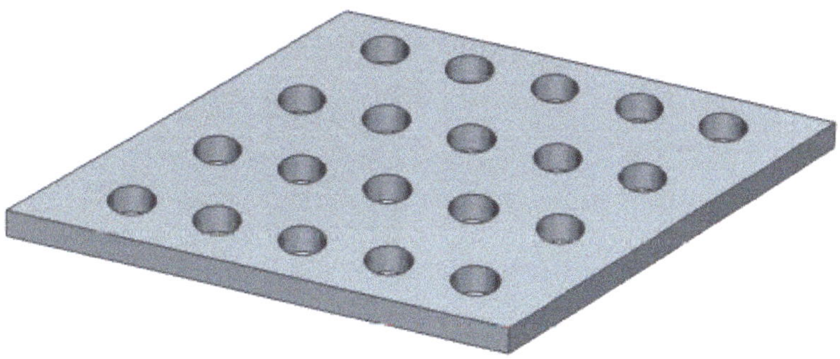

Circular Layout

On the **Pattern Feature** dialog, select **Layout > Circular** to pattern the selected features in a circular fashion. Select the feature to pattern from the model geometry. Under the **Rotation Axis** section, click **Specify Vector** and select the X, Y, or Z-axis to define the axis of the rotation. Usually, the axis of rotation is perpendicular to the plane/face on which the selected feature is placed. Click on a point to define the location of the rotation axis.

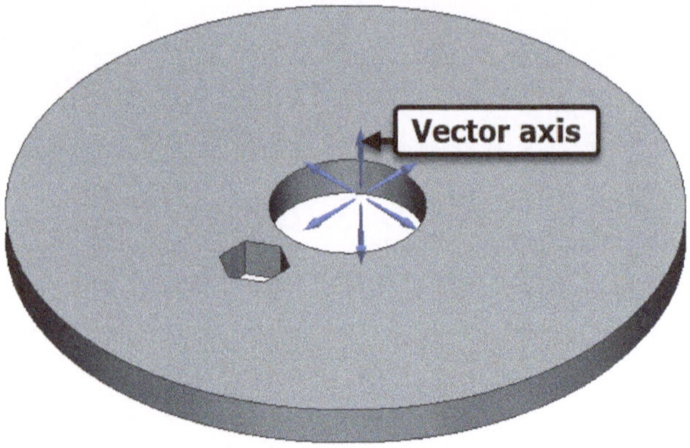

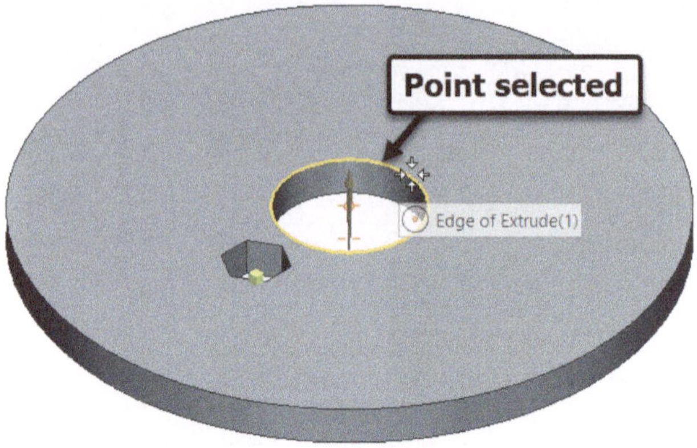

Under the **Angular Direction** section, select **Spacing > Count and Span**. Type-in values in the **Count** and **Span Angle** boxes.

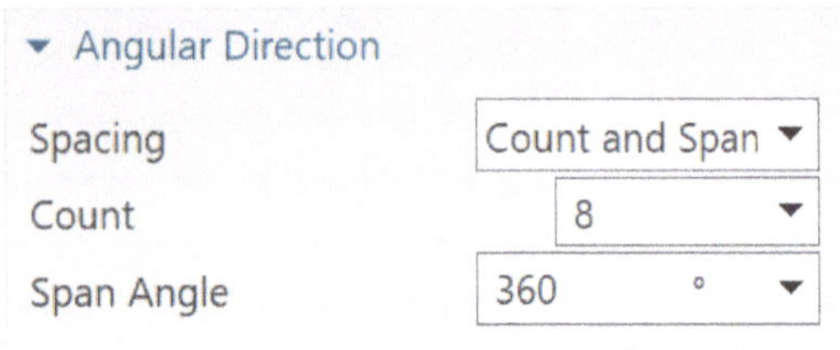

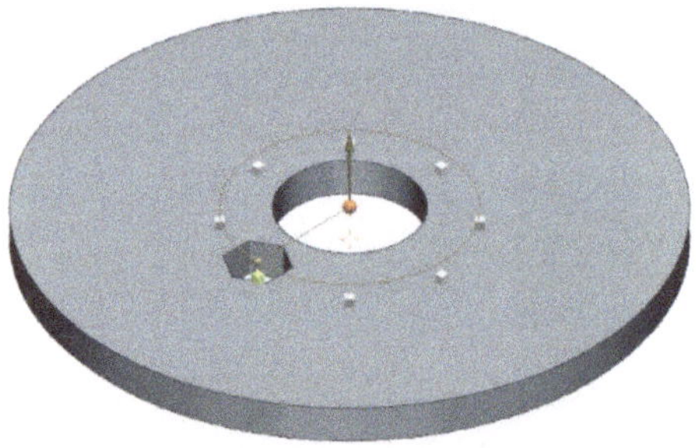

Select **Spacing> Count and Pitch**, if you want to type-in the count and the angle between individual instances.

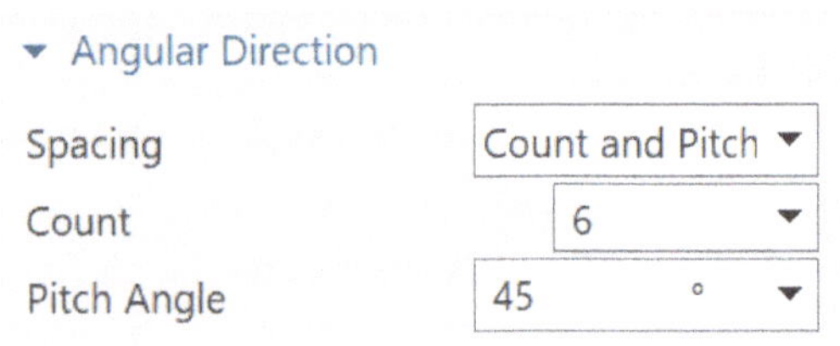

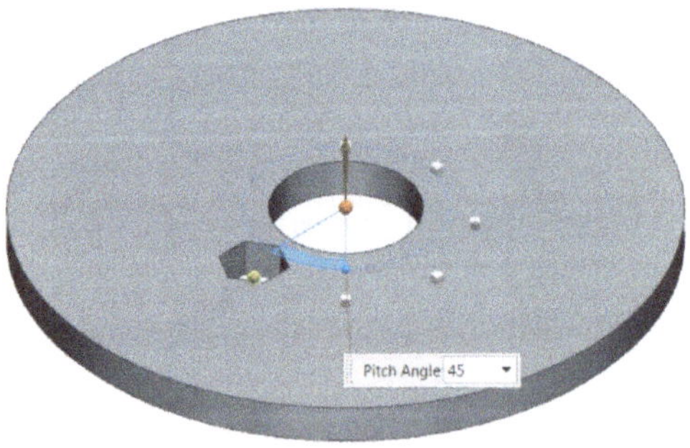

Select **Spacing > Pitch and Span**, if you want to type-in the angle between individual instances and the total angle of the circular pattern.

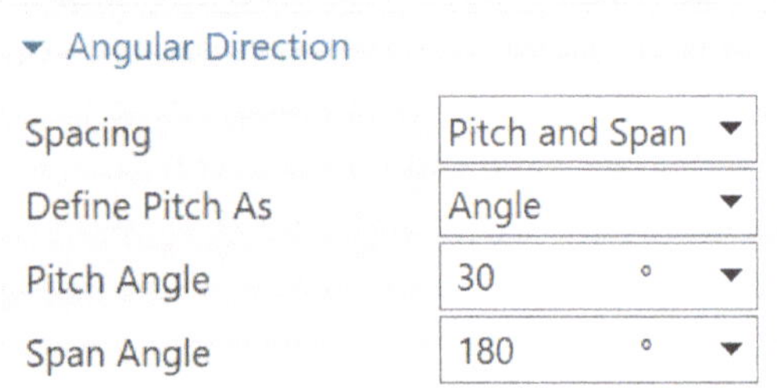

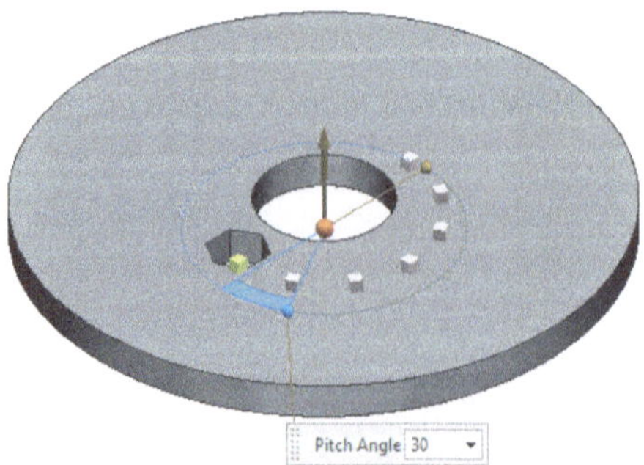

Under the **Orientation** section, select **Orientation > Same as Input** to pattern the feature with the original orientation. Select **Orientation > Follow Pattern** to change the orientation of the instances, as they are patterned circularly. Click **OK** to complete the circular pattern.

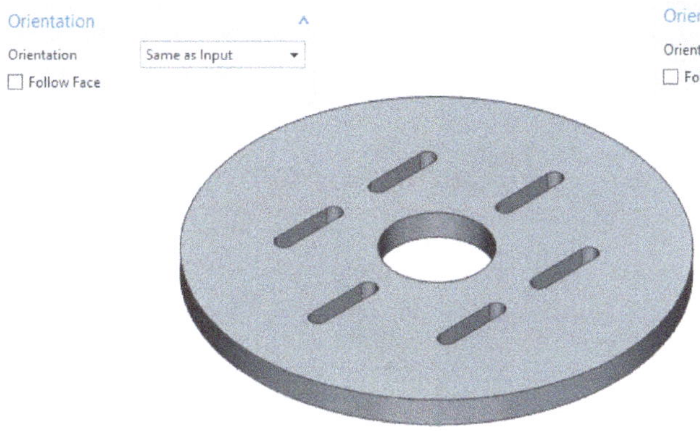

Create Concentric Members

The **Pattern Feature** command has options to radiate the circular pattern. On the **Pattern Feature** dialog, expand the **Radiate** section and check the **Create Concentric Members** option to view the options to radiate the circular pattern. Select **Spacing > Count and Pitch**, and type-in values in the **Count** and **Pitch** boxes. The **Count** and **Pitch** values specify the number of concentric members and distance between them, respectively. On your own, examine the other options in the **Spacing** drop-down as they are explained earlier in the **Linear Layout** section. Select/deselect the **Include First Circle** option to show or hide the first circle of the pattern.

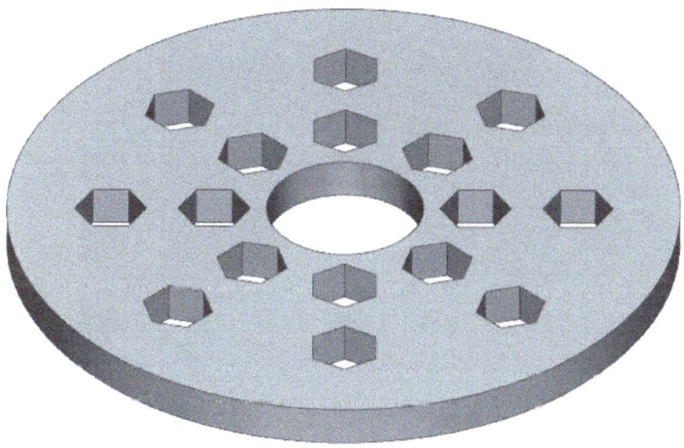

Along Layout

The **Along** option creates a pattern along a selected curve or edge. On the **Pattern Feature** dialog, select **Layout > Along** , and then click on the feature to pattern. Under the **Direction 1** section, click **Select Path** and select a curve or edge. For this example, select the **Offset** option from the **Path Method** drop-down. If the path has continuous tangent curves, then select **Curve Rule > Tangent Curves** on the **Sketch Scene Bar**. Now, you can select the path in a single click.

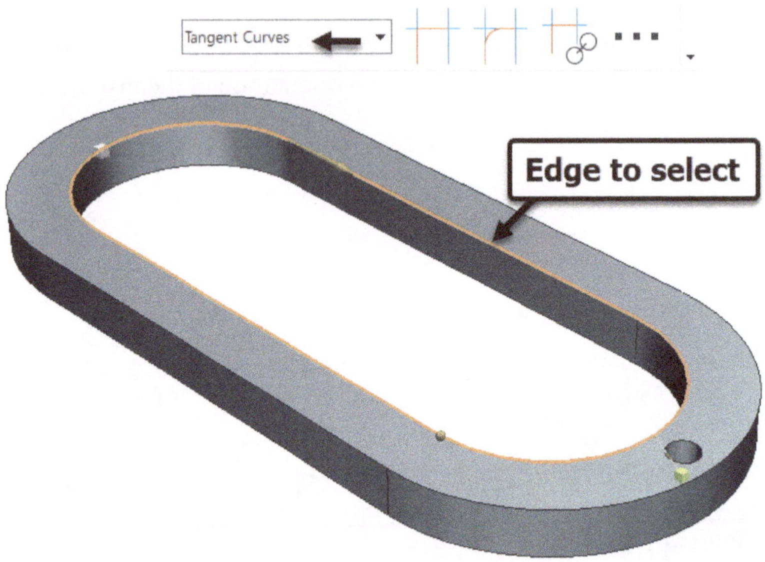

Under the **Direction 1** section, select **Spacing > Count and Span**. Type-in values in the **Count** and **%Span By** boxes. You have to enter **100** in the **%Span By** box to create pattern along the complete curve.

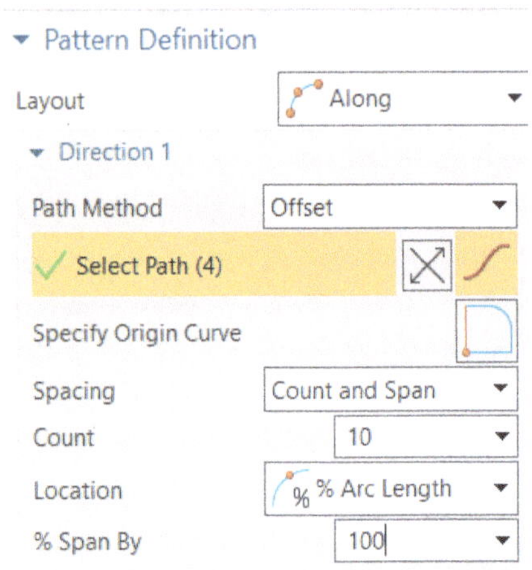

Helical Layout

The **Helix** option creates a pattern along a helical path. Select the feature to pattern from the model geometry and select **Layout > Helix** . Under the **Rotation Axis** section, click **Specify Vector** and define the axis of the helical pattern. Select a point to define the position of the axis. Under the **Rotation Axis** section, click the **Reverse Direction** button to reverse the axial pattern, if required. Under the **Angular Definition** section, define the **Direction** and select **Helix Size By > Count, Helix Pitch, Turns**. Type-in values in the **Count, Helix Pitch, Turns** boxes. Click **OK** to complete the helical pattern.

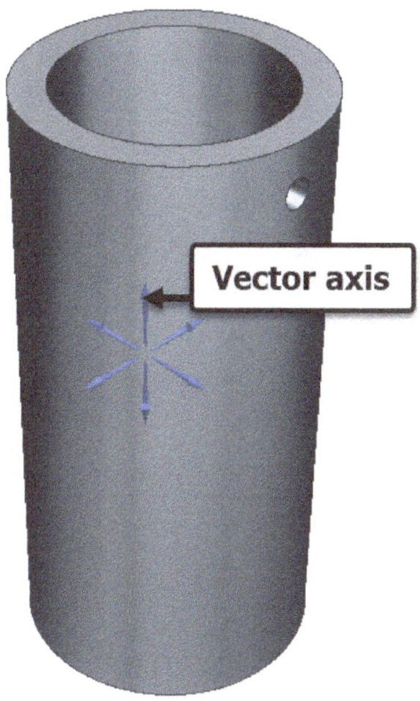

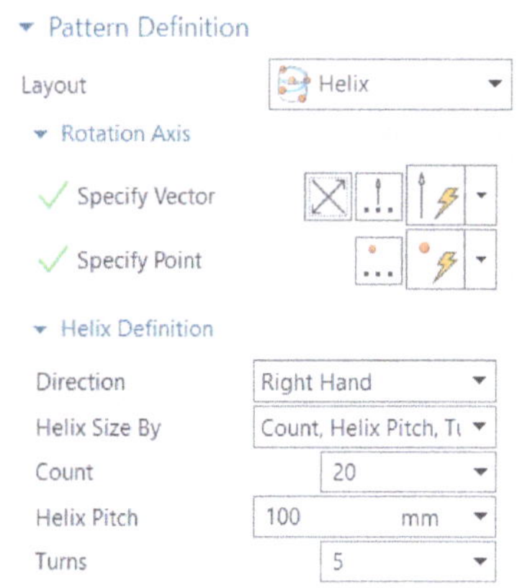

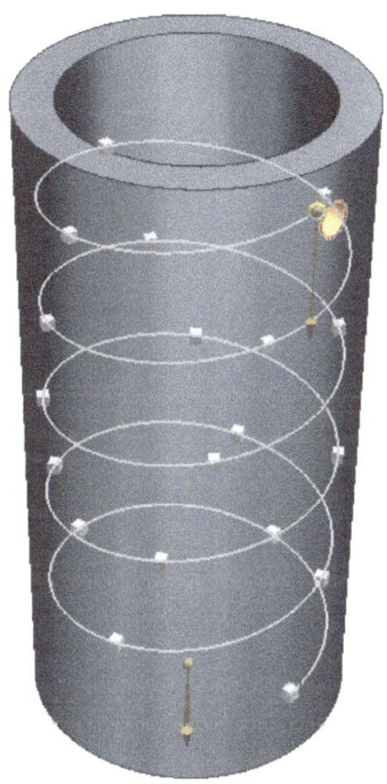

Axial Layout

The **Axial** option is used to create a repeated arrangement of features or bodies around a defined **rotation axis**. Instead of copying features in a linear direction, this tool distributes them radially, much like placing objects around the circumference of a circle or along a cylindrical surface. Select the feature to pattern from the model geometry and select **Layout > Axial**. Under the **Rotation Axis** section, click **Specify Vector** and define the axis of the helical pattern. Select a point to define the position of the axis. Under the **Rotation Axis** section, click the **Reverse Direction** button to reverse the axial pattern, if required.

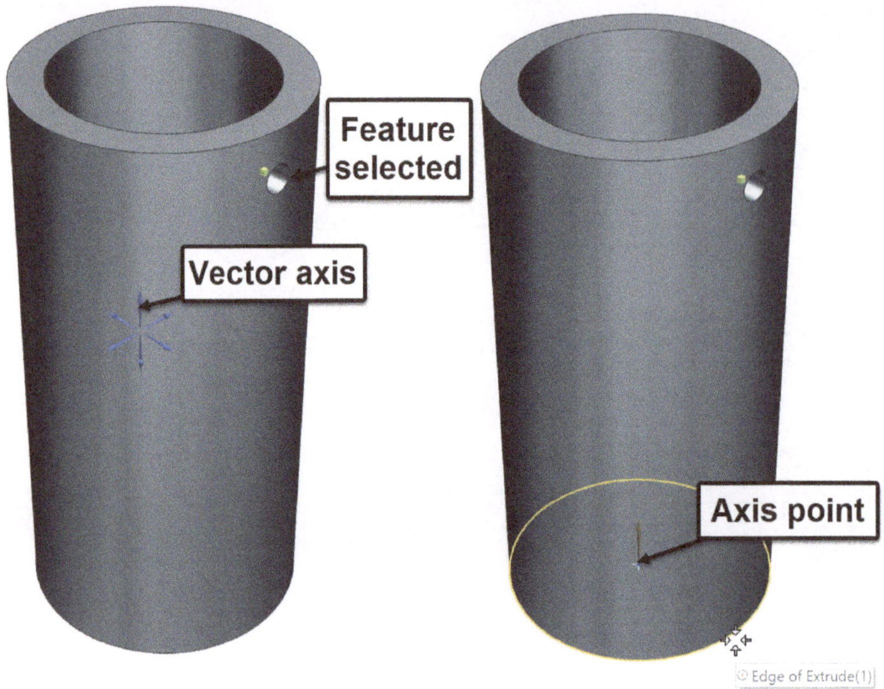

Under the **Angular Definition** section, define the **Spacing** by selecting the **Count and Span**, **Count and Pitch**, **Pitch and Span**, or **List** option. These options control how the instances of a feature are arranged around the rotation axis. The **Count and Span** option lets you define the number of instances (**Count**) along with the total angular sweep (**Span Angle**), and NX distributes them evenly across that span.

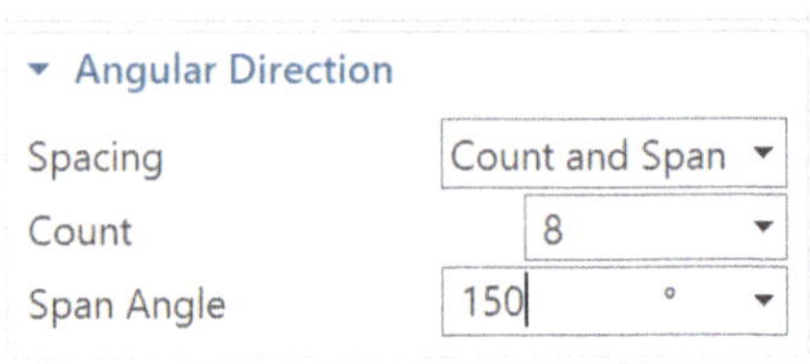

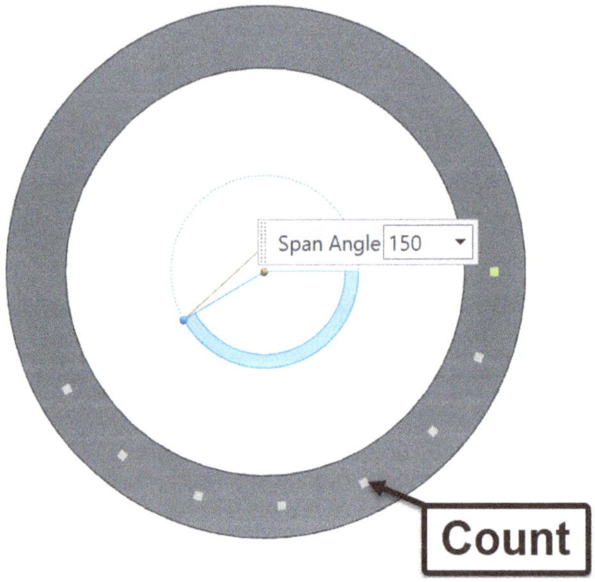

With **Count and Pitch**, you enter the number of instances (**Count**) and the **Pitch Angle** (spacing between each one), so the system places them step by step until the count is met.

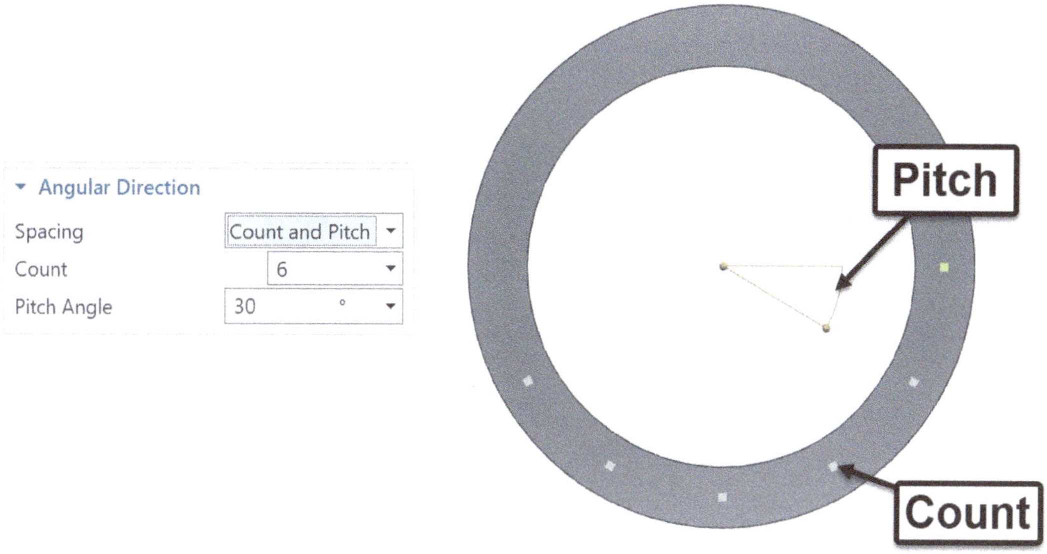

The **Pitch and Span** option requires you to specify the pitch and the overall **Span Angle**, and NX calculates how many instances fit within that range. You can specify the pitch by specifying the **Pitch Angle** or **Distance**.

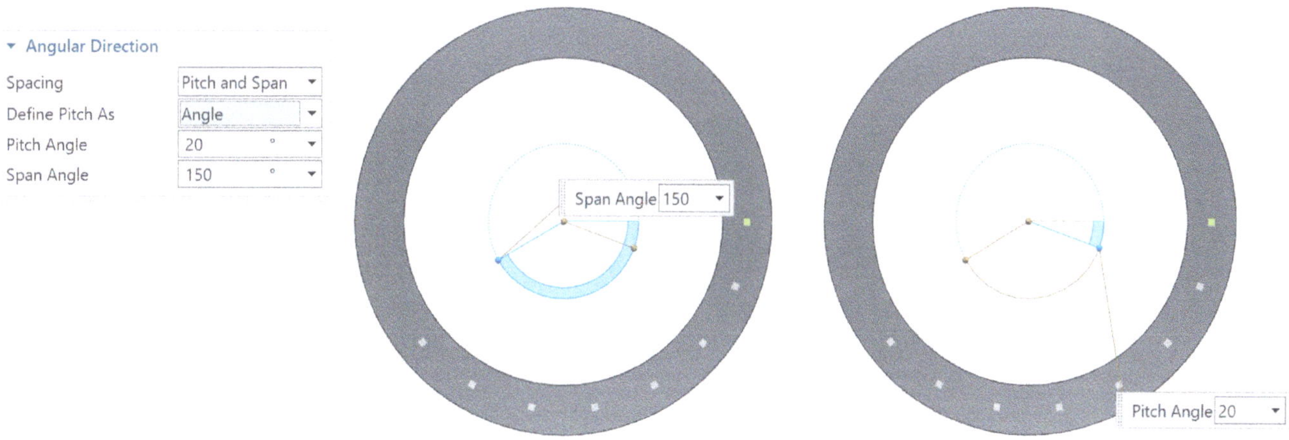

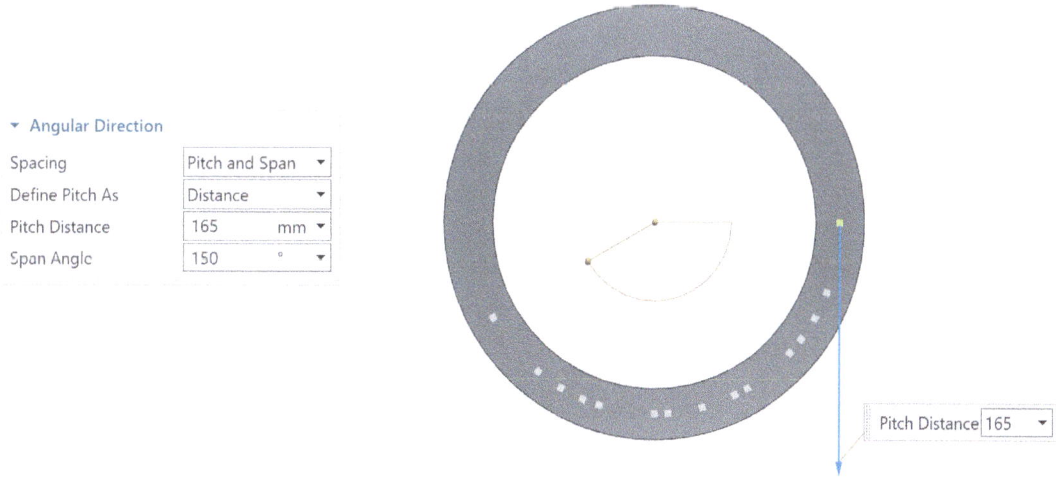

The **List** option gives you full flexibility, allowing you to manually enter the exact angles where each instance should be placed, which is useful when the distribution is not uniform.

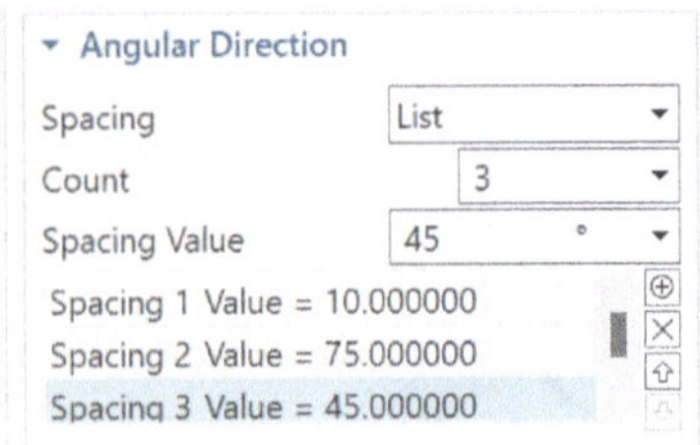

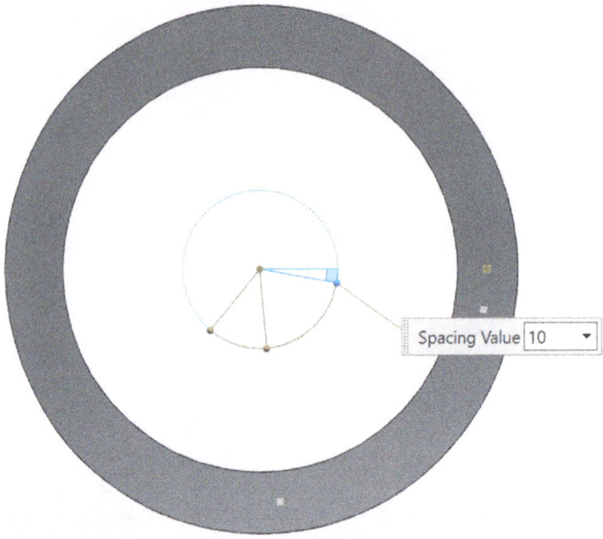

In the **Axial Direction** section, the **Spacing** drop-down controls how instances are distributed along a chosen vector.

Count and Pitch creates a uniform axial pattern with a specified instance count (**Count**) and a fixed center-to-center pitch (**Pitch Distance**); the overall span is whatever those two values produce.

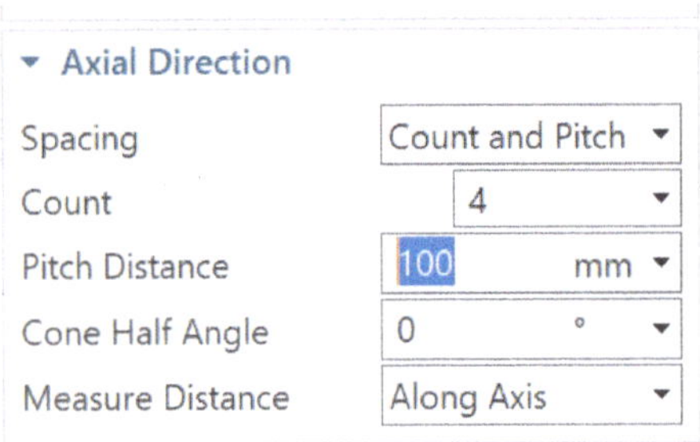

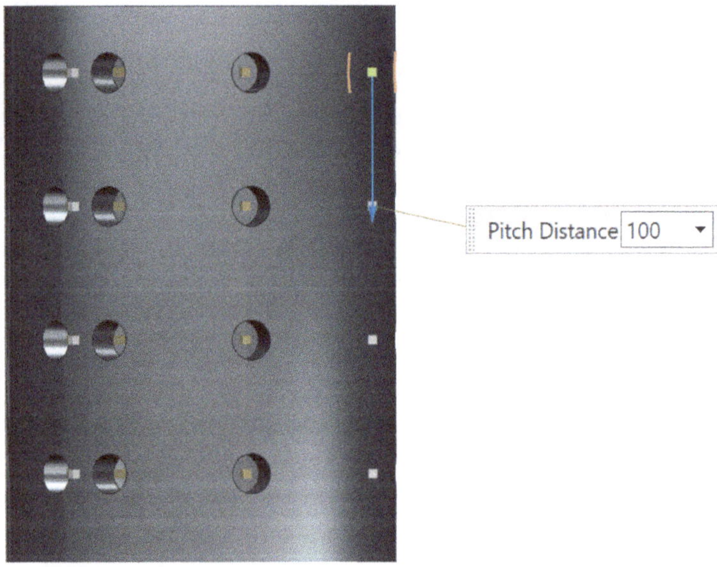

The **Cone Half Angle** box defines the taper when patterning on a conical surface (angle between cone axis and side); 0° behaves like a cylinder, non-zero values follow the cone's taper.

The **Measure Distance** drop-down is used when creating the axial pattern along the conical surface. It has two options: **Along Axis** and **Along Angle**. The **Along Axis** option measures pitch as a projection along the selected axis so each step is equal along that axis, even if the faces underneath are sloped or curved.

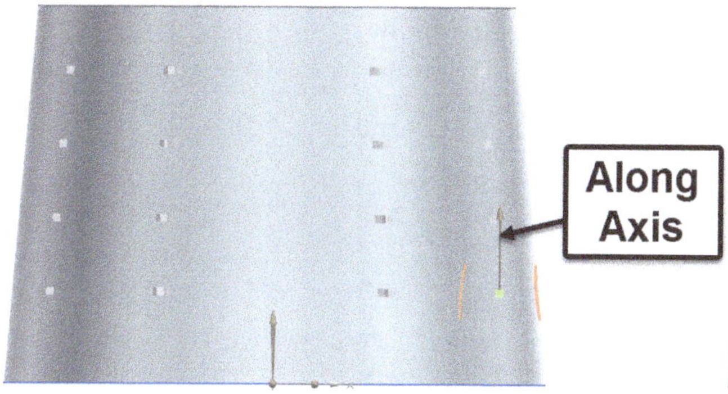

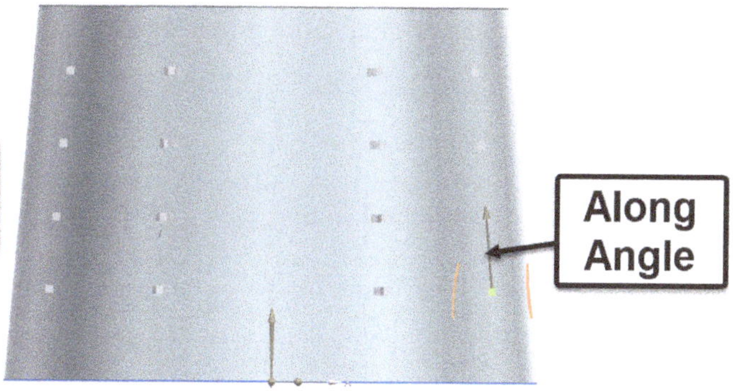

With **Count and Span**, you specify the total number of instances (**Count**) along with the **Span Distance**. NX then calculates the pitch automatically and distributes the instances evenly within that span.

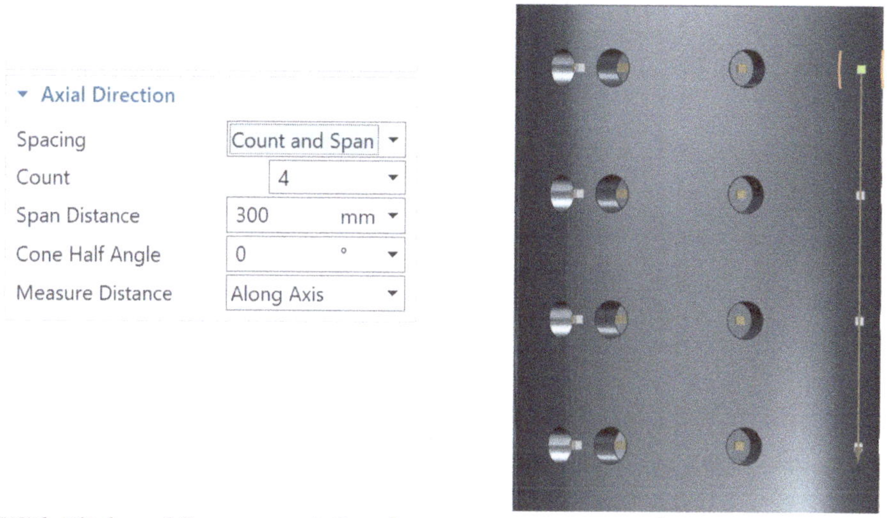

With **Pitch and Span**, you define the center-to-center pitch (Pitch Distance) and the overall span (Span Distance). Based on these inputs, NX determines how many instances can be accommodated within the span and provides the resulting count.

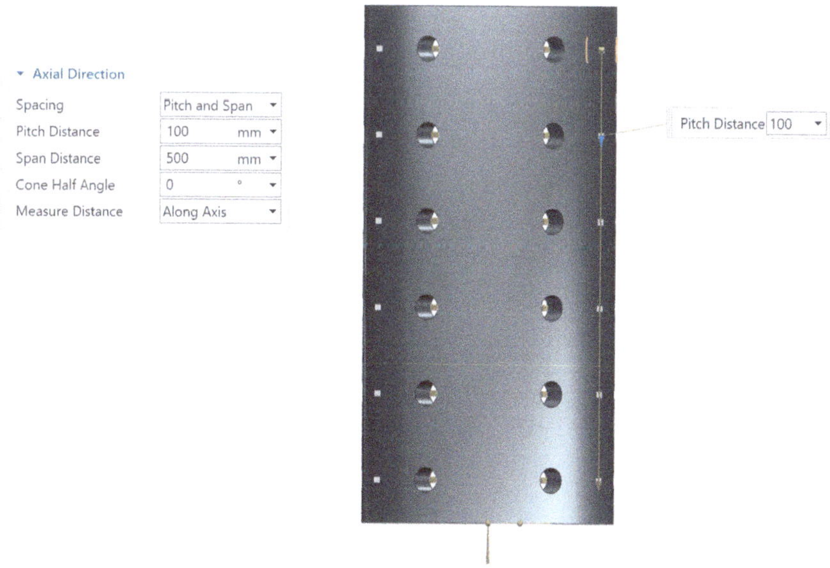

Use **List** when a non-uniform arrangement is required. Using this option, you can enter explicit distances for each instance relative to the original, allowing irregular spacing to be defined individually.

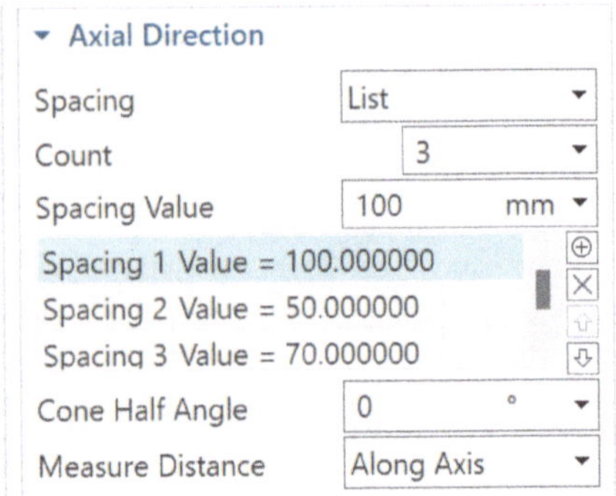

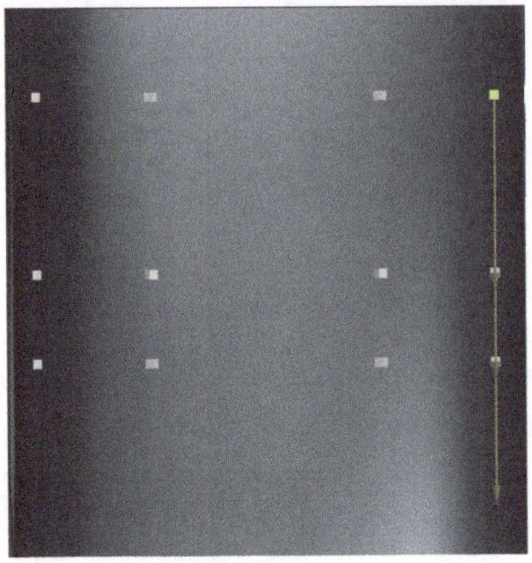

Examples

Example 1 (Millimetres)

In this example, you will create the part shown below.

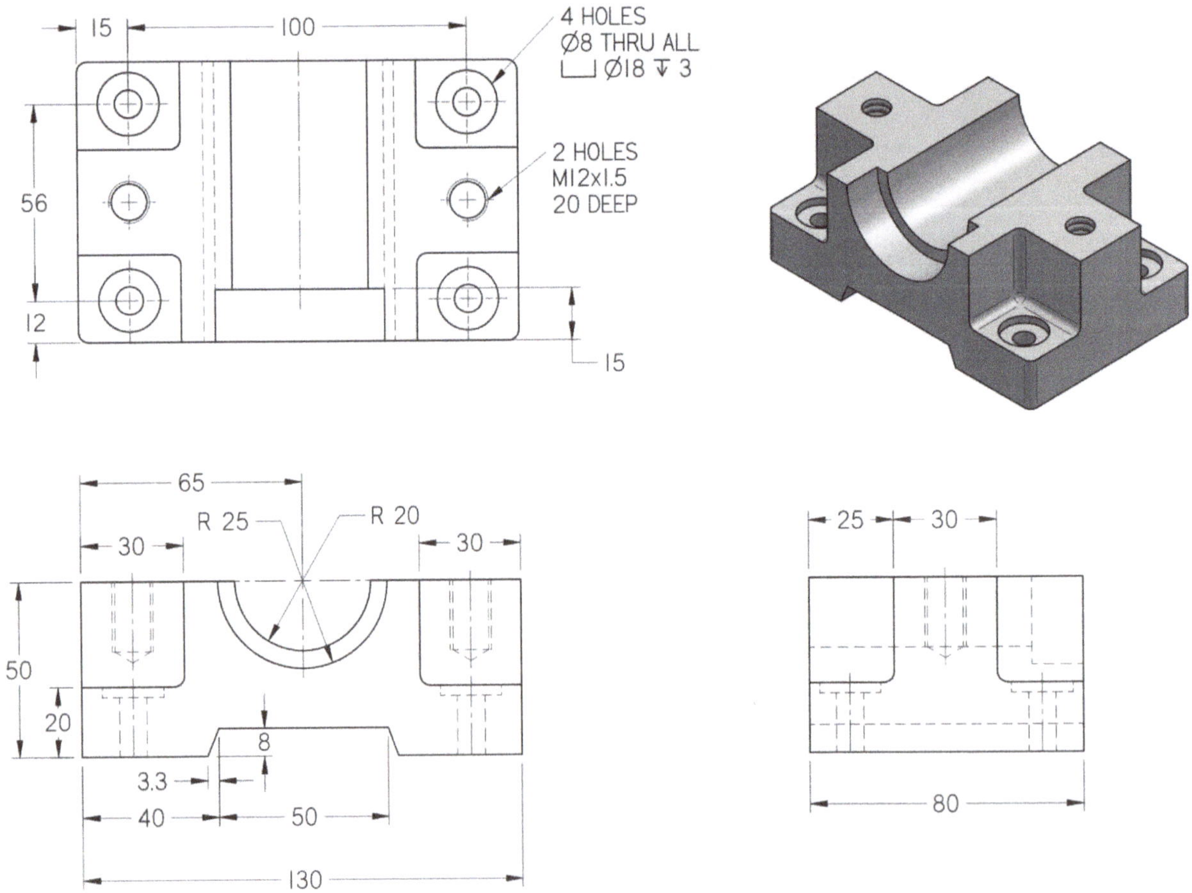

1. Start **NX**.

2. Open a new file using the **Model** template. The units are millimeters.
3. Activate the **Extrude** command and click on the XZ plane.
4. Create a rectangular sketch, add dimensions to it, and then click **Finish** on the ribbon.
5. On the **Extrude** dialog, select **Start > Symmetric Value** and type-in **80** in the **Distance** box.

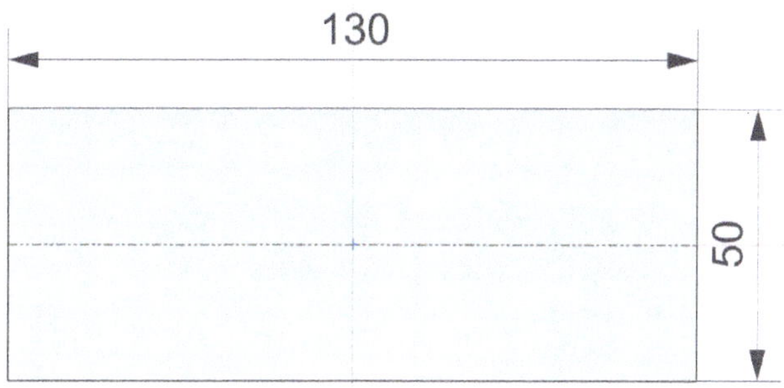

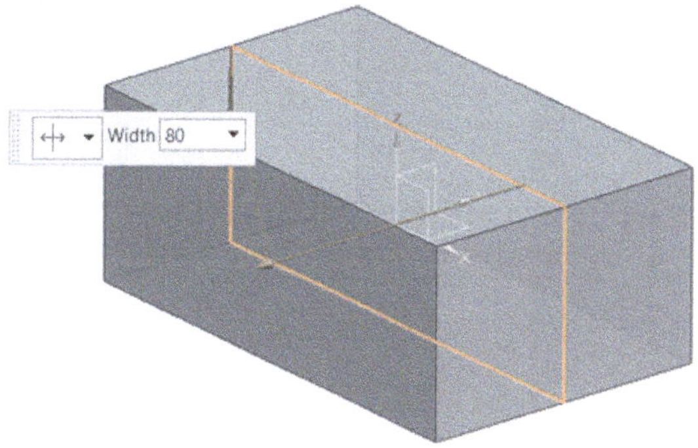

6. Click **Apply** to complete the *Extrude* feature.
7. Click on the top face of the part geometry at the location, as shown in the figure. Next, draw the sketch, as shown.
8. Create the *Cutout* feature of **30 mm** depth.

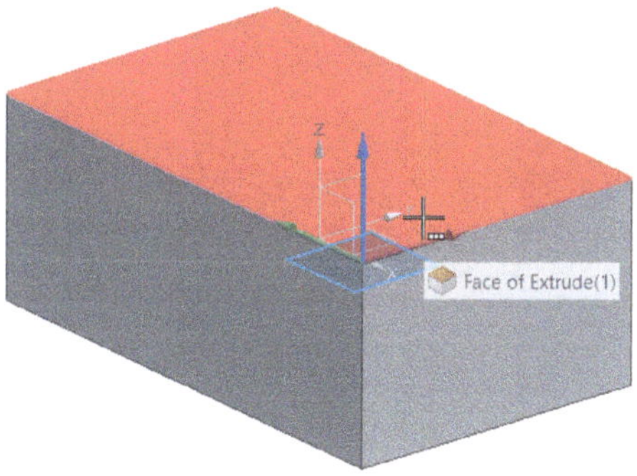

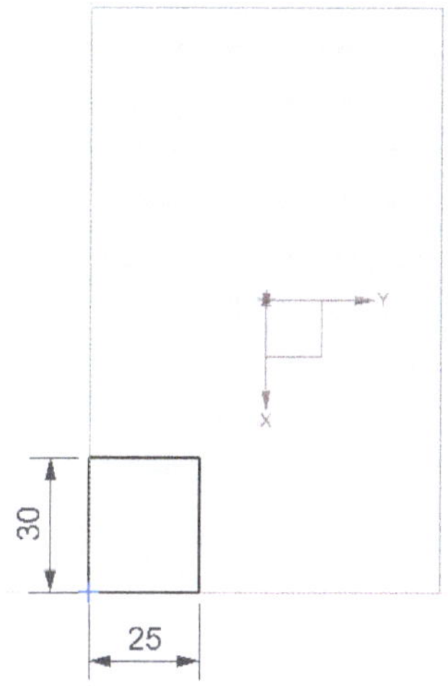

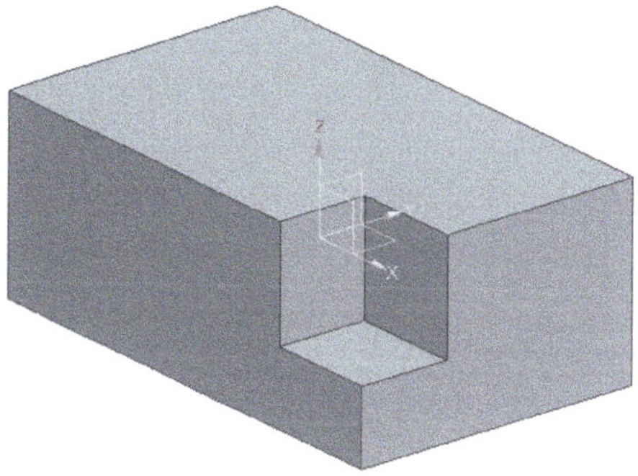

9. Activate the **Hole** command and place a counterbore hole on the *Cutout* feature.

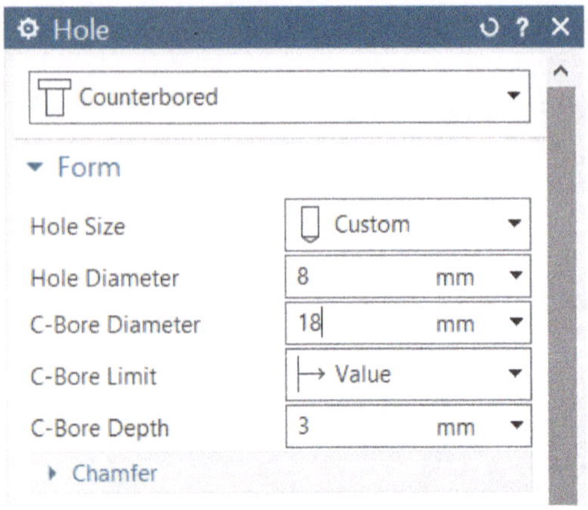

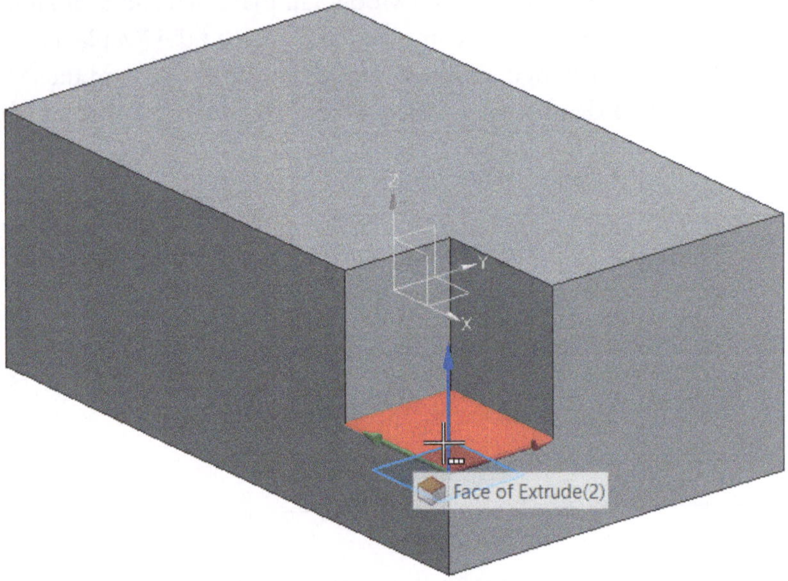

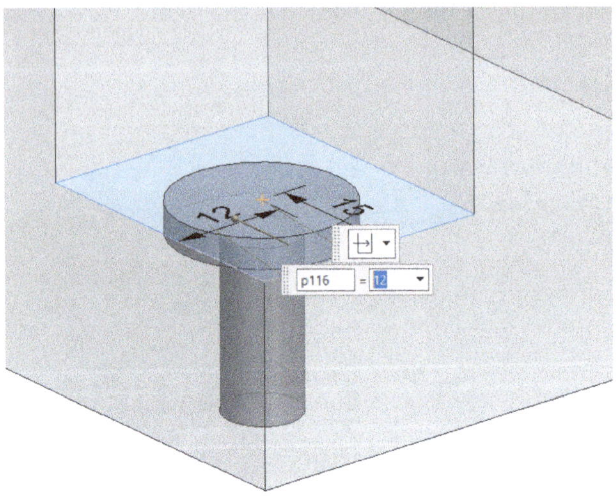

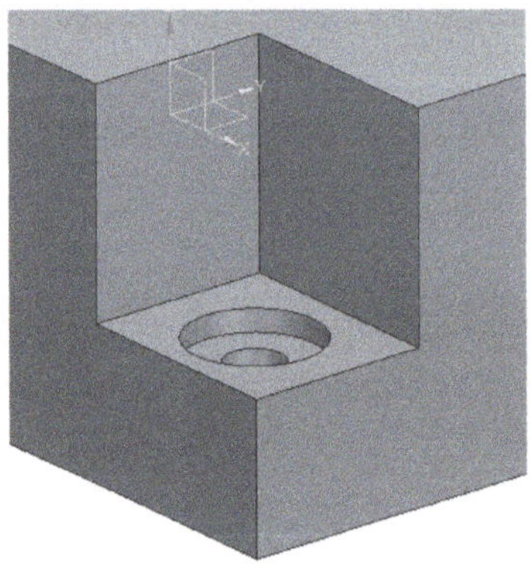

10. Click **Home > Base > Pattern Feature** on the ribbon. Next, click on the *Cutout* of the part geometry.
11. On the **Pattern Feature** dialog, select **Layout > Linear**.
12. Under the **Direction 1** section, click **Specify Vector,** and then click on the top front edge of the part geometry.
13. Under the **Direction 2** section, check the **Use Direction 2** option and click on the top side edge of the part geometry.

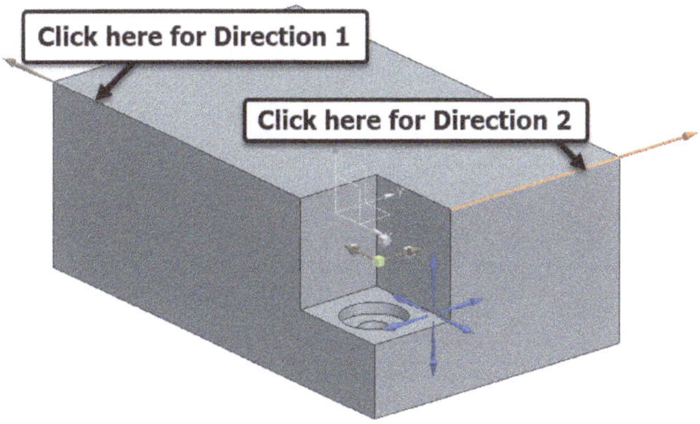

14. Under the **Direction 1** section, select **Spacing > Count and Span**.
15. Type-in **2** and **100** in the **Count** and **Span Distance** boxes, respectively.
16. Under the **Direction 2** section, select **Spacing > Count and Span**.
17. Type-in **2** and **55** in the **Count** and **Span Distance** boxes, respectively. Click **Apply** to complete the pattern feature.

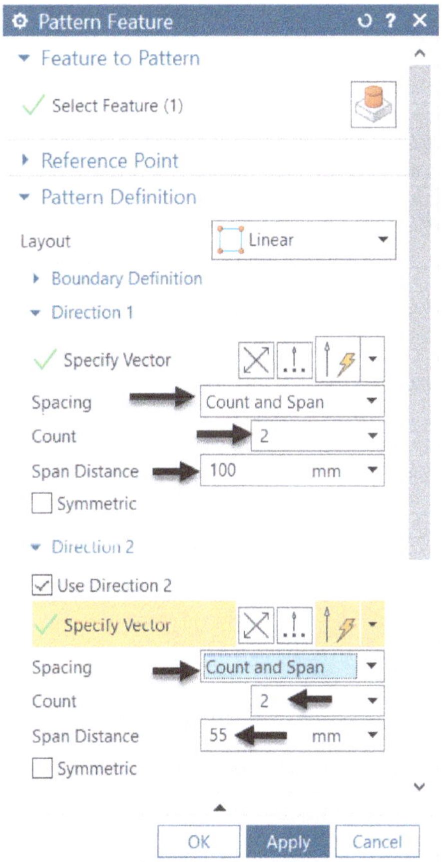

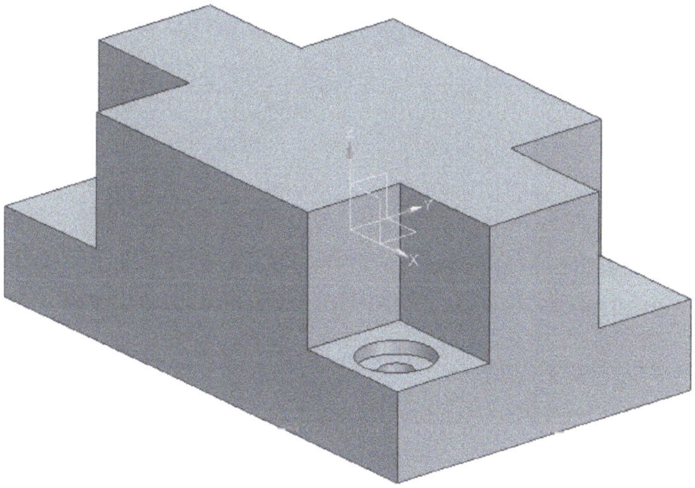

18. On the **Pattern Feature** dialog, select **Layout > Reference** .
19. Click on the counterbored hole of the part geometry.
20. Under the **Pattern Definition** section, select **Reference > Select Pattern** and then select the linear pattern from the model.
21. Select the dot displayed on the counterbored hole to define the base instance of the reference pattern.

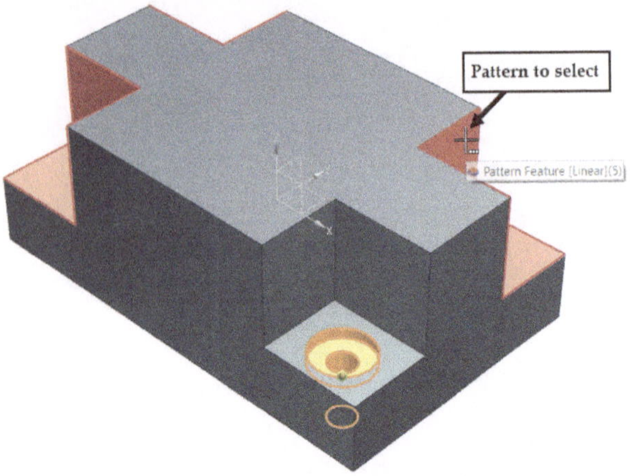

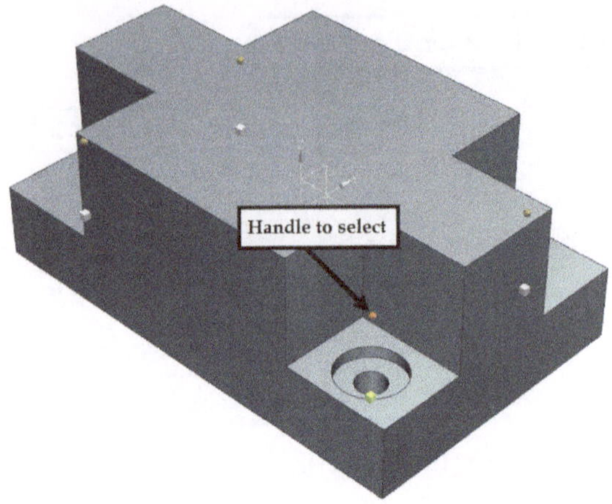

22. Under the **Pattern Method** section, select **Method > Simple**. Next, click **OK** to create the reference pattern.

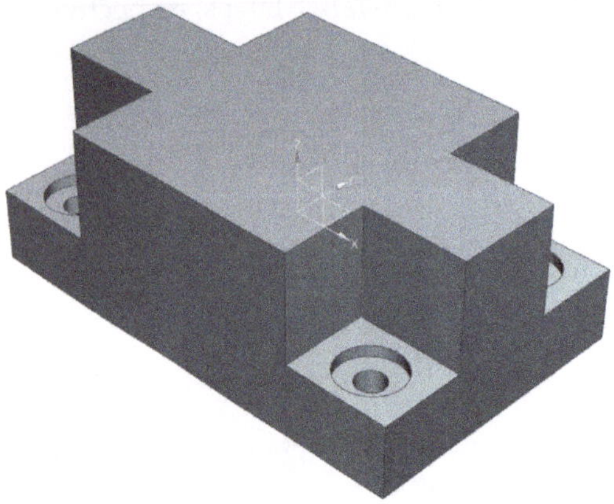

23. Activate the **Hole** command. On the **Hole** dialog, set the parameters in the **Form** section.
24. Under the **Direction** section, select **Hole Direction > Along Vector**.
25. Select the **Inferred Vector** option under the **Direction** section.
26. Select the Y-axis vector to define the direction in which the hole will be created.

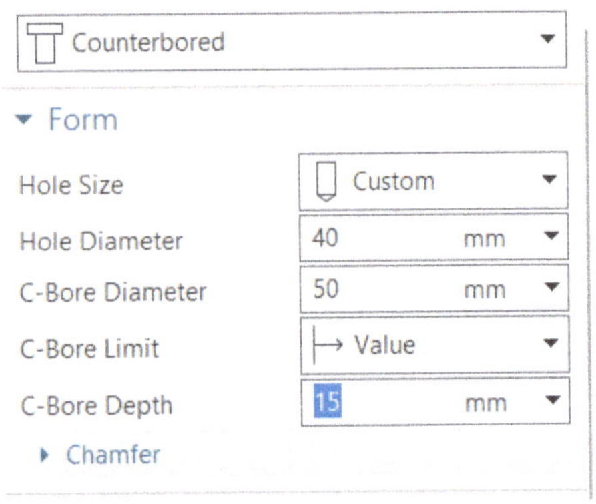

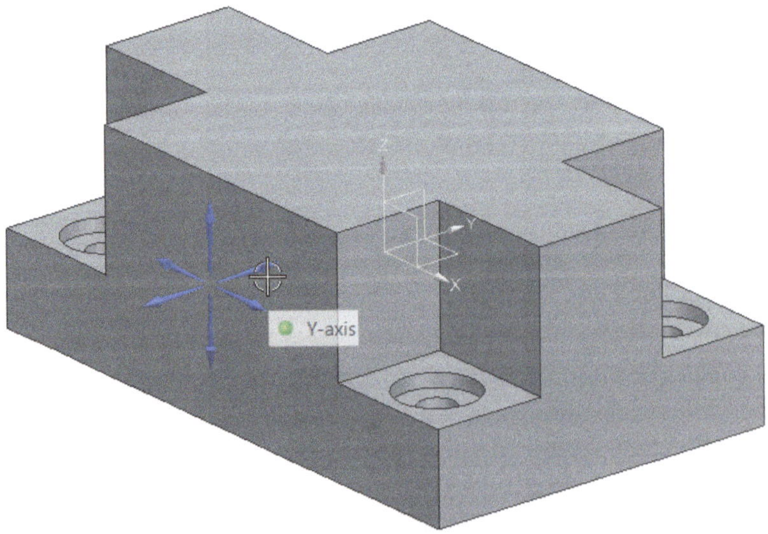

27. On the Sketch Scene Bar, click **Snap Point** drop-down > **Midpoint** and select the midpoint of the top front edge

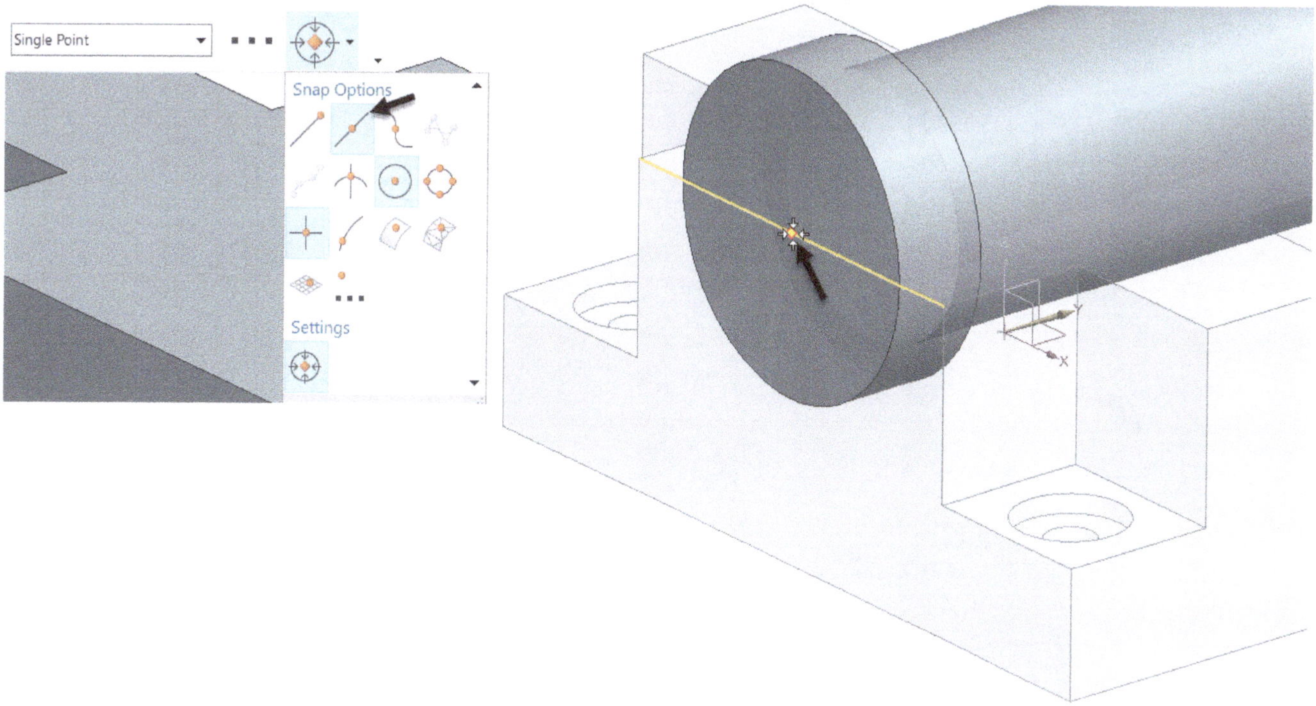

28. Click **Apply** to create the counterbore hole.

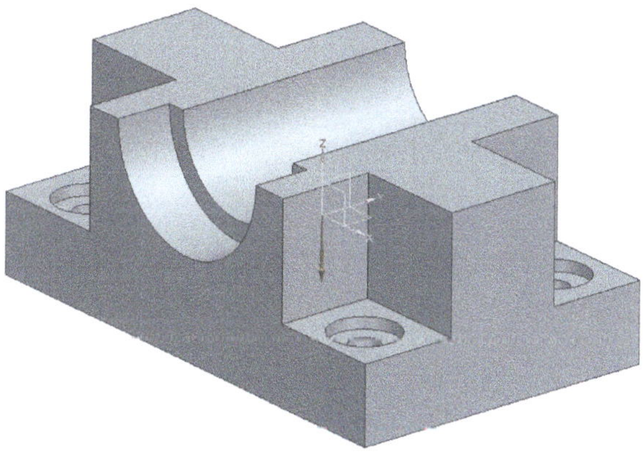

29. On the **Hole** dialog, select **Type > Threaded** .
30. Set the parameters in the **Form**, **Direction** and **Limit** sections, as shown in the figure.
31. Click on the top face of the part geometry.

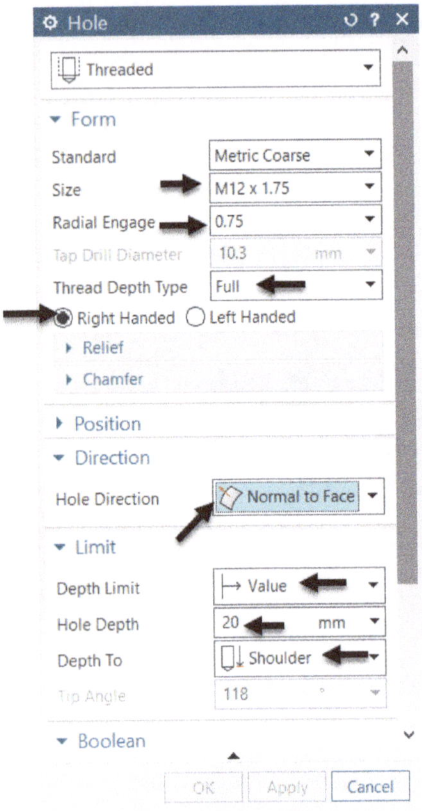

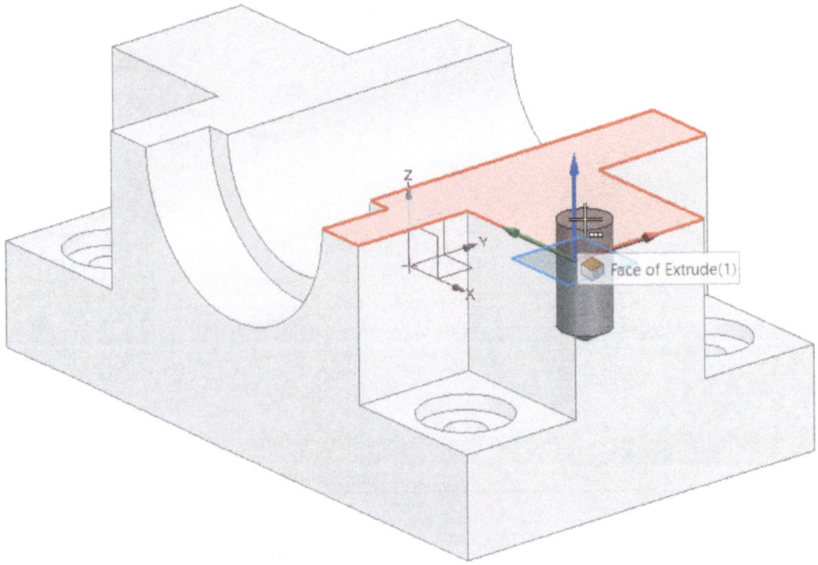

32. Change the location dimensions of the hole. Next, click **OK** to complete the threaded hole feature.

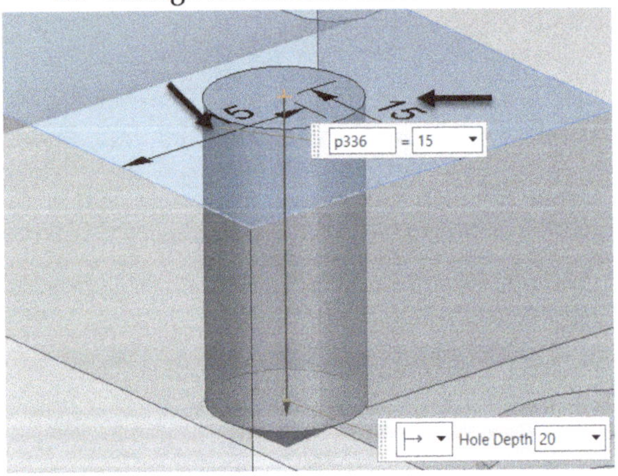

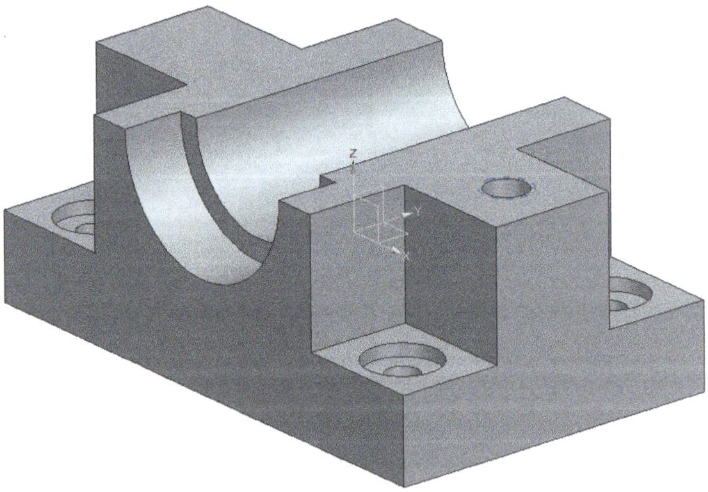

33. On the ribbon, click **Home > Base > Mirror Feature**.
34. Click on the threaded hole on the part geometry.
35. On the **Mirror Feature** dialog, expand the **Settings** section and check the **Maintain Thread Handedness** option.
36. Under the **Mirror Plane** section, click **Select Plane**, and then click on the YZ plane. Click **OK** to complete the mirror feature.

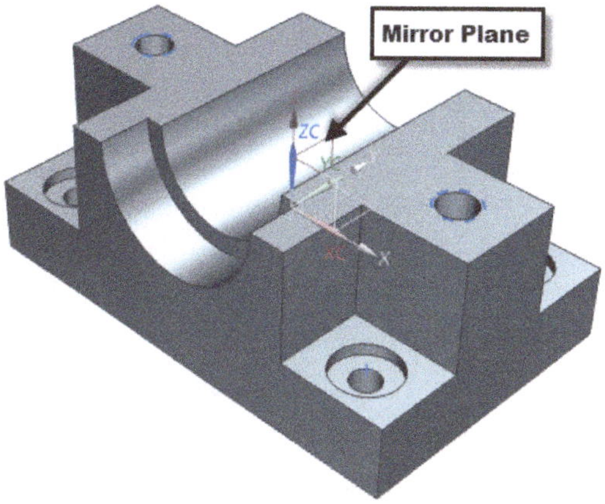

37. Activate the **Extrude** command and click on the front face of the part geometry.
38. On the ribbon, click **Home > Include > Include.** Next, select the horizontal and curved edges, as shown.
39. Activate the **Profile** command and create a closed loop, as shown.

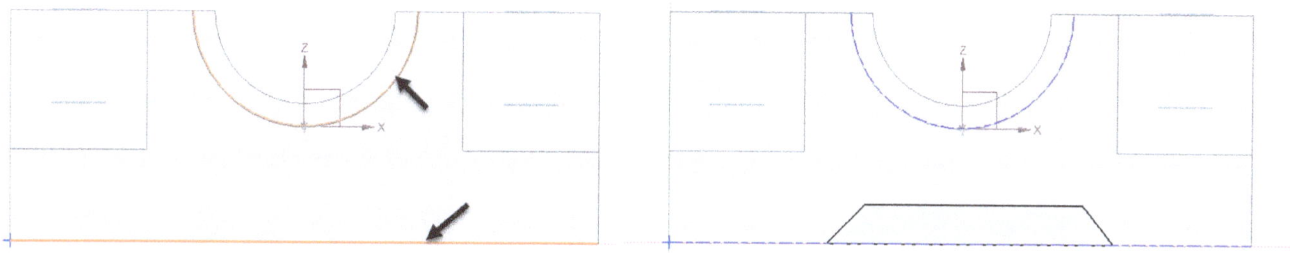

40. Activate the **Line** command and place the pointer on the included curved edge. Next, select the center point of the included edge.
41. Move the pointer vertically downward and click. Next, press ESC.
42. Select the newly created line and click the **Convert to Reference** icon on the Context toolbar.

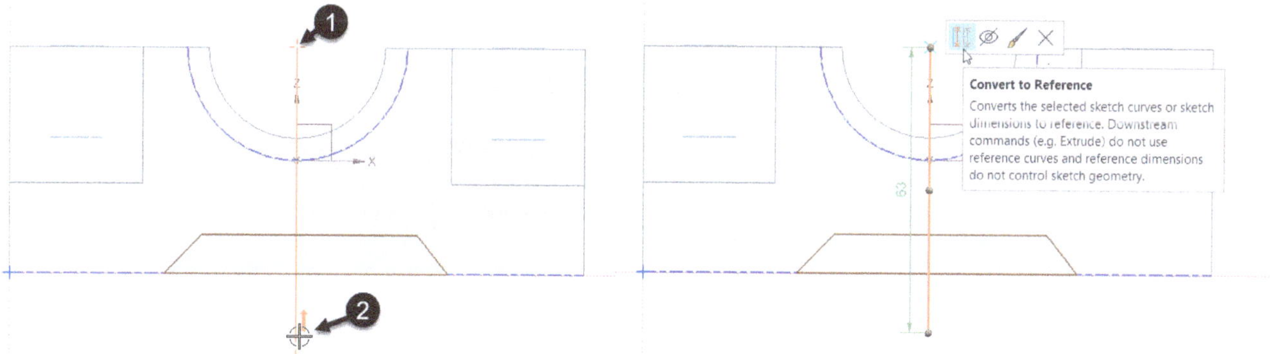

43. Add dimension to the sketch, and then press ESC.
44. Select the lower endpoint of the vertical reference line and the horizontal line of the sketch.
45. Click the **Make Midpoint Aligned** icon on the Sketch Scene Bar.
46. Select the two inclined lines and the vertical reference line. Next, click the **Make Symmetric** icon on the Sketch Scene Bar.

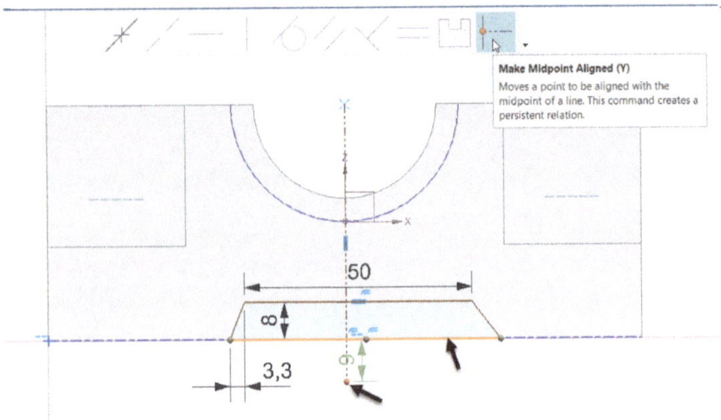

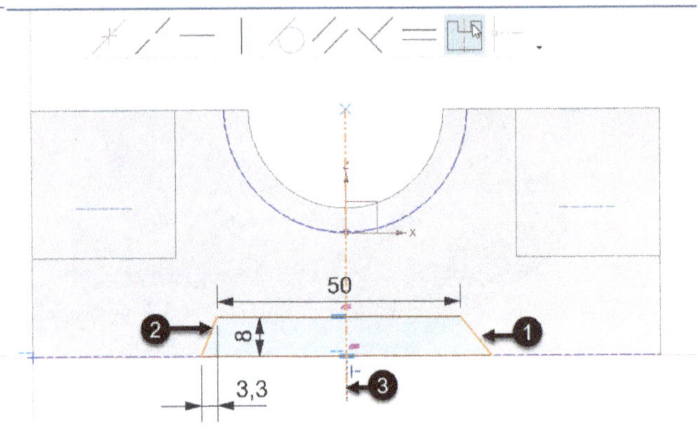

47. Select the two inclined lines and click the **Make Equal** icon on the Sketch Scene Bar.
48. Click **Finish** on the ribbon. Next, click the **Finish** button on the **Finish** message box.
49. On the **Extrude** dialog, select **End > Through all** from the **Limit** section.
50. Select **Boolean > Subtract** from the **Boolean** section.
51. Click the **Reverse Direction** button in the **Direction** section and click **OK**.

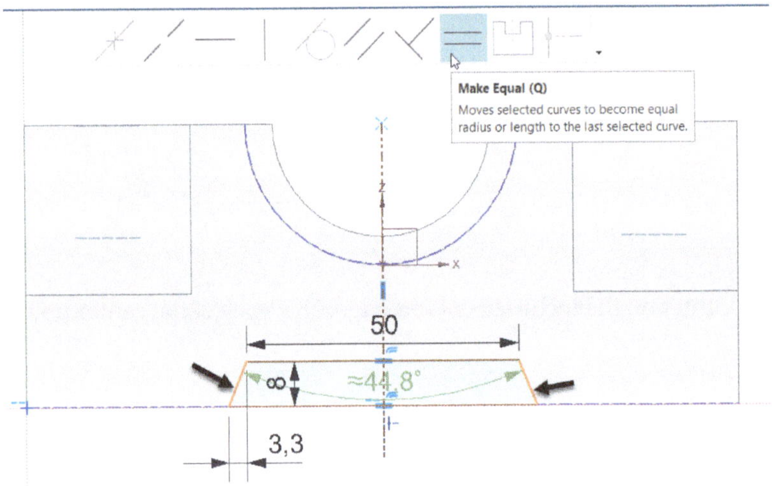

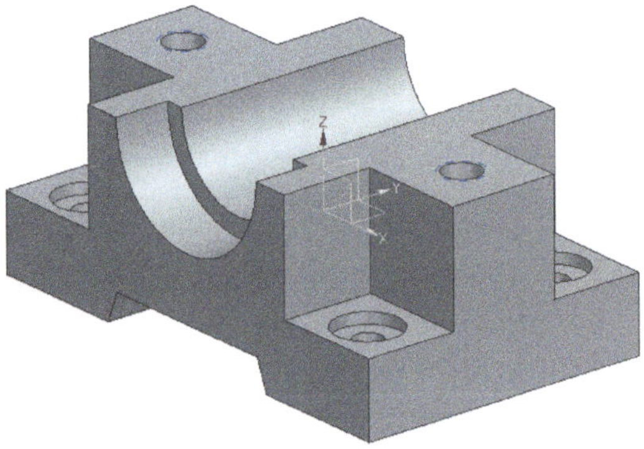

52. Blend the sharp edges of the geometry. The blend radius is 2 mm.

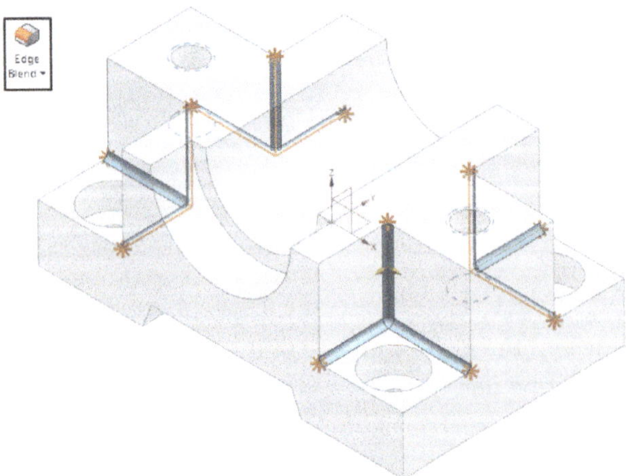

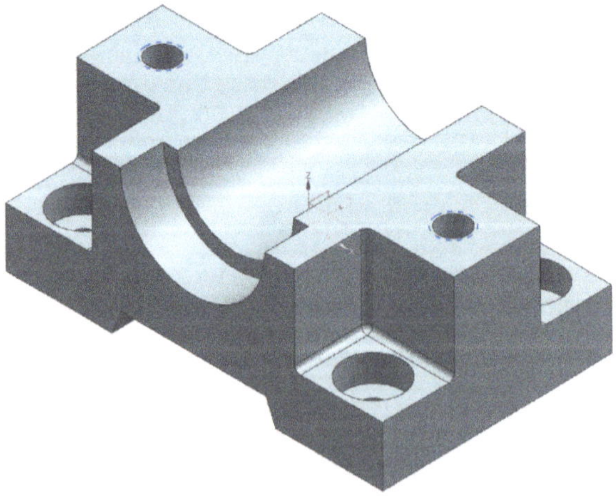

53. Save and close the part file.

Questions

1. Describe the procedure to create a mirror feature.
2. List any two layouts to create patterns.
3. What is the difference between the **Mirror Feature** and **Mirror Geometry** command?
4. Describe the procedure to create a helical pattern.
5. List the methods to define spacing in a linear pattern.

Exercises

Exercise 1 (Millimetres)

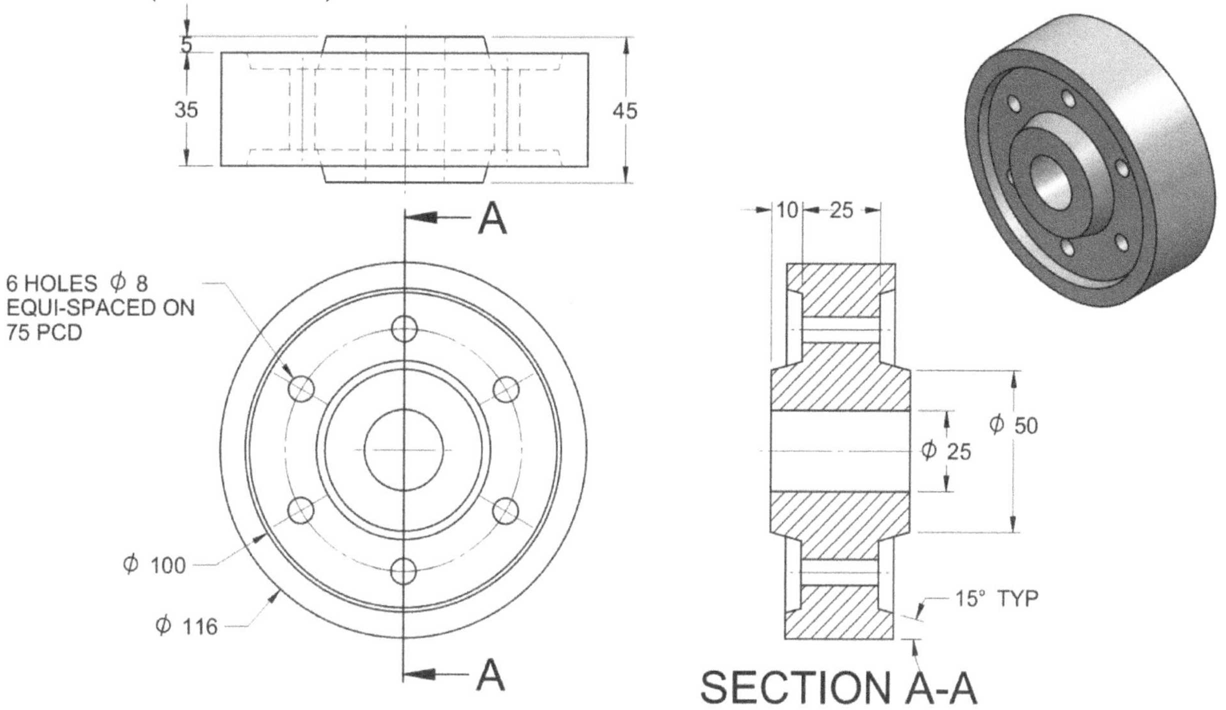

Exercise 2 (Inches)

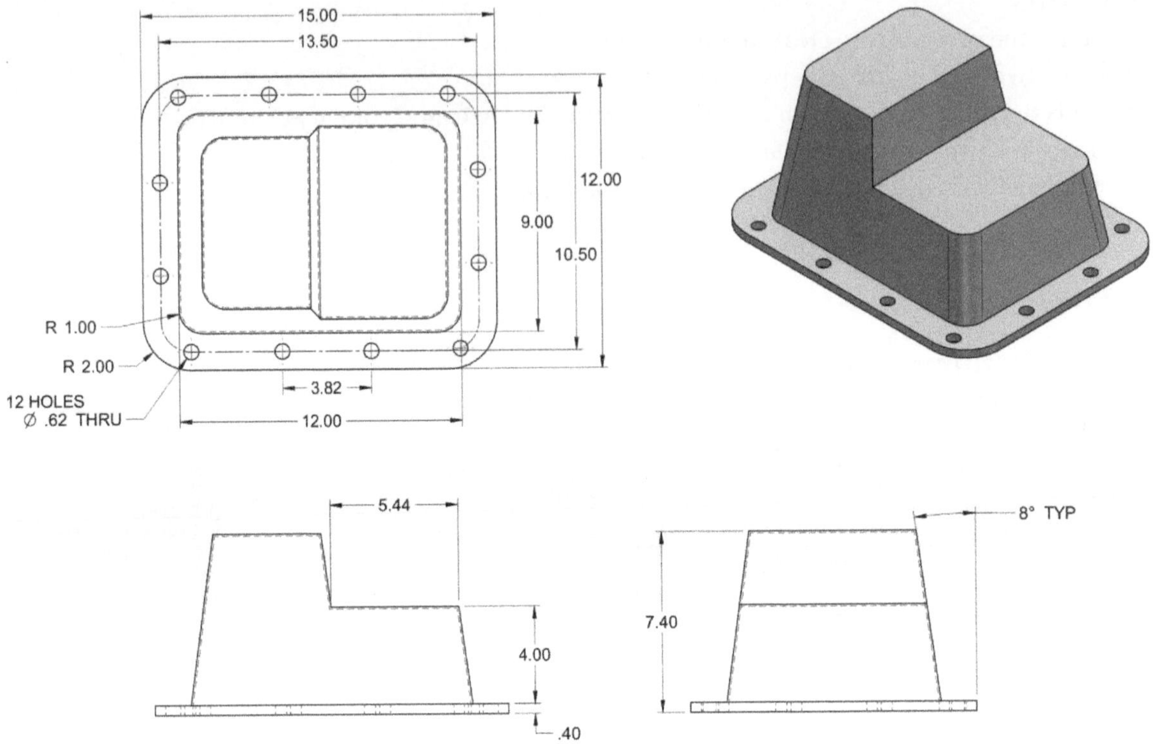

SHEET THICKNESS = 0.079 in

Chapter 6: Additional Features and Multibody Parts

NX offers you some additional commands and features which will help you to create complex models. These commands are explained in this chapter.

The topics covered in this chapter are:

- *Ribs*
- *Slots*
- *Multi-body parts*
- *Split bodies*
- *Boolean Operations, and*
- *Emboss features*

Rib

This command creates rib features to add structural stability, strength, and support to your designs. Just like any other sketch-based feature, a rib requires a two-dimensional sketch. Create a sketch, as shown in the figure, and activate the **Rib** command (click **Home > Base > More > Detail Feature > Rib** on the ribbon). Select the sketch; the preview of the geometry appears. You can add the rib material to either side of the sketch line or evenly to both sides. Set the **Dimension** type to **Symmetric** to add material to both sides of the sketch line. Type-in the thickness value of the rib feature in the **Thickness** box. You can click the **Reverse Rib Side** button to change the direction of the rib.

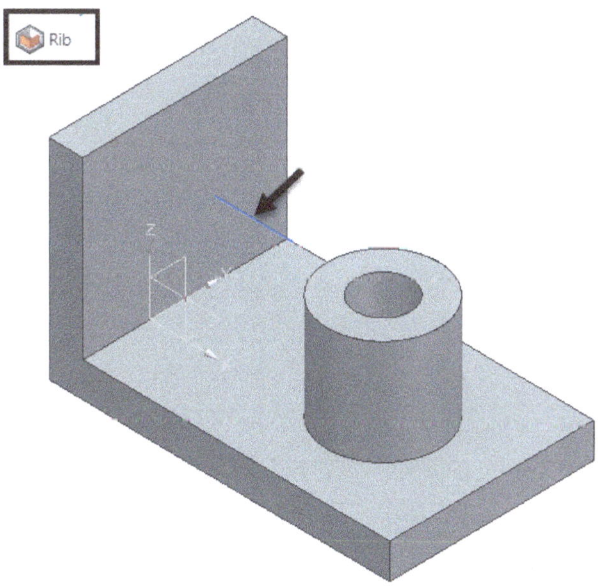

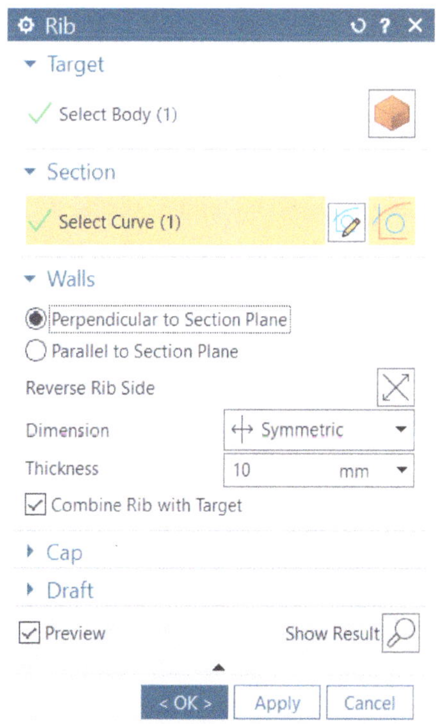

You can define the direction of the rib feature by using the **Perpendicular to Section Plane** or **Parallel to Section Plane** option.

Perpendicular to Section Plane

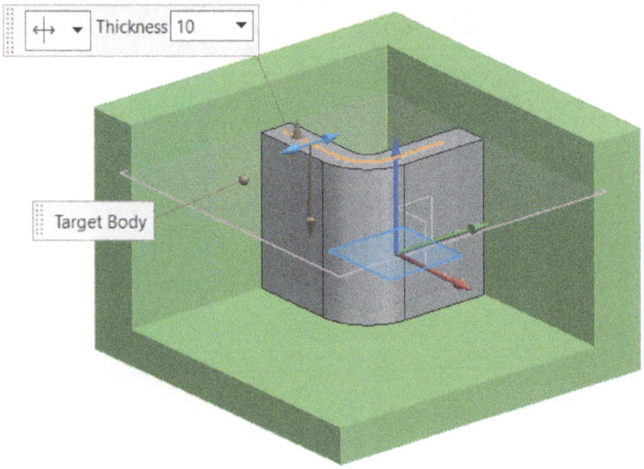

Parallel to Section Plane

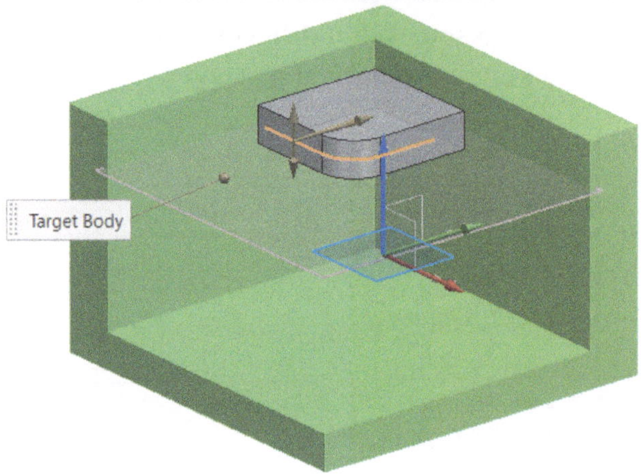

To draft to the rib feature, select **Draft > Draft > From Cap** on the **Rib** dialog, and then type-in a value in the **Angle** box. Note that the **Draft** section available only when you select the **Perpendicular to Section Plane** option.

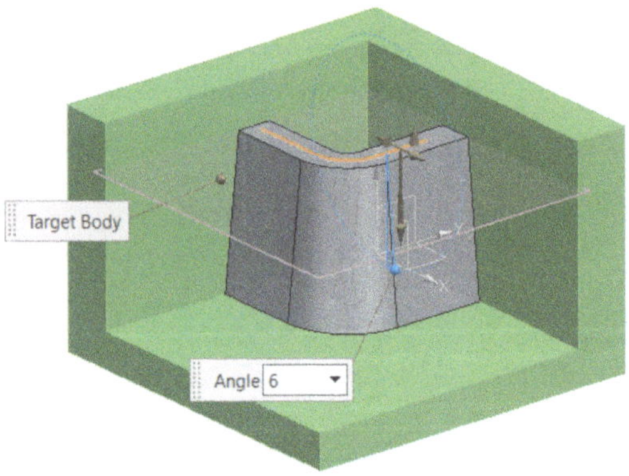

You can use a sheet body to cap the top face of the rib feature. To do this, select **Cap > Geometry > From Selected** on the **Rib** dialog and click on the sheet body, as shown.

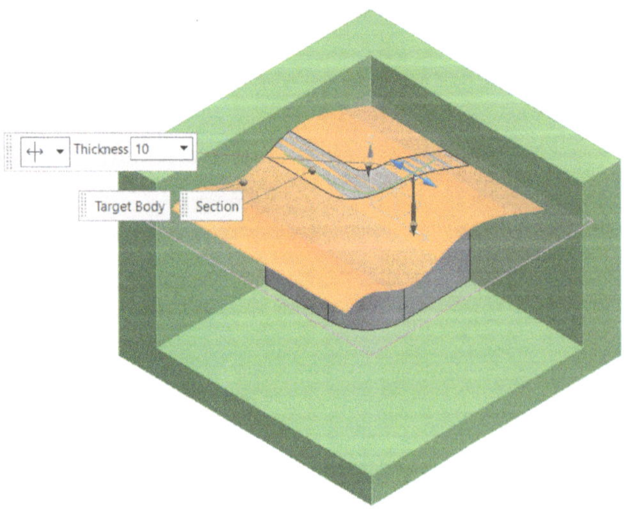

Multi-body Parts

NX allows the use of multiple bodies when designing parts. This opens the door to several design techniques that would otherwise not be possible. In this section, you will learn some of these techniques.

Creating Multibodies

The number of bodies in a part model can change throughout the design process. NX makes it easy to create separate bodies inside a part geometry. Also, you can combine multiple bodies into a single body. To create multiple bodies in a component, first, create a solid body, and then create any sketch-based feature such as extruded, revolved, or swept feature. While creating the feature, ensure that you set the **Boolean** type to **None**.

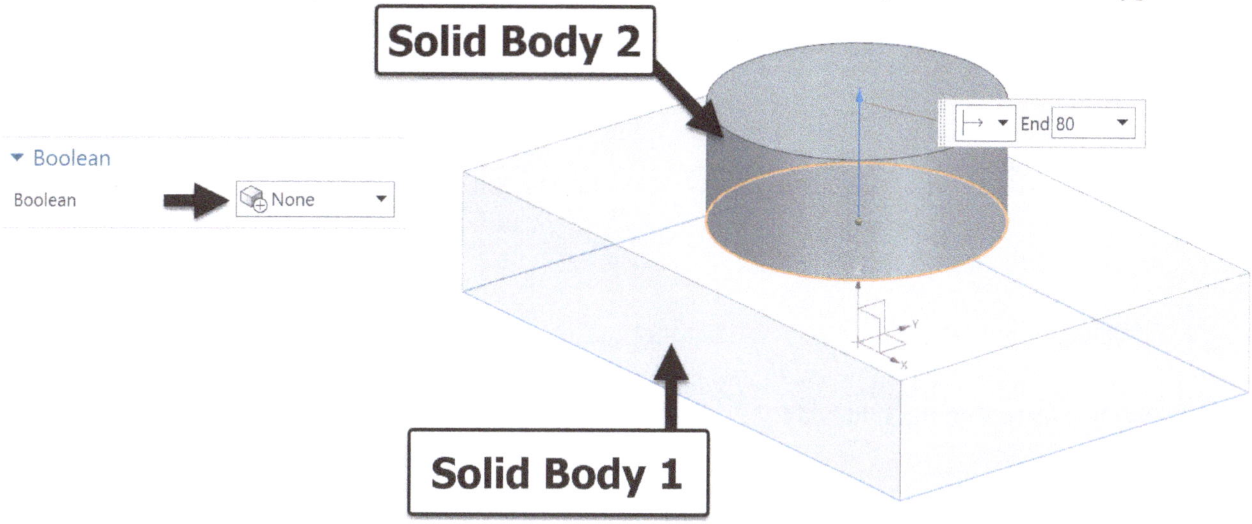

Split Body

The **Split Body** command can be used to separate single bodies into multiple bodies. This command can be used to perform local operations. For example, if you apply the shell feature to the front portion of the model shown in the figure, the whole model will be shelled. To solve this problem, you must split the solid body into multiple bodies (In this case, separate the front portion of the model from the rest).

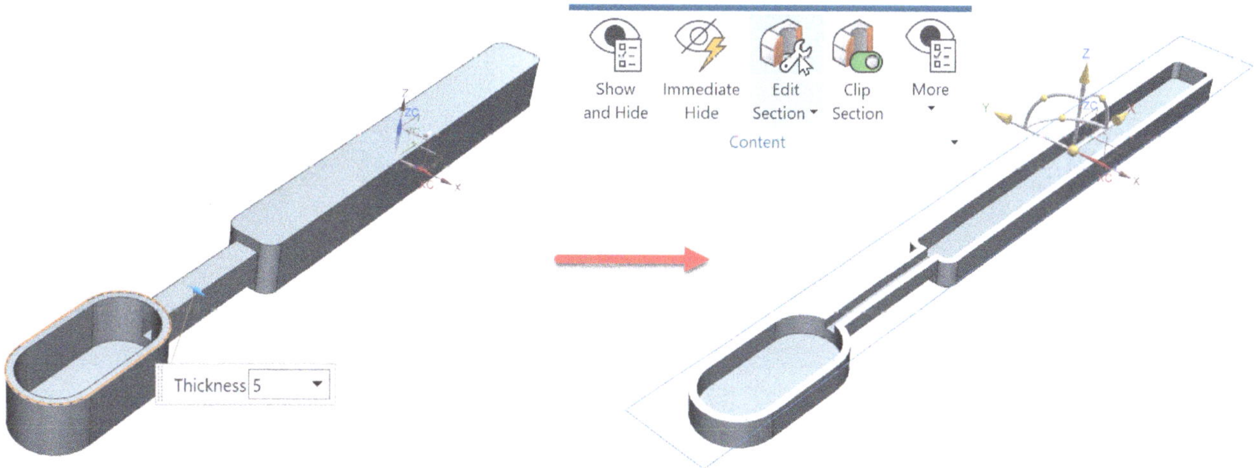

To split a body, you must have a splitting tool such as planes, sketch elements, surfaces, or bodies. In this case, a surface can be used as a splitting tool. Activate the **Split Body** command (click **Home > Base > More > Trim > Split Body** on the ribbon) and select the solid body from the graphics window. On the **Split Body** dialog, select **Tool >**

Tool Option > Extrude and click **Select Curve**. Click on the curved edge to define the section curve. As you click **OK**, an extruded surface will be created, and eventually, the body will be split into two separate bodies.

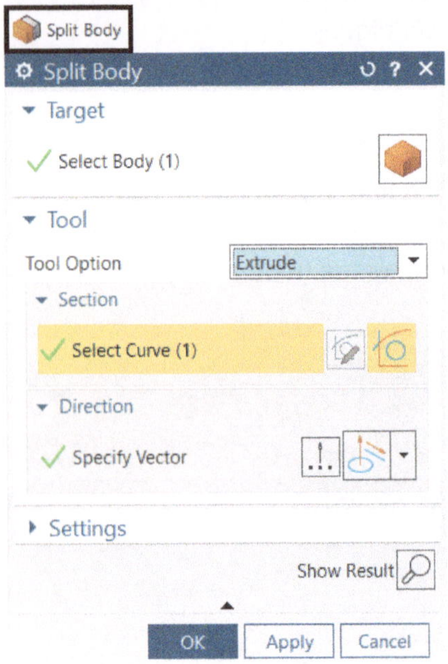

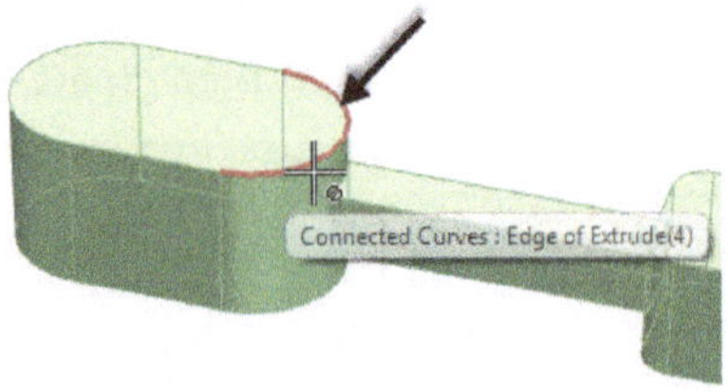

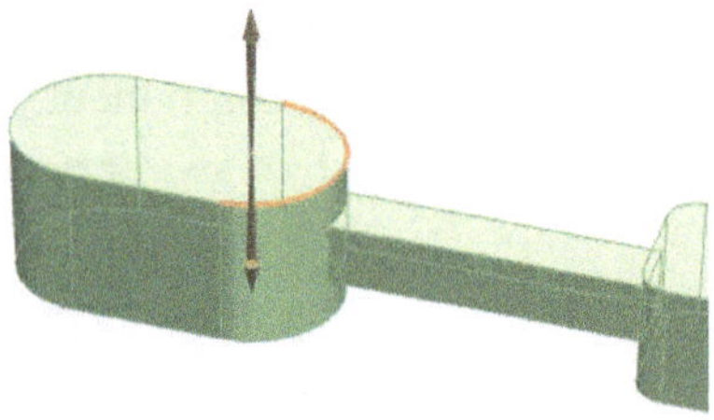

Now, create the shell feature on the split body.

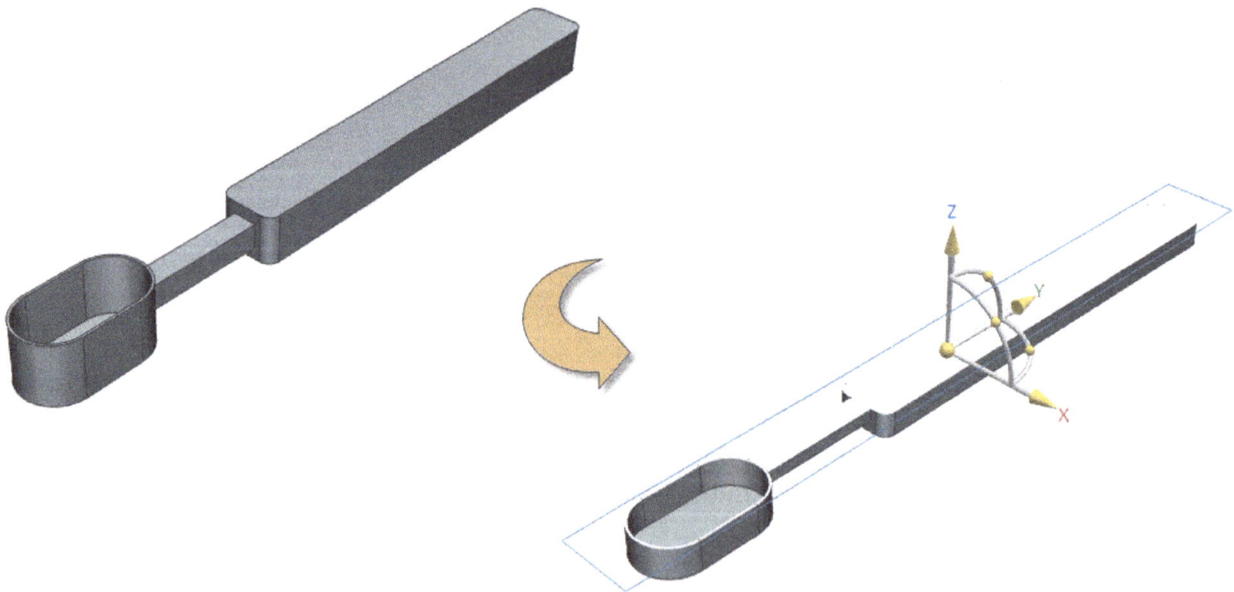

Unite

If you apply blends to the edges between two bodies, it will result in a different result, as shown in the figure. To solve this problem, you must combine the two bodies using the **Unite** command. Activate this command (click **Home > Base > Unite**  on the ribbon) and select the bodies. Click **OK** on the dialog to unite the bodies. Now, apply blends to the edges.

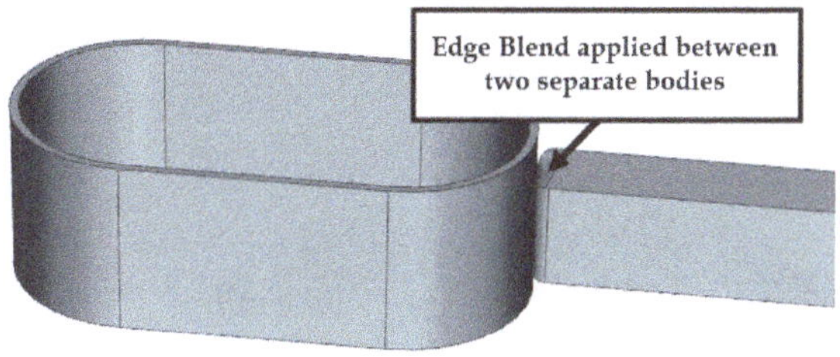

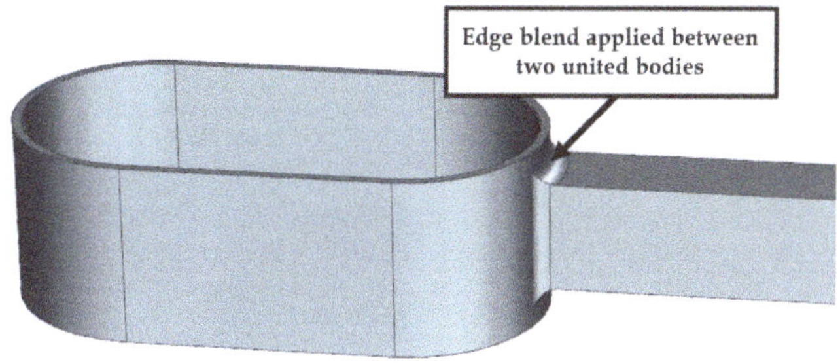

Intersect

By using the **Intersect** command, you can generate bodies defined by the intersecting volume of two bodies. Activate this command (click **Home > Base > Trim Body drop-down > Intersect** on the ribbon) and select two bodies. Click **OK** to see the resultant single solid body.

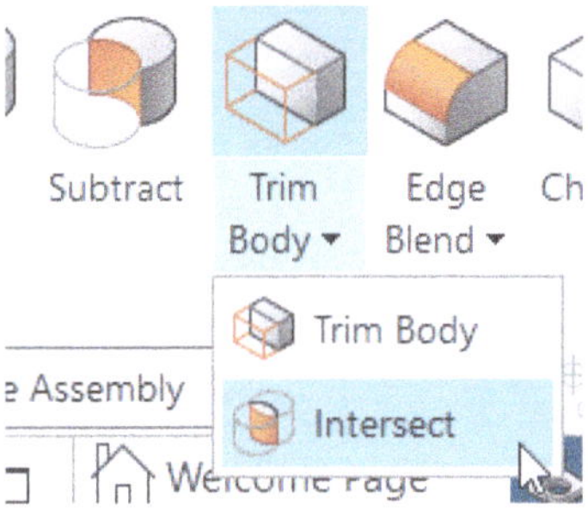

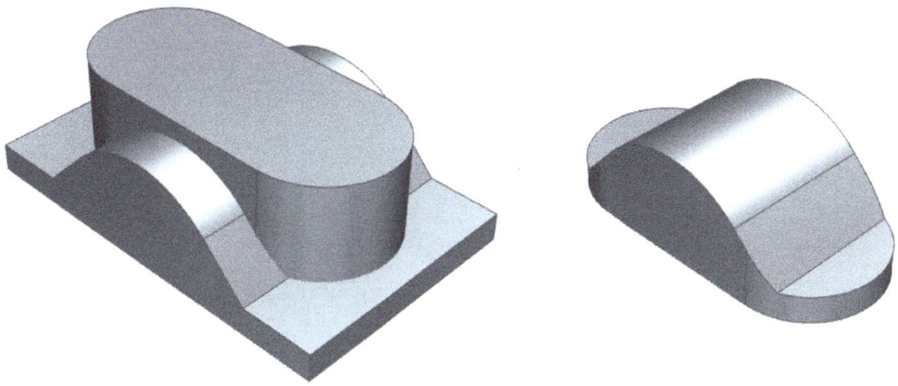

Subtract

This command performs the function of subtracting one solid body from another. Activate this command (click **Home > Base > Subtract** on the ribbon), and then select the target body and the tool body. Click **OK** to subtract the tool body from the target.

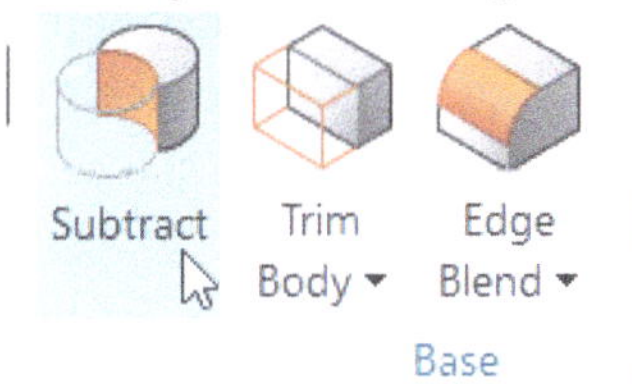

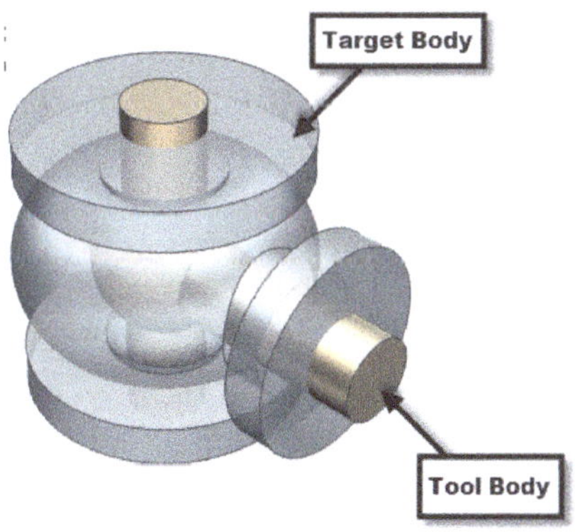

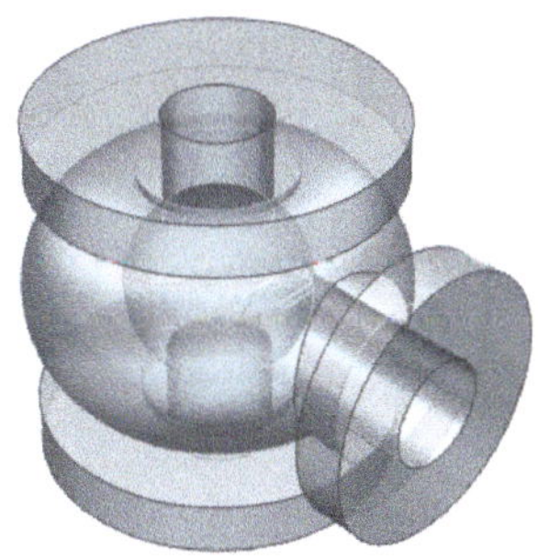

Emboss Body

This command allows you to change the shape of a solid body by using another solid body. The solid body that is changed is called the target body, and the solid body that causes the change is called the tool body. To do this, you must have two solid bodies in a component. Activate the **Emboss Body** command (click **Home > Base > More > Combine > Emboss Body** on the ribbon) and select the target and tool bodies. On the **Emboss Body** dialog, click **Select Region Object** and click on a portion of the tool body to define the side on which the body is embossed.

Type-in a value in the **Clearance** box. Next, check the **Thicken** option and type-in a value in the **Thickness** box. Click **OK** on the dialog to complete the emboss body.

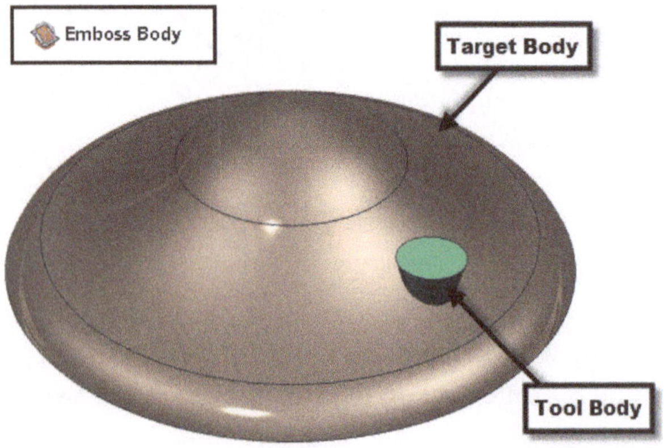

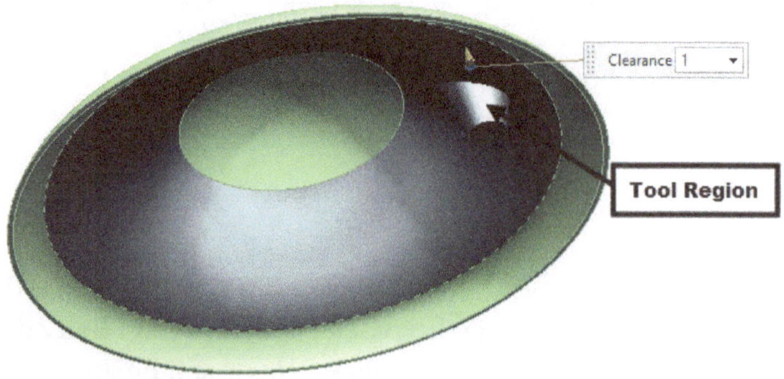

Swept Volume

This command removes the material or creates an intersection solid by sweeping the volume of a solid body along a planar or non-planar curve. To sweep a volume, first, create the target body and the tool path, and then create the tool body. Note that you should create the target and tool bodies as separate bodies (Set the **Boolean** option to **None**). The tool path should be created on the target face. The target face can be planar or non-planar. Also, note that the tool path and the axis of the tool body should intersect each other.

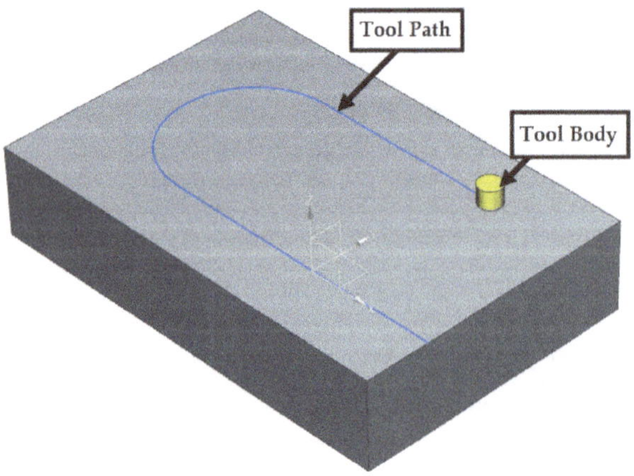

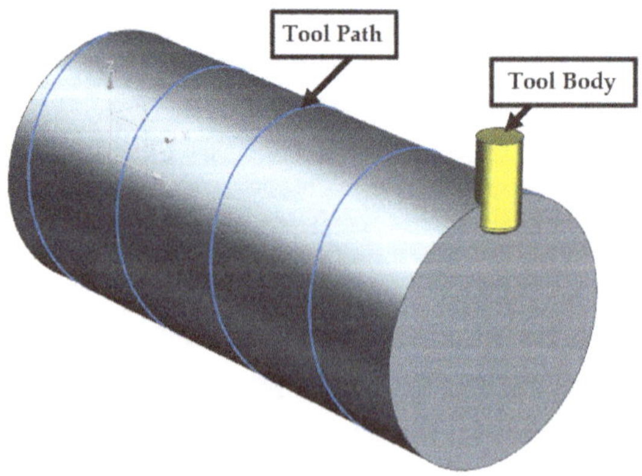

The tool body should be cylindrical or revolved solid with blended edges. However, you are not required to blend the edge of the tool body for the planar tool path. Examples of tool bodies are shown in the figure below.

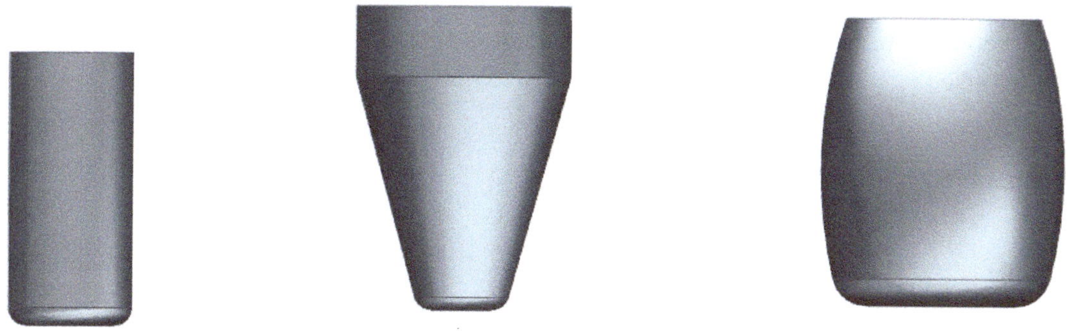

The following figure shows some examples of tool bodies that can be used for planar paths only.

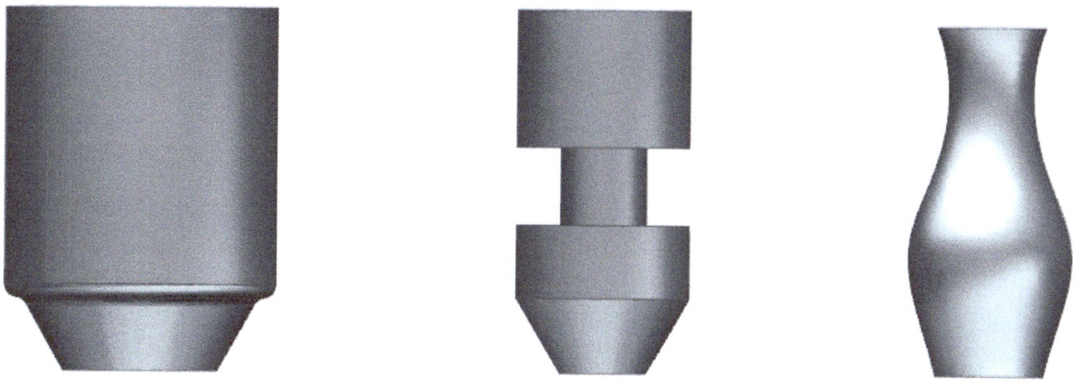

Sweeping Volume using Planar Tool Path

Activate the **Swept Volume** command (on the ribbon, click **Surface > Base > More > Sweep > Swept Volume**). Next, select the tool body and the planar tool path. On the **Swept Volume** dialog, expand the **Orientation** section, and specify the **Sweep Orientation**. Expand the **Boolean** section, and select **Boolean > Subtract** to remove material from the target body. Click **OK** to create the swept volume.

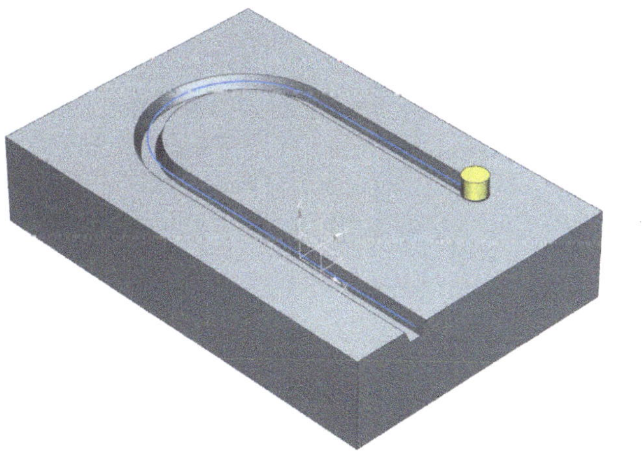

Sweeping Volume using Non-Planar Tool Path

Activate the **Swept Volume** command (on the ribbon, click **Surface > Base > More > Sweep > Swept Volume**). Next, select the tool body and the Non-planar tool path. On the **Swept Volume** dialog, expand the **Orientation** section, and select **Sweep Orientation > Normal To Path**. Click **Specify Lock Direction** and select the axis perpendicular to the tool body. Specify the **Boolean** type and click **OK**.

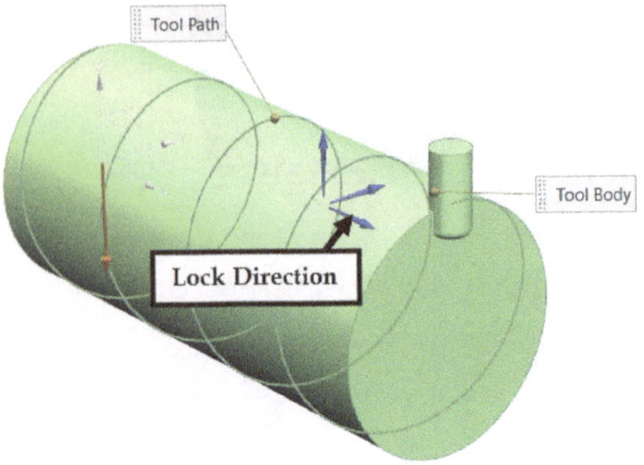

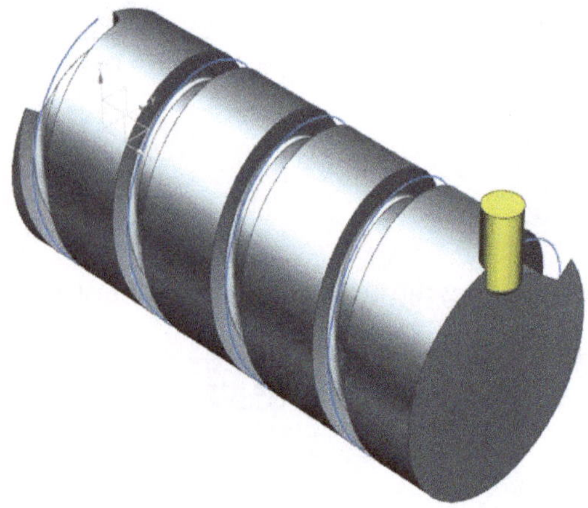

Creating Lattice

A lattice is a lightweight complex geometrical structural body created to strengthen the component using the **Lattice** command. It is like a framework that gives strength to designs while using less material. Lattice structures are often used in 3D printing to make parts that are both lightweight and durable. A lattice is created by tessellating (arranging) structural cells in two ways: **Unit graph** and **Conformal graph**.

Creating a Unit Graph Lattice

The Unit Graph lattice is created by arranging the structural cells within a closed volume defined by a solid body. Activate the **Lattice** command (on the Top Border Bar, click **Menu > Insert > Design Feature > Lattice > Lattice**) and select **Type > Unit Fill** from the **Lattice** dialog. Next, click on the solid body that you want to use as the boundary of the lattice. On the **Lattice** dialog, under the **Unit Cell** section, select an option from the **Cell Type** drop-down (there are fifteen cell types to select from the drop-down). You can preview the cell type by placing the mouse pointer on the options available in the **Cell Type** drop-down. Check the **Uniform Cube** option, if you want the cell to be uniform in all the directions. Next, specify a value in the **Edge Length** box.

On the **Body Creation** section, specify the **Rod Diameter** and **Tessellation Factor**. The tessellation factor is multiplied with the rod diameter to get the tessellation tolerance (pattern tolerance). On the **Seed Placement** section, click **Specify Orientation**, and then specify the orientation of the cells using the Dynamic CSYS (refer to **Chapter 3: Extrude and Revolve Features, Datum CSYS** section). Click **OK** to create the Unit Fill lattice. Hide the solid body to view the lattice.

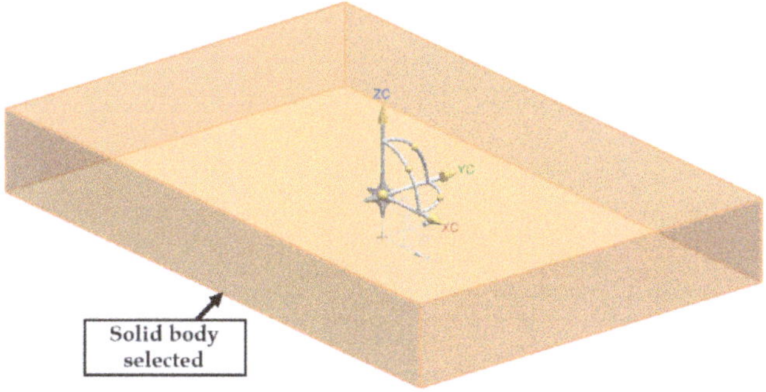

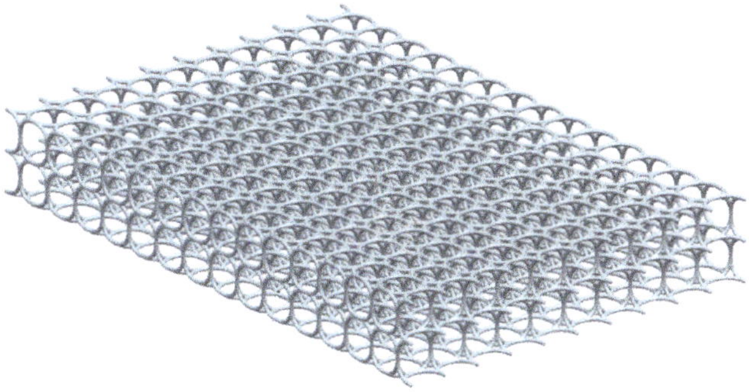

Creating a Conformal Lattice

The conformal lattice is created by arranging the cells in the boundary defined by a surface. You can also offset the lattice and create multiple layers of it. Activate the **Lattice** command (on the Top Border Bar, click **Menu > Insert > Design Feature > Lattice > Lattice**) and select **Type > Unit Conformal** from the **Lattice** dialog. Click on a face to define the boundary of the lattice. Select a **Cell Type** from the **Unit Cell** section and check the **Uniform Cube** option. Type in a value in the **Edge Length** box to define the size of the cell. In the **Graph** section, specify the number of layers in the **Layer** box. Next, type in a value in the **Offset** box if you want to offset the lattice from the selected boundary surface. On the **Body Creation** section, specify the **Rod Diameter** and **Tessellation Factor**. Click **OK** to create the conformal lattice.

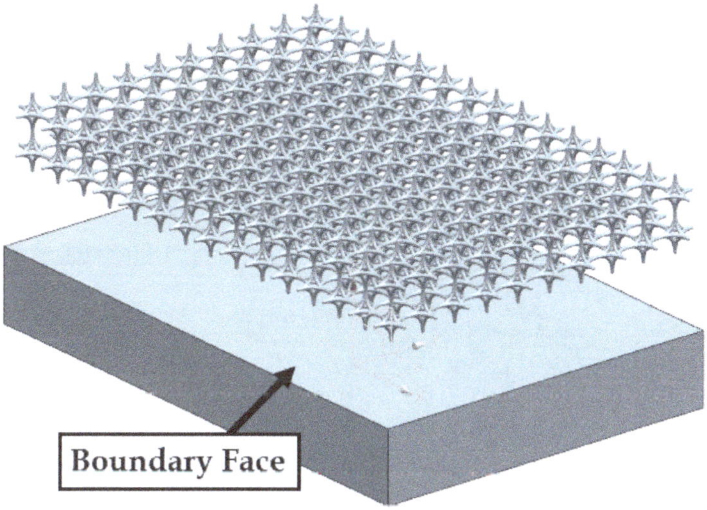

Cell Type: Octahedroid
Layers: 2
Offset: 20

Creating a Voronoi Lattice

The **Voronoi** option allows you to create a lattice pattern on a selected surface of an object. In addition to that, you can adjust the sizes of the holes and rods of the lattice. Activate the **Lattice** command (on the Top Border Bar, click **Menu > Insert > Design Feature > Lattice > Lattice**) and select **Type > Voronoi** from the **Lattice** dialog. Select a face on the object where you wish to apply the lattice pattern. Next, in the **Pore Size** section, select an option from the **Distribution** drop-down. There are three options in this drop-down: **Uniform**, **Variable**, and **Gaussian**.

The **Uniform** option creates all pores with the same size across the selected region, ensuring consistent and predictable behavior. You can define the pore size in the **Pore Size** section. The **Rod Diameter** in the **Body**

Creation section can then be specified separately, allowing you to adjust rod dimensions without altering the pore size rule.

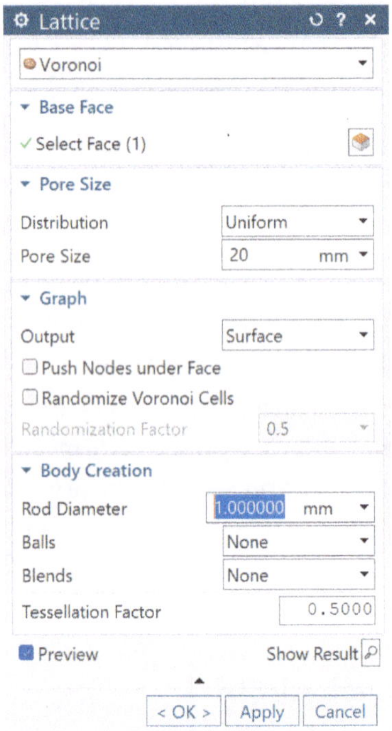

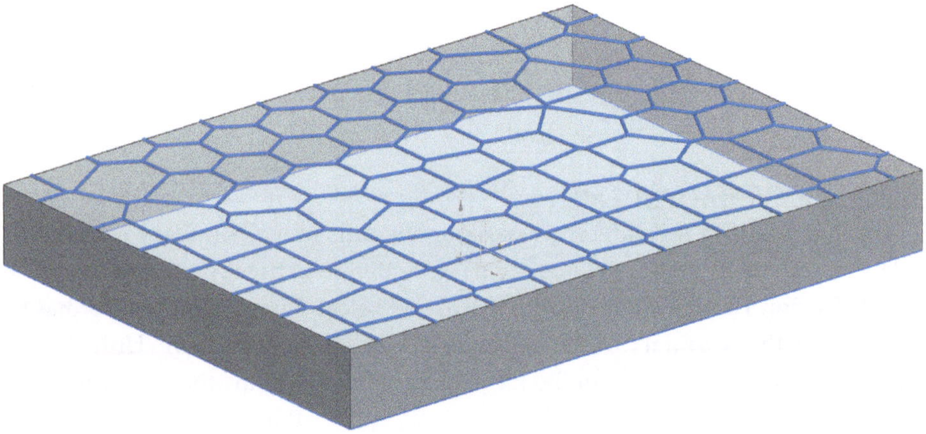

The **Variable** option allows pore size to change across the lattice by referencing specific faces or points, making it possible to introduce gradients in density or stiffness to meet local performance requirements. To set it up, first define the base face and set the **Distribution** to **Variable**. Then, use **Select Face or Point** to pick a face or point adjacent to the base face, and enter the required values for **Pore Size** and **Rod Diameter**.

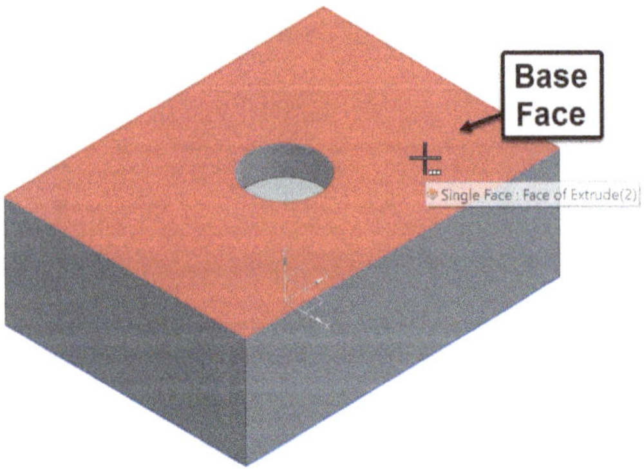

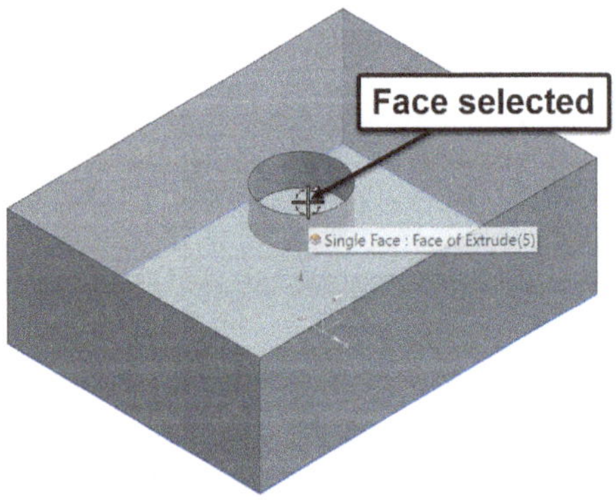

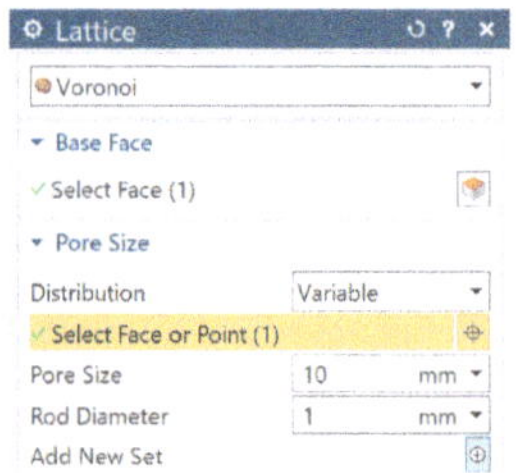

To add another control, click **Add New Set** in the **Pore Size** section, select a different adjacent face or point, and enter its corresponding values. The lattice then updates to reflect the varying pore sizes and rod diameters at the defined locations.

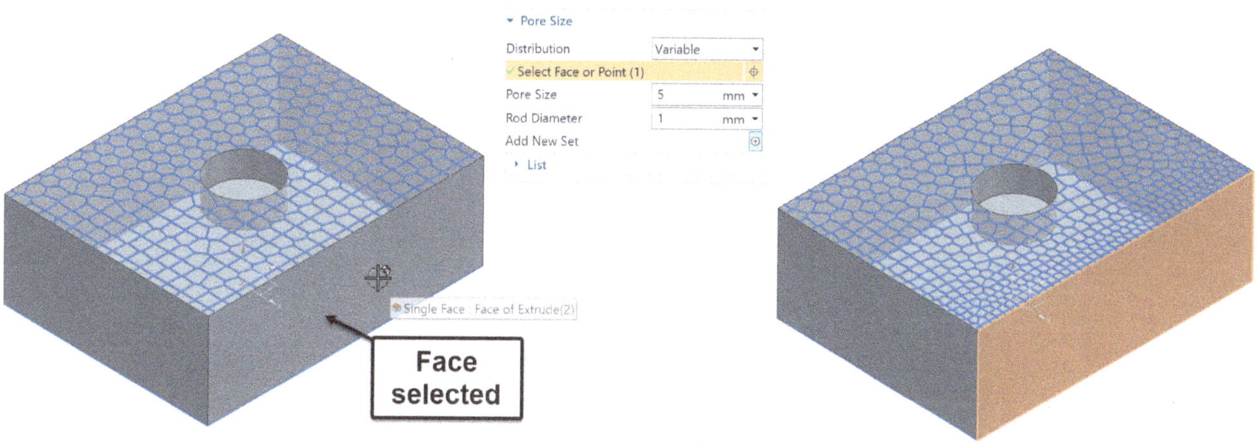

The **Gaussian** option allows you to create pore sizes that vary around a mean value using a normal distribution. This introduces controlled randomness into the lattice, producing a more natural or biomimetic appearance while still maintaining an overall target size.

To create a lattice with Gaussian pore distribution, choose **Gaussian** from the **Distribution** drop-down in the **Pore Size** section. Next, enter a value in the **Average** box, which sets the central pore size around which other pores will vary. Next, specify the **Standard Deviation** to control how much the pore sizes deviate from the average. To define limits, enter the **Minimum** value so that no pore is created smaller than this value. Similarly, type-in a value in the **Maximum** value to ensure no pore exceeds this size. Once these values are entered, click **OK**, and the lattice will generate with pore sizes distributed randomly but constrained within the specified range, centered around the **Average** value.

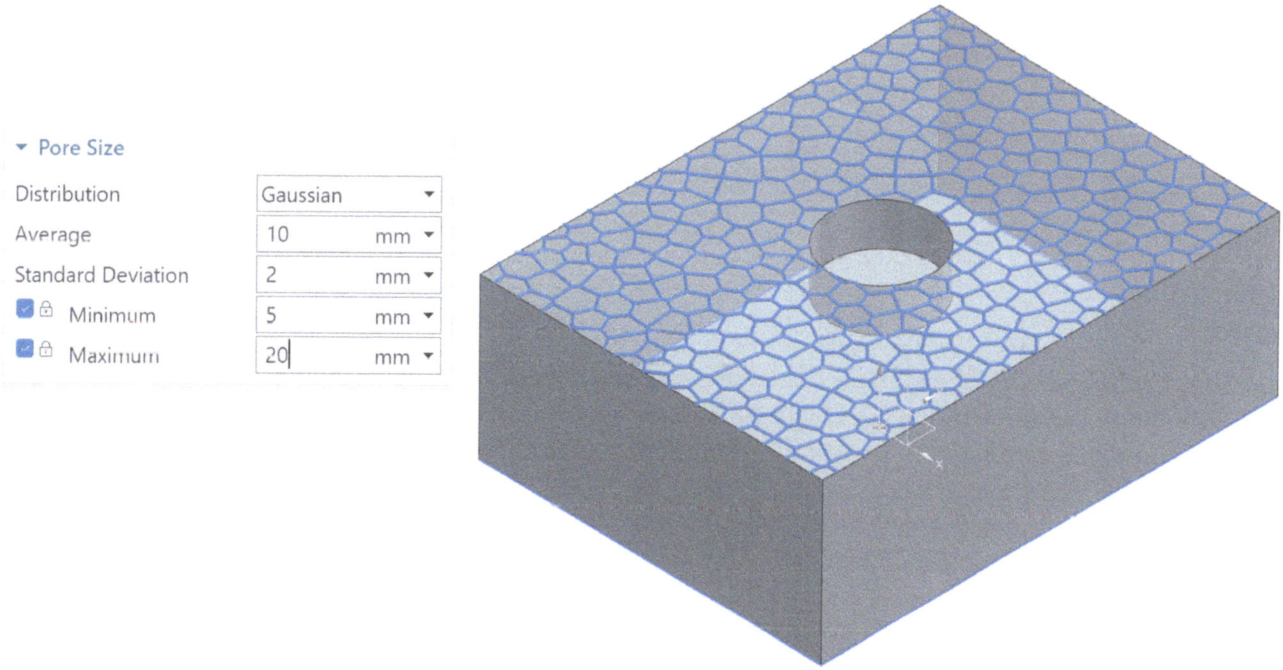

Examples

Example 1 (Millimetres)

In this example, you will create the part shown next.

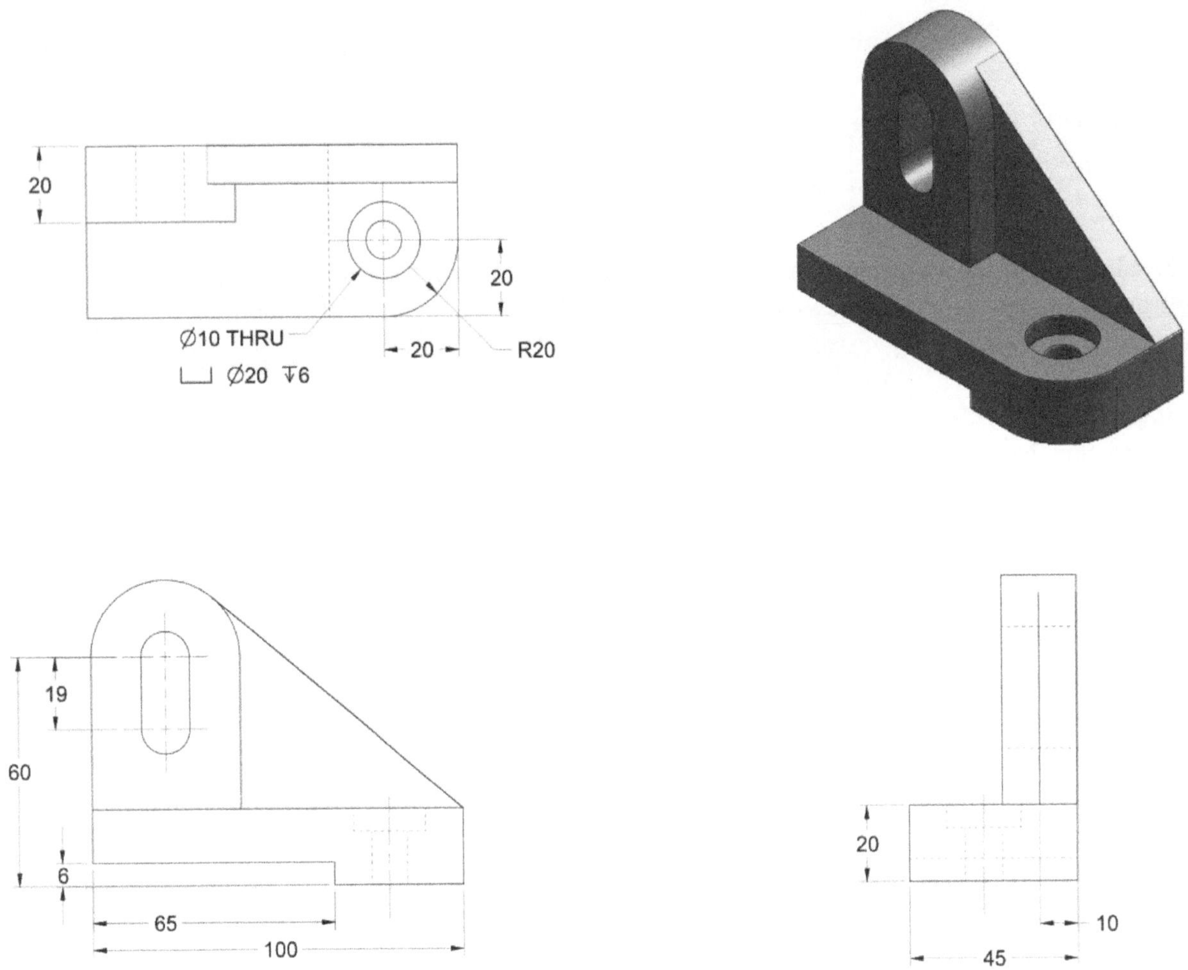

1. Start **NX** and open a part file using the **Model** template.
2. On the ribbon, click **Home > Base > Extrude**. Next, select the XY Plane from the Datum Coordinate System.
3. On the ribbon, click **Home > Curve > Rectangle**. Select the origin point of the sketch, move the pointer diagonally toward the bottom right corner, and click create the rectangle.
4. Add dimensions to the sketch, as shown. Next, click **Finish** on the ribbon.
5. On the **Extrude** dialog, type 20 in the **Distance** box available under the **End** drop-down in the **Limits** section. Next, click **OK**.

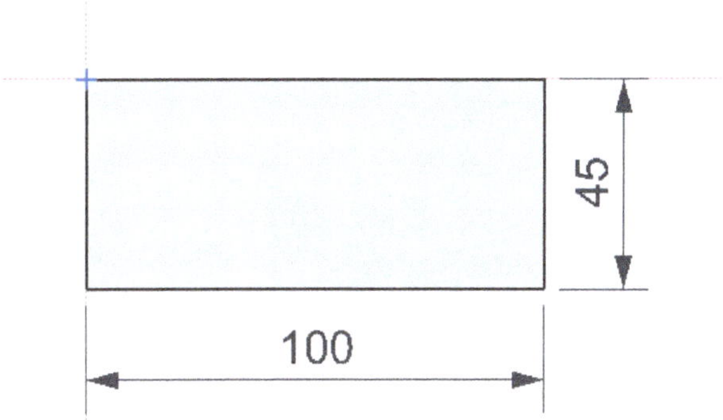

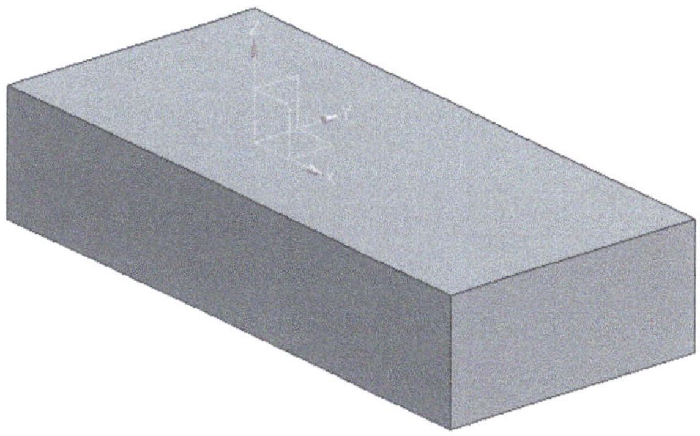

6. Activate the **Extrude** command (On the ribbon, click **Home > Feature > Extrude**). Select the XZ Plane from the Datum Coordinate System.
7. Activate the **Line** command and create the sketch, as shown (Refer to Chapter 2 for help).
8. Add dimensions to the sketch.
9. Click **Home > Include > Include** on the ribbon. Next, select the top horizontal edge of the model, and click OK.
10. Select the included horizontal edge and horizontal line of the sketch.
11. Select the **Make Collinear** icon on the Sketch Scene Bar.

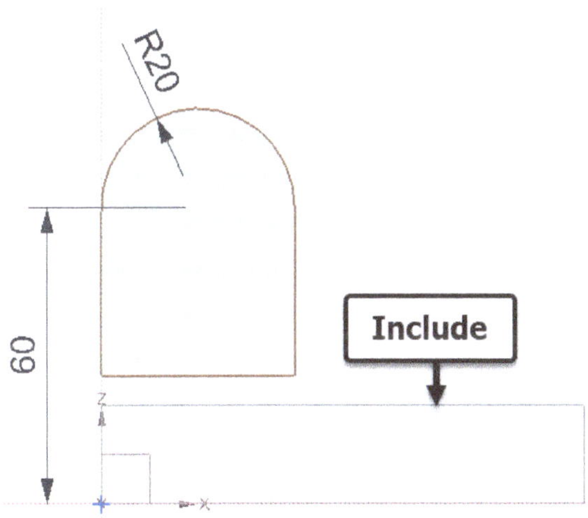

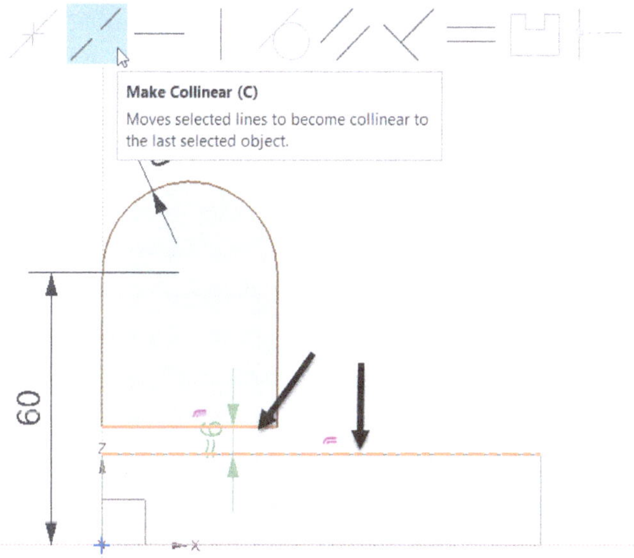

12. Select the arc and anyone of the vertical lines. Next, click the **Make Tangent** icon on the Sketch Scene Bar.
13. Next, click **Finish** on the ribbon.
14. On the **Extrude** dialog, type 20 in the **Distance** box available under the **End** drop-down in the **Limits** section. Expand the **Boolean** section and select **Boolean > Unite**. Click **OK**.

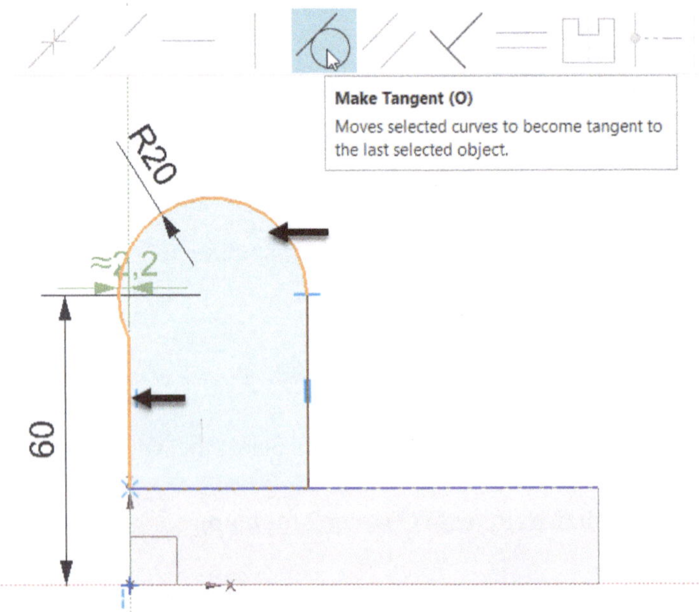

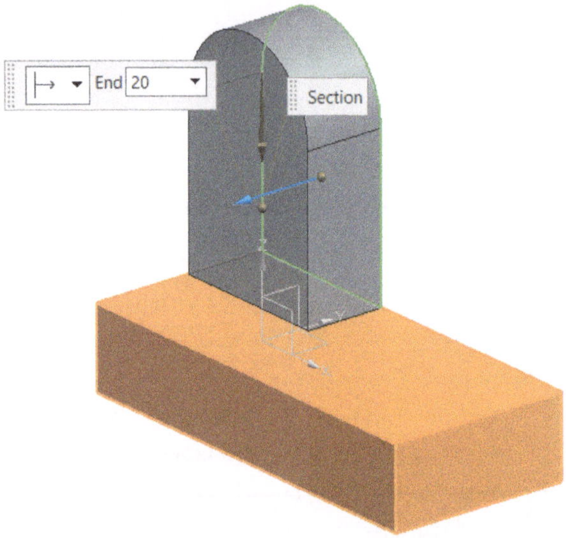

15. Activate the **Rib** command (On the ribbon, click **Home > Base > More > Detail Feature > Rib**). Click the **Select Curve** option and click on the XZ plane.
16. On the ribbon, click **Home > Include > Include**. Next, click on the curved edge of the model, and click **OK**.
17. Draw a line, which is tangent to the curved face of the second feature and connected to the top-right vertex of the first feature. Click **Finish** on the ribbon.

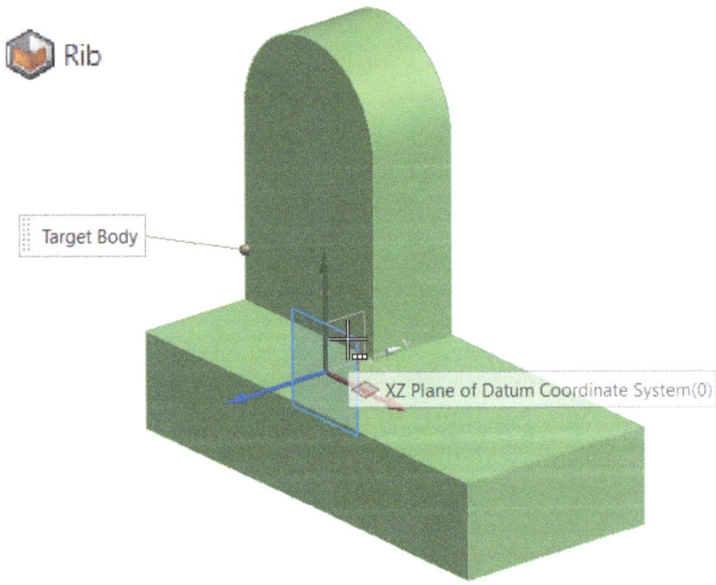

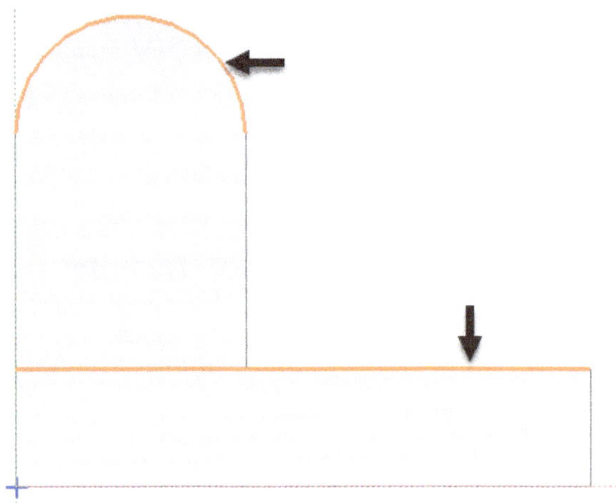

18. On the **Rib** dialog, under the **Walls** section, select **Parallel to Section Plane**.
19. Select **Dimension** > **Asymmetric,** and then type-in **10** in the **Thickness**.
20. Check the **Combine Rib with Target** option and click **OK** to create the rib.

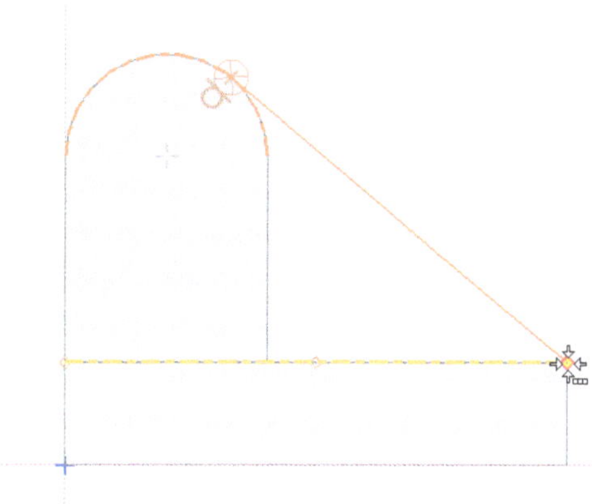

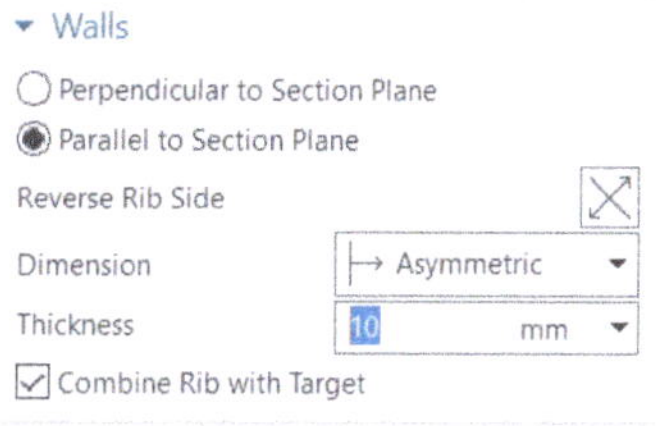

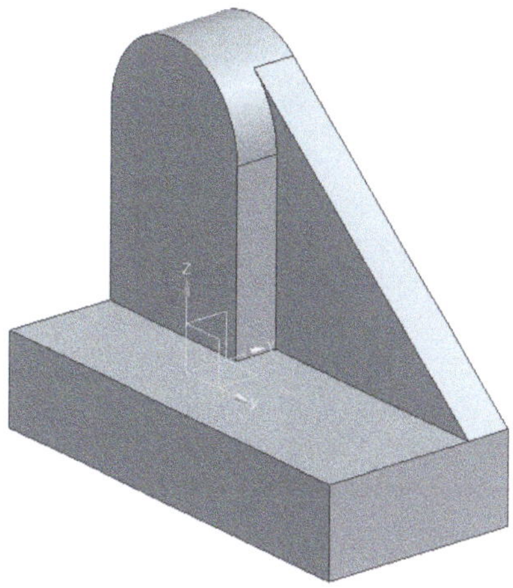

21. Activate the **Extrude** command (on the ribbon, click **Home > Base > Extrude**).
22. Click the **Reset** icon on the **Extrude** dialog.
23. Click on the front face of the second feature.
24. Sketch a slot using the **Line** command (refer to Chapter 2: Sketch Techniques to learn about the **Line** command). Click **Finish** on the ribbon.
25. On the **Extrude** dialog, under the **Limits** section, select **End > Through All**. Click the **Reverse Direction** icon in the **Direction** section, if the material is displayed outside the model.
26. Under the **Boolean** section, select **Boolean > Subtract**. Click **OK**.

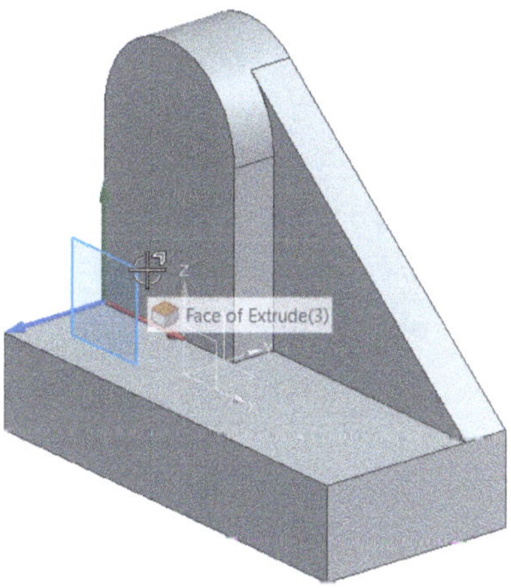

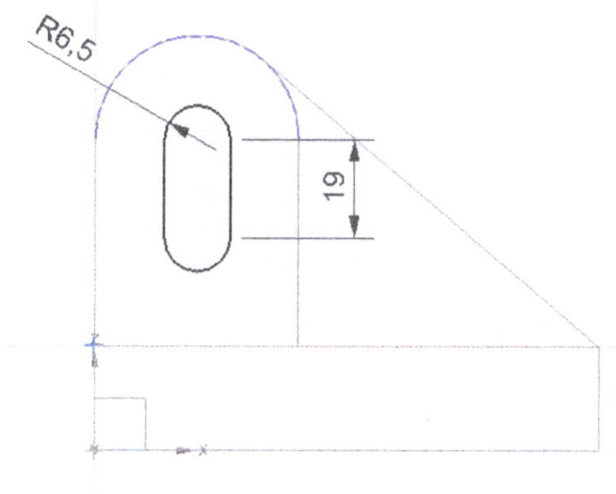

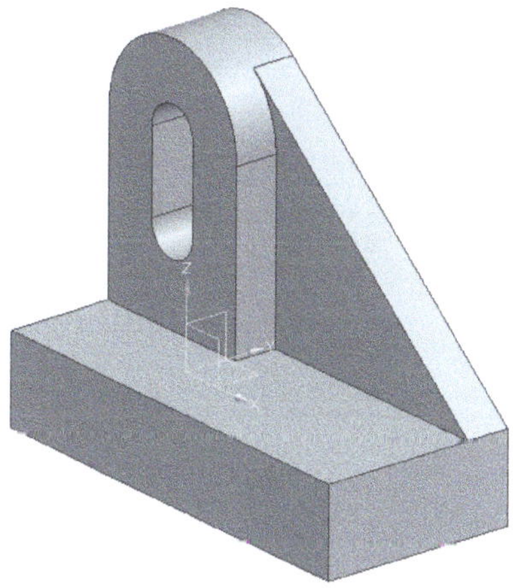

27. Add an edge blend of a 20 mm radius to the right vertical edge of the rectangular base.

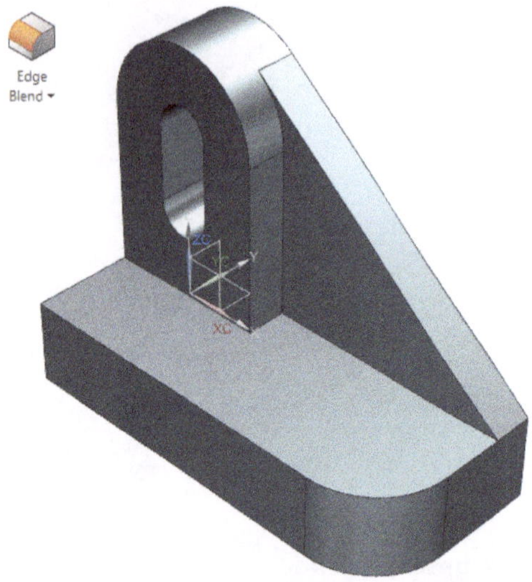

28. Activate the **Hole** command and create a counterbore hole concentric to the edge blend.

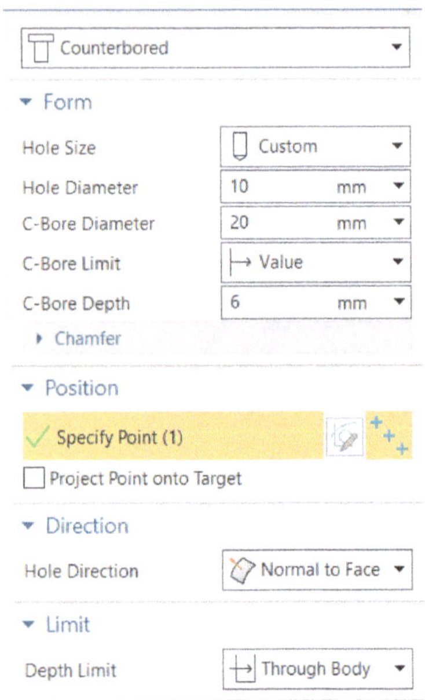

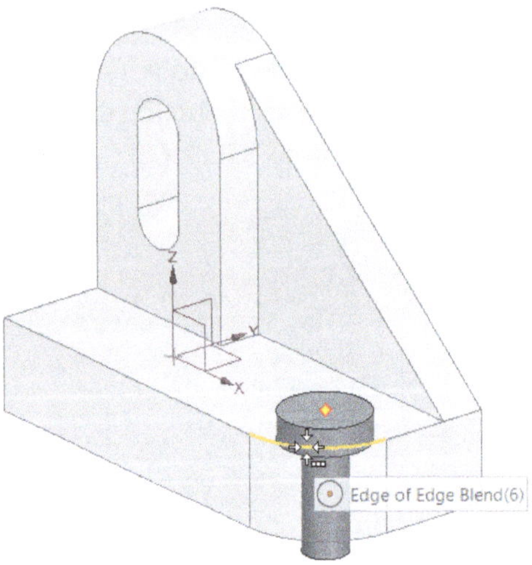

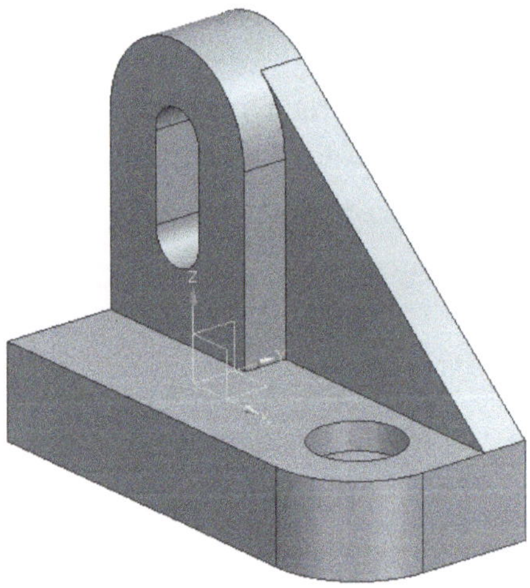

29. Construct an extruded cutout on the front face of the rectangular base.

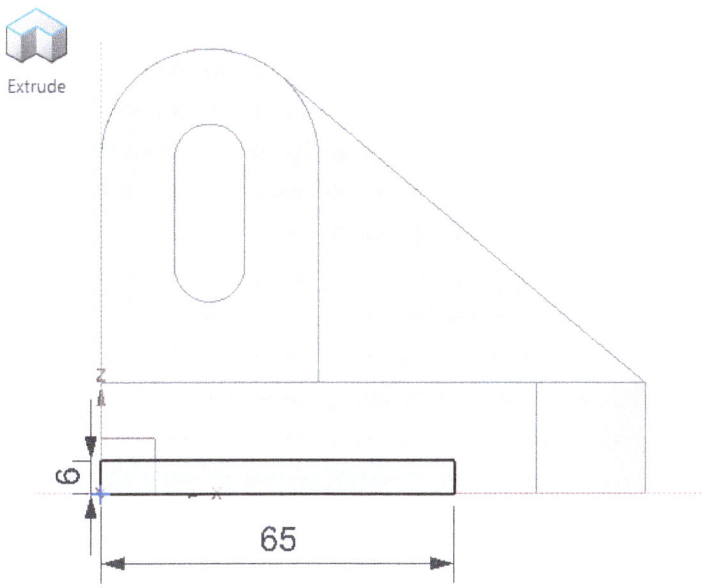

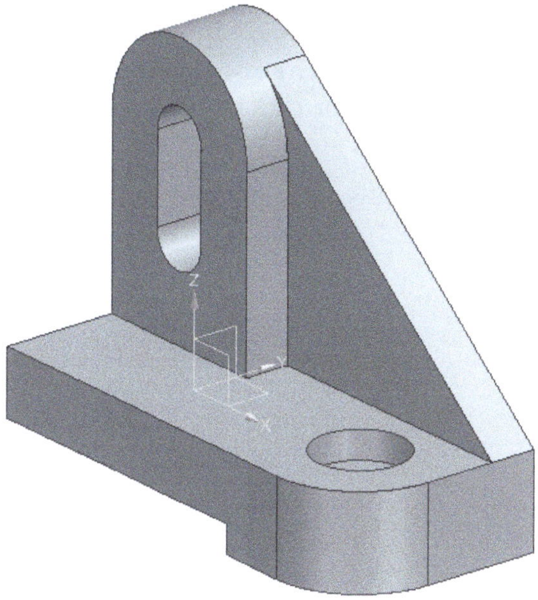

30. Save and close the file.

Example 2 (Inches)

In this example, you will create the part shown next.

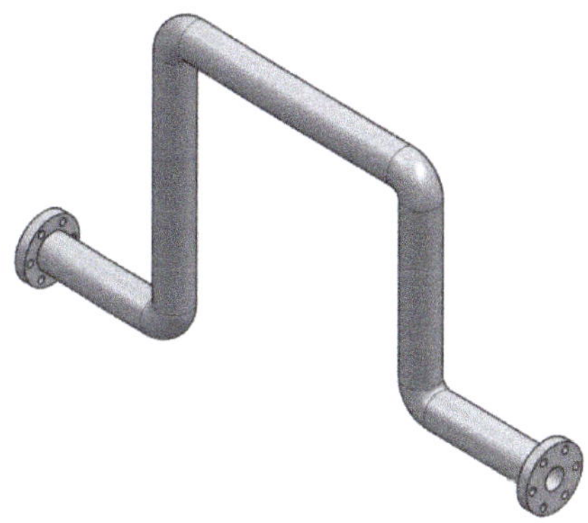

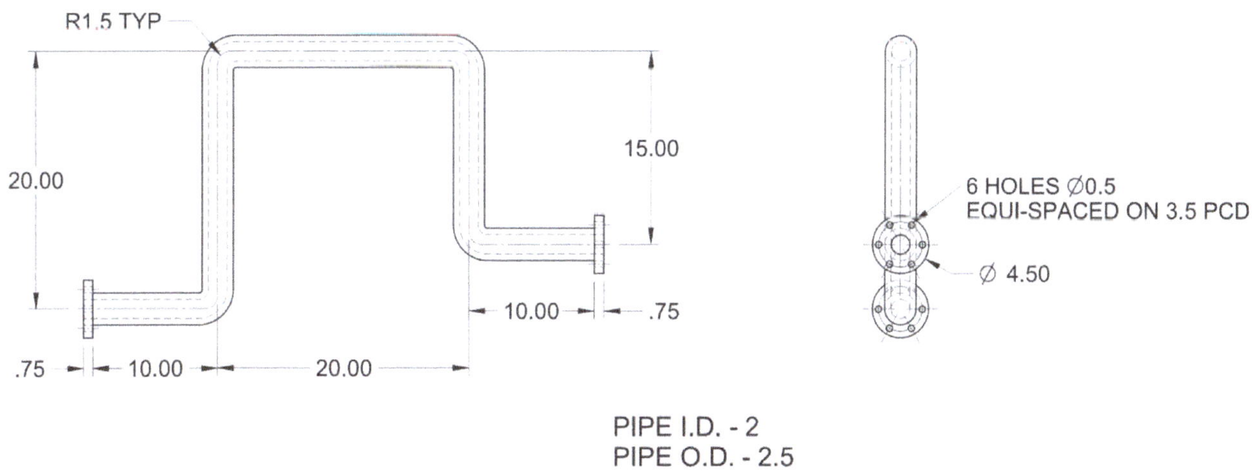

1. Start **NX**.

2. On the ribbon, click the **New** icon to open the **New** dialog.
3. On the **New** dialog, select **Units > Inches**. Next, click the **Model** template, and then click **OK**.
4. Draw the sketch shown in the figure on the Front plane.
5. On the ribbon, click **Finish** to complete the sketch.

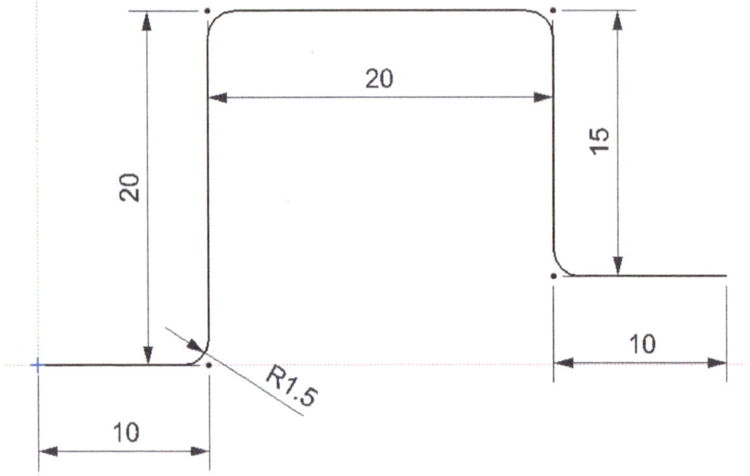

6. On the ribbon, click **Surface > Base > More > Sweep > Tube**.

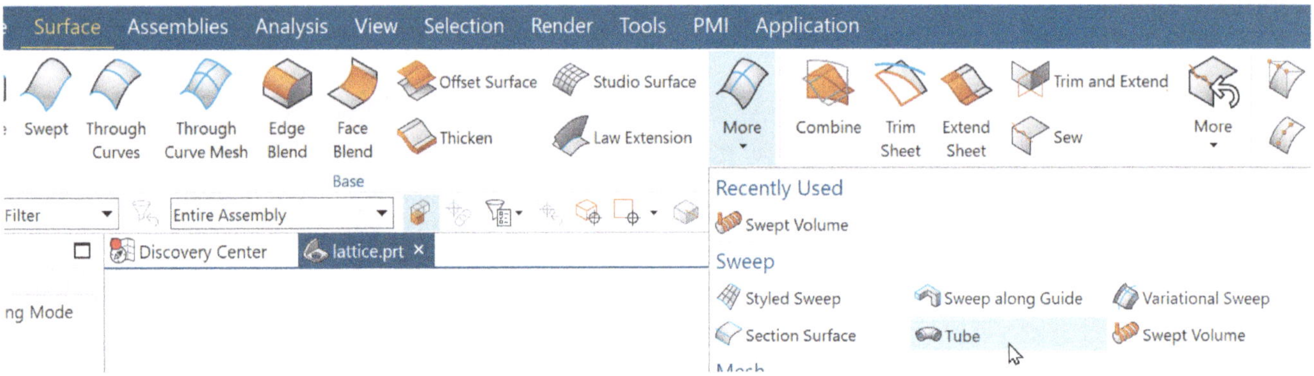

7. On the **Tube** dialog, type-in **2.5** and **2** in the **Outer Diameter** and **Inner Diameter** boxes, respectively.
8. Click on the sketch, and then click **OK** to complete the *Tube* feature.

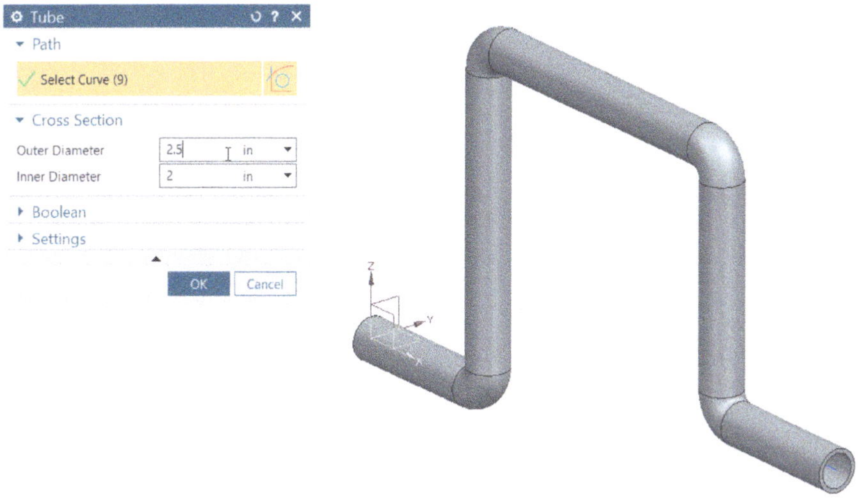

9. Activate the **Extrude** command and click on the front-end face of the *Tube* feature.
10. On the ribbon, click **Home > Include > Include** and click on the inner circular edge.
11. On the **Include** dialog, click **OK** to project the curve onto the sketch plane.
12. Draw a circle of 4.5 inches' diameter.

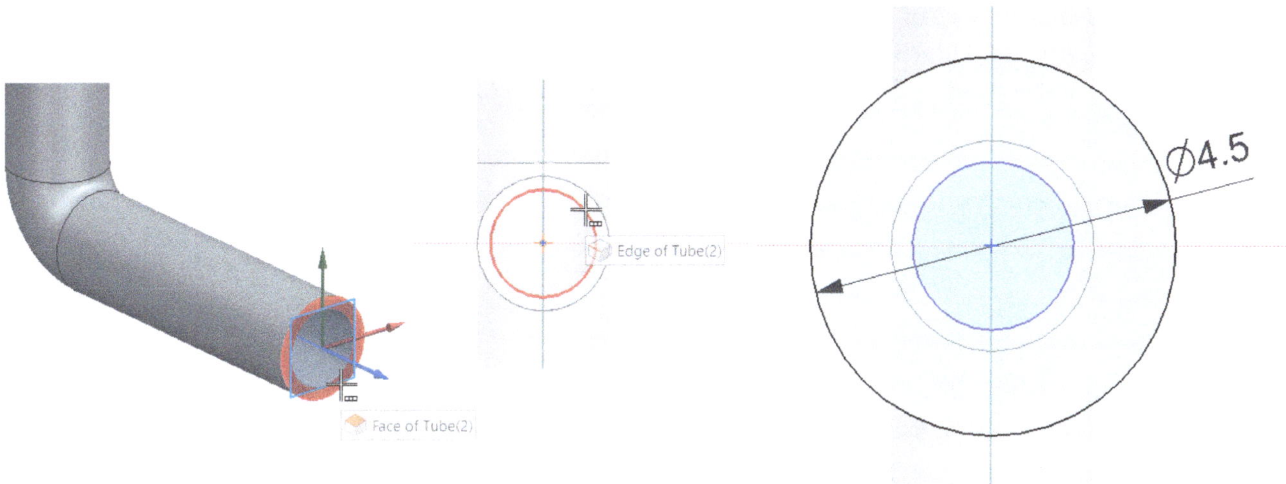

13. On the ribbon, click **Finish** to complete the sketch.
14. Type-in **0.75** in the **End** box attached to the preview. Click **OK** to complete the *Extrude* feature.

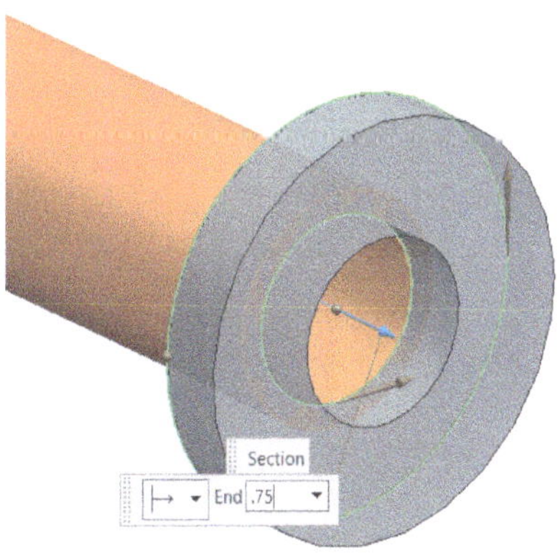

15. Create a hole of 0.50 diameter on the *Extrude* feature.

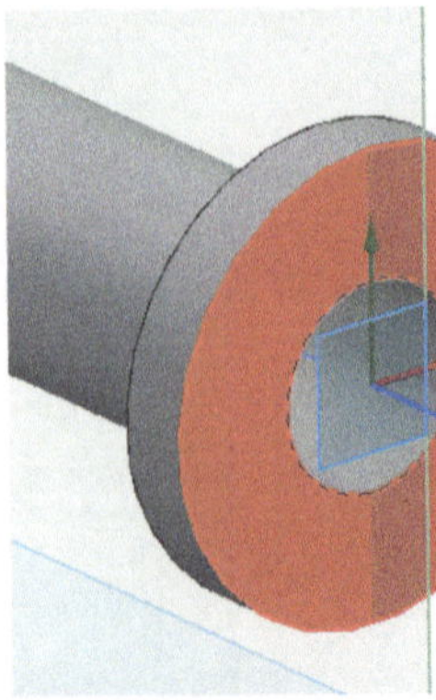

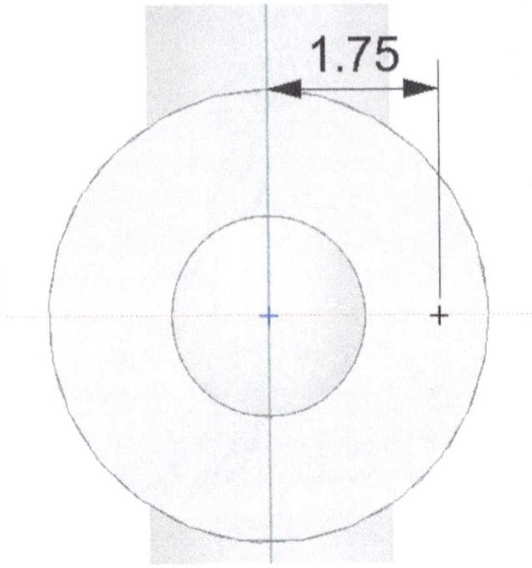

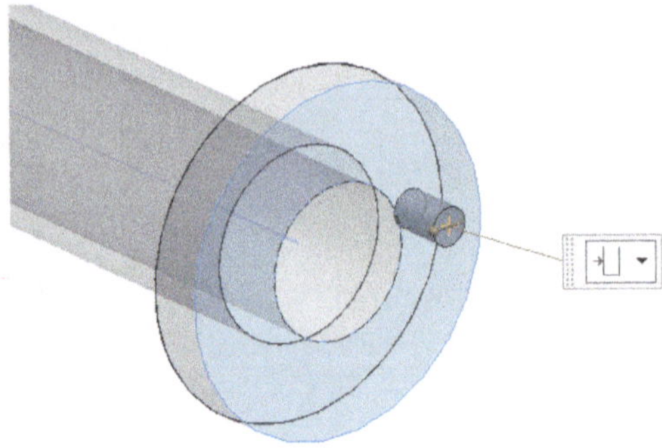

16. On the ribbon, click **Home > Base > Pattern Feature.**
17. Click on the hole on the part geometry.
18. On the **Pattern Feature** dialog, select **Layout > Circular**.
19. Under the **Rotations Axis** section, click **Specify Vector** and select the X-axis.
20. Click on a circular edge of the flange to define the pattern axis.
21. Under the **Angular Direction** section, select **Spacing > Count and Span**.
22. Type-in **6** and **360** in the **Count** and **Span** boxes, respectively. Click **OK** to pattern the holes in a circular fashion.

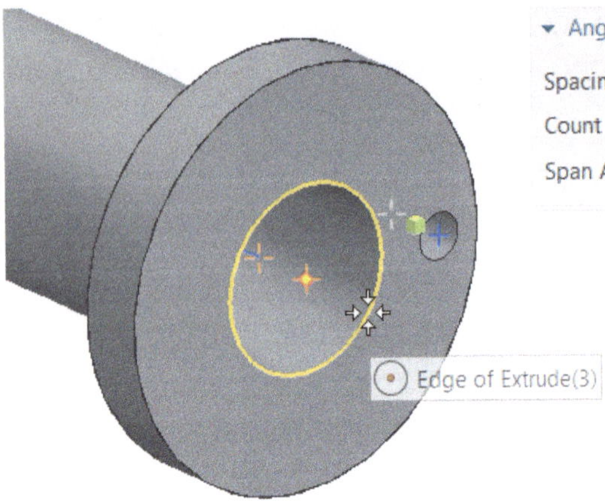

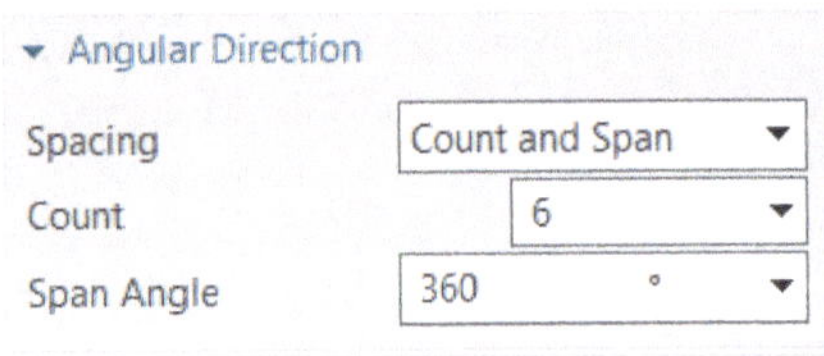

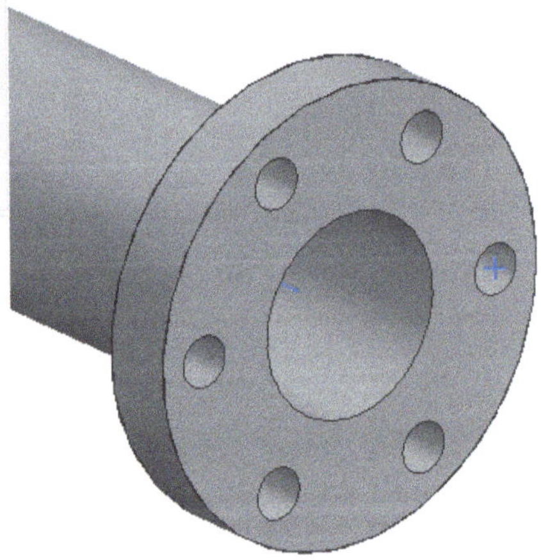

23. Change the model view orientation, as shown.
24. Create another flange and circular pattern.

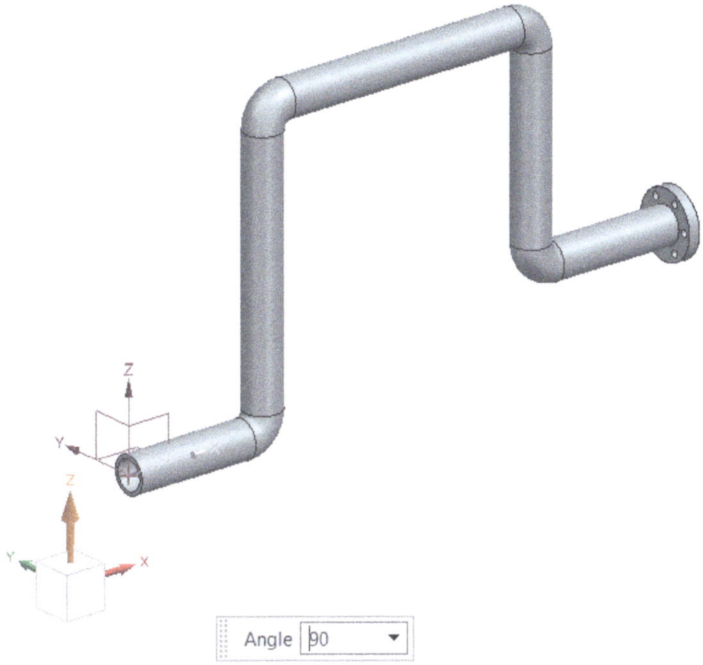

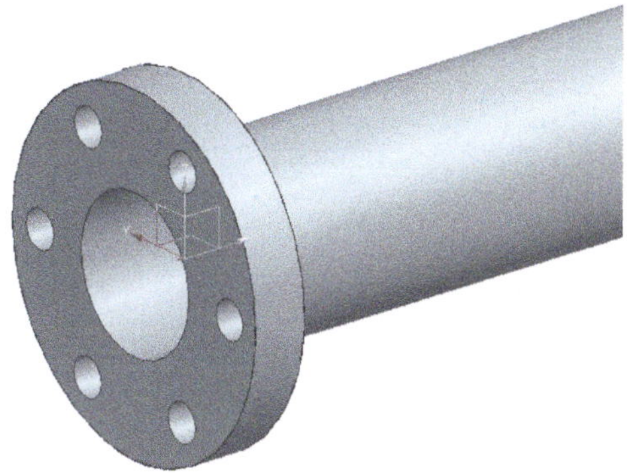

25. Save and close the part file.

Questions

1. What is the use of the **Rib** command?
2. Why do we create multi-body parts?
3. How do you split a single body into multiple bodies?
4. How do you add a draft to a rib feature?

Exercises

Exercise 1

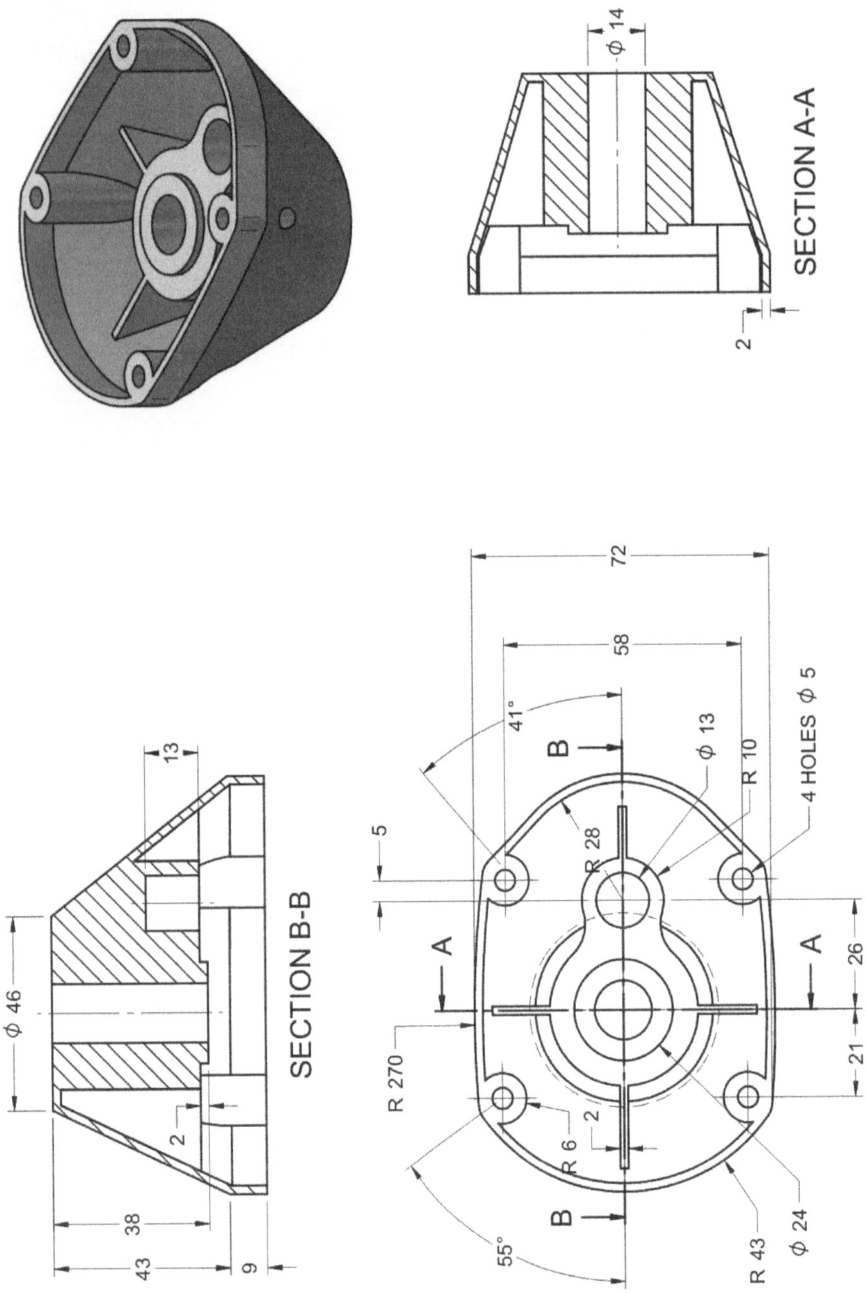

Exercise 2

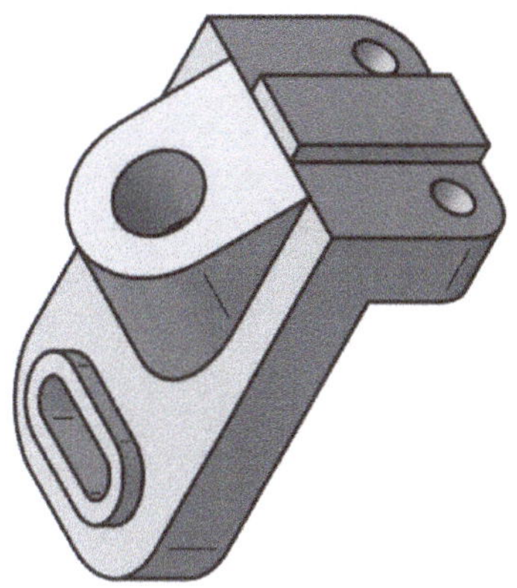

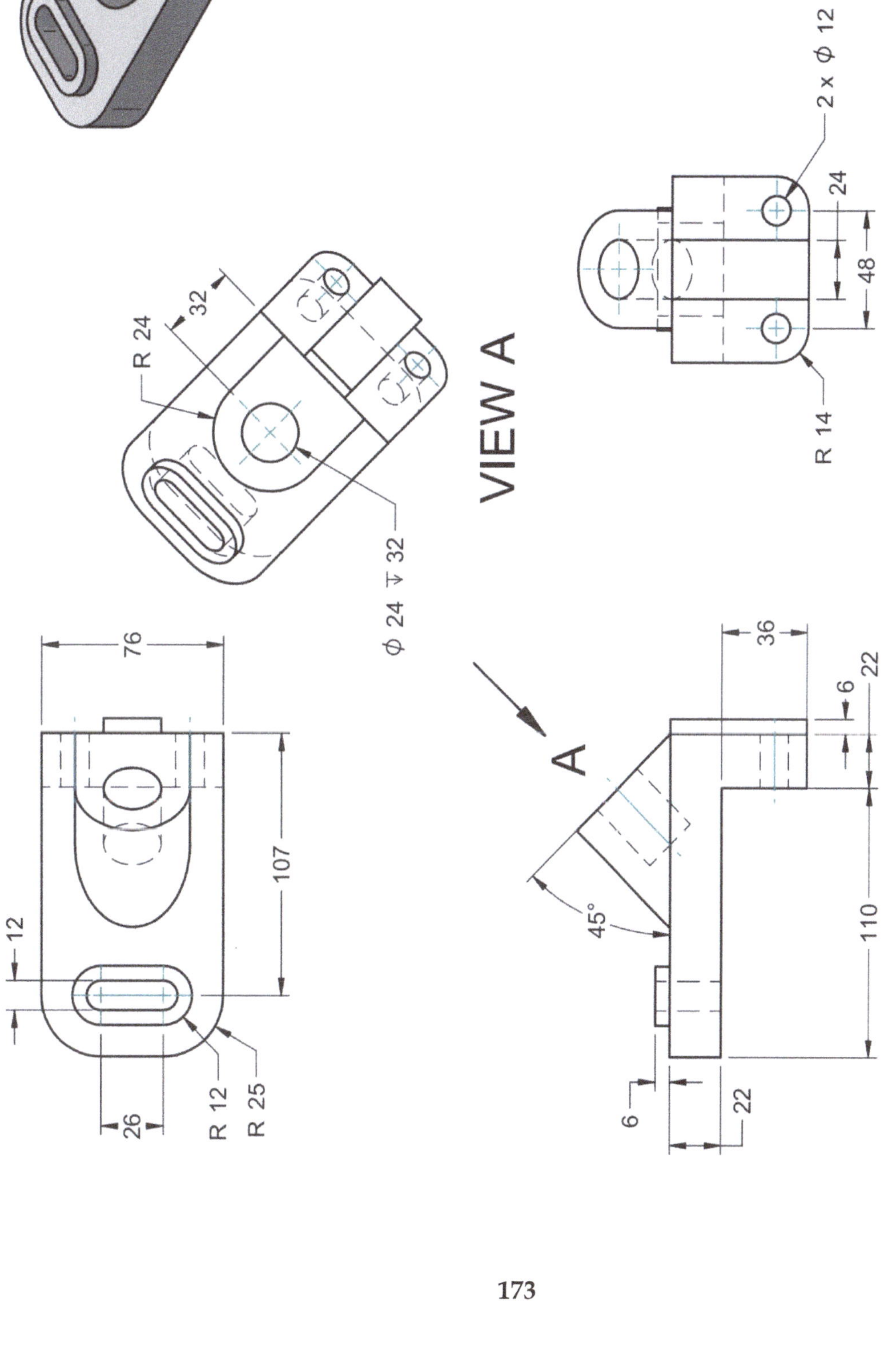
VIEW A
A
2 x ϕ 12
24
48
R 14
R 24
32
ϕ 24 ↧ 32
76
107
12
26
R 12
R 25
36
6
22
110
45°
6
22

Exercise 3 (Inches)

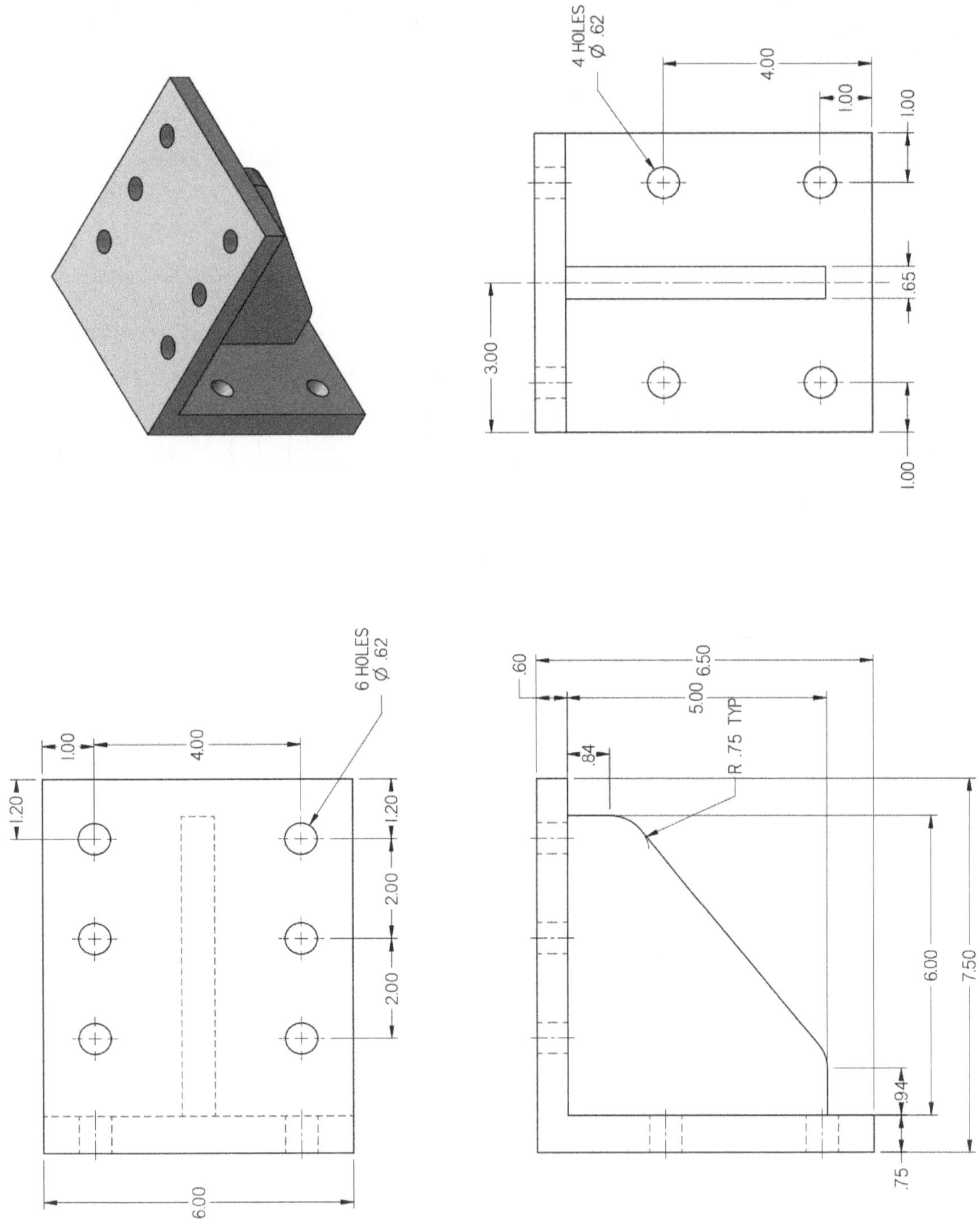

Chapter 7: Modifying Parts

In the design process, it is not required to achieve the final model in the first attempt. There is always a need to modify the existing parts to get the desired part geometry. In this chapter, you will learn various commands and techniques to make changes to a part.

The topics covered in this chapter are:

- *Edit Sketches*
- *Edit Feature Parameters*
- *Synchronous Modeling commands*

Edit Sketches

Sketches form the base of a 3D geometry. They control the size and shape of the geometry. If you want to modify the 3D geometry, most of the time, you are required to edit sketches. To do this, click on the feature to edit and select **Edit Sketch**. Now, modify the sketch and click **Finish** on the ribbon. You will notice that the part geometry updates immediately.

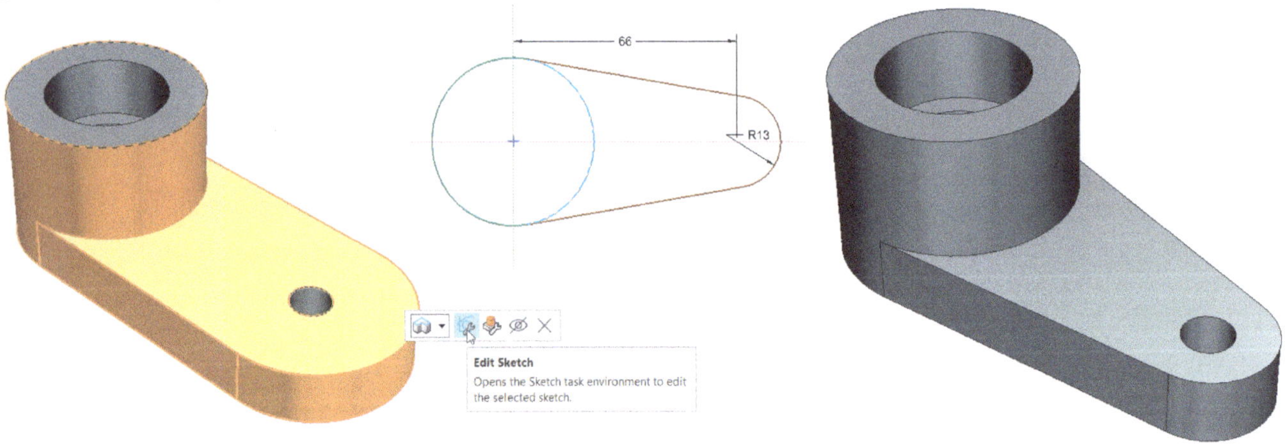

Edit Feature Parameters

Features are the building blocks of model geometry. To modify a feature, click on it and select **Edit with Rollback**. The dialog related to the feature appears. On this dialog, modify the parameters of the feature and click **OK**. The changes take place instantaneously. You can also modify a feature by simply double-clicking on it and changing the parameters.

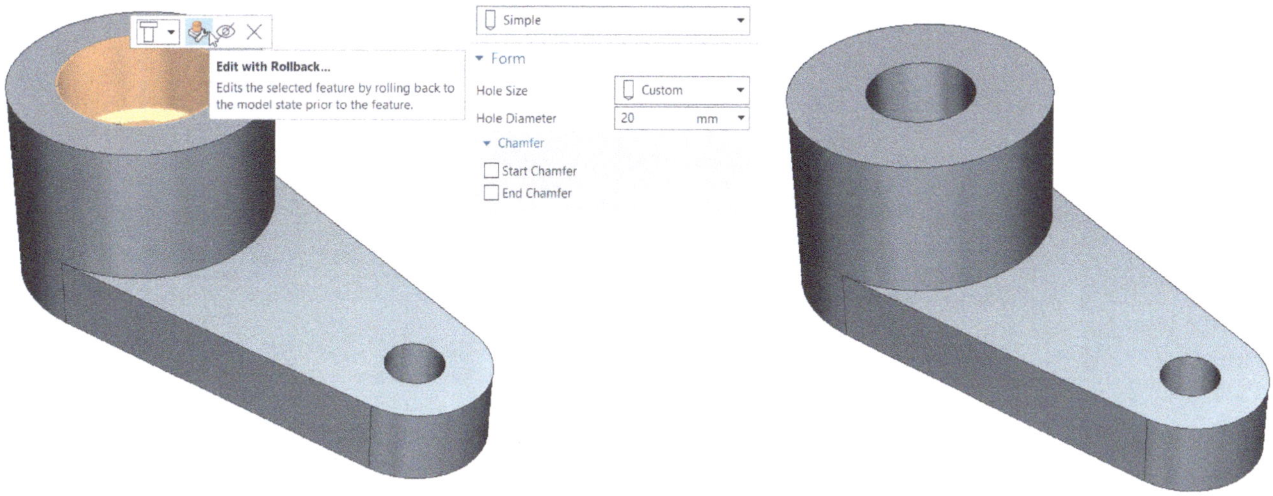

Suppress Features

Sometimes you may need to suppress the features of model geometry. To do this, click the right mouse button on the feature in the **Part Navigator** and select **Suppress** .

Synchronous Modeling Commands

NX allows you to modify the part geometry instantaneously using the Synchronous Modeling commands. These commands help you to move, rotate, copy, replace, and offset faces. In addition, you can define relations and dimensions between the faces of the model geometry. The following sections explain various Synchronous Modeling commands.

Move

This command moves a set of faces and adjusts the side faces to accommodate changes. Activate the **Move** command (on the ribbon, click **Home > Synchronous Modeling > Move**) and select a face. Drag the arrow that appears on the selected face, and then release the pointer to define the distance. You can also type-in a value in the **Distance** box.

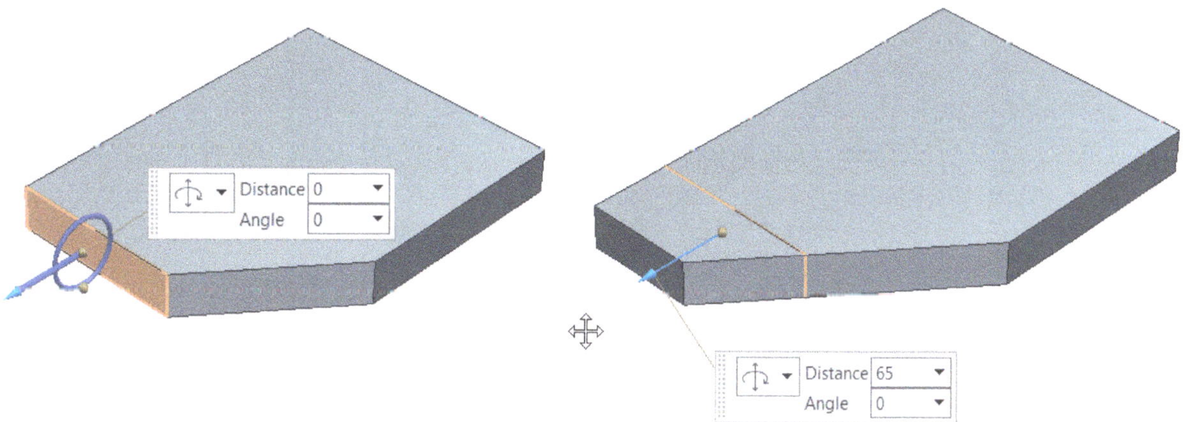

To rotate a face, select **Transform > Motion > Angle** on the **Move Face** dialog, and then select a vector axis. Click on a vertex to define the origin of the vector axis. Select the face to rotate and drag the angle handle.

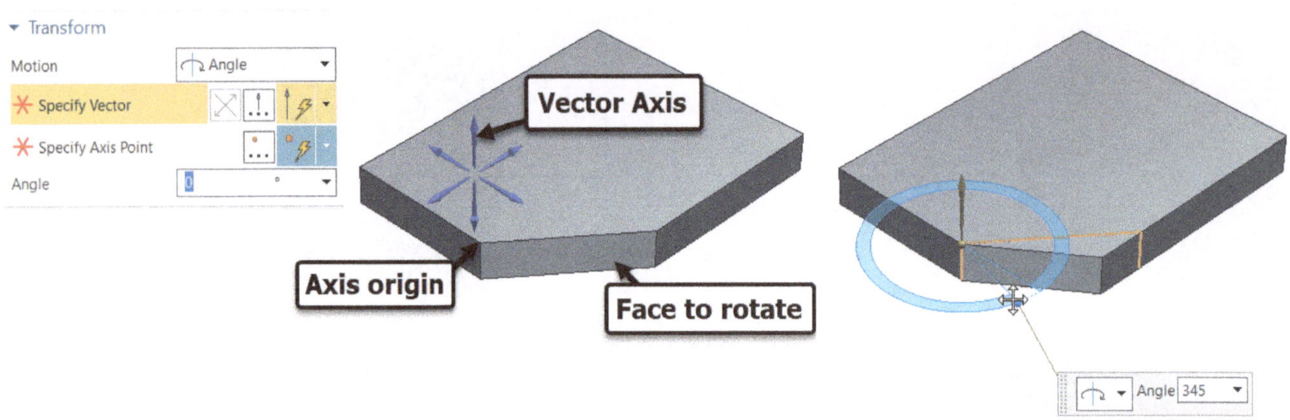

Use the **Cut and Paste** option to cut and paste a model face. To do this, activate the **Move** command, click on a model face, and then select **Settings > Move Behavior > Cut and Paste** on the **Move Face** dialog. Now, select **Transform > Motion > Distance**, and then select a vector axis to define the moving direction. Under the **Settings** section, check the **Heal** and **Paste** options, and then drag the arrow that appears on the selected face.

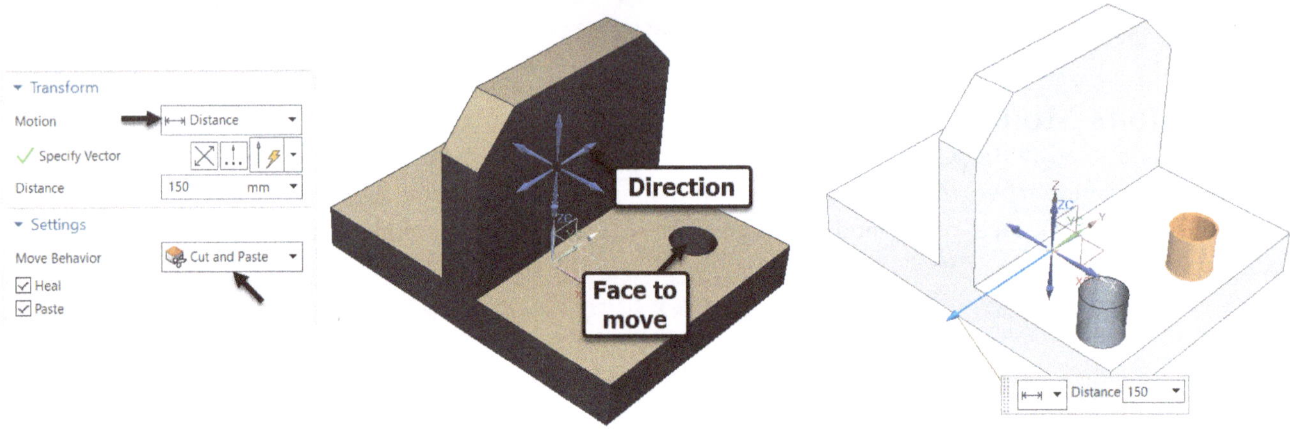

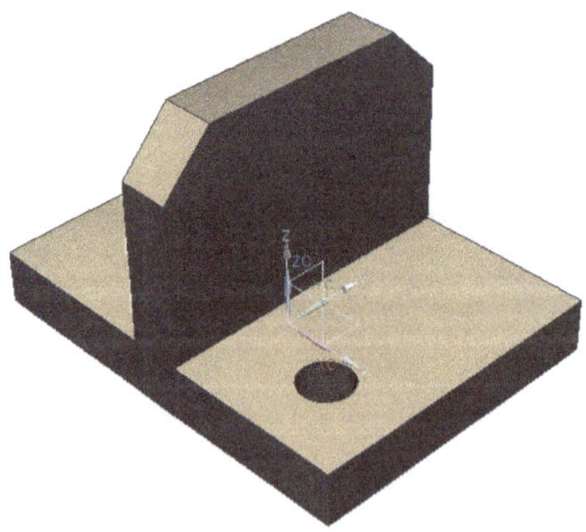

Pull Face

Use the **Pull Face** command (on the ribbon, click **Home > Synchronous Modeling > More > Pull Face**), if you want to pull the selected face and add new faces to the model. The new faces will be added perpendicular to the modified face.

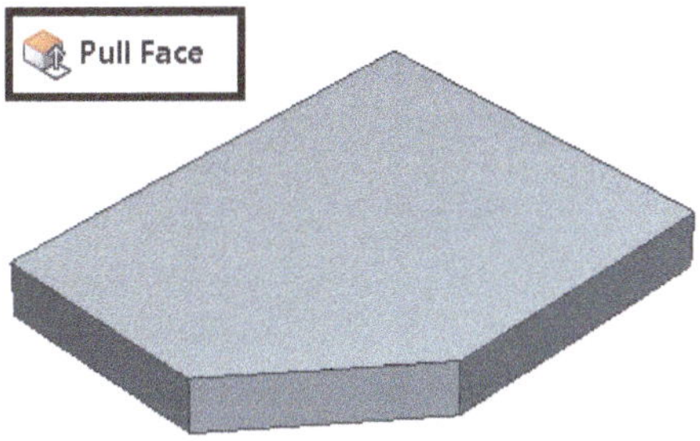

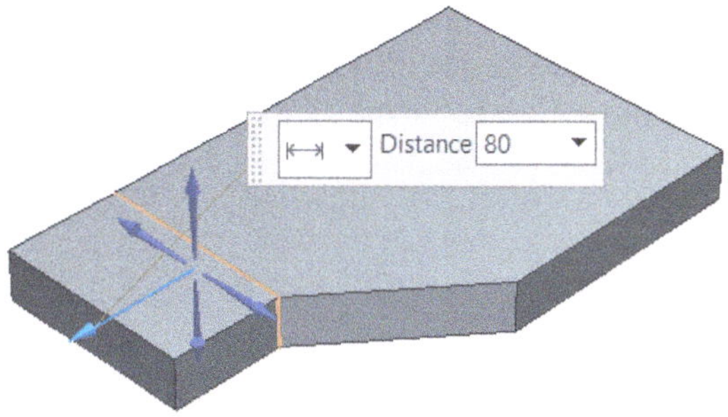

Offset

This command offsets a set of faces from the current position. Activate this command (click **Home > Synchronous Modeling > Offset** on the ribbon) and click on one or more faces. Drag the arrow that appears on the selected set or type-in a value in the **Distance** box.

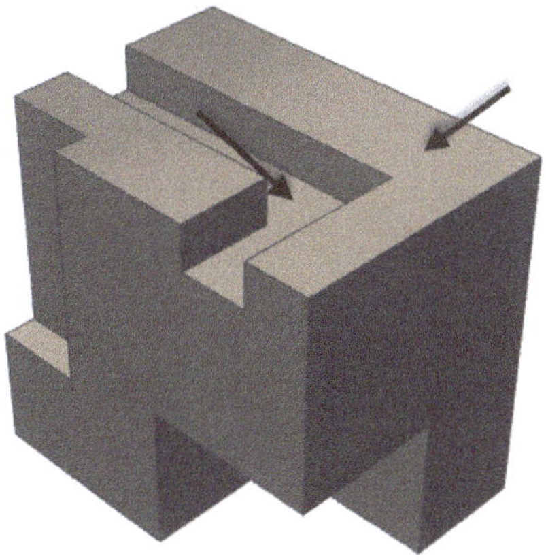

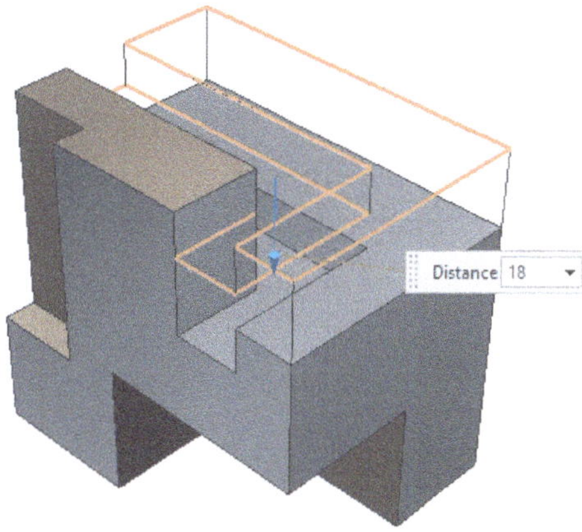

Replace

This command replaces a set of faces with another set of faces. Activate this command (click **Home > Synchronous Modeling > Replace** on the ribbon) and select the faces to replace. On the **Replace Face** dialog, under the **Replacement Face** section, click **Select Face** and select faces to replace with.

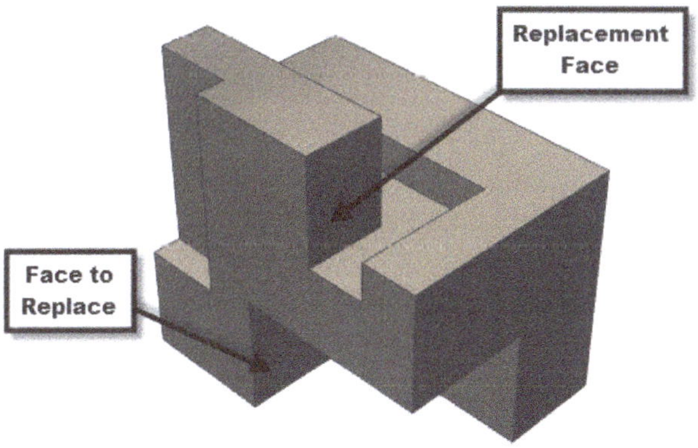

Make Coplanar

This command brings the selected faces onto one plane. Activate this command (click **Home > Synchronous Modeling > More > Relate > Make Coplanar** on the ribbon), and then select the first and second faces. Click **OK** to make the two faces coplanar.

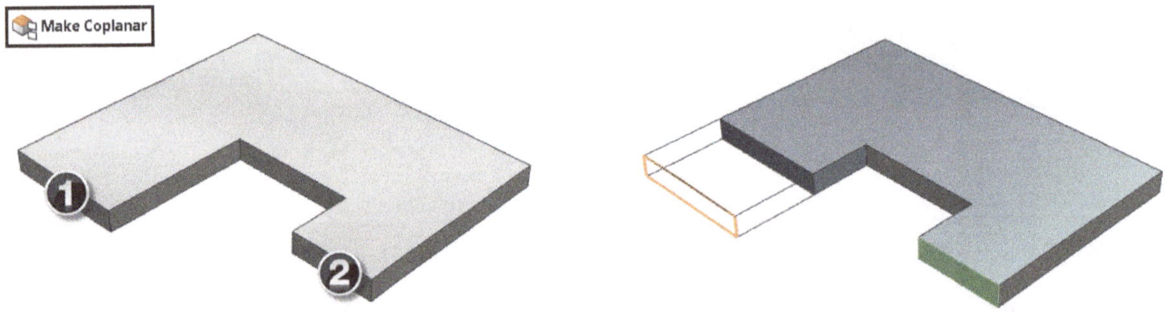

Make Coaxial

This command makes two cylindrical faces share the same centerpoint. Activate this command (click **Home > Synchronous Modeling > More > Relate > Make Coaxial** on the ribbon) and select the first and second cylindrical face. On the **Make Coaxial** dialog, under the **Settings** section, select **Overflow Behavior > Extend Change Face**; extends the cylindrical face of the hole such that it intersects with the top face of the boss. Click **OK** to make the first face concentric to the second face.

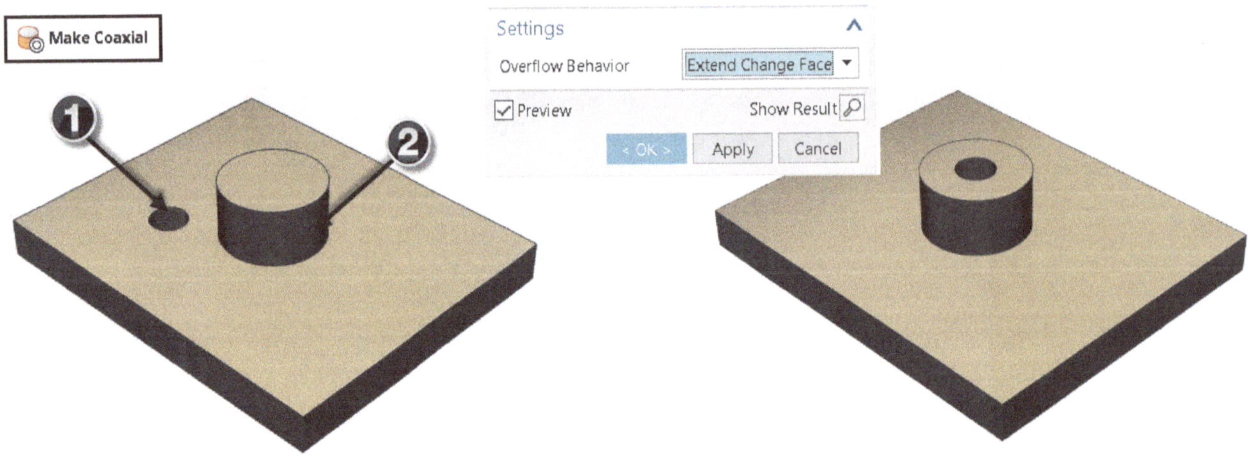

Make Symmetric

This command makes two faces symmetric about a plane. Activate this command (click **Home > Synchronous Modeling > More > Relate > Make Symmetric** on the ribbon), and select the first face. Click on the symmetric plane, and then the face to remain stationary. Click **OK** to make the faces symmetric.

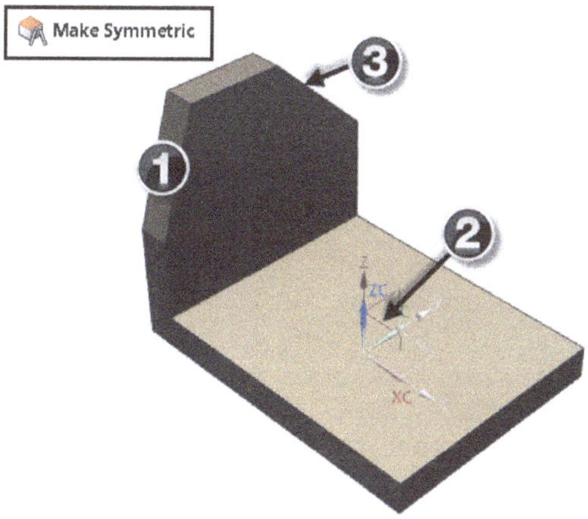

Make Offset

This command defines an offset distance between two faces. The selected faces should share a common face, which is perpendicular to both of them. Activate this command (click **Home > Synchronous Modeling > More > Relate > Make Offset** on the ribbon), select a face to define the motion face. Select a stationary face and type-in an offset value in the **Distance** box. Click **OK**; the first face will be offset from the second face by the value you specified.

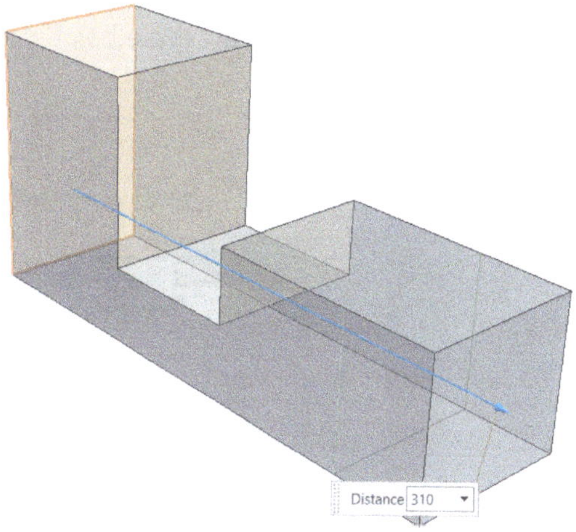

Linear Dimension

NX allows you to move a set of faces by adding a dimension and changing its value. To do this, activate the **Linear Dimension** command (click **Home > Synchronous Modeling > More > Dimension > Linear Dimension** on the ribbon) and select the origin object. Click on the object to move. Specify the measure direction by selecting a vector from the OrientXpress tool. Click to position the linear dimension. Now, type-in a value in the **Distance** box and click **OK**.

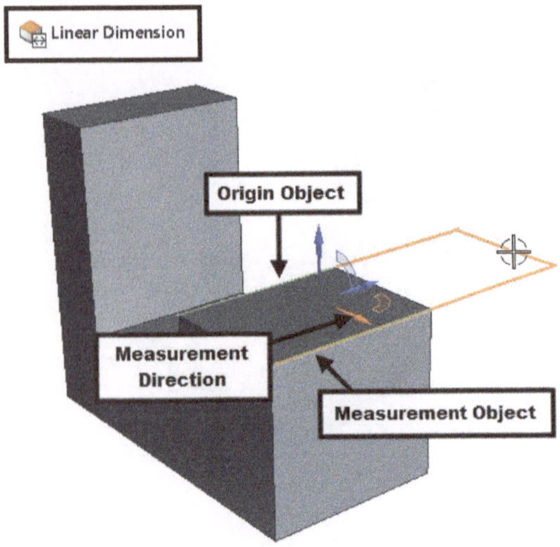

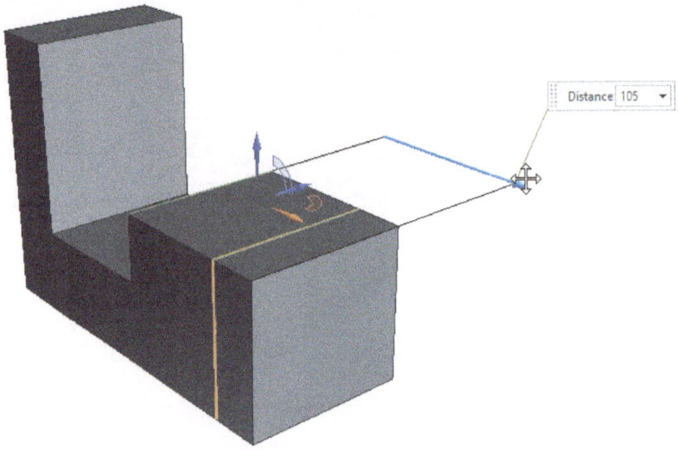

Angular Dimension

This command rotates a set of faces by adding a dimension and changing its value. Activate the **Angular Dimension** command (click **Home > Synchronous Modeling > More > Dimension > Angular Dimension** on the ribbon) and select the origin object. Select the measurement object and click to specify the location of the angular dimension. Type a value in the **Angle** box or drag the handle to rotate the measurement object.

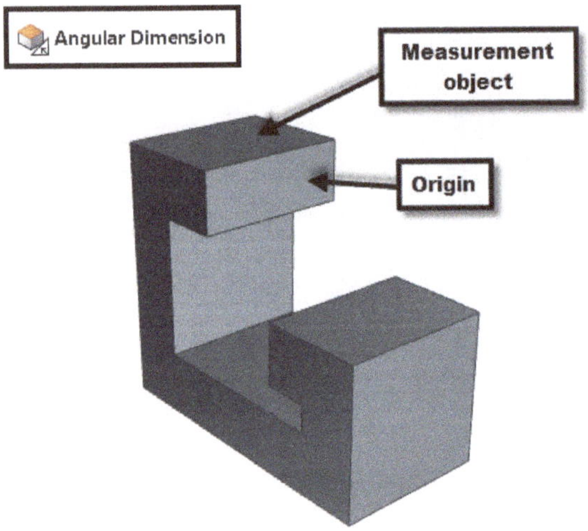

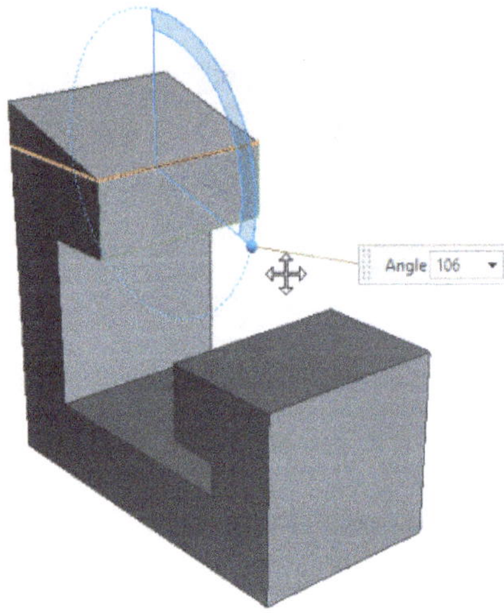

Make Parallel

The **Make Parallel** command (click **Home > Synchronous Modeling > More > Relate > Make Parallel** on the ribbon) makes two faces parallel to each other. The first face will be parallel to the second face.

Make Perpendicular

The **Make Perpendicular** command (click **Home > Synchronous Modeling > More > Relate > Make Perpendicular** on the ribbon) makes two faces perpendicular to each other. The first face will be perpendicular to the second face.

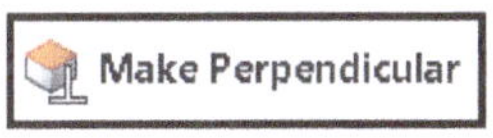

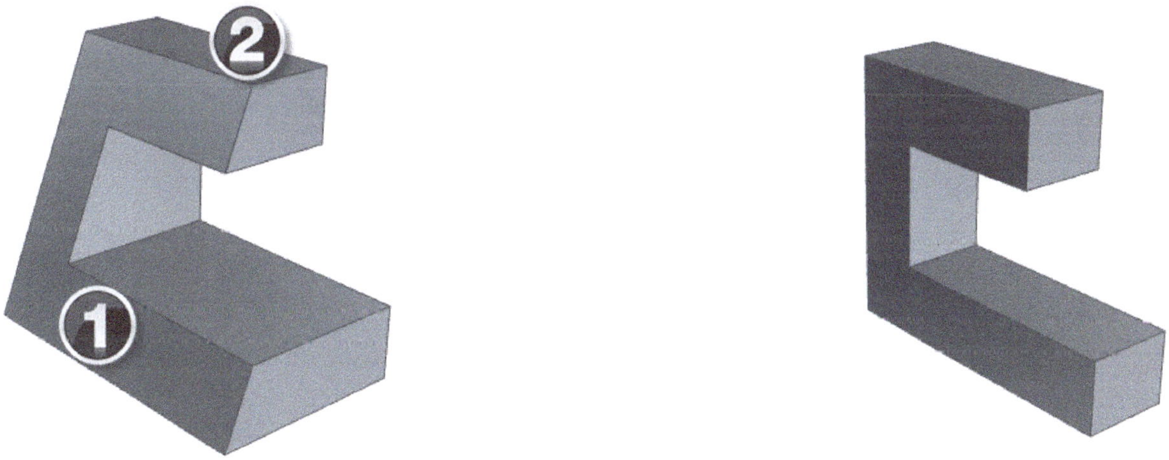

Label Notch Blend

The **Label Notch Blend** command (click **Home > Synchronous Modeling > More > Detail Feature > Label Notch Blend** on the ribbon) recognizes a curved face as a notch blend so that you can modify it using the synchronous modeling commands.

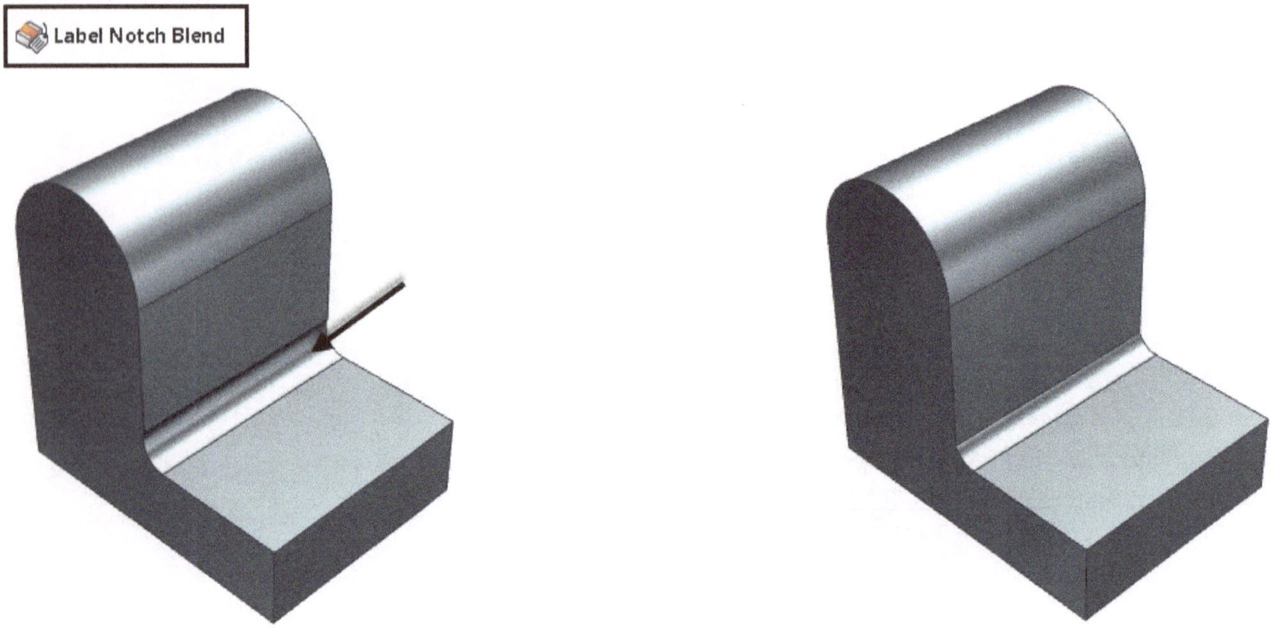

Resize Blend

The **Resize Blend** command (click **Home > Synchronous Modeling > Resize Blend** on the ribbon) increases or decreases the size of a blend.

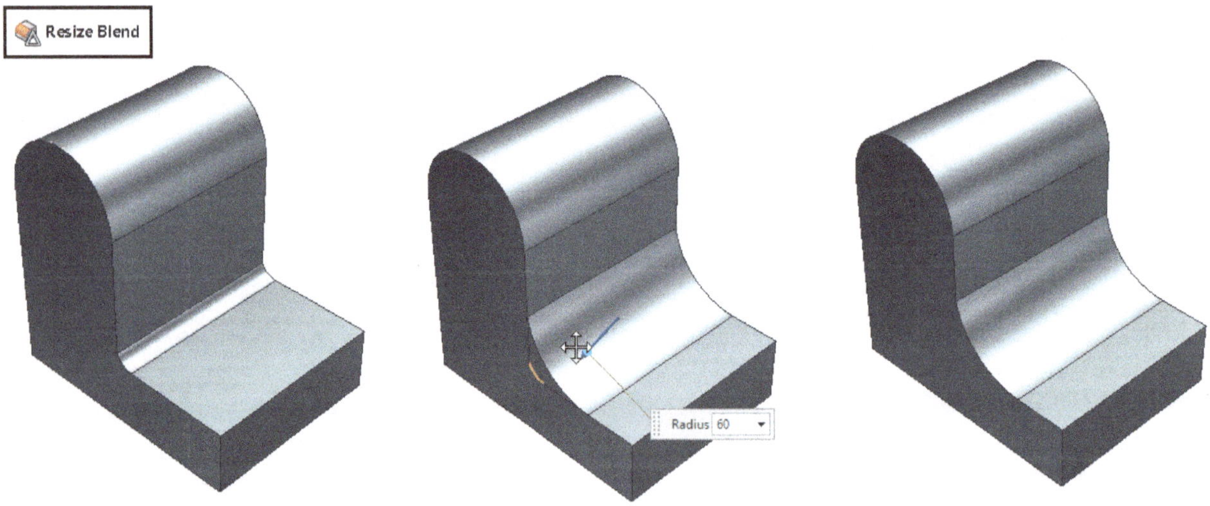

Replace Blend

This command converts a blend like a face into an actual blend feature. For example, if you have created blends by adding sketch fillets, then you must edit the sketch to edit the blends. To solve this problem, activate the **Replace Blend** command (click **Home > Synchronous Modeling > More > Optimize > Replace Blend** on the ribbon) and select the blend like faces. Click **OK,** and now you can modify the blend using the Synchronous modeling commands.

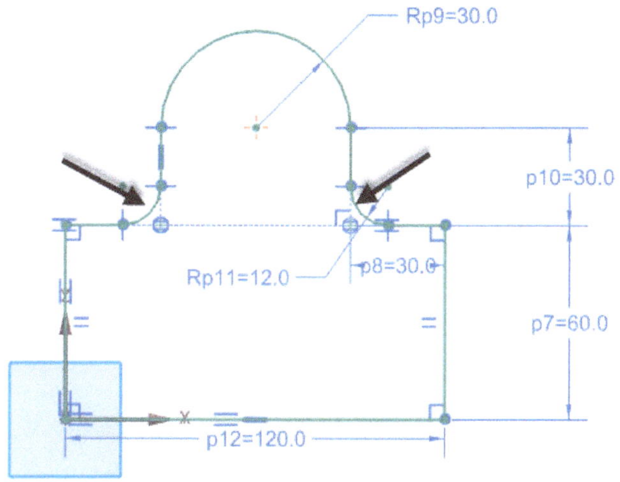

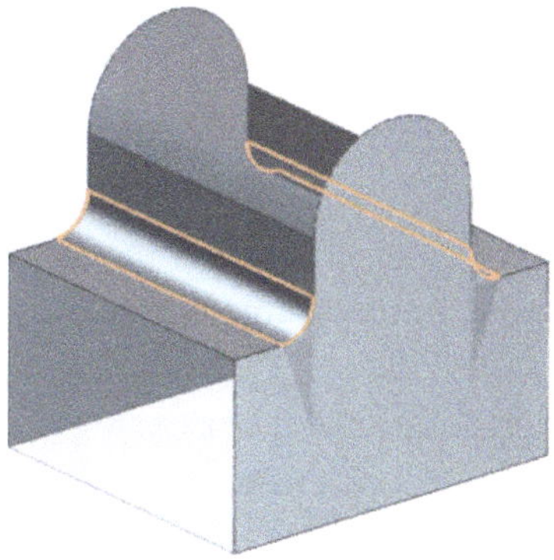

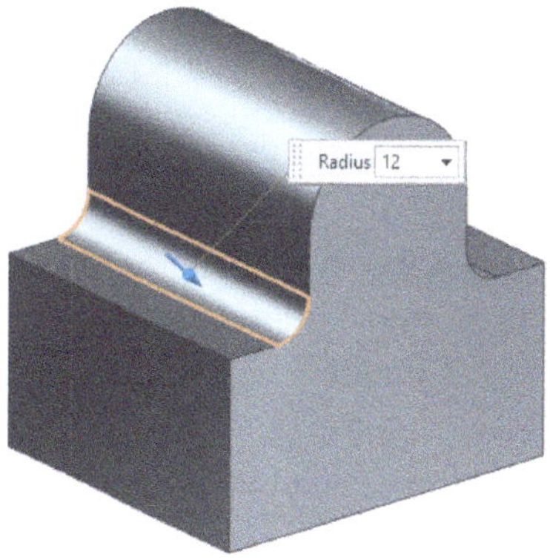

Reorder Blends

This command changes the order of intersecting blends. For example, if the blend 'B' overflows blend 'A,' then the **Reorder Blends** command results in blend 'A 'overflowing blend 'B.' Activate this command (click **Home > Synchronous Modeling > More > Detail Feature > Reorder Blends** on the ribbon) and click on the intersecting portion of the blends. Next, click **OK**.

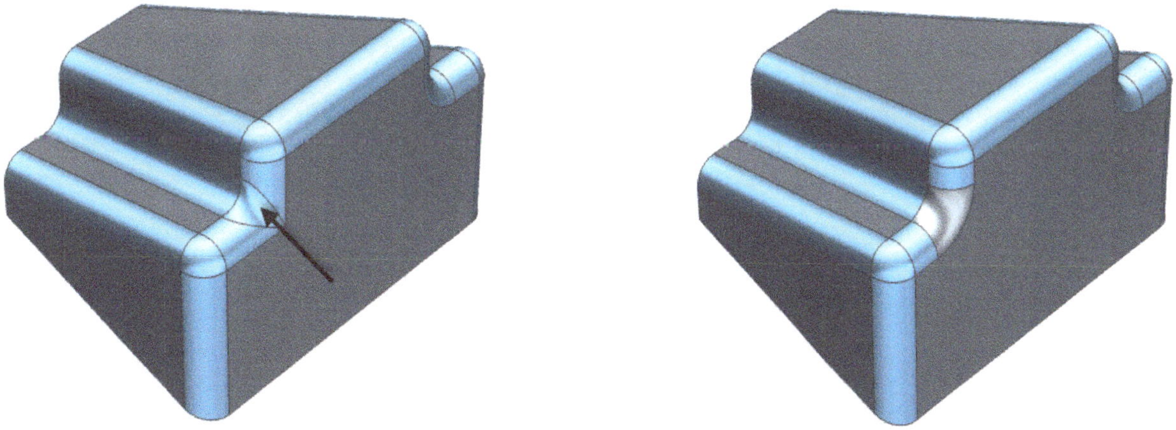

Label Chamfer

This command recognizes a bevel face as a chamfer. Activate this command (click **Home > Synchronous Modeling > More > Detail Feature > Label Chamfer** on the ribbon), and then select a bevel face. Click **OK** to recognize the selected face as a chamfer.

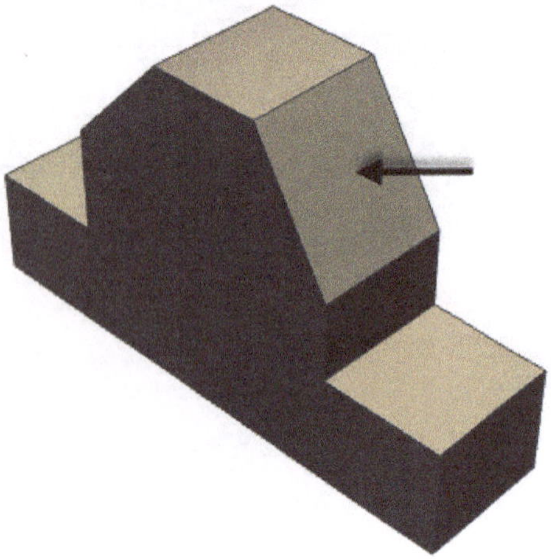

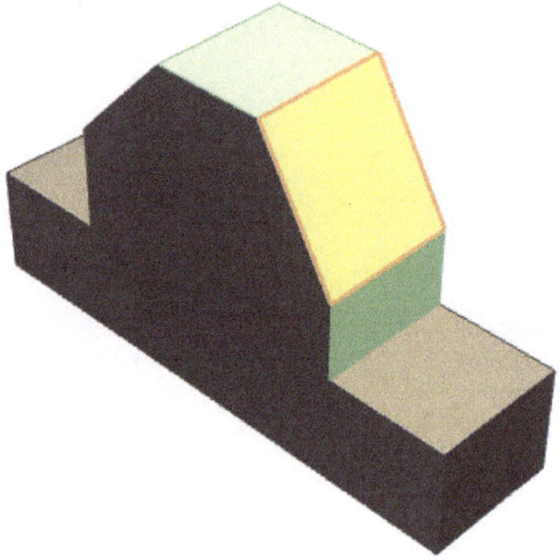

Resize Chamfer

This command changes the size of a chamfer. Activate this command (click **Home > Synchronous Modeling > More > Detail Feature > Resize Chamfer** on the ribbon), and then select a chamfer. On the **Resize Chamfer** dialog, set the **Cross-Section** type and specify the chamfer offset. For example, if you set the **Cross-Section** to **Symmetric Offset**, then you have to specify only one offset. Click **OK** to make the changes.

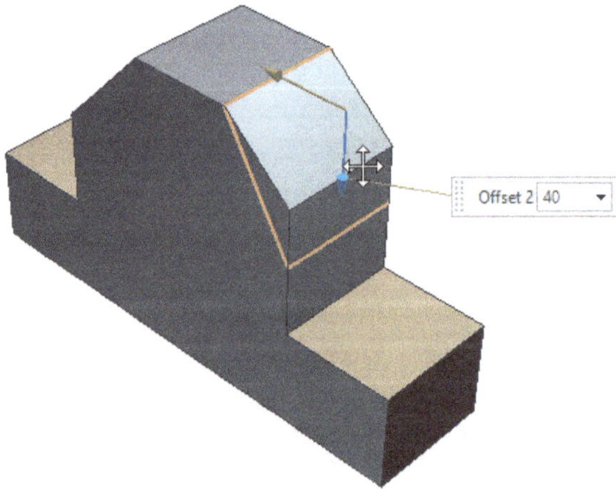

Make Tangent

The **Make Tangent** command (click **Home > Synchronous Modeling > More > Relate > Make Tangent** on the ribbon) makes two faces tangent to one another.

Radial Dimension

The **Radial Dimension** command (click **Home > Synchronous Modeling > More > Dimension > Radial Dimension** on the ribbon) modifies a cylindrical face by adding a dimension and changing its value.

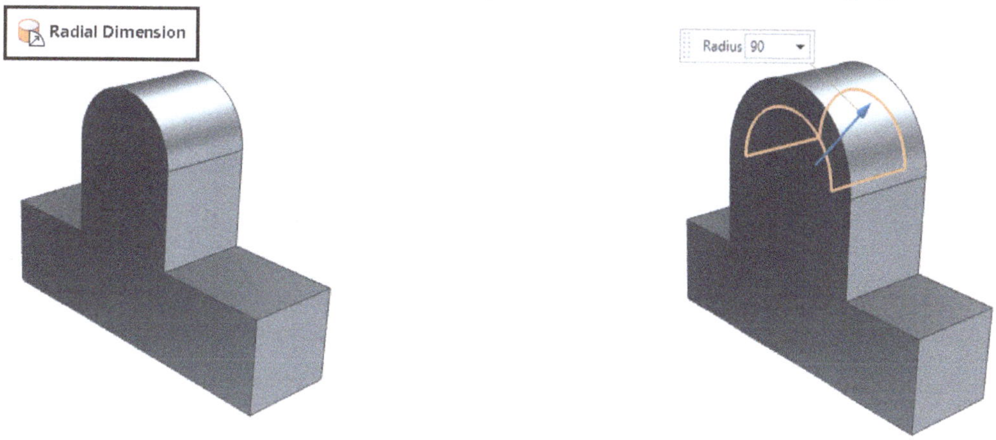

Radiate Face

The **Radiate Face** command (click **Home > Synchronous Modeling > More > Move > Radiate Face** on the ribbon) changes the diameter of a cylindrical face about its axis.

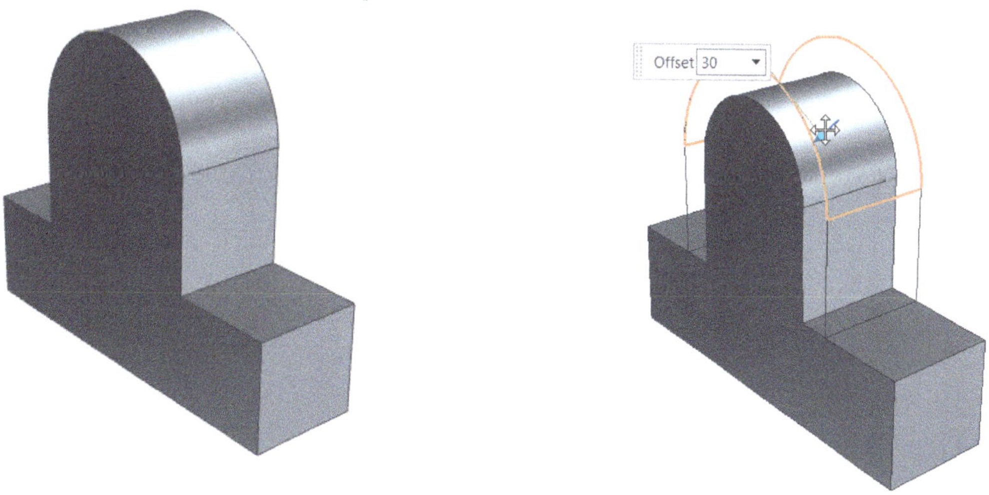

Edit Cross Section

If you want to create live sections and edit them, then activate the **Edit Cross Section** command (click **Home > Synchronous Modeling > More > Move > Edit Cross Section**) and select the faces on the model. On the **Edit Cross Section** dialog, click **Select Plane** and click on a datum plane to create the cross-section.

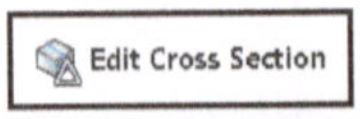

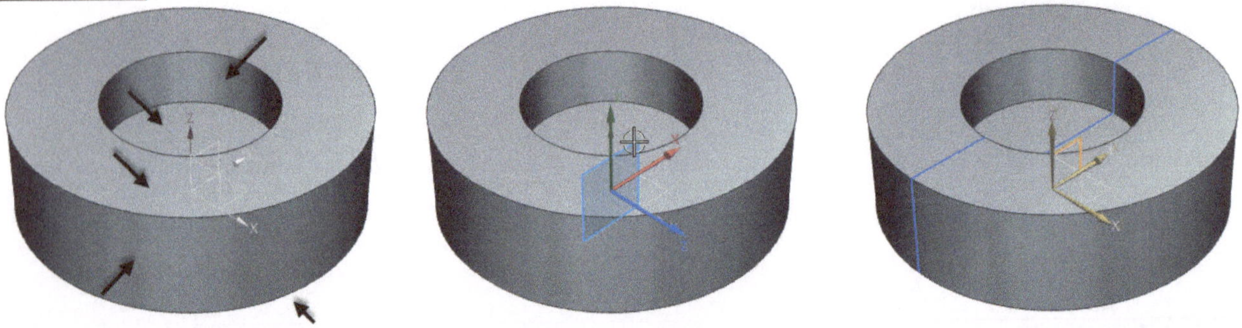

Now, click the **Edit Section Curve** button on the **Edit Cross Section** dialog to edit the cross-section. You can now drag the sketch elements or apply relations and dimensions to the sketch. After editing the sketch, click **Finish** on the ribbon, and then click **OK**.

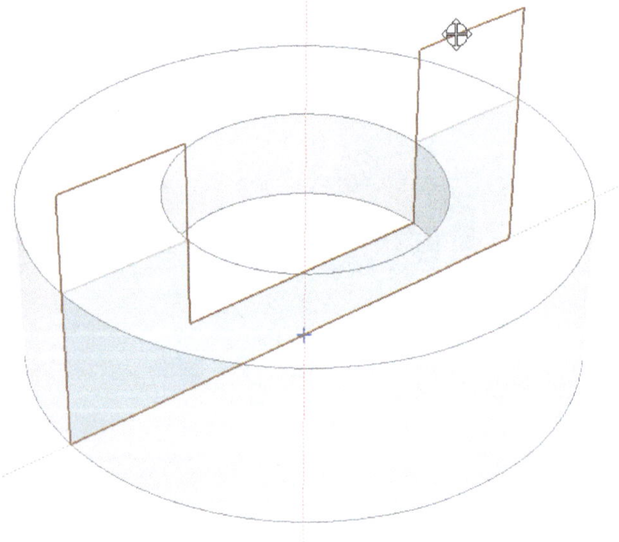

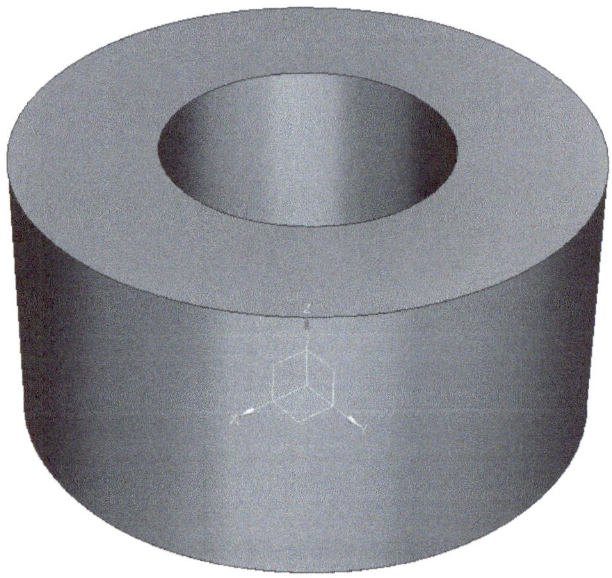

Delete

This command deletes the selected set of faces and adjusts the side faces. Activate this command (click **Home > Synchronous Modeling > Delete**  on the ribbon) and select **Type > Face** on the **Delete Face** dialog. Next, select the faces to delete. If you want to replace the deleted face with another face, then click **Select Face** under the **Cap Face** section, and then select a face to use as healing.

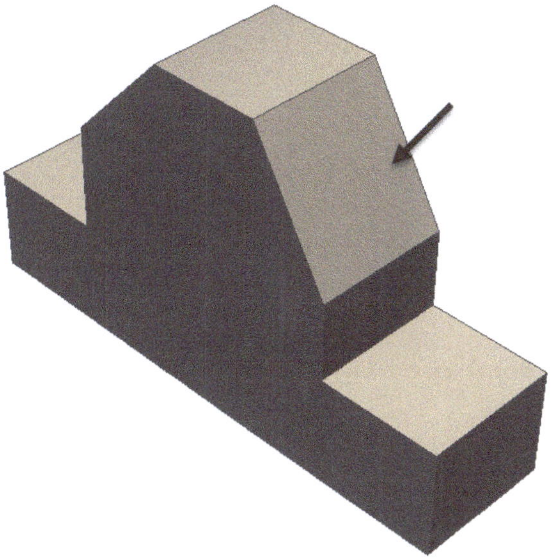

If you want to delete holes within a specific range of size, then select **Type > Hole** on the **Delete Face** dialog and type-in a value in the **Hole Size <=** box. Now, select a hole within the size range. You will notice the entire holes within the size range will be selected. Click **OK** to delete the holes.

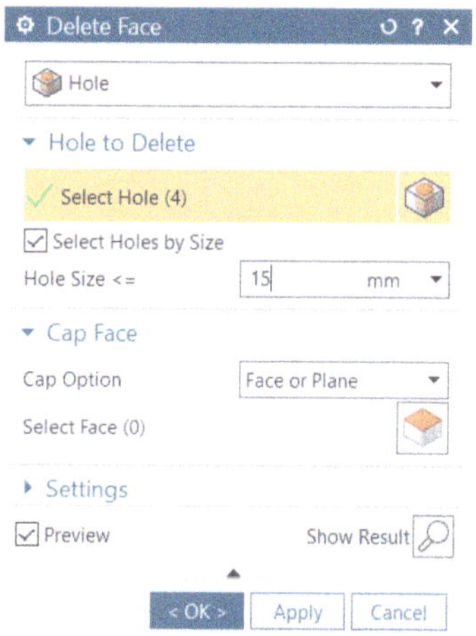

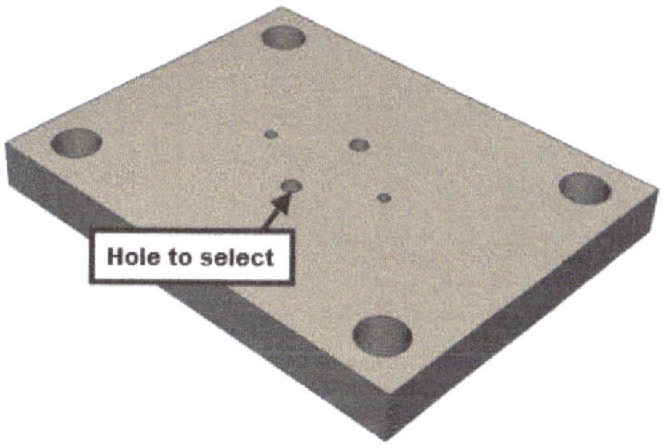

Likewise, you can delete blends using the **Blend Size** option.

Group Face

This command groups the selected set of faces. Activate this command (click **Home > Synchronous Modeling > More > Relate > Group Face** on the ribbon) and click on one or more faces. You can also drag a selection box to select multiple faces. Click **OK** to create a group. You can now copy and paste this group.

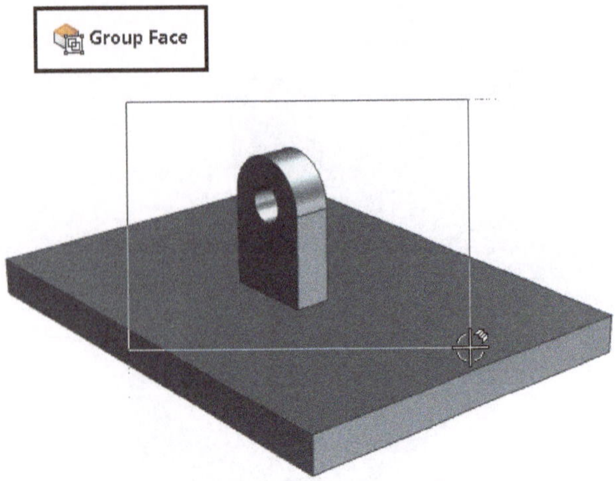

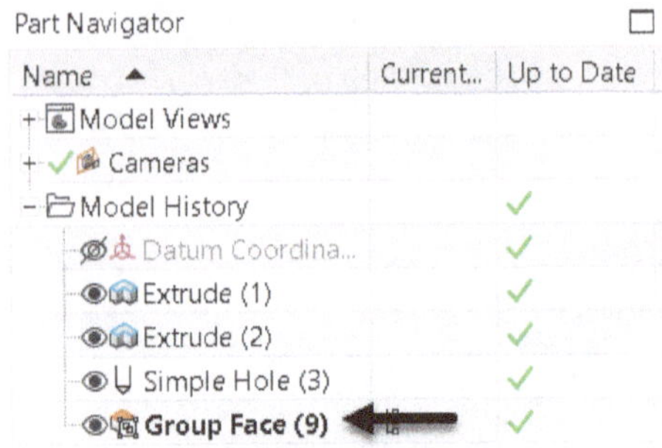

Copy Face

This command copies the selected set of faces or a group. Activate this command (click **Home > Synchronous Modeling > More > Reuse > Copy Face** on the ribbon) and select a face or group of faces. Click on the origin of the OrientXpress Tool to display the axes. Select axes to define the direction in which you want to move the copy.

Drag the arrow that appears on the selected set and click **OK**.

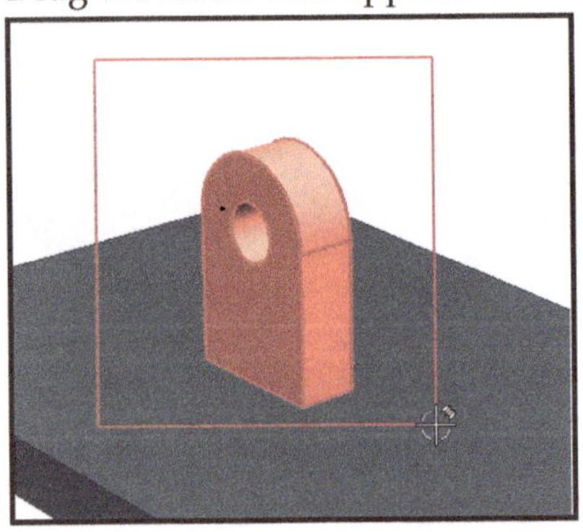

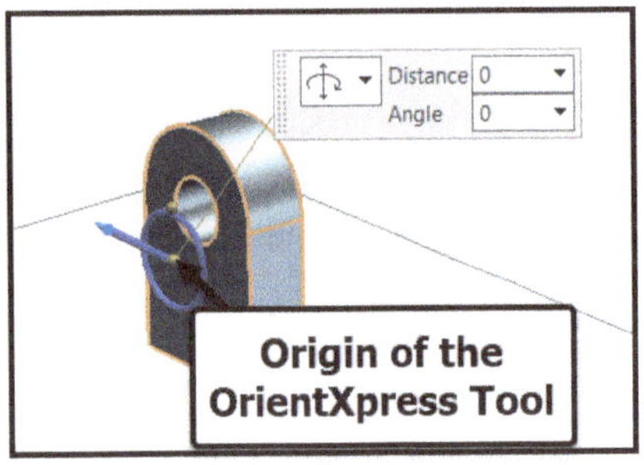

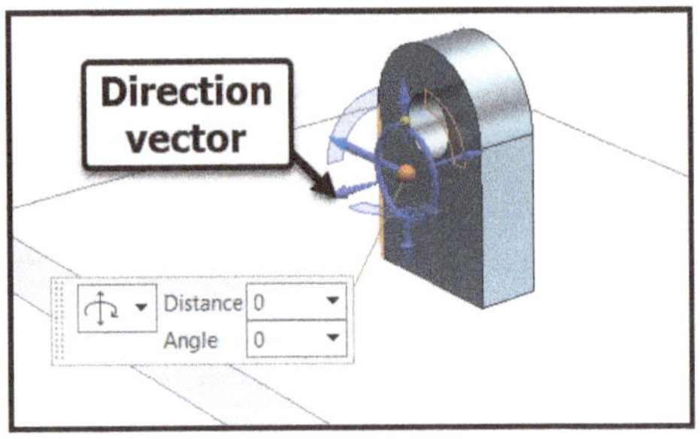

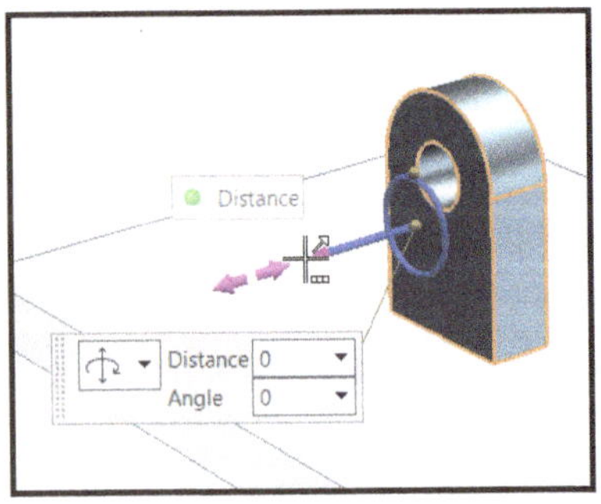

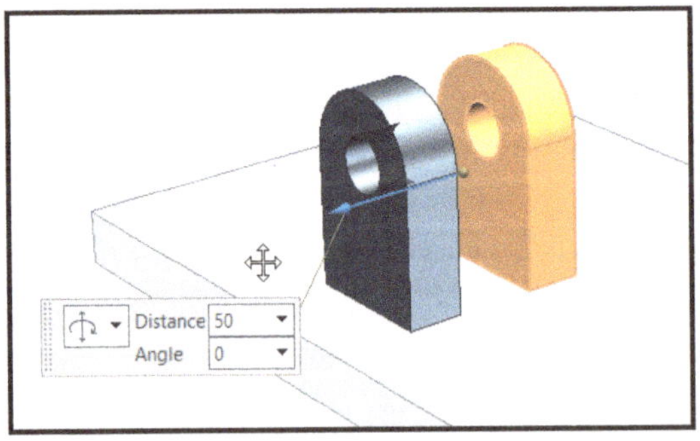

Paste Face

This command adds or subtracts a sheet body (surface body without any physical properties) to the model geometry. Activate this command (click **Home > Synchronous Modeling > More > Reuse > Paste Face**) and select the target body (solid). Next, click on the sheet body, and then click **OK**.

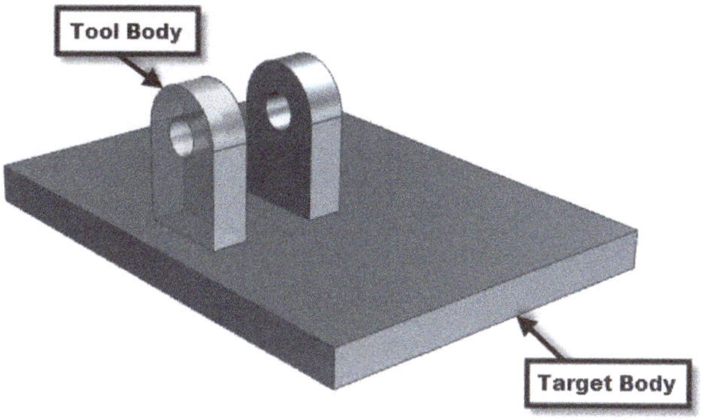

Mirror Face

This command copies and mirrors the selected set of faces across a plane. Activate this command (click **Home > Synchronous Modeling > More > Reuse > Mirror Face** on the ribbon) and select the faces connected to each other. You can drag a selection box to select multiple faces at a time. Next, on the **Mirror Face** dialog, under the **Mirror Plane** section, click **Select Plane**, and then select a datum plane. Click **OK** to mirror the faces.

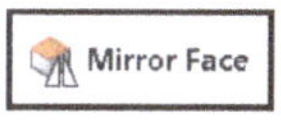

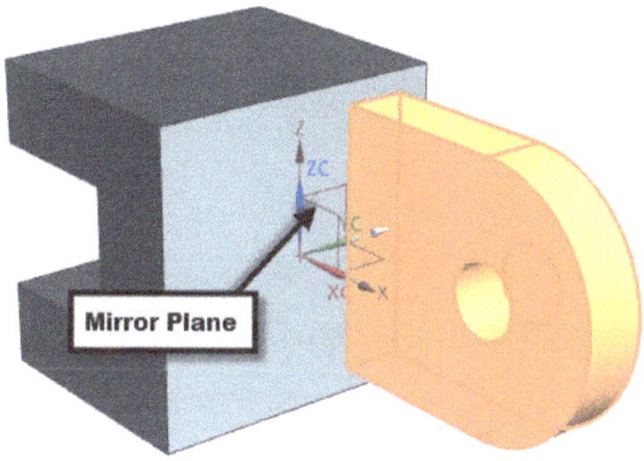

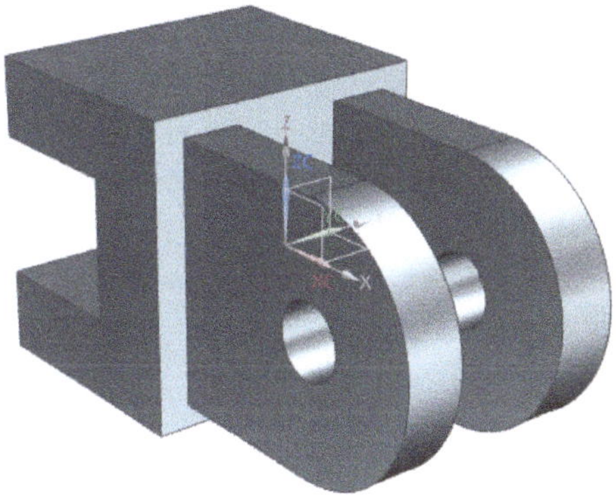

Examples

Example 1 (Millimetres)

In this example, you will create the part shown below, and then modify it using the Synchronous Modeling tools.

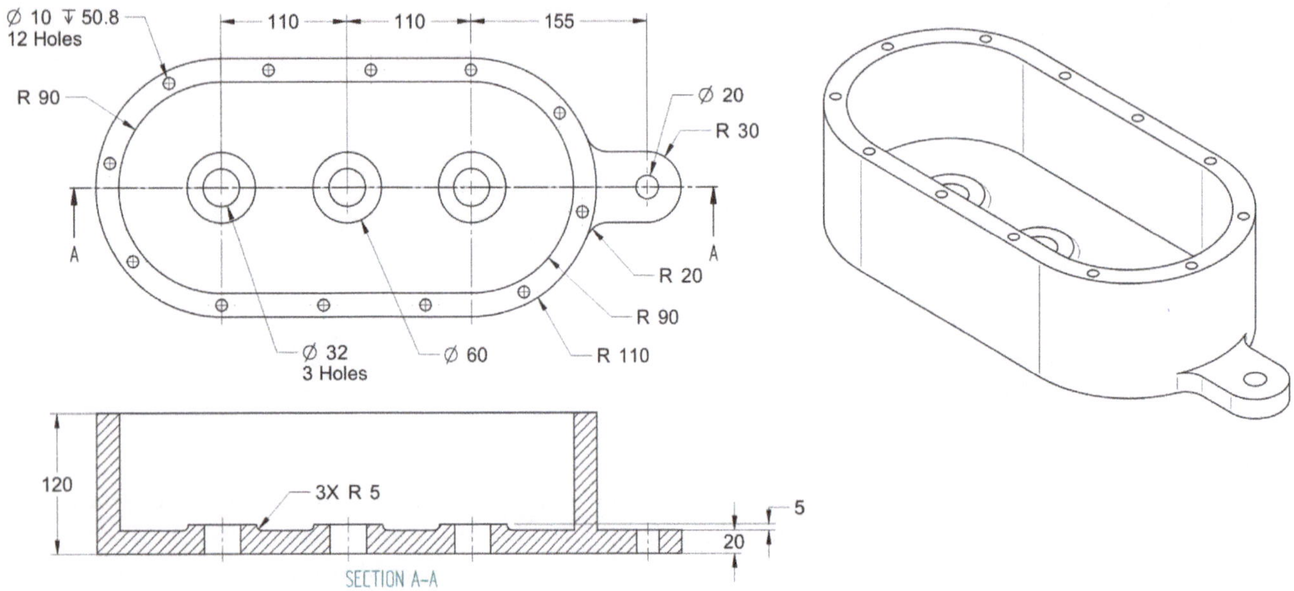

1. Start **NX** and open a part file using the **Model** template
2. Create the part using the tools and commands in NX. You can also download the part from the companion website.
3. Click on the 20 mm diameter hole. The context toolbar appears on the hole.
4. On the context toolbar, click **Edit with Rollback** to open the **Hole** dialog.
5. On the **Hole** dialog, set the hole **Type** to **Counterbored**. Set the **C-Bore Diameter** to 30 and **C-Bore Depth** to 10. Set the **Depth Limit** to **Through Body** and click **OK** to close the dialog.

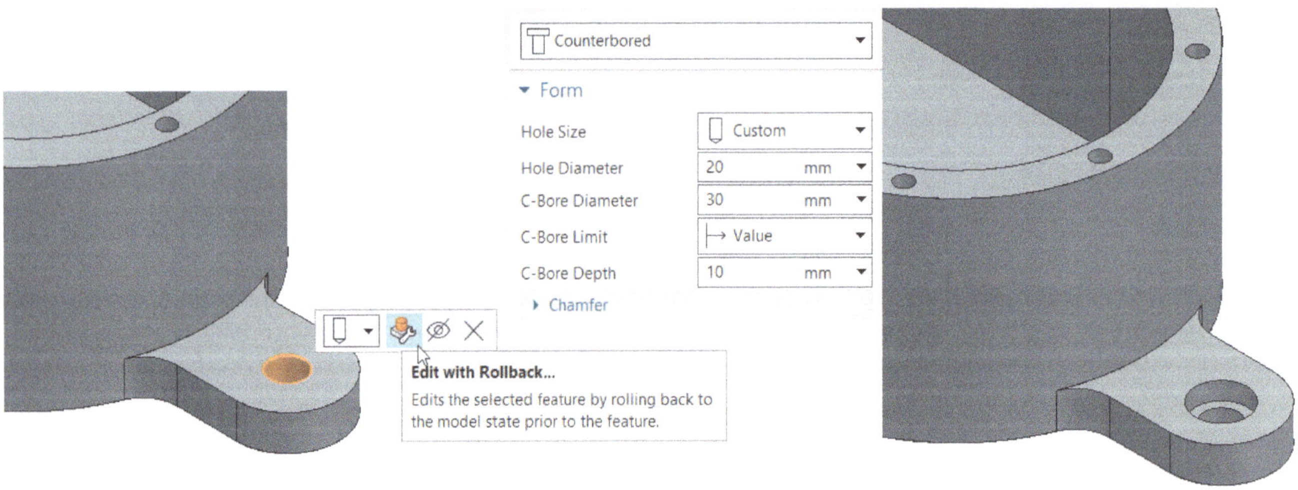

6. Activate the **Move** command (on the ribbon, click **Home > Synchronous Modeling > Move**) and click on the counterbore hole.
7. On the **Move Face** dialog, under the **Face Finder** section, select **Coaxial**.

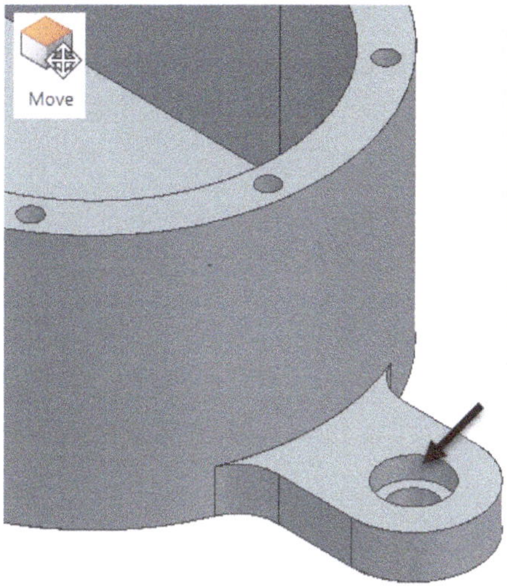

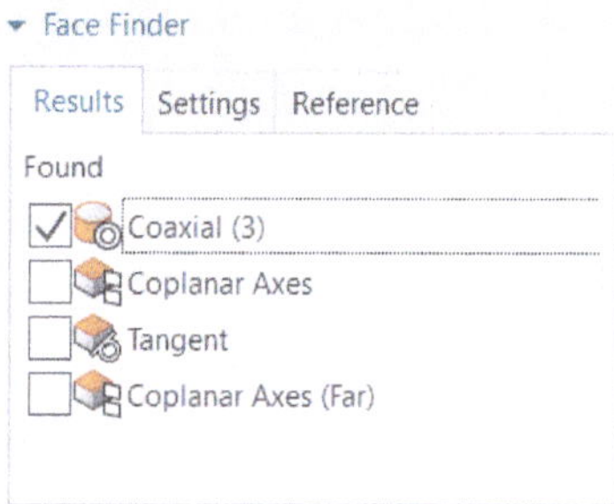

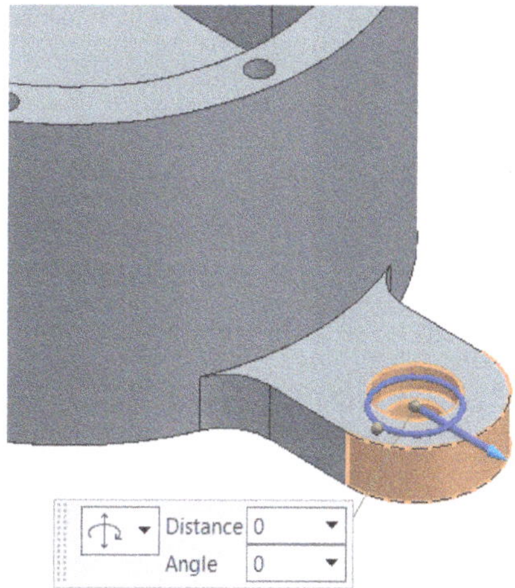

8. Drag the arrow that appears on the selected set, and then type-in 20 in the **Distance** box. Click **OK** on the dialog.

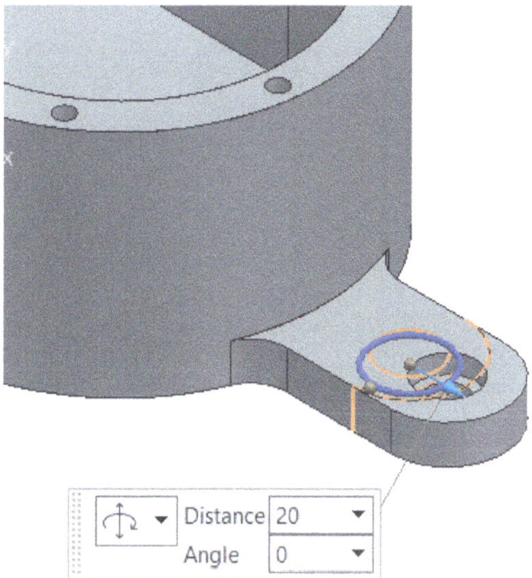

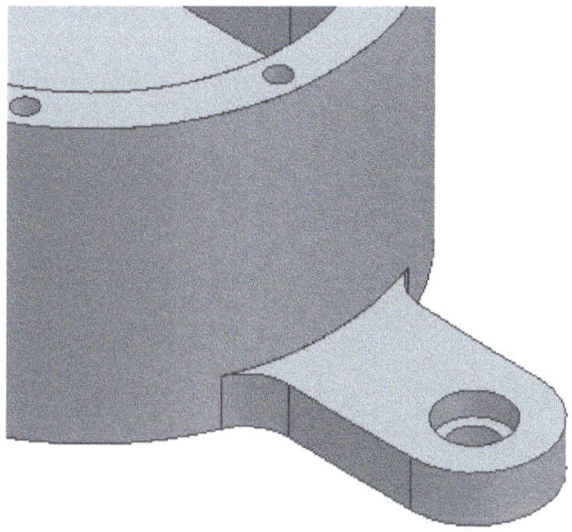

9. Activate the **Move** command and click on the side face of the bottom feature.
10. On the **Move** dialog, under the **Results** tab, check the **Symmetric** option.
11. Under the **Transform** section, select **Motion > Angle**.

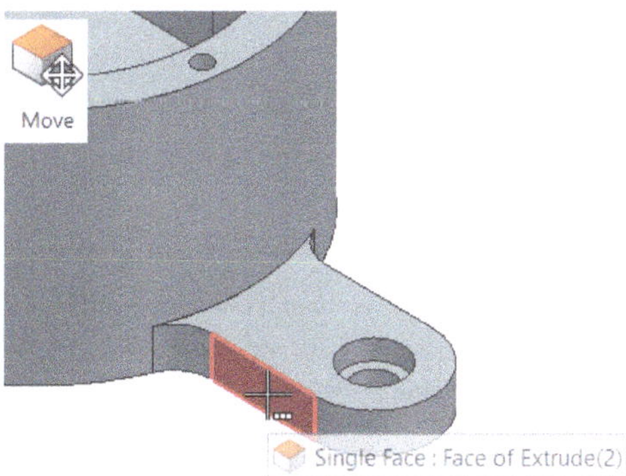

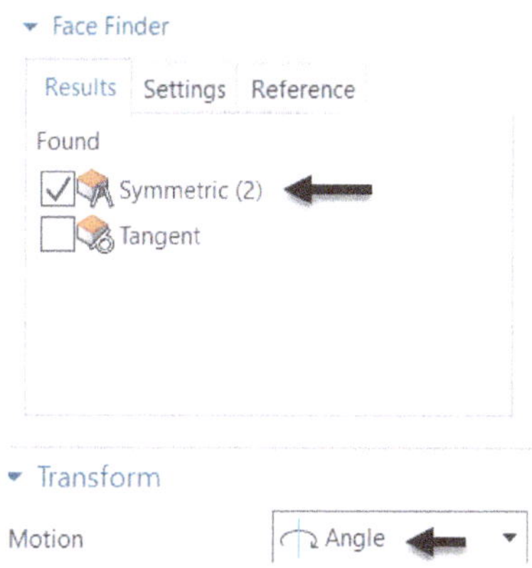

12. Click on the Z-axis vector to define the rotation axis, and then click on the vertex shown in the figure.

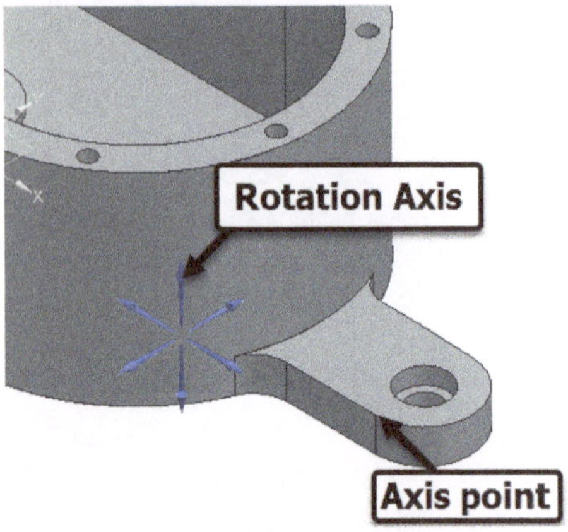

13. Click the spear handle and drag it.
14. Type-in 20 in the **Angle** box that appears on the geometry. Click **OK** to rotate the faces.

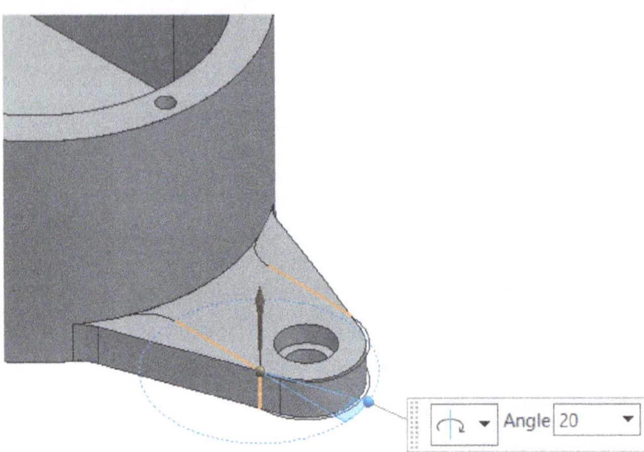

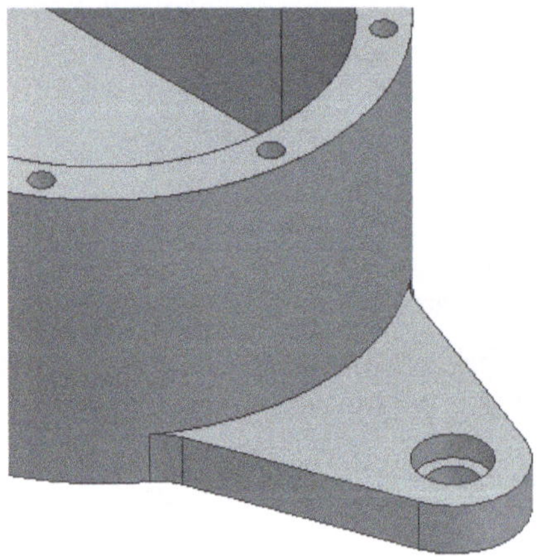

15. Select a hole from the **Pattern Feature (Along)** and select **Edit Parameters**.
16. On the **Pattern Feature** dialog, type-in 14 in the **Count** box and click **OK** to update the pattern.

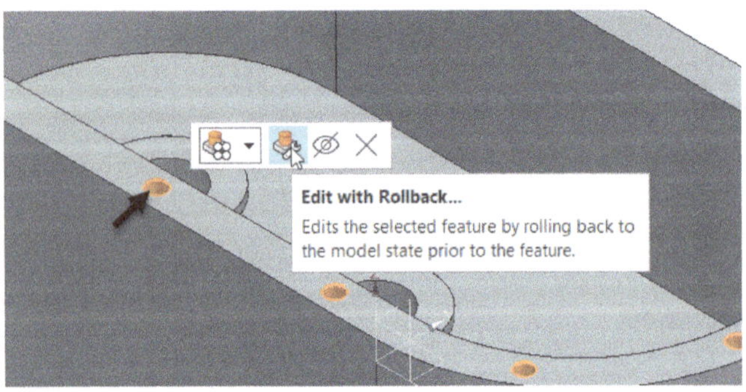

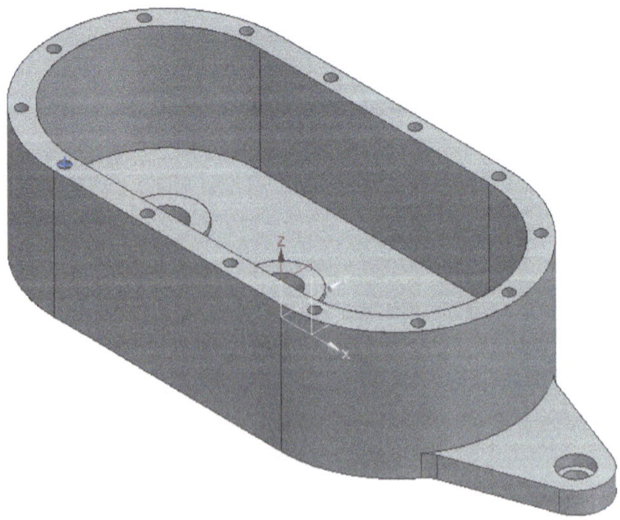

17. Activate the **Group Face** command (click **Home > Synchronous Modeling > More > Relate > Group Face**).

18. On the Part Navigator, select the **Pattern Feature** and **Simple Hole.**
19. Click on the top face of the geometry and click **OK**.

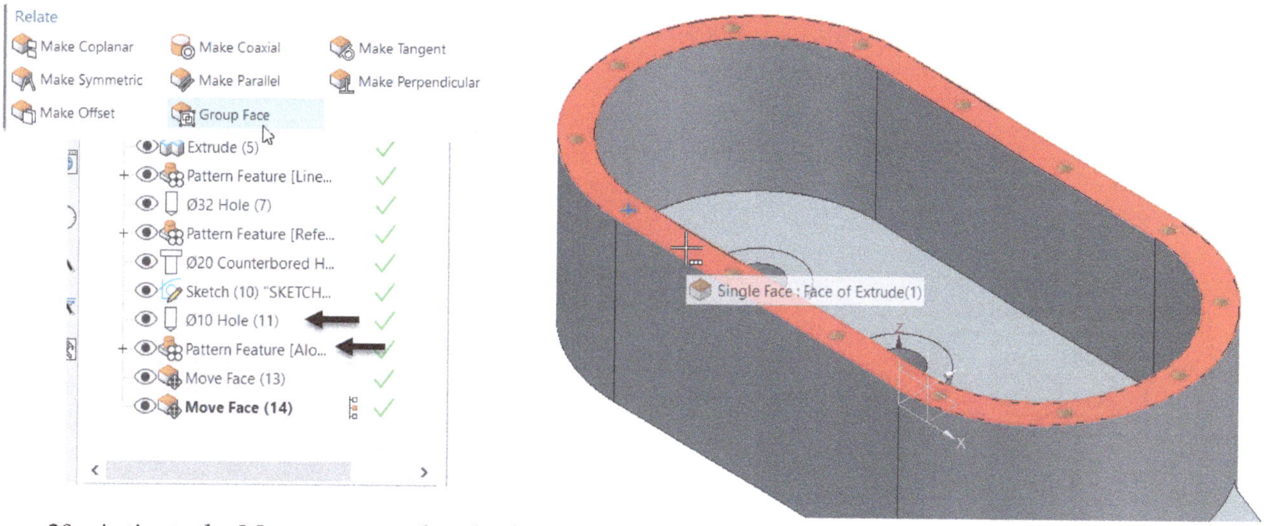

20. Activate the **Move** command and select **Group Face** from the **Part Navigator**.
21. On the **Move Face** dialog, select **Transform > Motion > Distance** and select the Z-axis vector.
22. Type-in -40 in the **Distance** box and click **OK** to update the model.

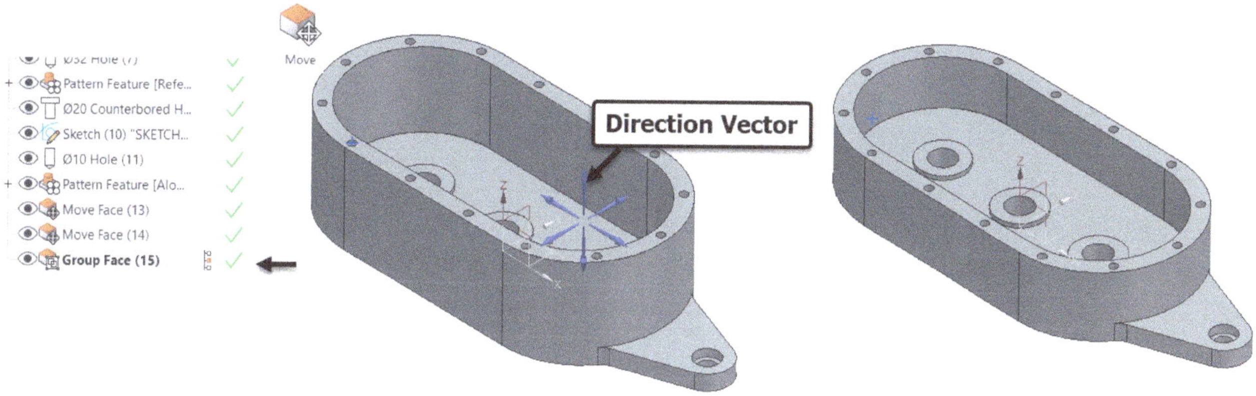

23. Save and close the file.

Questions

1. List any two face relationships.
2. List the uses of the **Move** command
3. How do you delete holes using the **Delete** command?
4. How do you modify revolved features using the **Edit Cross Section** command?
5. What is the difference between the **Make Offset** and **Offset Region** command?

Exercises

Exercise 1

Initial Part

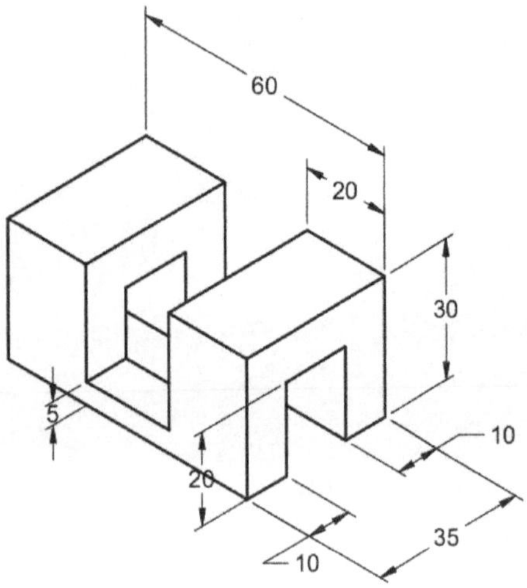

Modified Part

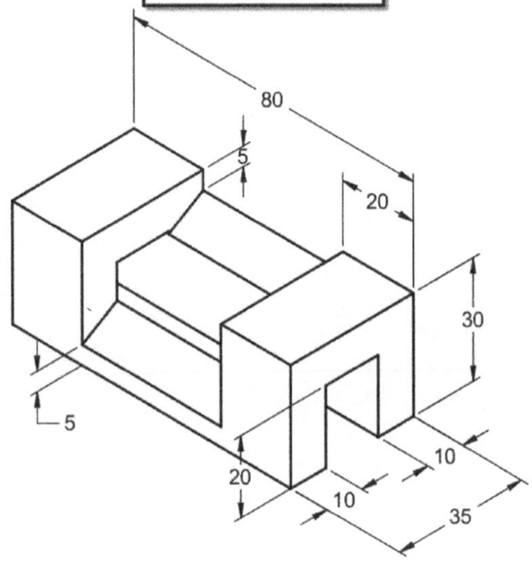

Chapter 8: Assemblies

After creating individual components, you can bring them together into an assembly. By doing so, it is possible to identify incorrect design problems that may not have been noticeable at the part level. In this chapter, you will learn how to bring components into the assembly environment and position them.

The topics covered in this chapter are:

- *Starting an assembly*
- *Inserting Components*
- *Adding Constraints*
- *Moving components*
- *Check Interference*
- *Remember Constraints*
- *Editing Assemblies*
- *Replace Components*
- *Pattern and Mirror Components*
- *Create Subassemblies*
- *Assembly Features*
- *Top-down Assembly Design*
- *Create Exploded Views*

Starting an Assembly

To begin an assembly file, you can use the **New** icon and select the **Assembly** template. Next, click **OK** to start the assembly file; the **Assemble** dialog appears on the screen.

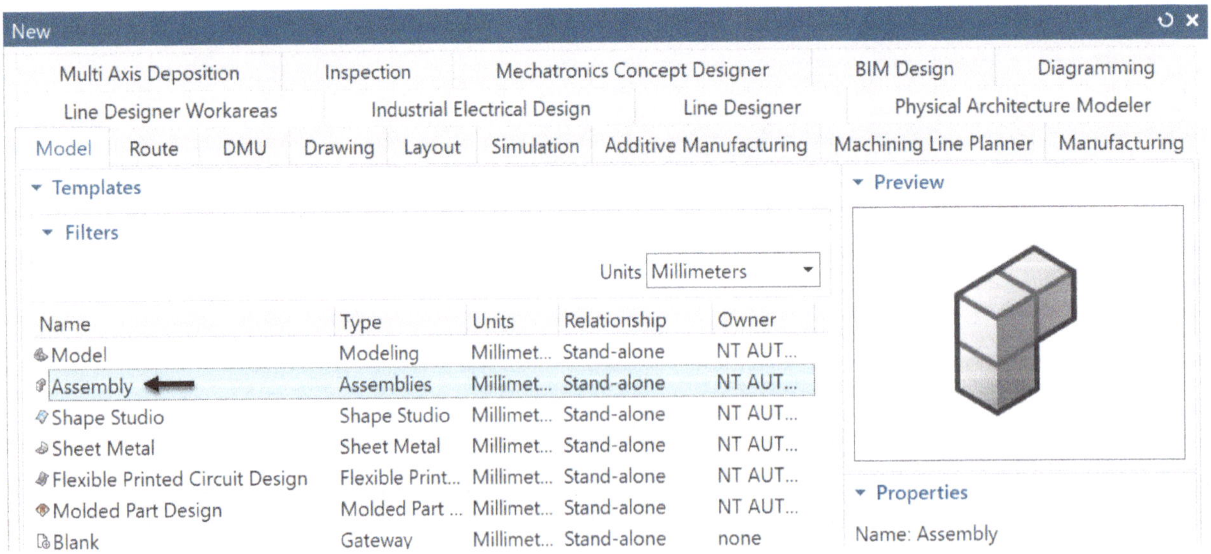

Now, you can insert components into the assembly by using the **Assemble** dialog. You can browse to the location of the components by using the **Open**  icon available on the **Assemble** dialog.

Another way to start an assembly is to create it while a part is open using tools available on the **Assemblies** tab of the ribbon. On the ribbon, click **Application > Design > Toolbox drop-down > Assemblies** if the **Assemblies** tab is not displayed.

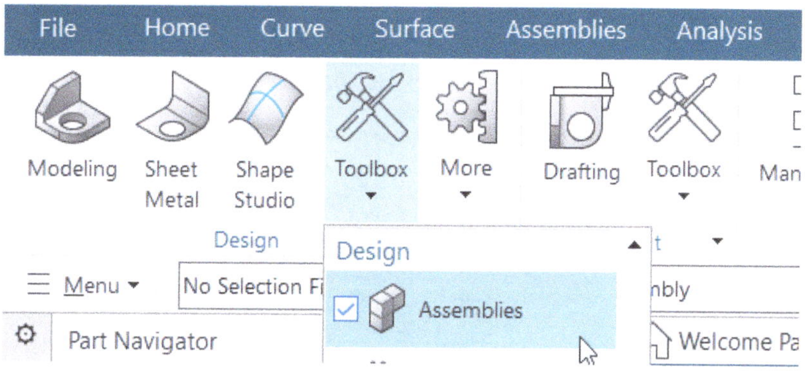

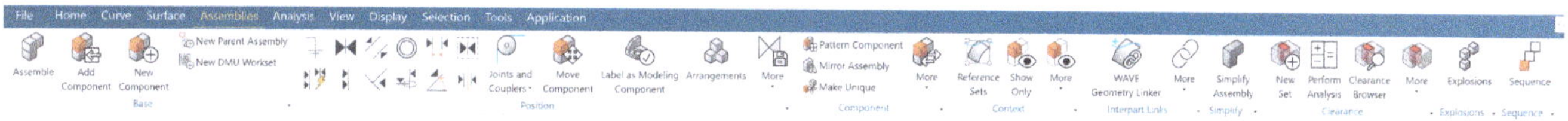

Inserting Components

There are two different methods to insert an existing part into an assembly. The first one is to insert using the **Assemble** dialog. The second way is to drag it directly from **Windows Explorer**. In the second method, you are not required to open the components in NX. You can simply drag-and-drop them into the assembly.

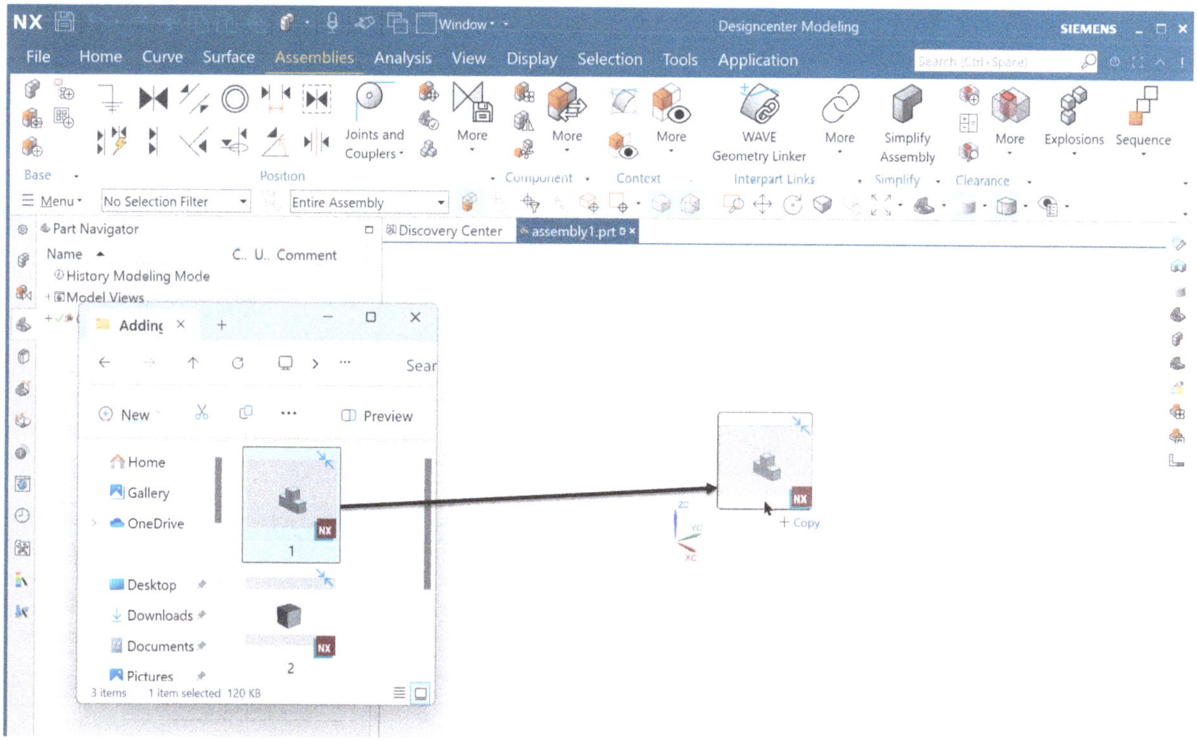

Add Component command

Activate the **Add Component** command (on the ribbon, click **Assemblies > Base > Add Component**) and click **Open** on the **Add Component** dialog. Go to the location of the first component and double-click on it. On the **Add Component** dialog, select **Location > Assembly Location > WCS** and click **OK** to position the component at the origin; the **Create Fix Constraint** message box appears. Click **Yes** on the **Create Fix Constraint** dialog to fix the component at the origin.

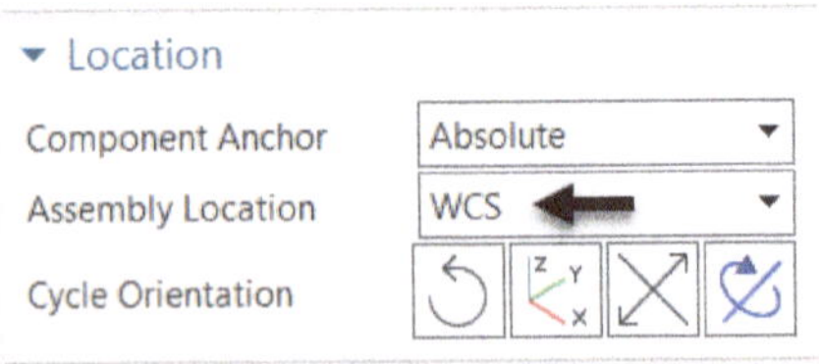

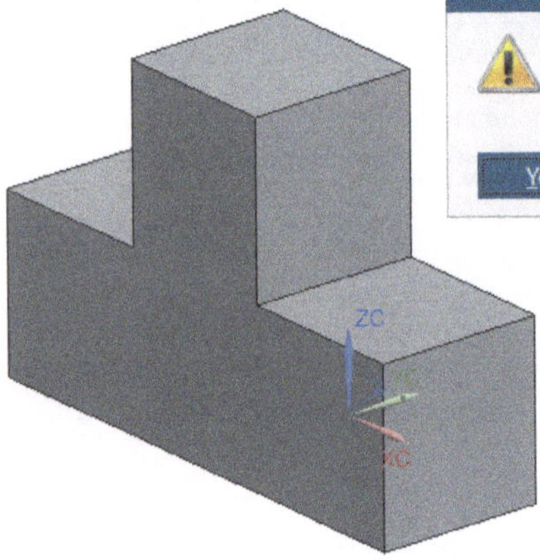

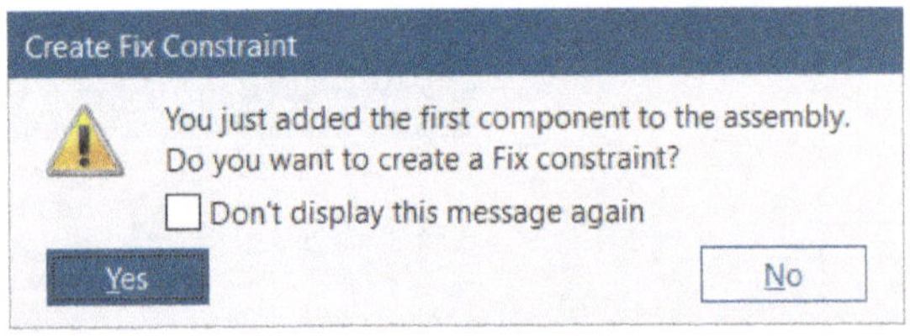

If you click the **NO** button, the component is placed at the origin, but it is free to move. You can check the degrees of freedom by using the **Show Degrees of Freedom** command. Activate this command (On the ribbon, click **Assemblies > Position > More > Show Degrees of Freedom**) and select the component to display the degrees of freedom.

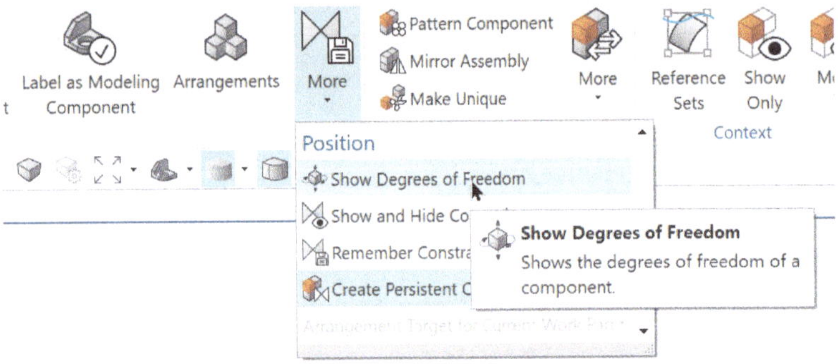

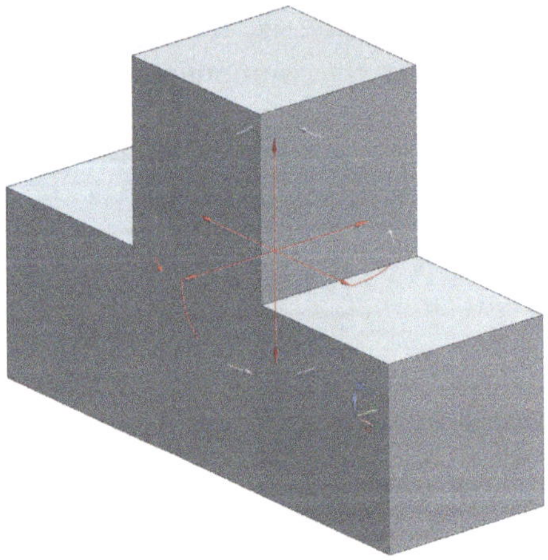

To remove the degrees of freedom, activate the **Fix** command (on the ribbon, click **Assemblies > Position > Fix**). Click on the first component. Click **OK** on the **Fix** dialog. Now, activate the **Show Degrees of Freedom** command and select the component. You can notice that the component is fixed at the origin.

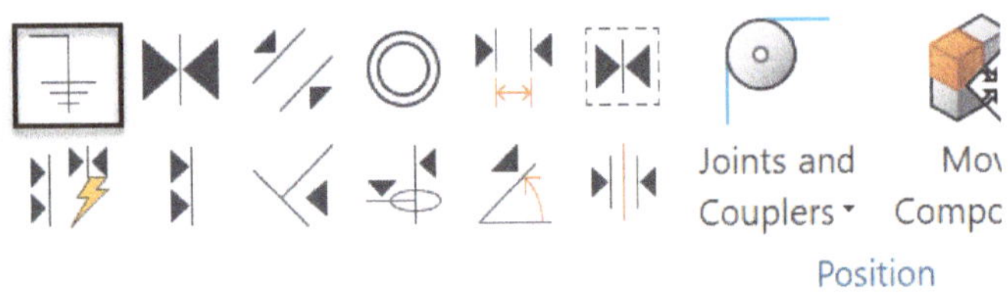

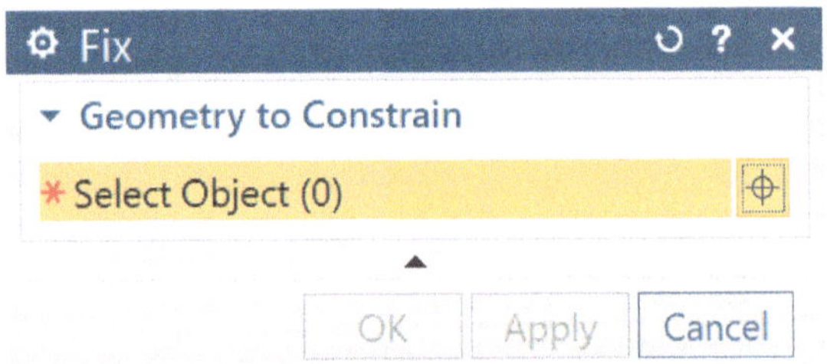

Note: Click ***Menu > View > Operation > Refresh*** *to update the view after applying the constraint.*

Now, activate the **Add Component** command and click the **Open** button on the **Add Component** dialog. Go to the location of the second component and double-click on it; the component is inserted into the assembly.

Move Component

On the **Add Component** dialog, under the **Placement** section, select the **Specify Orientation** option. Now, use the Dynamic CSYS to move the part. For example, to move the part in the X-direction, select the **XC** handle and move the part (press and hold the left mouse button and drag the pointer).

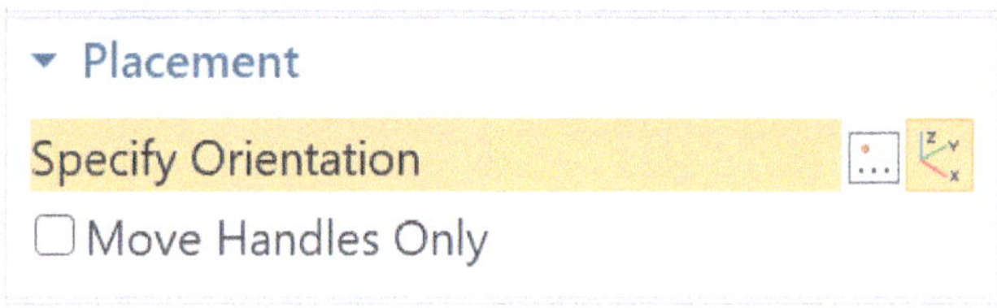

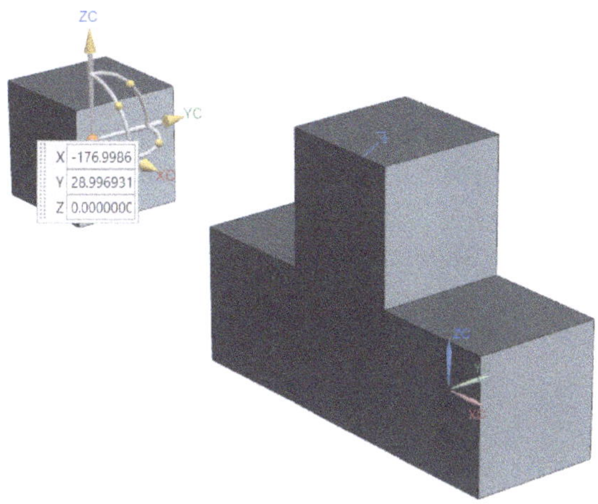

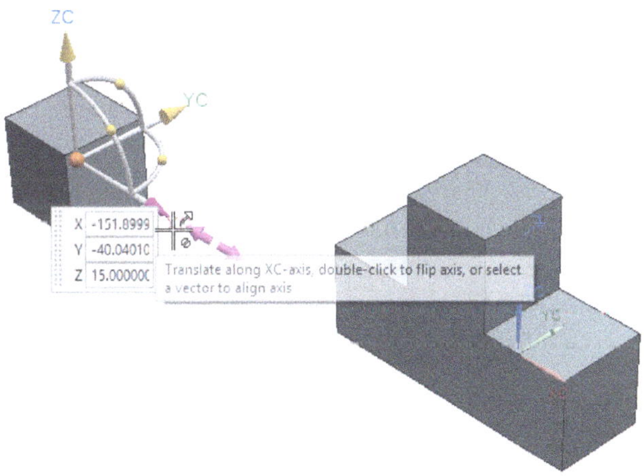

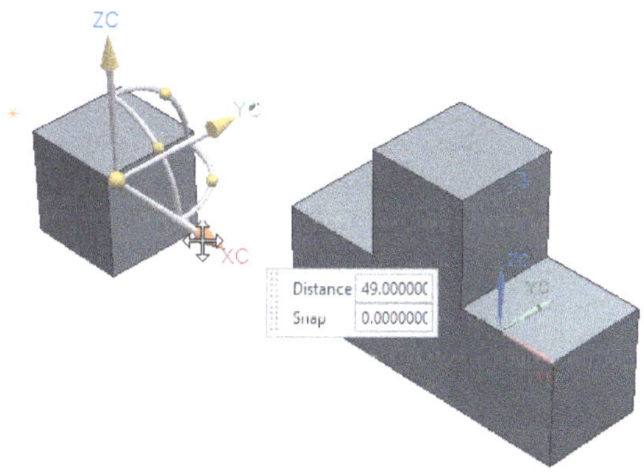

Use the rotate handles on the Dynamic CSYS to rotate the part about an axis. For example, to rotate the part about the X-axis, select the **Rotate about XC-axis** handle and rotate the part (press and hold the left mouse button and drag the pointer)

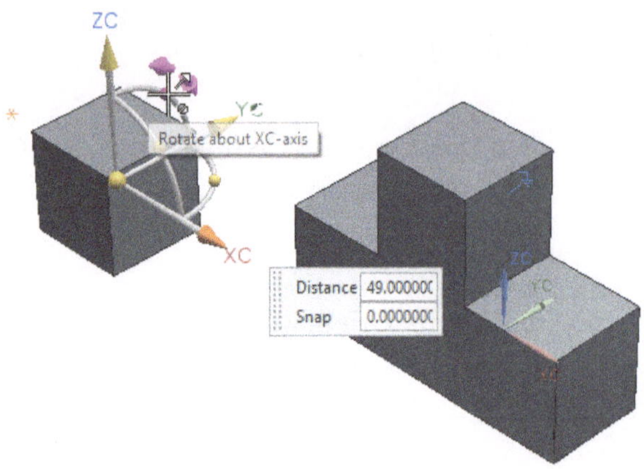

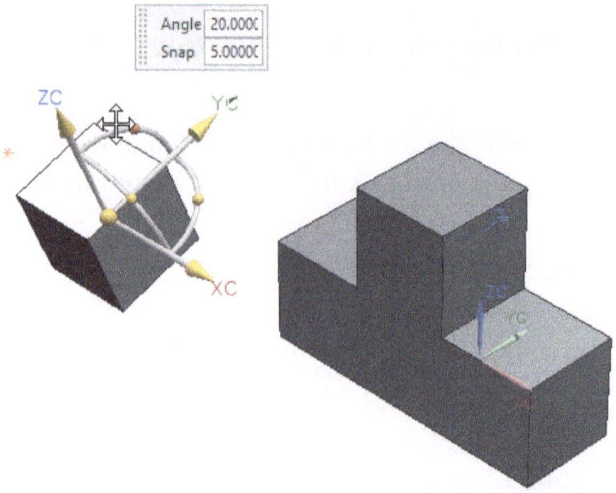

You can also move the component using the **Move Component** command. Add the component to the assembly using the **Add Component** command. Next, click **Assemblies > Position > Move Component** on the ribbon. Select the component to be moved. On the **Move Component** dialog, select **Transform > Motion > Dynamic**. Next, click the **Specify Orientation** option and move the component using the Dynamic Coordinate System. On the **Move Component** dialog, select **Settings > Collision Detection > Collision Action > Highlight Collision**. Now, when the moving part collides with any other part, both the components will be highlighted.

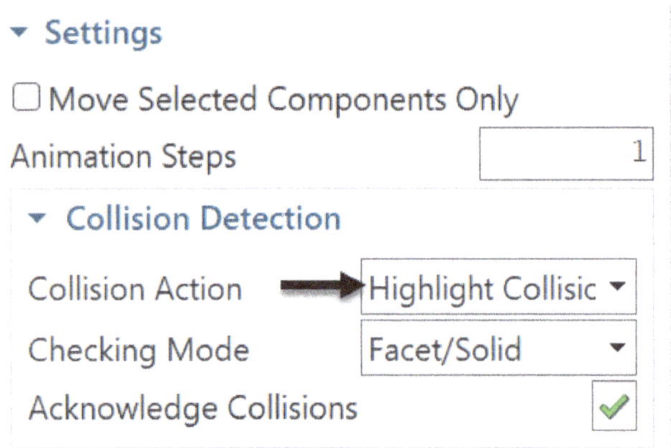

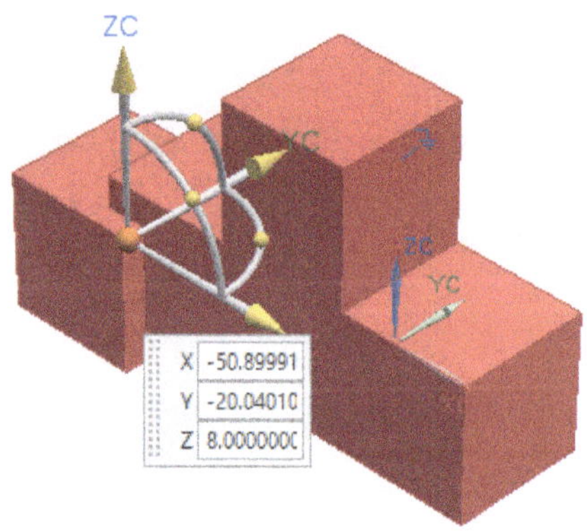

Use the **Stop Before Collision** option to stop the part when it collides with another part.

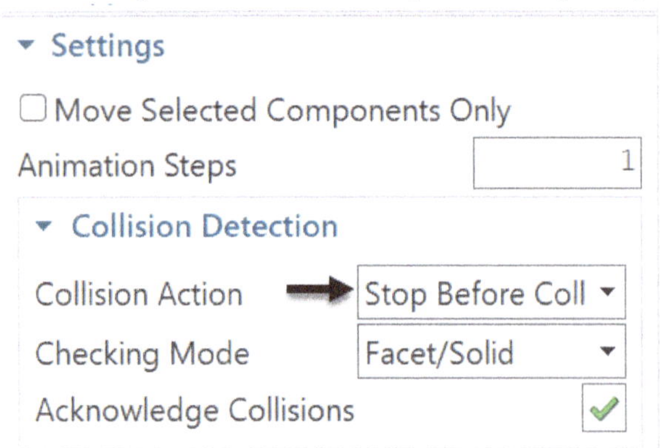

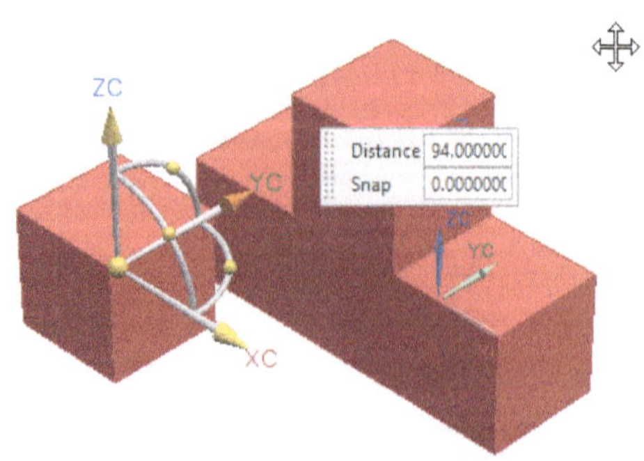

After completing the moving operation, click **OK** on the **Move Component** dialog to close it.

Adding Constraints

After inserting components into an assembly, you have to define constraints between them. By applying constraints, you can make components to flush with each other (or) two cylindrical faces concentric with each other, and so on. As you add constraints between components, the degrees of freedom will be removed from them. By default, there are six degrees of freedom for a part (three linear and three rotational). Eliminating degrees of freedom will make components attached and interact with each other as in real life. Now, you will learn to add constraints between components.

Touch Constraint

The **Touch** constraint makes two faces coincident and opposite to each other. Click **Touch** button in the **Position** group of the **Assemblies** tab of the ribbon. Select the face of the inserted part and then click on the face of the stationary part. The two selected faces will touch each other. Click **OK** on the **Touch** dialog.

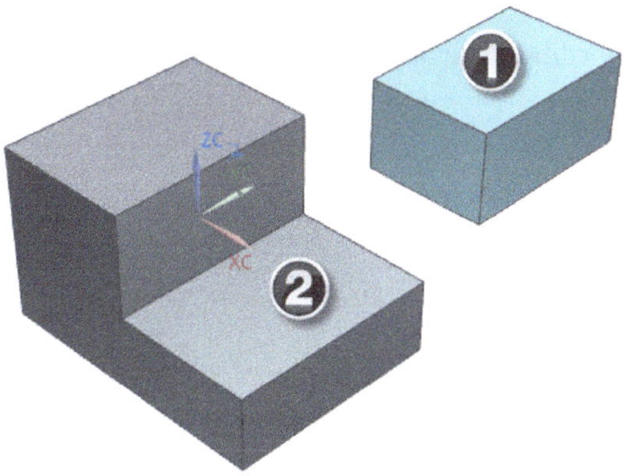

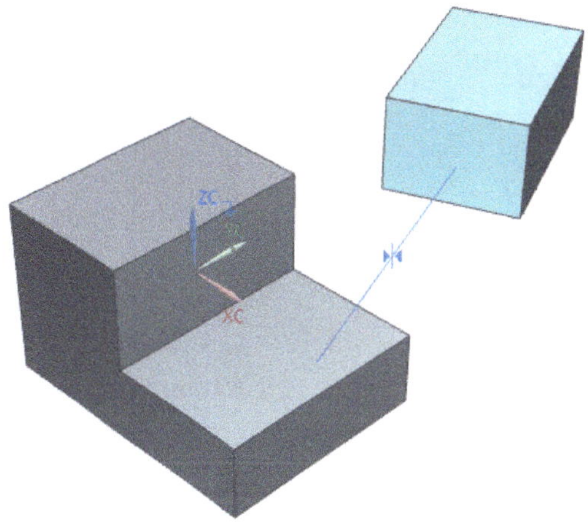

Similarly, select the second set of faces.

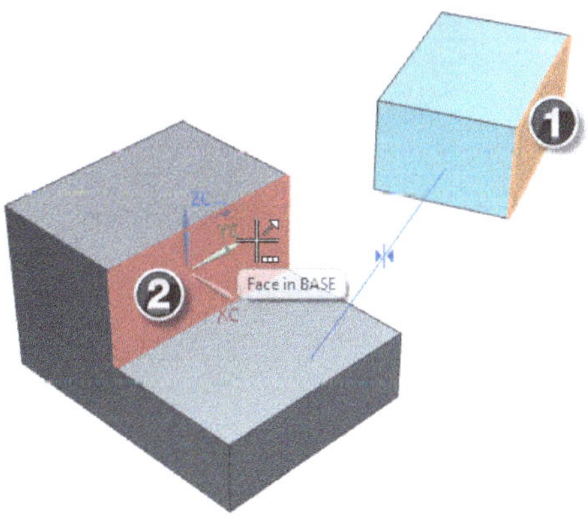

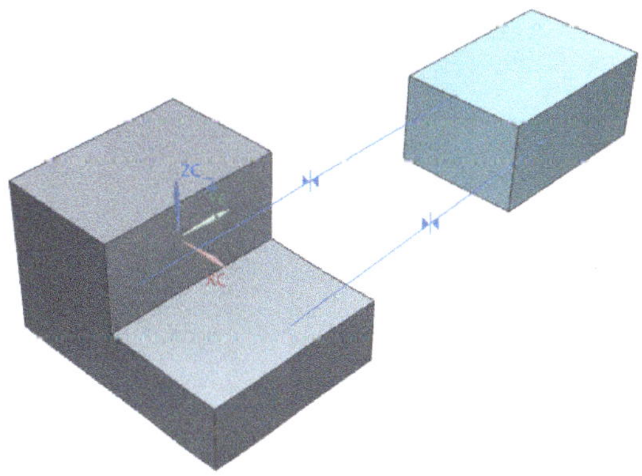

Align Constraint

The **Align** constraint makes two faces flush with each other. To add this constraint, insert the component into the assembly and click **OK** on the **Add Component** dialog. Next, Click **Align** button in the **Position** group of the

Assemblies tab of the ribbon. Select a face on the motion part, and then a face on the stationary part. Click **OK**; the two faces are levelled.

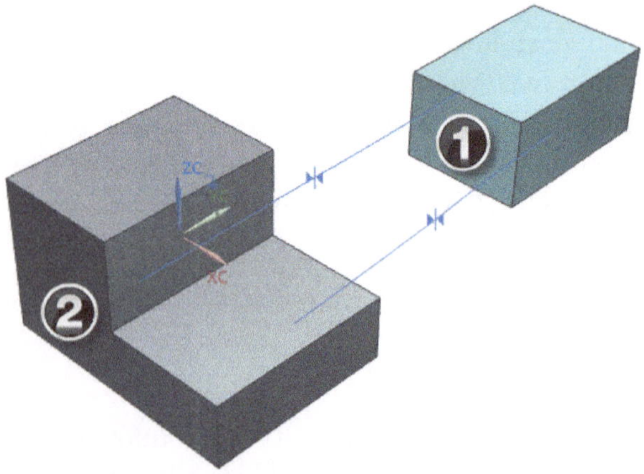

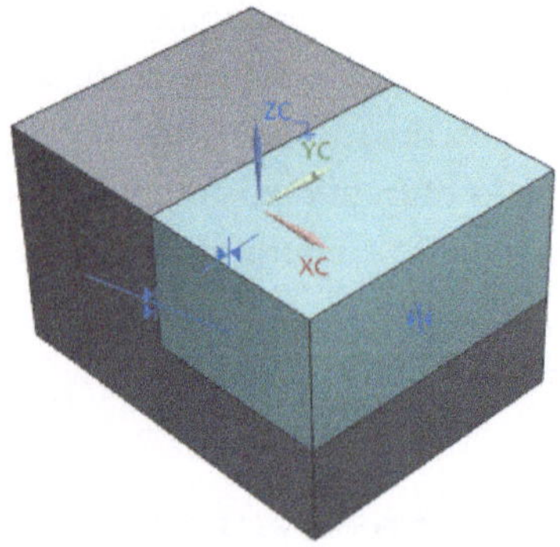

Auto Align

This command applies the **Align**, **Touch, Center/Axis** constraint between the two selected faces. Click **Auto Align**  button in the **Position** group of the **Assemblies** tab of the ribbon. Click on the face to be constrained. Next, click on the face of the fixed part.

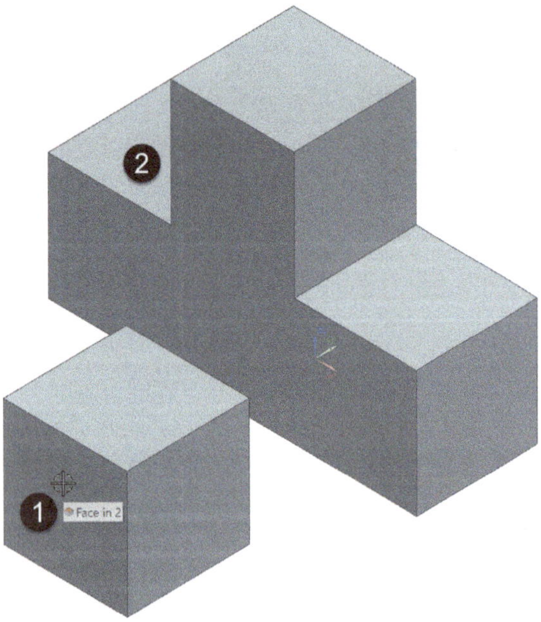

You can use the **Reverse Last Constraint** icon on the dialog to flip the part.

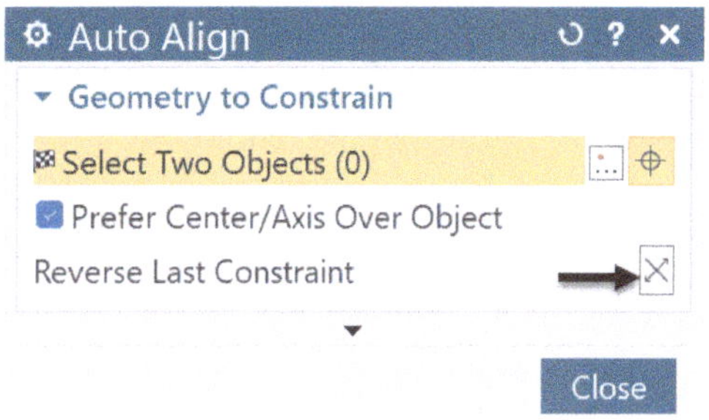

Select the second set of faces.

Select the third set of faces to constrain the part fully. Click **OK** to close the **Add Component** dialog. To confirm this, activate the **Show Degrees of Freedom** command and select the part.

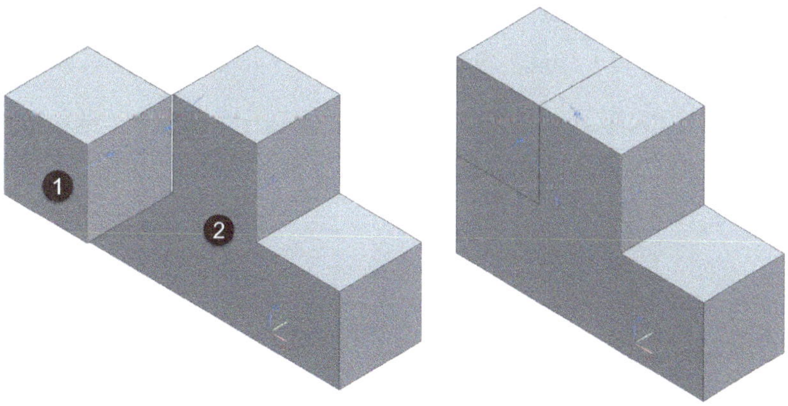

Prefer Center/Axis over object

The **Prefer Center/Axis over object** option makes the axes of two cylindrical faces coincide with each other. To do this, first activate the **Auto Align** command, and check the **Prefer Center/Axis over object** option. Next, click on a cylindrical face, linear edge, or axis of the placement part. Click on an element on the target part. The two cylindrical axes will be aligned together.

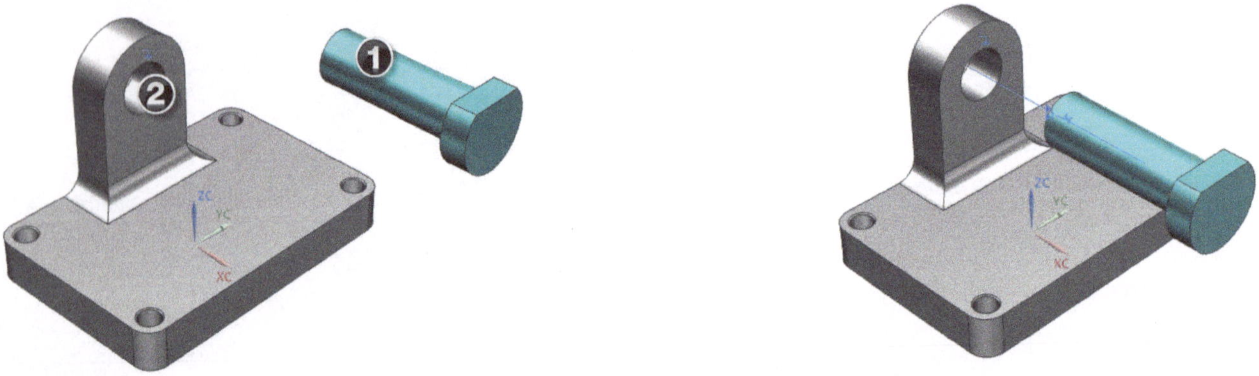

Align/Lock

If you want to align the axes of two cylindrical faces and lock the rotation, then the **Align/Lock** constraint will be useful. Click **Align/Lock** button in the **Position** group of the **Assemblies** tab of the ribbon. Next, select the axes of two cylindrical faces.

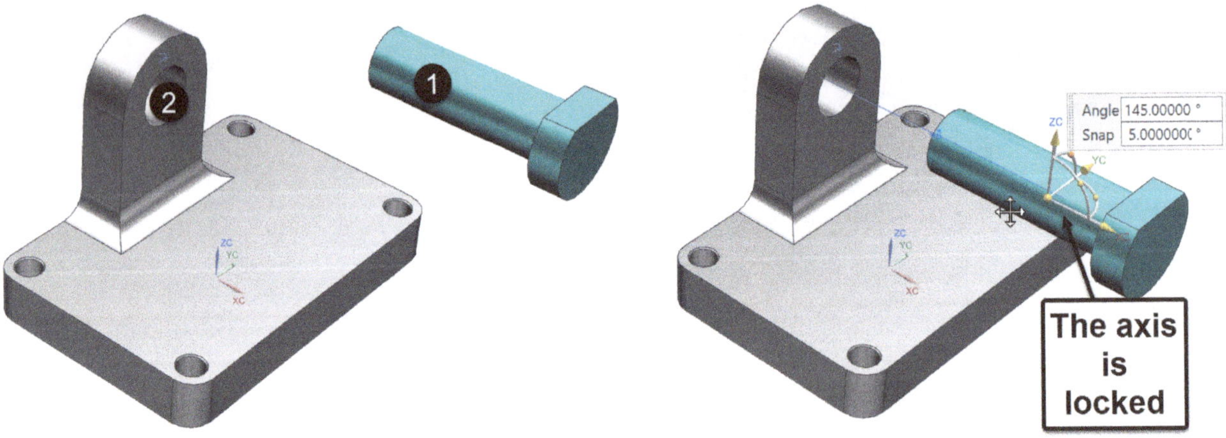

Concentric Constraint

The **Concentric** constraint helps you to make circular edges of two components concentric. To do this, click **Concentric** button in the **Position** group of the **Assemblies** tab of the ribbon. Click on the circular edges of the two components.

Angle Constraint

The **Angle** constraint is used to position faces at a specified angle. Click **Angle** button in the **Position** group of the **Assemblies** tab of the ribbon and select **3D Angle** from the drop-down available on the **Angle** dialog. Click on a plane or linear element of the first part. Next, click on a plane or linear element of the second part and type-in a value in the **Angle** box on the **Angle** dialog. Click **OK** to position the first part at the specified angle.

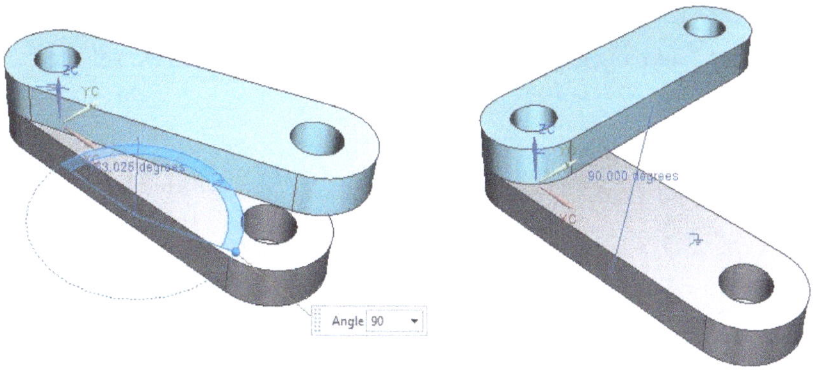

Parallel Constraint

The **Parallel** constraint makes an axis, face, or edge of one-part parallel to that of another part. Click **Parallel** button in the **Position** group of the **Assemblies** tab of the ribbon. Select a planar face, cylindrical face, linear edge, or axis of the first part. Next, click on an element of the second part. Two selected elements will be parallel to each other. Click **OK**.

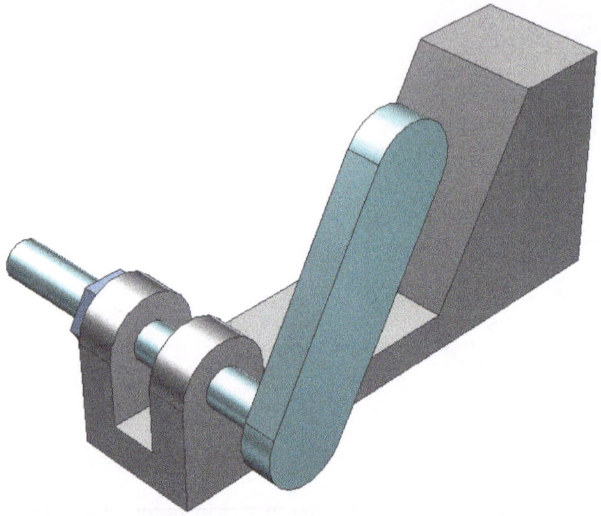

Perpendicular Constraint

The **Perpendicular** constraint makes an axis, face, or edge of a part perpendicular to that of another part. Click **Perpendicular** button in the **Position** group of the **Assemblies** tab of the ribbon. Select a planar face, cylindrical face, linear edge, or axis of the first part. Next, click on an element of the second part. Two selected elements will be perpendicular to each other. Click **OK**.

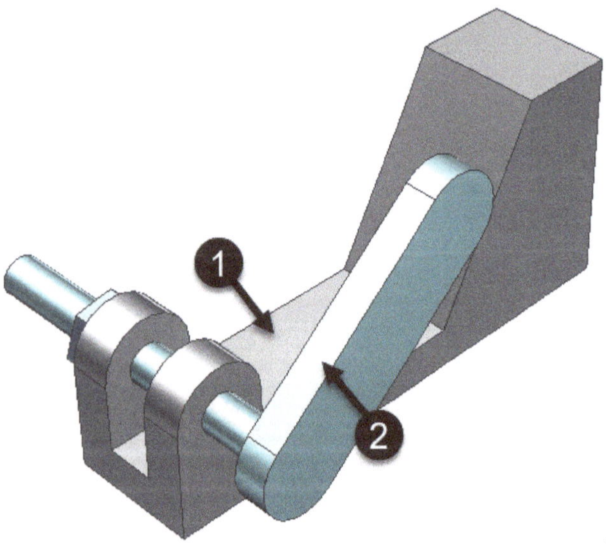

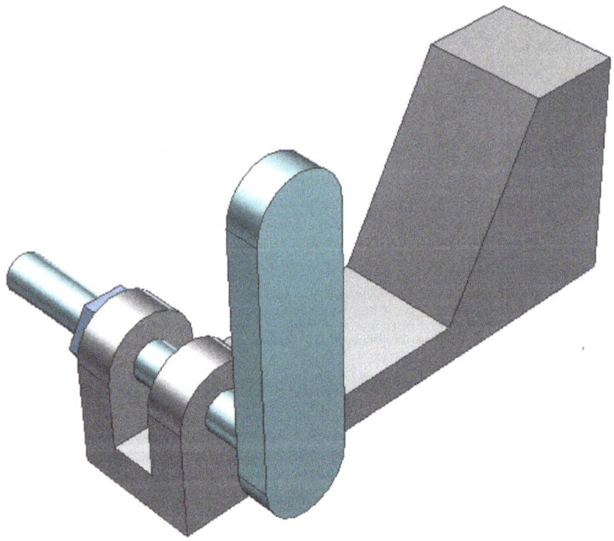

Distance Constraint

The **Distance** constraint offsets a component from another component. To do this, click **Distance** button in the **Position** group of the **Assemblies** tab of the ribbon. Next, click the planar faces of the two components. Next, type-in a value in the **Distance** box to define the distance between the selected faces. Notice the **Upper Limit** and **Lower Limit** options in the **Value** section. You can specify the maximum and minimum distance between the selected faces of the parts. Check the **Upper Limit** and **Lower Limit** options and specify the values in boxes located next to them. Next, click **OK** to apply the **Distance** constraint.

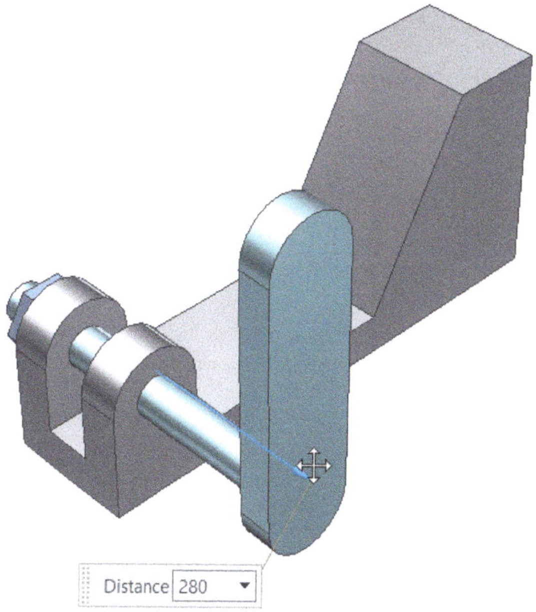

Next, click the **Constraint Navigator** tab on the **Resource Bar**. Next, right click on the **Distance** constraint and select **Make Driven**; the **Distance** constraint can be driven by another constraint or can be modified by the **Move Component** command.

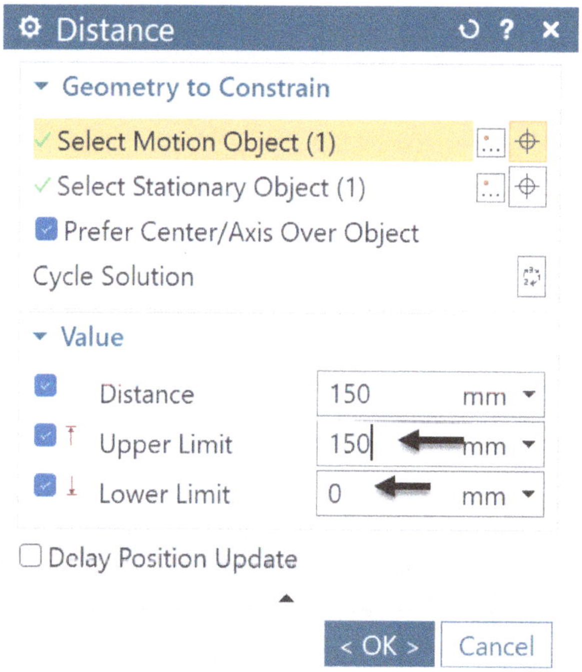

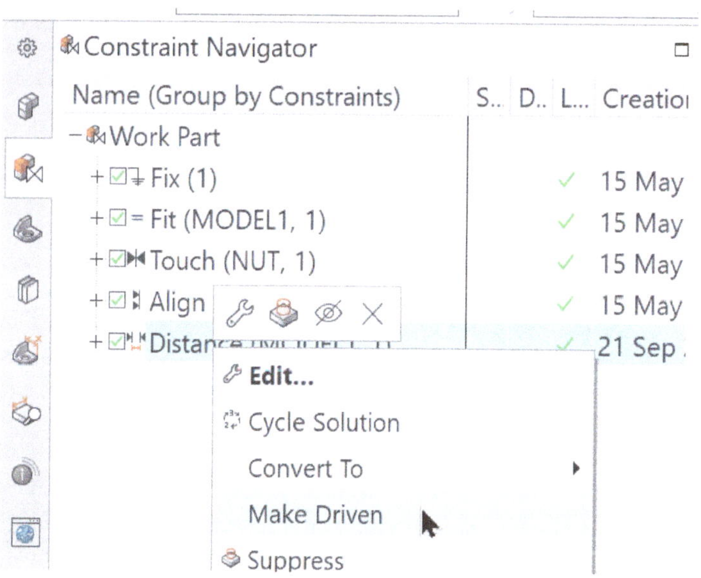

Activate the **Move Component** command (on the ribbon, click **Assemblies > Position > Move Component**). Select the component with the **Distance** constraint, and then click **Transform > Specify Orientation**. On the Dynamic Coordinate System, click on the axis, which points in the direction of the **Distance** constraint. Next, drag the handle and notice that the selected part can be moved only between the upper and lower limit of the **Distance** constraint. Click **Cancel** on the **Move Component** dialog, and then **Yes**.

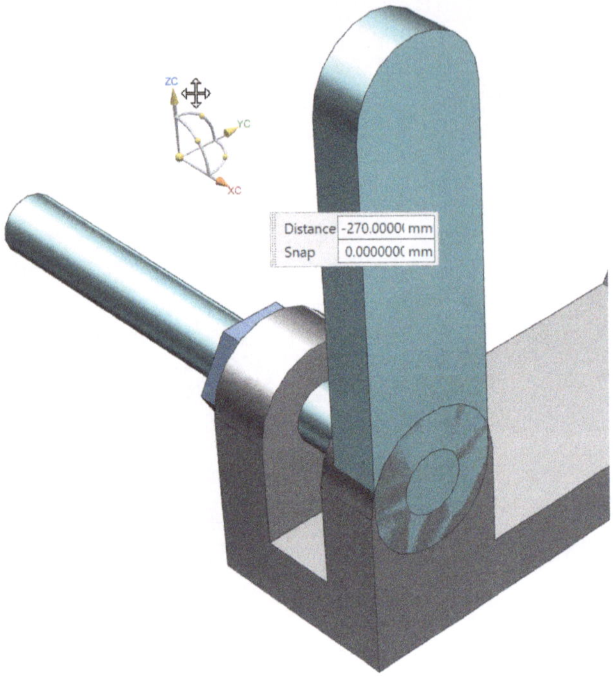

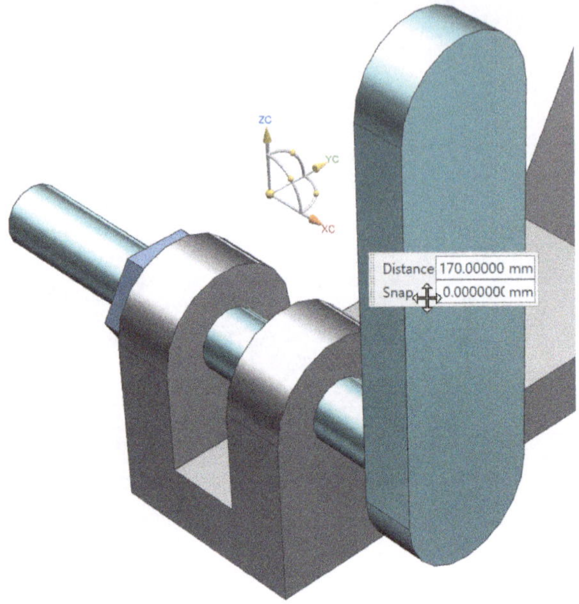

Center Constraint

The **Center** constraint allows you to center a part between two faces. Click **Center** button in the **Position** group of the **Assemblies** tab of the ribbon. On the **Center** dialog, select **1 to 2** from the **Type** drop-down. Select the first object to define the center, and then two references from the second component. Click **OK** to position the first part between the two references.

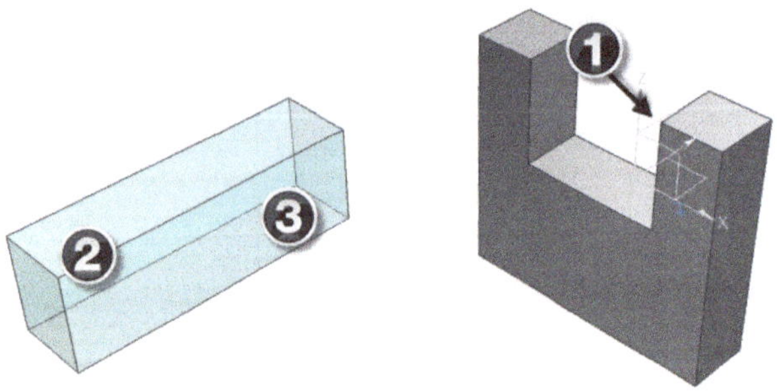

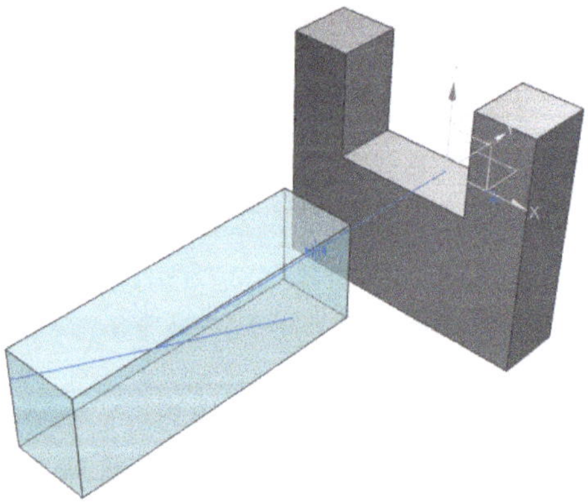

*If the Datum Coordinate System is not displayed in the assembly, click **Assemblies > Context > Replace Reference Set**. Next, select the component of which the Datum Coordinate System is to be displayed. Next, select the Entire Part option from **Replace Reference Set** dialog and click **OK**.*

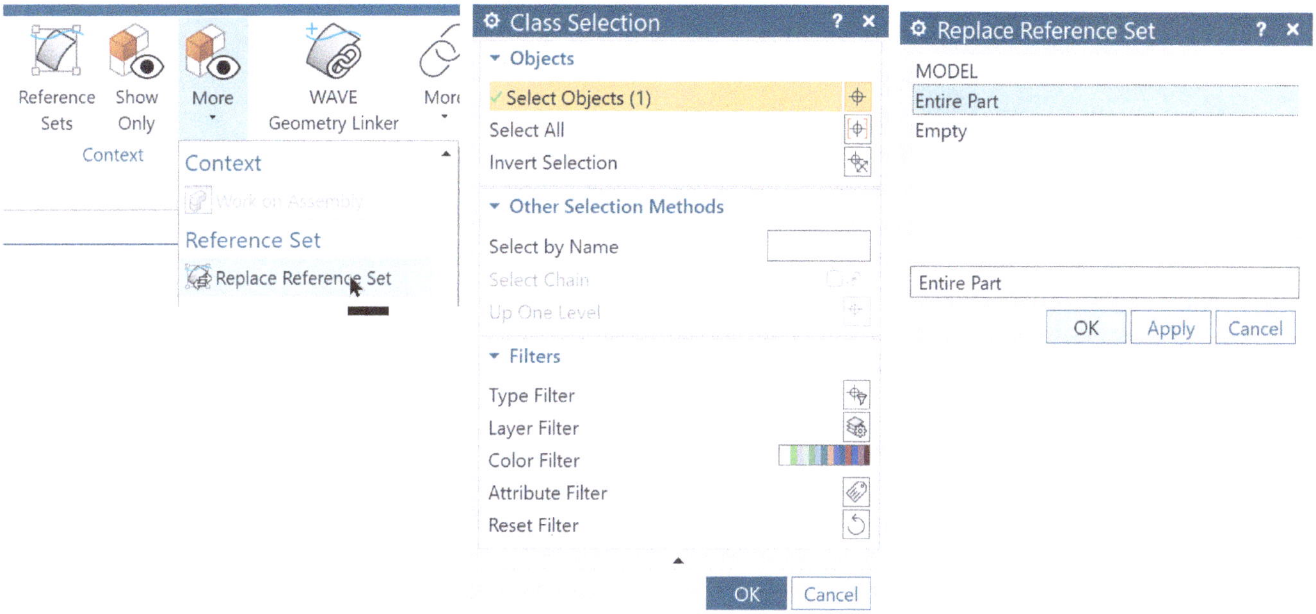

If you want to position a cylindrical part between two planar faces, then check the **Prefer Center/Axis Over Object**. Select the axis of the cylindrical object, and then click on two planar faces.

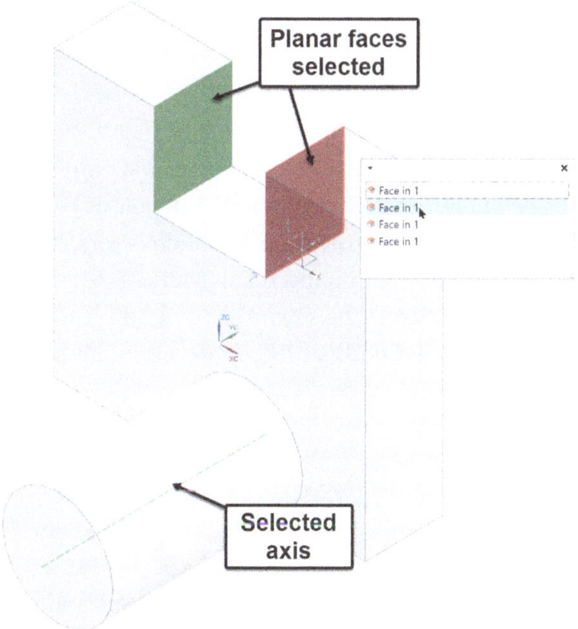

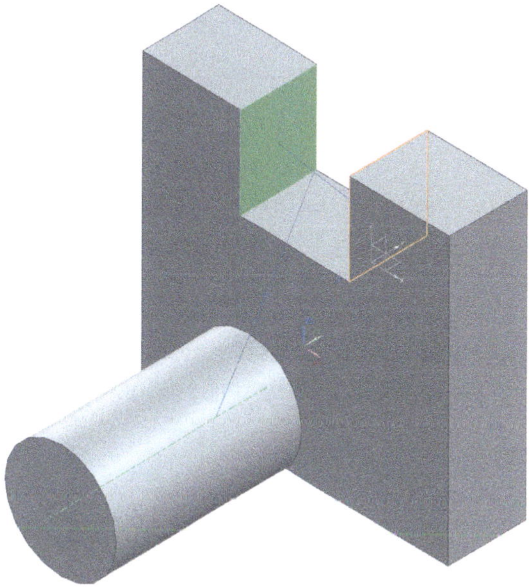

Bond Constraint

The **Bond** constraint makes components to form a rigid set. As you move a single part in a rigid set, all the other components will also be moved. To do this, Click **Bond**  button in the **Position** group of the **Assemblies** tab of the ribbon. Next, select the components from the assembly window and click **OK** on the dialog. The selected components will form a rigid set. Now, if you change the position or orientation of one part, all the other components in the rigid set will also be affected.

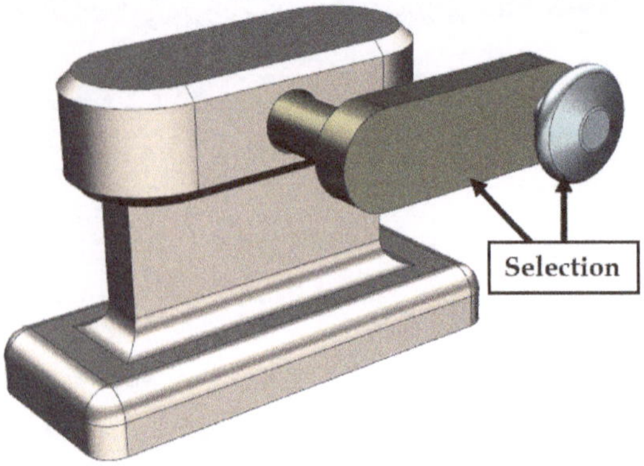

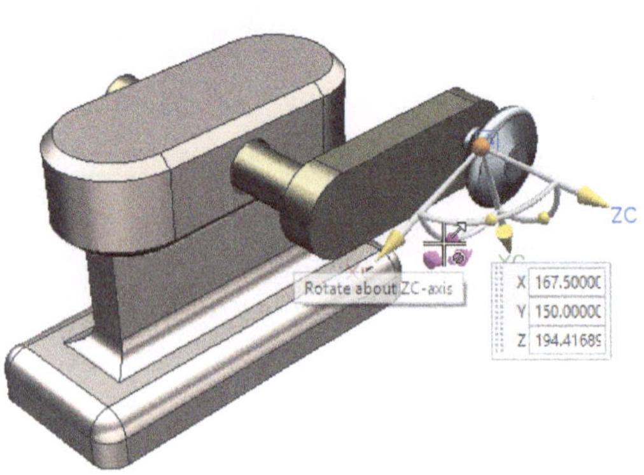

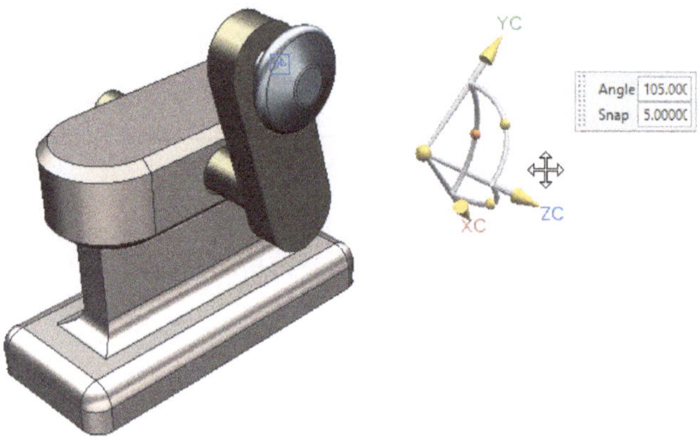

Simple Interference

In an assembly, two or more components can overlap or occupy the same space. However, this would be physically impossible in the real world. When you add relations between components, NX develops real-world contacts and movements between them. But sometimes interferences can occur. To check such errors, NX provides you with a command called **Simple Interference**. Activate this command (click **Menu > Analysis > Simple Interference** on the Top Border Bar) and select the first body. Select the second body and set the **Resulting Object** option to **Interference Body**. Click **OK** to create a solid body at the intersection. Hide the two components to view the intersecting portion.

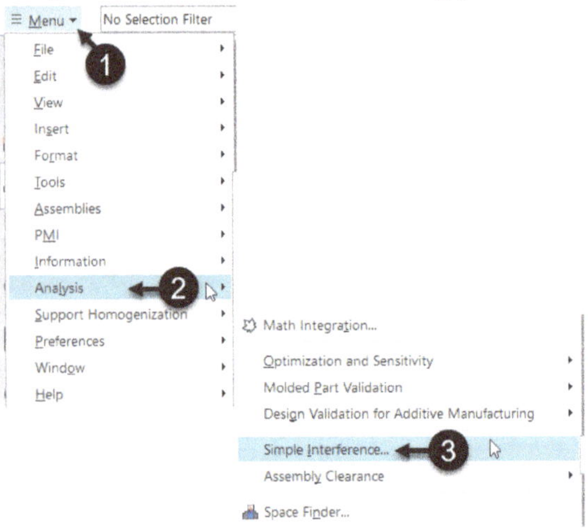

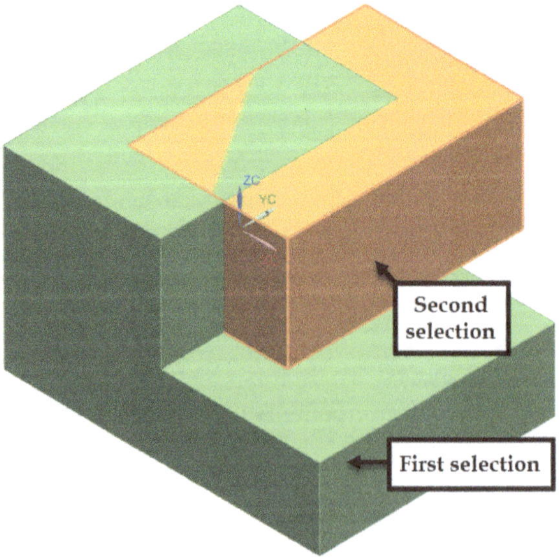

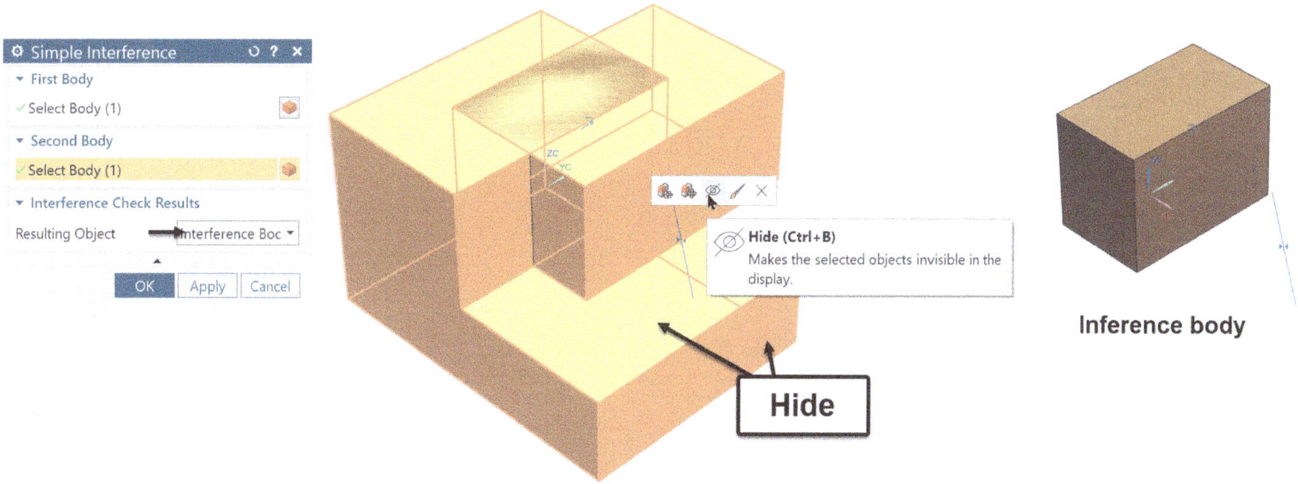

If you want to highlight the intersecting faces of the selected components, then set the **Resulting Object** option to **Highlighted Face Pairs** and select **Faces to Highlight > Cycle Through All Pairs**. Click the **Display Next Pair** button to view the next set of intersecting faces.

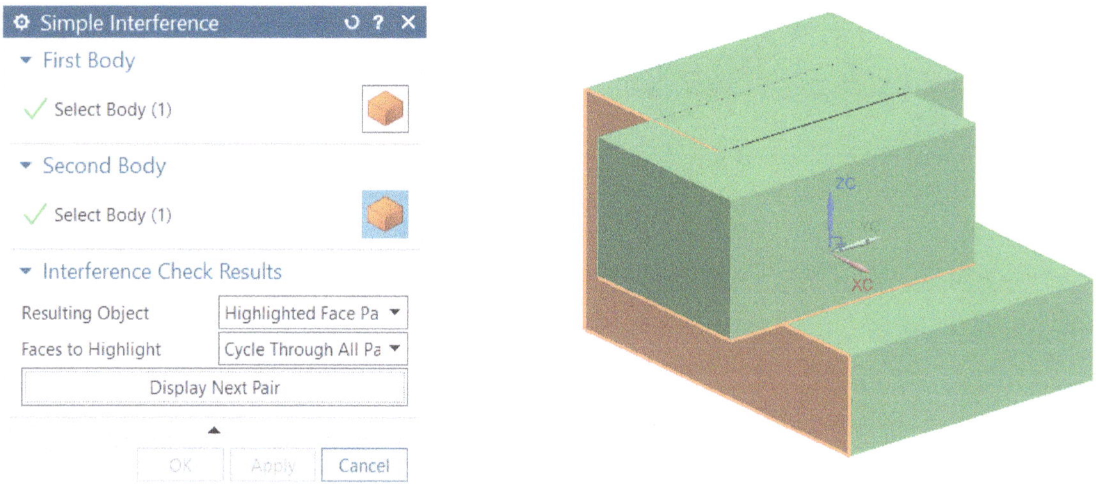

Remember Constraints

If you have an assembly in which you need to assemble the same part multiple times, it would be a tedious process. In such cases, the **Remember Constraints** command will drastically reduce the time used to assemble commonly used components. To use this command, first, you need to define a constraint or set of constraints between two components. For example, define the **Concentric** constraint between the screw and the hole.

Activate the **Remember Constraints**  command (click **Assemblies > Position > Remember Constraints** on the ribbon) and select the component (in this case, screw). On the **Assembly Navigator**, select the constraints associated with the selected component (in this case, the **Concentric** constraint) and click **OK** on the **Remember Constraints** dialog.

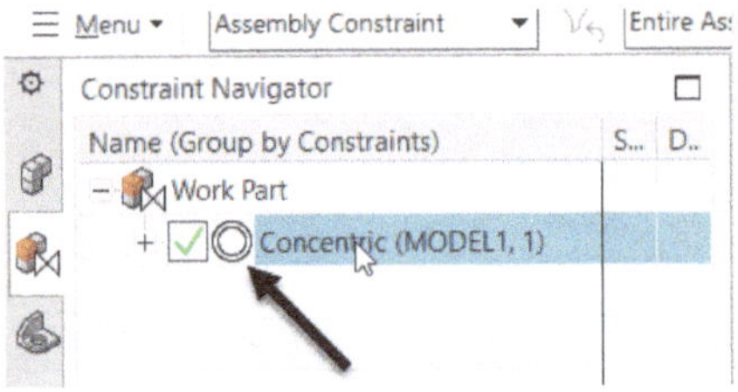

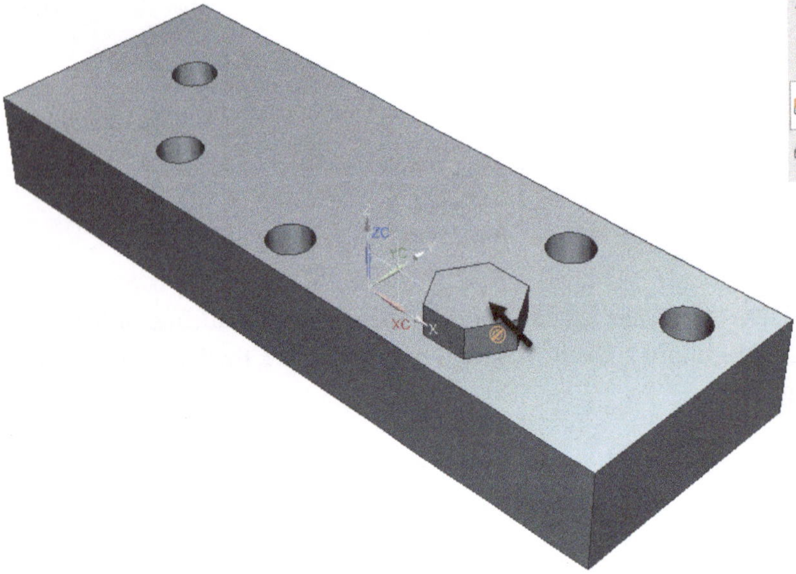

Now, activate the **Add Component** command and select the component (in this case, screw). On the **Add Component** dialog, click **OK**; the **Resolve Constraints** dialog pops up on the screen. Now, select a circular edge on the block and click **OK**. The screw will be inserted in the hole. Next, click **OK**. Likewise, insert screws in the rest of the holes and click **Cancel** to deactivate the **Resolve Constraints** dialog.

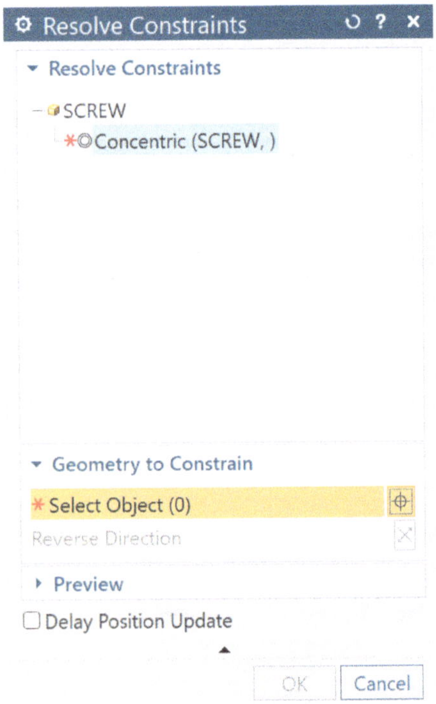

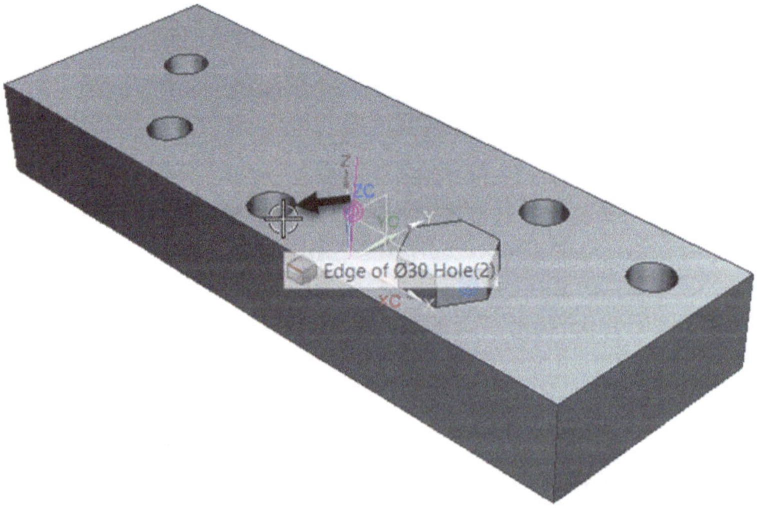

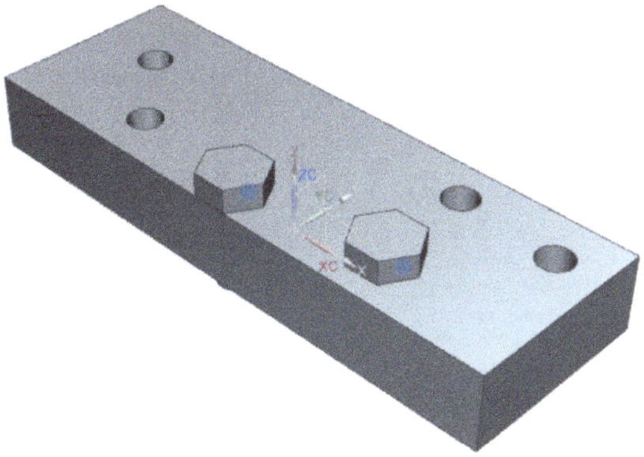

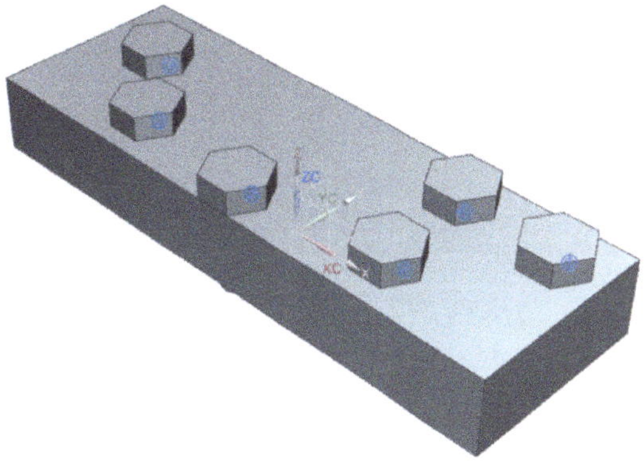

Editing and Updating Assemblies

During the design process, the correct design may not be achieved on the first attempt. There is always a need to go back and make modifications. NX allows you to accomplish this process very easily. To modify a part in an assembly, left-click on it and select **Make Work Part**, and then make changes to the part. Next, click **Assemblies > Context > More > Work on Assembly**. The part will be updated in the assembly, automatically.

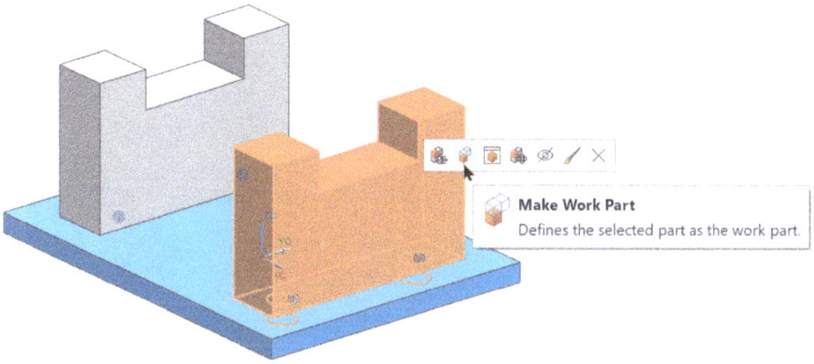

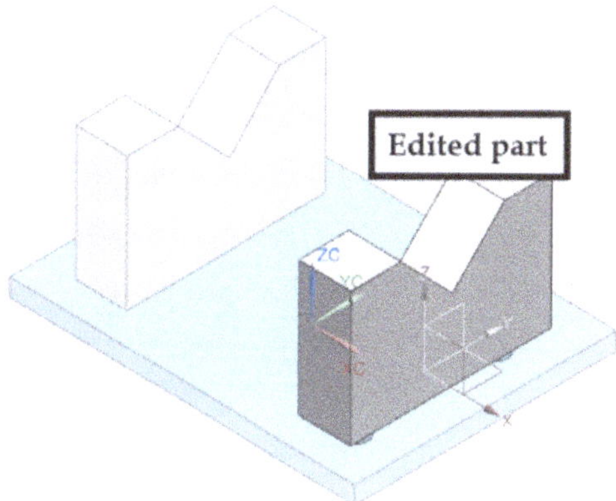

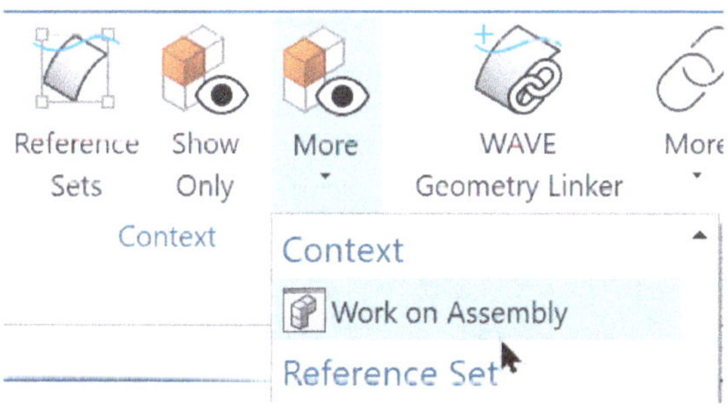

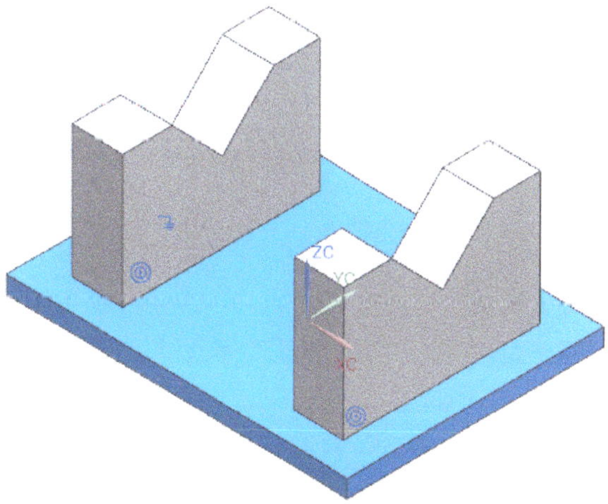

You can also redefine the existing constraints in an assembly. For example, if you want to change the faces that are aligned, then go to the **Assembly Navigator** and expand the **Constraints** section. Click the right mouse button on the **Align** constraint and select **Edit**. The aligned faces will be highlighted. Press the Shift key and deselect the face of the motion object, as shown. Now, select another face from the motion object and click **OK**.

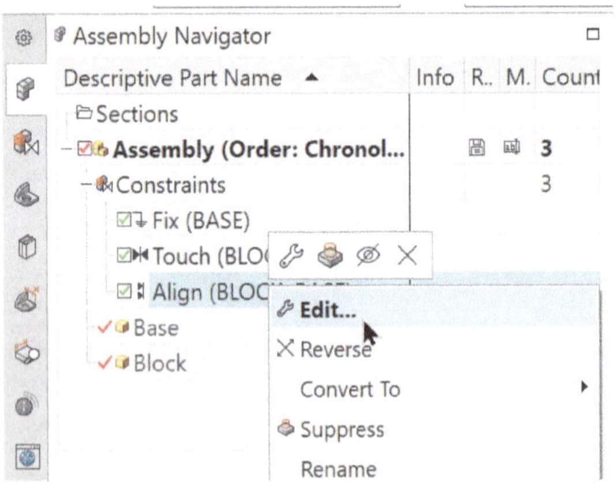

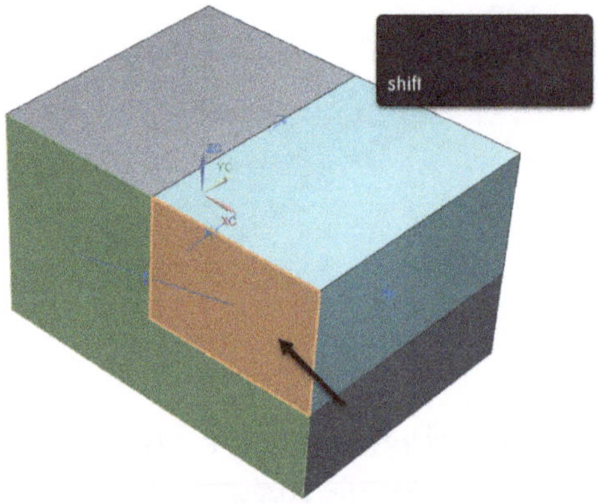

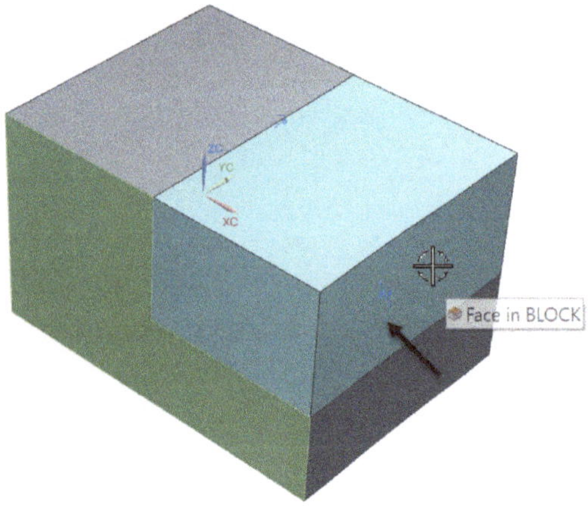

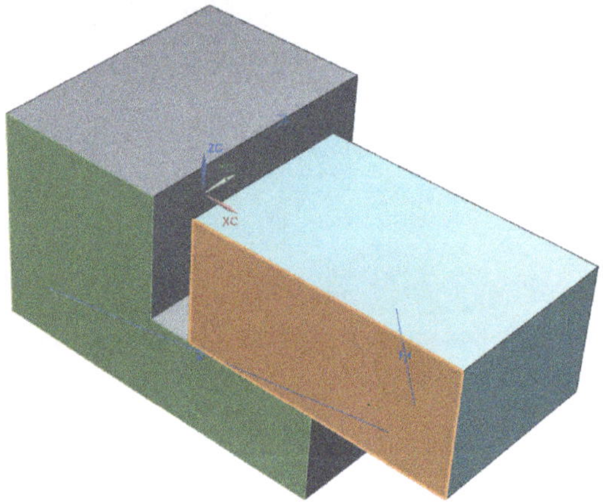

You can also convert an existing constraint into another type of constraint. For example, if you want to convert the **Align** constraint into **Distance** constraint, then click the right mouse button on it and select **Convert To > Distance**. Now, click the right mouse button on the **Distance** constraint and select **Edit** to change the distance value.

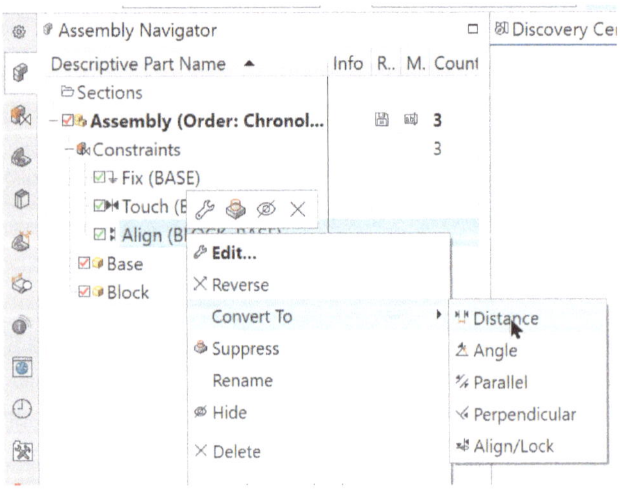

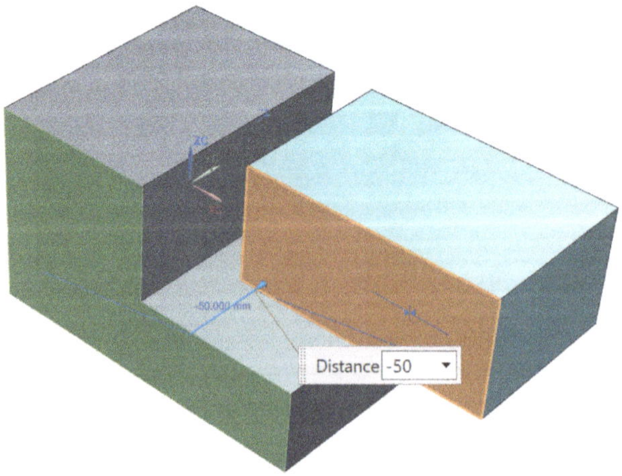

Likewise, you can delete, suppress, flip, or hide constraints.

Replace Component

NX allows you to replace any component in an assembly. To do this, go to the **Assembly Navigator** and click the right mouse button on the component to replace it. Select **Replace Component** to open the **Replace Component** dialog. On this dialog, click the **Browse** button and go to the location of the replacement part. Select the component and click **OK**. If the new component is not similar to the old component, then a message appears showing that the component to replace is not a version of the replacement part. Click **OK** to replace the component. Now, you can redefine the existing constraints or delete them and define new constraints. In this case, you can redefine the existing constraints.

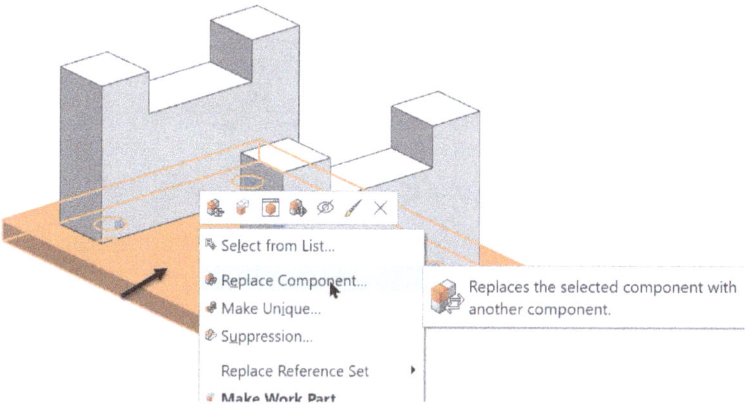

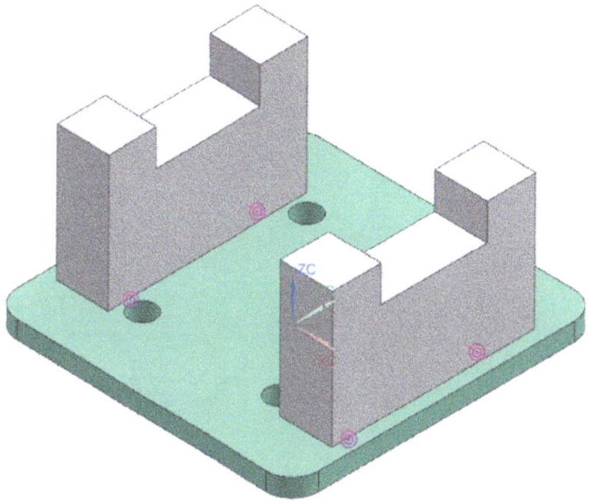

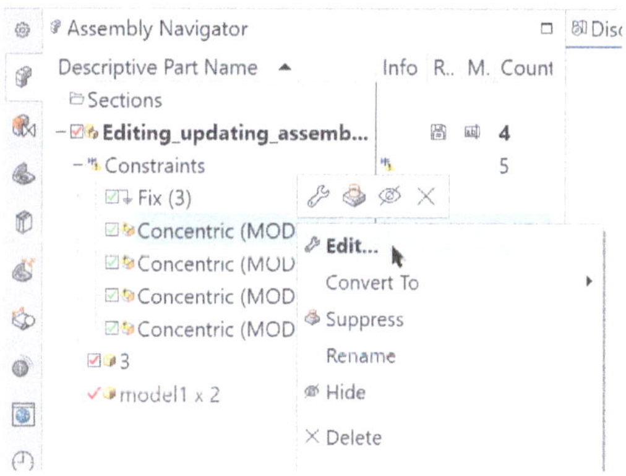

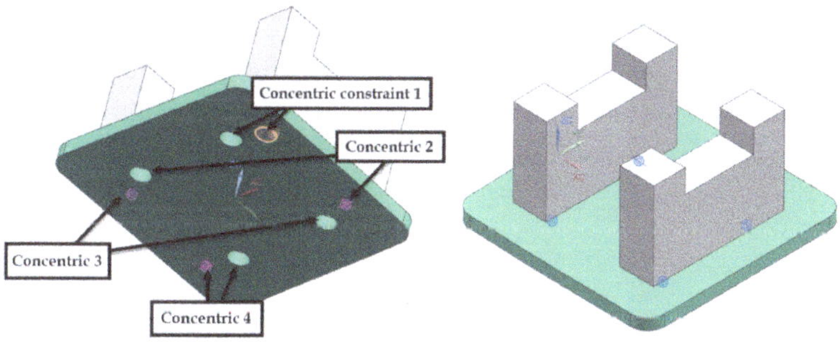

Pattern Component

The **Pattern Component** command allows you to replicate individual components in an assembly. However, instead of defining layouts of rectangular or circular patterns, you can select an existing pattern (**Pattern Feature**, **Pattern Face**, **Pattern Geometry**, or **Sketch Pattern Curve**) as a reference. For example, in the assembly shown in the figure, you can position one screw using constraints, and then use the **Pattern Component** command to place screws in the remaining holes.

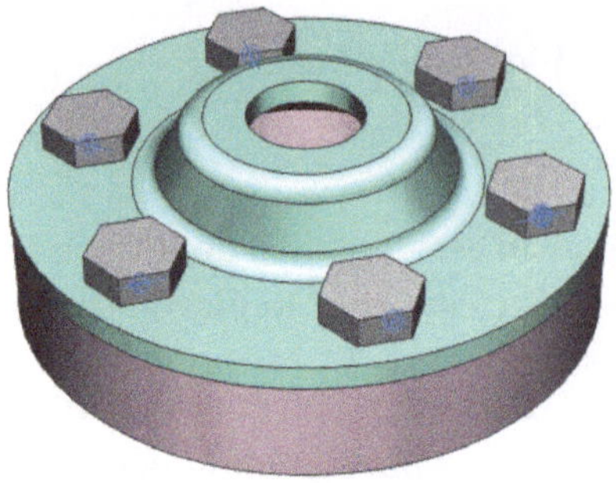

First, position the screw in one hole using the **Concentric** constraint. Next, activate the **Pattern Component** command (click **Assemblies > Component > Pattern Component** on the ribbon) and click on the part (In this case, screw) to include in the pattern. On the **Pattern Component** dialog, select **Layout > Reference**, and then click **OK**. The screw will be replicated using the existing pattern.

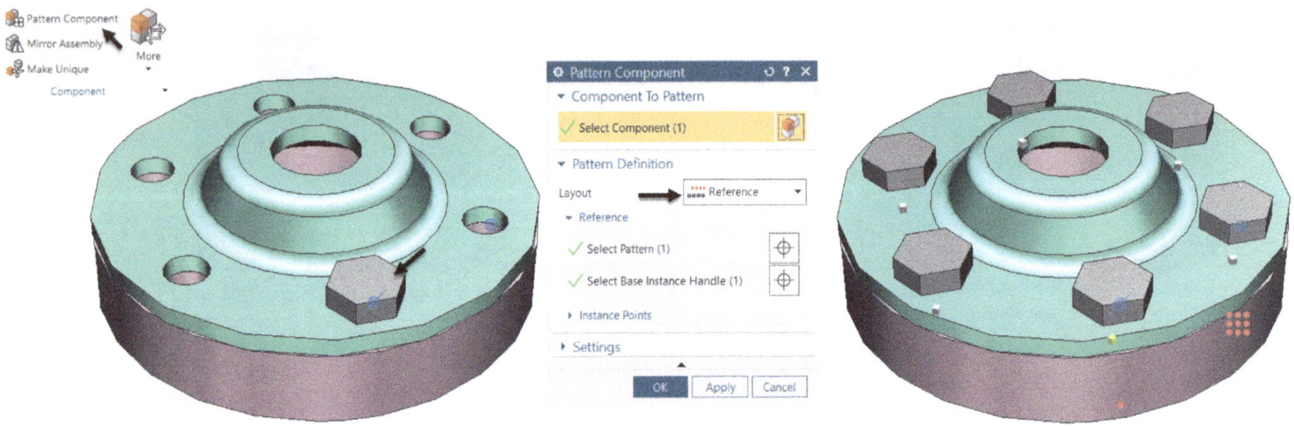

Mirror Assembly

When designing symmetric assemblies, the **Mirror Assembly** command will help you in saving time and capture design intent. To do this, first, you must display the datum planes of the base component. Click the right mouse button on the base component and select **Replace Reference Set > Entire Part**.

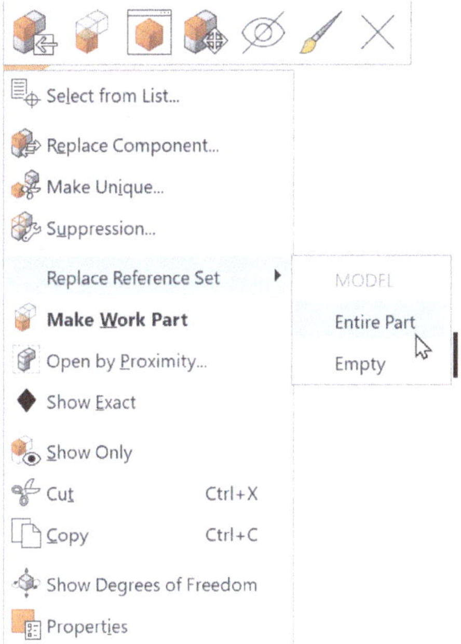

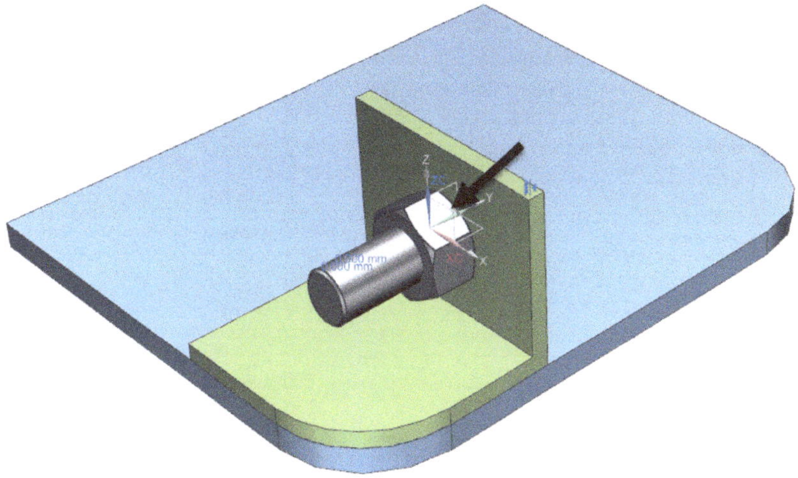

Now, activate the **Mirror Assembly** command (click **Assemblies > Component > Mirror Assembly** on the ribbon) and click **Next** on **Mirror Assemblies Wizard**. Press and hold the CTRL key and select the components to mirror and click **Next**. Click on a datum plane to mirror about, and then click **Next**. Leave **Naming Rule** to the default setting. Select **Add new parts to the specified directory** and click **Browse**. Go to the location of the current assembly folder and click **OK**. Click **Next** on the **Mirror Assemblies Wizard**.

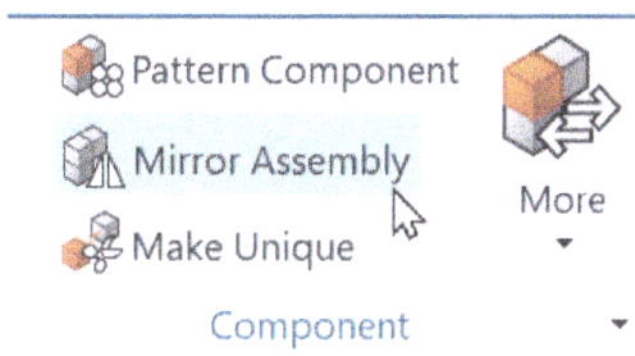

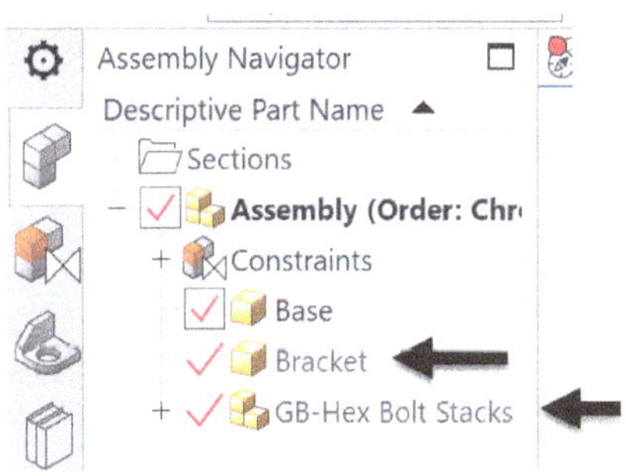

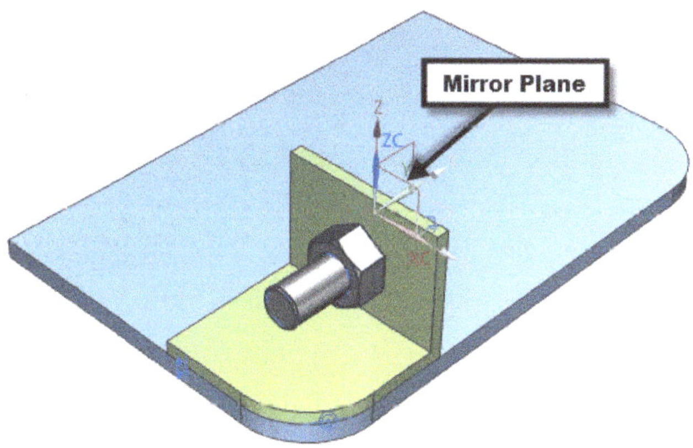

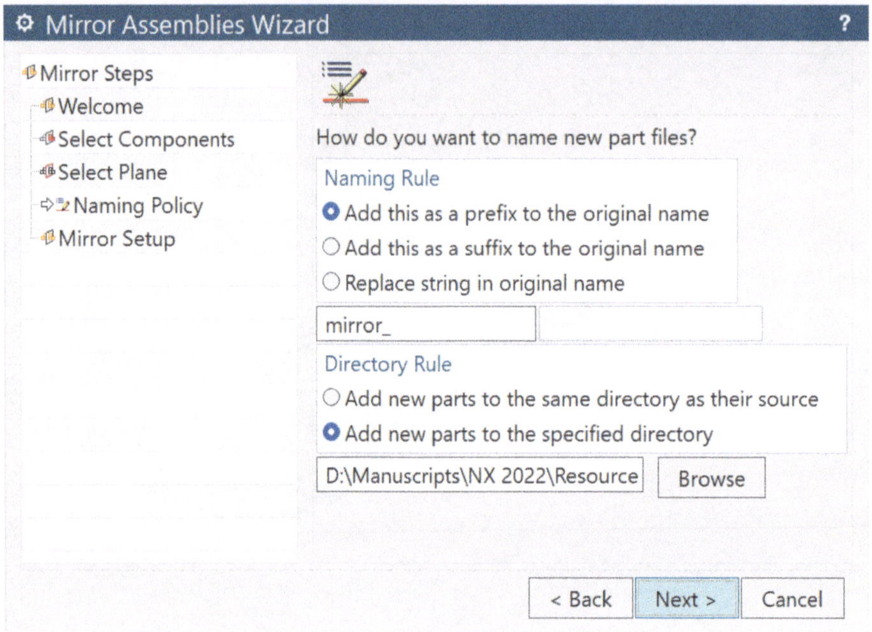

On the **Mirror Assemblies Wizard**, select the all the component to mirror, and then click the **Associative Mirror** icon. As you click **Next**, the **Mirror Components** message appears showing that this operation will create new part files and add them to the work part. Click **OK**.

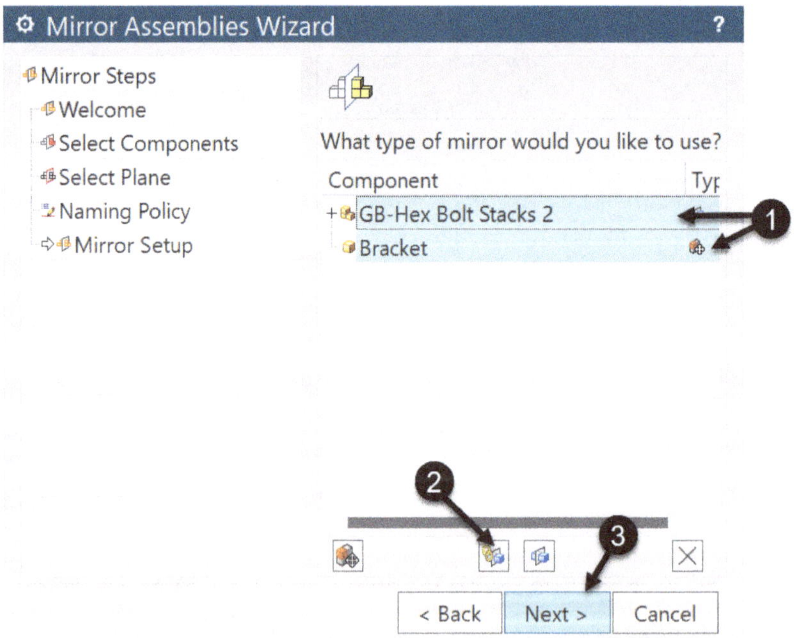

Review the mirror components and click **Next**. Click **Finish** to mirror the components.

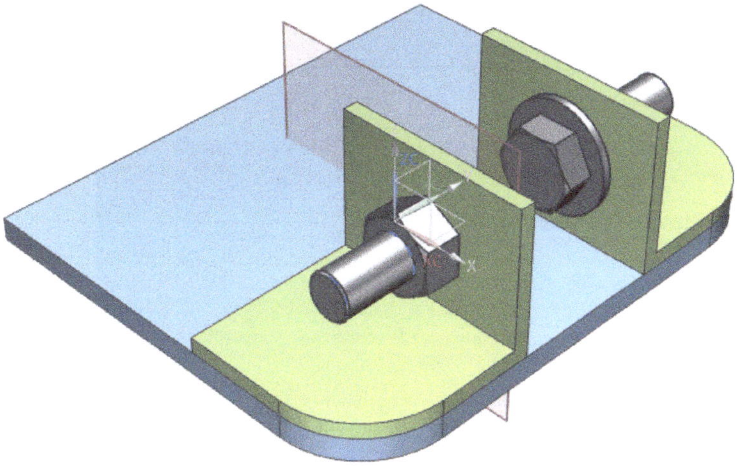

Sub-assemblies

The use of sub-assemblies has many advantages in NX. Sub-assemblies make large assemblies easier to manage. They make it easy for multiple users to collaborate on a single large assembly design. They can also affect the way you document a large assembly design in 2D drawings. For these reasons, it is important for you to create sub-assemblies in a variety of ways. The easiest way to create a sub-assembly is to insert an existing assembly into another assembly. You need to insert the assembly into an existing assembly using the **Add Component** command. Next, apply constraints to constrain the assembly. The process of applying constraints is also simplified. You are required to apply constraints between only one part of a sub-assembly and a part of the main assembly. In addition, you can convert a group of components into a sub-assembly and hide them. To do this, right-click on a sub-assembly and select **Hide**.

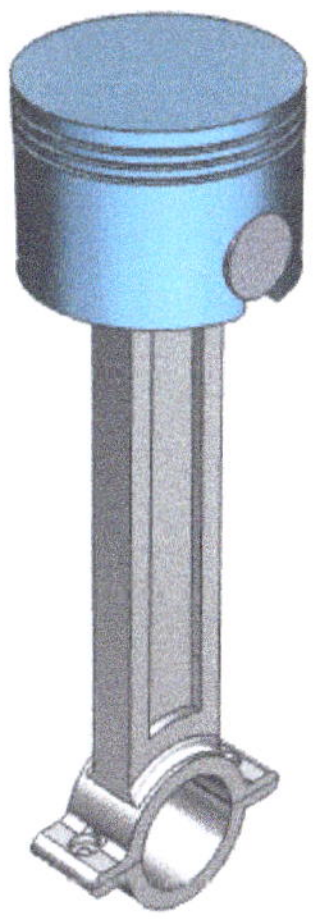

Sub-assembly

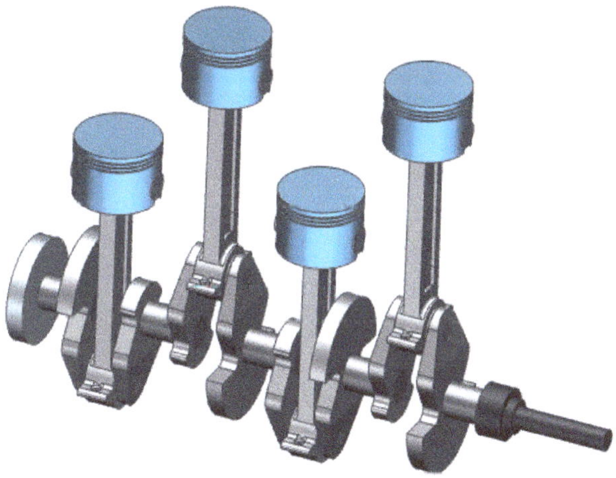

Main assembly

Assembly Cuts

Assembly cuts are the features that exist only in assemblies, i.e., instead of creating them at the part level, they are created at the assembly level. Most often, the features created at the assembly level are cuts and holes. These features are commonly created at the assembly level to represent post assembly machining. For example, to add a cut feature to the assembly shown in figure, create a solid body in the assembly file, and then activate the **Assembly Cut** command (click **Home > Base > More Gallery > Combine > Assembly Cut** on the ribbon or click **Menu > Insert > Combine > Assembly Cut** on the Top Border Bar); the **Assembly Cut** dialog pops up on the screen. Select the target bodies, and then click the **Tool** button on the dialog. Select the solid body to define the tool, and then click **OK**.

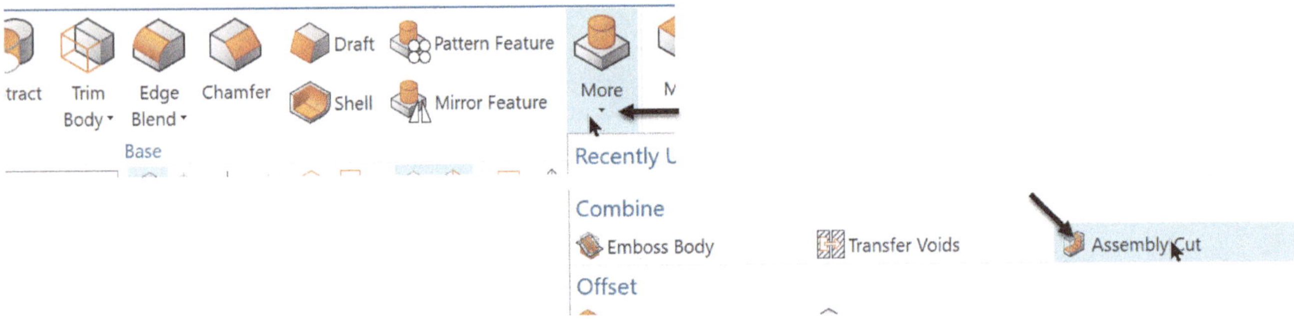

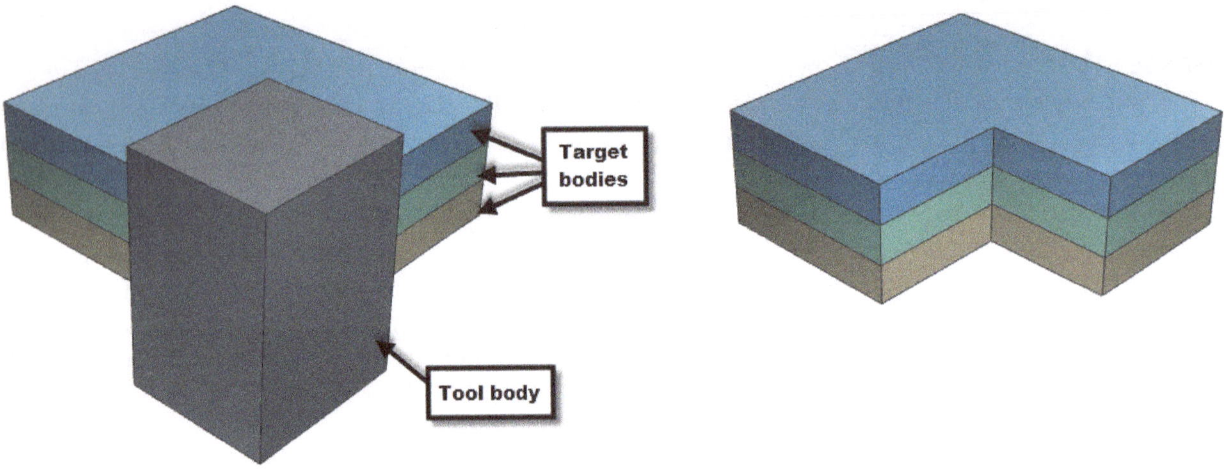

Now, open the individual part in another window. You will notice that the cut feature does not affect the part.

Top-Down Assembly Design

In NX, there are two methods to create an assembly. The method you are probably familiar with is to create individual components, and then insert them into an assembly. This method is known as Bottom-Up Assembly Design. The second method is called Top-Down Assembly Design. In this method, you will create individual components within the assembly environment. This allows you to design an individual part while taking into account how it will interact with other components in an assembly. There are several advantages to Top-Down

Assembly Design. As you design a part within the assembly, you can be sure that it will fit properly. You can also use reference geometry from the other components.

Creating a New Component

Top-down assembly design can be used to add new components to an already existing assembly. You can also use it to create entirely new assemblies. To create a part at the assembly level using the Top-Down Design, activate the **Create New** command (click **Assemblies > Base > New Component** on the ribbon). On the **New Component** dialog, define the required settings, and click **OK**. You will notice that the component will be listed in the Assembly Navigator. Double-click on the component to activate the part mode. Now, create the features of the part and then click **Assemblies > Context Control > Work on Assembly** to return to the assembly.

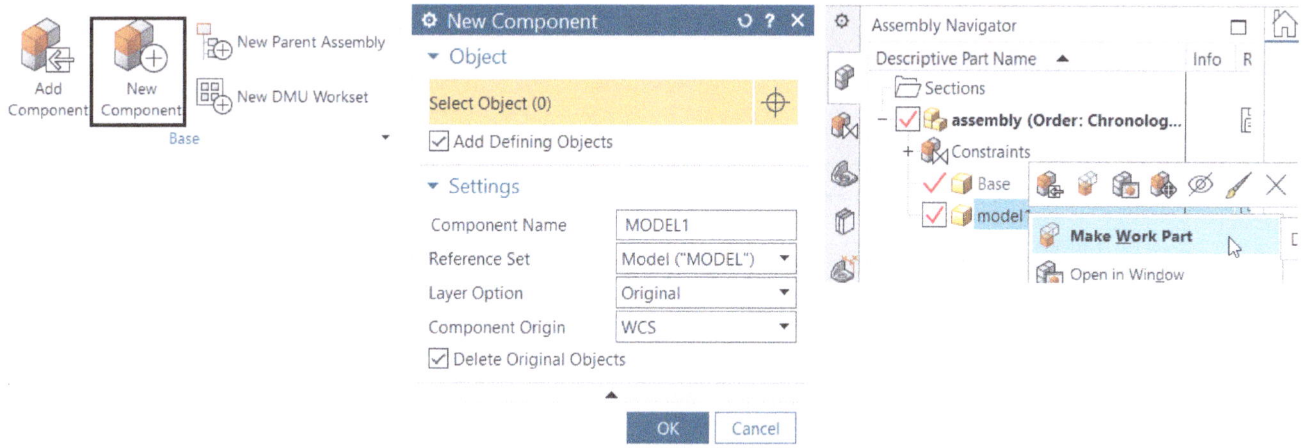

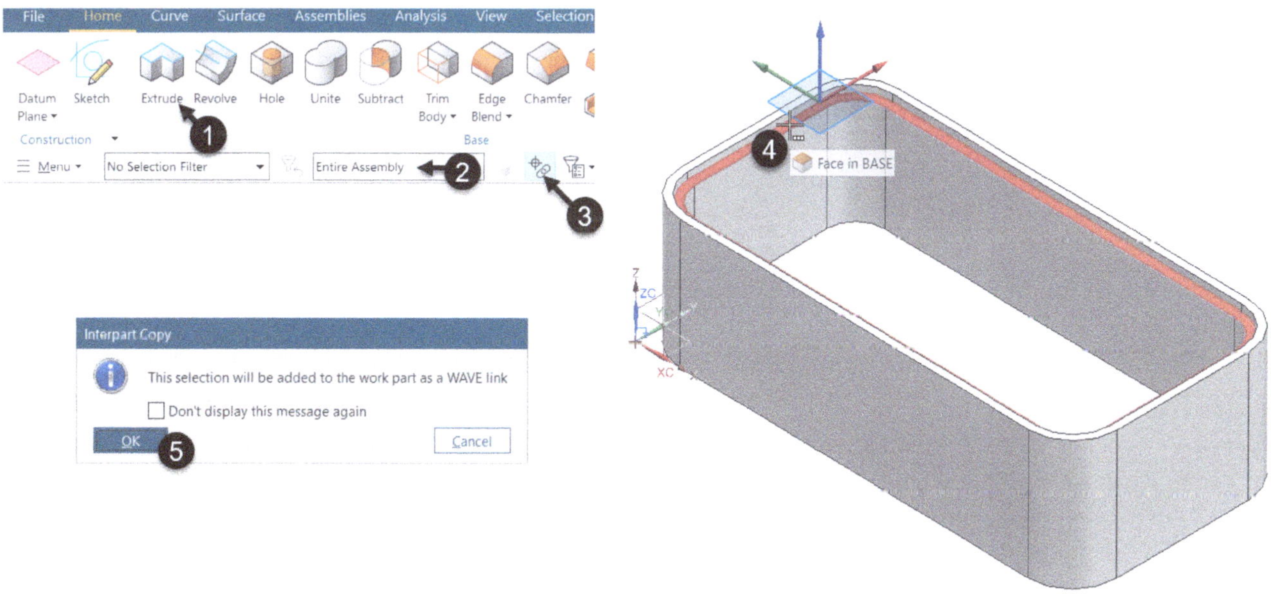

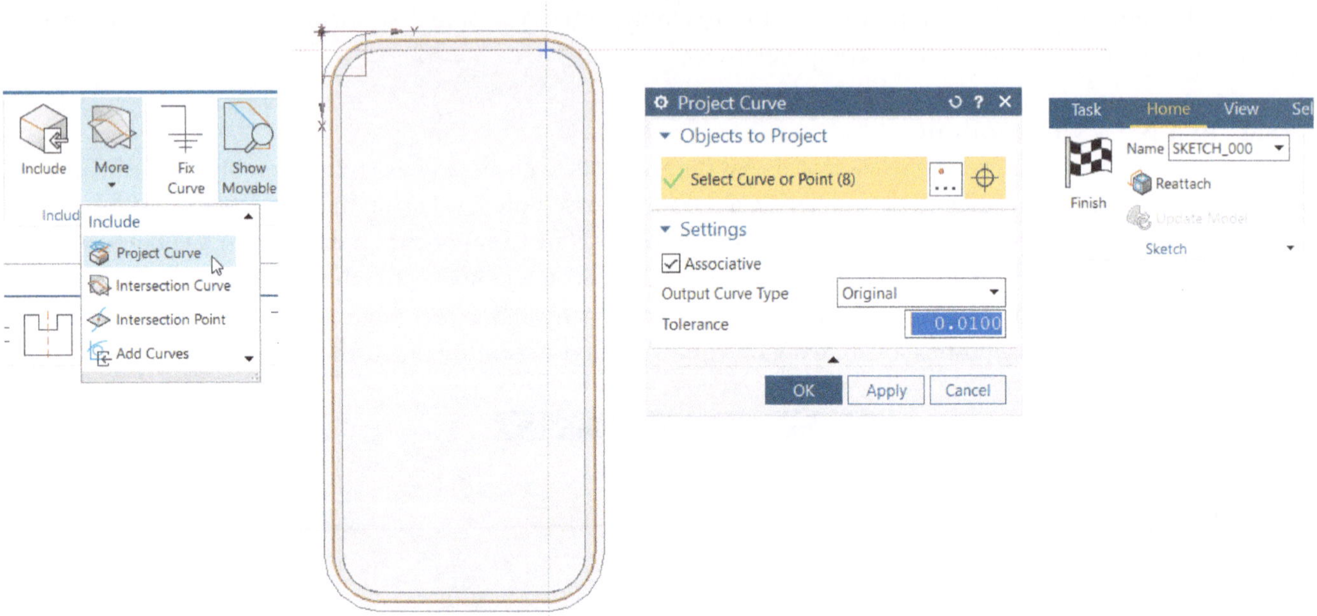

Now, if you change the parameters of the base component, the linked component will also change automatically.

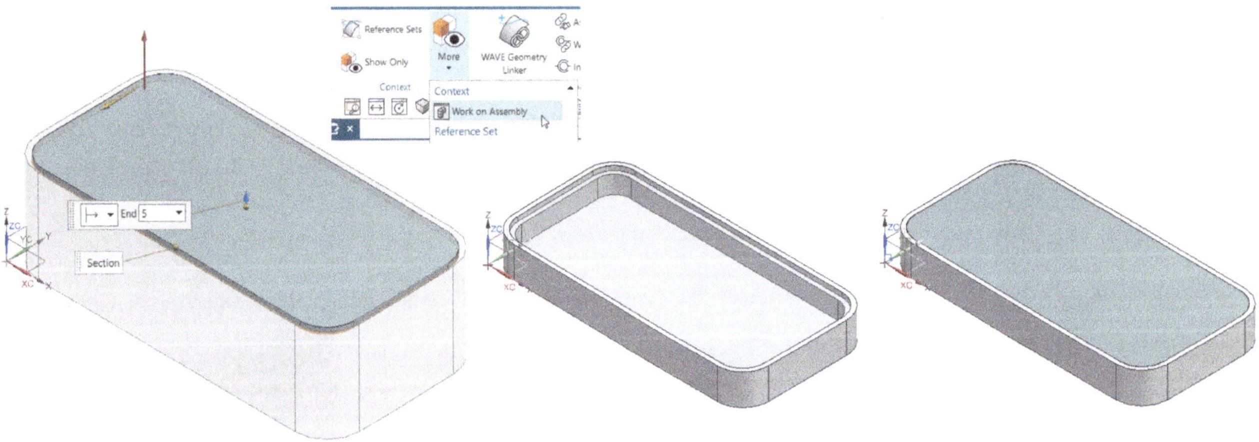

Click the **Save** icon on the Quick Access Toolbar; the **Named Parts** dialog appears. Enter the name of the newly created part and click **OK**.

Exploding Assemblies

It is very common to create an exploded view to document an assembly design properly. In an exploded view, the components of an assembly are pulled apart to show how they were assembled. To create an exploded view, activate the **Explosions** command (click **Assemblies > Explosions > Explosions** on the ribbon). Next, click the **New Explosion** icon on the **Explosions** dialog.

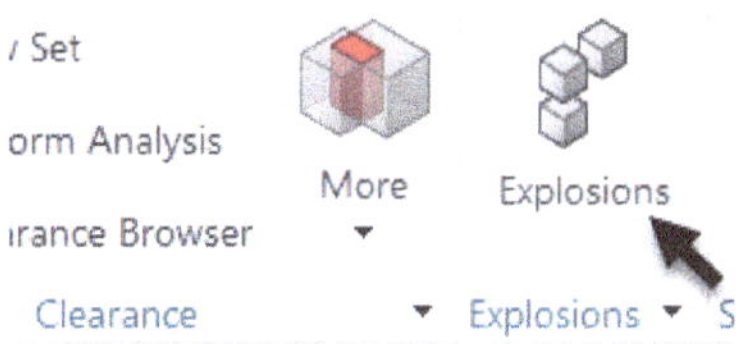

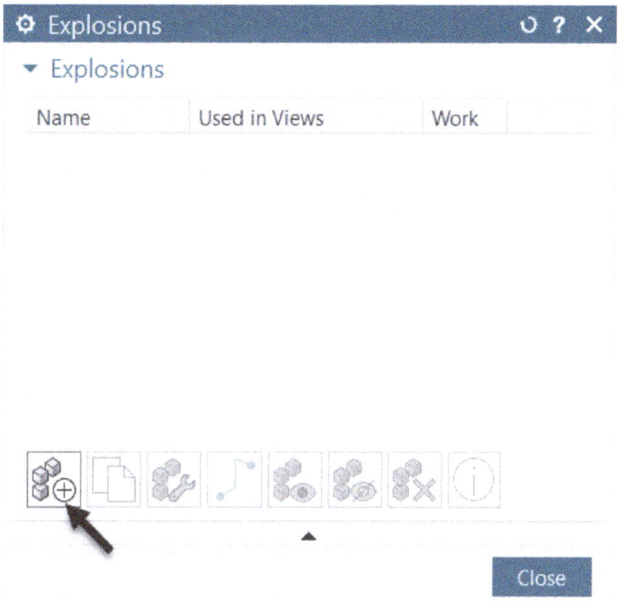

On the **Edit Explosion** dialog, select **Explosion Type > Automatic** from the **Move Components** section. Next, select all the components of the assembly by dragging a selection box. Enter a value in the **Auto-explode Distance** box and click the **Auto-explode**  icon; the components of the assembly are exploded automatically. Next, click **OK** to accept the explosion.

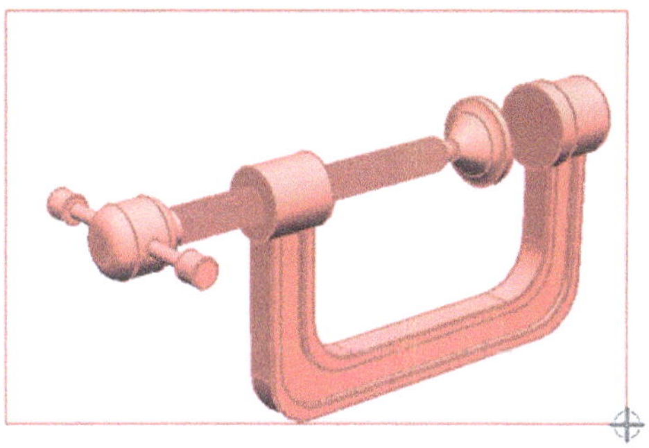

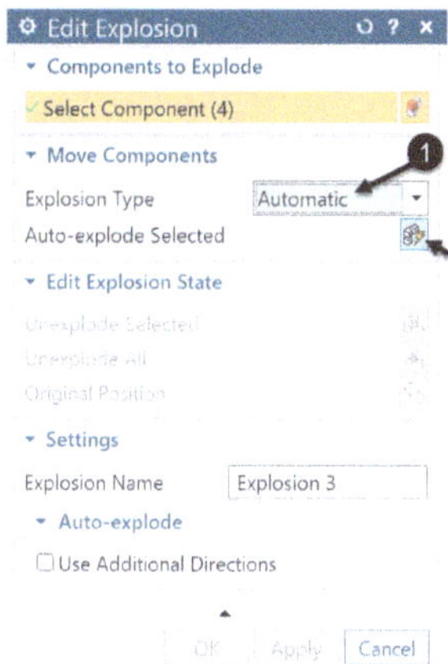

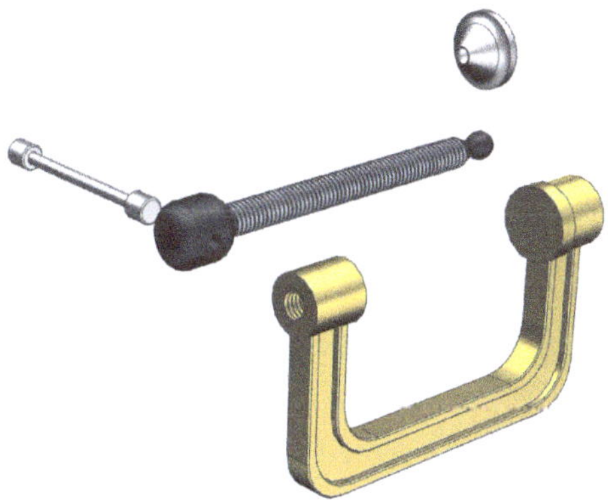

You will notice that the components are not exploded properly. To get the desired explosion, you need to use the **Edit Explosion** icon. Click the **Edit Explosion** icon on the **Explosions** dialog. Next, click the **Unexplode All** icon on the **Edit Explosion** dialog.

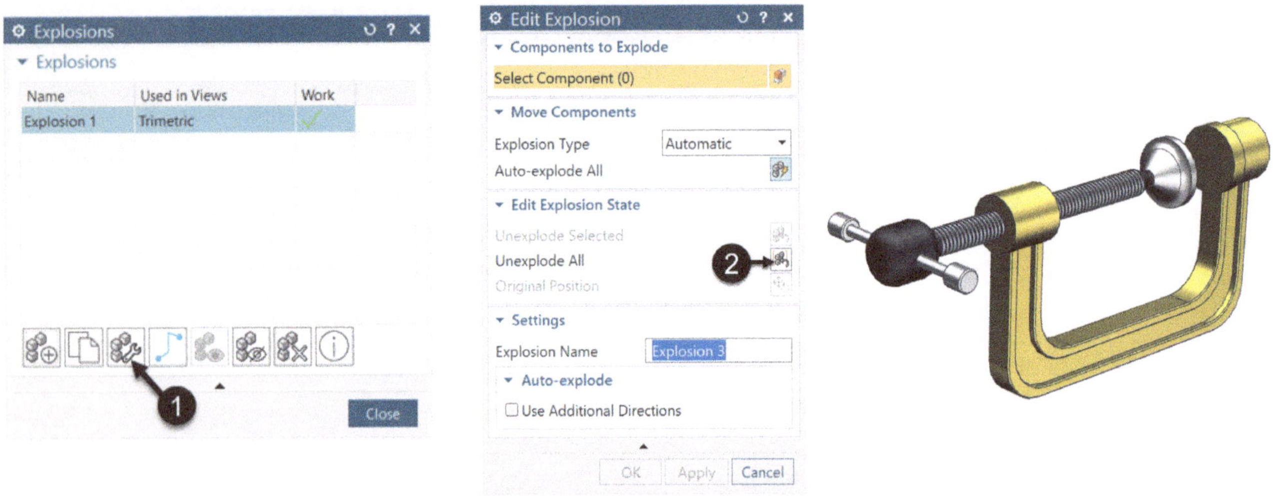

To explode an assembly manually, select **Explosion Type > Manual** from the **Move Components** section of the **Edit Explosion** dialog. Click on the components to be exploded, and then click the **Specify Orientation** option on the dialog. The Dynamic CSYS appears on the selected components. On the Dynamic CSYS, click on the X, Y, or Z handle to define the explosion direction. Type-in a value in the **Distance** box and click **Apply** to explode the selected components.

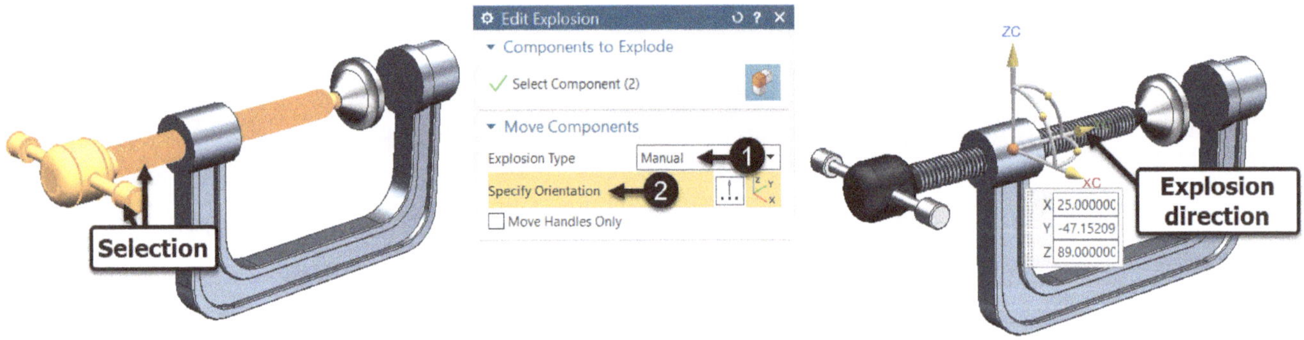

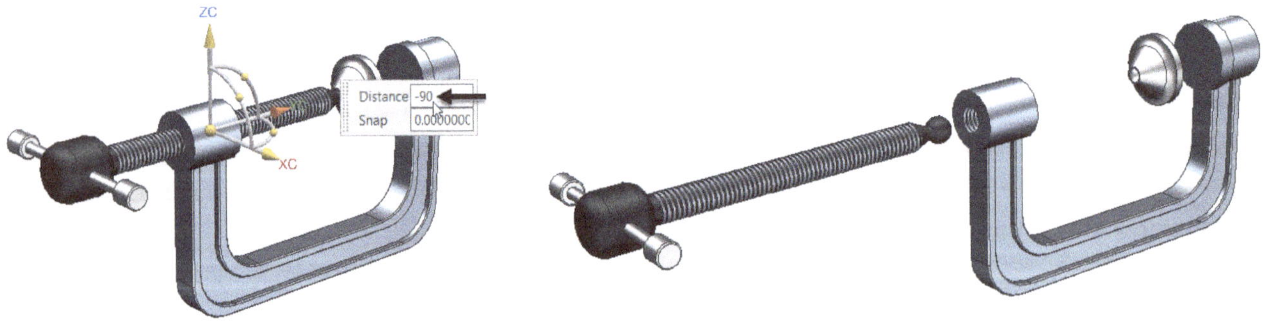

Likewise, explode the other components and click **OK**.

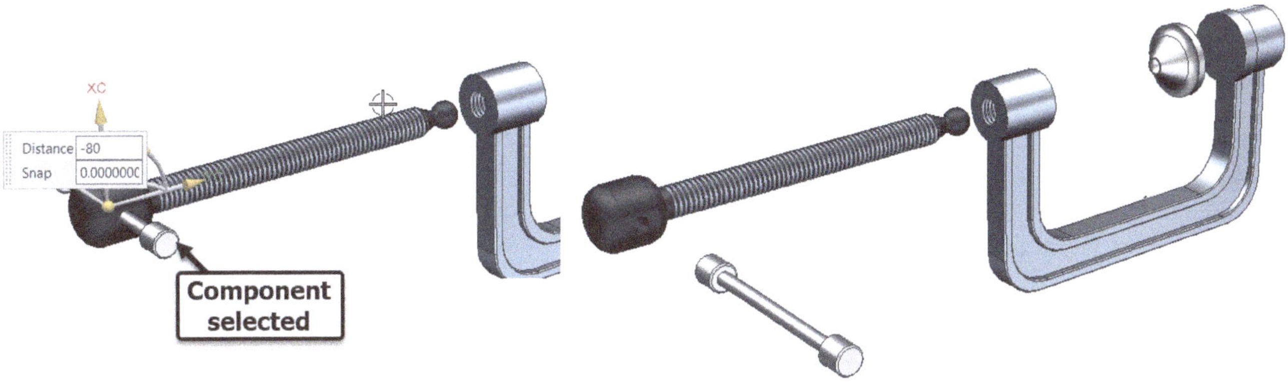

If you want to draw a trace line, click **Create Traceline** on the **Explosions** dialog and select the start and end points; a trace line appears between the selected points. Double-click on the arrow attached to the end-point to reverse the direction of the trace line. Next, click **Apply** on the **Tracelines** dialog.

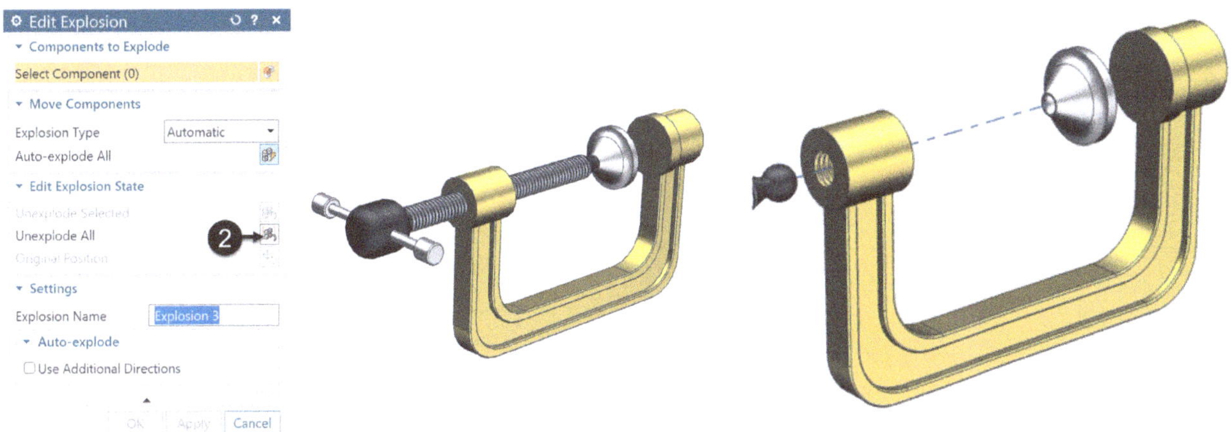

Likewise, create the other trace lines.

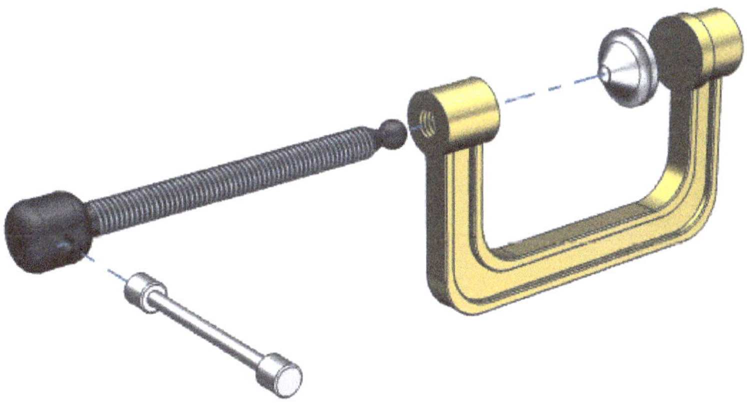

After the exploding the assembly, click **Hide Explosion in Visible View** on the **Explosions** dialog to come back to the work view. Next, click **Close** on the **Explosions** dialog.

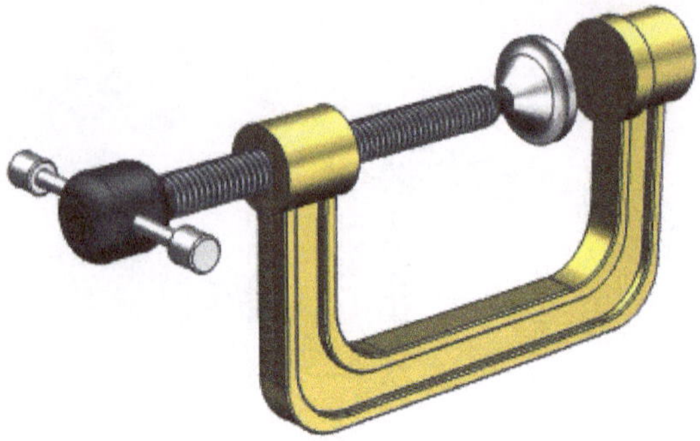

Examples

Example 1 (Bottom-Up Assembly)

In this example, you will create the assembly shown next.

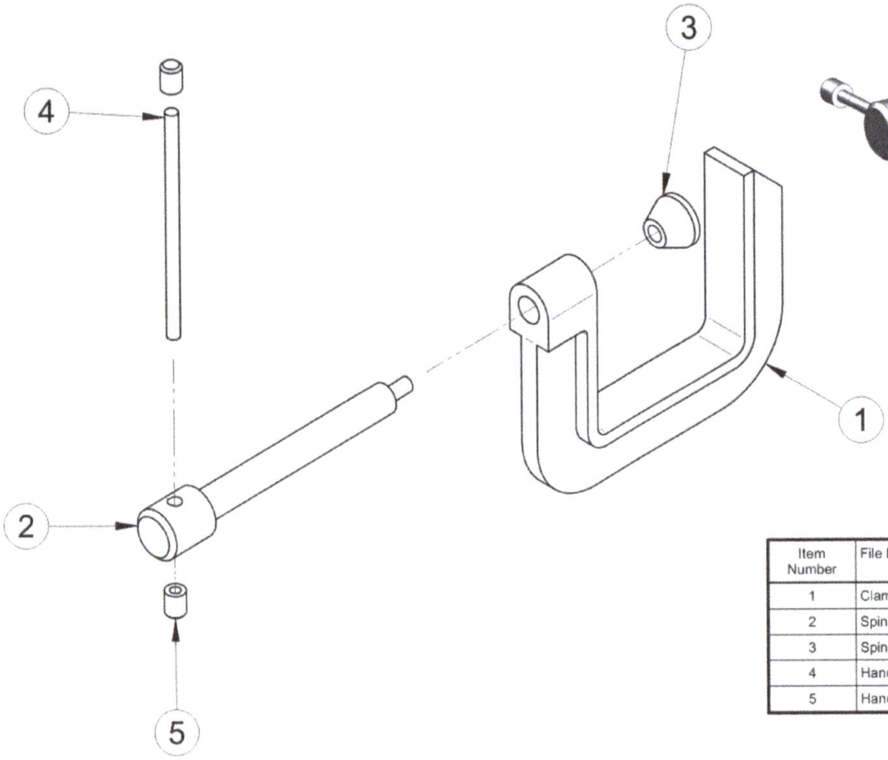

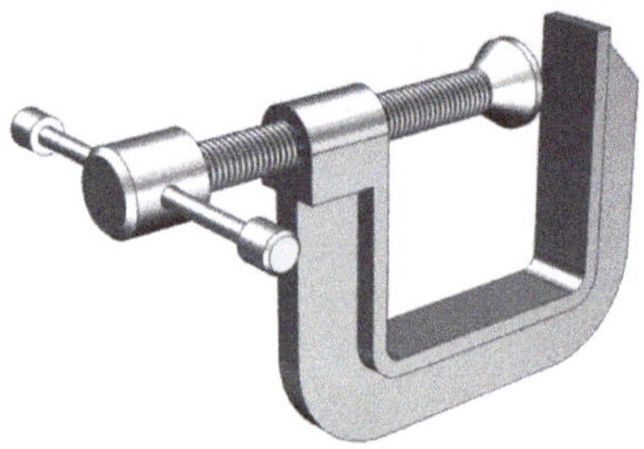

Item Number	File Name (no extension)	Quantity
1	Clamp Jaw	1
2	Spindle	1
3	Spindle Cap	1
4	Handle	1
5	Handle Cap	2

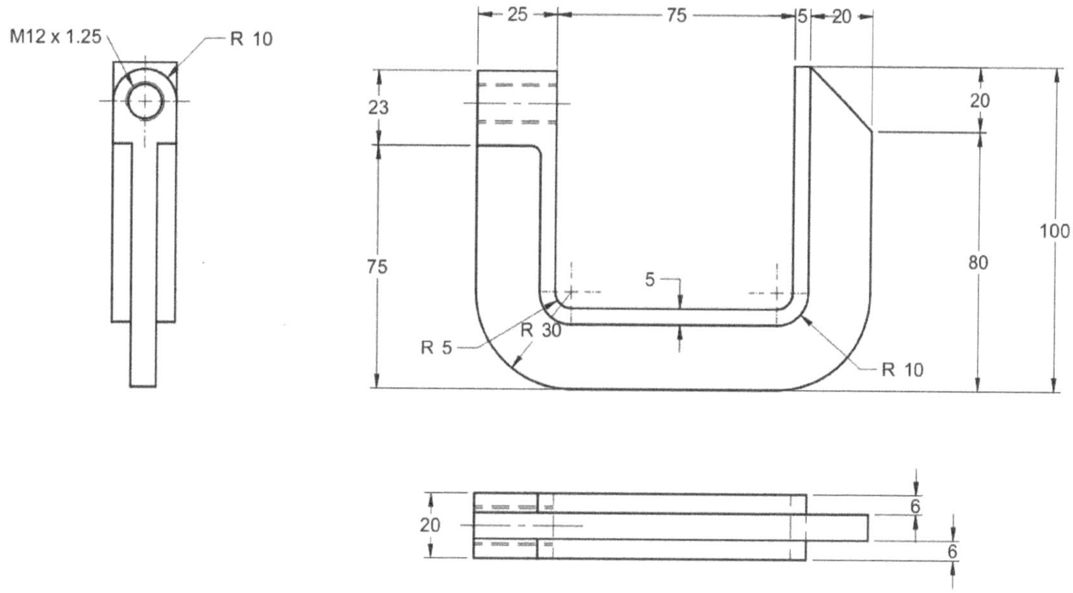

CLAMP JAW

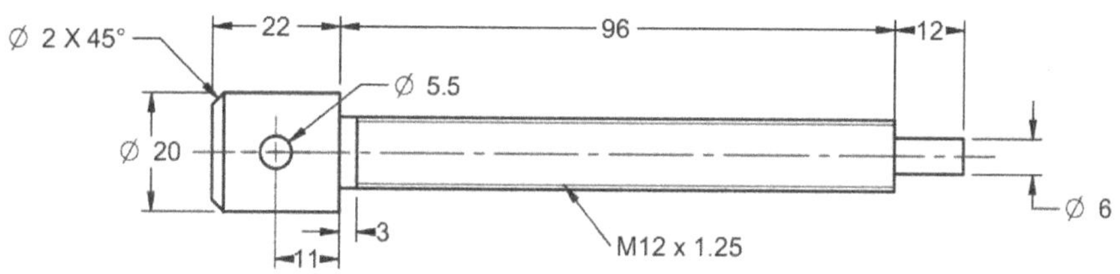

SPINDLE

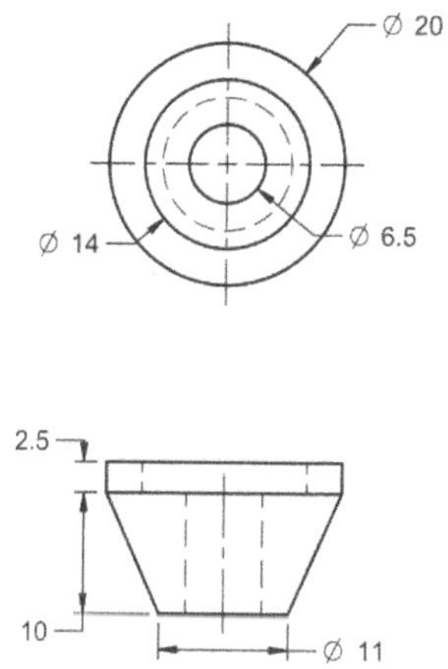

SPINDLE CAP

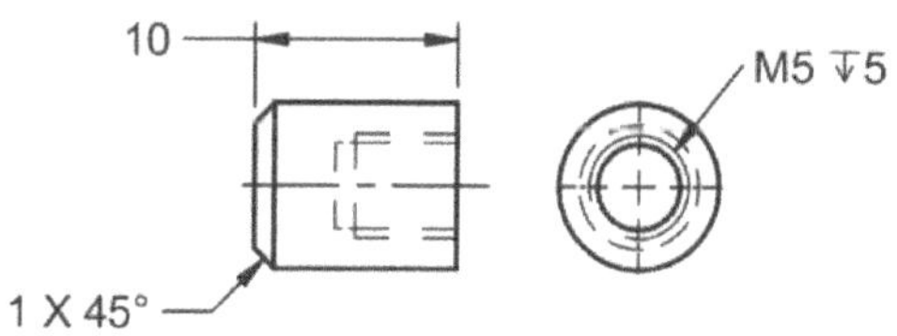

HANDLE CAP

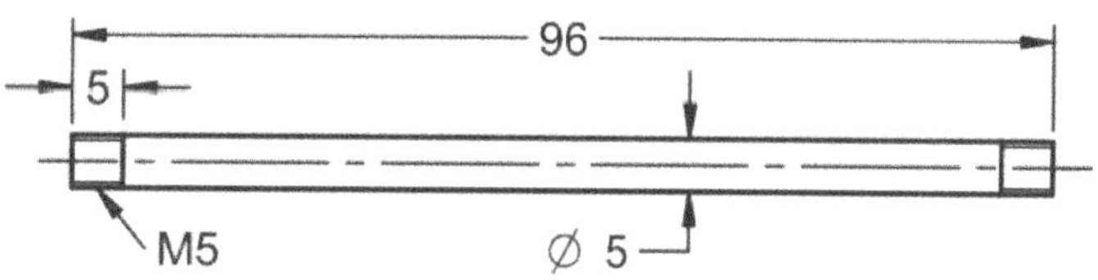

HANDLE

1. Start **NX**.

2. Create and save all the components of the assembly in a single folder. Name this folder as *G-Clamp*. Close all the files.
3. On the ribbon, click the **New** button to open the **New** dialog.
4. On the **New** dialog, select the **Assembly** template and click **OK**. Close the **Assemble** dialog.
5. Click **Assemblies > Component > Add Component** on the ribbon.
6. On the **Add Component** dialog, click the **Open** button and go to the *G-Clamp* folder. Select the *Clamp Jaw* and click **OK**.
7. On the **Add Component** dialog, under the **Location** section, select **Assembly Location > WCS**. Next, select **Placement > Constrain**. Next, click the **OK** and **Yes** buttons.

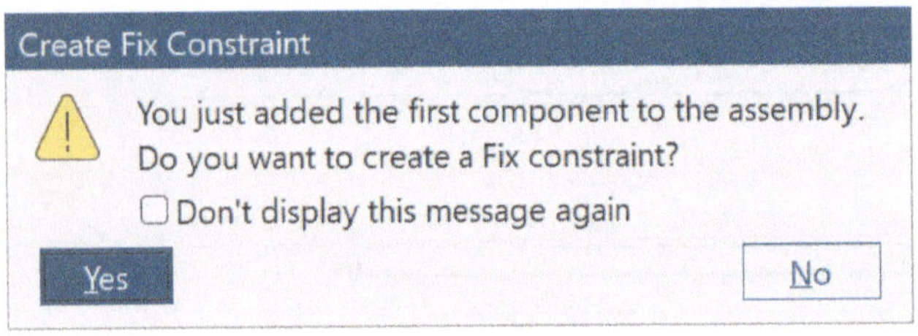

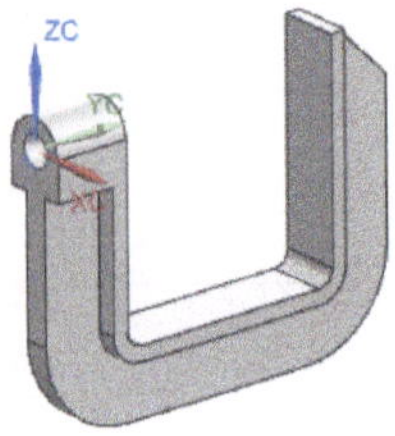

8. Activate the **Add Component** command (click **Assemblies > Component > Add Component** on the ribbon). On the **Add Component** dialog, click the **Open** button and go to the G-Clamp folder. Double-click on the *Spindle.prt* file.
9. Click and drag the move handles of the Dynamic CSYS to move the inserted component. Next, click **OK**.

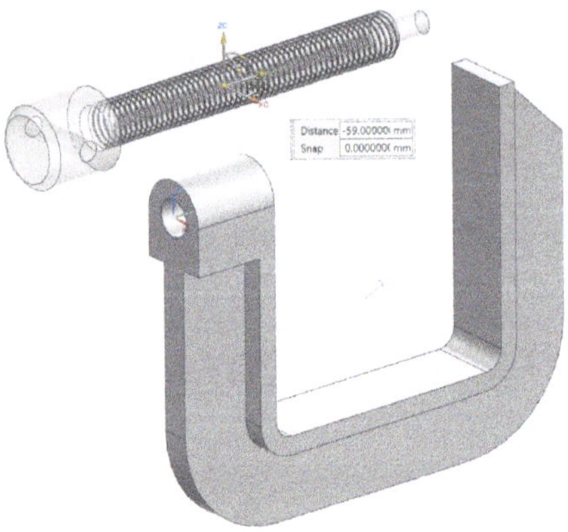

10. On the ribbon, click **Assemblies > Position > Auto Align**. Next, check the **Prefer Center/Axis Over Object** option.
11. Click on the cylindrical face of the *Spindle* and hole of the *Clamp Jaw*. Next, click **Close**.

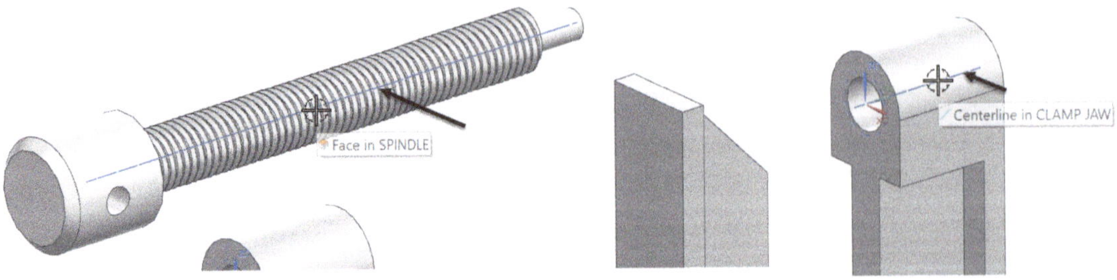

12. On the ribbon, click **Assemblies > Position > Distance** . Next, click on the back face of the *Spindle*.
13. Rotate the view and click on the flat face of the *Clamp Jaw*, as shown in the figure.
14. Type-in **40** in the **Distance** box and click **OK**.

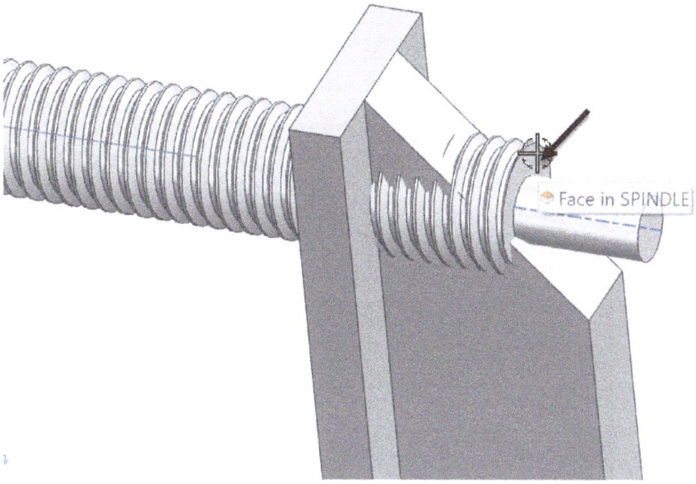

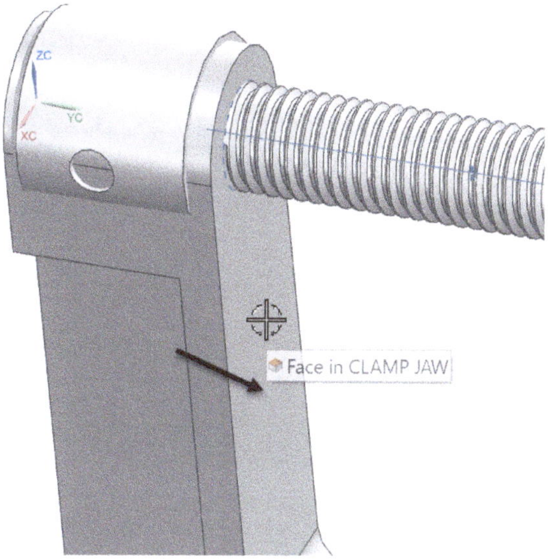

15. On the ribbon, click **Assemblies > Position > More > Show Degrees of Freedom** and select the *Spindle*. You can notice that the spindle is free to rotate.

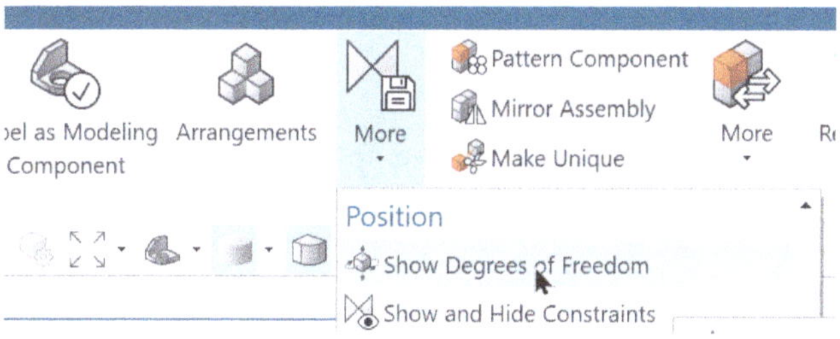

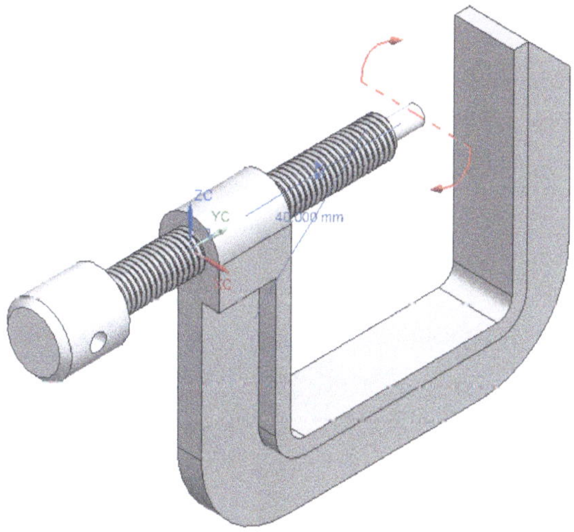

16. Right-click on the *Spindle* and select **Replace Reference Set** > **Entire Part**. All the datum planes of the spindle appear.

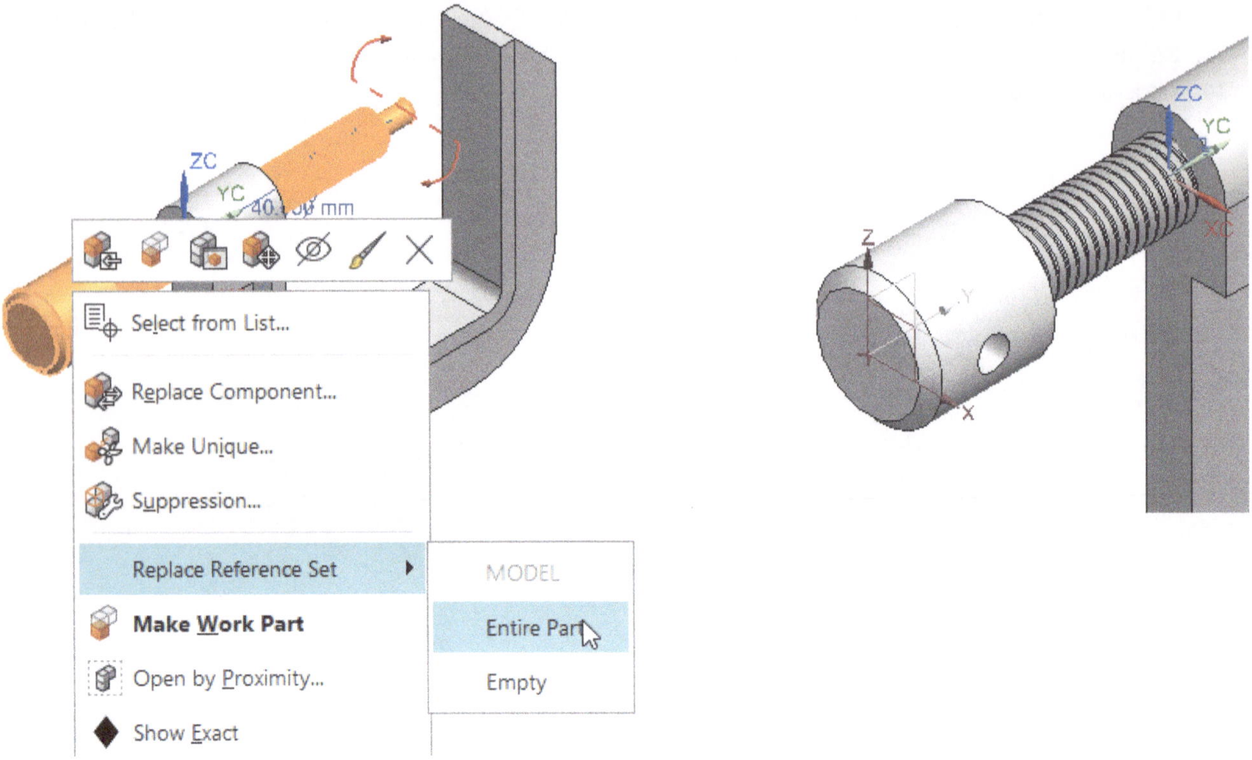

17. On the ribbon, click **Assemblies > Position > Parallel** .
18. Click on the XY plane of the *Spindle* and flat bottom face of the *Clamp Jaw*. Click **OK** to apply the parallel constraint.
19. On the Top Border Bar, click **Menu > View > Operations > Refresh**.
20. Now, activate the **Show Degrees of Freedom** command and select the spindle. You will notice that the spindle is fully constrained.

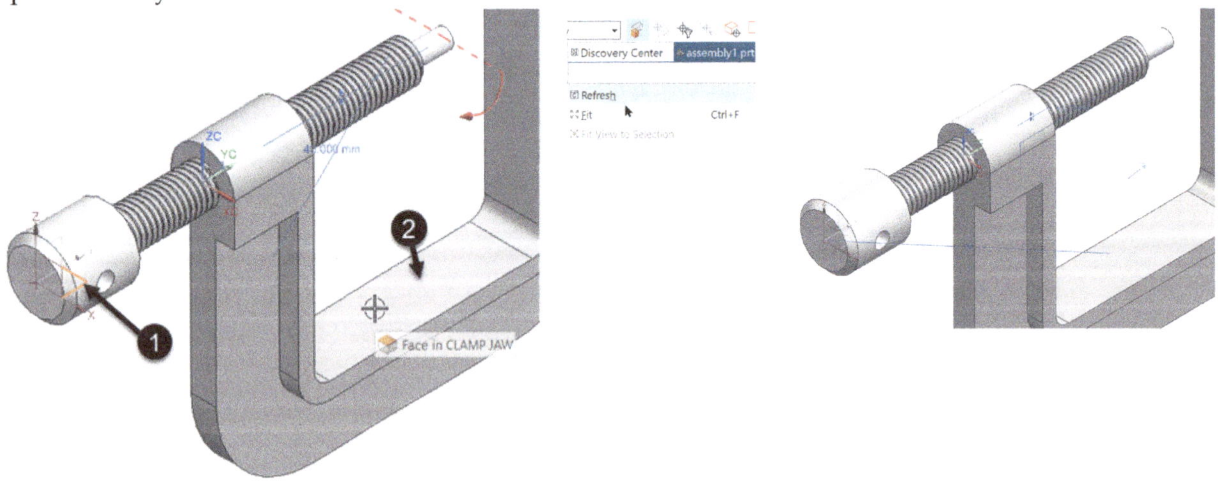

21. Activate the **Add Component** command (click **Assemblies > Base > Add Component** on the ribbon).
22. On the **Add Component** dialog, click the **Open** button and go to the *G-Clamp* folder. Select the *Spindle Cap.prt* file and click **OK**.

23. On the **Add Component** dialog, select **Settings > Reference Set > Entire Part**.
24. Drag the move handle of the Dynamic CSYS to move the *Spindle Cap*. Next, click **OK**.

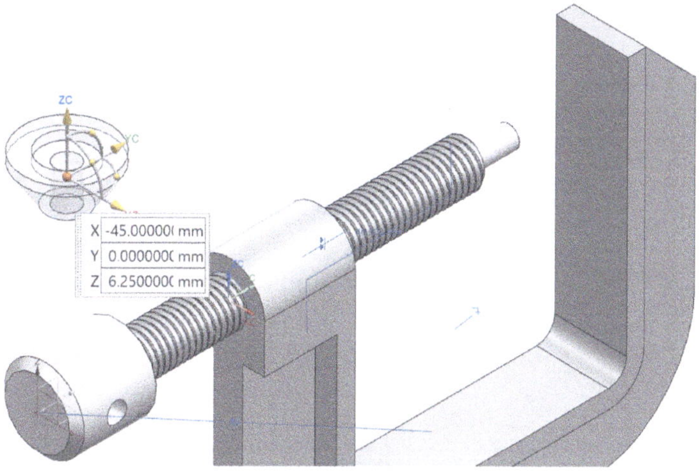

25. On the ribbon, click **Assemblies > Position > Concentric** . Click on the inner circular edge of the *Spindle Cap* hole.
26. Rotate the assembly and select the circular edge of the spindle, as shown. Click **OK**.

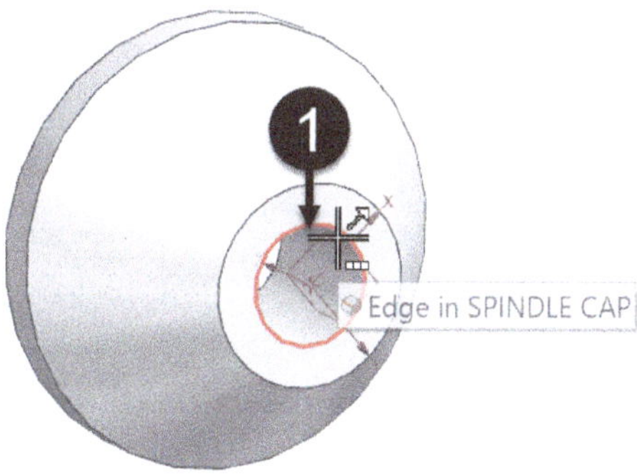

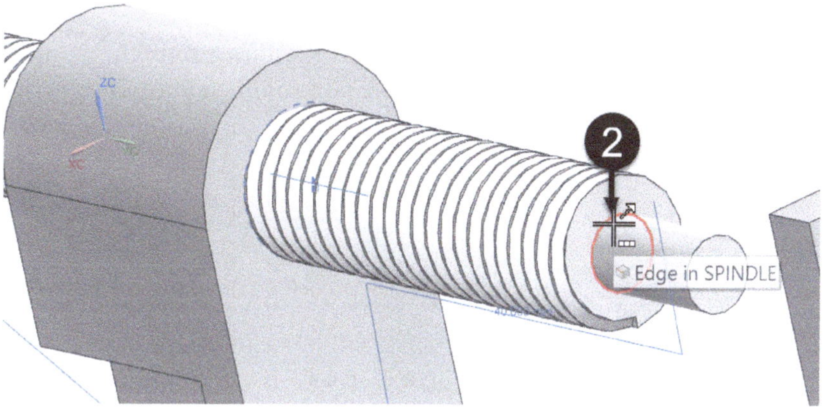

27. On the ribbon, click **Assemblies > Position > Align** .
28. Click on the YZ planes of the *Spindle Cap* and *Spindle*. Click **OK**.

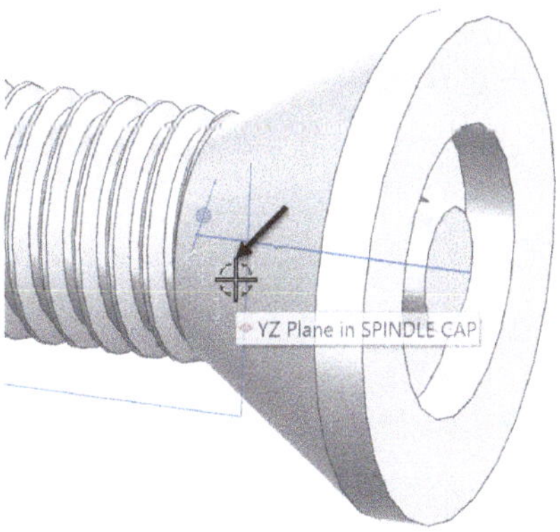

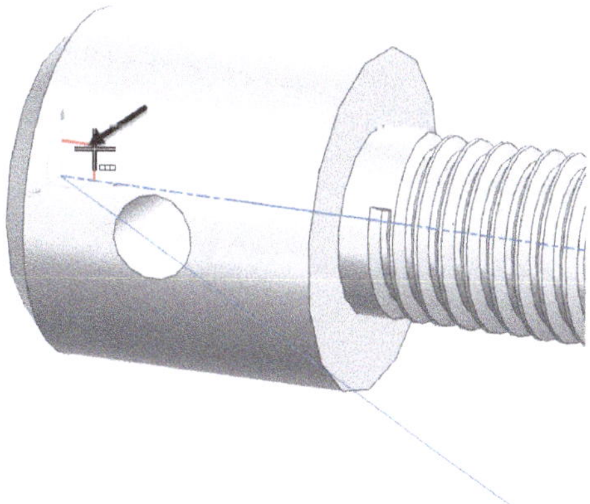

29. Activate the **Add Component** command and insert the *Handle*.
30. Drag the move handle of the Dynamic CSYS to move the *Handle*. Next, click **OK**.

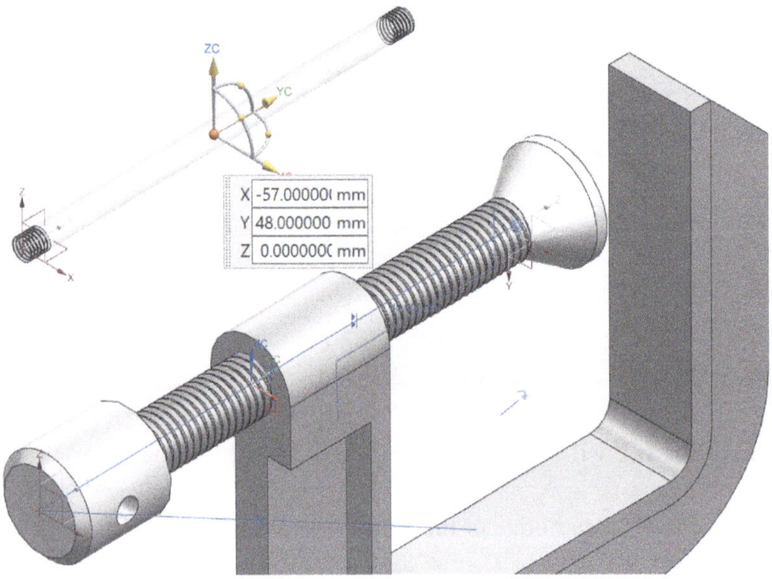

31. On the ribbon, click **Assemblies > Position > Center** and set the **Type** to **1 to 2**.
32. Click on the YZ plane of the *Spindle*, and then the end faces of the *Handle*.

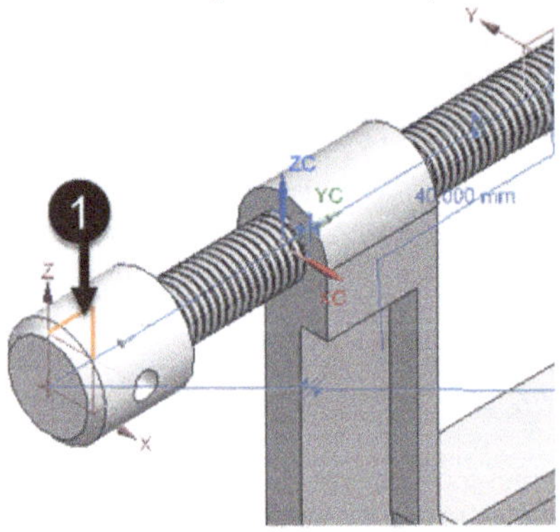

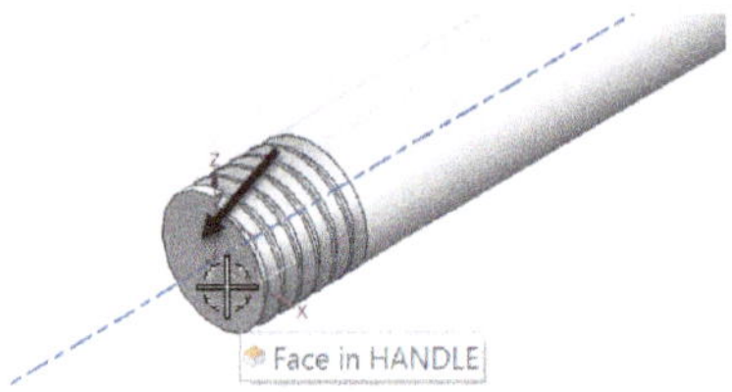

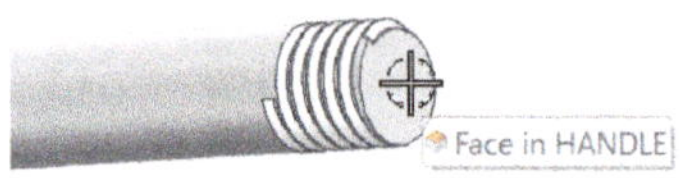

33. Click the **Reverse Direction** button if the Datum Coordinate Planes of the *Handle* are displayed on the left side, as shown. Next, click **OK**.

Before reversing the constraint

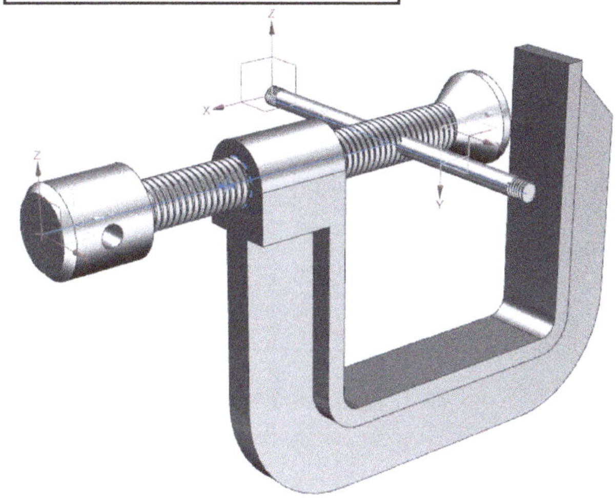

After reversing the constraint

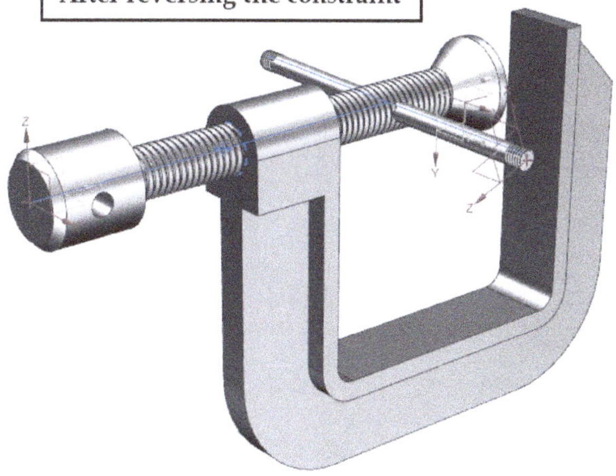

34. On the ribbon, click **Assemblies > Position > Align/Lock** and click on the centerline of the *Handle*.
35. Click on the centerline of the hole on the *Spindle*, and then click **OK**.

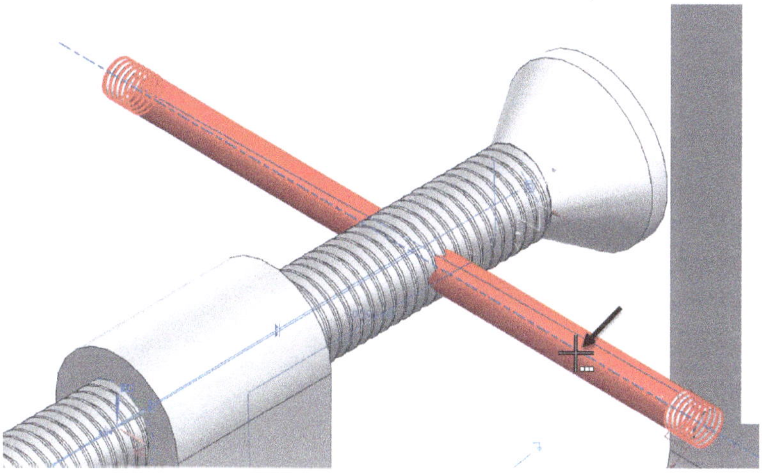

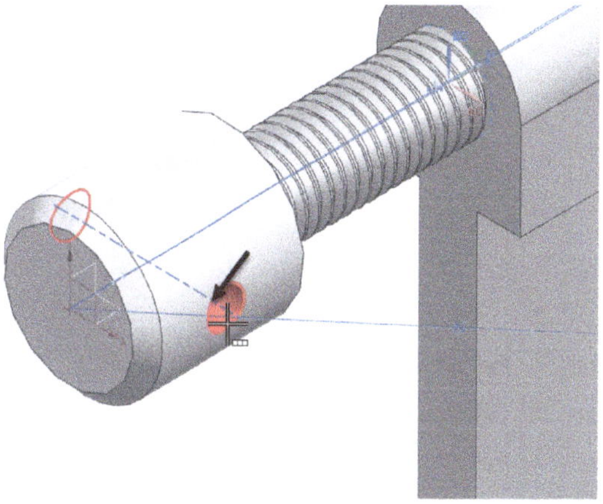

36. Activate the **Add Component** command and insert the *Handle Cap*.
37. Drag the move handle of the Dynamic CSYS to move the *Handle Cap*. Next, click **OK**.

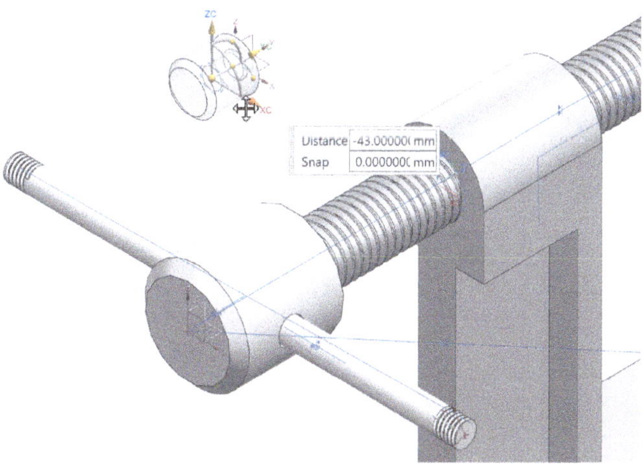

38. On the ribbon, click **Assemblies > Position > Concentric** and click on the innermost circular edge of the hole of the *Handle Cap*.
39. Click on the circular edge of the *Handle*. Next, click **OK**.

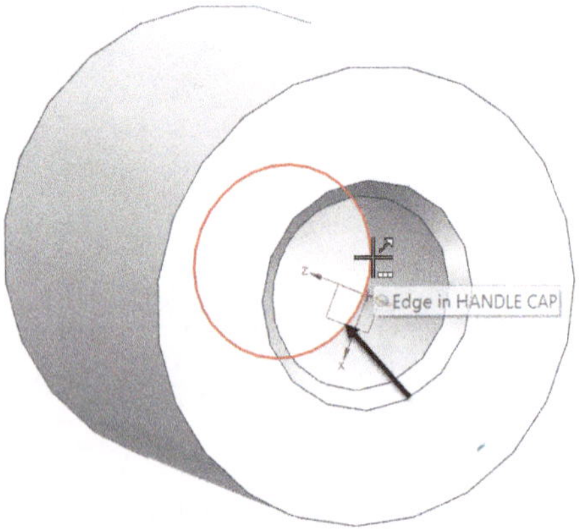

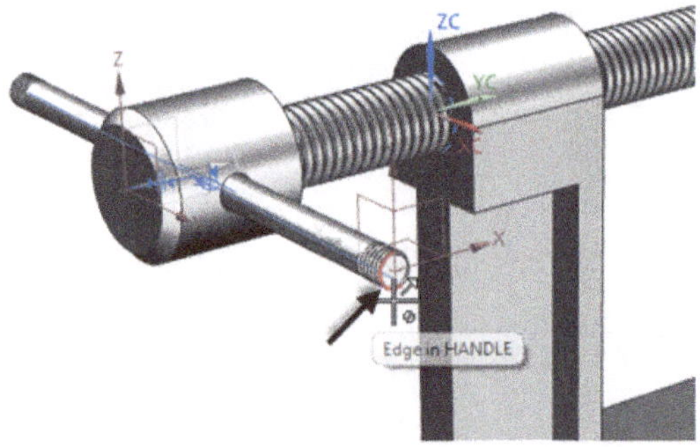

40. On the ribbon, click **Assemblies > Position > Align** .
41. Click on the YZ planes of the *Handle* and *Handle Cap*, and then click **OK**.

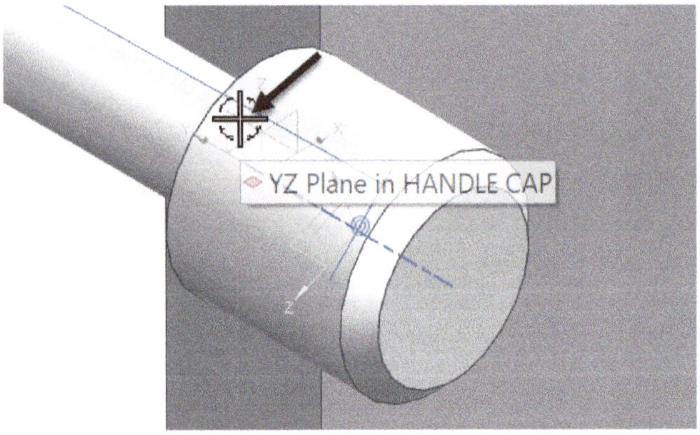

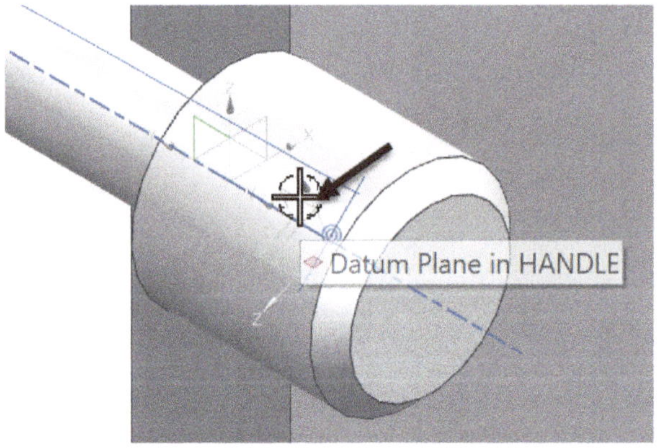

42. Activate the **Remember Constraints** command (on the ribbon, click **Assemblies > Position > More > Remember Constraints**) select the *Handle Cap*.
43. On the **Assembly Navigator**, expand the **Constraints** section, press the Ctrl key, and select the **Concentric** and **Align** constraints located at the bottom. Click **OK**.

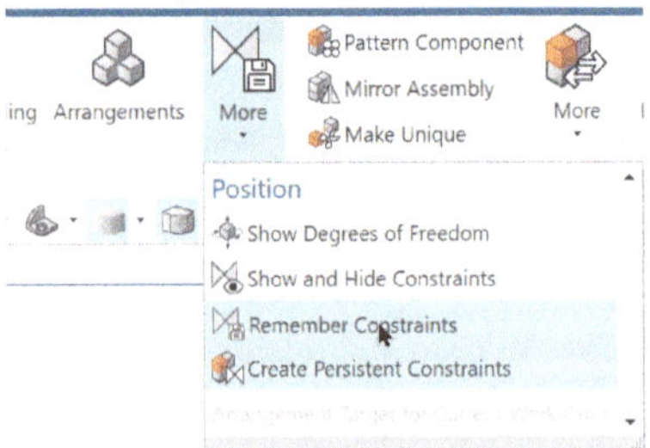

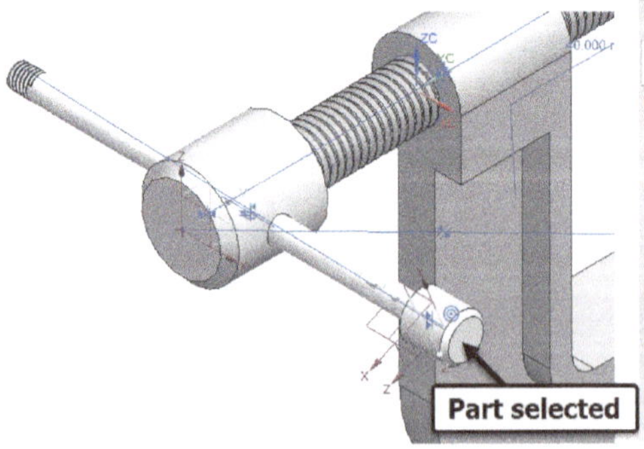

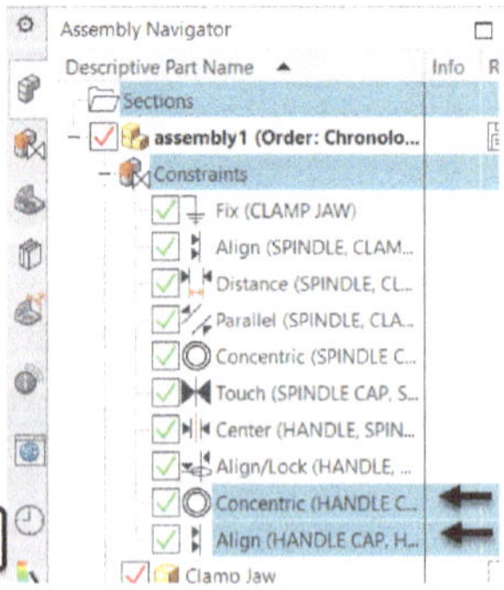

44. Activate the **Add Component** command and insert the *Handle Cap*.
45. Drag the move handle of the Dynamic CSYS to move the *Handle Cap*. Next, click **OK**.
46. Next, click **OK** on the **Add Component** dialog; the **Resolve Constraints** dialog pops up on the screen. In addition, the **Align** constraint is active, and YZ plane of the *Handle Cap* is selected.
47. Click on the YZ plane of the *Handle*. The **Concentric** constraint is active, and the inner circular edge of the *Handle Cap* hole is selected.

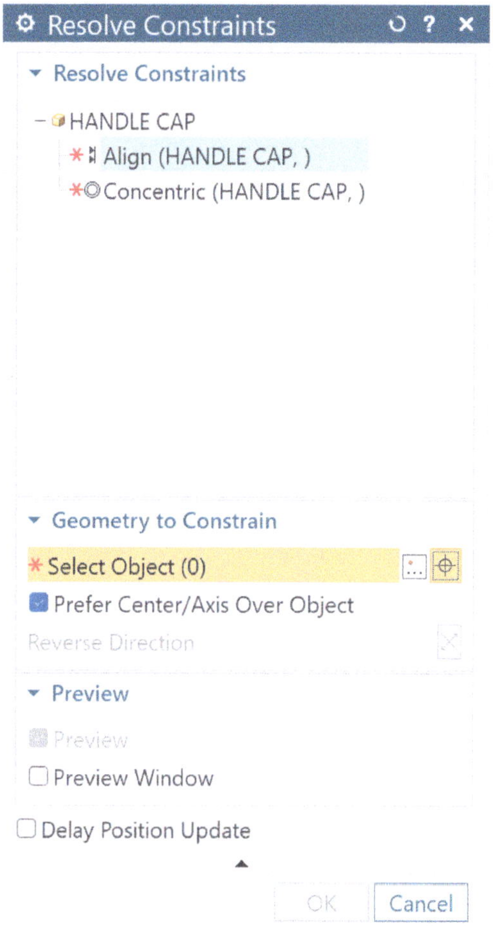

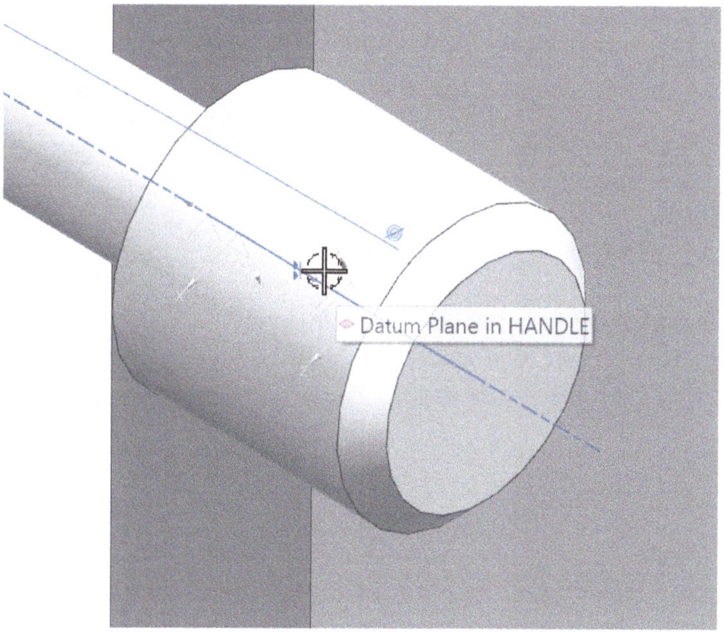

48. Rotate the assembly view and click on the circular edge of the *Handle*.
49. Click the **Reverse Constraint** button on the **Redefine Constraint** dialog, if the *Handle Cap* is displayed in reverse direction. Click **OK**.

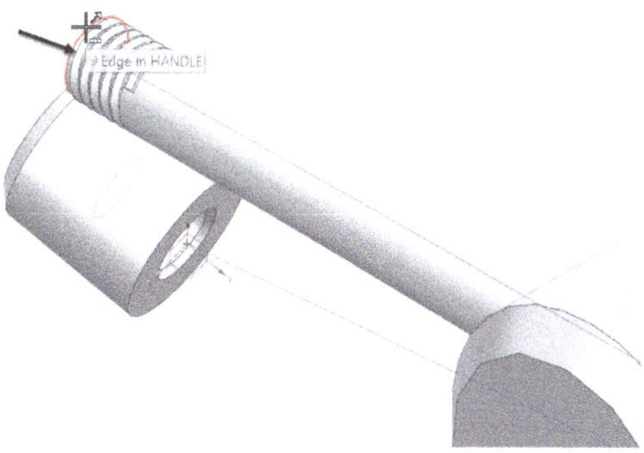

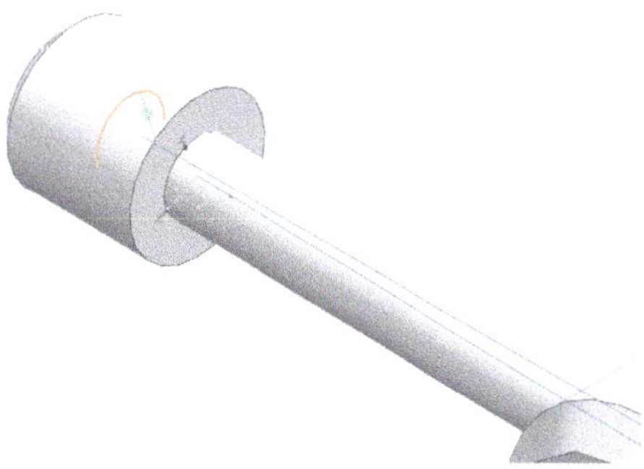

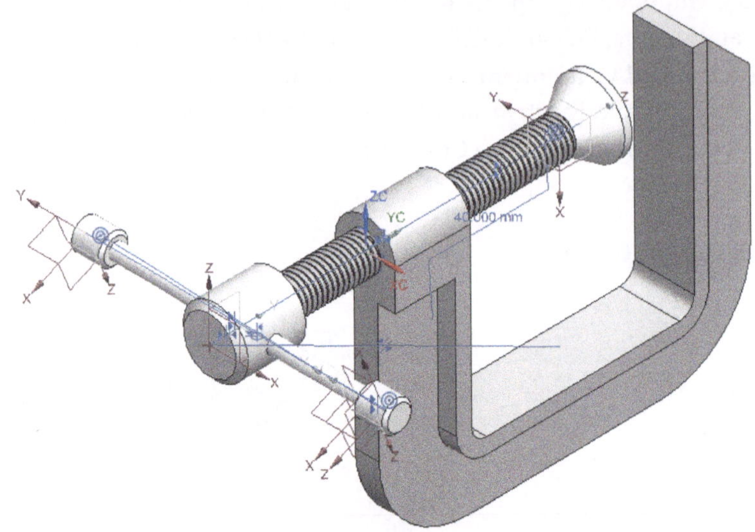

50. Save and close the assembly.

Example 2 (Top-Down Assembly)

In this example, you will create the assembly shown next.

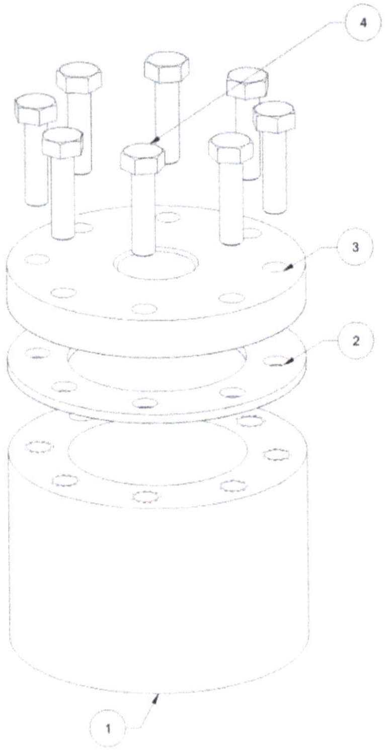

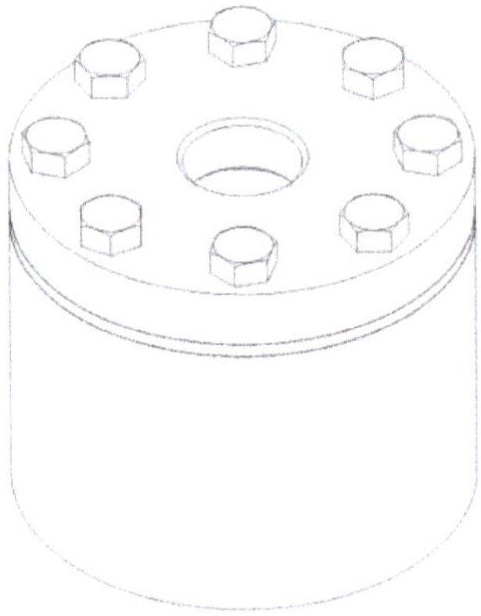

PC NO	PART NAME	QTY
4	HEX BOLT, AM,M8X1.25X30	8
3	COVER PLATE	1
2	GASKET	1
1	CYLINDER BASE	1

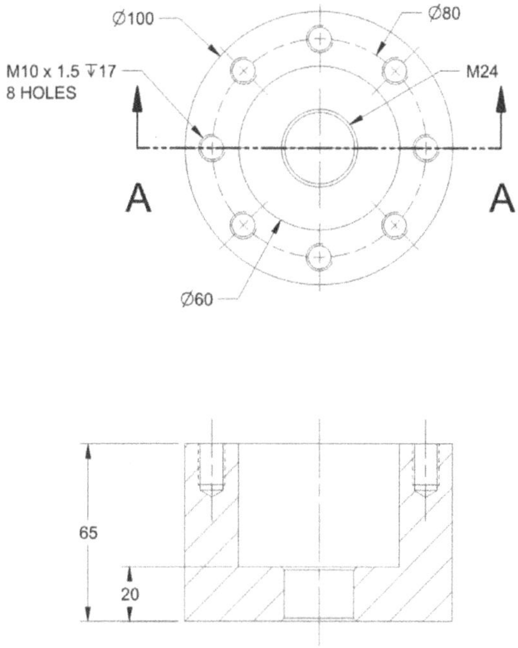

SECTION A-A

Cylinder Base

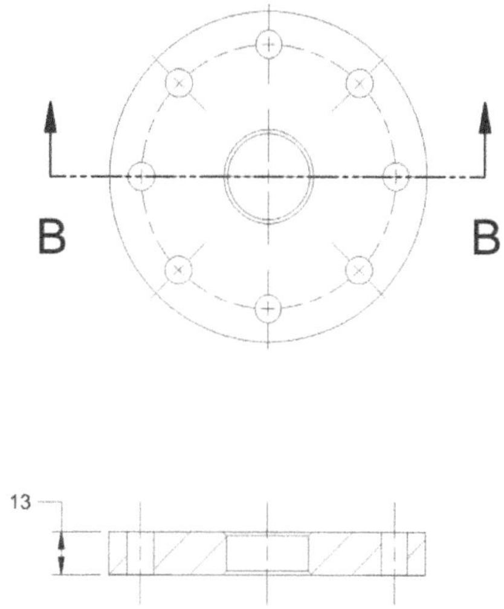

SECTION B-B

Cover Plate

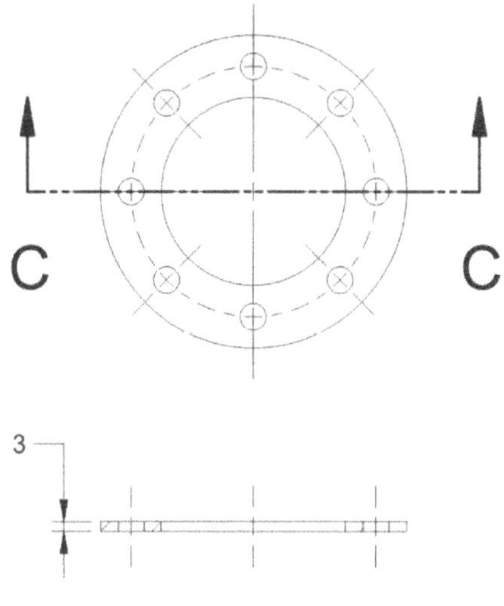

SECTION C-C

Gasket

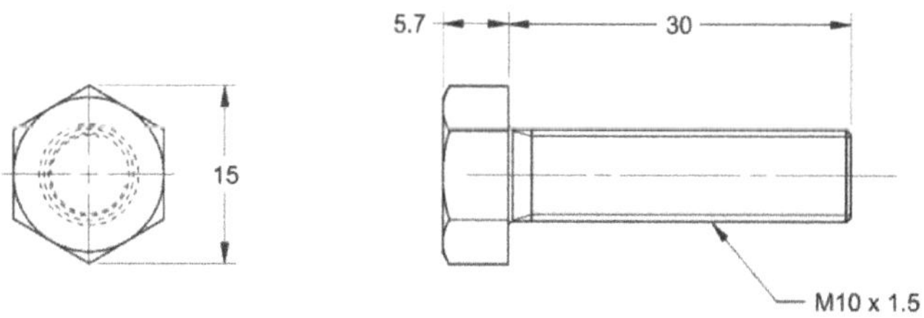

Screw

1. Create a new folder with the name the *Pressure Cylinder*.
2. Start **NX**.
3. On the ribbon, click the **New** button to open the **New** dialog.
4. On the **New** dialog, select the **Assembly** template and click **OK**.

5. Close the **Assemble** dialog.
6. Create a sketch on the Front Datum plane, as shown.
7. Activate the **Revolve** command (on the ribbon, **Home > Feature > Revolve**). Select the sketch and create the revolved feature.

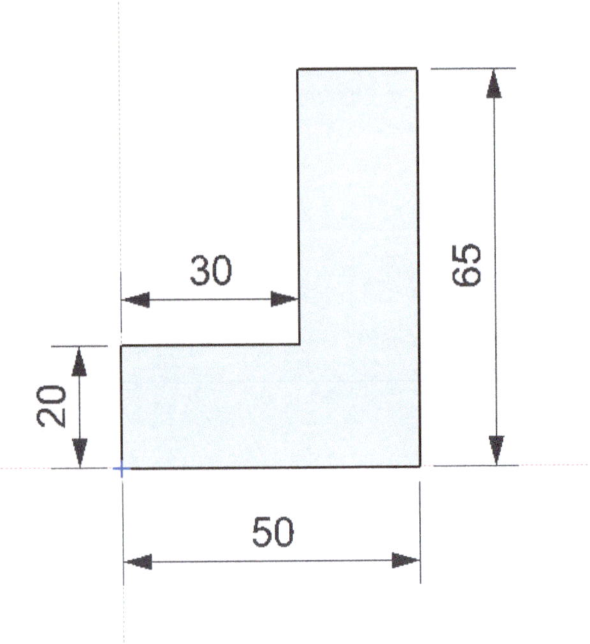

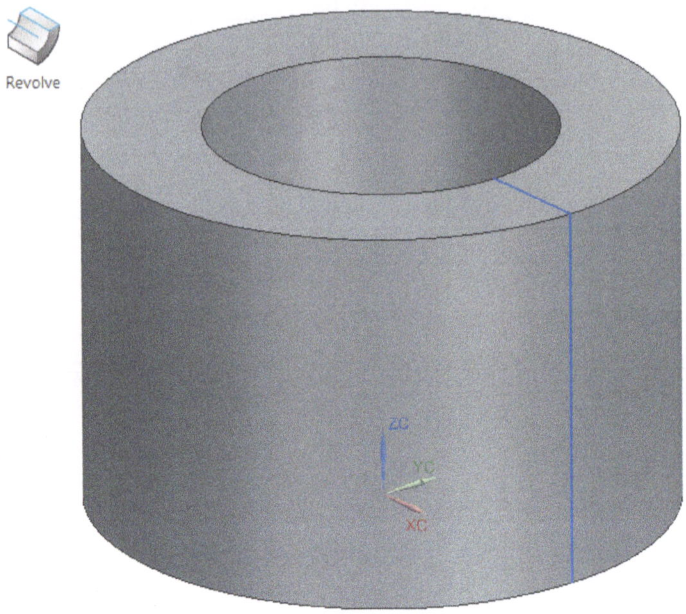

8. Activate the **Hole** command (on the ribbon, **Home > Base > Hole**). On the **Hole** dialog, select **Type > Threaded Hole**.
9. Click on the top face of the model; a point is placed on the selected face. Change the location dimensions of the point, as shown.

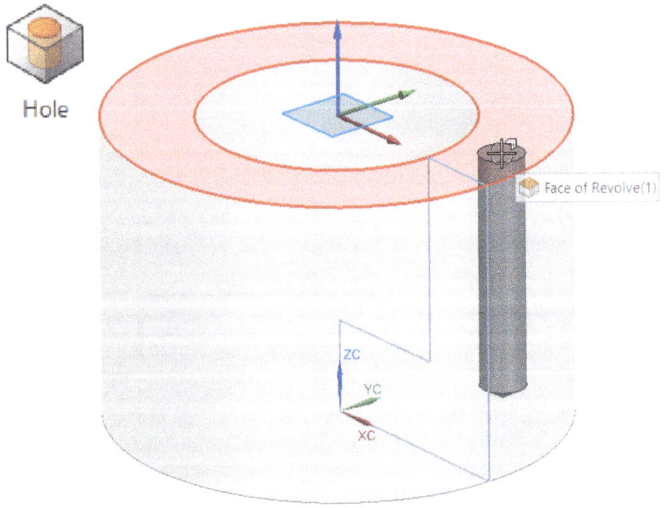

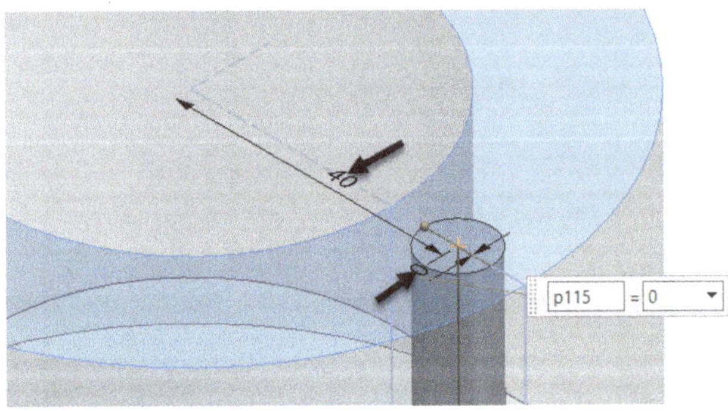

10. On the **Hole** dialog, set the options in the **Form** and **Limit** sections, as shown. Click **OK** to complete the hole feature.

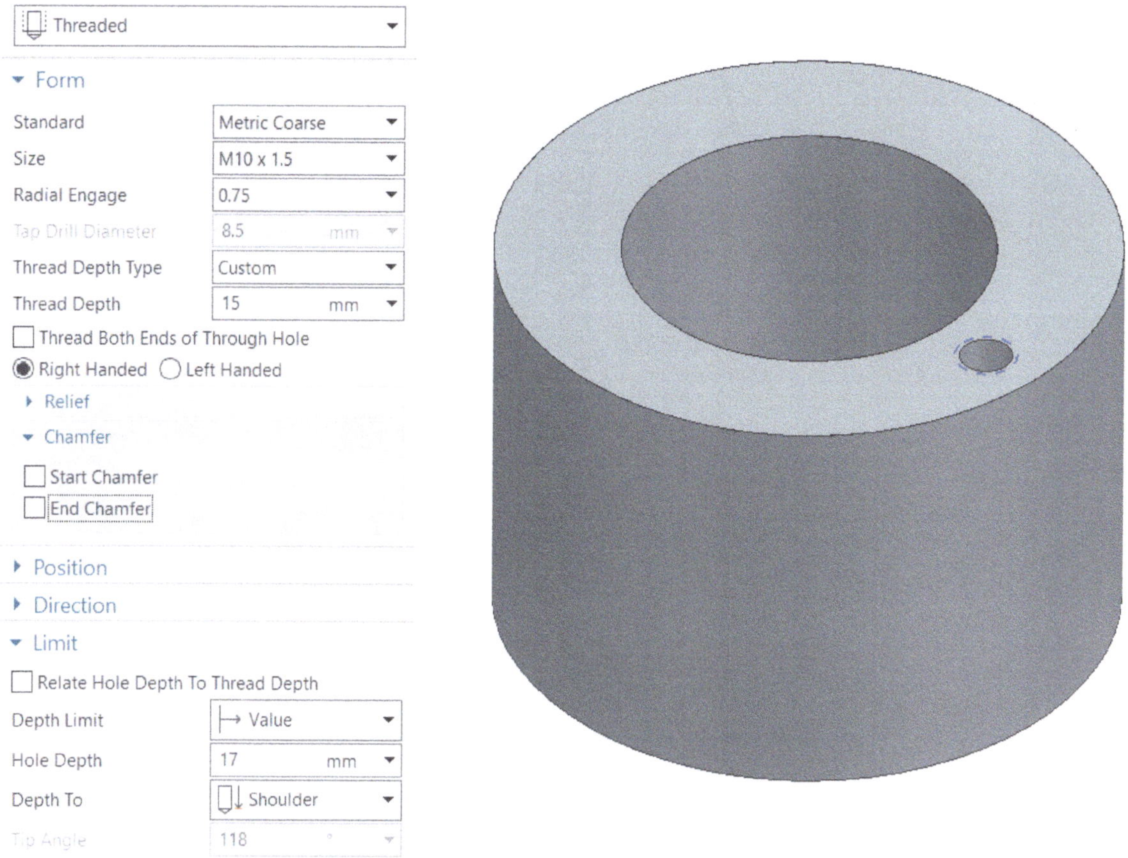

11. Activate the **Pattern Feature** command (on the ribbon, click **Home > Base > Pattern Feature**).
12. On the **Pattern Feature** dialog, select **Layout > Circular**.
13. Select the hole feature from the model.
14. Click **Specify Vector** under the **Rotation Axis** section, and then select the cylindrical portion of the model.
15. Select **Spacing > Count and Span** under the **Angular Direction** section.
16. Set **Count** = 8 and **Span Angle** = 360 degrees under the **Angular Direction** section, and then click **OK**.

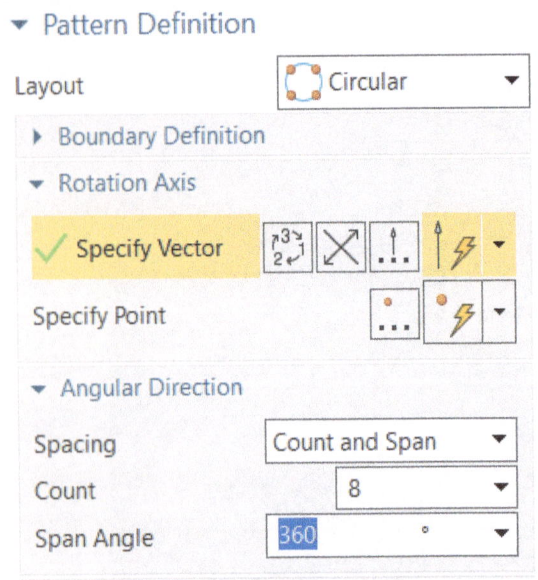

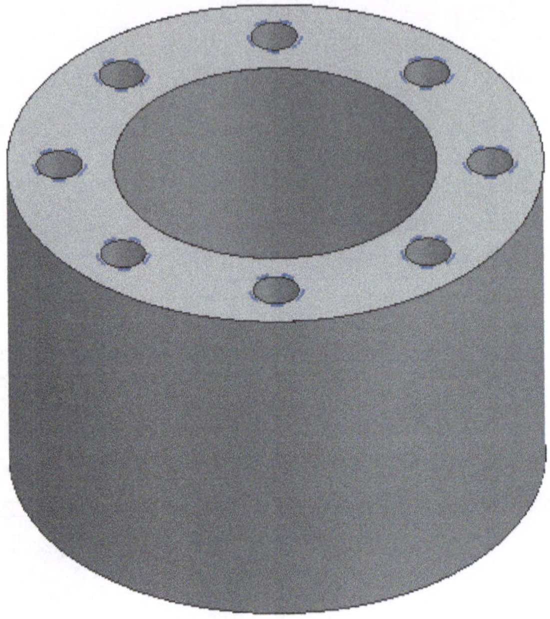

17. On the ribbon, click **Assemblies > Base > New Component** to open the **New Component** dialog.

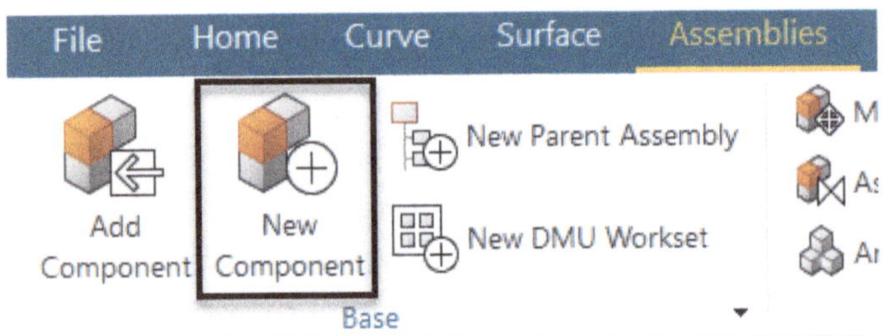

18. On the **New Component** dialog, expand the **Settings** section and type-in *Cylinder base* in the **Component name** box. Next, select the model geometry and click **OK**.
19. Activate the **New Component**  command (on the ribbon, click **Assemblies > Base > New Component**). The **New Component** dialog pops up.
20. Type-in *Gasket* in the Component **Name** box and click **OK**.
21. Click the **Assembly Navigator**  tab on the Resource Bar.
22. On the **Assembly Navigator**, double-click on the component located at the bottom of the tree.
23. On the Top Border Bar, deactivate the **Allow Automatic Work Part Change** icon.

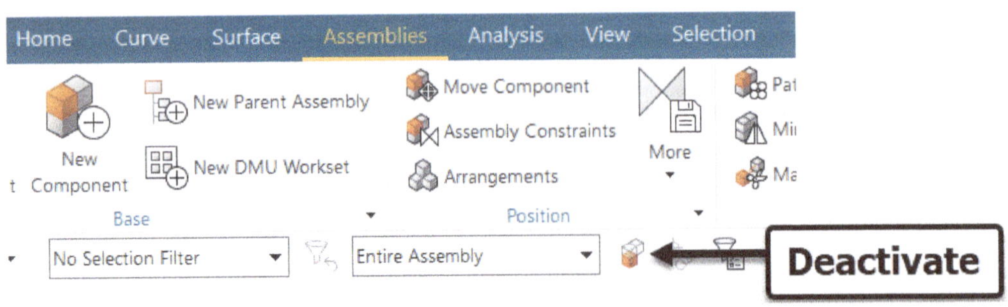

24. Activate the **Extrude** command (on the ribbon, click **Home > Base > Extrude**).

25. On the Top Border Bar, set the **Selection Scope** to **Entire Assembly**, and then activate the **Create Interpart Link** button.

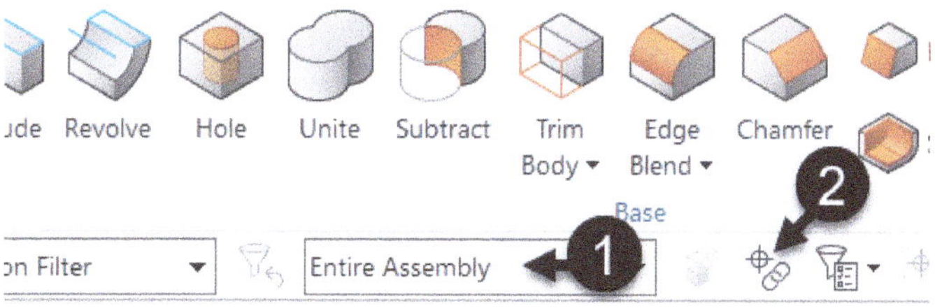

26. Click on the top face of the cylinder base. The **Interpart Copy** message pops up on the screen. Click **OK**; an interpart link is created between the **Gasket** and **Cylinder base**.

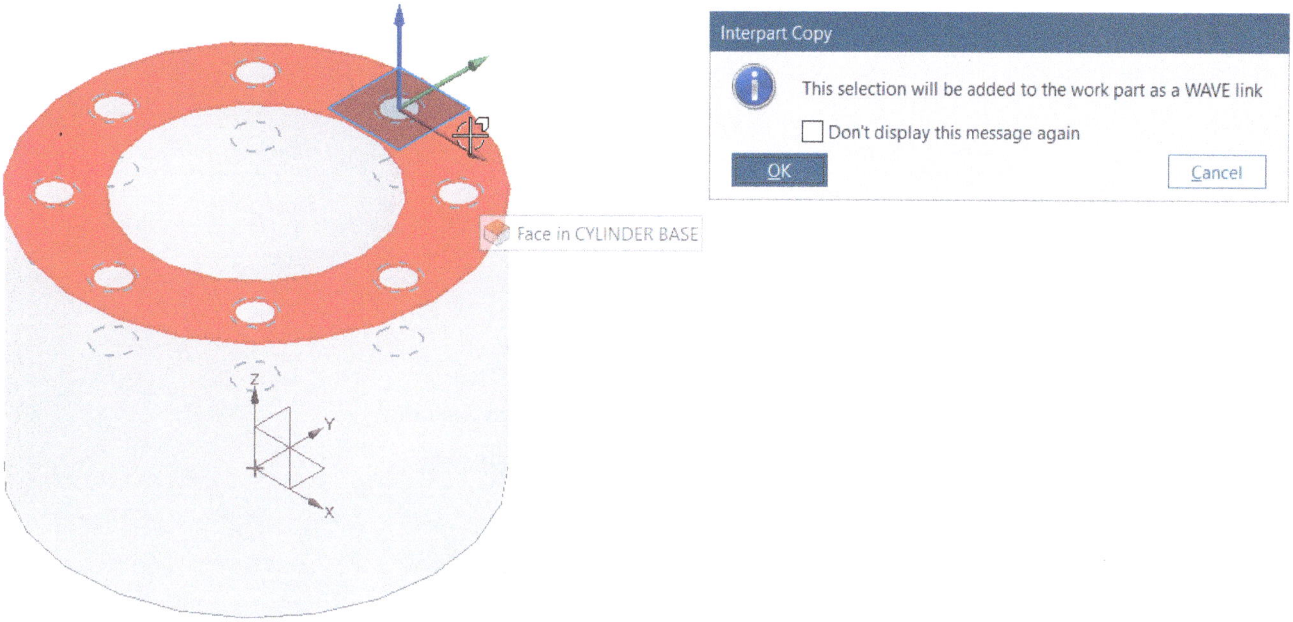

27. On the ribbon, click **Home > Include > Project Curve**. Set the **Curve rule** to **Face Edges** and click on the top face of the cylinder base. Click **OK** on the **Project Curve** dialog to project all the edges of the top face.

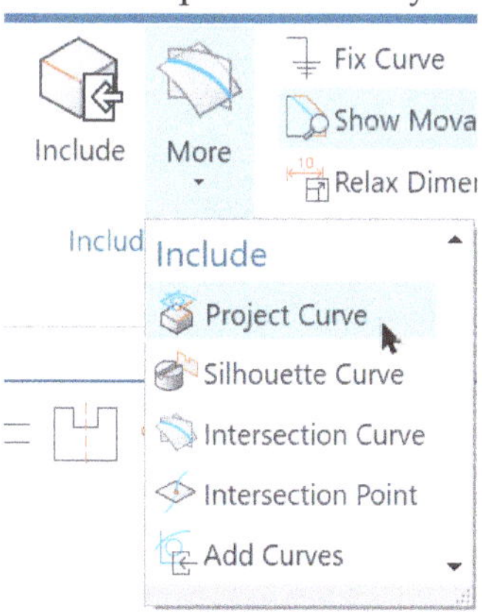

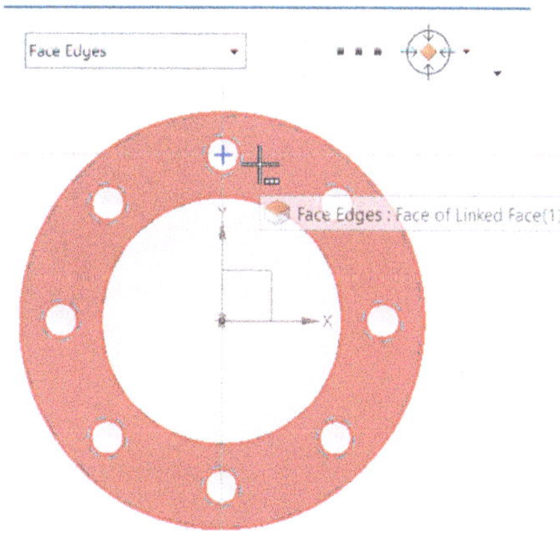

28. Click **Finish** on the ribbon and extrude the sketch up to 3 mm depth.

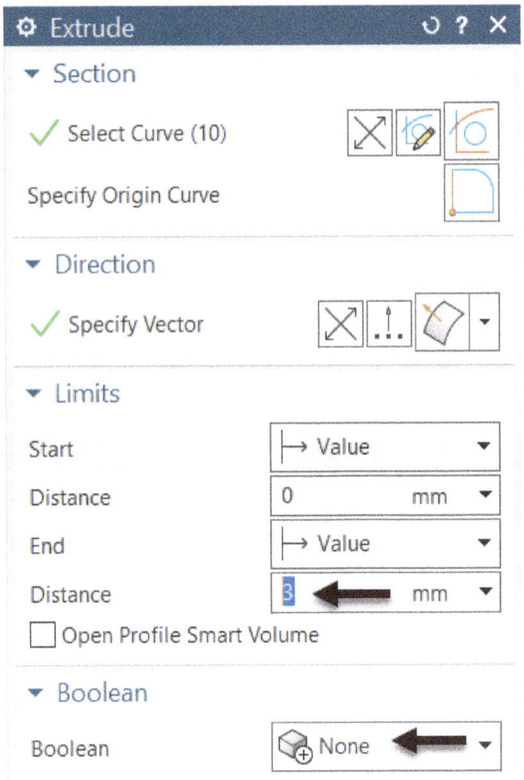

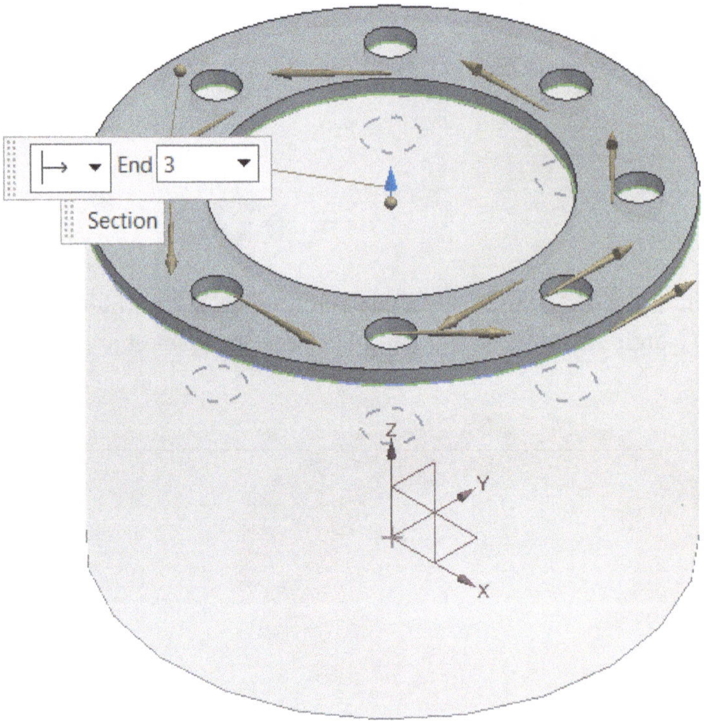

29. On the ribbon, click **Assemblies > Context > More > Work on Assembly**.

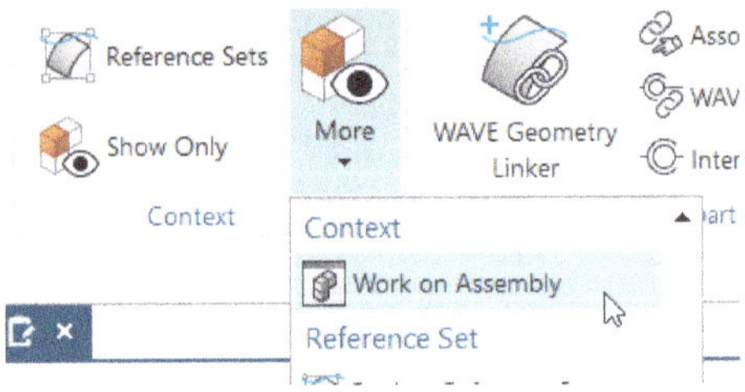

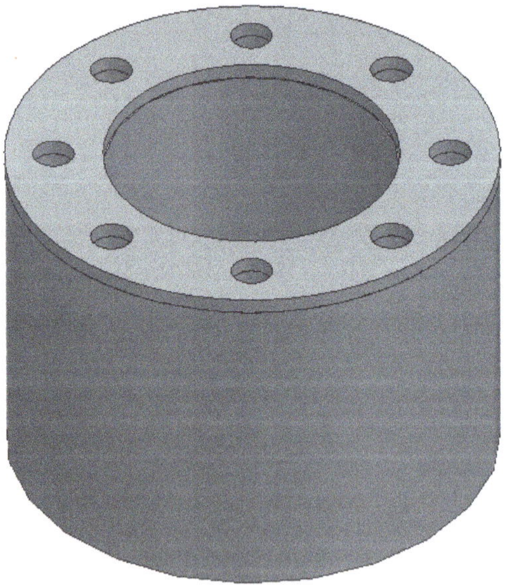

30. Activate the **New Component**  command and type *Cover plate* in the **Component Name** box. Next, click **OK**.
31. In the **Assembly Navigator**, double-click on the component located at the bottom of the tree to activate the part mode.
32. On the Top Border Bar, deactivate the **Allow Automatic Work Part Change**  icon.

33. Activate the **Extrude** command and click the top face of the Gasket. Make sure that the **Create Interpart Link** icon is selected on the Top Border Bar.
34. Activate the **Project Curve** command and select **Curve Rule > Single Curve** on the Top Border Bar.
35. Select the outer edge and the edges of the hole pattern, and then click **OK**.
36. Click **Finish** on the ribbon.
37. Type 13 in the **End** box attached to the extrusion and click **OK**.

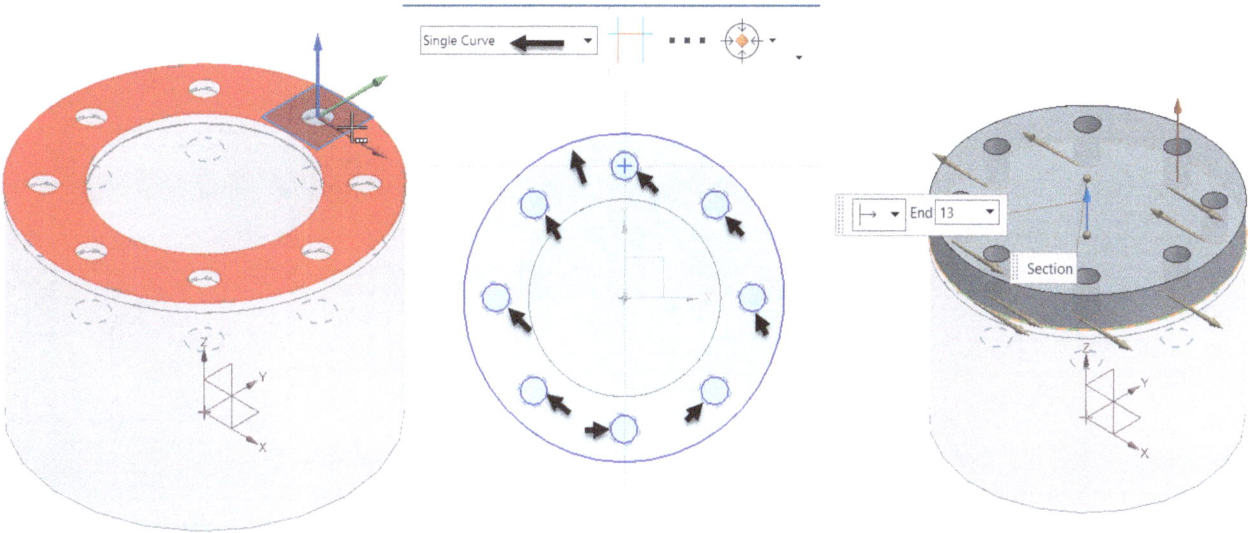

38. On the ribbon, click **Assemblies > Context > Work on Assembly**.
39. On the ribbon, click **Home > Base > Hole**.
40. On the **Hole** dialog, select **Type > Hole Series**. Set the **Screw Size** to M24 and create a hole on the top face.

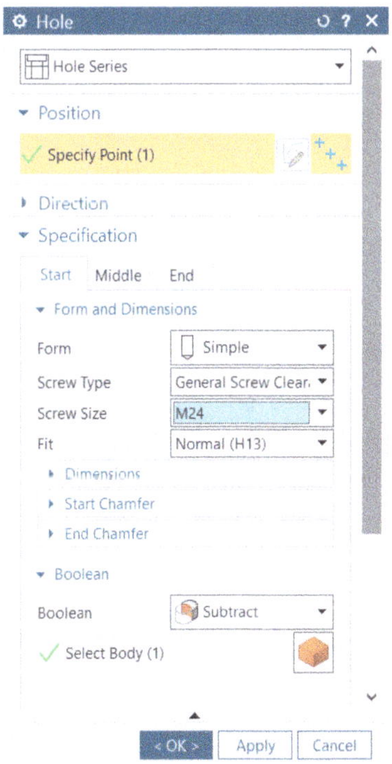

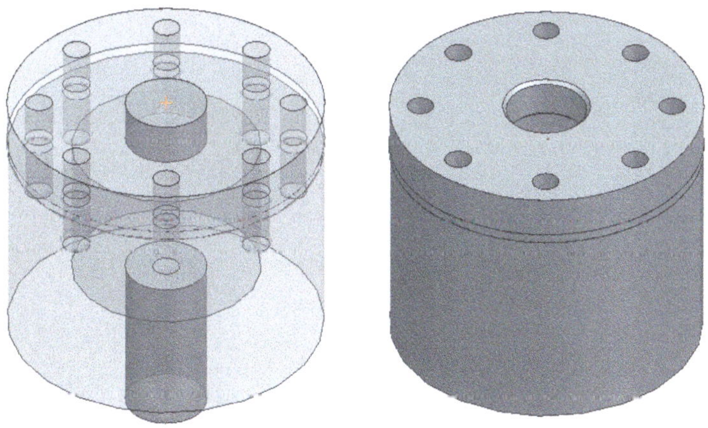

41. On the ribbon, click **Tools > Reuse Library > Fastener Assembly**.

42. On the **Fastener Assembly** dialog, check the **Find Coaxial Hole** option and click on the cylindrical face of any one of the small holes.
43. You will notice a fastener assembly in the **Hole** section of the **Fastener Assembly** dialog. Click **OK**.

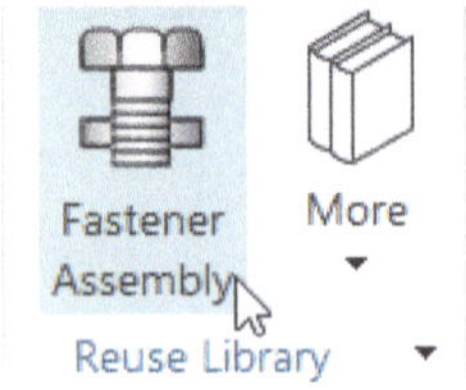

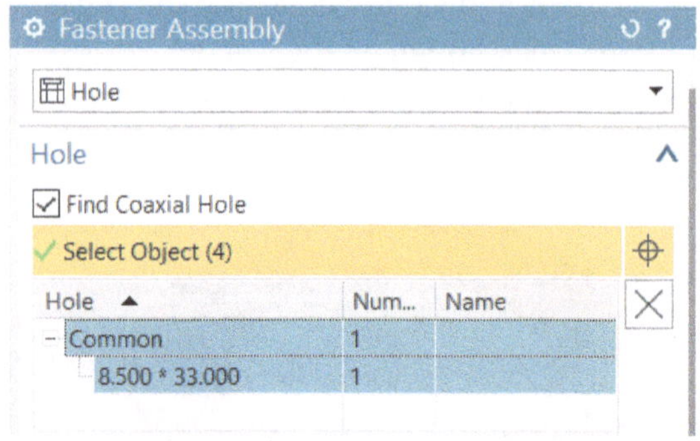

44. On the **Configure Fastener Assembly** dialog, set the **Standard** to **ANSI Metric**.
45. Under the **Fastener Configuration** section, delete **Top Stacks** and **Bottom Stacks** and click **OK**.

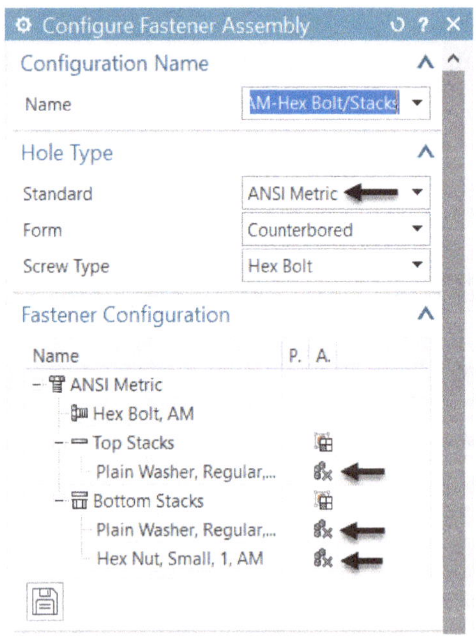

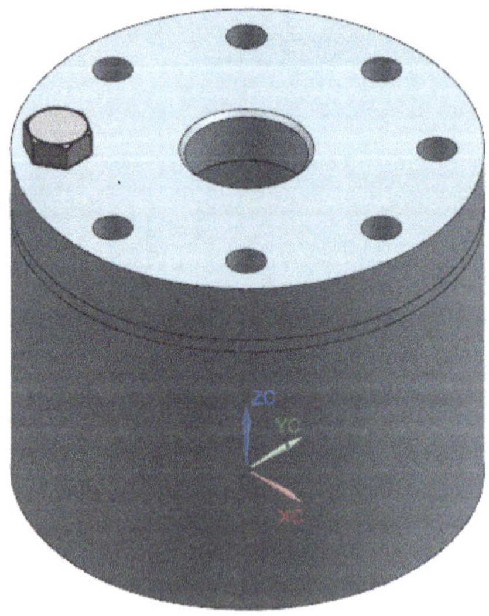

46. On the ribbon, click **Assemblies > Component > Pattern Component**.
47. On the **Assembly Navigator**, select the bolt assembly.

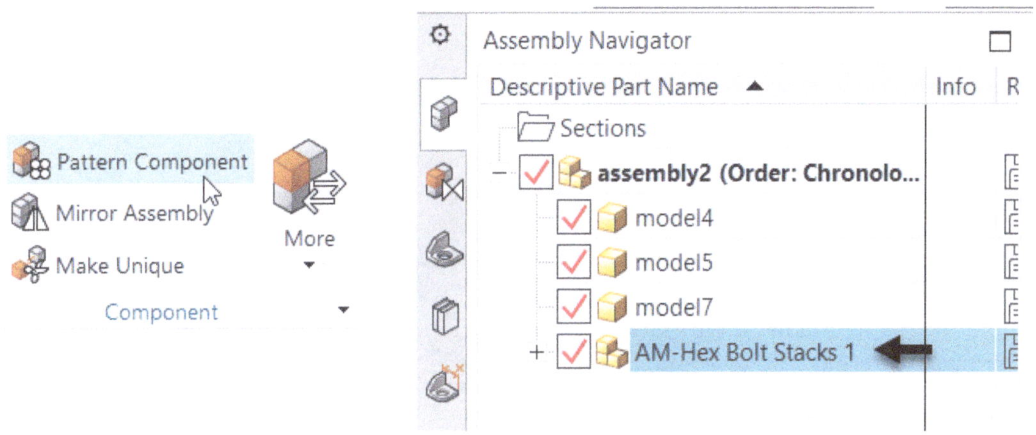

48. On the **Pattern Component** dialog, set the **Layout** type to **Circular**.
49. Set **Spacing** to **Count and Span** and type-in **8** and **360** in the **Count** and **Span Angle** boxes.
50. Under the **Rotation Axis** section, click **Specify Vector** and select the Z-axis vector from the triad.
51. Select the center point of the cover plate and click **OK** to pattern the bolts.

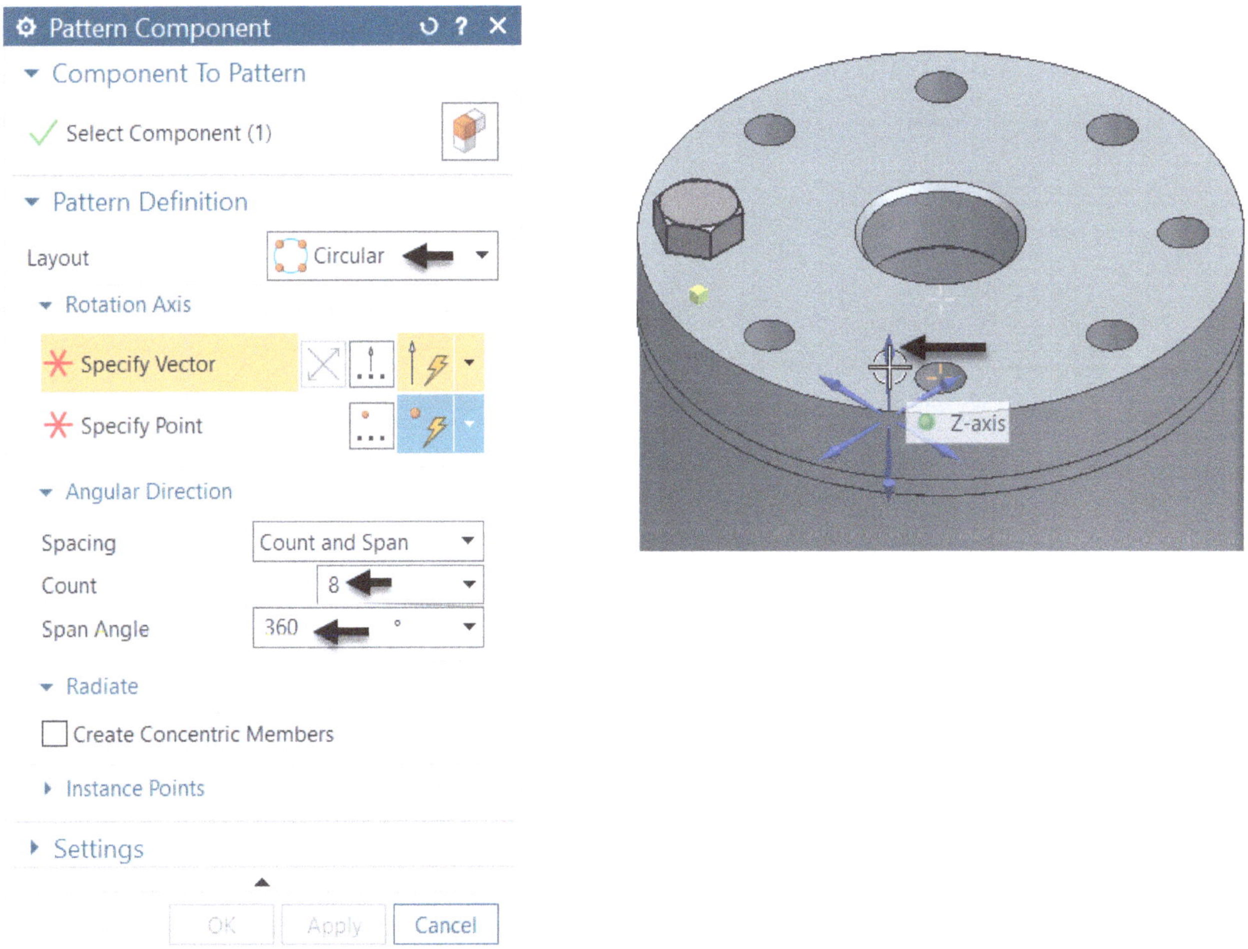

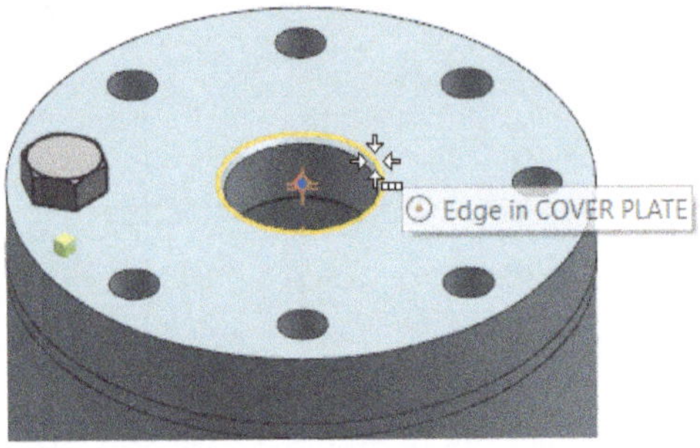

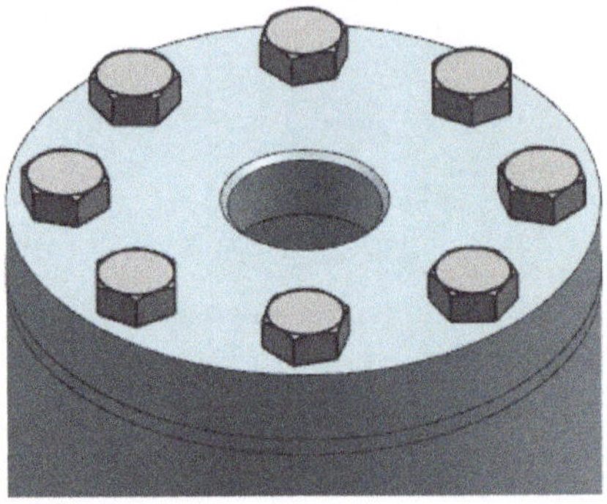

52. On the ribbon, click **Assemblies > Explosions > Explosion**.
53. Click **New Explosion** on the **Explosions** dialog.
54. Select **AM-Hex Bolt Stacks 1x 8** from the **Assembly Navigator**.

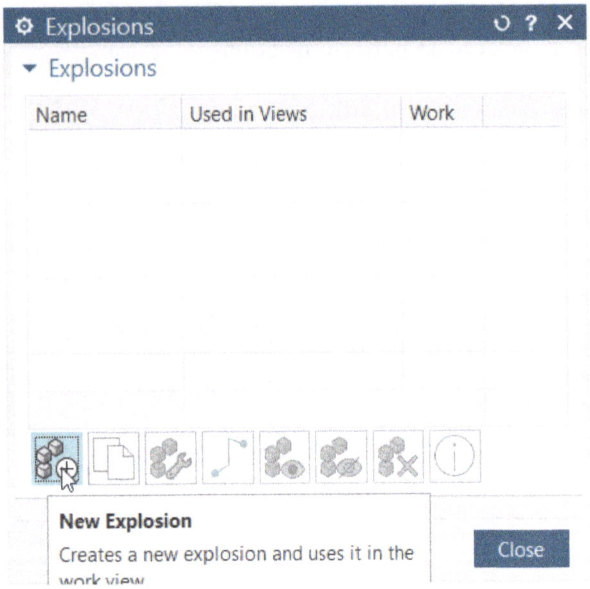

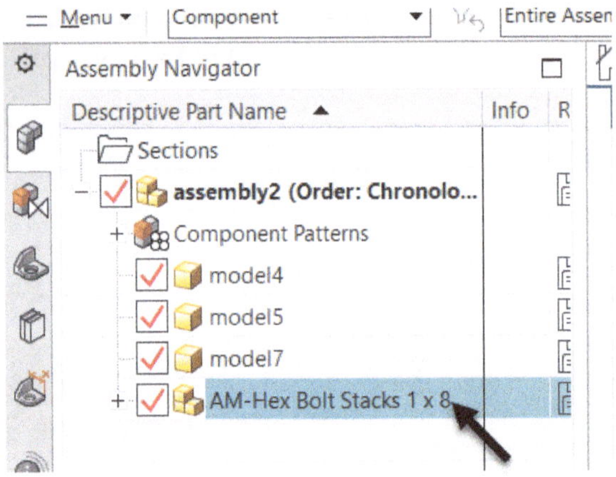

55. On the **Edit Explosion** dialog, select **Manual** from the **Explosion Type** drop-down available in the **Move Components** section.
56. Click the **Specify Orientation** option and select the Z handle on the Dynamic CSYS.
57. Type-in 100 in the **Distance** box and press ENTER. Next, click **Apply** on the **Edit Explosion** dialog.

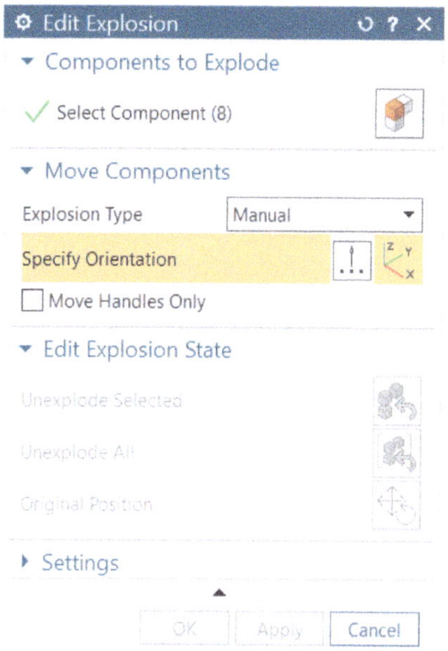

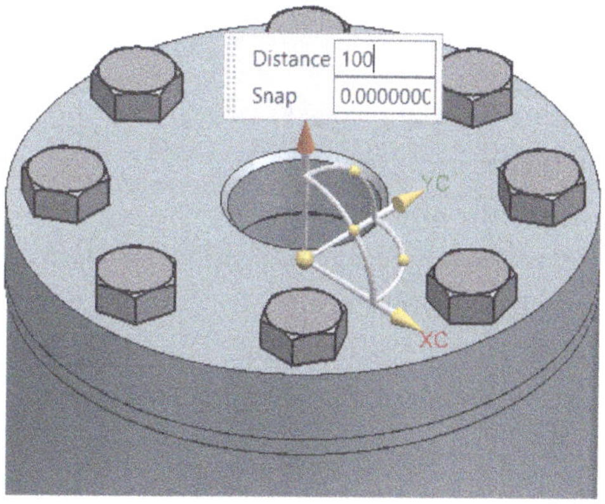

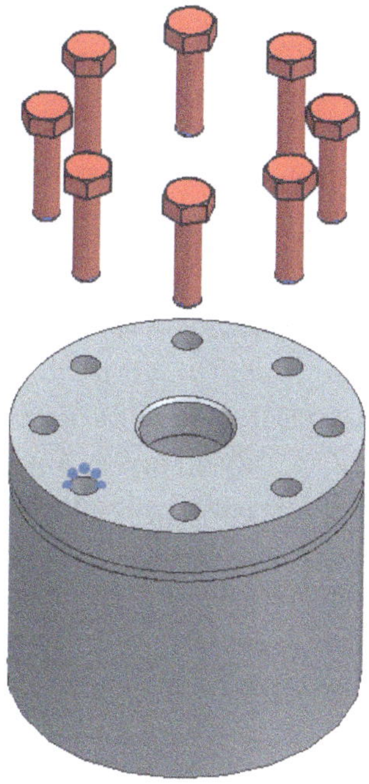

58. Select the cover plate and click the **Specify Orientation** option.
59. Select the Z handle on the Dynamic CSYS. Next, type-in 50 in the **Distance** box and press ENTER.
60. Click **Apply** and select the gasket from the assembly. Next, click the **Specify Orientation** option.
61. Select the Z handle on the Dynamic CSYS. Next, type-in 30 in the **Distance** box and press ENTER.
62. Click **OK** on the **Edit Explosion** dialog. Next, click **Close** on the **Explosions** dialog.

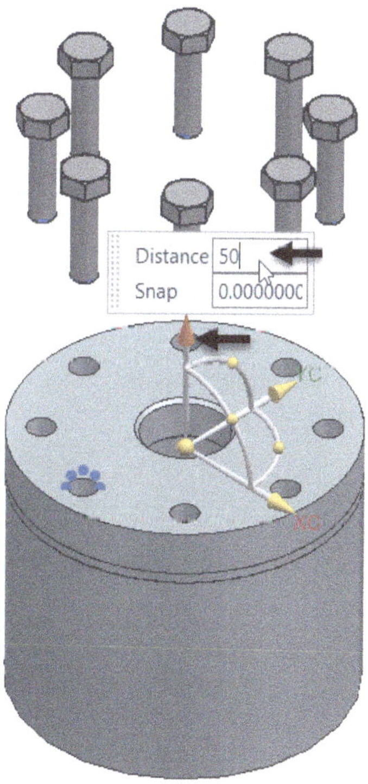

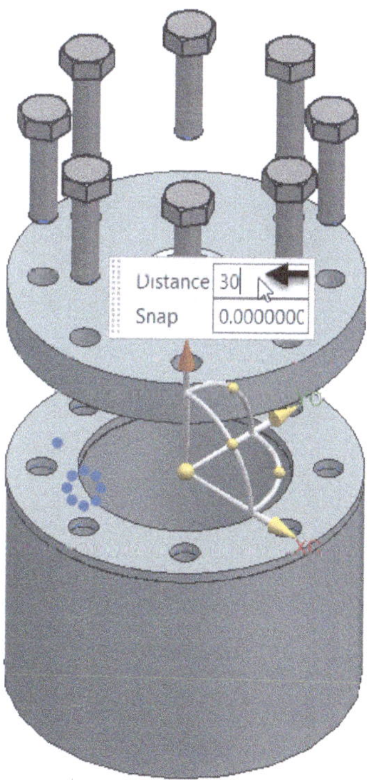

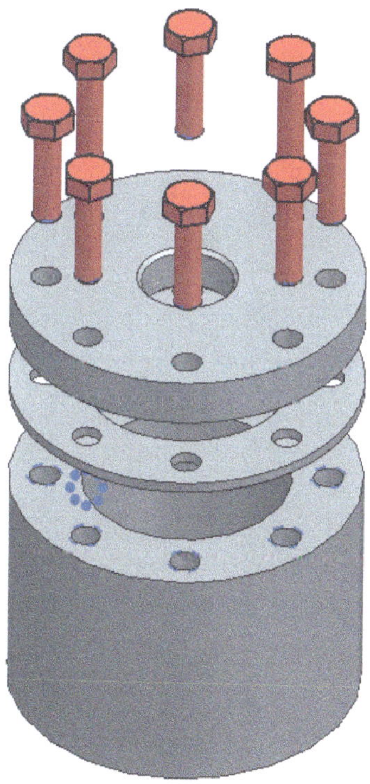

63. Click the **Save** icon on the **Quick Access Toolbar**.

64. On the **Name Parts** dialog, select the part file located on the top. Next, type **Cylinder base** in the **Name** box.
65. Select the second part file from the top. Next, type **Gasket** in the **Name** box.
66. Select the third part file from the top. Next, type **Cover plate** in the **Name** box.
67. Select the assembly file and then type **Pressure Cylinder** in the **Name** box. Next, click **OK**.
68. Close the assembly file.

Questions

1. How to start an assembly from an already opened part?
2. What is the use of the **Remember Constraints** command?
3. List the advantages of Top-down assembly approach.
4. How to create a sub-assembly in the assembly environment?
5. Briefly explain how to edit components in an assembly.
6. Why do we prefer the manual explosion type to automatic explosion type?
7. How to show or hide reference planes of a part?
8. How to add fasteners to an assembly?
9. How to redefine constraints in NX?
10. What is the use of **Align/Lock** constraint?

Exercise 1

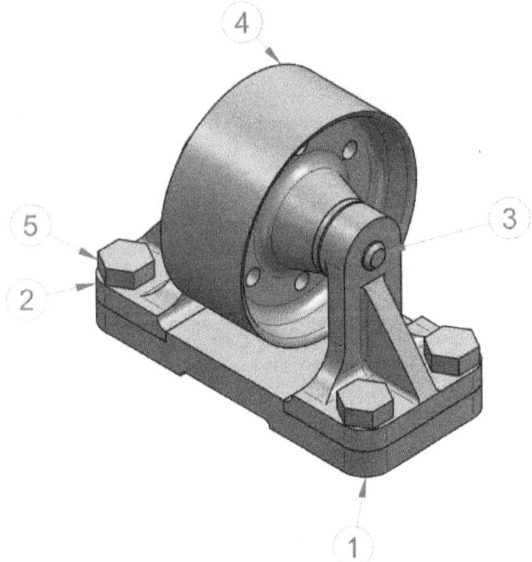

Item Number	File Name (no extension)	Quantity
1	Base	1
2	Bracket	2
3	Spindle	1
4	Roller-Bush assembly	1
5	Bolt	4

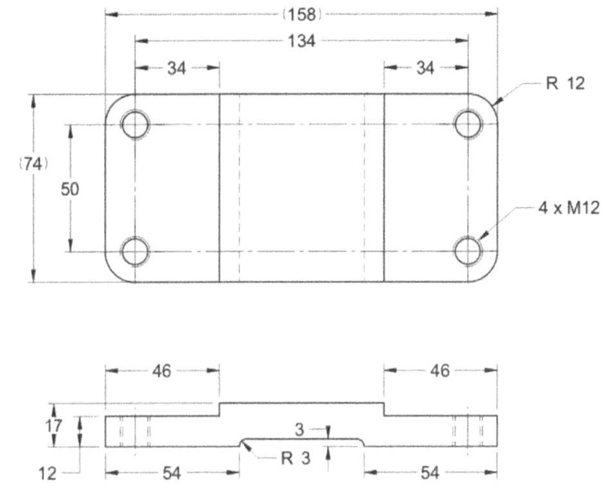

Base

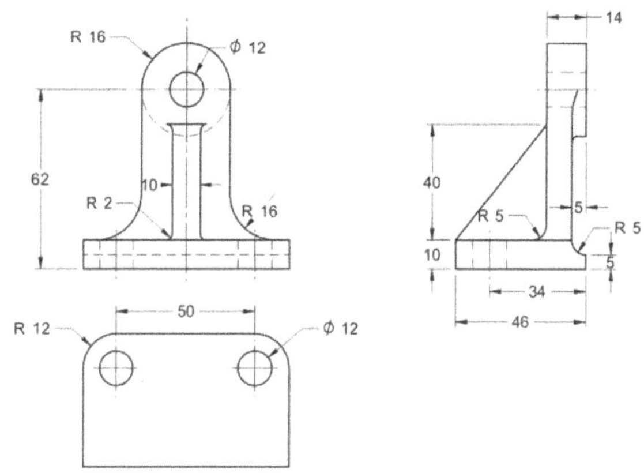

Bracket

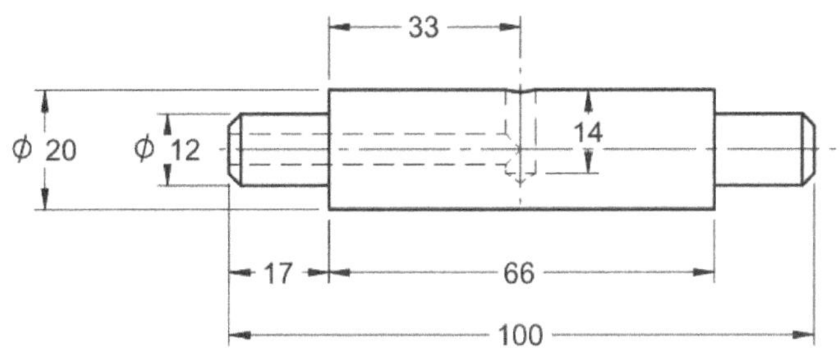

SPINDLE

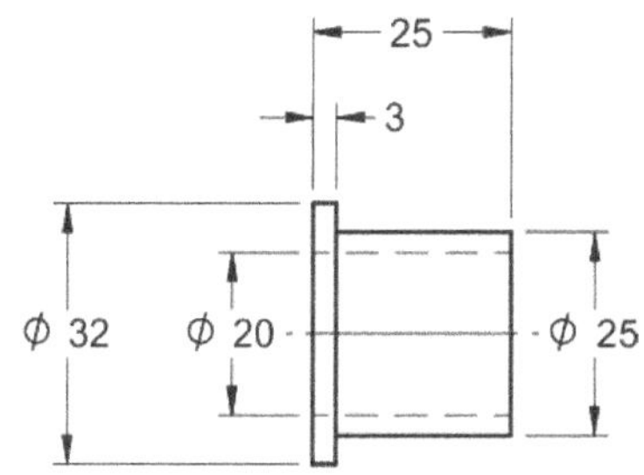

BUSH

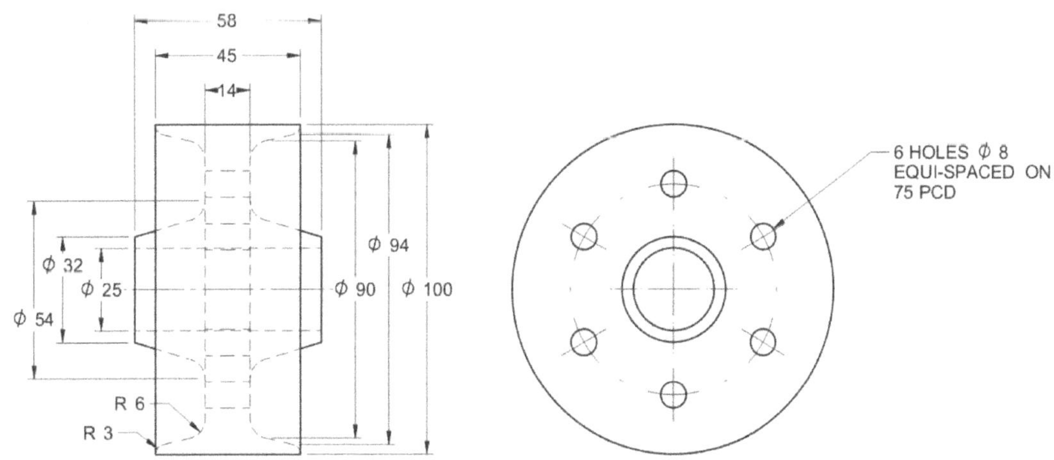

Roller

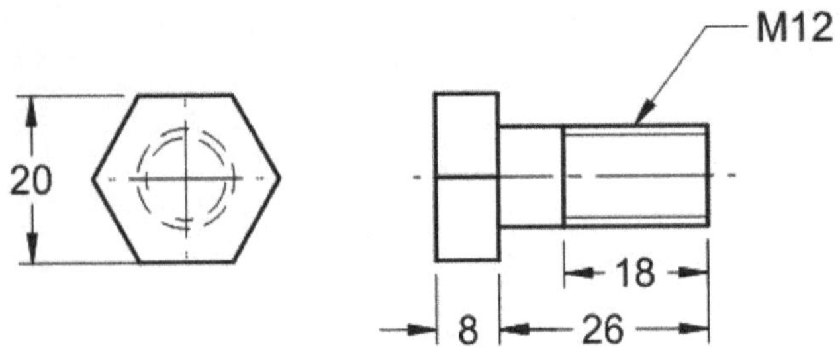

Bolt

Chapter 9: Drawings

Drawings are used to document your 3D models in the traditional 2D format, including dimensions and other instructions useful for the manufacturing purpose. In NX, you first create 3D models and assemblies and then use them to generate the drawing. There is a direct association between the 3D model and the drawing. When changes are made to the model, every view in the drawing will be updated. This relationship between the 3D model and the drawing makes the drawing process fast and accurate. Because of the mainstream adoption of 2D drawings of the mechanical industry, drawings are one of the three main file types you can create in NX.

The topics covered in this chapter are:

- *Create model views*
- *Projected views*
- *Auxiliary views*
- *Section views*
- *Detail views*
- *Break-out Section views*
- *View Breaks*
- *Display Options*
- *View Alignment*
- *Parts List and Balloons*
- *Retrieve Dimensions*
- *Maintain Alignment*
- *Remove Alignment*
- *Ordinate Dimensions*
- *Center Marks*
- *Centerlines*
- *Automatic Centerlines*
- *Bolt Circle Centerlines*
- *Callouts and Leaders*
- *Notes*

Starting a Drawing

To start a new drawing, click the **New** icon on the ribbon, and then click the **Drawing** tab on the **New** dialog. On the **Drawing** tab, set the **Units** value and click on a drawing sheet template. Click **OK** to start the drawing. Next, type-in values in the **Populate Title Block** dialog, and then click **Close**.

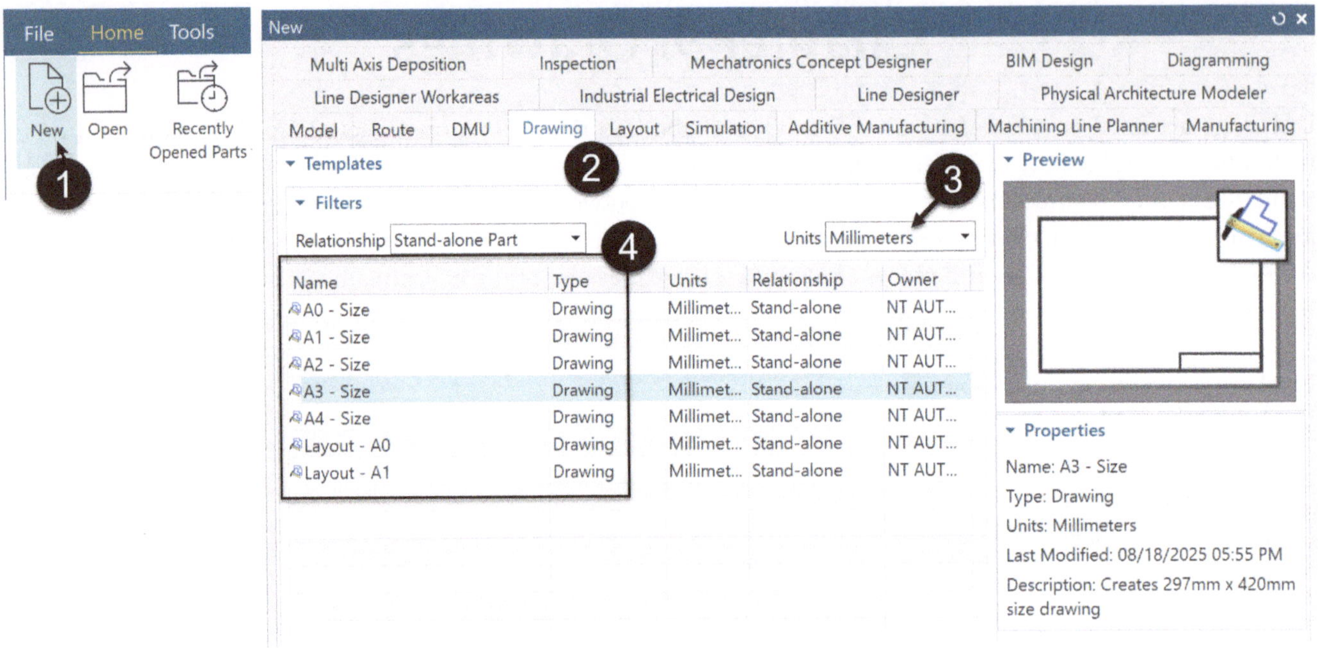

If you already have a part opened, you can click **Application > Document > Drafting** on the ribbon. On the **Sheet** dialog, click **Use Template** to access different sheet templates. Select any one of the sheet templates from the list. If the Sheet dialog does not appear, click **Home tab > Sheet drop-down > Edit Sheet.**

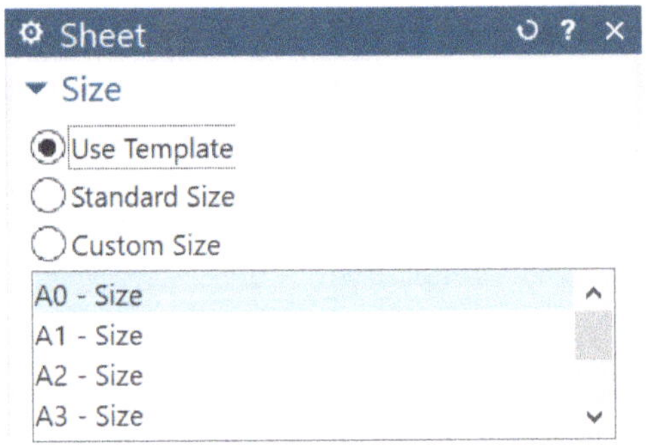

Click **Standard Size** to start a drawing by using standard sheet sizes. The drawing will start without a border and title block. Click **Custom Size** to start a drawing using your own sheet size.

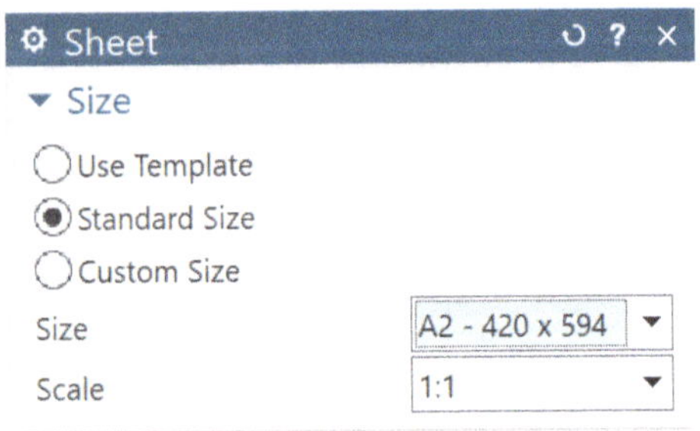

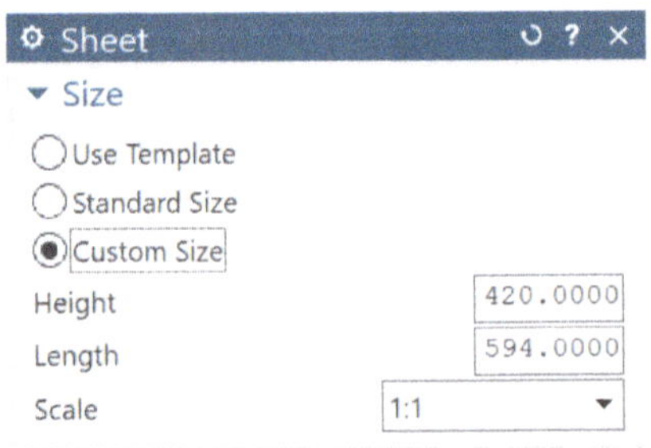

Under the **Settings** section (click the reset icon if this section is not displayed), set the **Units** and **Projection** type. Check the **Always Start Drawing View Command** option to start creating drawing views. If you uncheck this option, then you have to create the drawing views manually. Click **OK** to start a new drawing.

View Creation Wizard

There are different standard views of a 3D part, such as front, right, top, and isometric. In NX, you can create these views using the **View Creation Wizard** command. This command is not visible by default. Click the down-arrow located on the **View** group and select **View Creation Wizard** to display it. Next, click **Home > View > View Creation Wizard** on the ribbon. Next, select the **Open** button from the bottom of the dialog, browse to the part location, and double-click on it. On the **View Creation Wizard** window, click **Next** to navigate to the **Options** page.

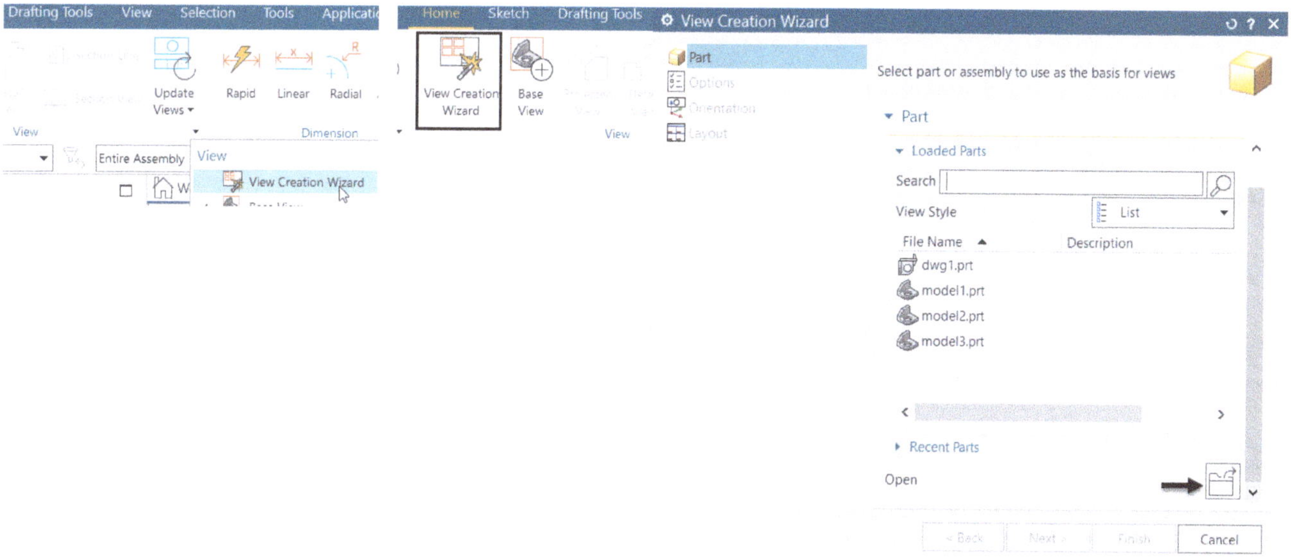

On the **Options** page, set the options related to view boundary, hidden lines, centerlines, silhouettes, view labels, and preview style. If you want to access additional settings related to the drawing views, then click **Settings** to open the **Settings** dialog. This dialog has various pages such as **Configuration**, **General**, **Angle**, **Visible Lines**, **Hidden Lines**, and so on. You can access the individual pages by selecting the corresponding options from the tree located on the left side of the dialog. Click **OK** after changing the settings on this dialog. On the **Options** page, click **Next** to navigate to the **Orientation** page.

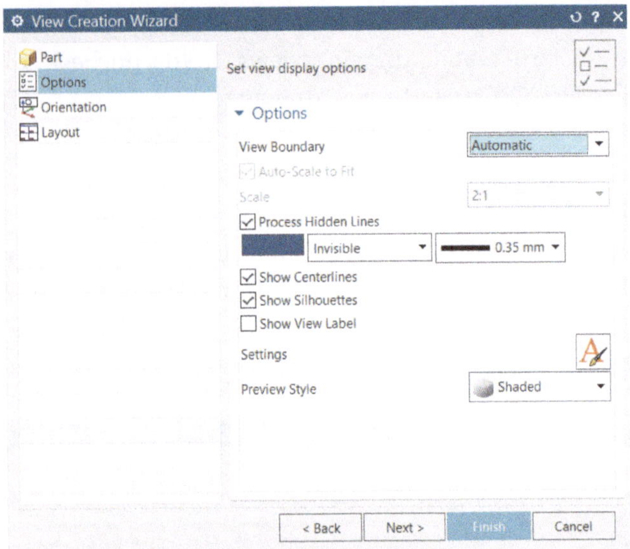

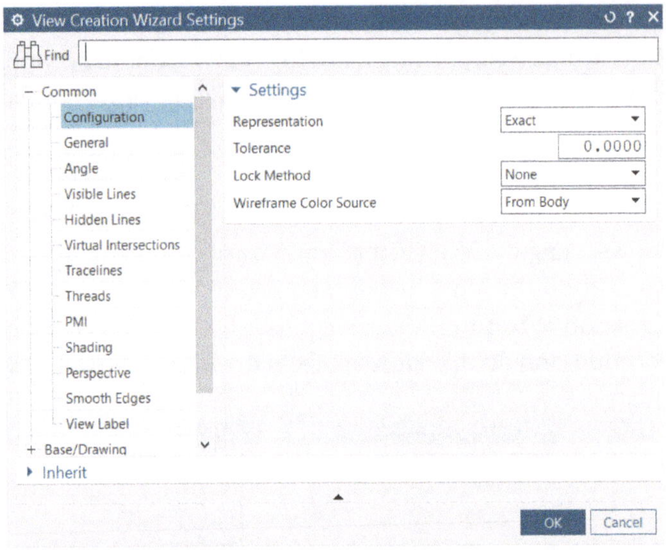

On the **Orientation** page, select the first view from the **Model Views** section. You can select from the standard orientations (Top, Front, Right, Back, Bottom, Left, Isometric, or Trimetric) of the model available in this section. If you want a different orientation, then click **Customized View**  to open the **Orient View** window. In this window, use the vector axes 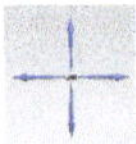 to reorient the model view, and then click **OK**. On the **Orientation** page, click **Next** to navigate to the **Layout** page.

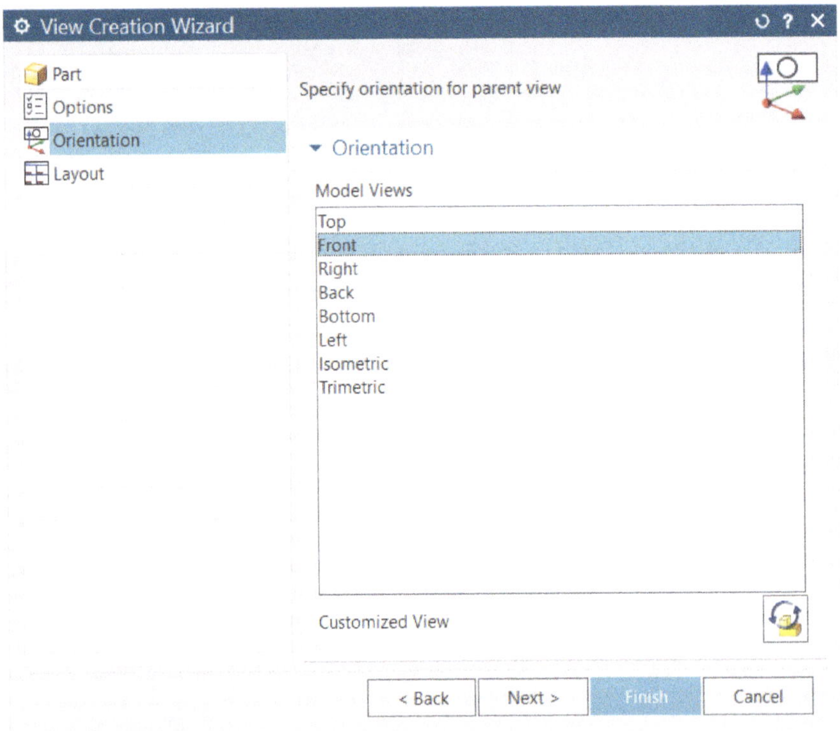

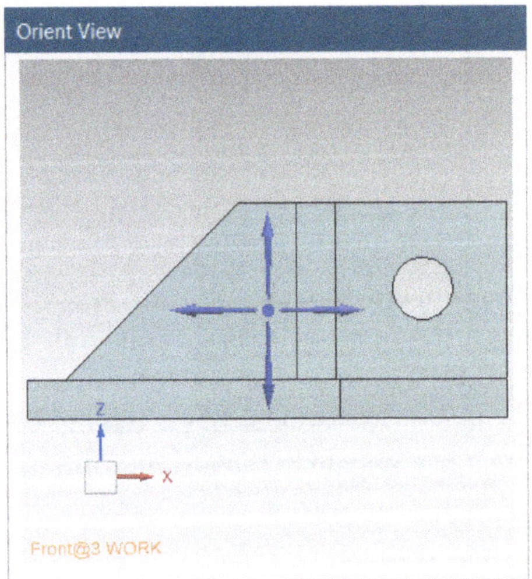

On the **Layout** page, click on the icons that represent the standard views that are to be created. After selecting the standard views, click **Finish** to create views. Click and drag the views to position them.

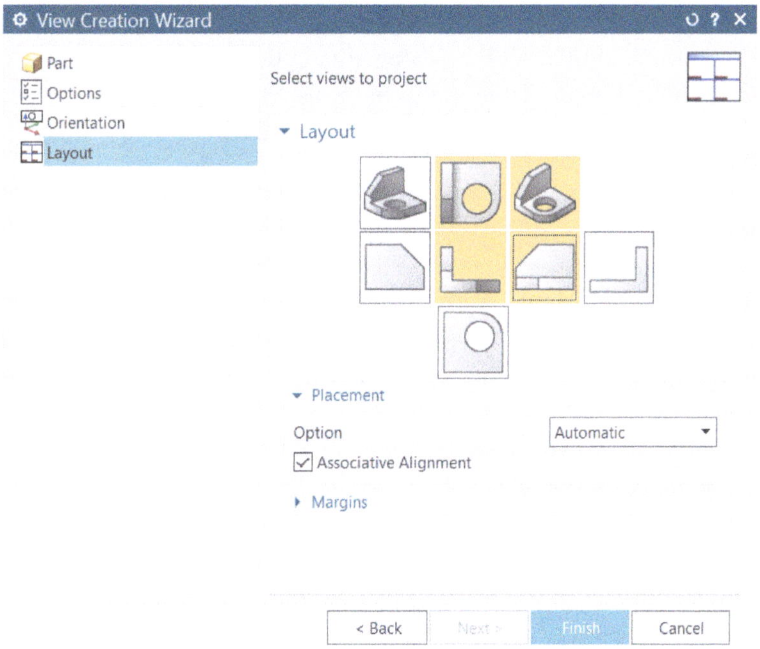

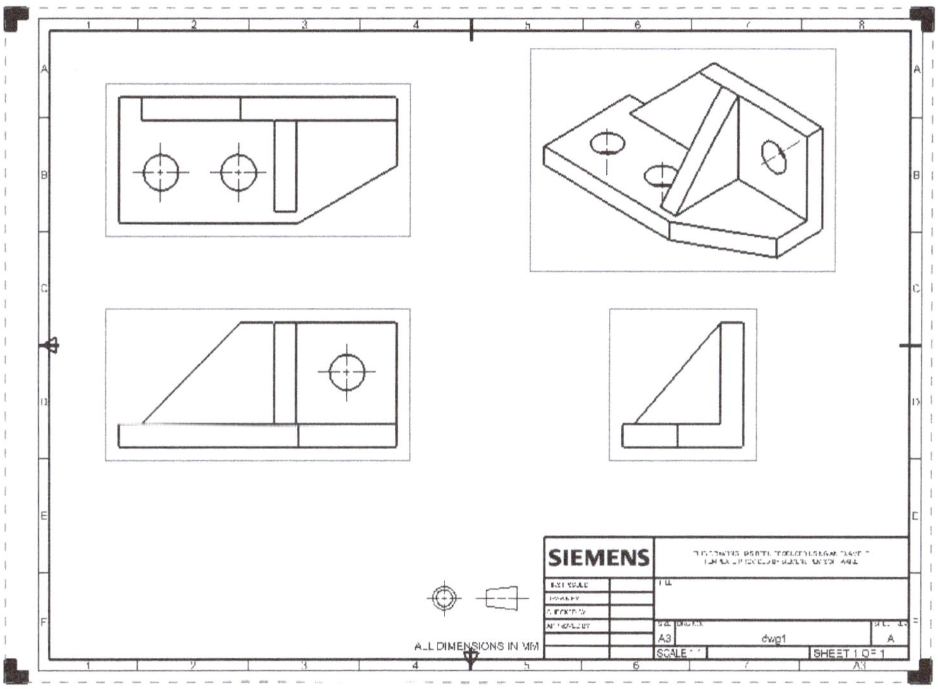

Base View

Unlike the **View Creation Wizard** command, the **Base View** command allows you to create a single view of the drawing. You can later project this view to create other views. Activate this command (On the ribbon, click **Home >View > Base View**). Next, expand the **Part** section on the **Base View** dialog and click **Open**. Next, browse to the location of the part/assembly and double-click on it.

On the **Base View** dialog, select the model view (Top, Front, Right, Back, Bottom, Left, Isometric, or Trimetric) to use from the **Model View** section, and then set the **Scale** value in the **Scale** section. Click on the drawing sheet to position the first view. Now, you can create other views by projecting the base view. Close the dialog or create the projected views. The **Projected Views** are explained in the next section.

Projected View

After you have created the first view in your drawing, a projected view is one of the simplest views to create. Activate the **Projected View** command (click **Home > View > Projected View** on the ribbon). After activating the command, move the pointer in the direction you wish to have the view projected. Next, click on the sheet to specify the location. On the **Projected View** dialog, click **Close** to deactivate this command.

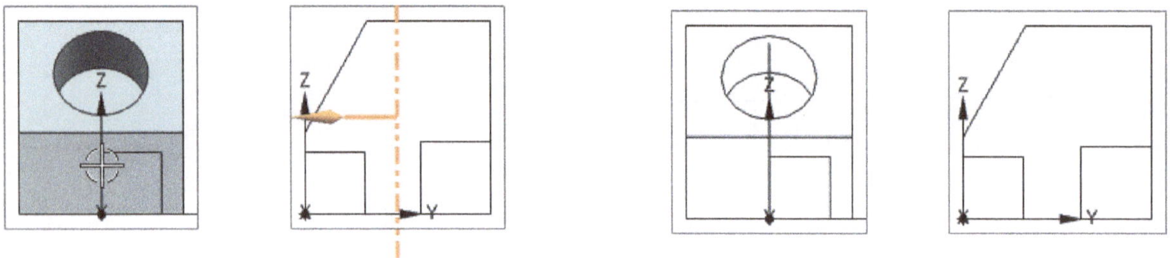

Auxiliary View

Most of the parts are represented by using orthographic views (front, top, and/or side views). But many parts have features located on inclined faces. You cannot get the true shape and size for these features by using the orthographic views. To see an accurate size and shape of the inclined features, you need to create an auxiliary view. You can create an auxiliary view by projecting the part onto a plane other than horizontal, front, or side planes. To create an auxiliary view, first, activate the **Projected View** command. On the **Projected View** dialog, under the **Hinge Line** section, select **Vector Option > Defined**. Now, click the angled edge of the model to establish the direction of the auxiliary view. Under the **View Origin** section, click **Specify Location** and drag the mouse to the desired location. Use the **Reverse Projected Direction** button in the **Hinge Line** section to reverse the projection direction, if needed. Click to locate the view and close the **Projected view** dialog.

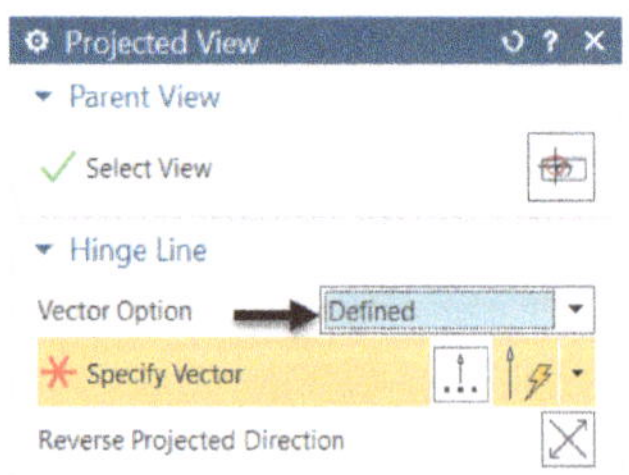

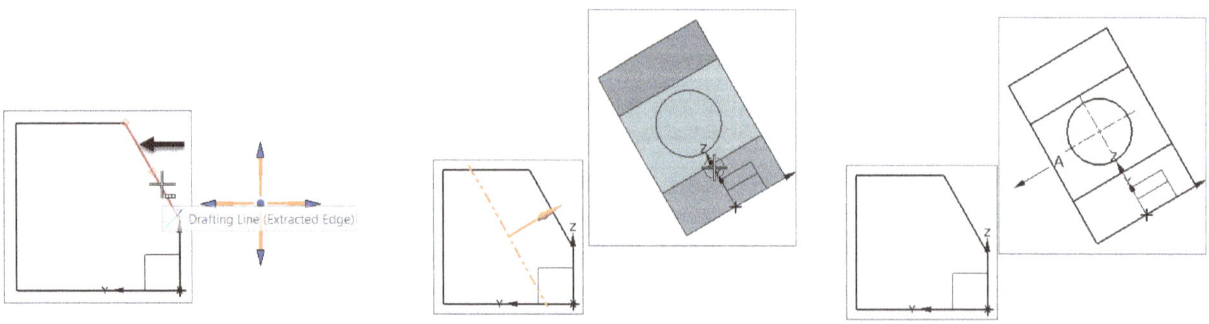

Section View

One of the common views used in 2D drawings is the section view. Creating a section view in NX is very simple. Activate the **Section View** command (On the ribbon, click **Home > View > Section View**) and select the view to section. Now, define the location of the section line by selecting a point on the view. Move the pointer on either side of the view, and then click to position the section view.

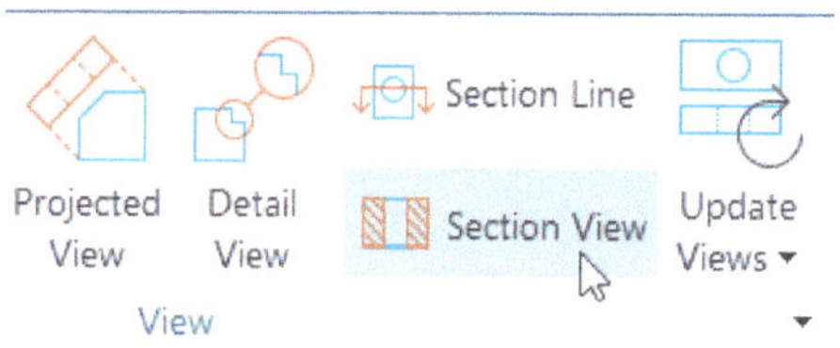

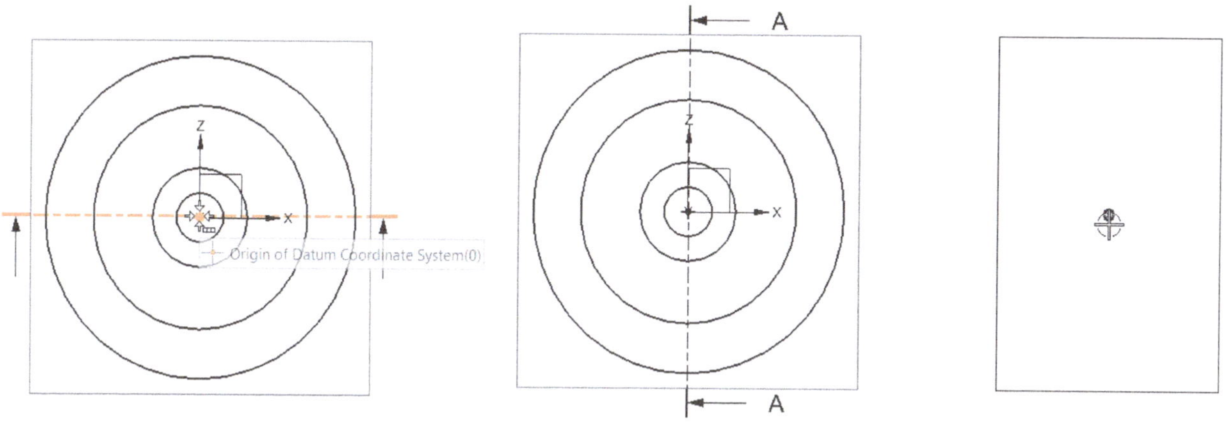

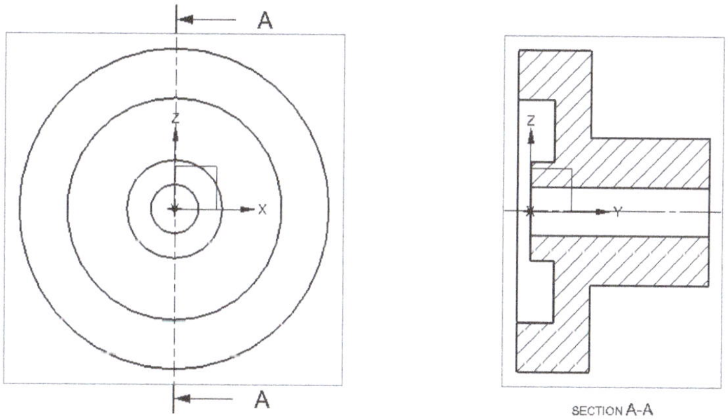

SECTION A-A

If you want to convert the single segment section line into a multi-segment one, then click the right mouse button on the section line and select **Edit**. On the **Section Line** dialog, click the **Specify Location** option in the **Section Line Segments** section and select points on the parent view.

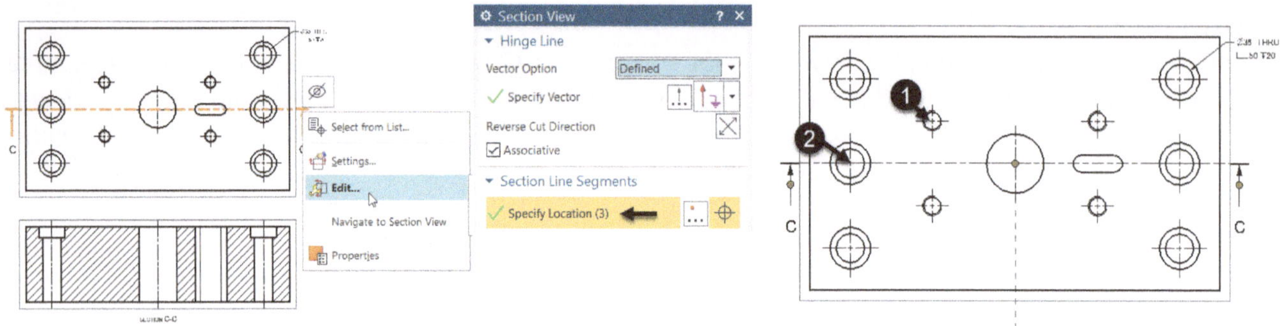

Click **Close** on the dialog. To update the section view, click on the section view and select **Update**.

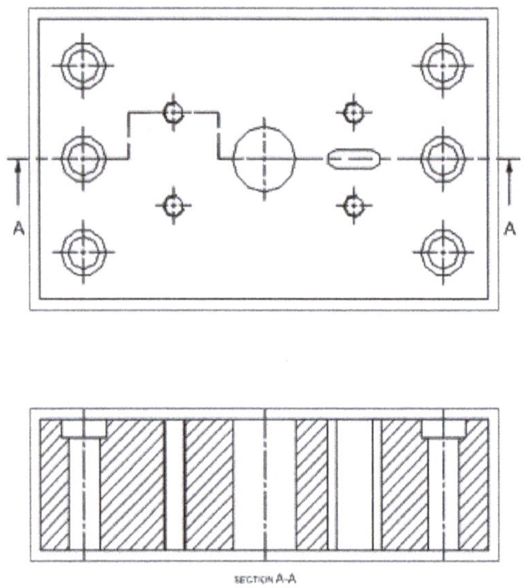

Half Section View

If you want to create a half section view, activate the **Section View** command (on the ribbon, click **Home > View > Section View**). On the **Section View** dialog, select **Method > Half**. Now, select a point on the view to define the cut position. Select another point to define the bend position of the half-section line. Move the pointer and click to position the half-section view.

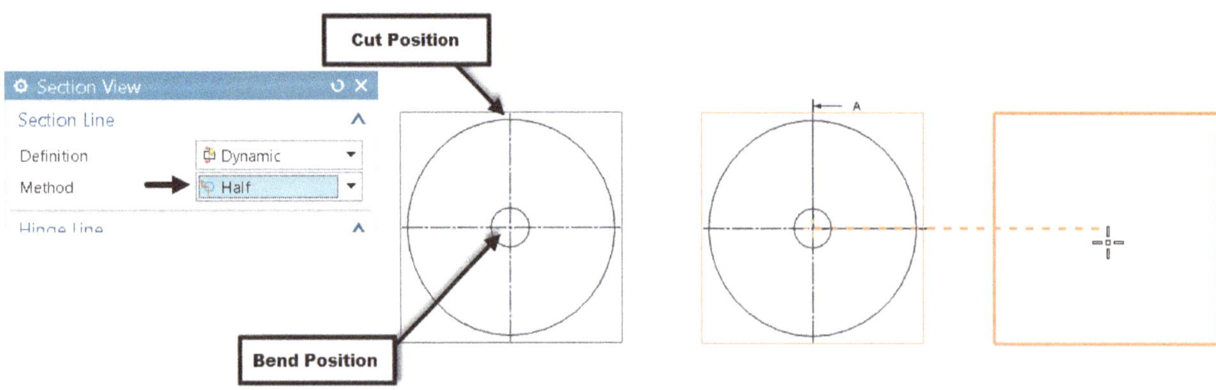

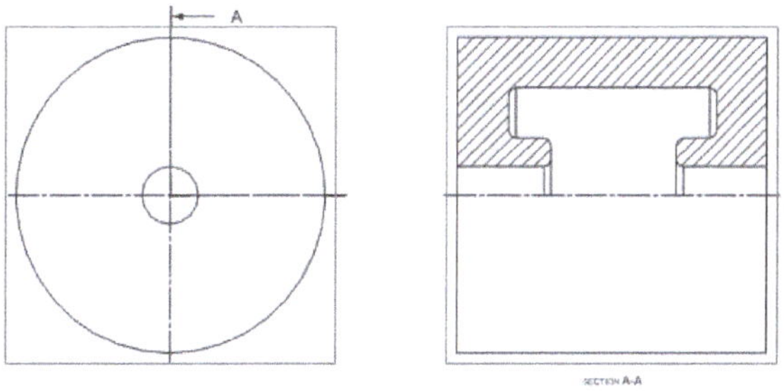

Revolved Section View

Use the **Section View** command to create a revolved section view. Activate this command (on the ribbon, click **Home > View > Section View**) and click the **Reset** icon on the **Section View** dialog. On the **Section View** dialog, under the **Section Line** section, select **Method > Revolved** . Define the rotation point and positions of the first and second-line segments. Move the pointer and click to position the revolved section view.

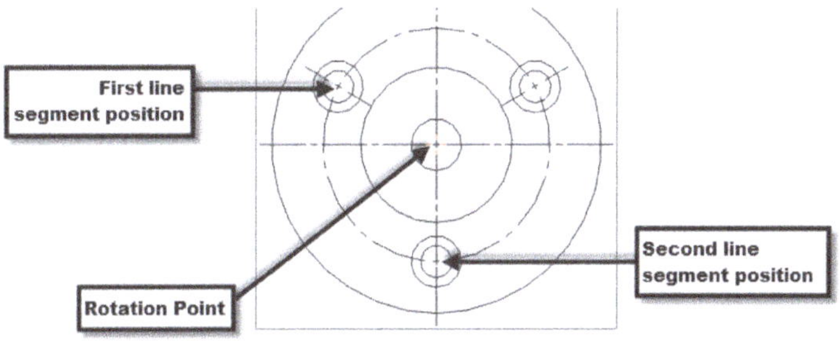

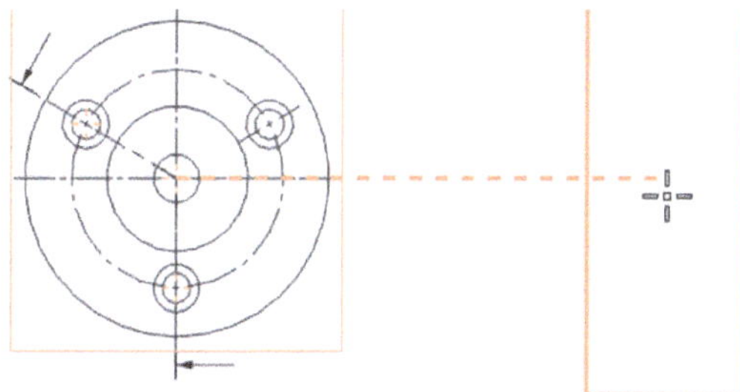

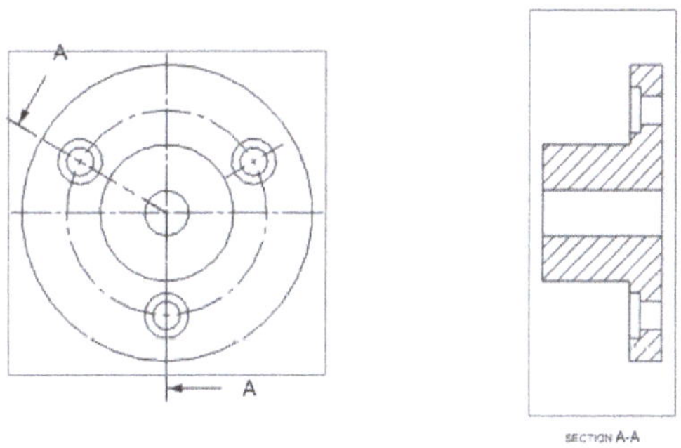

Point to Point Section View

Use the **Section View** command to create a point-to-point section view. Point-to-point section views are views that include multi segment section lines but no bend segments. You can to generate both folded and unfolded point-to-point section views. Activate this command (on the ribbon, click **Home > View > Section View**) and click the **Reset** icon on the **Section View** dialog. On the **Section View** dialog, under the **Section Line** section, select **Method > Point to Point** . Specify the direction of the section view by selecting a vector, as shown.

In the **Section Line Segments** section, check the **Create Folded** option. Select the center points of the hole circles, as shown. To position the view on the drawing sheet, click the **Specify Location** option in **View Origin** section and drag it to the desired location. Finally, click to place the view on the drawing sheet.

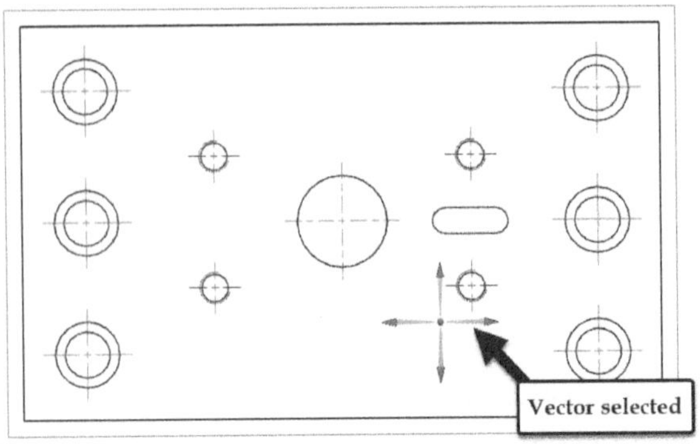

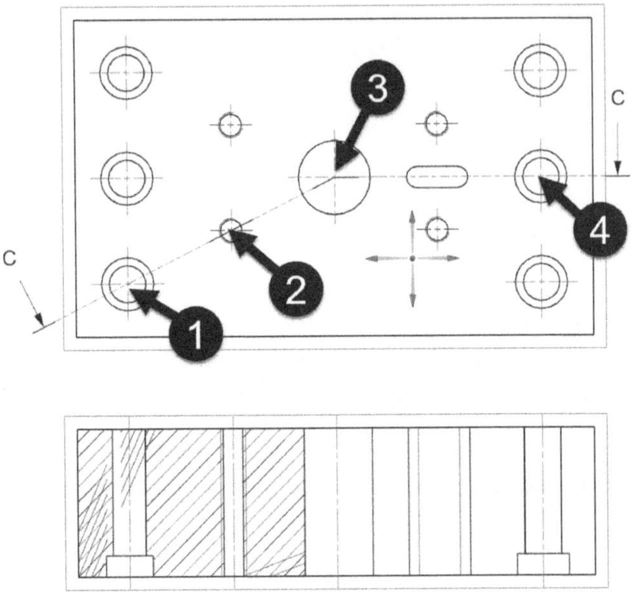

SECTION C-C

If you want to create an unfolded **Point to Point** section view, then uncheck the **Create Folded** option in the **Section Line Segments** section before specifying the location of the section view.

Unfolded Point to Point Section View

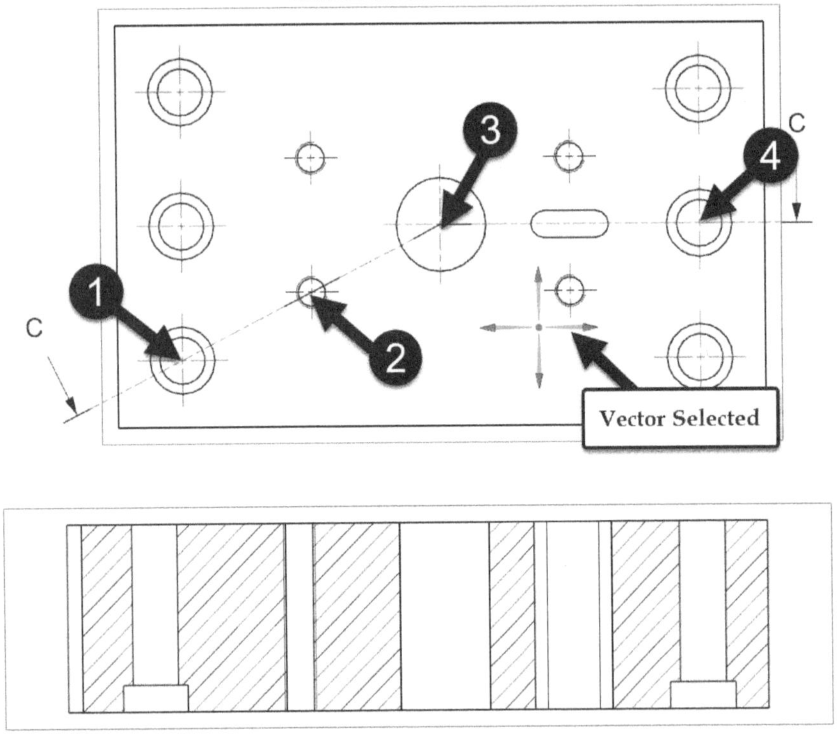

SECTION C-C

Section Line

The **Section Line** command allows you to create independent section lines that can be used in conjunction with the **Section View** command to generate section views. While you can create a section line interactively when using the **Section View** command, the **Section Line** command provides more control by enabling you to use sketch tools to define the section line. With the stand-alone section line, you have the flexibility to create various types of section views, including **Simple**, **Stepped**, **Revolved**, **Half**, and **Point to Point**. Activate the **Section Line** command (click **Home > View > Section Line** on the ribbon) and click on a drawing view. Now, you have to draw the section line. To do this, activate the **Line** command and select **Entire Assembly** from the **Selection Scope** drop-down available on the Top Border Bar.

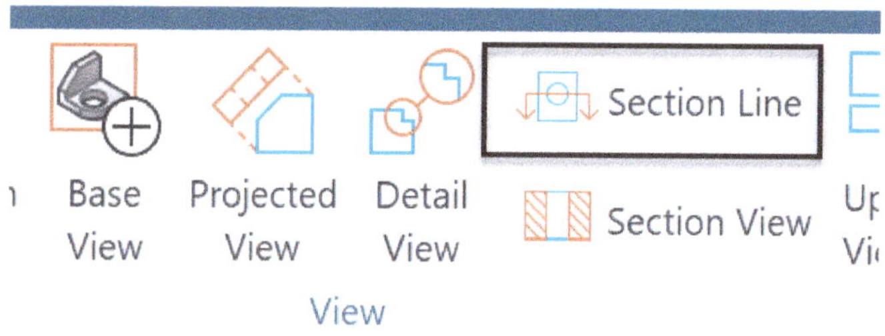

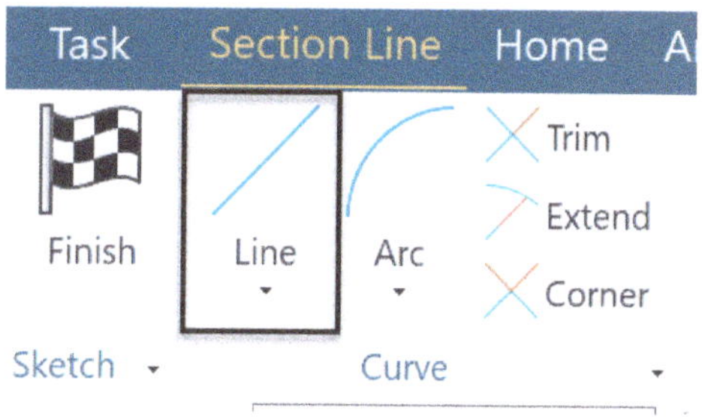

Specify the start point of the section line by selecting the **midpoint of the left vertical edge**. Then, move the pointer to the right and select the **endpoint of the horizontal centerline of the hole**. Next, move upward and select the **left endpoint of the centermark of the small hole**. Continue by moving horizontally to select the **right endpoint of the centermark**. From there, move vertically downward and click when the pointer aligns with the **centermark of the large central hole**. Finally, move the pointer to the right and select the **midpoint of the right vertical edge**. Click **Finish** on the ribbon.

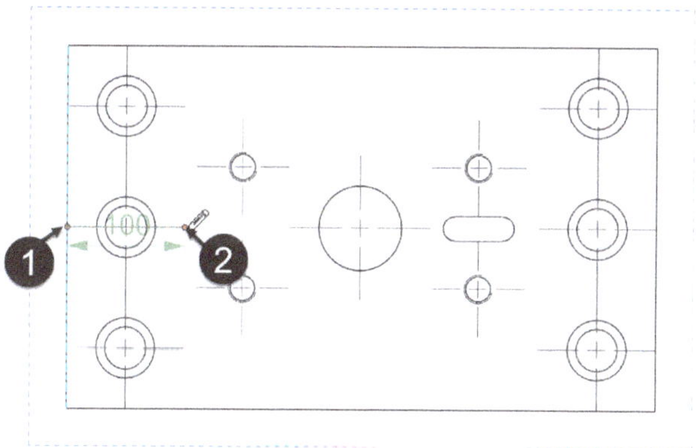

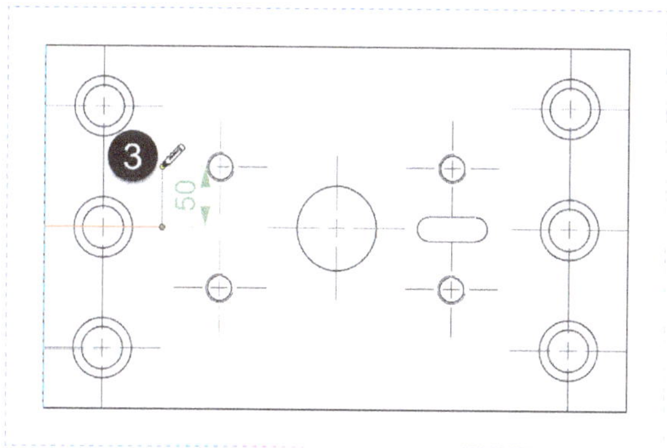

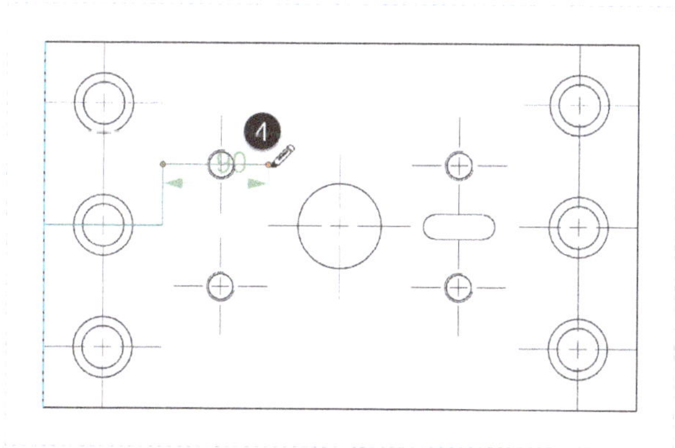

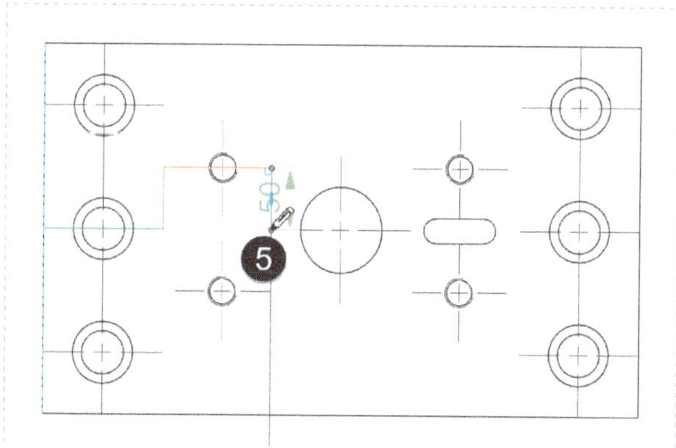

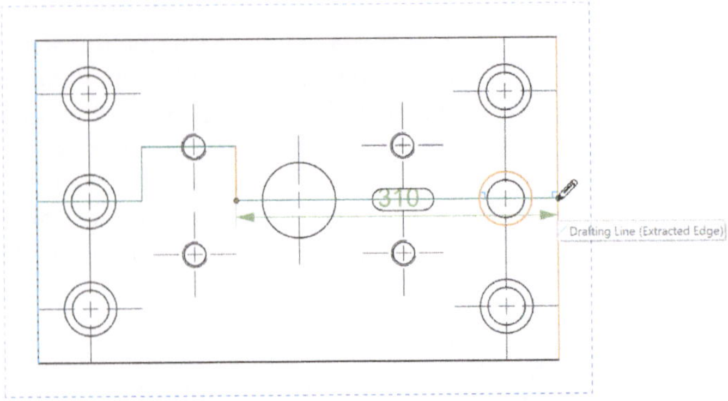

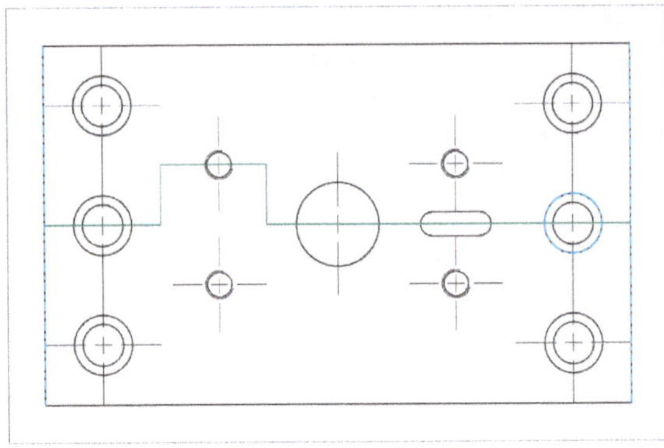

On the **Section Line** dialog, select the desired section method from the **Method** drop-down and click **OK**.

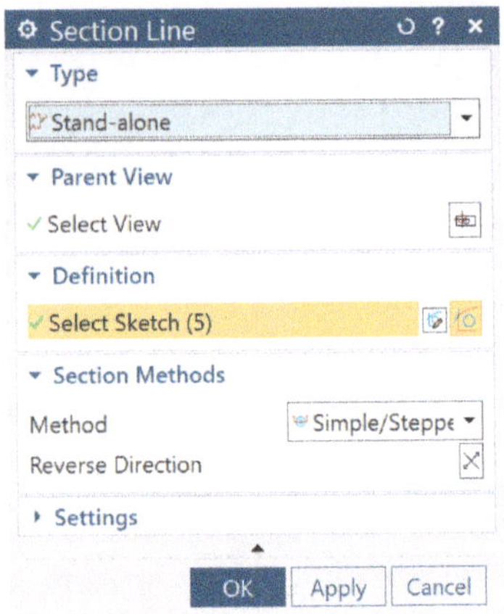

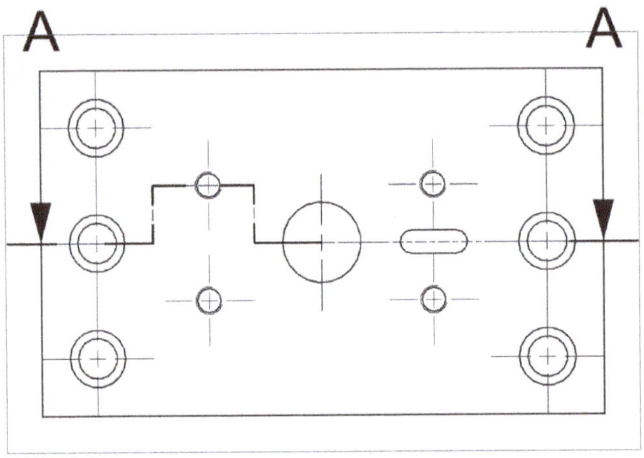

Activate the **Section View** command (click **Home > View > Section View** on the ribbon) and select **Definition > Select Existing** from the **Section view** dialog. Next, click on a section line. Move the pointer and click to position the section view.

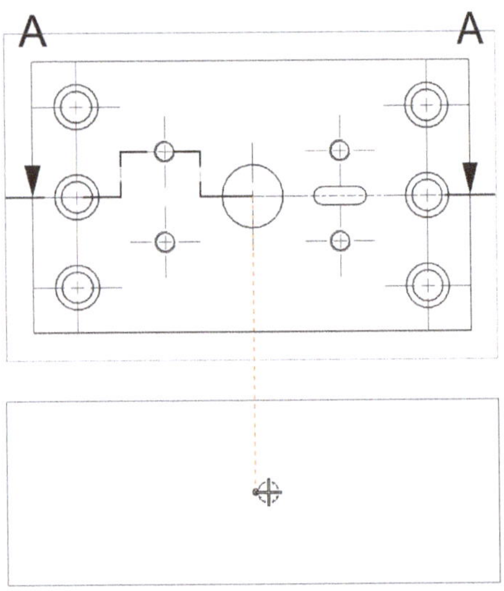

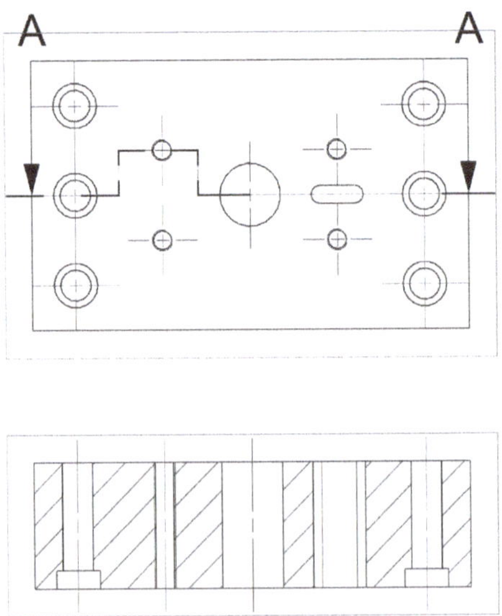

SECTION A-A

Section in View

After creating a section view of an assembly, you can choose to exclude one or more components from the section cut. For example, to exclude the piston of a pneumatic cylinder, activate the **Section in View** command (on the ribbon, click **Home > View > Edit View** drop-down > **Section in View** on the ribbon) and select the section view. On the **Section in View** dialog, under the **Body or Component** section, click **Select Object** and select the object from any one of the views. Under the **Action** section, select **Make Non Sectioned** and click **OK**.

Note: *If the **Section in View** command is not available in the **Edit View** drop-down, then click the down arrow located at the bottom right corner of the View group of the ribbon. Next, select **Edit View** drop-down **> Section in View** from the drop-down; the **Section in View** command will be added to the **Edit View** Drop-down.*

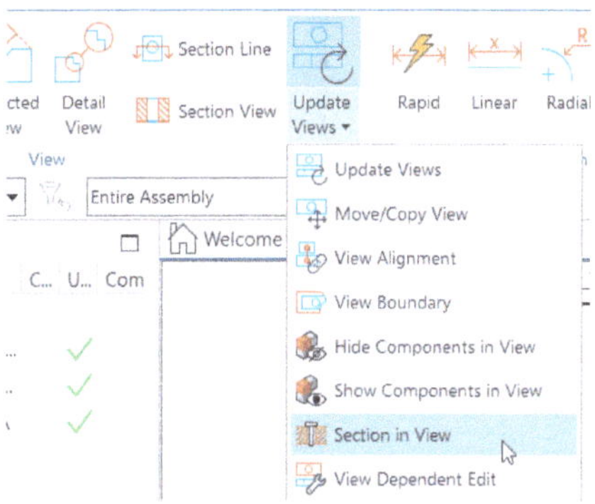

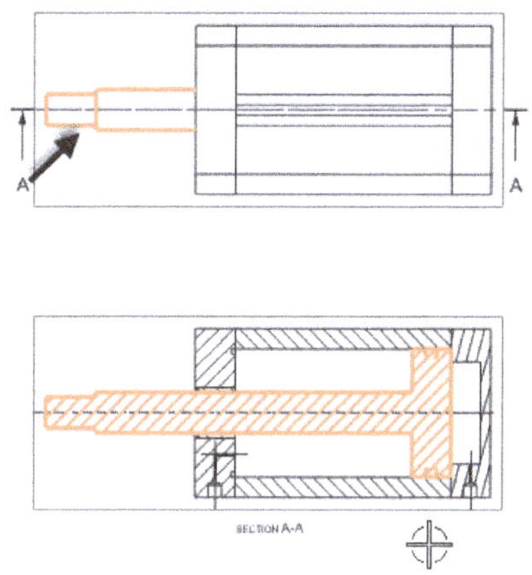

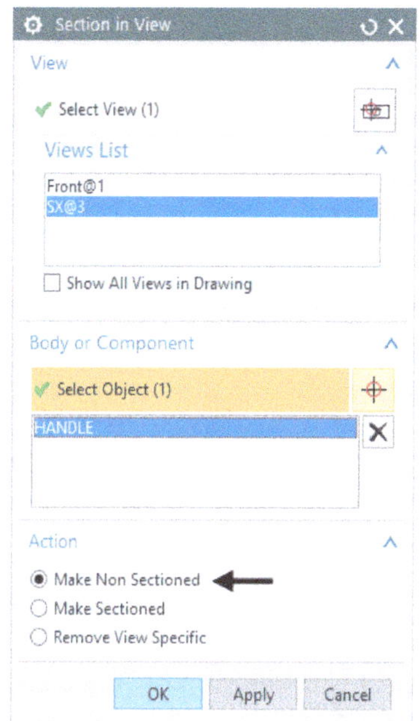

On the ribbon, click **Home > View > Update Views**. On the **Update Views** dialog, select the section view and click **OK**.

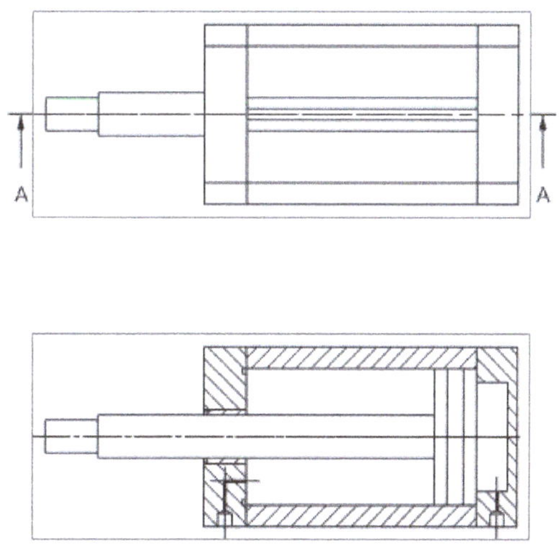

Unfolded Point and Angle section View

The **Unfolded Point and Angle section View** command generates an unfolded section view by utilizing a sequence of points and angles specified on the parent view. To create this view, click **Home > View > Detail**

Unfolded Point and Angle section View  on the ribbon. Select the parent view from the drawing sheet. Select an edge from the parent view to define the hinge line of the section view. Next, click **Apply**.

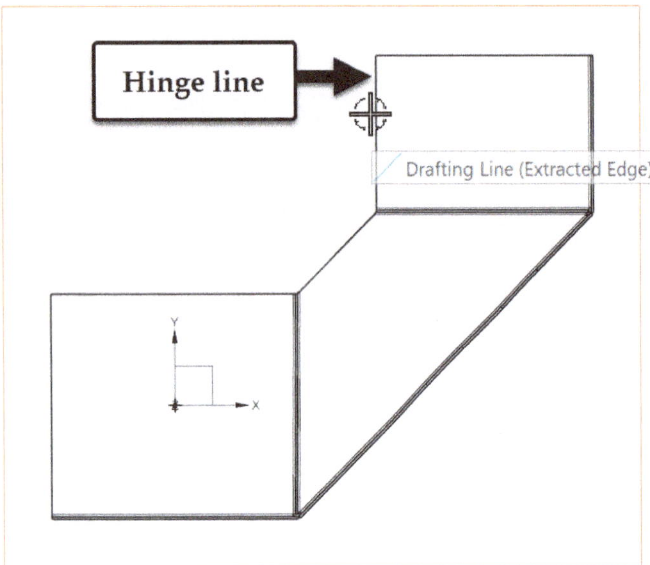

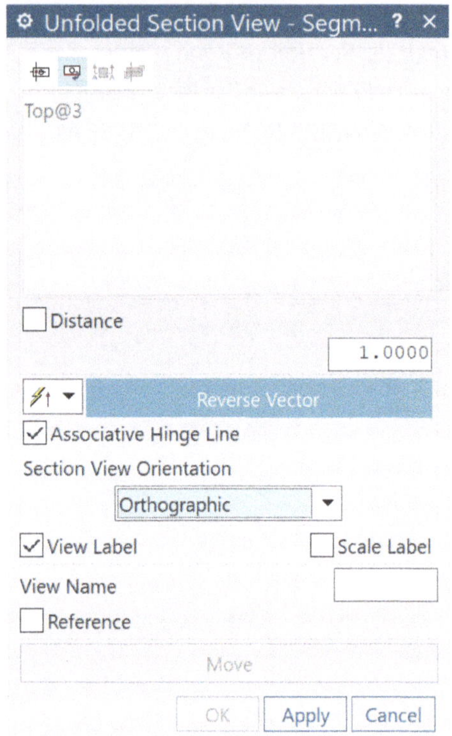

Select **Cut Position** or **Arrow Position** from the **Section Line Creation** dialog and select a point from the drawing view; the cut position or arrow position of the first section line is defined. Select a point from the drawing view to specify the second cut position. Type-in a value in the **Angle** box available on the **Section Line Creation** dialog and press ENTER.

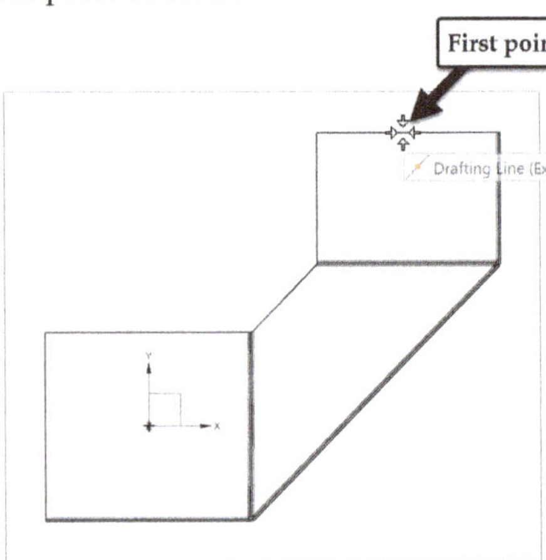

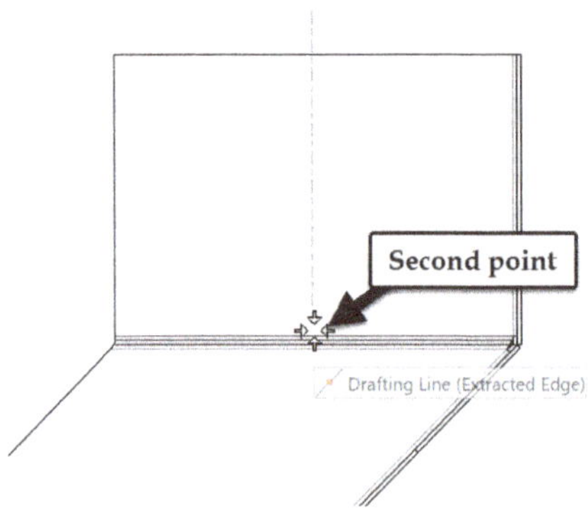

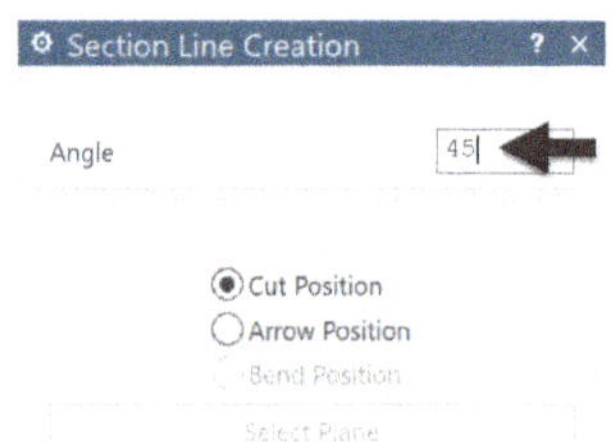

Select a point from the parent view to define the third cut position. Type-in a value in the **Angle** box and press ENTER.

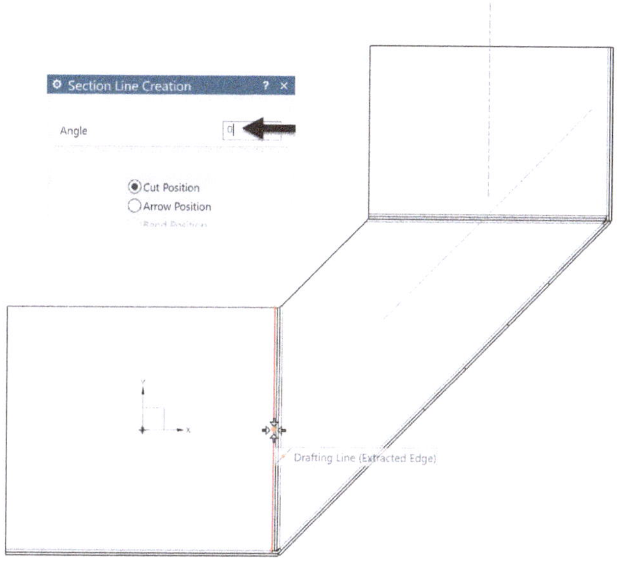

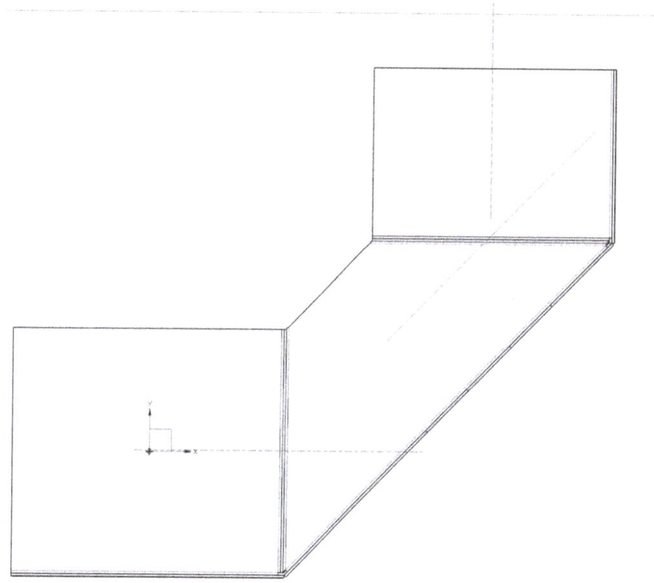

Click **OK** on the **Section Line** dialog. Move the pointer and click to specify the location of the section view.

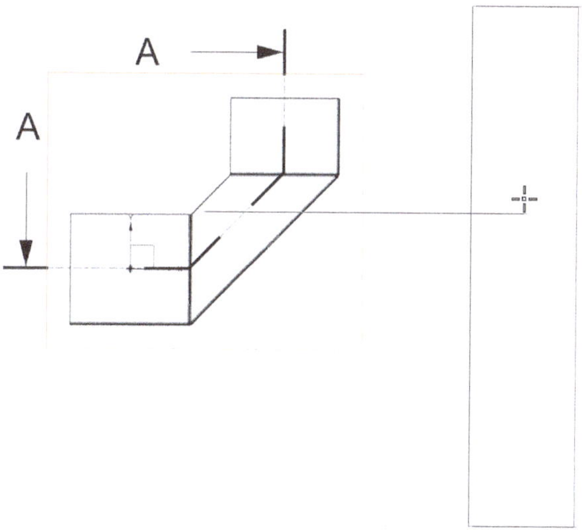

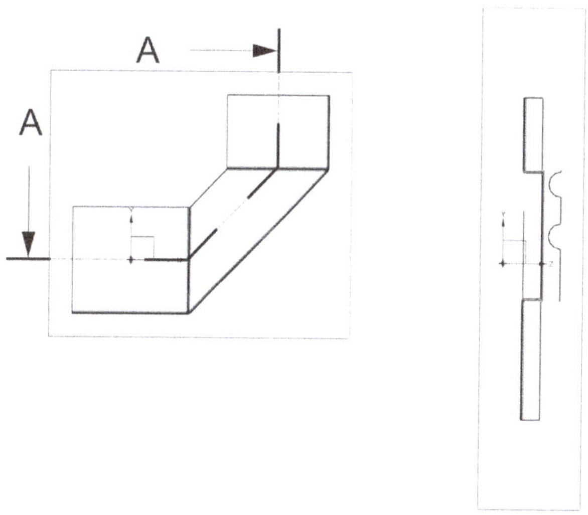

SECTION A-A

Detail View

If a drawing view contains small features that are difficult to see, a detailed view can be used to zoom in and make things clear. To create a detailed view, activate the **Detail View** command (click **Home > View > Detail View** on the ribbon); this automatically activates the circle tool. Draw a circle to identify the area that you wish to zoom in. Once the circle is drawn, set the **Scale** value on the **Detail View** dialog. Next, move the pointer and click to locate the view; the detail view will appear with a label.

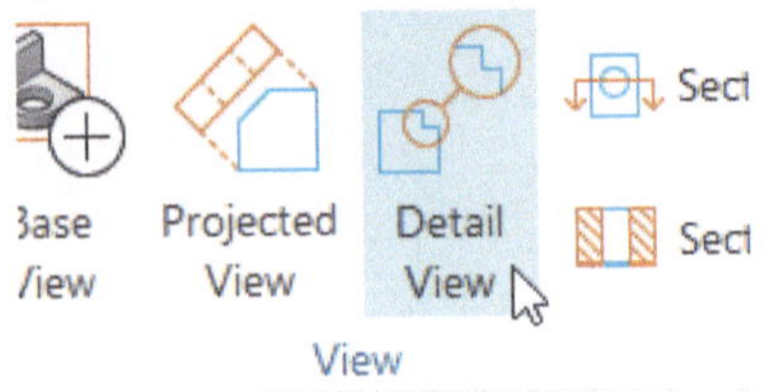

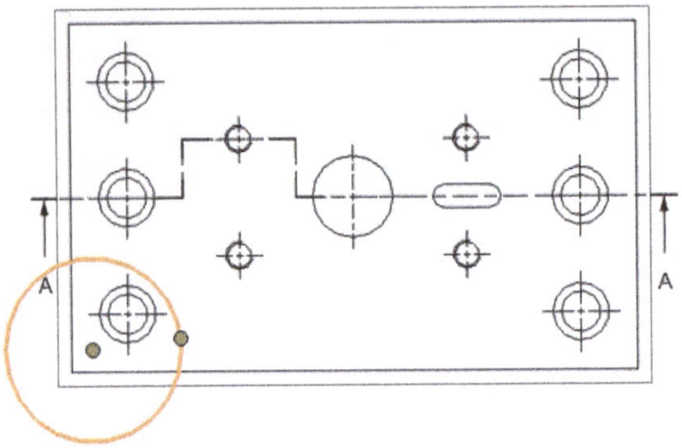

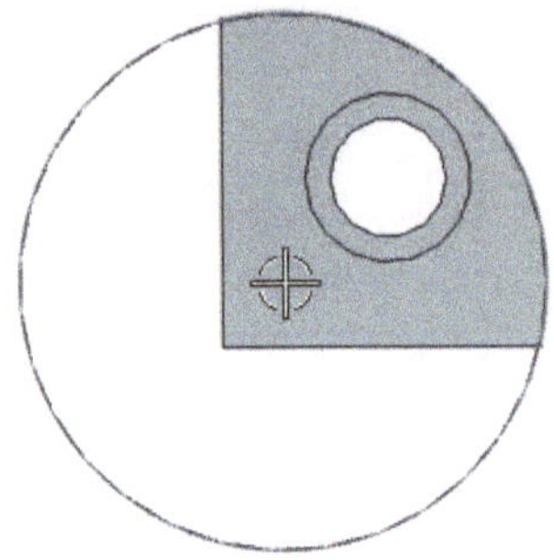

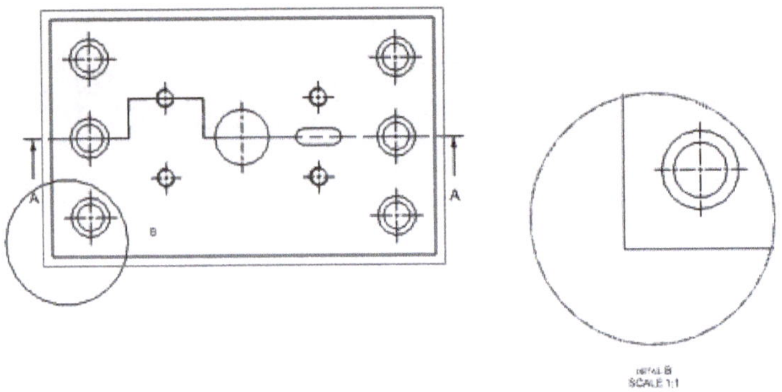

Add Break Lines

You can add break lines to a drawing view, which is too large to fit on the drawing sheet. They break the view so that only important details are shown. To add break lines, activate the **View Break** command (on the ribbon, click **Home > View > View Break**) and select the view. On the **View Break** dialog, select **Regular** from the **Type** drop-down. Click once on the drawing view to locate the beginning of the break. Next, select another point on the drawing view to locate the end of the break. On the **View Break** dialog, expand the **Settings** section and type-in a value in the **Gap** box. Select the view break style that you need from the **Style** drop-down.

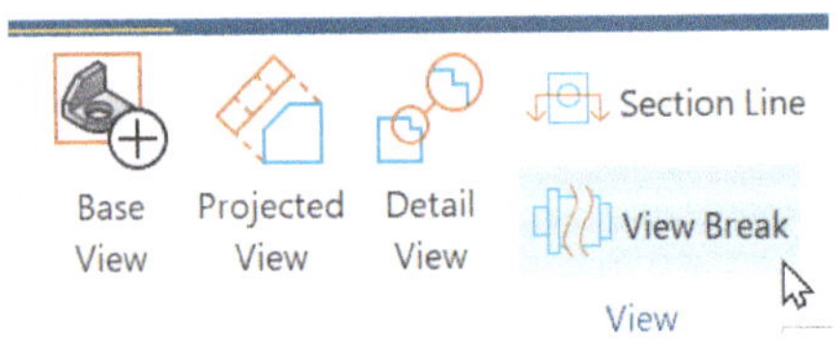

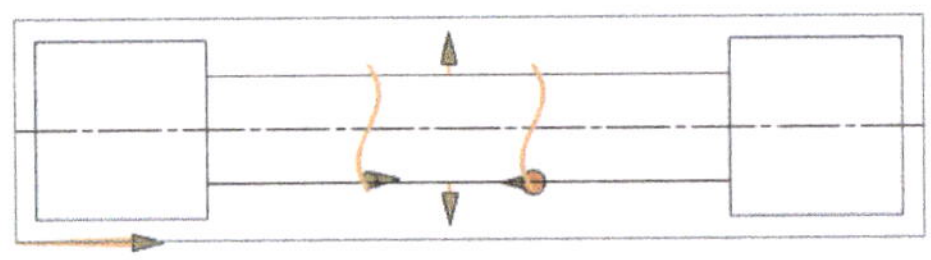

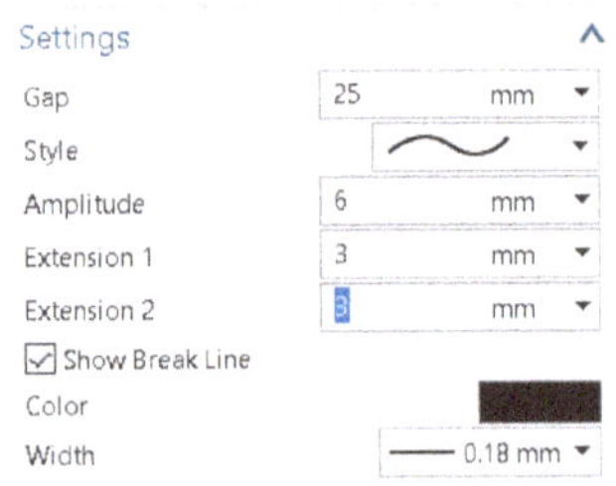

Click **OK** to add break lines.

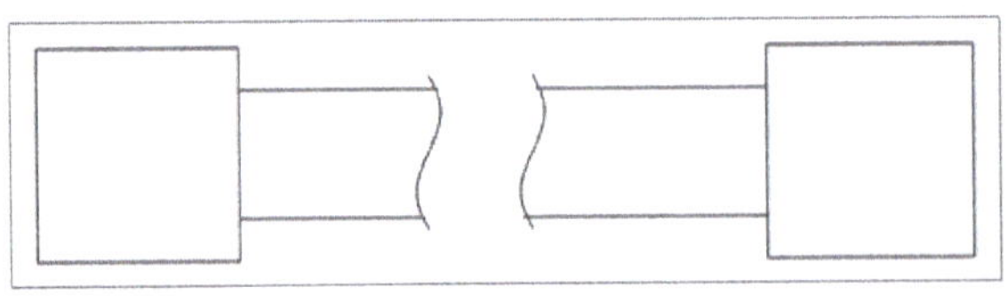

Note that you cannot add sketch curves such as section lines to a drawing view with a View Break. You need to add them before creating the view break.

Adding a Single-Sided Break Line to a View

To add a single-sided break line to a view, begin by activating the **View Break** command. In the **View Break** dialog, select **Type > Single-Sided**  . Then, choose an anchor point from the master view to specify the location of the break line within the view. Once selected, the break line will be displayed accordingly. Adjust the position of the break line by clicking and dragging the handle that appears on the line. Alternatively, you can enter a specific value in the **Offset** box for precise positioning. Further customization of the break line can be done by expanding the **Settings** section. Here, you can specify various settings such as **Style**, **Amplitude**, **Extension 1**, **Extension 2**, **Color**, and **Width**.

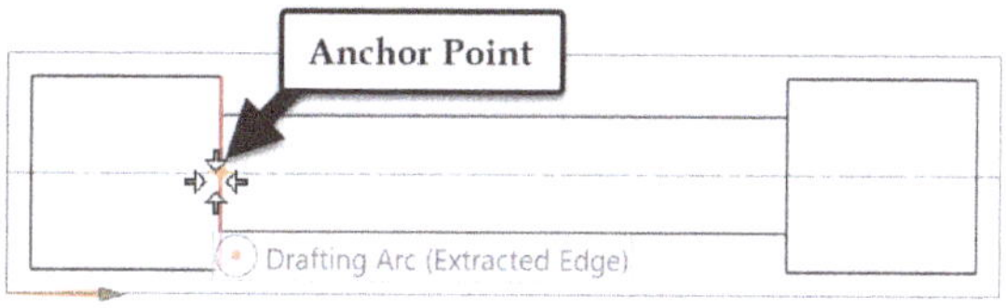

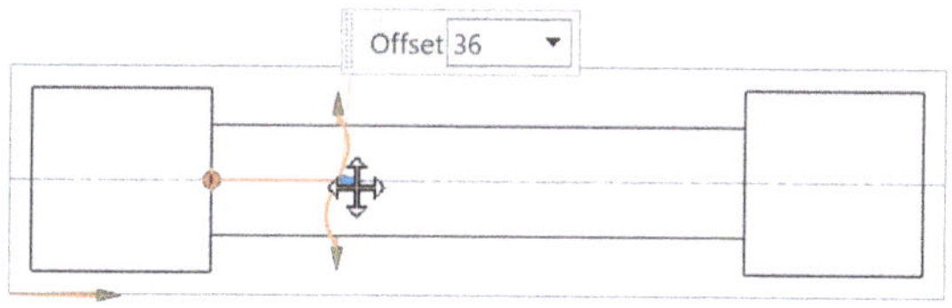

Click **OK** to add a single-sided break line to the view.

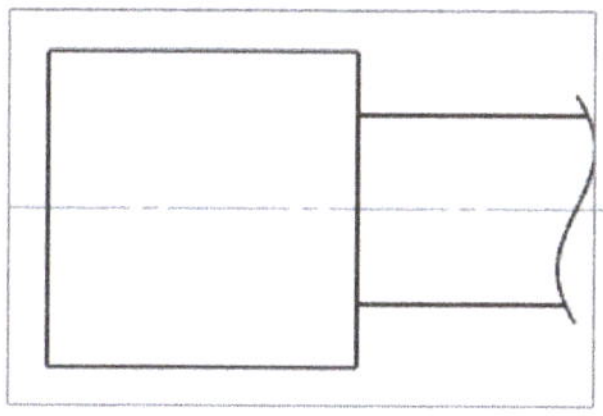

Note that the existing horizontal dimension will be hidden when add a Single-sided view break.

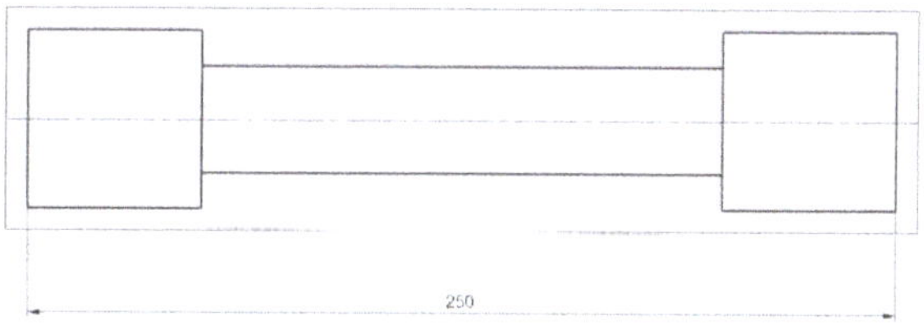

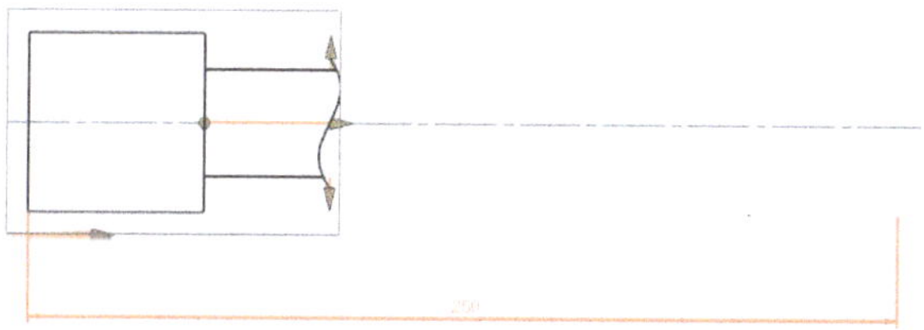

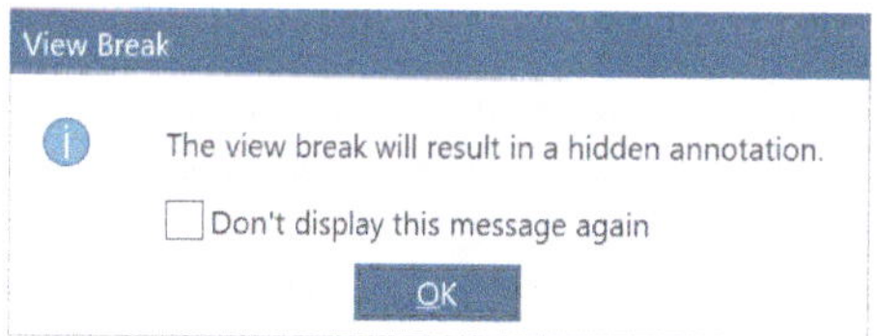

However, you can make the horizontal dimension to be visible by changing the Single-sided view break to a regular one. To do this, right-click on the break line and select **Edit**. Next, select **Type > Regular** from the **View Break** dialog. Next, specify the anchor point of the second break line. Click and drag the handle displayed on the break line to offset it. Modify the parameters in the **Settings** section if required and click **OK**.

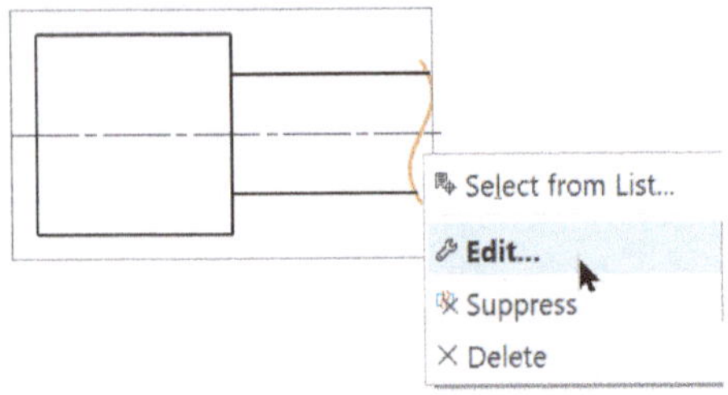

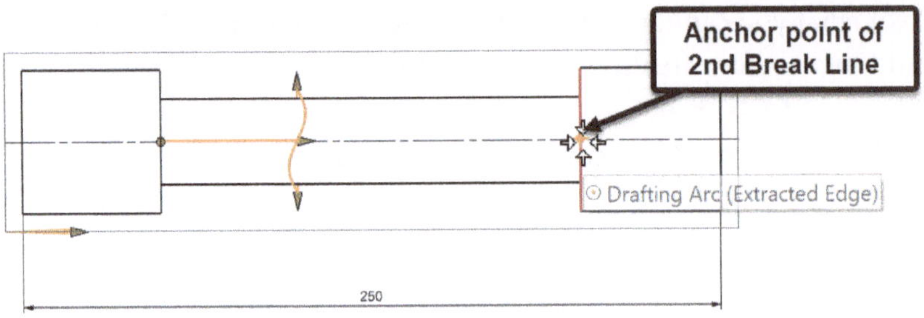

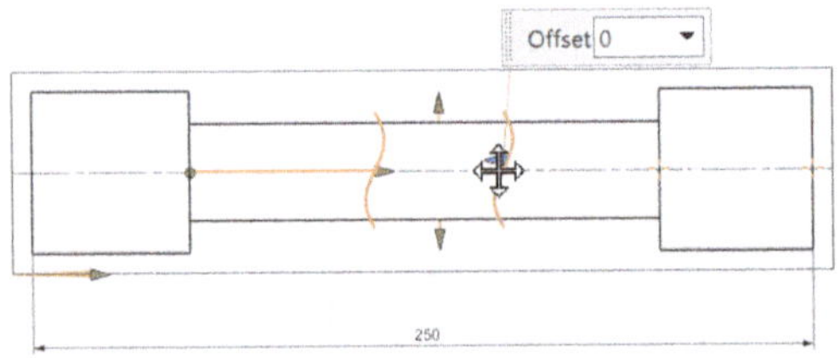

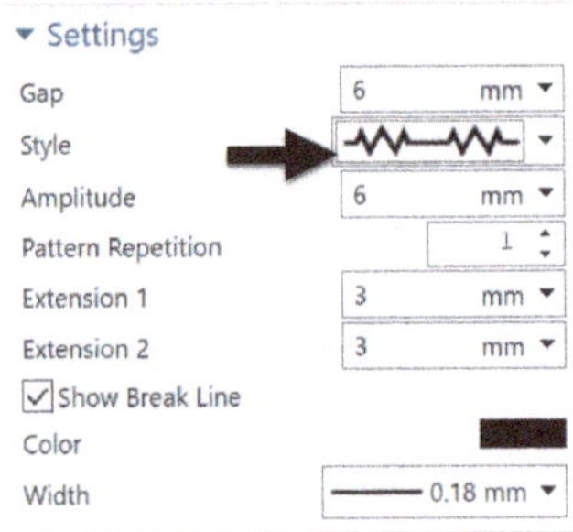

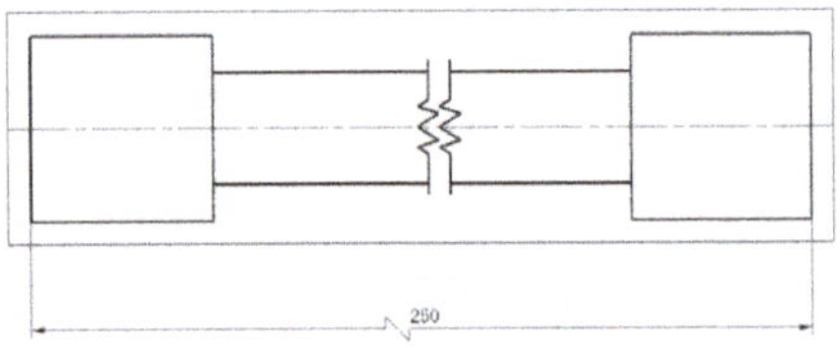

Break-out Section View

The **Break-out Section View** command alters an existing view to show the hidden portion of a part or assembly. This command is very useful to show the parts, which are hidden in an assembly view. You need to have a closed profile to breakout a view. For example, if you want to show the piston inside the pneumatic cylinder, click on the right-side view and select **Active Sketch View**.

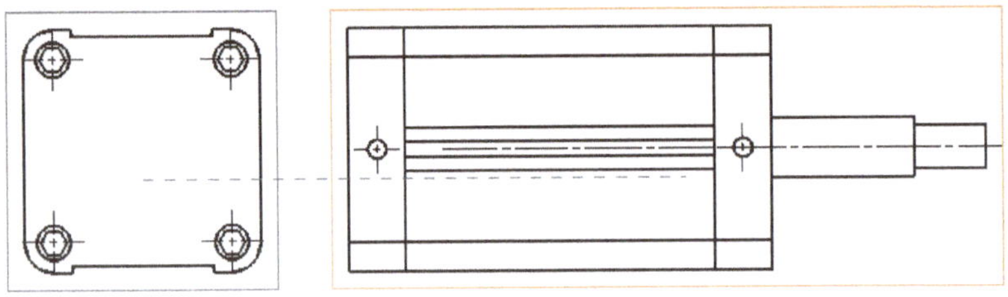

Use the sketch commands available on the ribbon and draw a closed profile on the view. Click **Finish Sketch** on the ribbon.

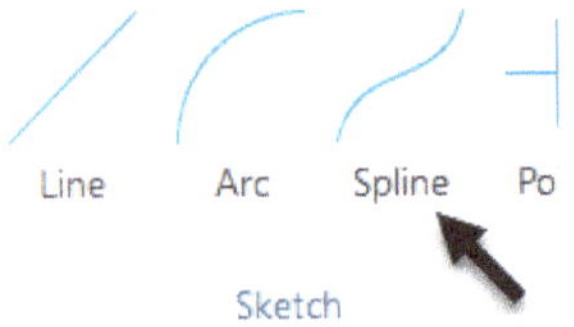

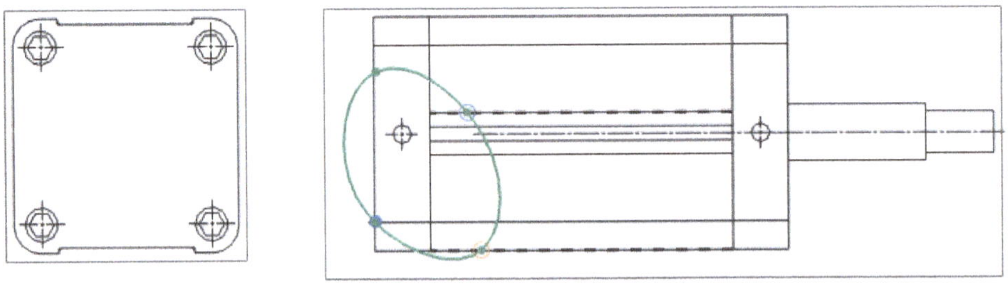

Activate the **Break-out Section View** command (click **Home > View > Break-out Section View** on the ribbon) and select the view. Define the base point on the other view. On the **Break-out Section** dialog, click **Reverse Vector** to reverse the extrusion direction.

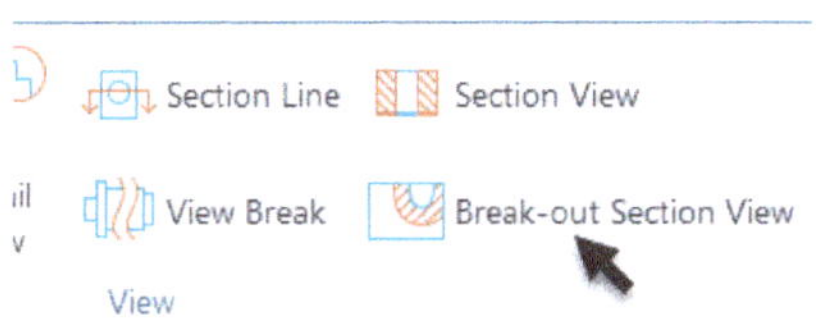

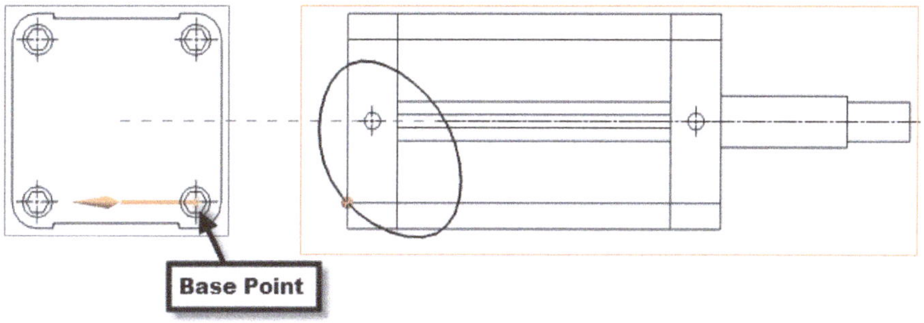

On the **Break-out section** dialog, click **Select Curves** and select the sketched profile. Click **Apply** to create the break-out section view.

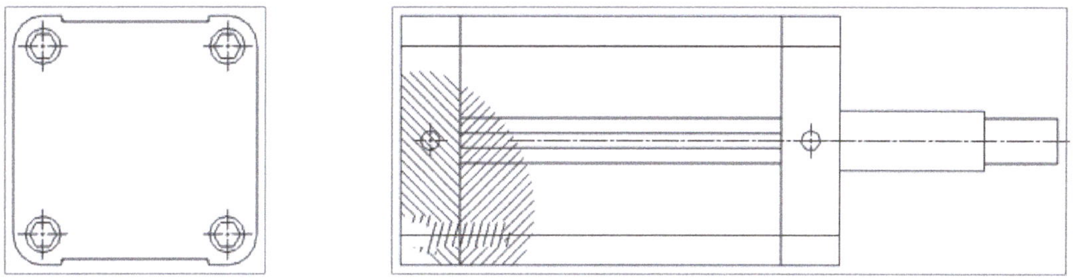

Exploded View

You can display an assembly in an exploded state as long as the assembly already has an exploded view defined (refer to **Chapter 8: Assemblies > Exploding Assemblies** section). If you want to add an exploded view to drawing, open the assembly file, and switch to the **Drafting** application (Click **Application > Document > Drafting**). Activate the **Base View** command and ensure that the assembly file is selected. On the **Base View** dialog, select **Model View > Model View to Use > Trimetric**. Under the **Scale** section, set the **Scale** value and click on the drawing sheet. Click **Close** on the **Projected View** dialog.

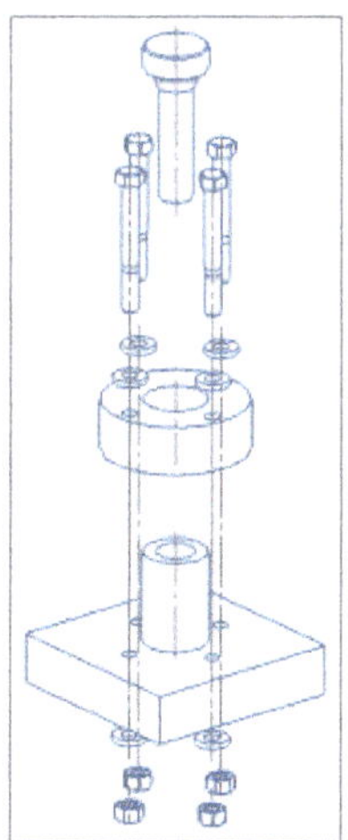

Display Options

When working with NX drawings, you can control the way a model view appears by using the display options. Select a view from the drawing sheet and click the **Settings** icon on the context toolbar. On the **Settings** dialog, select **Common > Shading**. Set the **Rendering Style** to **Fully Shaded** and click **OK**. The rendering style of the view will be changed.

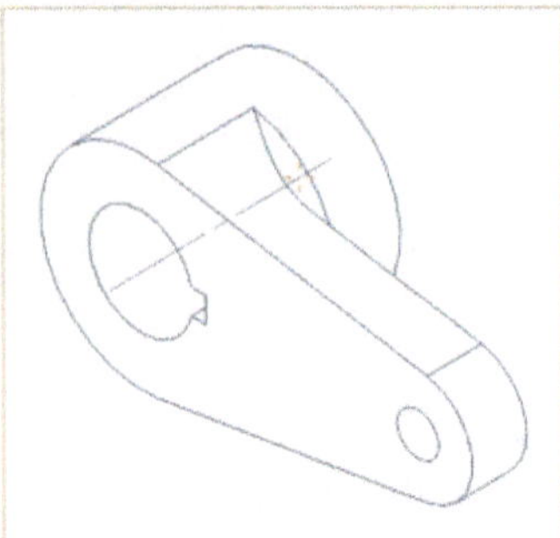

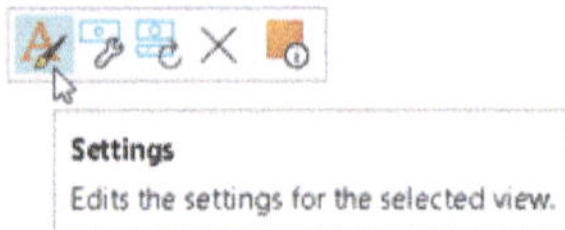

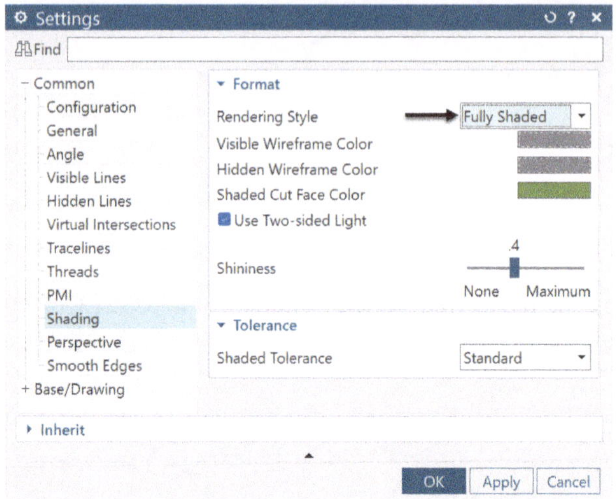

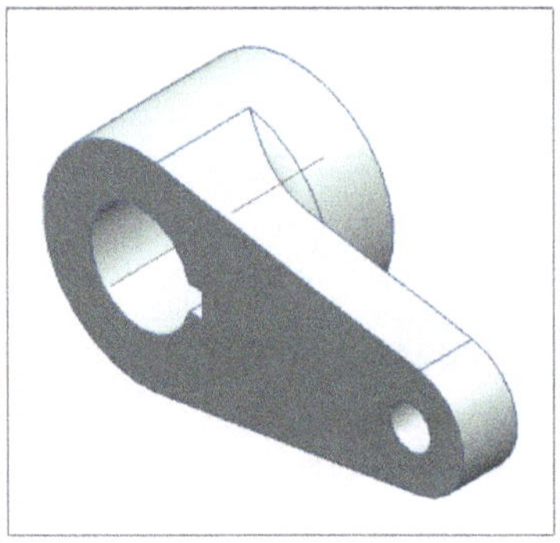

If you want to modify the display of hidden lines, then select the view and click **Settings**. On the **Settings** dialog, select **Common > Hidden Lines**. On the **Hidden Lines** page, check the **Process Hidden Lines** option. Set the line type to **Hidden** and click on the color swatch next to the line type drop-down. On the **Color** dialog, select the color and click **OK** twice.

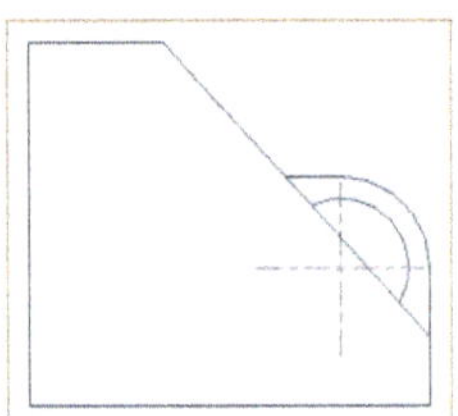

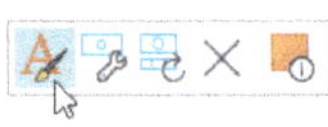

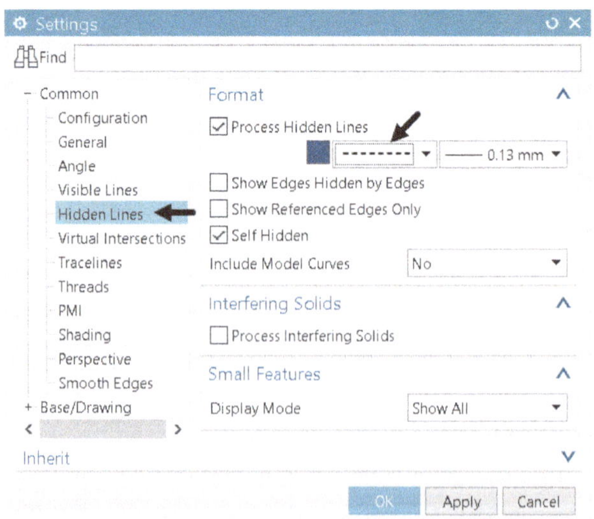

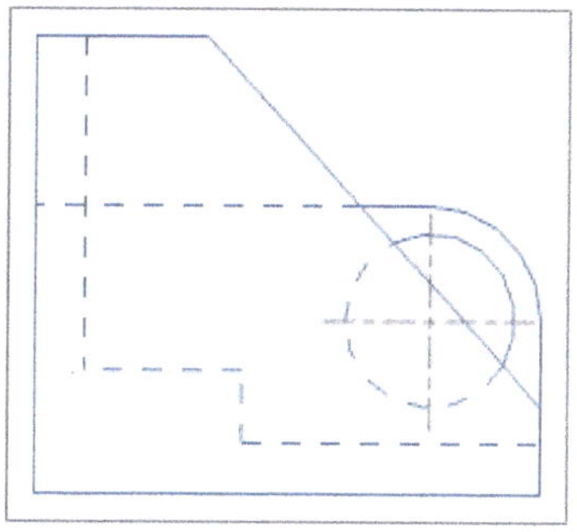

View Alignment

There are views that are automatically aligned to a parent view. These include auxiliary views and projected views. If you move down a view, the parent view associated with it will also move.

You need to break the alignment between them to move the view separately. Click the right mouse button on the view and select **View Alignment**. On the **View Alignment** dialog, under the **List** section, select the view and uncheck the **Associative Alignment** option in the **Placement** sub section of the **Alignment** section. Click **OK**.

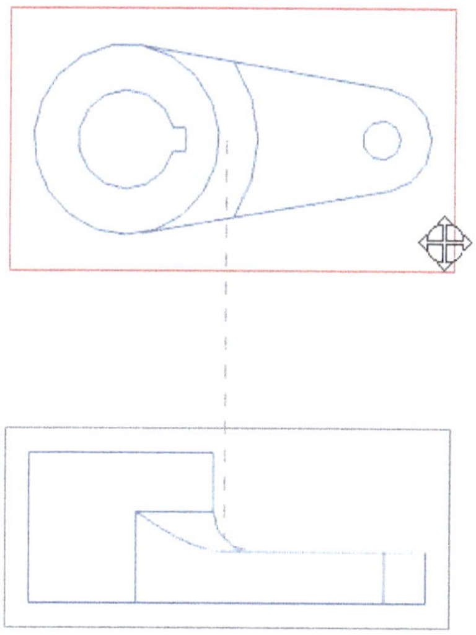

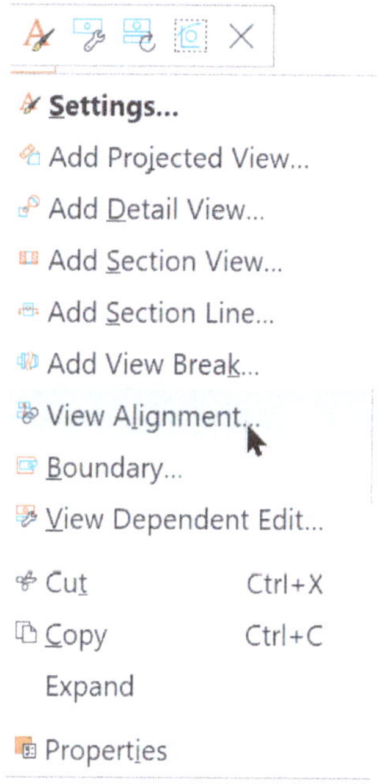

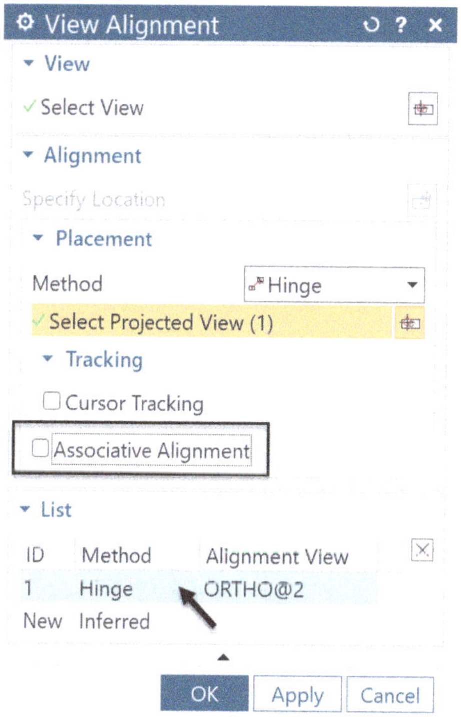

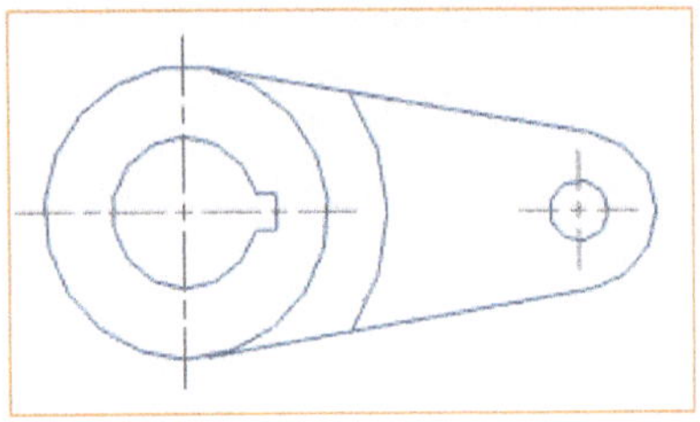

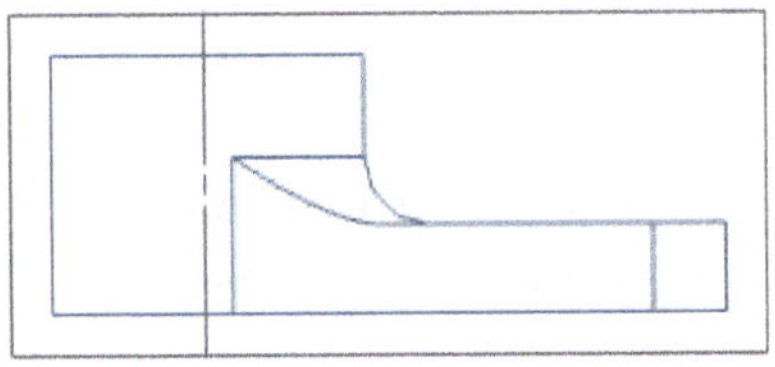

If you want to create an alignment between the views, click **Home > View > Edit View Drop-down > View Alignment** on the ribbon. Click on the view to align and select the alignment method from the **Placement** section. For example, select **Vertical** from the **Method** drop-down available in the **Placement** section. Next, select the parent view and click **OK**; both the views are aligned to each other, horizontally.

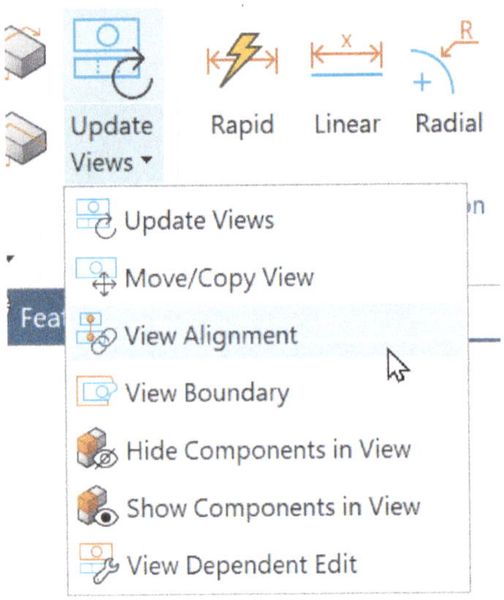

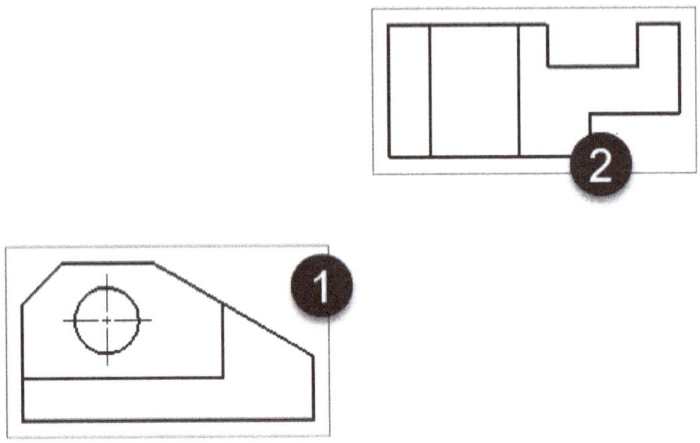

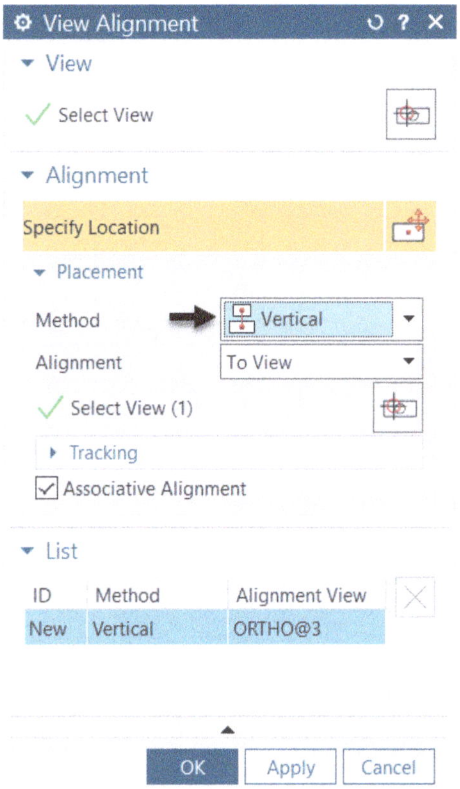

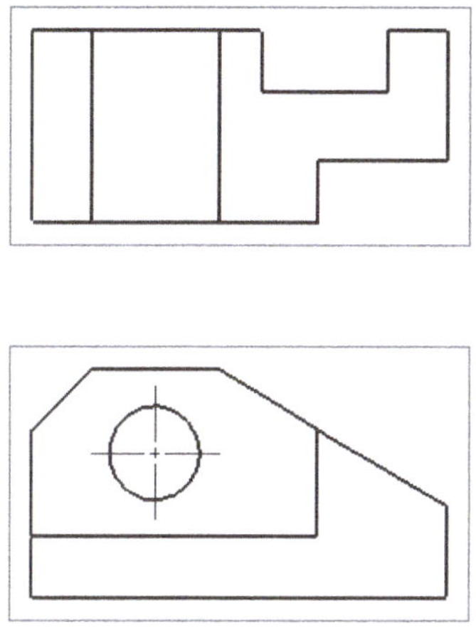

Parts List and Balloons in an Assembly Drawing

Creating an assembly drawing is very similar to creating a part drawing. However, there are few things unique in an assembly drawing. One of them is creating parts list. A parts list identifies the different components in an assembly. Generating a parts list is very easy in NX. First, you need to have an assembly view placed in the drawing. Next, you have to set your own preferences for the part list. To do this, click **File > Preferences > Drafting**. On the **Drafting Preferences** dialog, click **Table > Parts List > Workflow** and set the preferences of the Parts list and balloons. Click **OK** to close the dialog.

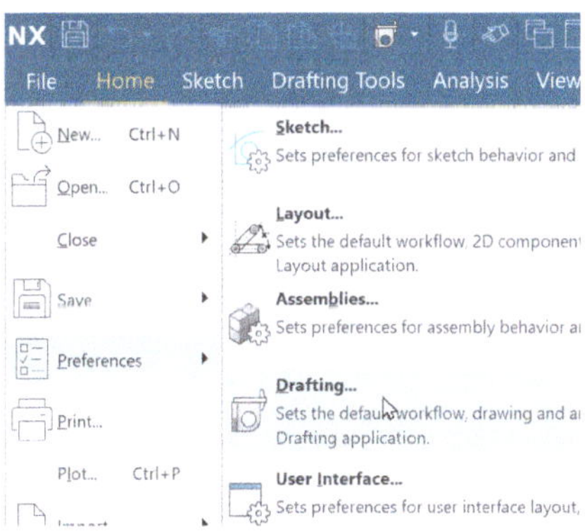

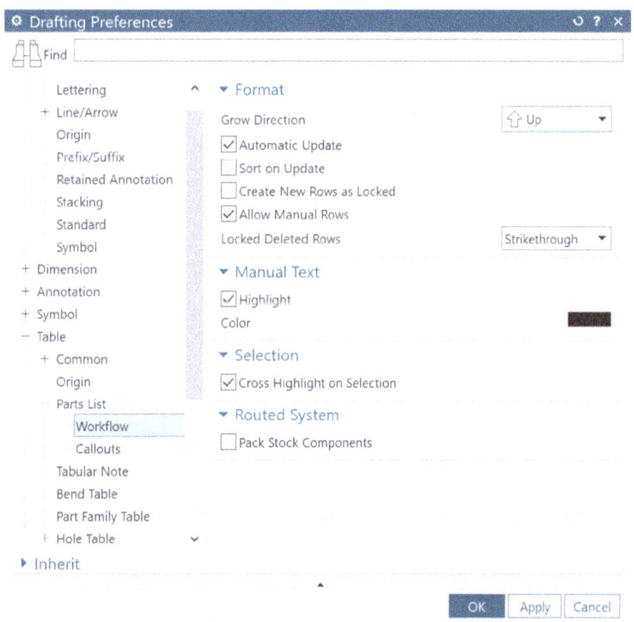

Now, click **Home > Table > Parts List** on the ribbon, and then click on the drawing sheet.

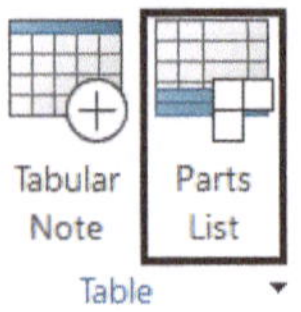

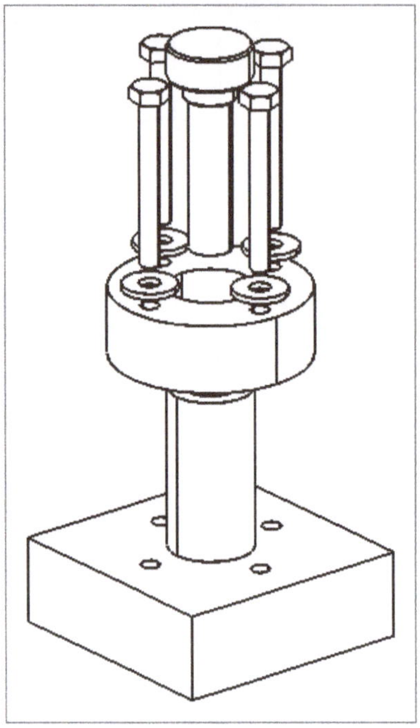

5	BOLTED_CONNECTI ON	4
4	FLAT WASHER REGULAR_AM_B18. 22M - PLAIN WASHER, 12 MM, REGULAR	4
3	SHOULDER SCREW	1
2	SPACER	1
1	BASE	1
PC NO	PART NAME	QTY

Select the Parts list and click the **Edit** icon on the context toolbar. Next, select the **Scope > Top Level Only** on the **Contents** section on the **Parts List** dialog.

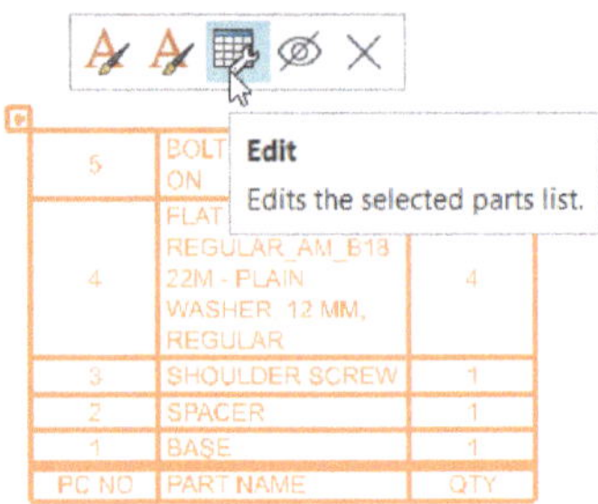

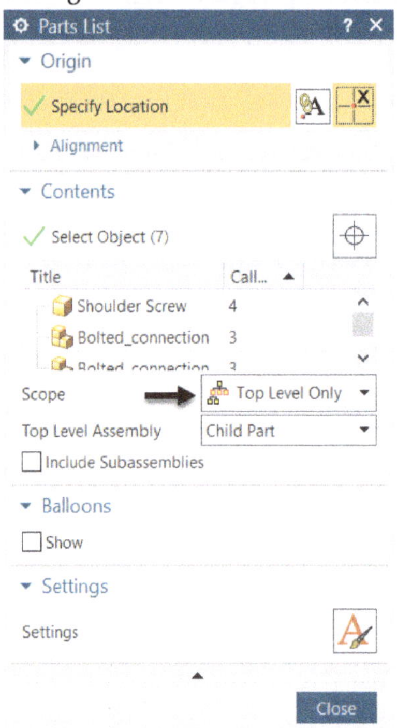

4	SHOULDER SCREW	1
3	BOLTED_CONNECTI ON	4
2	SPACER	1
1	BASE	1
PC NO	PART NAME	QTY

To add balloons to the assembly drawing, check the **Show** option in the **Balloons** section. Next, select the assembly view from the drawing sheet. Click **Close** on the **Parts List** dialog.

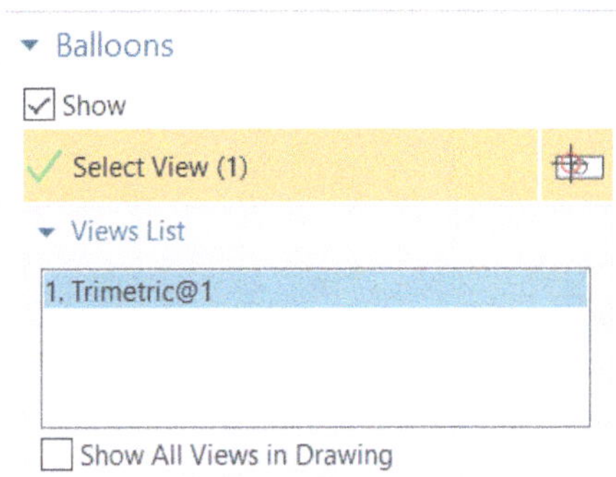

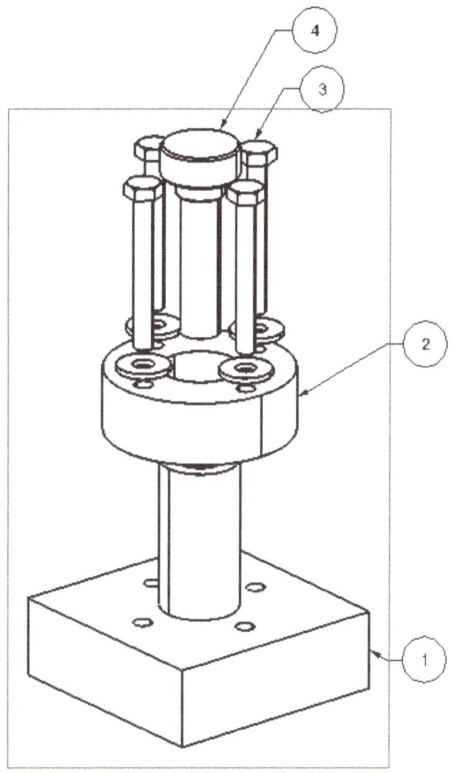

4	SHOULDER SCREW	1
3	BOLTED_CONNECTI ON	4
2	SPACER	1
1	BASE	1
PC NO	PART NAME	QTY

Dimensions

NX provides you with different types of commands to add dimensions to the drawing. However, before adding dimensions to a drawing, you must define some dimension preferences. These preferences control the display of the dimensions. To do this, click **File > Preferences > Drafting**. On the **Drafting Preferences** dialog, expand the **Dimension** section and modify the options that control the display of the dimensions. Expand the **Common** section and set the **Lettering** and **Line/Arrow** preferences. Click **OK** to apply the preferences.

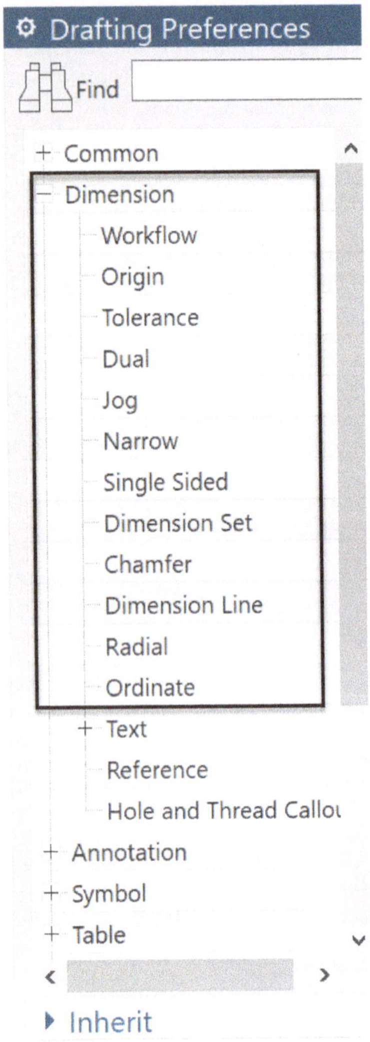

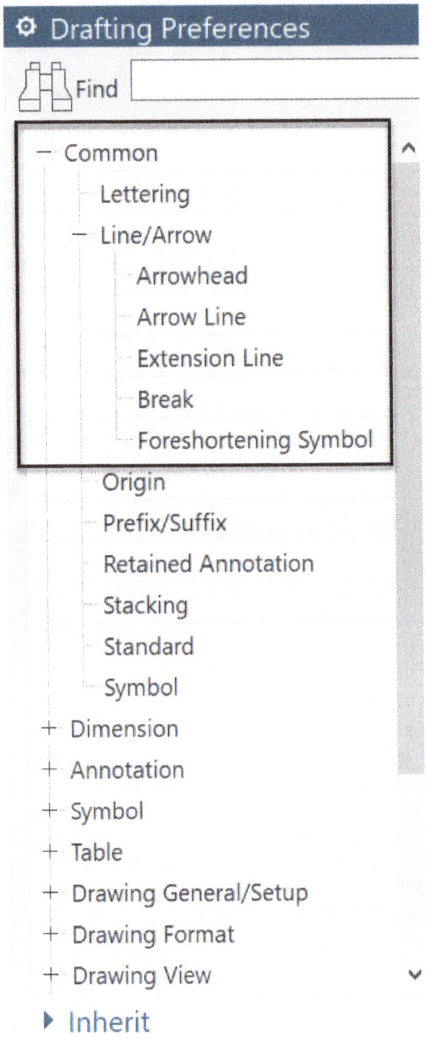

If you want to add dimensions, which are necessary to manufacture a part, activate the **Rapid Dimension** command and add them to the view. You can use this command to add all types of dimensions, such as length, angle, and diameter, and so on. This command creates a dimension based on the geometry you select. For instance, to dimension a circle, activate the **Rapid Dimension** command (on the ribbon, click **Home > Dimension > Rapid**) and then click on the circle. Next, move the pointer and click again to position the dimension.

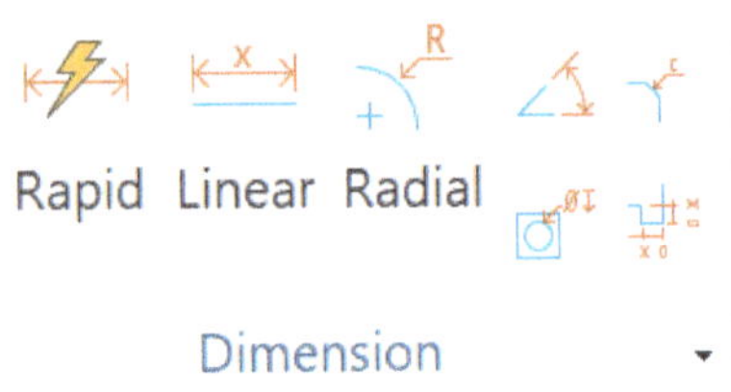

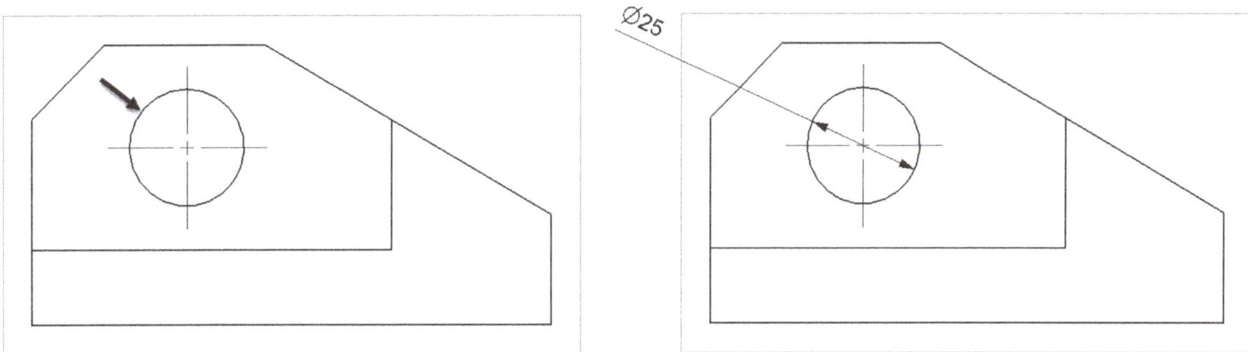

If you want to create a linear dimension, activate the **Rapid Dimension** command. Next, select **Measurement > Method > Inferred** on the **Rapid Dimension** dialog. Select a linear edge and position the dimension.

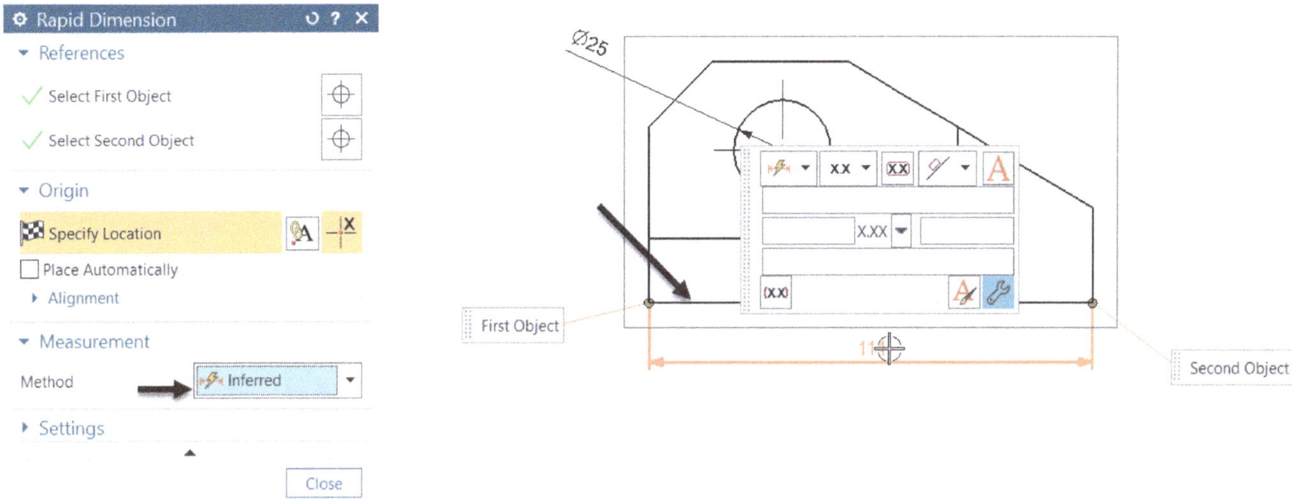

On the **Rapid Dimension** dialog, click **Close** to deactivate the **Rapid Dimension** command.

Ordinate Dimensions

Ordinate dimensions are another type of dimension that you can add to the drawing. To create them, activate the **Ordinate** command (click **Home > Dimension > Ordinate** on the ribbon). On the **Ordinate Dimension** dialog, select **Type > Single Dimension** and then click on any endpoint of the drawing view to define the ordinate or zero references. Now, click on a point or edge of the drawing view. On the **Ordinate Dimension** dialog, under the **Baseline** section, check the **Activate Perpendicular** option to create ordinate dimensions in both the directions. Move the pointer and click to place the coordinate dimension. Next, check the **Place Automatically** option from the Origin section. Next, select the remaining points from the drawing view.

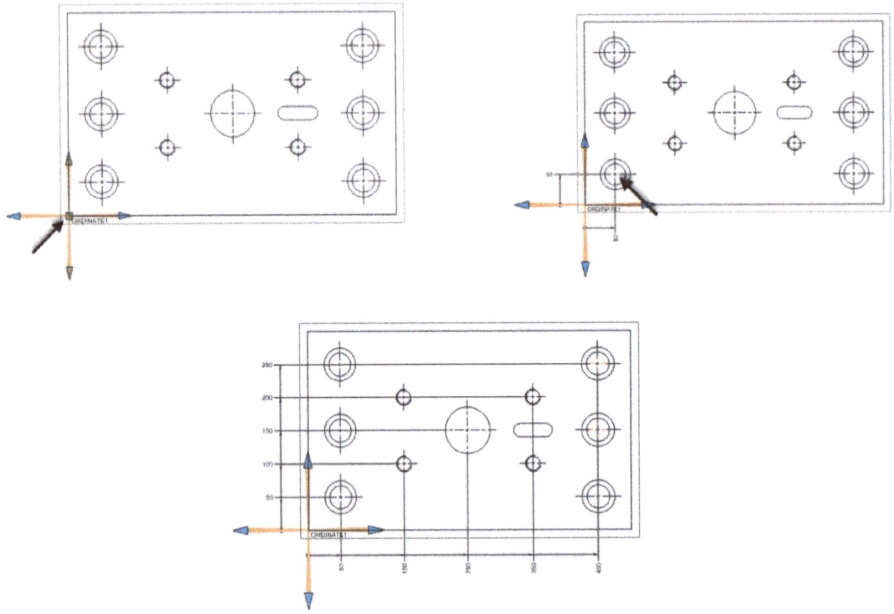

If you want to add multiple ordinate dimensions at a time, then select **Type > Multiple Dimensions** on the **Ordinate Dimensions** dialog and define the ordinate or zero references. Now, click on multiple points or drag a rectangle selection box to select multiple points. If you want to select only the center points of holes, then check the **Select Only Arc Centers** option on the **Ordinate Dimension** dialog and drag a rectangular selection box. On the dialog, expand the **Margins** section and click the **Define Margins** button. Now, select the ordinate point to define the margin. On the **Define Margin** dialog, type-in values in the fields available under the **Settings** section. Click **OK** and **Close** to add ordinate dimensions to the drawing.

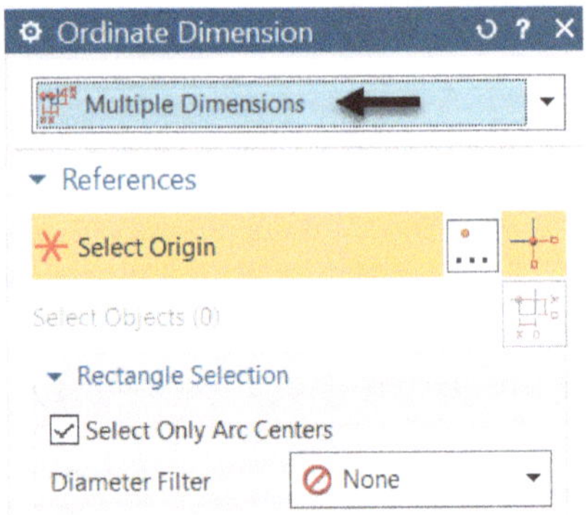

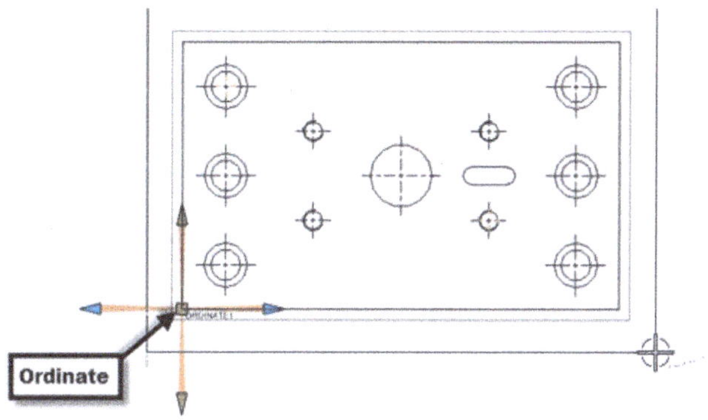

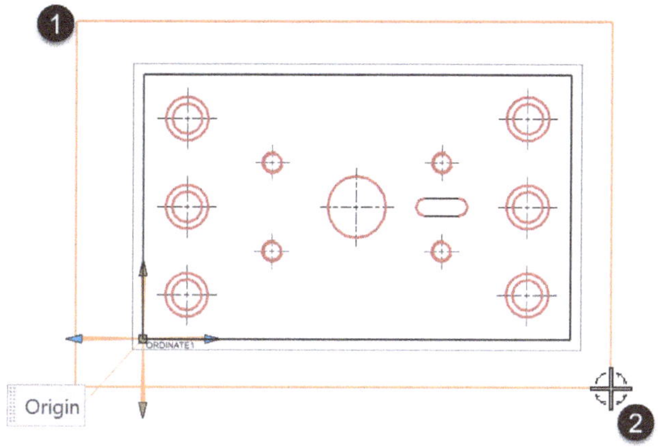

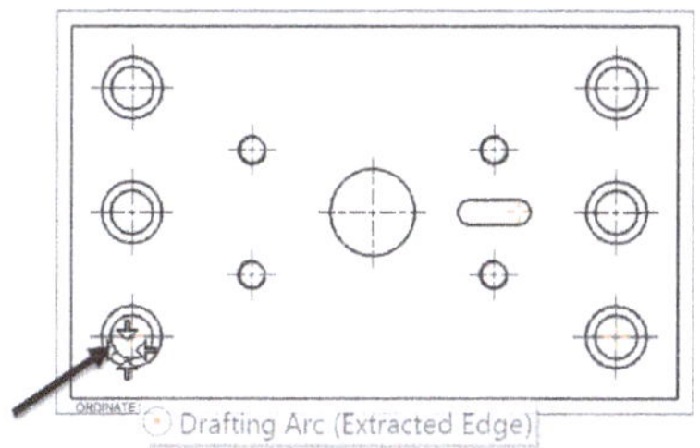

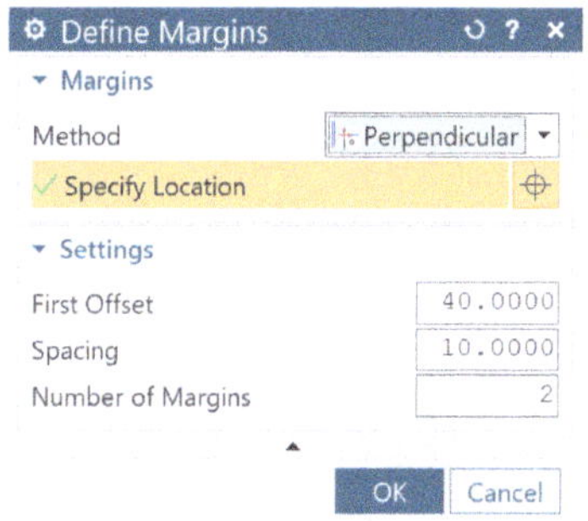

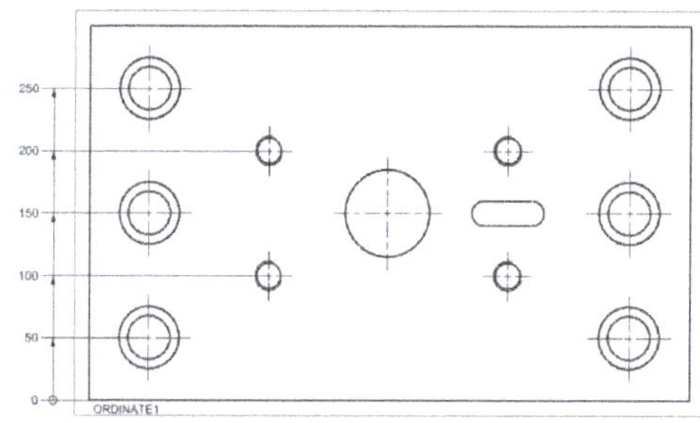

Adding Hole Callouts

If you want to add a hole callout, then activate the **Hole and Thread Callout** command (on the ribbon, click **Home > Dimension > Hole and Thread Callout**). On the **Hole and Thread Callout** dialog, select **Method > Radial** and select a hole feature. Next, position the hole callout and lose the **Hole and Thread Callout** dialog.

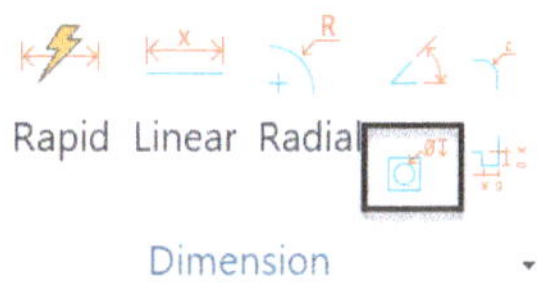

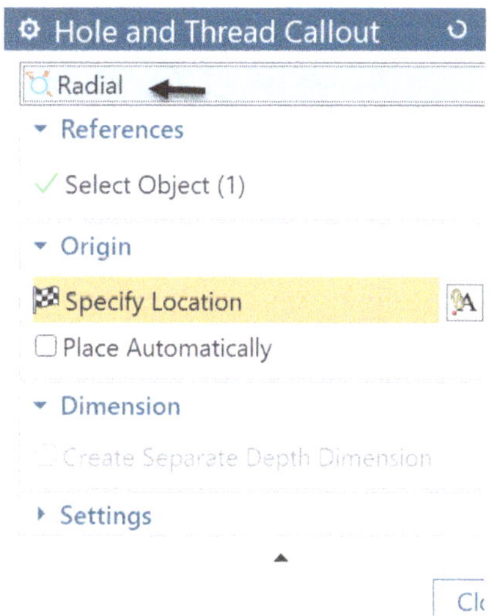

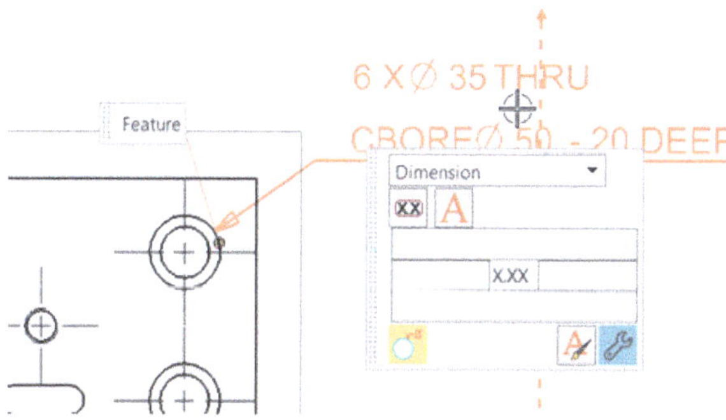

Center Marks and Centerlines

Centerlines and Centermarks are used in engineering drawings to denote hole centers and lines. Centerlines are automatically created while you create drawing views. However, if you want to create centermarks and centerlines manually, then uncheck the **Show Centerlines** option on the **Options** page of the **View Creation Wizard**. If you create views individually, then open the **Settings** dialog (click the **Settings** icon on the **Base View** dialog) and uncheck the **Create with Centerlines** option on the **General** page.

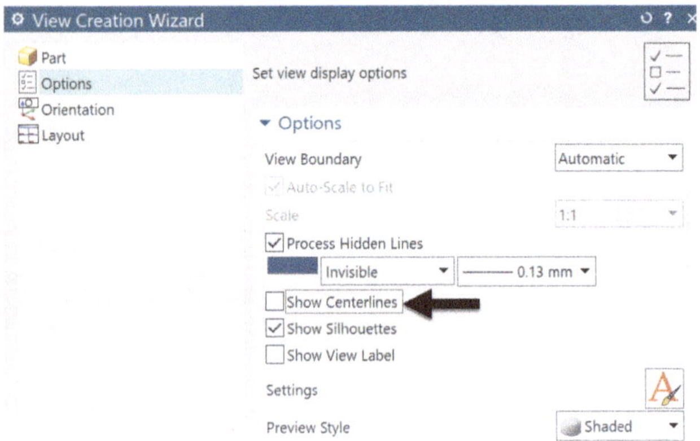

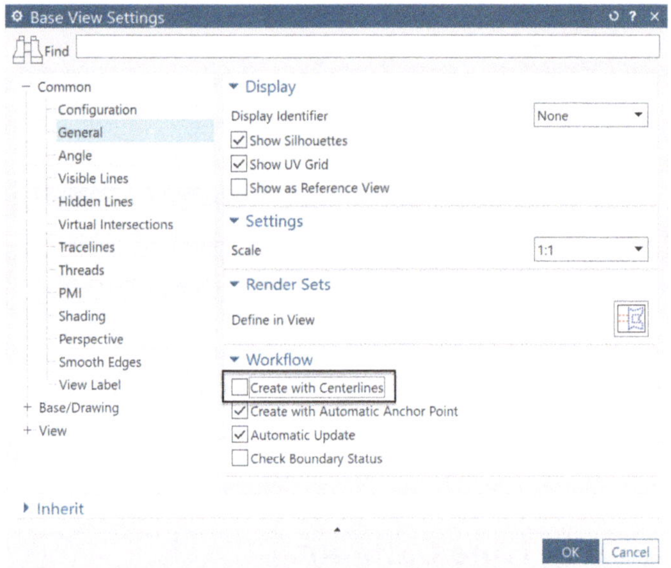

To add center marks to the drawing, activate the **Center Mark** command (click **Home > Annotation > Center Mark** on the ribbon) and click on the hole circles. Click **OK** on the **Center Marks** dialog to add center marks to the circles.

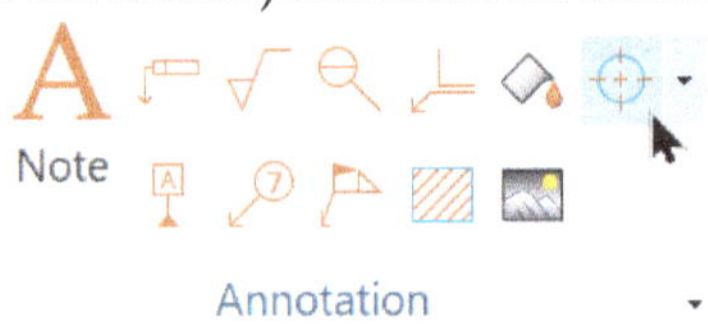

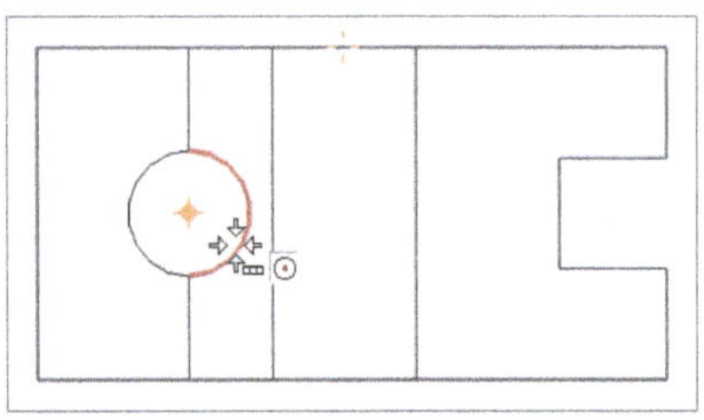

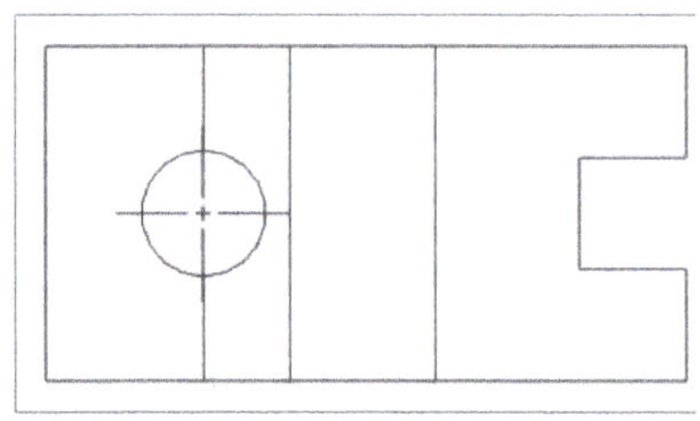

To add centerlines to a 2D view, activate the **2D Centerline** command (click **Home > Annotation > Centerline Drop-down > 2D Centerline** on the ribbon). Click on two parallel edges of the drawing view. Click **OK** to create a centerline between the two lines.

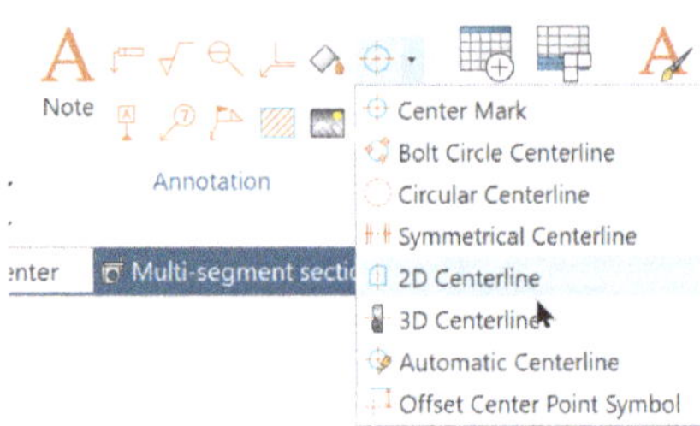

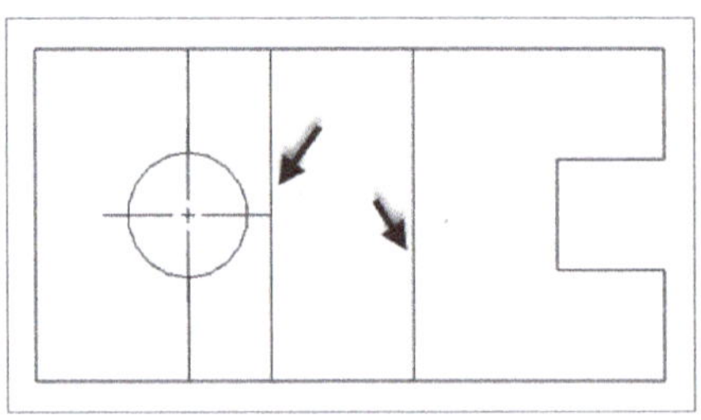

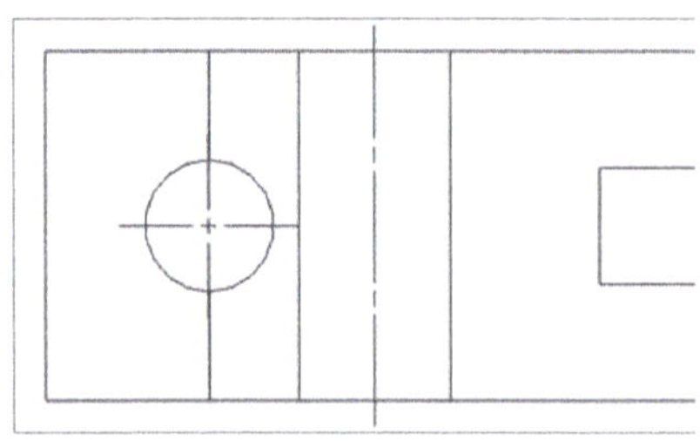

Likewise, you can add centerlines to an Isometric view by activating the **3D Centerline** command (click **Home > Annotation > Centerline Drop-down > 3D Centerline** on the ribbon) and selecting the cylindrical face of the view. Click **OK** on the **3D Centerline** dialog after selecting the cylindrical face.

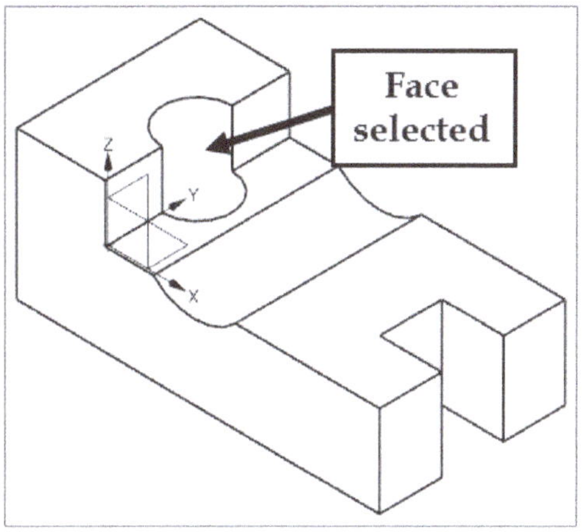

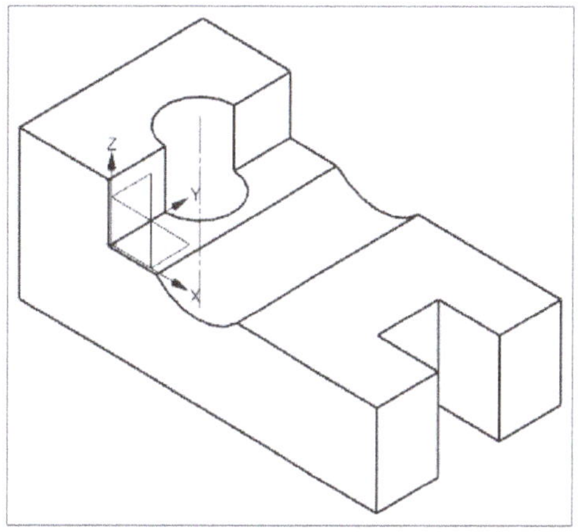

Bolt Circle Centerline

The **Bolt Circle Centerline** command (click **Home > Annotation > Bolt Circle Centerline** on the ribbon) allows you to add center marks to the holes arranged in a circular fashion. Activate this command and select **Type > Center Point** on the **Bolt Circle Centerline** dialog. Click for the center of the bolt circle. Drag the pointer and click for the radius point. Click on the center points of the circles located on the bolt circle. Click **OK** on the **Bolt Circle Centerline** dialog.

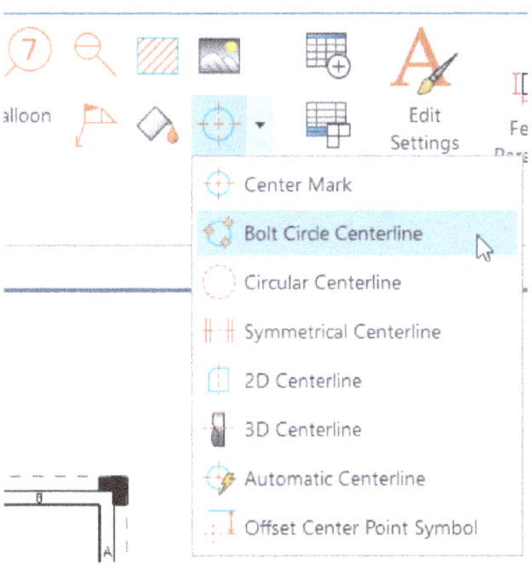

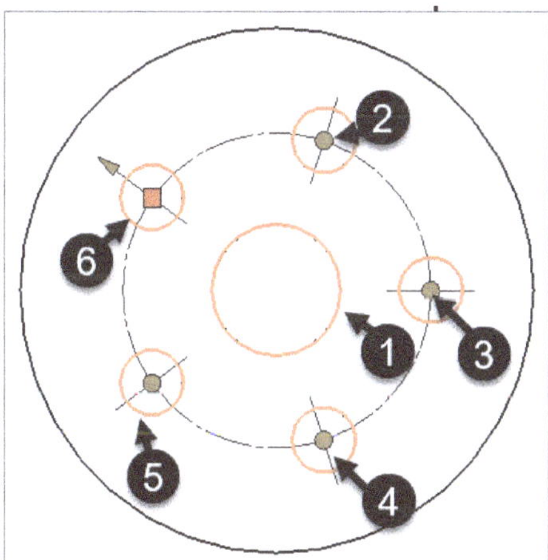

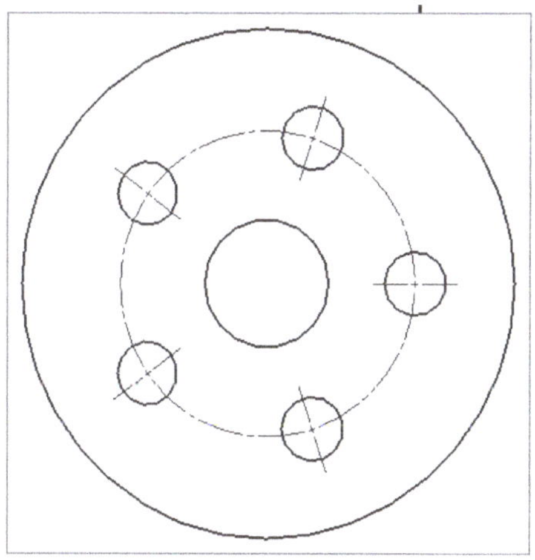

Notes

Notes are an important part of a drawing. You add notes to provide additional details, which cannot be done using dimensions and annotations. To add a note or text, activate the **Note** command (click **Home > Annotation > Note** on the ribbon). On the **General** tab, on the **Formatting** panel, select the font and font size. Next, type text in the **Text Input** section on the Note dialog and then click on the drawing sheet to specify its location.

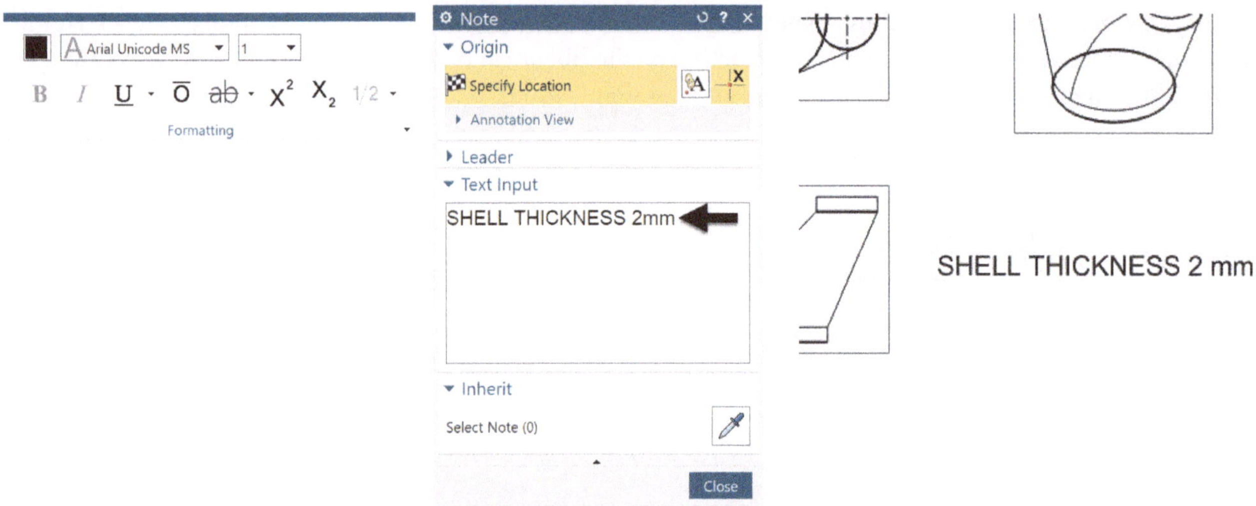

Examples

Example 1

In this example, you will create a 2D drawing of the parts shown below.

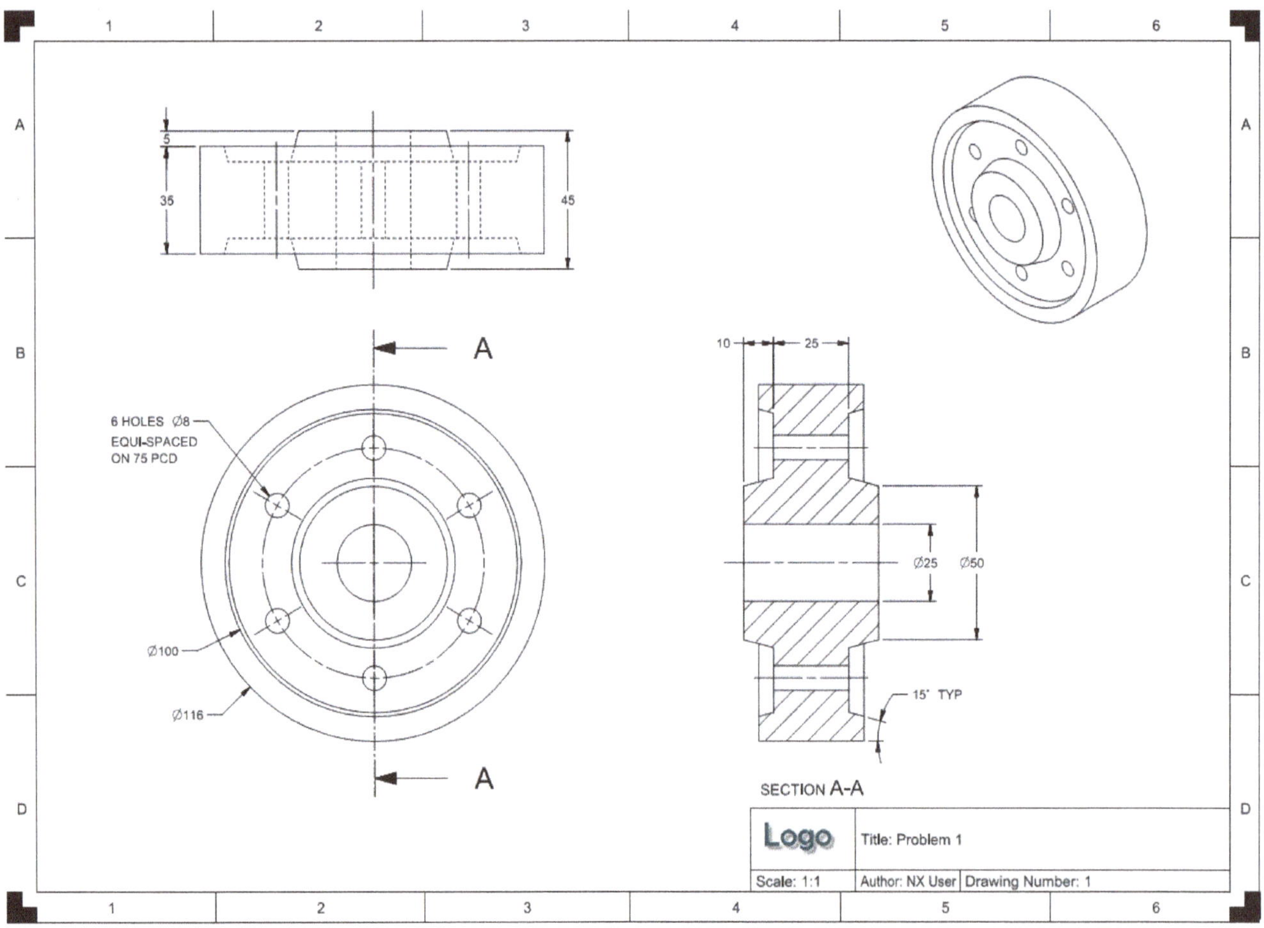

Start a New drawing and create a drawing template

1. Close the NX application window, if it is opened.
2. Type NX in the search bar located on the taskbar; NX appears in the search results.
3. Click the right mouse button on NX and select **Run as administrator**. Next, click the YES button.
4. On the ribbon, click the **New** button.
5. Click the **Model** tab on the **New** dialog.
6. On the **New** dialog, double-click on the **Model** template.
7. Click **Application > Document > Drafting** on the ribbon.

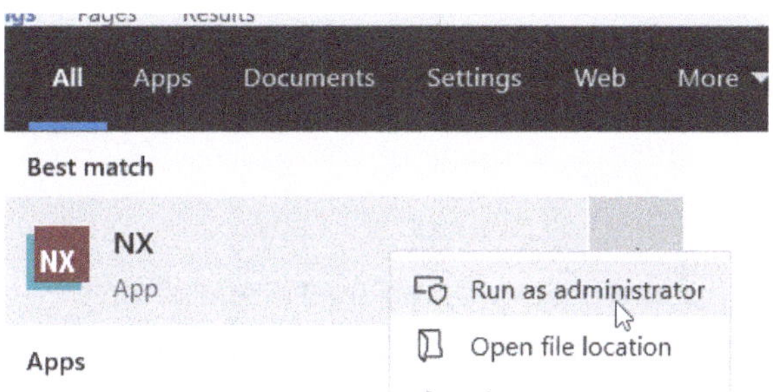

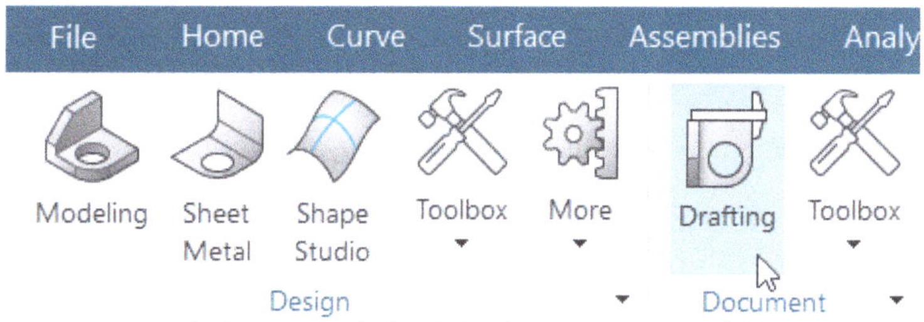

8. On the **Sheet** dialog, select **Standard Size**.
9. Set **Size** to **A3 – 297 x 420**.
10. Set **Scale** to **1:1**.
11. Under the **Settings** section, set **Units** to **Millimeters**.
12. Select 3rd **Angle Projection** 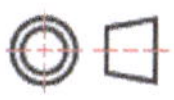 and uncheck **Always Start Drawing View Command**.
13. Click **OK** to open a blank sheet.

Set Drafting Standard

1. On the Top Border Bar, click **Menu > Tools > Drafting Standard**.
2. On the **Load Drafting Standard** dialog, select **Standard > ASME**, and then click **OK**.

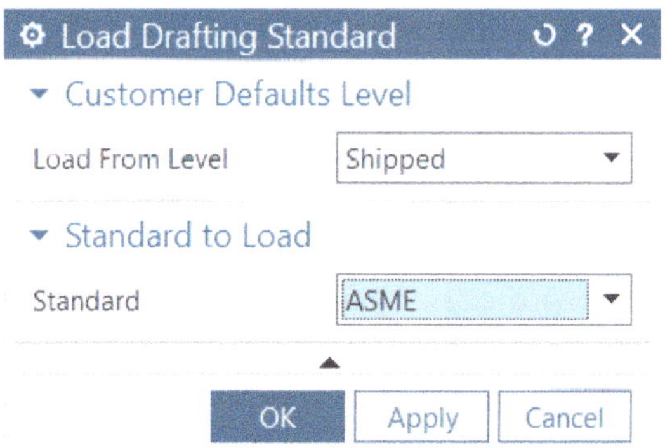

Adding Borders and Title Block

1. On the ribbon, click **Drafting Tools > Drawing Format > Borders and Zones**.
2. On the **Borders and Zones** dialog, leave the default settings, and click **OK**.

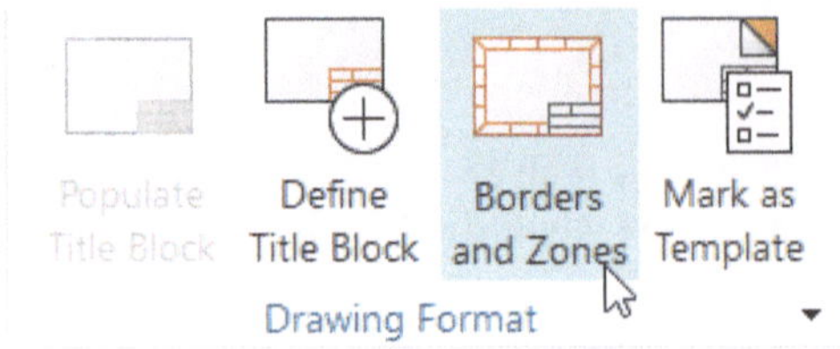

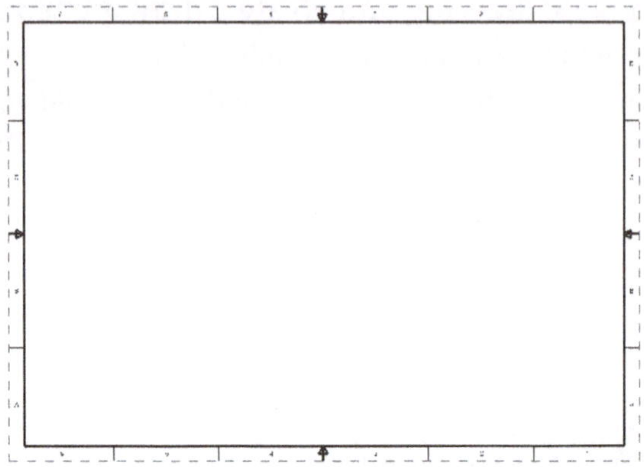

3. On the ribbon, click **Home > Table > Tabular Note**.
4. Click the **Settings** button on the **Tabular Note** dialog.
5. On the **Tabular Note Settings** dialog, click **Common > Section** from tree view. Under the **Format** section, select **Alignment Position > Bottom Right**. Next, click **Close**.
6. Under the **Table Size** section, set **Number of Columns** to **3** and **Number of Rows** to **2**.
7. Type-in **50** in **Column Width** box.
8. Click on the bottom right corner of the sheet border. Click **Close** on the **Tabular Note** dialog.

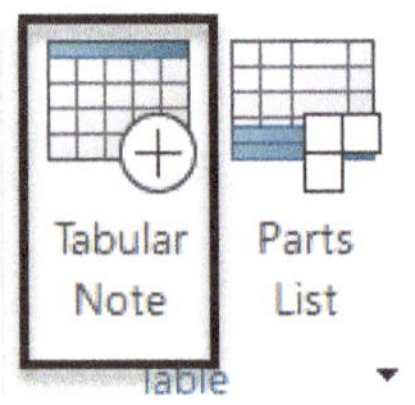

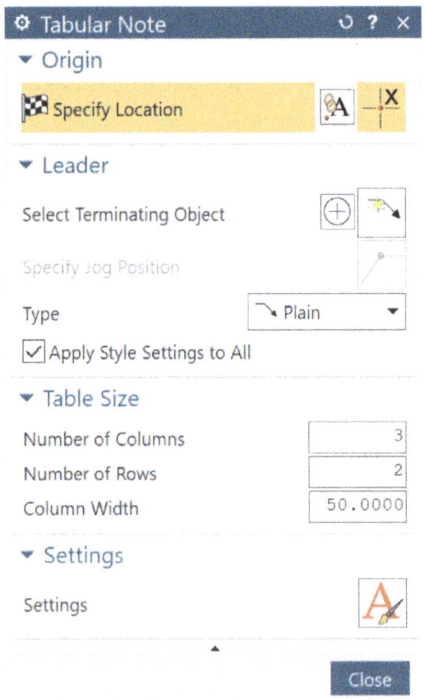

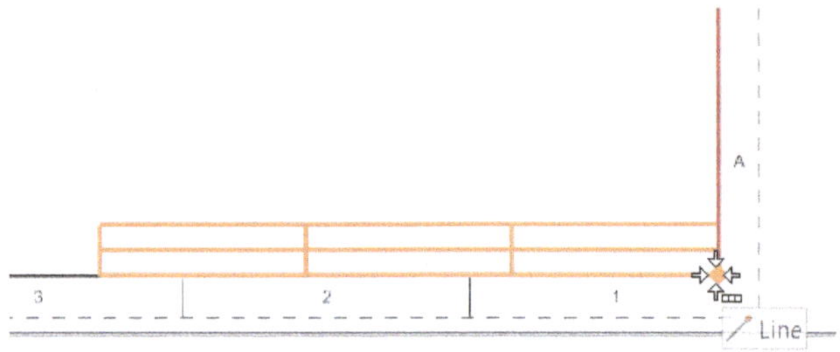

9. Click on the left vertical line of the tabular note.
10. Press the left mouse button and drag toward the right. Release the left mouse button when the column width is changed to 35.

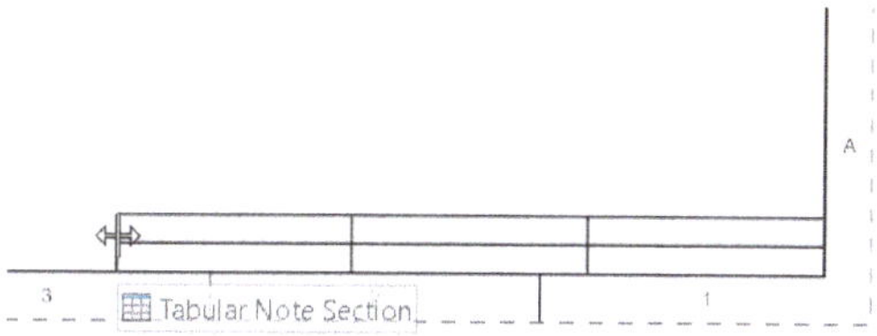

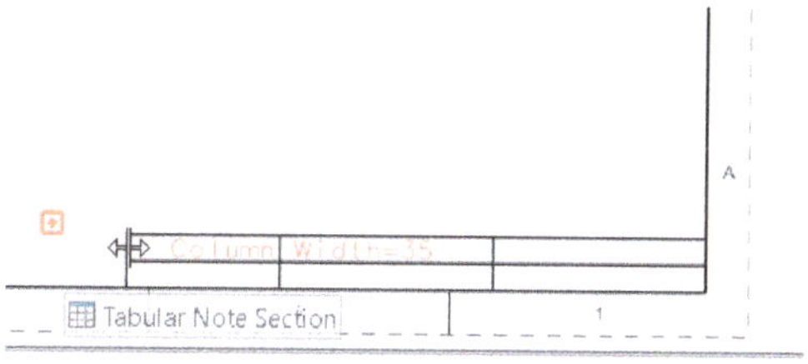

11. Likewise, change the width of the second and third columns.

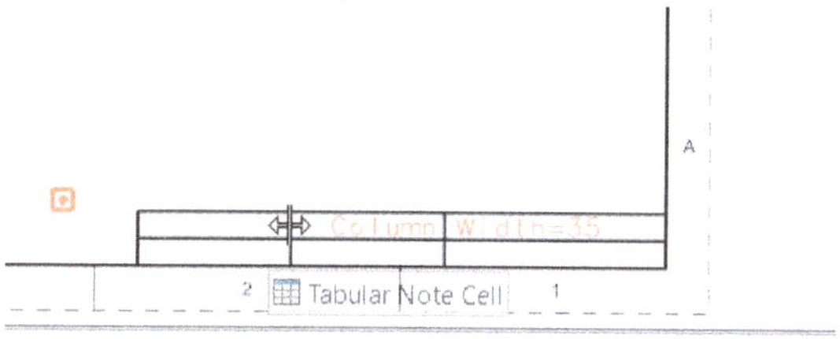

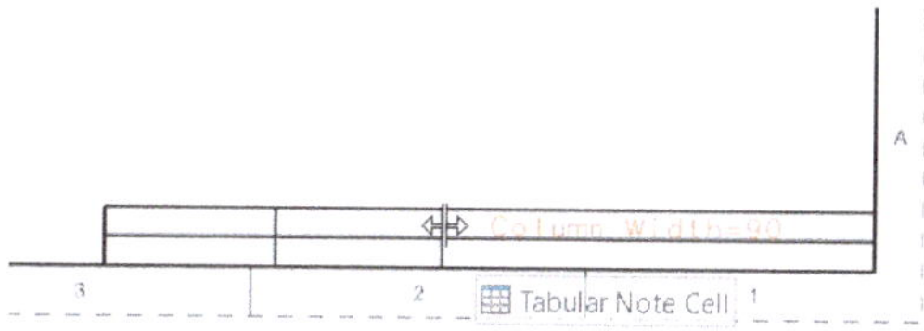

12. Change the height of the top row to 20. Next, click **Yes**.
13. Click inside the second cell of the top row. Press the left mouse button and drag it to the third cell.

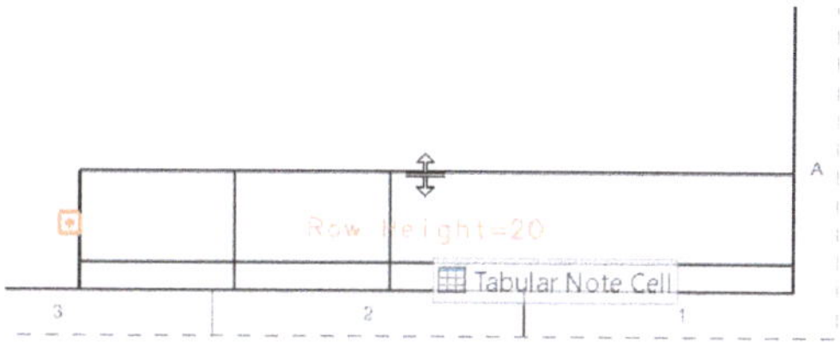

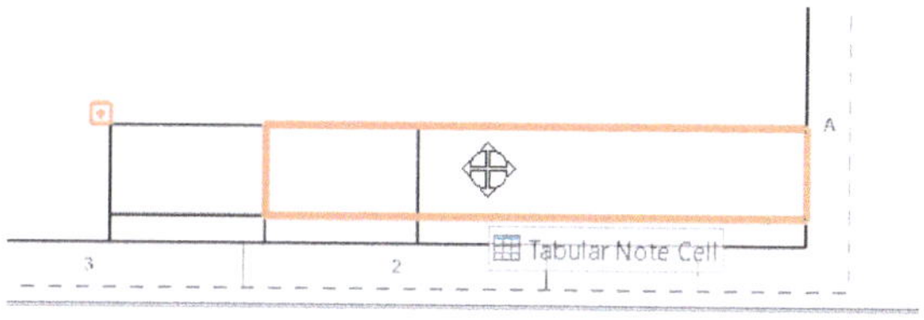

14. Click the right mouse button and select **Merge Cells**.

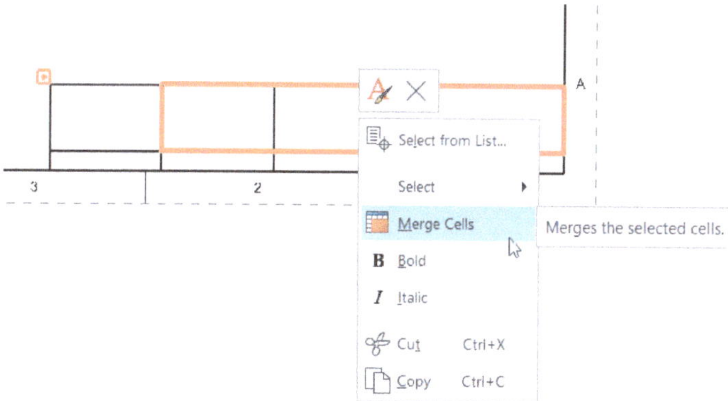

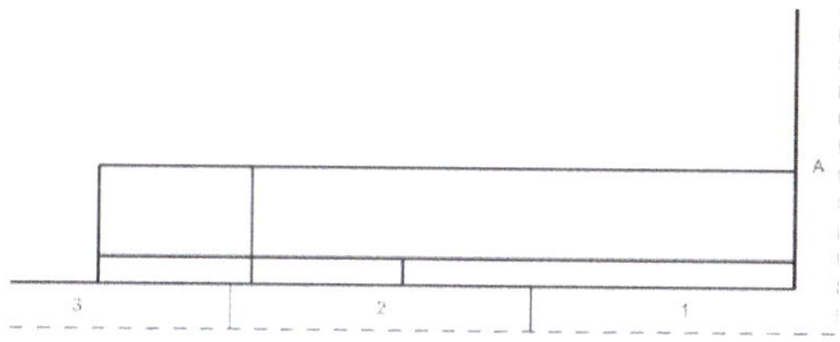

15. Click in the merged cell of the top row. Select **Settings**.
16. On the **Settings** dialog, select Prefix/Suffix from the left side. Next, type-in **Title:** in the **Prefix** box and press the Spacebar. Click **Close**.

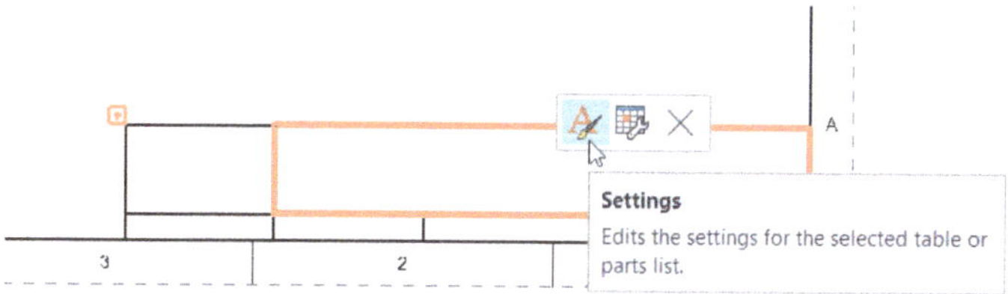

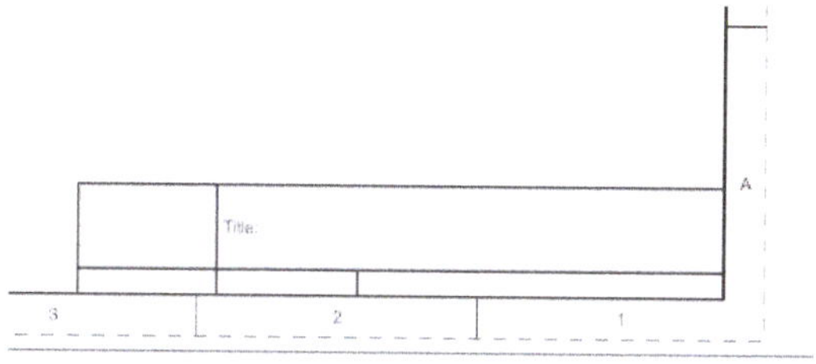

17. Likewise, add prefixes to other cells, as shown.
18. Click the right mouse button in the top-left cell of the table, and then click **Import > Image**.

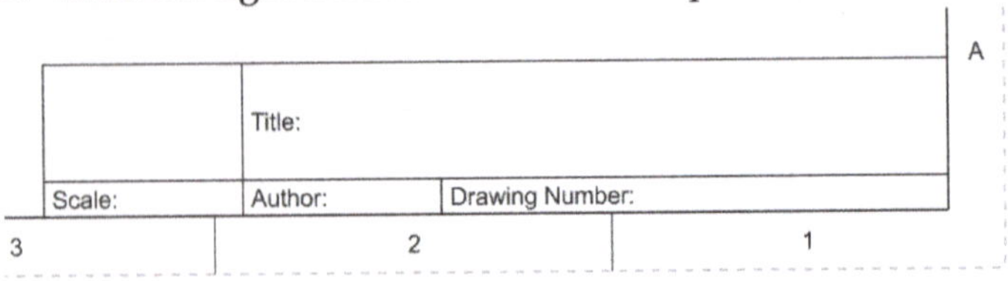

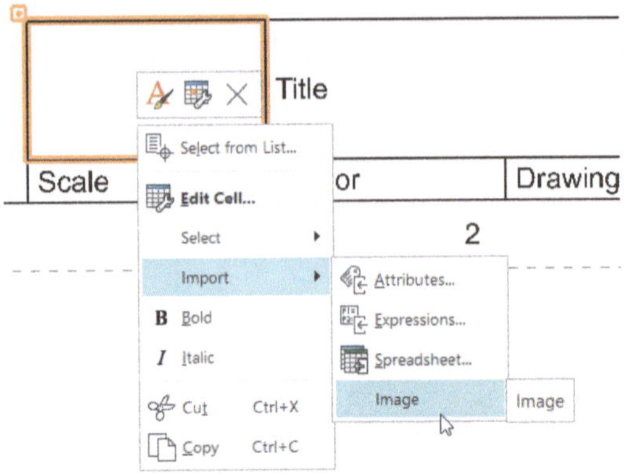

19. Select your company logo image and click **OK.**
20. On the ribbon, click **Drafting Tools > Drawing Format > Define Title Block.**
21. Click on the table, and then click **OK.**
22. On the ribbon, click **Drafting Tools > Drawing Format > Mark as Template.**

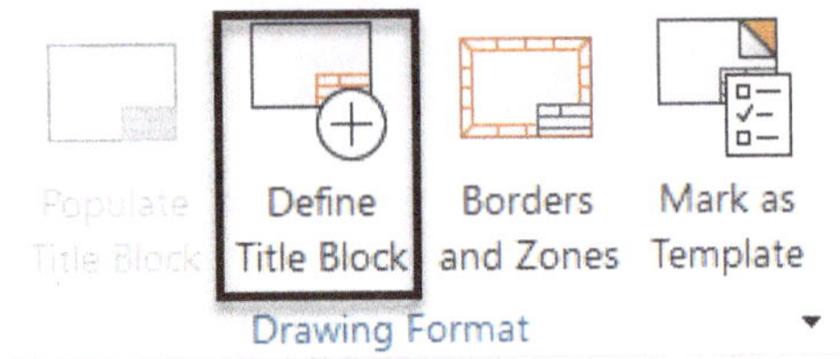

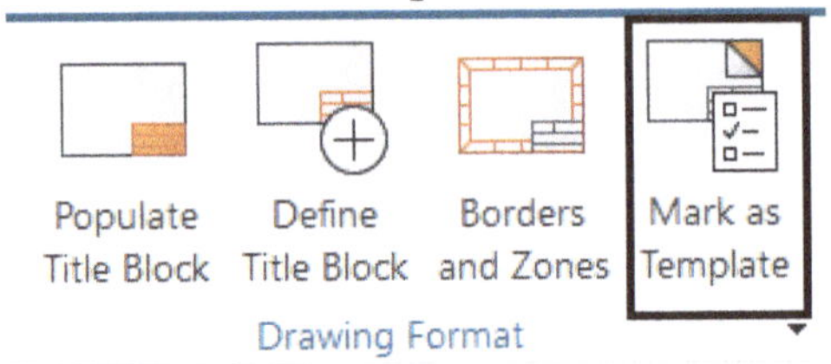

23. On the dialog, select **Mark as Template and Update PAX File.**
24. Under the **PAX File Settings** section, type-in **Sample Template** in the **Presentation Name** box.
25. Select **Template Type > Reference Existing Part.**
26. Click the **Browse** icon.
27. Go to *C:\Program Files\Siemens\NX2506\DRAFTING\templates*
28. Click **ugs_drawing_templates**, and then click **OK.**
29. On the **Input Validation** box, click **Yes.**
30. Click **OK** twice.
31. Save and close the file.

Start a new drawing using the Sample Template

1. On the ribbon, click the **New** icon to open the **New** dialog. On this dialog, click the **Drawing** tab and select **Relationship > Reference Existing Part.**
2. Under the **Templates** section, select **Sample Template.**
3. Under the **Part to Create a Drawing of** the section, click the **Browse** button.
4. On the **Select CAD Source Part** dialog, click **Open**. Go to the location of Exercise 1 of Chapter 5 and double-click on it.
5. Click **OK** twice.
6. On the **Populate Title Block** dialog, select **Label2** from the **List** and type-in Example 1.
7. Likewise, select the other labels and type in values, as shown.

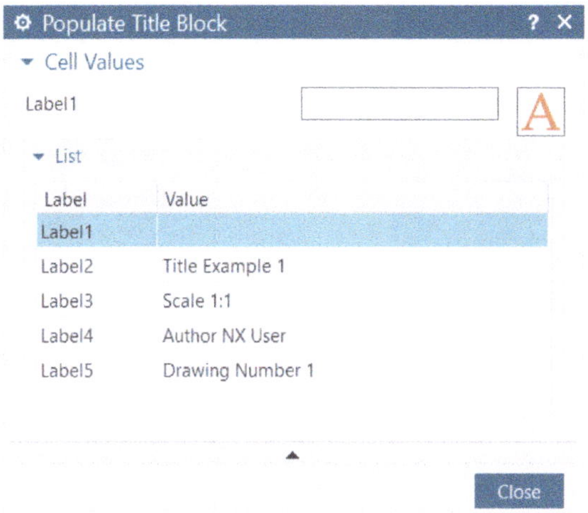

8. Click **Close**.

Generating Drawing Views

1. On the **Base View** dialog, select **Model View to Use > Front** from the **Model View** section.
2. Select **Scale > 1:1** from the **Scale** section.
3. Click the **Settings**  button in the **Settings** section.
4. On the **Base View Settings** dialog, select the **General** option from the tree displayed at the left side.
5. Uncheck the **Create with Centerlines** option under the **Workflow** section.

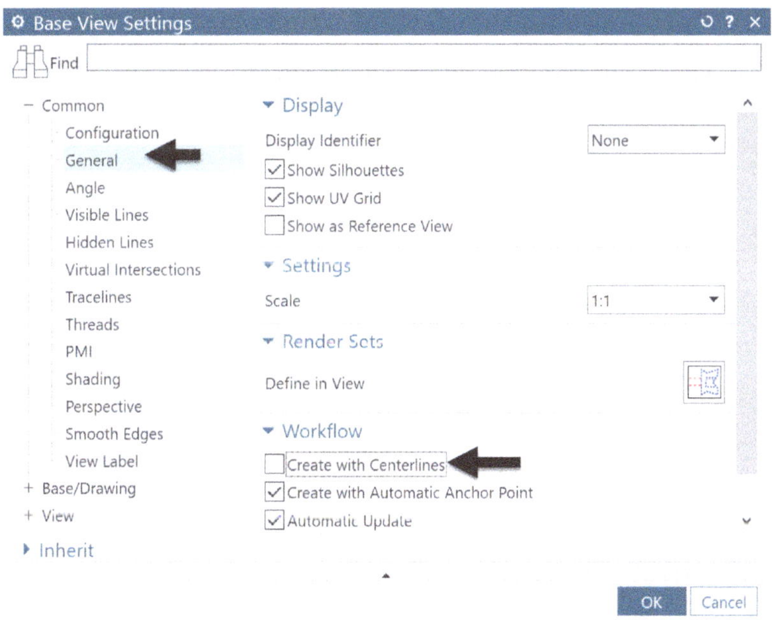

6. Select the **Hidden Lines** option and make sure that the **Process Hidden lines** option is selected.
7. Select **Invisible** from the drop-down located below the **Process Hidden Lines** option.

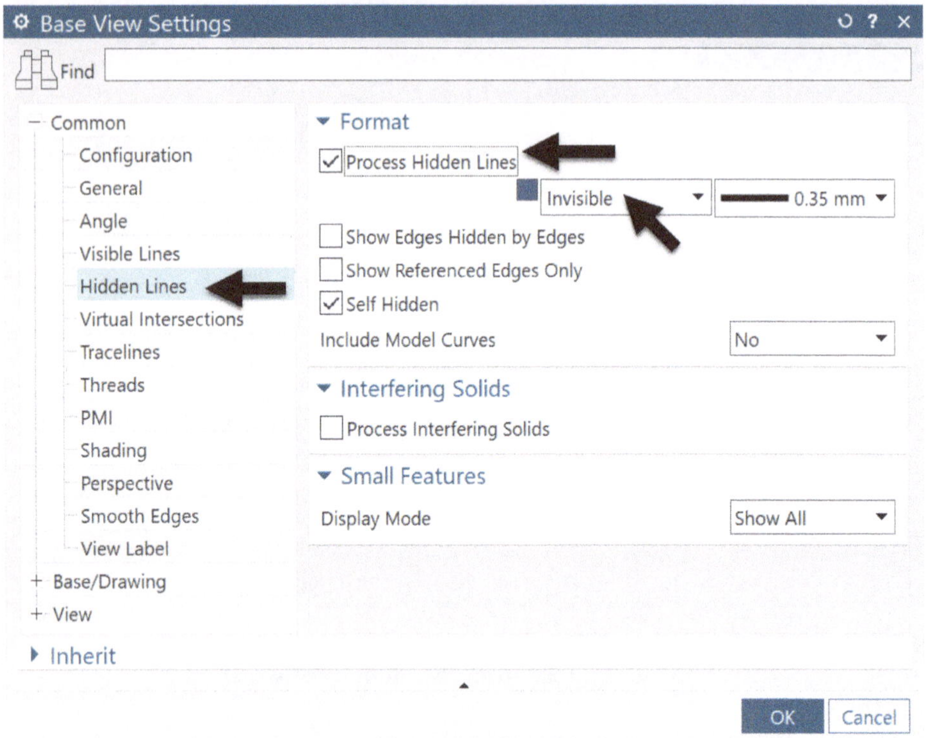

9. Click **OK** on the **Base View Settings** dialog.
10. Click to define the location of the view, as shown next.
11. Move the pointer upward and click to position the projected view. Next, close the **Projected View** dialog.

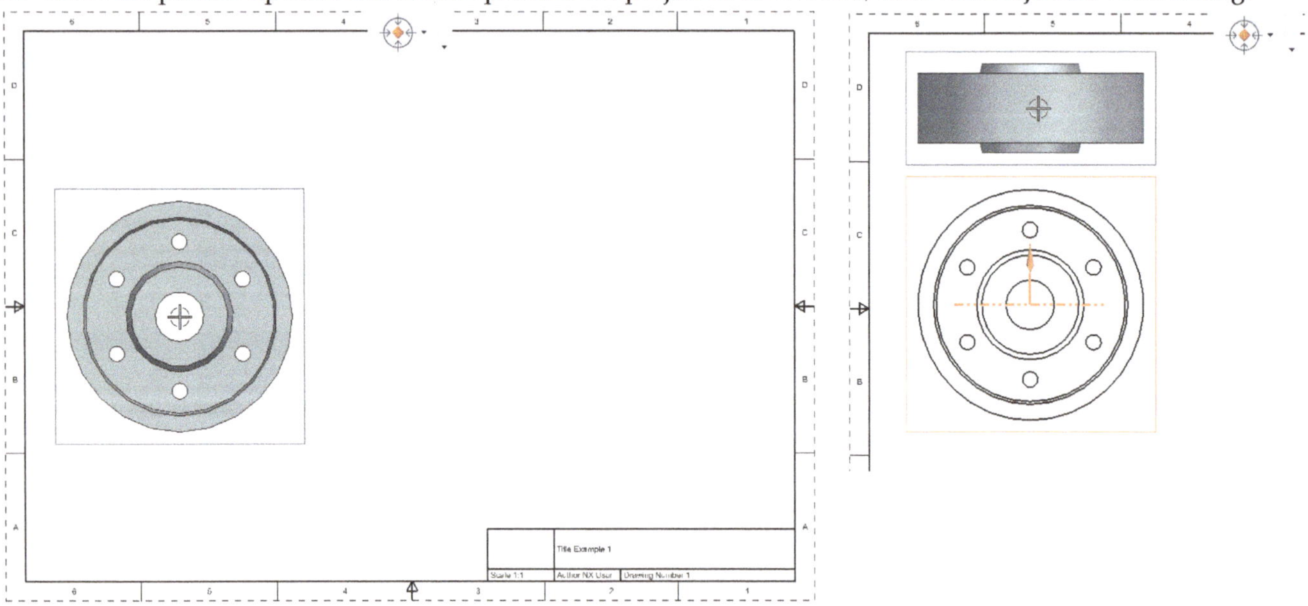

12. On the ribbon, click **Home > View > Base View**  . Next, select **Model View to Use > Isometric** from the **Model View** section of the **Base View** dialog.
13. Select **Ratio** from the **Scale** drop-down available in the **Scale** section.
14. Type **1** and **1.5** in the boxes available below the **Scale** drop-down.
15. Click at the top-right corner of the drawing sheet. Next, close the **Projected View** dialog.

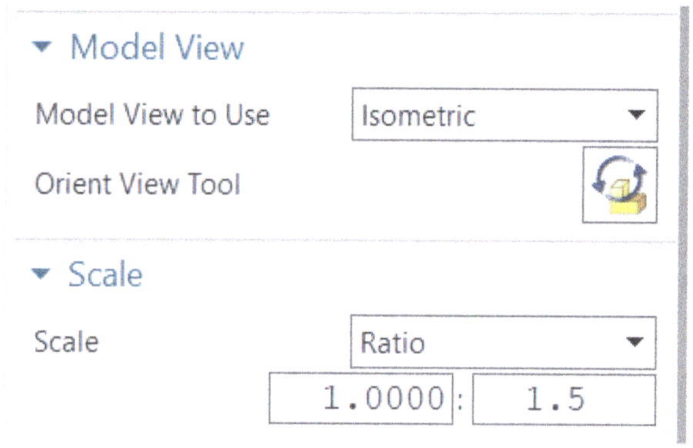

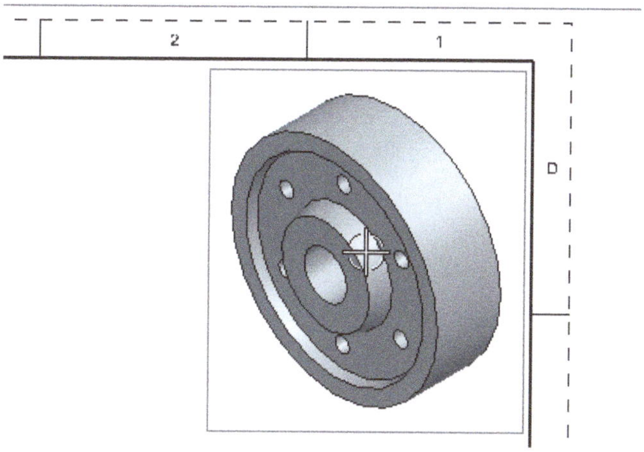

Show the Hidden lines of the Top view

1. Click on the top view and select **Settings**.

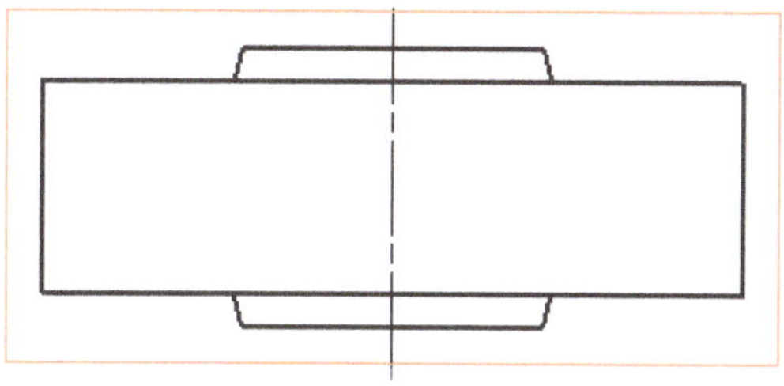

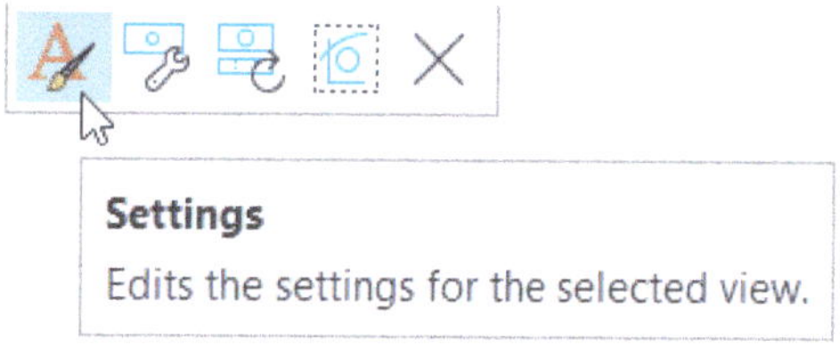

2. On the **Settings** dialog, select **Common > Hidden Lines**. Check the **Process Hidden Lines** option and set the hidden line type to **Dashed**. Change the color of the hidden line to black and click **OK**.

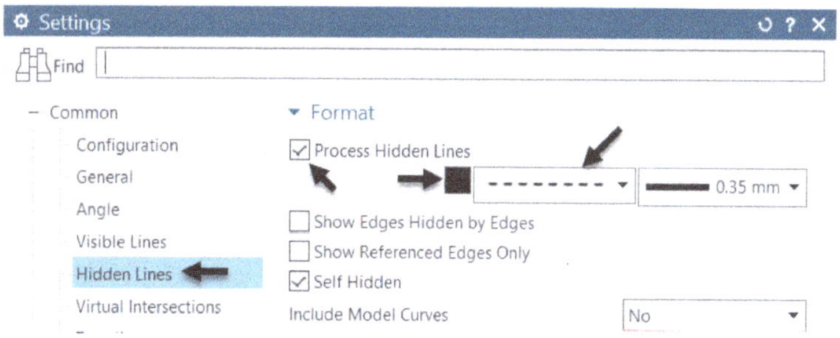

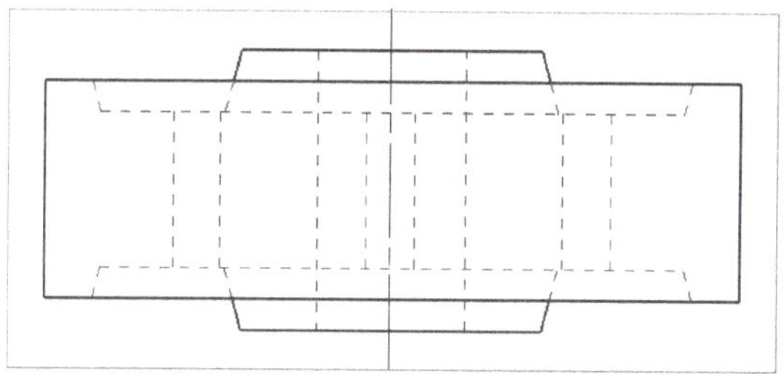

Create the Section view

1. On the ribbon, click **Home > View > Section View** .
2. On the **Section View** dialog, click the **Reset** icon.
3. Click the **Settings** button under the **Setting** section. On the **Section View Settings** dialog, select **Section Line** from the tree view. Next, select **Type > Arrows Away from Line** from the **Display** section. Click **OK**.
4. Select the center point of the front view and move the pointer toward the right. Click to position the view. You will notice that the centerlines appear on the section view, automatically. Click **Close** on the **Section View** dialog.

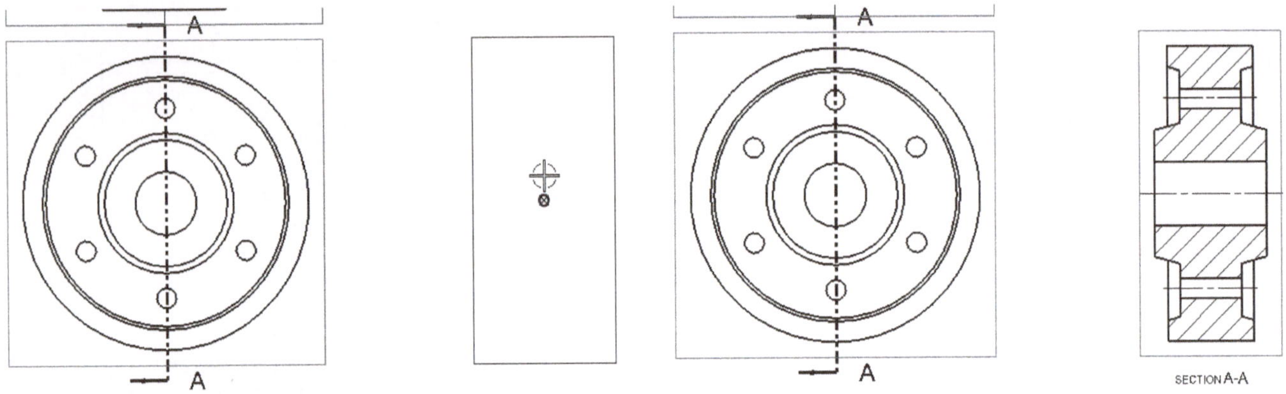

Add Centerlines, Centermarks, and Bolt Circle Centerlines

1. On the ribbon, click **Home > Annotation > Centerline Drop-down > Automatic Centerline**.
2. Click on the top view, and then click **OK**.

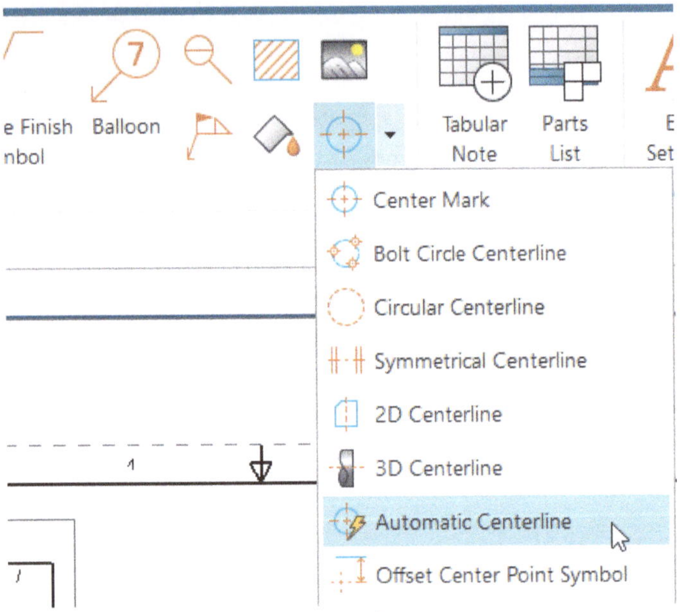

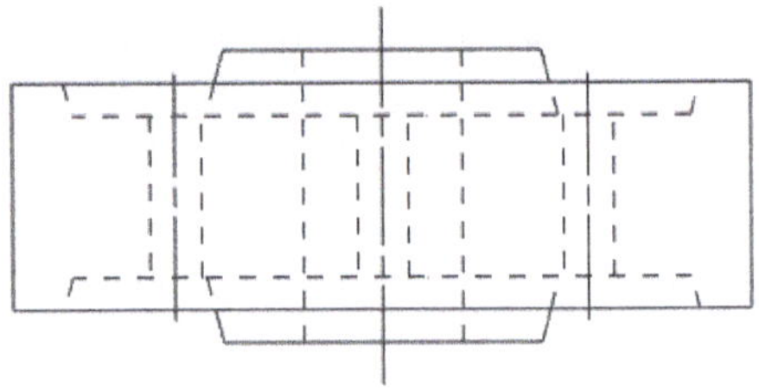

3. Activate the **Center Mark** command (click **Home > Annotation > Center Mark** on the ribbon).
4. Click on the hole located at the center of the front view, and then click **OK**.

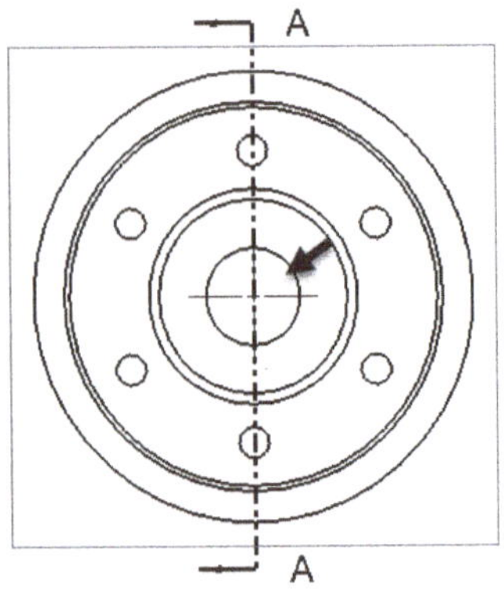

5. Activate the **Bolt Circle Centerline** command (click **Home > Annotation > Centerline Drop-down > Bolt Circle Centerline** on the ribbon) and select **Type > Center Point** from the **Bolt Circle Centerline** dialog.

6. Click on the hole located at the center of the front view. Drag the pointer and click on any one of the small holes.
7. Click on other circles located on the front view, and then click **OK**. This creates a bolt circle centerline.

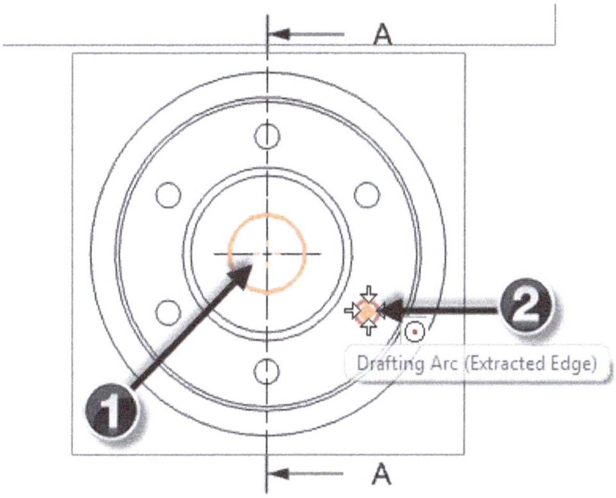

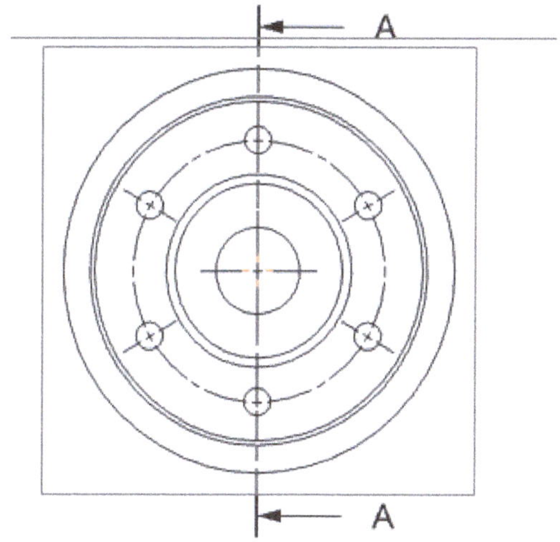

8. Activate the **Rapid Dimension** command and apply dimensions to the top view.

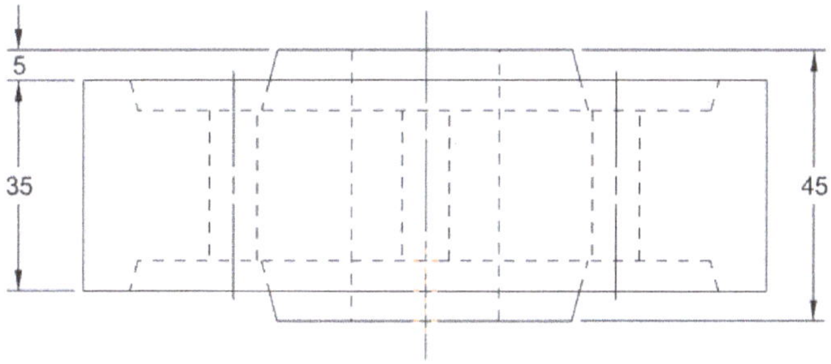

9. On the **Rapid Dimension** dialog, under the **Measurement** section, select **Method > Cylindrical** .
10. On the section view, select the end-points of the innermost horizontal edges. Drag the pointer and position the diameter dimension.
11. Likewise, create another diameter dimension.

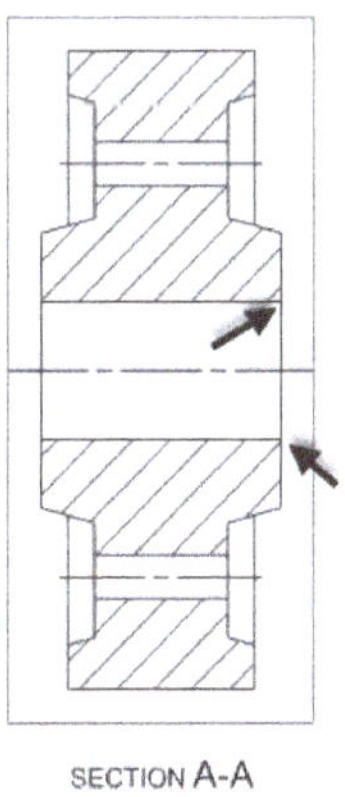

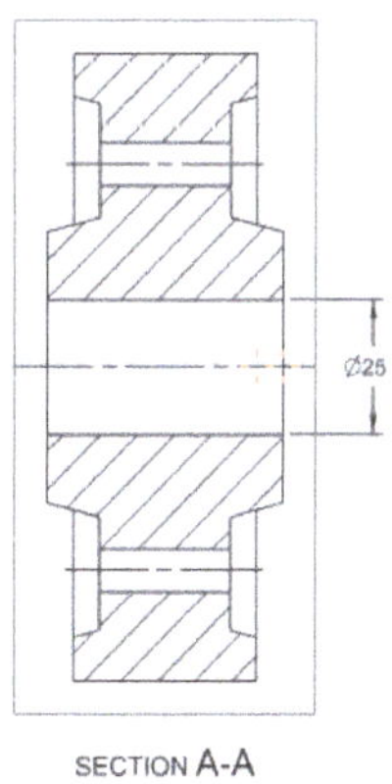

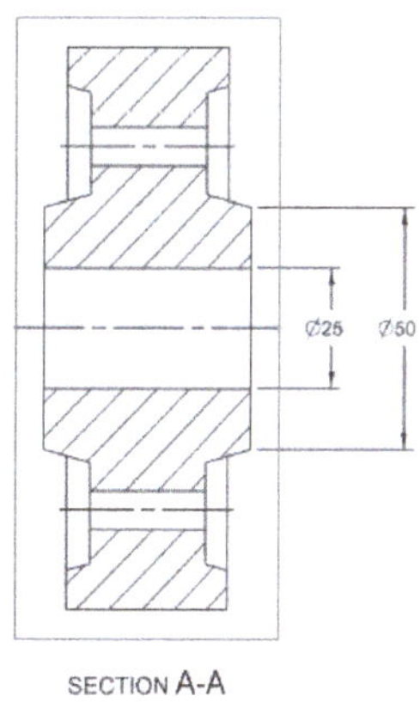

12. Activate the **Angular** command (on the ribbon, click **Home > Dimension > Angular**) click on the inclined edge and lower horizontal edge of the section view. Drag the pointer and click to position the angle dimension. Press Esc to deactivate the **Angular** command.

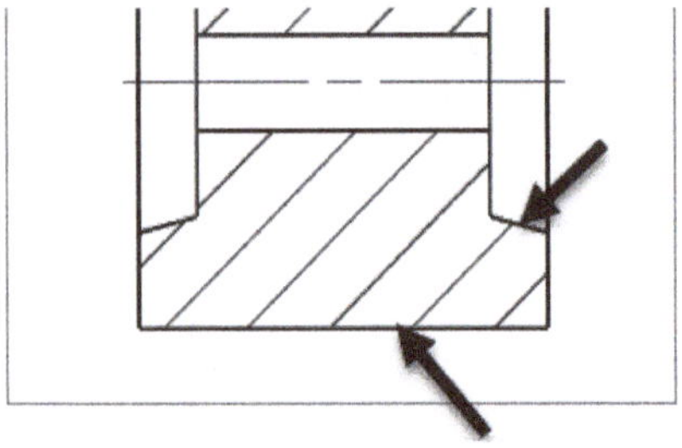

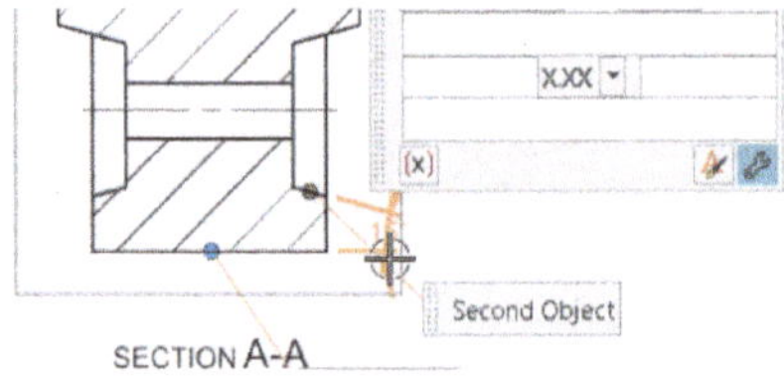

13. Click on the angle dimension and drag it upward.
14. Double-click on the angular dimension to open a palette.
15. On the palette, type-in **TYP** in the suffix box. Click **Close** on the **Angular Dimension** dialog.

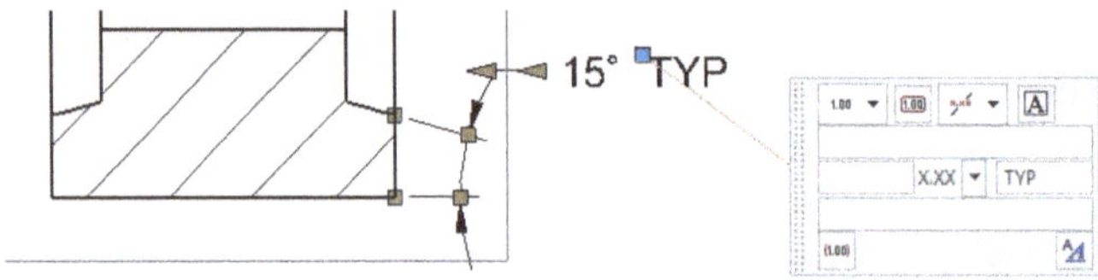

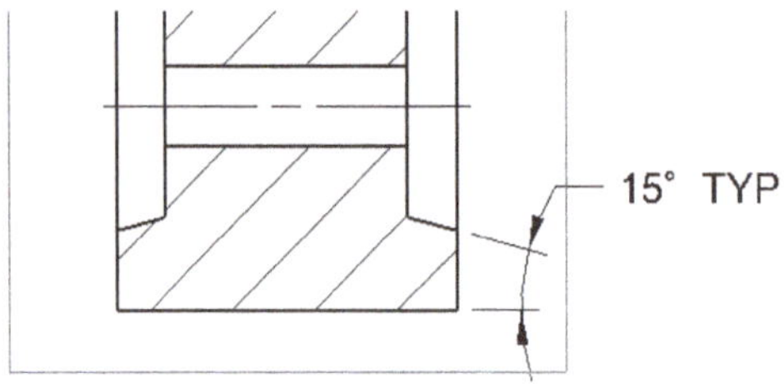

16. Activate the **Rapid Dimension** command and select **Measurement > Method > Diametral** on the **Rapid Dimension** dialog.
17. Click on the small hole of the front view and create a diameter dimension. Close the dialog.

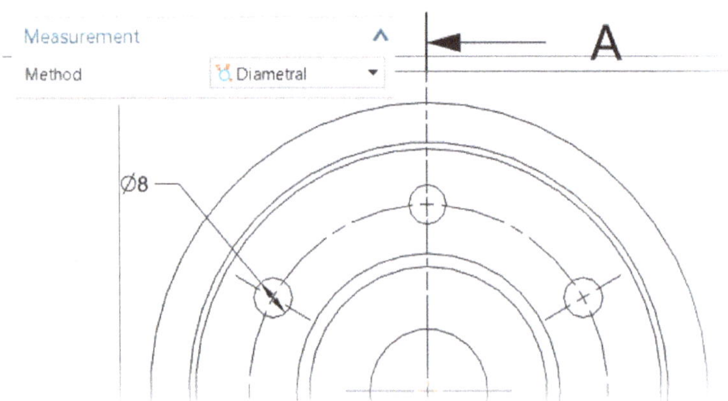

18. Double-click on the diameter dimension to open a palette.

19. On the palette, click the **Edit Appended Text** button to open the **Appended Text** dialog.
20. On the **Appended Text** dialog, select **Text Location > Before** and type-in **6 HOLES** in the **Formatting** box.
21. Select **Text Location > Below** and type-in **EQUI-SPACED ON 75 PCD** in the **Formatting** box. Click **Close** on the dialog.
22. On the palette, click **Arrows Out Diameter**, and click **Close** on the **Radial Dimension** dialog.

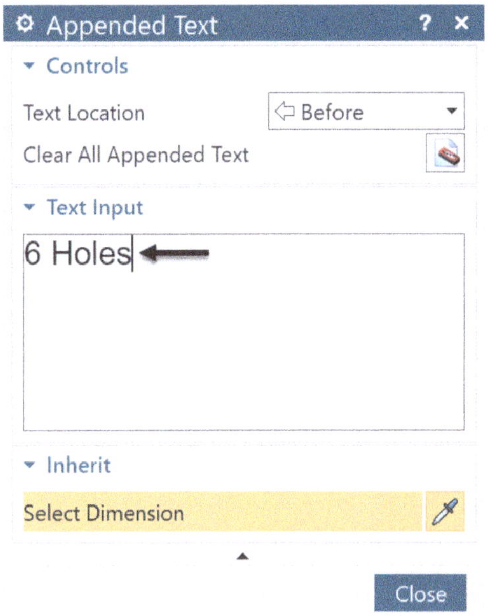

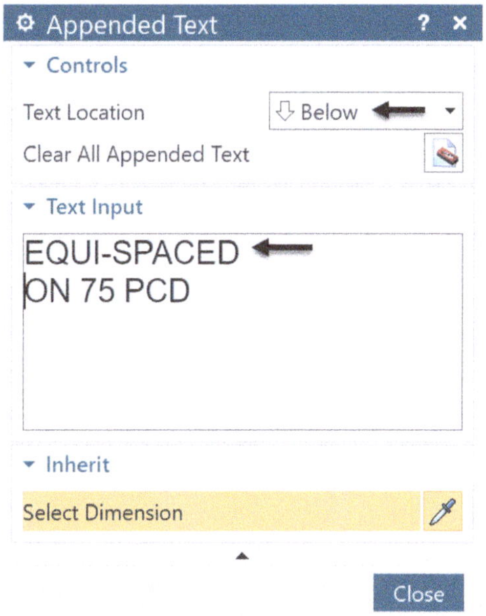

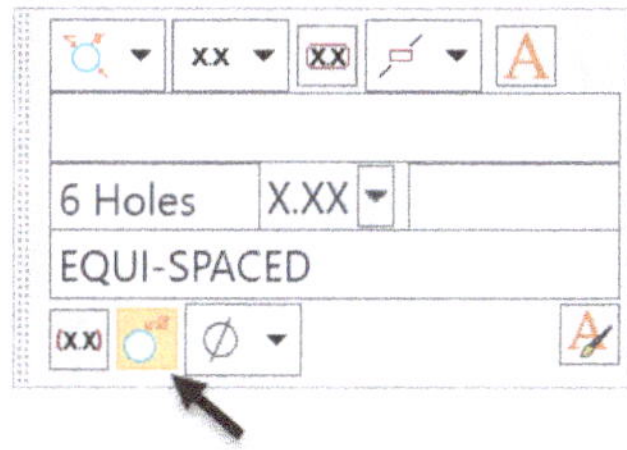

23. Create other dimensions in the drawing.

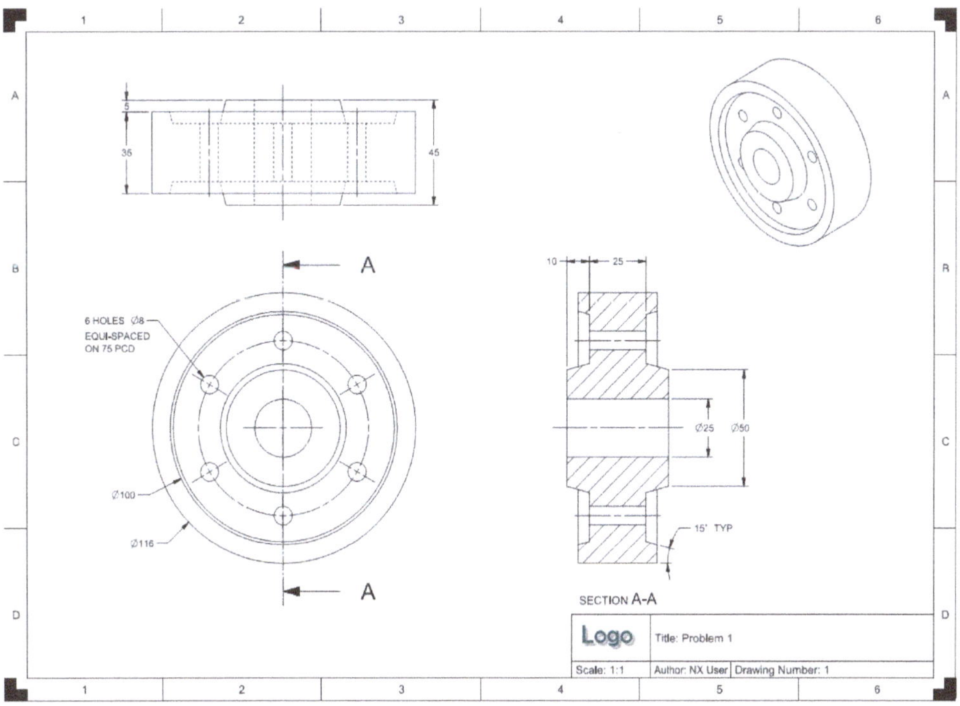

24. Save and close the drawing.

Example 2

In this example, you will create an assembly drawing shown below.

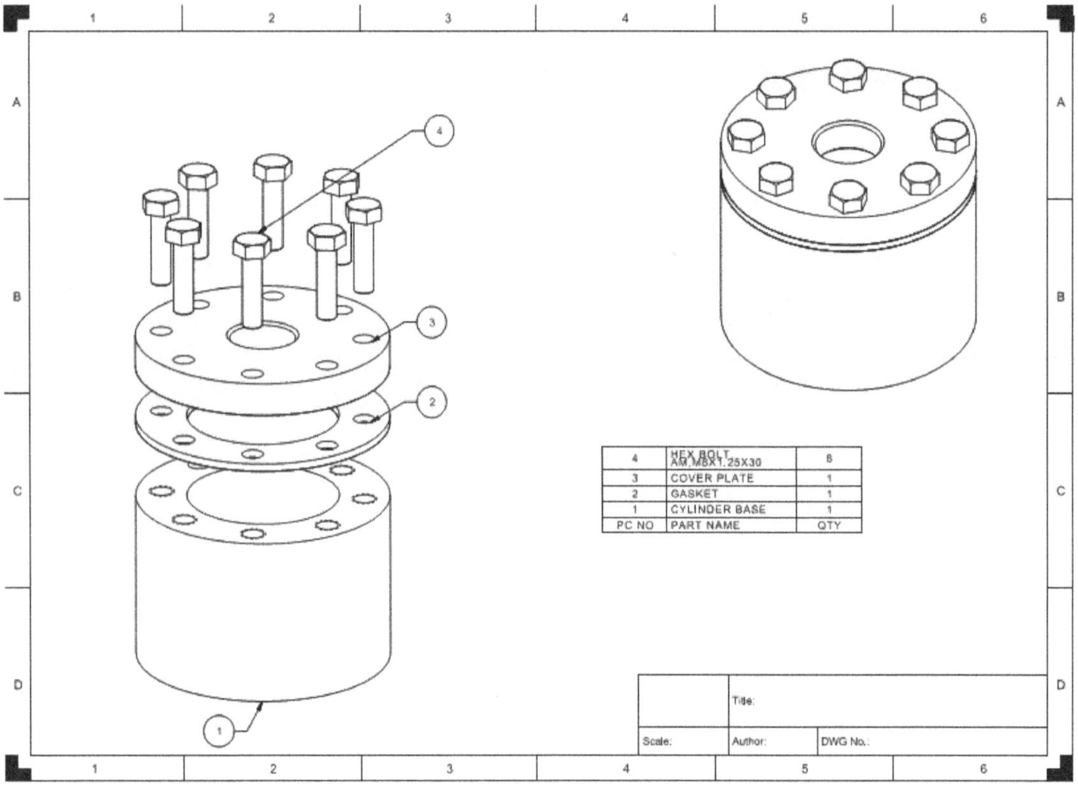

1. Open the Pressure Cylinder.prt file that you have created in Chapter 8.
2. Click **Application > Document > Drafting**.
3. On the **Sheet** dialog, select **Standard Size**.
4. Set **Size** to **A3 -297 x 420**.
5. Set **Scale** to **1:1**.
6. Under the **Settings** section, check the **Always Start View Creation** option, and then select the **Base View Command** option.
7. Click **OK**.
8. On the **Base View** dialog, under the **Model View** section, select **Model View to Use** > **Isometric**.
9. Under the **Scale** section, select **Scale > 1:1**.
10. Click on the top right side of the drawing sheet.
11. Click **Close** on the **Projected View** dialog.

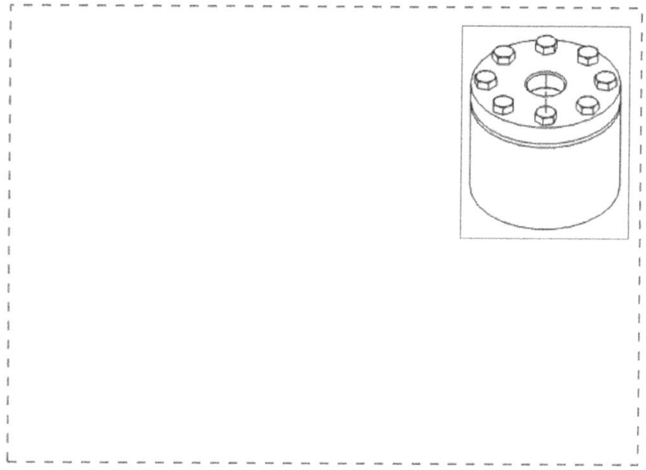

Generating the Exploded View

1. On the ribbon, click **Home > View > Base View**.
2. On the **Base View** dialog, select **Model View to Use >Trimetric**.
3. Click on the left side of the drawing sheet.
4. Click **Close**.

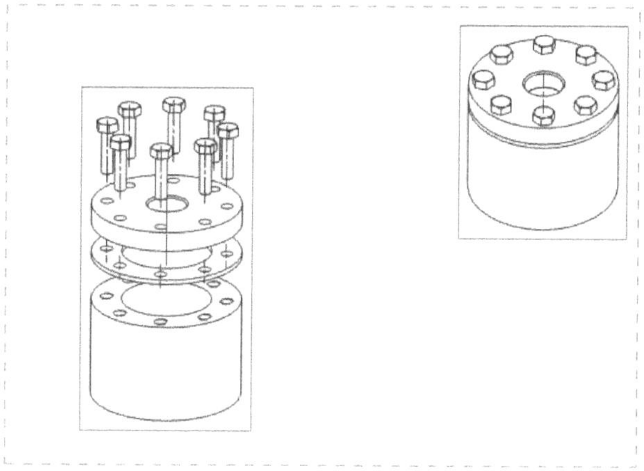

Generating the Part list

1. To generate a part list, click **Home > Table > Parts List** on the ribbon.
2. Place the part list at the bottom-right corner.
3. Select the Parts list from the drawing sheet and click the **Edit** icon on the context toolbar.
4. On the **Parts List** dialog, select **Scope > Leaves Only** from the **Parts List** dialog. All the individual parts of the assembly are listed in the parts list.

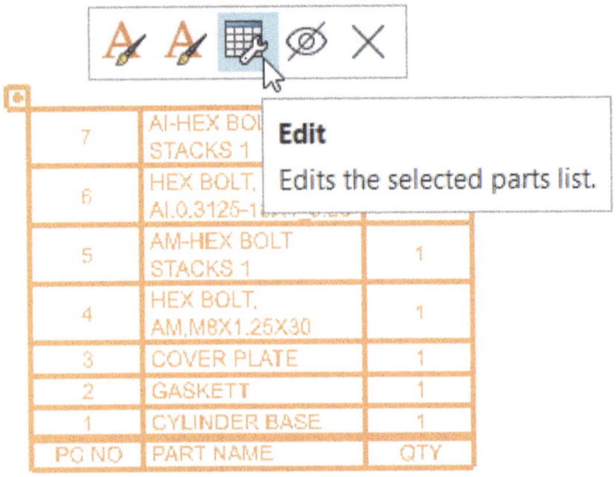

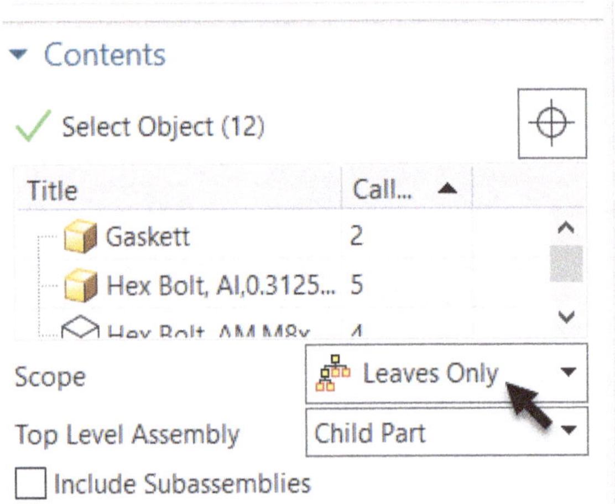

5. Expand the **Balloons** section and check the **Show** option.
6. Select the Trimetric@2 from the View List.
7. Close the **Parts List** dialog.

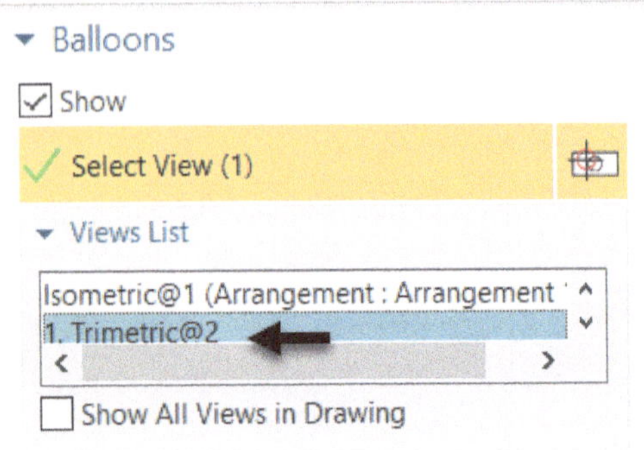

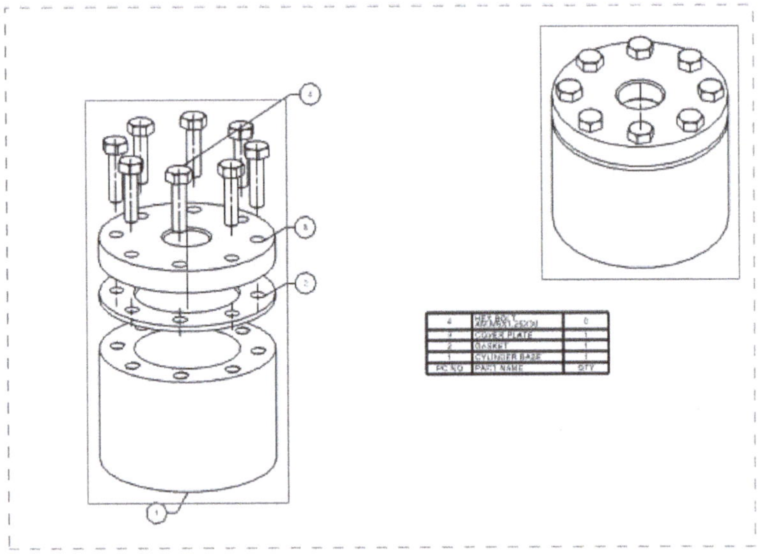

8. Add borders and title block to the drawing.
9. Save and close the file.

Questions

1. How to create drawing views using the **View Creation Wizard** command?
2. How to show or hide hidden edges of a drawing view?
3. How to change the display style of a drawing view?
4. How to update the drawing views when the part is edited?
5. How to control the properties of dimensions and annotations?
6. List the commands used to create centerlines and center marks.
7. How to add symbols and texts to a dimension?
8. How to add break lines to a drawing view?

9. How to create revolved section views?
10. How to create an exploded view of an assembly?
11. Which command is used to apply different types of dimensions?

Exercises

Exercise 1

Create orthographic views of the part model shown next. Add dimensions and annotations to the drawing.

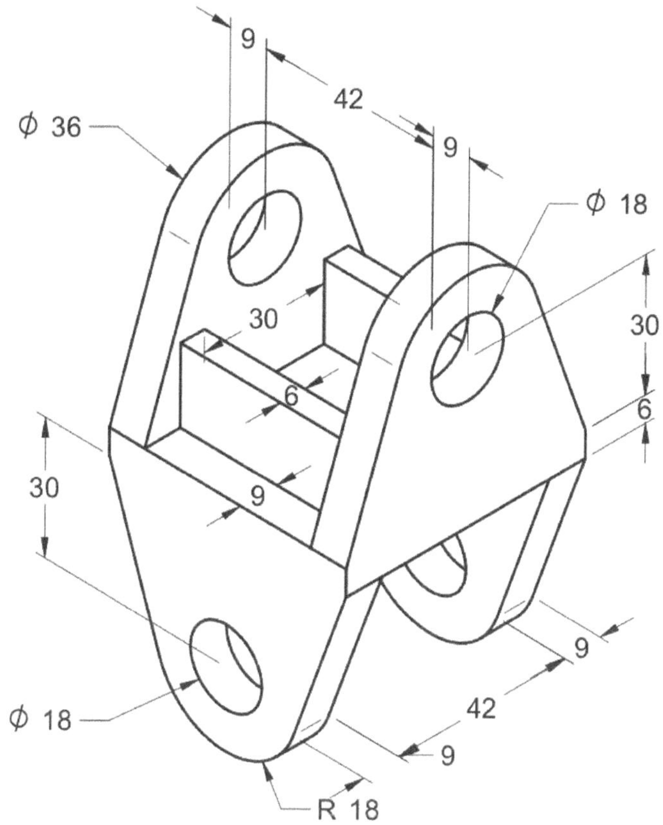

Exercise 2

Create orthographic views and an auxiliary view of the part model shown below. Add dimensions and annotations to the drawing.

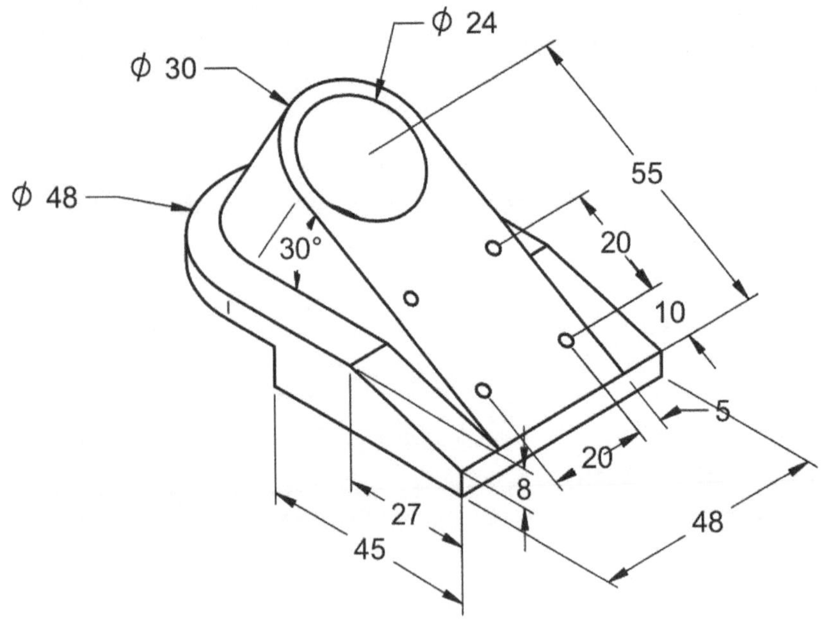

Φ 24
Φ 30
Φ 48
55
20
30°
10
5
20
8
27
45
48

Chapter 10: Sheet Metal Design

You can make sheet metal parts by bending and forming flat sheets of metal. In NX, sheet-metal parts can be folded and unfolded, enabling you to show them in the flat pattern as well as their bent-up state. There are two ways to design sheet-metal parts in NX. Either you can start the sheet-metal part from scratch using sheet-metal features throughout the design process (or), you can design it as a regular solid part and later convert it to a sheet-metal part. Most commonly, you design sheet-metal parts in the Sheet Metal environment from the beginning. In this chapter, you will learn both the approaches.

The topics covered in this chapter are:

- *Tabs*
- *Flanges*
- *Bend Allowance*
- *Bend Tables*
- *Counter Flanges*
- *Hems*
- *Close 2-Bend Corners*
- *Bends*
- *Jogs*
- *Dimples*
- *Louvers*
- *Drawn Cutouts*
- *Beads*
- *Gussets*
- *Etches*
- *Embosses*
- *Cuts*
- *Convert to Sheet Metal*
- *Rip Corners*
- *Flat Pattern*
- *Export to DXF or DWG*

Starting a Sheet Metal part

To start a new sheet metal part, click **Home > Standard > New** on the ribbon. On the **New** dialog, click the **Model** tab, and then double-click on the **Sheet metal** template.

Sheet Metal Part Properties

The most common Sheet Metal Part Properties are the type of material and bend allowances. You can define these properties by clicking **File > Preferences > Sheet Metal.** On the **Sheet Metal Preferences** dialog, select **Parameter Entry > Value Entry** and type-in values in the **Material Thickness**, **Bend Radius**, **Relief Depth**, and **Relief Width** boxes. These parameters are illustrated in the following figure.

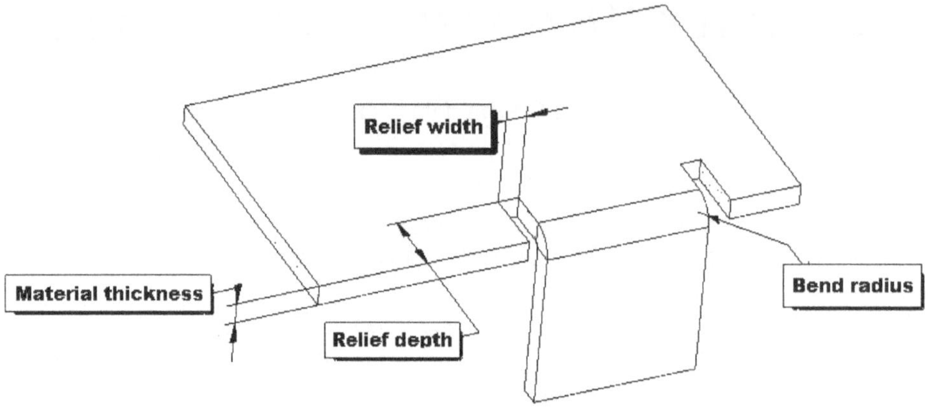

Next, type-in a value in the **Neutral Factor Value** box. The **Neutral Factor** is the ratio that represents the location of the neutral sheet measured from the inside face with respect to the thickness of the sheet metal part. The **Neutral Factor** defines the bend allowance of the sheet metal part. The standard formula that calculates the bend allowance is given below.

$$BA = \frac{\pi(R + KT)A}{180}$$

BA = Bend Allowance

R = Bend Radius

K = Neutral Factor = t/T

T = Material Thickness

t= Distance from inside face to the neutral sheet

A = Bend Angle

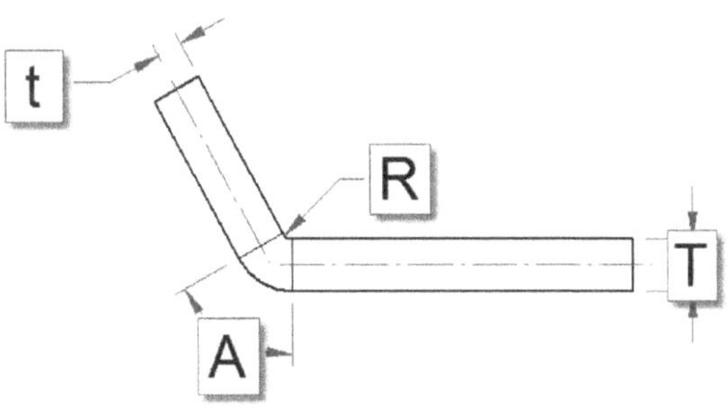

You can also define the bend allowance by using a bend table or your own bend allowance formula. To enter a bend allowance formula, select the **Formula** option from the **Method** drop-down available in the **Bend Definition Method** section, and type-in a value in the box. Click **OK** after specifying values on the **Sheet Metal Preferences** dialog.

Tab

The tab is a basic type of sheet metal feature. To create a tab, create a closed sketch on a plane. You can also create a sketch with internal loops. Next, activate the **Tab** command (On the ribbon, click **Home > Basic > Tab**). Click on the internal and external loops of the sketch, and then click **OK** on the **Tab** dialog.

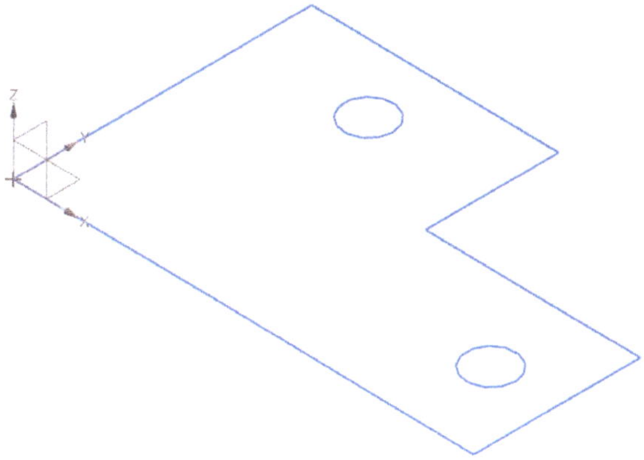

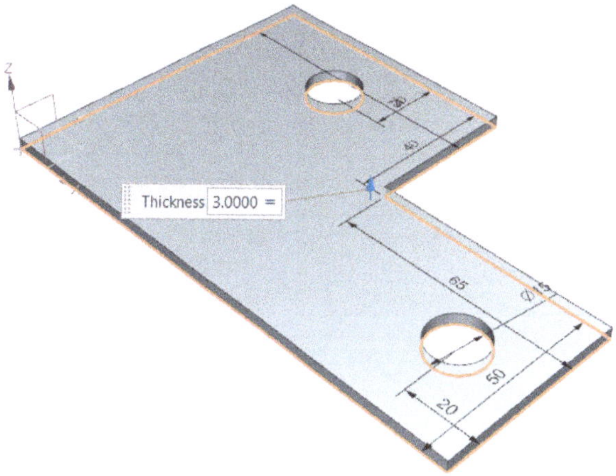

Flange

The second feature after creating a tab is a flange. You can create this feature along an edge or multiple edges of a sheet metal part. In order to create a flange, all you need is to activate the **Flange** command (On the ribbon, click **Home > Base > Flange**), and then click an edge of the tab feature. The flange preview appears on the selected face. Click the arrow attached to the preview and drag the pointer to change the length of the flange.

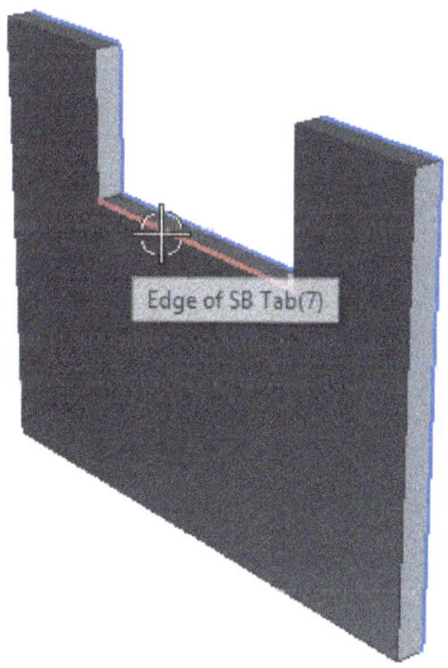

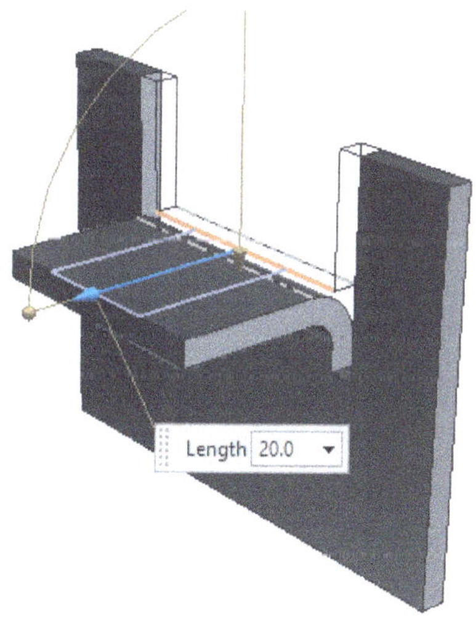

On the **Flange** dialog, select the required **Width Option** to define the flange width. The default width option is **Full**. The remaining width options are discussed next.

The **At Center** option creates a flange at the center of the selected edge.

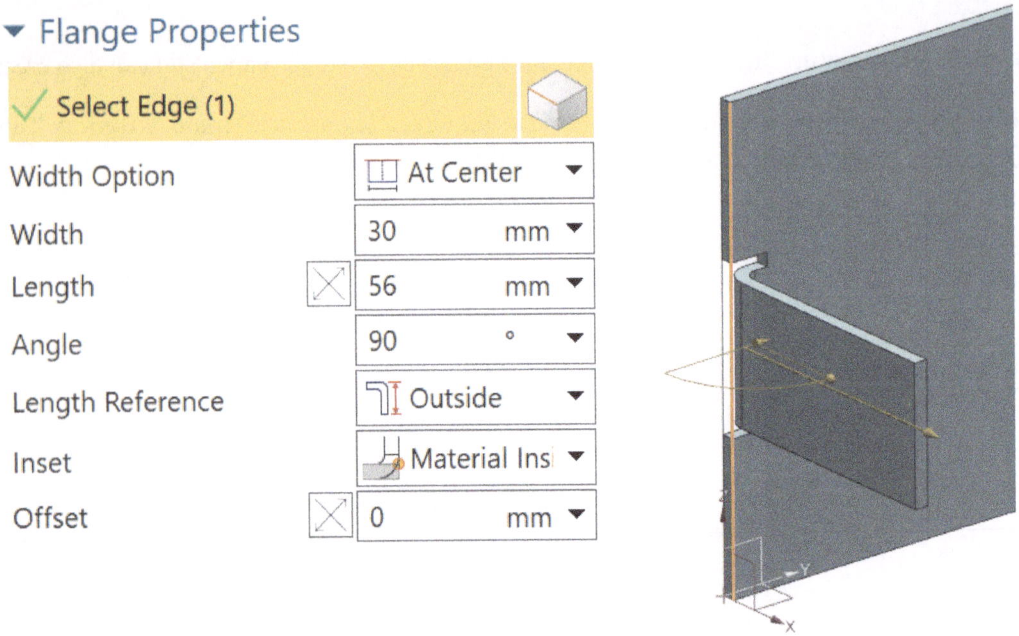

The **At End** option creates a flange at an endpoint of the selected edge. Select this option from the **Width Option** drop-down, and then click **Specify Point.** Next, select an endpoint to locate the flange.

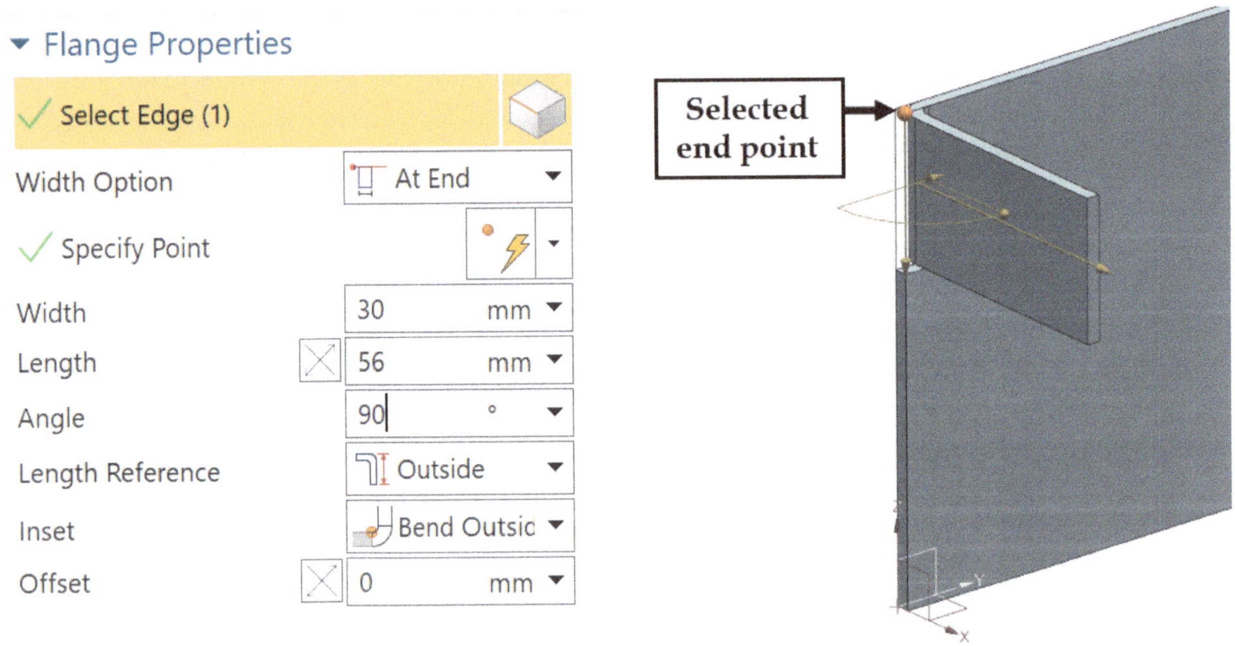

The **From End** option creates a flange at a distance from the selected endpoint of the edge. You need to select an endpoint of the selected edge. Next, type in a value in the **Distance 1** box to define the start point of the flange.

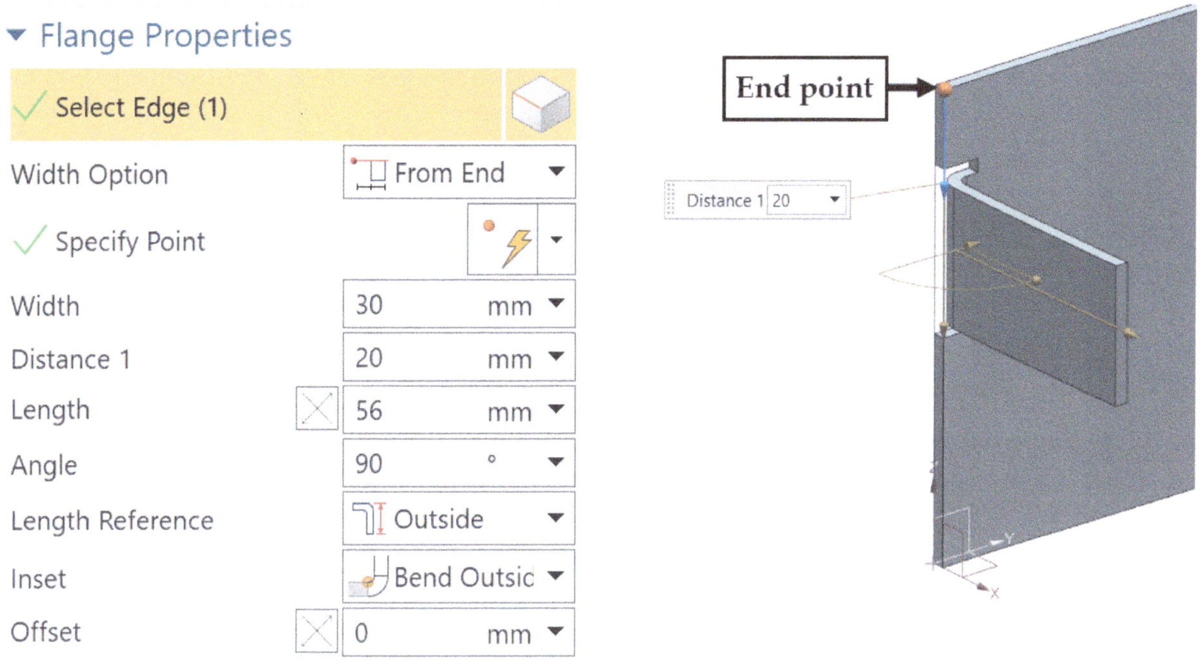

The **From Both Ends** option creates a flange by offsetting it from both the endpoints of the selected edge. You need to specify the values in the Distance 1 and Distance 2 boxes. The flange will be created between both the end of the selected.

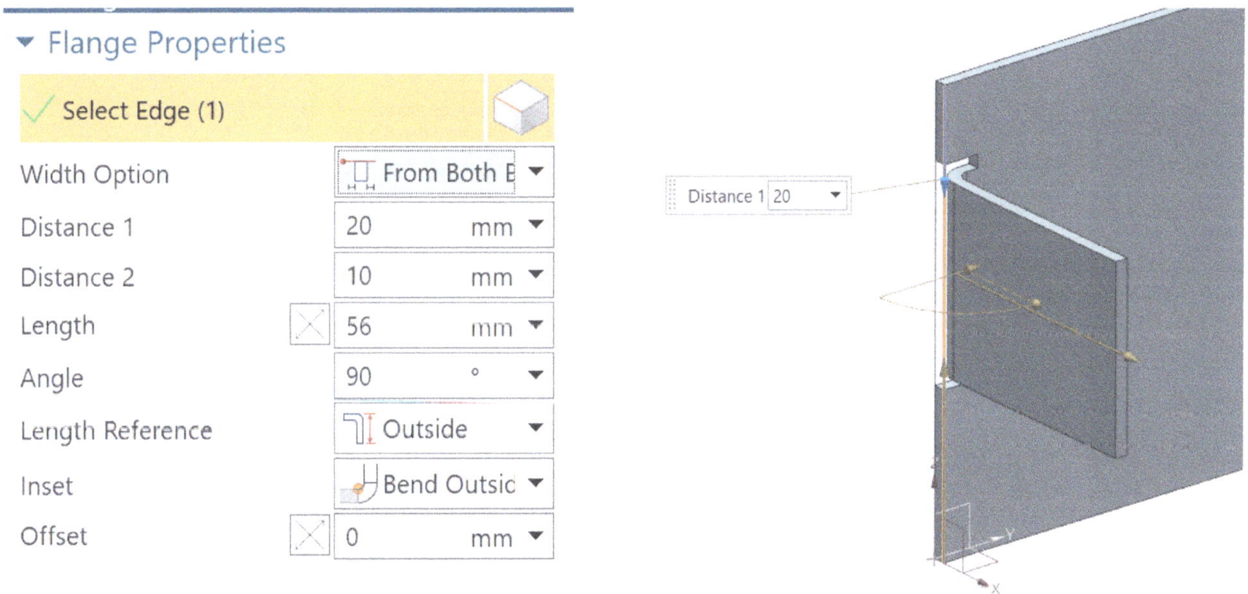

Type-in a value in the **Angle** box available in the **Flange Properties** section to create the flange at an angle.

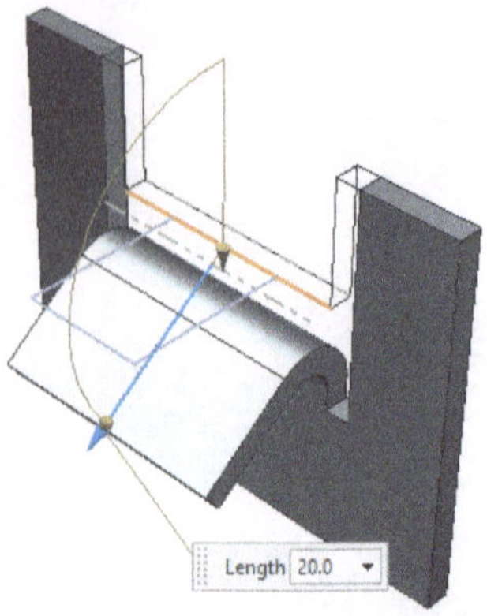

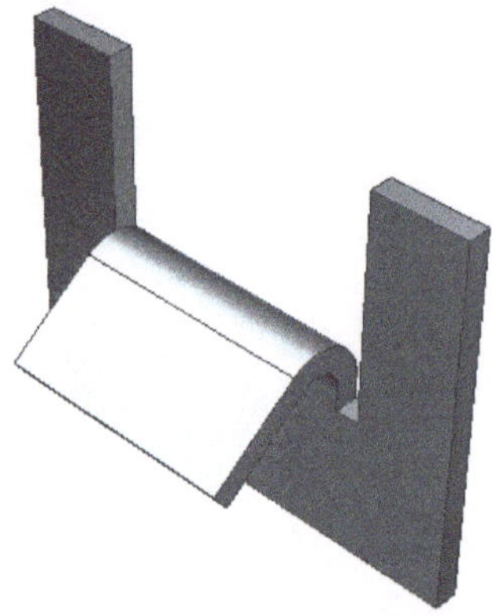

Under the **Flange Properties** section, select **Length Reference > Inside** to define the flange length from the inside face of the supporting tab. Select **Length Reference > Outside** to define the flange length from the outside face of the supporting tab. Select **Length Reference > Web** to exclude the bend from the flange length.

Define the material side using the **Inset** drop-down menu. The three types of material sides: **Material Inside**, **Material Outside**, and **Bend Outside** are shown below. The **Material Inside** option matches the outer face of the flange with the edge on which the flange is created. The **Material Outside** option matches the inner face of the flange with the edge on which the flange is created. The **Bend Outside** option starts the flange bend from the edge selected to create the flange. The **Material Inside OML** option flushes the outer face of the flange with the opposite side of the selected edge.

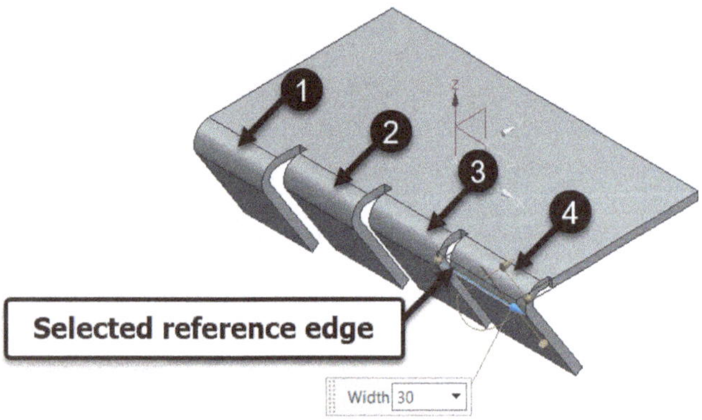

1. **Bend Outside**
2. **Material Outside**
3. **Material Inside**
4. **Material Inside OML**

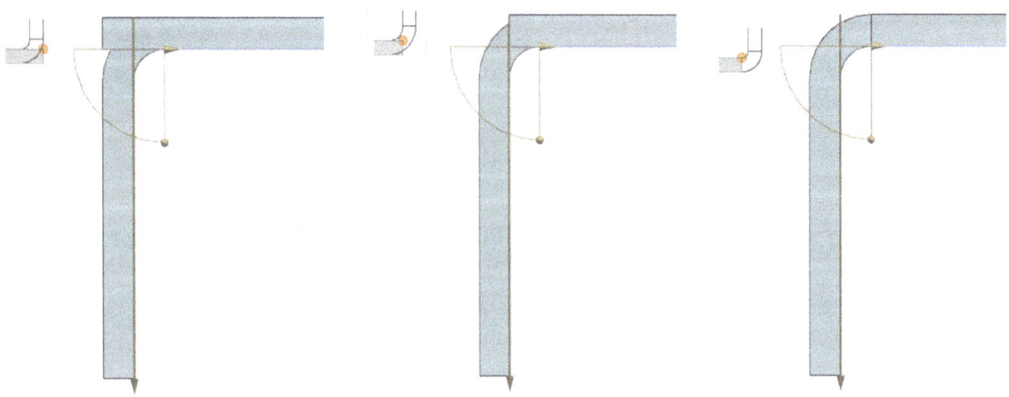

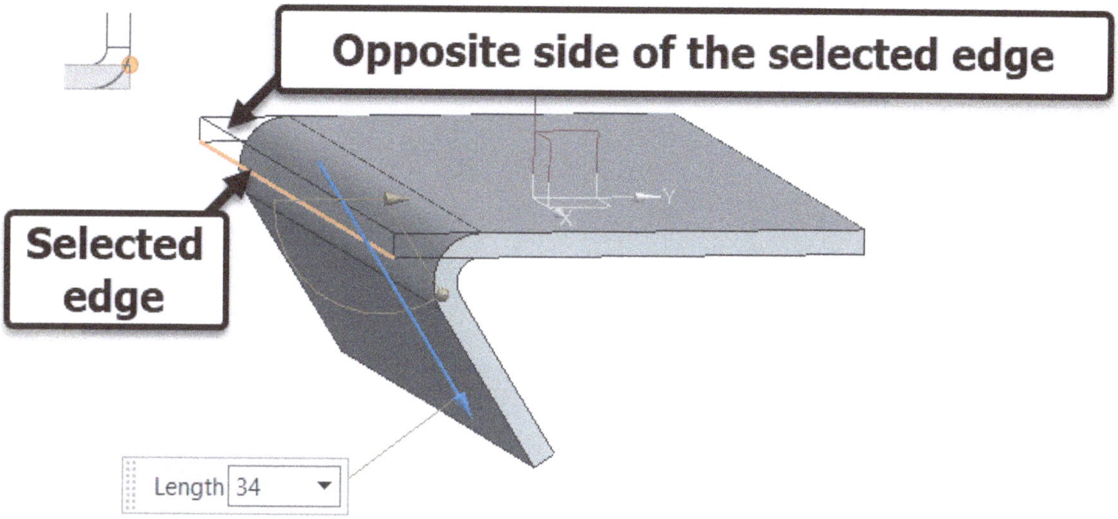

Type in a value in the **Offset** box, if you want to offset the flange from the selected edge.

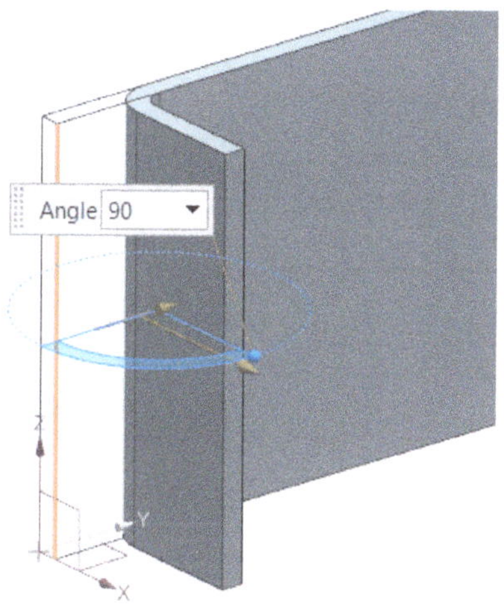

The **Geometry Properties** section has two options: **Use Geometry Mirror and Pattern** and **Miter** options. The **Use Geometry Mirror and Pattern** option helps you to mirror or pattern the flange geometry without considering the feature parameters. The **Miter** option avoids the intersection of two flanges by creating a miter at the corner at which two flanges meet.

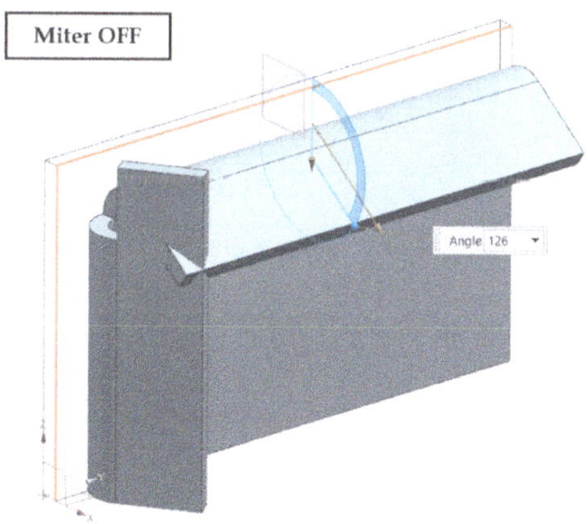

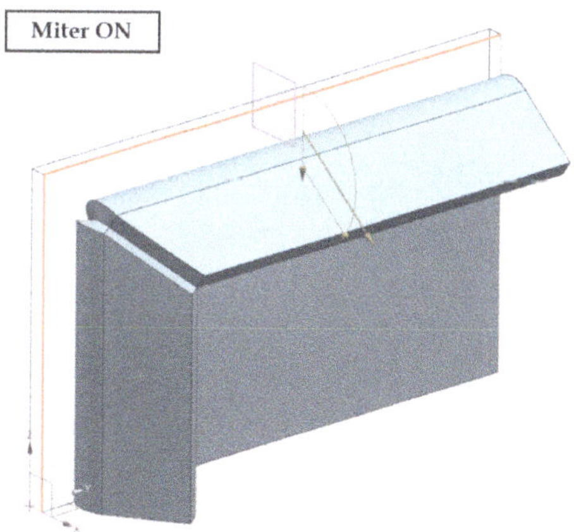

On the **Flange** dialog, you can override the sheet metal properties under the **Bend Parameters** and **Relief** sections. For example, to change the **Bend Radius** value, click **Launch Formula Editor** = > **Use Local Value**. Now, type-in a new bend radius value.

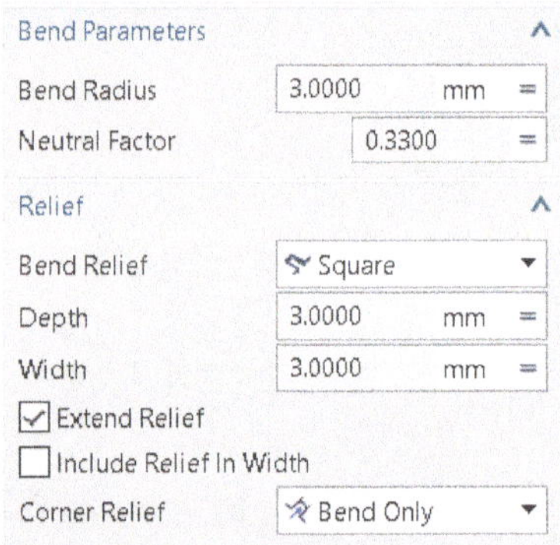

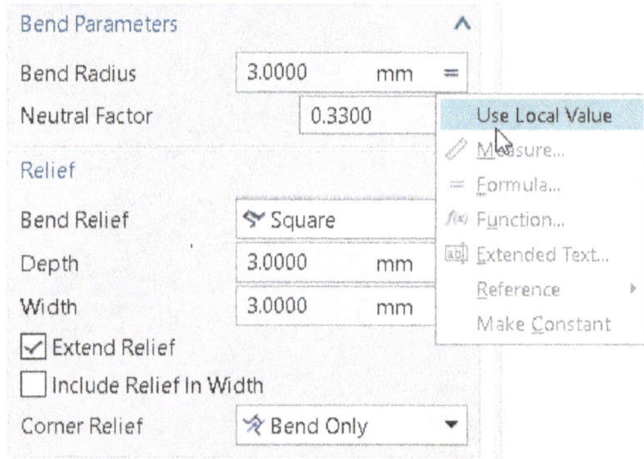

The **Bend Relief** drop-down allows you to specify the bend relief to the base face of the flange. There are three options in this drop-down: **Square**, **Round**, and **None**. The following figure shows the three types of blend reliefs. After selecting the required bend relief type, specify the **Depth** and **Width** values.

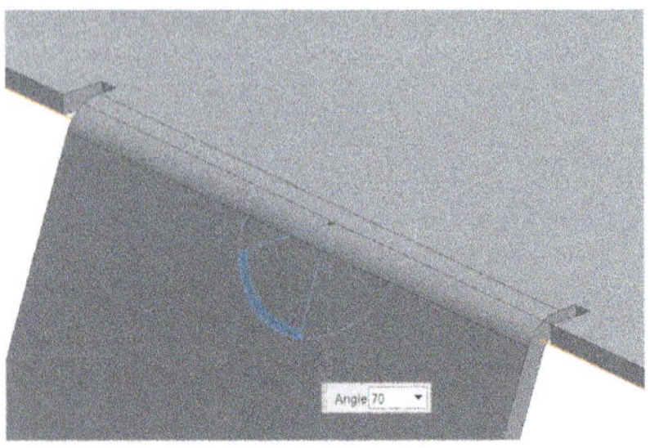

Square

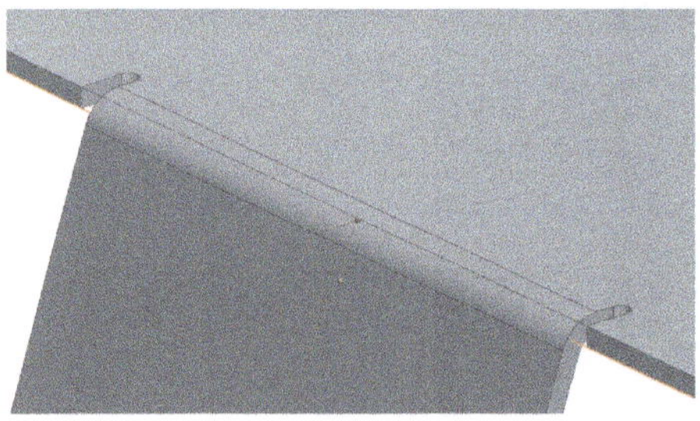

Round

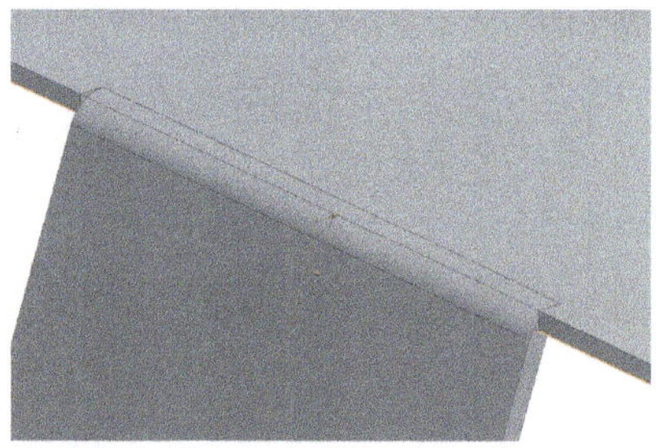

None

Check the **Extend Relief** option if you want to extend the bend relief up to the edge of the part.

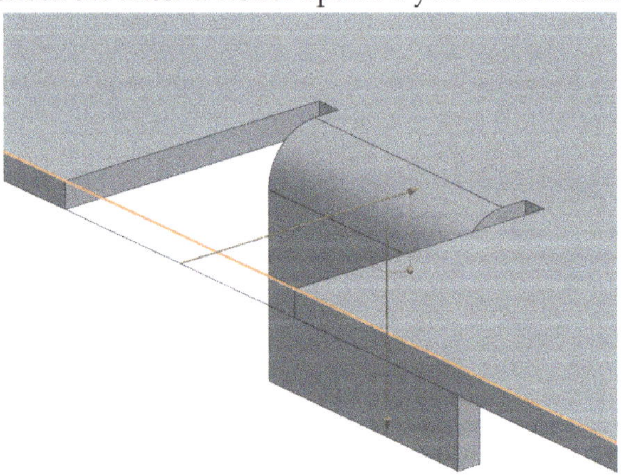

Extend Relief ON

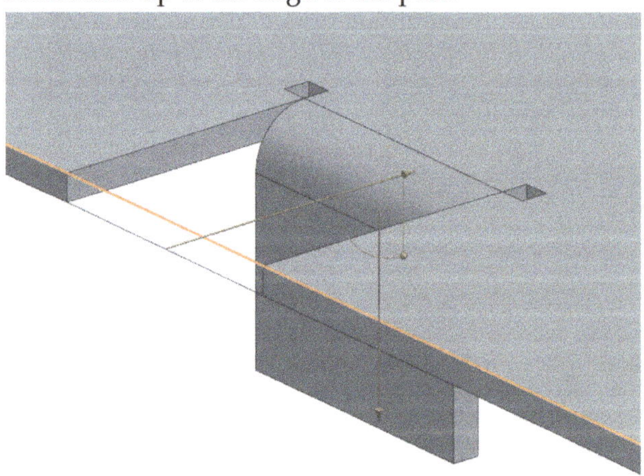

Extend Relief OFF

Check the **Include Relief in Width** option if you want to include the width of the relief in the width of the flange.

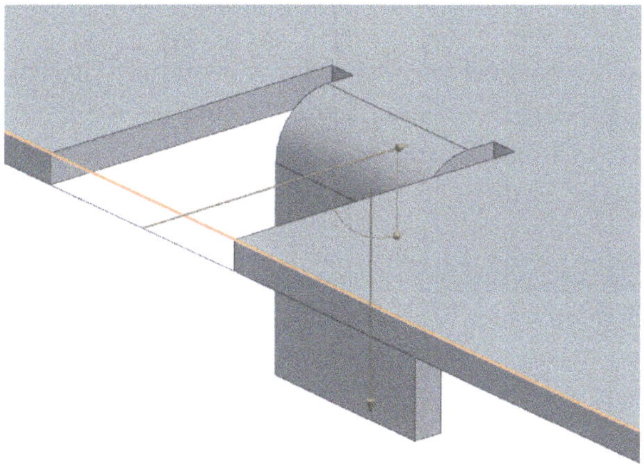

Include Relief in Width OFF

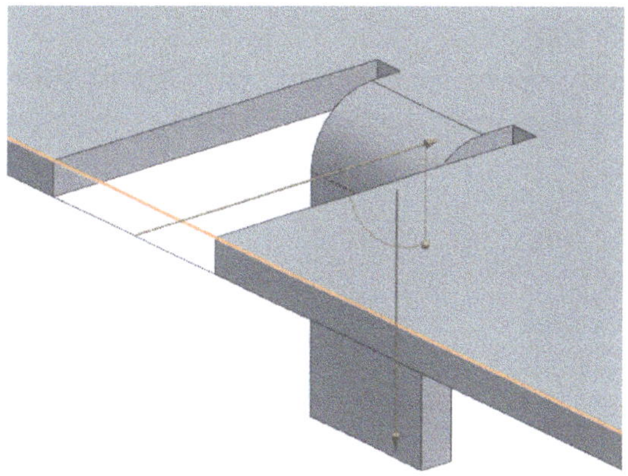

Include Relief in Width ON

From the **Corner Relief** drop-down menu, select an option to define the type of corner relief. Corner relief is to be provided when two flanges meet at a corner. The following figure shows the three types of corner reliefs. The **Bend Only** option applies the relief is exclusively to the bend section of the neighboring features. The **Bend/Face** option applies relief to not only the bend but also the face portions of the neighboring feature. The **Bend/Face Chain** option extends relief to the entire chain of bends and faces of the neighboring features.

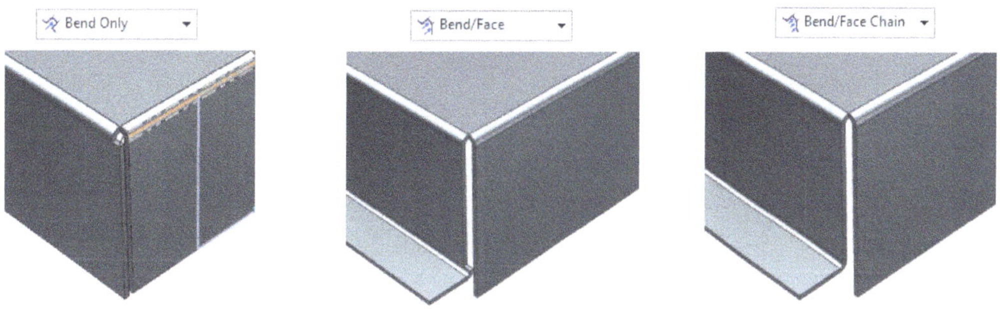

On the **Flange** dialog, select **Reference Plane > Match Face > Until Selected** to create the flange up to a selected face. Next, select a planar face from the graphics window; the outer face of the flange matches with the selected face.

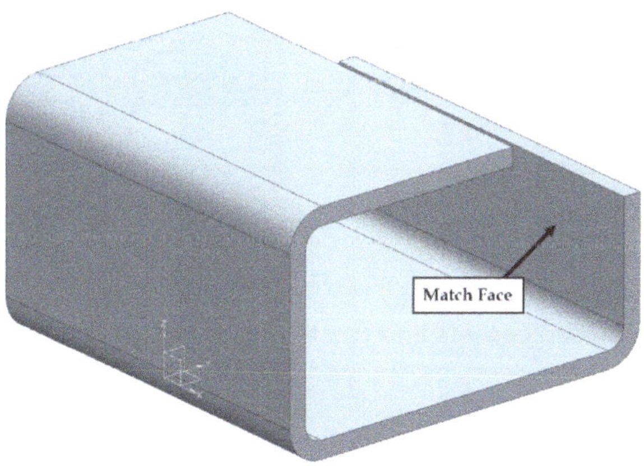

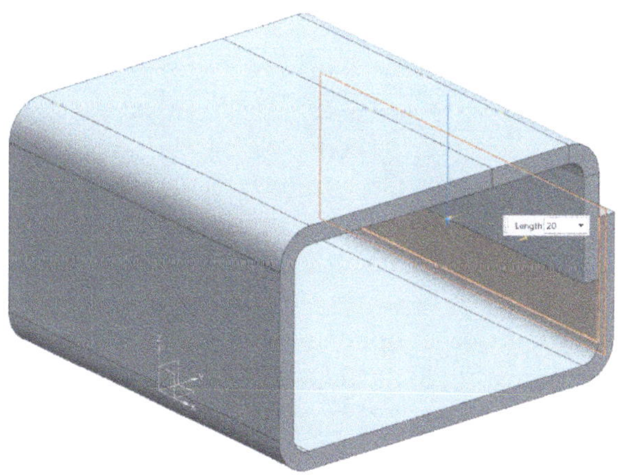

Click **OK** on the **Flange** dialog to complete the flange feature.

Closed Corner

The **Closed Corner** command allows you to control the appearance of sheet metal seams. For example, when two flanges meet at a corner, this command allows you to close the gap between them. In addition to that, it applies a corner treatment. Activate this command (click **Home > Corner > Closed Corner** on the ribbon) and click on two bends that meet at a corner. On the **Closed Corner** dialog, select the required corner treatment.

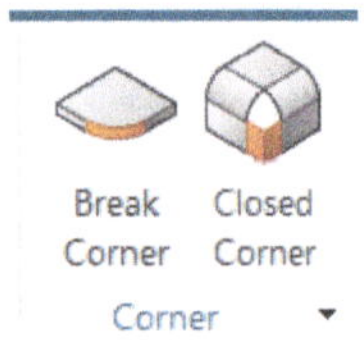

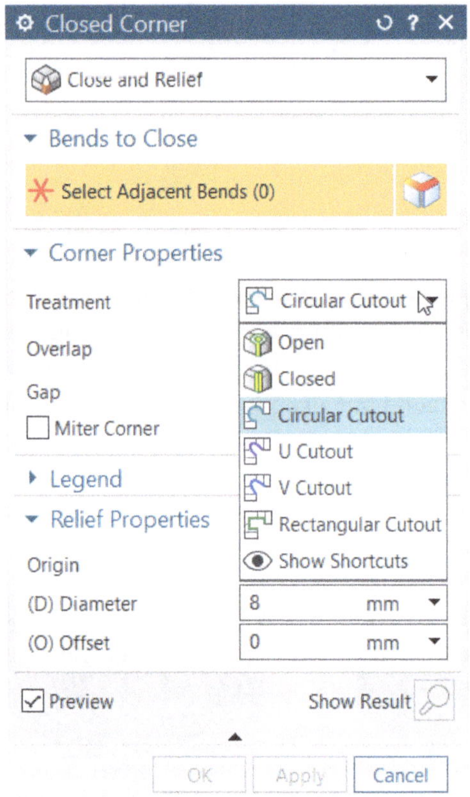

There are six types of corner treatments available in the **Treatment** drop-down menu, as shown below.

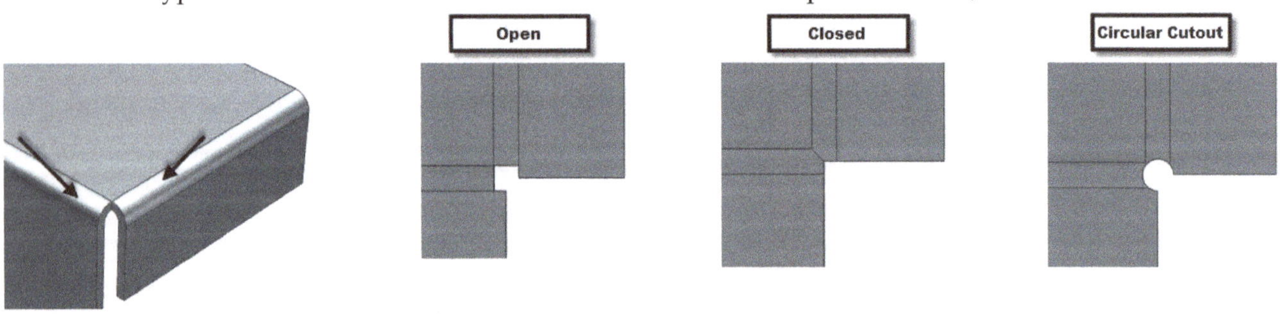

The **Miter Corner** option removes rough edges and bumps at the closed corners and creates a gaps so that you can create a cut in the flattened state easily.

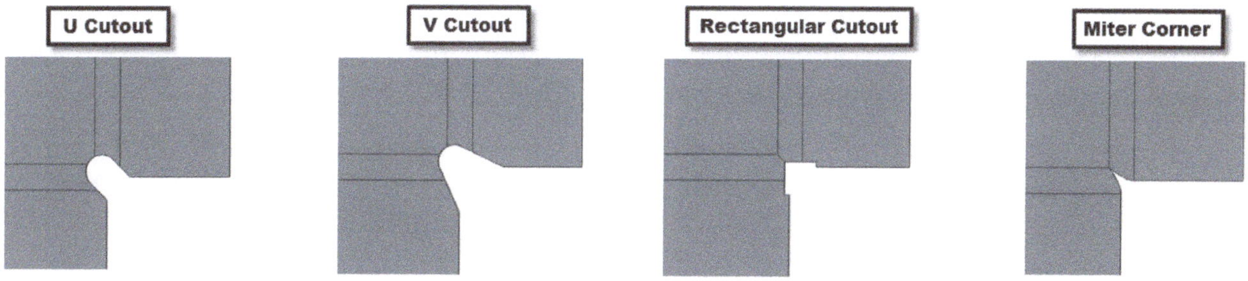

In the **Corner Properties** section, click **Overlap > Side 1** or **Side 2** to overlap one flange on the other – next, type-in a value in the **Overlap Ratio** box.

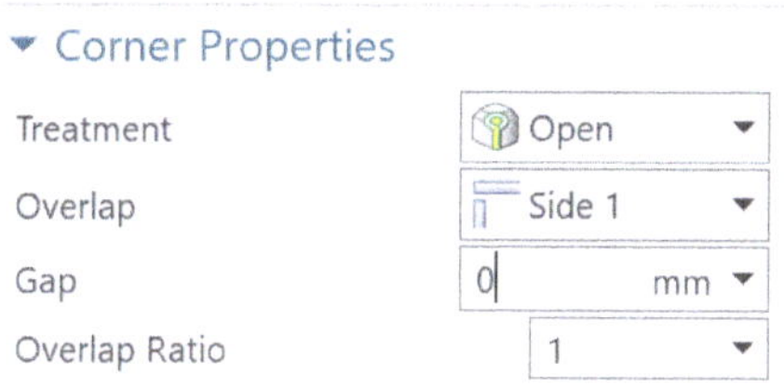

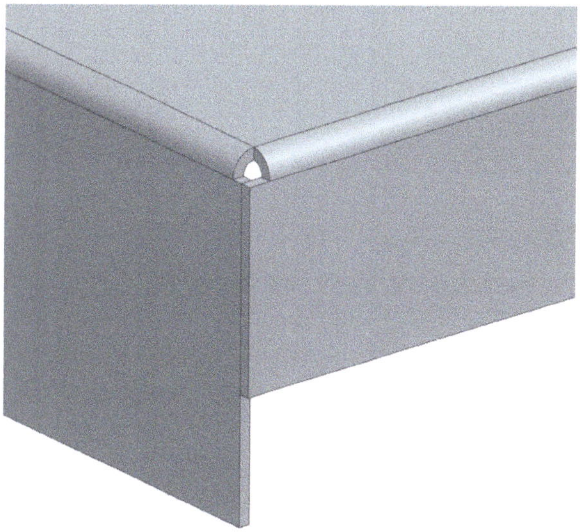

Contour Flange

The contour flange is another basic type of sheet metal feature. In order to create a contour flange, you need to have an open sketch. Activate the **Contour Flange** command (click **Home > Base > Contour Flange** on the ribbon) and click on elements of an open sketch. Drag the arrow or type-in a value in the **Width** box to define the width of the contour flange. Press Enter to create the contour flange feature.

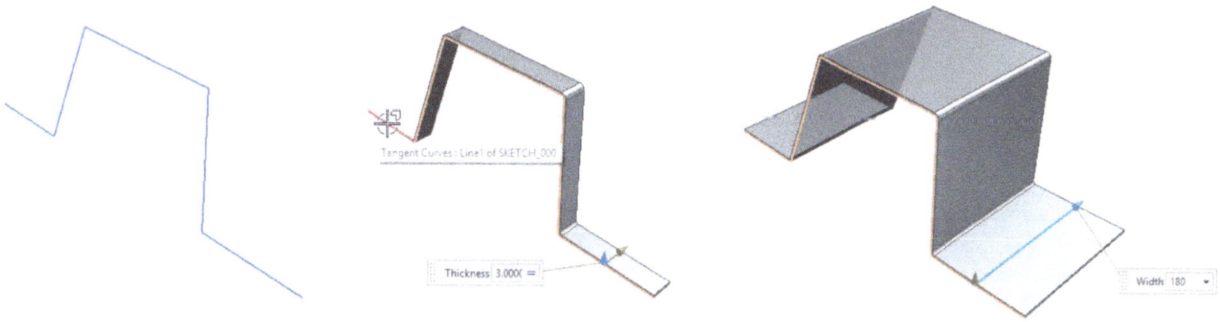

Creating a Rolled Sheet Metal part

You can use the **Contour Flange** command to create a rolled sheet metal part. To do this, create a sketch using the **Arc** command. Next, create a contour flange using the sketch.

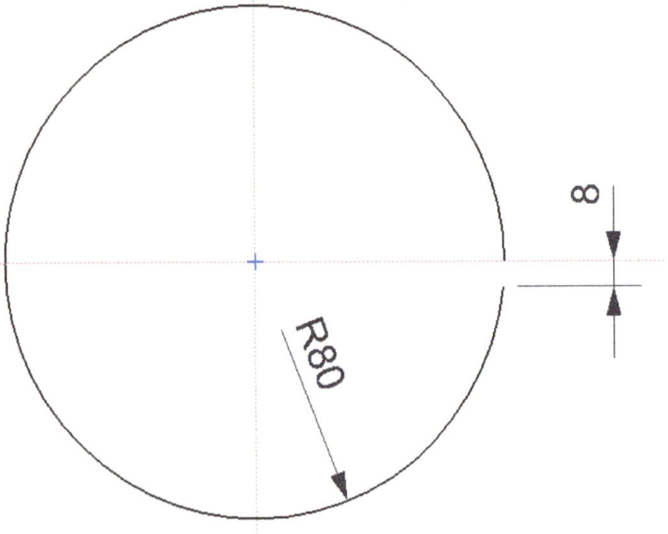

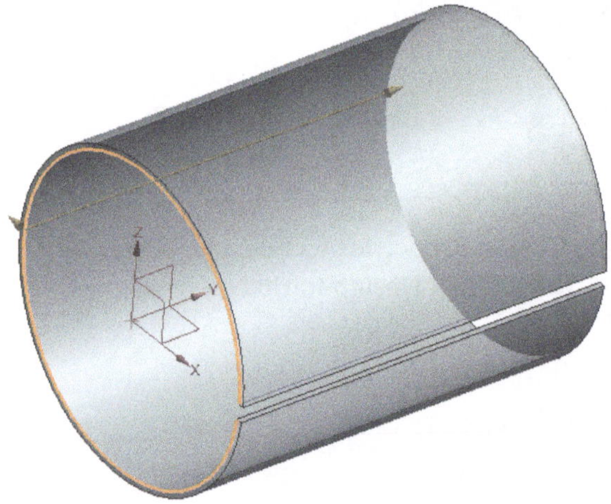

Creating a Secondary Contour Flange

You can also add contour flanges to a base tab. Activate the **Contour Flange** command and click an edge of the *Tab* feature. A plane appears normal to the selected edge. Type-in a value in the % **Arc Length** box to define the position of the plane and click **OK**; a sketch will be started. Draw an open profile of the contour flange feature and click **Finish** on the ribbon. On the **Contour Flange** dialog, select **Width > Width Option > Finite** to define a finite distance of the contour flange.

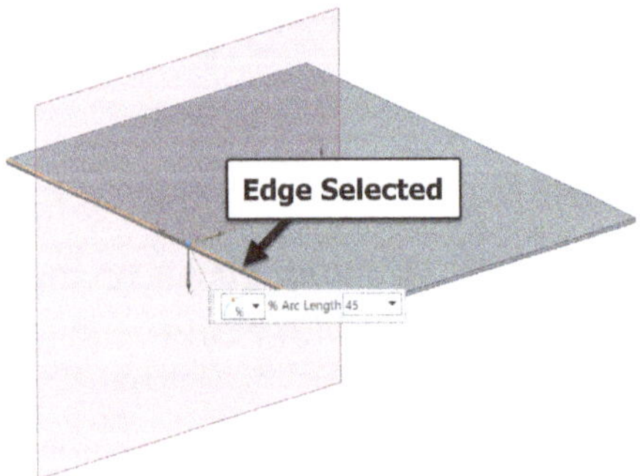

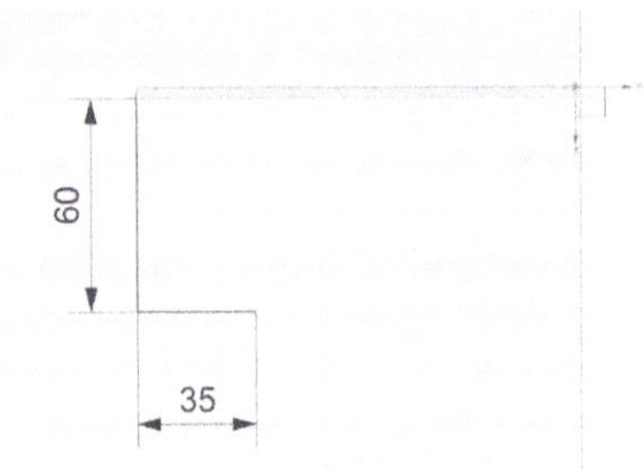

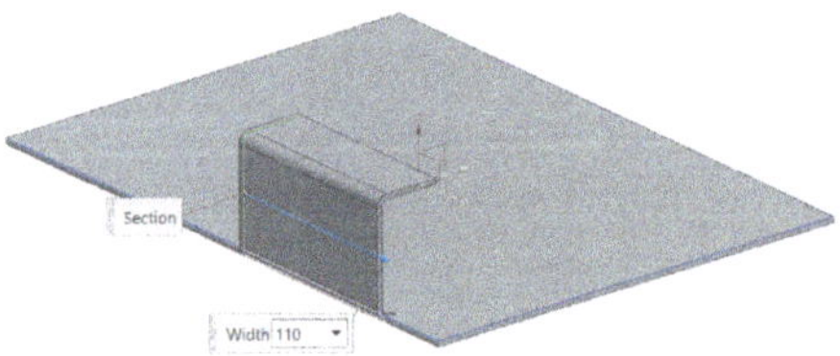

Select **Width Option > Symmetric** to create the contour flange on both sides of the profile. Select **Width Option > To End** to create the contour flange up to the end of the selected edge.

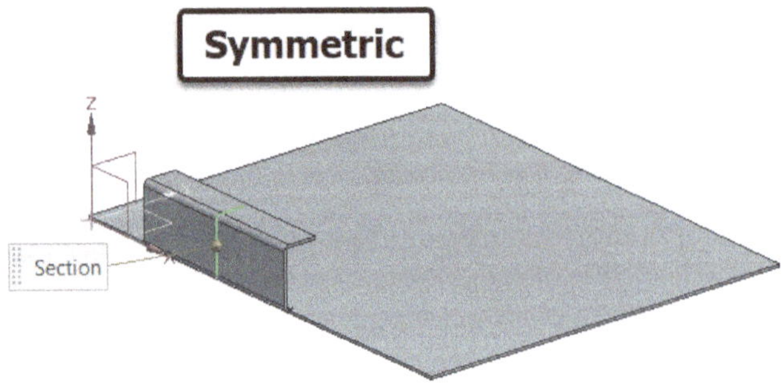

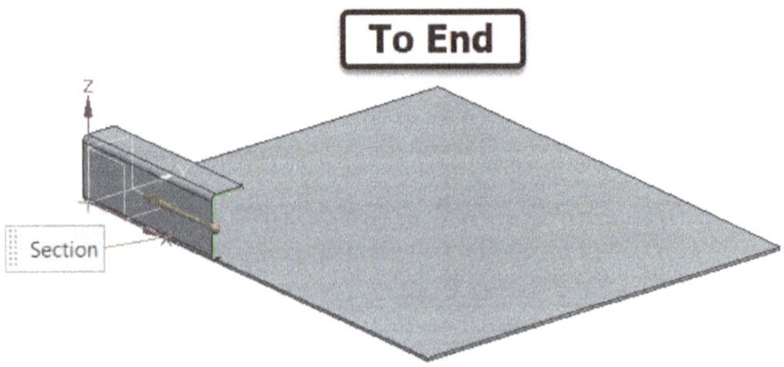

Select **Width Option > Chain** and select **Select edge** from the **Width** section. Next, click on the edges connected to the selected edge. The contour flange preview appears along the selected chain of edges.

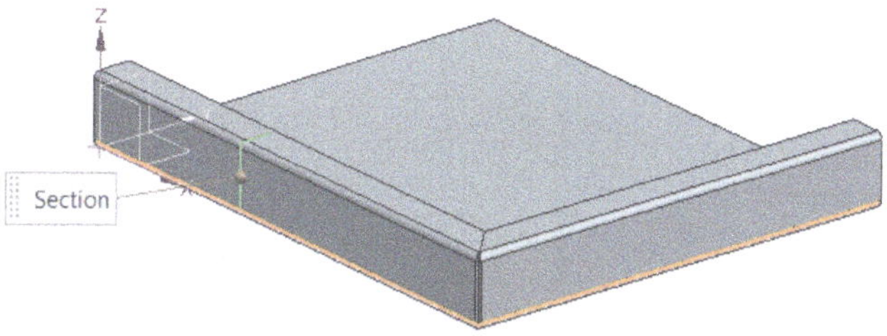

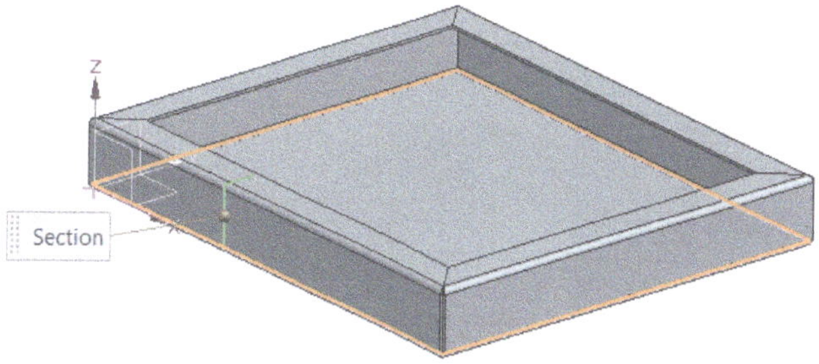

If you want to apply treatments at the corners of the contour flanges, then select **Corner > Close Corner**. The options in the **Treatment** drop-down are explained earlier in the **Closed Corner** command. Also, notice the **Miter Corner** option below the **Treatment** drop-down. Note that this option is available only when the **Treatment** type is set to **Closed, Circular Cutout, U Cutout**, or **V Cutout.** The **Miter Corner** option applies a miter to the closed corner. The following image displays a closed corner with and without miter.

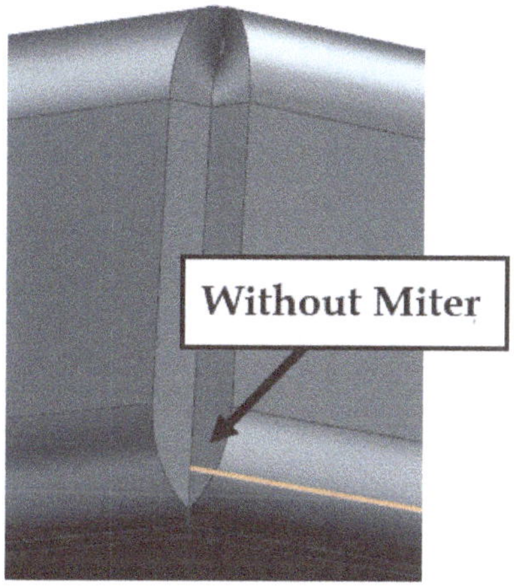

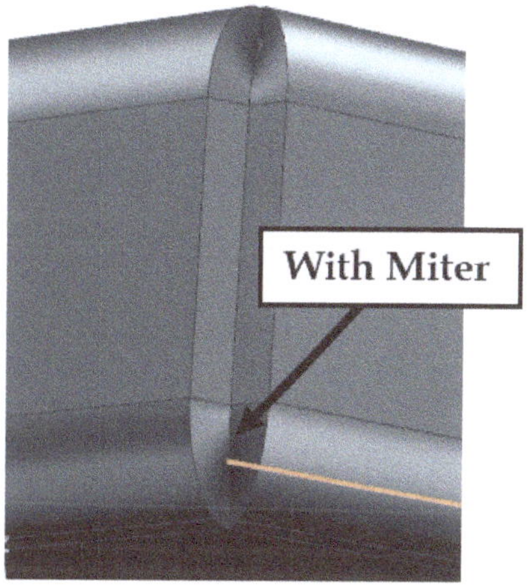

The **Blend Miter** option blends the sharp corners of the miter. The following image shows a closed cutout with a blended miter.

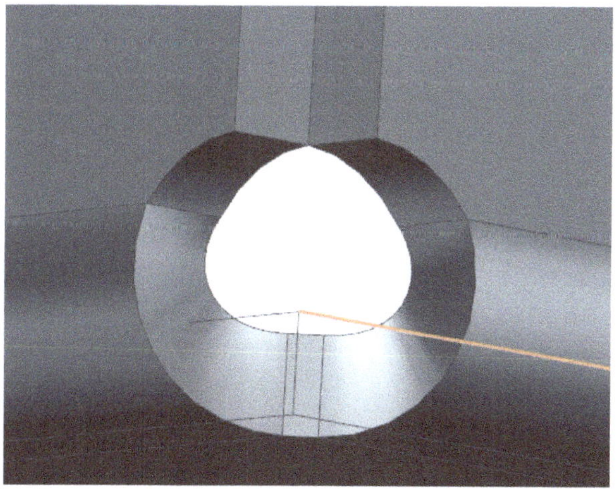

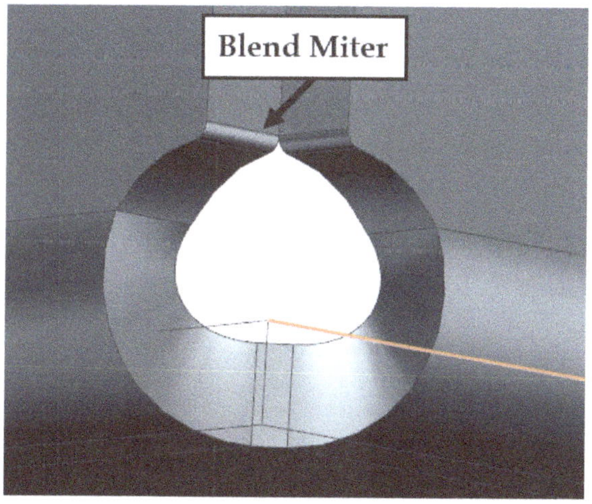

On the dialog, expand the **Miter** section and check the **Miter Corners** option to apply miter to the ends of the contour flange. Next, select an option from the **Cutout** drop-down: **Normal to Thickness Face** and **Normal to Source Face**. Type in a value in the **Angle** box and click **OK** to complete the contour flange.

Normal to Thickness Face

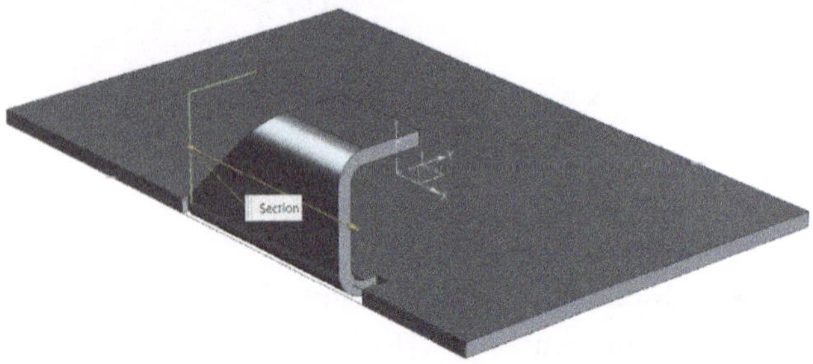

Normal to Source Face

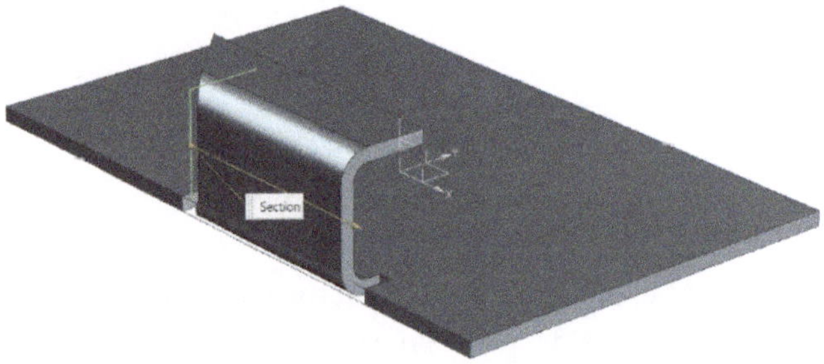

Hem

The **Hem** command folds an edge of a sheet metal part. To add a hem, activate the **Hem** command (click **Home > Bend > More > Hem** on the ribbon) and select the edge you need to fold over.

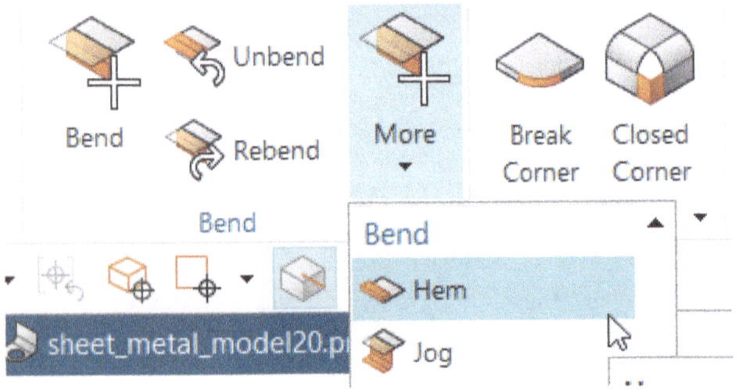

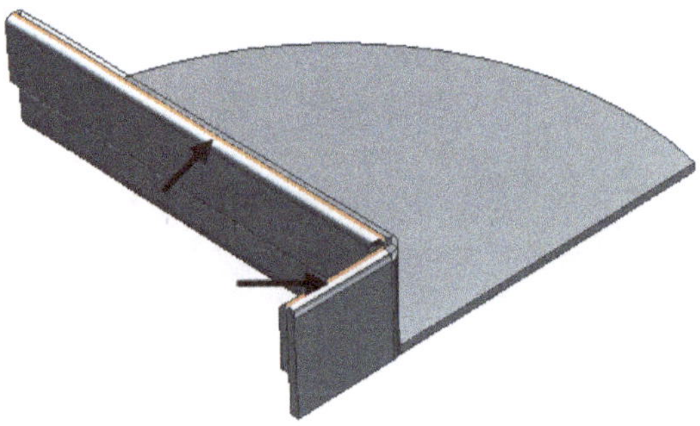

On the dialog, the **Inset** drop-down menu controls whether to add the material inside or outside of the existing edge.

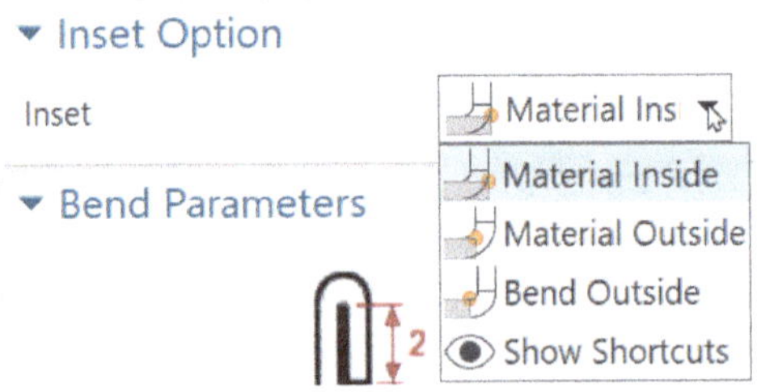

On the **Hem** dialog, select a hem type from the **Type** drop-down menu and define its parameters. The following figure shows different hem types.

Closed

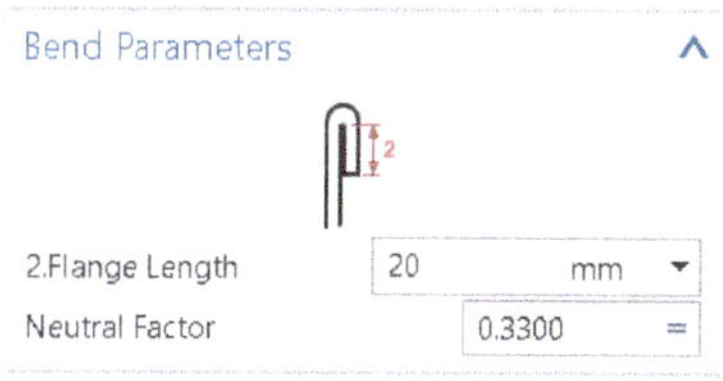

Open

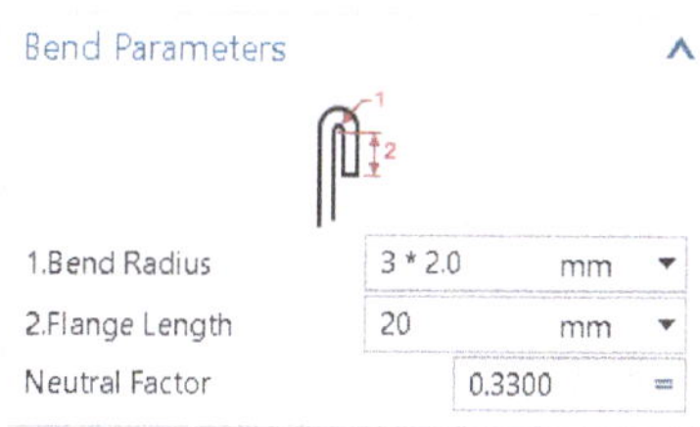

S-Type

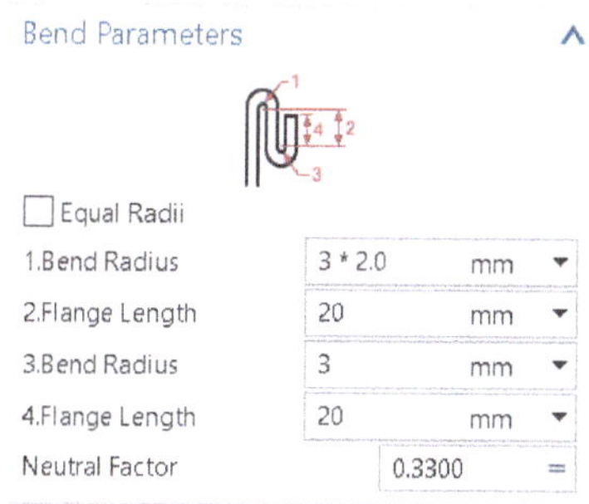

Curl

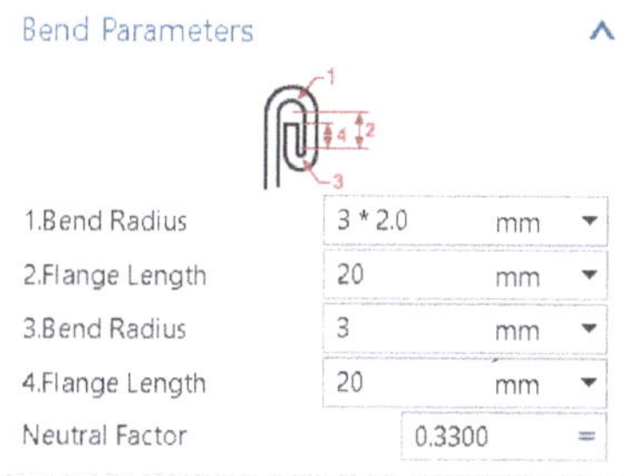

Open Loop

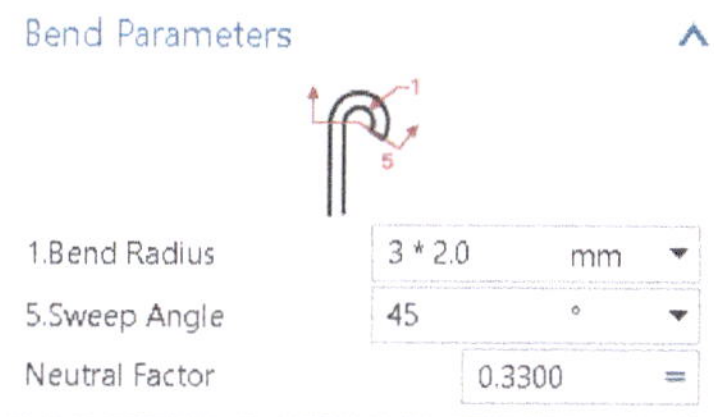

Closed Loop

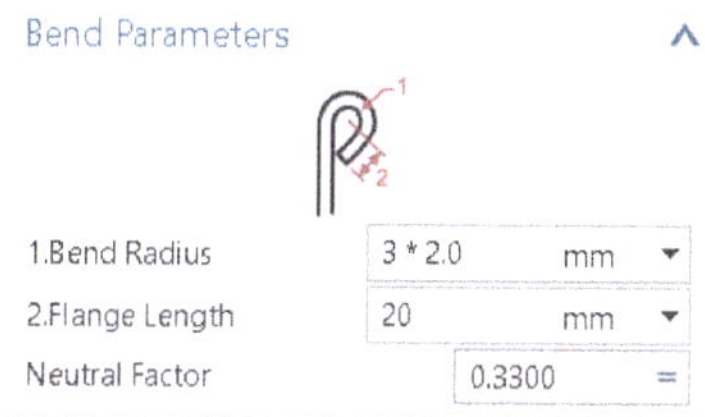

Centered Loop

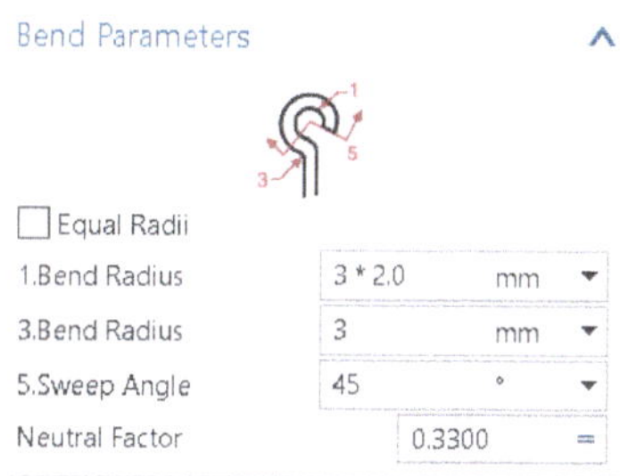

If you want to bevel the end faces of the hem, then expand the **Miter** section and check the **Miter Hem** option. Type-in a value in the **Miter Angle** box. Click the **OK** button to complete the hem feature.

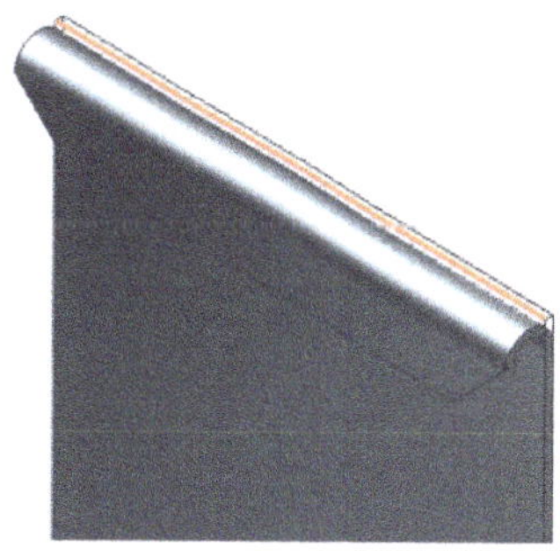

Bend

In addition to adding flanges and contour flanges, you can also bend a flat sheet using the **Bend** command. Activate the **Bend** command (click **Home > Bend > Bend** on the ribbon) and click on the face to bend. Draw a sketch line on the flat sheet and click **Finish** on the ribbon. The flat sheet bends along the sketch line. On the **Bend** dialog, click the **Reverse Side** button to flip the bend side if you want to reverse the side to be bent. Type-in a value in the **Angle** box to change the folding angle. Click the **Reverse Direction** to reverse the folding direction. Select an option from the **Inset** drop-down menu to define the material side of the bend feature. Click **OK** to complete the bend feature.

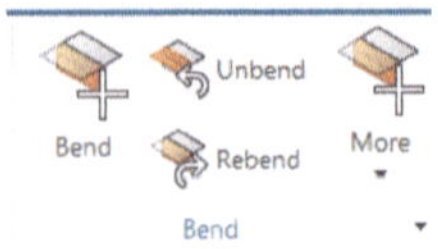

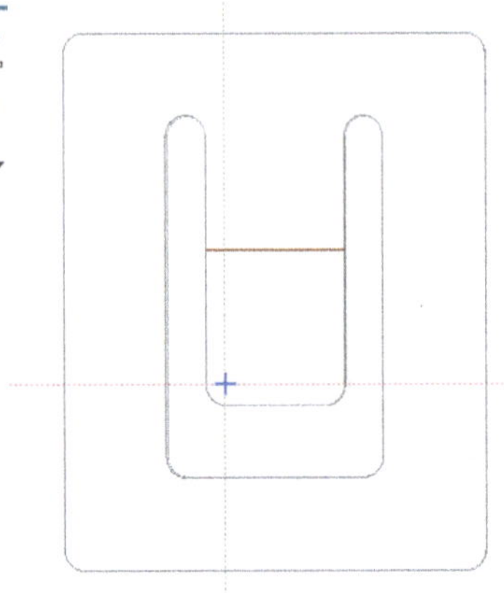

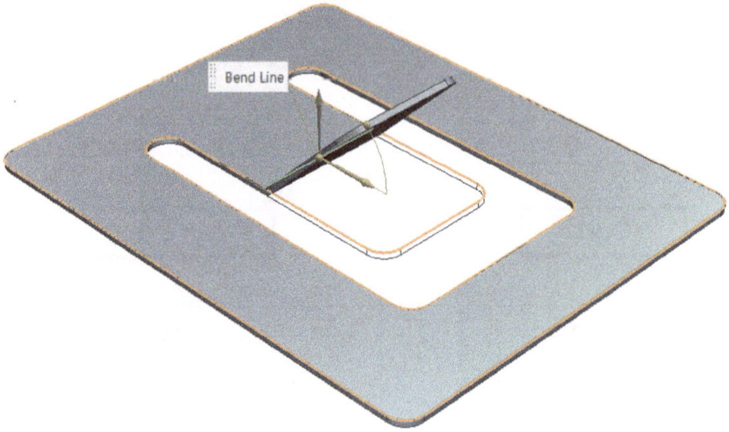

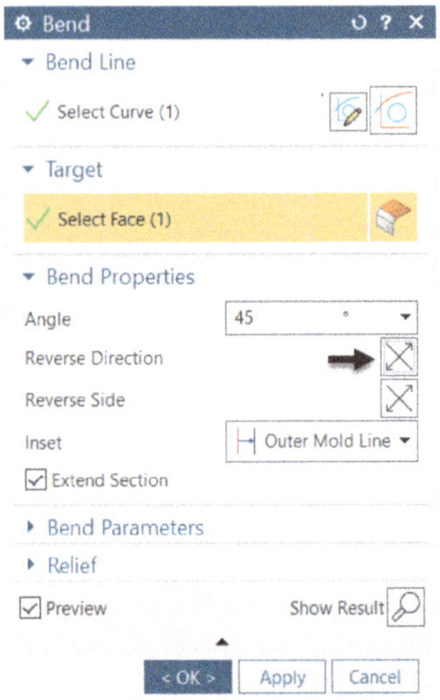

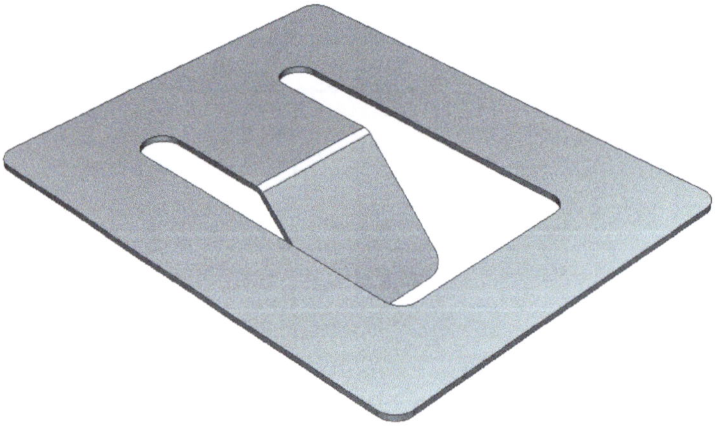

Jog

The **Jog** command adds a jog or offsets to a flat sheet. Activate the **Jog** command (click **Home > Bend > More > Jog** on the ribbon) and click on a face to add the jog. Draw a line defining the location of the jog, and then click **Finish** on the ribbon. A preview of the jog feature appears. Type-in a value in the **Height** box to define the jog height. On the **Jog** dialog, click the **Reverse Side** button to flip the jog side. Click the **Reverse Direction** button to reverse the jog direction.

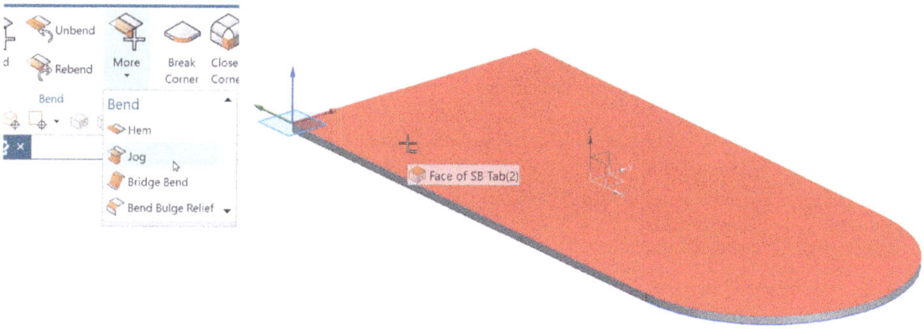

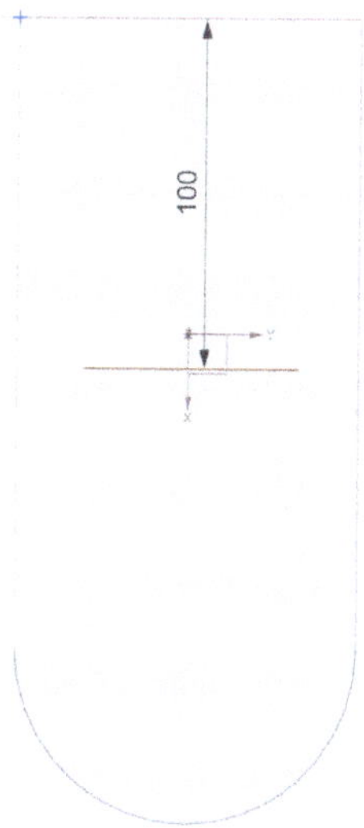

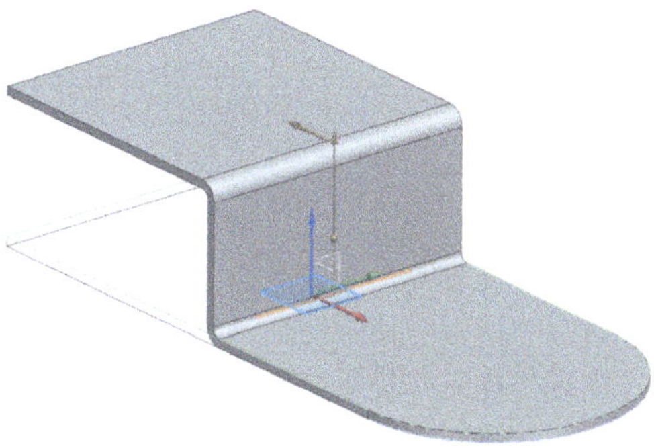

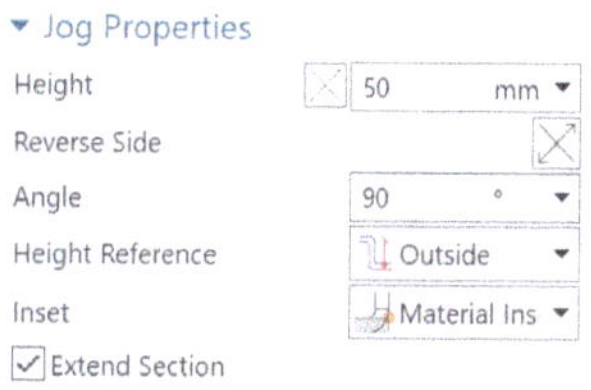

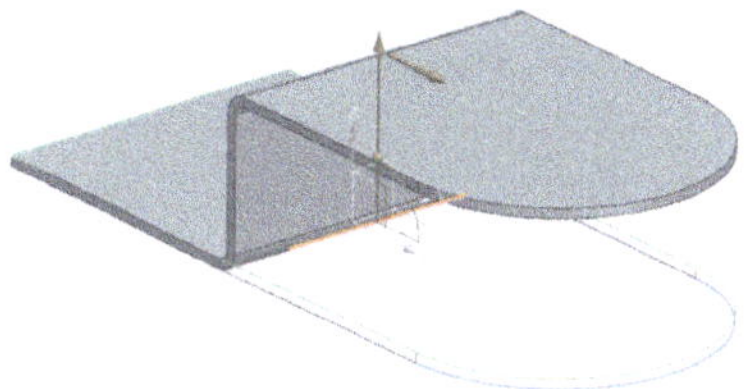

Under the **Jog Properties** section, select a measurement point from the **Height Reference** drop-down menu. The following figure illustrates both the measurement points.

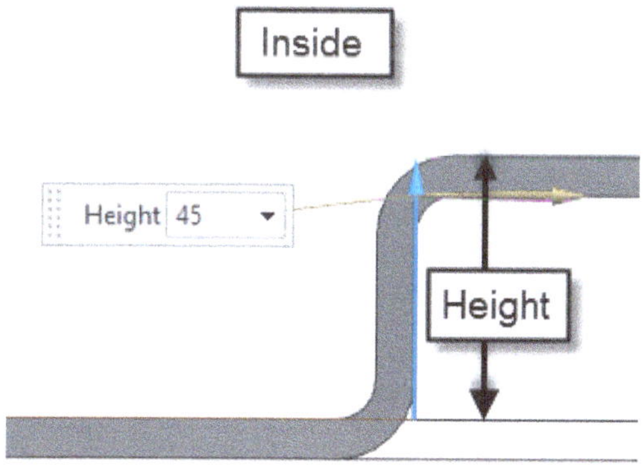

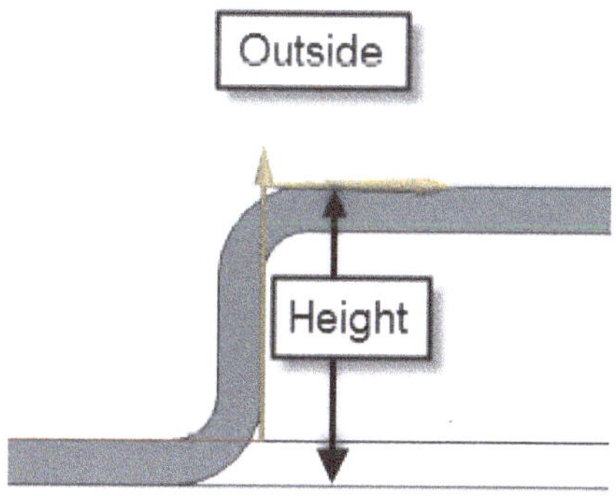

The **Extend Section** option extends the sketch profile up to the side edge of the sheet metal part. If you uncheck this option, it results in a jog, as shown in the figure.

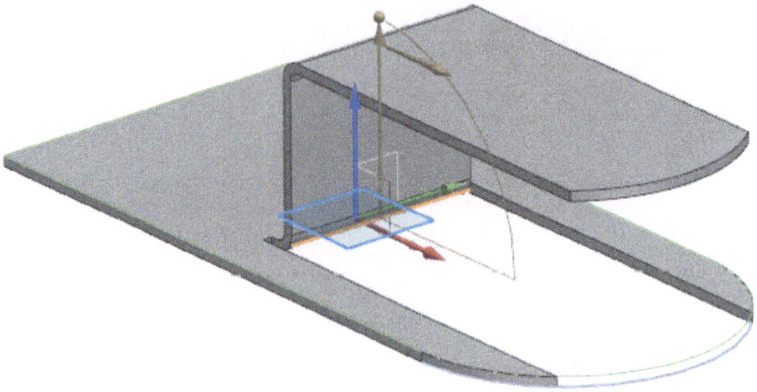

Click **OK** to create the Jog.

Dimple

The **Dimple** command adds a dimple to a flat sheet by deforming it. Activate the **Dimple** command (click **Home > Punch > Dimple** on the ribbon) and click on the face to add dimple. Draw a closed sketch and click **Finish** on the ribbon. A dimple shape appears in the sketch region. On the **Dimple** dialog, click the **Reverse Direction** button to change the dimple direction. Type-in a value in the **Depth** box to define the depth of the dimple feature.

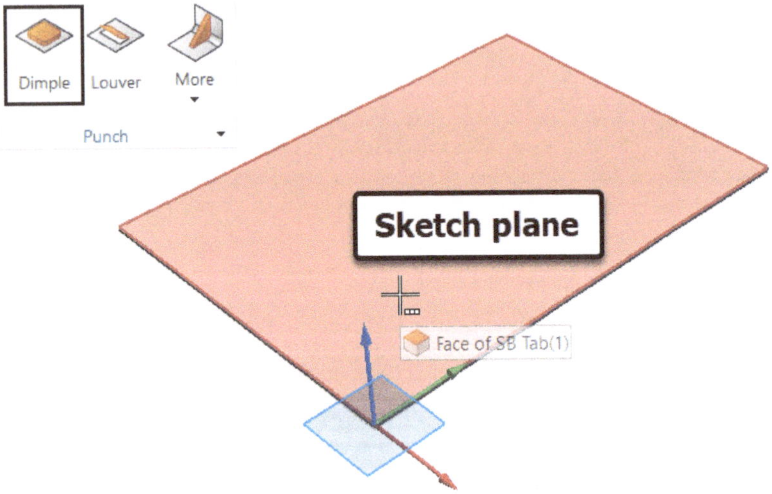

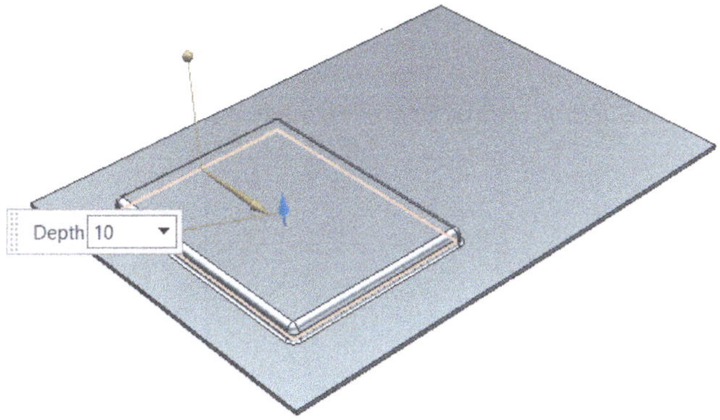

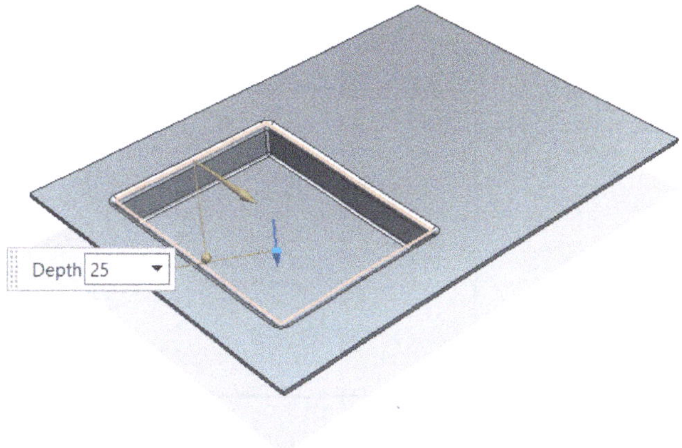

On the **Dimple** dialog, type-in the values of **Side Angle**, **Punch Radius**, **Die Radius**, and **Corner Radius**.

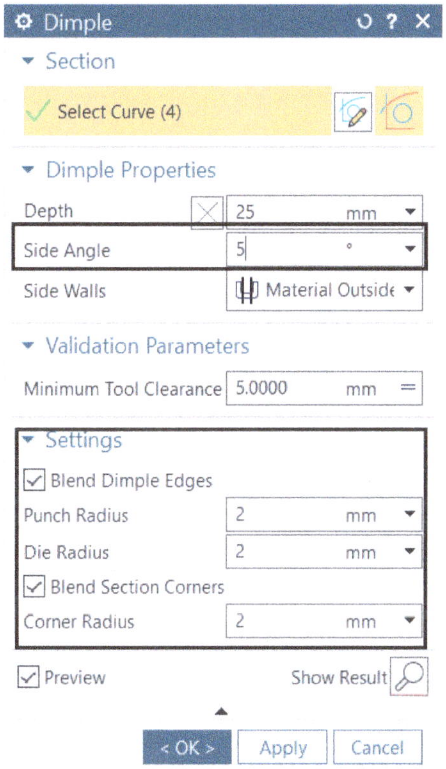

Use the **Side Walls** drop-down menu to define the material side of the dimple feature. You can select **Material Outside** or **Material Inside**.

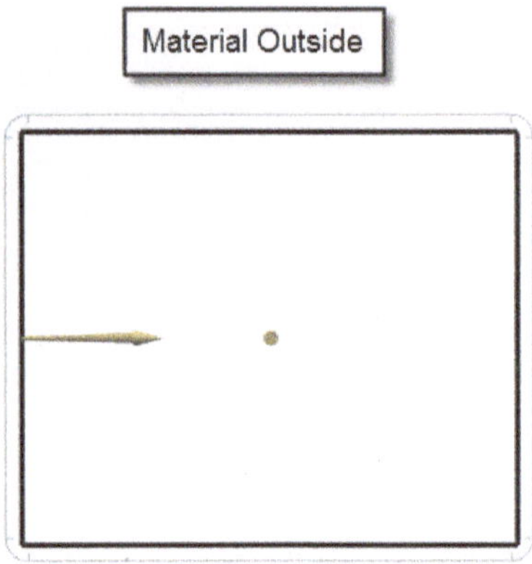

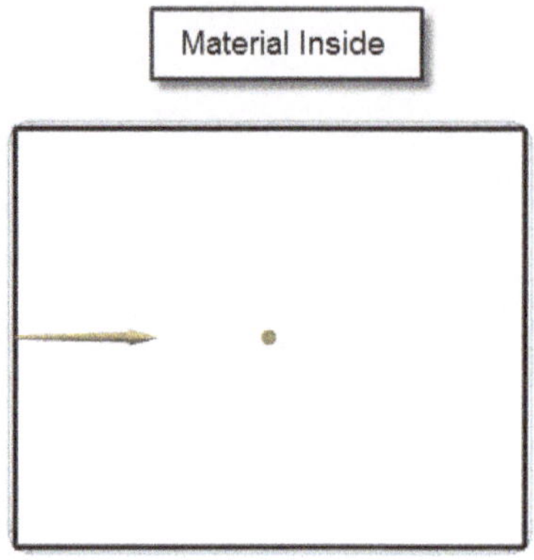

Drawn Cutout

The drawn cutout and dimple features are almost alike, except that an opening is created in case of a drawn cut out. Activate the **Drawn Cutout** command (click **Home > Punch > More > Drawn Cutout** on the ribbon) and click on the face to add drawn cutout. Draw a closed sketch and click **Finish** on the ribbon. On the **Drawn Cutout** dialog, click the **Reverse Direction** button to change the cutout direction. Type-in a value in the **Depth** box to define the depth of the drawn cutout feature.

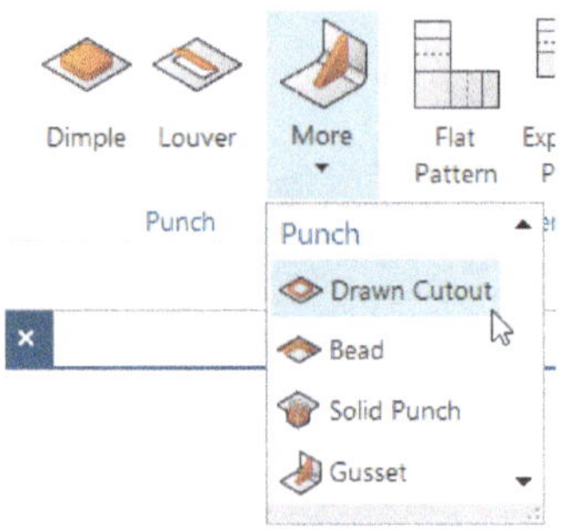

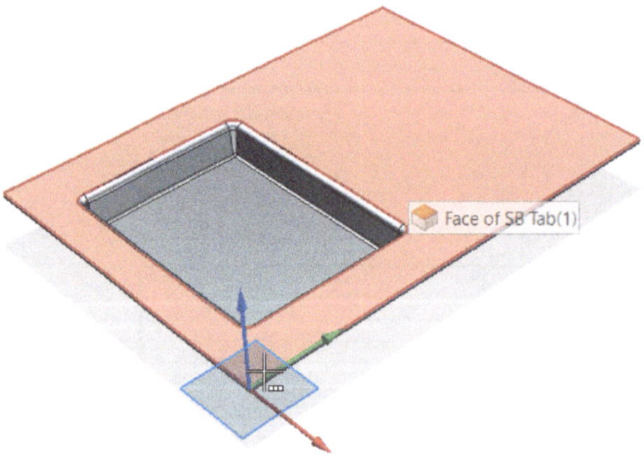

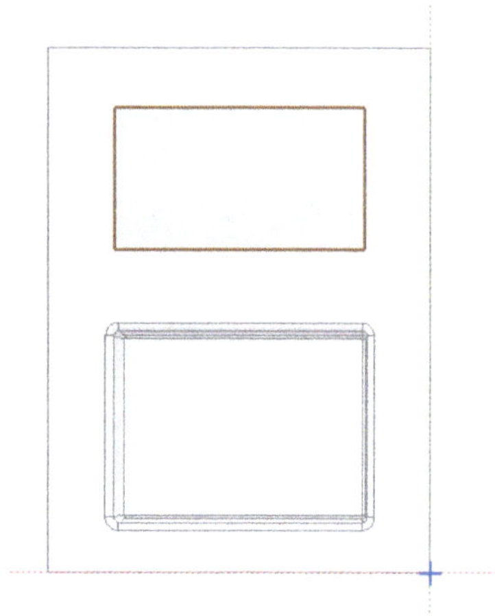

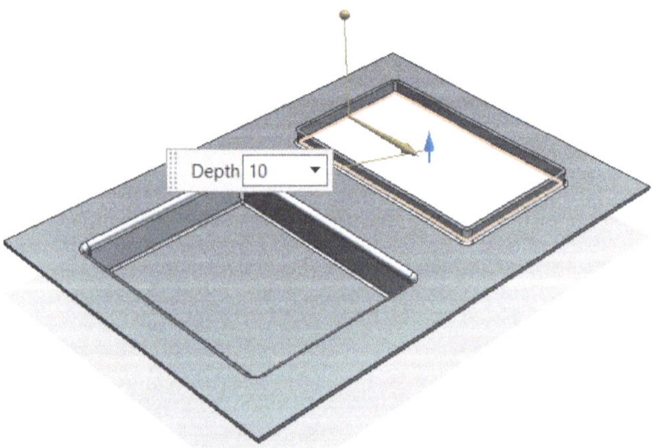

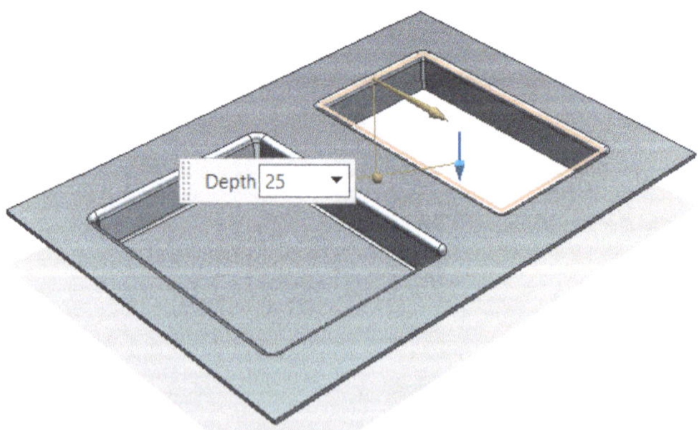

On the dialog, type-in values of **Side Angle**, **Die Radius**, and **Corner Radius**.

From the **Side Walls** drop-down menu, select **Material Outside** or **Material Inside**. This determines whether the sidewalls will appear inside or outside the sketch profile. Click **OK** on the dialog to complete the drawn to cut out.

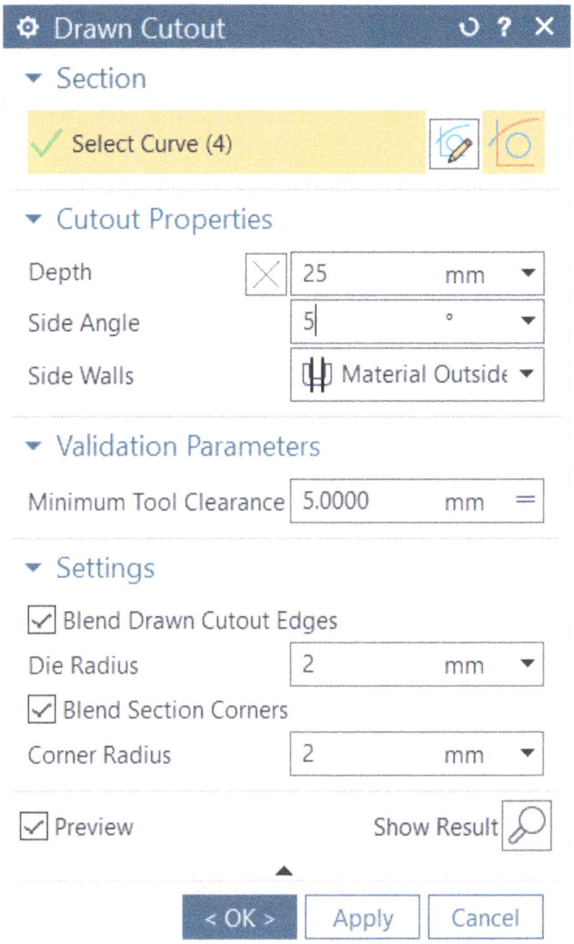

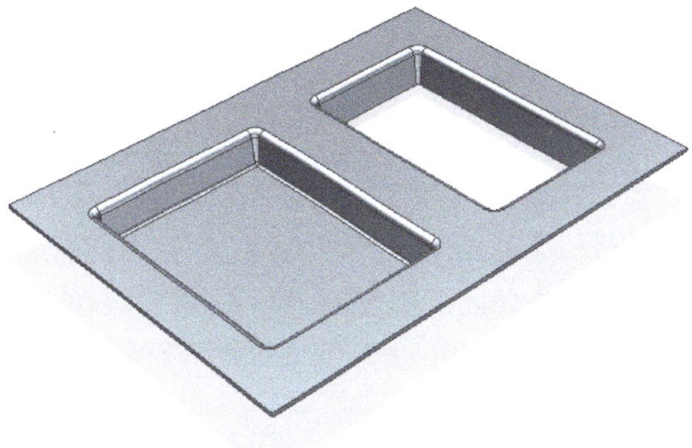

Bead

The **Bead** command creates a bead feature, which stiffens the sheet metal part. In order to create a bead feature, first, you must have a sketch, which defines the bead size and shape. If the sketch has curved edges, then ensure that they are tangent continuous. Activate the **Bead** command (click **Home > Punch >More > Bead** on the ribbon) and click on the sketch. On the **Bead** dialog, click the **Reverse Direction** button to flip the bead feature.

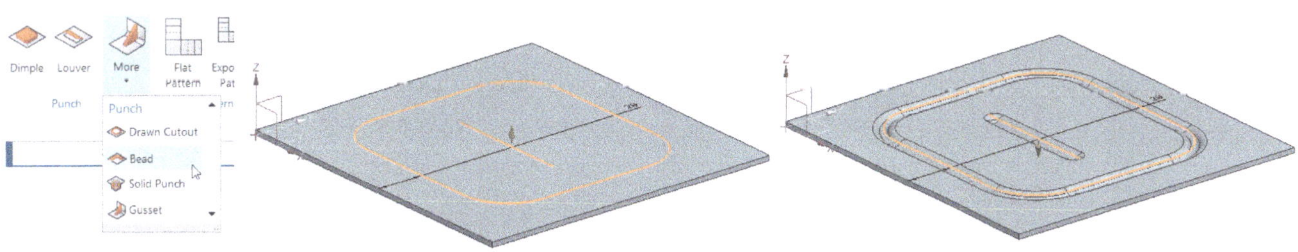

On this dialog, under **Bend Properties**, select the cross-section type and define the size parameters. There are three different cross-section types, as shown.

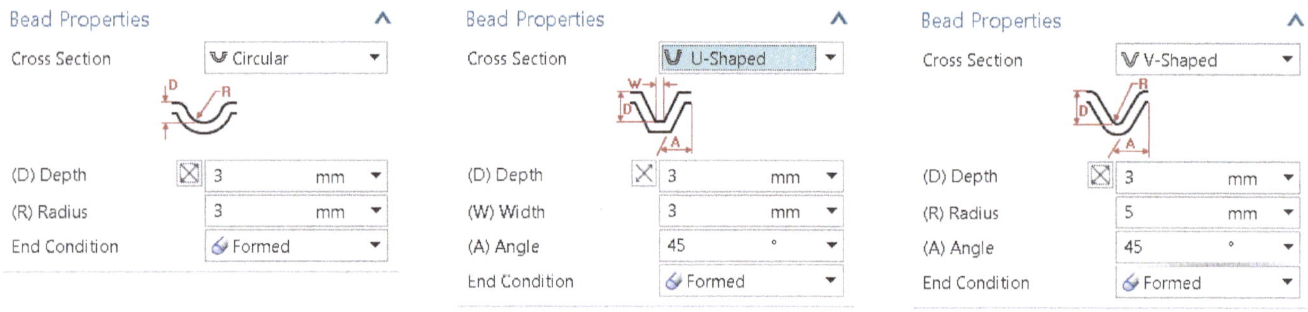

From the **End Condition** drop-down menu, select **Formed, Lanced, Punched,** or **Tapered** (available only for the V-Shaped cross-section). These end conditions are shown in the following figure.

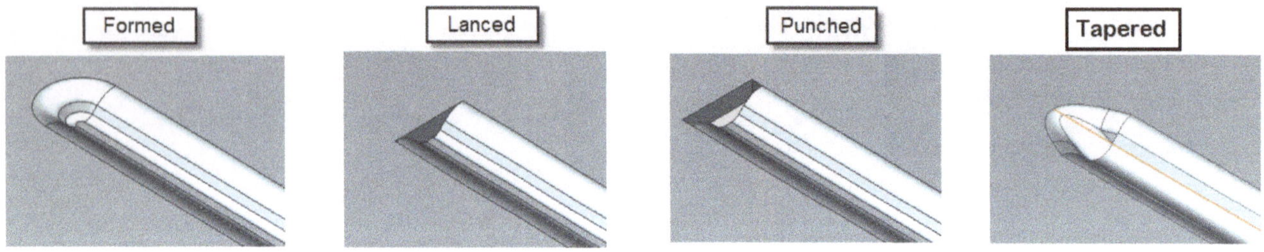

Under the **Settings** section, check the **Blend Bead Edges** option to apply rounds to the edges of the bead feature. Type-in values in the **Die Radius** and **Punch Radius** boxes. Note that the **Punch Radius** box is available only for the U-Shaped cross-section. Click **OK** to complete the bead feature.

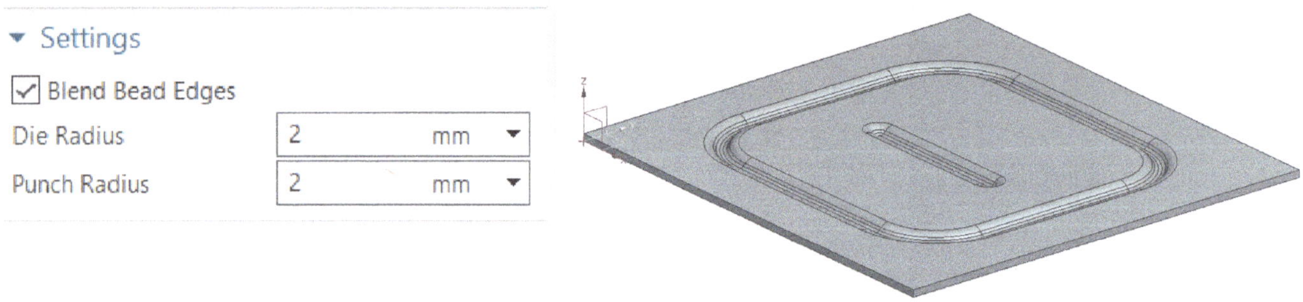

NX allows you to create beads across bends. First, you must unbend the sheet metal part using the **Unbend** command. Activate the **Unbend** command (On the ribbon, click **Home > Bend > Unbend**) and click on the face to remain stationary. Click on the bend and click **OK** to unbend the sheet metal part.

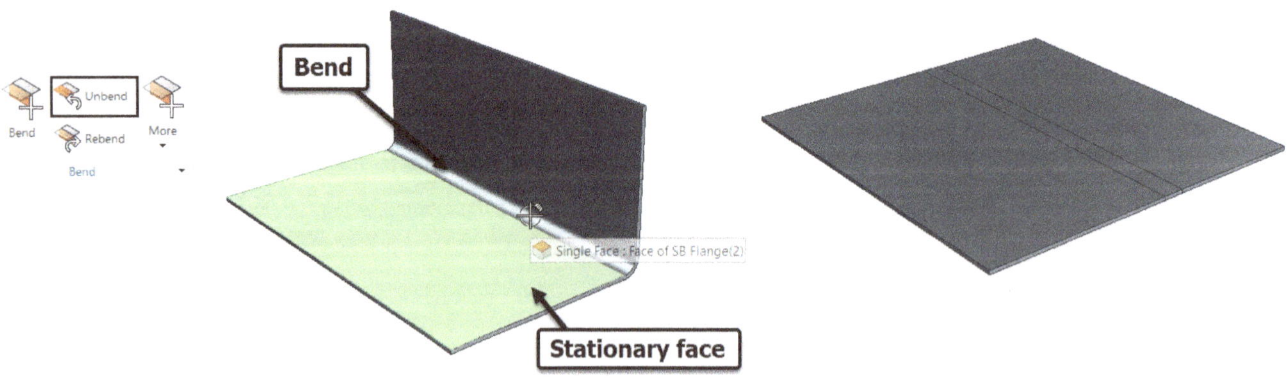

Activate the **Bead** command and click on the face to add beads. Draw bead profiles and click **Finish** on the ribbon. Define the bead parameters on the **Bead** dialog and click **OK**.

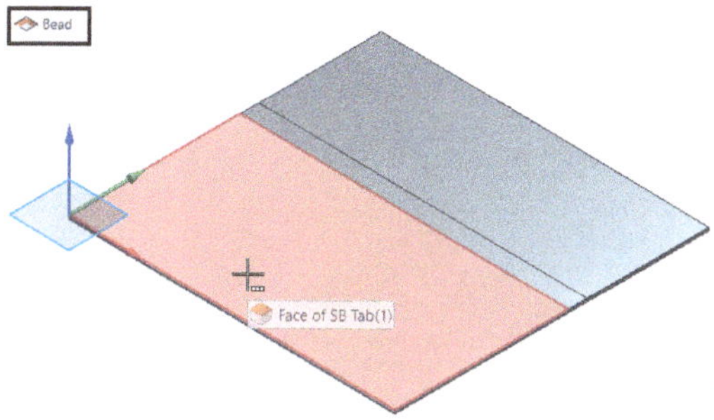

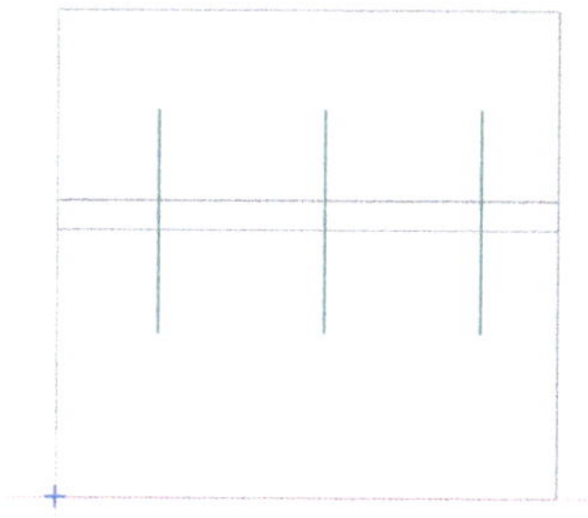

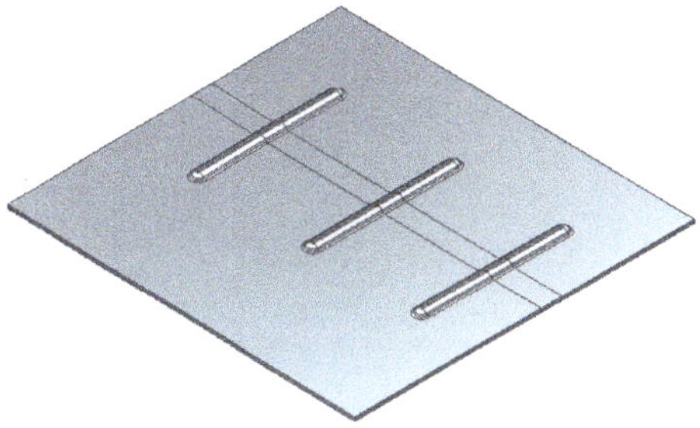

Now, activate the **Rebend** command (On the ribbon, click **Home > Bend > Rebend**) and click on the bend. On the **Rebend** dialog, click **OK** to rebend the sheet metal part.

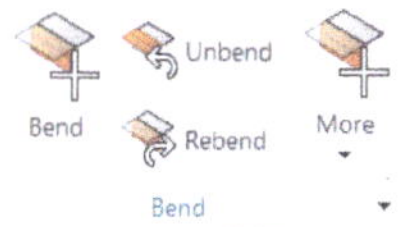

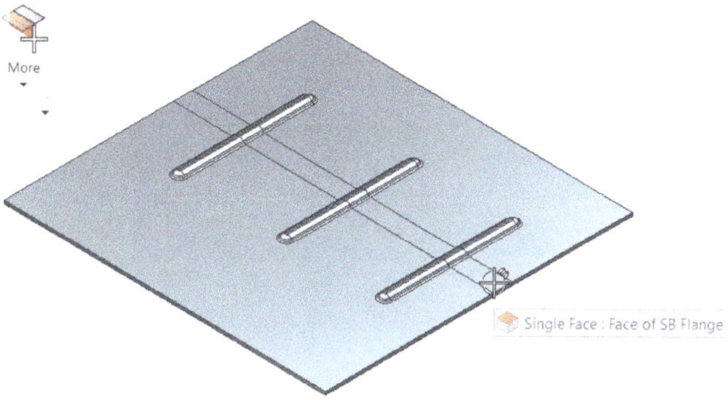

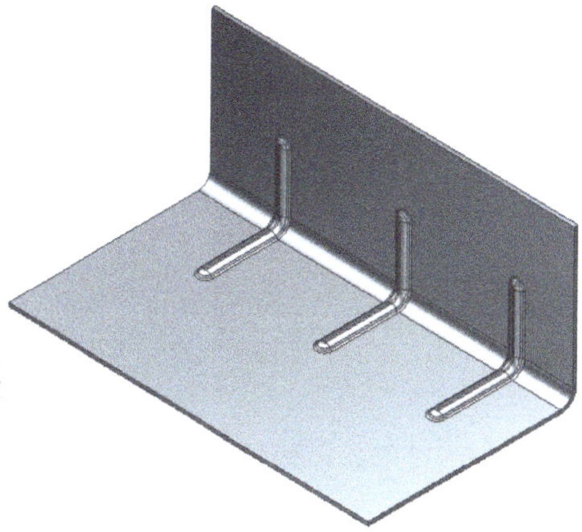

Louver

NX provides you with the **Louver** command, which makes it easy to create louvers. Activate this command (click **Home > Punch > Louver** on the ribbon) and click on a face. Draw a line on the selected face and click **Finish** on the ribbon. On the **Louver** dialog, type-in a value in the **Depth** box. Click **Reverse Direction** next to the **Depth** box to reverse the depth direction. Type-in a value in the **Width** box to define the width of the louver. Click **Reverse Direction** next to the **Width** box to reverse the width. You should ensure that the louver depth should be less than or equal to width minus the material thickness.

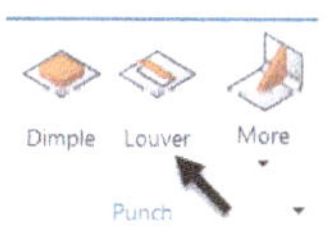

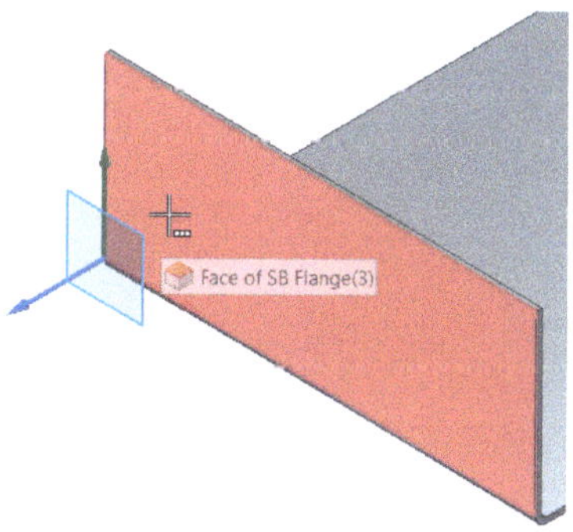

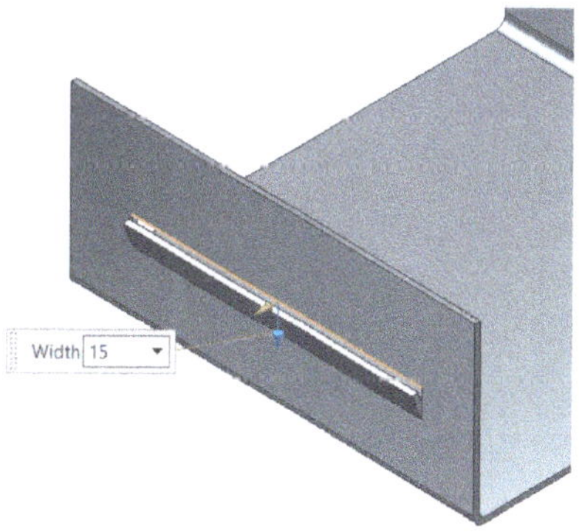

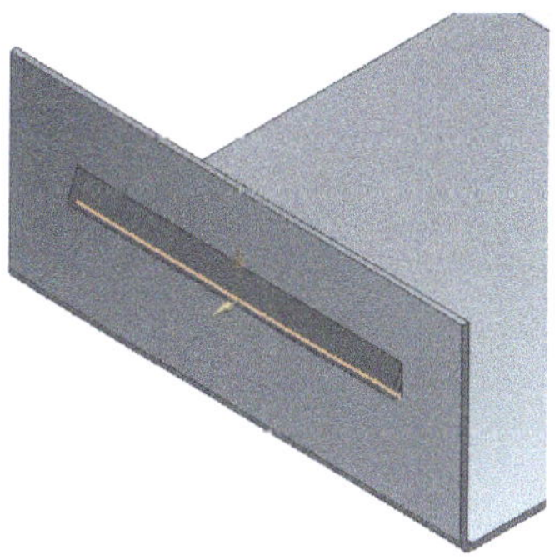

On the **Louver** dialog, define the end condition of the louver from the **Louver Shape** drop-down menu. The following figure shows the two end conditions.

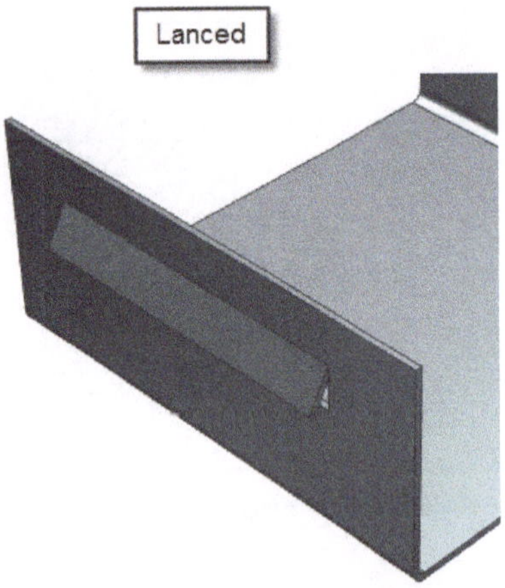

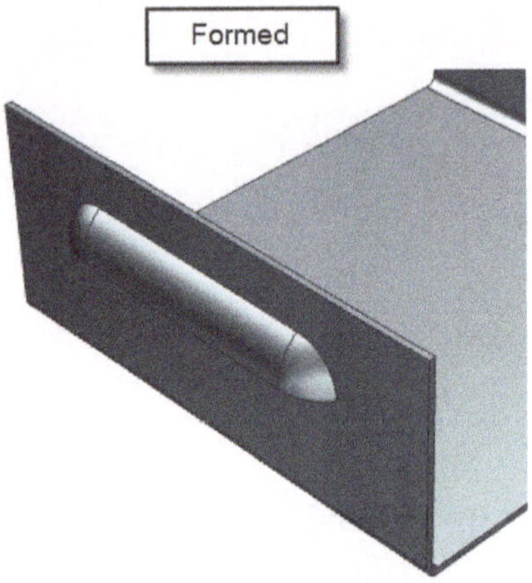

Under the **Settings** section, check the **Blend Louver Edges** option and type-in a value in the **Die Radius** box to round the edges of the louver. Click **OK** to complete the louver feature.

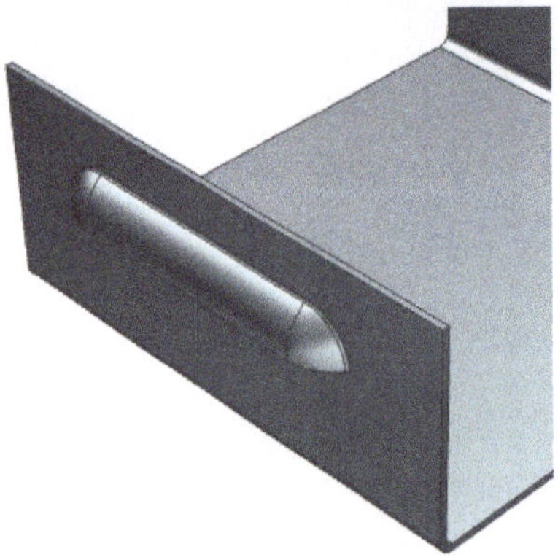

Gusset

Gussets are stiffening features created across a bend to reinforce the sheet metal part. Activate the **Gusset** command (click **Home > Punch > More > Gusset** on the ribbon) and click on a bent face. Select a point on the edge of the selected bend face; a gusset feature appears along with a plane. Drag the plane to define the location of the gusset.

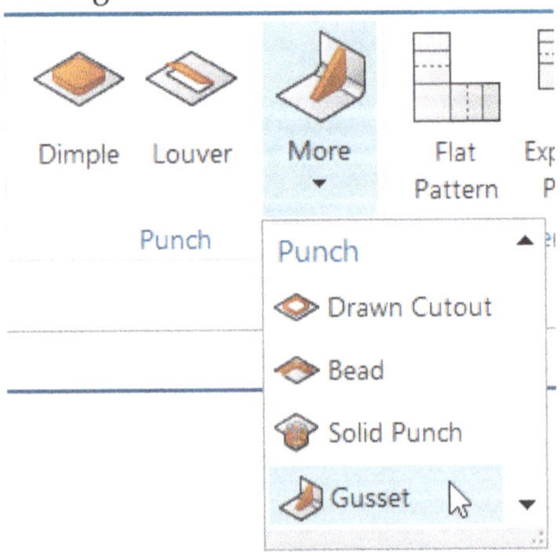

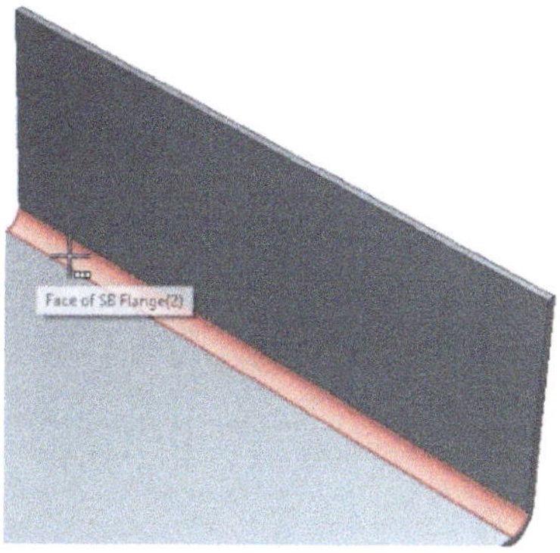

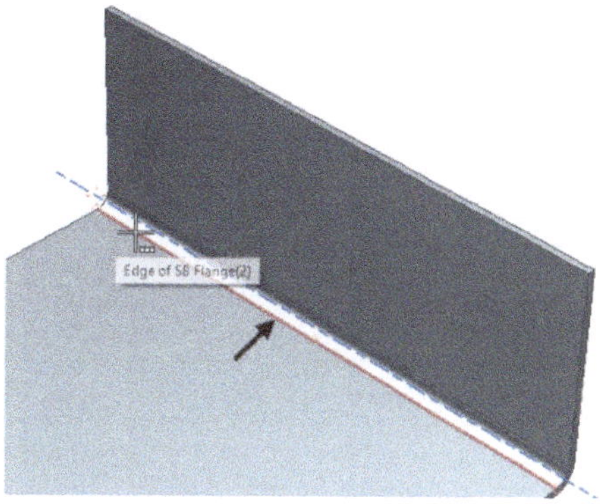

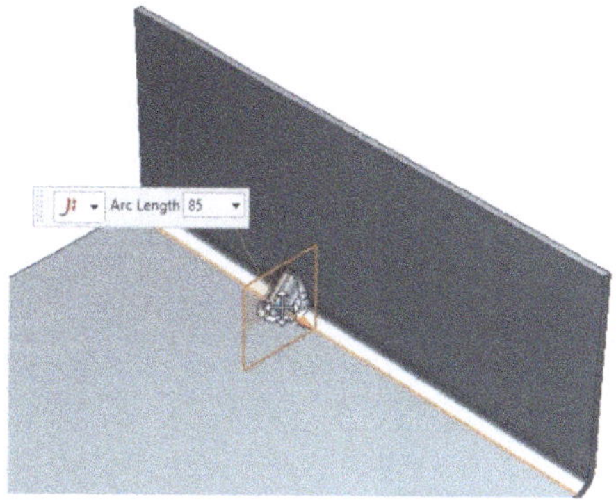

Under the **Shape** section, select the gusset form from the **Form** drop-down and type-in a value in the **Depth** box. Type-in values of **Width**, **Side Angle**, **Punch Radius,** and **Die Radius**.

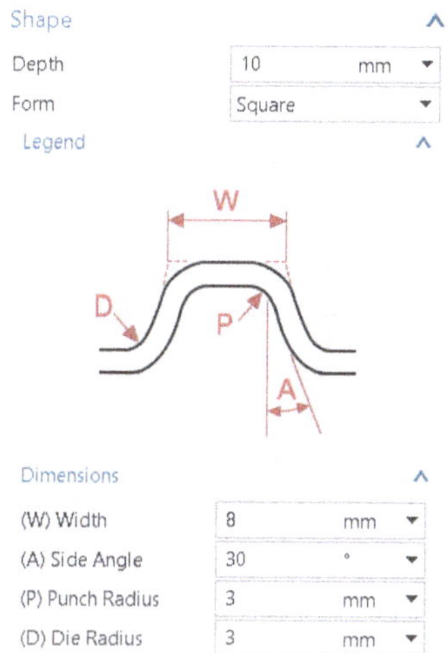

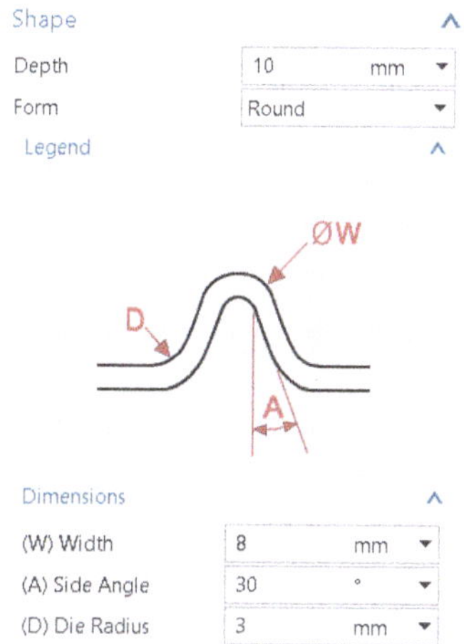

Click **OK** to complete the gusset feature.

In addition to creating a gusset with an automatic profile, NX allows you to create a gusset with a user-defined profile. On the **Gusset** dialog, select **Type > User Defined Profile**  and click on the edge of the bend. A plane appears normal to the edge. Click **OK** and draw a sketch. On the ribbon, click **Finish** to create the gusset with the custom profile. Under the **Section** section, use the **Width Side** drop-down menu to define the side of the gusset feature.

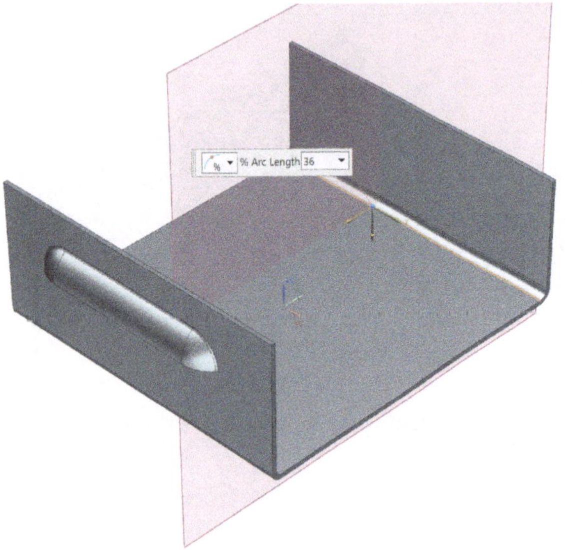

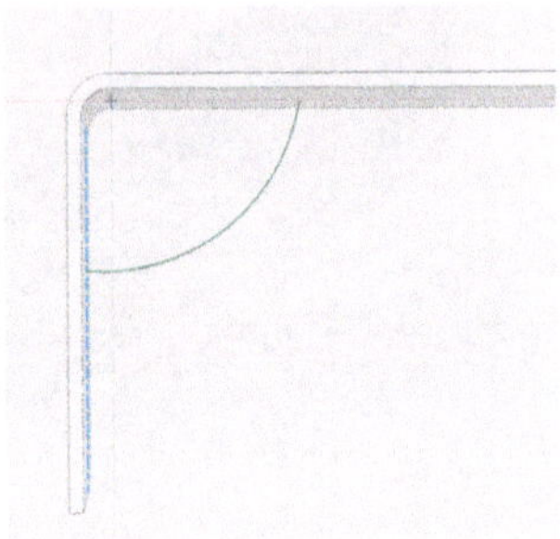

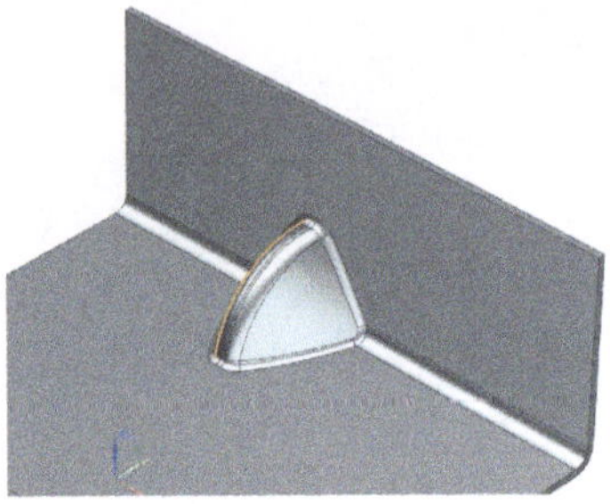

Normal Cutout

More often, it is necessary to remove material from a sheet metal part. To do so, you must use the **Normal Cutout** command. First, draw a sketch, and then activate the **Normal Cutout**  command (On the ribbon, click **Home > Base > Normal Cutout**). Click on the sketch and select the extent type from **Cutout Properties > Limits**. Type-in a value in the **Depth** box in case the **Limits** is set to **Value**. You can also set the **Limits** to **Between**, **Until next**, or **Through All**. These options are explained in *Chapter 3: Extrude and Revolve Features*. On the dialog, click **OK** to create the cutout.

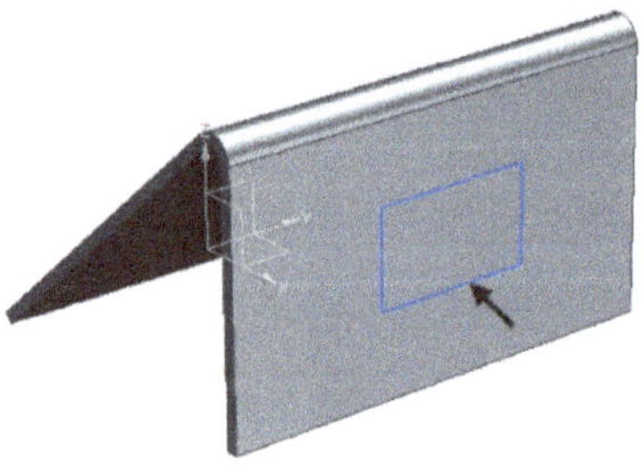

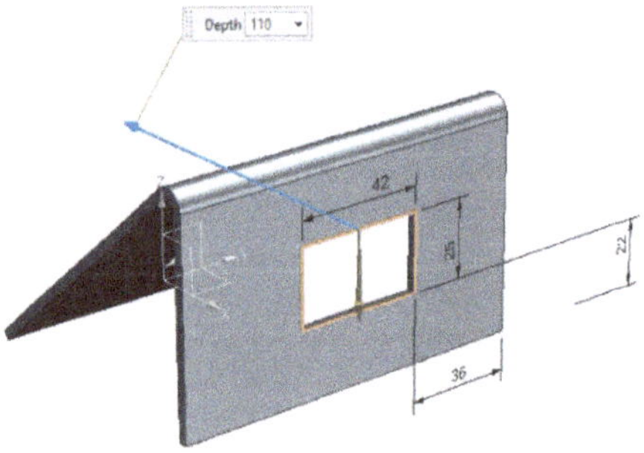

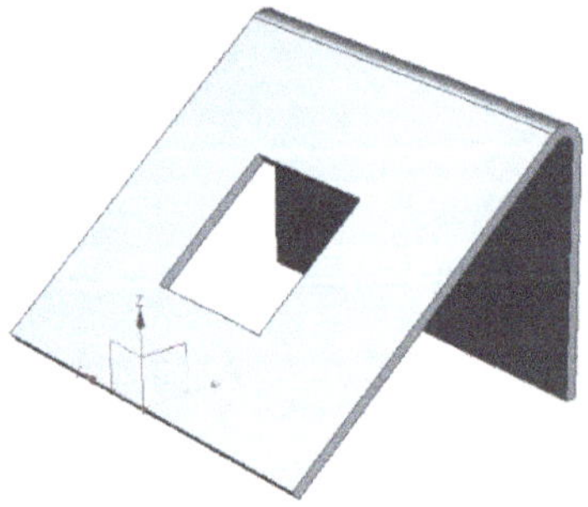

Cutting across Bends

If you want to create a cut across a bend, you must unbend the sheet metal part and draw a sketch.

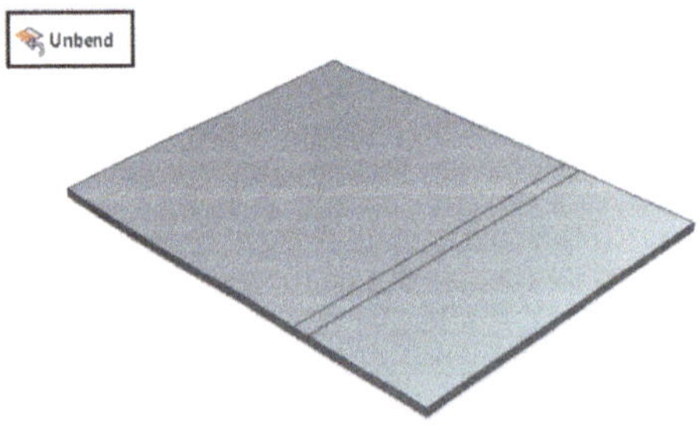

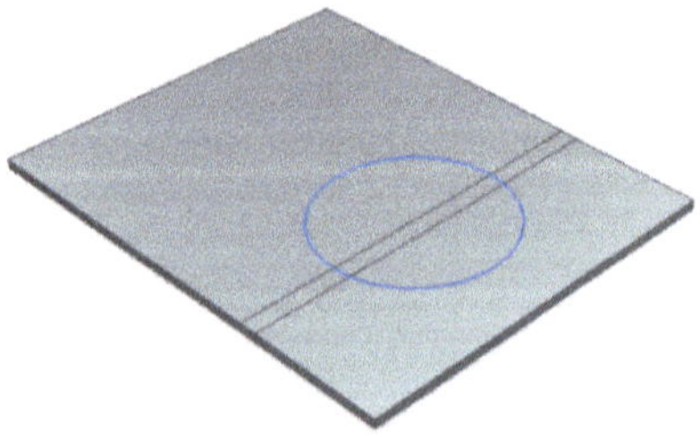

Activate the **Normal Cutout** command and create a cut across the bend. Use the **Rebend** command and fold the sheet metal part.

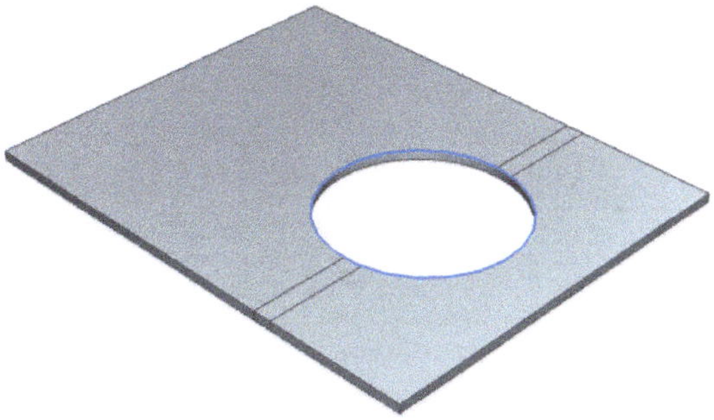

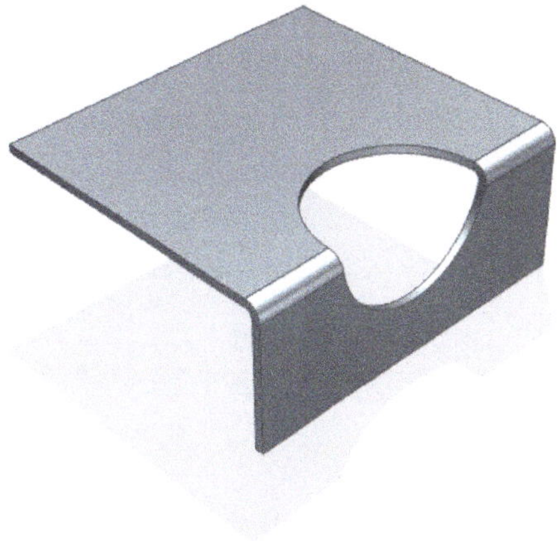

Break Corner

The **Break Corner** command rounds or chamfers the sharp corners of a sheet metal part. Activate this command (click **Home > Corner > Break Corner** on the ribbon) and click on the corner edges of the sheet metal part. If you want to break all the corners of the sheet metal part, then drag a selection window across the geometry. This will select all the corners of the sheet metal part.

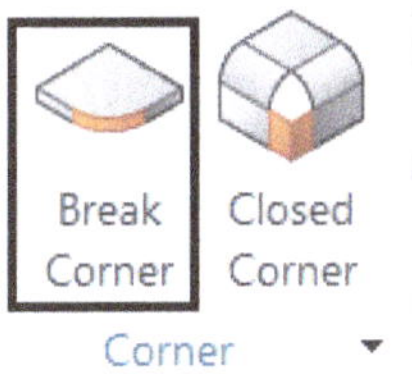

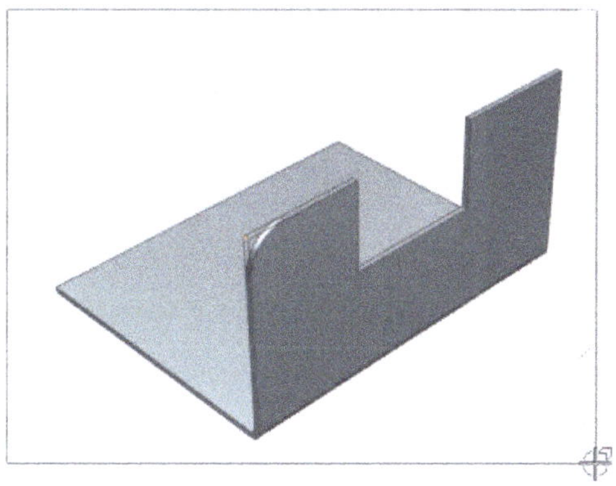

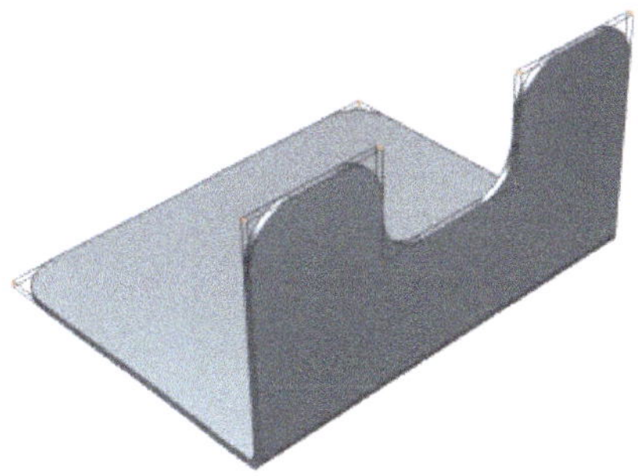

On the **Break Corner** dialog, select **Method > Chamfer** to apply a chamfer to the corner edges. Type-in a value in the **Radius** or **Distance** box. Click **OK** to complete the break corner feature.

Flat Pattern

The **Flat Pattern** command flattens the part so that you can easily display the manufacturing information. Activate the **Flat Pattern** command (click **Flat Pattern > Flat Pattern** on the ribbon) and click on a base sheet. On the **Flat Pattern** dialog, select **Orientation Method** > **Edge** in the **Orientation** section. Select an edge to define the x-axis of the flat pattern. Click **OK** to create the flat pattern.

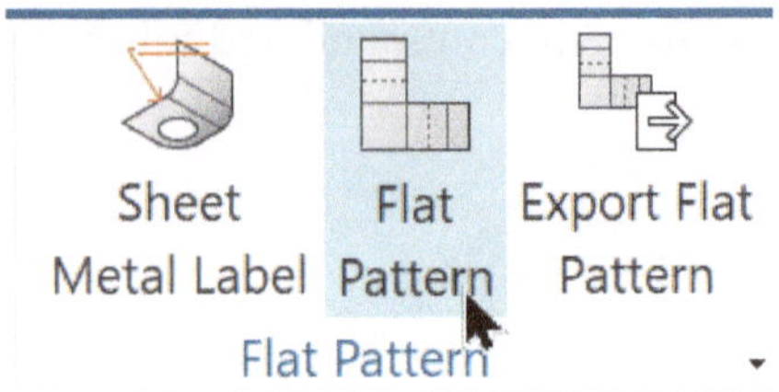

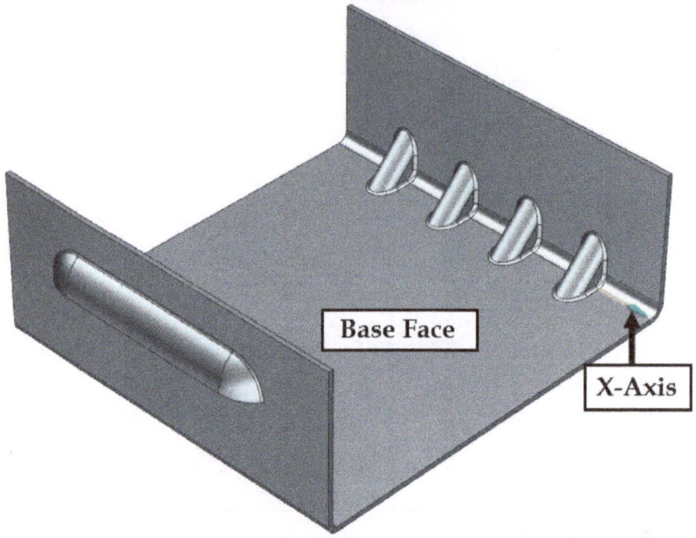

On the Top Border Bar, click **Menu > View > Layout > New** to open the **New Layout** dialog. On this dialog, select **FLAT-PATTERN** and click **OK**. The flat pattern appears. To switch back to the modeling mode, open the **New Layout** dialog, select **Isometric**, and click **OK**.

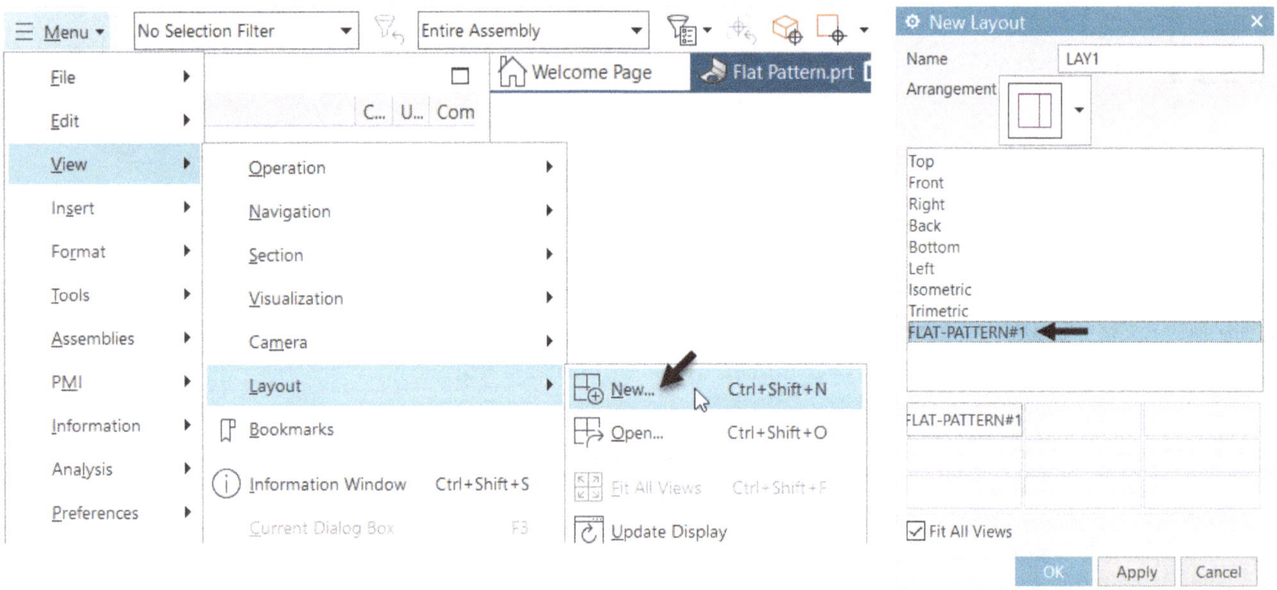

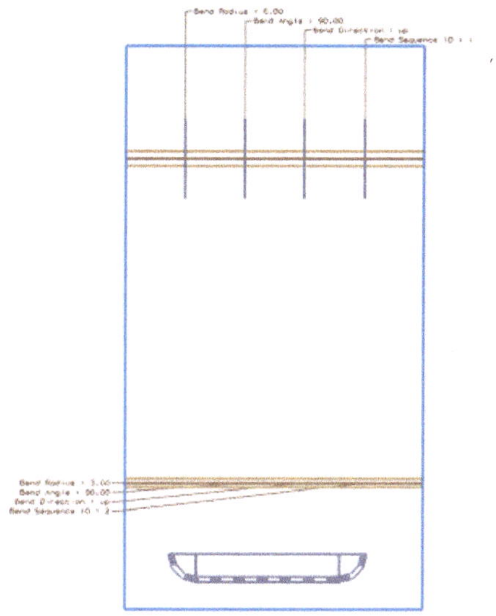

Flat Solid

Besides creating a flat pattern, NX allows you to create a flattened Solid of a sheet metal part. Activate the **Flat Solid** command (On the ribbon, click **Home > Flat Pattern > Flat Solid**) and click on the base face of the sheet metal part. Under the **Orientation** section, select **Orientation Method > Edge** and click on the edge to define the x-axis of the flat solid. Click **OK** to create the flat solid.

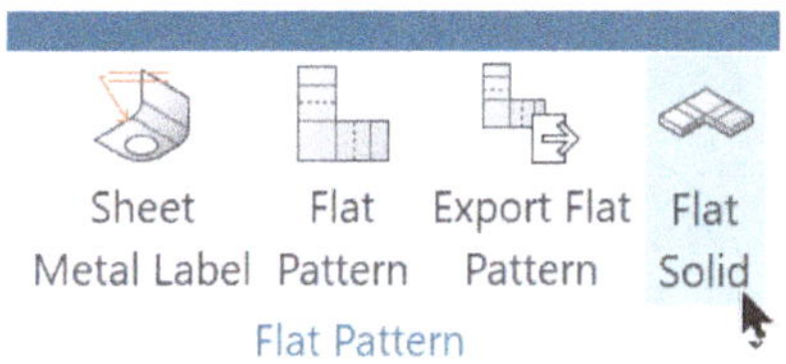

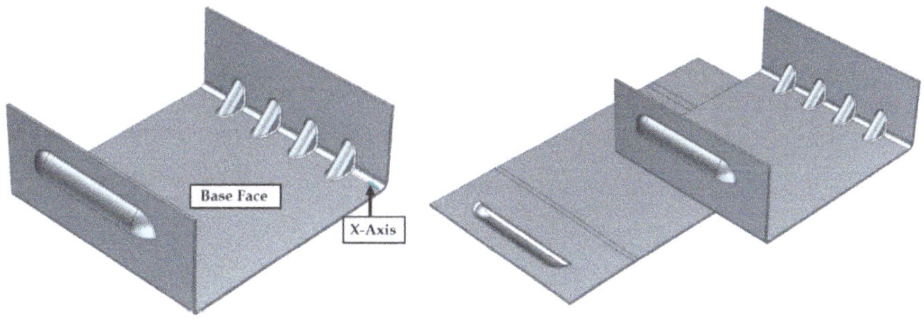

Lofted Flange

The **Lofted Flange** command creates a lofted flange that can be unfolded into a flat pattern. Create two sketches on planes parallel to each other. Ensure that the sketches are not closed. In addition, the openings should be in the same direction.

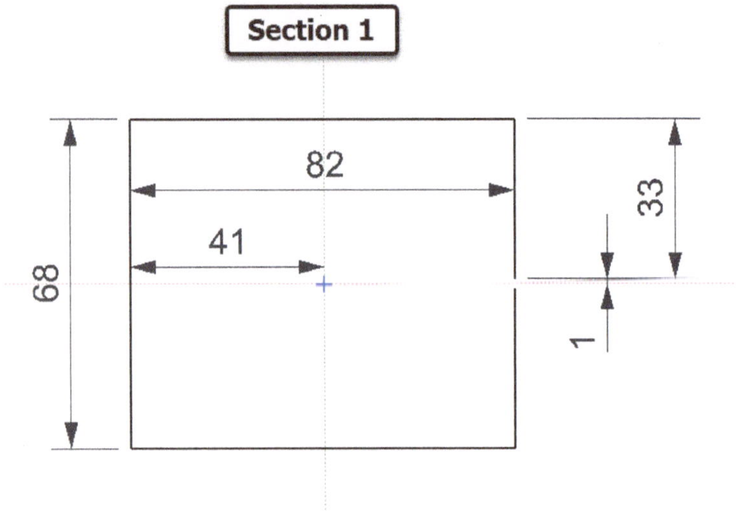

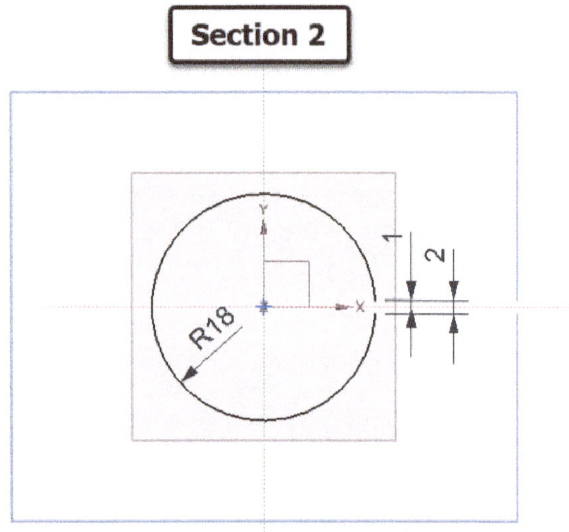

Activate the **Lofted Flange** command (click **Home > Base > Contour Flange** drop-down **> Lofted Flange** on the ribbon) click on the first cross-section. On the **Lofted Flange** dialog, under the **End Section**, click **Select Curve**. Click on the second cross-section.

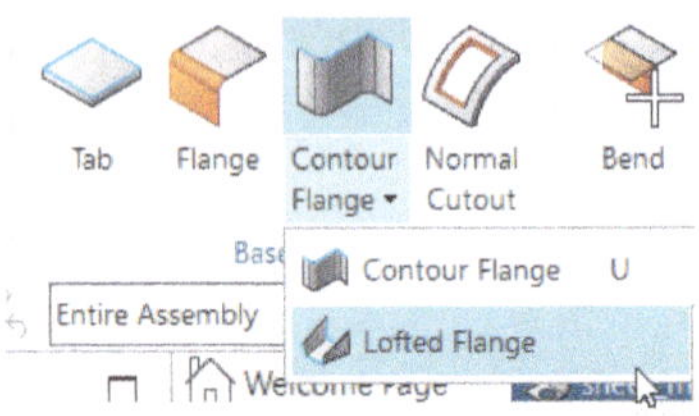

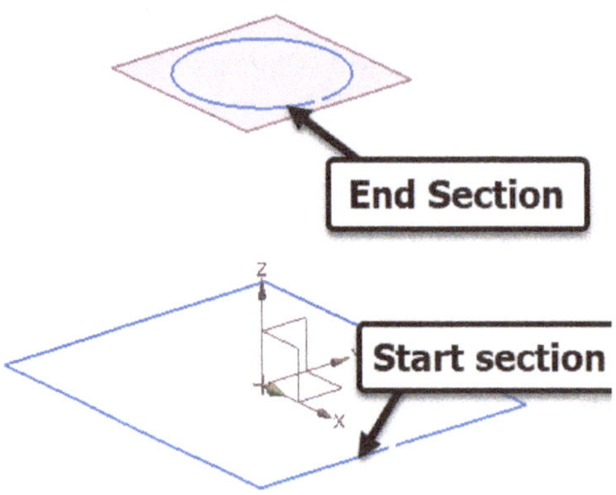

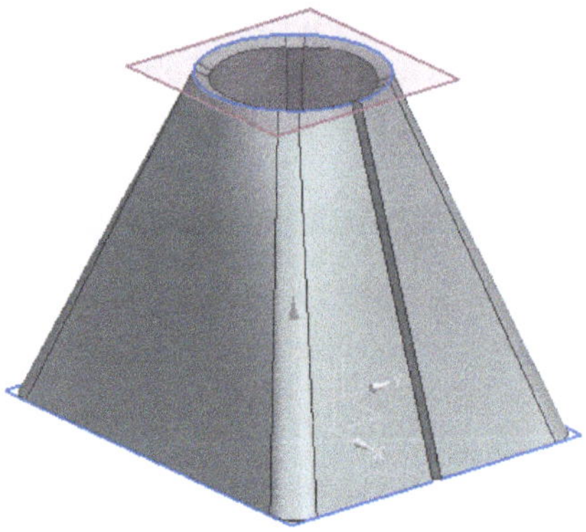

Expand the **Bend Segments** section and select an option from the **Bending Method** drop-down. There are three options available in this drop-down: **Formed**, **Advanced**, and **Bends**. The **Formed** option creates irregular faces that do not conform to the standard geometric shapes of planes, cylinders, or cones. The **Advanced** option creates regular faces that adhere to the standard geometric shapes of planes, cylinders, and cones. They have straightforward and well-defined forms.

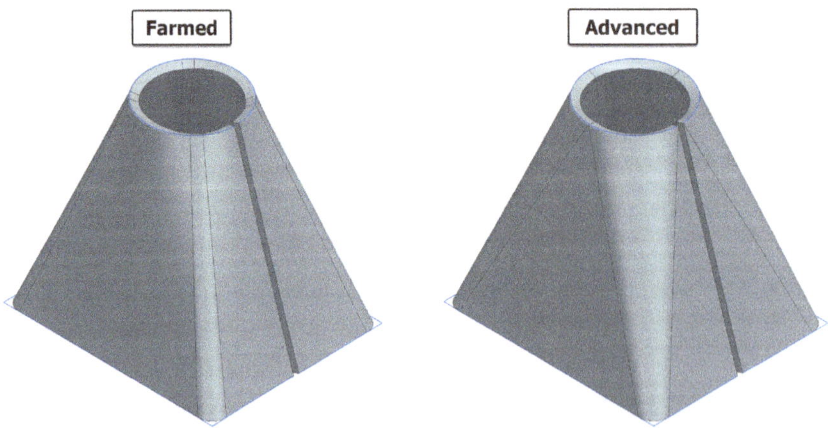

The **Bend** option creates a lofted sheet metal feature in the combination of planar faces and cylindrical bends.

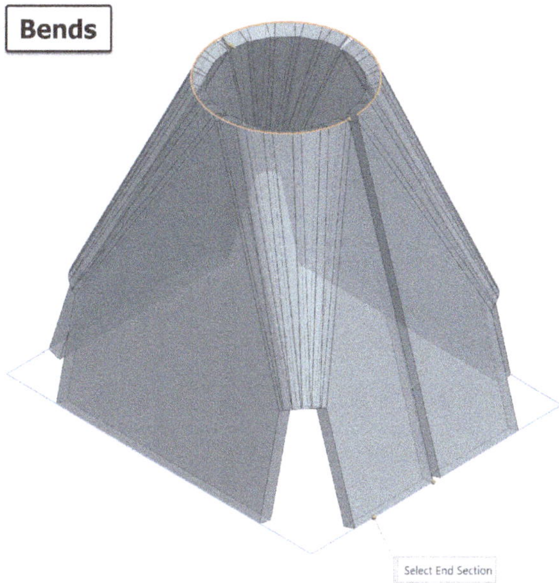

Use the **Divide Parameter** drop-down to specify how each bend region can be subdivided. There are four options in this drop-down: **Bend Segments**, **Chord Height**, **Segment Length**, and **Segment Angle**.

The **Bend Segments** option divides the bend region into a number of segments using the value that enter in the **Number of Bend Segments** box. The following example shows the flat pattern of the lofted sheet metal part with **Number of Bend Segments=12.**

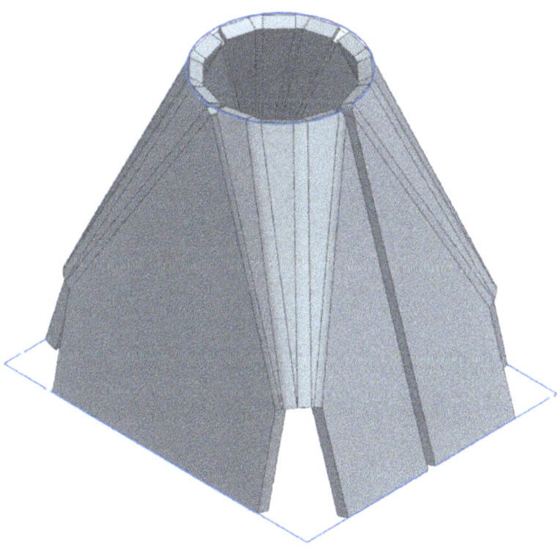

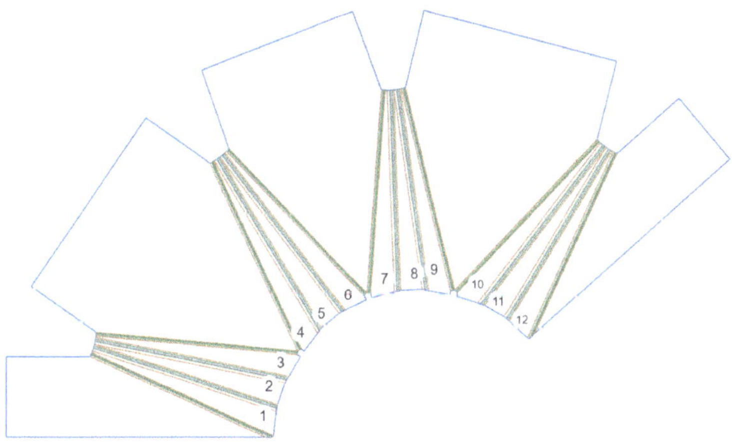

The **Chord Height** option uses the **Maximum Chord Height** value to divide the bend region into segments. The **Maximum Chord Height** is the maximum distance between the planar surface of the bend and the curve.

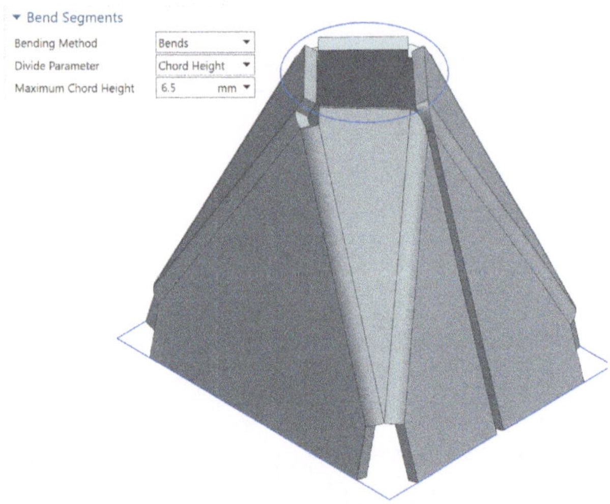

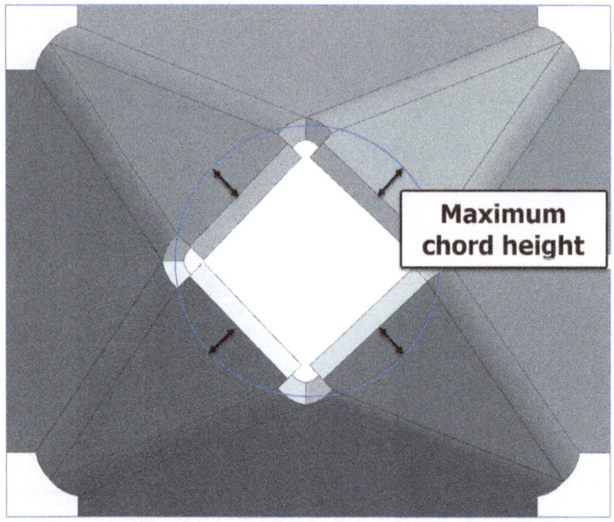

The **Segment Length** option uses the **Maximum Segment Length** value to divide a conical or cylindrical region. The **Maximum Segment Length** is the distance between the two bend segments located next to each other.

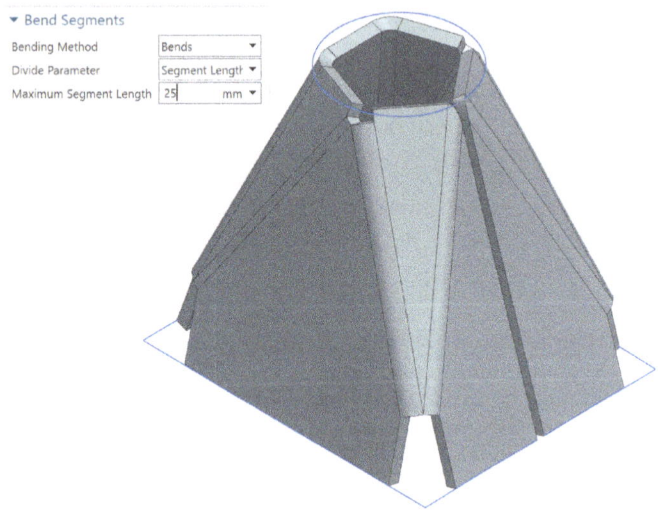

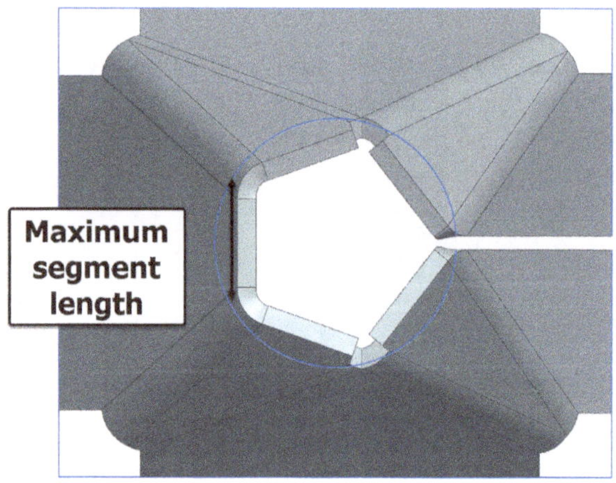

The **Segment Angle** option uses the **Maximum Segment Angle** value to divide a conical or cylindrical region. The **Maximum Segment Angle** is the angle between the two bend segments located next to each other.

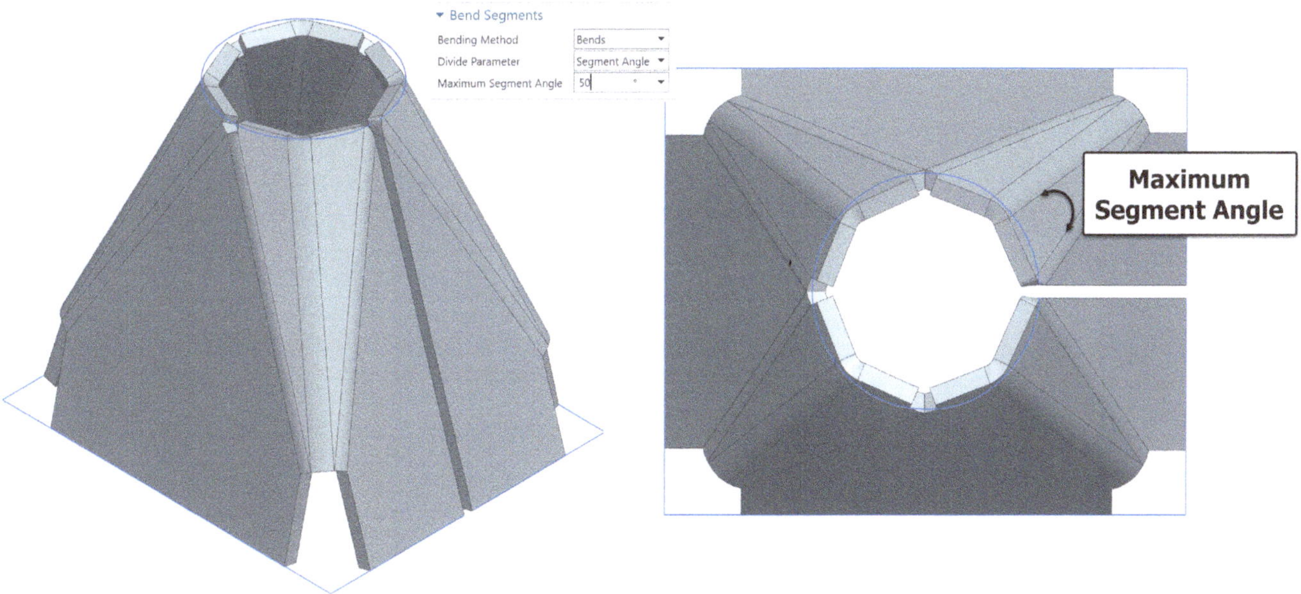

Expand the **Relief** section and select an option from the **Auto Relief** drop-down. The options in this drop-down will add reliefs to multi bend segments so that the resulting model can be flattened with ease. Click **OK** to complete the lofted flange.

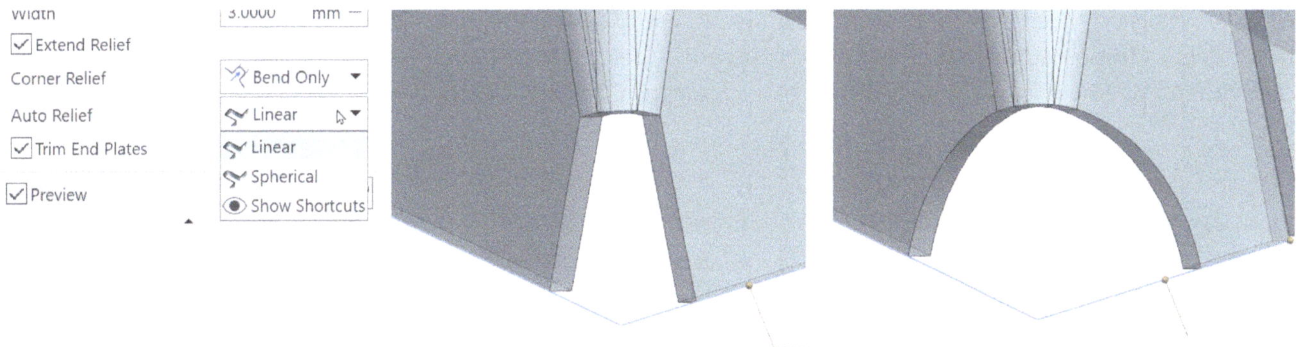

Create the flat pattern of the sheet metal part.

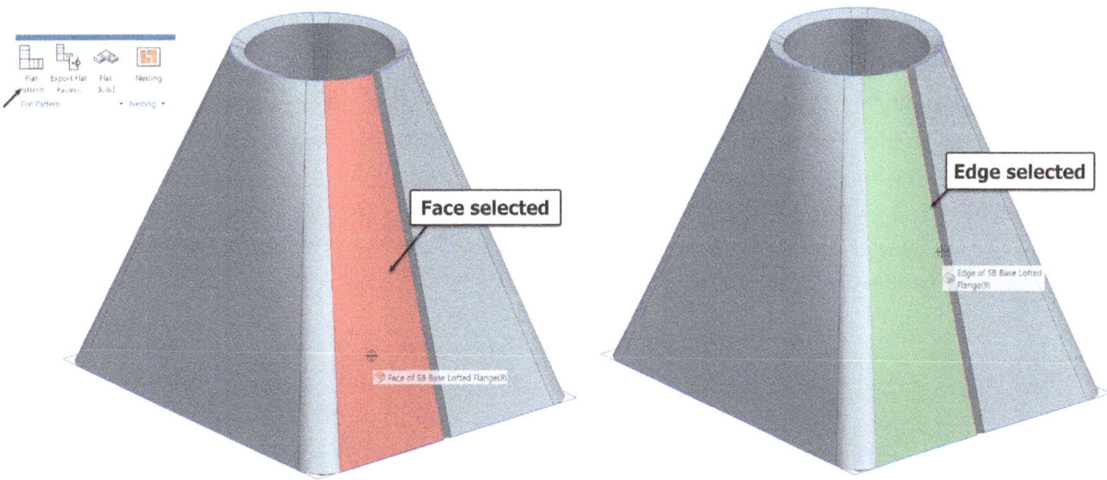

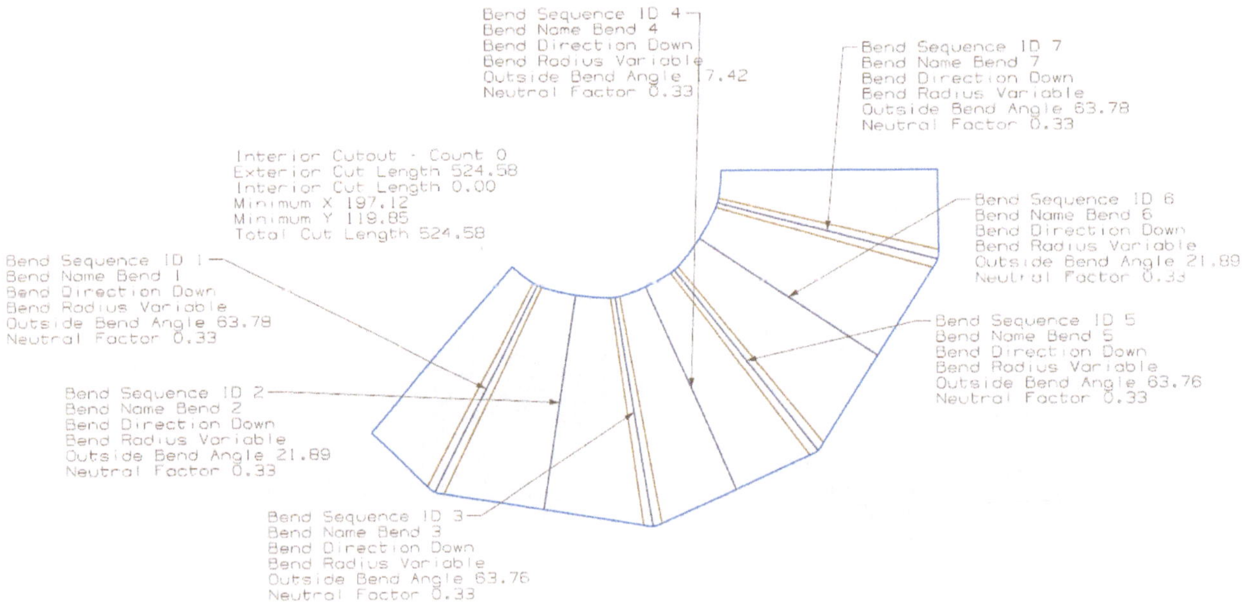

Sheet Metal from Solid

The **Sheet Metal from Solid** command creates a sheet metal part from a set of planar faces of a solid body. First, create a solid body using the **Extrude** command, and then activate the **Sheet Metal from Solid** command (On the ribbon, click **Home > Convert > Sheet Metal from Solid**). Click on the planar faces of the solid body, which connect each other. The **Sheet Metal from Solid** message appears. Click **OK** to preview the sheet metal.

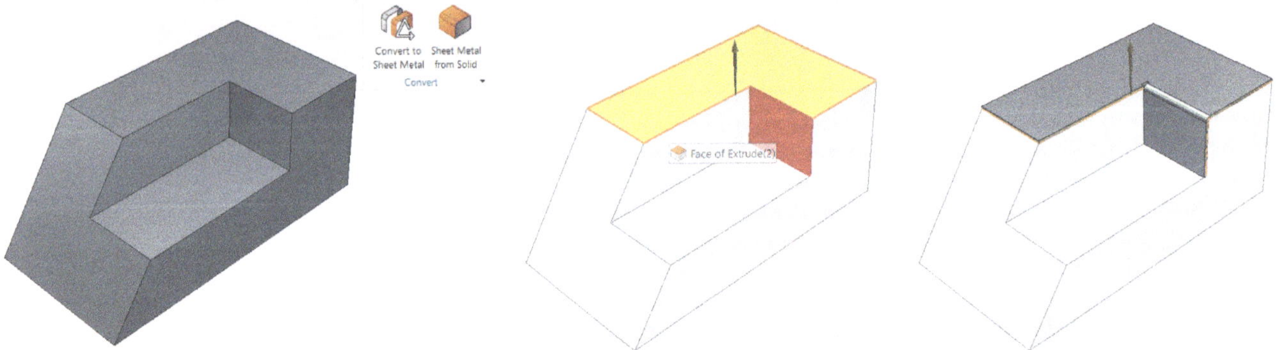

Click on the other faces connected to the previously selected faces. If an **Alert** message appears, then you have to select the bent edge manually. For example, if you click on the right-side face of the solid body, then an alert message appears asking you to select appropriate bend edges. On the **Sheet Metal from Solid** dialog, under the **Parameters** section, click **Select Bend Edge**. Click on the edge connecting the two faces.

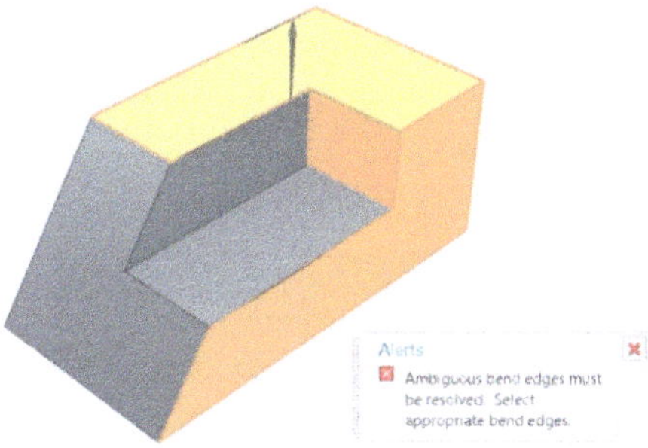

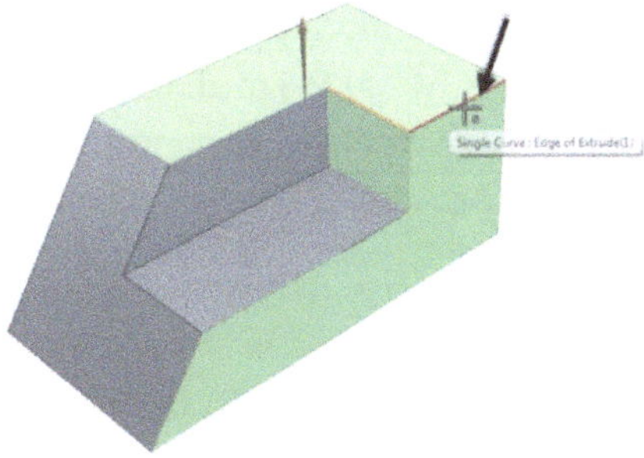

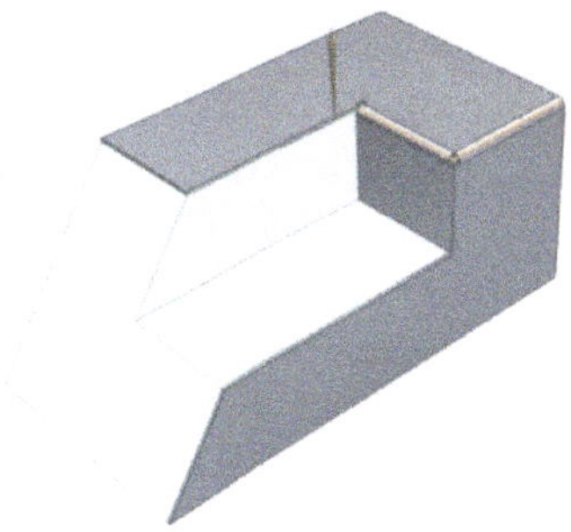

On the dialog, click **Select Web face** and start selecting the other planar faces. If an alert message appears, then select the bend edges manually. Hide the solid body to view the completed sheet metal part.

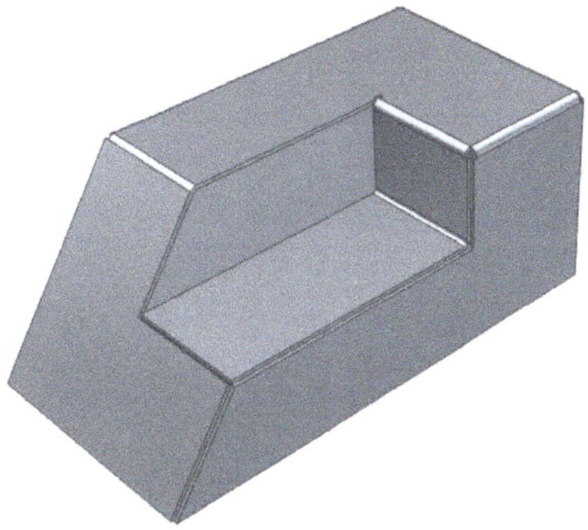

Convert to Sheet Metal Wizard

NX has a special command called **Convert to Sheet Metal Wizard**, which automates the process of converting an already existing part into a sheet metal part. First, create a part in the Modeling environment, and then shell it using the **Shell** command. Next, click **Application > Design > Sheet Metal** on the ribbon.

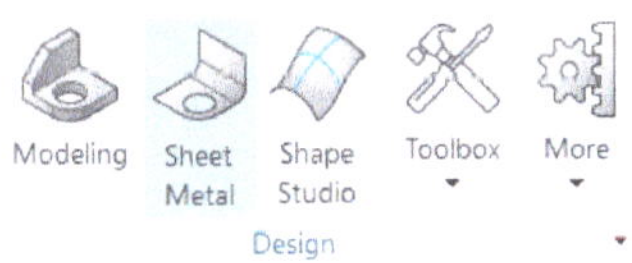

On the ribbon, click the down-arrow located on the **Convert** group and select the **More Gallery** option. On the ribbon, click **Home > Convert > Convert to Sheet Metal Wizard**. Click on the edges to rip off. On the dialog, click the **Next** button and click on the horizontal face. Click **Next**. Expand the **Relief** section and define the **Bend Relief**. Click **Finish** to complete the conversion process.

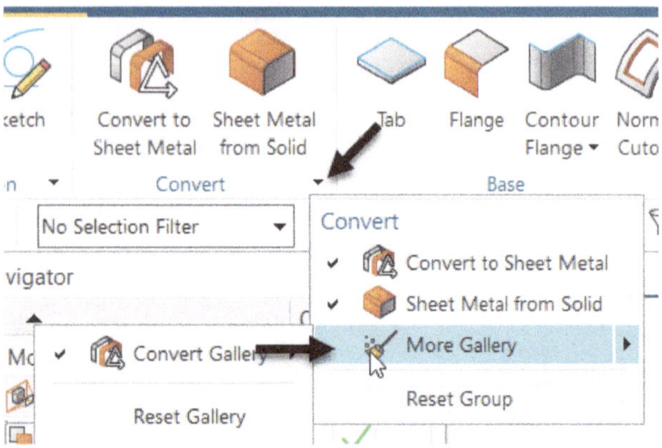

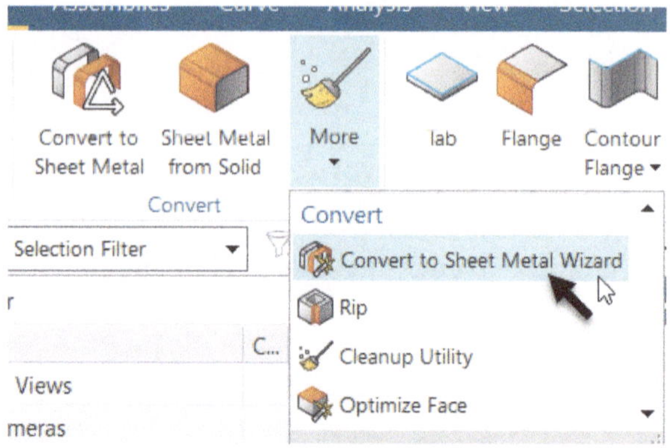

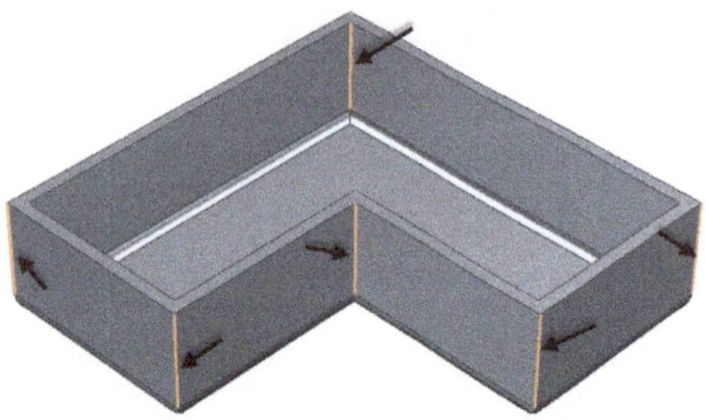

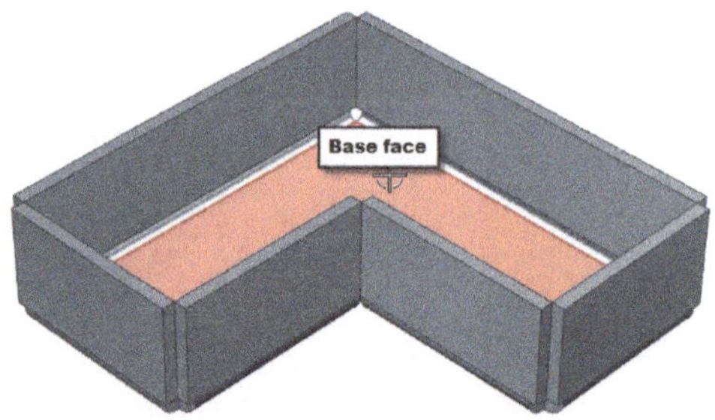

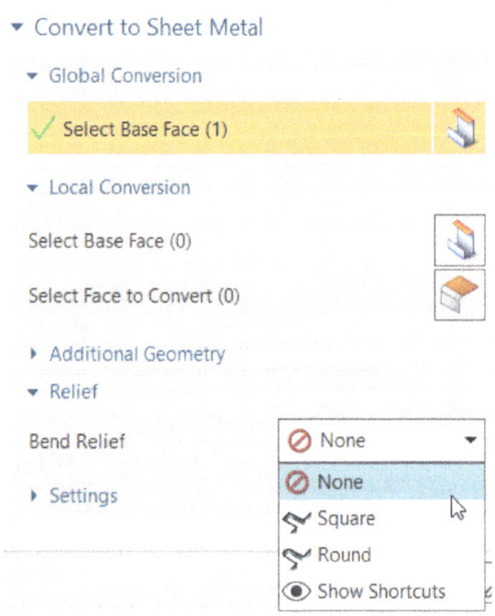

Resize Bend Radius

The **Resize Bend Radius** command changes the radius of a bend. Activate this command (On the Top Border Bar, click **Menu** > **Insert > Resize > Resize Bend Radius**). On the **Resize Bend Radius** dialog, from the **Type** drop-down menu, select **Fixed Tab/Flange Position**. Click on a bend face and type-in a value in the **Bend Radius** box. If you select **Type > Fixed Unfolded Length**, then you must select a stationary face.

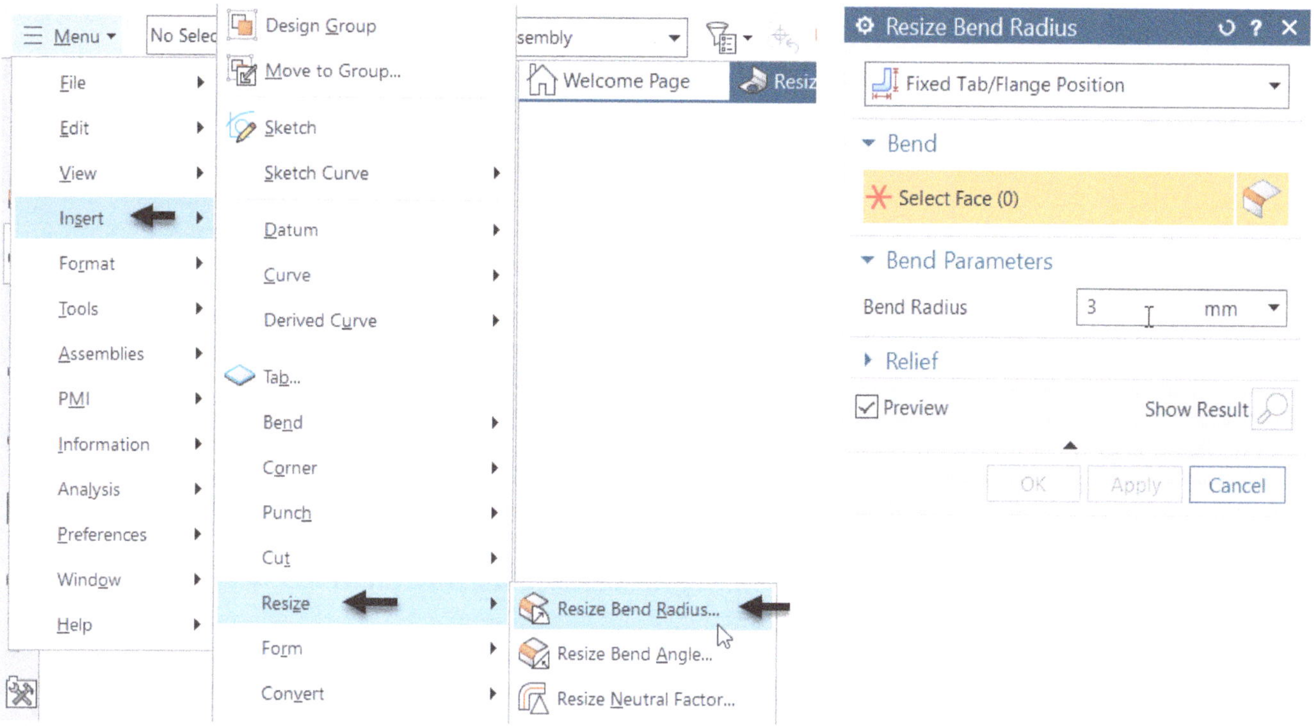

Resize Bend Angle

The **Resize Bend Angle** command changes the angle of a bend. Activate this command (On the Top Border Bar, click **Menu** > **Insert > Resize > Resize Bend Angle**) and click on the face to remain stationary. Click on the bend face and type-in a new value in the **Angle** box. Check the **Keep Radius Fixed** option, if you do not want to change the bend radius value with the angle. Click **OK** to complete resizing the bend angle.

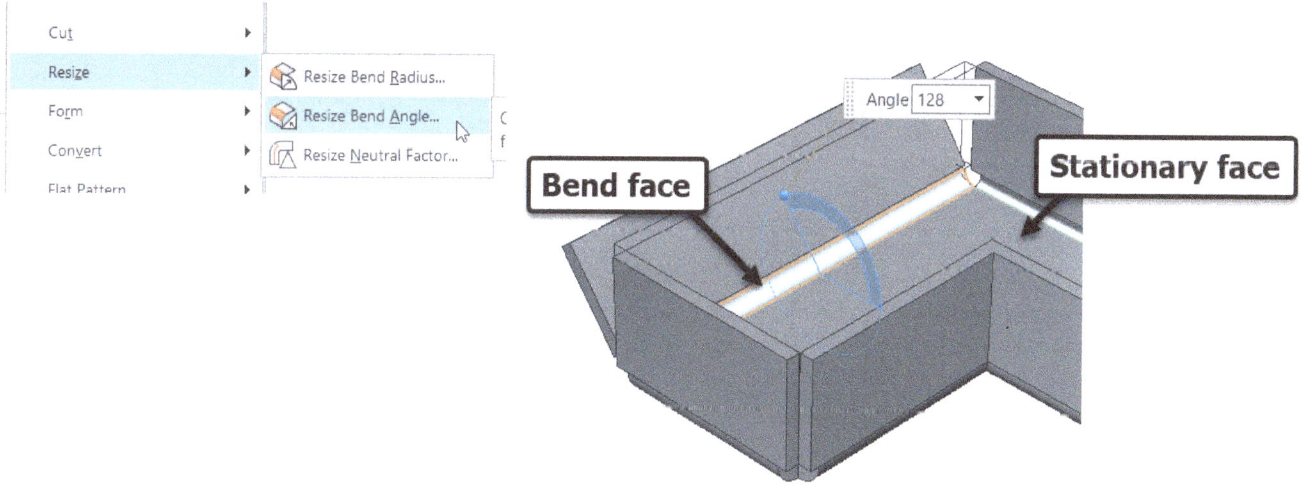

Resize Neutral Factor

The **Resize Neutral Factor** command changes the Neutral factor value of a sheet metal part. The neutral Factor defines the bend allowance of a sheet metal part. Activate this command (On the Top Border Bar, click **Menu** > **Insert > Resize > Resize Neutral Factor**) and click on a bent face. Click the **Launch the formula editor** = icon next to the **Neutral Factor** box, and then select **Use Local Value**. Type-in a value in the **Neutral Factor** box and click **OK**.

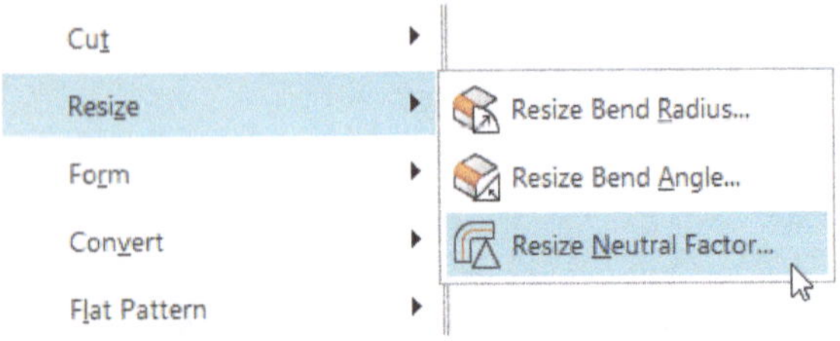

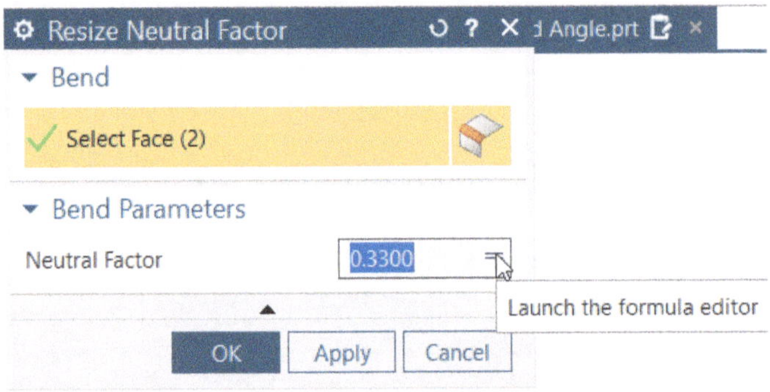

Sheet Metal Drawings

Creating drawings of a sheet metal part is the same as creating any other drawing. However, there are some options specific to the sheet metal flat pattern. You can access these settings under the **Flat Pattern View** section of the **Drafting Preferences** dialog. To do this, open Drawing file and click **File** tab > **Preferences > Drafting** to open the **Drafting Preferences** dialog.

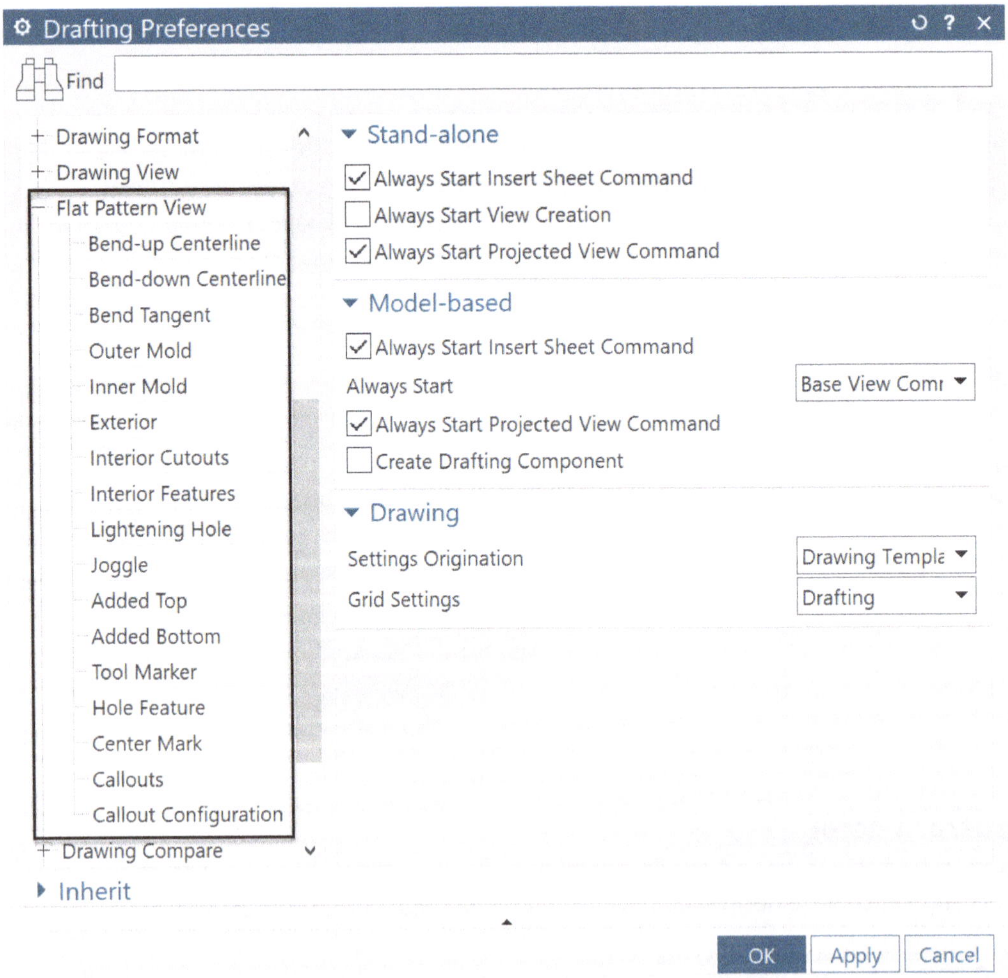

To insert a flat pattern view into the drawing, activate the **Base View** command (on the ribbon, click **Home > View > Base View**) and select the sheet metal part. On the **Base View** dialog, under the **Model View** section, select **Model View to Use > FLAT-PATTERN#1**. On the dialog, set the **Scale** value and click to place the view. You will notice that lines represent the bends.

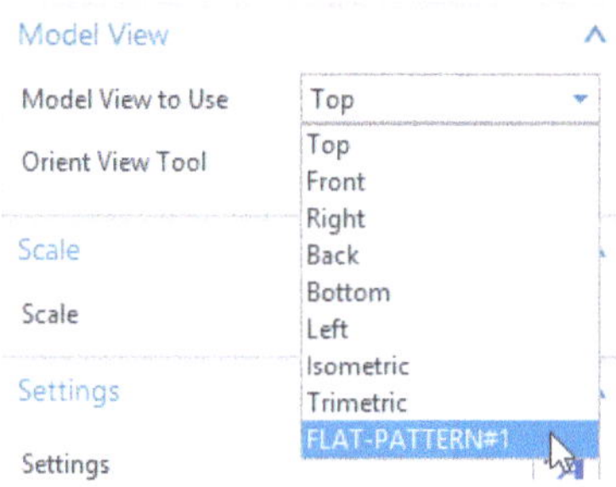

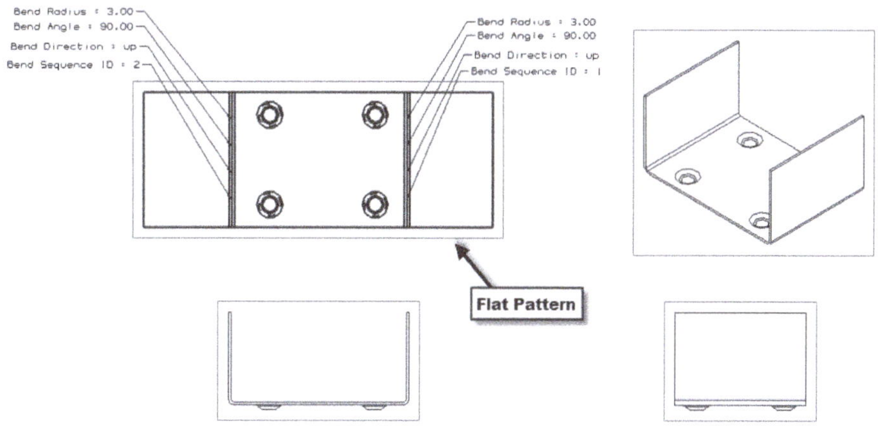

To add a bend table, click **Home > Table > Bend Table** on the ribbon, and then click on the flat pattern view. Click on the sheet to position the bend table.

2	Bend 2	3.00	90.00	up	90.00
1	Bend 1	3.00	90.00	up	90.00
ID	Name	Radius	Angle	Direction	Included Angle

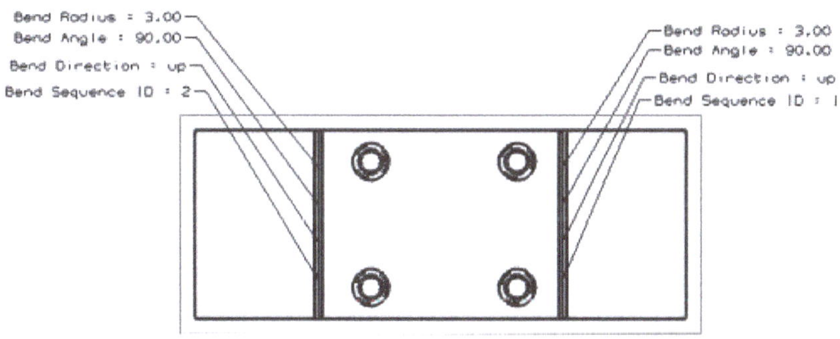

Export Flat Pattern

In addition to creating drawings, you can directly export a sheet metal to DXF or Trumpf GEO formats. All you have to do is click **Flat Pattern > Export Flat Pattern**. On the **Export Flat Pattern** dialog, select **Type > DXF** and specify the output file location. Under the **Flat Pattern Geometry Types** section, check the geometry types to export. Under the **Settings** section, select the **DXF Revision** type.

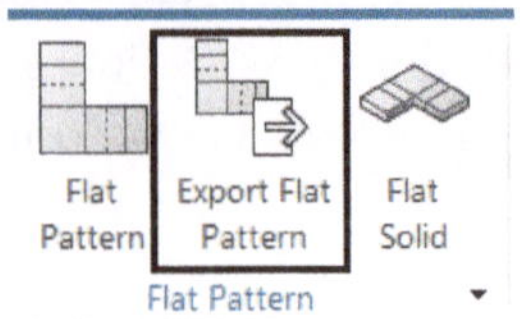

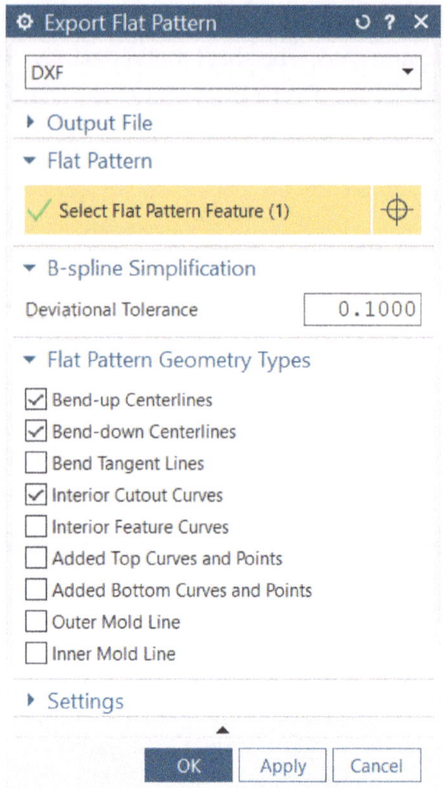

Under **Part Navigator**, click on the **Flat Pattern** feature to export, and then click **OK**.

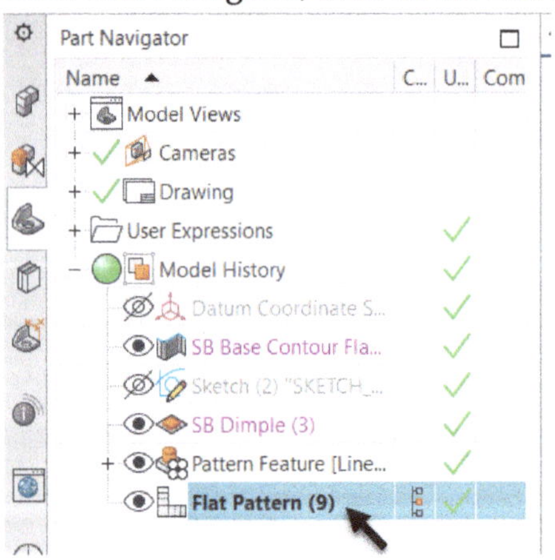

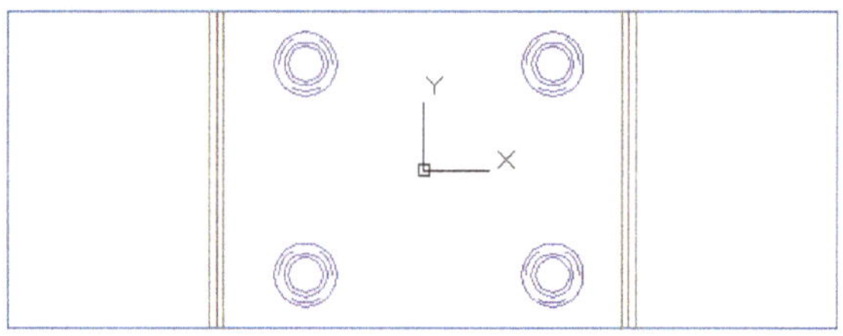

Examples

Example 1

In this example, you will construct the sheet metal part shown below.

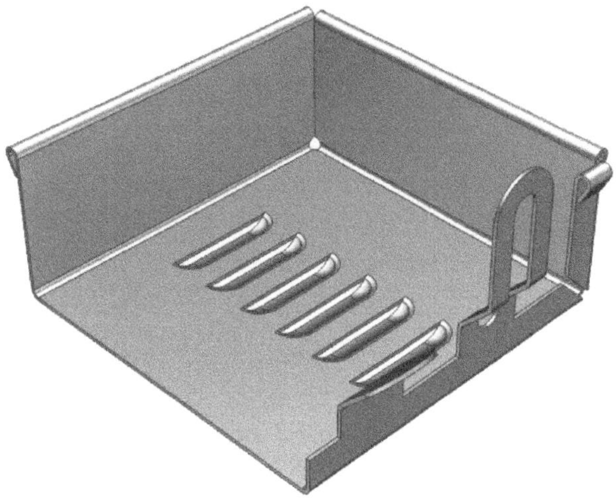

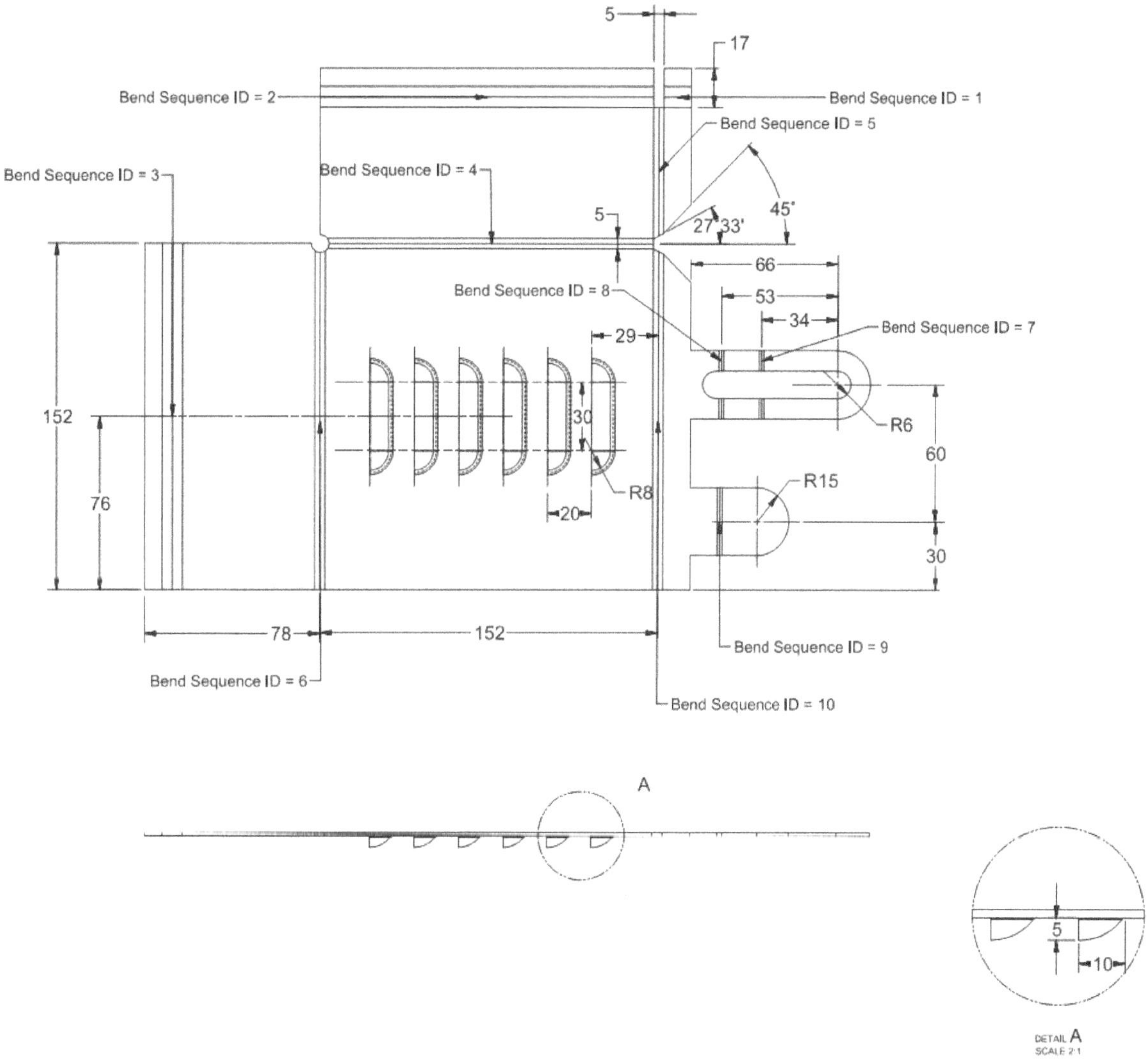
5
17
Bend Sequence ID = 2
Bend Sequence ID = 1
Bend Sequence ID = 5
Bend Sequence ID = 3
Bend Sequence ID = 4
5
45°
27°33'
66
53
34
Bend Sequence ID = 8
Bend Sequence ID = 7
29
R6
152
30
60
76
R8
R15
20
30
78
152
Bend Sequence ID = 9
Bend Sequence ID = 6
Bend Sequence ID = 10
A
5
10
DETAIL A
SCALE 2:1

10	Bend 10	2.40	90.00	up	90.00
9	Bend 9	2.40	45.00	down	135.00
8	Bend 8	2.40	45.00	down	135.00
7	Bend 7	2.40	45.00	up	135.00
6	Bend 6	2.40	90.00	up	90.00
5	Bend 5	2.40	90.00	up	90.00
4	Bend 4	2.40	90.00	up	90.00
3	Bend 3	2.00	208.05	down	-28.05
2	Bend 2	2.00	208.05	down	-28.05
1	Bend 1	2.00	208.05	down	-28.05
ID	Name	Radius	Angle	Direction	Included Angle

1. Start **NX**.
2. On the ribbon, click the **New** button to open the **New** dialog.
3. On the **New** dialog, select **Units > Millimeters** and click **Sheet Metal**. Click **OK**.
4. On the **Top Border Bar**, click **Menu > Preferences > Sheet Metal**.
5. On the **Sheet Metal Preferences** dialog, under **Part Properties**, select **Parameter Entry > Type > Material Selection**. Click **Select Material**.
6. On the **Select Material** dialog, select **Aluminiun_6061** from the **Available Materials** section and click **OK**.
7. On the **Sheet Metal Preferences** dialog, under the **Parameter Entry** section, select **Type > Value Entry**.
8. On the **Sheet Metal Preferences** dialog, type-in **2.4** in the **Relief Depth** and **Relief Width** boxes. Click **OK**.
9. On the ribbon, click **Home > Base > Tab** and click on the XY plane.
10. Create a sketch and click **Finish** on the ribbon. On the **Tab** dialog, click **OK** to create the tab feature.

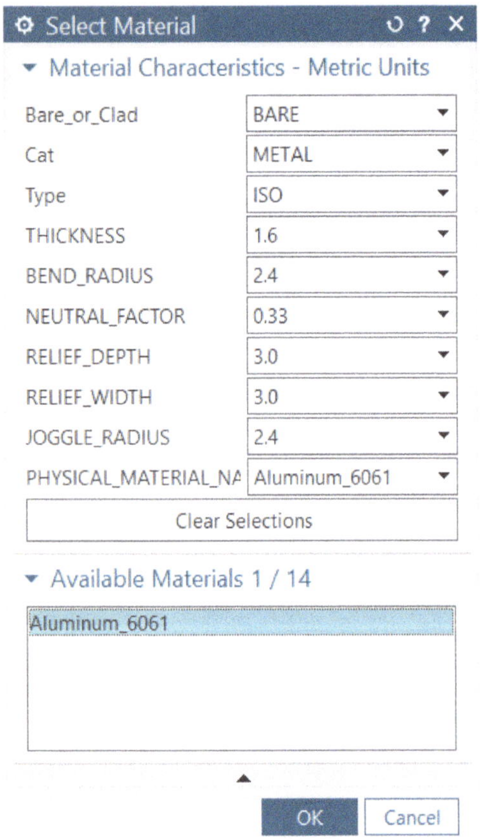

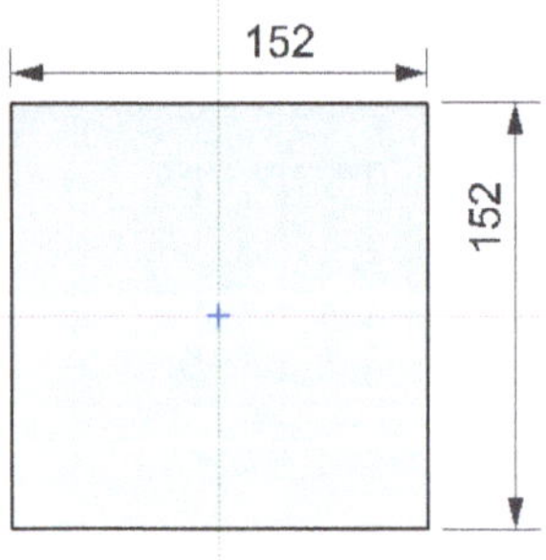

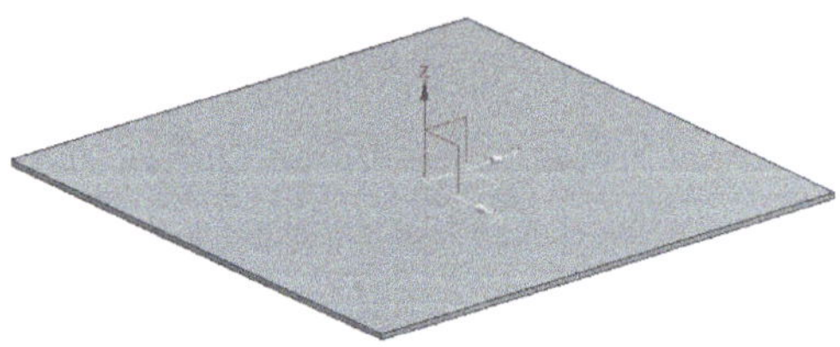

11. On the ribbon, click **Home > Base > Flange** 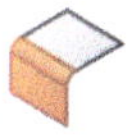 and click on the back edge.
12. On the **Flange** dialog, under **Flange Properties**, select **Length Reference > Outside**. Select **Inset > Material Outside**.
13. Type-in **65** in the **Length** box. Click **OK** to create the flange.

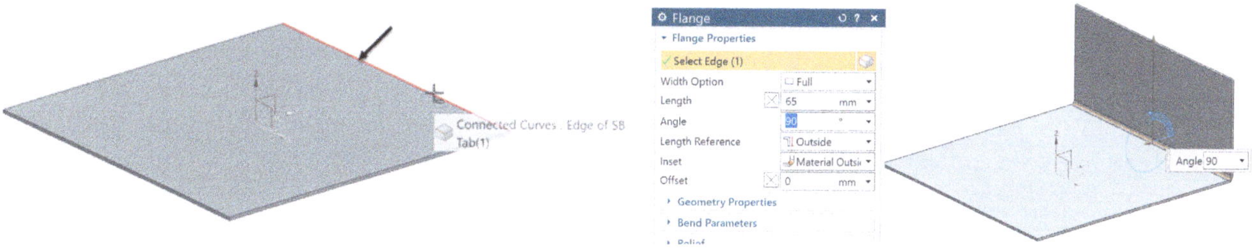

14. Create another flange on the left side. The flange length is 65 mm.

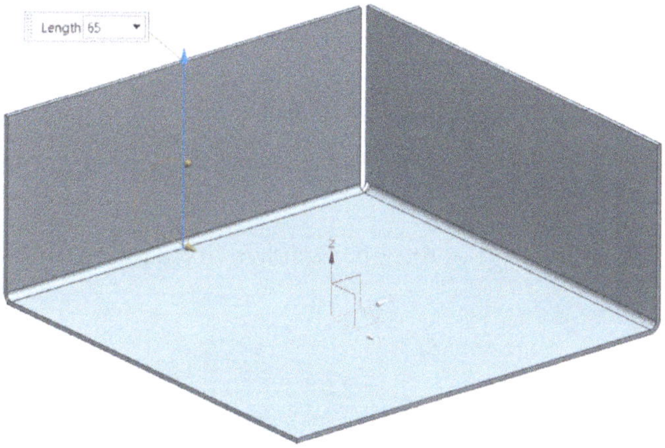

15. On the ribbon, click **Home > Base > Contour Flange**.
16. On the **Contour Flange** dialog, select **Section > Sketch Section** and click on the right edge of the tab feature.

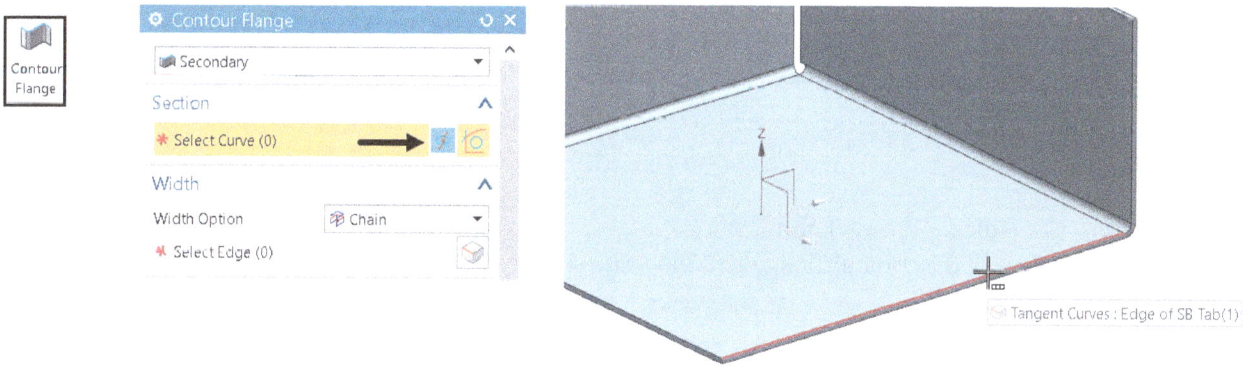

17. In the %**Arc Length** box, type-in **0** and click **OK**.
18. Draw a line of **15** mm length and click **Finish** on the ribbon.

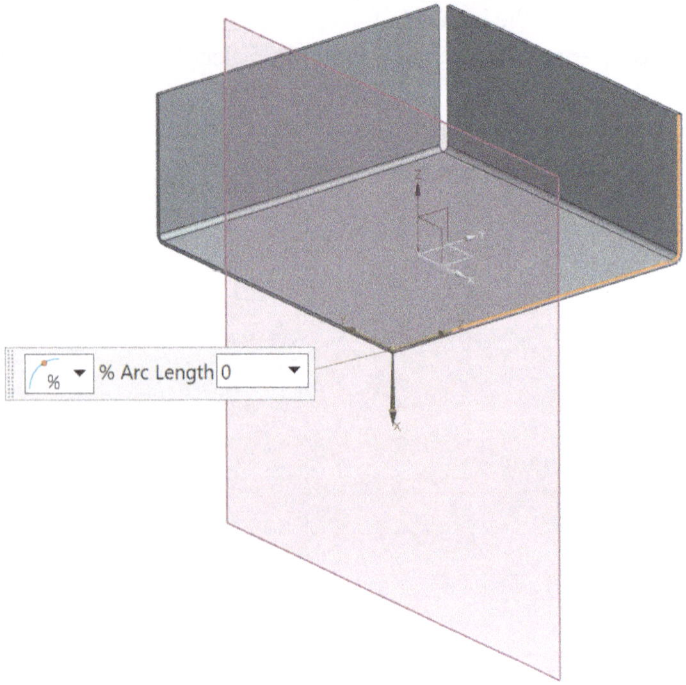

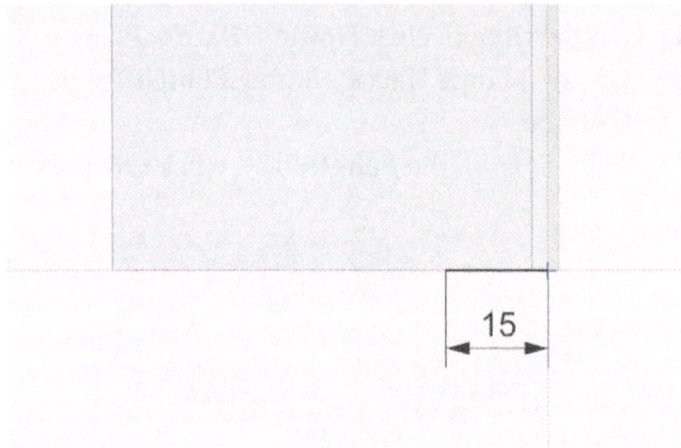

19. On the **Contour Flange** dialog, select **Width Option > Chain**.
20. Click **Select Edge** from the **Width** section and click on the edge of the tab, as shown in the figure. Click **OK** to complete the flange.

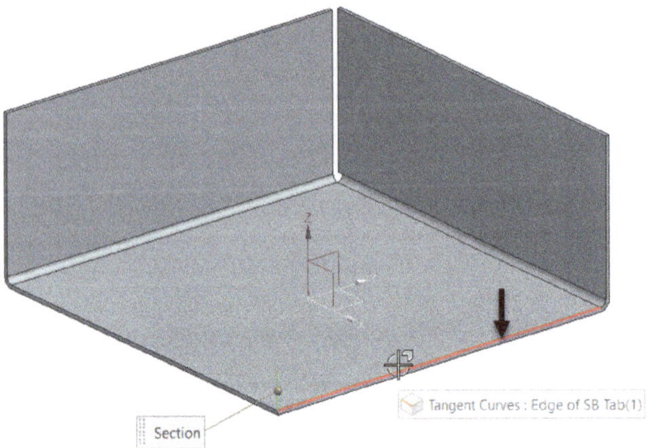

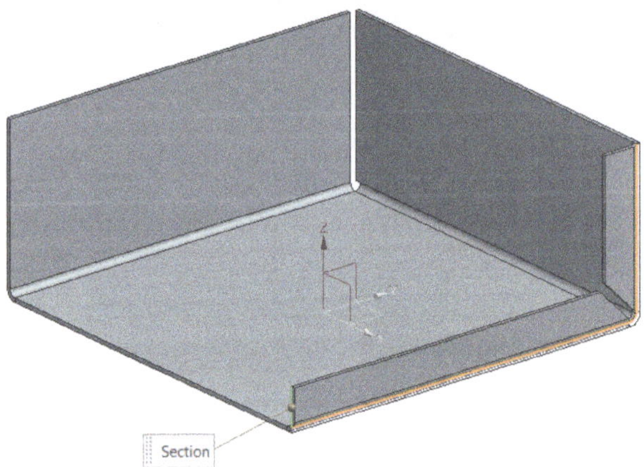

21. On the ribbon, click **Home > Base > Tab.**
22. Click on the outer face of the contour flange and draw the sketch shown below.
23. Click **Finish** on the ribbon.

24. On the **Tab** dialog, select **Type > Secondary** , and then click **OK** to create a tab feature.

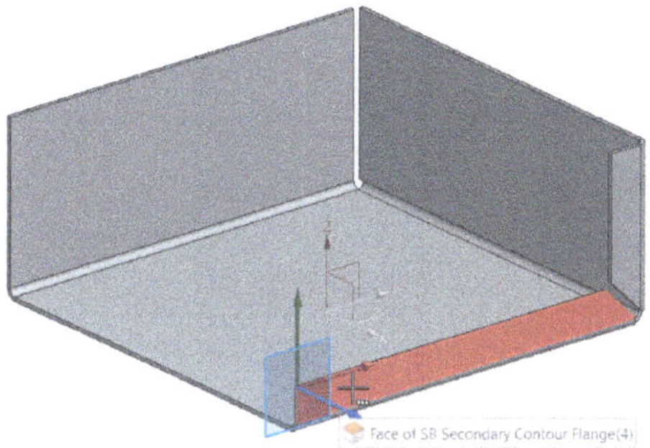
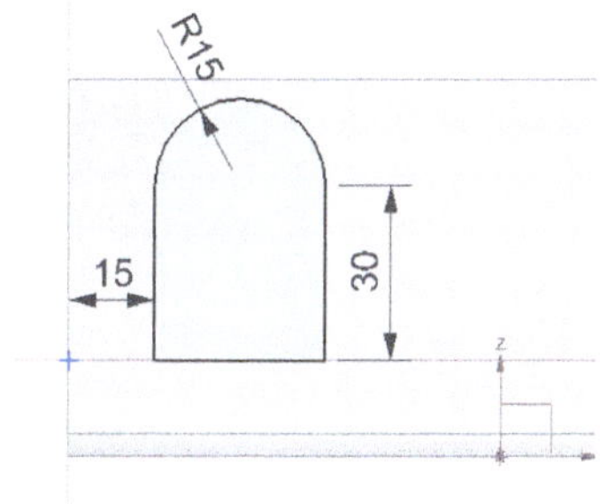

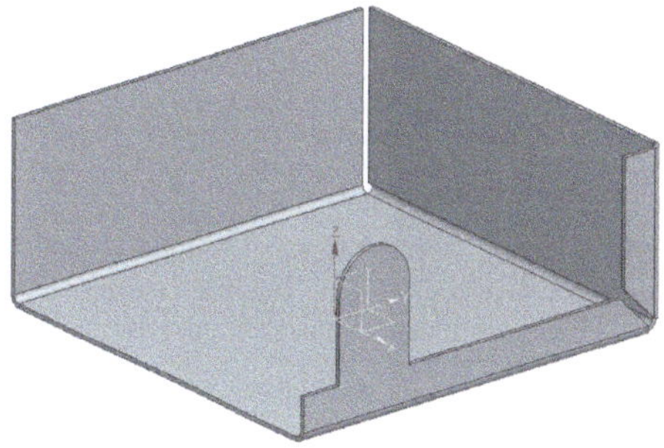

25. Activate the **Sketch** command, and then select **Sketch Type > On Plane** . Next, click on the outer face of the newly created tab, and then click **OK**.
26. Draw a horizontal line at 12 mm distance from the top edge of the contour flange. Next, click **Finish** on the ribbon.
27. Activate the **Bend** command (On the ribbon, click **Home > Bend > More > Bend**) and click on the line.
28. On the **Bend** dialog, type-in **45** in the **Angle** box.
29. Use the **Reverse Side** button to make sure that the output matches that shown below. Next, click **OK** to bend the tab feature.

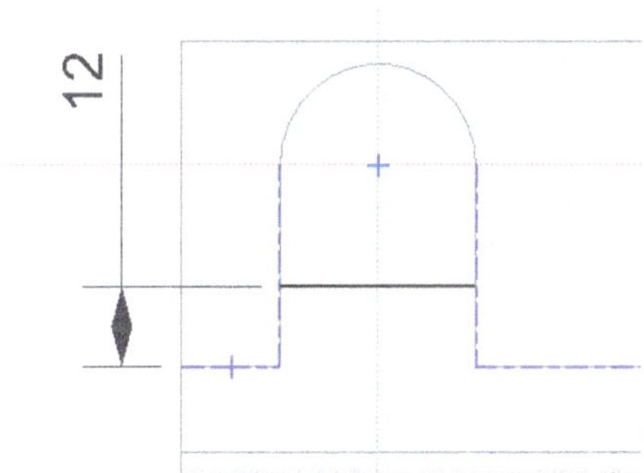

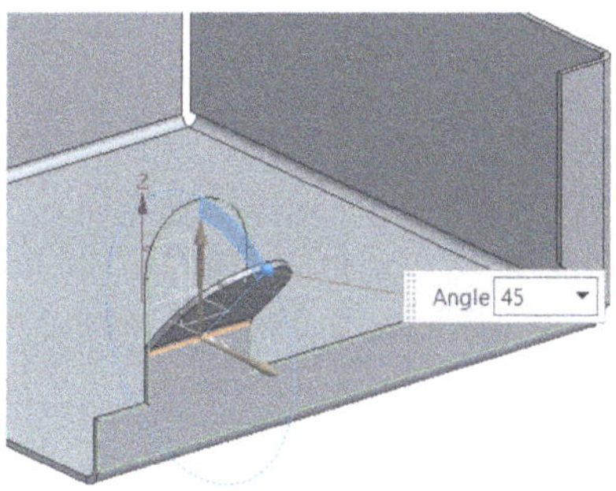

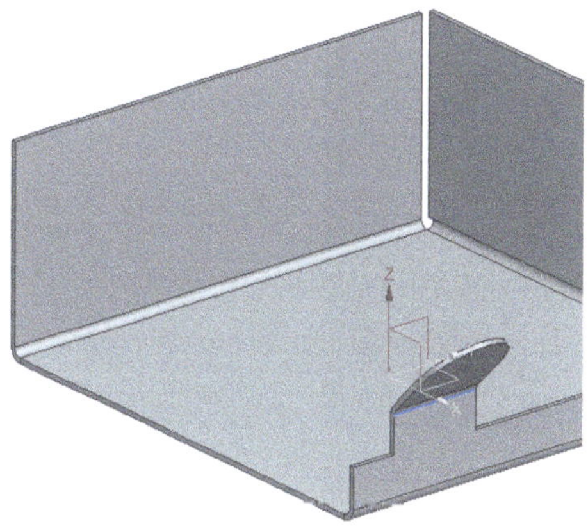

30. Draw another sketch on the outer face of the contour flange.
31. Activate the **Tab** command and create a tab feature using the sketch.

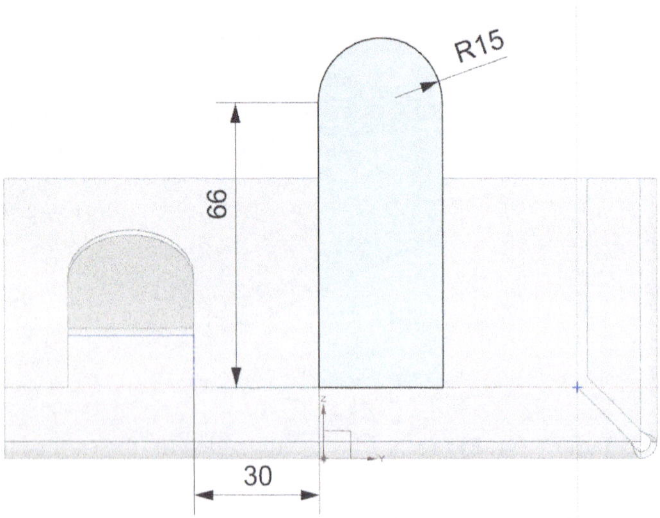

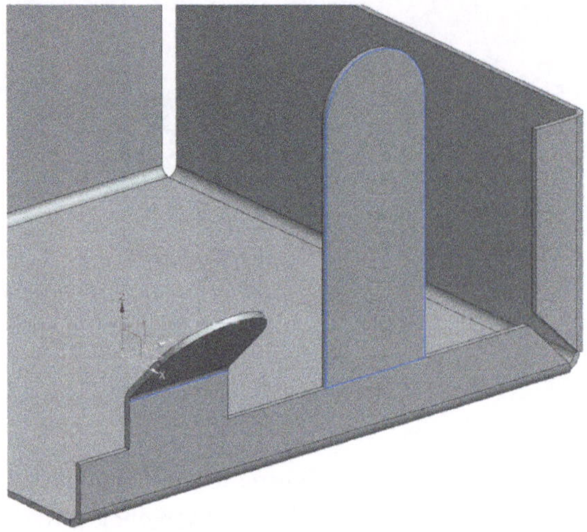

32. Draw a line on the outer face of the tab feature. Next, add a 15mm dimension between the line and the top edge of the contour flange feature. Click **Finish** to exit the sketch.
33. On the ribbon, click the **Group Options** (down-arrow) located on the **Bend** panel.
34. Select the **More Gallery** option.
35. Activate the **Jog** command (click **Home > Bend > More > Jog** on the ribbon) and click on the sketched line.

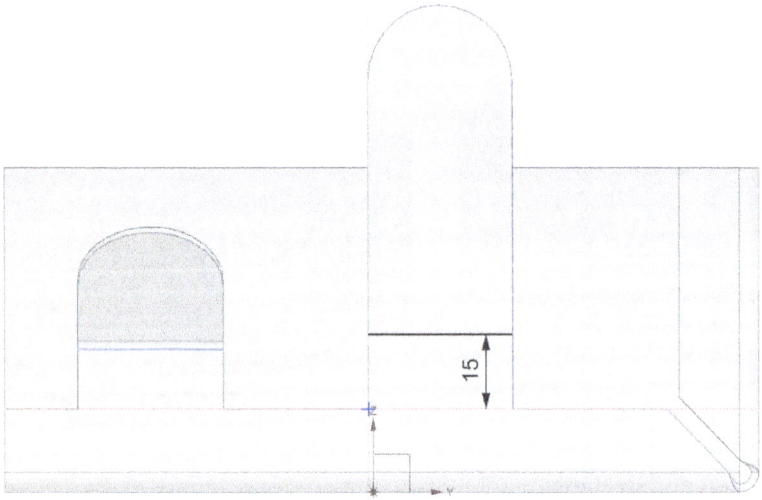

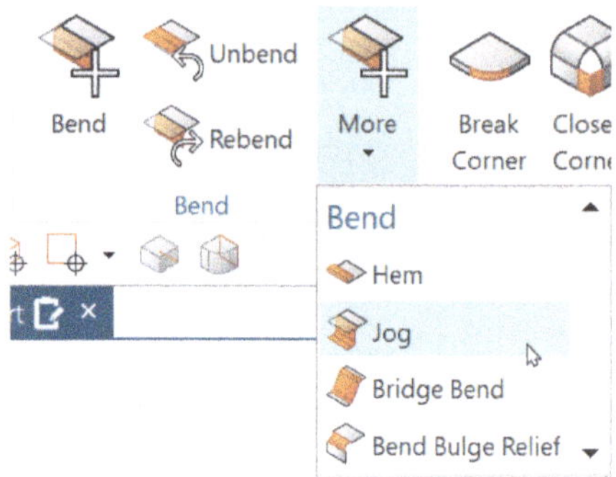

36. On the **Jog** dialog, select **Height Reference > Outside** and **Inset > Material Outside**.
37. Use the **Reverse Side** button to make sure that the output matches that shown below.
38. Make sure that the **Extend Section** option is selected.
39. Type-in **10** and **45** in the **Height** and **Angle** boxes and click **OK** to add jog to the tab feature.

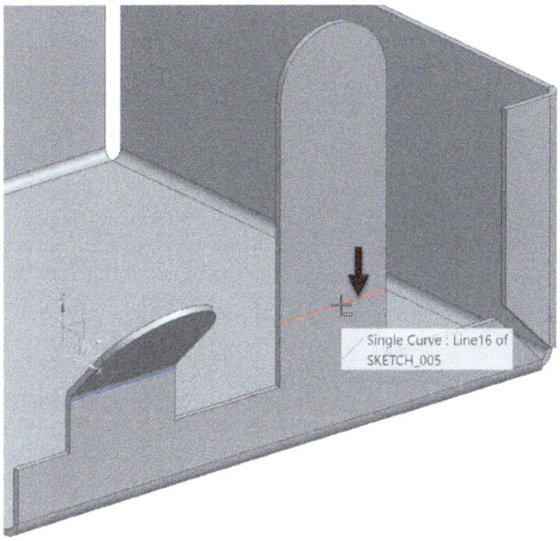

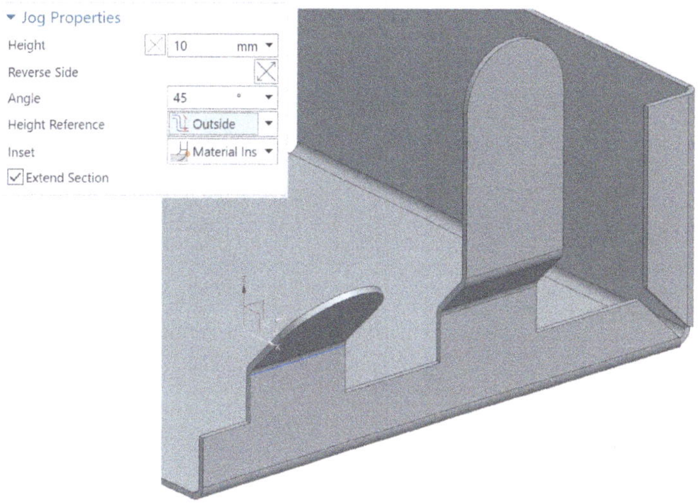

40. On the ribbon, click **Home > Bend > Unbend**.
41. Click on the outer face of the contour flange feature to define the stationary face.
42. Click on the lower bend of the jog feature. Click **Apply** to unbend the jog.

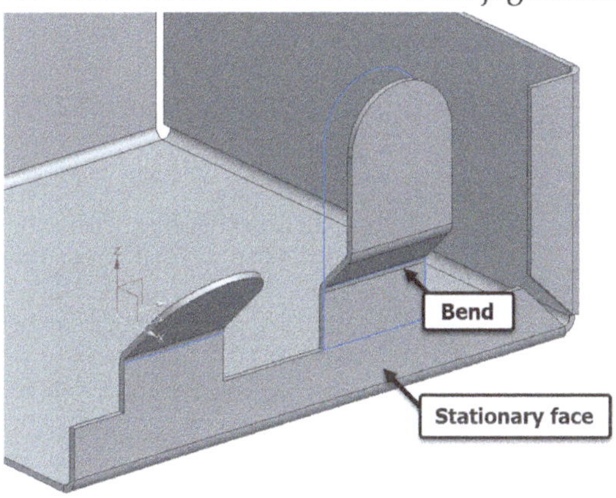

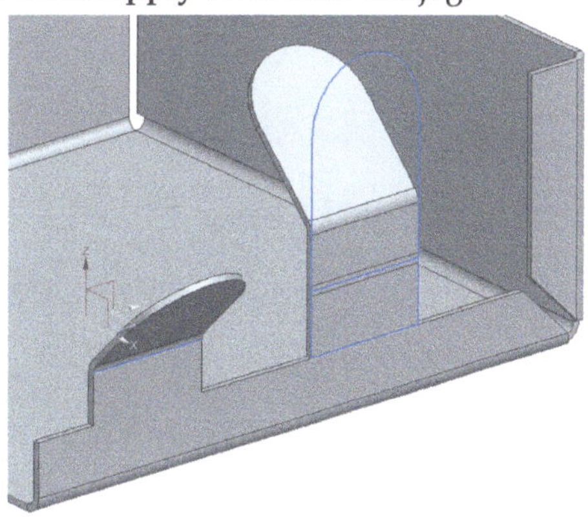

43. Click on the face located between two bends of the jog to define the stationary face.
44. Click on the upper bend and click **OK**.

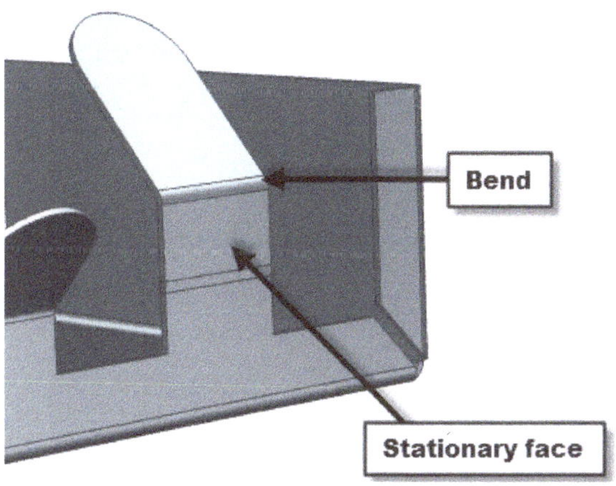

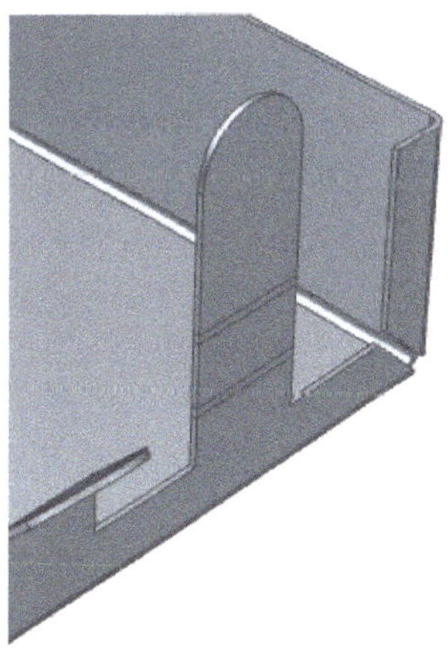

45. On ribbon, click **Home > Base > Normal Cutout**.
46. Click on the outer face of the unbent jog feature. Create the sketch and click **Finish** on the ribbon.

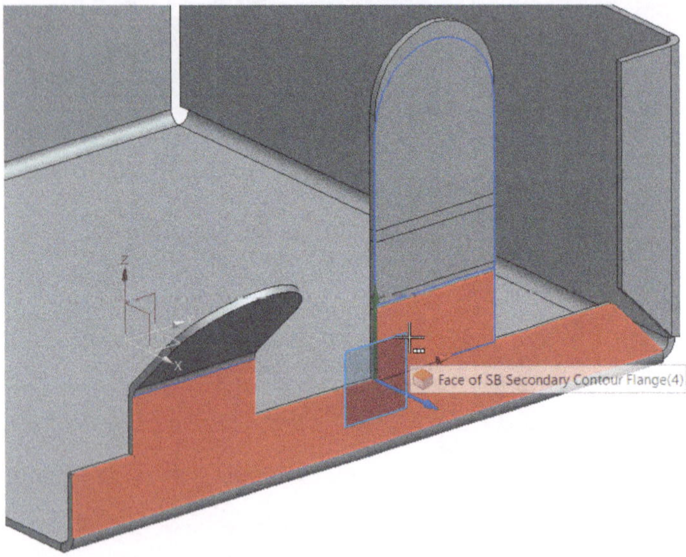

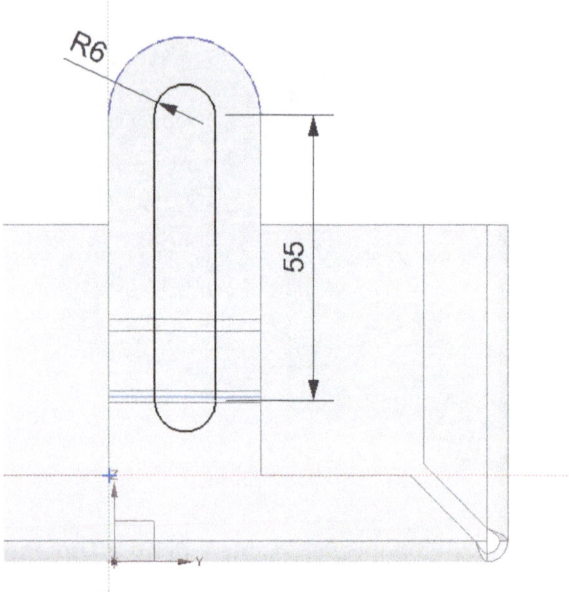

47. On the **Normal Cutout** dialog, select **Limits > Until Next**. Select **Cut Method > Thickness**, and then click **OK** to complete the normal cutout feature.

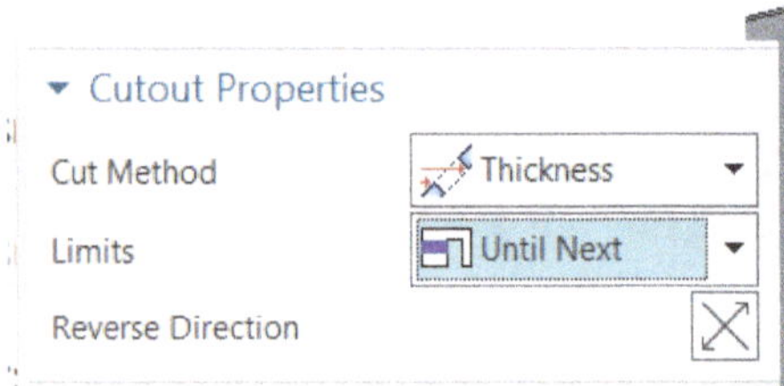

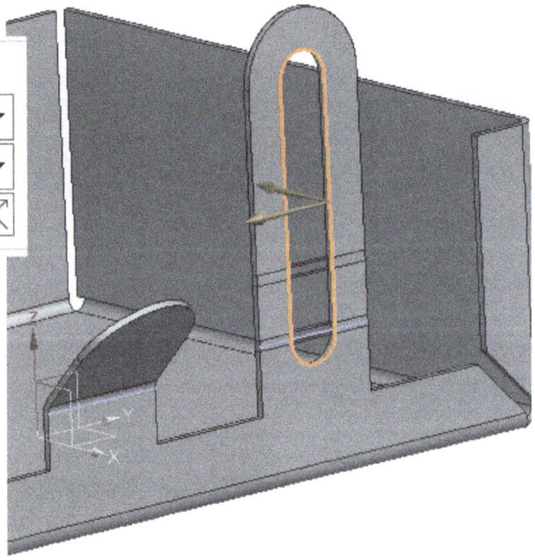

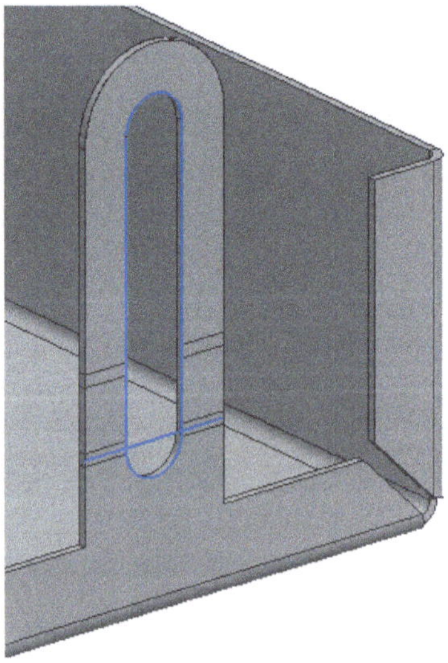

48. On the ribbon, click **Home > Bend > Rebend** and click on the lower bend face of the jog feature. Click **Apply** to rebend the feature.

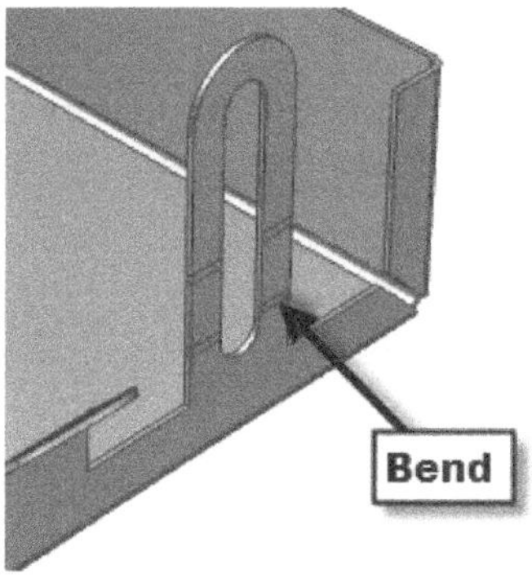

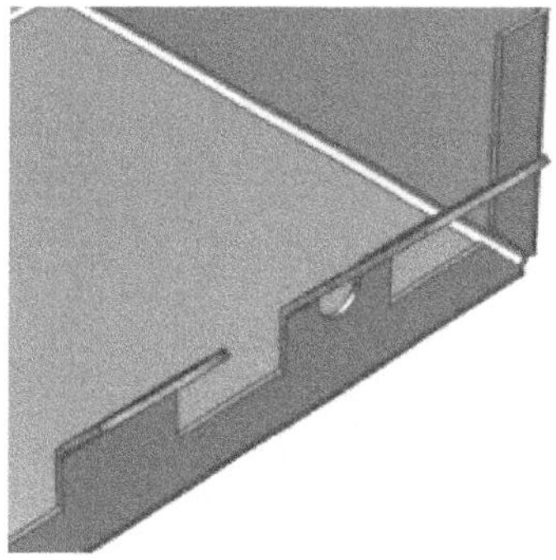

49. Click on the upper bend face, and click **OK**.

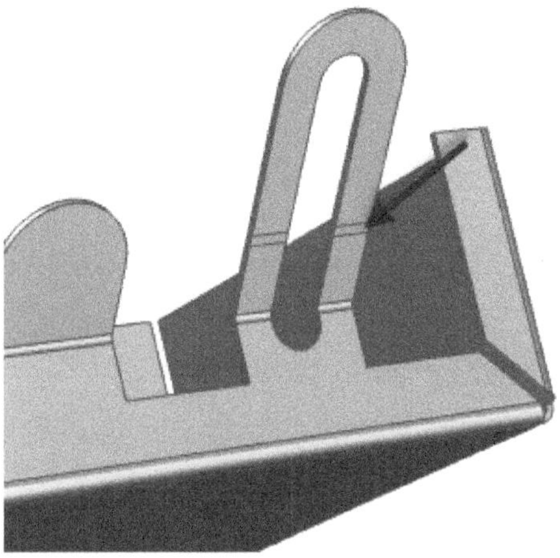

50. Activate the **Closed Corner** command (click **Home > Corner > Closed Corner** on the ribbon) and click on the bends of the flange features.
51. On the **Closed Corner** dialog, select **Type > Close and Relief**. Under the **Corner Properties** section, select **Treatment** > **Circular Cutout**.
52. Under the **Relief Properties** section, set the **(D) Diameter** value to 8 mm. Click **OK** to close the bends.

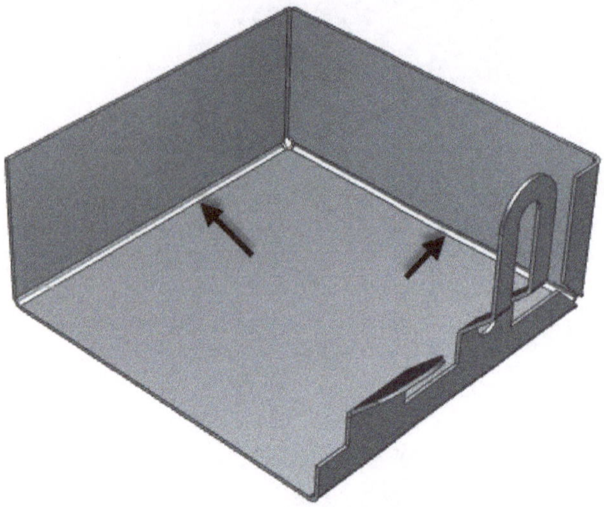

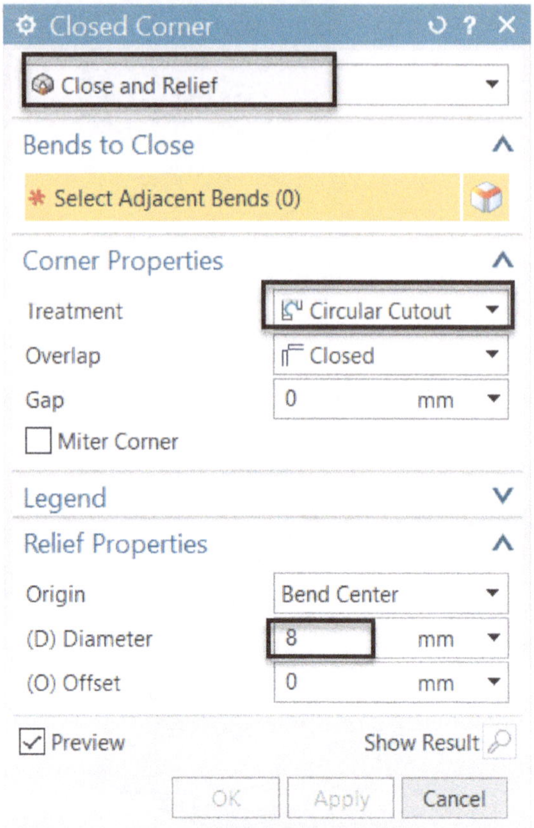

53. Activate the **Hem Flange** command (On the ribbon, click **Home > Bend > More > Hem Flange**)
54. On the **Hem Flange** dialog, select **Type > Closed Loop**.
55. Under **Inset Options**, select **Inset > Material Outside**.
56. Set **Bend Radius** to 2 and **Flange length** to 8.
57. Click on the outer edge of the left-side flange and click **Apply**.

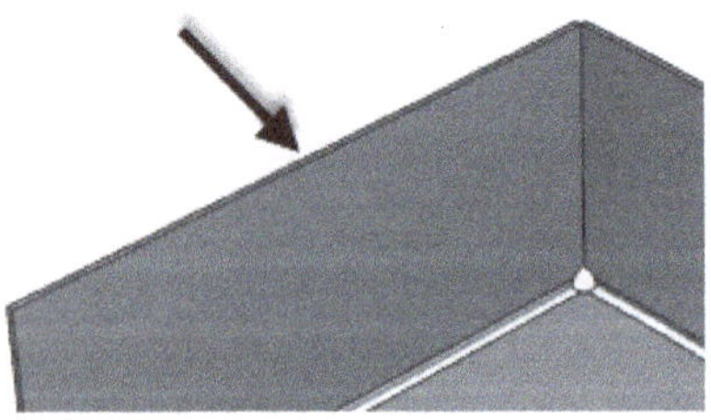

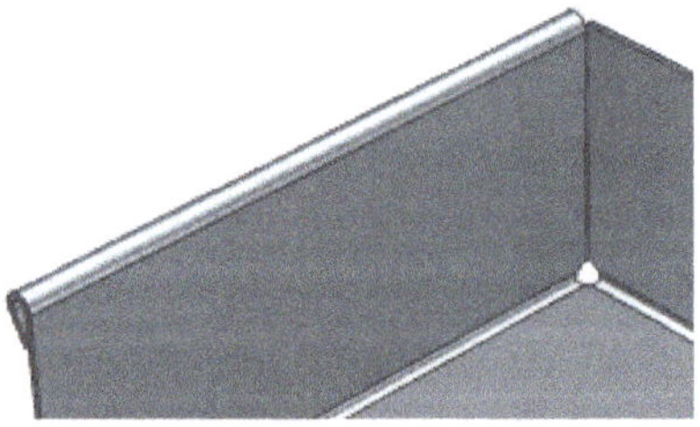

58. Click on the outer edge of the backside flange and click Apply. Next, click on the outer edge of the contour flange, and then click **OK** to create the hem features.

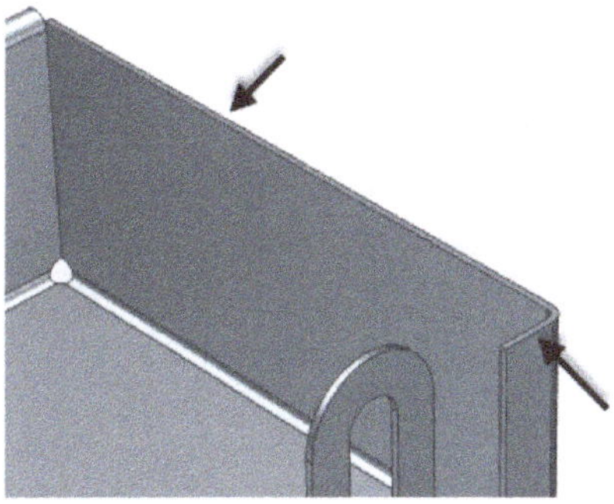

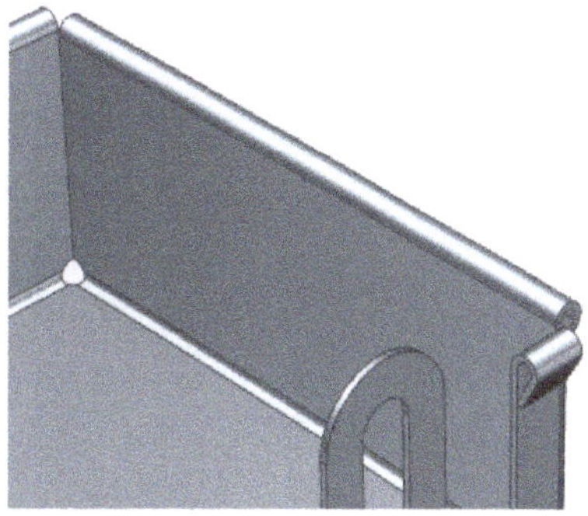

59. Activate the **Louver** command (click **Home > Punch > Louver** on the ribbon) and click the **Reset** icon on the **Louver** dialog.
60. Click on the top face of the tab feature.
61. Draw the sketch shown in the figure and click **Finish** on the ribbon.

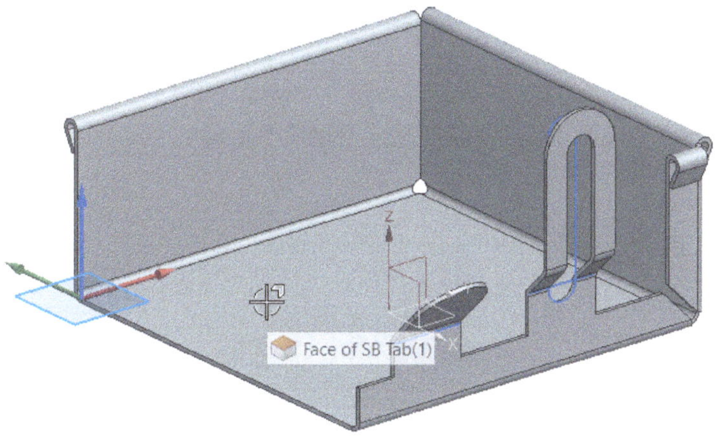

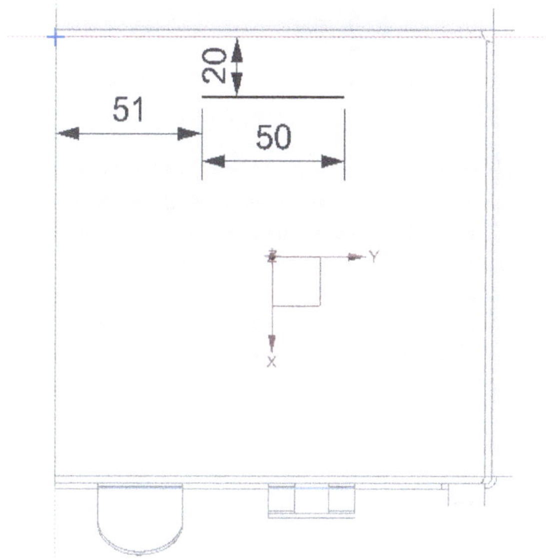

62. On the **Louver** dialog, type-in **5** in the **Depth** box and click the **Reverse Direction** button next to it.
63. Type-in **10** in the **Width** box.
64. Under the **Louver Properties** section, select **Louver Shape > Formed**.
65. Expand the **Louver** dialog and check the **Round Louver Edges** option under the **Rounding** section. Type-in **1** in the **Die Radius** box and click **OK** to create the louver.

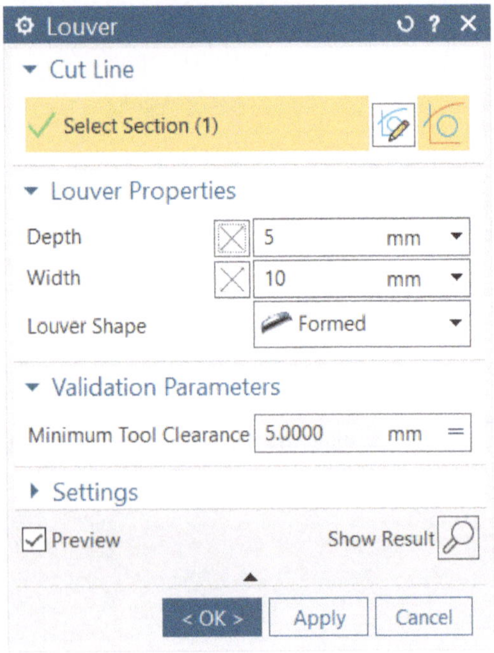

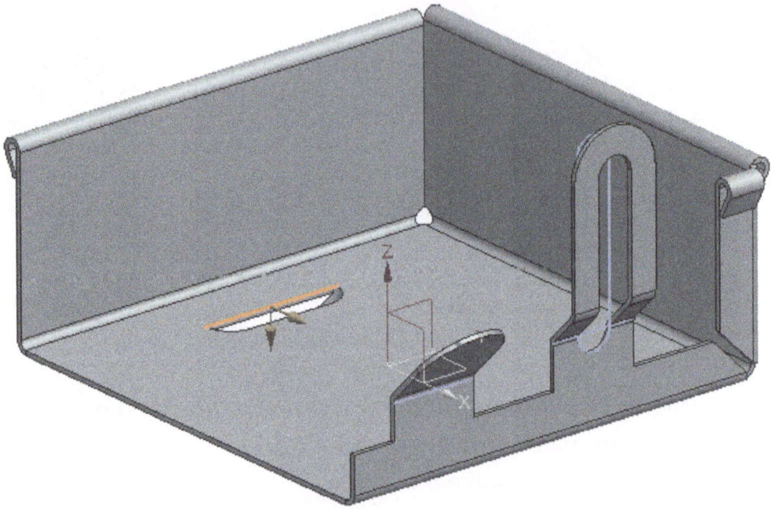

66. Activate the **Pattern Feature** command (On the Top Border Bar, click Menu > **Insert > Associative Copy > Pattern Feature**) and click louver feature.
67. On the **Pattern Feature** dialog, select **Layout > Linear.**
68. Under the **Direction 1** section, click **Specify Vector** and click on the X-axis vector.

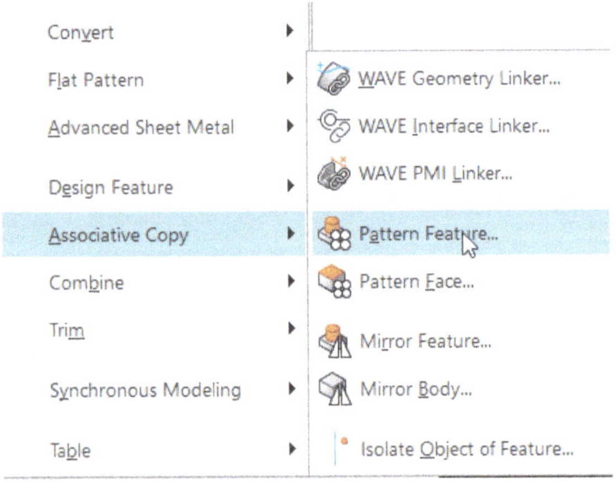

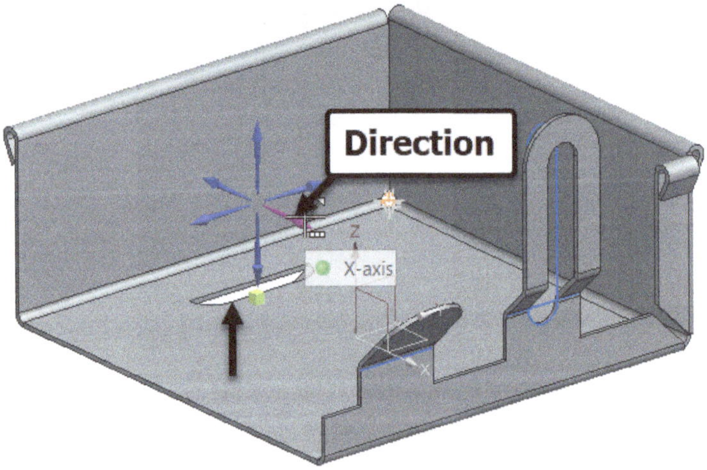

69. Under the **Direction 1** section, select **Spacing > Count and Span**. Type-in 6 and 100 in the **Count** and **Span Distance** boxes.
70. Under the **Pattern Method** section, select **Method > Variational**.
71. Click **OK** to create the linear pattern of the louver.

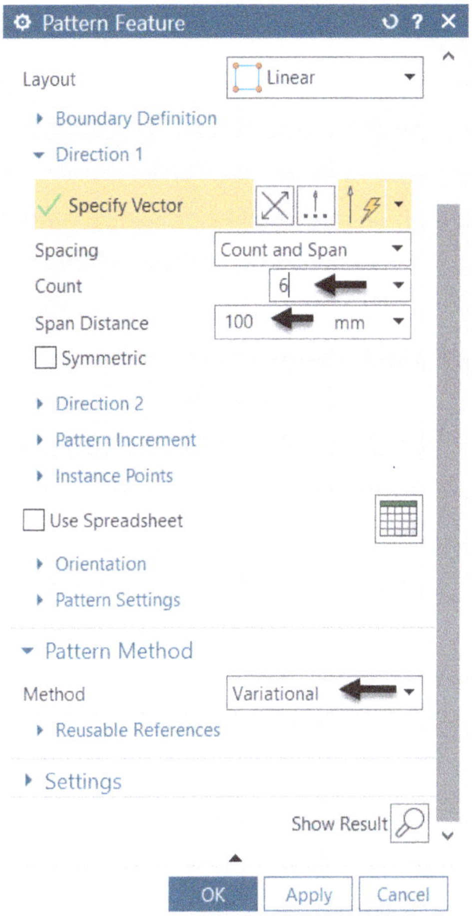

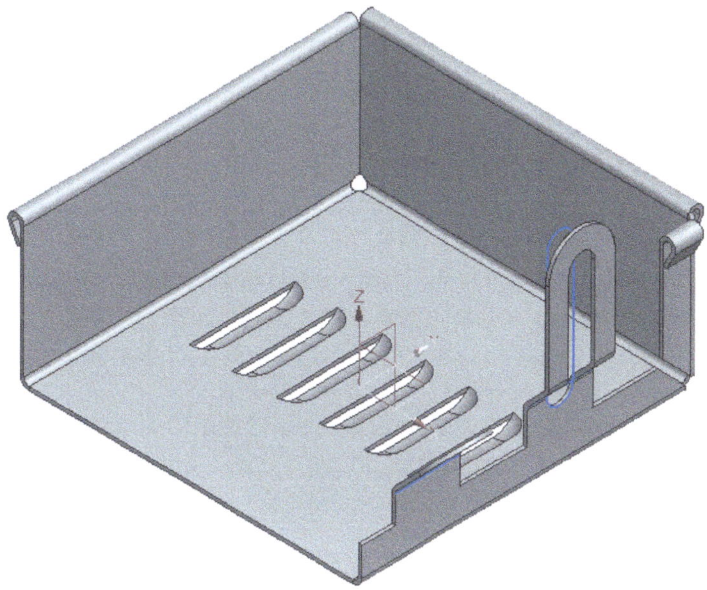

72. On the ribbon, click **Home > Flat Pattern > Flat Pattern**.
73. Click on the top face of the tab feature. On the **Flat Pattern** dialog, under the **Orientation** section, select **Orientation Method > Default**. Next, click **OK** on the **Flat Pattern** dialog to create a flat pattern. Next, click **OK** on the **Sheet Metal** message.
74. On the Top Border Bar, click **Menu > View > Layout > New**.
75. On the **New Layout** dialog, click FLAT-PATTERN#1 and click **OK** to view the flat pattern.

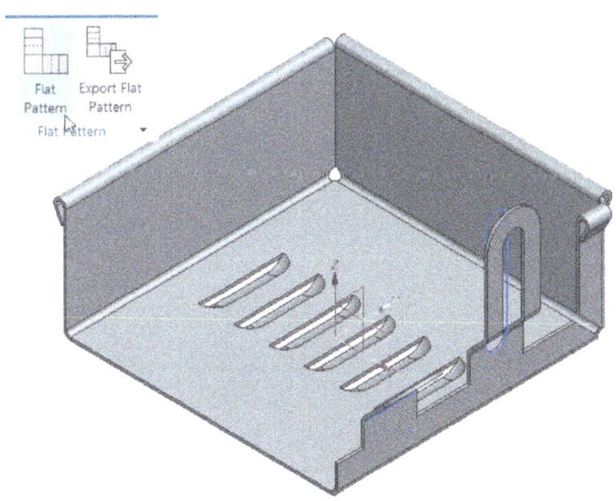

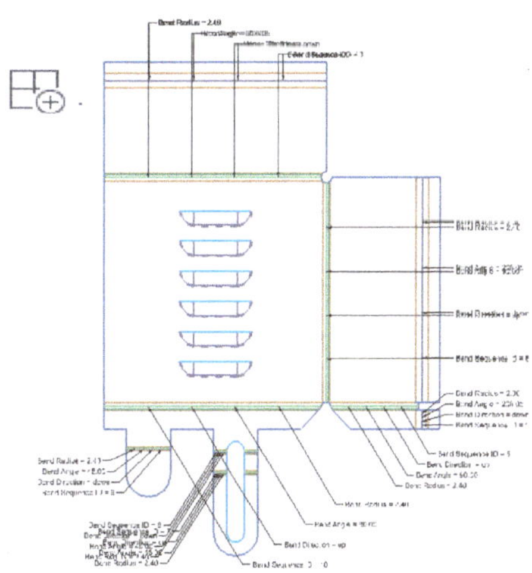

76. On the Top Border Bar, click **Menu** > **View > Layout > Replace View**. On the **Replace View with** dialog, click **Isometric**, and then click **OK**.
77. Save and close the sheet metal part.

Questions

1. How to insert a flat pattern into a drawing?
2. Describe parameters that can be specified on the **Sheet Metal Preferences** dialog.
3. Define the term 'Neutral Factor.'
4. List any two sheet metal part preferences that can be overridden when creating a feature.
5. What is the use of the **Normal Cut** command?
6. Which command is used to apply rounds and chamfers to the corners of a sheet metal part?
7. List the types of hems that can be created in NX?
8. What does the **Close Corner** command do?
9. What are the corner treatment options available when closing a corner?
10. What is the difference between a dimple and drawn cutout?

Exercises

Exercise 1

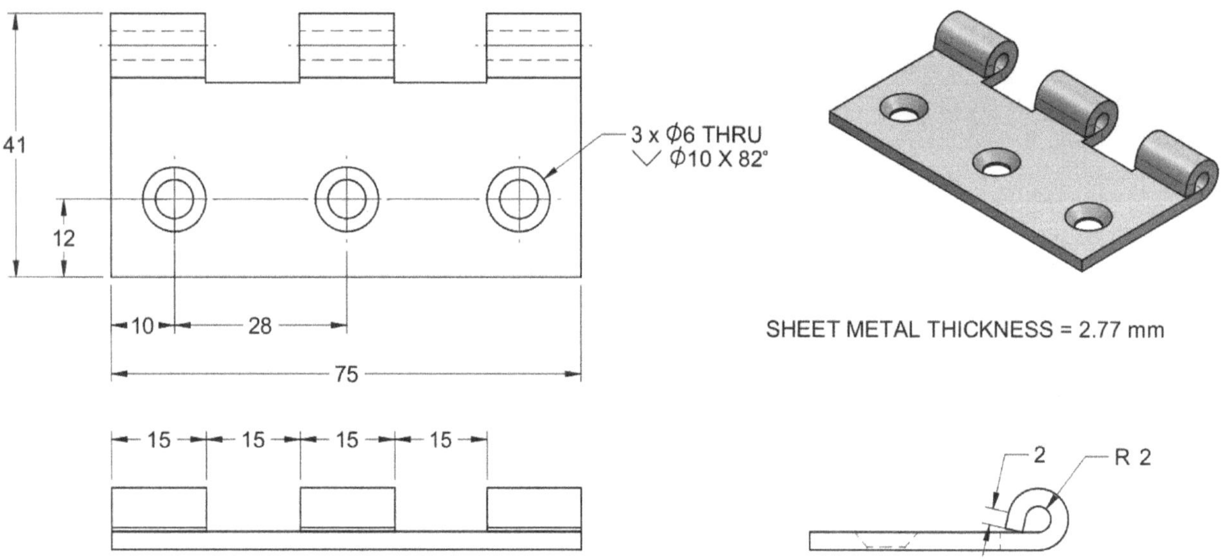

Exercise 2

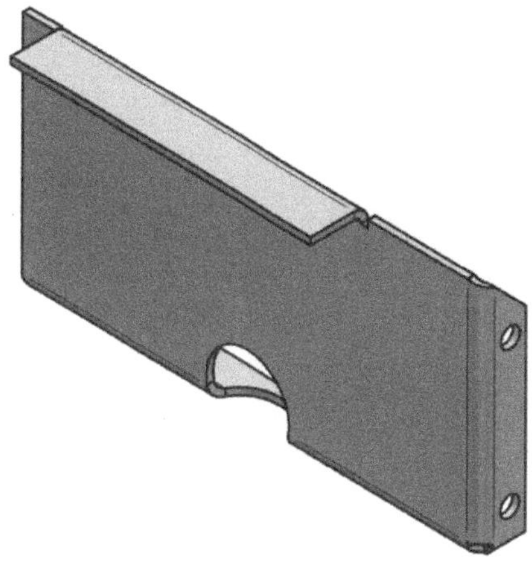

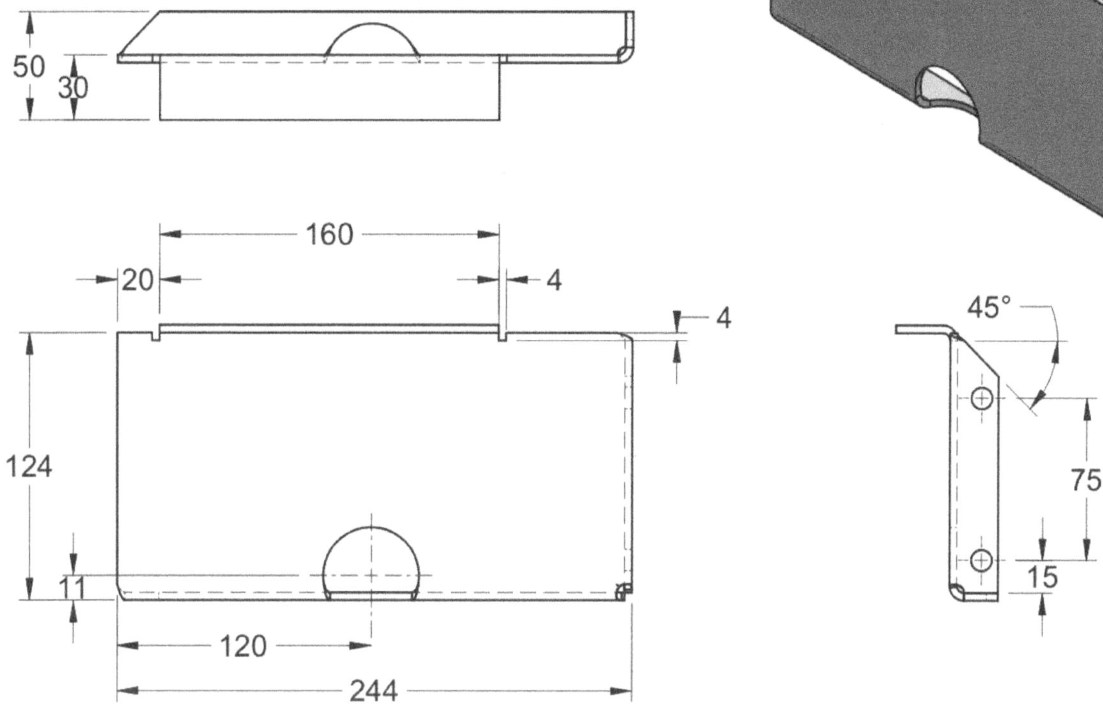

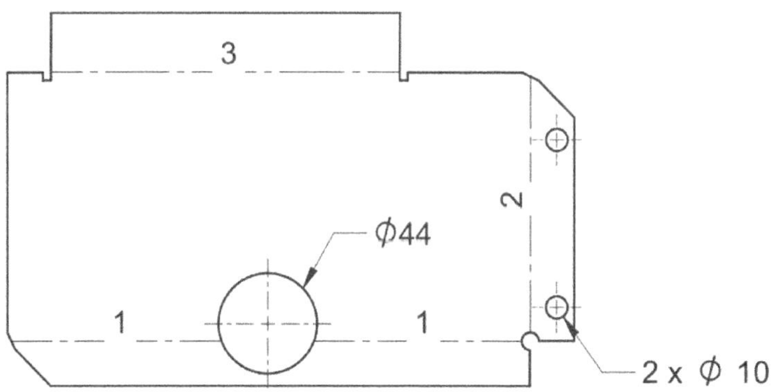

Sequence	Feature	Radius	Angle	Direction	Included Angle
1	Bend 1	3.58 mm	90.00 deg	Down	90.00 deg
2	Bend 2	3.58 mm	90.00 deg	Down	90.00 deg
3	Bend 3	3.58 mm	90.00 deg	Up	90.00 deg

Chapter 11: Surface Design

The topics covered in this chapter are:

- *Basic surfaces*
- *Swept command*
- *Sweep along Guide*
- *Styled Sweep*
- *Ruled*
- *Through Curves*
- *Through Curve Mesh*
- *Studio*
- *Bounded Plane*
- *Four Point Surface*
- *Swoop*
- *Transition*
- *Bridge Surface*
- *Face Blend*
- *Law Extension*
- *Offset Surface*
- *Variable Offset*
- *Offset Face*
- *Extract Geometry*
- *Trimmed Sheet*
- *Trim and Extend*
- *Extension Surface*
- *Untrim*
- *Delete Edges*
- *Patch Openings*
- *Sewing Surfaces*
- *Thicken*
- *Trim Body*
- *X-Form*

NX Surfacing commands can be used to create complex geometries that are very difficult to create using standard extruded features, revolve features, and so on. Surface modeling can also be used to edit and fix the broken imported parts. In this chapter, you learn the basics of surfacing commands that are mostly used. The surfacing commands are available in the **Surface** tab.

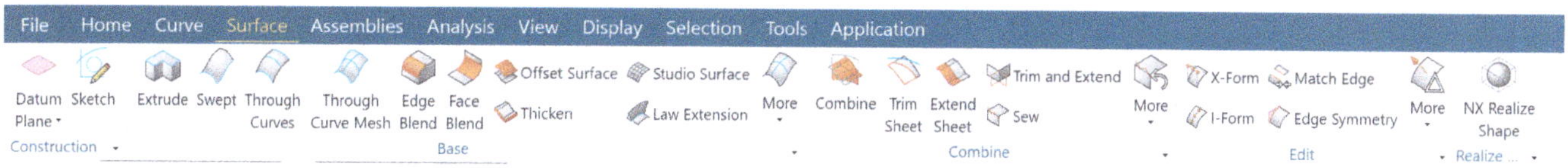

If the **Surface** tab is not displayed by default, you can customize the Ribbon. Click the right mouse button on the empty area of the ribbon and select **Surface.** In order to create a surface model, you must set the **Body Type** to **Sheet**. You can do this by clicking **Menu > Preferences > Modeling** on the Top Border Bar. On the **Modeling Preferences** dialog, set the **Body Type** to **Sheet** and click **OK.**

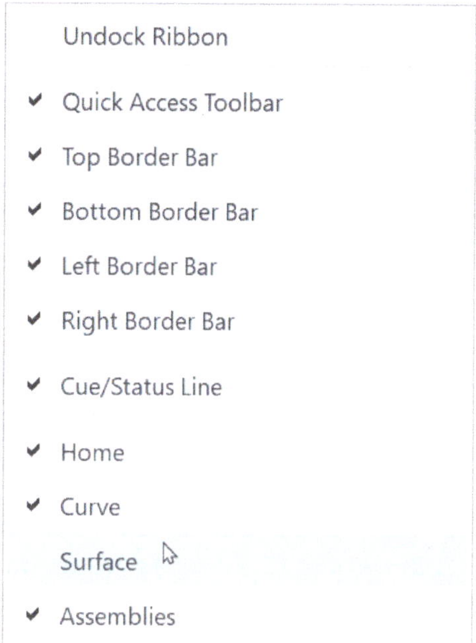

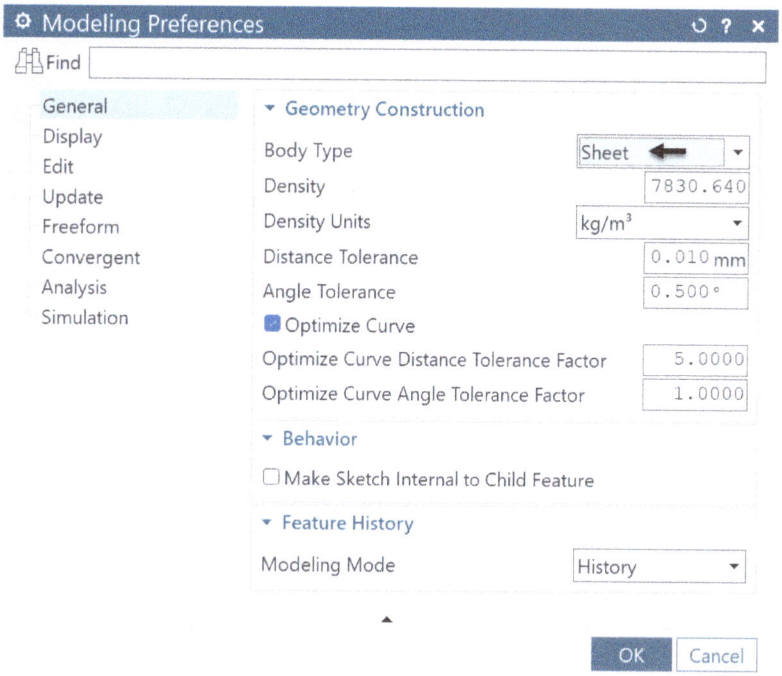

NX offers a rich set of surface design commands. A surface is an infinitely thin piece of geometry. For example, consider a cube shown in the figure. It has six faces. Each of these faces is a surface, an infinitely thin piece of geometry that acts as a boundary in 3D space. Surfaces can be simple or complex shapes.

In solid modeling, when you have created solid features such as an Extruded feature or a Revolved feature, NX creates a set of features (surfaces) that enclose a volume. The airtight enclosure is considered as a solid body. The advantage of using the surfacing commands is that you can design a model with more flexibility.

Extruded Surface

To create an extruded surface, first, create an open or closed sketch and activate the **Extrude** command. Select the sketch and type-in a value in the **Distance** box available below the **End** drop-down. Click **OK** to create the extruded surface. You will notice that the extrusion is not capped at the ends.

Note: *You need to make sure that the **Body Type** is set to **Sheet** in the **Modeling Preferences** dialog.*

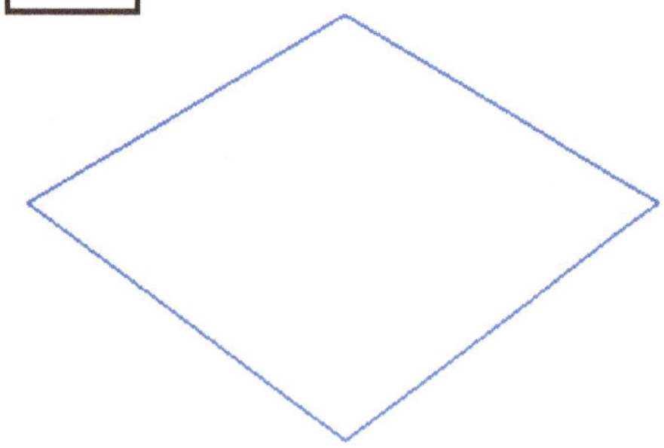

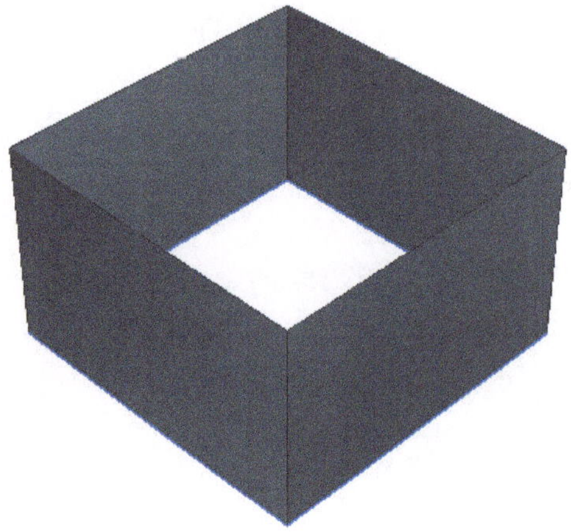

Revolved Surface

To create a revolved surface, first, activate the **Revolve** command and select a plane. Next, create an open or closed profile and click Finish on the ribbon. On the **Revolve** dialog, under the **Axis** section, click **Specify Vector** and select the axis. Type-in the angle of revolution in the **End** box and click **OK**.

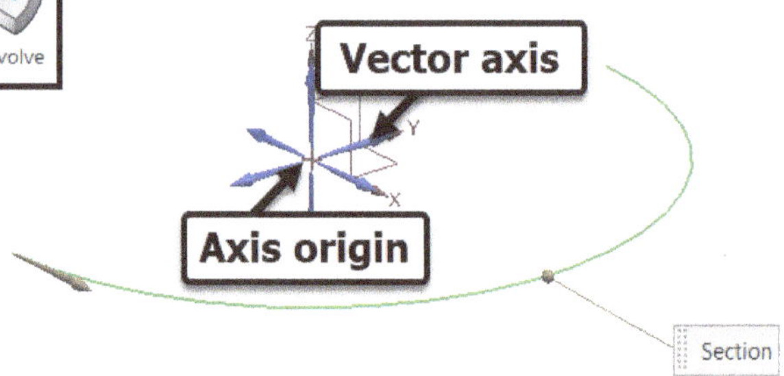

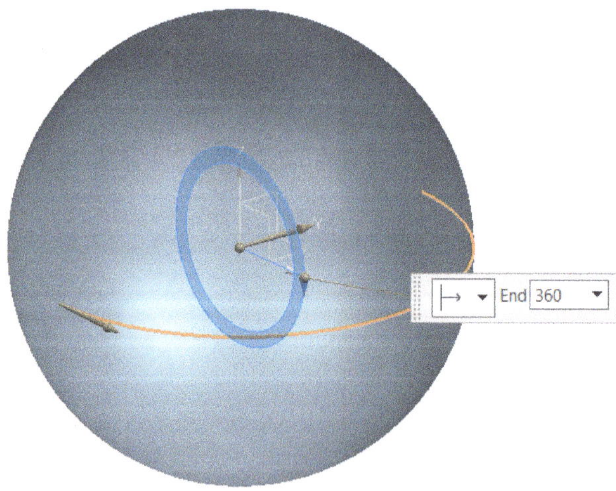

Even if you create an enclosed surface, NX will not recognize it as a solid body. You can examine this by activating the **Show Mass Properties Panels**  command (on the ribbon, click **Analysis > Mass Properties > Show Mass Properties Panels**). Next, click the **Assembly Navigator** tab and expand the Mass Properties section. You will notice that there no mass properties displayed under this section.

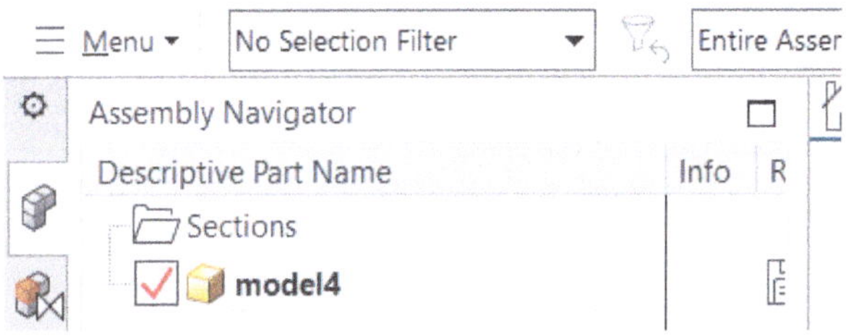

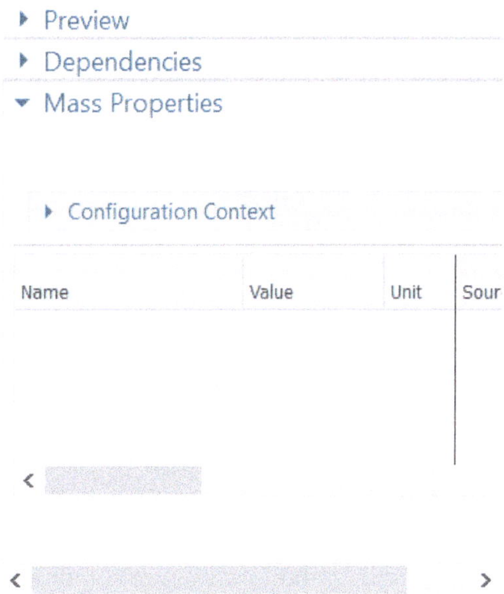

Swept

This command creates a surface or a solid body by sweeping one or more cross-sections along guide curves. It also provides various options to control the shape along with the guides. To create a swept surface or swept solid body, first create the cross-sections and guide curves. You must ensure that the guide curves and cross-sections are well connected. Activate the **Swept** command (on the ribbon, click **Surface > Base > Swept** ) and select the first cross-section. Click the middle mouse button and click on the second cross-section. Under the **Guides** section, click **Select Curve** and select the first guide curve. Click the middle mouse button and click on the second guide curve. Click **OK** to complete the swept body.

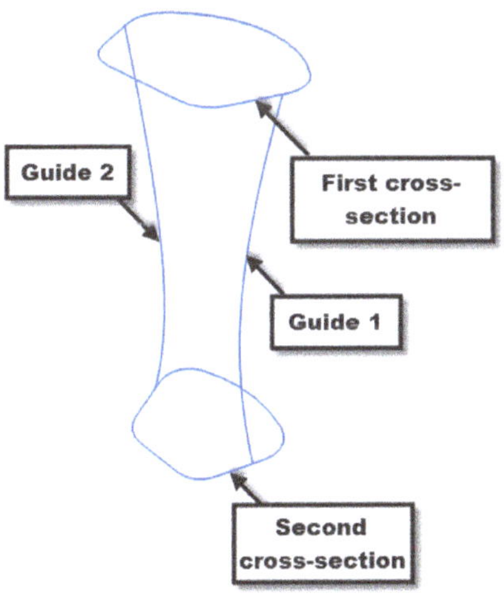

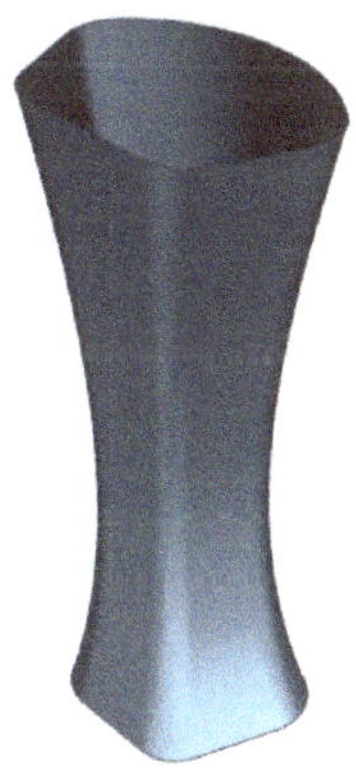

Sweep along Guide

This command creates a surface or solid body by sweeping a section along a guide curve. First, create a sweep profile and a guide curve, and then activate the **Sweep Along Guide** command (on the ribbon, click **Surface > Base > More > Sweep > Sweep Along Guide**). Click on the section curve, and then click **Guide > Select Curve** on the **Sweep Along Guide** dialog. Click on the guide curve, and then click **OK**.

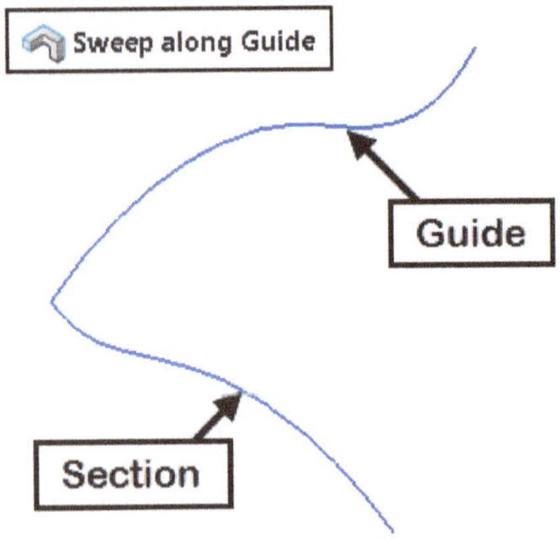

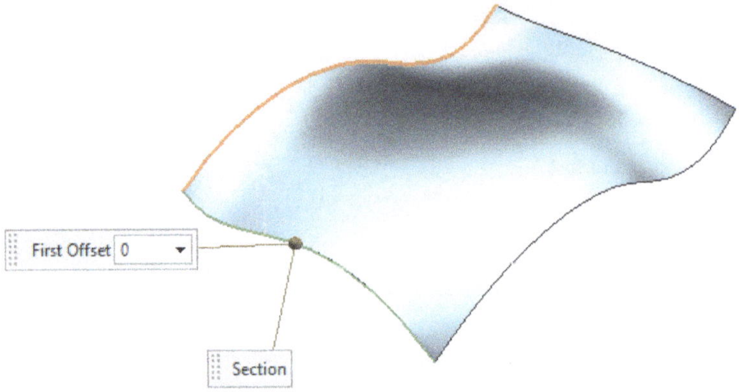

Styled Sweep

This command creates a smooth surface by sweeping section curves along the guide curves. You can use four different kinds of sections and guide curve combinations to create a styled sweep surface. Activate this command (on the ribbon, click **Surface > Base > More > Sweep > Styled Sweep**) and select **Type > 1 Guide** on the **Styled Sweep** dialog. Click on the section curve, and then click **Guide Curves > Select Guide Curve**. Click on the guide curve and click **OK** to create the styled sweep surface.

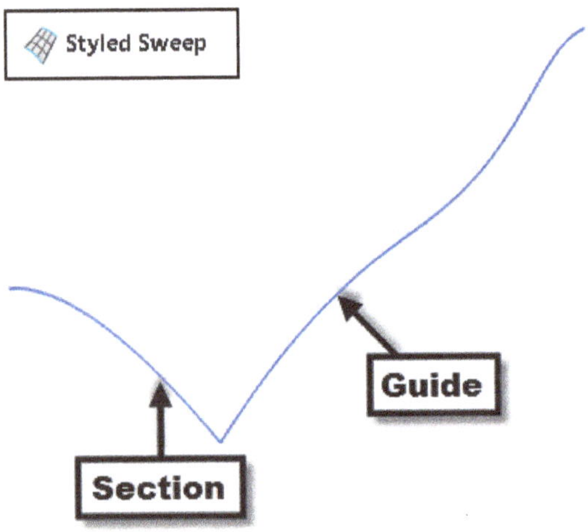

On the **Styled Sweep** dialog, select **Type > 1 Guide, 1 Touch,** and click on the section curve. Click **Guide Curves > Select Guide Curve**, and then click on the guide curve. Click **Select Touch Curve**, and then click on the touch curve. Click **OK**.

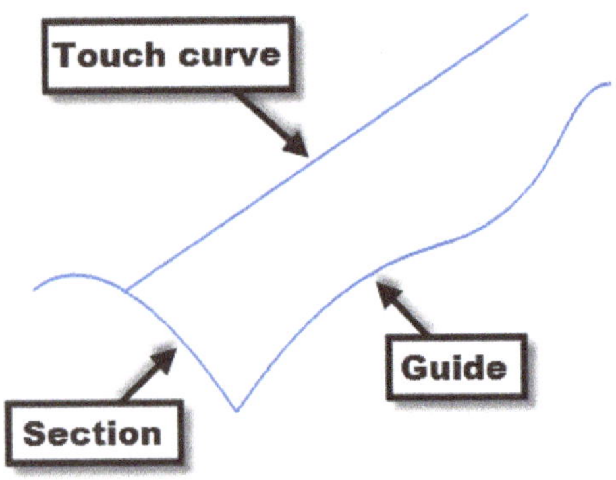

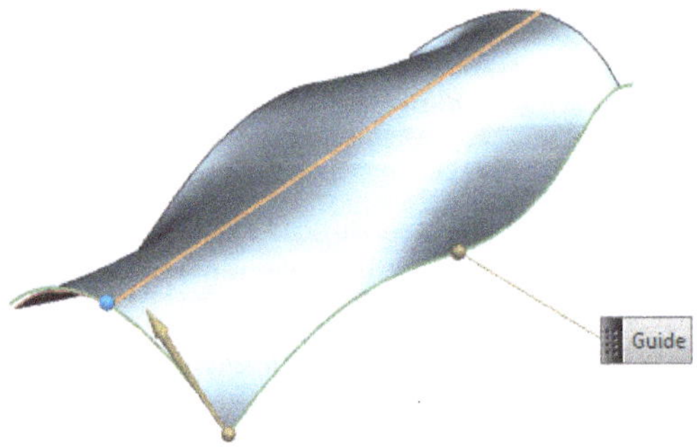

On the **Styled Sweep** dialog, select **Type > 1 Guide, 1 Orientation,** and select the section, guide, and orientation curves.

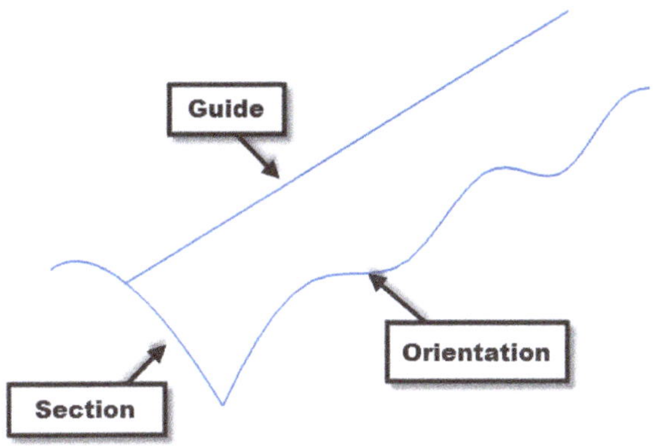

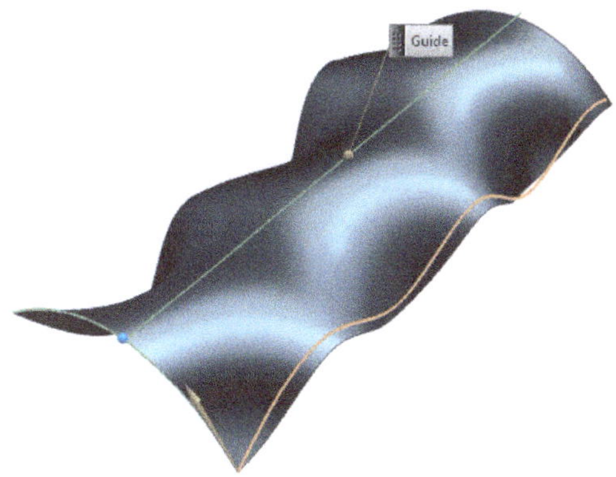

On the **Styled Sweep** dialog, select **Type > 2 Guides** and select the section and two guide curves.

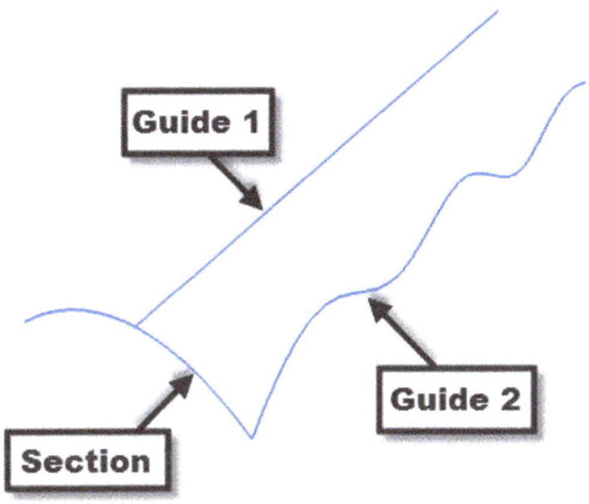

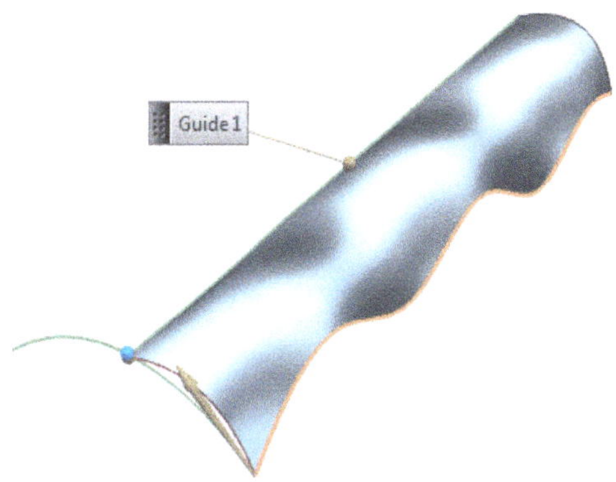

Ruled

The **Ruled** command creates a linear surface between two cross-sections. Activate this command (on the ribbon, click **Surface > Base > More > Mesh > Ruled**) and click on the first cross-section. If it has multiple segments, select **Curve Rule > Connected Curves** on the Sketch Scene Bar, and then click on a segment. The whole cross-section will be selected. On the **Ruled** dialog, under the **Section 2** section, click **Select Curve**, and then select the second section.

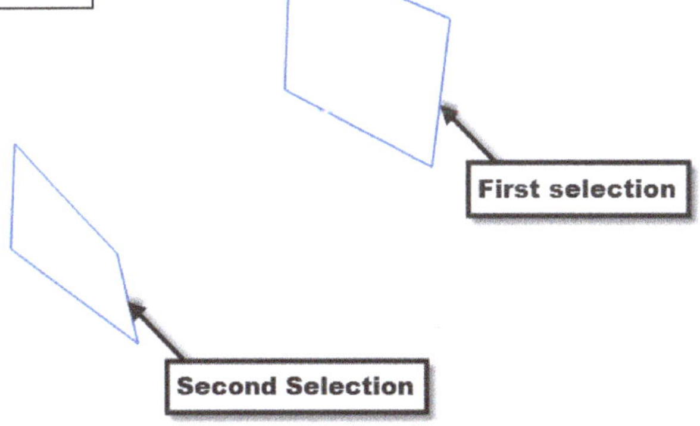

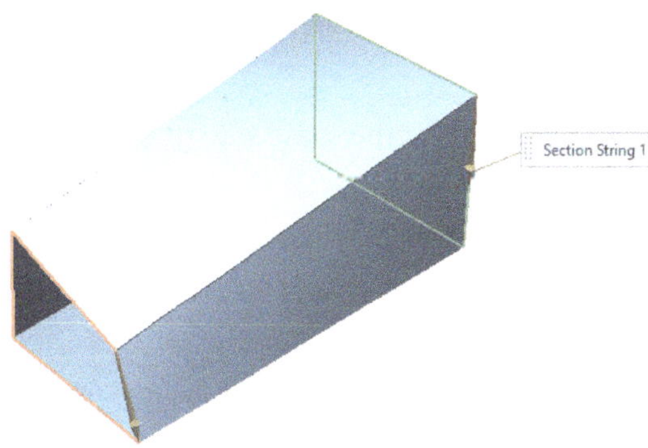

While selecting the cross-section, you must ensure that origin points are in the same direction. Otherwise, a twisted result may appear, as shown.

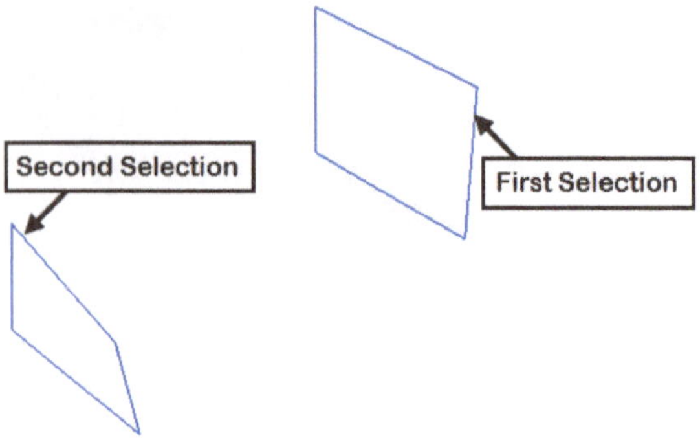

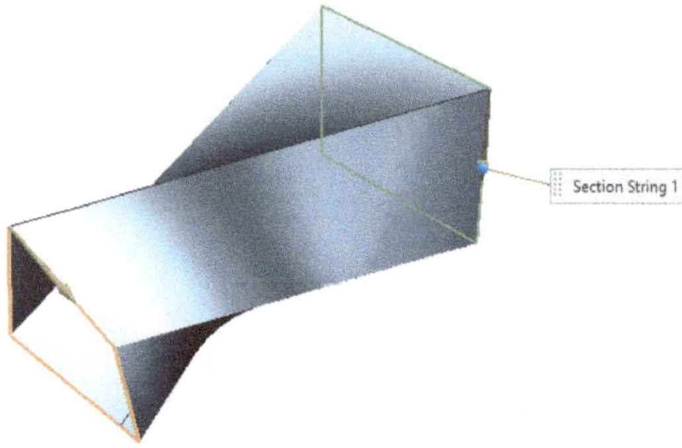

However, if you do happen to make a mistake, then select **Alignment > Alignment > By Points** on the **Ruled** dialog. Points appear on the vertices of the cross-sections. Drag the points to fix any unwanted twisting.

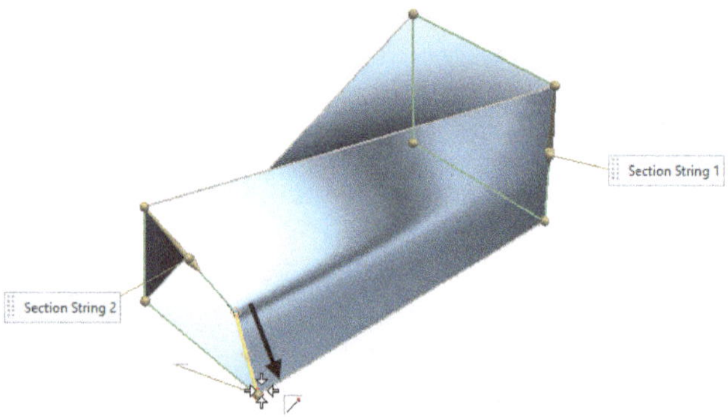

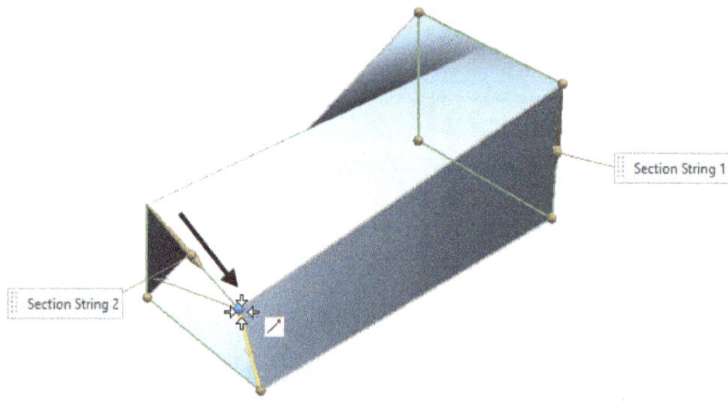

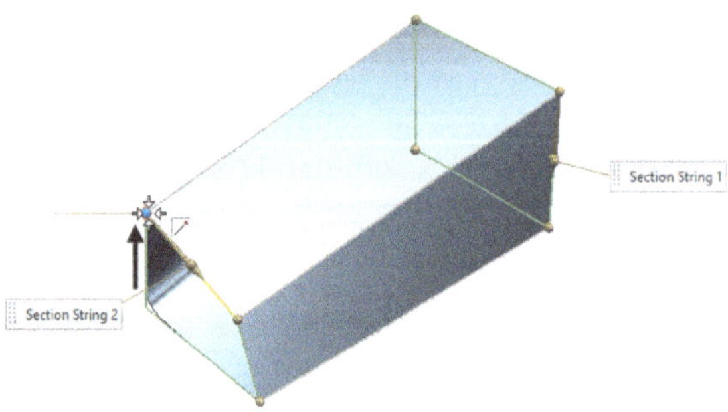

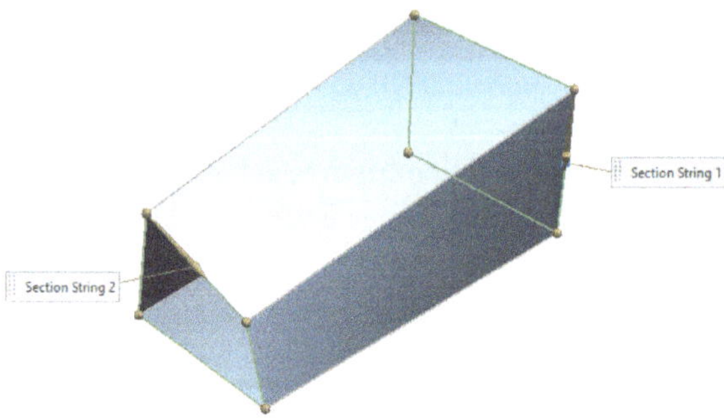

In addition to that, you can also reselect the origin curve of the second section matching that of the first one. To do this, click **Section 2 > Specify Origin Curve** and select the curve from the second section. Make sure that the selected curve is on the same side of the origin curve of the first section.

Through Curves

This command creates a solid or surface body through multiple cross-sections. The shape of the geometry adjusts automatically to pass through the cross-sections. First, create cross-section on different planes. The cross-sections can be closed, or open curves, or points, and they are not required to be on parallel planes. Next, activate the **Through Curves** command (on the ribbon, click **Surface > Base > Through Curves**) and select the first cross-section. Click the middle mouse button and select the second cross-section. Next, click the middle mouse button to accept the selection. Likewise, select the remaining cross-sections. While selecting the surfaces, ensure that arrows are pointing in the same direction. Next, click **OK**.

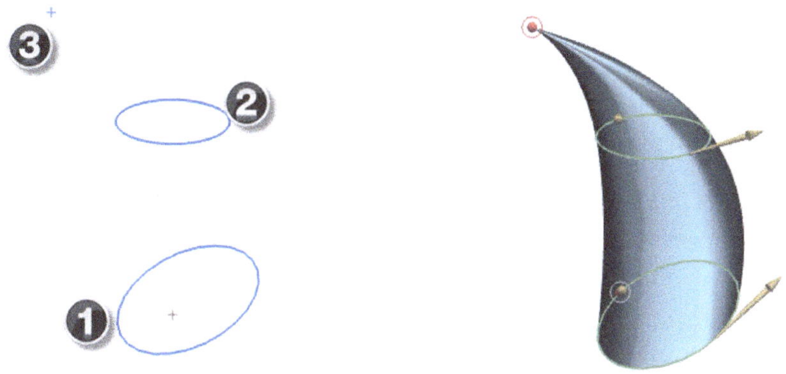

Through Curve Mesh

The **Through Curve Mesh** command creates a surface from a mesh of cross-sections and guide curves. Create sections and guide curves and ensure that they are well connected. Activate the **Through Curve Mesh** command (on the ribbon, click **Surface > Base > Through Curve Mesh**) and select the first primary curve. Click the middle mouse button and select the second primary curve. Ensure that the arrows point in the same direction. To do this, you must click on the same side of both the curves. Likewise, select the other primary curves. Likewise, use the **Cross Curves > Select Curve** option and select the cross curve. By mistake, if the primary and cross curves are not well connected, then a message appears showing that they do not intersect with each other. In that case, expand the **Settings** section and increase the **Tolerance** values.

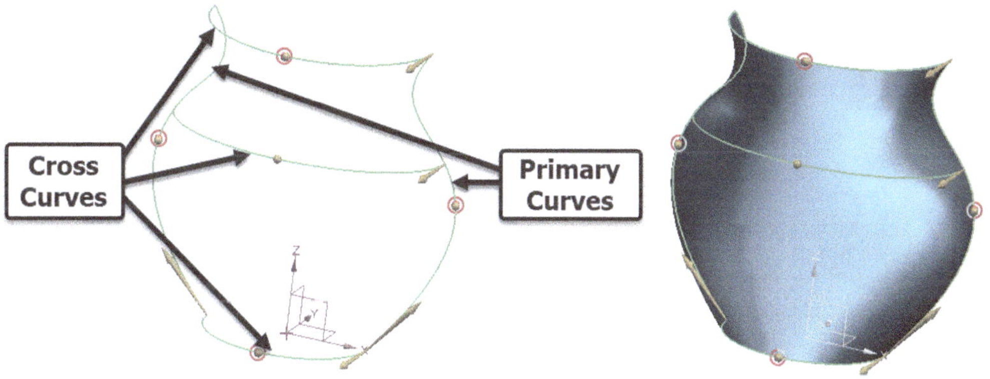

Studio Surface

This command creates a surface, which sweeps through any number of sections and guide curves. The process to create this kind of surface is similar to that of through curve, through curve mesh, or swept surfaces. However, there would be a slight variation in the result obtained. First, create sections and guide curves and activate this command (on the ribbon, click **Surface > Base > Studio Surface**). Select one or more section curves by clicking the middle mouse button after each selection. After selecting the section curves, click in the **Guide (Cross) Curves** section and select the guide curves.

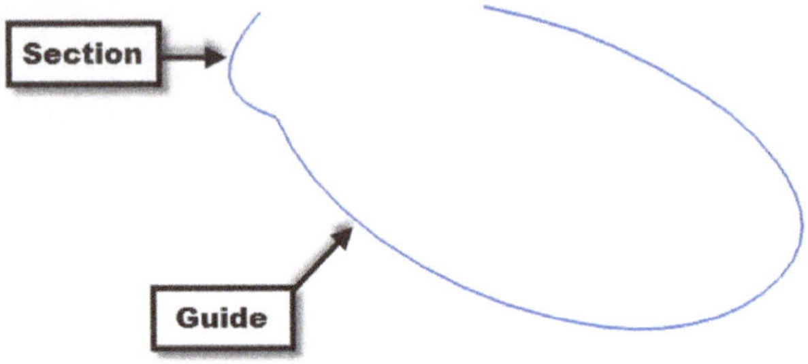

Bounded Plane

To create a bounded plane surface, Activate the **Bounded Plane** command (on the ribbon, click **Surface > Base > More > Fill > Bounded Plane**) and select a closed sketch or closed loop of edges. Click **OK** to create the Bounded Plane surface.

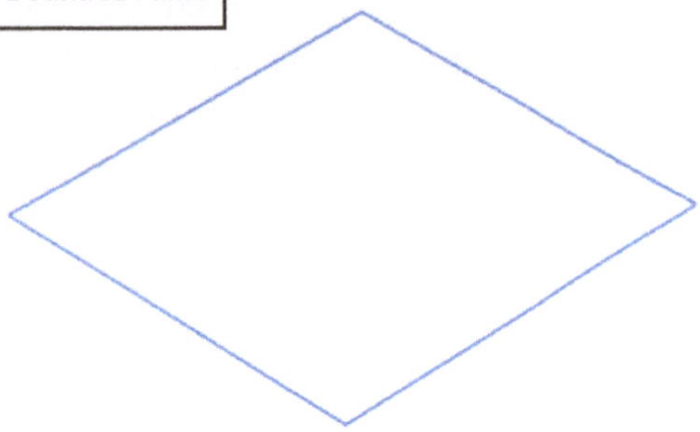

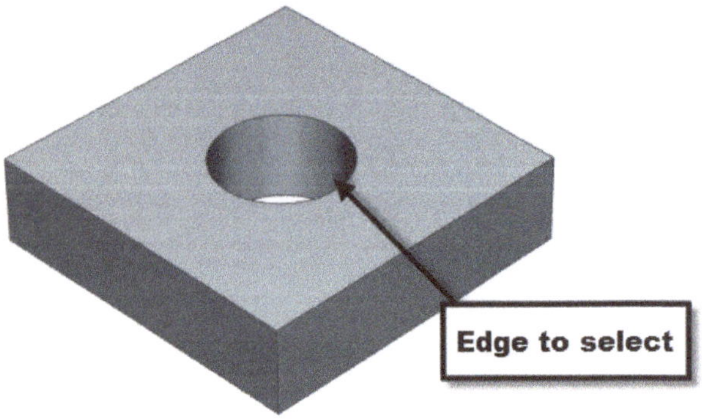

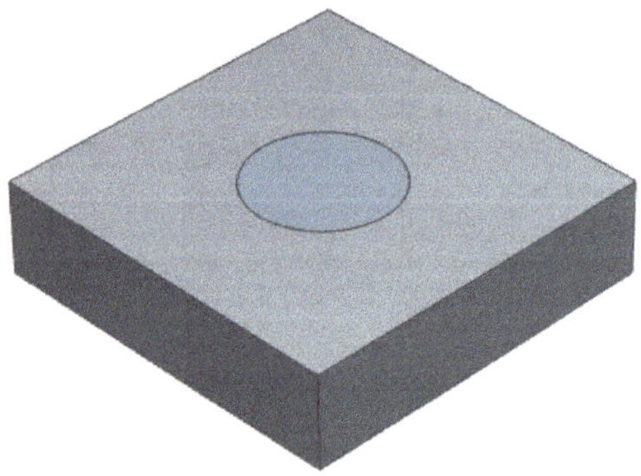

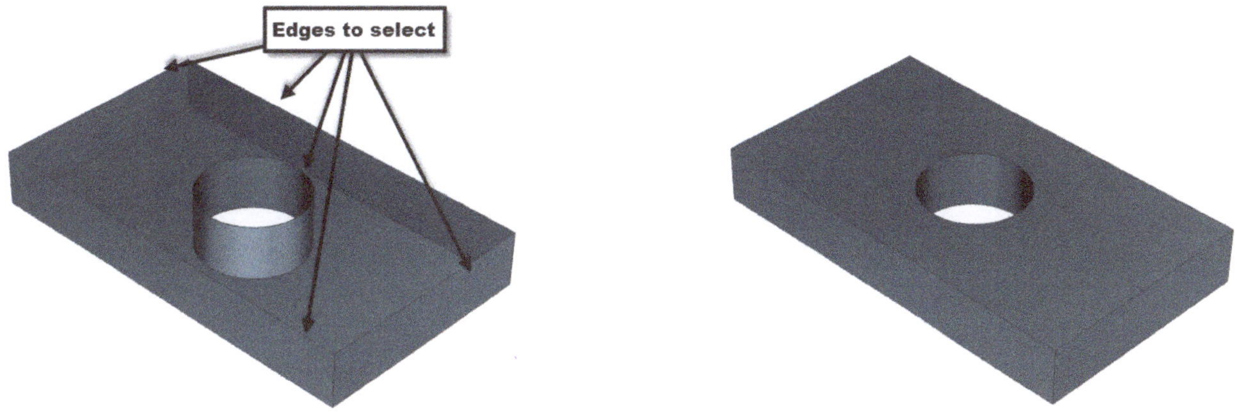

Four Point Surface

This command creates a surface by using four points that you specify. Activate this command (click **Surface > Base > More > Fill > Four Point Surface** on the ribbon) and select four points. Click **OK** to create the four-point surface.

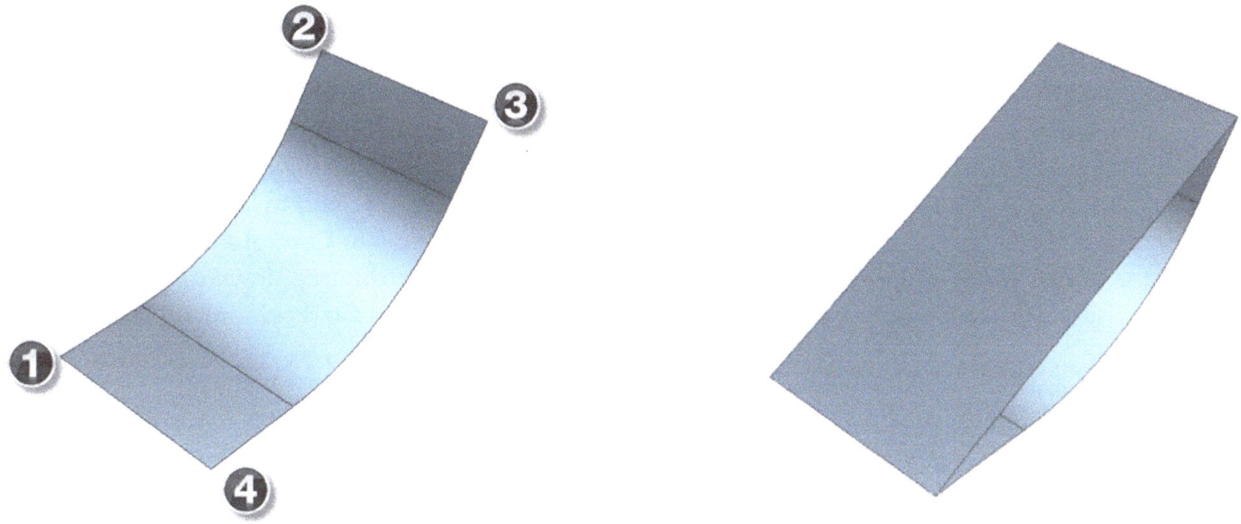

Bridge Surface

The **Bridge Surface** command creates a surface bridging the gap between two surfaces. This can be tangent or curvature, continuous in both directions. To create a bridge surface, activate the **Bridge Surface** command (On the ribbon, click **Surface > Base > More > Blend > Bridge**) and select the first and second edges.

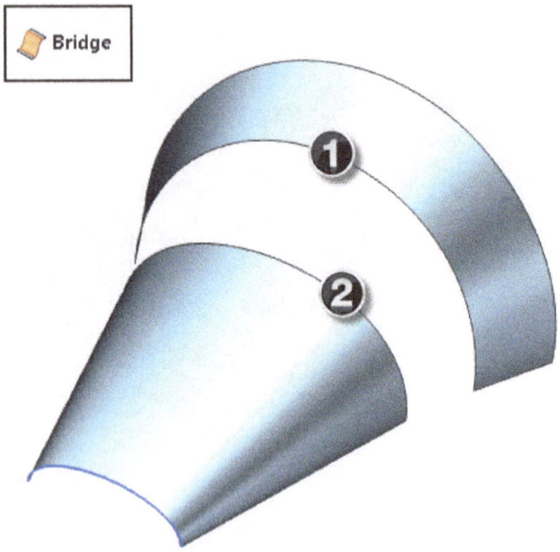

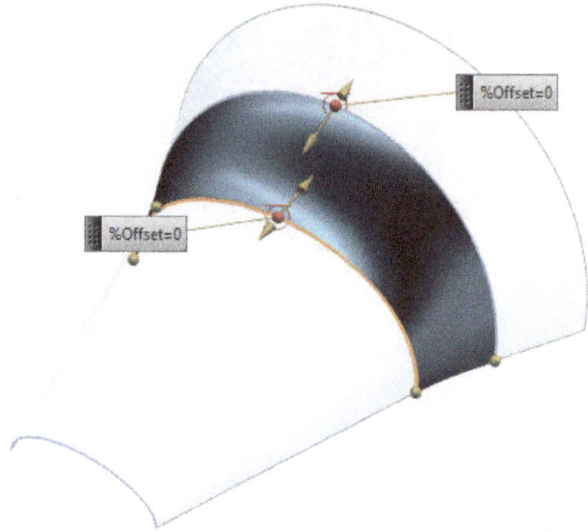

To avoid the twist, make sure that you click on the same side of the two curves. If a twist is created, then click the **Reverse Direction**  button on the **Bridge Surface** dialog.

You can specify the way in which the boundary surface will be connected to the selected edges. To do this, expand the **Shape** section on the **Bridge Surface** dialog. Select **Edge 1 Continuity > G1 (Tangent)** to maintain tangency between the first edge and the bridge surface. Next, select an option from the **Tangent Control** drop-down. There are two options available in this drop-down: **Constant** and **Linear**. The **Constant** option allows you to control the tangency by specifying single for each selected edge. The Linear option allows you to specify the start and end values of the selected edges to control the tangency. For example, select **Tangent Control > Constant** and type-in a value in the **Edge 1 Constant** box located below expand the **Tangent Control** drop-down to define the tangent length. Likewise, set the continuity type of the second edge. You can also select **G0 (Position)** or **G2 (Curvature)**.

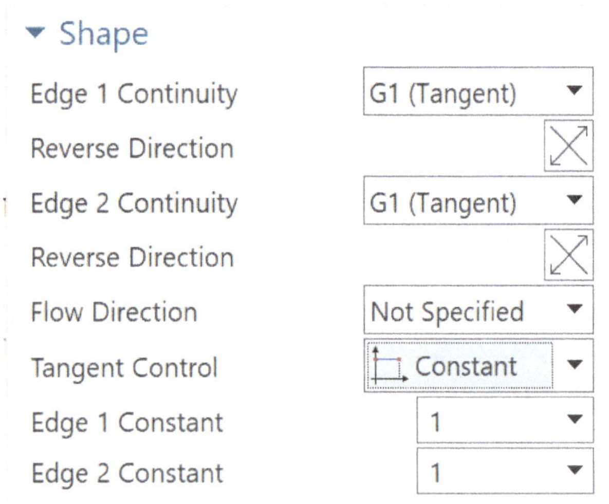

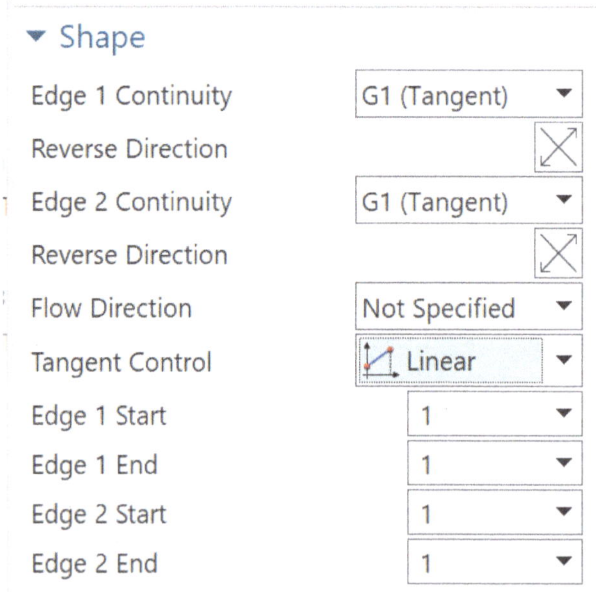

Next, set the **Flow Direction** of the first and second edges. You can select **Isoparametric** or **Perpendicular** or leave it **Not Specified.** If you want to create a partial bridge surface, then use the options in the **Edge Limit** section. You can drag the **%Start** and **%End** sliders in this section to position the start and endpoints of the bridge surface. If you want to offset the bridge surface, then drag the **%Offset** slider.

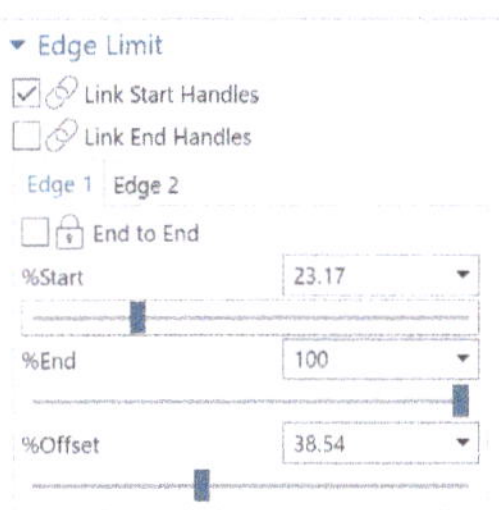

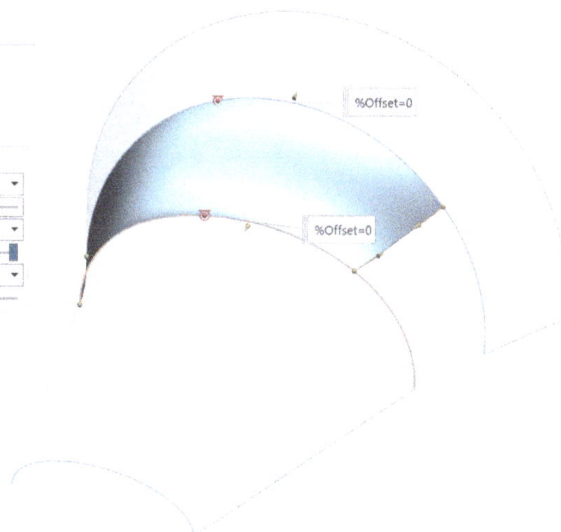

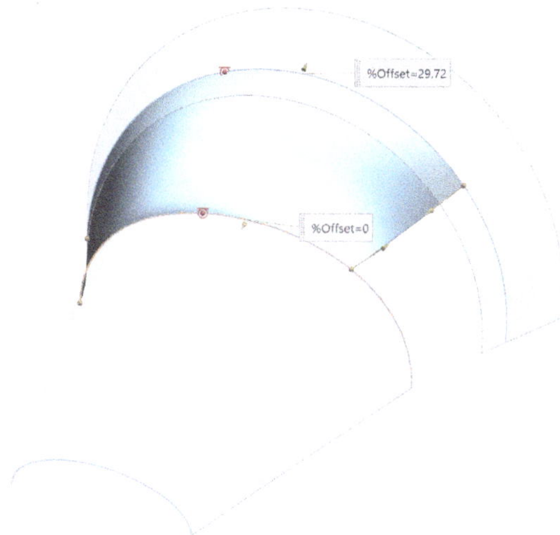

After you have the desired output, click **OK** to create the bridge surface.

Face Blend

Face blends have several uses. They can span across gaps between faces, they can be useful in blending complex surfaces, and they can be defined by a boundary curve instead of a radius. For example, you can create a face blend, which spans across a gap between two faces. To do this, activate the **Face Blend** command (on the ribbon, click **Surface > Base > Face Blend**) and select **Type > Two-face**. Select the first face chain, and then click **Select Face 2.** Select the second face chain and type-in a value in the **Radius** box under the **Cross Section** section. Ensure that the arrows point in the same direction. Make sure that the radius is more than or equal to the distance between two surfaces.

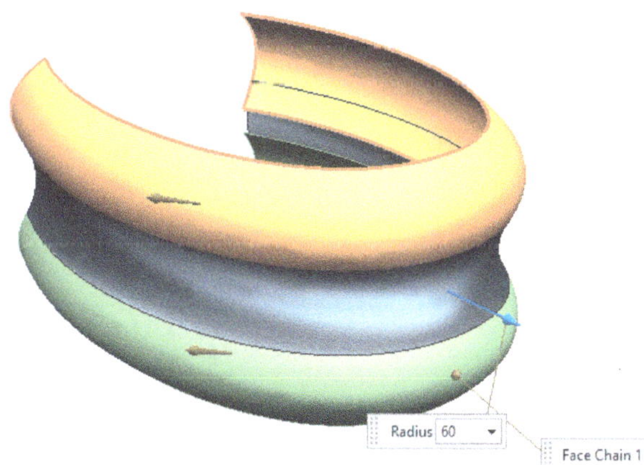

When you need to create a blend between two faces and a supporting face at the middle, select **Type > Three-face** on the **Face Blend** dialog. Use the options under the **Faces** section to select the three faces, and then click **OK.** Note that you need to select **Face rule > Single Face** on the Sketch Scene Bar while selecting the faces.

Law Extension

The **Law Extension** command allows you to create surfaces attached to the edges of existing surfaces. Activate this command (on the ribbon, click **Surface > Base > Law Extension**) and select an edge from the geometry. On the **Law Extension** dialog, click **Face > Select Face**, and then select the face attached to the selected edge. The preview of the extension surface appears.

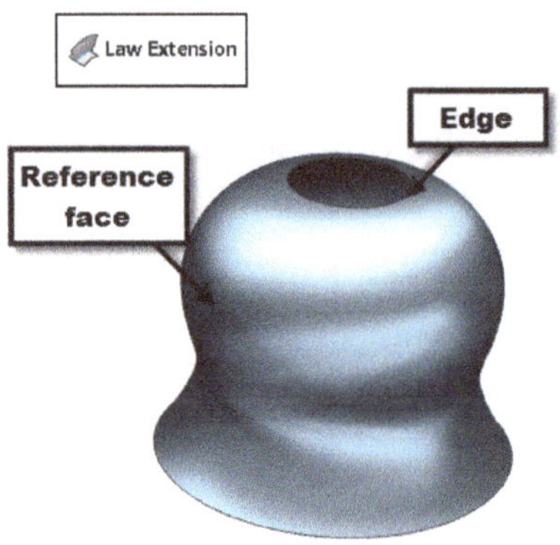

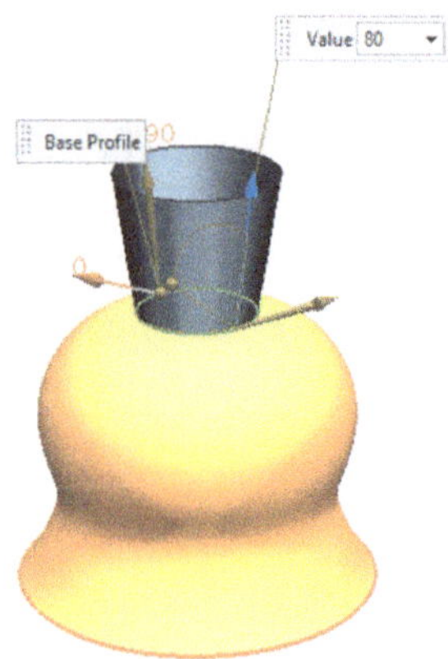

Now, type-in a value in the **Value** box under the **Length Law** section (or) drag the arrow handle that appears on the selected edge. You can also use the laws available in the **Law Type** drop-down to change the length of the extension surface. Go to the NX help file to get more information about these law types. To manipulate the angle of the extension surface, type-in the **Value** box under the **Angle Law** section (or) drag the angle handle. Click **Apply**.

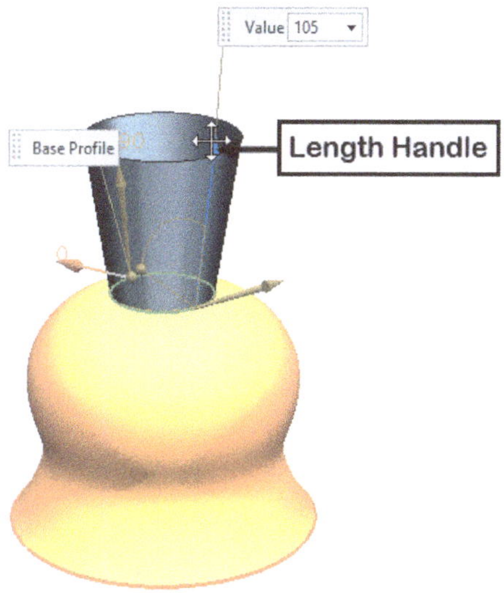

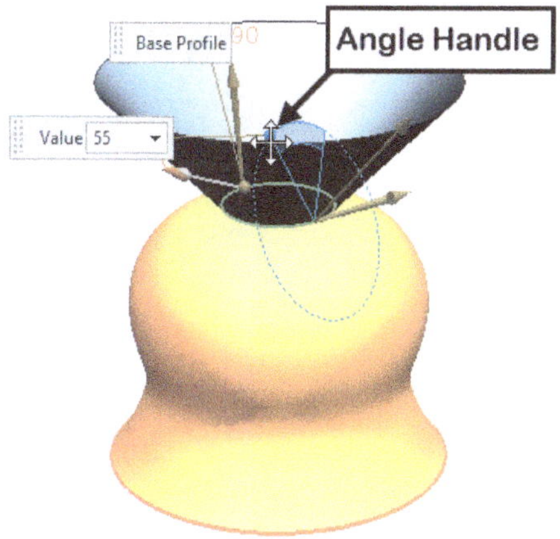

On the **Law Extension** dialog, select **Type > Vector**, and then click on edge to extend. On the dialog, click **Reference Vector > Specify Vector** and select a vector axis. The extension surface appears perpendicular to the selected vector. You can change the length and angle of the extension surface. Next, click **OK** to create the law extension surface.

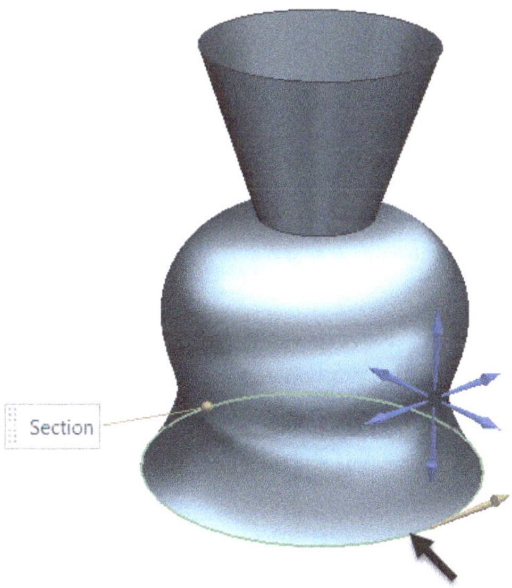

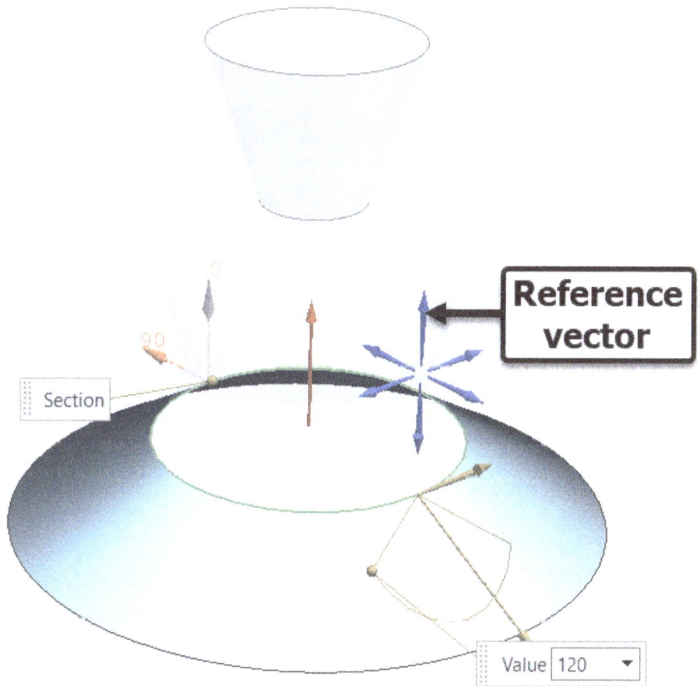

Offset Surface

To create an offset surface, activate the **Offset Surface** command (click **Surface > Base > Offset Surface**  on the ribbon) and select the faces to offset. Note that you need to select **Face rule > Single Face** on the Sketch Scene Bar while selecting the faces. Next, type-in a value in the **Offset 1** box.

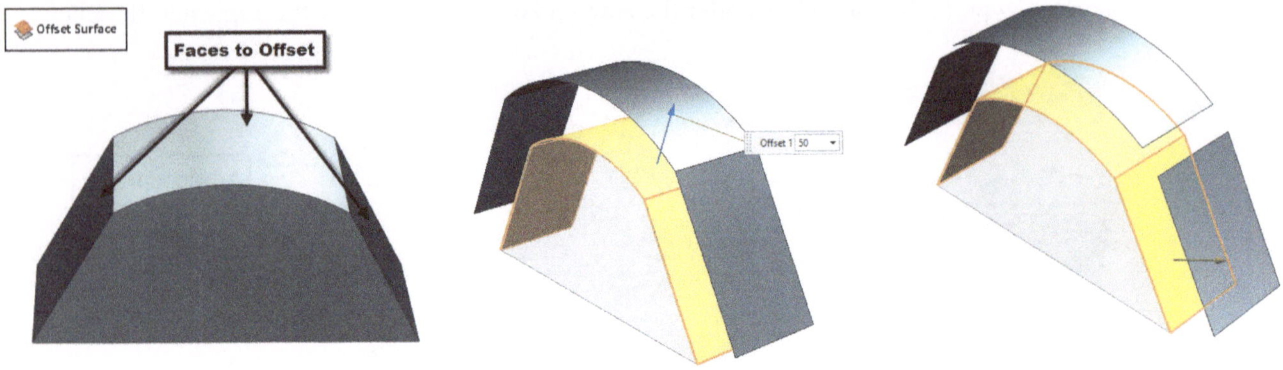

On the **Offset Surface** dialog, under the **Feature** section, select **Output > One Feature for Each Face** to offset faces. This results in offset surfaces, which are detached from each other. Click **OK** to create the offset surfaces.

Offset Face

The **Offset Face** command makes it easy to change the geometry by offsetting a set of faces. For example, if you want to offset the front face of an imported solid, activate the **Offset Face** command (on the ribbon, click **Home > Base > More > Offset > Offset Face)** select the face to move. Drag the arrow that appears on the selected face (or) type-in a value in the **Offset** box. You can click **Reverse direction** ⊠ to reverse the direction of the offset. Click **OK** to offset the face.

Extract Geometry

In some cases, you may need to extract the surfaces of the solid body. You can use the **Extract Geometry** command (click **Home > Base > Copy > Extract Geometry** on the ribbon) to extract the surfaces of the solid body. Activate this command and select **Type > Face** on the **Extract Geometry** dialog. Click on the face of the solid body, and then click **OK**. Hide the solid body to see the extracted surfaces.

Trimmed Sheet

This command trims a portion of a surface using a trimming tool. The trimming tool can be a surface, plane, or a sketched entity. Activate this command (click **Surface > Combine > Trim Sheet** on the ribbon) and select the target body. You must select the target body by clicking on the portion to keep. On the **Trim Sheet** dialog, under the **Boundary** section, click **Select Object**, and then click on the trimming tool. Click **OK** to trim the surface.

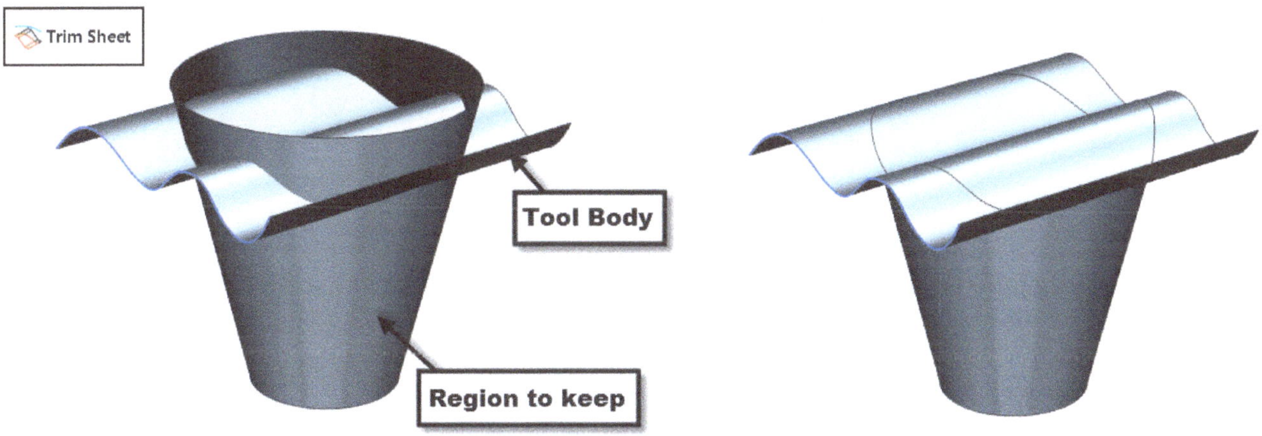

You can also trim a surface using a sketch. Activate the **Trim Sheet** command and select the target body. On the dialog, click **Boundary > Select Object**, and then click on the sketch. You will notice that the trimming boundary is created normal to the surface. If you want the trimming boundary to be normal to the curve plane, then select **Projection Direction > Normal to Curve Plane**.

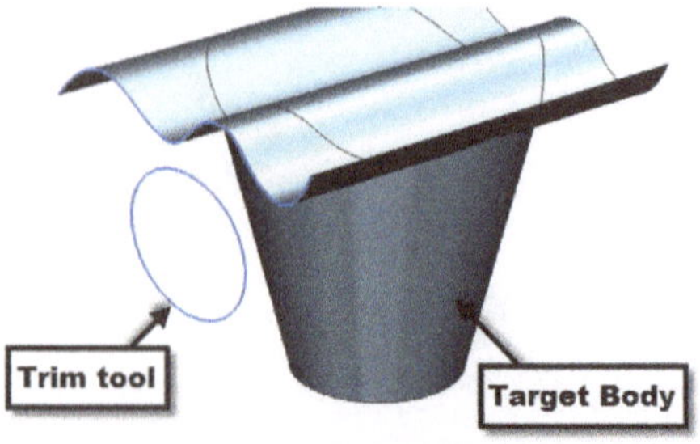

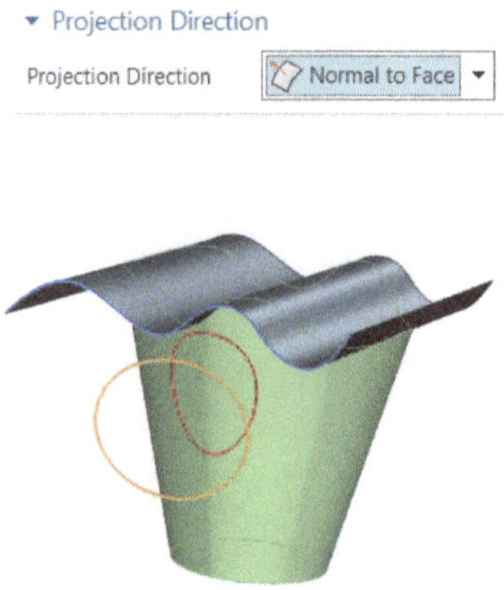

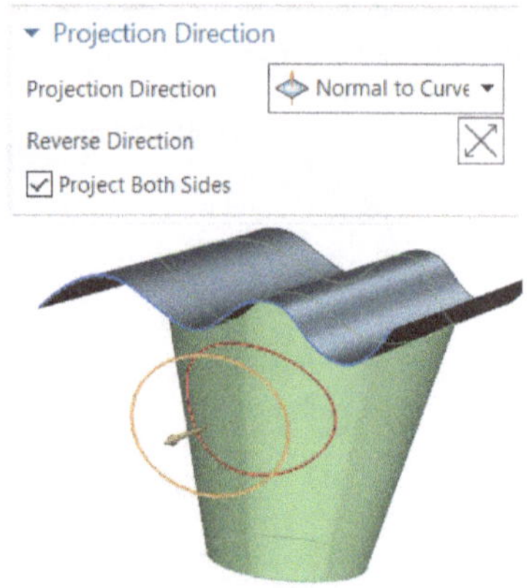

You will notice that the trim boundary is created at the backside of the surface as well. If you want to trim only the front portion of the surface, click **Region > Select region** on the **Trimmed Sheet** dialog and click inside the trim boundary at the backside. Now, click **OK** to trim the surface.

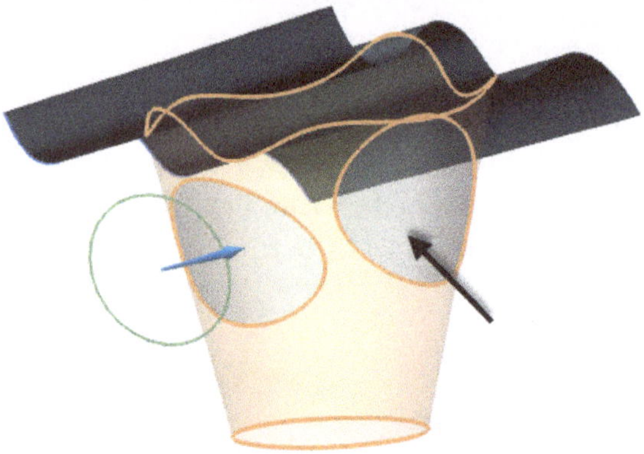

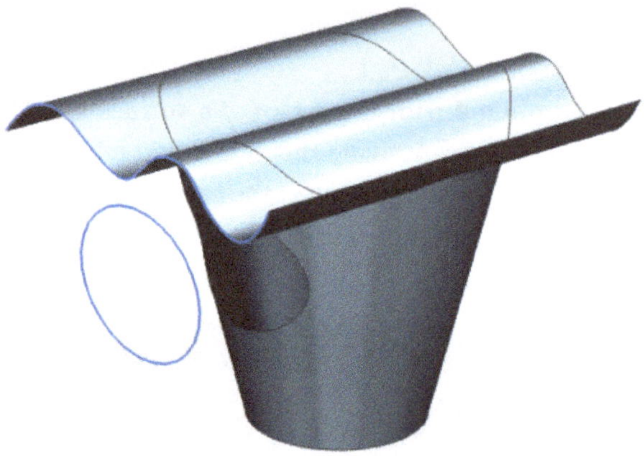

Trim and Extend

This command trims or extends a set of surfaces by the distance that you specify or up to another surface. Activate this command (on the ribbon, click **Surface > Combine > Trim and Extend**) and select **Type > Make Corner** on the **Trim and Extend** dialog. Click on edge to extend and click **Tool > Select Face or Edge**. Click on the surface to trim. Under the **Desired Results** section, select **Arrow Side > Delete** to trim the side in which the arrow is pointing. Click **OK** to create a corner.

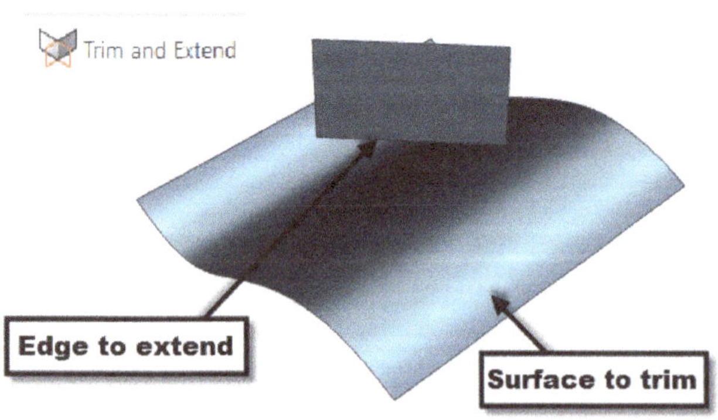

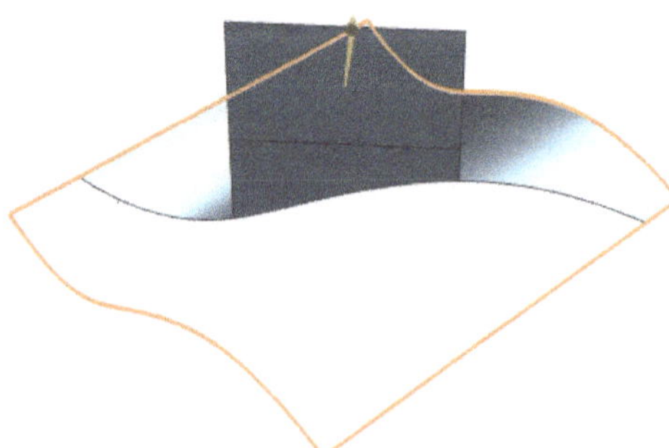

Combine

The **Combine** tool is used to combine multiple surfaces into a single surface and trim the unwanted portions. You can also combine multiple surfaces to form a closed volume.

Combining Surfaces into a Closed Volume

Activate the **Combine** command (On the ribbon, click **Surface > > Combine > Combine**) and click on the surfaces that form a closed volume. On the **Combine** dialog, click the **Find Volume** button. Click **OK** to create a closed volume.

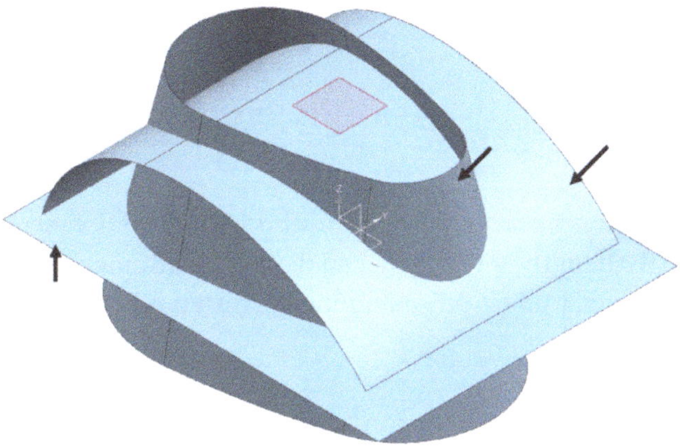

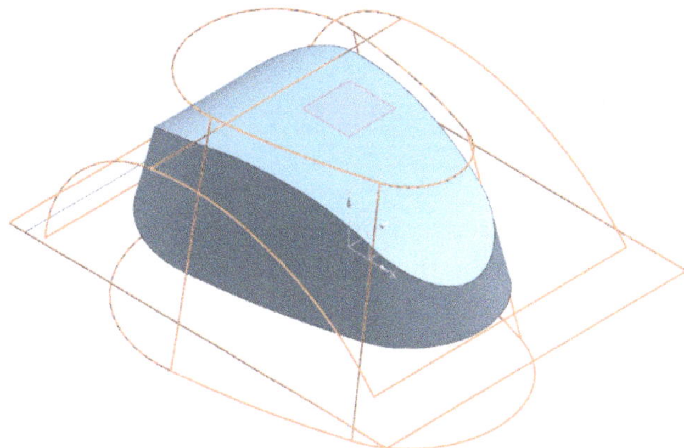

Combining surfaces

Activate the **Combine** command (On the ribbon, click **Surface > Combine > Combine**) and click the **Reset** icon on the **Combine** dialog. On **Combine** dialog, under the **Region** section, select the **Keep** option. Next, click on the surfaces to combine, and then click **OK**.

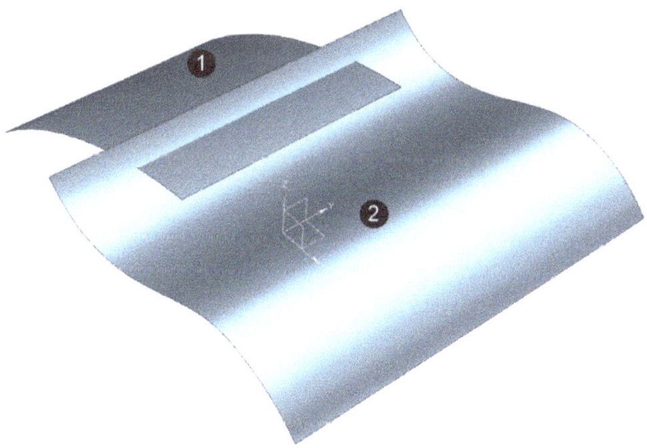

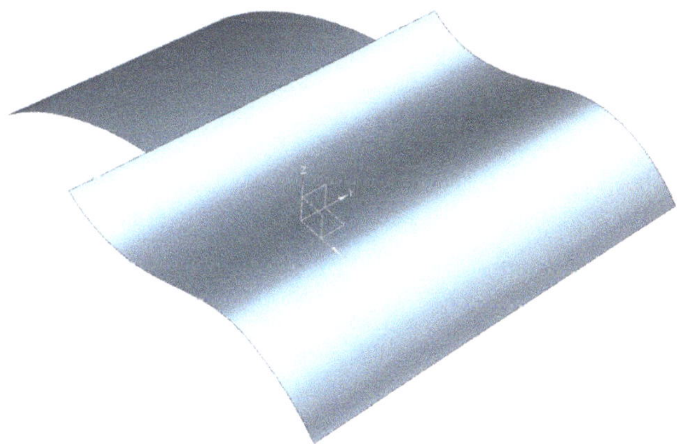

Extension Surface

During the design process, you may sometimes need to extend a surface. You can extend a surface using the **Extension Surface** command. Activate this command (On the ribbon, click **Surface > Base > More > Flange > Extension Surface**) and click the surface to extend. While selecting the surface, you must ensure that you click near the edge to be extended.

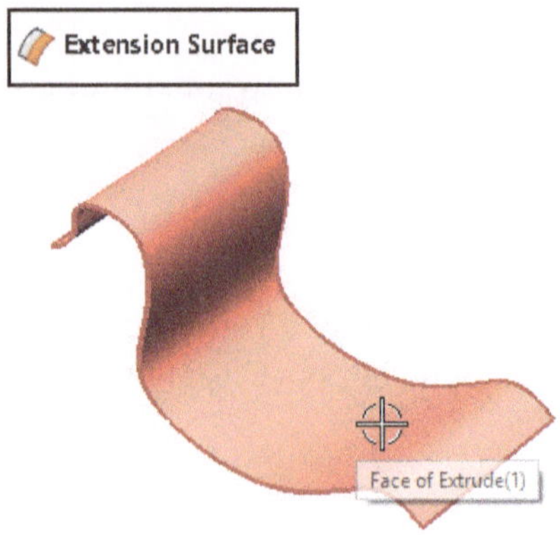

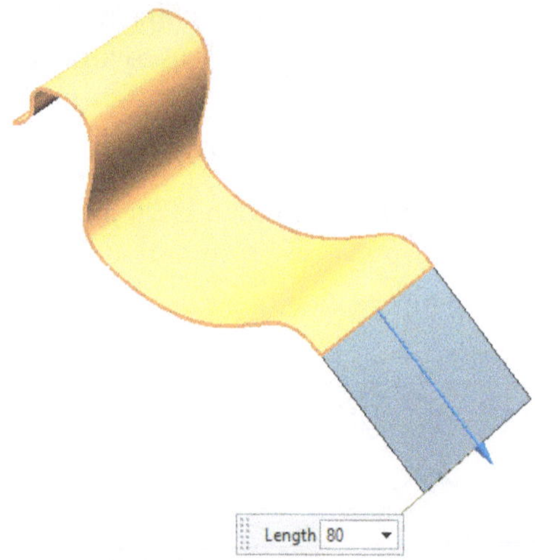

After selecting an edge, you can define the distance of the extension surface by using the options in the **Distance** drop-down (**By Length** and **By Percentage**). If you select the **By Length** option, you can define the distance by entering a value in the **Length** box. If you select the **By Percentage** option, you can define the distance by entering a value in the % **Length** box.

When the surface you have selected is not planar, you can decide the type of extension by using the **Method** options. Use the **Circular** option to extend the surface by maintaining the curvature of the original surface. If you select the **Tangential** option, the extended surface will be created tangent to the original surface.

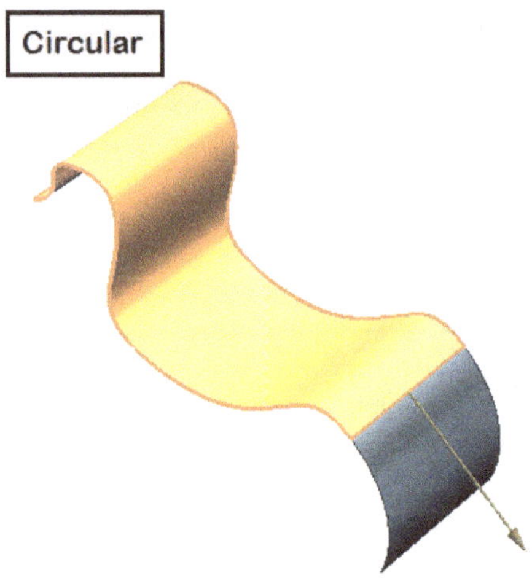

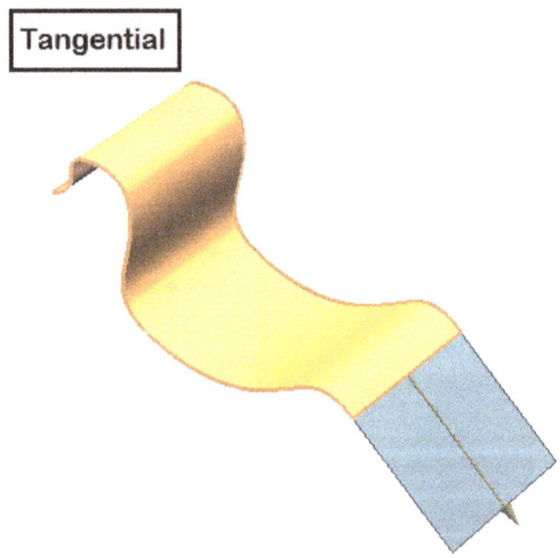

If you want to extend the corners of a surface, then select **Type > Corner** on the **Extension Surface** dialog and click near the corner to extend. Type-in values in the %**U Length** and %**V Length** boxes or drag the arrow handles to define the extension length in both the directions. Click **OK** after specifying the settings.

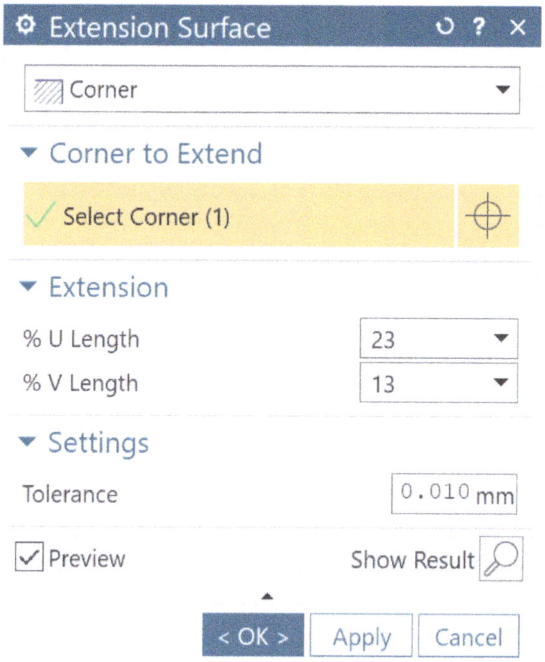

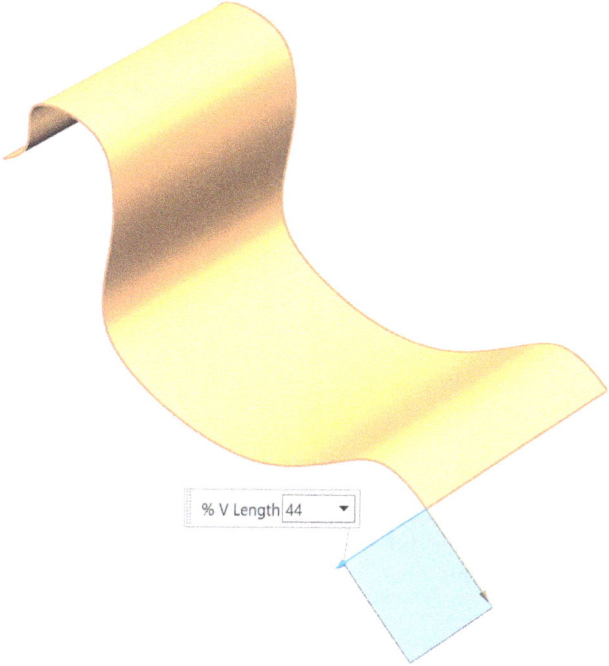

Untrim

You can untrim a trimmed surface using the **Untrim** command. Activate this command (on the ribbon, click **Surface > Combine > More > Trim > Untrim**) and click on the trimmed surface. On the **Untrim** dialog, check the **Hide Original** option and click **OK**.

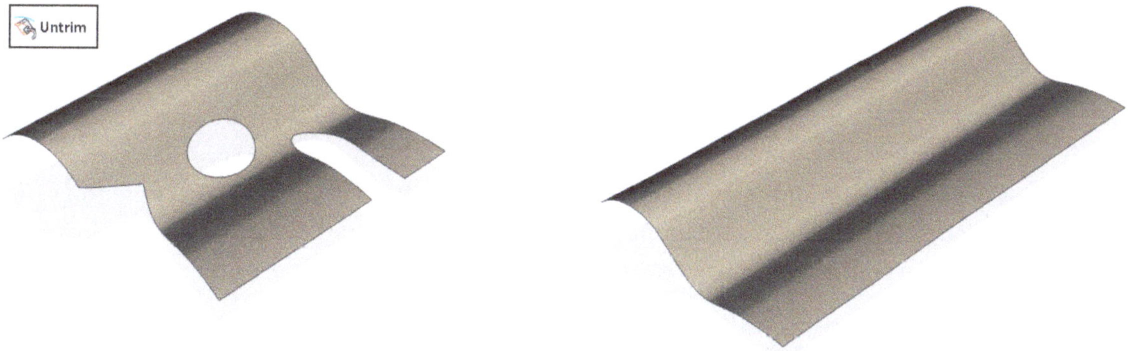

Delete Edge

You can also delete the individual edges of the surface using the **Delete Edge** command. Activate this command (on the ribbon, click **Surface > Combine > More > Trim > Delete Edge**) and click on the edges of the surface body. Click **OK** to delete the edges.

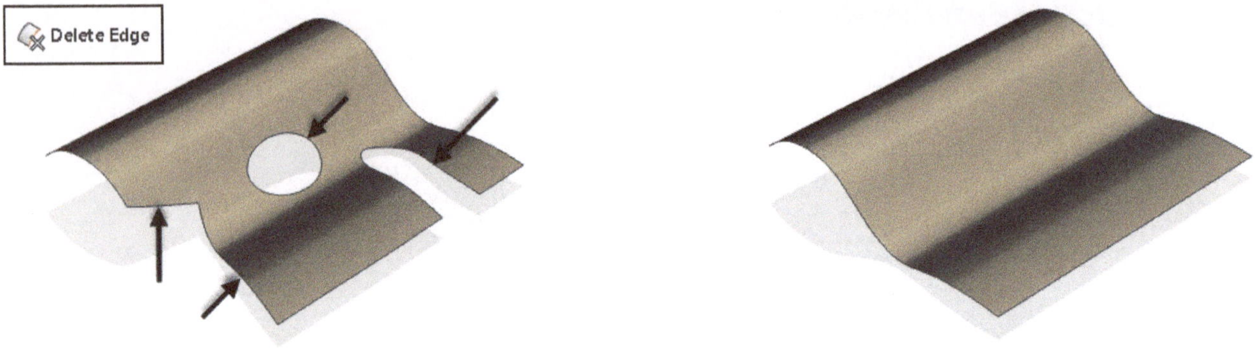

Patch Openings

The **Patch Openings** command can be used to patch holes in models. As a patching tool, the **Patch Openings** command is more robust than deleting holes or untrimming. It provides more discrete control over the definition of the resultant patch. For example, consider the model shown in the figure. You can see that a face is missing. In a case like this, both the **Delete Edge** and **Untrim** commands fail to fill this gap. The **Patch Openings** command will be used in this case.

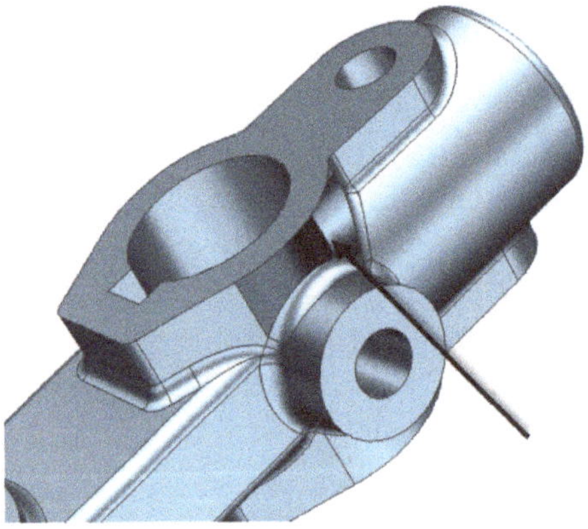

Activate the **Patch Openings** command (on the ribbon, click **Surface > Base > More > Patch Openings**) and select **Type > N-sided Area Patch**. Select all the faces connected to the open face, and then click **Opening to Patch > Select Edge**. Select the edges of the opening and click **OK**.

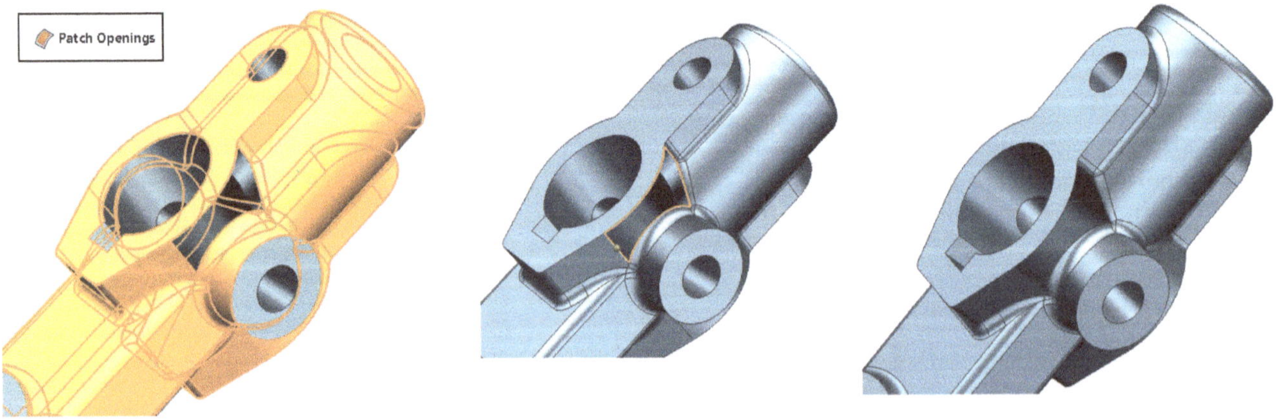

Fill Surface

The application of the **Fill Surface** command is similar to that of the **Patch Openings**, **Delete Edges**, and **Untrim** commands. In addition to filling the openings, this command has some additional options to control the shape of the fill surface. To fill the opening of a solid or surface body, activate the **Fill Surface** command (On the ribbon, click **Surface** tab > **Base** panel > **More > Fill** > **Fill Surface**) and expand the **Settings** section on the **Fill Surface** dialog. In the **Settings** section, specify the **Default Edge Continuity** type (select **G0 (Position)** for this example). Select the edges of the opening and notice the preview of the fill surface.

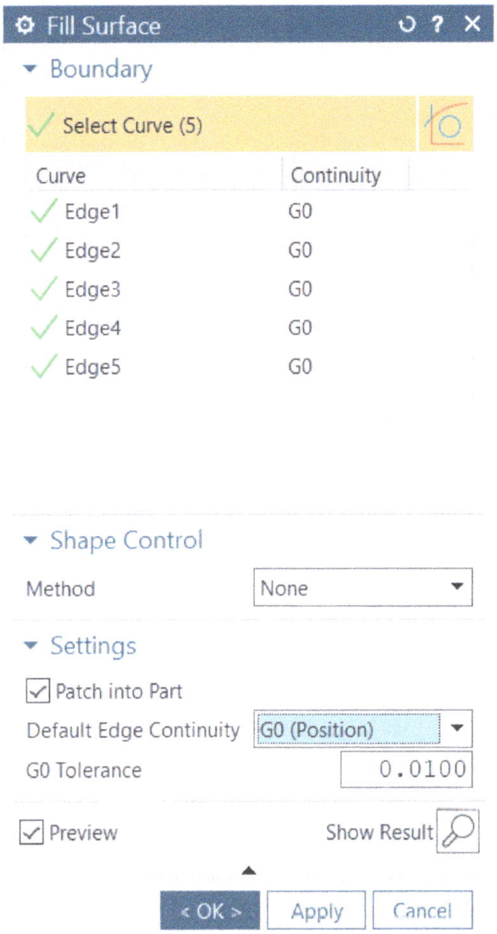

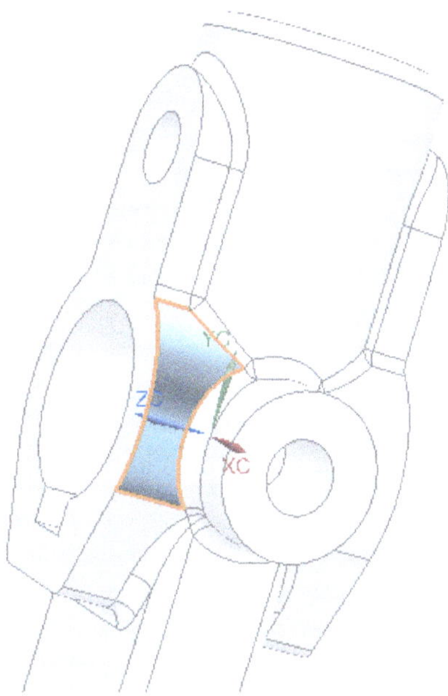

Under the **Shape Control** section, select **Method > Fullness** and notice that a dot appears on fill surface along with an arrow handle. This dot is called the control point. You can change the position of the control point by clicking and dragging it. You can offset the control point by dragging the arrow attached to it (or) dragging the **Control Point Offset** slider in the **Shape Control** section. After achieving the required shape, click **OK** to create the fill surface.

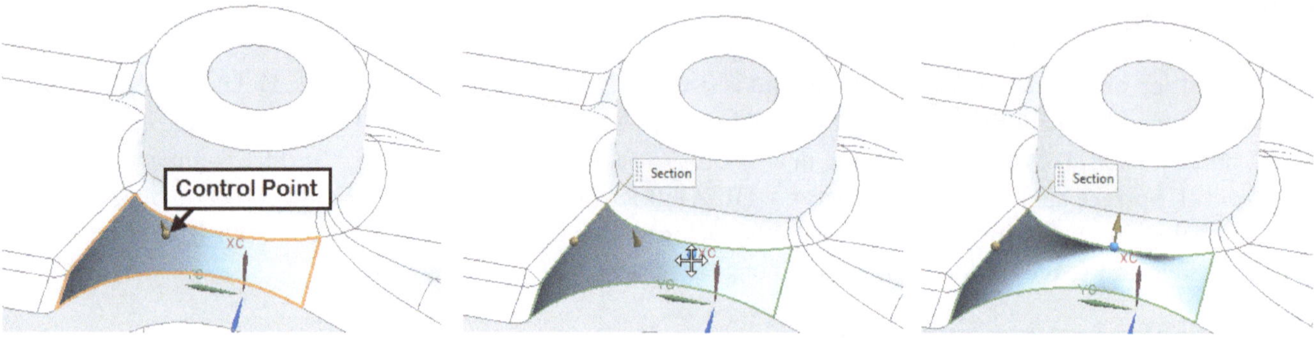

You can also use the curves to control the shape of the fill surface. To do this, select **Method > Fit to Curves** from the **Shape Control** section. Select the boundary and control curves. Click **OK**.

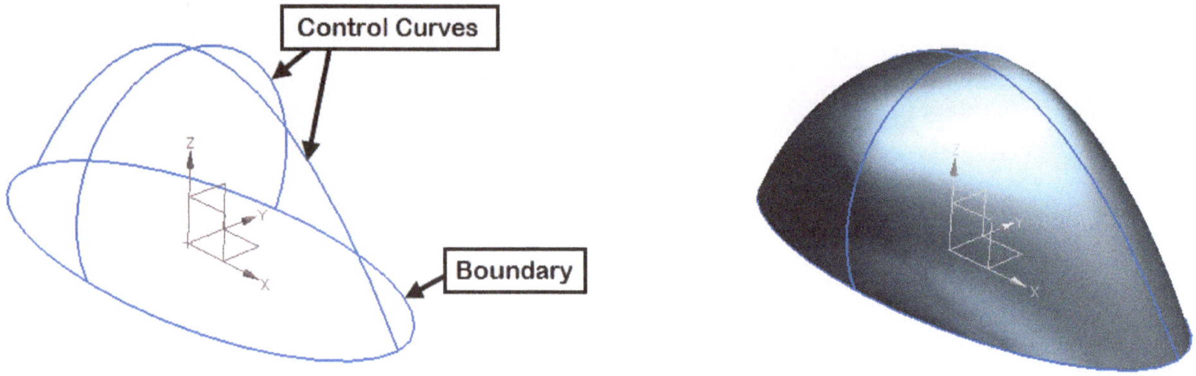

Sewing Surfaces

The surfaces that are created act as individual surfaces unless they are sewed together. The **Sew** command lets you combine two or more surfaces to form a single surface. To sew surfaces, activate the **Sew** command (click **Surface > Combine > Sew** on the ribbon) and select the surfaces to sew.

The value you type in the **Tolerance** box of the **Settings** section defines the tolerance gap. All the surfaces within the tolerance gap will be sewed. Click the **OK** button to sew the surfaces.

Thicken

Creating a solid from a surface can be accomplished by simply thickening a surface. To add thickness to a surface, activate the **Thicken** command (on the ribbon, click **Surface > Base > Thicken**) and click on the face of the surface geometry. Enter the thickness value in the **Offset 1** box.

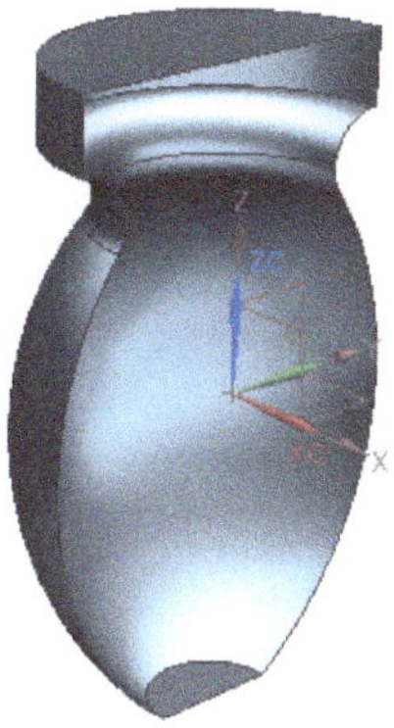

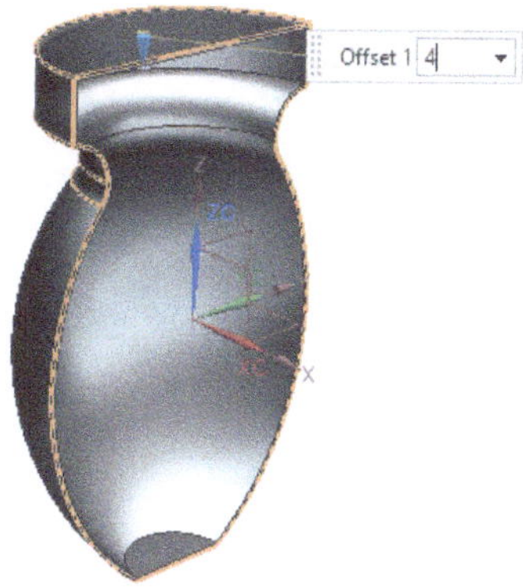

If you want to keep a region of your surface body open, then click **Region Behavior > Region to Peirce > Select Boundary Curve** on the **Thicken** dialog. Click on the face to remain open.

If you want a different thickness for a region, then click **Region of Different Thickness > Select Boundary Curve** on the dialog. Click on the region to have different thickness, and then drag the arrow handle to add different thickness to it.

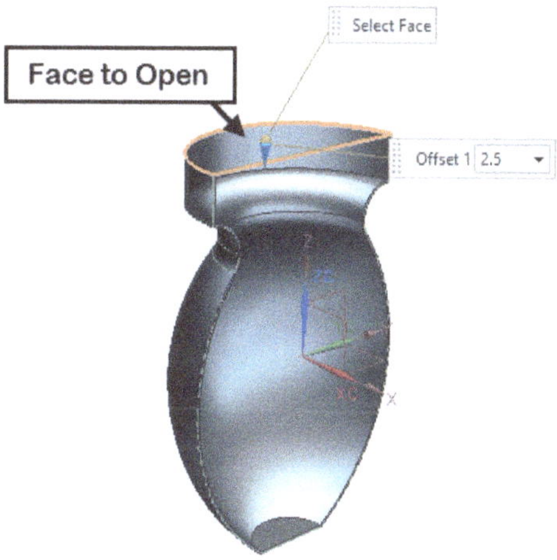

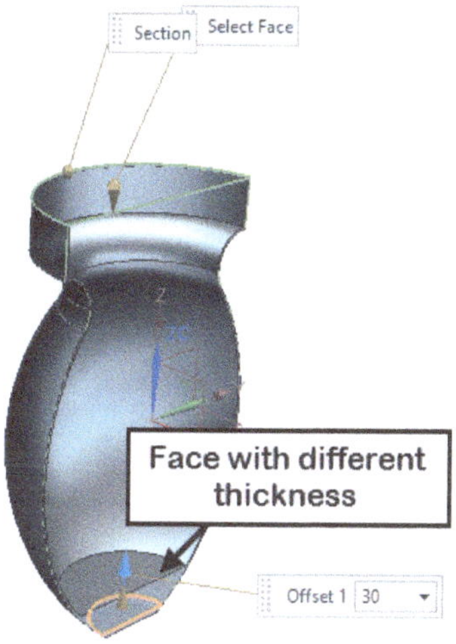

Trim Body

You can trim a solid with a surface using the **Trim Body** command. For example, you can trim the solid shown in the figure using a surface and create a complex face on the top.

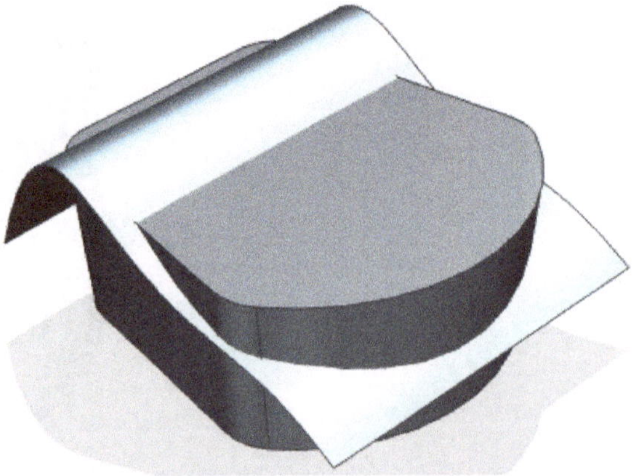

To trim solid using a surface, activate the **Trim Body** command (on the ribbon, click **Home > Base > Trim Body**) and select the target body. On the **Trim Body** dialog, click **Select Face or Plane** and select the tool body. If you want to reverse the trim direction, then click the **Reverse Direction** button. Click **OK**. Next, hide the tool body to view the result.

X-Form

The **X-Form** command is a powerful feature that is used to create ergonomic shapes. This command allows you to push and pull on a surface to create complex shapes that are otherwise difficult to produce. An X-form can be applied to any face. It can be a surface or a face of a solid body.

To create an X-form surface, activate the **X-Form** command (on the ribbon, click **Surface > Edit > X-Form**) and select a face. On the **X-Form** dialog, under the **Parameterization** section, specify the **Degree** and **Patches** values. A mesh appears on the selected surface. You will also notice the poles on the mesh.

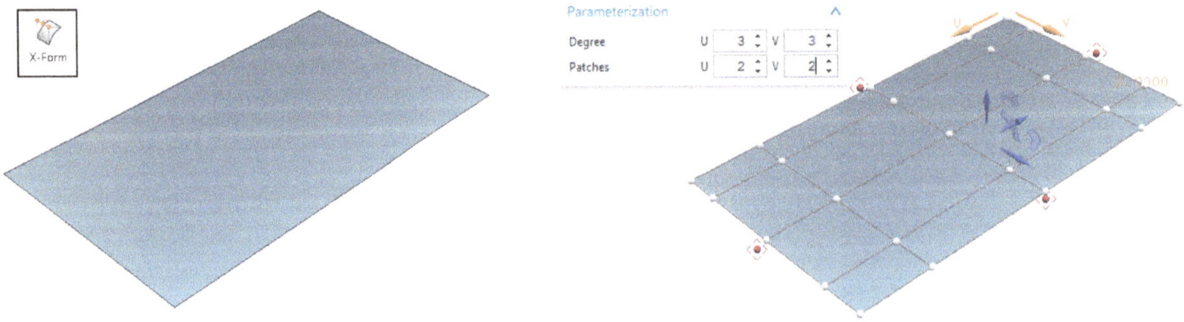

You can drag these poles to change the shape of the face.

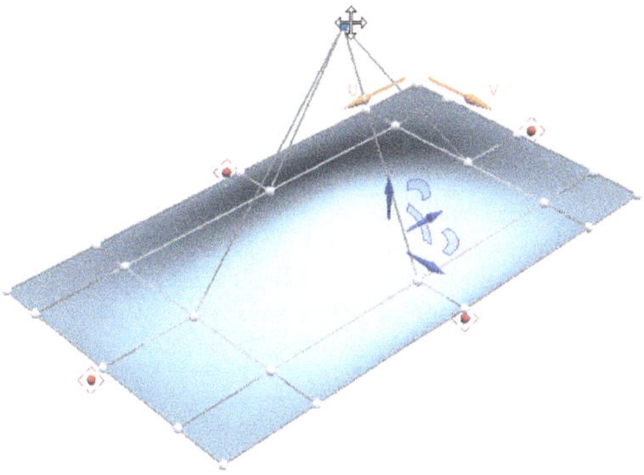

You can use the OrientXpress tool to push and pull on the surface along the three directions (X, Y, and Z). For example, if you want to pull the surface along the Z-direction, select the Z-axis vector and drag the poles. This pushes or pulls the surface along the Z-direction. In addition, you can also select the rows to manipulate the surface. To do this, select **Pole Selection > Manipulate > Any** on the **X-Form** dialog, and then drag the rows.

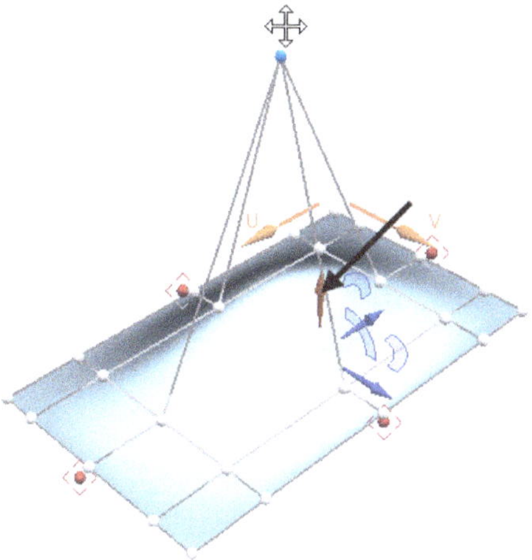

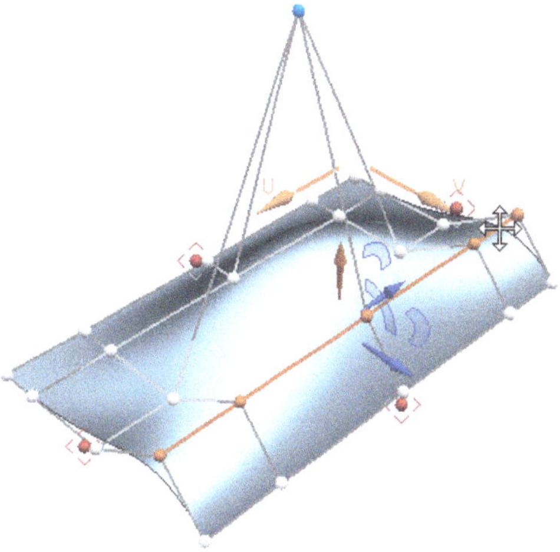

I-Form

Use the **I-Form command** to modify a face by adding isoparametric curves, which can then be adjusted in any direction to reshape the surface. This tool provides a flexible way to give the face a dynamic and customized form. You can directly select and manipulate the control poles or polygons of any face type, whether it is a B-surface or a non-B-surface, without the need to extract, untrim, refit, replace, or convert the geometry.

Each modification you apply builds progressively on the face, allowing for controlled transformation. For example, you might first adjust the U-direction isoparametric curves and then refine the surface further by editing the V-direction curves. This incremental approach gives you precise control over the surface design.

On the ribbon, click **Surface > Edit > I-Form**  and select a face. Next, specify the isoparametric curves on the Iso Curves section of the **I-Form** dialog. For example, select **Direction > U**, **Location > Uniform**, and then type 5 in the **Number** box. Next, you need to add constraint points on the isoparametric curves. To do this, activate **Select Iso Curves** in the **Iso Curve Shape Control** section of the dialog box and select the three isoparametric curves in the graphics window where you want to insert constraint points. In case you don't select any curves, constraint points will be added to all of them. Type **4** in the **Number** box available in the **Iso Curve**

Shape Control section. Next, click and drag the control points you wish to move. You can also use the OrientXpress tool to drag the control points along the selected direction. In case you haven't specified a drag direction (e.g., by using the OrientXpress tool), each constraint point will move along its surface normal direction. Once you've completed your adjustments, click **OK** to apply the changes.

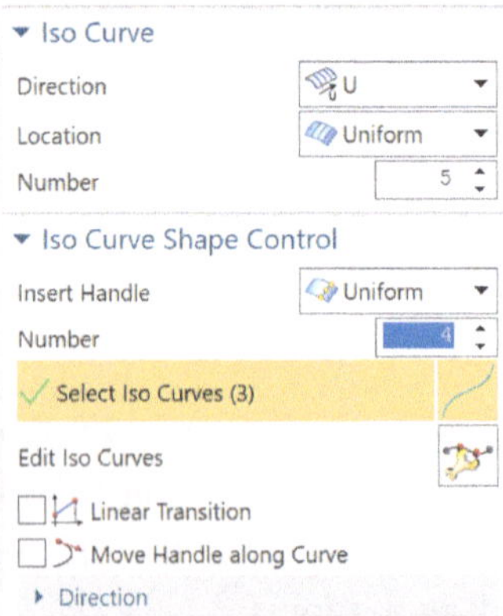

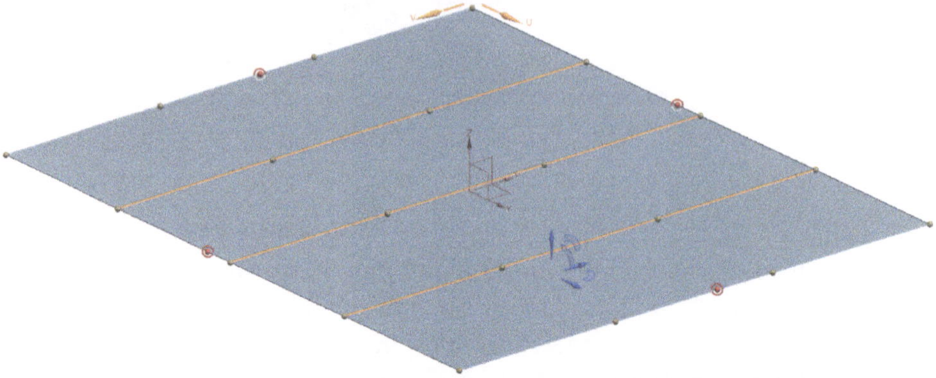

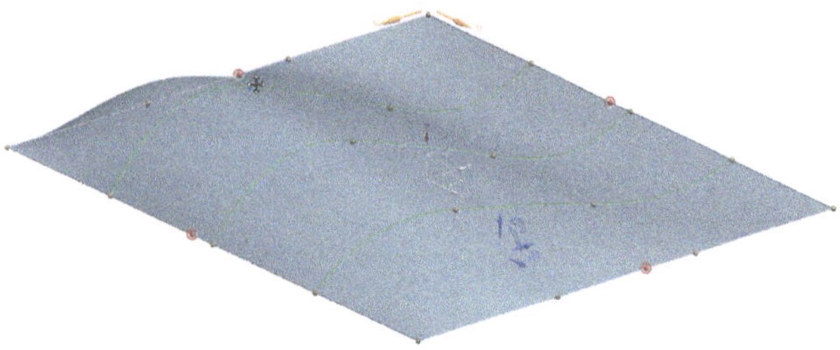

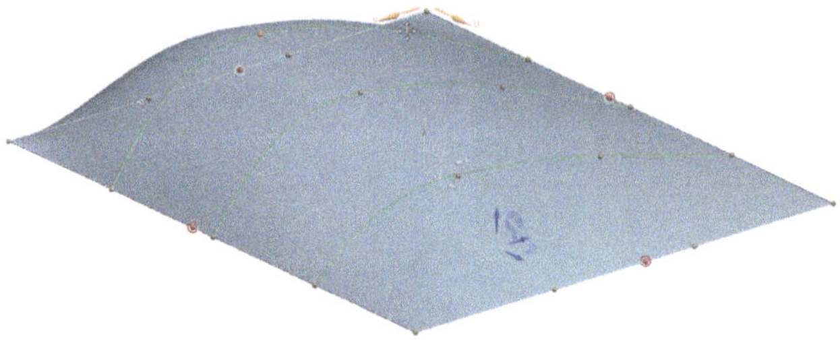

Example

In this example, you will construct the model shown below.

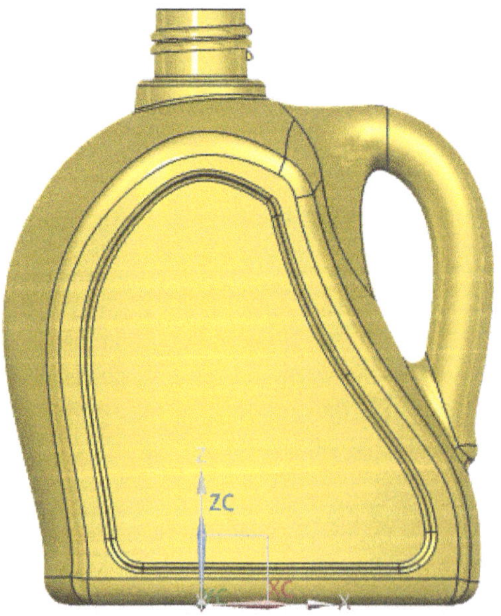

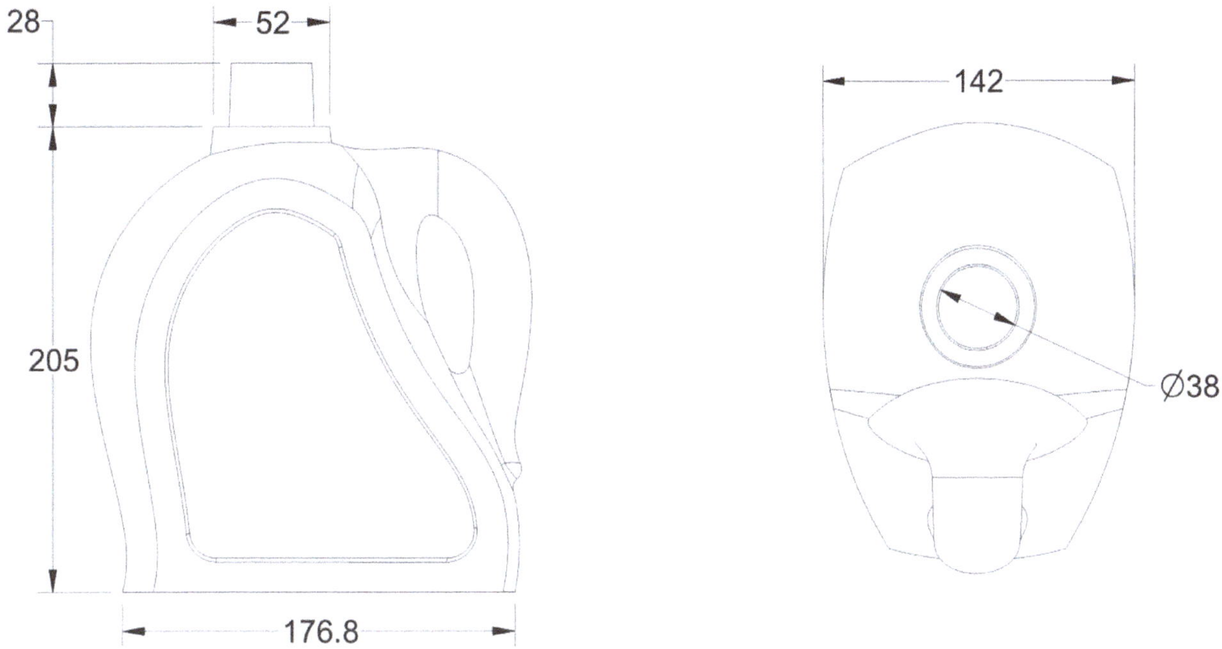

Drawing the layout sketch

1. Start **NX**.
2. Start a new part file using the **Model** template.
3. Click **File > Preferences > Modeling.** On the **Modeling Preferences** dialog, set the **Body Type** to **Sheet** and click **OK**.
4. Start a sketch on the XZ plane.
5. Activate the **Line** command (on the ribbon, click **Home > Curve > Line**) and create the horizontal and vertical lines, as shown.
6. Make the horizontal and vertical lines collinear to the X-axis and Y-axis, respectively.

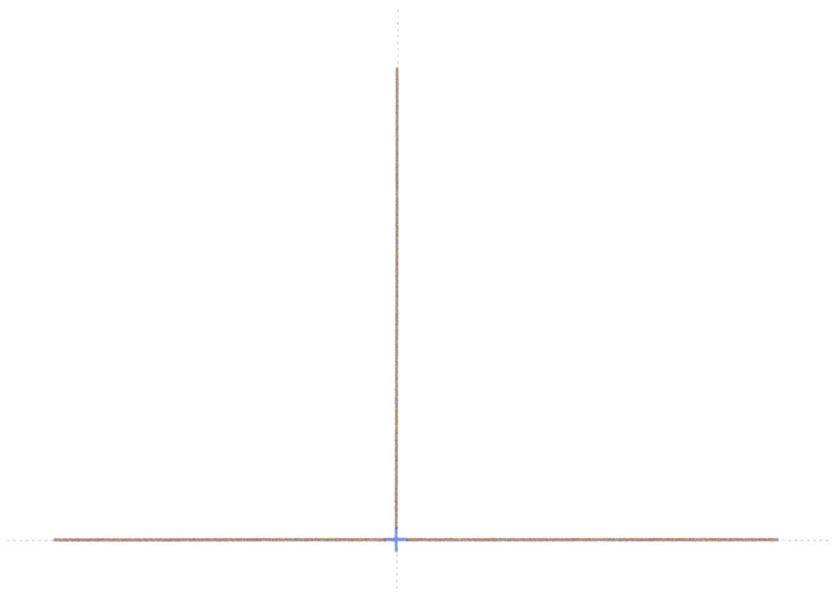

7. Select the vertical line and click the **Convert to Reference** button on the contextual toolbar.
8. Activate the **Spline** (on the ribbon, click **Home > Curve > Spline**) command.
9. On the **Studio Spline** dialog, select **Type > Through Points** and specify the points, as shown.
10. Leave the default settings on the dialog, and then click **OK**.

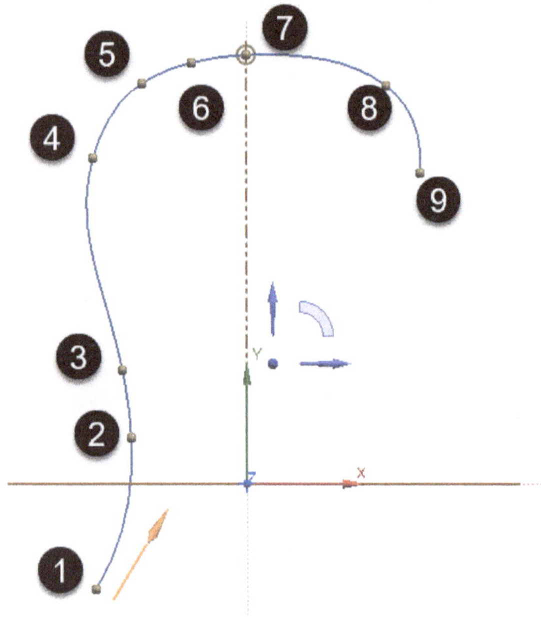

11. Add dimensions to the sketch.

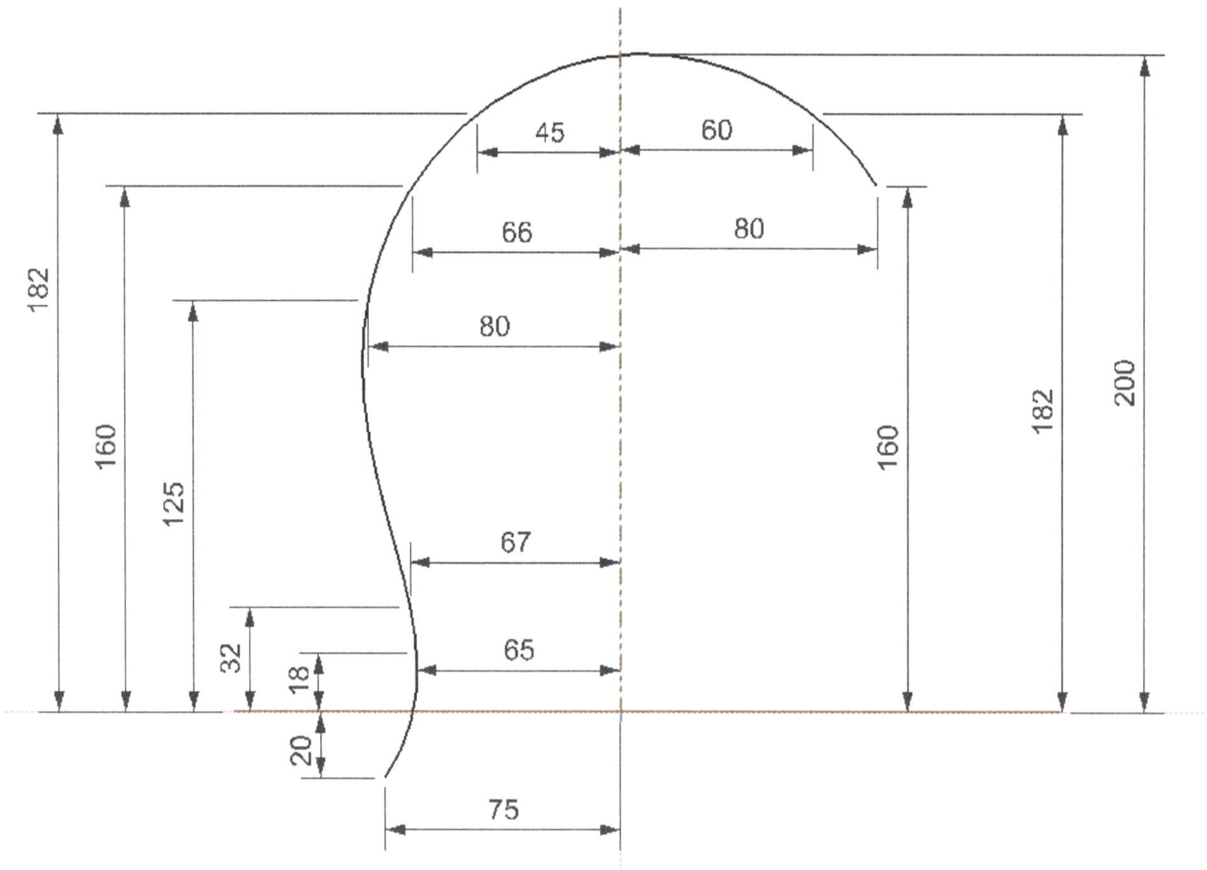

12. Click on the horizontal line and select **Convert to Reference** on the contextual toolbar.
13. Click **Home > Sketch > Finish** on the ribbon.
14. Start a new sketch on the XZ-Plane.
15. Activate the **Studio Spline** command and draw another spline curve similar to the one shown in the figure.

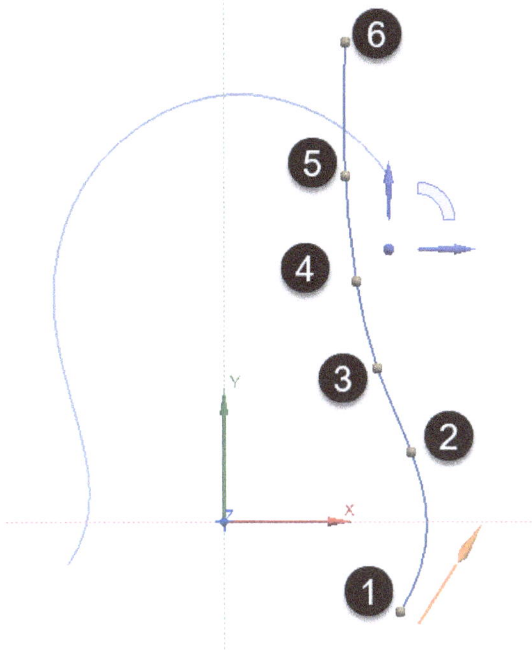

16. Add dimensions to the spline.

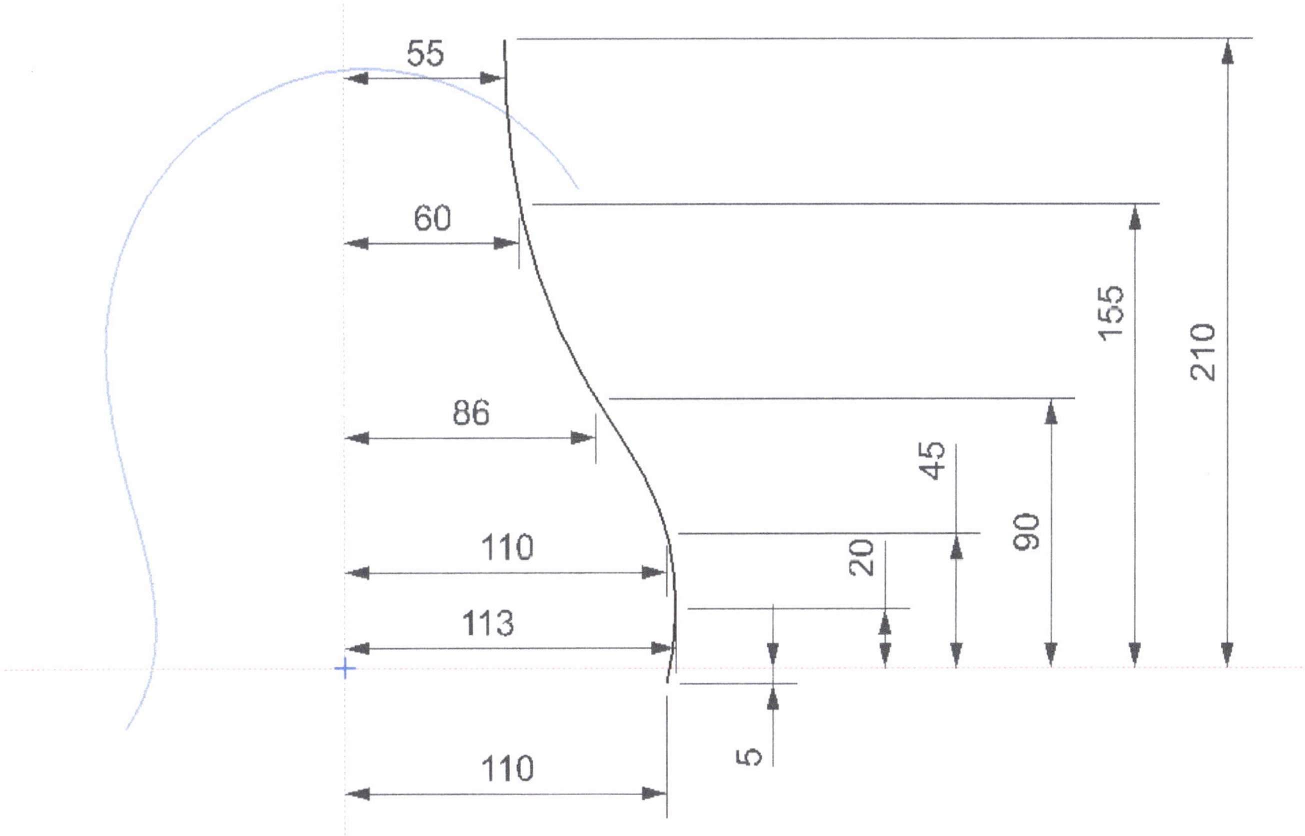

17. Click **Home > Direct > Finish** on the ribbon.
18. Start a new sketch on the XZ-Plane.
19. Create another spline similar to the one shown below.

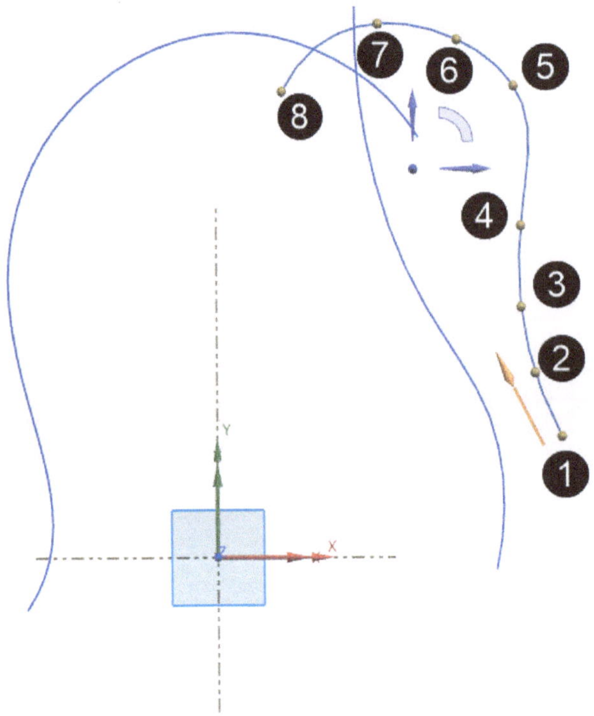

20. Add dimensions to the spline.

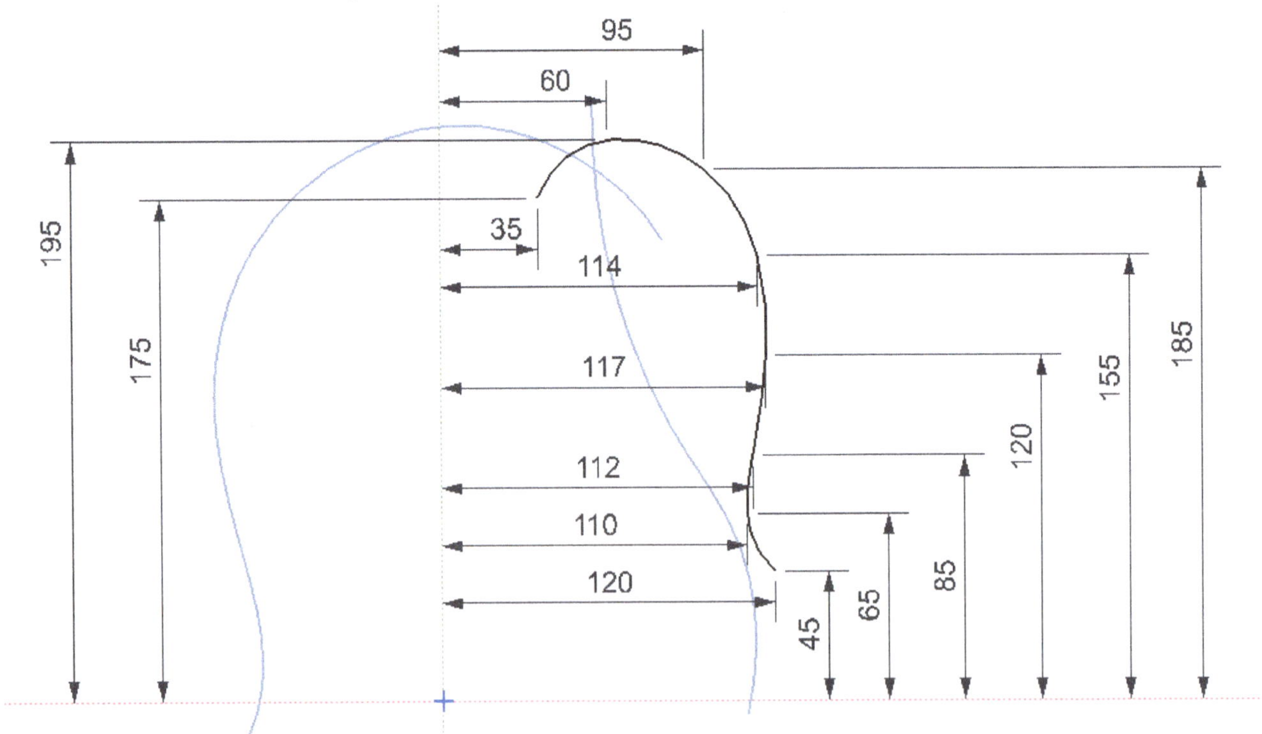

21. Finish the sketch.

If you find it difficult to create the layout sketch, then you can download it from our website.

Creating the Front Surface

1. Create an arc on the XY Plane and add dimensions to it. Note that you need to make the endpoints of the arc symmetric about the horizontal axis. Finish the sketch.

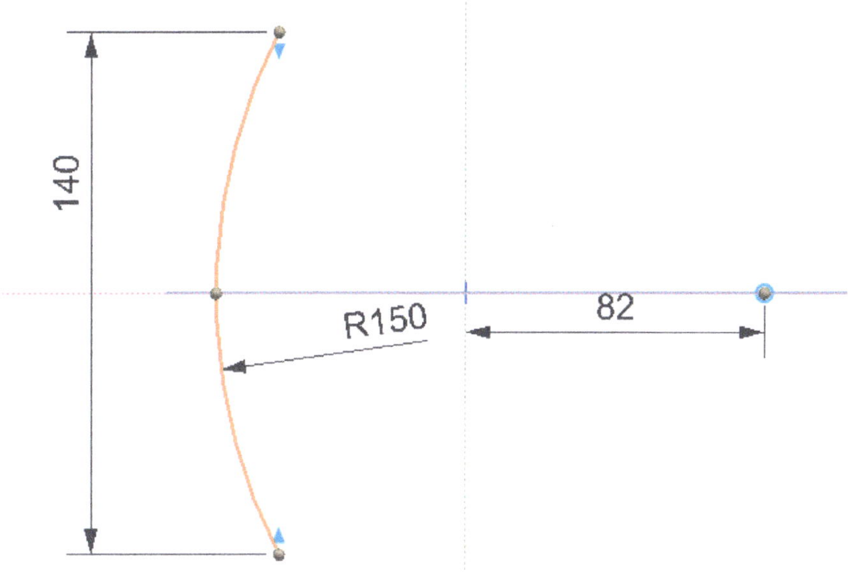

2. Create an arc on the Right Plane and add dimensions to it. Note that you need to make the endpoints of the arc symmetric about the Y-axis. Finish the sketch.

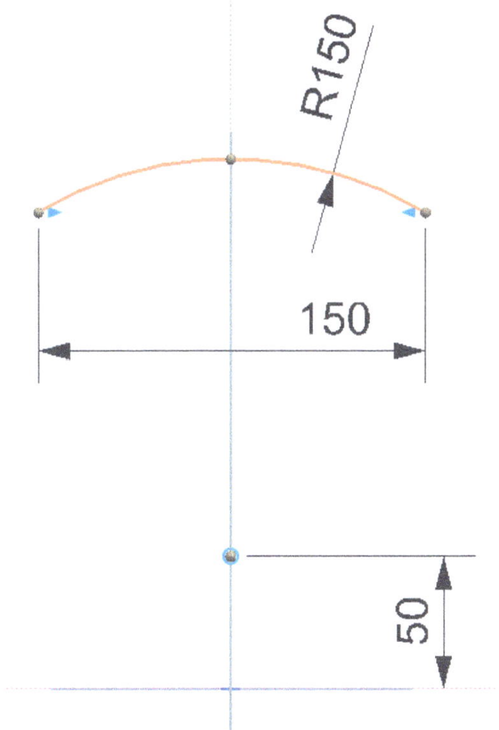

3. Create a datum plane normal to the front face spline.

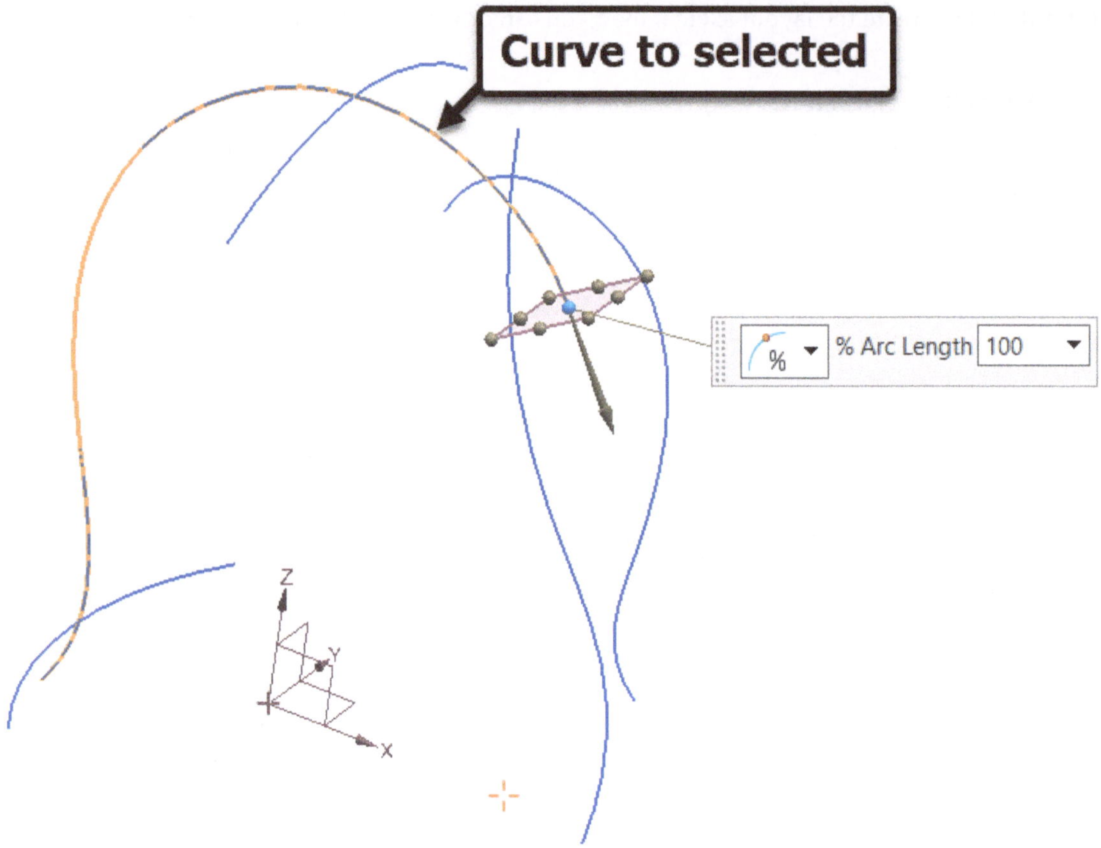

4. Create an arc on the plane normal to the curve.

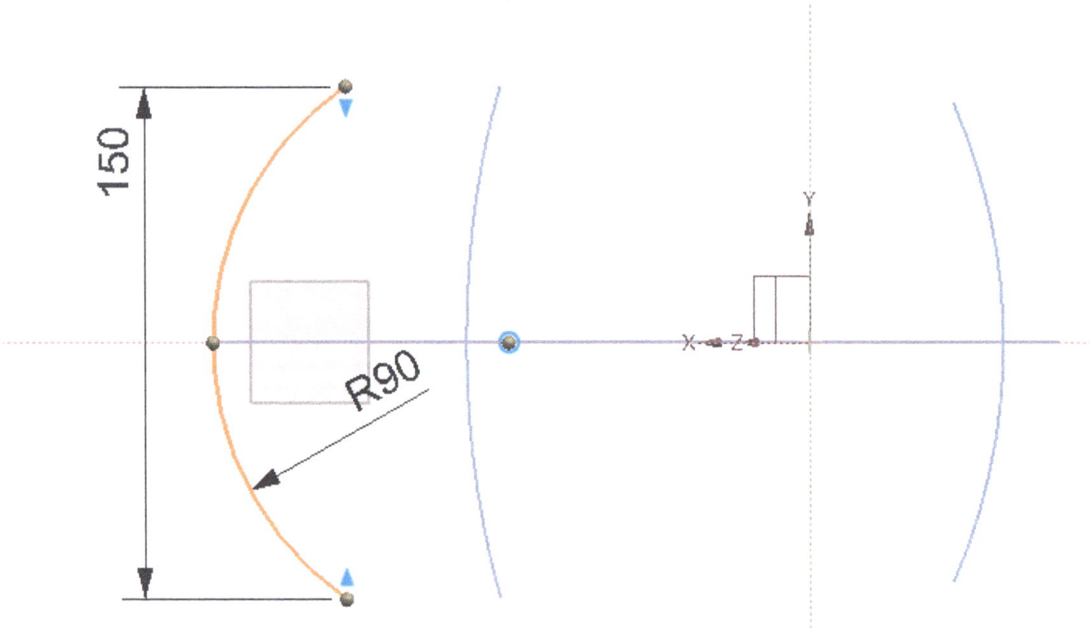

5. Change the orientation to Isometric, and then click **Home > Include > Include**.
6. Select the endpoint of the spline and click **OK**.
7. Select the arc and the include point. Next, click the **Make Coincident** icon on the Sketch Scene Bar.

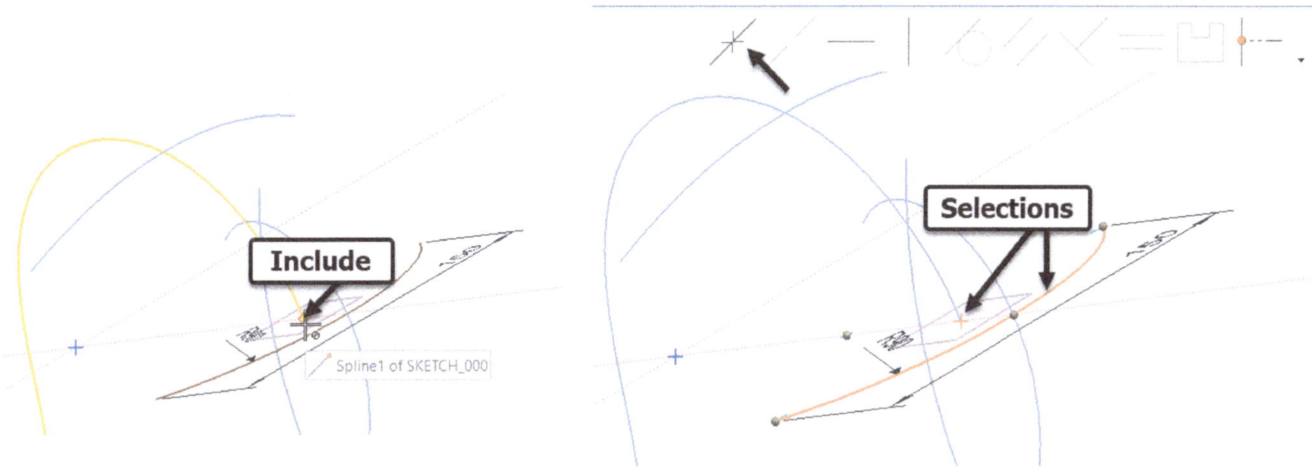

8. Click **Home > Sketch > Finish**.
9. Activate the **Studio Surface** command (on the ribbon, click **Surface > Base > Studio Surface**) and click on the spline to define the section curve.
10. On the dialog, click **Guide (Cross) Curves > Select Curve** and select the first guide curve.
11. Click the middle mouse button and select the second guide curve. Likewise, select the third guide curve.
12. On the **Studio Surface** dialog, expand the **Output Surface Options** section and select **Alignment > Arc Length**. Next, click **OK** to create the studio surface.

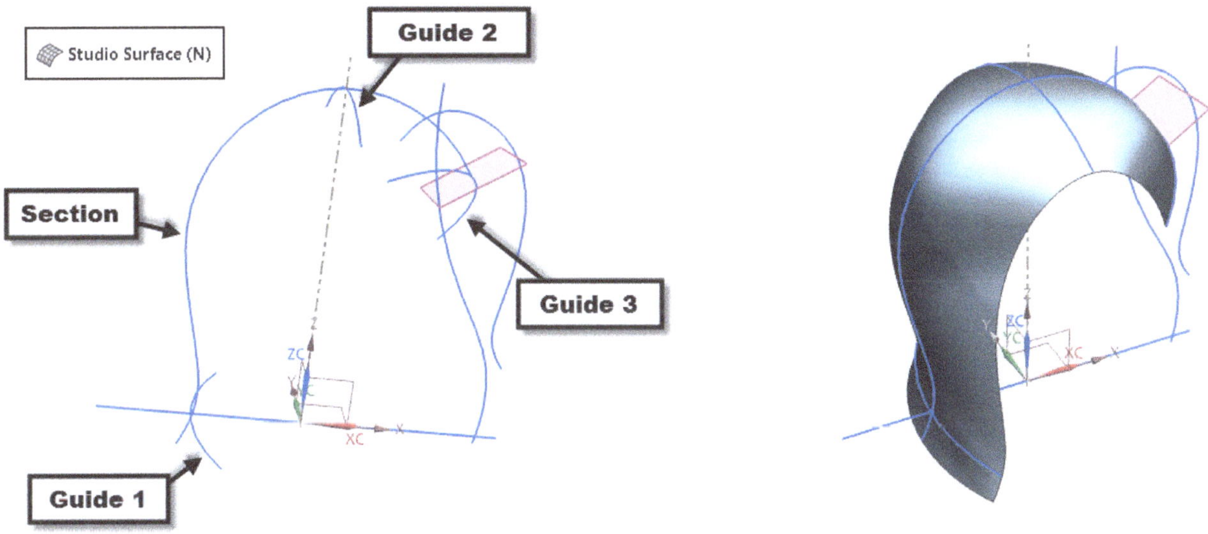

13. Save the file. As you are creating a complex geometry, it is advisable that you save the model after each operation.

Creating the Label surface

1. Start a sketch on the Top plane, and then draw a horizontal arc.
2. Add dimensions and relations to the sketch, as shown below.

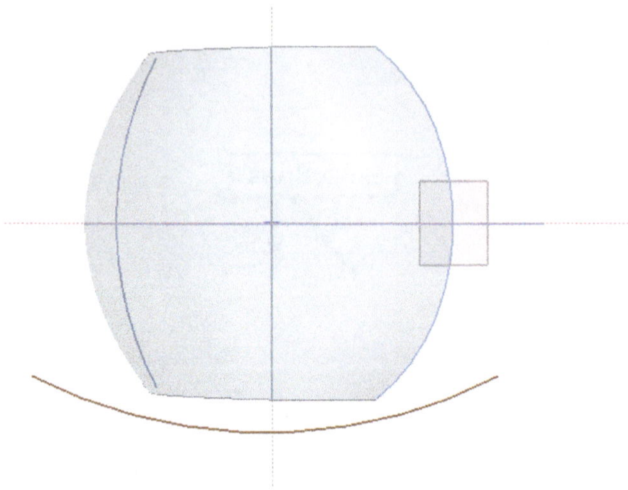

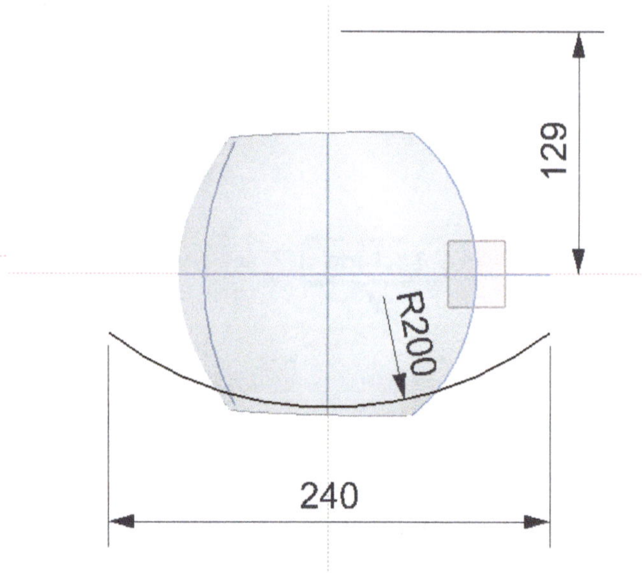

3. Click **Home > Sketch > Finish**.
4. Activate the **Extrude** command (on the ribbon, click **Surface > Base > Extrude**) and extrude the arc up to 220 mm distance. Ensure that **Boolean** is set to **None**.
5. Activate the **Mirror Feature** command (on the ribbon, click **Home > Base > Mirror Feature**), and then mirror the extruded surface about the XZ plane.

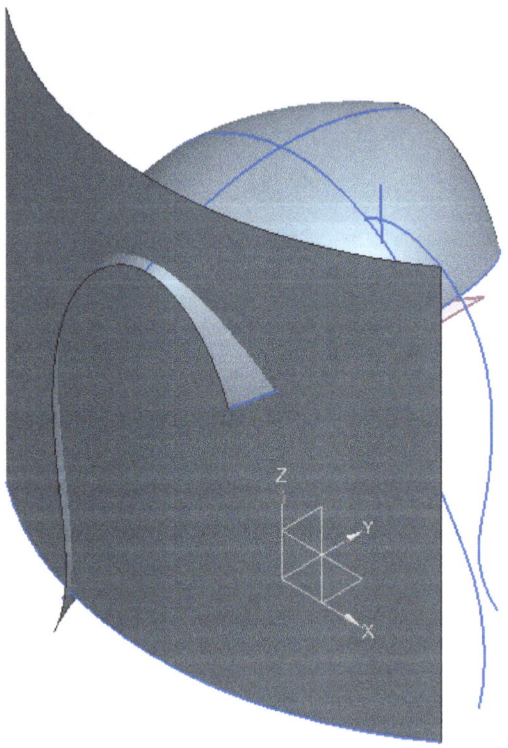

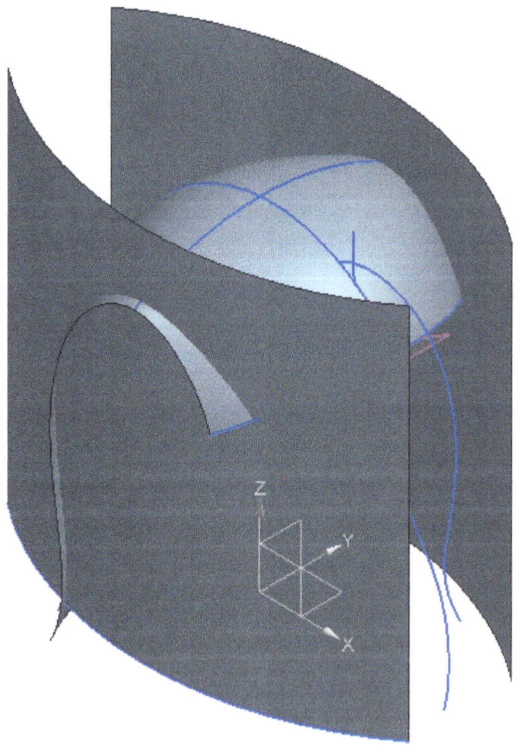

Creating the Back surface

1. Create an arc on the XY plane. Finish the sketch.

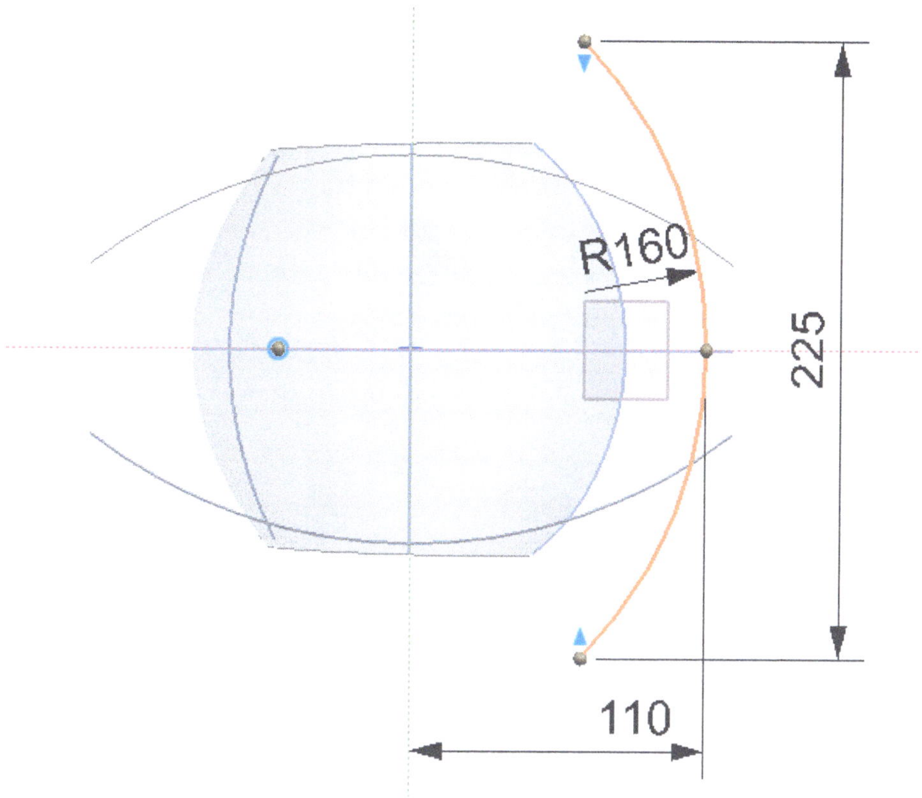

2. Activate the **Studio Surface** command (Click **Surface > Base > Studio Surface** on the ribbon).
3. Select the section from the graphics window, as shown.
4. On the **Studio Surface** dialog, click **Guide (Cross) Curves > Select Curve**, and then select the guide curve, as shown. Next, click **OK** to create the studio surface, as shown.

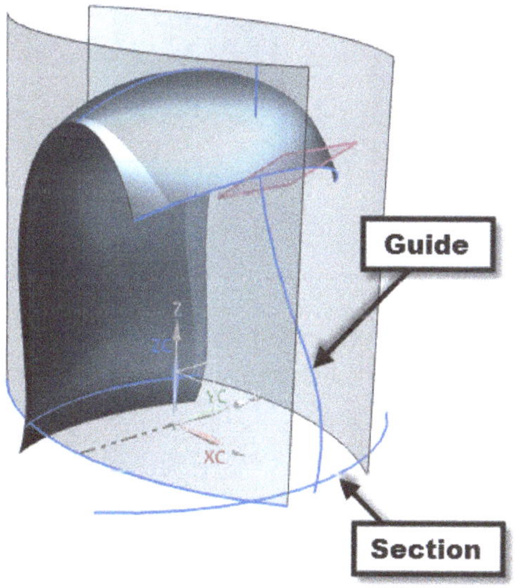

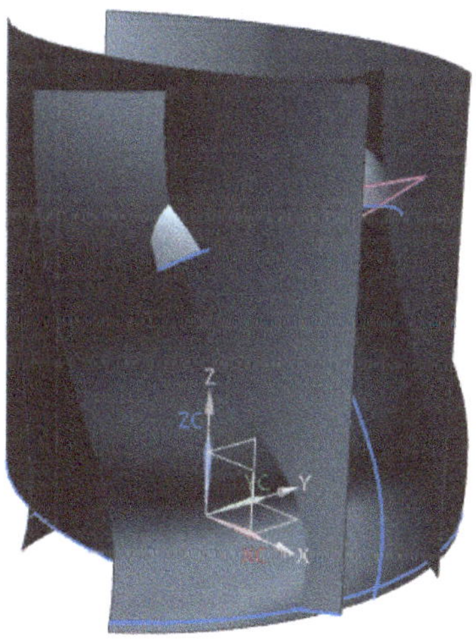

Trimming the Unwanted Portions

1. Activate the **Trim and Extend** command (on the ribbon, click **Surface > Combine > Trim and Extend**) and select **Trim and Extend Type > Make Corner**.
2. Select the target body and click **Tool > Select Face or Edge**.

3. Click on the tool body and click the **Reverse Direction** buttons under the **Tool** and **Target** sections such that they are pointing inwards.
4. Click **Apply**; the two surfaces are trimmed and stitched together.

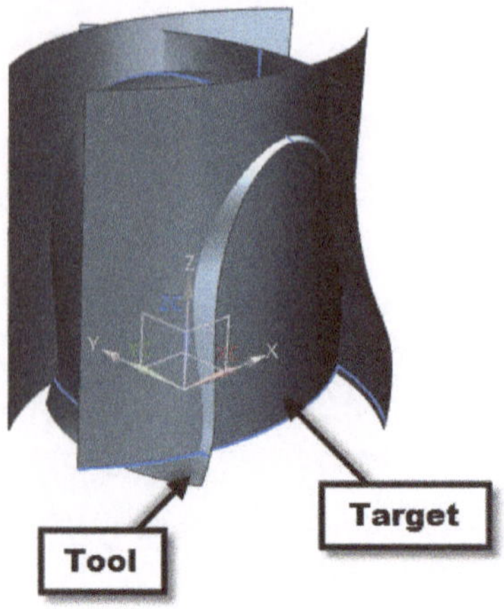

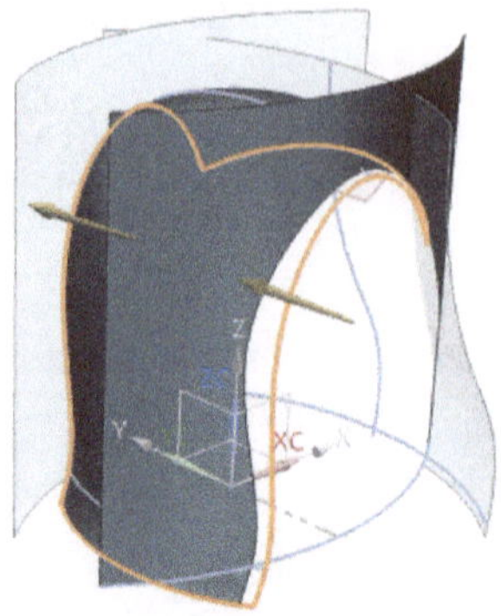

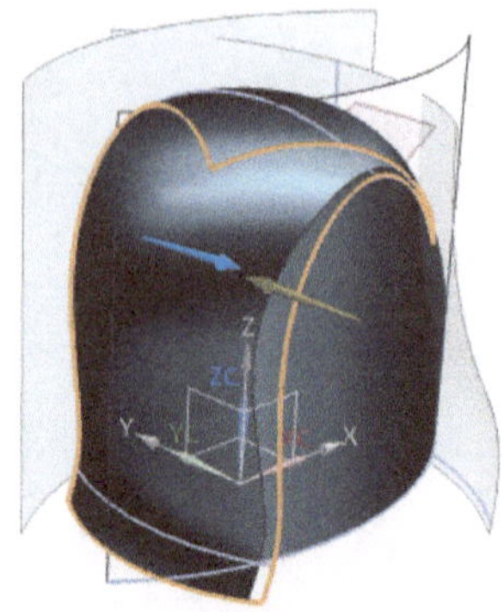

5. Likewise, trim the mirrored surface body by using the front face as a tool body. Click the **Apply** button selecting the target and tool bodies.

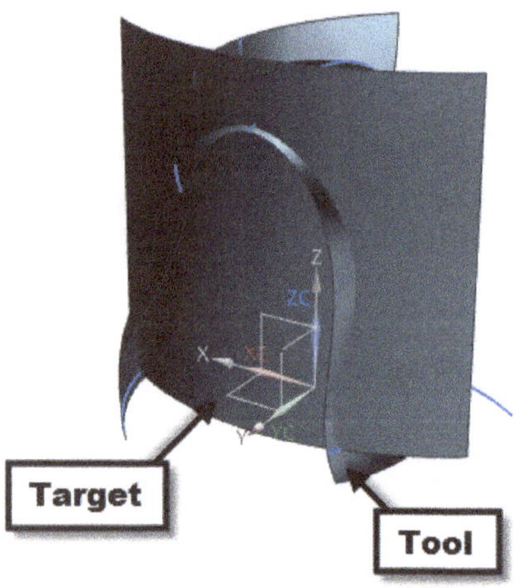

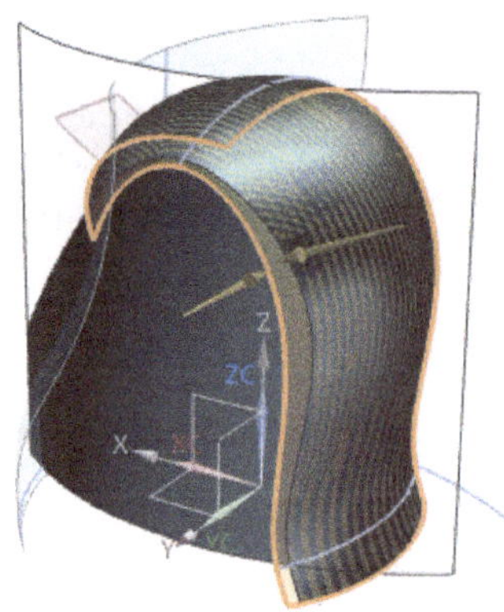

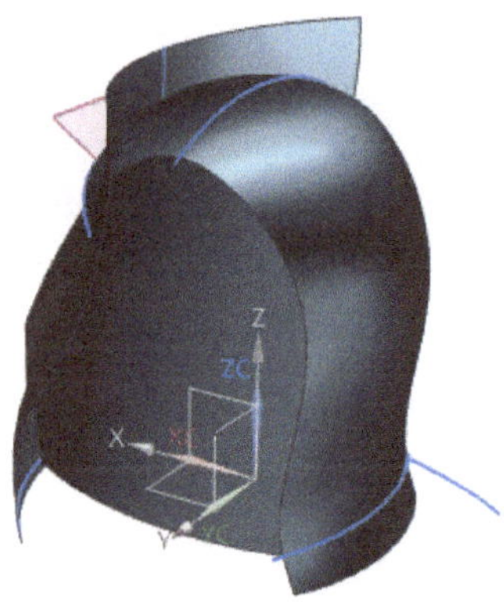

6. Select the back surface to define the target body.
7. On the **Trim and Extend** dialog, click **Tool > Select Face or Edge**, and then select the label surface.
8. Make sure that the arrows on the target and tool bodies point inward. You can change the arrow directions by double-clicking on them or using the **Reverse Direction** buttons in the **Target** and **Tool** sections.
9. Click **OK** after the desired preview appears. Notice that the selected surfaces are trimmed and stitched together. This makes all the surfaces to act as a single surface body.

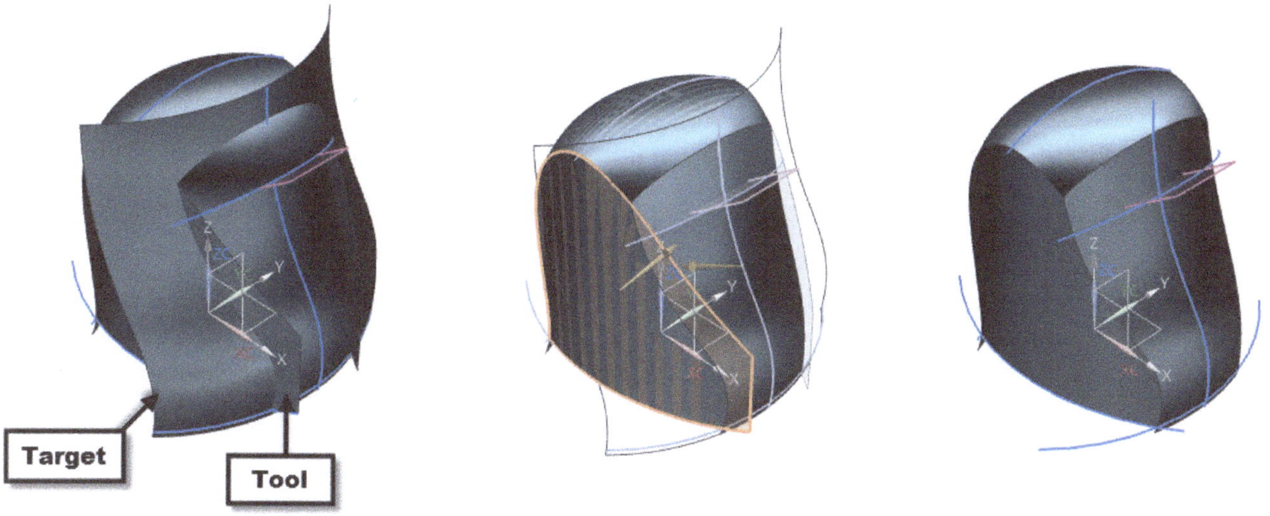

10. Activate the **Trim Sheet** command (on the ribbon, click **Surface > Combine > Trim Sheet**) and click on the surface body.
11. On the **Trim Sheet** dialog, click **Boundary > Select Object**, and then select the XY Plane from the Datum Coordinate System.

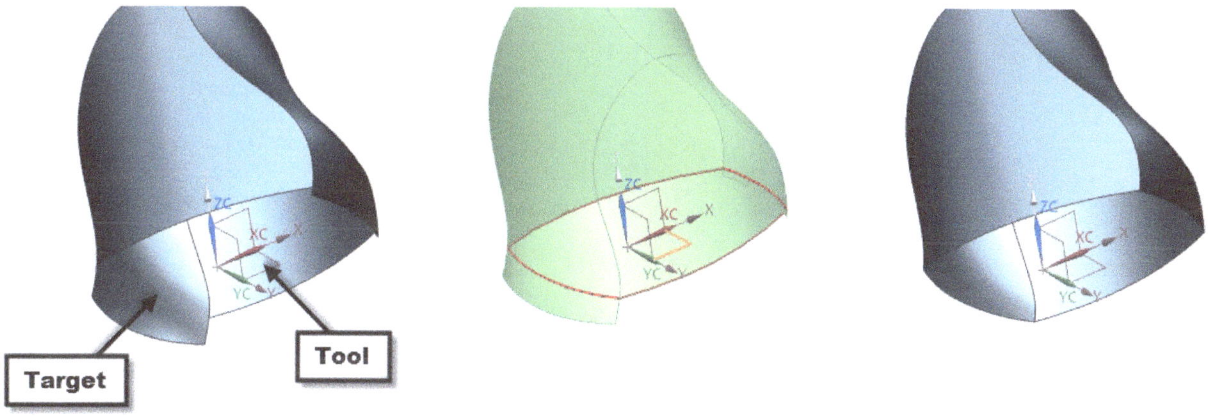

12. Click **OK** to trim the sheet.

Creating the Handle Surface

1. Activate the **Datum Plane** command and click on the lower end-point of the spline. Click **OK** to create the plane normal to the spline.

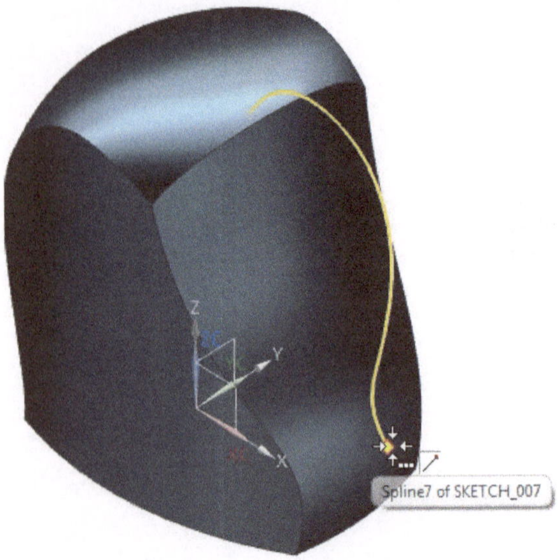

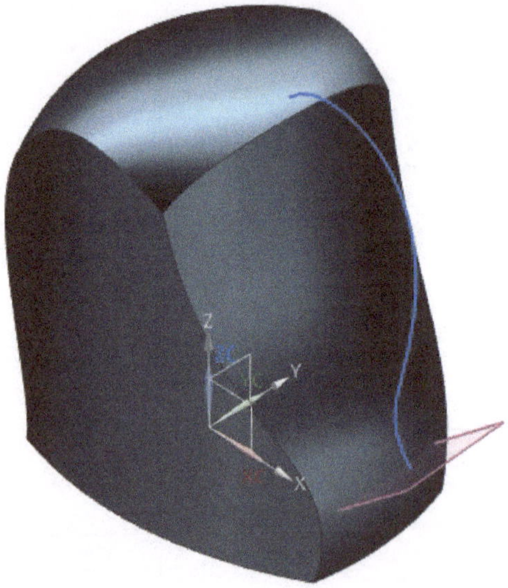

2. Start a sketch on the plane normal to the spline.
3. Activate the **Ellipse** command and create an ellipse on the sketch plane.
4. Create two lines between the ellipse and its center. Apply the **Horizontal** relation to one line and the **Vertical** relation to another.

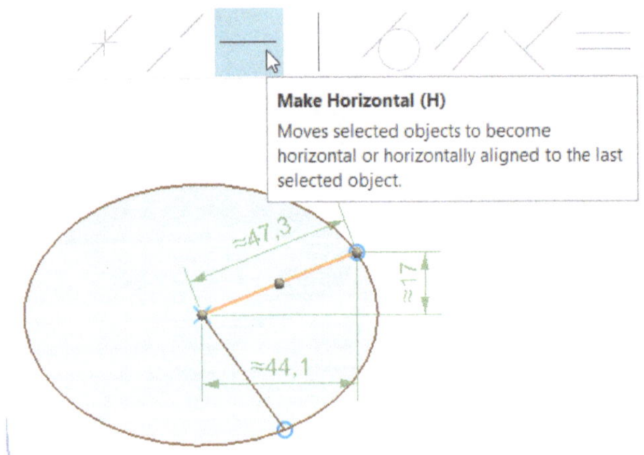

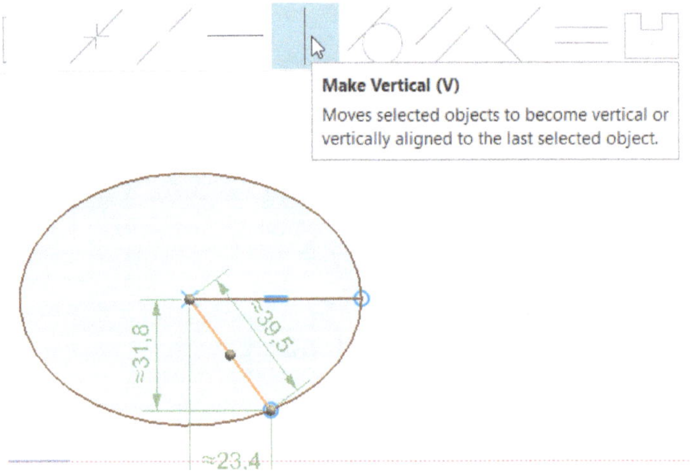

5. Select the horizontal line and the ellipse. Click the **Make Parallel** icon on the Sketch Scene Bar. Next, select the two lines and click **Convert to Reference** on the Context toolbar.

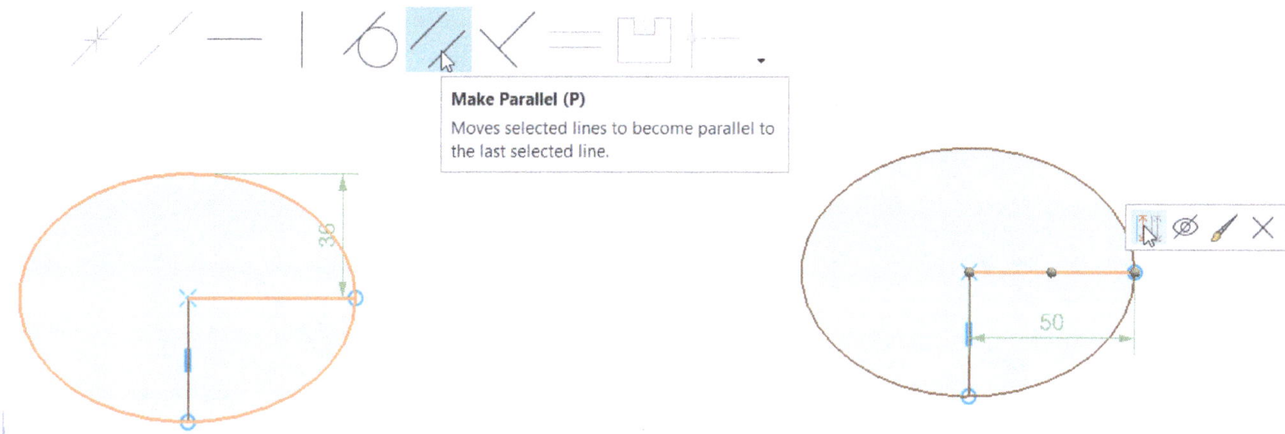

6. Apply 12 and 18 mm linear dimensions to the horizontal and vertical reference lines, respectively.
7. Rotate the model and click **Home > Include > Include** on the ribbon.
8. Select the endpoint of the spline, as shown. Next, click **OK** on the **Include** dialog.
9. Select the included point and the ellipse. Next, click the **Make Coincident** icon on the Sketch Scene Bar.

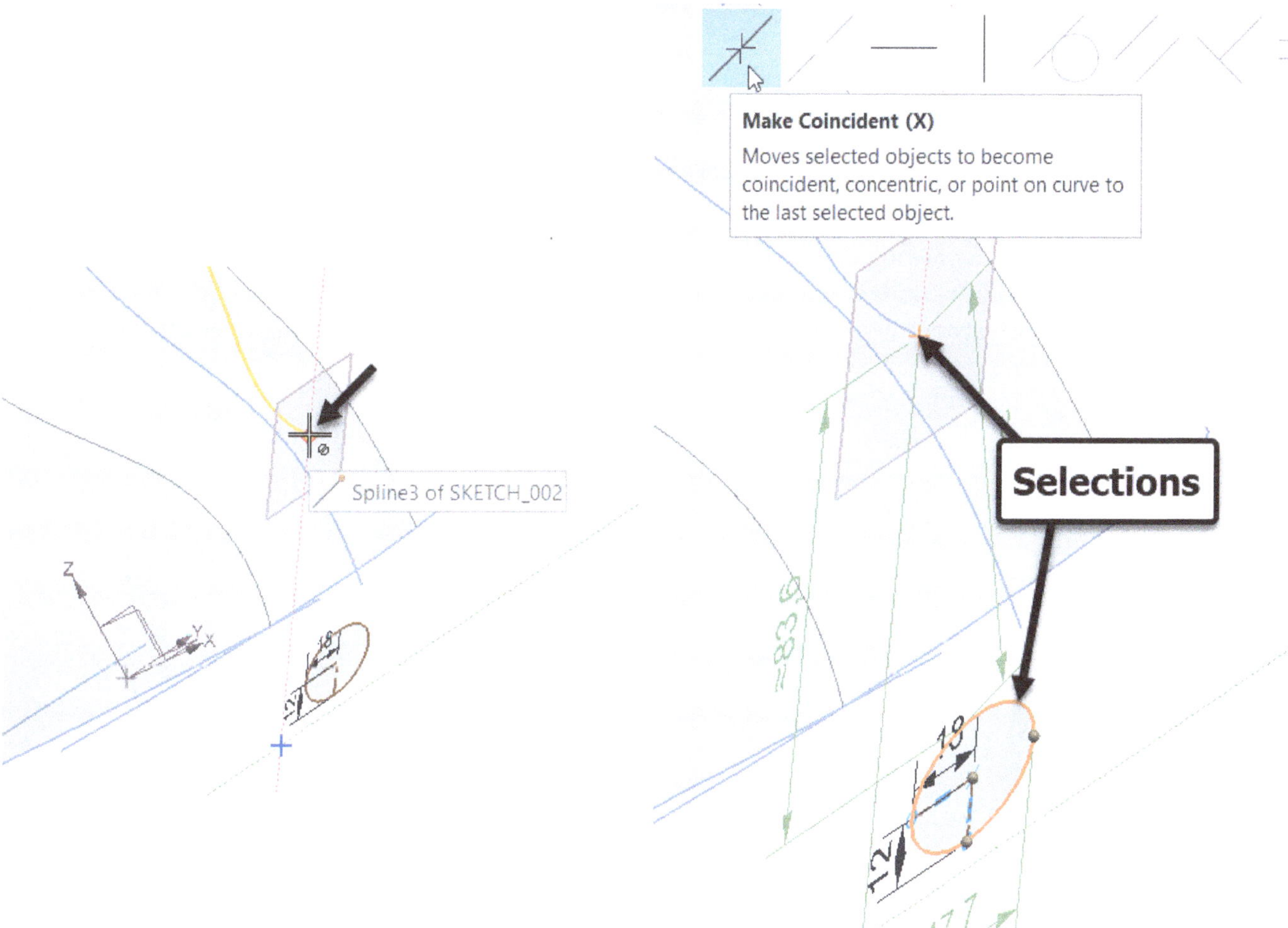

10. Select the vertical reference line and the vertical axis of the sketch.
11. Select **Make Collinear** icon on the Sketch Scene Bar. Next, finish the sketch.

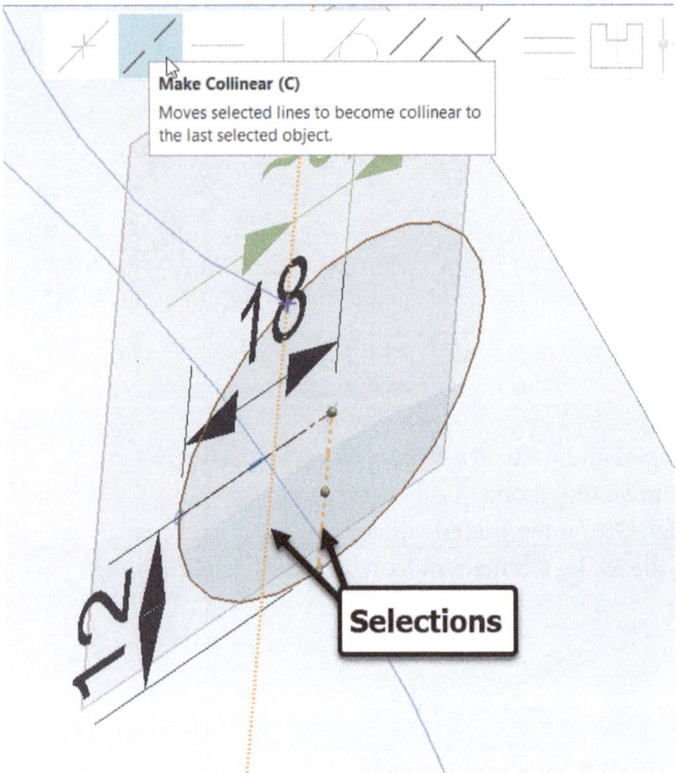

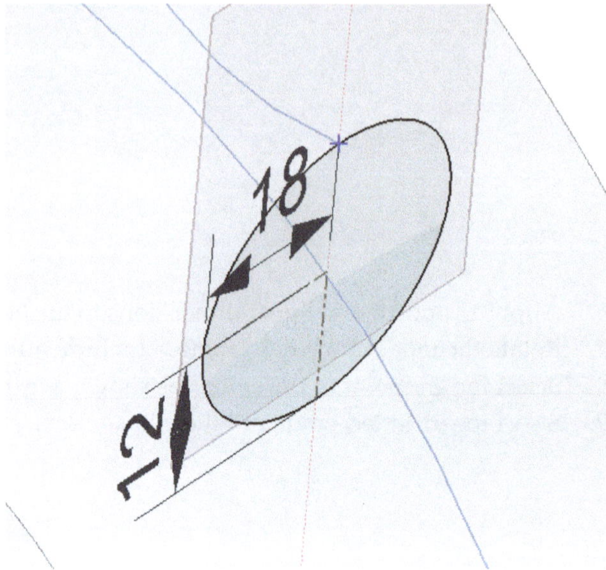

12. Activate the **Swept** command (on the ribbon, click **Surface > Base > Swept**) and click on the section curve.
13. On the **Swept** dialog, click **Guides > Select Curve**, and then select the guide curve.
14. On the **Swept** dialog, expand the **Settings** section, and then select **Body Type > Sheet**. Click **OK** to create the handle surface.

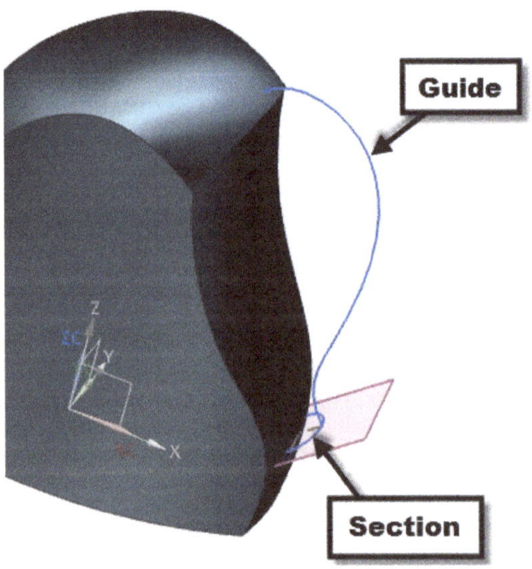

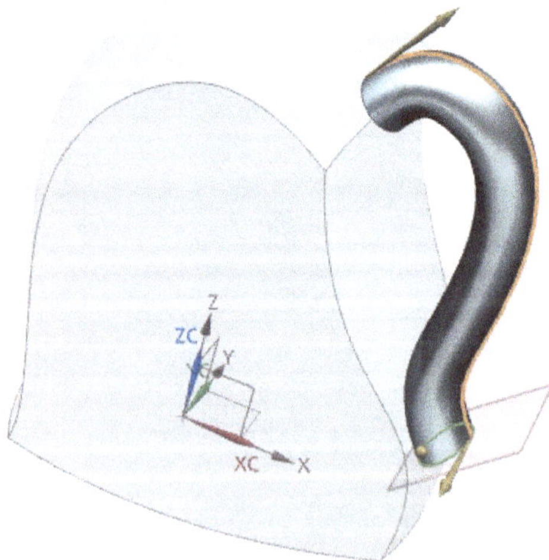

Blending the Front and back faces

1. Activate the **Face Blend** command (on the ribbon, click **Surface > Base > Face Blend**) and select **Type > Two - face** on the **Face Blend** dialog.

2. On the Sketch Scene Bar, select the **Face Rule > Single Face**.
3. Click on the front face, and then click **Select Face 2**.
4. Click on the back face and type-in 25 in the **Radius** box. Leave the default settings on the dialog and click **OK**.

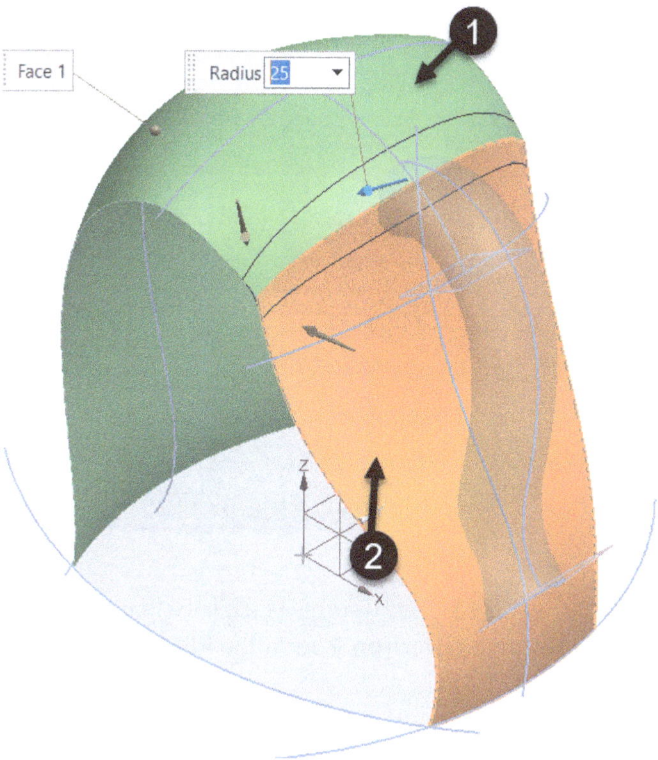

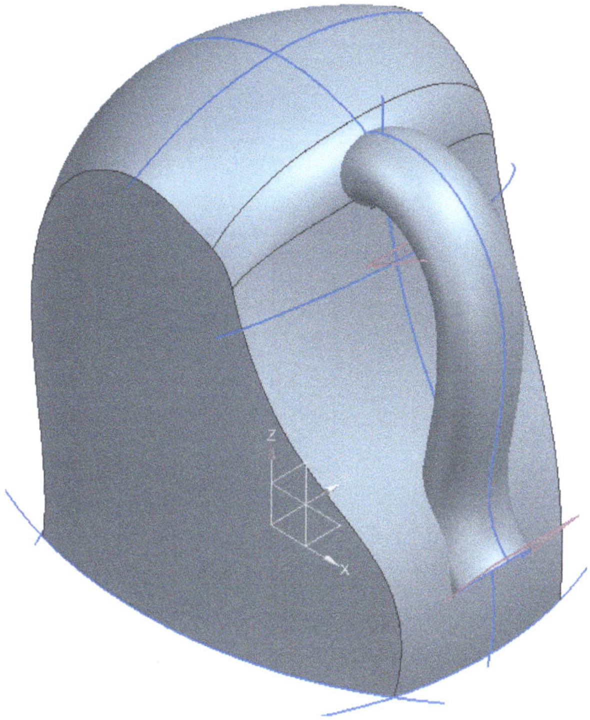

Trimming the Handle

1. Create a vertical line on the XZ Plane and finish the sketch.
2. Activate the **Trim Sheet**  command and click on the Handle surface.
3. Click **Boundary > Select Object** and select the vertical line.
4. Select **Projection Direction > Normal to Curve Plane** and select the **Project Both Sides** option. Next, click **OK**.

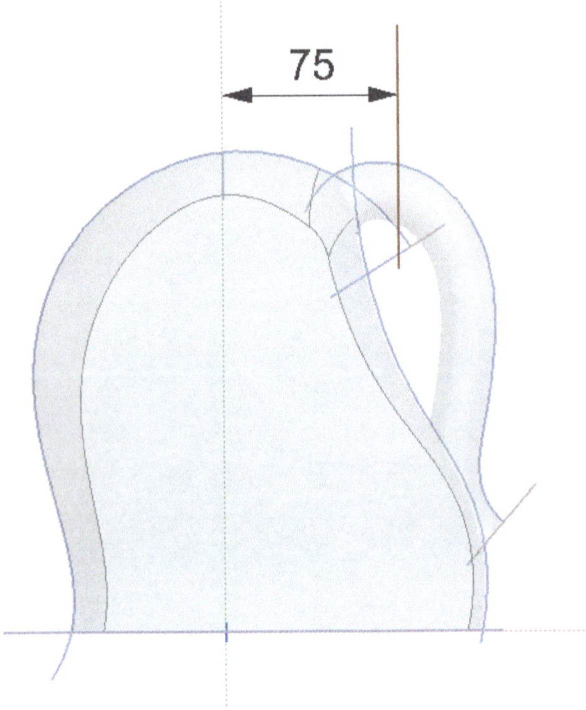

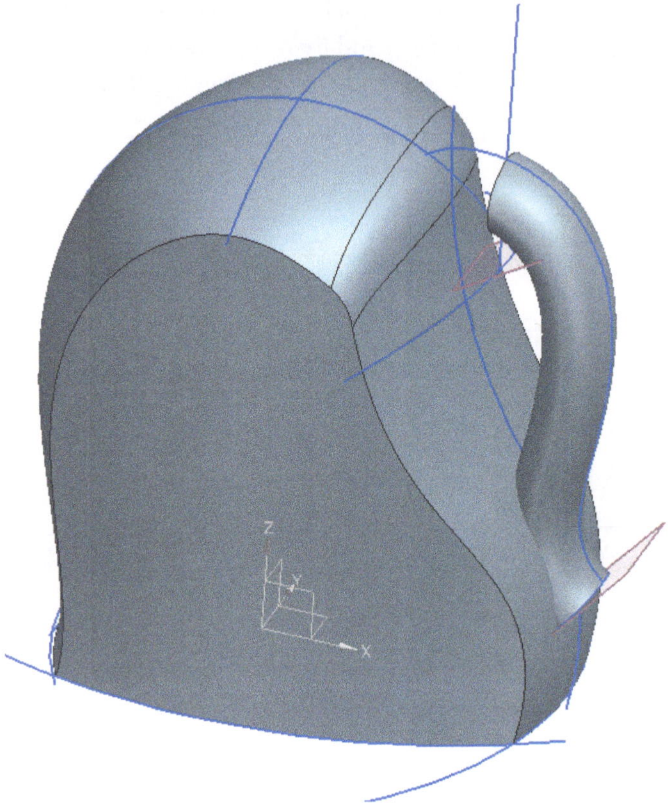

5. Create a datum plane, which is normal to the spline and located at the top end-point. Make sure that the arrow points downwards while creating the datum plane. Use the **Reverse Direction** icon in the **Plane Orientation** section, if required.

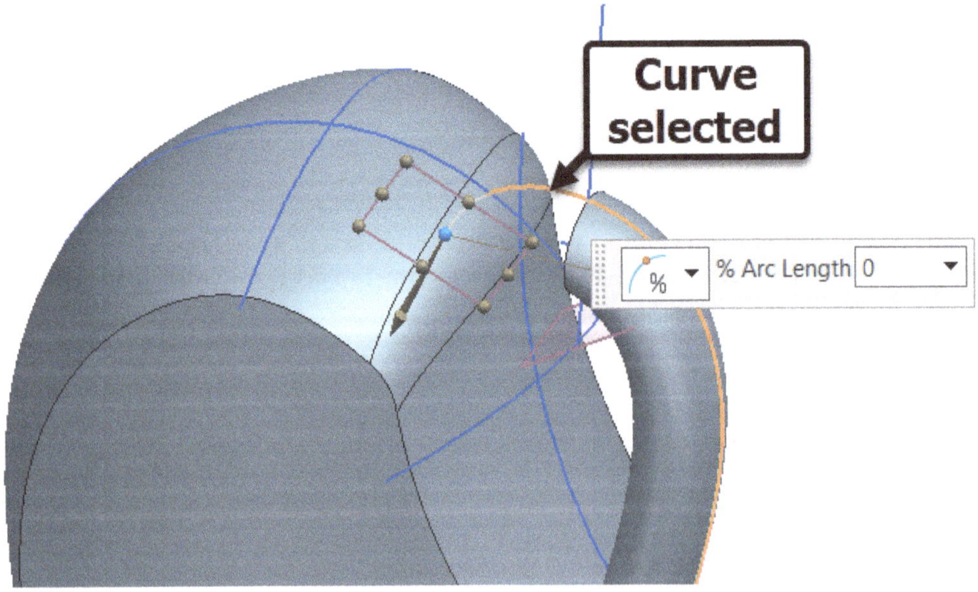

6. Start a sketch on the normal to the path and draw an ellipse. Next, fully constrain the ellipse using the steps given the ***Creating Handle Surface*** section of this example.
7. Add dimensions to the ellipse, as shown. Next, click **Direct Sketch1 > Finish Sketch**.

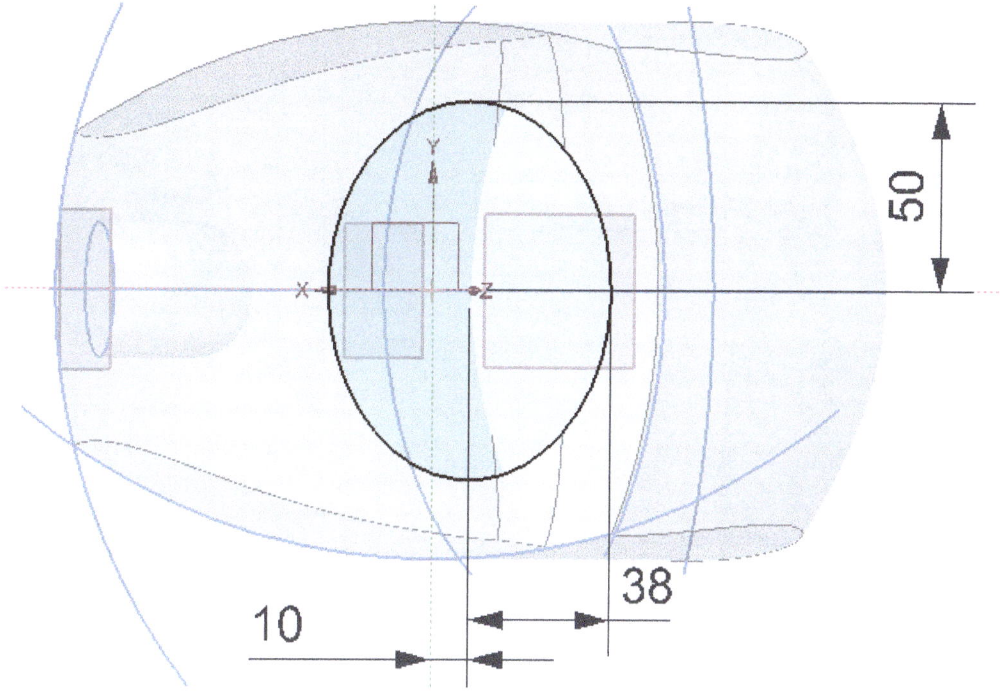

8. Activate the **Trim Sheet** command (on the ribbon, click **Surface > Combine > Trim Sheet**) and click on the surface body.
9. Click **Boundary > Select Object** and select the elliptical sketch.
10. On the **Trimmed Sheet** dialog, select **Projection Direction > Normal to Curve Plane**. Next, click **OK**.

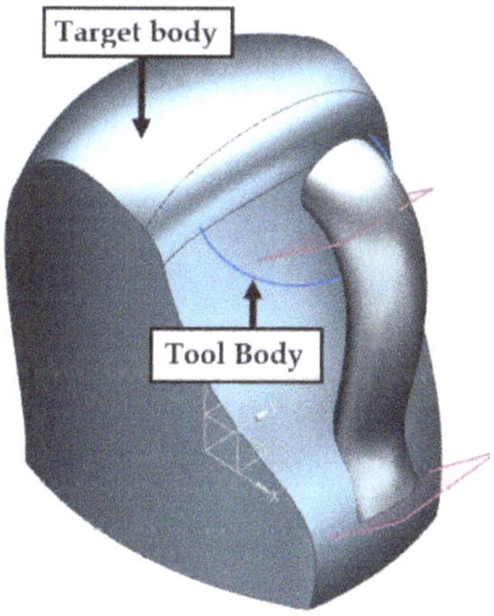

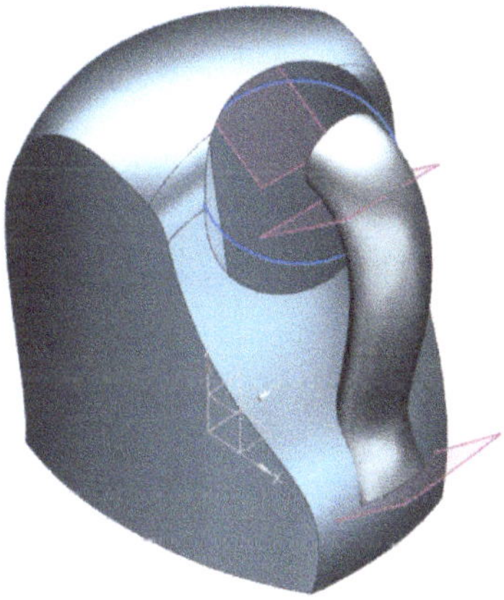

Blending the Top handle

1. Activate the **Through Curves** command (on the ribbon, click **Surface > Base > Through Curves**) and click on the edges of the trimmed opening one-by-one in the clockwise direction.
2. On the **Through Curves** dialog, under the **Sections** section, click **Select Origin Curve** and click at the point, as shown.
3. Click the middle mouse button and select the top edge of the handle. Click the **Reverse Direction** button to ensure that both the arrows point in the same direction.

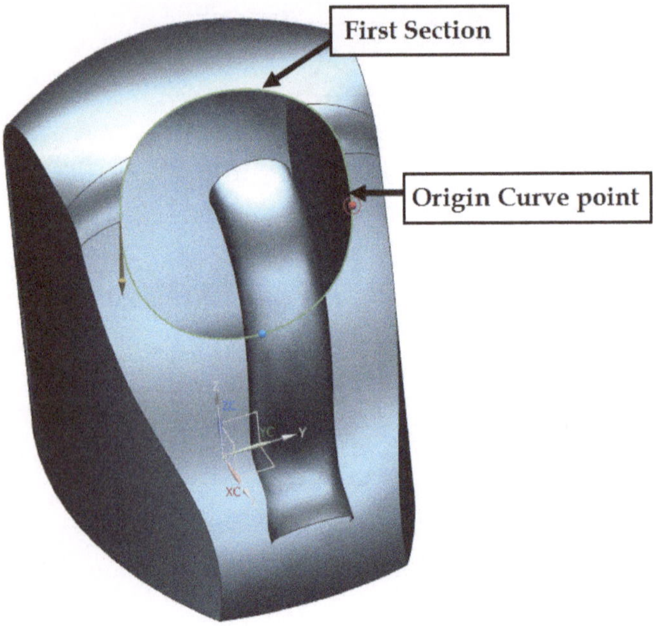

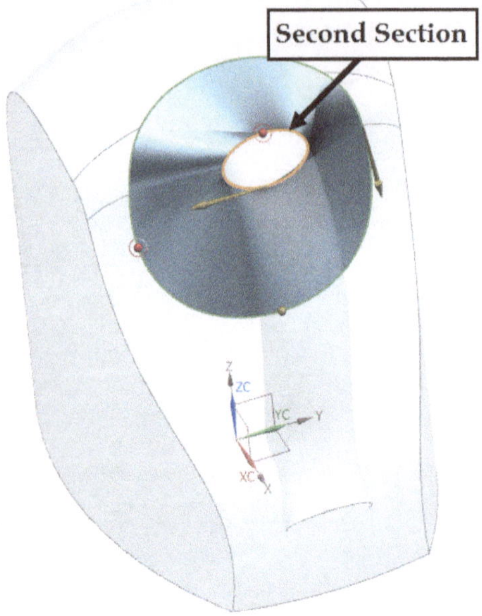

4. Under the **Continuity** section, select **First Section > G1 (Tangent)** and click on the surfaces connected to the first section.
5. Select the **Last Section > G1 (Tangent)** and click on the surface connected to the second section.

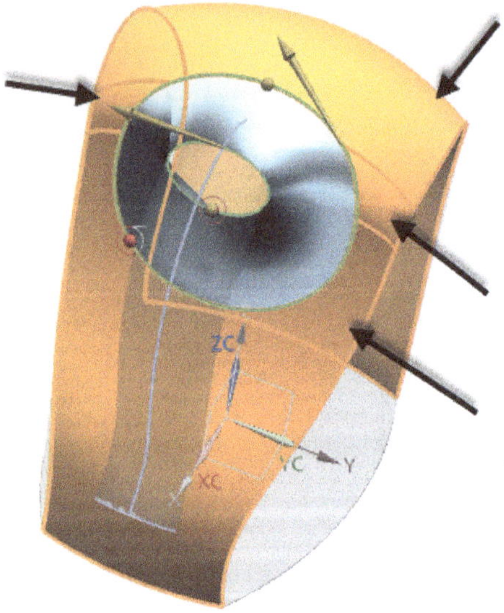

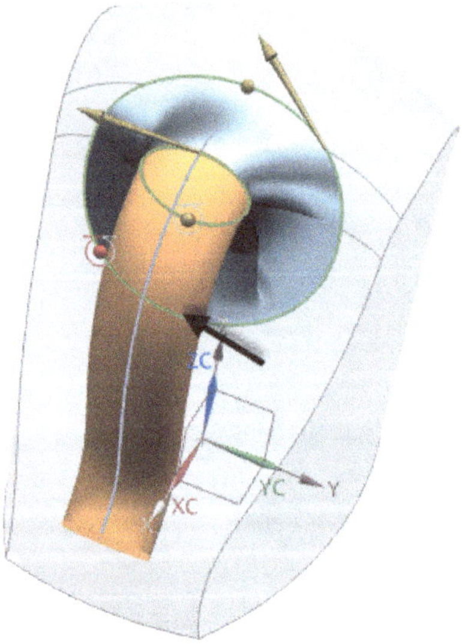

6. Select **Flow Direction > Perpendicular**.
7. Under the **Alignment** section, select **Alignment > By Points**.
8. Drag the first Point handle and position it, as shown.
9. Drag the second Point handle and position it, as shown.

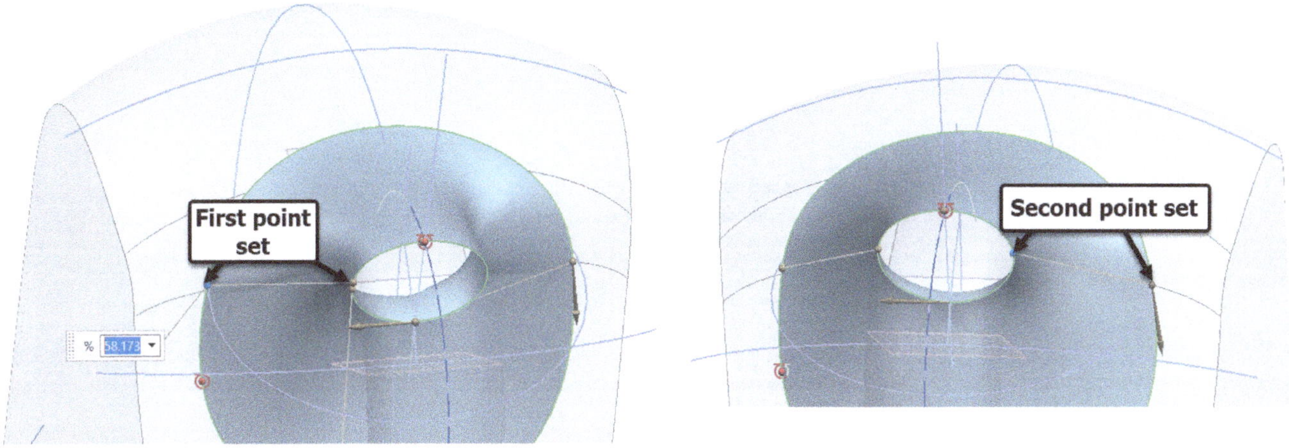

10. Click **OK** to blend the handle surface.

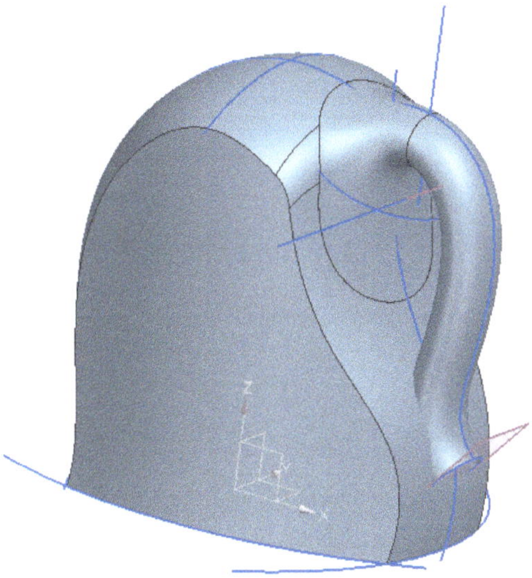

Blending the Bottom handle

1. Start a sketch on the XZ Plane and draw a line, a shown. Assume the dimension of the line.
2. On the ribbon, click **Home > Include > Include**. Next, select the spline curve and click **OK**.

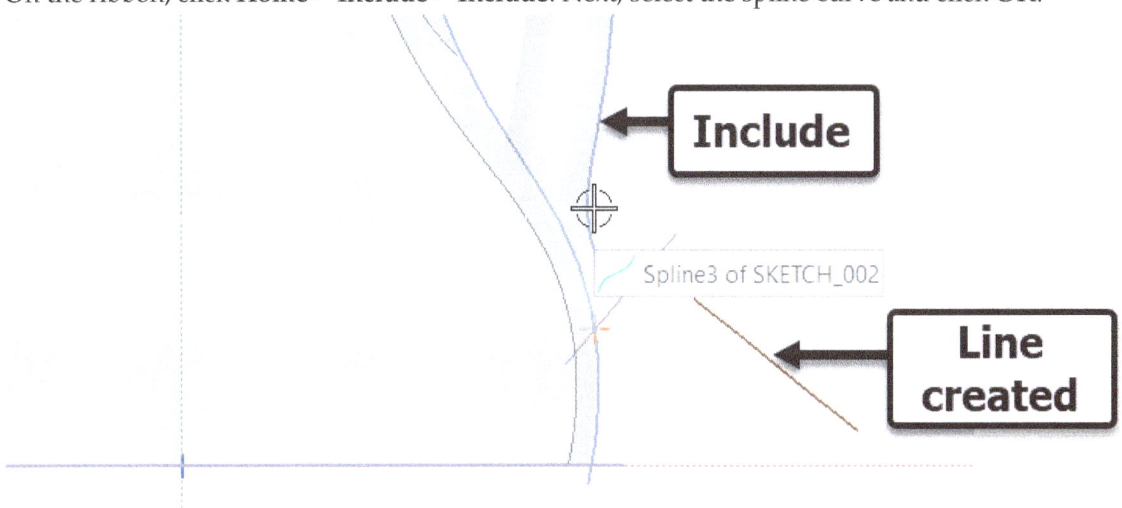

3. Select the created line and the spline curve of the handle surface. Next, click **Make Tangent** on the **Sketch Scene Bar**.

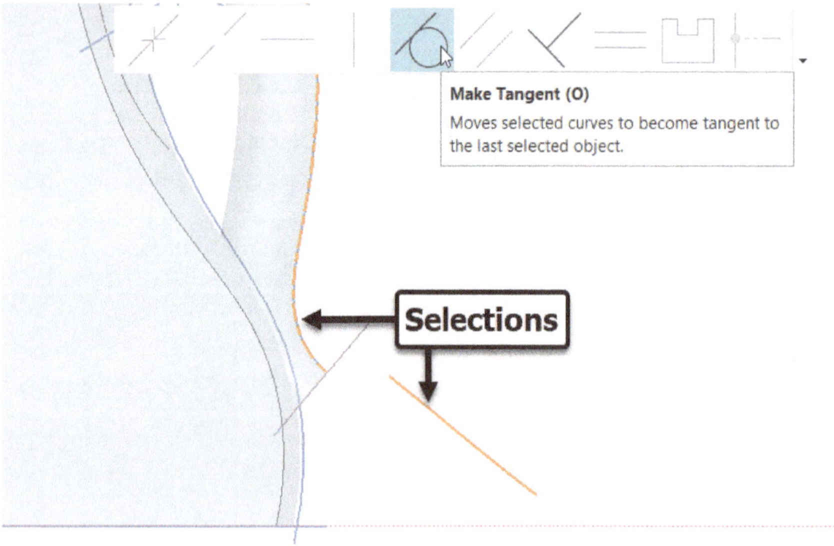

4. Click the **Finish** button on the ribbon.

5. Activate the **Datum Plane** command and select **Type > At Angle**.
6. Click on the XZ Plane and the line tangent to the spline. Click **OK** to create the datum plane.

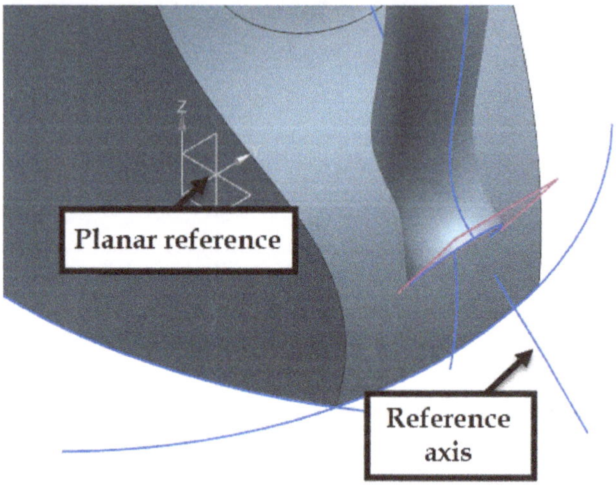

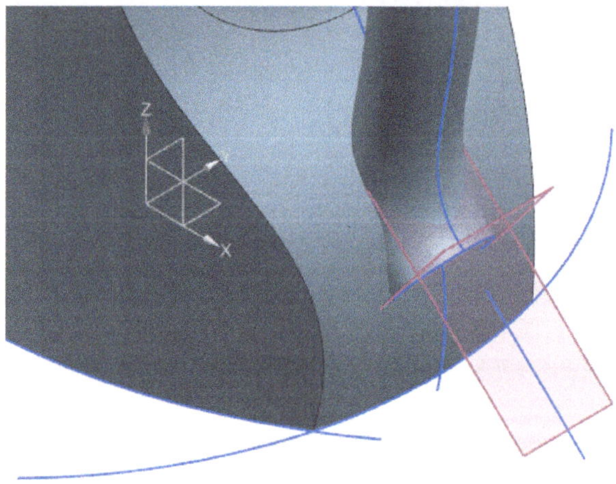

7. Create an ellipse on the new plane and fully constrain it using relations and dimensions.

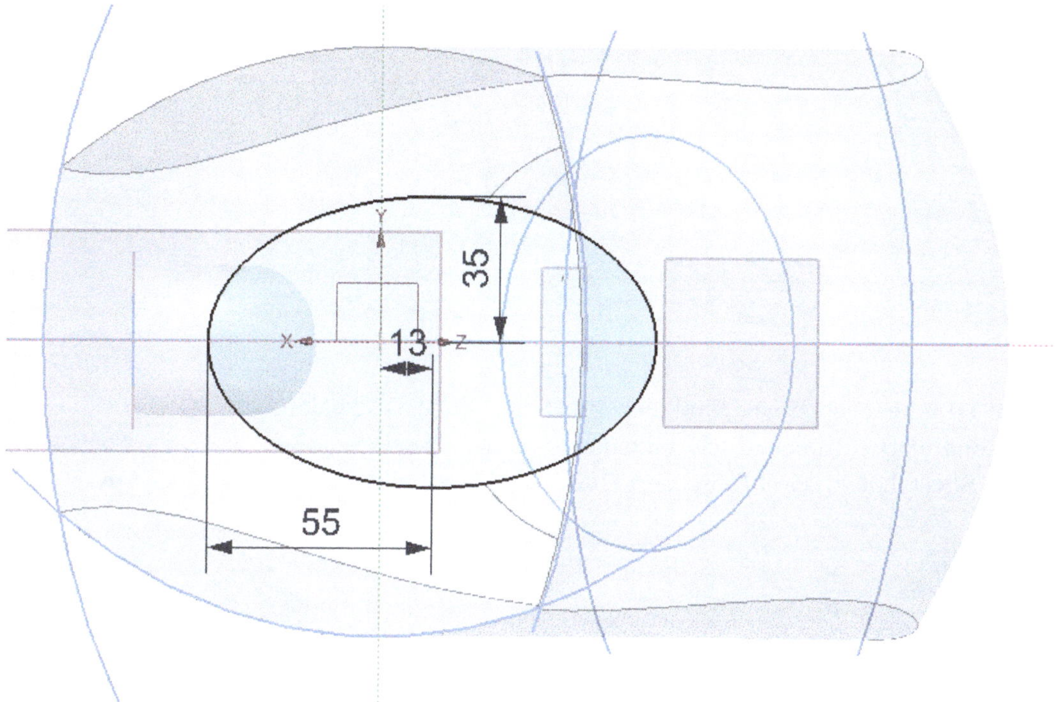

8. Extrude the sketch up to an arbitrary distance (approximately 60 mm) in both directions.

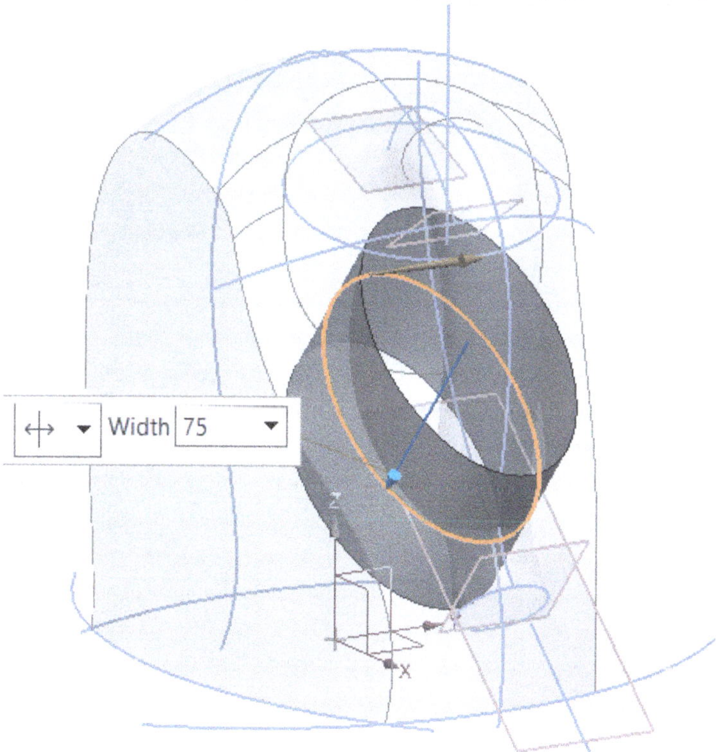

9. Create a line on the tangent plane and add dimension to it, as shown. Next, click **Finish** on the ribbon.

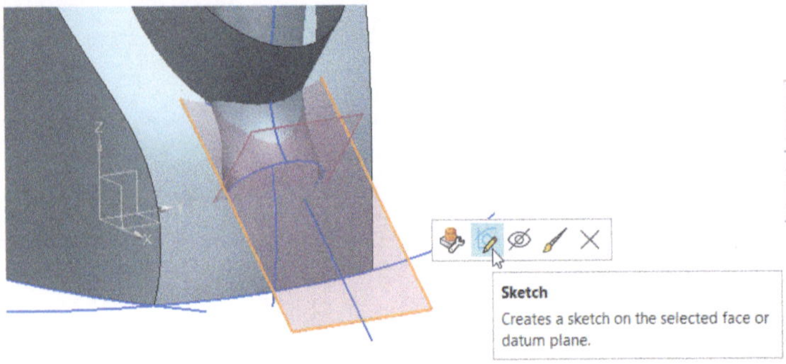

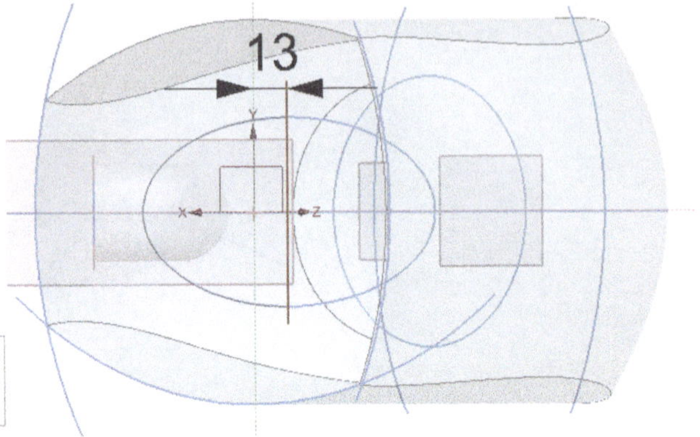

10. Activate the **Trim Sheet** command, and then select the elliptical extrusion.
11. Click in the **Boundary** section and select the newly created sketch.
12. On the **Trim Sheet** dialog, select **Projection Direction > Normal to Curve**. Next, click **OK**.

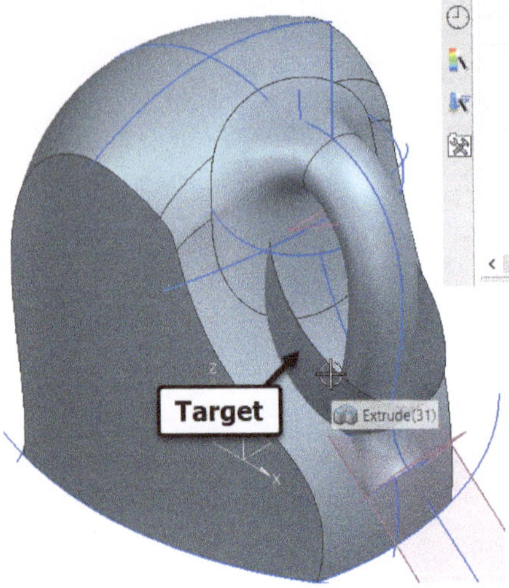

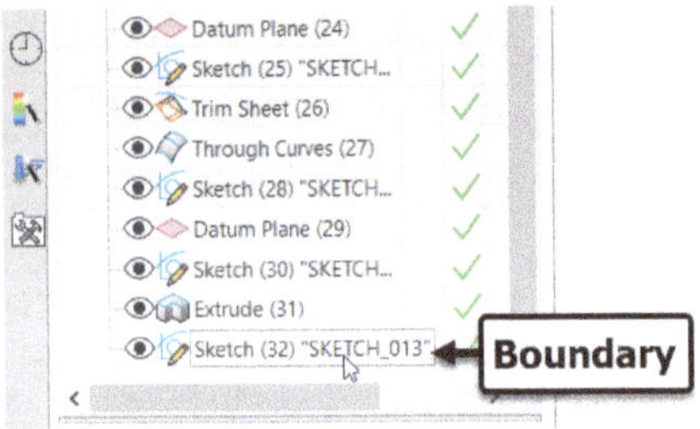

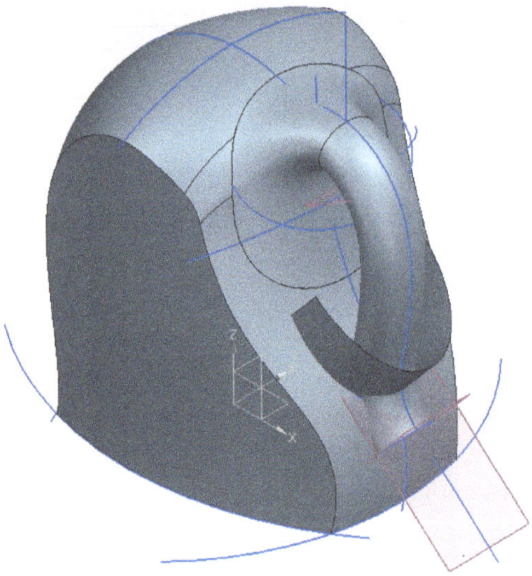

13. Activate the **Trim and Extend** command and select **Type > Make Corner**.
14. Click on the handle surface to define the target, and then click **Tool** > **Select Face or Edge**.
15. Click on the extruded surface to define the tool. Click the **Reverse Direction** button under the **Tool** section. Also, make sure that the arrow on the tool body points upwards.

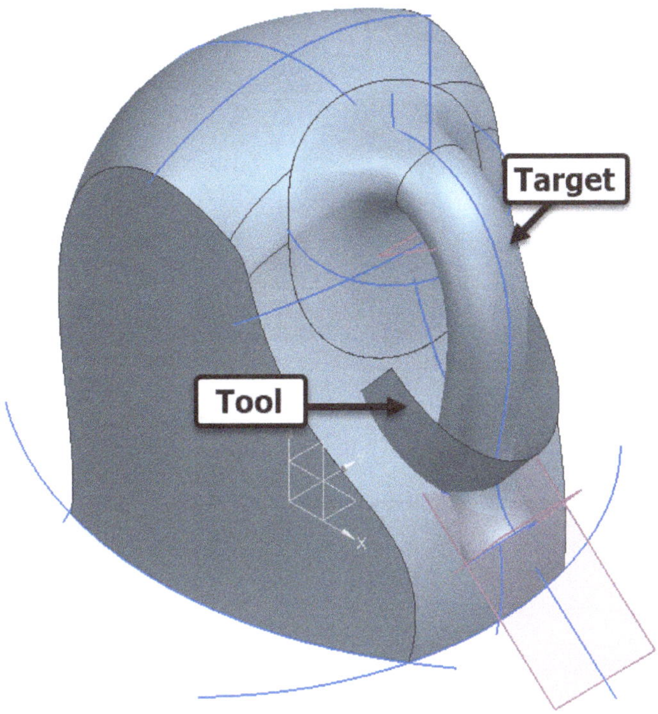

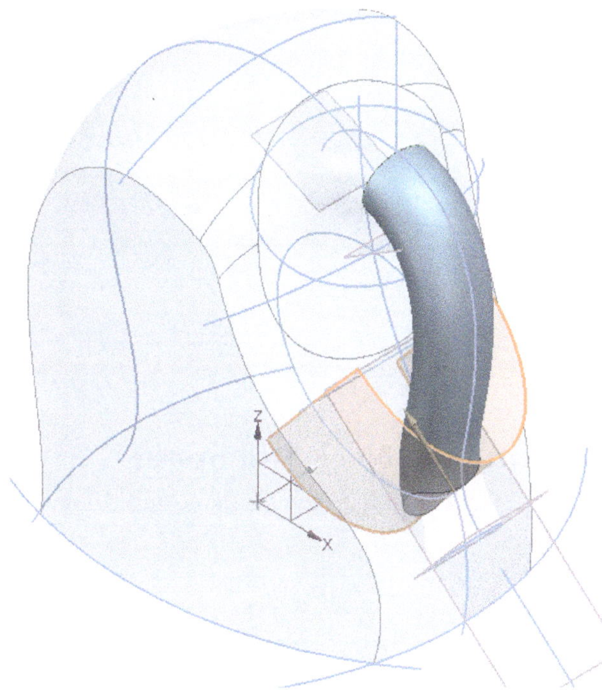

16. Click **Apply**.
17. Rotate the model and click on the inside portion of the handle.
18. Click **Tool > Select Face or Edge**, and then select the main surface body to define the tool.
19. Click the **Reverse Direction** buttons under the **Target** section. Click **OK**.

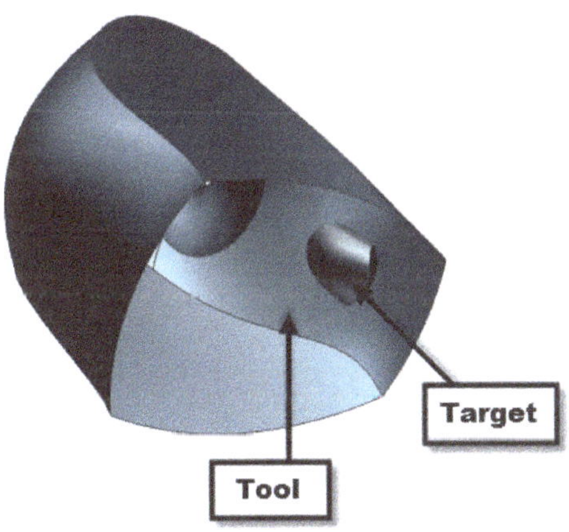

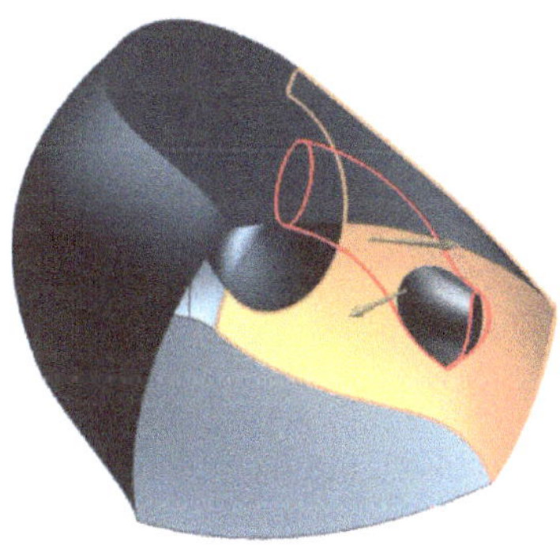

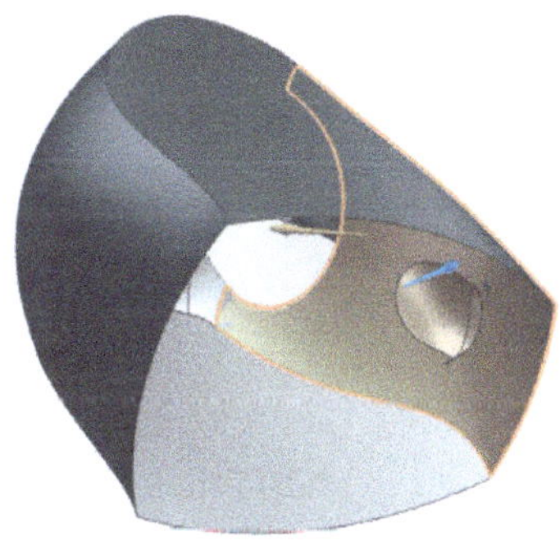

20. Activate the **Edge Blend**  command and blend the edge of the handle. The blend radius is 6 mm.
21. Blend the intersection between the main surface and handle. The blend radius is 5 mm.

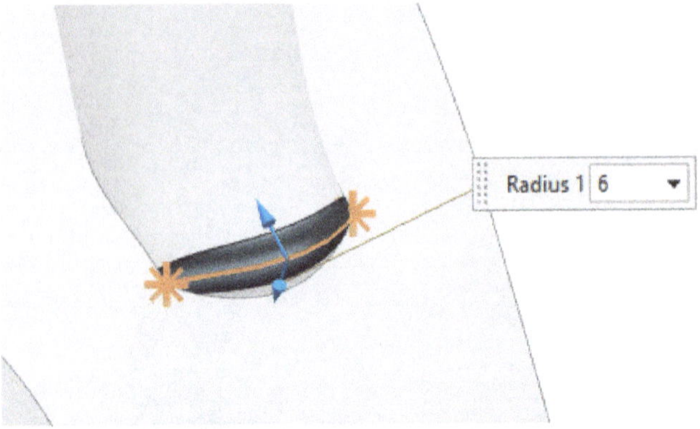

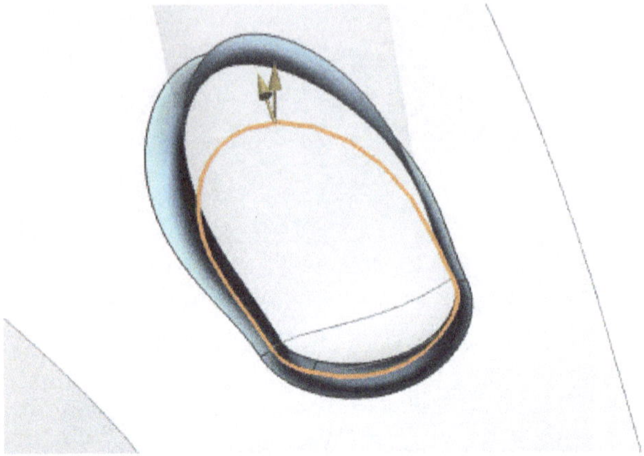

Creating the Neck and Spout

1. Start a sketch on the XZ Plane and draw the sketch for the revolved surface.

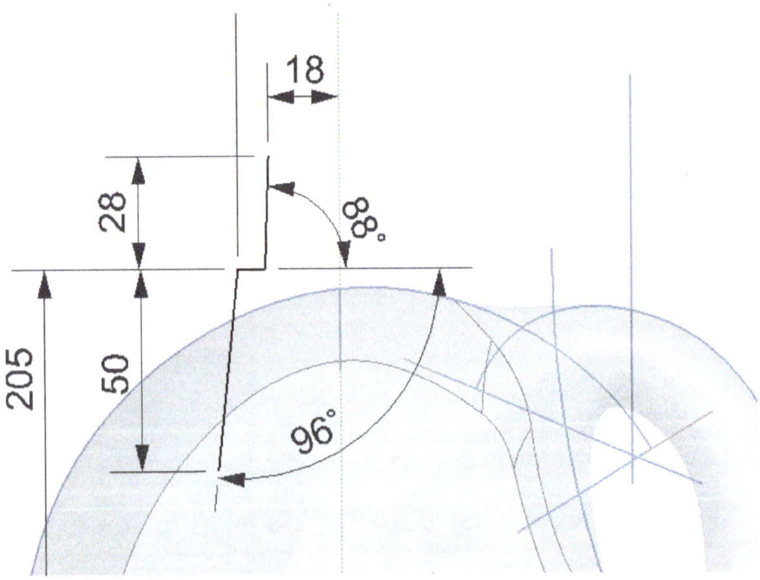

2. Finish the sketch and create a revolved surface. Make sure that the **Body Type** in the **Settings** section is set to **Sheet**.

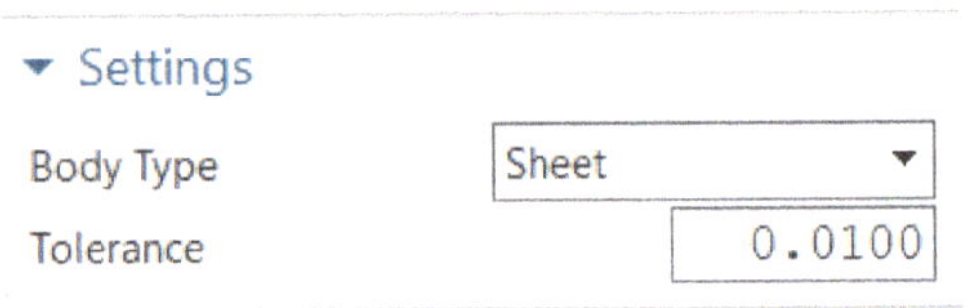

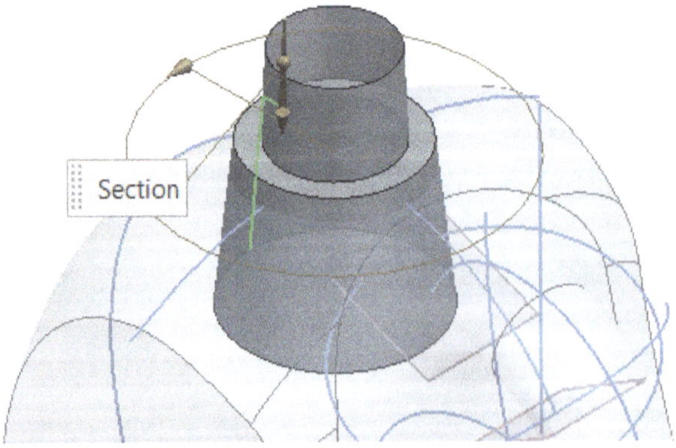

3. Activate the **Trim and Extend** command and trim the unwanted portions of the revolved and main surface.

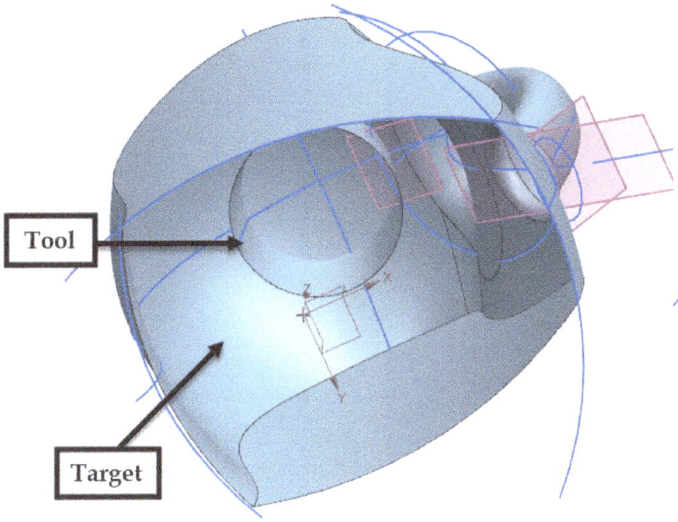

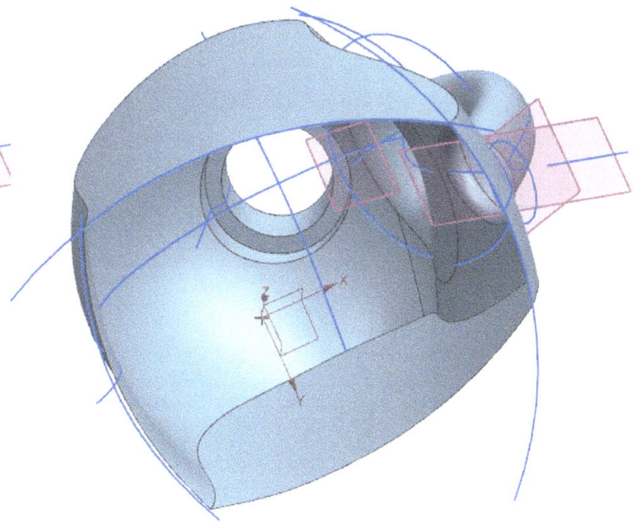

Creating the Bottom Face

1. Hide all the sketches.
2. Activate the **Bounded Plane** command (on the ribbon, click **Surface > Base > More > Fill > Bounded Plane**) and click on the edges at the bottom of the surface model.
3. Click **OK** to create the bounded plane surface.

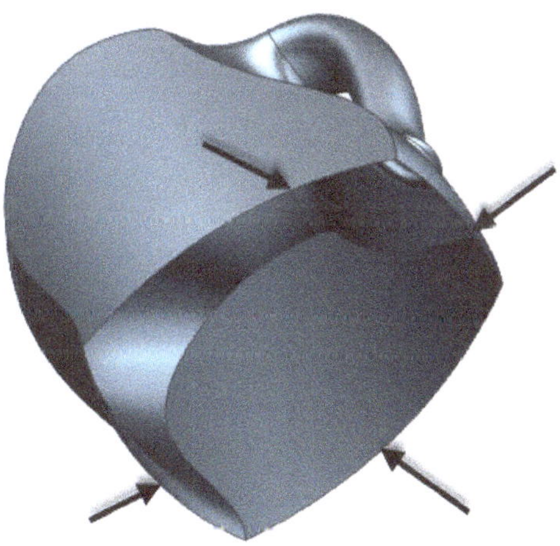

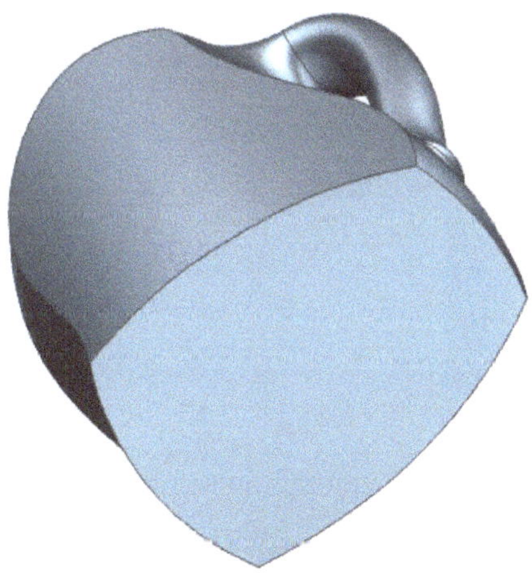

Creating the Emboss on the Label Face

1. Start a sketch on the XZ Plane.
2. On the ribbon, click **Home > Include > More > Project Curve**. Next, select the edges of the label face and click **OK**.

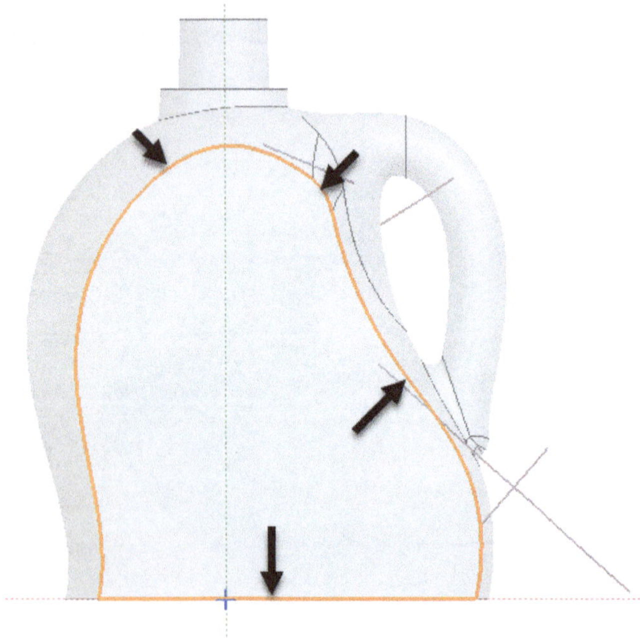

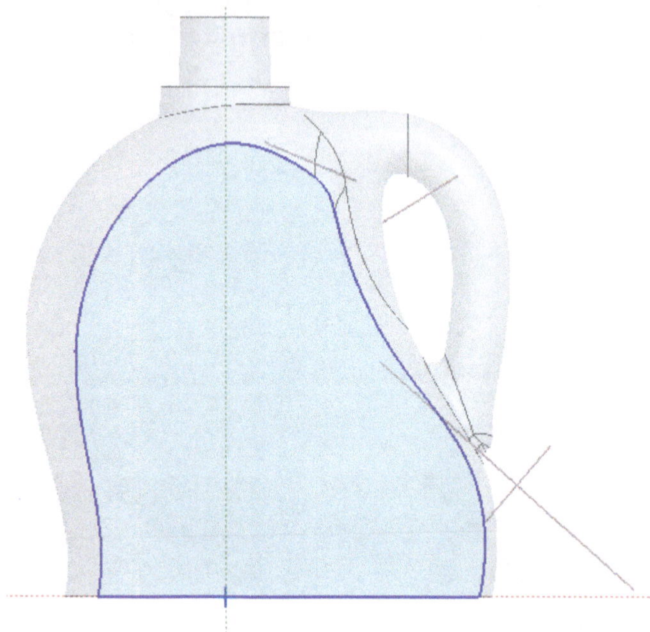

3. Activate the **Offset Curve** command (on the ribbon, click **Home > Curve > Offset Curve**). Next, click the **Reset** button located at the top right corner of the **Offset Curve** dialog.
4. Expand the **Settings** section and check the **Create Persistent Relation** option.
5. On the Sketch Scene Bar, set the **Curve Rule** to **Tangent Curves** and click on any one of the boundary edges of the label face.
6. Type-in **15** in the **Distance** box. Click **Apply** to offset the curve. Ensure that the offset curve is created inside.

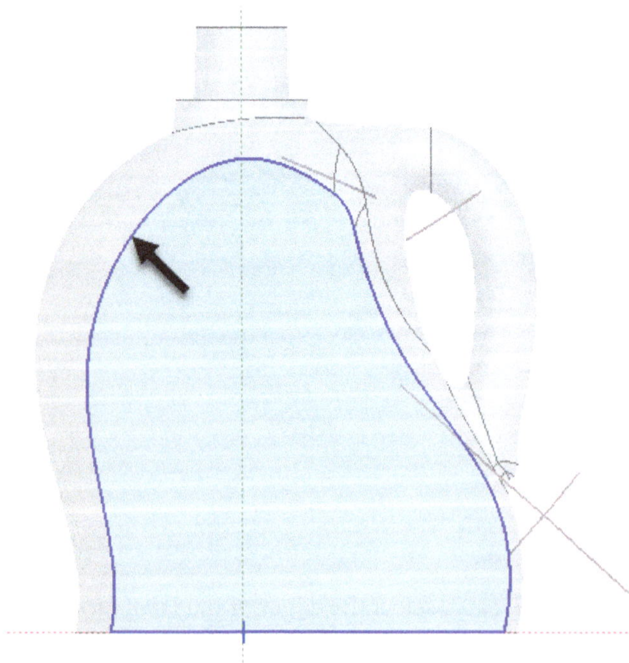

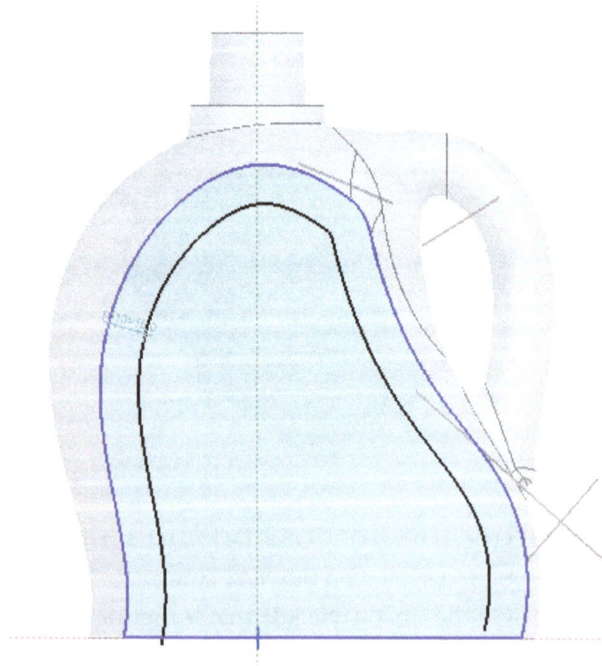

7. Click on the bottom horizontal edge. Next, type 15 in the **Distance** box. Click the **Reverse Direction** button on the **Offset Curve** dialog. Click **OK**.

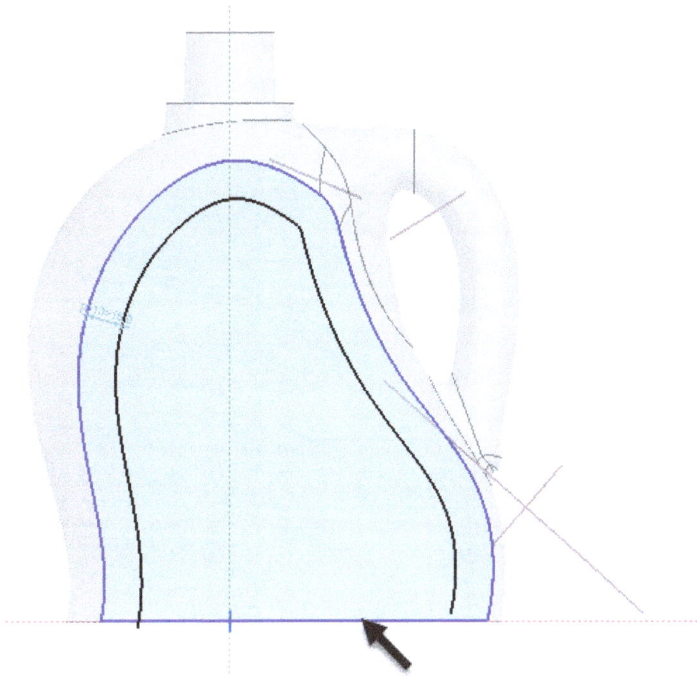 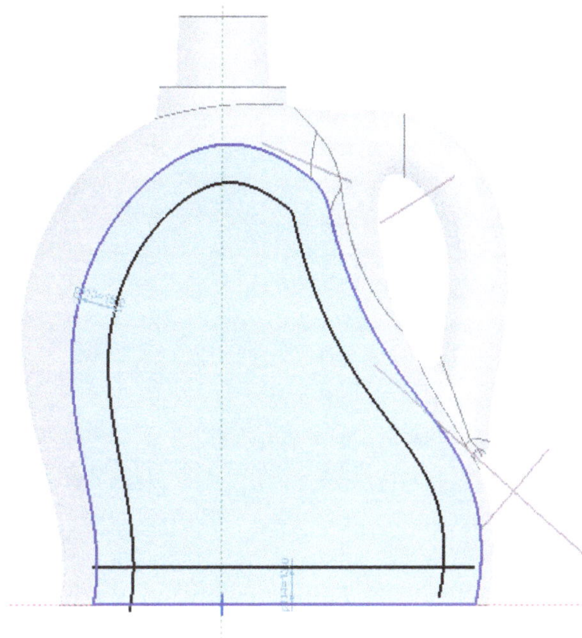

8. Add 12 radius fillets at the bottom, and then trim the unwanted portions.

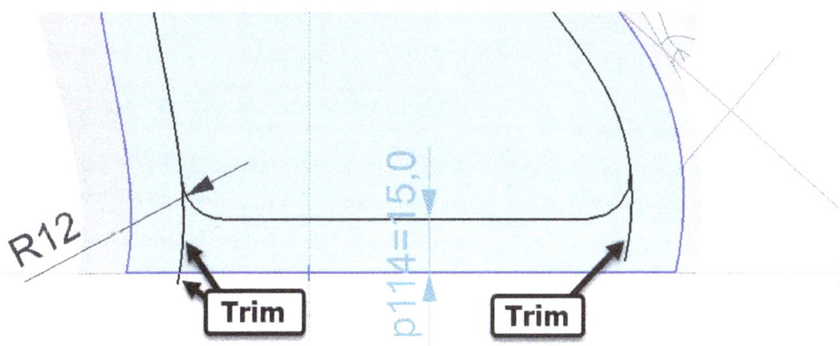

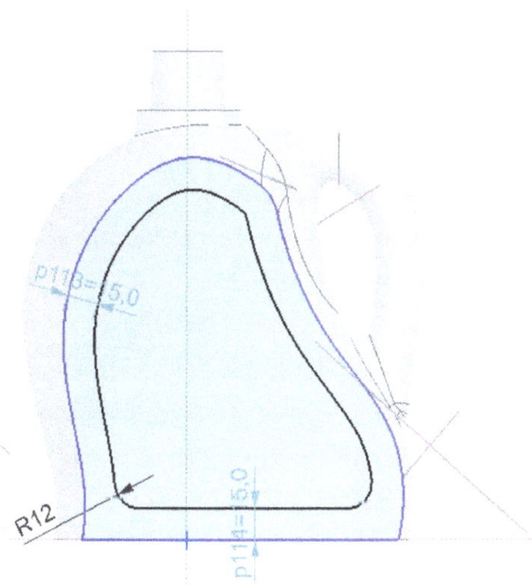

9. Select the projected edges. Next, select the **Convert to Reference** option from the context toolbar.
10. Finish the sketch.

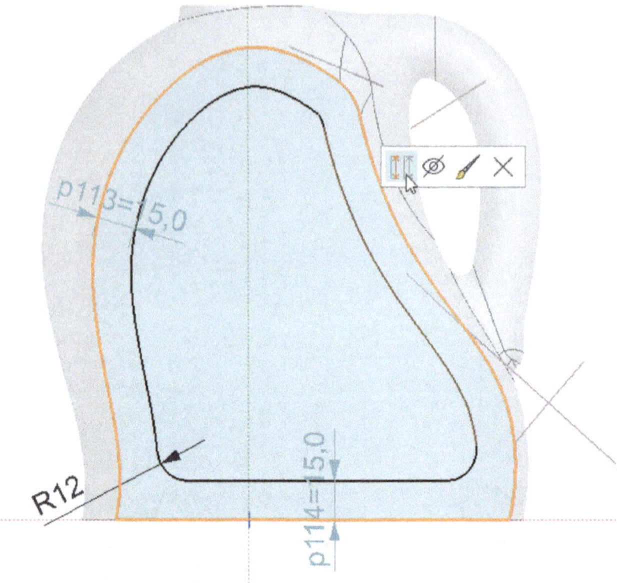

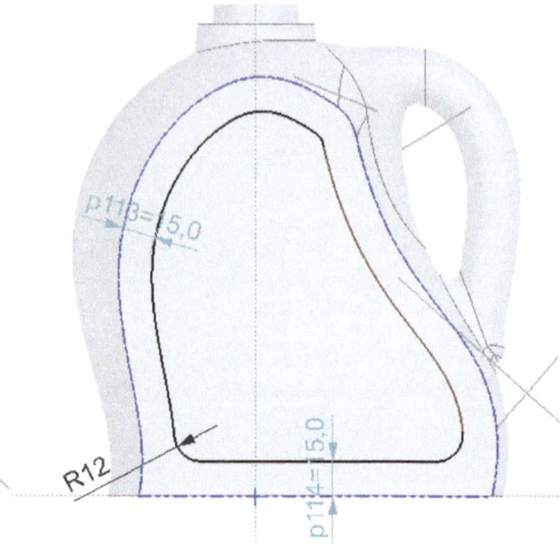

11. Activate the **Emboss** command (on the ribbon, click **Home > Base > More > Detail Feature > Emboss**) and select the sketch.
12. On the **Emboss** dialog, click **Face to Emboss > Select Face** and click on the label face.
13. Under the **End Cap** section, select **Geometry > Embossed Faces**.
14. Select **Location > Translate** and type-in 3 in the **Distance** box.
15. Under the **Draft** section, type-in 30 in the **Angle 1** box and click **OK**.

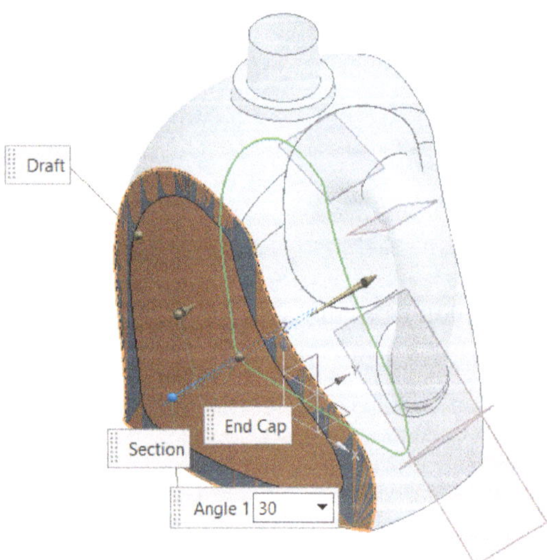

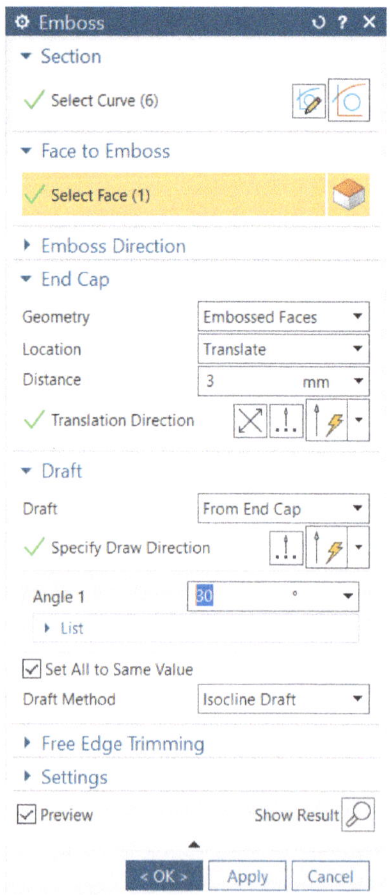

16. Likewise, create emboss on the label face on the opposite side (click the **Reverse Direction** button in the **End Cap** section).

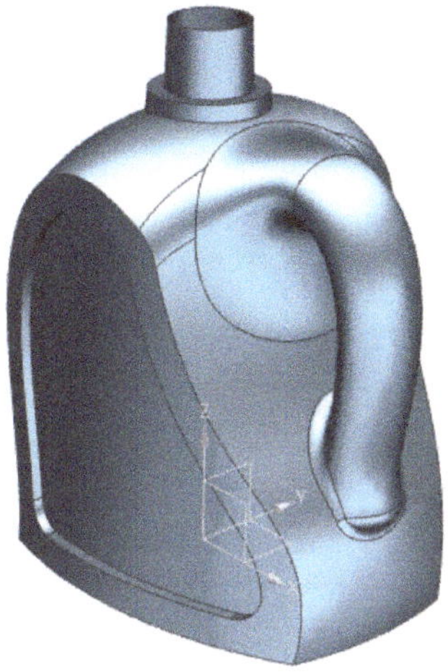

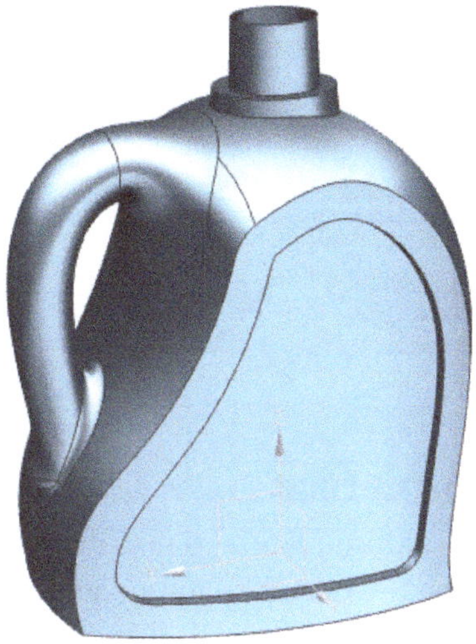

Blending the Label Faces

1. Activate the **Edge Blend** command and select the edges of both the label faces
2. On the **Edge Blend** dialog, type-in **10** in the **Radius 1** box, and click **OK**.

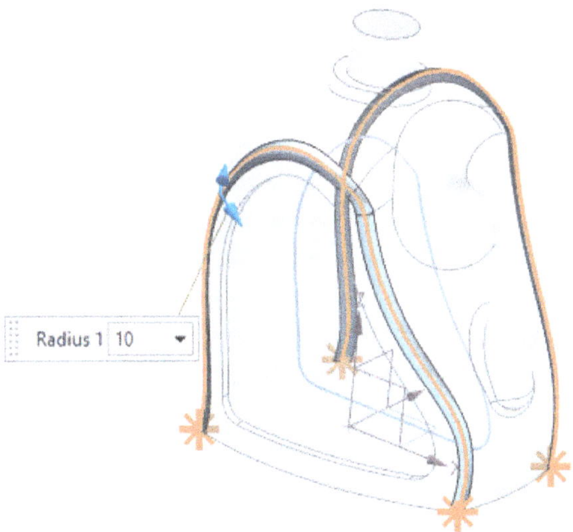

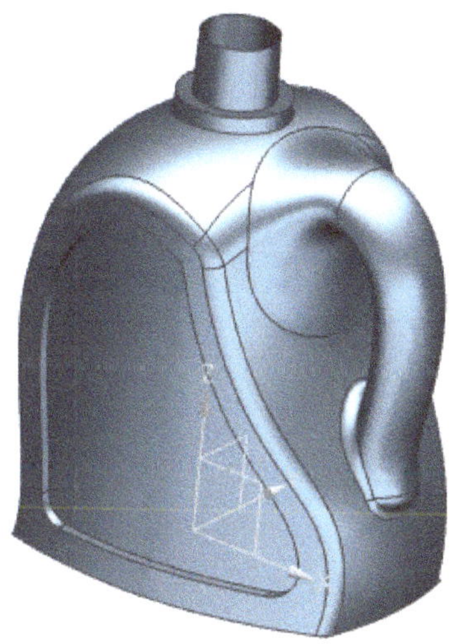

3. Activate **Face Blend** command (on the ribbon, click **Surface > Base > Face Blend**) and select **Type > Two-face** on the dialog.
4. Click on the bottom face, and then click **Select Face 2**.
5. Click on the label face and type-in 7 in the **Radius** box under the **Cross-Section** section. Make sure that the arrows point inside the model. Click **OK**.

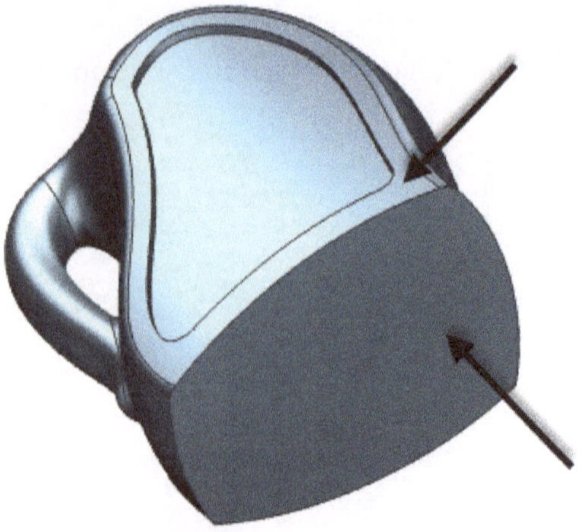

Embossing the bottom face

1. Construct a parallel datum plane at 5 mm distance below the bottom face.
2. Start a new sketch on the parallel datum plane.
3. Activate the **Offset Curve** command and set the **Curve Rule** on the Sketch Scene Bar to **Single Curve**.
4. On the Top Border Bar, set the **Selection Scope** to **Within Work Part Only**.
5. Click on the inner boundary edges of the bottom face, as shown.
6. Type-in 10 in the **Distance** box and click the **Reverse Direction** button. Click **OK** to project and offset the edges.
7. On the ribbon, click **Home > Edit > Corner**. Next, select the offset edges at the corners, as shown.
8. Click **Close** on the **Corner** dialog.

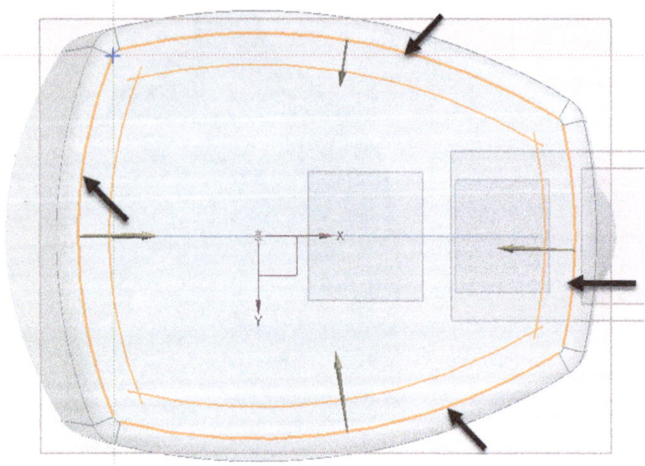

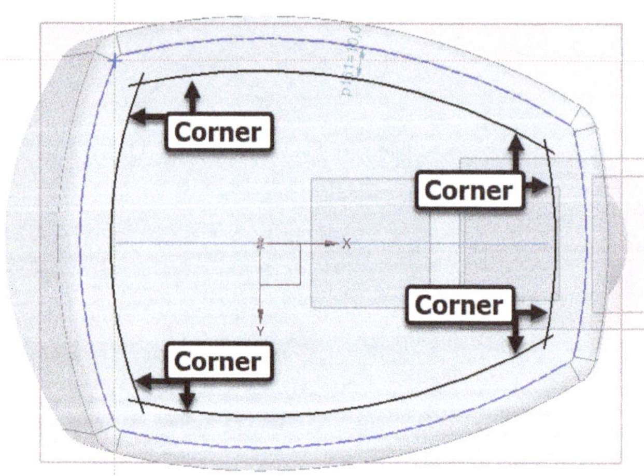

9. Add 12 mm fillets to the corners and trim the unwanted edge portions. Finish the sketch.

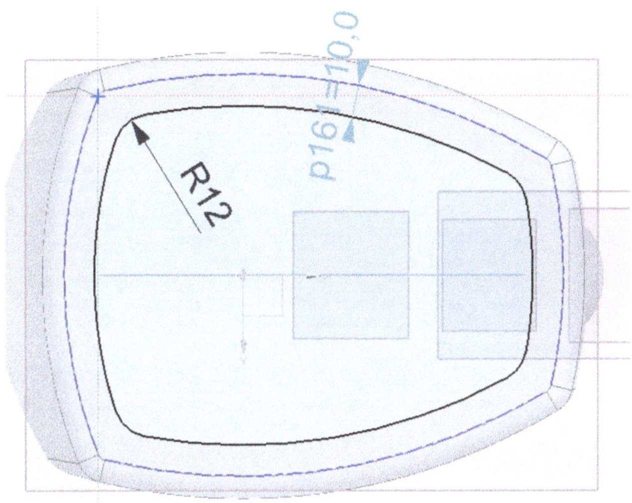

17. Activate the **Emboss** command (on the ribbon, click **Home > Base > More > Detail Feature > Emboss**) and click the **Reset** button located at the top right corner of the **Emboss** dialog. Next, click on the sketch.
10. On the **Emboss** dialog, click **Face to Emboss > Select Face** and click on the bottom face.
11. Under the **End Cap** section, select **Geometry > Embossed Faces**.
12. Select **Location > Offset** and type-in 2.5 in the **Distance** box. Next, click the **Reverse Direction** icon.
13. Under the **Draft** section, type-in 50 in the **Angle 1** box. Click **OK** to add embossing.
14. Activate the **Edge Blend** command and blend the sharp edges of the embossed features. The blend radius is 2 mm.

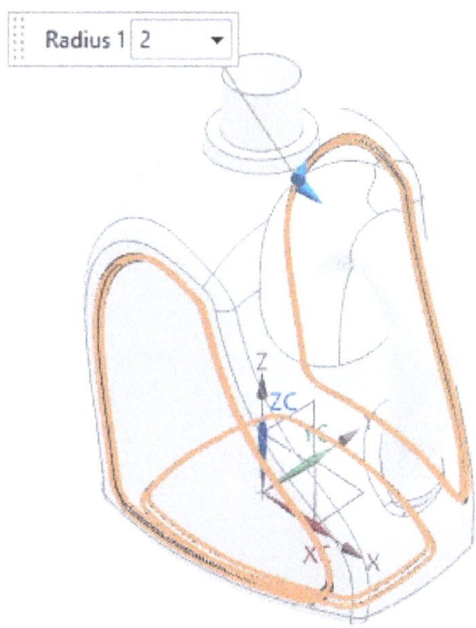

Sewing the Surfaces

1. Activate the **Sew** command (on the ribbon, click **Surface > Combine > Sew**) and click on the main surface body.
2. Click on the Through Curves surface, and then click **OK**.

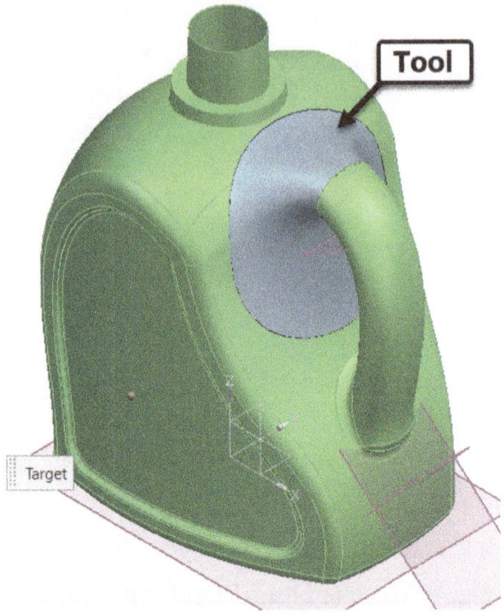

Adding thickness to the model

1. On the ribbon, click **View > Content > Edit Section** and select **Section Plane > Set Plane to Y** on the **View Section** dialog. Click **OK**.

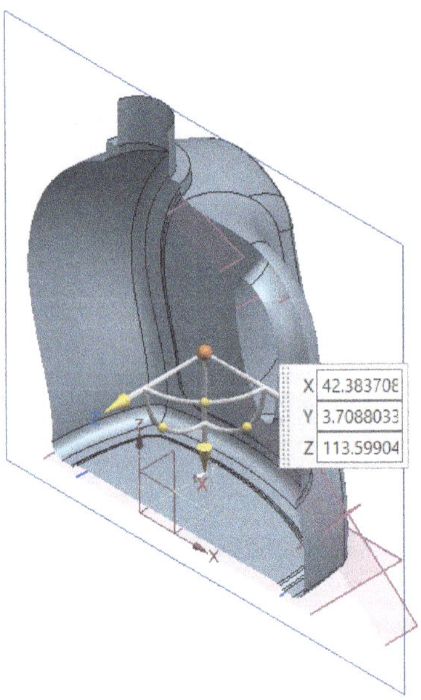

2. Activate the **Thicken** command (on the ribbon, click **Surface > Base > Thicken**), and click on the surface body.
3. On the **Thicken** dialog, type-in 1.5 in the **Offset 1** box.
4. Under the **Region Behavior** section, click **Region of Different Thickness > Select Boundary Curve**, and select the neck and spout region.
5. Type-in 2.5 in the **Offset 1** box under the **Region of Different Thickness** section. Click **OK**.

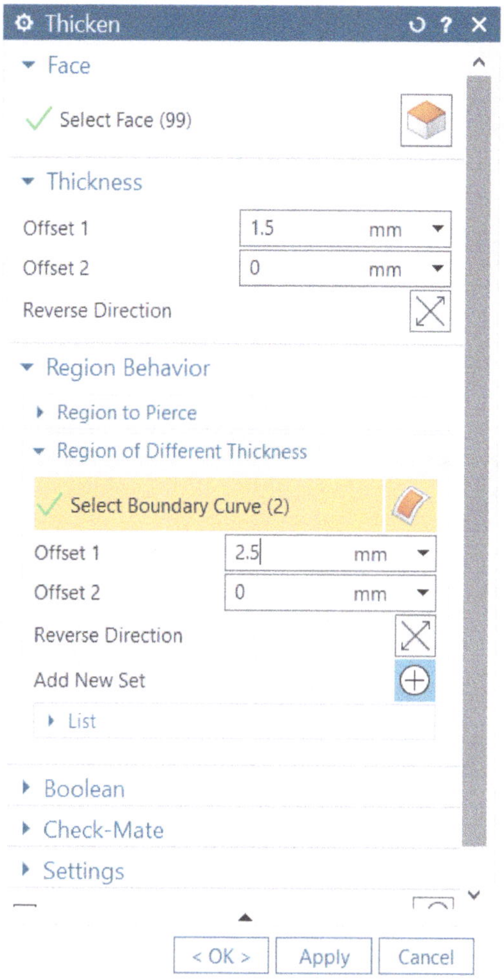

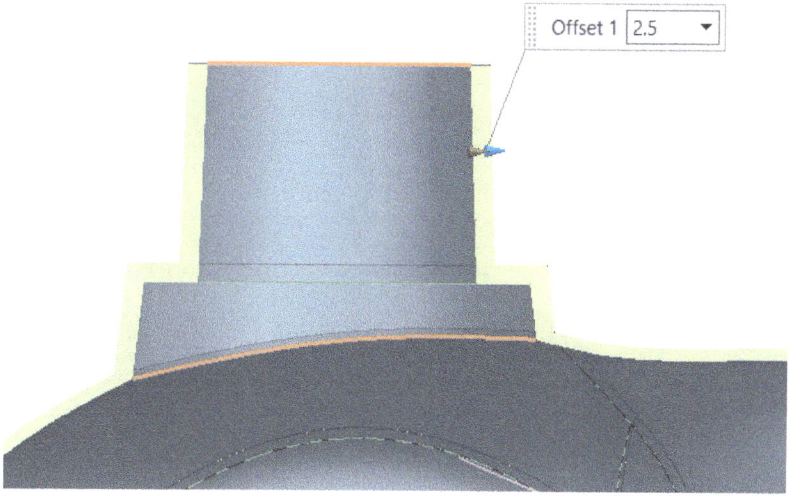

6. Hide the Sew surface on the Part Navigator.

7. On the ribbon, click **View > Content > Clip Section** .

8. Activate the **Edge Blend**  command, and then blend the sharp edges of the neck and spout.

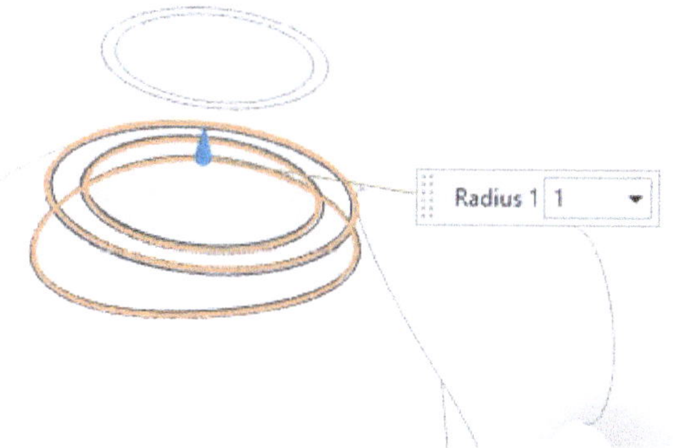

Creating threads

1. Activate the **Datum Plane** command, and then create a plane offset from the neck surface. The offset distance is 20 mm.

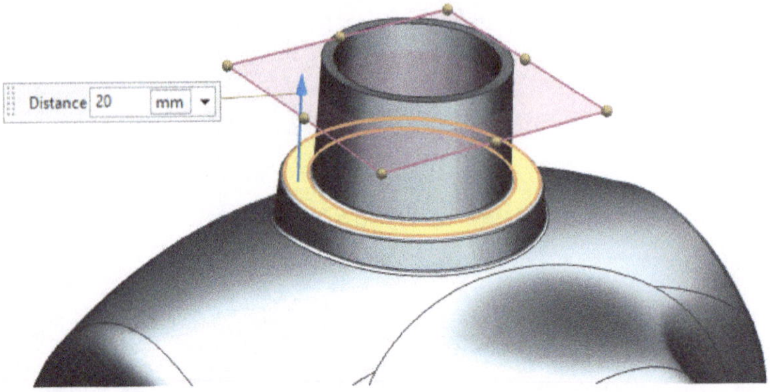

2. Create another offset plane at a 10 mm distance.

3. Activate the **Intersection Curve** command (on the ribbon, click **Curve > Derived > Intersection Curve**) and select the outer face of the spout.
4. Click the middle mouse button and select the two planes. Click **OK**.

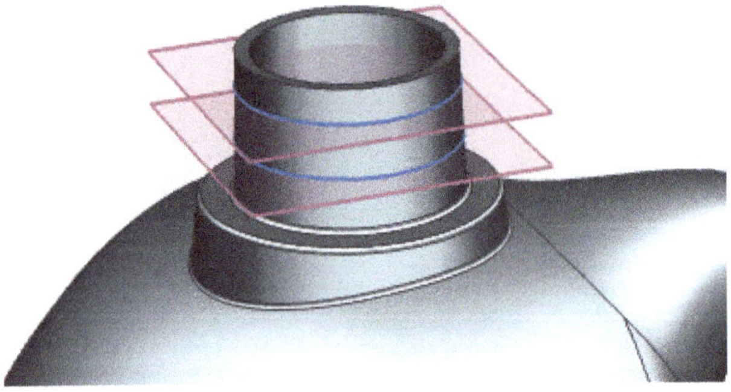

5. Activate the **Helix** command (on the ribbon, click **Curve > Advanced > Helix**) and select the center point of the lower intersection curve.

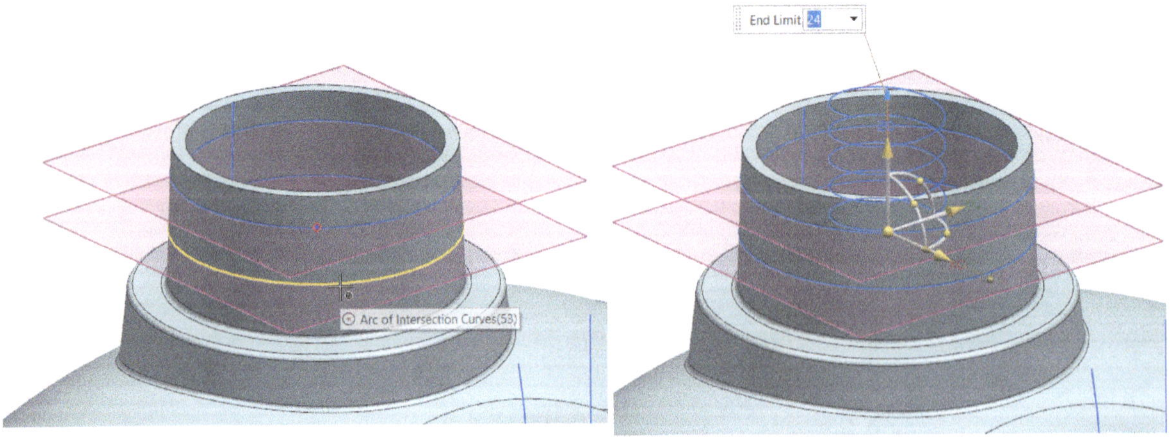

6. On the **Helix** dialog, under the **Size** section, select **Law Type > Linear**.
7. Click the down arrow next to the **Start Value** box and select **Measure**. On the **Measure** dialog, select **Object to Measure > Object** and click on the lower intersection curve.
8. On the callout, select the **Diameter** option from the drop-down, as shown. Next, click the **Creates a measurement expression on OK** icon next to the diameter value.

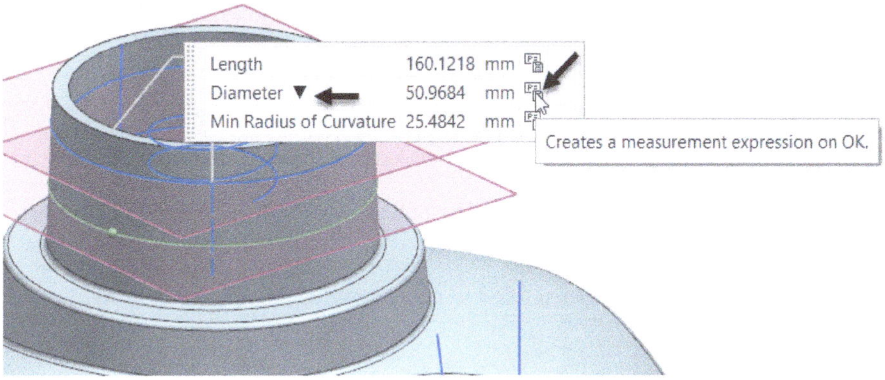

9. Click **OK** on the **Measure** dialog.
10. Click the down arrow next to the **End Value** box and select **Measure**. On the **Measure** dialog, select **Object to Measure > Object** and click on the upper intersection curve.
11. On the callout, select the **Diameter** option from the drop-down, as shown. Next, click the **Creates a measurement expression on OK** icon next to the diameter value.
12. Click **OK** on the **Measure** dialog.
13. Type-in 5 in the **Value** box under the **Pitch** section.
14. Under the **Length** section, select **Method > Turns**. Type-in 2 in the **Turns** box and click **OK**.
15. Hide the intersection curves and datum planes.
16. Create a datum plane normal to the helix.

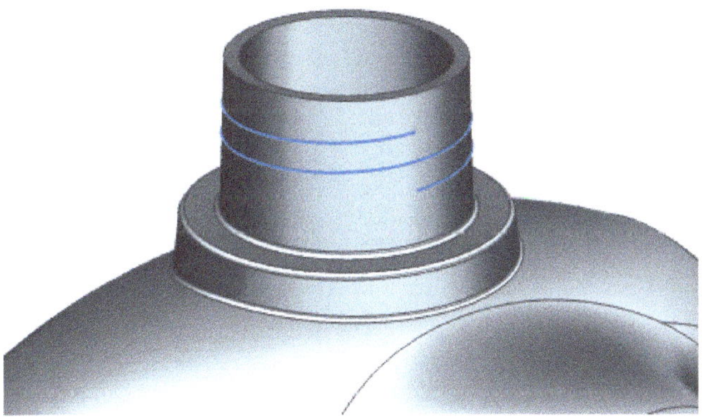

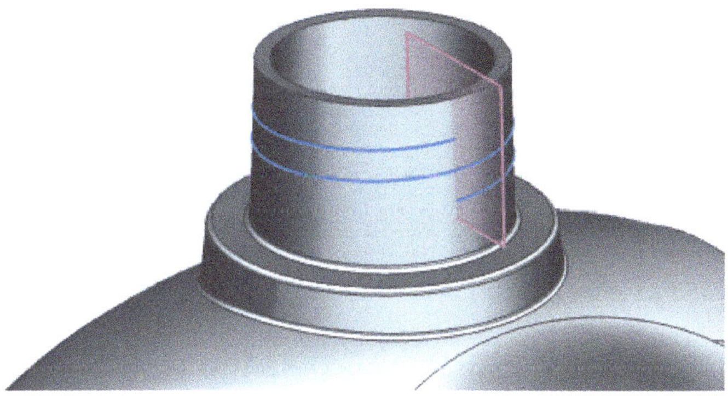

17. Draw a sketch on the plane normal to the helix. Finish the sketch.

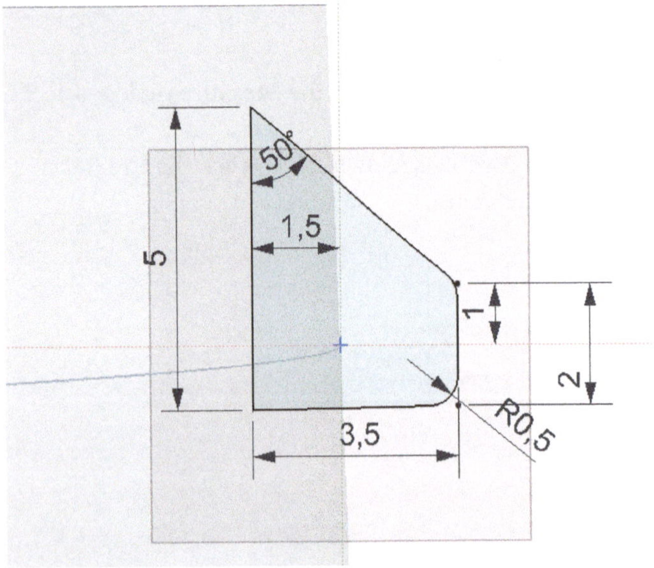

18. Activate the **Swept** command (on the ribbon, click **Surface > Base > Swept**) and click the **Reset** icon.
19. Select the cross-section. Next, click **Guides > Select Curve** and select the helix.
20. Under the **Section Options** section, select **Orientation Method > Face Normal**. Select the outer face of the spout.
21. Under the **Settings** section, set the **Body Type** to **Solid**. Click **OK**.
22. Unite the thread body with the main body.

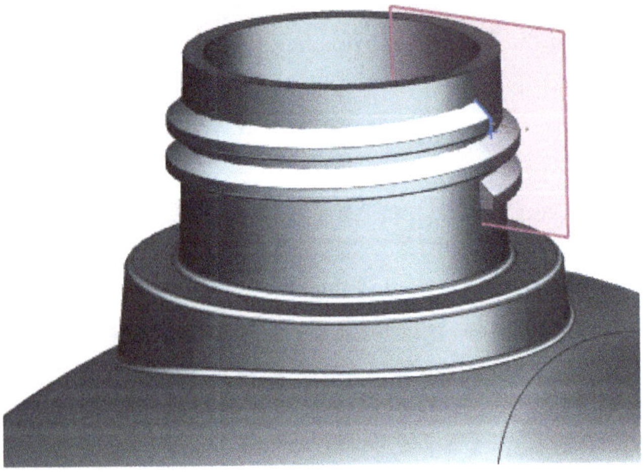

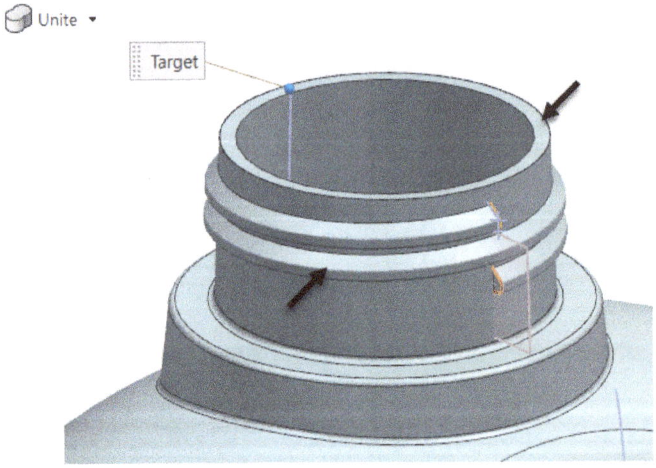

Measuring the Volume of the bottle

1. Activate the **Measure** command (on the ribbon, click **Analysis > Measure > Measure**) and click on the **Unite** feature in the Part Navigator. The measurements of the bottle appear. View the Volume of the bottle and click **OK** on the **Measure** dialog.

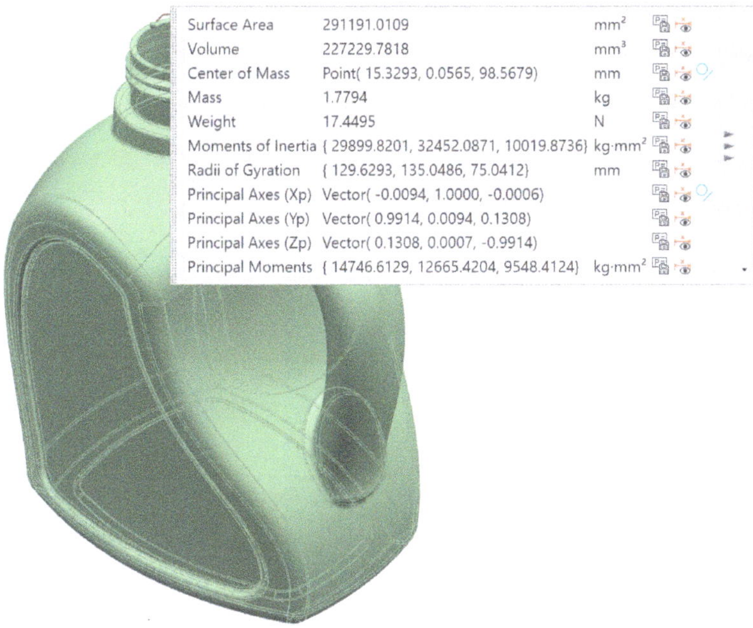

2. Select the geometry and click **View >True Shading Setup > True Shading Editor** 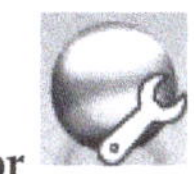 .
3. On the **True Shading Editor** dialog, **Object Specific Materials > Yellow Glossy Plastic**  on the ribbon. Next, select the model from the graphics window.
4. Click **OK** on the **True Shading Editor** dialog.

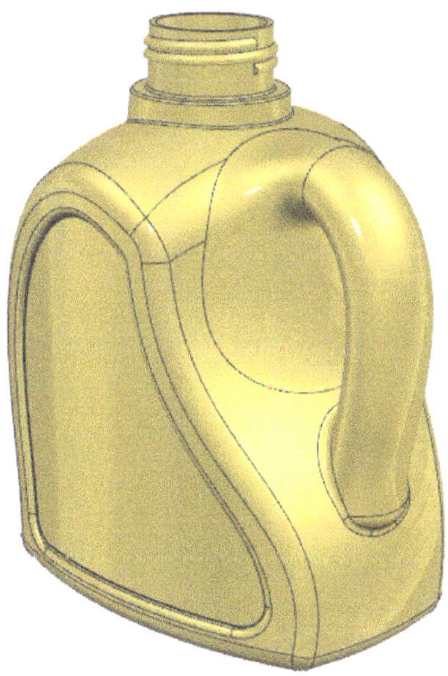

5. Save and close the file.

Questions

1. What is the use of the **Sew** command?
2. How many types of face blends can be created in NX?

3. Why do we use the **Patch Openings** command?
4. What are the commands that can be used to delete the openings on a surface?
5. Which commands can be used to bridge the gap between two surfaces?
6. Name the command that can be used to perform a variety of surface operations.
7. How to add multiple thicknesses to a surface body?
8. List the commands used to extend surfaces from an edge.
9. Why do we use the **Face Blend** command?
10. List the commands used to offset faces.

Exercise 1

Create the model shown next.

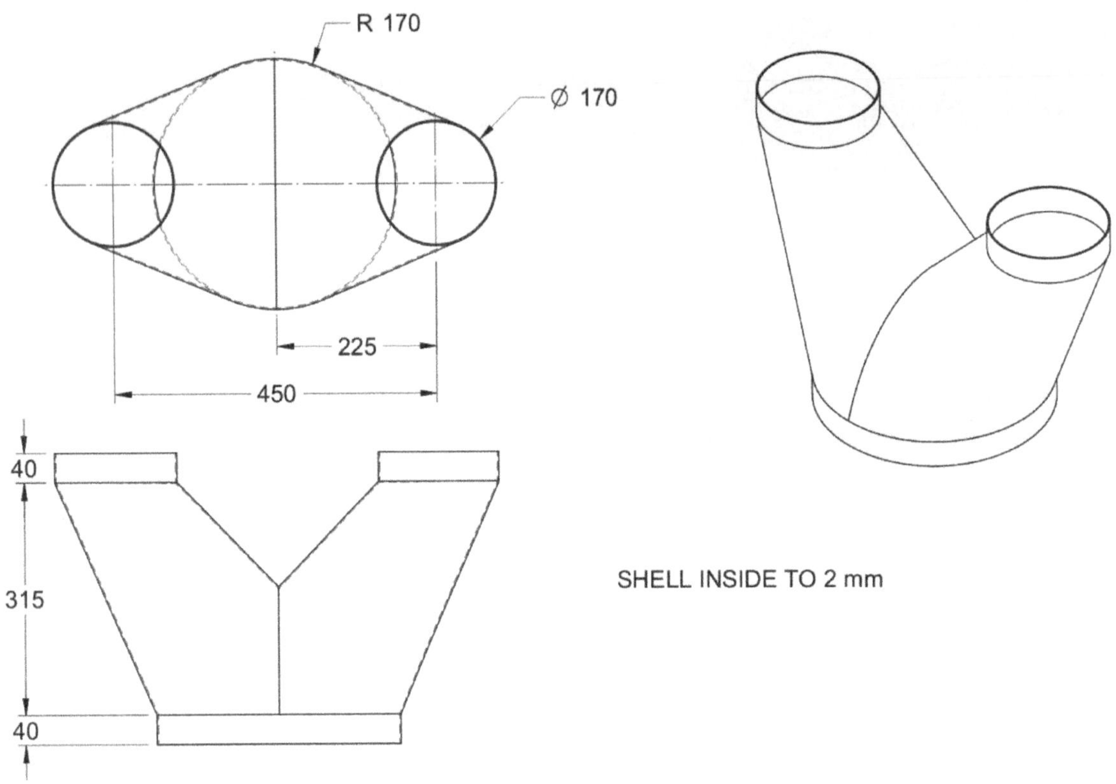

Chapter 12: NX Realize Shape

NX Realize Shape environment allows you to create organic smooth solid or surface models by manipulating and subdividing the primitive shapes such as spheres, blocks, cylinders, and so on.

The topics covered in this chapter are:

- *Primitive Shapes*
- *Transform Cages*
- *Extrude Cages*
- *Revolve Cage*
- *Fill*
- *Tube Cage*
- *Loft Cage*
- *Sweep Cage*
- *Set Continuity*
- *Start Symmetric Modeling*
- *Mirror Cage*
- *Copy Cage*
- *Subdivide Face*
- *Bridge Face*
- *Split Face*
- *Merge Face*
- *Delete*
- *Sew Cage*
- *Project Cage*

Activating the NX Realize Shape Environment

On the ribbon, click **Surface** tab > **Realize Shape > NX Realize Shape**  to activate the **NX Realize Shape** environment. The tools available on the **Home** tab of the NX Realize Shape environment are shown in the below figure.

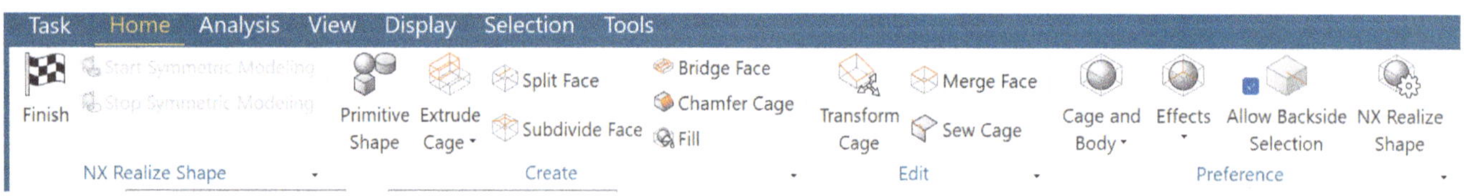

Creating Primitive Shapes

In the NX Realize Shape environment, first you create primitive shapes and then refine them into finished models. The primitive shapes are simple geometric models such as a sphere, cylinder, block, and so on. They are completely airtight closed surfaces. The **Primitive Shape** command helps you to create different primitive shapes. The procedures to create different primitive shapes are explained next.

Creating a Sphere

To create a sphere, activate the **Primitive Shape** command (on the ribbon, click **Home > Create > Primitive Shape**), and then select **Type > Sphere** on the **Primitive Shape** dialog. The sphere appears at the origin of the Datum Coordinate System. You can also select a different point in the graphics window to define the location of the sphere (or) use the Dynamic CSYS to define the location of the sphere. Type-in a value in the **Size** box available on the **Primitive Shape** dialog to define the size of the sphere (or) click and drag the arrow handle that appears on the sphere in the graphics window.

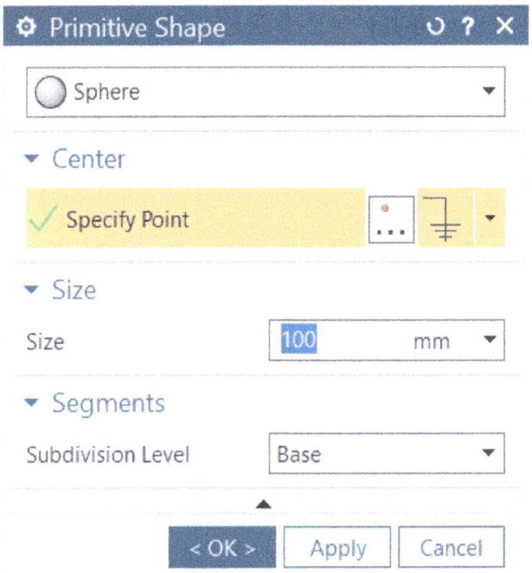

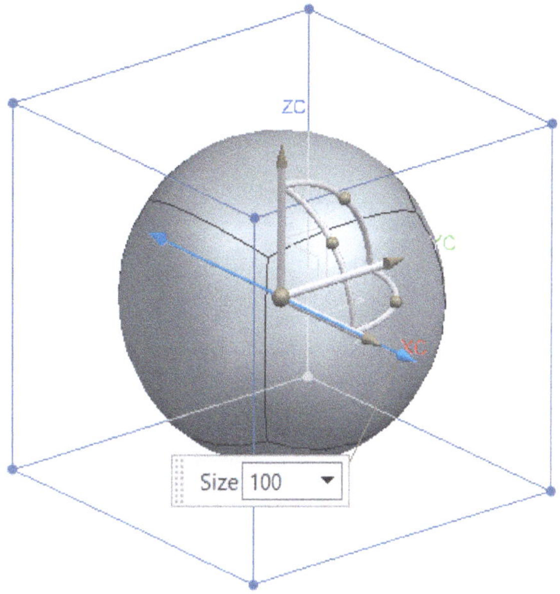

Next, you need to define the number of segments by selecting an option from the **Subdivision Level** drop-down (**Base**, **First**, and **Second**). The **Base** option creates a sphere with six segments. The **First** option creates a twenty-four segmented sphere. The **Second** option creates a ninety-six segmented sphere. Click **OK** to create the sphere.

Base

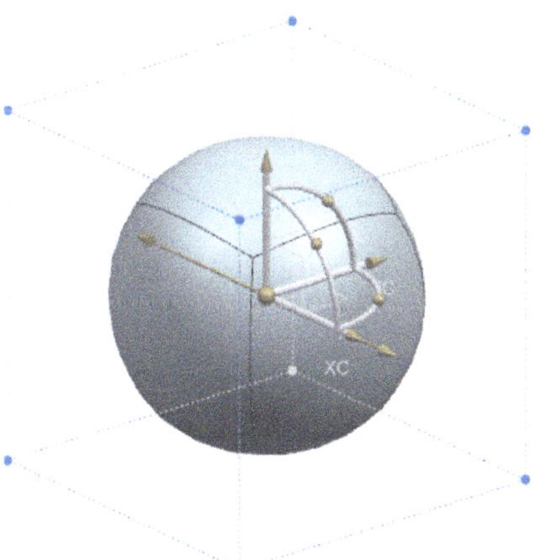

First

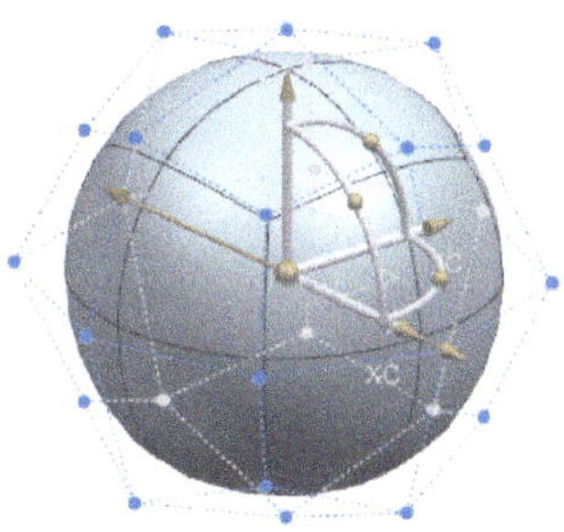

Second

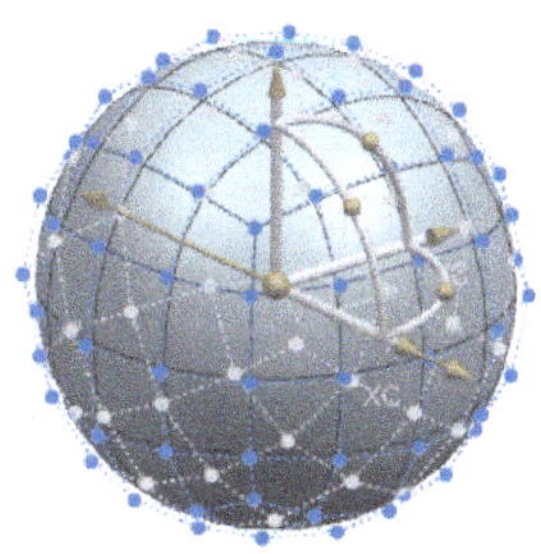

Creating Cylinder

To create a cylinder, activate the **Primitive Shape** command (on the ribbon, click **Home > Create > Primitive Shape**), and then select **Type > Cylinder** . Next, specify the location of the cylinder by using any one of the options available in the **Specify Point** drop-down. Next, type in a value in the **Size** and **Height** boxes available on the **Primitive Shape** dialog (or) click and drag the horizontal and vertical arrows to define the diameter and height of the cylinder.

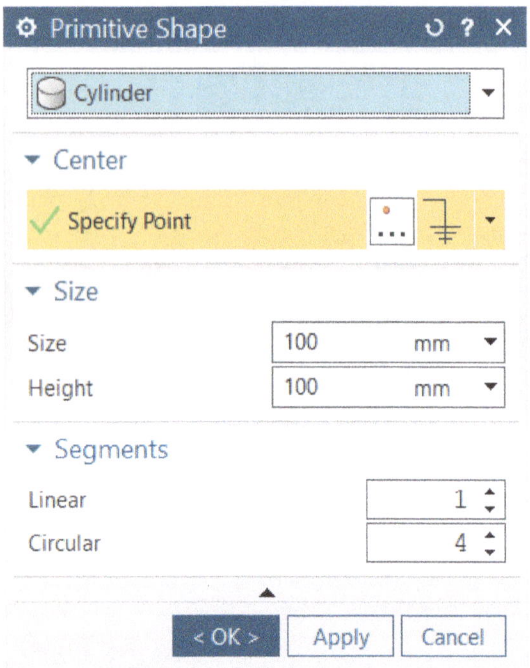

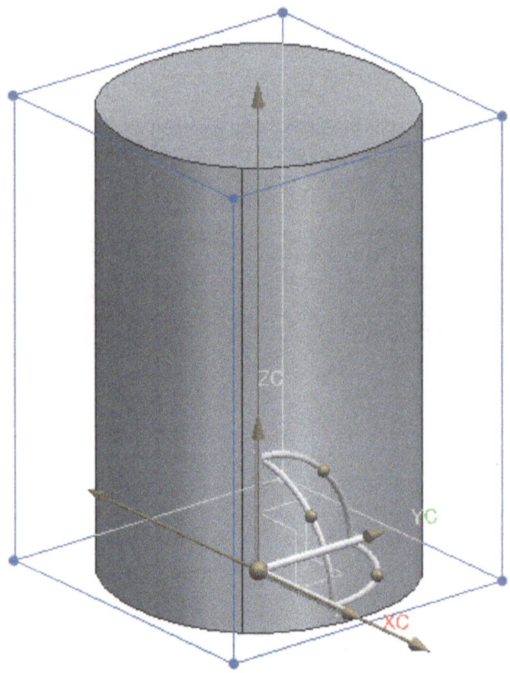

Next, specify the number of segments in the linear and circular direction by entering values in the **Linear** and **Circular** boxes available in the **Segments** section. Note that the number of segments in the circular direction should be between three and thirty-six. Click **OK** to complete the cylindrical shape.

Linear: 3
Circular : 4

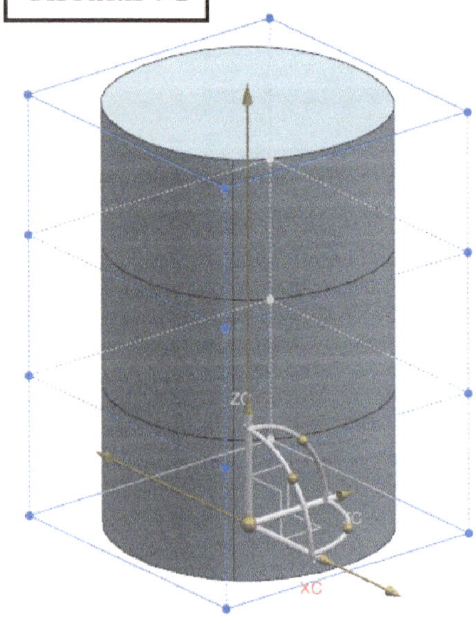

Linear: 4
Circular : 6

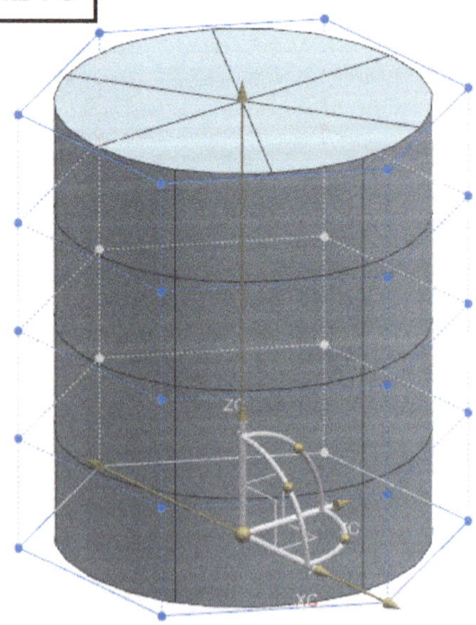

Creating a Block

To create a block, activate the **Primitive Shape** command (on the ribbon, click **Home > Create > Primitive Shape**), and then select **Type > Block** . Specify the location of the block, and then type-in values in the **Length (XC)**, **Width (YC)**, and **Height (ZC)** boxes available on the **Primitive Shape** dialog (or) drag the arrows available on the edges of the block to define the block size.

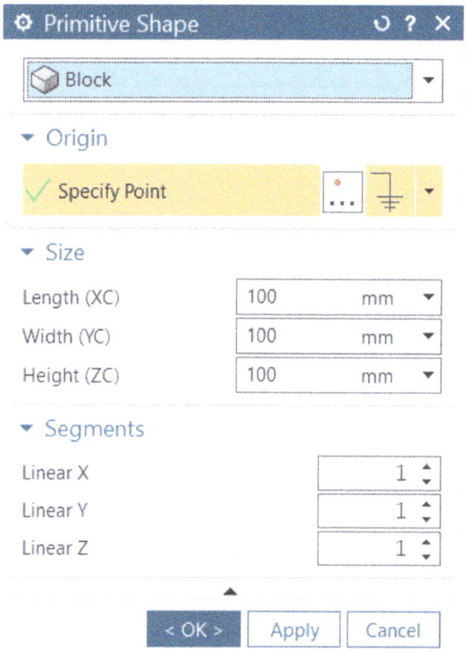

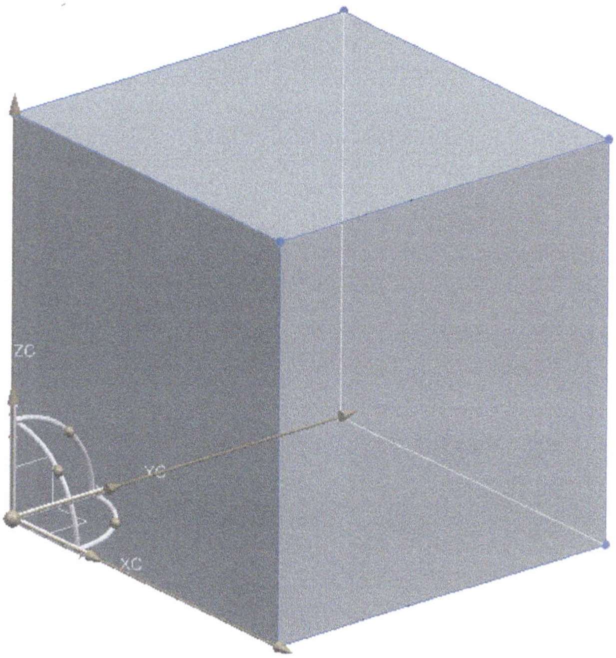

Next, type-in values in the **Linear X**, **Linear Y**, and **Linear Z** boxes to add segments along the X, Y, and Z directions, respectively. Click **OK** to complete the block.

Creating Torus

To create a torus, activate the **Primitive Shape** command (on the ribbon, click **Home > Create > Primitive Shape**), and then select **Type > Torus** . Type-in a value in the **Outer** box in the **Size** section of the **Primitive Shape** dialog (or) drag the **Outer** diameter handle to change the outer diameter of the torus. Likewise, change the inner diameter of the torus by entering a value in the Inner box or dragging the Inner diameter handle.

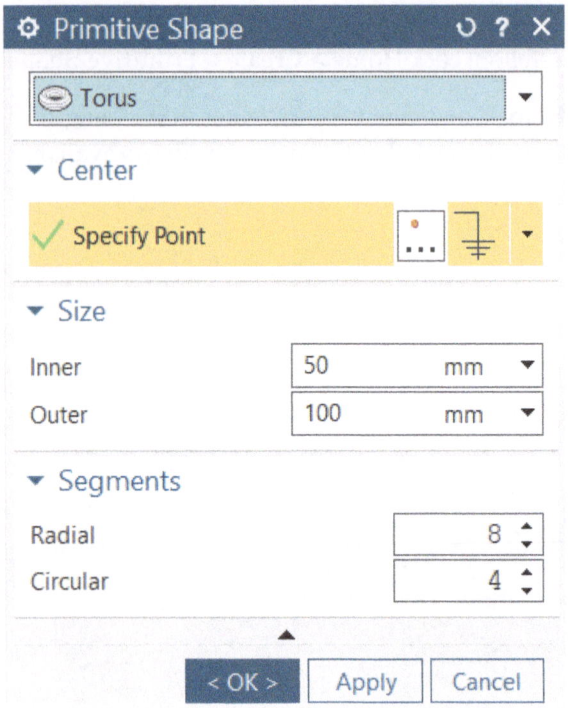

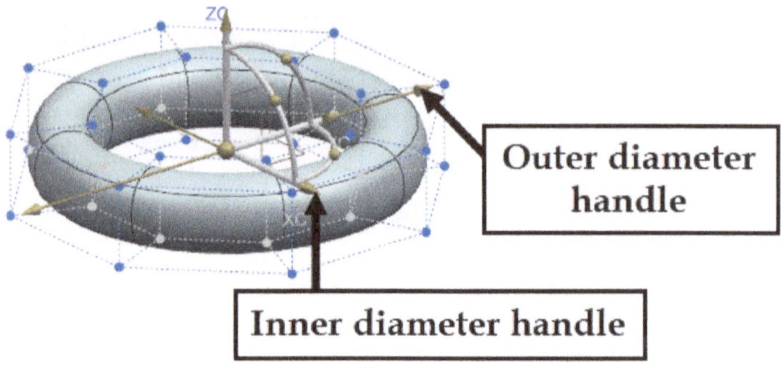

Next, specify the number of segments in the radial and circular directions by entering values in the **Radial** and **Circular** boxes, respectively. Next, click **OK** on the **Primitive Shape** dialog.

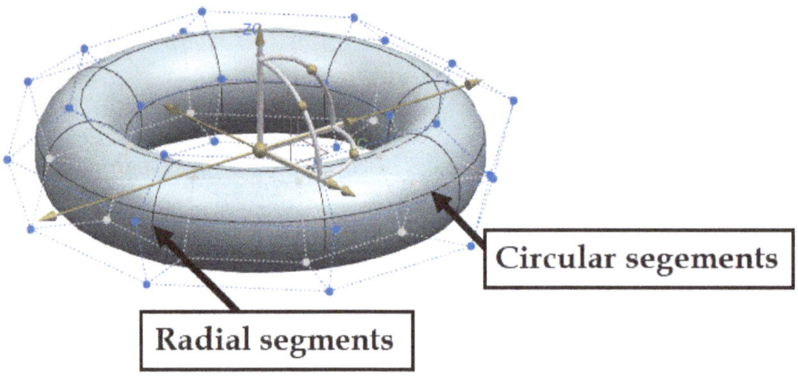

Creating a Circle

To create a circle, activate the **Primitive Shape** command (on the ribbon, click **Home > Create > Primitive Shape**), and then select **Type > Circle** . Next, specify the size of the circle and number of segments in the **Size** and **Circular** boxes, respectively. Use the Translate or Rotate handles of the Dynamic CSYS displayed on the circle to change its location and orientation. Click **OK** to create the circle.

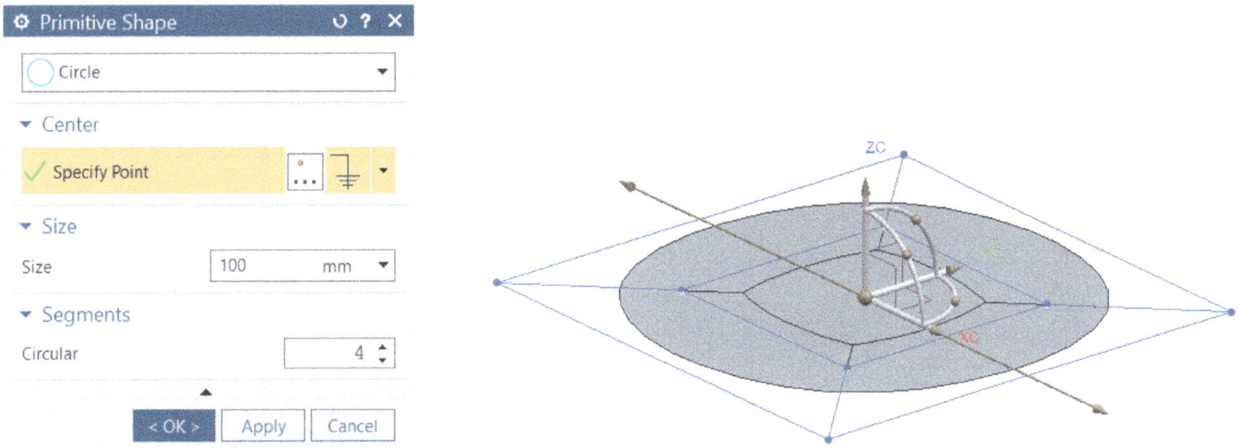

Creating a Rectangle

To create a rectangle, activate the **Primitive Shape** command, and then select **Type > Rectangle**. Next, specify the **Length (XC)** and **Width (YC)** values to define the size of the rectangle. Type in values in the Linear X and Linear Y boxes to divide the rectangle into a number of segments along the X and Y directions.

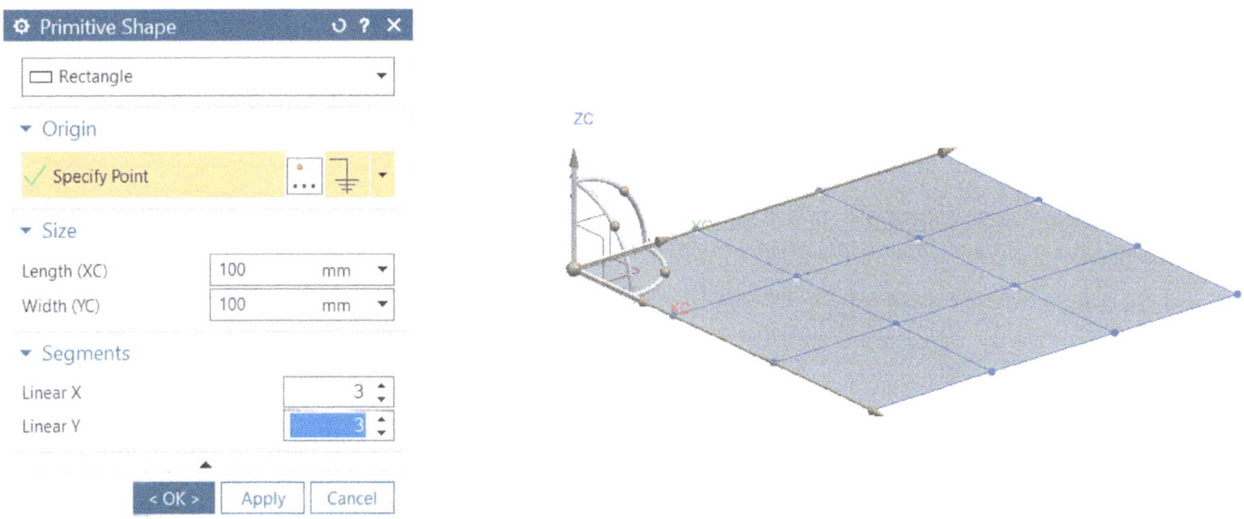

The Transform Cage command

After creating the freeform primitive shapes, you need to use the **Transform Cage** command to manipulate them. For example, create a block, as shown below.

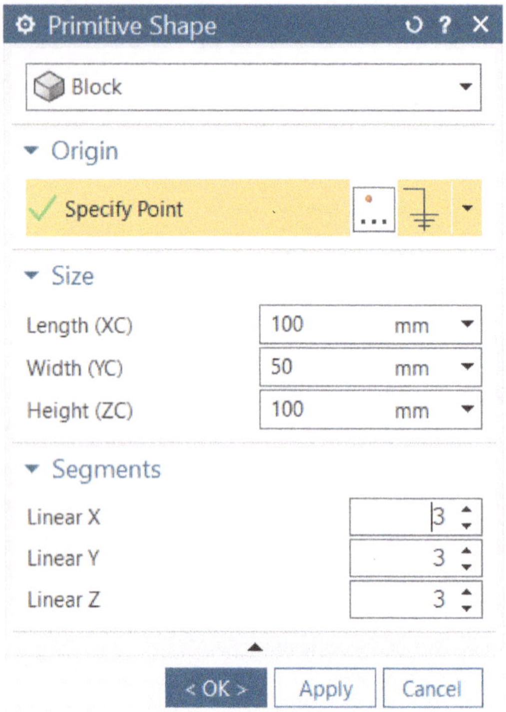

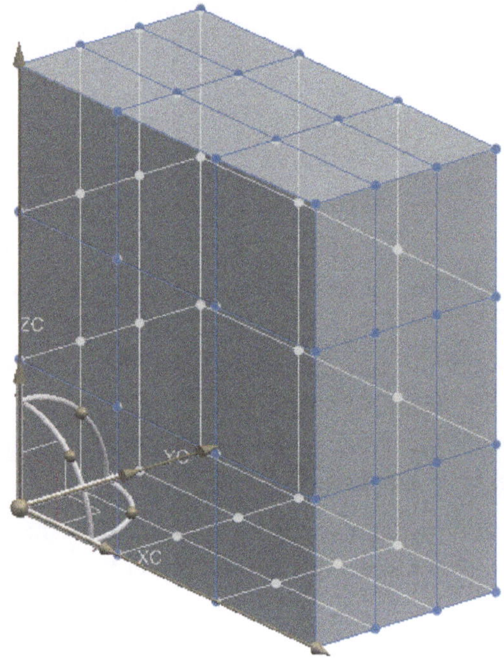

Next, activate the **Transform Cage** command (on the ribbon, click **Home > Modify > Transform Cage**). On the Top Border Bar, the **Selection Filter** drop-down has four filters: **Cage Edge**, **Cage Face**, **Cage Vertex**, and **Control Cage**. For example, if you set **Selection Filter** to **Cage Edge**, you will be able to select only the edges of the cage. The **Selection Rule** drop-down on the Sketch Scene Bar has six options: **Single Object**, **Loop**, **Matrix**, **Region**, **Sharp Edges**, and **Weighted Edges**. You can also set the **Selection Rule** options in addition to the Selection Filters.

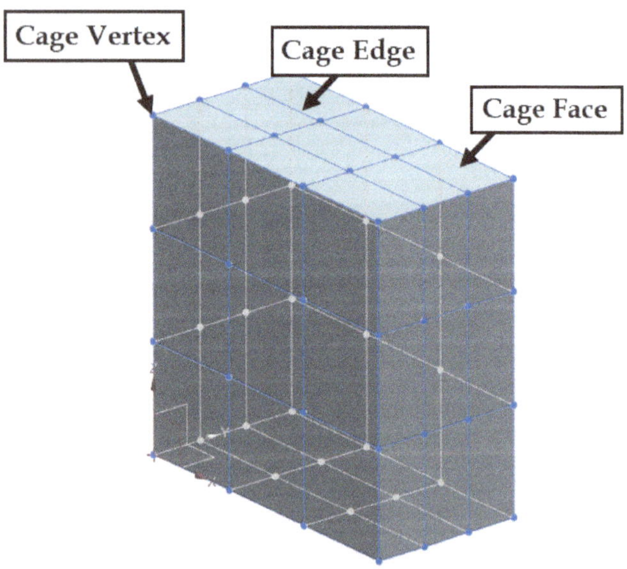

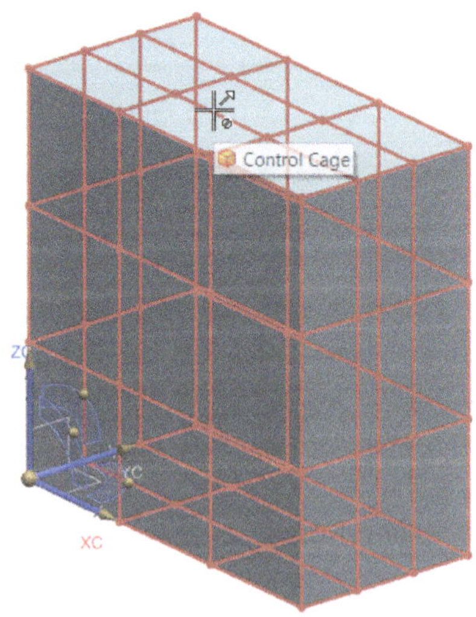

On the Sketch Scene Bar, select **Selection Rule > Loop** and click on the cage edge, as shown; the entire loop is selected. Next, drag the selected loop by holding the left mouse button and release it, as shown. Click **Apply** on the **Transform Cage** dialog.

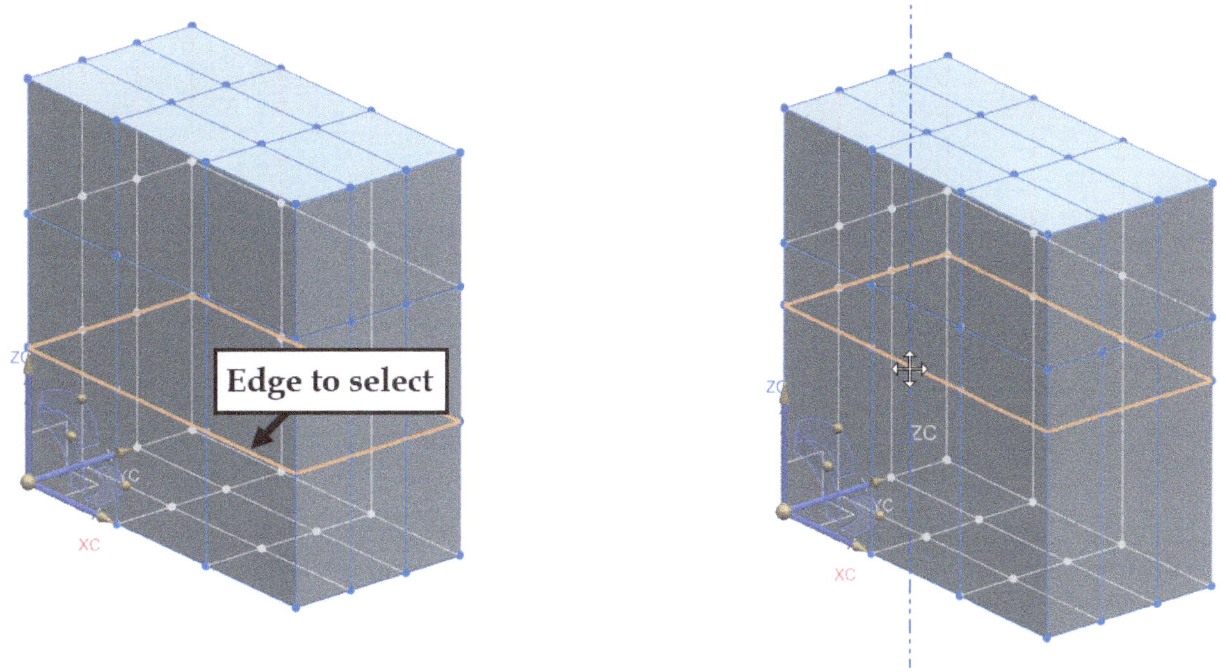

On the Sketch Scene Bar, click **Selection Rule > Region**. Next, change the view orientation to **Right**. On the **Transform Cage** dialog, click the **Transform** tab and make sure that the **Relocate Tool to Selection** and **Reorient Tool to Selection** options are selected. Click and drag a selection window across the upper portion of the block, as shown; the entire region is selected. Also, notice that the transform handle is displayed in the selected region. Click on the YZ-Rotate handle and drag the pointer to rotate the region. Click **Apply** on the **Transform Cage** dialog.

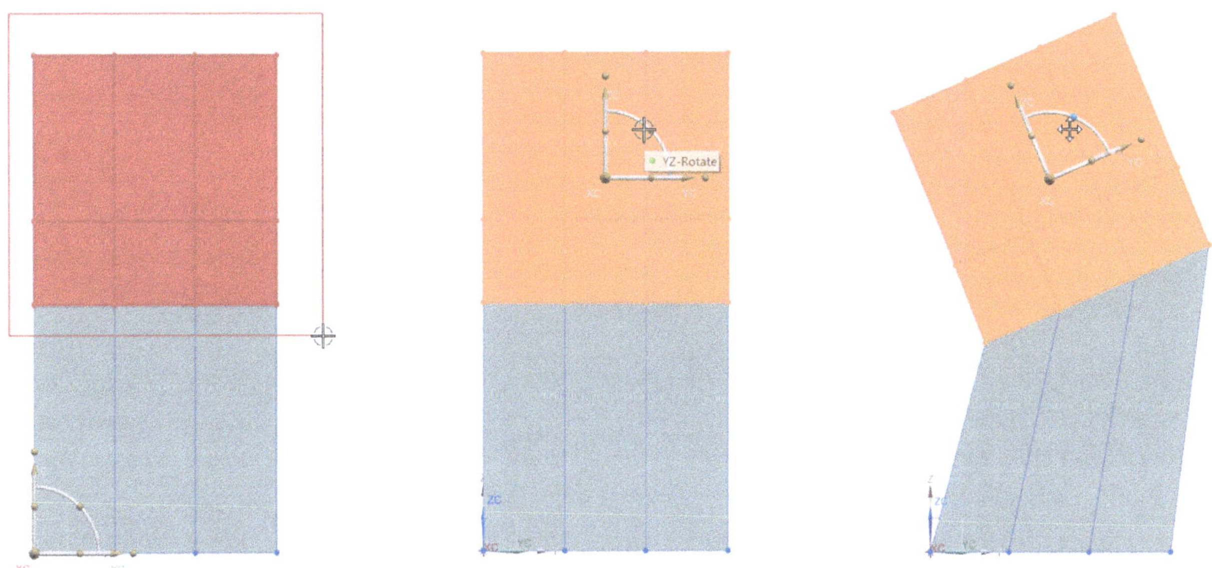

On the Top Border Bar, set **Selection Filter** to **Cage Face** and select **Selection Rule > Single Object**. Next, change the view orientation to **Isometric**. On the **Transform Cage** dialog, click the **Transform** tab and make sure that the **Relocate Tool to Selection** and **Reorient Tool to Selection** options are selected. Next, select **Scaling > Uniform**

on the dialog. Click on the cage faces on the top face of the block, as shown. Click and drag the scale handle, as shown; the selected faces are scaled.

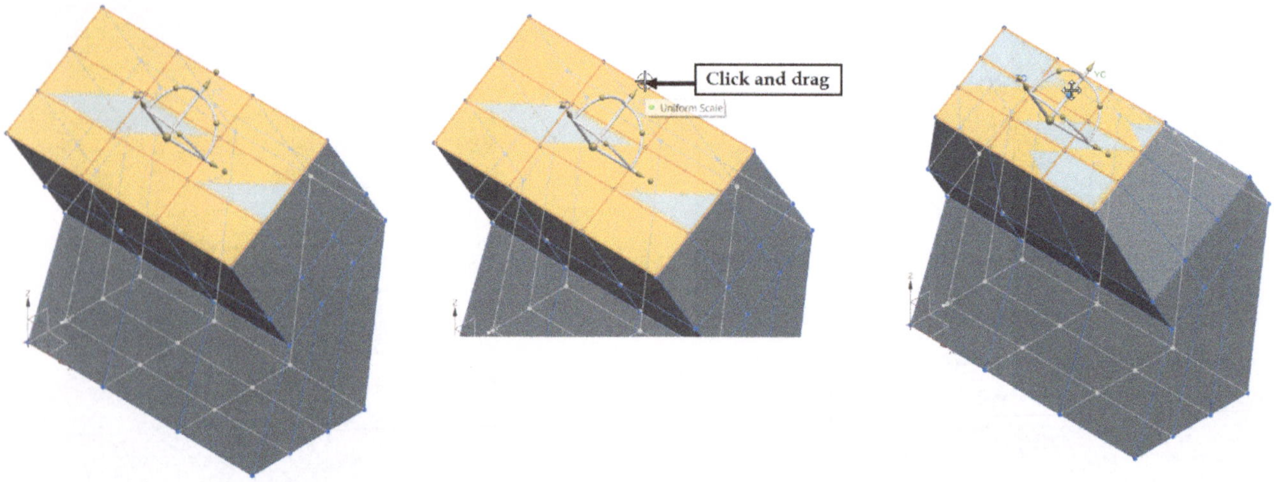

The Extrude Cage command

The **Extrude Cage** command is used to extrude the cage faces, cage edges, or curves. This command is practically illustrated in the following example. First, create a block using the **Primitive Shape** command, as shown. Next, activate the **Extrude Cage** command (on the ribbon, click **Home > Create > Extrude Cage**) and click the **Reset** icon. Click on the center face on the top face of the block, and then drag the Distance handle displayed on the selected face. Notice that there is a smooth transition at the bottom of the extrusion. On the **Extrude Cage** dialog, expand the **Settings** section, and select the **Sharp** option; the edges at the bottom are sharpened.

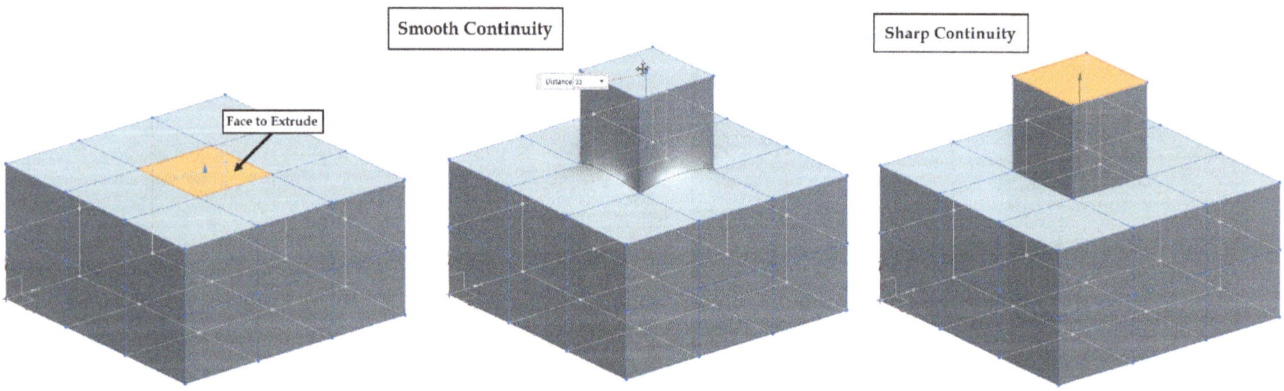

Click **Apply** on the dialog; notice that the Distance handle is displayed on the top face. Click and drag the Distance handle up to some distance, and then click **Apply**. On the **Extrude Cage** dialog, click the **Transform** tab and drag the Z-Translate handle up to some distance. Next, click and drag the YZ-Rotate handle to rotate the face, as shown. Again, click and drag the Z-Translate handle, and then click **OK**.

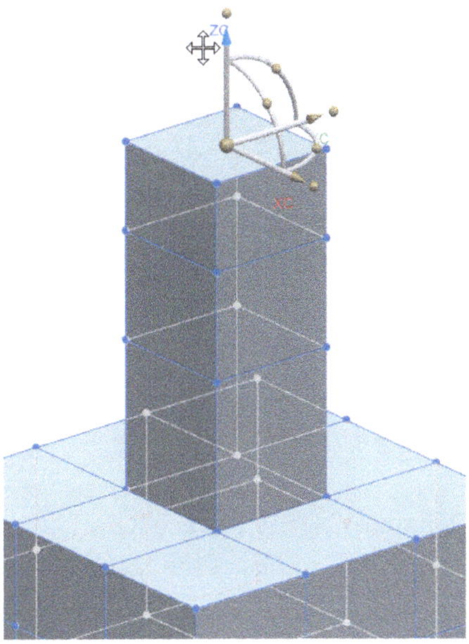
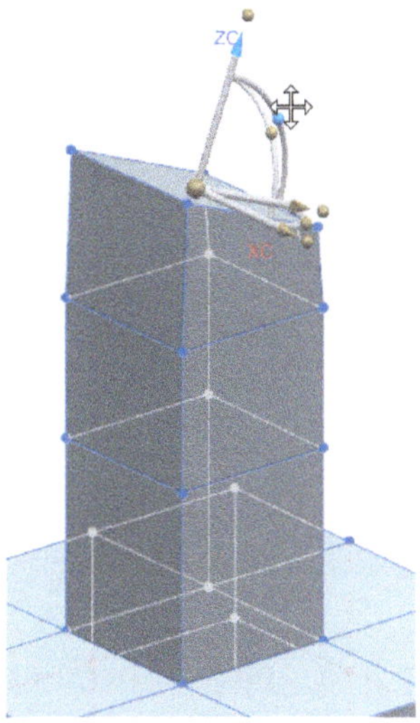
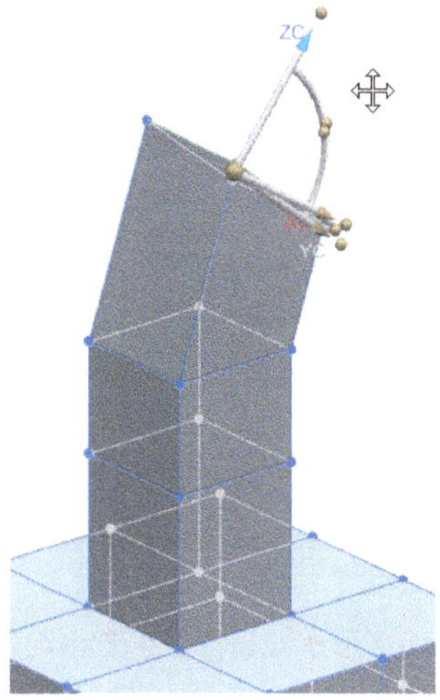

Extruding a Planar Face

Create a rectangle using the **Primitive Shape** command. Next, activate the **Extrude Cage** command and select all the faces of the planar face. Click and drag the Distance handle to add thickness to the face. Next, click **OK**.

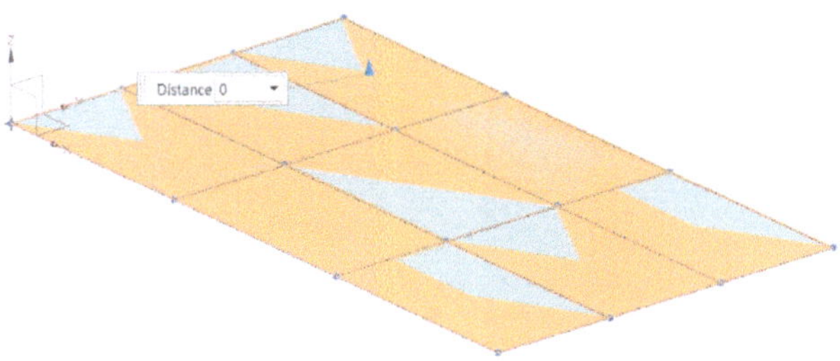

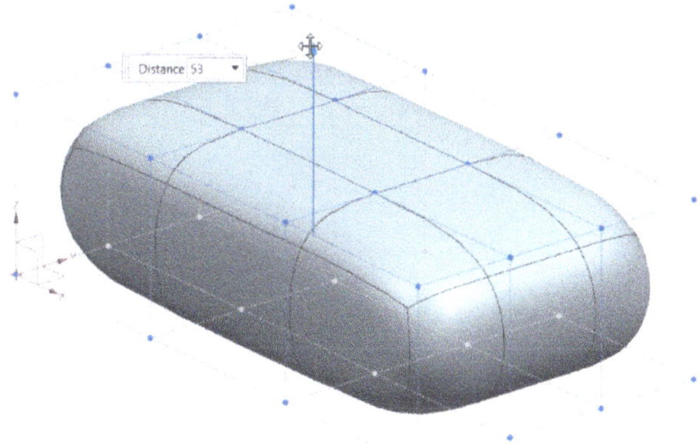

Extruding the Cage Edges

Create a rectangle using the **Primitive Shape** command. Next, activate the **Extrude Cage** command (on the ribbon, click **Home > Create > Extrude Cage**) and click on the cage edges, as shown. On the **Extrude Cage** dialog, click the **Drag Linear** tab and select **Direction > Perpendicular**. Click and drag the Distance handle to extrude the cage edge. Click **Apply** on the dialog.

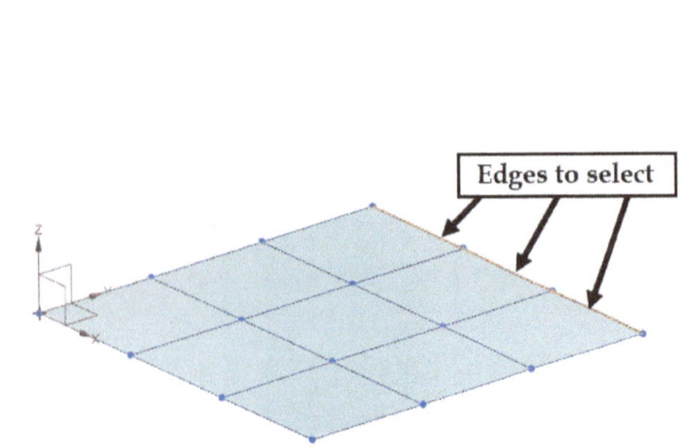

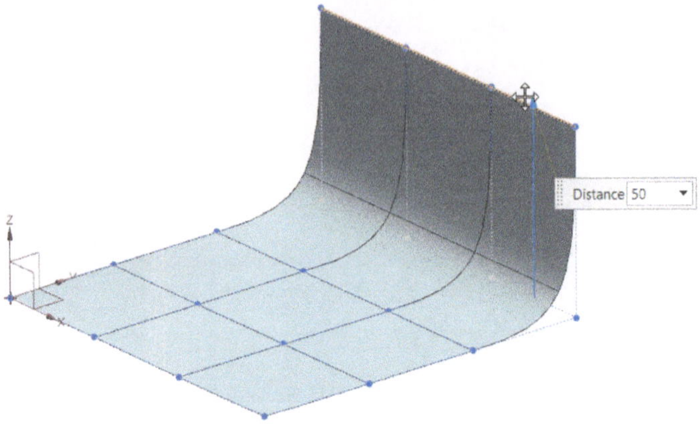

Click the **Transform** tab of the dialog and drag the Y-Translate handle of the Dynamic CSYS. Click the XZ - Rotate handle and drag to rotate the selected edge. Likewise, you can also use the scale handles of the Dynamic CSYS to modify the selected edges.

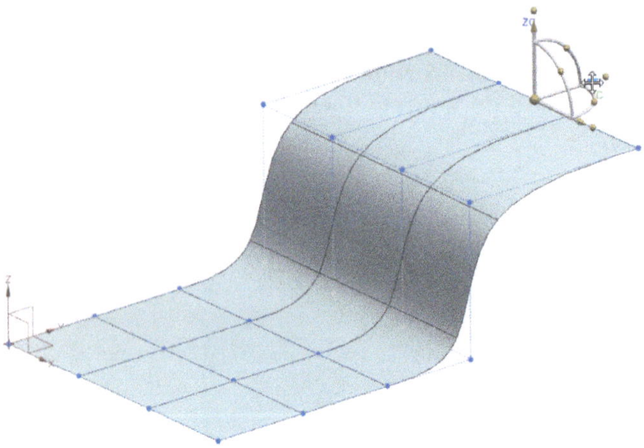

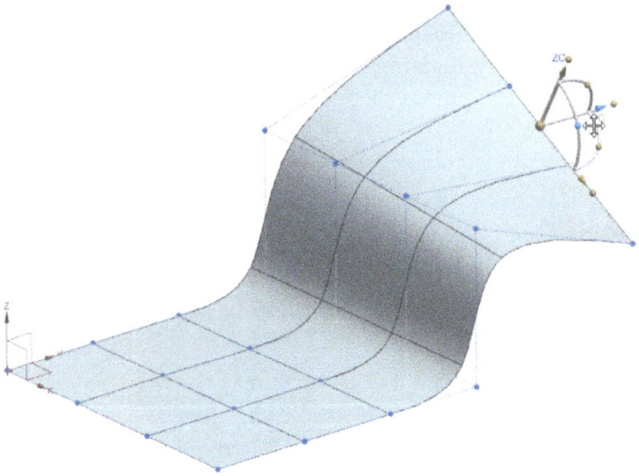

The Revolve Cage command

The **Revolve Cage** command revolves a polyline or cage edges to create cage faces. This command is practically illustrated in the following example. Activate the **Cage Polyline** command (Top Border Bar, click **Menu > Insert > Cage Polyline**) and click the **Reset** icon on the **Cage Polyline** dialog. Next, click the **YC-ZC** icon in the **Drawing Plane** section of the **Cage Polyline** dialog. On the Top Border Bar, click **Orient View** drop-down **> Right**. Specify the points of the polyline, as shown. Next, click **OK** to create the cage polyline.

Activate the **Revolve Cage** command (on the ribbon, click **Home > Create > Extrude/Revolve** Drop-down **> Revolve Cage**) and click the **Reset** icon on the **Revolve Cage** dialog. Select the cage polyline from the graphics window. On the **Revolve Cage** dialog, click **Specify Vector** under the **Axis** section and then select Z-axis from the vector triad displayed in the graphics window. Click on the origin point of the Datum Coordinate system to specify the location of the axis. Next, specify the **Start Angle** and **End Angle** of the revolved cage. Expand the **Segmentation** section and type in a value in the **Number of Segments** box. Note that the number of segments should be three or more. Click **OK** to create the revolved cage.

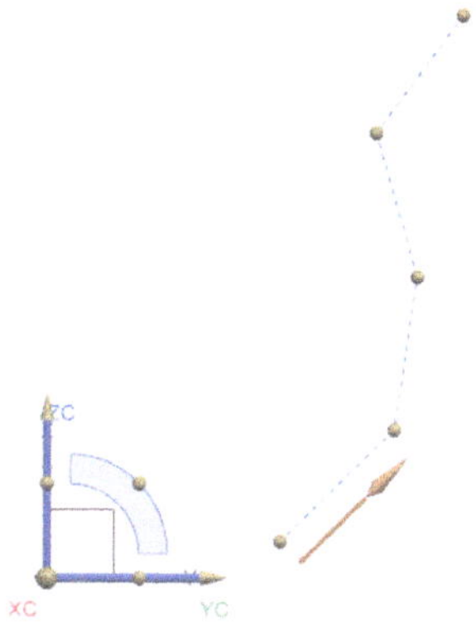

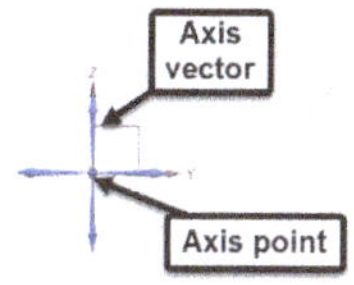

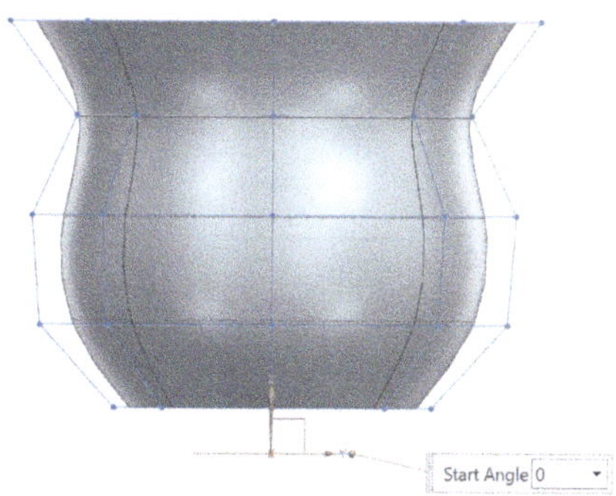

The Fill command

The **Fill** command adds a new face to the cage using two or more cage edges. Activate this command (on the ribbon, click **Home > Create > Fill**) and click on the open edges of a cage. On the **Fill** dialog, expand the **Settings** section and set **Continuity** to **Smooth**. Next, click **OK**.

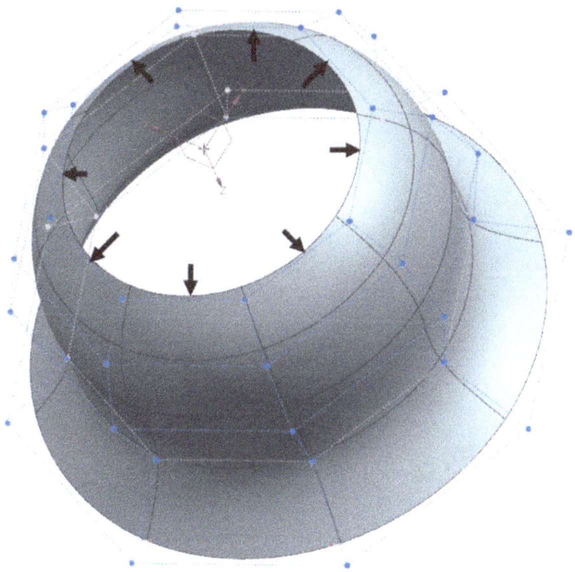

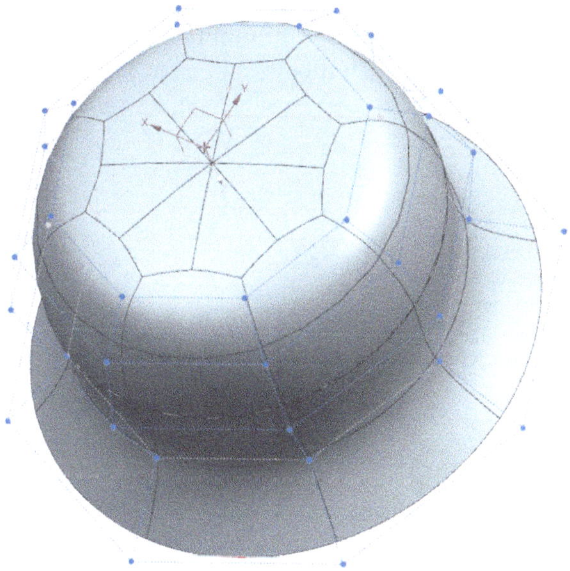

The Tube Cage command

The **Tube Cage** command creates a tube with a control cage using a polyline as its path. Activate this command (on the ribbon, click **Home > Create > Tube Cage**), and select **Type > Single Path**. Next, click on a polyline. On the **Tube Cage** dialog, under the **Cross Section** section, specify the **Size** and **Number of Segments**. Click **OK** to create the tube cage.

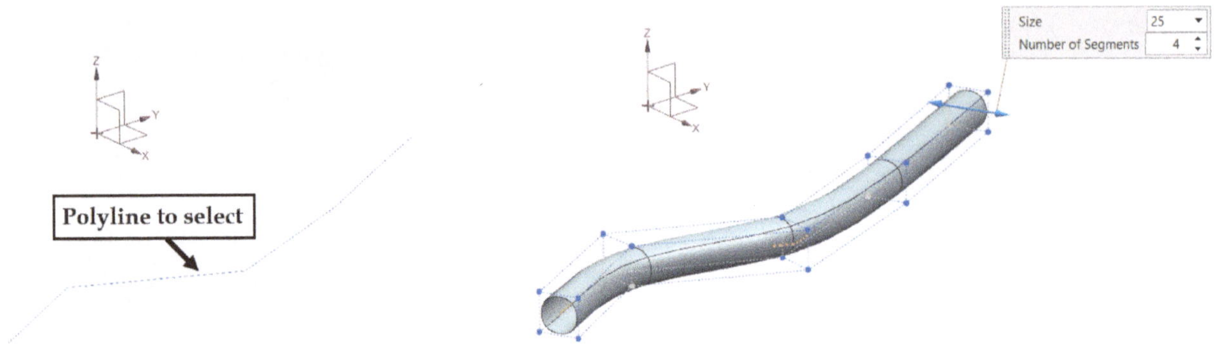

Creating a Branched Tube Cage

Activate the **Tube Cage** command and select **Type > Branched Path**. Next, select the branched polyline, as shown. On the **Size** section of the **Tube Cage** dialog, specify the values in the **Node Size**, **Rod Size**, and **Fallout Distance** boxes, respectively. The **Node Size** value adjusts the size of the nodes located at the intersections of paths. The **Rod Size** value defines the diameter of the tube. The **Falloff Distance** value defines the distance of transition from nodes to rods.

Specify the **Cross Section** and **Rod** values in the **Segments** section. The **Cross Section** value specifies the count of cage segments to generate around the tube's cross-section. The **Rod** value establishes the count of cage segments to generate along each tube rod.

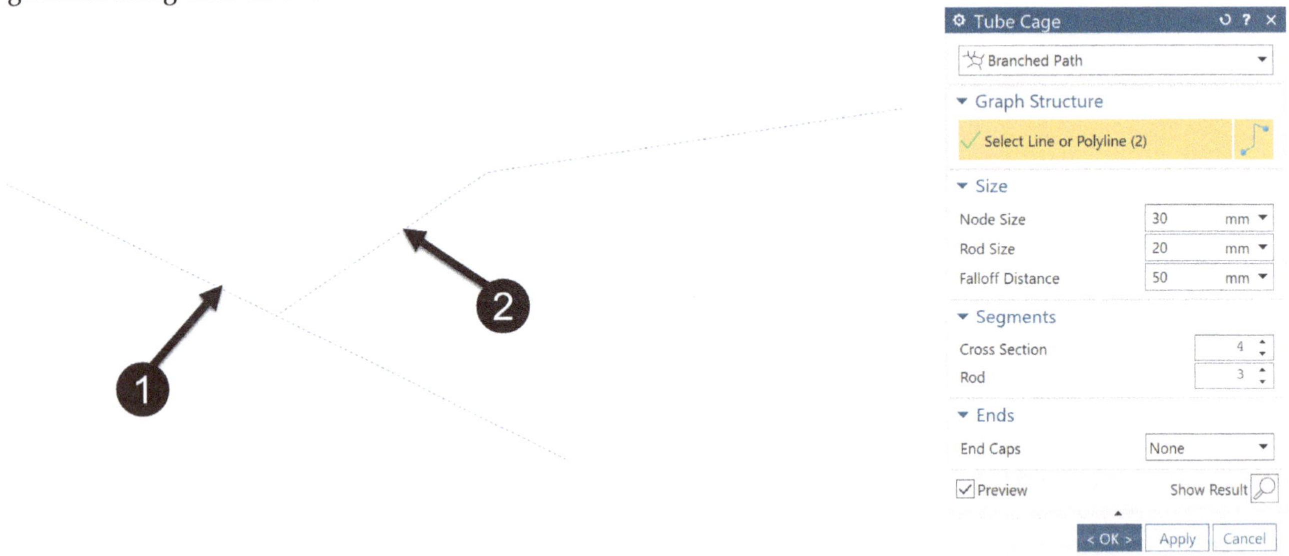

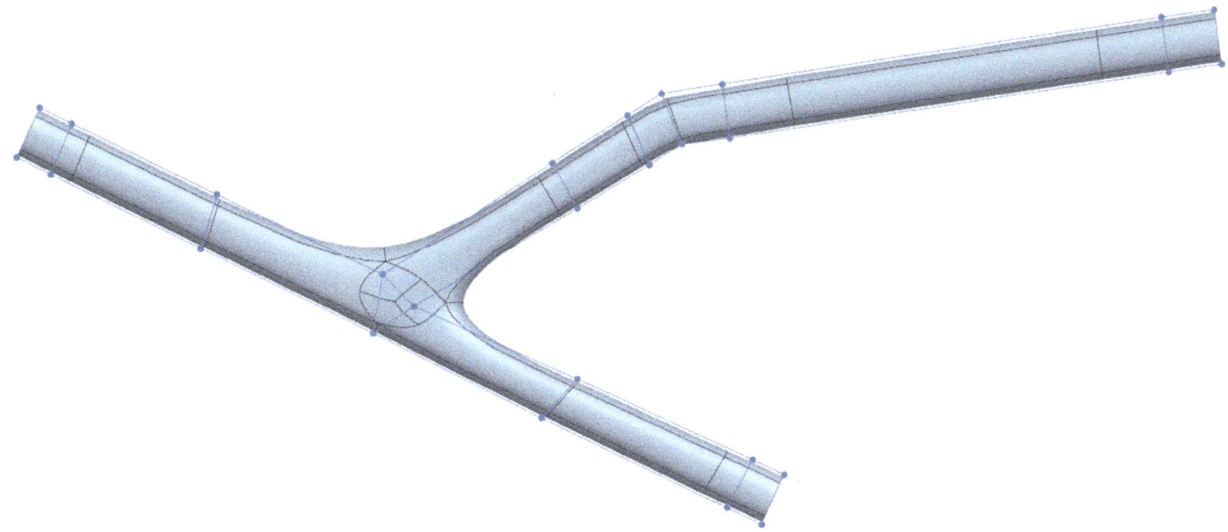

In the **Ends** section, select an option from the **End Caps** drop-down (**Flat** or **Round**). Click **OK** to create the branched tube cage.

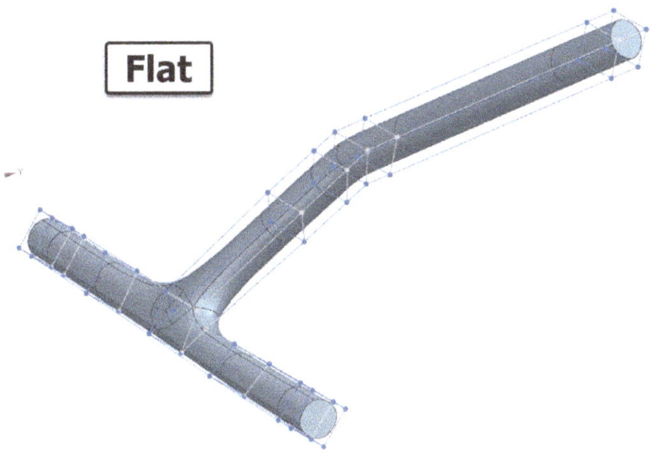

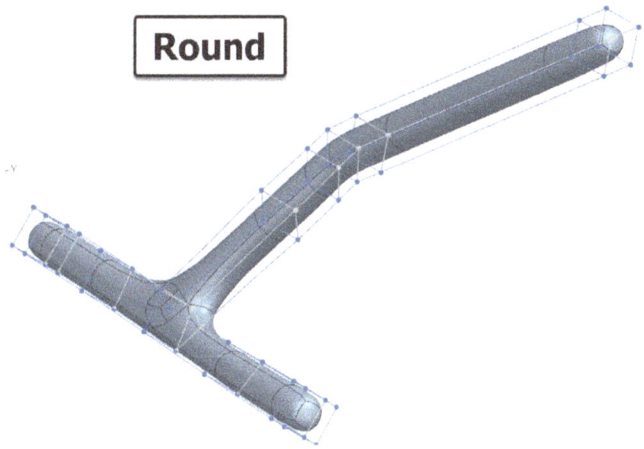

The Loft Cage command

The **Loft Cage** command creates a lofted surface with a control cage using two or more polylines. First, you need to create two or more polylines in the graphics window. You can use the **Cage Polyline,** or **Extract Cage Polyline** commands to create polylines. In this example, the **Extract Cage Polyline** command is used to create cage polylines. Likewise, create sketches on the two datum planes, as shown.

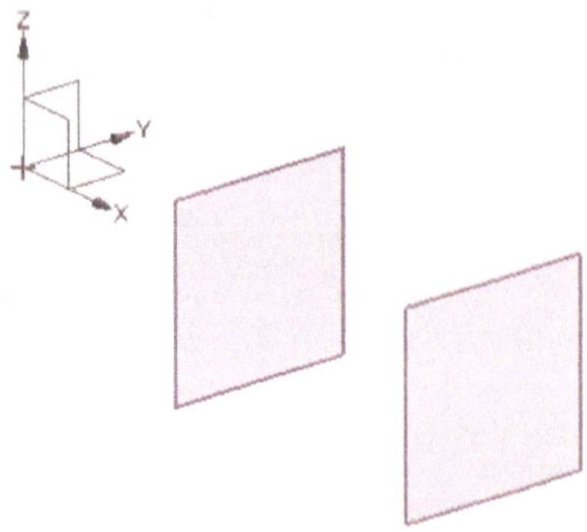
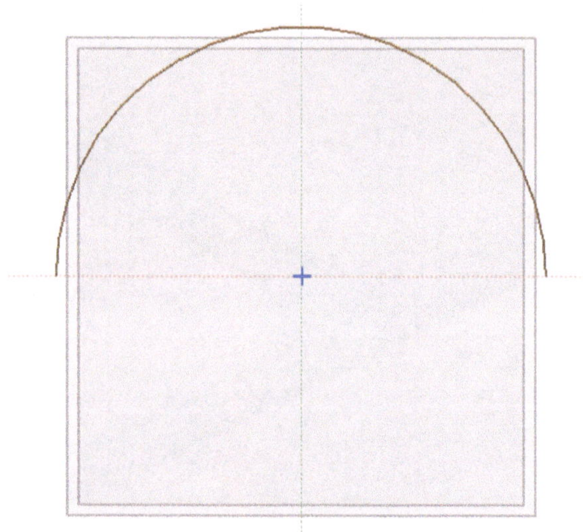

Click **Surface > Realize Shape > NX Realize Shape** on the ribbon. Next, activate the **Extract Cage Polyline** command (On the Top Border Bar, click **Menu > Insert > Extract Cage Polyline**) and select the first sketch from the graphics window. Next, set the **Number of Segments** value to **3**. Click **Apply**. Likewise, convert the remaining curves to polylines.

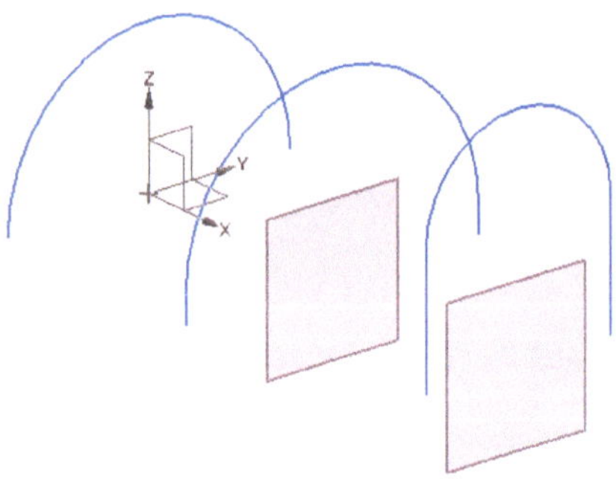
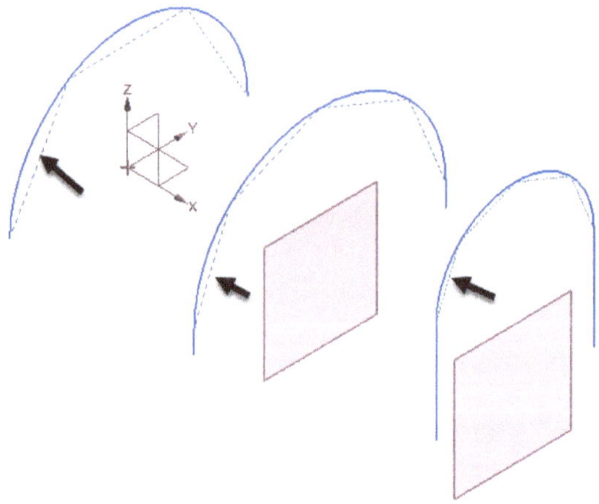

Activate the **Loft Cage** command (on the ribbon, click **Home > Create > Loft Cage**), and click on the first polyline. Next, click the **Add New Set** icon and click on the second polyline. Likewise, click the **Add New Set** icon and click on the third polyline. Make sure that the arrows on the selected polylines point in the same direction. Use the **Reverse Direction** icon if they are in different directions. Next, expand the **Segmentation** section and set the **Number of Segments** value to 3. Click **OK** to create the loft cage.

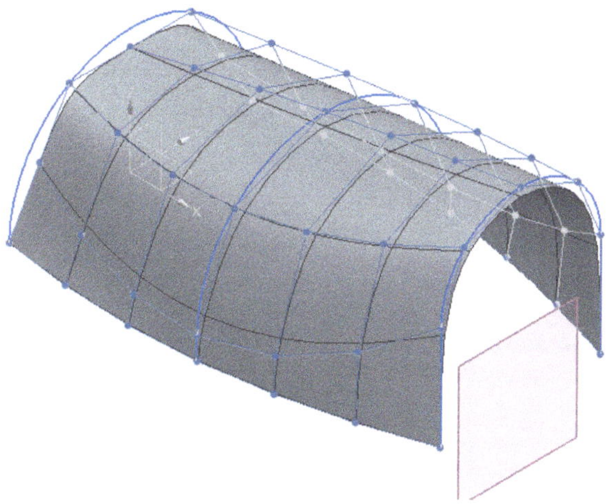

The Sweep Cage command

The **Sweep Cage** command is similar to the **Swept** command except that this command creates a surface along with a control cage. Activate this command (on the ribbon, click **Home > Create > Sweep Cage**) and click on the polyline to be swept. On the **Sweep Cage** dialog, under the **Guides (2 Maximum)** section, click **Select Face Edge or Polyline** click on the polyline to define the first guide polyline. Next, click the **Add New Set** icon and select another polyline to define the second guide. Make sure that the arrows on the selected guides point in the same direction. Use the **Reverse Direction** icon in the **Guides** section to change their direction. Click **OK** to create the swept cage.

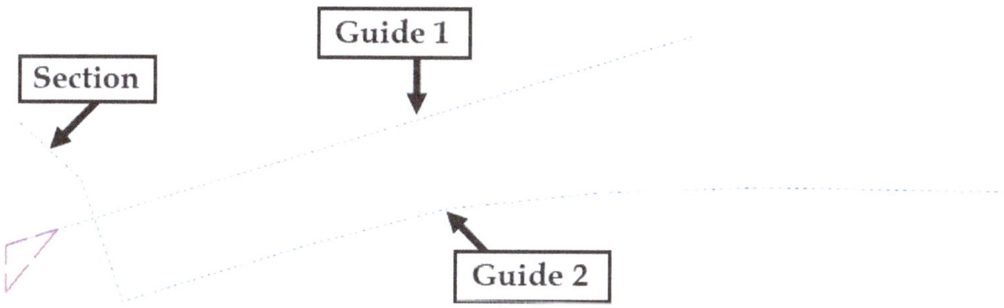

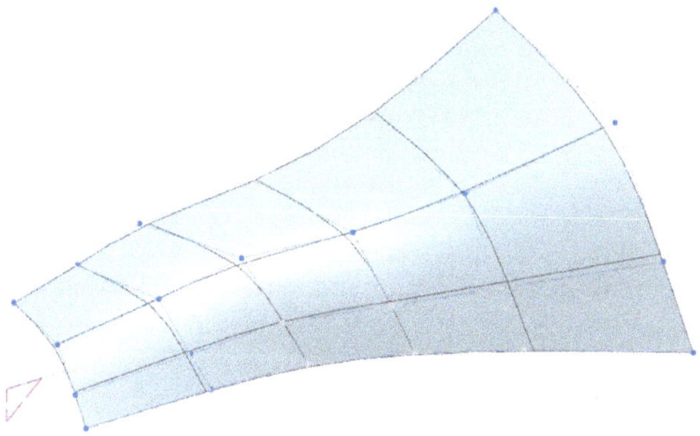

The Set Continuity command

The **Set Continuity** command helps you to smoothen or sharpen the edges of the cage. Activate this command (on the ribbon, click **Home > Edit > More > Set Continuity**) and select a cage edge to set the continuity. You can also drag the selection window across the entire model to select all its edges. Next, select the **Smooth** or **Sharp** option from the **Continuity** section of the **Set Continuity** dialog, and then click **OK**.

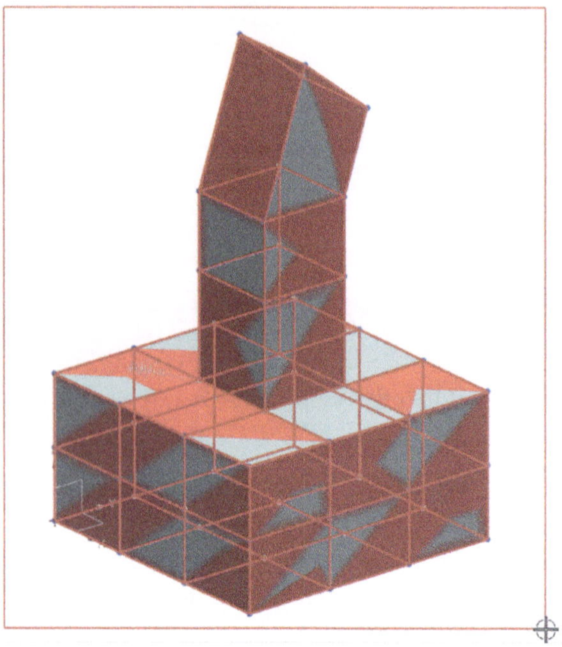

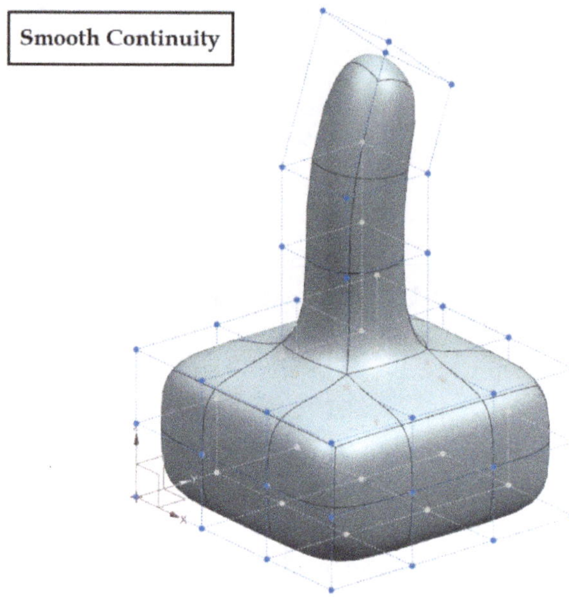

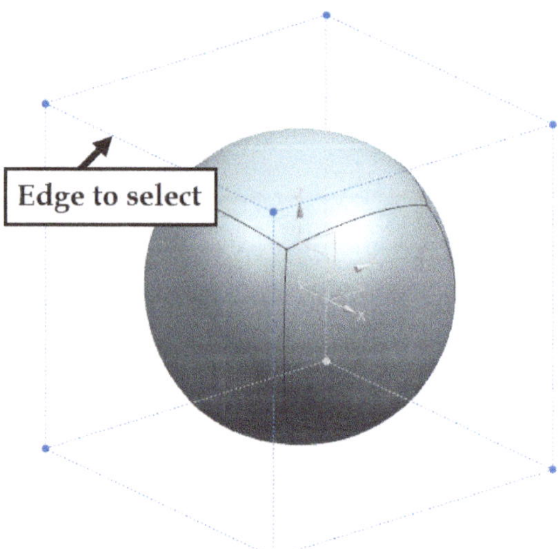

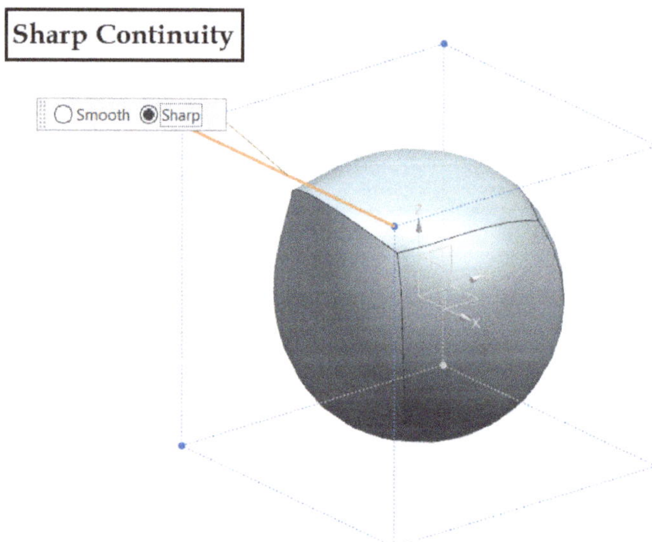

Start Symmetric Modeling

The **Start Symmetric Modeling** command helps you to create B-surface models that are symmetrical about a plane. Activate this command (on the ribbon, click **Home > NX Realize Shape > Start Symmetric Modeling**) and select a plane from the graphics window to define the symmetric plane. Click the **Switch Side** icon to change the side to be manipulated. Next, click **OK** to start symmetric modeling.

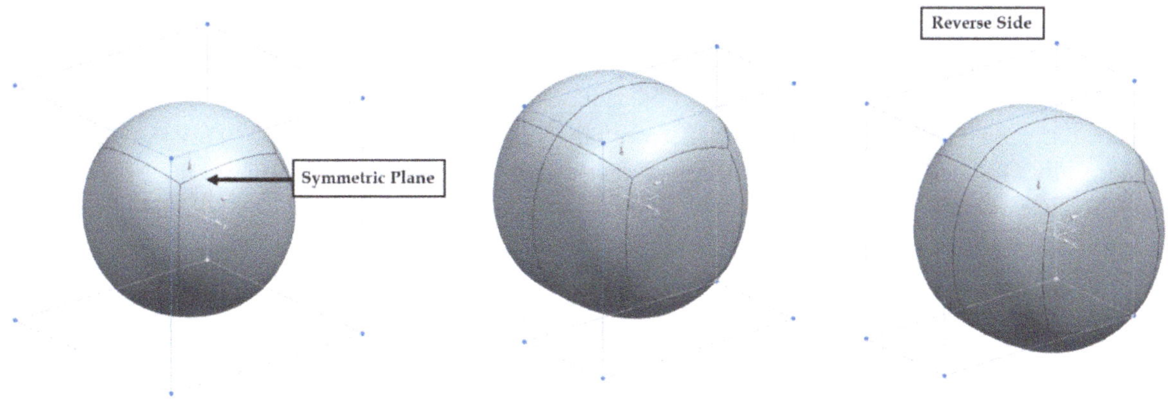

Now, activate the **Transform Cage** command and manipulate the cage edge, as shown; the cage is modified symmetrically.

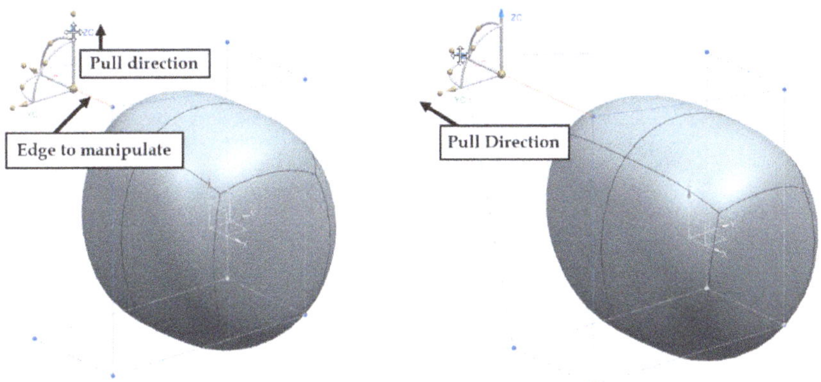

You can use the **Stop Symmetric Modeling** command to stop manipulating the model symmetrically. Activate this command (on the ribbon, click **Home > NX Realize Shape > Stop Symmetric Modeling**) and notice that the cage is displayed on both sides of the model. You can manipulate the model independe1ntly on both sides.

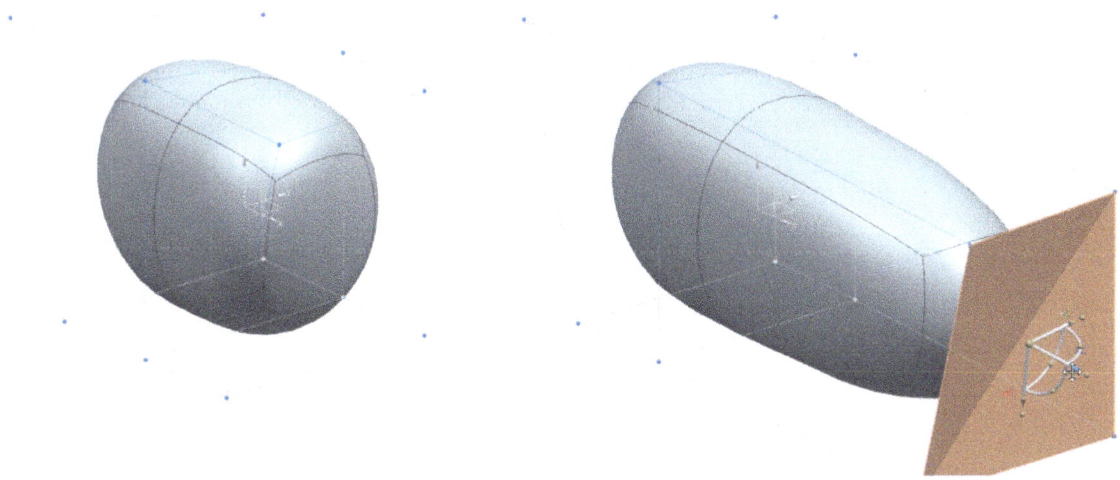

Select Projection Edge

The **Select Projection Edge** option is useful while creating a symmetrical body using an open surface. This option is practically illustrated in the following example. First, create a circle using the **Primitive Shape** command, as shown. Next, click **Home > Edit > Transform Cage** on the ribbon. Click on the inner cage face of the circle, as shown. On the **Transform Cage** dialog, click the **Transform** tab. Next, click on the translate handle of the Dynamic CSYS pointing in the direction perpendicular to the selected cage face. Press and hold the left mouse button and drag the pointer in the direction perpendicular to the cage face; the cage face is manipulated, as shown. Click **Apply** on the **Transform Cage** dialog.

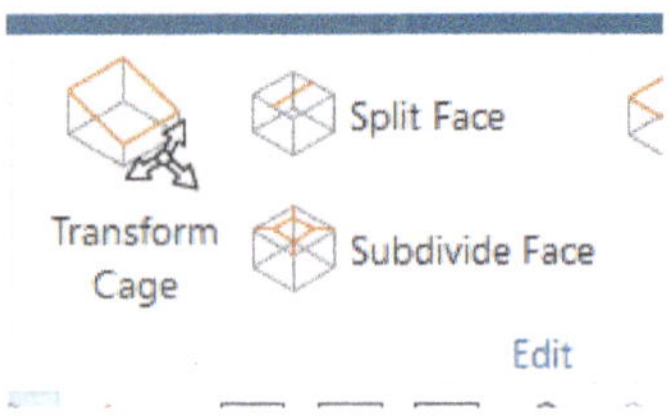

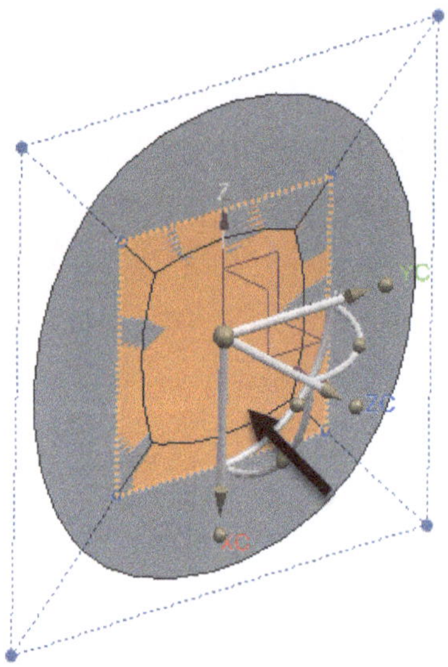

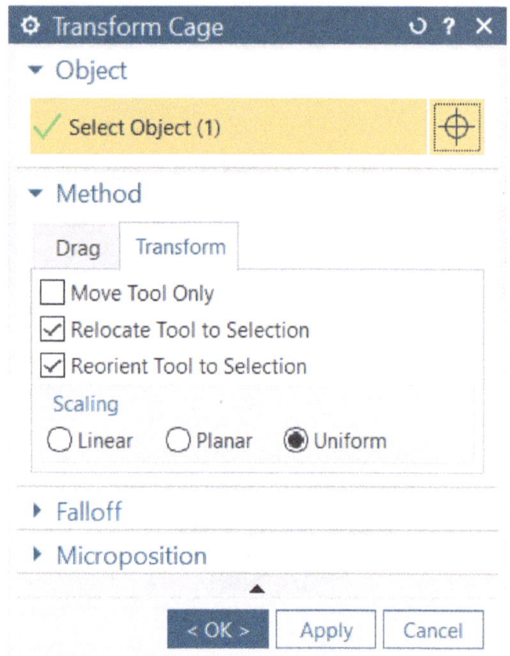

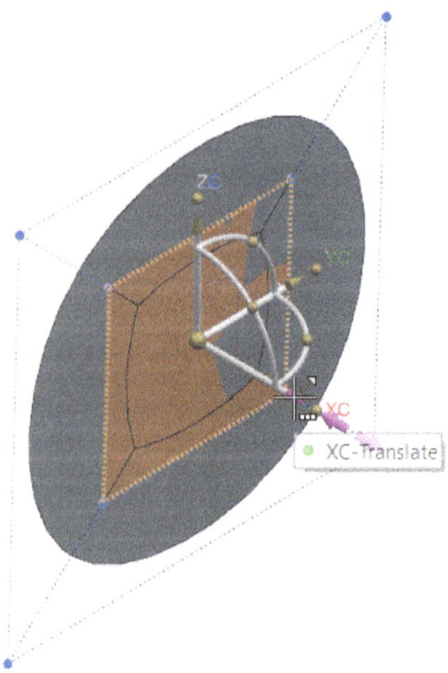

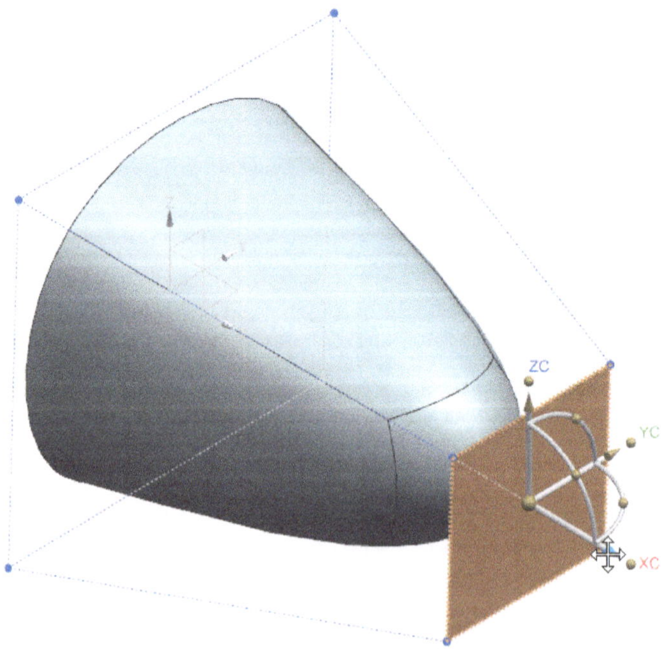

Click on the left top edge of the cage, and then drag the ZC handle of the Dynamic CSYS upward. Click **OK** on the **Transform Cage** dialog. On the Top Border Bar, click **Menu > Insert > Datum Plane**, and then click on the YZ Plane of the Datum Coordinate System; a datum plane appears. Click and drag the datum plane toward left up to a random distance. Click **OK** on the **Plane** dialog.

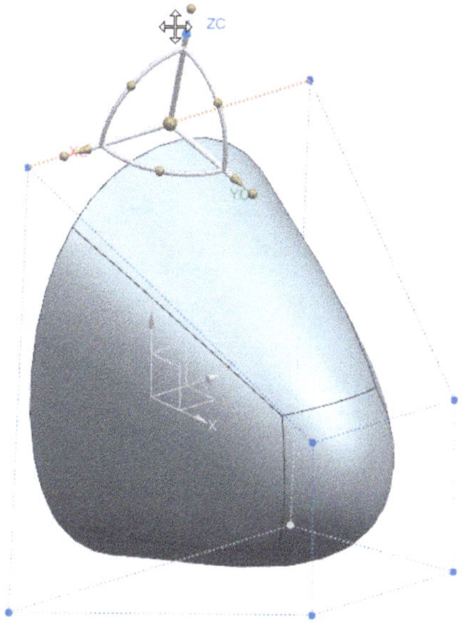

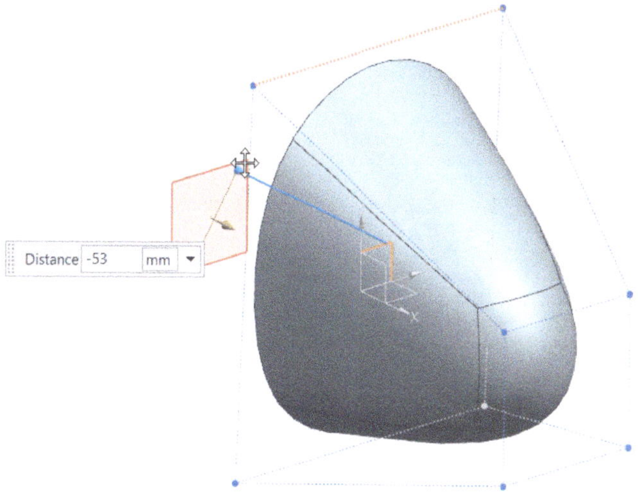

On the ribbon, click **Home > NX Realize Shape > Start Symmetric Modeling**, and then click on the newly created plane. Make sure that the arrow on the plane points towards the model (use the **Switch Side** icon to change the arrow direction). Click **OK** and notice that the surface body is mirrored without any connection.

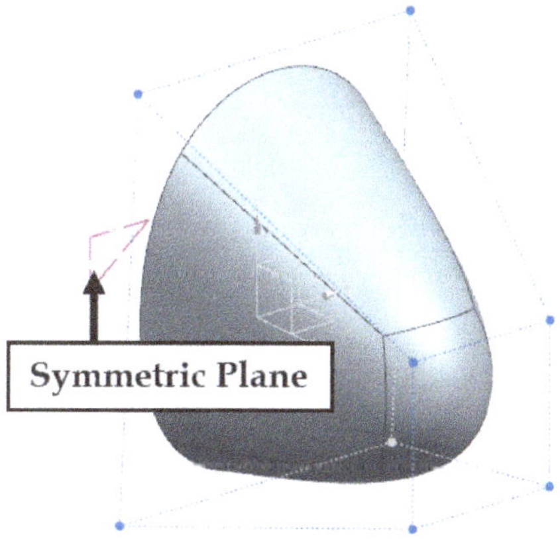

Without Projecting the open edges

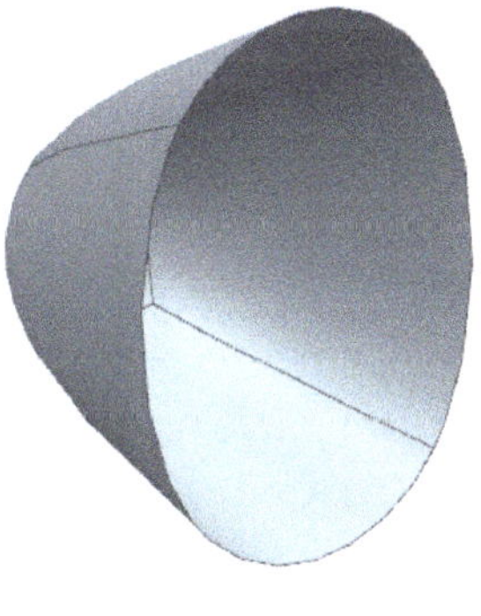

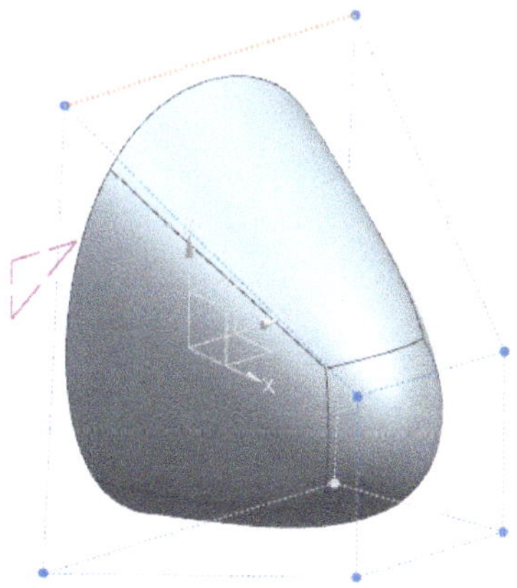

On the Quick Access Toolbar, click the **Undo** icon (or) press Ctrl+Z on your keyboard. Next, click the **Start Symmetric Modeling** icon on the **NX Realize Shape** panel. Select the datum plane from the graphics window to define the symmetric plane. On the **Start Symmetric Modeling** dialog, click **Select Projection Edge**, and then select the open edges of the cage, as shown. Click **OK** on the **Start Symmetric Modeling** dialog; the selected edges are projected on to the symmetric plane.

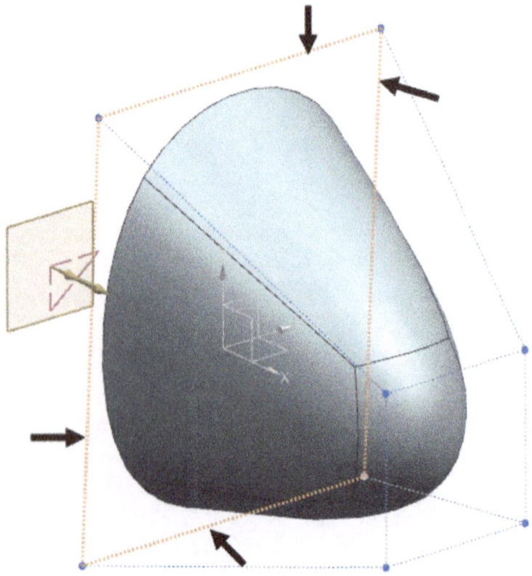

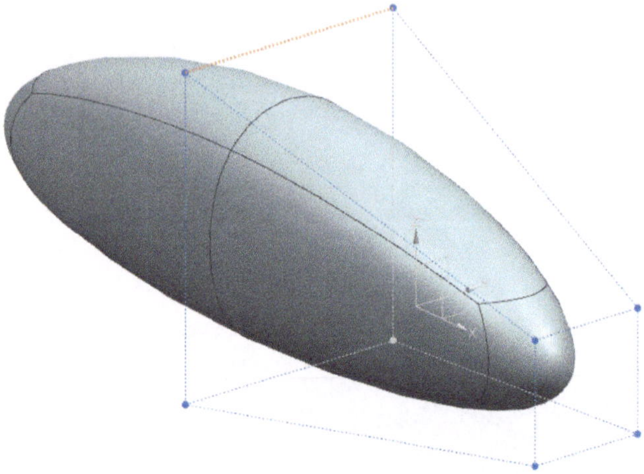

Click on a cage edge and transform it, as shown.

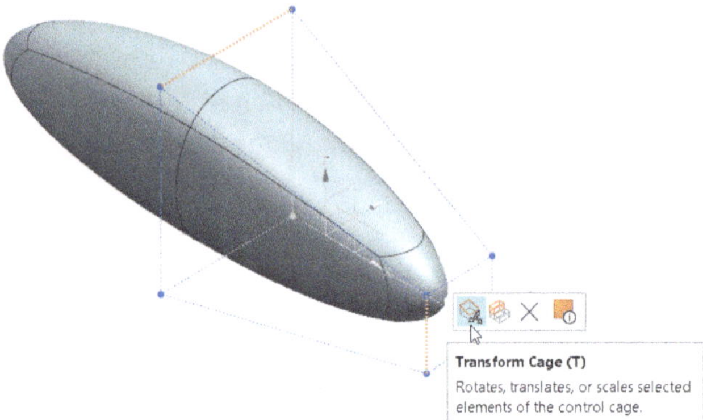

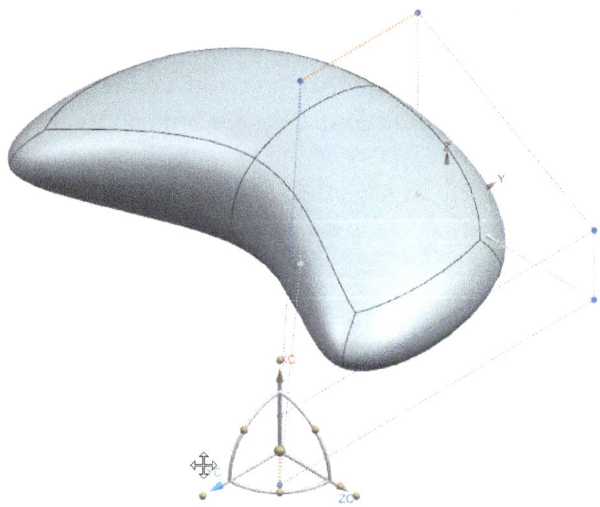

Mirror Cage

The **Mirror Cage** command helps you to create a mirror copy of the selected surface body. This command is similar to the **Start Symmetric Modeling** command except that there is no associative link between the original body and the mirrored copy. This command is practically illustrated in the following example. First, create a rectangle using the **Primitive Shape** command, as shown. Click on the cage vertex of the rectangle, and then select the **Transform Cage** icon from the Context toolbar. Press and hold the left mouse button on the selected vertex, and then drag it upwards. Release the mouse button, and then click **OK** on the **Transform Cage** dialog.

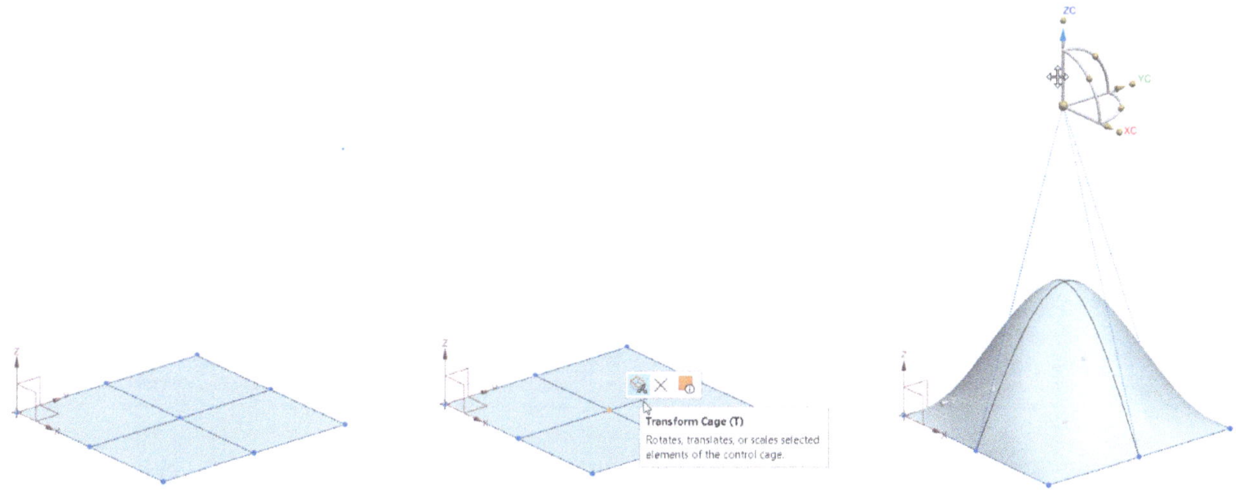

Activate this command (on the ribbon, click **Home > Create > Mirror Cage**) and select **Selection Rule > Region** from the Sketch Scene Bar. Next, select a cage face of the surface body to be mirrored. Next, select a plane from the graphics window to define the mirror plane. Click **OK** to mirror the cage.

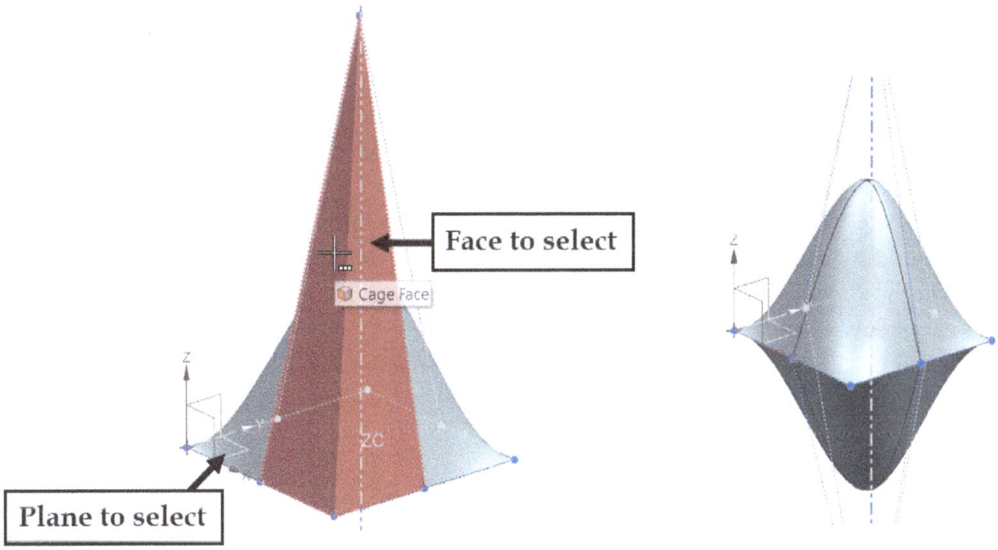

Copy Cage

The **Copy Cage** command creates a copy of the selected cage faces, edges, or entire cage. The following example is one of many ways in which this command can be used. Activate the **Primitive Shape** command and create a rectangle, as shown.

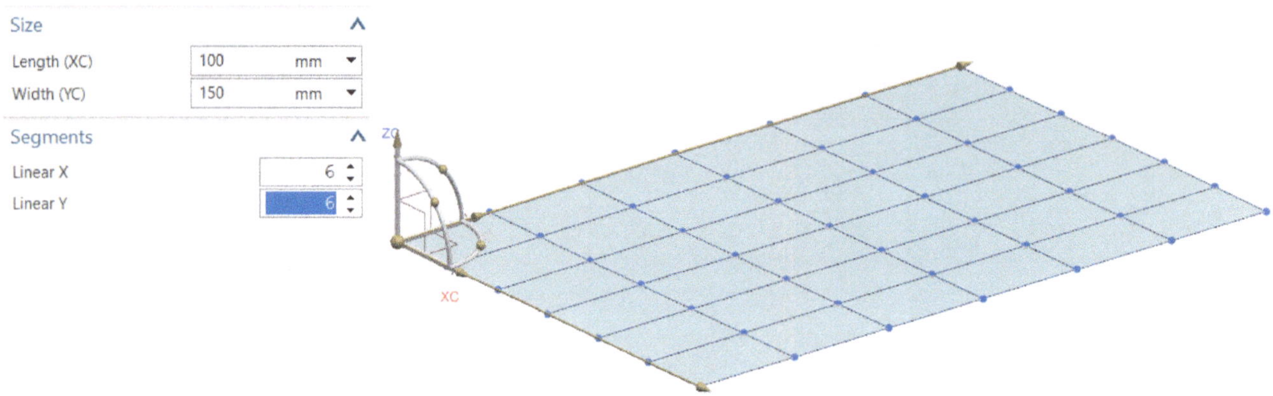

Activate the **Extrude Cage** command and drag a selection window across the rectangle. Next, click and drag the Distance handle up to 50 mm and click **OK**.

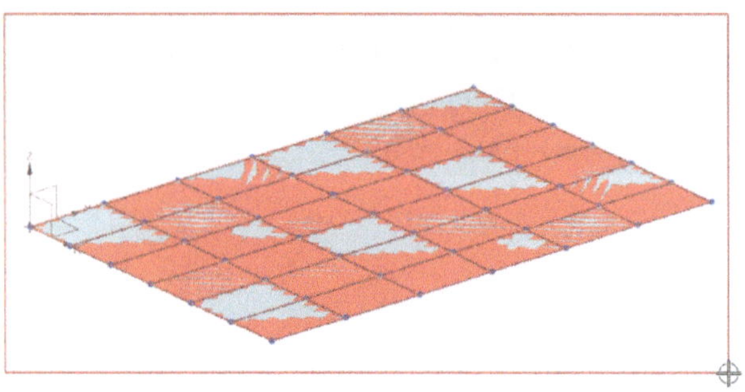

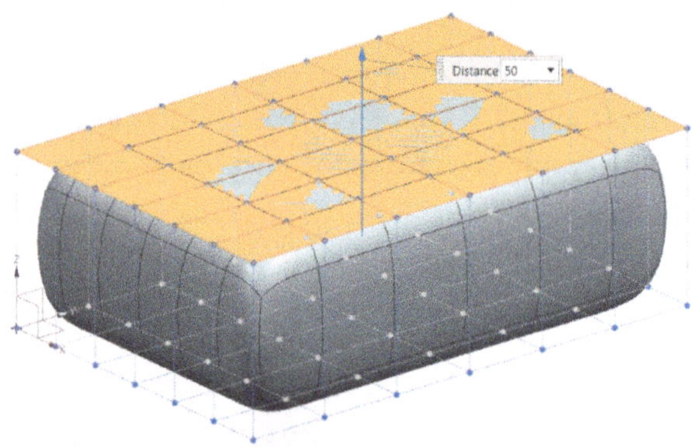

Activate the **Copy Cage** command (on the ribbon, click **Home > Create > Copy Cage**). On the Sketch Scene Bar, set **Selection Rule** to **Loop**, and then click on the two faces of the cage, as shown; the loops associated with the selected faces are selected. On the **Copy Cage** dialog, under the **Result** section, set the **Number of Copies** to **1**. Click **OK** to copy the selected cage faces.

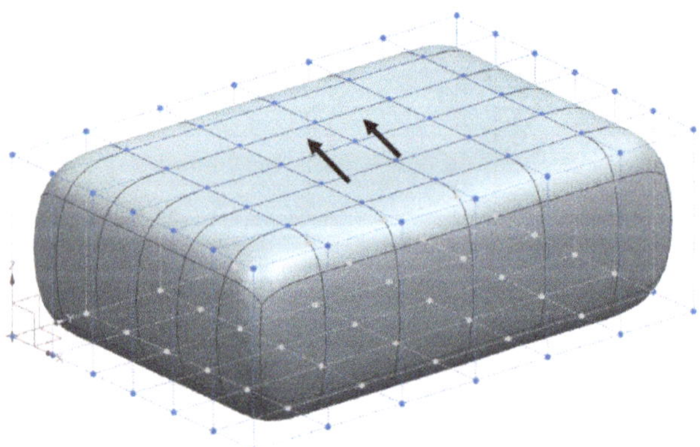

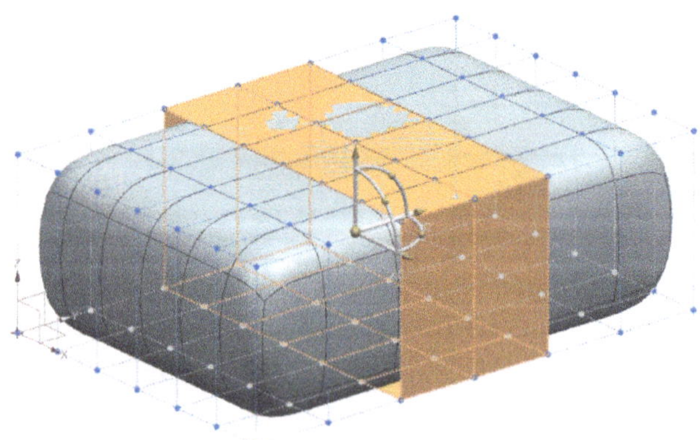

Activate the **Extrude Cage** command and set the **Selection Rule** to **Loop**. Click on the two faces of the copied surface, as shown; the entire copied surface is selected. Click and drag the **Distance** handle up to **10** mm in the upward direction. Click **OK**.

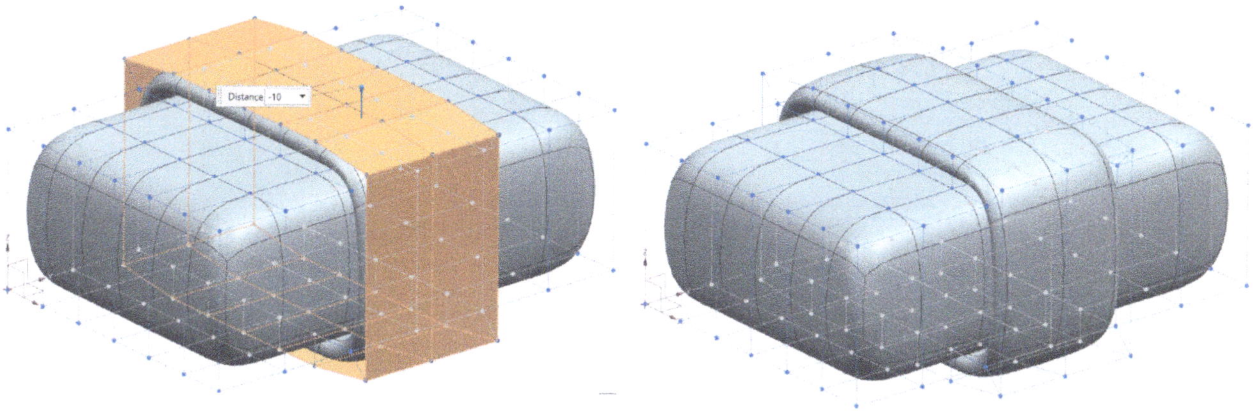

Subdivide Face

The **Subdivide Face** command subdivides the selected face by offsetting its edges. Activate this command (on the ribbon, click **Home > Edit > Subdivide Face**) and click on a face to subdivide. Drag the **Percentage** handle or enter a value in the **Percentage** box in the **Offset** section of the **Subdivide** dialog; the edges of the face will be offset in the inward direction based on the **Percentage** value. Click **OK** and notice that the selected face is subdivided into five faces.

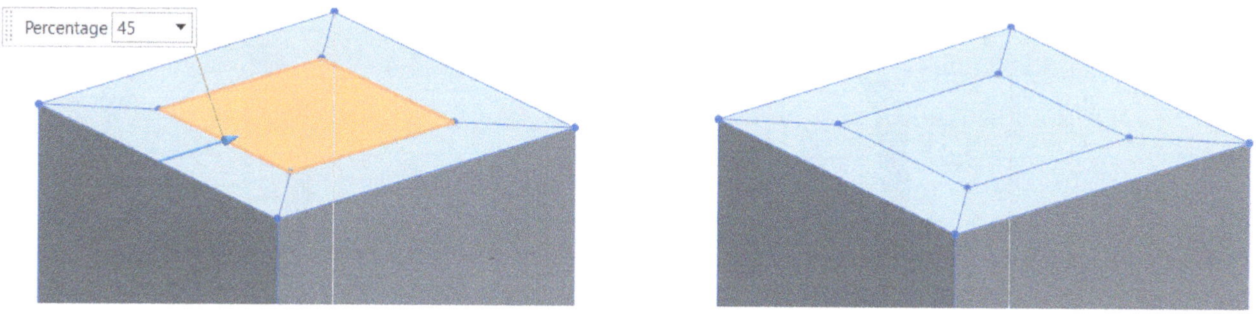

Subdividing Faces that are Perpendicular to each other

Subdividing two faces which are perpendicular to each other produces a different result. Activate the **Subdivide Face** command and select the two faces that are perpendicular to each other. Drag the **Percentage** handle to offset the edges of the faces. Notice that the common edge of the two perpendicular faces is not offset.

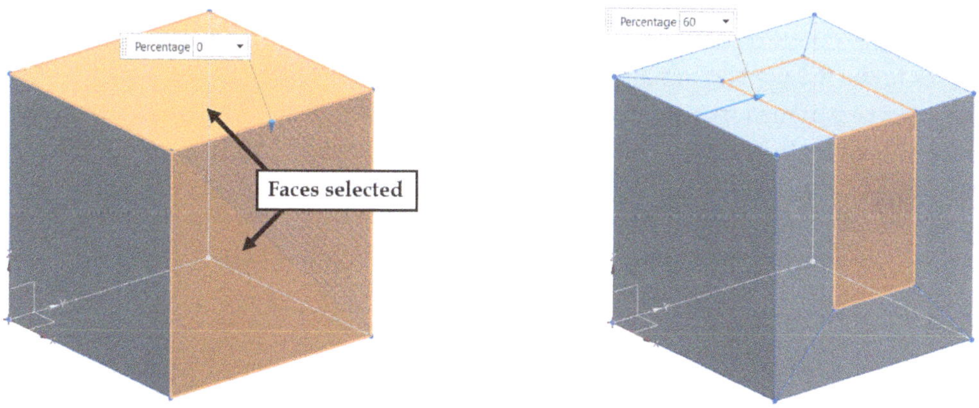

Likewise, select three faces that are perpendicular to each other and notice a different result.

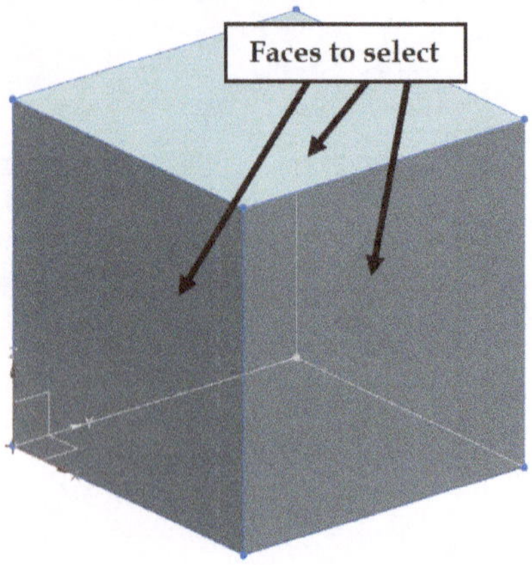

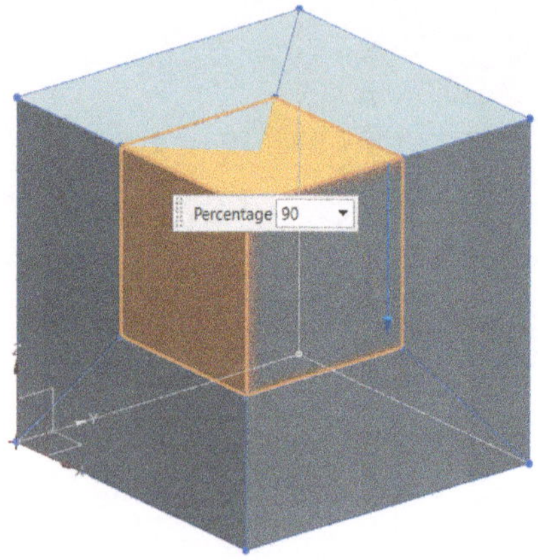

Bridge Face

The **Bridge Face** command creates a closed tunnel-like surface between two faces. The following example illustrates the use of this command. First, create a torus with the specifications, as shown. Next, create a sphere of 100 mm size at the center of the torus.

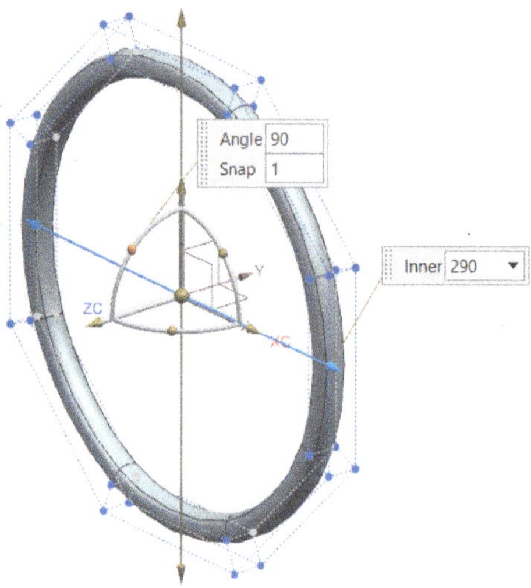

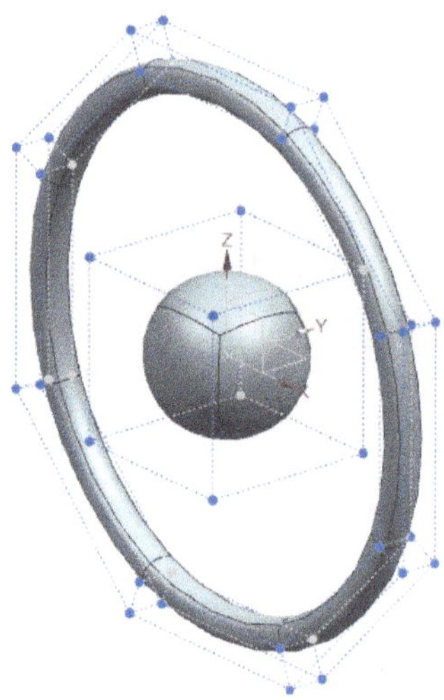

Activate the **Bridge Face** command (on the ribbon, click **Home > Create > Bridge Face**) and click on the right face of the sphere, as shown. On the **Bridge Face** dialog, click **Select Object** under the **Face Set 2** section. Rotate the model and click on the inner face of the torus, as shown. On the **Bridge Face** dialog, under the **Segmentation** section, change the **Number of Segments** value to **2**. Expand the **Settings** section and select **Smooth**. Click **Apply** to create a bridge face between the selected face.

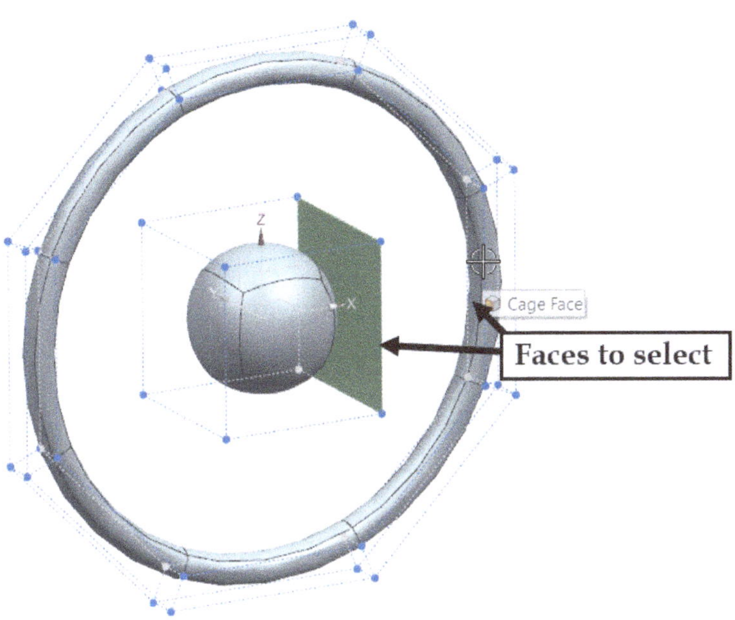

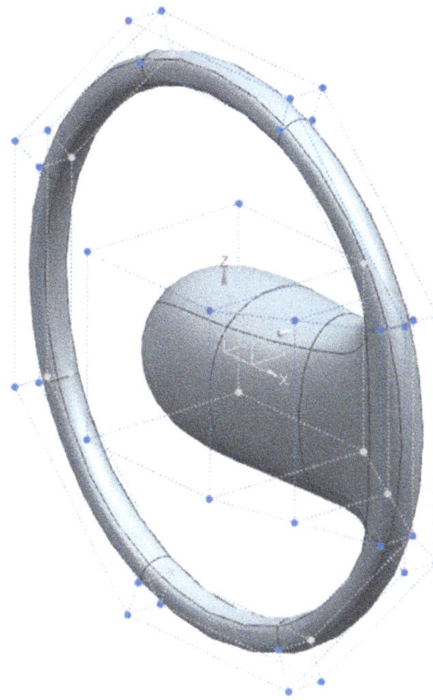

Likewise, bridge the left and bottom faces of the sphere with the torus.

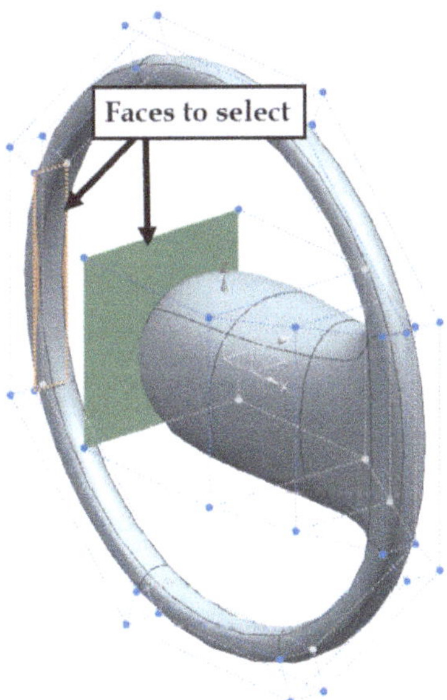

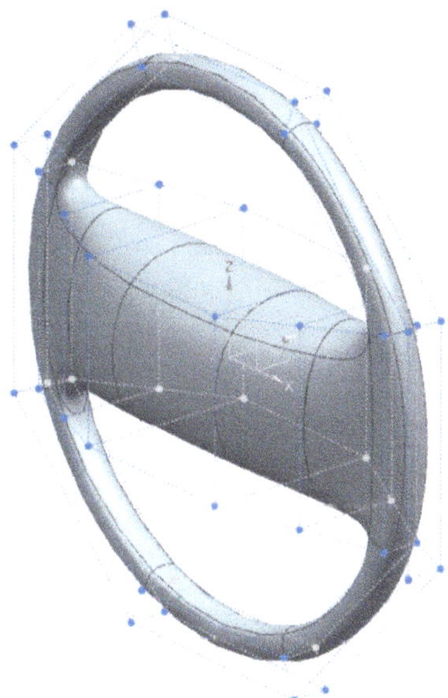

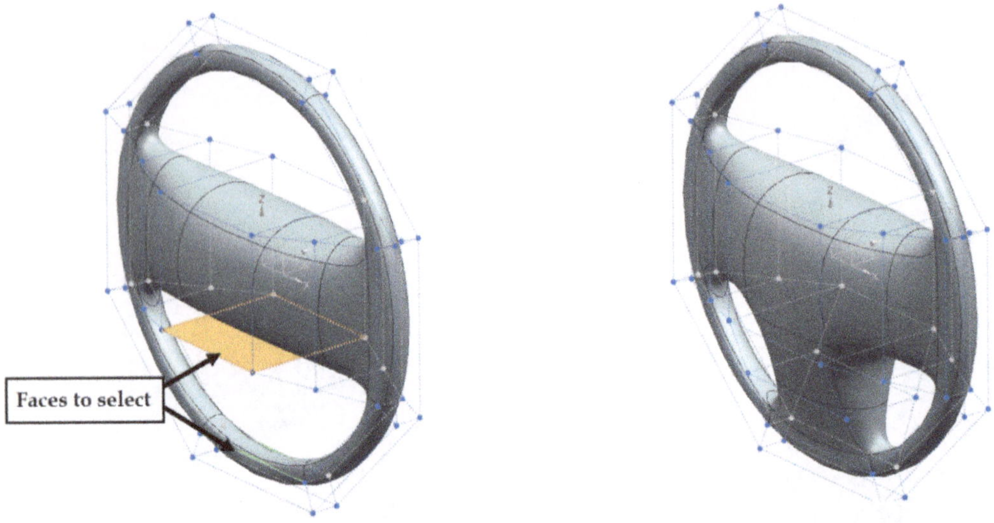

Subdivide the center faces on the front and backside of the model, as shown.

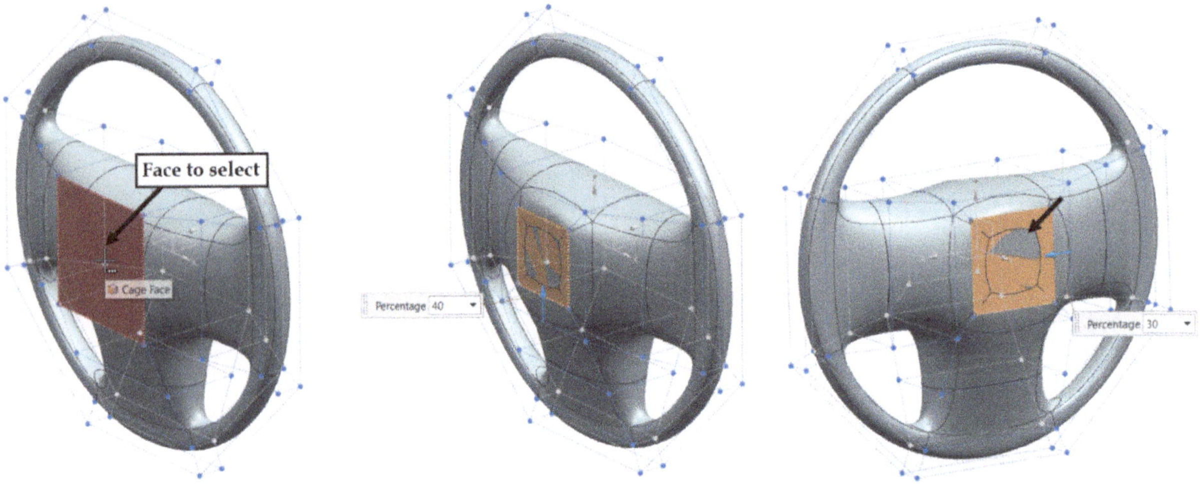

Activate the **Bridge Face** command and select the subdivided center face on the front side. Next, click **Select object** in the **Face Set 2** section of the **Bridge Face** dialog. Rotate the model and select the subdivided center face on the backside. Expand the **Segmentation** section and change the **Number of Segments** value to **1**. Click **OK** to create a tunnel between the two selected faces.

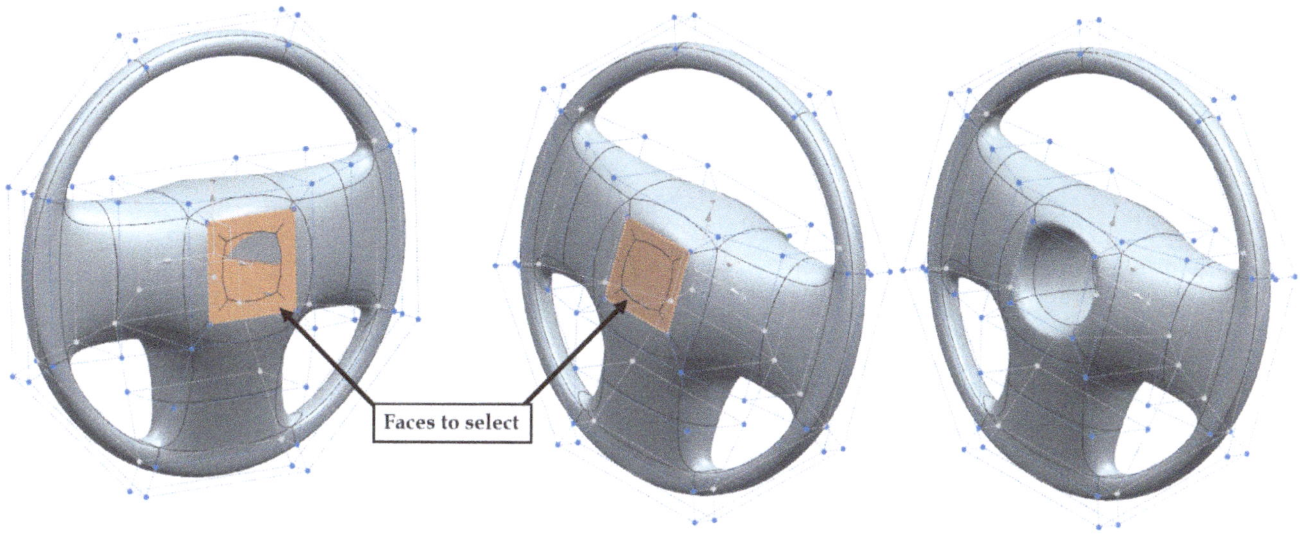

Split Face

The **Split Face** command splits a cage face into multiple faces uniformly or through selected points. The following example illustrates the use of this command. First, create a cylinder with the specifications, as shown.

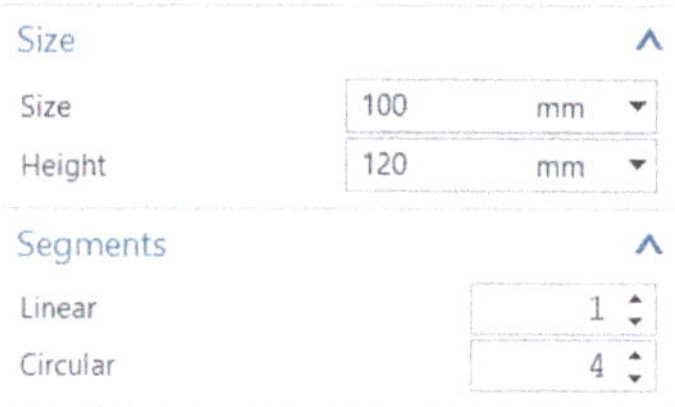

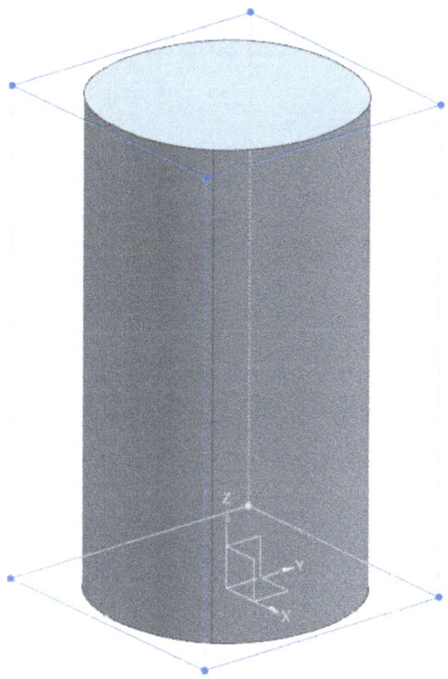

Activate the **Split Face** command (on the ribbon, click **Home > Create > Split Face**), and then select **Type > Uniform** on the **Split Face** dialog. Click on the face to split, and then click **Select Reference Edge** from the **Split** section. Select an edge of the selected cage face, and then specify the number of splitting edges in the **Number** box. Click the **Show Result** icon.

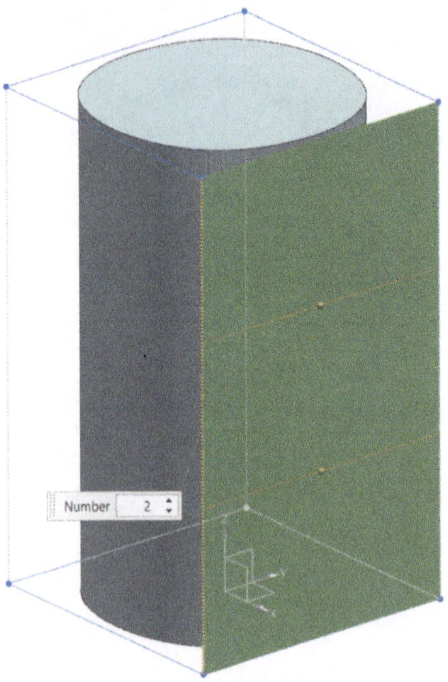

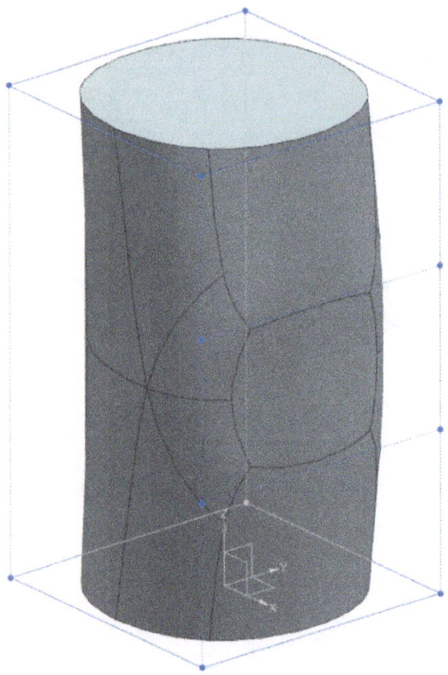

Notice that the adjacent faces of the split face are affected. Click the **Undo Result** icon to undo the changes. On Sketch Scene Bar, set the **Selection Rule** to **Loop**. On the **Split Face** dialog, under the **Face** section, click **Select Face.** Click on the side face of the previously selected face; all the cylindrical faces of the cage are selected. Click **Apply** to split the selected cage faces.

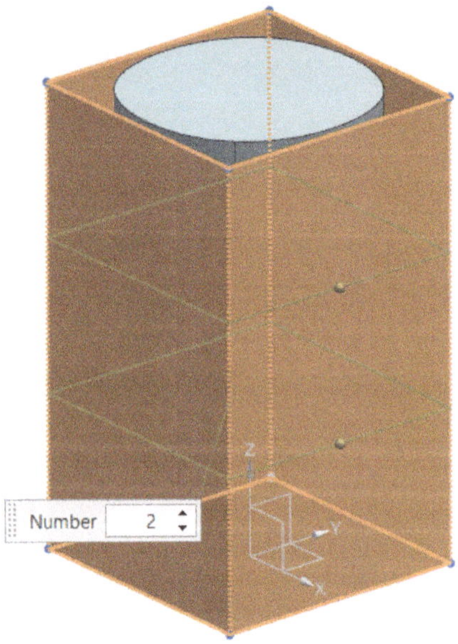

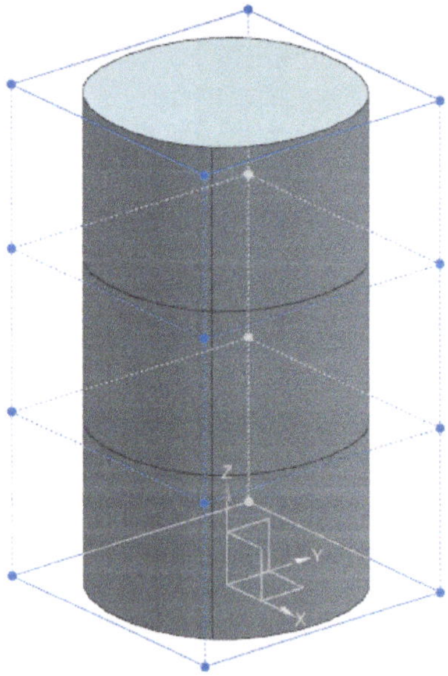

On the **Split Face** dialog, select **Type > Along Polyline**, and then select the midpoints of the cage edges, as shown.

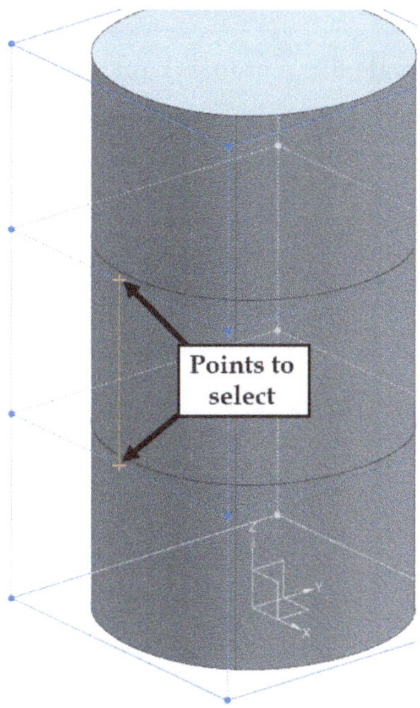

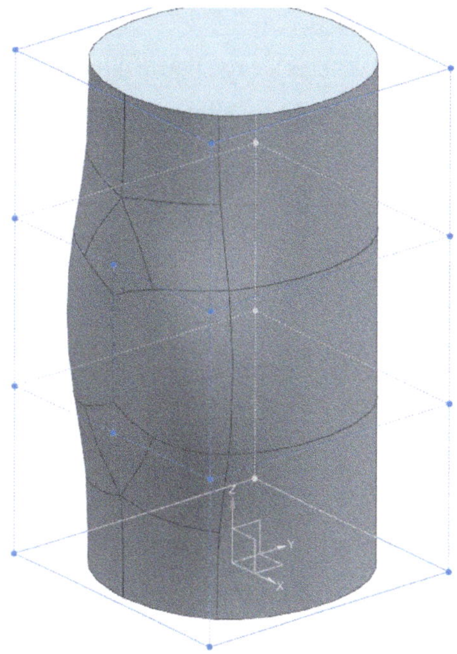

Merge Face

The **Merge Face** command merges two or more faces of the cage to simplify the design. Activate this command (on the ribbon, click **Home > Modify > Merge Face**) and click on the faces to merge. Next, click **OK**.

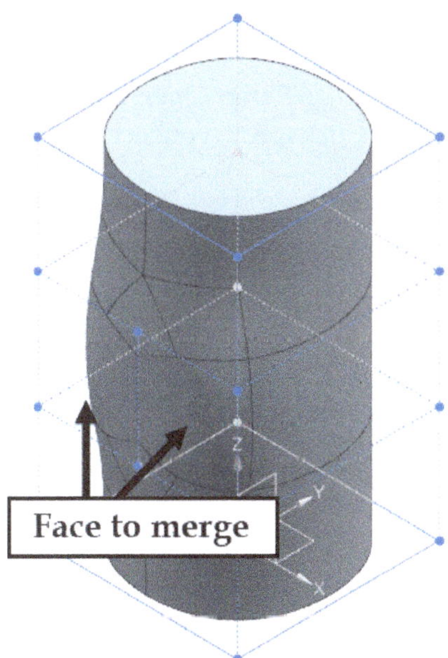

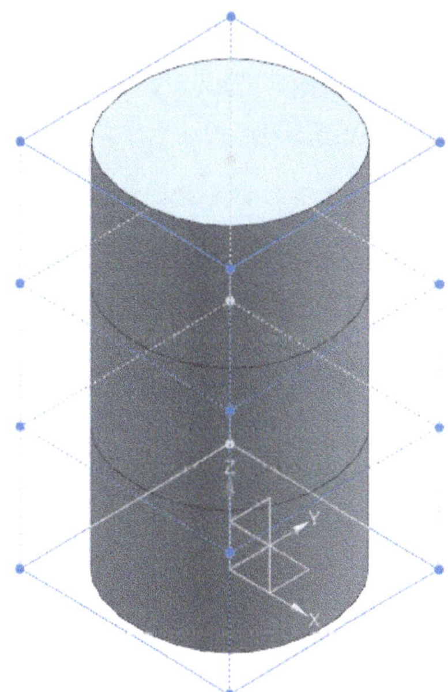

Delete

The **Delete** command deletes a cage point, edge, face, or the entire cage. Activate this command (on the Top Border Bar, click **Menu > Edit > Delete**) and select the objects to delete. Click **OK** to delete the face.

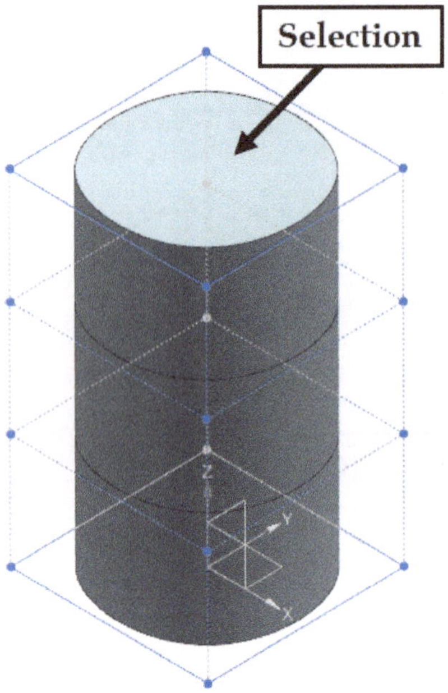

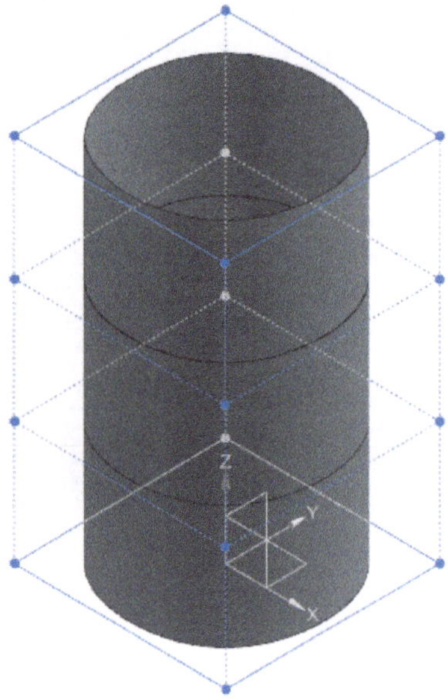

Sew Cage

The **Sew Cage** command connects the open edges of two control cages. Activate this command (on the ribbon, click **Home > Edit > Sew Cage**) and click on the first set of the open edges. Next, click **Select Open Edges** in the **Side 2** section of the **Sew Cage** dialog. Select the open edges of the second side. Click **OK** to connect the selected open edges

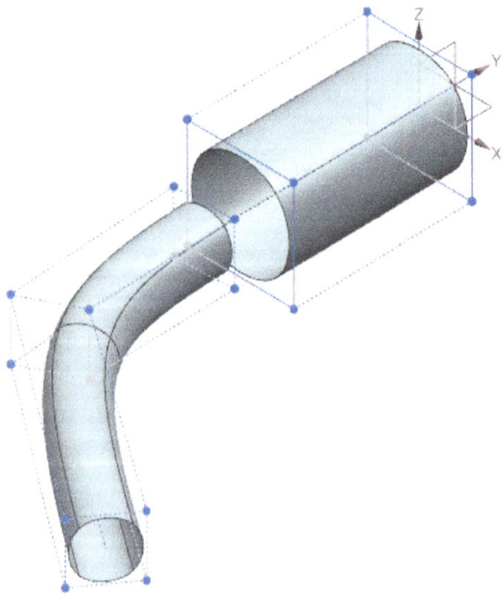

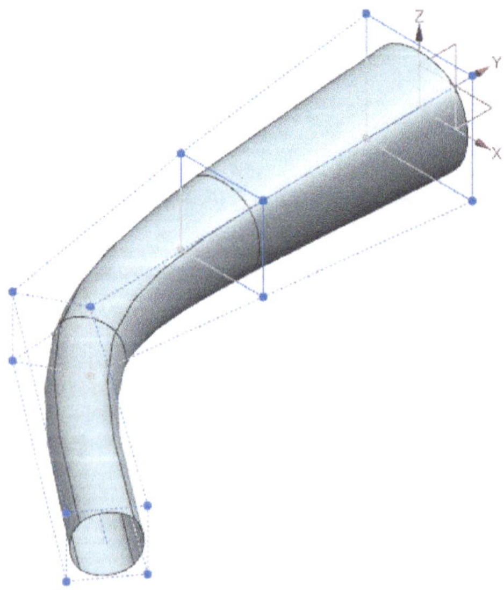

Set Weight

The **Set Weight** command sets weights on the selected edge or face. The edges are sharpened by a weight factor that you specify in the **Percentage** box. Activate this command (on the ribbon, click **Home > Edit > More > Set Weight**) select the edges to set weight. Next, click and drag the **Percentage** dragger to specify the weight factor. Click **OK** on the **Set Weight** dialog. On the ribbon, click **Home > Preferences > Show Weight** to display the weight factor on the edges.

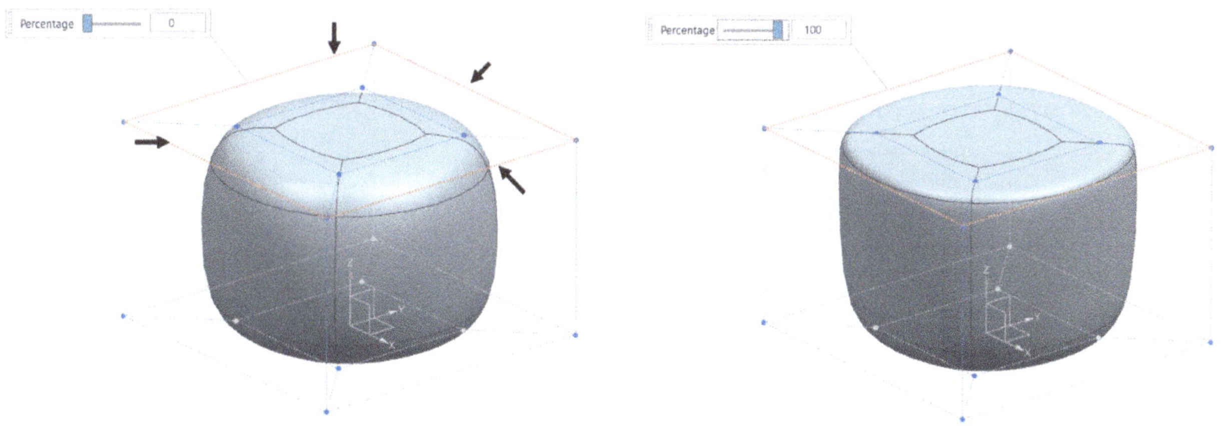

Project Cage

The **Project Cage** command projects the elements of the cage (edge, face, or vertex) up to a selected target element. The target element can be a planar face or a linear element. Activate this command (on the Top Border bar, click **Menu > Edit > Project Cage**) and select **Type > To Target**. Next, select the **Target Type** (**Curve** in this example) and click on the target element. Select the cage face to the project.

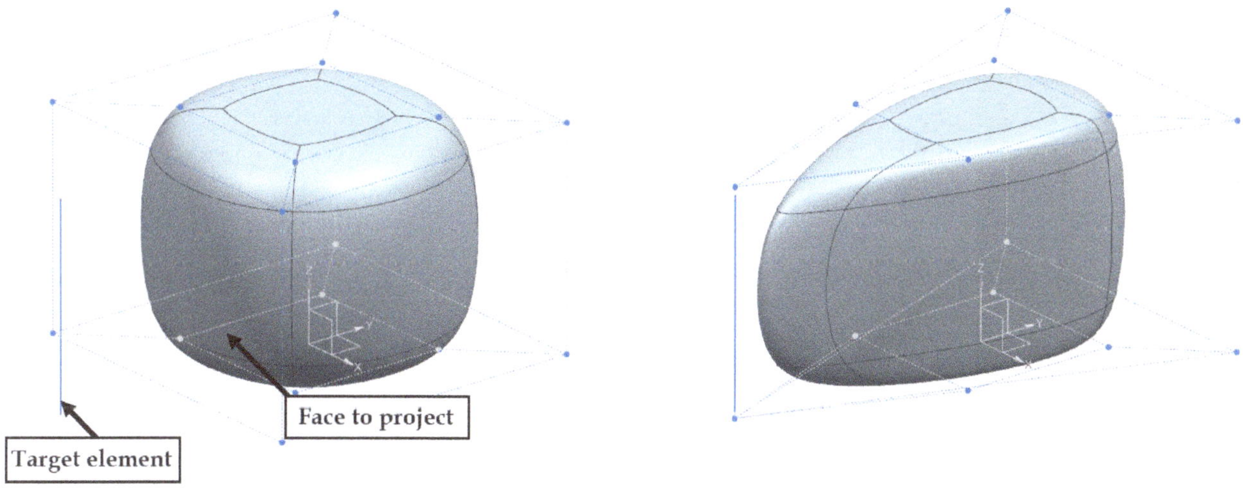

Section Tube

With the help of the **Section Tube** command, you have the ability to generate a tube cage in proximity to a convergent body. The convergent bodies are imported geometries that are not converted NX format. You can add additional geometry to them using the NX modeling command.

For example, first import the convergent body using the Import option. To do this, click **File > Import > STL**. Next, click the Browse button on the **STL Import** dialog, browse to the location of the STL file, and double-click on it. On the **STL Import** dialog, select **Facet Body Output Type > Convergent**. Leave the other default settings and click **OK**.

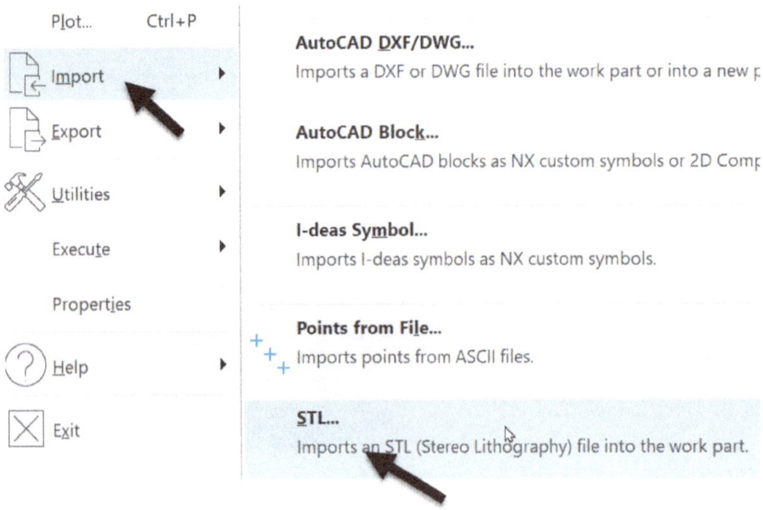

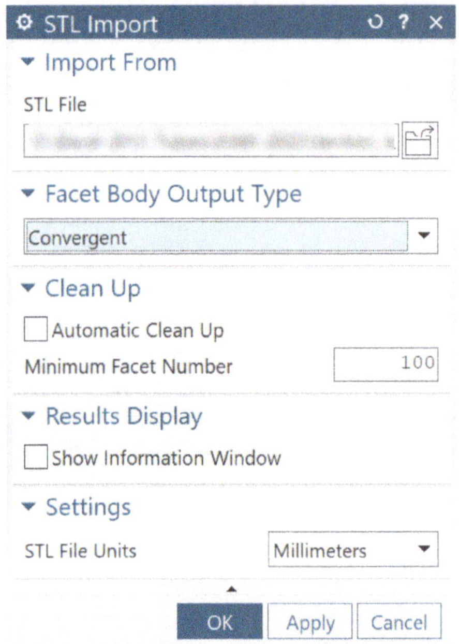

On the ribbon, click **Surface > NX Realize Shape** to activate the Realize shape environment. On the ribbon, click **Home > Create > Section tube** and select the first point from the facet vertices of the convergent geometry, as shown. On the **Section Tube** dialog, under the **Sections** section, check the **Show Tool** option; the manipulator tool is displayed on the section plane. You can use the handles on this tool to move, rotate, or scale the section plane. On the Segments section, enter a value in the Circular box. The **Circular** box determines the number of segments you desire for each cross-section, ranging from 3 to 36 segments.

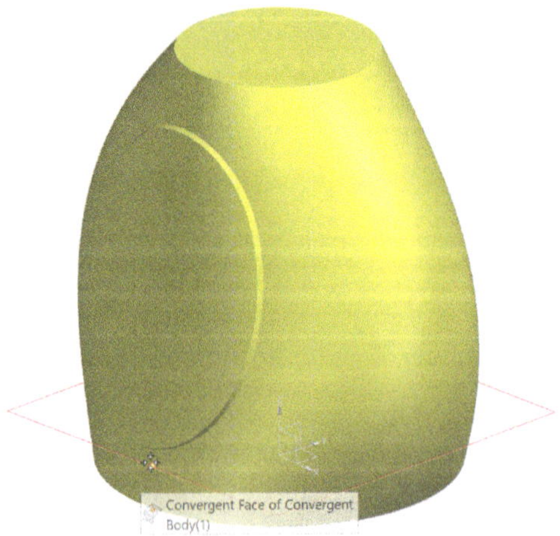

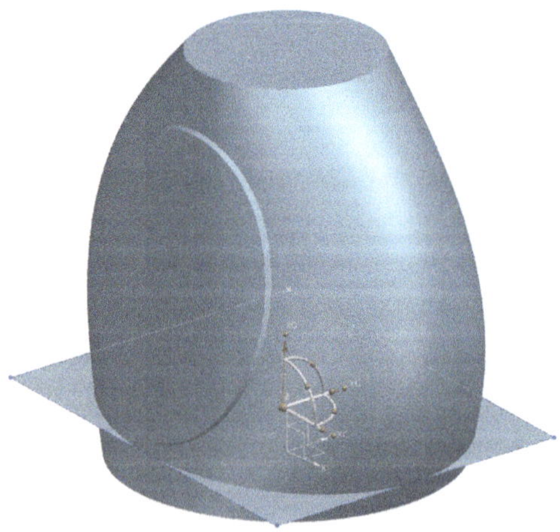

Likewise, select the desired points along the convergent body until the control cage is fully formed. Click **OK** on the **Section Tube** dialog. Next, hide the Convergent Body in the Part Navigator to display the control cage.

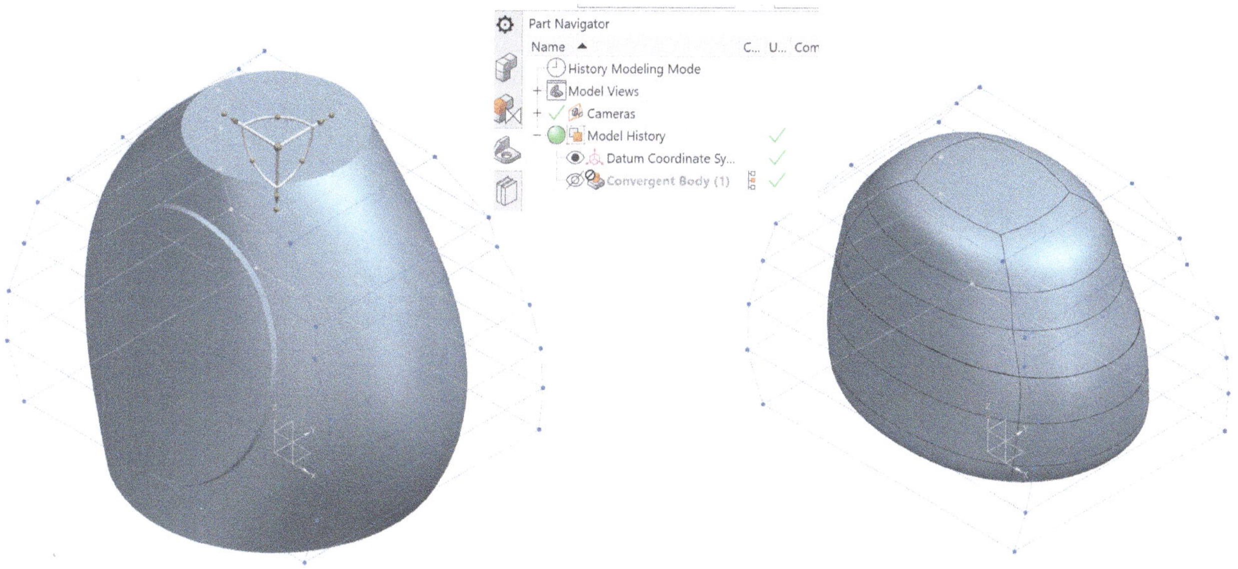

Cage From Facet Body

With the help of the **Cage From Facet Body** command, you have the ability to generate an entire control cage by selecting a region from a convergent body. On the ribbon, click **Home > Create > Cage From Facet Body** 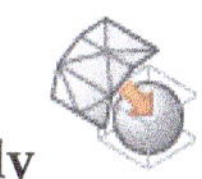 and select a facet from the convergent geometry, as shown. Next, specify the average face size of the control cage in the **Average Size** box available in the **Face Size** section.

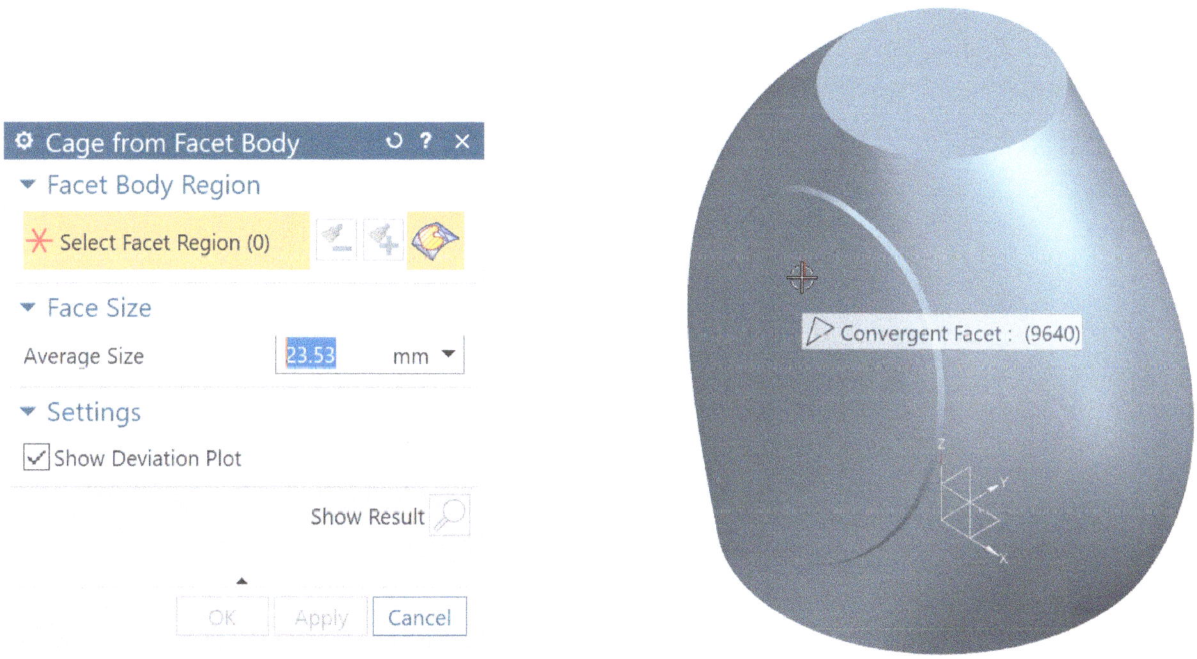

In the **Cage From Facet Body** dialog, expand the **Settings** section and check the **Show Deviation Plot** option and click the **Show Result** button; a clear visual representation of the deviations between the input regions and the resultant subdivision faces of the output cage is presented. Click **OK** to create the control cage.

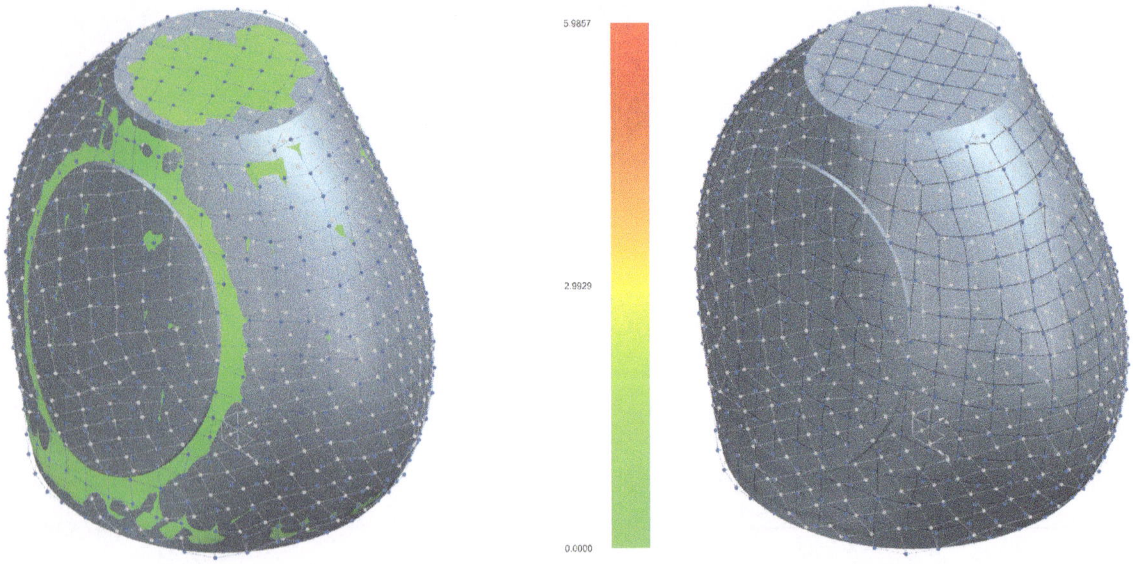

Draw Cage

With the help of the **Draw Cage** command, you can create a control cage by selecting the vertices from a reference body. On the ribbon, click **Home > Create > Draw Cage** 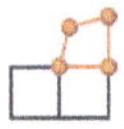 and select **Face Shape > Quad**. The **Quad** option allows you to create control cage faces with four sides each. The **Polygon** option allows you to form control cage faces with any desired number of sides (n-sided). Next, select four points on the reference geometry, as shown. Notice that another rubber band line is attached to the cursor. Specify the two points in the sequence, as shown.

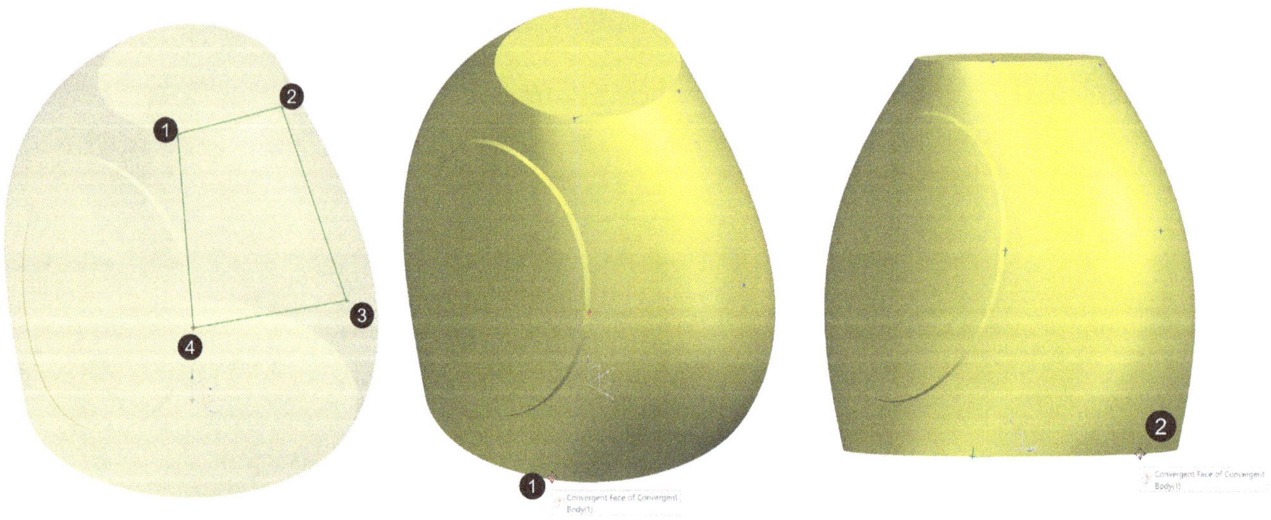

Click the **Reset Start Point** icon in the **Vertices** section of the **Draw Cage** dialog. Next, specify the new start point of the cage, as shown. Select the other three points of the cage face, as shown. Click **OK** to create the cage.

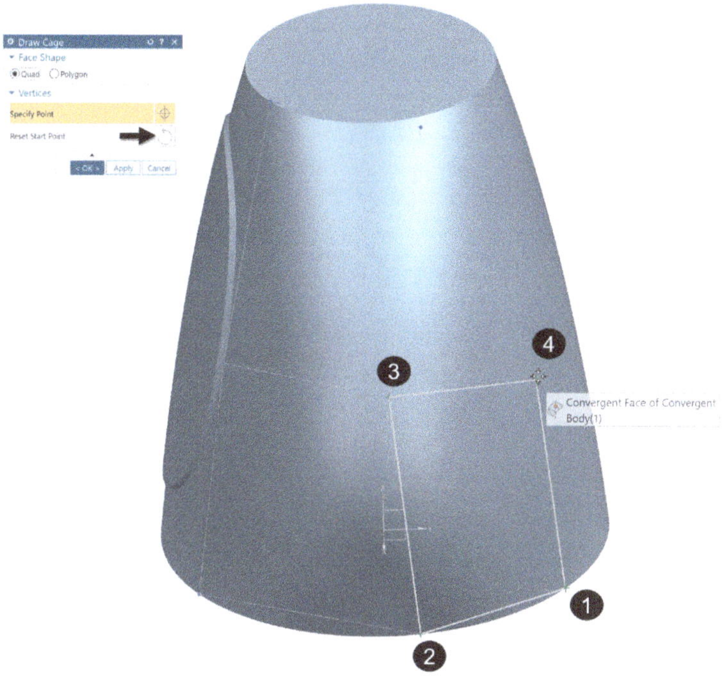

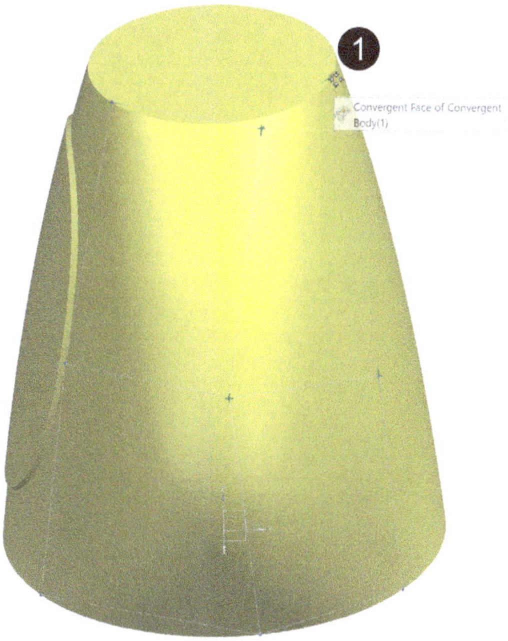

Hide the reference geometry to view the subdivision surface.

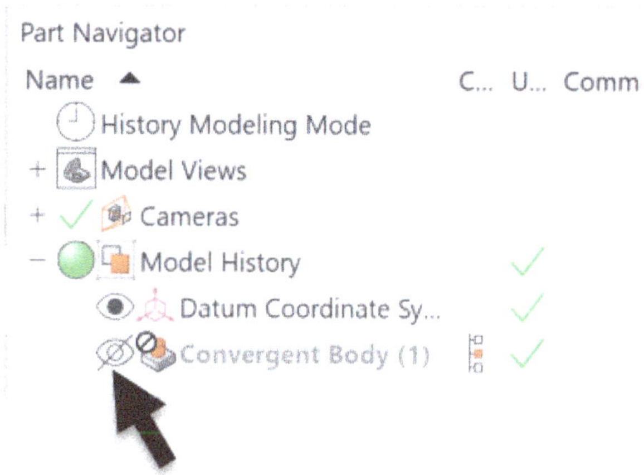

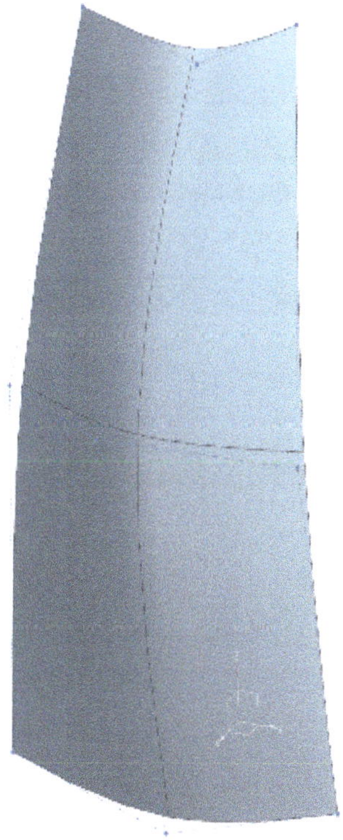

Example 1

In this example, you will construct the model shown below.

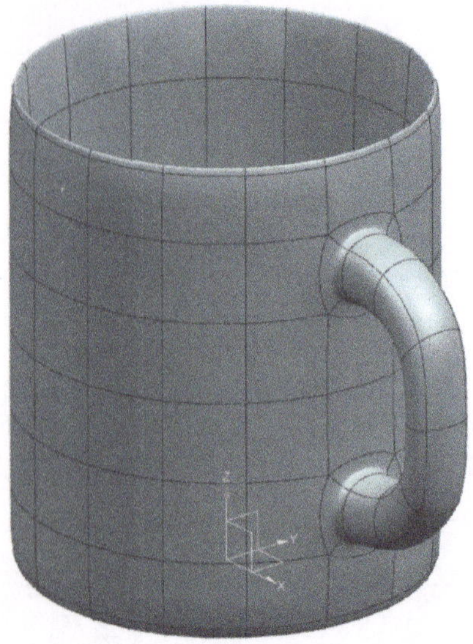

Activating the NX Realize Shape Environment

1. Start **NX**.
2. Start a new part file using the **Model** template.
3. On the ribbon, click **Surface > NX Realize Shape > NX Realize Shape** .

Creating a Cylinder Shape

1. On the ribbon, click **Home > Create > Primitive Shape** .
2. Click the **Reset** icon on the **Primitive Shape** dialog. Next, select **Type > Cylinder** .
3. Under the **Size** section, type 80 and 90 in the **Size** and **Height** boxes, respectively. Next, type 6 and 16 in the **Linear** and **Circular** boxes of the **Segments** section. Click **OK** to create the cylinder.

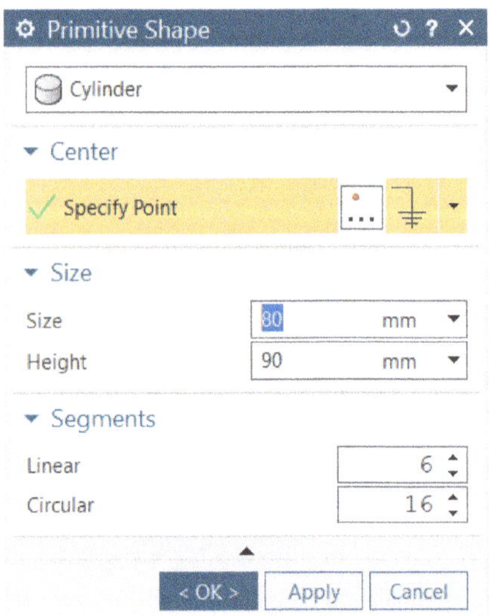

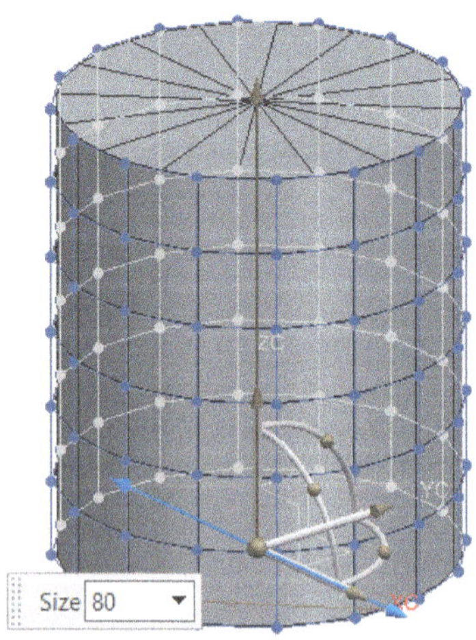

Adding Symmetry to the model

1. On the ribbon, click **Home > NX Realize Shape > Start Symmetric Modeling**. Click the **Reset** icon on the **Start Symmetric Modeling** dialog.
2. Click on the XY plane of the Datum Coordinate System. Type 45 in the **Distance** box and then press Enter; a plane is created in the middle of the model. Leave the default options and click **OK** to make the model symmetric about the newly created plane.

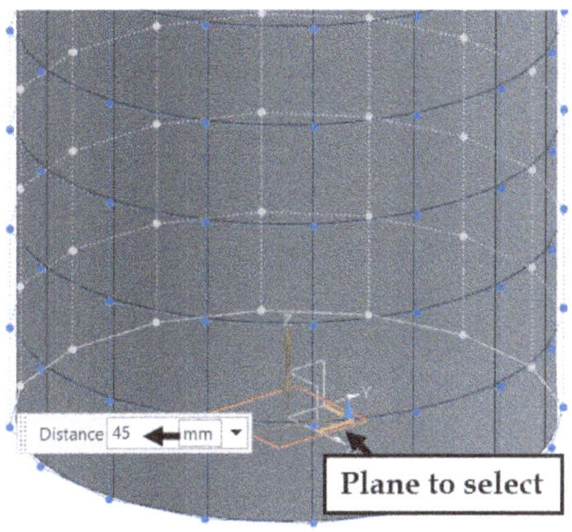

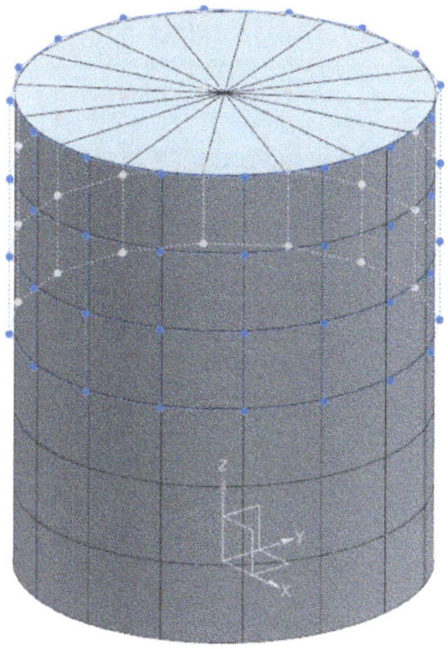

Subdividing Top Face

1. On the ribbon, click **Home > Edit > Subdivide Face**. Click on the top face of the model. Type **8** in the **Percentage** box and click **Apply** to subdivide the face.

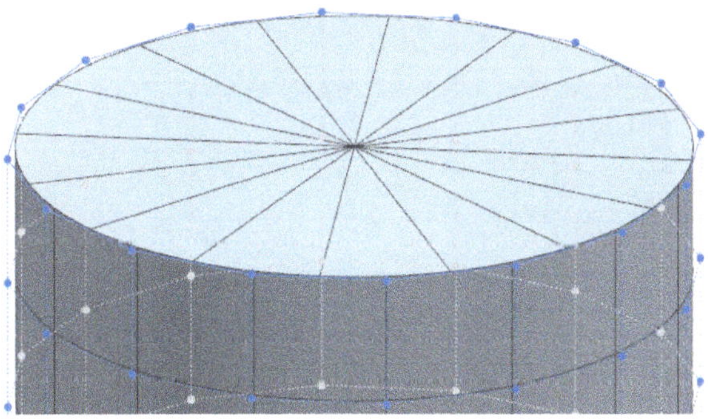

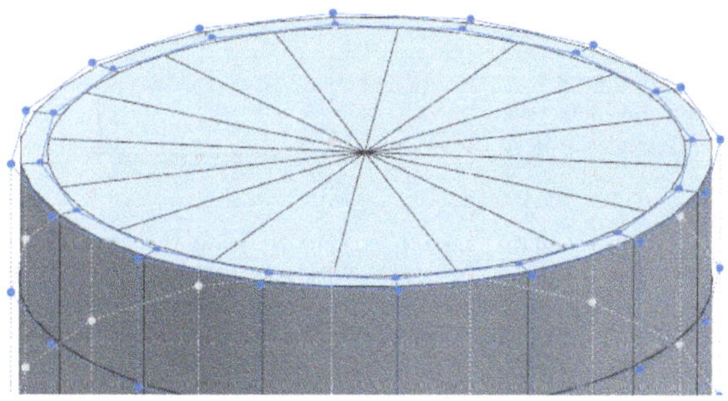

2. Likewise, subdivide the inner face of the top surface. The Percentage value is 15.

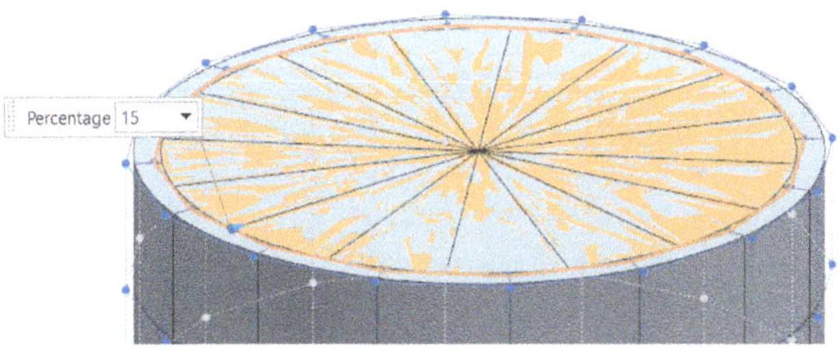

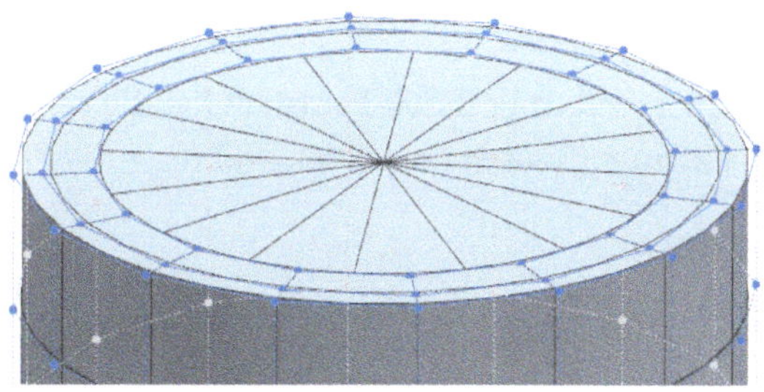

Creating the Handle

1. Right-click and select **Orient View > Right**. Next, activate the **Subdivide Face** command (on the ribbon, click **Home > Edit > Subdivide Face**). Click on the cage face, as shown. Type **10** in the **Percentage** box, and then click **OK**.

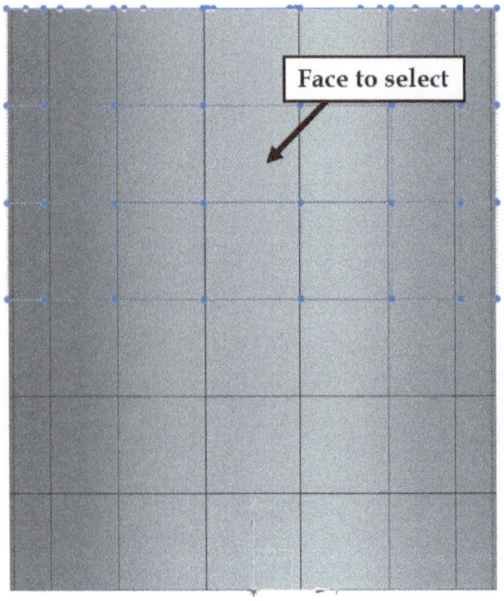

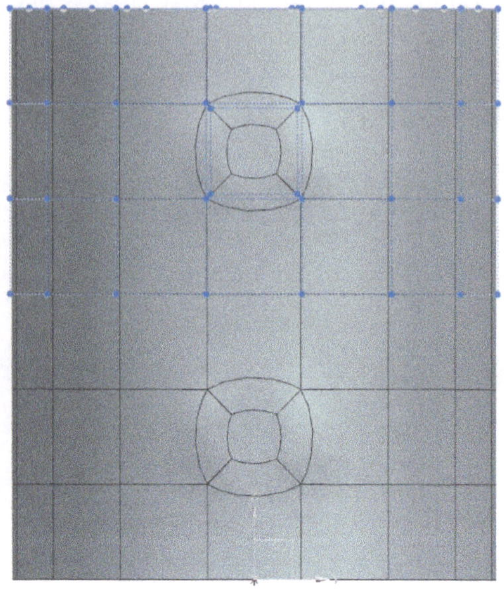

2. On the ribbon, click **Home > Create > Extrude Cage**. Click the **Reset** icon on the **Extrude Cage** dialog. Click the **Transform** tab on the **Extrude Cage** dialog. Click on the subdivided face.
3. Right-click and then select **Orient View > Front**.

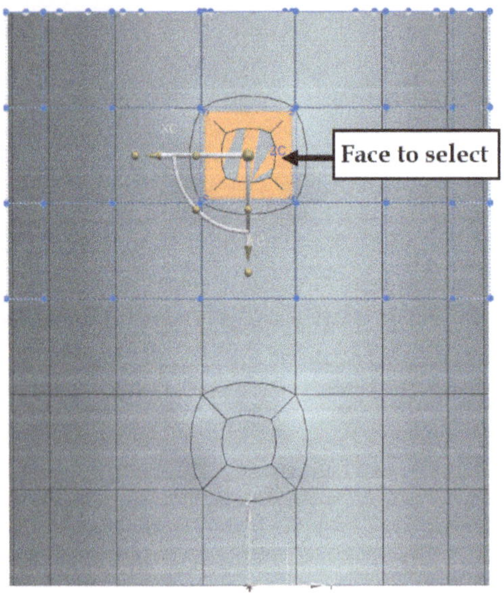

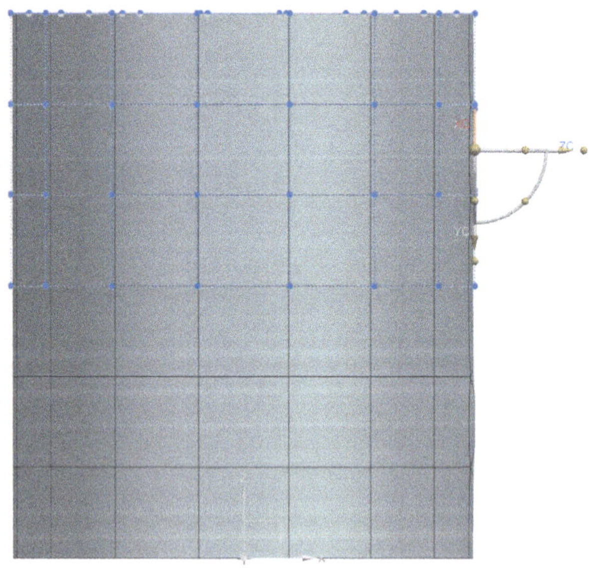

4. Click and drag the Z-Translate handle of the transform tool up to a small distance. Click **Apply** on the **Extrude Cage** dialog. Click and drag the YZ-Rotate handle, as shown.

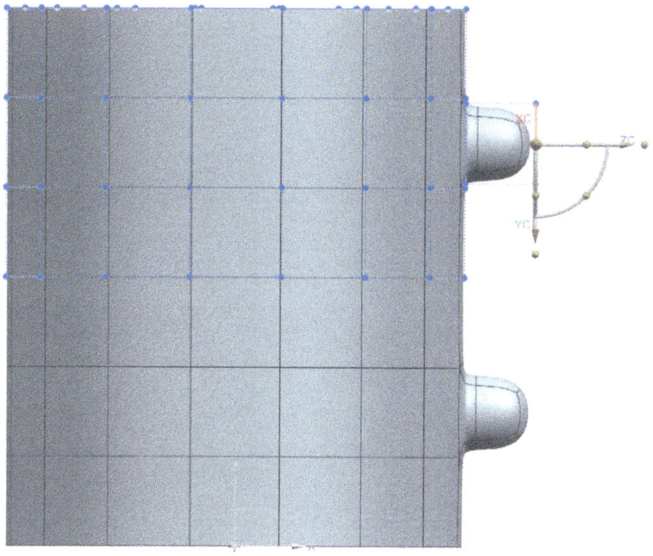

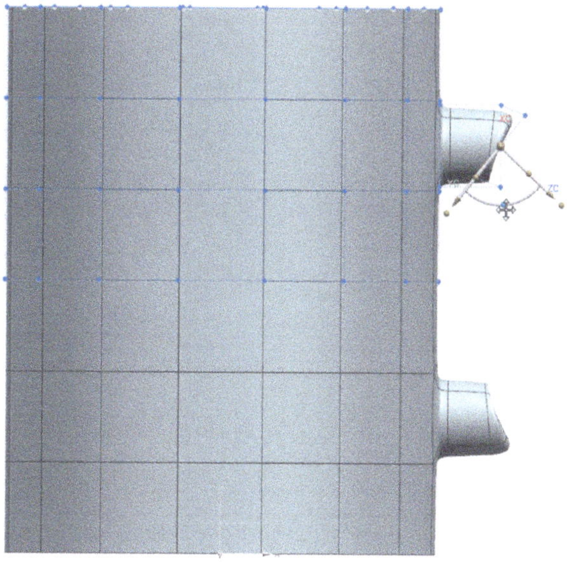

5. Click and drag the Z-Translate handle, as shown. Click **OK** to complete the extrude cage process.

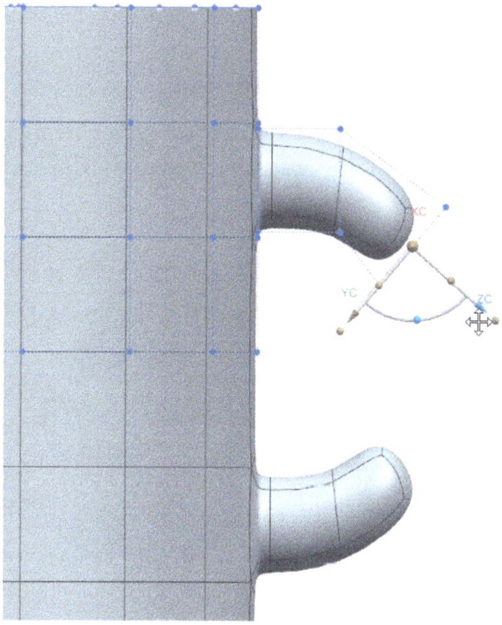

6. On the ribbon, click **Home > NX Realize Shape > Stop Symmetric Modeling**. Next, right-click and select **Orient View > Trimetric**.
7. On the ribbon, click **Home > Create > Bridge Face**. Click the **Reset** icon on the **Bridge Face** dialog. Click on the end face of anyone of the extruded cages. Click **Select object** in the **Face Set 2** section, and then click on the end face of the remaining extruded cage. Expand the **Segmentation** section set the **Number of Segments** value to **2**. Click **OK** to bridge the end faces.

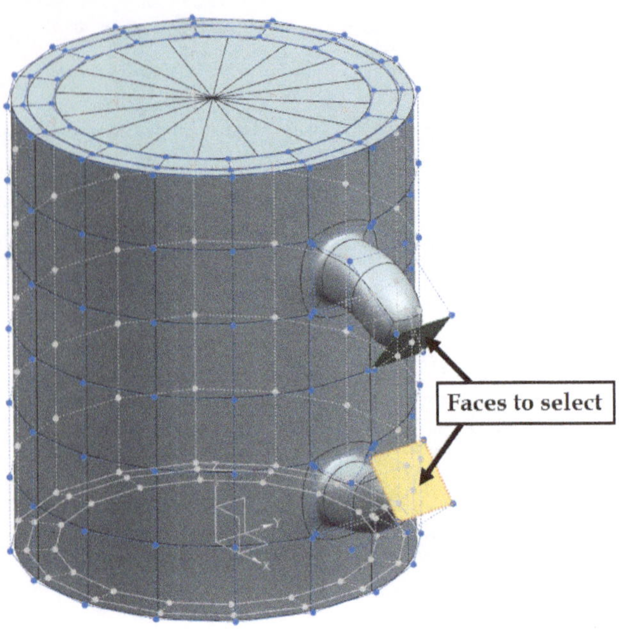

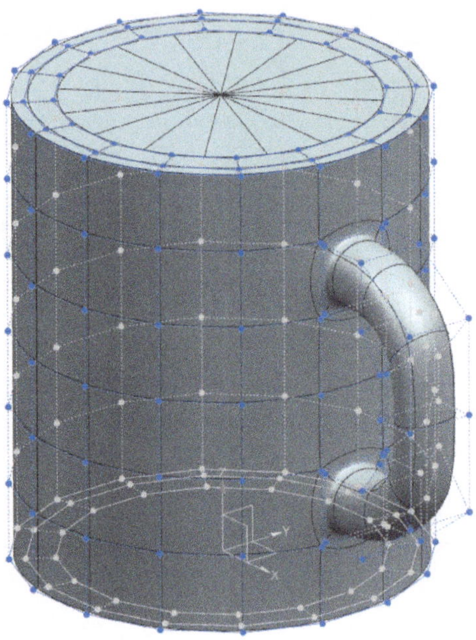

Shelling the Mug

1. On the ribbon, click **Home > Create > Extrude Cage**. Next, type **5** in the **Number of Segments** box.
2. Click on the center face and the faces surrounding it on the top surface. Next, right-click and select **Orient View** > **Front**. Click and drag the **Z-Translate** handle of the transform tool downwards, as shown. Click **OK** to shell the model.

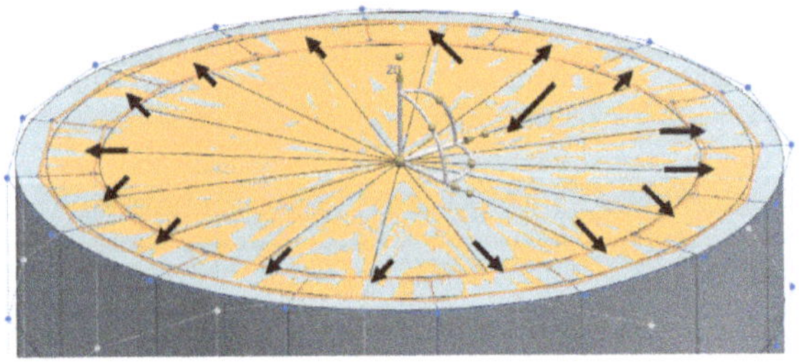

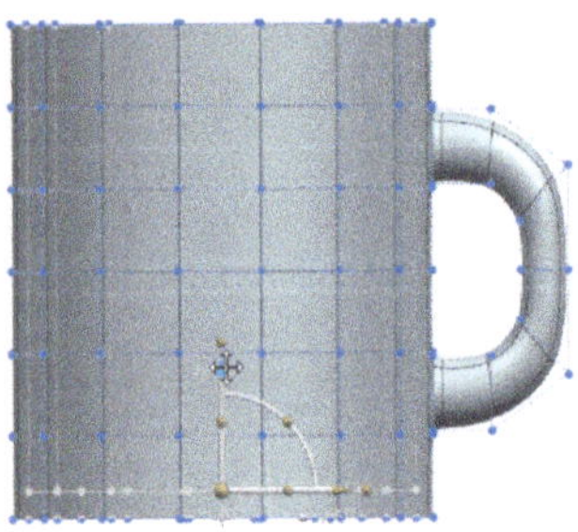

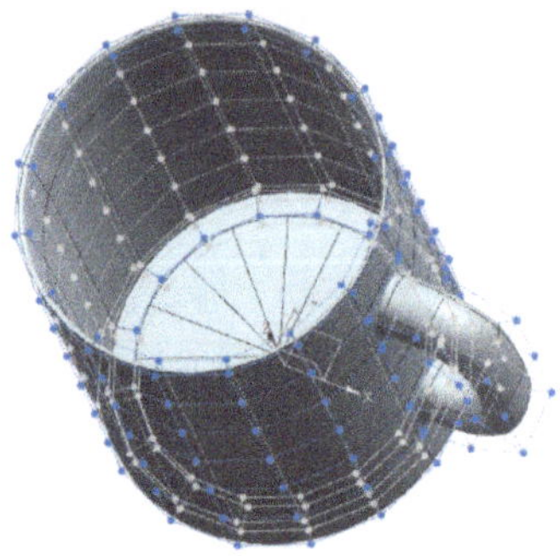

Creating a Bump at the bottom

1. On the ribbon, click **Home > Edit > Transform Cage**. Click the **Reset** icon on the **Transform Cage** dialog. Click the **Transform** tab on the dialog. Rotate the model such that the bottom face is visible. Next, click on the center face at the bottom.
2. Click on the Z-Translate handle of the transform handle. Type -2 in the **Distance** box, and then click **OK**.

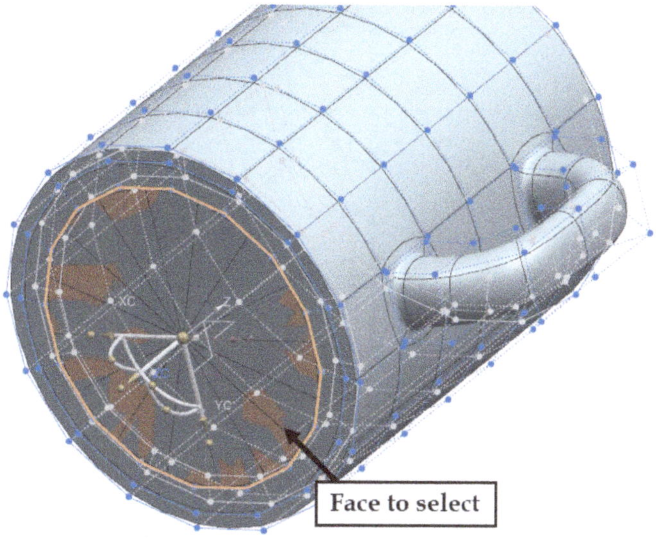

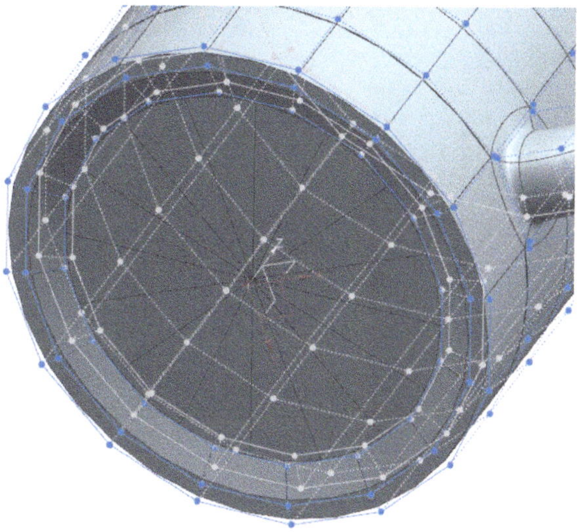

3. On the ribbon, click **Home > Edit > More > Set Continuity**. Create a selection window across the entire model.
4. On the **Set Continuity** dialog, select **Continuity > Smooth**. Click **OK**.

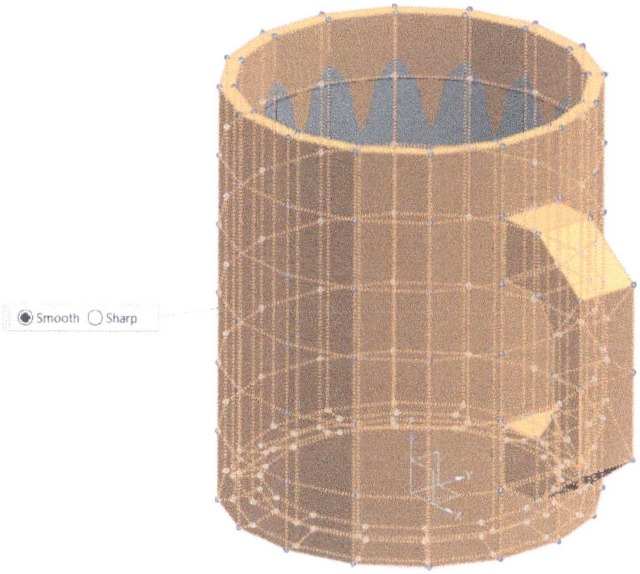

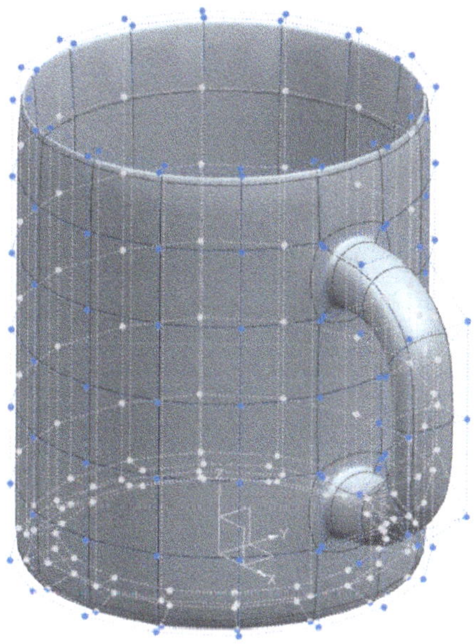

5. On the ribbon, click **Home > NX Realize Shape > Finish**.
6. Save and close the part file.

Example 2

In this example, you will construct the part shown below.

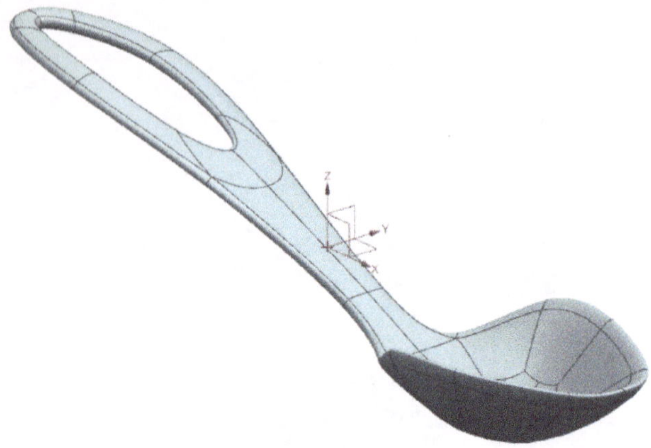

Importing the Raster Image

1. Download the image files related to *Example 2* of *Chapter 12: NX Realize Shape* from the companion website.
2. Start **NX**.
3. Start a new part file using the **Model** template.
4. On the ribbon, click **Tools > Utilities >Raster Image** . Click the **Reset** icon on the **Raster Image** dialog. Click on the XY plane of the Datum Coordinate System.
5. Click the **Choose Image File** icon and select the Top_View.jpg file. Select **Orientation > Basepoint > Middle Center** . Check the **Preview** option, and then click the **Flip Horizontal** icon.
6. Check the **Lock Aspect Ratio** option in the **Size** section. Next, select **Scaling Method > User Defined** and then type **150** in the **Width** box.
7. Expand the **Image Settings** section, and then select **Transparency > Pixel Color**. Click on the white portion in the **Transparency** window. Next, click **OK** to insert the image file.

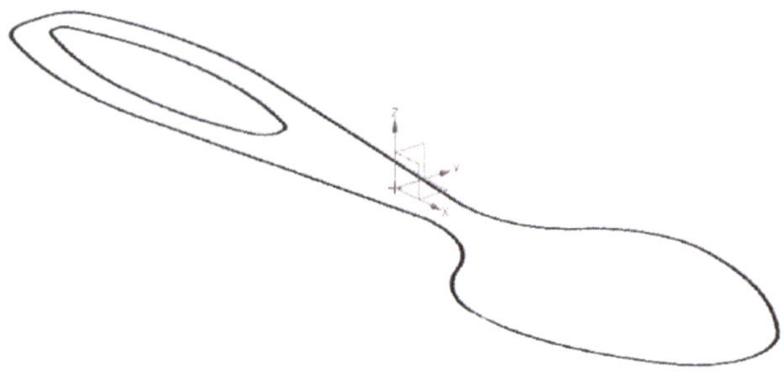

8. Likewise, insert the Front_view.jpg file on the XZ Plane.

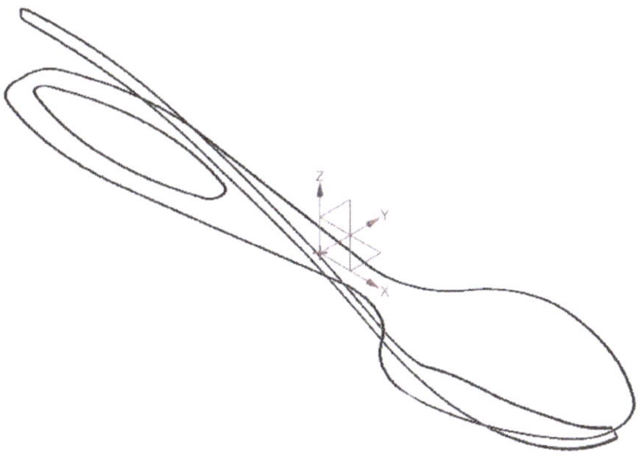

Creating and Manipulating the Circle

1. On the ribbon, click **Home > Surface > Surface > NX Realize Shape** .
2. Right-click and select **Orient View** > **Top**.
3. On the ribbon, click **Home > Create > Primitive Shape** . On the **Primitive Shape** dialog, select **Type > Circle**. Type-in 42 and 8 in the **Size** and **Circular** boxes, respectively.
4. Click and drag the move handle displayed on the circle to position it at the location, as shown. Click **OK** to create the circle.

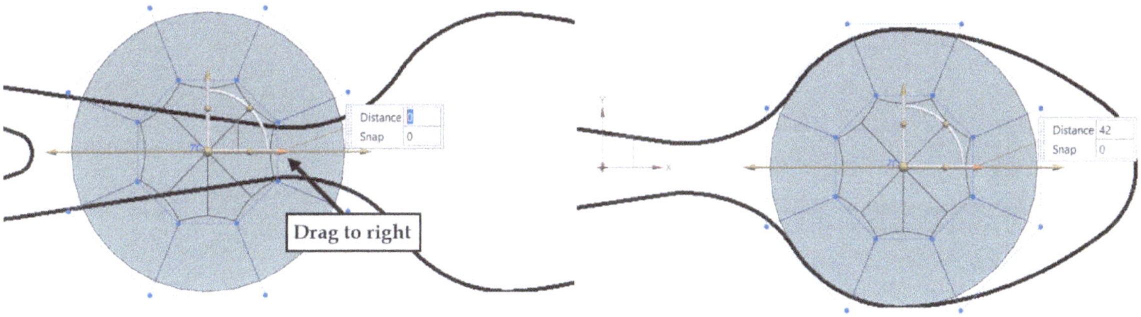

5. On the ribbon, click **Home > Edit > Transform Cage** . Click the **Reset** icon on the **Transform Cage** dialog. Click the **Transform** tab and select the right cage edge, as shown. Click and drag the Y-Translate up to the image outline, as shown. Click **OK**.

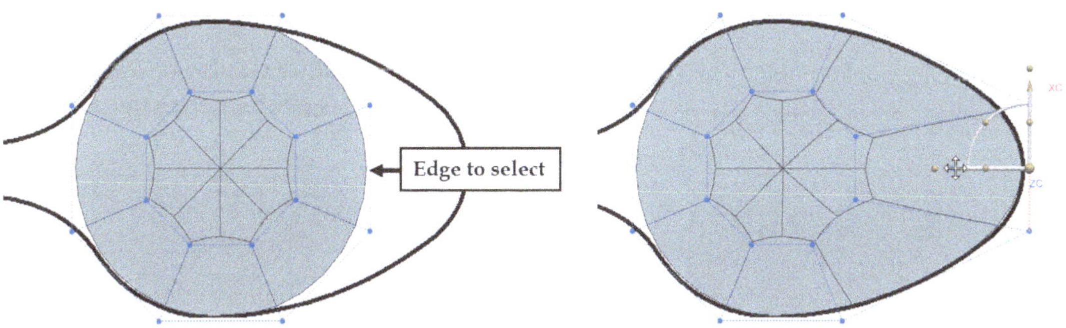

6. On the ribbon, click **Home > Create > Extrude Cage**, and then click the **Reset** icon on the **Extrude Cage** dialog. Select the edges, as shown. Next, click and drag the **Distance** handle up to the left end of the image. Click **OK**.

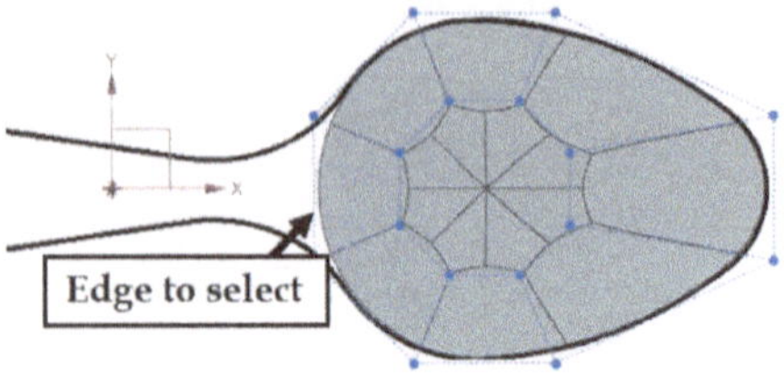

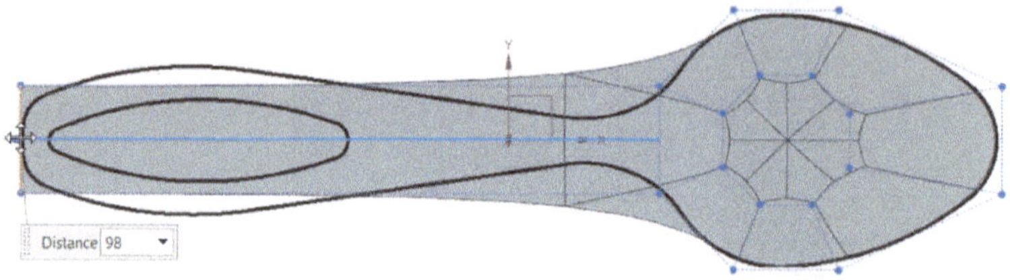

7. On the ribbon, click **Home > Edit > Split Face**. Click the **Reset** icon on the **Split Face** dialog. Select **Type > Uniform**.
8. Click on the extruded face to define the face to split. Next, click **Select Reference Edge** in the **Split** section of the dialog, and then select the horizontal cage edge, as shown. Type **3** in the **Number** box, and then click **OK**.

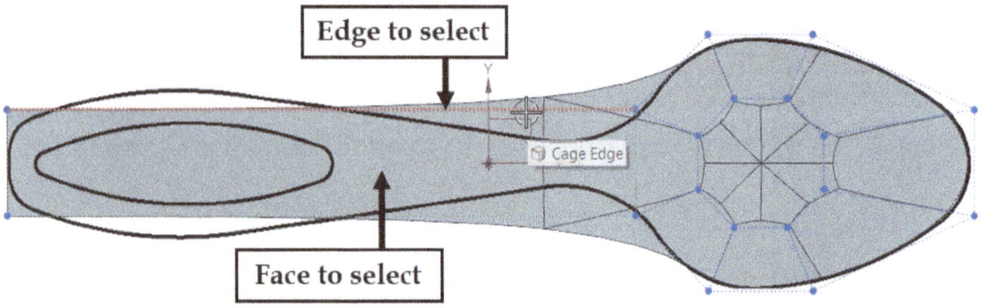

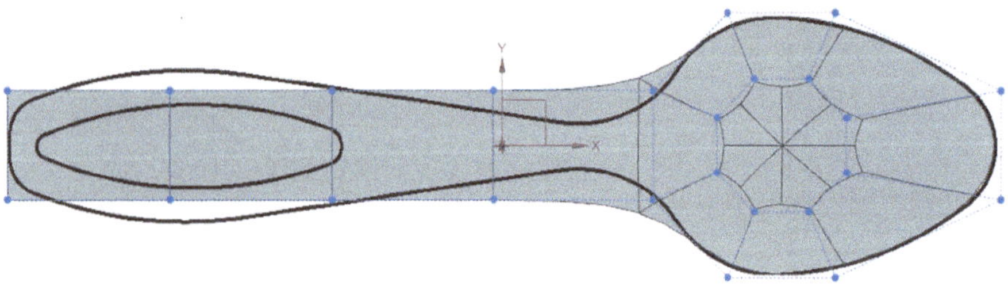

9. On the ribbon, click **Home > NX Realize Shape > Start Symmetric Modeling**. Click the **Reset** icon on the **Start Symmetric Modeling** dialog. Click on the XZ Plane of the Datum Coordinate System. Click **OK** to start symmetric modeling.

10. On the ribbon, click **Home > Edit > Transform Cage**. Click the **Reset** icon on the **Transform Cage** dialog. Click the **Transform** tab and select the cage edge, as shown. Click and drag the Y-Translate up to the position, as shown.

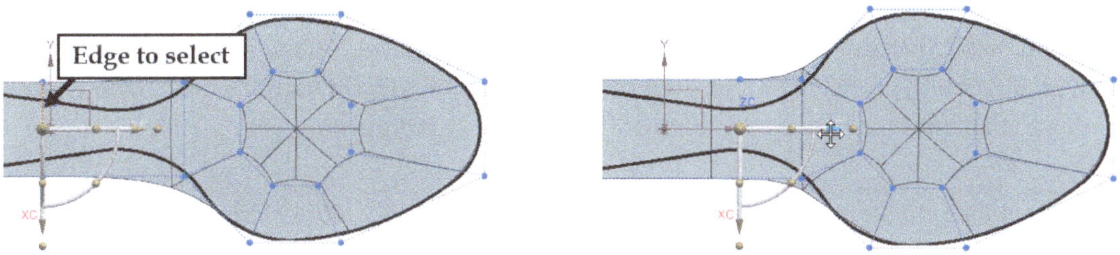

11. Click and drag the X-Scale handle downwards; the selected cage edge is scaled, as shown. Click **Apply**.

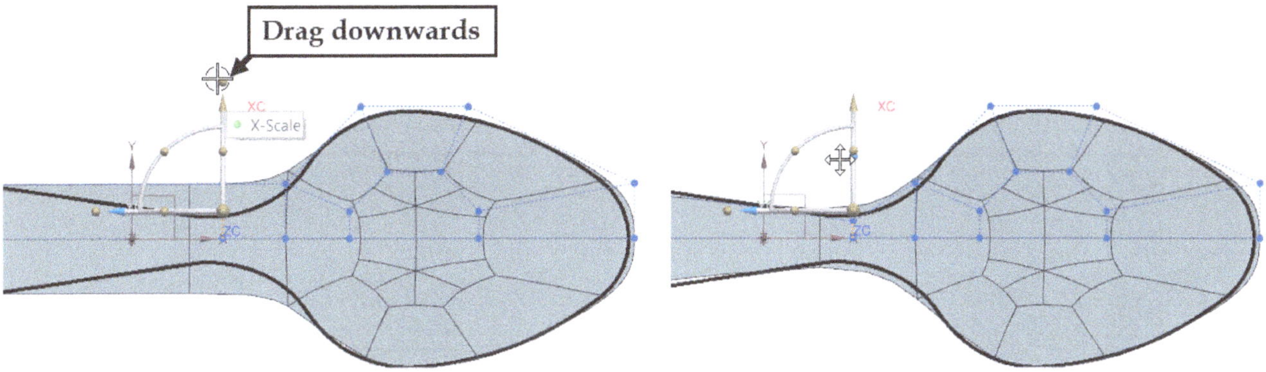

12. Select the cage edge and drag the X-Scale handle upwards, as shown. Click **Apply**.

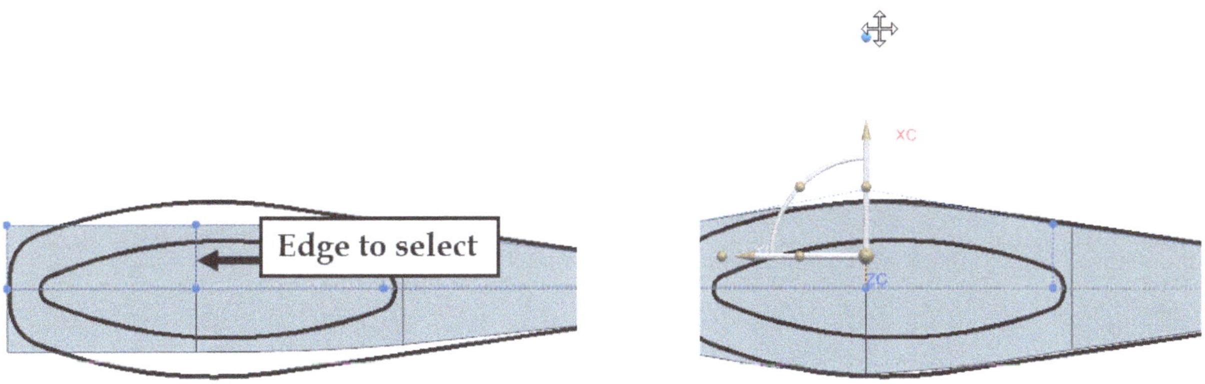

13. Likewise, scale the leftmost edge of the cage, as shown. Click **OK**.

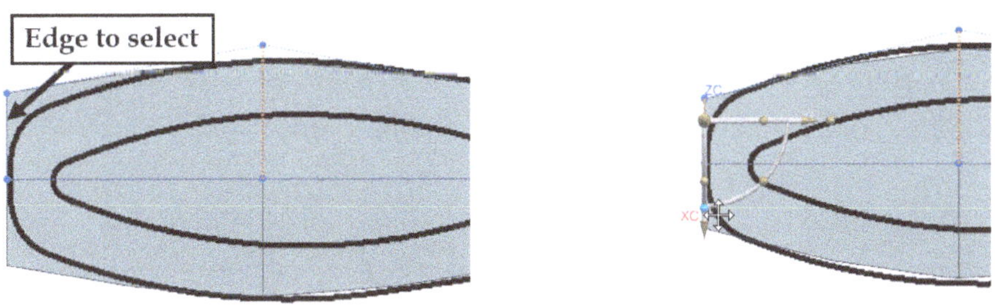

14. Change the view orientation to the Trimetric. On the ribbon, click **Home > Edit > Transform Cage** . Click the **Transform** tab on the **Transform Cage** dialog. Next, select the cage face, as shown.
15. Change the view orientation to Front. Click and drag the Z-translate handle upward. Release the mouse button when the cage coincides with the lower edge of the image. Click **Apply**.

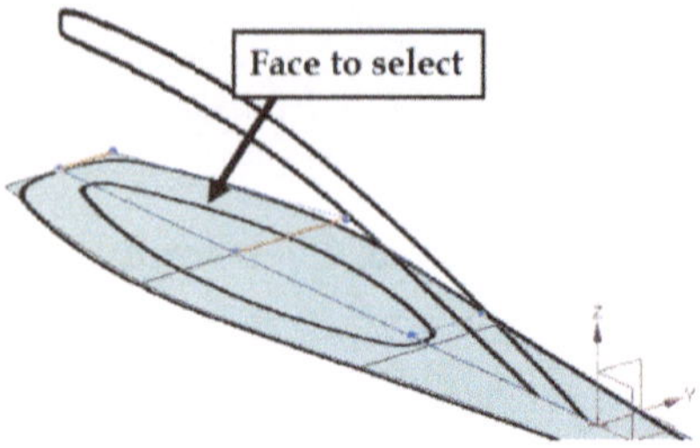

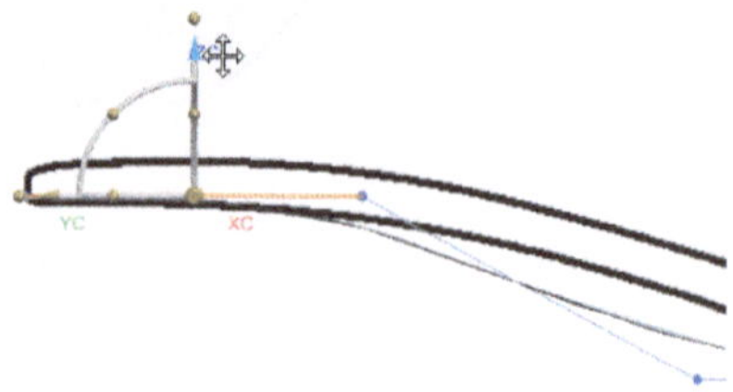

16. Change the view orientation to Trimetric. Click on the cage face, as shown.
17. Change the view orientation to Front. Click and drag the YZ-Rotate handle toward the left to change the angle of the face.

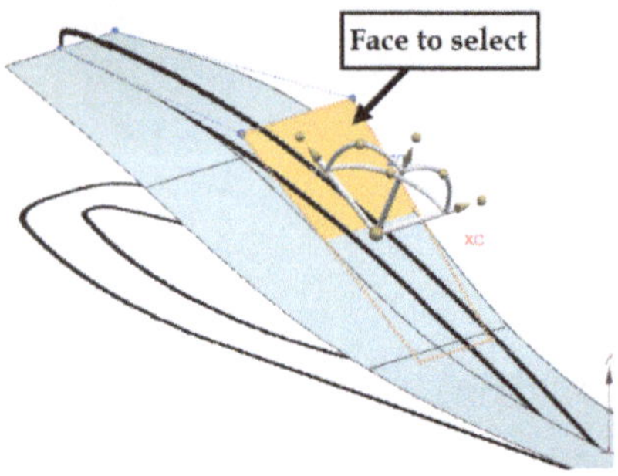

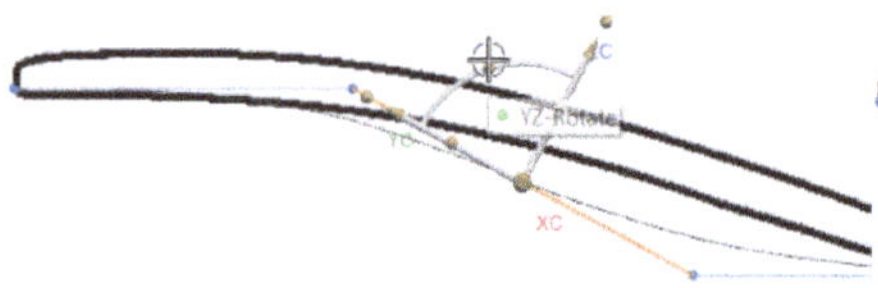
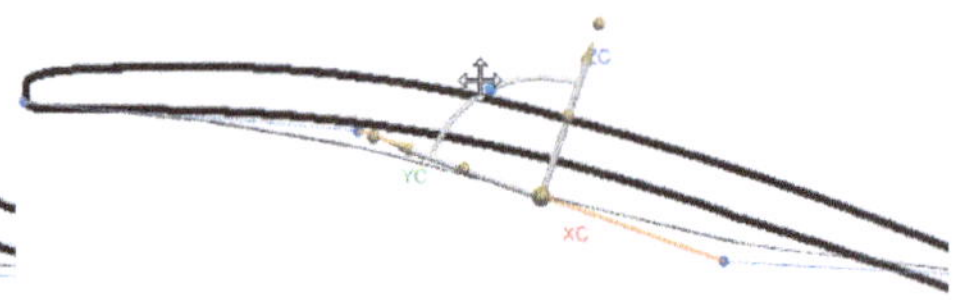

18. Click and drag the Z-Translate handle upward such that the face coincides with the lower edge in the image. Click **Apply**.
19. Change the view orientation to Trimetric. Click on the cage face, as shown. Next, change the view orientation to Front.
20. Click and drag the YZ-Rotate handle toward the right. Next, drag the Z-Translate handle downward. Click **Apply**.

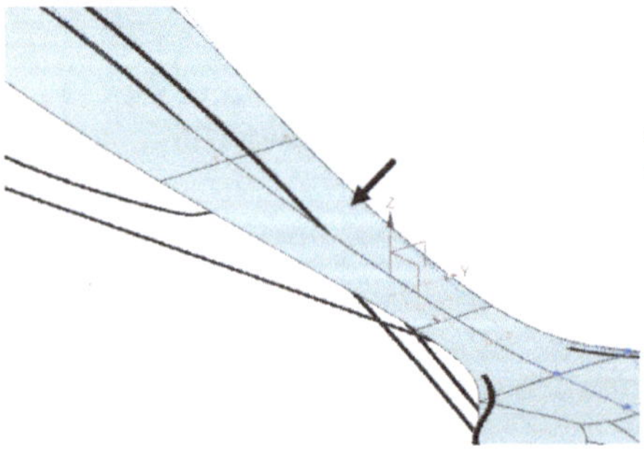

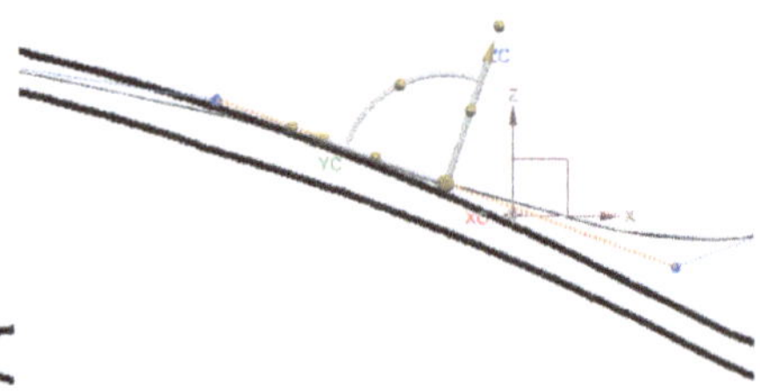

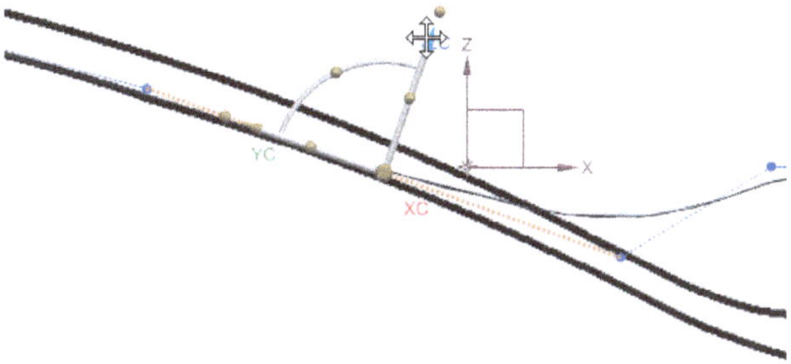

21. Likewise, transform the next face such that it is aligned to the lower edge of the image. Click **Apply**.

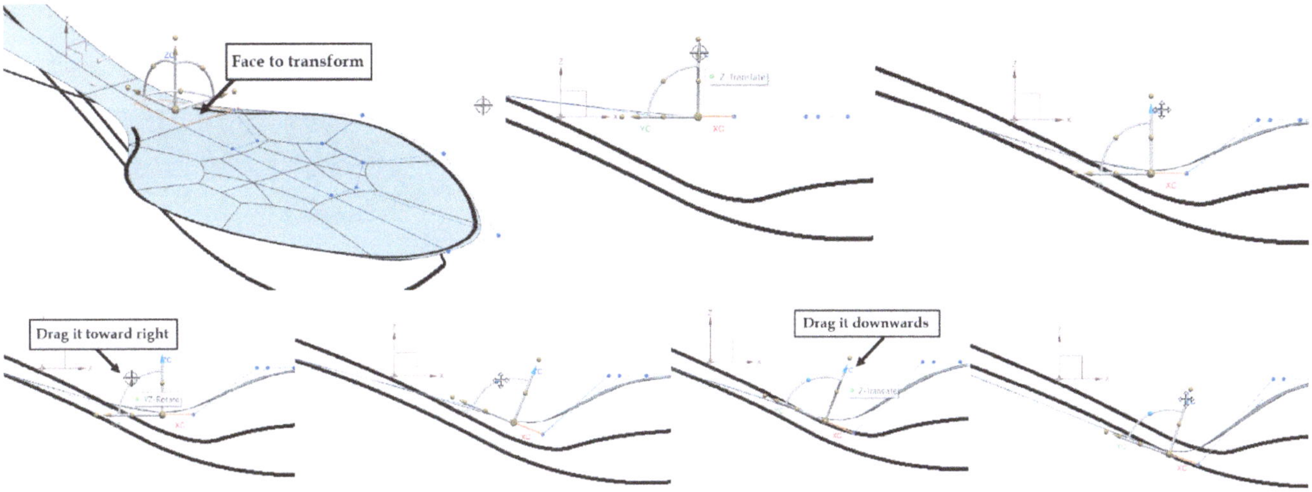

22. Modify the cage face adjacent to the previously modified face, as shown. Click **Apply**.

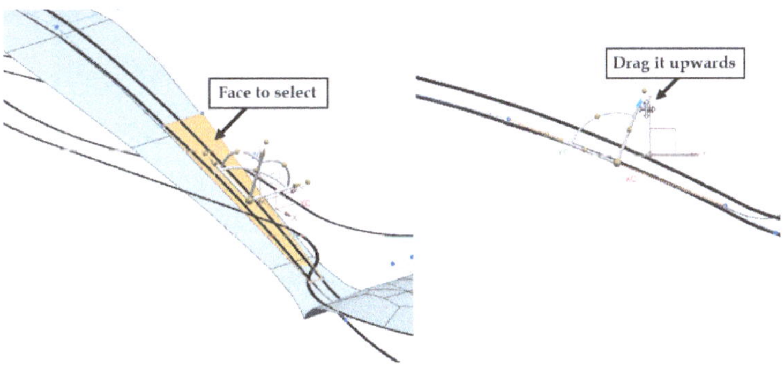

23. Transform the remaining faces to align them with the lower edge of the image. Click **OK**.

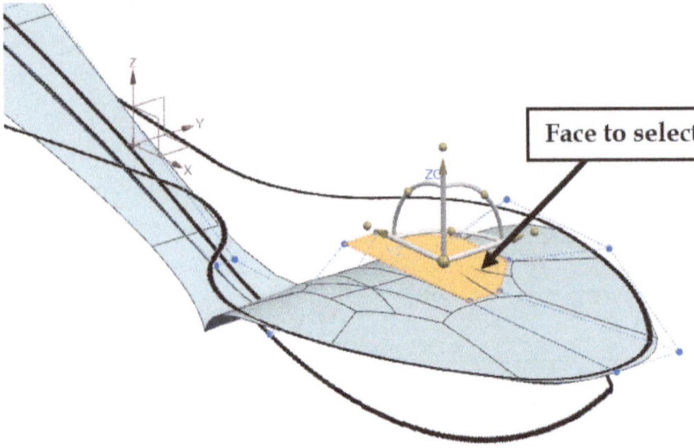

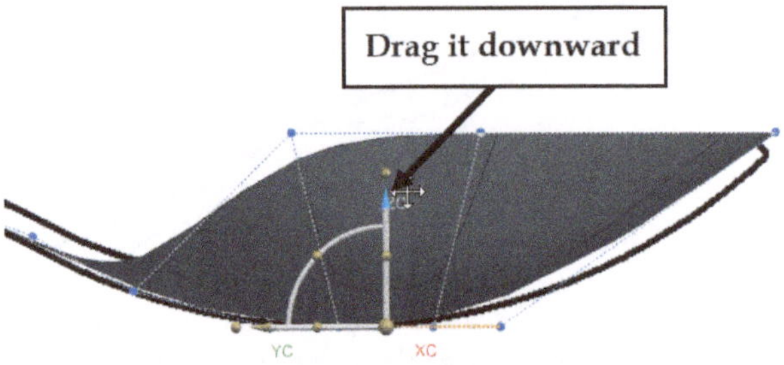

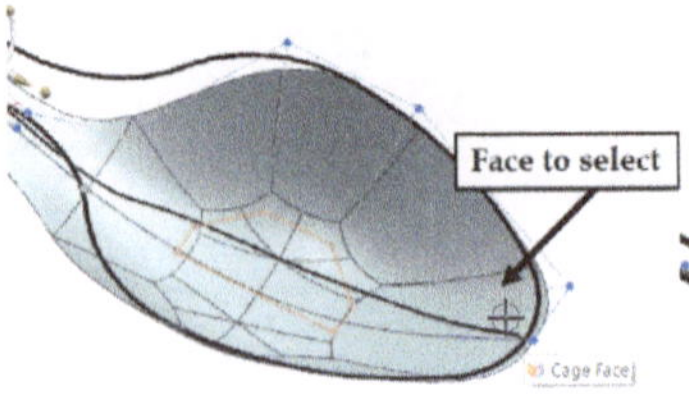

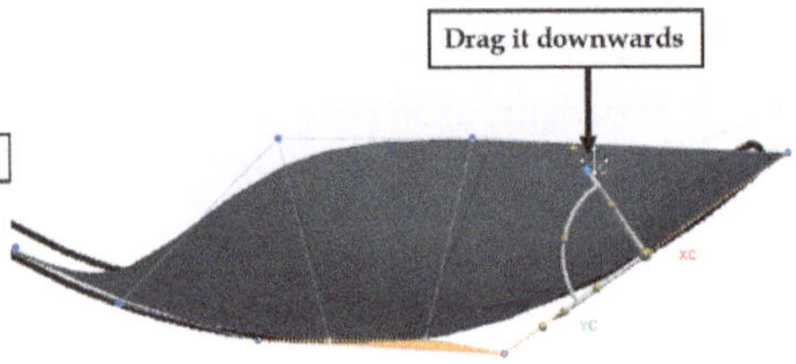

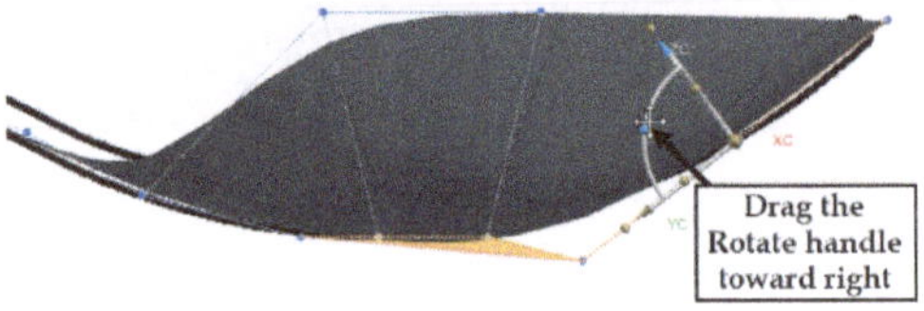

24. On the ribbon, click **Home > Create > Extrude Cage**. On the Sketch Scene Bar, select **Selection Rule > Region**. Click any one of the faces of the cage; all the faces are selected. Type 3 in the **Distance** box and click **OK**.

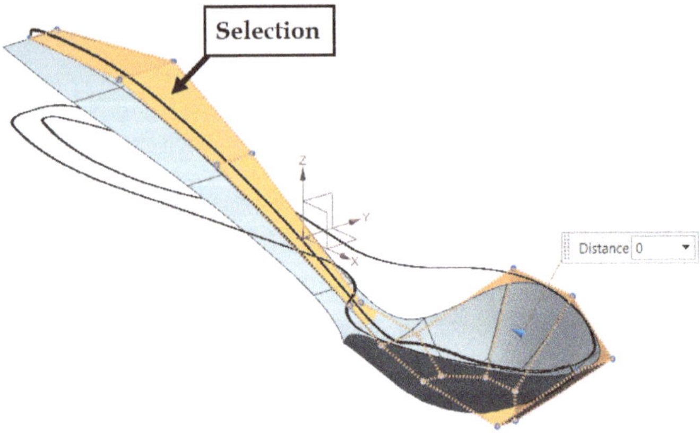

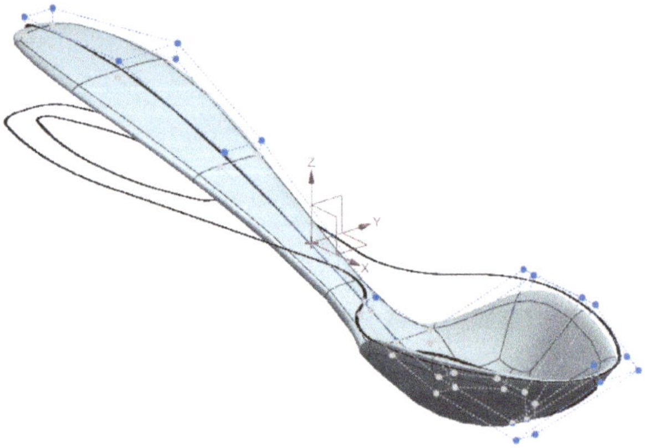

Creating a Cutout

1. On the ribbon, click **Home > Edit > Subdivide Face**. Select the faces of the cage, as shown. Type 40 in the **Percentage** box and click **Apply**.

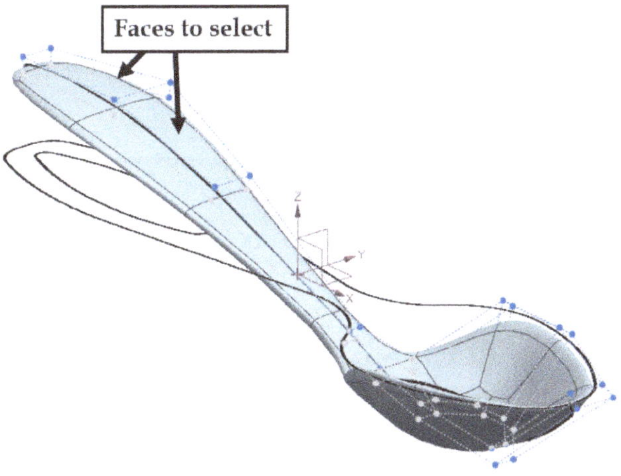

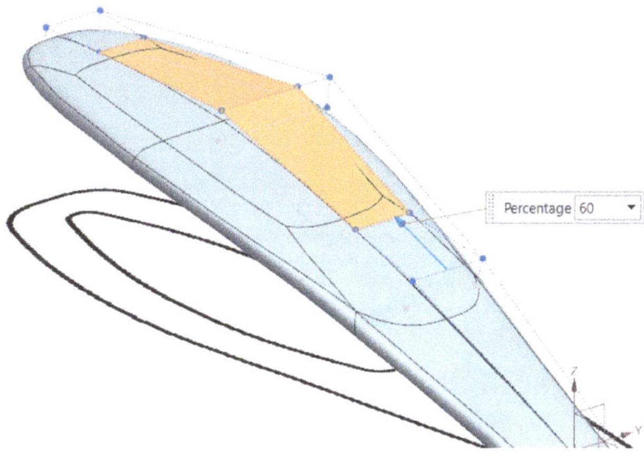

2. Rotate the model and click on the corresponding faces on the bottom side, as shown. Type **60** in the **Percentage** box and click **OK**.

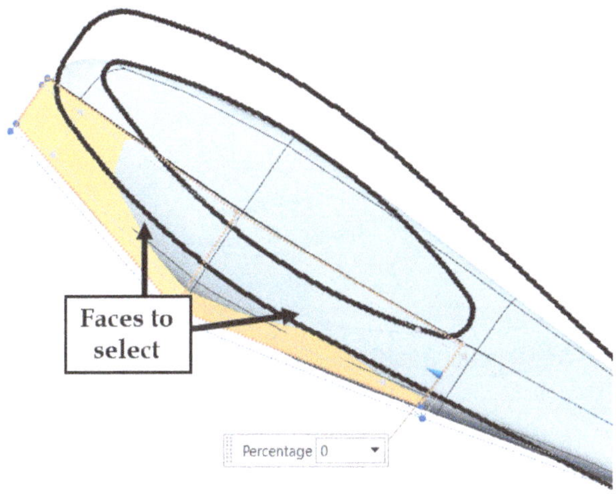

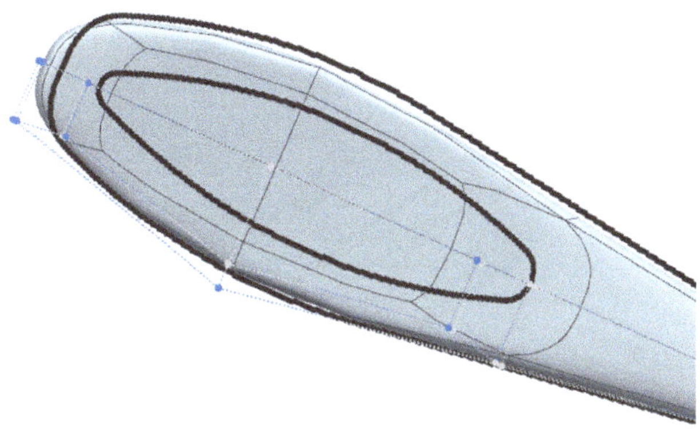

3. On the ribbon, click **Home > Create > Bridge Face**. Click the **Reset** icon on the **Bridge Face** dialog. Click on the cage faces on the top side of the model.
4. On the **Bridge Face** dialog, click **Select object** in the **Face Set 2** section. Rotate the model and select the two faces on the bottom side, as shown. Click **OK**.

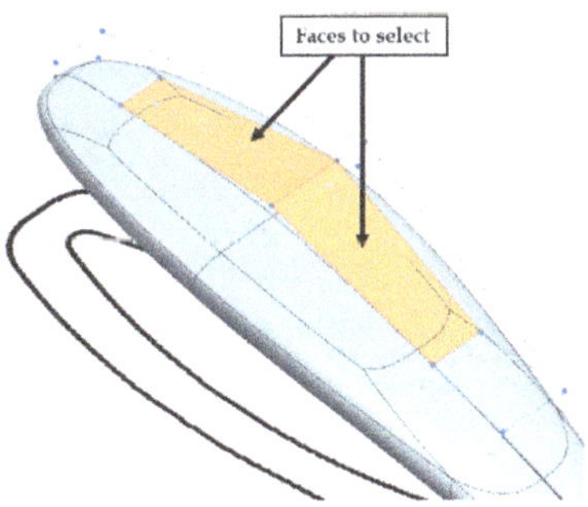

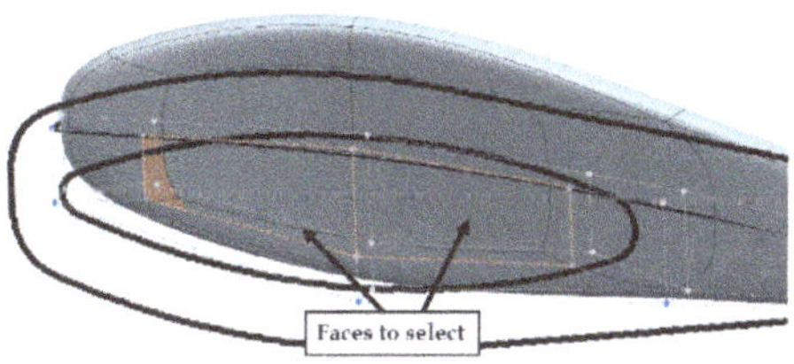

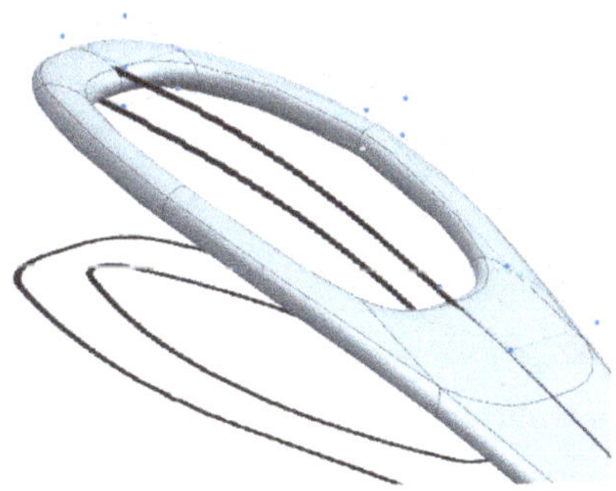

5. On the Top Border Bar, select **Selection Filter > Cage Edge**.
6. Click on the edge of the cage, as shown. Click the **Transform Cage** icon on the Context toolbar. Click the **Transform** tab on the **Transform Cage** dialog.

7. On the Top Border Bar, select **Orient** drop-down > **Top**. Drag the X-Translate handle toward the left, as shown. Click **Apply**.

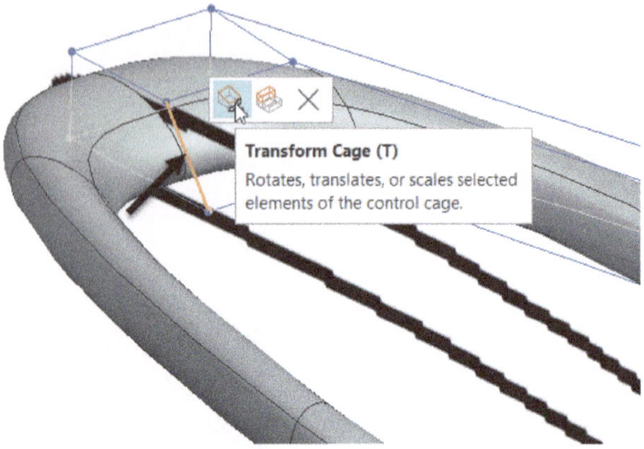

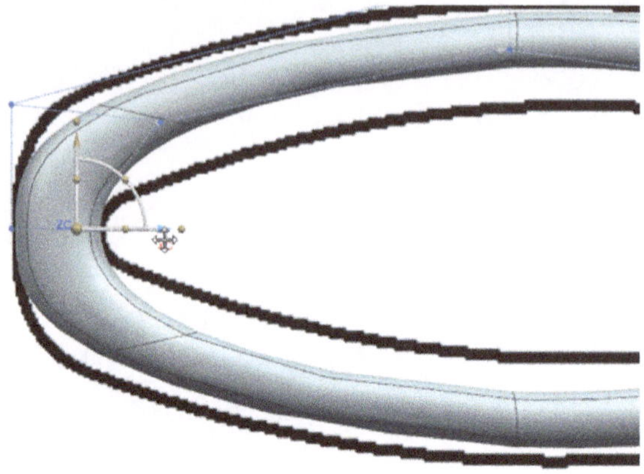

8. Likewise, transform the other edges of the bridged face.

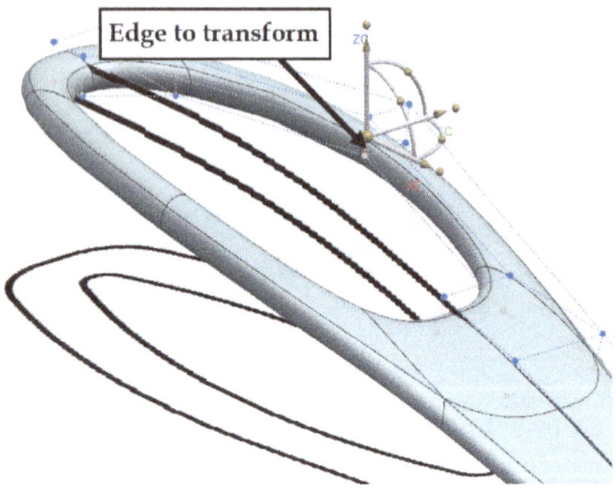

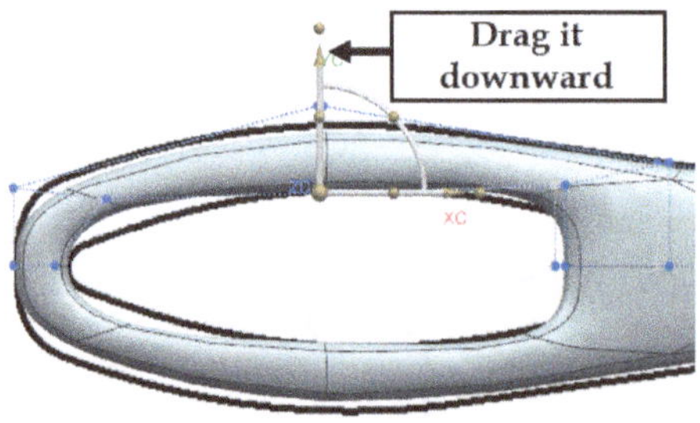

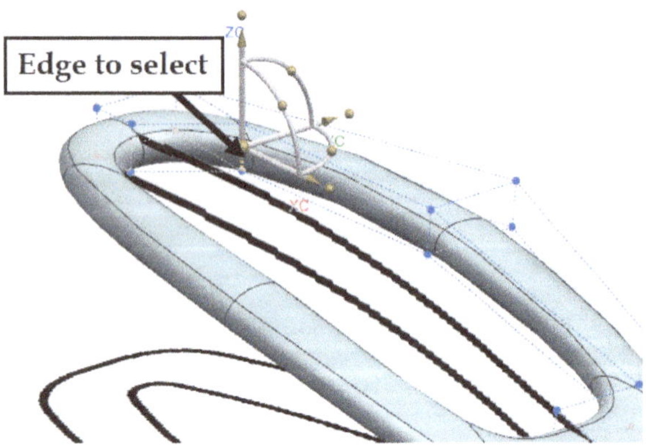

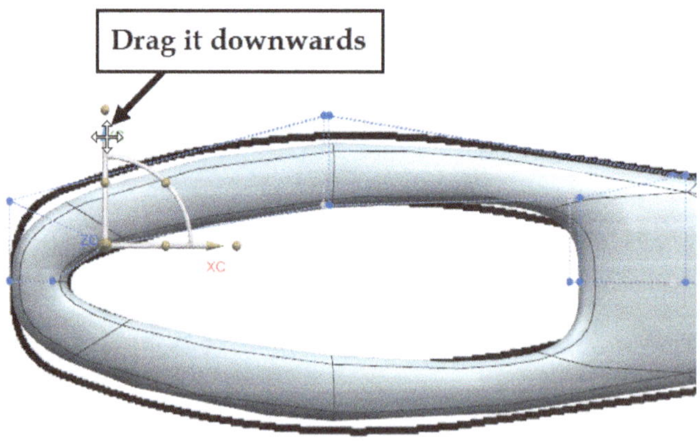

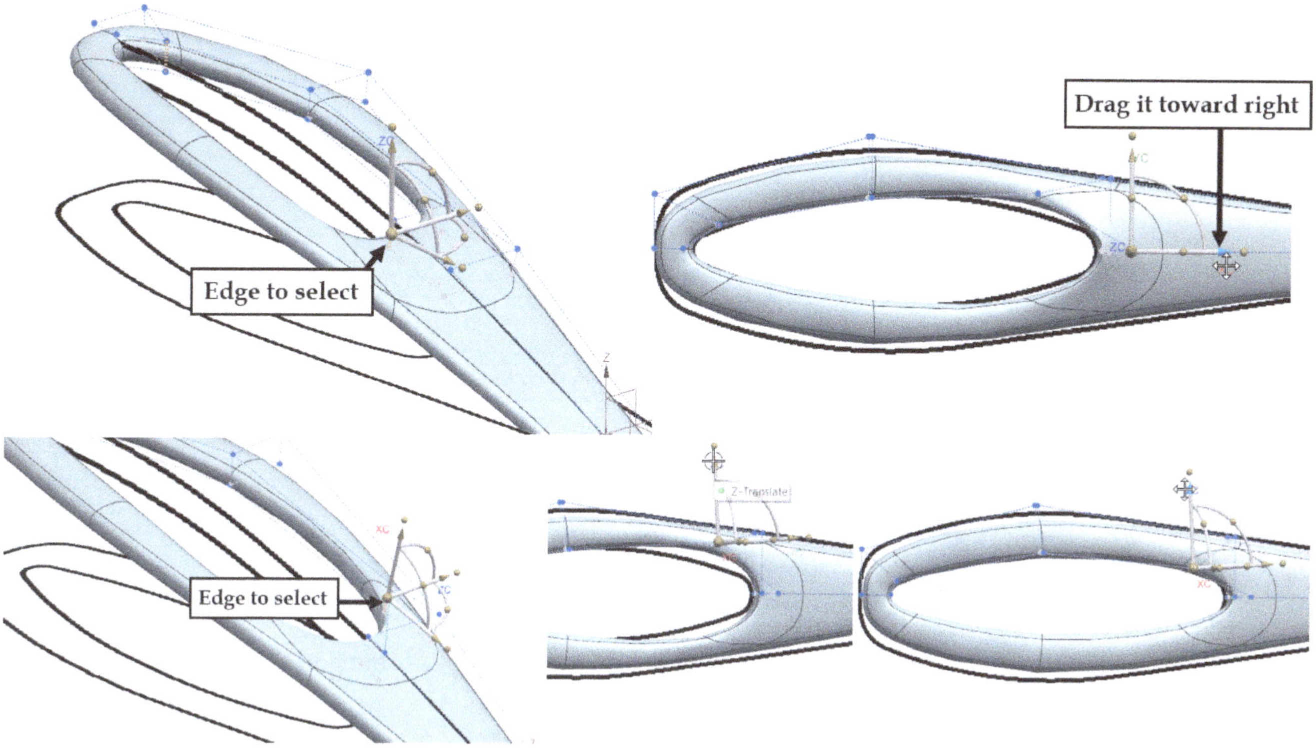

9. Right-click and select **Orient** View > **Front**. Activate the **Transform Cage** command and uncheck the **Reorient Tool to Selection** option in the **Transform** tab.
10. Select the cage edge, as shown. Click and drag the XZ-Rotate handle toward the right.
11. Click and drag the Z-Translate handle downward, and then click **OK** on the **Transform Cage** dialog.

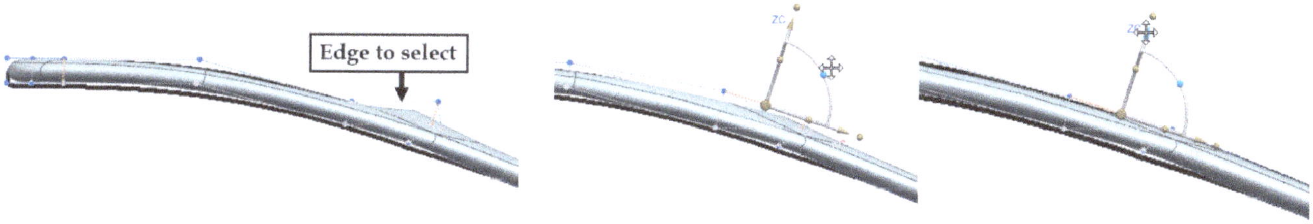

12. On the ribbon, click **Home > NZ Realize Shape > Finish**.
13. On the ribbon, click **View** > **Content** > **Show and Hide**. On the **Show and Hide** dialog, click the Hide icon next to the **Raster Images** option. Next, close the **Show and Hide** dialog.

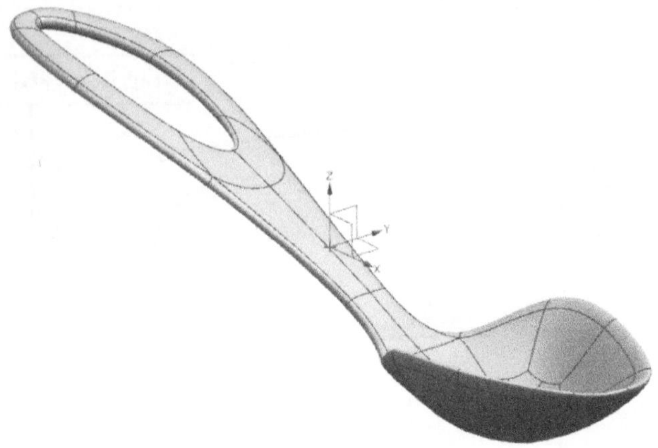

14. Save and close the file.

Questions

1. Explain how to bridge faces.
2. What are primitive shapes that you can create using the **Primitive Shapes** command?
3. Give one example of where you can use the **Bridge Face** command.
4. What is the difference between symmetric modeling and Mirror cage?
5. What are the two procedures to create cage polylines?
6. How can you change the size of a face using the **Transform Cage** command?
7. What is the difference between the **Subdivide Face** and **Split Face** command?

Index

9 788199 428973

Printed at Repro India Ltd.